W9-AGF-486

SUCCESS! SUCCESS! SUCCESS!

The Book of Inside Secrets

BOARDROOM CLASSICS
55 Railroad Avenue, Greenwich, CT 06830

First Printing 10 9 8 7 6 5 4 3 2 1

Library of Congress Cataloging-in-Publication Data
Success! Success! Success! The Book Of Inside Secrets
p.cm.
Includes index.
ISBN 0-88723-106-3

55 Railroad Ave., Greenwich, CT 06830

Printed in the United States of America

Contents

4 • COMMUNICATION SECRETS

5 • SELF-IMPROVEMENT

6 • GETTING ORGANIZED

7 • FINDING A JOB

8 • GETTING AHEAD ON THE JOB

9 • DEVELOPING GOOD WORK HABITS

10 • RELATIONSHIPS

11 • YOUR HOME

12 • BUYING/RENTING A HOME

13 • SMART MONEY MANAGEMENT

14 • YOUR CAR

15 • INSURANCE AND BANKING SAVVY

16 • THE NEW INVESTOR

17 • TAXES

18 • STAYING HEALTHY

19 • HEALTHY HEALING

20 • NUTRITION

21 • FITNESS

22 • BETTER SLEEP

23 • COPING WITH EMERGENCIES

24 • SELF-DEFENSE

29 • FUNTIME

30 • TRAVEL SMARTS

1

Life Lessons

Life Lessons from Ben Franklin

Benjamin Franklin was perhaps the most awesome of our nation's amazing founding fathers.

By his own efforts, he rose from a boyhood of poverty and only two years of formal schooling to become one of America's richest men and a world-renowned author and publisher, scientist and inventor, statesman and diplomat.

But above all, he was a genius at persuasion. Ben Franklin's achievements rested on a foundation of native brilliance and hard work. His incredible success in so many fields, however, was only possible because he was a master salesman. By studying his life and work I discovered his secrets of salesmanship.

I sum up Ben Franklin's formula for sales success by using the acronym *TALKING*... where every letter stands for one of the seven keys for successful persuasion...

•Timing. Franklin was a master of timing. As a printer's apprentice eager to go into business for himself, he decided to become Philadelphia's leading expert in the latest printing techniques in use in London. Unable to afford the trip himself, he made an audacious suggestion to the governor of Pennsylvania—that he should finance Franklin's journey.

Young Ben argued that he would then be able to provide the colony with exceptional printing services...but he was careful to make his case as persuasive as possible by approaching the governor at the most strategic moment—right after he had finished a hearty meal in the colony's best restaurant.

Lesson: For every successful salesman, it's not good enough to have the *right message*...you must also choose the *right moment.*

•Appreciation. Franklin knew the surprising fact of life that people are likely to want to help you with a big favor if they've already done you a small one. He used this psychological knowledge to great effect when he was in France during the Revolutionary War, trying to raise funds for Washington's Continental Army.

The French finance minister, Count Vergennes, refused to see Franklin, who was otherwise an especially popular figure in the royal court. Franklin reasoned that Vergennes was jealous of the attention being showered on Franklin.

Franklin's strategy: He wrote to Vergennes asking to borrow an obscure book from his personal library. Flattered that he had something that Franklin lacked, Vergennes was glad to lend him the book. After this, the two began a useful diplomatic relationship.

Lesson: Anyone who wants someone else to *accommodate* his request should learn to *appreciate* the other one's problems.

•Listening. Franklin was a master at listening closely. This enabled him instantly to take advantage of any opening in the conversation.

Once, at a ball in France, King Louis remarked to Franklin upon a certain lady and the physical features revealed by her low-cut gown. Ben instantly responded: *But you in France can endow our American government, which suffers from the same problem as the lady—an uncovered deficit.*

Lesson: Every good salesman must learn to listen well enough to his customer to find out what he needs and how best to sell it to him—and then to feed back his own words, using *them* to sell him.

•Knowledge. Franklin always realized that knowledge was power. He set up the first library in America and never stopped learning himself. The aged Franklin, universally acknowledged as America's elder statesman, once heard that a town in Massachusetts wanted to erect a bell tower in his honor. He wrote back that he was flattered but suggested that they should use the money instead to set up a library.

Opportunity: Every salesman should take advantage of the knowledge available at libraries—and every other research aid available—to find out where his customers are coming from...and how to get them where he wants them to go.

•Integrity. Franklin was a masterful diplomat—but he never misrepresented his fundamental beliefs. Even as the American minister at the French court, he never sought to disguise his republican beliefs. When playing chess with the French monarch, he began by removing the two kings from the board, joking to the startled Louis XVI that *in America, we have no need of kings.*

Lesson: For salesmen, as for everyone, in the long run honesty is the best policy.

•Need. Franklin realized that the three most persuasive words in the English language are *I need you.* He used their powerful appeal from his youth, when he had to find lodging, to his later prosperity, when he sought to raise funds for public libraries and hospitals.

Lesson: Every persuader should know that when you must ask people for something, the best way to convince them is to show them that they are uniquely qualified to give it to you.

•Giving. Franklin was a master of compromise. He knew that if you want *everything* your own way, you may lose it all. And he was able to exert tremendous influence because he always sought ways to improve his ideas by combining them with those of other people.

Franklin was a strong believer in majority rule. But he was the one who broke a deadlock at the Constitutional Convention by agreeing that the United States should have both a House of Representatives based purely on population and a Senate with just two members from each state, regardless of its population.

Lesson: Every salesman needs to learn the value of giving...nobody ever lost an arm or leg by lending an ear. If you insist on everything, you may wind up with nothing.

Bottom line...

When Thomas Jefferson was sent as the new American minister to France, Count Vergennes asked if he was Franklin's replacement. Jefferson replied, "I have come to succeed Dr. Franklin. No one could ever replace him."

When asked the secret of Franklin's triumph as a diplomat, Jefferson said that it was that he had never heard of Franklin directly contradicting someone else.

The overwhelming lesson of salesmanship taught by Ben Franklin is that the aim of persuasion is not to confront other people, but to appreciate their points of view and try to move them gently in your direction.

Source: James C. Humes, a former legislator and diplomat who wrote and performed a one-man show about Benjamin Franklin. He is the author of *The Ben Franklin Factor: Selling One to One,* William Morrow and Co., 1350 Avenue of the Americas, New York 10019.

Lessons in Life from George Washington

George Washington, the first president of the US, taught Americans what to expect from their leaders. He set an example that has served the nation well for more than 200 years. Washington's personality and behavior can teach us many lessons—in statesmanship and also in life.

Strength...

Washington stood six-feet three-inches tall, head and shoulders above most of his countrymen. At that time, the average American male was five-feet six-inches tall, about three inches shorter than now.

Washington had huge hands and took pride in his physical strength. He put that strength to good use throughout his unusually active life. He was a businessman and farmer, soldier and statesman—often simultaneously. But he recognized the distinction between strength and force.

Example: When Washington campaigned for election to the Virginia State Assembly in 1755, one of his speeches offended a proud man named William Payne. The hot-tempered Payne grabbed a hickory branch and knocked the much bigger Washington to the ground. The next day Washington visited Payne's favorite tavern and demanded to see him. Payne thought he was going to be challenged to a duel. Instead, Washington apologized, retracted his offending comment and asked to shake hands in friendship.

Lesson: The true test of strength is not indulging your natural aggressive instincts but being able to conquer them.

Self-improvement...

As a youth, Washington wanted to become a member of the fashionable Virginia aristocracy and win fame and fortune. He observed very closely the way his high-placed friends and relatives acted and dressed. And he read widely to make up for the deficit in his skimpy formal education.

After he inherited a substantial estate at Mount Vernon, Virginia, from a relative and then came into wealth in 1759 by marrying Martha Custis, the richest woman in Virginia, Washington worked to improve the estate by experimenting with new agricultural techniques and machines, and tested 60 different crops.

As he matured, Washington combined his own ambitions for material advancement with continuous efforts to develop his own character.

Example: Washington had a fierce temper that he struggled his entire life to control. As president, one of his worst moments came when he received news of the fate of an army expedition sent to subdue a group of warring Indian tribes in Ohio. Because of the ineptitude of Major General Arthur St. Clair, who commanded the expedition, two-thirds of the 1,400 men had been killed or wounded.

Washington's immediate reaction was a furious outburst of swearing. But within a few minutes, he controlled his temper and declared that St. Clair would be given a fair hearing.

Lesson: Before you can lead others well, you must learn to lead yourself.

Price of fame...

As president, Washington was probably the most famous man of his time...as a general, his small army of colonials defeated the mightiest army in the world...as a statesman, he was charged with leading a newborn nation based on the unprecedented idea of the freedom of the individual.

Everywhere Washington went, he was met by his countrymen's adulation and foreigners' curiosity. He accepted his historic role but suffered because he was unable to enjoy a private life—outside the one with his closest family members.

Example: Washington's adopted granddaughter, Nelly Custis, described how he would laugh heartily when she described her youthful pranks. But her friends—and even Washington's relatives—were so awed by him that they were afraid to laugh or speak naturally in his presence. When Washington entered a room full of children who were enjoying a lively conversation, they would often be struck dumb. He would stay for a short while and then leave, frustrated and disappointed.

Lesson: Fame is a mixed blessing. A small amount gratifies the ego...but in large doses, it makes life difficult.

Humility...

Washington's military exploits against the French and Indians made him well known when he was still in his 20s.

However, he was acknowledged as the leader of the American cause against the British 20 years later because of the practical economic measures he sponsored...and the judgment he showed as a delegate to the Continental Congress.

After being unanimously chosen as commanding general of the new Continental Army in 1775, Washington left the meeting room, telling Patrick Henry: "From the day I enter upon the command of the American armies, I date my fall and the ruin of my reputation."

Before his first election to the presidency in 1789, he explained his ambition *to live and die on [his] own plantation.* He reluctantly agreed to run for a second term only when it became clear that he was the only person who could hold the country together.

Washington resolutely refused a third term, setting a precedent broken only by Franklin D. Roosevelt and now prohibited by a constitutional amendment.

After he left office in 1797, Washington returned to his beloved Mount Vernon to live the farming life he had always wanted. A constant stream of admirers visited...and each was impressed by the same character traits.

Example: English comedian John Bernard, touring the young United States in 1798, came across an overturned carriage with a woman lying beside it, unconscious, on a rural Virginia road. Bernard saw an elderly man straining to help the woman and free the carriage from the half-ton of luggage burying it.

After they had finished their work, the elderly man invited Bernard to recover at Mount Vernon ...and he realized that the savior was George Washington. Bernard was impressed by Washington's thoughtful remarks—but even more by his behavior, so different from that of most country gentlemen, who would have sent their servants to help. The former president had pitched in himself.

Lesson: Greatness is measured by action, not reputation.

Source: Richard Norton Smith, author of *Patriarch: George Washington and the New American Nation* (Houghton Mifflin, 215 Park Ave. S., New York 10003). He is former director of the Herbert Hoover Presidential Library and now executive director of the Ronald Reagan Center for Public Affairs in Simi Valley, California.

Lessons in Life from John Adams

John Adams, the second president of the United States, was one of the greatest of our nation's founding fathers. Thomas Jefferson and John Adams both died on July 4, 1826—the 50th anniversary of the signing of the Declaration of Independence. And eulogists across the nation saluted both equally as giants in the struggle for American independence.

Most Americans today recognize Jefferson's greatness, but few are aware of Adams's stature. Many people confuse John Adams with his second cousin Samuel Adams, the fiery anti-British orator who organized the Boston Tea Party...or confuse him with his son, John Quincy Adams, the sixth president.

That is unfortunate, because the life of John Adams can show all Americans how to strike a balance between public and private obligations...realism and idealism...and loyalties to friends and personal principles.

Adams in history...

In the Continental Congress, John Adams was a delegate from Massachusetts and the leading advocate of American independence.

As chairman of the committee to draft the Declaration of Independence, he assigned the actual writing task to Thomas Jefferson, Virginia's delegate.

Elected president of the US in 1796, Adams faced the difficult task of following the majestic and revered George Washington. He confronted a major challenge facing the still young United States—to preserve its neutrality between France and Britain, the warring superpowers of the era.

That course required Adams to put the good of the country ahead of his personal ambitions and steer a lonely course with no political allies. His Federalist party was dominated by Alexander Hamilton, who strongly favored the British. The opposition Republicans, led by Vice President Jefferson, favored the French.

Vigorously opposed by both sides, Adams was still able to save the country from war. However, he was not embraced by his own party and did not win a second term in the White House. Although he lost the election, historians today recognize that he led the nation wisely.

• *Lesson:* Resisting pressure from individuals while acting in the best interest of the whole may not be immediately rewarding, but it will be appreciated over the long term.

Realism and self-understanding...

John Adams was never afraid of self-evaluation. He was keenly aware of his own faults. He recognized that he possessed an internal feeling of superiority...tended to be petty and quarrelsome...and was overly ambitious. He thought deeply about how to overcome these flaws.

Assuming that his shortcomings were shared by most men, Adams argued that the new American nation would only flourish if its institutions made allowances for human imperfections...encouraged people to channel their personal ambitions for public good...and contained checks and balances to make change take place at a sensible and slow pace. He favored political *evolution* over *revolution.*

Others—like Jefferson—had a more idealistic and populist attitude. They were thrilled when the French Revolution broke out—assuming that when men were free they would automatically be good. Adams was horrified. He foresaw the bloodshed and social upheaval that followed the revolution.

Over the next 200 years, the disastrous aftereffects of revolutions in France, Russia and China proved Adams right. And today, American society is suffering serious damage because old institutions—including the family—have broken down and there is nothing better to replace them.

• *Lesson:* Enduring change often takes time. Instead of rushing evolution, study and learn from the smaller changes that take place as you move toward your larger goals.

Personal relationships...

Many politicians—today as well as 200 years ago—do not form close personal relationships. They have few true friends...are committed only to their careers...and try to avoid emotional involvement. *Their slogan:* "Don't get mad—get even."

Adams was not like that. He had very strong feelings and was not afraid to show them. But he had a powerful warmth and an intellectual honesty and openness that led to deep and lasting friendships.

Example: After he lost the 1800 election to Jefferson, Adams was so upset that he left Washington, DC before Jefferson was sworn in as his successor. He was the only sitting president who did not attend his successor's inauguration. He spent the next decade vigorously defending his actions and attacking his political opponents.

But after 1812, he reconciled with Jefferson. Despite their continuing political differences, the two began a long and friendly correspondence that lasted for the rest of their long lives.

• *Lesson:* True friendship can transcend political differences. It's possible to disagree without being disagreeable.

Relationships with women...

Adams was no feminist. He opposed allowing women to vote in Massachusetts, and dismissed abstract arguments for women's rights. But he did not look down on women.

He had an extremely close relationship with his wife Abigail, sympathizing with her trials as

First Lady, and formed a strong bond with his daughter-in-law Louisa Catherine. He treated intellectually able women as his equals...and even thought them superior to men. He wrote: *I have a...terror of learned ladies...I can scarcely speak in their presence...I have always come off mortified at the discovery of my inferiority.*

In this respect he was more egalitarian than Jefferson, who believed that all men were created equal, but paid little attention to women. Jefferson restricted his daughters' education to music, art and "womanly" topics, while Adams believed in educating women as seriously as men so they could introduce their children to philosophy, literature and history as taught at his alma mater, Harvard.

• *Lesson:* If you truly respect others, you encourage them to reach their full potential.

Adams and slavery...

Adams strongly opposed slavery all his life. During the struggle for independence he recognized the time was not right to challenge the South to give up slavery, but argued that the issue would eventually have to be dealt with... and predicted it could lead to civil war.

In his old age, Adams vigorously opposed the Missouri Compromise of 1820, which allowed slavery to spread beyond the borders of the South...while Jefferson, the champion of individual liberty and theoretical foe of slavery, remained a slave owner all his life. Later, John Quincy Adams continued his father's anti-slavery tradition as a leading abolitionist in Congress after his term as president.

• *Lesson:* To see what someone really believes, don't just listen to what they say...look at what they do and the legacy they leave.

Source: Joseph J. Ellis, PhD, Ford Foundation Professor of History at Mount Holyoke College in Holyoke, Massachusetts. He is the author of *Passionate Sage: The Character and Legacy of John Adams,* W.W. Norton & Co., 500 Fifth Ave., New York 10110.

Life Lessons from Thomas Jefferson

Author of the Declaration of Independence, founder of the University of Virginia and our nation's third president, Thomas Jefferson was a cerebral politician—a sublime intellect. He was also an exemplar of great pragmatic wisdom, as shown by these anecdotes related by his most famous biographer.

• *Lesson:* Never relinquish your dreams. Jefferson was a young man when he first conceived of founding a university. But not until the eighth decade of his life was he able to realize this ambitious dream. Long after lesser men would have given up, and despite long years of frustration and affliction with heart disease and probably colon cancer, Jefferson pursued his goal with a zeal that belied his old age—and ultimately triumphed.

• *Lesson:* Respect your adversaries. Jefferson endured many fierce political rivalries. Yet no matter how contentious the disagreements, Jefferson always accorded his rivals the utmost respect. When he lost a political battle, he refused to hold a grudge, believing that doing so was simply a waste of time. And when he prevailed, he withstood the temptation to trumpet his victory. Instead, he sought to credit the contributions of his rivals and to help soothe their wounded egos.

When Jefferson became president, Alexander Hamilton—perhaps Jefferson's fiercest rival —wrote to a friend, *While I have not wanted him to become president, I must admit he is an honest man.* Jefferson respected Hamilton as well. At Monticello, two busts face each other across a room. One is of Jefferson, the other of Hamilton.

• *Lesson:* Think rationally, but heed your heart. As a political leader, Jefferson was widely admired for his cool logic and rationality. But he thought that the best decision-makers were those who consulted both their heads and their hearts. Jefferson knew, for instance, that the notion of rebelling against mighty England seemed foolhardy. But the patriots were so eager for revolution that breaking with England seemed not only possible, but inevitable.

• *Lesson:* Be tolerant of others' beliefs. Jefferson today has something of a reputation for being an opponent of religion. In fact, while his beliefs were unorthodox, he himself was deeply religious. He was also extremely tolerant of others' beliefs—so long as these beliefs were truly heartfelt. He was similarly tolerant of differing political beliefs—again, so long as they were heartfelt. Jefferson agreed with Learned Hand, the great judge, who wrote, *The spirit of liberty is the spirit which is not too sure that it is right.* Jefferson was confident enough to fight for his beliefs, yet sufficiently philosophical to know that no one has a monopoly on truth.

• *Lesson:* Be independent, but don't fear conformity. While Jefferson was known as an independent thinker, he was never different just for the sake of being so. For him, avoiding conformity was no less a trap than conformity itself. He refused to join what he called the "herd of independents."

• *Lesson:* Don't give in to self-pity. Upon his wife's death, a grieving Jefferson retired to Monticello, where for two years he allowed himself only minimal social contact. The reclusive life failed to ease his grief. Indeed, he grew so depressed that some family members believed him headed for a breakdown. Only upon the resumption of a busy social life was Jefferson finally able to shake his prolonged sadness. Never again did he allow himself or his daughters to withdraw from the world, no matter how great their difficulties.

• *Lesson:* Be a lifelong student. A gifted linguist, scientist and logician as well as an astute politician, Jefferson was, in the opinion of many, the smartest chief executive in history. While native intelligence accounted for much of his intellectual strength, his appetite for learning played a key role. Jefferson regularly read several books at once, and he insisted upon rereading his favorites. He mastered Latin, Greek, German and French in order to read important works in the original. Most important, he never stopped pursuing his education, tutoring himself wherever and whenever possible. Once, during a six-week European trip, Jefferson not only taught himself Spanish but also read the major Spanish classics.

Jefferson even compiled his own version of the Bible. Yet despite his focus on reading, Jefferson was no bookworm. Throughout his life he made it a point to listen to and learn from those around him, including children and servants as well as distinguished colleagues.

• *Lesson:* Do your share and much more, if necessary. While Jefferson is duly credited with founding the University of Virginia, his actual contribution to the school was far greater. He laid out the curriculum, hired the faculty and selected library books. Once, upon learning that an instructor hired to teach four languages knew only three, Jefferson insisted that the instructor be ready to teach all four languages the following year.

• *Lesson:* Live within your means. Jefferson the President was probably the finest fiscal manager in our nation's history. Yet a handful of unwise decisions kept Jefferson the private citizen on the brink of financial ruin.

He chose to build his beloved Monticello on land that while pretty, was steep and rocky and therefore poorly suited for cultivation. He continued to indulge his appetite for fine food, wine, books and other luxuries long after prudence dictated that he stop. He assumed he would inherit a fortune—yet all his father-in-law left was debts. And, a friend for whom Jefferson reluctantly co-signed a bank note defaulted on the loan. *Result:* Jefferson's heirs lost Monticello.

• *Lesson:* Always help others. Jefferson remained friendly and approachable throughout his long life, even as President. Once, President Jefferson and several companions were fording a deep stream on horseback. A man standing on the bank watched as several of the riders headed across the river, then stopped Jefferson and asked for a ride. Without a moment's hesitation, Jefferson hauled the man onto his horse and carried him across. Later, astonished witnesses asked the man if he had known his benefactor's identity. *No,* replied the man. *Then why did you pick him and not one of the others?* asked one of the witnesses. *Because,* said the man, *he looked like he'd be willing to help.*

• *Lesson:* Be efficient—but take time for important things. Even as President, Jefferson insisted upon answering his own mail. He thought people deserved the courtesy of a personal reply...and knew that writing strengthened both his mind and his connection to friends and constituents. Yet in other areas of his life, Jefferson emphasized efficiency. He organized his days along a very tight schedule. He invented a rotating book holder that let him read several books at once. He even placed his bed in an alcove between his bedroom and his office. When he awoke with an idea, he could jump straight out of bed and into his office.

Source: Alf J. Mapp, Jr., eminent scholar emeritus and Louis I. Jaffe professor of history at Old Dominion University, Norfolk, Virginia. Mapp is the author of two books on Jefferson, including *Thomas Jefferson: Passionate Pilgrim,* Madison Books, 4720 Boston Way, Lanham, Maryland 20706.

Lessons from George Orwell

With the collapse of the Soviet Union, it may seem that the world of the 1990s has at last gone beyond the message of George Orwell's writings, especially his two most famous novels, *1984* and *Animal Farm.*

But even after the fall of communism and the world's largest totalitarian government, Orwell still has something very important to teach us, as we try to create a global future for ourselves different from the past. His core ideas are timeless and account for his lasting popularity and tremendous readership—his books have been translated into 68 different languages. *Animal Farm* and *1984* together have sold more than 60 million copies.

• *Lesson:* Individuals are more important than systems. Orwell's political outlook had a much more personal element than is true of most political thinkers. Orwell's focus was on the human element. He was constantly aware of how the individual's rights and feelings would always rise above any theory, any plan, any system. That brought him under attack from the intellectuals, who also had a stake in the theories. *Their view:* Because Orwell was not theoretical enough, there was somehow a flaw in his thinking.

• *Lesson:* Every system has its flaw. Orwell taught us to be skeptical of theories and systems and of the "isms" that people are constantly trying to sell us—grand solutions to social or political problems.

These systems often fail because of the very thing Orwell pointed out...they don't take into account the individuality of real people. Orwell wanted us always to remember that every human system has its flaw. You can never create any theory or system that can accommodate all the thousands of different ways that people can try to outwit a theory or thwart it in some way. Any system that has no room for differences will be repressive.

• *Lesson:* Take into account the practical realities. Americans have always been pragmatic. That may be the reason why we've accomplished as much as we have. We suffer when we become too obsessed with theory. Certainly during the Cold War, I think we magnified communism. It turned out to be a paper tiger. The Russian economy has collapsed—and yet for years we held them up as great thinkers and warriors. We were wrong.

When Americans are pragmatic, when we roll up our shirtsleeves and look carefully at a situation, not from a theoretical point of view, but just simply asking how we can make something work, we do pretty well.

• *Lesson:* It's important—and possible—to be decent. This is a very old-fashioned concept, which intellectuals scoff at.

Orwell used the word *decent* over and over again.

He talked often about the decency of the common man. By that, he simply meant trying to do the right thing. He didn't mean taking a sanctimonious or self-righteous point of view, telling others that they should do this and shouldn't do that.

Orwell said that at the base of all society, of all civilization, there had to be some concept of what's right and what's wrong—that some things are good for us and some are bad. Our task is to know the difference.

Orwell lived what he preached...

Orwell lived what he preached. Usually people who preach moral values don't follow their own advice—and we are very wary of them.

When Orwell said that he thought it was important to fight for democracy against fascism, he followed through on it. Even before Hitler began to march across Europe, Orwell went to Spain to fight in the Spanish Civil War with the army that was trying to stop the fascist-supported forces of General Franco. He got a bullet through his throat for his troubles and almost died.

Throughout his life, Orwell sacrificed personal comfort and safety in order to stand up for the things that he believed were right.

The message he gives to the rest of us: Make up your own mind as to what you think is right or wrong and stand by it. Don't be afraid of losing or failing—*face failure.* Your life won't last forever that way, but it will be a life you can be proud of.

That's hard for us to follow, because most of us prefer living comfortably, without having to make sacrifices. Orwell believed that you establish in your own mind what you think is decent, and then you practice what you believe with integrity. You don't back down, you don't engage in hypocrisy.

Craftsman...

Anyone who has ever had to pick up a pen or sit down at a keyboard and write could learn something from Orwell. He was a skilled and melodious writer.

Many people who preach democratic values do so in a rather elitist prose style. Orwell tried very hard to make his writing accessible to a wide variety of people.

Trying to be very clear and very straightforward is extremely difficult. When you read Orwell's writing, it's deceptively easy on the surface. If you were to look at his manuscripts, however, you would see how difficult it was for him to achieve that surface simplicity.

He constantly revised. He was trying to get just the right word for just the right state of mind or feeling.

Many writers make the mistake of forgetting that there's someone on the other end who's going to read what they've written. If you're too easy on yourself while you write, you're probably going to make it harder on someone else.

Big Brotherism is still a threat...

Orwell wasn't describing just a Soviet-style system, or even a fascist-style system. He was describing totalitarianism in all its forms. Totalitarian tendencies can exist even in a society that on the surface seems free.

We all know that there are various Big Brothers—maybe also Big Sisters. There are people in our lives—in government, in business—who try to make us do things we don't want to do, to serve them rather than serve the interests of the whole. The methods those people employ on a smaller scale are no different from the ones that Orwell talks about in *1984*.

Big Brother in *1984* was probably American. Orwell divided the world into three huge zones of influence—Oceania, Eurasia and Eastasia. Winston Smith lives in Oceania—whose currency is the dollar. It is North and South America combined. This American empire stretches from the US across the Atlantic to Britain, which has now been renamed Airstrip One. The Americans use the island of Great Britain as a huge aircraft carrier. That isn't farfetched, because when the Cold War started we established huge air bases in Britain, which are still there. When we struck Libya, the planes took off from outside Oxford, England.

This illustrates how accurate Orwell was in his predictions of what would happen. He said that if the working-class people—the *proles*—ever woke up and realized that there are more of them than there are on the side of the Big Brother types, they would be able to pull the system down. If you think about it, that's exactly what happened. The people went out into the streets and pulled down the Berlin Wall with their hands. They surrounded the tanks in Moscow and protected Yeltsin and Gorbachev.

I don't think we'll ever be able to stop fighting to protect our privacy and individual rights, because someone's always out there trying to take them away from us—for their own interests or those of the larger group. As long as individual freedom and privacy are an issue, *1984* is still relevant.

It illustrates the way people allow—or can allow—those rights to be taken away, and then wake up and realize what they've lost. Orwell believed that with any institution, we need to be constantly vigilant about what we're giving up to authority.

If another relevancy is needed for *1984,* we can't overlook the fact that even though the Soviet Union has fallen there still are totalitarian states around the world.

China remains as bad as any Orwellian state. We've still got those kinds of societies to deal with.

Read Orwell...

Many of his other works, including *Down and Out in Paris and London* and *Homage to Catalonia,* and his other novels and essays, may be ordered through your local bookstore.

Source: Michael Shelden, PhD, professor of English at Indiana State University, and author of *Orwell: The Authorized Biography.* HarperCollins, 10 E. 53 St., New York 10022.

Life Lessons from Eleanor Roosevelt

While it is unclear what sort of national example Hillary Clinton will set, the life of Eleanor Roosevelt argues persuasively that the truly important ingredients for a fulfilling life are compassion, intelligence and grit.

As a beloved First Lady...as an indefatigable champion of the disadvantaged...and as someone who overcame numerous personal struggles, Eleanor Roosevelt has much to teach us...

• *Lesson:* Act upon your convictions and ignore your critics. Eleanor Roosevelt was never afraid to stand up for what she believed in. Over the years, she lent emotional and financial support to a number of unpopular causes, including housing for the poor, relief for Jewish refugees and civil rights for African-Americans. Reporters and political rivals belittled these efforts, arguing that women had no place in political affairs.

Yet no matter what was written or said or drawn about her—for she was a favorite target of political cartoonists—Eleanor Roosevelt never wavered in her commitment to what she believed to be right. "Every woman in public life, she once explained, needs to develop skin as tough as rhinoceros hide." Only one thing about these attacks bothered her—their effect on her friends and family. In 1940, she wrote to a friend, *I am sorry these attacks are causing my friends so much anguish, but I intend to keep on saying what has to be said.* This rare combination of courage and compassion is, I believe, Eleanor Roosevelt's greatest legacy.

• *Lesson:* Transform your misfortunes into compassion for others. Eleanor Roosevelt was born into the kind of family that is now called dysfunctional. When Eleanor was only four, her beautiful but emotionally remote mother told her young daughter, "You have no looks." Four years later, Eleanor's mother died. Eleanor's father— the younger brother of President Theodore Roosevelt—was an alcoholic given to irresponsible and occasionally bizarre behavior. He died when Eleanor was 10.

A child raised under such conditions might easily have grown up to be cold and withholding. But Eleanor matured into an unusually warm and generous woman, full of compassion for those on the margins of life. I was lucky enough to meet her in the late 1950s, and when we were introduced, she smiled, took my hand and looked me straight in the eye. She did the same with everyone she met because she truly loved all people. Wherever she went and whenever she spoke, people knew instantly that her view of the world included them.

• *Lesson:* Overcome your prejudices. Despite their long tradition of philanthropy, the family into which Eleanor Roosevelt was born was marked by intolerance and bigotry. Her early letters reveal her own strong dislike of some groups. Yet unlike other members of her family and her social class, Eleanor Roosevelt retained an open mind...and slowly but surely her attitudes began to change. She cultivated friendships with a large and disparate group of people, including several groups considered "off-limits" by other members of her class.

• *Lesson:* Be steadfast and loyal. The marriage of Eleanor and Franklin Roosevelt was not without its share of problems. Franklin Roosevelt was not always faithful to his wife, and she appears to have had affairs as well.

Yet even after their ardor had cooled, the Roosevelts continued to honor and respect one another. Franklin continually involved Eleanor in his work, and she continued to give full support to his political career. They knew their union was imperfect, but their mutual respect and admiration remained for both of them a source of great emotional strength.

• *Lesson:* Help others as directly as possible. For generations, Eleanor Roosevelt's family had devoted itself to philanthropic and charitable work. Her grandfather helped found both the Children's Aid Society and the Museum of Natural History. So it came as no surprise when, as a young woman, Eleanor Roosevelt took up charity work.

But instead of doing something "safe," such as fund-raising, she chose to lend a hand directly, by working in a settlement house on Manhattan's Lower East Side. This decision horrified her family, who feared she was exposing herself to disease and hardship. But Eleanor continued to work in the settlement house for some time, and she even made it a point to take her suitor Franklin to see the conditions under which poor Americans were forced to live. Eleanor's commitment to the poor touched not only her life and the lives of those she helped, but also helped develop the nascent political policies of a future president.

• *Lesson:* Be proud, but modest. Even after years as a beloved First Lady, Eleanor Roosevelt remained humble and unassuming. Once, upon arriving at an airport, she spied a red carpet and school band...and noted there must be someone important on board, not considering that the display might be for her.

Source: Blanche Wiesen Cook, PhD, professor of history and women's studies at John Jay College and the Graduate Center of the City University of New York. She is vice president for research at the American Historical Association and the author of *Eleanor Roosevelt: Volume One, 1884–1933*. Viking Penguin, 375 Hudson St., New York 10014.

Lessons in Life from Harry Truman

When Harry Truman became President of the United States, few people anywhere in the world expected much of him. But just a few years later, Winston Churchill was calling him the man who saved Western civilization.

Truman's life shows how a seemingly average man was able to change the nation...and the world.

He got to the White House without the help of inherited wealth, personal glamour, influential family connections or higher education. Yet he was the President who...

...put a stop to traditional American isolationism.

...introduced the strategy of containment of the Soviet Union.

...pushed through the Marshall Plan to rebuild Western Europe.

...ended segregation in the US armed forces and the federal Civil Service.

His achievements teach us a series of traditional lessons in life that have been forgotten by many today.

• Hard work. Truman's father, an unsuccessful businessman who eventually returned to farming, taught young Harry how to work hard. And for his whole life, Truman put all he had into everything he did, rising early and working hard well into the night.

When serving in the Senate, he arrived so early that he became the first senator ever issued a key to the building. He learned so much about World War II defense programs that his Committee on War Production inspired major improvements in defense industries, saved millions of taxpayer dollars and gave him a national reputation that helped him become Vice President.

When he suddenly became President, many people didn't think that he could fill Roosevelt's shoes...but when they saw how he tackled the job, they quickly changed their minds.

Lesson: If you really want to move up, be prepared to buckle down.

•Persistence. Before he entered politics, Truman had a long record of failure. As a young man working on the barely profitable family farm, he made unsuccessful efforts to become a speculator in land...in zinc mines... in oil leases ...and he was a 38-year-old bankrupt haberdasher when he first ran for political office. But he never let fear of failure discourage him.

•When Tom Pendergast, the Kansas City Democratic boss and Truman's political mentor, was convicted on corruption charges, Truman faced an almost impossible race for his second Senate term against the man who sent Pendergast to jail. But he persevered...and won an upset victory.

•In the famous 1948 Presidential race against Thomas E. Dewey, Truman's friends...advisers ...all the pundits...were sure he couldn't win. The only man who believed he could was Truman himself. He put on such a gallant fight that millions of people voted for him even though they expected him to lose...and he pulled off the most famous upset victory in US political history.

Lesson: Don't think of yourself as a failure—despite temporary setbacks...you can bounce back to greater heights than before.

•Education. Truman had only a high school education. But he never stopped learning.

•In World War I, he was able to compete successfully in math-intensive artillery school... then was assigned to teach math and engineering to other officers, graduates of top colleges.

•Truman was a voracious reader, and his knowledge of history gave him a perspective on the nation's problems extending beyond the next election. The containment policy introduced by Truman contributed to the eventual collapse of world communism 45 years later.

Lesson: The worth of your education isn't measured by what school you went to or how long you stayed there...it's whether you keep thinking after you leave.

•Loyalty. No "kiss-and-tell" memoirs were written by people close to Truman. Unlike many later Presidents, he inspired lasting loyalty...not fear...in those who worked for him.

•During World War I, Truman commanded 200-odd tough, undisciplined soldiers. He used tough discipline to whip them into a crack artillery battery...but looked after their welfare like a father. Long after the war, many of his "boys" volunteered for his campaigns... and they marched in his inaugural parade.

•When Kansas City political boss Tom Pendergast died in disgrace after serving his jail term, shunned by all, newly inaugurated Vice President Truman flew to Kansas City to honor the memory of his first political supporter.

Lesson: If you want others to be loyal to you, show loyalty to them.

•Family values. Harry Truman really practiced what today's politicians preach when they invoke traditional family values. He relied on his family for emotional support...and his family could rely on him.

•As a 21-year-old in 1905, he left a promising position with a Kansas City bank when his father needed him to work on the family farm. Without complaint, he came immediately and stayed for 12 years. He worked long hours at unpleasant and often menial tasks, until World War I.

•He fell in love with Bess Wallace as a young man in Sunday school, but couldn't persuade her to marry him until he was 33 years old. After their marriage, because Bess was attached to her mother, the couple moved into the Wallace home. And even when he moved to the White House, his mother-in-law came along.

Lesson: Strong family ties not only provide great support...but also require personal sacrifices.

•Self reliance. The famous sign on Truman's desk said "The Buck Stops Here"...and it was true. He dug deeply into every subject that concerned him and was never afraid to take advice, but when the time came to decide, he made the decision himself.

•Before British rule over Palestine ended in 1948, the State Department advised Truman very strongly that the US should not support establishment of a fragile, tiny, new Jewish state surrounded by violently hostile Arab countries. Truman agonized over the issue for months as it was developing. Then he made his decision...and recognized the State of Israel just 11 minutes after it was proclaimed.

•During the Korean War, General Douglas MacArthur carried out a brilliant counterattack, driving the North Koreans back behind their original lines. But MacArthur disregarded orders to change his strategy following massive Chinese involvement in the war...so Truman dismissed him, in spite of the public storm it would provoke because of the General's fame.

•Truman came from a family very sympathetic to the Confederate side in the Civil War, and he was uneasy about social integration between the races. But he knew he was President of all the people, and he fought vigorously in favor of civil rights...seriously splitting the Democratic party in an election year.

Lesson: Always listen to what the experts have to say. But you're the one who must make the decision, so don't be afraid to use your own judgment.

Bottom line...

Harry Truman grew up 100 years ago. He lived by the values he learned then...hard work, persistence, self-reliance, loyalty to family, friends and nation. Those 19th-century values aren't fashionable today. But as the 21st century approaches, they still have much to offer to individuals...and nations.

Source: Irwin Unger, PhD, professor of history at New York University and Pulitzer Prize-winning author of six books on modern American history.

Lessons in Life from Henny Youngman

Internationally famous comedian Henny Youngman is close to 90 and still as funny as ever. Moreover he continues to be as active on the comedy circuit as he's been all his life. *Bottom Line/ Personal* found him at his "office"—a VIP table at the Friar's Club in New York, complete with his own telephone—and asked him for the secrets of his long-lived success. *Here's what he had to tell us...*

•Find out what you want to do—and learn all about that business. Few people take the time to find what they are really good at. And ...they're so busy working and paying the family bills that they don't take the time to think and grow.

In my case, none of the adults around me recognized what I was really good at when I was a kid. In fact, I was thrown out of my classes because I was funny—and therefore disruptive to the class.

Now, you may ask yourself—I certainly have—why couldn't the teachers have laughed at me? Why couldn't they have figured out that my being funny was a talent, not a menace? Why didn't they tell my parents, "This kid is funny. Let's develop that." Instead, they sent me out of class because I made everybody laugh.

•Your greatest talent may be something that's right under your nose, but you don't see it. Your real talent may be the very thing everybody complains about. It could also be a talent for something no one around you recognizes as a way to make a living. When I was a kid, I never even dreamed that you could make a living being a comedian. My mother wanted me to be the violinist, Jascha Heifetz—only I couldn't, because Jascha Heifetz was Jascha Heifetz already.

Once, we were both on the *Ed Sullivan Show,* and afterwards I took his violin by mistake. It was a Stradivarius, worth big, big dollars—and all the police were out looking for me. That's the closest I ever came to being Jascha Heifetz. I still play the violin—badly—in all my shows. It's a great prop.

•Get experience. Whatever you're selling, whatever you're doing, you've got to have something to talk about. You've got to have merchandise to put on the shelf.

If you're going to be successful, you have to know what you're doing. You can't blame everything on luck. There's no such thing as luck, all by itself. Luck is where you find it—but you have to find it. Meanwhile, get as much experience as you can, so you'll be ready for luck when you run into it.

I was lucky at certain points along the way. I started out as a musician—I had a band. People came in late—and I made fun of them, and everybody laughed. I was funny.

One night the boss said, "The emcee didn't show up, Henny. I have a big banquet here. Get on and tell your jokes. Save my life." I was so good that I let the band go—and I became a comic.

•Be persistent. If you keep going, you will eventually run into what you really want to do. There's always somebody that needs you somewhere. You can't give up easily.

In my own case, I didn't get discouraged because I didn't have the gift to become a major violinist—or a band leader. My family and friends certainly lived through some difficult times listening to me practice. I used what I had and when a different opportunity came along, I was open to it.

•*Nem de Gelt*—get the money. It has many layers of meaning. The most obvious is, don't believe all the baloney that people tell you when they're describing what they're going to do for you soon. If there's no money that comes with it, it isn't real.

There's a modern version of this that says, *Wait until the check is in your hands.* But, let me tell you, that's not good enough. Back in the 1930s, during the Great Depression, I learned a lot of lessons that are useful to us all today too: A check can bounce...the money counts...you've got to pay the rent...get whatever you can get, with reason...and keep going until somebody finally gives you what you want.

•Don't let your pride get in your way. About half a century ago, I was on the *Kate Smith Show,* earning a thousand dollars a week. In the 1930s, a thousand dollars a week was a small fortune! I did that for two years before I decided to leave. I thought I would be able to ask for the same amount from other clients. I sat around for weeks with no takers.

Finally, one night at Lindy's restaurant, a friend who had heard me moaning and complaining about how tough times were told me I had to decide whether I wanted to keep my pride and starve to death in grand style...or whether I was willing to swallow my pride and work for what people were willing to pay.

It didn't take long to make that decision. I got a job at $350 per week working in a club owned by Billy Rose. And just a short time later I got another job for $750 a week, that I could hold at the same time. So by working for what people were willing to pay, I ended up making what I wanted to after all!

•If you like what you're doing, keep doing it. If you've got something good going—and you enjoy it, and you're in demand, and you're healthy enough to do it—why retire? I'm against the practice of retiring people at the age of 65. I really enjoy what I do—putting on my show...making the deals.

•*Mensh tracht, Gott lacht.* A Yiddish proverb, but it's not a Yiddish lesson—it's a lesson about life. It says: *Man plans, God laughs.*

In other words, life is an accident. Plan ahead as much as you want...plot out your career moves as though it were an arithmetic problem if you enjoy doing that sort of thing. Fate may have something else in mind. It might be great, it might be terrible, but hang on—see how it turns out.

I'm close to 90, and I still don't know why all these wonderful things happened. It's been like a dream. Sometimes I wonder what would have happened if I had done things differently—if I had been a little bit better student, or a better fiddle player. But if I had, I wouldn't have had this fascinating life in show business.

The best I could wish for you is—when you get to be my age—you should be so active...so involved...and so happy.

Source: Henny Youngman, author of *Take My Life, Please!* William Morrow and Company, 1350 Avenue of the Americas, New York 10019.

From David Brown: Lessons in Living Life To its Very Fullest

When David Brown was a young man, the number-one best seller was *Life Begins at Forty,* by Walter B. Pitkin.

Today, that view is outmoded...it's *puberty* that begins at 40. Life doesn't get better until after 50...and it gets even better later on, Brown says in his new book, *The Rest of Your*

Life is the Best of Your Life: David Brown's Guide to Growing Gray (Disgracefully).

The years between 65 and 75 have been the best years of his life...best for work, best for making money, best for making love.

While he admits that he had a lot of fun before 50—as his friend Alan J. Lerner put it, he's glad *he's not young anymore.* Youth is too fragile, too easily intimidated, unsure of itself.

At 75, David Brown likes himself, and now he says and does what he wants—without worrying much about what others may think. The sense of freedom one can have after passing 50 is exhilarating.

Simple rules for staying young...

•Don't retire. Brown intends to work until his death. What keeps him going is his involvement in work. The work is the machine, the motive.

Almost everybody he knows who feels young, vital and sexy—no matter what his/her age—is working. He is certain that if he stopped working and started getting up late, his machine would slow down...and stop.

With his friends Richard and Lili Zanuck, David Brown produced the movie *Cocoon.* They discovered that the older actors they selected to play retirees—Hume Cronyn, Jessica Tandy, Jack Gilford, Maureen Stapleton, Don Ameche, Gwen Verdon—looked too young to play their own ages. They had to be aged with makeup and taught to limp and bend over. They had kept on working and never had time to grow old!

How powerfully retirement can affect your health was shown by a recent study of airline pilots. When they retired at age 55, this group of pilots was in certifiably good health. At the time Brown wrote his book—only a few years later—their mortality rate was higher than that of the general public.

Many people hate their work, he observes, and can't wait for "the machine to stop." But if you retire from one thing, you can always go on and do something you really love.

•Start planning your second career while you're in your first one. Brown believes that when you get a job, you should start looking for the next one—or for the next career—however covertly you do it. If you're 35, prepare to deal with getting fired when you're 55 or 60. If you don't get fired, the planning won't hurt you. But you must start thinking creatively while there's time. Identify what interests you, and what you can develop on the outside as an independent person.

It's very tough for people who work in companies to do this because they've been programmed to depend upon the system. They come to work knowing they'll be required to do certain tasks that have been laid down for them.

But so many companies now are in a desperate state. Those that can't pay their bills pare down their work forces. The economists are saying that most of those who are being let go will not be rehired. What is going on, in Brown's opinion, is not a temporary shrinkage. It's a basic restructuring. So always keep your eye on your options 10 or 20 years down the road.

•Be prepared to start over. What can you do if you are a company man who didn't want to stop working—but got retired?

Brown says he would cut his standard of living, possibly by moving to a much less costly place. Next, he would look around to see what services were needed. Is a messenger service required? Is there something else that isn't being provided in the community?

Then he would go and try to raise money... a modest amount of capital. In other words, he would try to get someone else interested in staking him to a business, after he had done some careful research.

When Brown and Richard Zanuck founded their own movie-production company—after being thrown out of executive posts that they thought they had for life—they decided that never again would they let their lives be controlled by others. But—they weren't certain that they would succeed on their own.

Twice in his fifties, Brown was jobless, a former top executive reduced to collecting unemployment insurance and sending out résumés. What saved him was his refusal to face facts.

If he had held onto his old job, Brown, as an over-65 employee, would have had to retire long ago. Launching out on his own was the best thing that ever happened to him, he feels.

•Worship your body. Even if your body doesn't look as good to you as it did in your twenties, his best advice is to take good care of your body. You won't get far without it. This means paying attention to what you eat and drink, to how much exercise you get, and to the right kind of medical care.

An old friend of his, a gerontologist at Rockefeller University, says that the best recipe for a long, healthy life is to eat half of what you do now...exercise regularly...and make love every day.

Watching your weight is just common sense, and it may have life-extending virtues, too. Experiments at Cornell University and UCLA have shown that underfed mice lived longer than mice who were fed as much as they wanted. Most of the men and women he knows who have reached the age of 80 or more are thin. But don't get too thin, he cautions. There's no advantage to being emaciated. Moderation in all things is a good rule.

The same goes for exercise. There's no medical evidence that hard exercise extends life, and some doctors believe it shortens it. On the other hand, the authors of *Total Fitness in Thirty Minutes a Week* say 10 minutes of peak effort every day gives you 80% of the cardiovascular conditioning benefits of hours of exercise.

About medical care: Remember, doctors aren't gods. If you get a diagnosis that is ominous, or if your doctor wants to do a little fancy tailoring on your interior, get a second opinion. And maybe a third.

One phenomenally successful producer, David Geffen, dropped out of the entertainment business for three years, after being told he was dying of cancer. He wasn't. The diagnosis was wrong.

Actress Peggy Cass came out of surgery to discover that the wrong knee had been operated on.

You can save yourself a lot of worry by being your own medical consultant. Pay attention to how your body feels and what it needs. Make sure you understand and agree with any medical treatment that's suggested.

Finally, there's the question of drinking. As early as your late forties you will notice a decrease in your ability to consume alcohol. Brown has found that even a small amount—a few drinks—can cause his voice to slur and his mind to fog...even though he feels as if he is sharper than ever.

Drinking can also release sudden and inexplicable combativeness, repressed aggressions and paranoia. Brown came closest to wrecking his marriage and friendships while drinking, even drinking moderately. Avoid alcoholic beverages entirely when there is pressure or tension...or when you're tired.

•Keep your friends—including friends of the opposite sex. People who stay young all their lives never stop being interested in the opposite sex. There is hardly a day or an hour when Brown is not aware of the women around him. Whether you're married or single, friends of the opposite sex can be a joy and a rejuvenation.

Brown says his wife, *Cosmopolitan's* pioneering editor, Helen Gurley Brown, cautions older men to beware of women who are too young. Women closer to your own age understand life better—and they are much more interesting than younger women. And Brown agrees.

Source: David Brown, producer of *The Sting, Jaws, Cocoon* and other successful films. He is the author of *The Rest of Your Life is the Best of Your Life: David Brown's Guide to Growing Gray (Disgracefully),* Barricade Books, 1530 Palisade Ave., Fort Lee, New Jersey 07024.

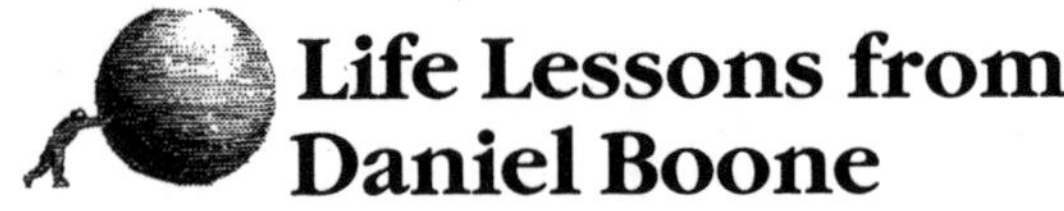

Life Lessons from Daniel Boone

Daniel Boone (1734-1820) was the most famous of the heroic pioneers who led the conquest of the American frontier. He lived in a long-gone era, the time of the birth of the United States, when most of America was still an untamed wilderness. But his life can teach us much about how to approach the challenges we face today.

A long and active life...

Boone lived until age 86 at a time when the average life expectancy was far less than it is now...but he never worried about security. Each time civilization caught up with his family, he moved them further west to settle in a new wilderness, beginning again from scratch.

As a hunter and explorer, he survived the dangers of wild animals and exposure to the elements. As a militia officer in numerous campaigns, he survived battles and sieges...led a daring rescue of his daughter from hostile Indians...for several months during the War of Independence was himself held captive.

He always retained his enthusiasm for an active life. As Boone grew older, he suffered severe rheumatism, the legacy of years spent outdoors in cold and wet conditions...but never stopped hunting, his life-long passion.

Boonestory: When Boone could no longer carry his gun, he went on hunting trips with his wife...she carried the gun. When he became too weak to pursue large animals, he set traps for beaver...at times only able to do that when he was carried.

• *Lesson:* Longevity is tied to limitless enthusiasm and activity.

Between two cultures...

Boone was born to a Quaker family in Pennsylvania. Although he was not a churchgoing man in his adult life, he never lost his attachment to the Quaker values of peace and tolerance.

The Indians taught Boone how to survive in the forest, track animals and live off the land. They taught him enough woodsmanship to make him the premier explorer of his time... the man who marked and laid out the Wilderness Trail to Kentucky, which was later traveled by more than 200,000 emigrants.

Nevertheless, Boone fought alongside his countrymen to wrest control of the land from the Indians...but unlike many Americans, he appreciated the Indian way of life and made friends among them.

Boonestory: During the American Revolution, Shawnee warriors, supported by the British, captured Captain Boone and a group of fellow settlers. Boone's diplomatic skills prevented a massacre of his outnumbered men, and Blackfish, the Shawnee chief, adopted Boone as his own son.

Boone escaped and returned to lead the defense of Boonesborough, the Kentucky settlement he had founded a number of years before. He almost succeeded in forging an equitable peace treaty with Blackfish, but not before the Indians attacked the settlement.

After the war, other men with less tolerant attitudes charged Captain Boone with treason during his captivity, and he was court-martialed by the Kentucky militia. He was not only acquitted...but was promoted to Major.

In his old age, Boone renewed his friendship with his old Indian foes and stated: "I am very sorry to say that I ever killed any Indians, for they have always been kinder to me than the whites."

• *Lesson:* It is possible to accept the worth of other cultures without abandoning your own.

Pioneer women...

The frontier was not settled by men alone... while they were exploring, hunting or warring, their wives had to run the household and often singlehandedly raise their large families.

Daniel Boone and his wife Rebecca were married for 56 years...had 10 children...and brought up six orphaned cousins, too. Boone was away for months...sometimes years...at a time, and Rebecca was left in charge in both times of peace and war.

Boonestory: Once, with the Indians on the warpath and Boone away with the militia, Rebecca and the children left their farm to join others who had taken refuge in a small fort. One day, the women noticed that the men assigned to defend the fort were loafing around outside.

Rebecca, her two oldest daughters and some other wives armed themselves, crept out of the fort, fired a fusillade, ran back inside the fort and bolted the gates. The men locked outside ran around in a state of panic while the women laughed. Later, Boone was put in charge of the fort's defenses, and he improved discipline there.

• *Lesson:* Marriage is an enterprise that succeeds when husbands and wives are equal partners.

Commerce and frontier values...

In his lifetime, Daniel Boone acquired thousands of acres of land...some by purchase, some in exchange for services, and some by government grants. He ended up with almost none of it because his strong ethical values did not fit in the unscrupulous world of commerce that replaced the fair frontier he had known.

As the man who knew the land best, Boone chose and surveyed many tracts of land for others and for himself. But his technical surveying skills did not match the questionable business practices and sharp legal stratagems used by the speculators who followed the pioneers, and he —and those who used his services—lost their lands.

His strong ethical principles compelled him to pay back all his debts...so he lost even more land.

In his old age, he petitioned the federal government to recognize his right to land he had been granted by the Spanish before Louisiana was acquired by the US...and his petition was rejected.

Boonestory: One insolent trickster was Gilbert Imlay, who promised to pay Boone for 10,000 acres of excellent land in Kentucky. After Boone assigned him the rights to the property, Imlay ran off to England without paying...but first signed over the land to a third party. Ironically, Imlay later wrote a book praising Boone and inspired Lord Byron to include a tribute to "General Boone, backwoodsman of Kentucky" in his famous epic poem, *Don Juan.*

• *Lesson:* Encounters with lawyers and speculators can be more brutal than those with wild animals.

Accepting life...

Daniel Boone had a long life, but a hard one. He had financial problems that left him in constant debt...frequent injuries—and also chronic pain from his exposure to the elements...two sons killed by Indians and three daughters who died in their 30s. But he did not despair of life.

Boonestory: A popular folk tale about Boone describes an occasion when he and his brother, Squire, are camped on the riverbank, trapped in a heavy rain and huddling together under a horse blanket. Squire does not understand how Daniel is able to take it without complaining.

When the rain ends, they leave and soon discover nearby a camp recently abandoned by Indians. Daniel tells Squire, "What fretted you so much was really the means of Providence for our salvation. But for the storm, we should have run into the very jaws of our enemies."

• *Lesson:* Don't be quick to complain. Sometimes a new situation can be more trouble than it's worth.

Source: John Mack Faragher, professor of history at Mount Holyoke College. He is the author of *Daniel Boone: The Life and Legend of an American Pioneer,* Henry Holt and Co., 115 W. 18 St., New York 10011.

2 Secrets of Success

How to Avoid the Most Common Obstacles To Success...Love... Happiness

Life is often difficult enough without us standing in our own way, blocking our path to career success, satisfying relationships and the attainment of our personal goals. Yet many of us exhibit particular behaviors and cling to particular beliefs that keep us from getting precisely what we want out of life. *Seven most common obstacles...*

1. Poor time management.

The ineffective time manager doesn't know how to prioritize his/her time. He will often come late for meetings or personal appointments and will hand in things past their deadlines. That's not because he's a procrastinator but because he just doesn't have a realistic feel for how much time things take.

Other possibilities: Job dissatisfaction...or passive-aggressive behavior, which in this case means trying to control events by showing up late and holding up progress. *Solutions...*

•Plan activities the night before so you can prepare for what needs to be done.

•Get a time-and-project organizer to help you anticipate and plan for future activities.

•Look at your watch frequently so you can begin to gauge where your time-management skills are off.

•Build in down time to unwind as well as help you plan future work time better.

2. Disorganization.

People who have a disorganization problem don't know how to control the paper on their desks and can't distinguish between important material and junk.

They feel an irrational discomfort about getting rid of things and have an irrational need to read and know everything. They are forever promising themselves that someday they'll get to those newspapers and magazines, but they never do...and the mess accumulates and swallows them up.

Solution: Stop being a collector. Start prioritizing and acting on everything that comes across your desk or into your home. Toss out all unnecessary papers, and file those you need. The key is to act *immediately.*

3. Unassertiveness.

Unassertive people have trouble saying no to requests...and they don't express annoyance because they fear negative evaluations or being disliked. If they're angry at someone, rather than express their anger directly they will engage in passive-aggressive behavior, such as moodiness or lateness, which is particularly destructive on the job.

Solutions...

• Examine the values with which you were raised. *Example:* Did you grow up believing that being assertive meant being impolite...or that it's wrong to express anger?

• Learn the necessary social and career skills. Do you know the best ways to start a conversation...state your opinions...negotiate a deal?

• Learn to overcome your fear of criticism or rejection. *Helpful:* With a friend, rehearse a difficult situation and deliberately respond differently from the way you naturally would. See how it feels to ask for that raise—while maintaining eye contact and without being apologetic. If a friend isn't available, use a tape recorder and replay your replies.

4. "Awfulizing".

The awfulizer has a fertile catastrophic imagination and always assumes the worst will happen. These anxious, fearful people constantly ask themselves "what if" questions: "What if I don't get the job?"..."What if he/she notices that I'm balding?"

Solutions...

• Shift the degree of intolerability in your mind and recognize that while there may be things in life that are uncomfortable, there's very little that people can't endure.

• Examine the probabilities. In any given situation, ask yourself, "What are the actual chances that the worst will occur?" If you begin to do this regularly, you'll realize the unlikelihood of the horrible outcome you're anticipating.

• Actively challenge your beliefs. If you catch yourself engaging in "what if?" thinking, write down any evidence you have that you won't be able to handle the upcoming situation. This will help you see how silly your fears are.

• Recall past successes. Remind yourself that whatever is coming up is simply a variation on something you've already done.

5. Perfectionism.

Perfectionists can't stand being viewed as wrong or inadequate in any way. And because the perfectionist believes he must do everything perfectly, it can lead to procrastination out of fear of doing an imperfect job.

Solutions...

• Accept the reality that all humans are fallible. We're constantly making mistakes—it's part of our nature.

• Deliberately do some things imperfectly... to prove to yourself that you'll survive.

Example: I have one client who's a perfectionist when it comes to her dressing—she wastes a tremendous amount of time changing clothes, matching accessories and running home from wherever she is if she spots a run in her pantyhose. As an exercise, I've had her deliberately go to work with a run in her pantyhose or with mismatched shoes and purse.

Until you've actually risked being imperfect, you won't make those fundamental philosophical changes crucial to overcoming the problem.

6. Demandingness.

This is the irrational belief that you always deserve to be treated right. Every problem in life is blamed on unfair people or an unfair world. These men and women feel that they're special somehow and entitled to a break because they've always been a good spouse, parent, child, or employee.

Solutions...

• Understand that, in reality, the world operates quite independently from what you want or demand.

Example: A woman discovers that her husband has been philandering. She's devastated because she feels she was such a good, self-sacrificing wife for years. *How could he do this to me?* she asks. That question presupposes that being a good wife will guarantee protection from anything hurtful a husband can do ...but the reality is quite different.

• Look at the big picture. The economy is bad and that's why nobody in your office—not even you—got a raise last year.

• Eliminate the words *should, ought* and *must* from your vocabulary. These are words that set up absolutist thinking. You'll be a lot happier once you start "desiring" and "preferring" things rather than "demanding" and "requiring" them.

7. *Discomfort anxiety.*

These people just can't bear hassles. Anything that disrupts the smooth running of their day is perceived as insurmountable. They can't stand to hear bad news or confront somebody on a difficult issue. So they regularly practice "discomfort dodging"—palming off unpleasant tasks onto others or avoiding the problems altogether in the hope they'll just go away.

Example: An executive flips through her stack of phone messages when she gets to work in the morning and routinely gives all the unpleasant ones to her secretary to handle...or stashes them permanently at the bottom of the pile.

Solution: Try systematic desensitization, the treatment of choice for people who suffer from discomfort anxiety. First, practice relaxing using any common relaxation skill you feel comfortable with—tensing and relaxing the muscles, etc.

Then, while you're completely relaxed, practice "seeing" yourself doing whatever unpleasant activities you regularly avoid. If done often enough, the relaxation will neutralize the anxiety, and in time you should be able to carry out the task in real life.

Source: Psychologist Barry Lubetkin, PhD, director of the Institute for Behavior Therapy in New York. His most recent book is *Why Do I Need You to Love Me in Order to Like Myself?,* Longmeadow Press, 201 High Ridge Rd., Stamford, CT 06904.

Key to Effectiveness: Keep Alert!

In today's 24-hour world, workers are given extensive training, equipped with very reliable automated machinery and provided with comfortable surroundings. But that doesn't guarantee effective performance around the clock.

Bizarre example: In the cockpit of a Boeing 707 en route to Los Angeles, the entire crew fell asleep while the autopilot continued to fly the plane westward...far over the Pacific Ocean. When air traffic controllers on the ground noticed the wayward plane, their verbal inquiries went unanswered. The desperate controllers averted disaster when they managed to wake up the crew by triggering loud chimes in the cockpit.

Alertness is key to effective performance...

That near-disaster was caused by the failure of one critical human factor—*alertness.* Like so many systems today, the airplane was designed to perform so well automatically that it was hard for the pilots to remain alert.

But alertness is vital for people to perform effectively. Only in that state are people fully aware of their surroundings...able to think clearly...consider all options...make sensible decisions.

Physiological basis...

To physiologists, alertness represents a desirable state of balance between two human nervous systems.

One of these nervous systems—*the sympathetic nervous system*—automatically triggers the fight-or-flight response...heart pounding... blood pressure rising...pupils dilating...hair standing on end.

It represents a peak of alertness vital for dealing with emergency situations...but it usually can't be sustained for too long.

Minimum alertness occurs when the body is highly relaxed...under control of the *parasympathetic nervous system.* Consider someone dozing by the fire after a heavy meal...heart beating slowly...blood pressure dropping... pupils constricting. It is essential for the body and mind to rest sometimes...but a state of total relaxation is bad news if you're supposed to be working...studying...even observing.

In a state of alertness, the brain is engaged and ready to react appropriately to evolving situations. But we're often not alert when we need to be because our external environment or our internal state—or a combination of both—work to disengage our brain.

Nine switches of alertness...

Research into the physiology of alertness has shown there are nine switches that control alertness. We can improve our alertness by learning what they are and how to switch them on or off. *They are:*

1. Sense of danger, interest or opportunity. Nothing switches us faster from drowsiness to alertness than awareness of imminent danger. The brain can also be awakened in a less extreme way by other forms of stimulation.

Helpful: If you're in a meeting about a subject that's not too exciting and feel yourself dozing off, try to stimulate yourself. Ask questions...make comments...take notes...bring others into the discussion.

2. Muscular activity. Vigorous exercise can improve alertness for an hour or more. Many people performing tasks where alertness is vital cannot move around—pilots, drivers, nuclear-plant operators. But they can find other types of muscular activity to help keep them alert.

Helpful: Stretch in place...chew gum...take periodic breaks to walk around.

3. Time of day on the biological clock. Humans have their own biological clock that tells when it's time to wake and to sleep. If you're on shift work or traveling between different time zones, it's not easy to adjust your built-in clock to match the environment.

Helpful: If you're running a meeting with people from all over the country or the world, be aware of their biological clocks. Try to schedule a compromise time that helps as many as possible stay awake. Remember that people feel drowsy after lunch and are most alert when their body tells them it's mid-morning or late afternoon.

4. Sleep bank balance. Alertness depends on how long it is since we last slept. It is possible to restore the balance in our sleep bank by a good single night's sleep or by a number of brief naps at strategic intervals.

Interesting: A short nap of 10–15 minutes provides more benefit than one of 30–40 minutes, which leaves you drowsy. Research has shown that people can work 22 hours a day for extended periods if they get a 20-minute nap every four hours.

5. Ingested nutrients and chemicals. Stimulation by food, drink or chemicals can improve our alertness. In moderation, it may be sensible, but it's often a poor way to cope. Two or three cups of coffee are fine to help you stay awake, but any more than that stays in the system and makes it hard to sleep after work, and it makes you more tired the next day. Similarly, people who pop too many stay-awake pills develop insomnia and then become dependent on sleeping pills.

Helpful: A 10-minute coffee break. But if you have the choice, a 10-minute nap is better.

6. Environmental light. Bright light keeps people alert, but to be truly effective, it must be about the level of natural light at dawn—about the level of a hospital operating room, which is twice as bright as a well-lit office. This level of light doesn't just help you see well, it stimulates the brain. Today, exploiting light for alertness is on the technological frontier.

7. Environmental temperature and humidity. We all know that a cold shower wakes us up...a warm bath puts us to sleep...and that when driving on a boring highway, one of the best ways to wake up is to open the window and get a blast of cold air.

8. Environmental sound. The rolling surf at the beach or the smooth rushing of a mountain stream can lull us to sleep. These are examples of "white noise" that is also generated by machines that people use to help them go to sleep...and resembles the background noise produced by much equipment found in industrial control rooms where operators are expected to stay awake at night.

Helpful: In control rooms, try to use irregular sources of sound that vary in pitch and intensity...allow workers to listen to stimulating radio programs when possible.

9. Environmental aroma. Although this switch has not been scientifically investigated as much as the other eight switches, there are intriguing reports that aromas like peppermint may help alertness.

With an awareness of how these nine switches work, you can improve your own alertness. By learning to put them in the "off" position, you can learn how to relax better, as well.

Source: Martin Moore-Ede, MD, PhD, associate professor of physiology at Harvard Medical School, director of the Institute for Circadian Physiology. He is the founder and CEO of Circadian Technologies, consultants to industry worldwide on enhancing alertness in the workplace and author of *The Twenty-Four-Hour Society: Understanding Human Limits in a World that Never Stops*, Addison-Wesley, Jacob Way, Reading, MA 01867.

Positive Reappraisal

Reformulate negative thoughts through positive reappraisal. If you find yourself thinking, "I can't do this," change it to, "This will be a challenge, but I'll go at it—one step at a time." Instead of a negative self-message, this gives you one of being innovative and capable. Instead of "I don't want to get out of bed," say, "I'll feel better after a warm shower." The self-message is that you can help yourself. *Key:* Recognizing negative thoughts so you can rethink them.

Source: *Living with Rheumatoid Arthritis*, by Tammi Shlotzhauer, MD, clinical associate professor of medicine, Rochester Medical Center, Rochester, NY. The Johns Hopkins University Press, 2715 N. Charles St., Baltimore 21218.

Mastery...Quick-Fix Thinking...and Us

We live in a time of instant gratification. We're told to take this pill for fast relief, or go on that quick weight-loss diet or buy a lottery ticket and become a millionaire overnight. Yet our addiction to quick-fix thinking is leading us to social and personal disaster.

George Leonard, a pioneer in work to develop the human potential, is working now to push us all to abandon our continuing search for quick results...and return to a more natural rhythm of life. He is finding more and more that fulfillment comes through what he calls *mastery,* the process of savoring the doing. *We asked him more about his views...*

What do you mean by a natural rhythm of life?

Studies of learning curves show us that in the course of learning anything, your knowledge increases a little...then plateaus for a while, then goes up and down again...and then hits another plateau, but at a higher level.

For people to gain control of their lives they must realize that they're on a path of endless learning and growth. There's no such thing as getting to the top and staying there without further effort.

What is the key to mastering something?

You have to return again and again to the discipline or task...and stick to your work even when you appear to be going nowhere.

Mastery requires doing the best you can to improve—without pushing yourself *too* hard. You have to be willing to stay on the plateau as long as necessary.

Example: I was fortunate in my middle years to have found the practice of aikido, a martial-arts discipline, very difficult and totally resistant to the art of the quick fix.

When I first started with aikido, I assumed that I would steadily improve, but after a year and a half of practice, I was forced to recognize that I was on a plateau of rather formidable proportions. I was shocked and disappointed, but somehow I managed to persevere.

After a few more exhilarating spurts and disappointing plateaus, I found myself thinking, *Oh good, another plateau. I can just stay on it and keep practicing and sooner or later there will be another spurt.* It was one of the warmest moments on my journey toward the black belt I eventually earned.

Most people see practice as a being a burden. What's your approach to it?

Practice is a path. In Chinese, the word is *tao* and in Japanese, *do.* Practice is the road upon which you walk—your path in life.

The great sports figures of our time are masters of their practice—and they love to practice.

Example: Larry Bird, who, without a doubt, was one of the best basketball players, was not all that talented. He owed his success to regular, intense practice—which he loved to do.

We call law and medicine practices, but today that's rarely the case. Modern law today isn't so much a practice as a get-rich-quick vehicle—and you can't call medicine a practice if you hardly know your patients.

In your job, the road to mastery will provide promotions, money and opportunity to excel. But the key is loving your work and being willing to hang in there through the tough times.

Why is mastery so difficult for Americans?

Because of our soured values as a country. We used to learn values from the village elders, rituals, religion and the family. Today we learn values from television and other media, which teach us that the ideal rhythm of life is a series of climactic moments.

Examples: In a cake commercial, you'll see glowing, happy faces around the cake and a child blowing out the candles, but you won't see any of the work that goes into baking. Or you'll see young people relaxing after a bicycle race by drinking diet soda, but you won't see the effort that went into the race. Or on sitcoms, you see complicated social and psychological problems dramatized, then magnificently solved in 22 minutes.

Television has established a rhythm in our culture that values the climax above everything and believes one climax should follow another.

Trying to maintain the rhythm of life as a perpetual high leads to such tragedies as our drug epidemic. Cocaine is the ultimate quick fix.

Quick-fix thinking has pervaded our society at every level. Modern medicine attempts to solve almost every problem with a drug or operation. Modern business sacrifices long-term planning and development to produce quick profits. Education has gone into a sharp decline because no one has the patience to master difficult subjects such as math or foreign languages.

The quick weight loss diet is one of the best examples of the quick fix...and long-term weight control is one of the best examples of mastery. To keep weight off you have to permanently change your lifestyle, not just go on some fad diet for a few months.

What are the most common pitfalls on the road to mastery?

• Obsessive goal orientation. The desire of most people for quick, sure and highly visible results is the deadliest enemy of mastery.

• A conflicting way of life. The traveler whose main path of mastery coincides with career and livelihood is fortunate. Others must find space and time outside of regular working hours for their practice. *Keys:* Be realistic about balancing job, family and path...enlist the support of family and friends. *How to find the time:* Stop watching TV.

• Lack of instruction. For mastering most skills, there's nothing better than being in the hands of a master teacher, either one-on-one, or in a small group. But there are also books, films, tapes and other good instruction available.

• Vanity. To learn something new of any significance, you have to be willing to look foolish. Even after years of practice you may still take pratfalls.

• Inconsistency. Consistency of practice is the mark of the master. *Helpful:* Establish a regular time and place to practice. But if you should happen to miss a few sessions, don't use that as an excuse to quit.

• Perfectionism. We set such high standards for ourselves that neither we, nor anyone else, could ever meet them. We fail to realize that mastery is not about perfection. It's about a process, a journey.

• Dead seriousness. Without laughter, the rough and rocky places on the path might be too painful for us to bear. Humor not only helps to lighten your load, it also broadens your perspective.

Source: George Leonard, author of *Mastery: The Keys to Long-Term Success and Fulfillment,* Penguin USA, 375 Hudson St., New York 10014.

How to Make Your Dreams Work for You

Dreams can help us understand our feelings, attitudes and beliefs—even those hidden from our conscious minds. They can help build intimacy between friends and families... and help us find our way in times of personal crisis... and even warn us of serious illness. *To put your dreams to work for you:*

• Prime yourself for dreaming. All humans dream, but some have trouble recalling their dreams. For best recall, try a period of relaxation before bedtime.

Helpful: Soothing music, bathing or meditating.

Avoid: Alcohol, drugs and caffeine, all of which suppress dreaming.

Next, mentally review the day's events, especially those that elicited strong emotions in you. Focus on the faces of people closest to you. As you drift off, say to yourself that you will recall your dreams in the morning.

Upon waking, lie still for a few minutes. Keep your eyes closed or unfocused and remain in your sleeping posture. Use a regular alarm clock (tone or bell). Music alarms are distracting and can impair dream recall.

• Keep a dream journal. A series of dreams will be more helpful than a single one. A dream journal helps you spot recurring characters, situations and emotional themes that would otherwise remain hidden.

Procedure: After waking and lying still for several minutes, jot down the main points of your dream in your journal. This journal can be a special notebook or a simple pad of paper.

In either case, it must be kept at your bedside.

Don't worry about writing style. The goal is not to write a beautiful story, but to record the key details. Be sure to record all your dreams, even those that seem fragmentary, trivial, illogical or morally repugnant. Do not censor yourself.

Besides the dream's key elements, each journal entry should include your feelings during the dream and upon waking...the insights and hunches you have about your dream...peculiar traits and, if possible, the identities of your dream characters...details about the dream's ending...and a title by which to remember the dream. Conclude by summarizing the dream's main themes and by listing any ideas or strategies for making changes in your life, as suggested by the dream.

• Explore dreams on your own. Find a comfortable place, where you will not be disturbed. Pick a dream from your journal, then close your eyes and pretend you are reliving the dream. Imagine that the events and feelings of the dream were really happening. Then, open your eyes and jot down any feelings, associations or insights that come to mind.

At this point, several exercises often prove productive...

• Automatic writing. Set a timer for five minutes, then jot down as many ideas as you can before the bell sounds. Don't worry about making sense.

• Dream dialogue. Choose two characters or objects from a dream and write a dialogue between them. Write as fast as you can. Do not censor yourself or put down your pen.

• Dreaming the dream onward. "Reenter" your dream in a daydream and continue your dream beyond its original ending. If the original ending is negative or unresolved, imagine a more positive ending. A man troubled by a dream of being chased by a bear might dream the dream onward until the bear was trapped or killed.

• Share your dreams with others. Doing so not only helps you make sense of dreams, it also deepens the emotional bonds between you and those around you.

Helpful: After each daydreaming exercise, relate your dream to a friend or spouse, or even to a dream discussion group. Use the present tense to make the dream as vivid as possible.

Key questions: Are there links between your dream and any personal relationships, events or turning points in your life? Do these links suggest a course of action? Ask your listener for his/her ideas.

Caution: Dream discussion is fruitful only in an emotionally supportive setting, in which participants focus not upon a formal analysis of *dream content,* but upon an *appreciation* of dream imagery. *Bottom line:* View your dreams —and ask others to view your dreams—the same way you would view paintings in an art museum.

• Avoid "cookbook" dream interpretations. Dreams are full of distorted reality and bizarre symbols that defy easy interpretation.

Many people search for a single "correct" interpretation. In fact, dream symbols hold not one correct interpretation, but many...and the best way to understand these symbols is to explore your own associations. A dream about a knife might symbolize one thing to a frustrated housewife, for example, but quite another to a surgeon.

Helpful: The tingle test. Describe your dream to someone else, then ask for his interpretation. If the interpretation evokes no particular emotional response in you, odds are that particular interpretation holds no specific relevance for you. However, an interpretation that elicits a "tingle" in your body is on target. It warrants further exploration.

On rare occasions, people diagnosed with serious illnesses report having had warning (prodromal) dreams. In one instance, a patient discovered that he had throat cancer after dreaming of a feeling of heat in his neck. Usually, however, dreaming of a serious illness or accident does not mean you actually will get sick or hurt. Dreaming of losing your teeth, for example, may suggest you need to visit the dentist...but it's more likely that loose teeth are merely symbolic of a feeling of loss or powerlessness.

• Put your dreams to work. Humans dream more frequently and with greater intensity during times of transition or crisis—marriage, divorce, the death of a loved one, mid-life, etc.

While no one knows precisely why this is so, one plausible explanation is that when strong feelings overwhelm our conscious mind, our unconscious (dreaming) mind begins to work overtime. Even when we try to "paper over" these powerful emotions, our dreams are there to point out strong emotions that need to be "processed" before we can move on with our lives.

Once you have mastered the basics of dream work, you can begin using your dreams to help resolve your problems, whether it's a simple day-to-day aggravation or an emotional crisis.

How it's done: First, spend some time consciously exploring ways to resolve the problem. This process of conscious exploration can be done on your own, or with a therapist or trusted friend. Consider as many options as possible.

Next, write an "incubation question" in your dream journal. This question, designed to encourage dreams that relate to your specific problem, should be open-ended.

Examples: How do I feel about this career change? Why am I still grieving over my husband's death?

Caution: Avoid narrowly focused, yes-or-no questions.

As you fall asleep, focus upon this question. Repeat this "incubation ceremony" each night until a dream that seems to address this problem occurs.

Then, treat this dream as you normally would, using your dream journal, daydreaming exercises...and sharing the dream with others. With a little practice, you will learn to spot clues in your dreams on how best to respond to your problem.

Example I: Just before her wedding, a woman dreamed that she needed a $10,000 heart operation. At first this dream seemed to have no particular significance. The woman was healthy. Then she realized that $10,000 was the cost of the wedding...and that she was, in one sense, going to have a $10,000 "heart procedure." This dream showed her she was nervous about her marriage, and that she needed to discuss her feelings.

Example II: A restaurateur was so unhappy in her work that she had developed an ulcer. Yet she did not know why she was unhappy. Then, a series of dreams in which she screamed at her employees made her realize that she was really angry at them...and suggested that she needed to express this anger and set new performance standards at the restaurant. These changes enabled her to get over her anger—and her ulcer.

Source: Alan B. Siegel, PhD, an adult and child psychologist in private practice in San Francisco. Dr. Siegel, who has led dream workshops for 15 years is the author of *Dreams That Can Change Your Life: Navigating Life's Passages Through Turning Point Dreams,* Jeremy P. Tarcher, 5858 Wilshire Blvd., Los Angeles 90036.

There Are Great Virtues In Stubbornness

Stubbornness is one of those qualities we find terribly annoying in others and are reluctant to admit to in ourselves.

But stubbornness may be underrated as a valuable defense—and coping mechanism. Stubbornness is not only helpful when it comes to dealing with bad times, it's a must for success.

To find out more about the important part this personality trait plays in our lives, we interviewed psychiatrist and admitted stubborn person, Dr. Sue Chance.

Why do people think stubbornness is negative?

It's a matter of degree. They think tenacity is okay, but when it's carried to an extreme, it becomes stubbornness, and that's a negative.

I think there are other ways of looking at stubbornness. What you call it matters less than the purpose it serves. If being stubborn can help us survive some hard knocks, then it's a virtue as far as I'm concerned.

It takes a lot of stubbornness to persist in the face of rejection, to believe in yourself and your own talents despite what others tell you. But that's what it takes to succeed. Stubbornness, not talent, is often the difference between someone who actually achieves his goals and someone who sits around and talks about what he's going to accomplish one day.

In what situations does stubbornness help people survive hard knocks?

In any adverse situation. When you tell yourself that you're going to hold on for dear life until the bad times pass, that's stubbornness.

Stubbornness applies whether the problem is physical or emotional. It's having the courage to say, *I'll be damned if this is going to beat me.* My stubbornness helped me survive my son's suicide. *I just held on*—and assumed if I stayed alive long enough, the worst would pass. It did. I was just too stubborn to give up.

Is that stubbornness or bravery?

To me bravery implies taking action in difficult circumstances. Tenacity and stubbornness is just holding on, battening down the hatches and toughing it out.

If it's such a survival mechanism, why is stubbornness considered a negative trait?

It's a negative trait when you apply it to someone else. We don't think of ourselves, generally, as stubborn. We call other people stubborn if they hold onto something that we think they should let go of.

Stubbornness *can* be a serious problem in interpersonal relationships. If what you're hearing in your relationships is a lot of feedback about how stubborn you are, you need to think about what it is you're doing to elicit that response.

Stubbornness in relationships may be a sign of selfishness and lack of consideration and caring about the other person. It can indicate failure of empathy.

Stubbornness is a positive only when it's you dealing with yourself. It's positive to stubbornly adhere to what you believe, or stick to goals that you think are worthwhile, or just survive the slings and arrows of life.

Doesn't stubbornness make you resistant to change?

My stubborn patients may stubbornly resist change, but when they finally do make changes, they're more likely to maintain them.

I'd rather work with someone who is stubborn at the core because they'll hang on through the hard stuff. They'll be able to tolerate the anxiety of treatment.

I'm very leery of instantaneous changes. The classic example is the alcoholic who says he'll never drink again. You know he's going back —soon. He hasn't done the hard work it takes to change repetitive behavior.

I prefer the person who says he isn't sure, he knows it's going to be difficult but he's willing to give it a try. That person's got a much better chance because that's how we make changes—slowly, with great reluctance and great effort.

Example: Recovering alcoholics who have some sobriety behind them. They were stubborn enough to make a major change in their lives and consequently are able to look at making other major changes.

How should parents handle stubbornness in children?

Use it as an opportunity for communication. If you ask a child who's being stubborn what's going on, he'll often have an explanation that will make sense to you. Don't make it a battle of wills. Ask your child what the underlying problem is.

Example: We moved from Georgia to Texas when my son was starting the third grade. I got a call from his teacher that he wouldn't do anything in class. He wouldn't even take out his books. When I pressed him about what the problem was, it turned out that what looked like stubbornness was actually shame and fear. He couldn't read the books the class was using because there was a drastic difference in the quality of the education from Georgia to Texas. They were way ahead of him. We put him back a half year until he caught up and then everything was fine.

Is stubbornness something you're born with?

Stubbornness seems to be an innate character trait rather than something you learn.

Example: Newborns' hands grip so strongly they can lift their own weight. They're not physically strong, but they do have a strong instinct to survive. That survival instinct is stubbornness.

How can people foster positive stubbornness in themselves?

Most of the time we program ourselves for failure. Our parents and society teach us how to criticize ourselves.

Typical messages: Don't be conceited... What makes you think you can succeed where others have failed?... You're not so special. We get all this negative programming.

Be sure to give equal time to positive programming.

Tell yourself: I'm going to give it my best. If people want to disagree with me, I'll listen to them, and learn if I can, but sometimes there will just be a difference of opinion and I'm going to take mine over theirs.

Don't pay attention to people who think you should only do what's easy. There's no such thing as *instant success.*

Foster your stubbornness and turn it into drive. Stubbornness can even be a substitute for believing in yourself.

Many of us weren't raised to have a very high opinion of ourselves, but we wind up succeeding through sheer stubbornness. Refusal to give up and the desire to prove yourself against all odds is a powerful motivator.

Source: Psychiatrist Sue Chance, MD, who has a private practice in Dallas. Dr. Chance writes a regular column for the *Psychiatric Times.* She is the author of *Stronger Than Death,* which addresses how family and close friends can survive the suicide of a loved one, W.W. Norton, New York.

Championship Factors

Championship factors apply in all life, not just athletics. Self-analysis—know your strengths and weaknesses...self-competition—concentrate on doing your best, not beating others... confidence—set tough but reasonable goals... toughness—accept risk and try to win instead of just trying not to lose...have a game plan—talent alone is not enough.

Source: *Runner's World,* 33 E. Minor St., Emmaus, PA 18098.

Self-Esteem Builder

Talking to yourself helps build self-esteem. *Helpful:* Give yourself a pat on the back for a job well done...compliment yourself...applaud your achievements. *Important:* Speak these positive messages out loud so you think and hear them.

Source: *51 Ways to Save Your Job: Your 30-Minute Guide to Job Security* by Paul Timm, PhD, professor of management at Brigham Young University. Career Press, 180 Fifth Ave., Hawthorne, NJ 07507.

Practical Paths To Personal Success

The traditional routes to career success don't always work anymore. The time when smart people with impressive academic credentials could link up with big companies and enjoy a non-stop ride to the top is over.

It takes much more to get ahead today. You've got to be shrewd in promoting yourself and your ideas.

Once you choose a company in which to work...

• Get noticed. In many good companies, top executives simply don't have the time to get to know most of the people who work for them. That puts the burden on *you* to make the most of the opportunities. If you have 10 minutes to make a presentation to top management, realize that they may be the most important minutes in the 10 years you've worked for the company.

Example: IBM's Tom Watson, Sr., once promoted a salesman he'd never met to sales manager on the basis of a brief presentation the man made.

When you know key people will be watching, do your homework and prepare for the occasion as though your career depends on it ...because it does.

And if you're offered two positions, take the one with more visibility, unless there's a compelling reason not to.

• Develop your people skills. Learn what motivates people. This applies equally in relations with subordinates, peers and superiors. Learn to *read* people so that you are able to anticipate their actions.

People skills make self-promotion easier. They also enhance your other talents and make up for some you lack.

Example: Ross Johnson, CEO of RJR Nabisco, was no expert at products and marketing. But he knew people and could regularly talk the board of directors into agreeing with his position.

Although there's no magic way to develop these skills, it helps to watch others who have them. *Notice how they...*

• Ask *others* for opinions.

• Make a point to be useful to others.

• Remember special occasions—birthdays, anniversaries, etc.

If you think you need help in developing people skills, look into seminars that focus on these skills.

Identify with a product...

Identifying your career with a hot product can be a fast route to personal success.

Above all, look for products or services that solve problems. They stand the best chance of being winners.

Example: Edwin Land discovered the potential for an instant camera when his young daughter asked why she couldn't see a picture right after she took it.

Read everything you can get your hands on —the major business and financial press, newsletters, journals, consumer magazines, etc. *Aim:* To find out what's going on *beyond* your own company's current product or service line.

Example #1: Lee Iacocca didn't design the Mustang. But he knew enough about people's tastes to know it would sell. In the process, of course, he promoted himself.

Example #2: More recently, smart managers at GM joined the Saturn project. They knew that if the project turned out to be a winner, so would their careers.

It's a myth that once you're past 40 or 50 it's better to stick with your current career path than to change directions. *Reality:* It's hardly ever too late. In fact, a person who changes direction late in life usually has a wealth of experience to help steady the new course.

Classic example: Ray Kroc, a long-time head of McDonald's, didn't sell a hamburger until he was 52.

The power of ideas...

Developing a successful idea can give you a fast ride to the top. Ironically, however, even great ideas aren't always easy to sell.

Example: Ken Olsen, head of Digital Equipment Corp., rejected the idea of making a personal computer until it was too late for the company to enter the lucrative field.

Some basic concepts to keep in mind when selling your ideas...

•Keep ideas simple. Consumers back away from anything complex, regardless of how useful it may be.

Example: Prodigy, the computer database, is marketed with such complex descriptions that relatively few people understand it well enough to subscribe.

•Keep ideas timely. Even great ideas won't work if the market isn't ready.

•Consider taking your idea elsewhere if your own company isn't interested. Ironically, many executives will listen to an outsider's idea with more enthusiasm than they would to one that comes from within. Once your company has rejected an idea, you usually have nothing to lose by taking it elsewhere.

Example: When Al Neuharth couldn't get his company, *The Miami Herald,* interested in the concept for *USA Today,* he took it to Gannett. And even though the paper has struggled, the concept worked well enough to earn him that company's chairmanship.

Source: Jack Trout and Al Ries, authors of *Horse Sense,* McGraw-Hill, 11 W. 19 St., New York 10011.

The Six Thinking Hats

We all think many different kinds of thoughts —from positive to negative and everything in between. One way to become a better thinker is to separate these different kinds of thinking and use each one separately, instead of in a jumper, as we usually do.

How it works...

One of the biggest traps in thinking is that we categorize people according to *type.* This limits people to expressing views that are expected of them.

Example: Someone who is identified as a negative personality is always expected to come up with negative ideas.

By pretending to switch hats, everyone can come up with a wide spectrum of thoughts on the same subject. Wearing the hats also helps overcome ego—another big hangup in thinking.

Example: If a person opposes an idea, he/she usually won't look for any points in favor of it. But if he's wearing a positive thinking hat, it becomes a game to find the positive side.

This gives people the freedom to remove their egos from the thinking process and think in many different ways.

My six hats...

• *White hat:* Objective thinking. *Memory jog:* White...paper...neutral...objective.

While you wear the white hat, you concentrate on the facts. You can also point out any gaps in that information. White-hat thinking does not involve arguments, views or opinions.

• *Red hat:* Feelings. *Memory jog:* Red...fire ...anger (seeing red)...emotions.

While you wear the red hat, you can express hunches and intuitive feelings. You may not be able to explain your feelings...they may be based on experiences you can't put your finger on.

In many discussions—particularly in business—we're not supposed to include our feelings. But we put them in anyway...disguised as logic. The red hat lets us express our feelings openly.

Example: A head of research at DuPont often asks for three minutes of red-hat thinking at the start of a meeting. He wants to know how everyone feels about a project...without having to explain or justify their feelings.

Telling someone, "You've got your red hat on," is a way to let him know he's expressing his feelings when he's trying to be objective.

• *Black hat:* Caution. *Memory jog:* Black... gloomy...negative...the color of a judge's robes.

While wearing the black hat, you can think about logical negatives—why something is illegal, why it won't work, why it won't be profitable, why it doesn't fit the facts or experience.

Although some peole get the impression that black-hat thinking is bad, it's at least as useful as any of the other kinds of thinking.

Black-hat thinking can be used as a way to get people to *stop* being negative. *Good state-*

ment: "That's great black-hat thinking...but now let's try our green hats."

• *Yellow hat:* Logical, positive thoughts. *Memory jog:* Yellow...sunny...positive.

While you wear the yellow hat, you *must* be logical.

Example: A family is considering moving to the country. Yellow-hat thinking involves looking at logical considerations—lowering housing costs, better schools, etc. Just saying that it would be nice to have a change is red-hat thinking.

Note: The black and yellow hats are both judgment hats. *Black says:* Let's look at the difficulties and dangers. *Yellow says:* Let's look at the feasibility, benefits and savings.

• *Green hat:* Creativity. *Memory jogs:* Green ...grass...fertile growth...energy.

While you wear the green hat, you're free to generate new ideas, alternatives and possibilities.

Example: A couple planning a vacation puts on their green hats and brainstorms possibilities—the wilder the better. These aren't ideas they've checked or thought seriously about... they're just ideas.

Normally when we're discussing something, it's very difficult to slip in creative ideas. Wearing the green hat is a way of making off-the-wall ideas acceptable.

• *Blue hat:* Objective overview. *Memory jog:* Blue...cool...the color of a clear sky, which is above everything else.

While you wear the blue hat, you tell yourself or others which of the other five hats to wear. It's like conducting an orchestra.

Blue-hat statement: "We haven't gotten anywhere by being logical. Putting on my blue hat, I suggest we have some red-hat thinking to clear the air."

The blue hat says: Let's look at our objectives and values. It lets you lay out your goals, evaluate how far you've gotten, summarize the results and reach a conclusion.

How to use the hats...

You can use the hat concept to think about any issue. You can use it by yourself, with one other person or in a group. *Good statements:*

• Let's try some green-hat thinking for three minutes to generate some different ideas.

• It seems you're just wearing your black hat...why don't you take it off now?

• That's all red-hat thinking...we need to put on our white hats for a while and consider the facts.

• Putting on my black hat, I want to talk about the difficulties, dangers and problems we might face with this.

• Wearing my red hat, this is how I feel about it.

• Here's a provocative idea I got while wearing my green hat.

To stimulate creativity at a meeting, ask everyone to put on his green hat for three minutes and come up with some creative ideas. This will allow even the most unimaginative member of the group to indulge his creative side. *Note:* Make it a rule that anyone can call for some green-hat time.

Make it feel like a game to get people to play along. If everyone else is wearing a yellow hat, someone who's still expressing black-hat ideas is going to feel very silly. Make sure that every idea that is brought up is analyzed under each hat. Once you've narrowed your options down to three or four, go back and do one more yellow- and black-hat check on each. At the end of this process you will have a well-thought-out plan of what you want to do.

Source: Edward DeBono, PhD, the leading international authority on the teaching of thinking as a skill. He has held faculty appointments at Oxford, Cambridge and Harvard. His Six Thinking Hats program is used by such companies as IBM, Du Pont and Prudential.

Norman Vincent Peale's 10 Rules for Getting Along with People

• Remember their names.

• Be comfortable to be with. Don't cause strain in others.

• Try not to let things bother you. Be easy-going.

•Don't be egotistical or know-it-all.

•Learn to be interesting so that people will get something stimulating from being with you.

•Eliminate the "scratchy" elements in your personality, traits that can irritate others.

•Never miss a chance to offer support or say "Congratulations."

•Work at liking people. Eventually you'll like them naturally.

•Honestly try to heal any misunderstandings and drain off grievances.

•Develop spiritual depth in yourself and share this strength with others.

Source: *Time Talk,* Time Management Center, Grandville, MI.

What's Your Personality Style?

Your personality determines the way you think, feel and behave—all the qualities that make you uniquely you.

Everyone is a combination of many personality styles. But most people have their strongest tendencies in one or two of them. Identifying your styles will help you make the most of your personality.

The 13 personality styles...

•Adventurous. Commonly a male style. Adventurous people are wanderers, real mavericks who will plunge into almost anything. They think every new experience is interesting. Because adventurers are restless, they don't settle down easily. Although many people have elements of this style in their personality, it isn't as common as many of the others as a predominant style.

To be more effective: Try to use your head rather than always being ruled by your appetite for change. Think about what you want out of life five, 10, 20 years from now.

•Aggressive. Take-charge people who are comfortable with power and authority. They are highly disciplined, goal-directed and function well in difficult and dangerous situations. Aggressive people often enjoy competitive sports. *Trap:* Their need to dominate other people can cause problems in intimate relationships.

To be more effective: Even if you're the boss at work, quit trying to be the boss at home. Give people a chance to make their own mistakes. At least once a week, ask those people closest to you what you can do to be helpful to them.

•Conscientious. Hard workers—sometimes even workaholics. They're perfectionists, pragmatic people who love order and detail. *Trap:* Most conscientious people are cerebral and emotionally undemonstrative.

To be more effective: Because conscientious people are susceptible to many stress-related health risks, you should broaden your personal life and learn to relax.

•Devoted. Most often female, the caretakers of the world. They generally put the needs of others before their own. Devoted people feel safe and secure in a relationship with a dominant person who makes life's big decisions for them.

To be more effective: Stop and think about your own needs and assert them more often. Express your anger directly. Practice decision-making.

•Dramatic. A common personality style, particularly among people with careers in film, television and publishing. Dramatic people are *people people.* They're very sociable, emotionally effusive and spontaneous. They like being the center of attention, are interested in clothing and appearance and in seeking sexual pleasure. *Trap:* They may be too impulsive and inattentive to the practical side of life.

To be more effective: Count to 10 before you jump into something exciting. Force yourself to go home and balance your checkbook.

•Idiosyncratic. The world's eccentrics, the individualists who wear and do what they want and don't give a damn what others think. They're interested in fringe ideas—UFOs, ESP, New Age philosophies, etc. Idiosyncratic people are self-directed and independent. They require few close relationships.

To be more effective: Make it easier on yourself to function in the real world—compromise and do the things other people want you to do occasionally. People who insist on setting their own rules often fail in some of life's most important areas.

•Leisurely. What we call the *California types.* They put their personal priorities first. Leisurely people may be willing to work nine to five...but not one minute more. They like to relax and enjoy themselves and jealously guard their personal time.

To be more effective: Expand your priorities to include other people. Helping others is *not* hard work, when you consider the rewards. And stop procrastinating. If you do the things you have to do today you'll have more time to have fun tomorrow.

•Mercurial. Similar in some ways to dramatic people, mercurial people are also impulsive. Extremely intense, they yearn for new experience and will quickly jump into a new love or lifestyle. They are uninhibited, spontaneous, fun-loving and undaunted by risk.

To be more effective: Work on developing some detachment and restraint. It will help you feel more fulfilled and successful.

•Self-confident. The go-getters—ambitious, capable and successful. They have a lot of innate confidence. Donald Trump typifies this style. *Trap:* Many self-confident people are insensitive to the needs of others. They'll climb over anyone in their drive to succeed.

To be more effective: Develop a realistic sense of your own shortcomings. *Ask yourself:* What's *not* so great about me? How would my loved ones answer that question? Stop concentrating on your own goals and focus on the needs of those close to you for a while.

•Self-sacrificing. These people think that to live is to serve...to love is to give. They're generous to a fault, helpful, considerate, accepting, humble, long-suffering and rather naive and innocent. At its best and most noble, this is the selfless style of which saints and good citizens are made. *Trap:* At their worst, self-sacrificers can turn into guilt-pushing martyrs.

To be more effective: Work on establishing a better balance of give and take in your life. Focus more on yourself and less on others.

•Sensitive. Fearful worriers who concentrate on the potential pitfalls before they take any action. They'll pack four suitcases for a weekend trip to make sure they don't forget anything. Sensitive people are very self-conscious and worried about what others think. *Trap:* Although they like other people, they hold back because of their anxiety and lack of self-confidence.

To be more effective: Change one or more of your routines for the sake of change. Doing something you would prefer to avoid will help you overcome your anxiety about the future.

•Solitary. Loners who are perfectly content to be by themselves. Solitary people are usually even-tempered, unsentimental and unflappable. They're not feelers, they're doers and watchers. *Trap:* Because they don't have strong feelings themselves, they often can't understand other people's feelings.

To be more effective: Watch how people express their feelings and accept the fact that feelings are important to most people. Instead of retreating when pressured by people, tolerate your discomfort and stick around a little longer.

•Vigilant. We call this the *New York style*—it's most common in high-powered, competitive, urban areas. Vigilant people are very alert, very watchful and very wary. No one puts anything past them. Perceptive and aware of their environment, they are constantly sizing people up.

To be more effective: Try to remember that others may see your guardedness as a sign that you don't like them. Every time you find yourself wondering about someone's ulterior motives, think about other, better motives that could explain the same action.

Source: John M. Oldham, MD, associate chairman, department of psychiatry, Columbia University College of Physicians and Surgeons and acting director of the New York State Psychiatric Institute. He is coauthor, with Lois B. Morris, of *The Personality Self-Portrait: Why You Think, Work, Love and Act the Way You Do,* Bantam Books, 666 Fifth Ave., New York 10103.

The Perils of Success

There are dangers in being a big success at anything. No matter how good you are at what you do, it eventually becomes second nature.

Trap: People who don't continually update their knowledge—no matter how successful they are—become fearful of new ideas, creativity and risk-taking. *Result:* Their area of success becomes an area of mediocrity.

Problem: Hangers-on...

Some successful people wind up surrounded by people who make their living from winners' ideas. And because these hangers-on fear offending the successful ones, they become a group of yes-men, who insulate the winners from reality.

If that happens, if a successful person stops paying attention to what's really going on in his/ her business and the world, his position is in danger.

Example: In the 1970s, American carmakers, despite massive evidence to the contrary, refused to believe that car buyers wanted high-quality, economical cars, and continued to make low-quality gas-guzzlers.

Problem: Tunnel vision...

Once someone's life is defined by success in a particular field, his focus often gets narrower and narrower. Instead of taking new risks, branching out into new areas, he tackles only projects that repeat what he has already done well...and loses his edge.

Example: Roger Corman, a producer of successful horror films, never wavered from his original low-budget, high-gore formula. Although many of his protégés, film-school grads whom he hired cheaply to act and direct, have gone on to become famous Hollywood stars, Corman is still relatively unknown.

Problem: Continued demand...

Many successful products, ideas, etc., are spawned by the needs of the time and creative, aggressive energy.

Trap: Although the times change, the person who generated the success doesn't change along with them. His next project isn't based on what's needed now...but on what worked for him before.

The difference between doing something because there's an urgency about it and doing something because there's a continued demand for it represents a subtle shift.

Example: Many 1960s rock groups, like the Beach Boys, who were once vibrant and creative, have become caricatures of their former selves. Paunchy and graying, they perform stale renditions of their old hits...to audiences of people who don't want to change, either.

In some instances, a person who is quite successful in his own little corner of a particular field tries to gain recognition from the outside world. But his methods are so outdated he winds up looking ridiculous.

Example: A therapist with a successful practice sent me her manuscript for a book about therapy. I found that the basic theory and assumptions—even the character structures of the people she described—were all 20 years old. There was absolutely nothing new in the book. *What had happened:* Although she had been able to keep a practice going with her outdated methods, she certainly wasn't equipped to write a useful, up-to-date book.

What successful people need to know...

Assume that even if you're doing well... even if your services are in demand...even if you're growing and learning in your specialty, that you're getting out-of-date.

Assume that brilliant new processes and wonderful new people have emerged in your field while you've been busy at your "cobbler's bench."

Keep looking around. Keep seeking opportunities to expand in ways that weren't available when you became successful in the first place.

Example: The therapist mentioned above should have been reading about and attending workshops in the latest techniques. Then, if she still wanted to write a book about her methods, she could have acknowledged that, although the new techniques are good, her old-fashioned approach still works better for certain people.

Ask the people around you if you're resting on your laurels. Ask friends, family and co-workers to tell you things that you may not have noticed about what's going on in your business and in the world.

Helpful: Recognize that it's wise to encourage people to tell you things that may make you uncomfortable. Don't identify with your success. Once you start seeing yourself as Mr. Widget-Maker—rather than Joe who makes widgets, plays tennis and loves his family—you're in danger of losing your identity as a multifaceted individual.

Doing the same thing over and over, no matter how well, leads to disengagement and disinterest. Once you lose interest you start ignoring the changing environment, setting up a vicious cycle.

As soon as you start to feel disinterested, step outside your realm and make a shift in focus. Look for new challenges that may use what you're already good at...but will still get you to try something new.

Source: Martin G. Groder, MD, a psychiatrist and business consultant in Chapel Hill, North Carolina. His book, *Business Games: How to Recognize the Players and Deal With Them*, is available from Boardroom Classics, Greenwich, CT.

Simple System to Help You Operate at Your Highest Level

My *Intensive Journal* process combines one of the oldest methods of self-exploration—keeping a diary—with a new, highly structured format that enables journal-keepers to get to know themselves on ever-deeper levels. The process is designed to help people discover internal resources they didn't know they had.

Simple system...

Putting your day-to-day thoughts in writing automatically forces you to become more introspective. This helps you identify patterns in conscious and unconscious thinking.

As you work in your journal, the experiences of your life—times of exaltation and despair, moments of hope and anger, crises and crossroads, failures and successes—will gradually fit into place. You will discover that your life *has* been going somewhere, however blind you may have been to its direction.

Getting started...

The journal itself is just a large three-ring notebook filled with paper and divided into many sections. Don't think that you have to write something in each section each day. Some sections you'll want to write in quite frequently. Others may be saved for special occasions.

Although you should write in your journal as often as possible, writing should never be a chore. Once you've established a dialogue with your journal, your inner self will tell you when there are things to be written...and you'll naturally turn to your journal as a means of self-expression and discovery.

The major sections...

• Period log. This is where you'll make your first entry each time you write. Write about things that are going on in your life *now*. Now can be a short or a long period of time.

Example: For one person, *now* may reach back three years since he was involved in an automobile accident and was hospitalized. For another person, *now* may be merely a few weeks since he met a new friend, moved to a different city, began a new job or experienced another significant change in circumstances.

Ask yourself: Where am I now in my life? Write in a nonjudgmental way.

• Twilight imagery log. After you complete your basic entry in the period log, try to duplicate the twilight state between sleeping and waking. By working in that intermediate state of consciousness, you can reach consciousness levels that are difficult to contact any other way.

Meditation exercise: Sit quietly in a comfortable position. Relax. Close your eyes. Follow your breathing until you feel a great calm. On your mental screen, picture a deep well. Enter the well and go deeper and deeper. At the bottom of the well is a river. The waters are muddy but they begin to clear.

Examine the images that appear, then allow yourself to become a bit more alert and jot those images down. Then return to the twilight state. Keep moving back and forth jotting down the images.

Ask yourself: Do the images suggest anything?

•Daily log. These entries should focus the emotions you experienced during the day. Include only a minimum of descriptive material. The primary purpose of the daily log is to provide ideas for other sections of the journal.

Example: If you mention your father in the daily log, you might want to talk with him in the upcoming *Dialogue* section.

•Stepping-stones. List the dozen or so key events that have shaped your life. *Include:* Important times in your life from childhood—school, first love, marriage, divorce, parenthood, friendship, relocation. Explore the periods when possibilities were opening for you, when you had alternatives, when critical decisions were made or unmade.

Don't judge yourself. Make neutral observations about your life. *Purpose:* To recreate in the present the exact feelings you had when you were going through a momentous time. Our stepping-stones made us who we are today.

•Life-history log. When you don't want to be sidetracked from the section you're working in, but want to retain a memory that has arisen, record the thought briefly in this section. This will become a grab bag of memories that don't fit anywhere else.

•Intersections: Roads taken and not taken. Record here those experiences that marked an intersection in your life, where some kind of change became inevitable.

The choices you made at those intersections left many potential paths untouched and unexplored. Although those unlived possibilities have never been given their chance, you may still be waiting for an opportunity to do so.

Examples: You got married instead of pursuing an acting career...you took a corporate job instead of starting your own business.

Ask yourself: Can any of these roads still be traveled? How do I feel about doing it now?

•Dialogues. Having begun by recording and exploring much of your life history, it's time to deepen your relationship with the important aspects of your life and let them speak to you.

Create subsections. Start each with a focus statement. Write down what is or was positive or negative about your relationship with that aspect of your life, how it got to where it is and what your hopes are for it.

Next, as best you can, list at least a dozen stepping-stones for that person or part of your life. Do the twilight imagery meditation. Then write a dialogue where you express what you really mean to each other. Listen carefully to what the other party—living or dead, animate or inanimate, spiritual or material—has to say to you. *Subsections:*

•*Person.* Someone who is living or dead, with whom you had an important relationship.

Example: In a dialogue with your deceased father you may ask, *Why didn't you ever really love me?* He may answer, *I did, I was just too busy to express it.*

•*Work.* List the kinds of work you've done in your life. State the situation you find yourself in regarding that kind of work, and listen to what the work has to say.

Example: You may talk to the bills you've been avoiding at the office. They may respond, *You don't want to pay us because you want to be a kid and have Daddy pay the bills.*

•*The body.* List two or three important physical events for each decade of your life, then relax and write a conversation with your body.

Example: An overweight middle-aged woman wrote, *When I was young, I could throw any rag on you and look great. Now I can't find anything big enough to cover you.*

•Now: The open moment. This section is about your future. First, sum up your experiences writing in the journal. Then, focus on your future in the context of your life history.

Write whatever comes to you. It may be a prayer, a poem, a brief focusing phrase that gives you a reminder about the continuity of your life.

Again, although journaling is important, don't feel that you have to write each and every day. What's important is that you *are* writing-...and, in doing so, learning more and more about yourself.

Source: Psychologist Ira Progoff, PhD, who pioneered the Intensive Journal concept, now taught in workshops all over the country. Dr. Progoff is the author of a series of books about keeping an Intensive Journal.

How to Use Fantasy As A Creative Tool

An active fantasy life is as crucial to the mental health of adults as it is to children. We tend to think that as we grow up we must leave our fantasies behind. But without fantasy, we would never dare to push or grow psychologically. We would become bland and constricted half-people. Fantasy has many useful functions in our lives. Here are some of them:

• Fantasy lets us "try out" new roles. For example, anyone who contemplates a job or career change first fantasizes what it would be like to do other kinds of work.

• Fantasy is a way of testing concepts and ideas, from new products to financial systems.

• Fantasy helps us master negative emotions and events. If we're very depressed over a loss or other unhappy event, we can allow ourselves to feel better by imagining something that makes us feel good.

• Fantasy can relieve boredom or an unpleasant experience. We've all fantasized through a traffic jam.

• Fantasizing can mean the difference between life and death in truly traumatic situations—war, solitary confinement, etc. Diaries of concentration camp survivors and prisoners of war attest to this.

• In sex, fantasy has been touted as an enhancer of pleasure, and shared sexual fantasies can indeed do this. But unshared fantasy during sex can be one way of tuning out and avoiding intimacy with the other person.

• Love relationships are predicated on fantasy. We project onto the loved one our fantasy of the ideal lover. This is an obstruction in one way because it keeps us from seeing the real person, but if we didn't do it we wouldn't fall in love at all.

• Fantasy displaces fear. We displace frightening things through fantasy as adults, just as we did as children. Thus, we imagine that harmful things will happen elsewhere—that someone else will have a car accident or get cancer.

While fantasy has many benefits, it's important to temper fantasy with reality. When we retreat into a fantasy world untempered by reality, there is the real danger of becoming nonfunctional—not getting out of bed in the morning or not taking care of the routine matters that ensure our daily existence.

Source: Dr. Simone F. Sternberg, a psychotherapist and psychoanalyst in private practice in New York.

To Develop Genius

Geniuses are made by sheer hard work more often than by simple inborn talent. *Steps toward developing genius:*

• "Falling in love" with a particular subject.

• Sharpening skills with time and effort.

• Mastering a personal style, with the goal being excellence rather than praise.

Source: Study by education specialist Benjamin Bloom, University of Chicago, cited in *Success!*

Pushing Toward Peak Performance

You have undoubtedly had the experience at one time or another of finding yourself in a high-pressure situation and performing way above your usual level.

A few people—you could call them peak performers—seem able to turn on the superchargers almost at will. Studies reveal that to be a peak performer you must be:

• Deeply and unambiguously committed to your goals.

• Confident of your ability to perform well.

• In control of your actions.

The commitment connection is fundamental...

• If you're not doing what you really want to do, it's not likely that you will give your best attention and energy to what you do.

• True commitment requires that you be in touch with your true desires.

•Pay attention to your most unguarded daydreams. Take note of these with an open mind and, in a tranquil moment, reflect on what they're telling you about you innermost desires. Give them credence. Don't edit. As you begin to act in accordance with those desires, you should find your performance improving.

Build or enhance confidence by controlling fear...

•When you feel fear taking hold, extricate yourself immediately from the bog of undefined apprehension and get a firm grasp on the concrete realities of the situation.

•Measure the difficulty of the problem. Make a mental or written profile of exactly what has to be accomplished. It is almost invariably much less than your undefined fears projected.

•Rate the problem on a scale of one to 10. This further serves to put the problem into realistic perspective, making it concrete rather than abstract.

•Compare your problem with others you have handled successfully in the past. Reflect on past instances in which you have performed well on similar or even more difficult problems.

•Imagine the worst. Define as objectively as you can the worst possible consequences that could result from completely "blowing it."

•A reality check won't alter the reality, but it will help to interrupt the self-perpetuating cycle of fear that keeps you from doing your very best. It will help you to act.

The importance of control in high-pressure performance is largely a matter of momentum and efficient use of energy:

•Distinguish between elements you can control and those you can't, and focus on what you can do.

•Choose an action (a can-do) that is concrete, that can be embarked on immediately, and that is in your power to carry out. As one can-do follows another, the task will be rapidly completed and the problem solved.

Source: Robert Kriegel, PhD, coauthor with Marilyn Harris Kriegel, PhD of *The C Zone: Peak Performance under Stress,* Anchor Press/Doubleday, Garden City, NY.

Dangers in Perfectionism

Emotional perfectionists believe they should always be happy and in control of their feelings.

They believe they should never:

•Feel insecure...so they worry about shyness, thus adding to their anxiety.

•Feel ambivalent about a commitment... so they're unable to make a decision in the first place and then feel miserable about their vacillation.

•*More reasonable goal:* To have general control of emotions and accept emotional flaws as part of our humanity.

Source: Dr. David D. Burns, cognitive therapist, Presbyterian-University of Pennsylvania Medical Center, Philadelphia.

How to Change Type A Behavior

Here are some ways to modify dangerous Type A behavior:

•Walk and talk more slowly.

•Reduce deadline pressure by pacing your days more evenly.

•Stop trying to do more than one thing at a time.

•Don't interrupt other people in mid-speech.

•Begin driving in the slow lane.

•Simply sit and listen to music you like while doing nothing else.

Developing Your Own Image of Success

•Recognize that you have talents and skills that are ingredients of success. Focus on these and forget your bad points entirely.

•Concentrate your energy. *One way to focus energy:* Split up your day into the smallest possible segments of time. Treat each segment as independent and get each task done one at a time. This will give you the feeling of accomplishment and will fuel your energy.

• Take responsibility. Be willing to accept personal responsibility for the success of your assignments, for the actions of people who work for you, and for the goals you have accepted. Seize responsibility if it is not handed over easily. There are always company problems that are difficult to solve and that nobody has been assigned to—take them for starters.

• Take action instead of waiting to be told. Listen to other people's problems and link their ambitions to your goals. Then deliver what you promise.

• Nurture self-control. Don't speak or move hastily. Don't let personal emotions color decisions that must be hard and analytical. Before taking a major action, ask yourself, "What's the worst that can happen?" Let that guide your next step.

• Display loyalty. No matter how disloyal you feel, never show it. Show loyalty to your boss, your company, your employees. Be positive about yourself and about others. Never run anybody down.

• Convey a successful image. Move decisively—walk fast and purposefully, with good posture. Look as if you are on the way to something rather than moping along.

• When you sit, don't slump. Sit upright and convey alertness. Choose a chair of modest dimensions. A large chair makes you look small and trapped. The chair should have a neutral color and be of a material that doesn't squeak or stick to your body.

• Avoid large lunches—they deprive you of energy. Successful people tend to eat rather sparingly.

Source: Michael Korda, author of *Success! How Every Man and Woman Can Achieve It,* Random House, New York.

Are You Really as Ambitious as You Think You Are?

To test your ambition quotient, rate the following statements on a scale of 1 to 5 to indicate how much the statement applies to you. A rating of 1 means it doesn't apply at all, and 5 means it applies very much.

• I truly enjoy working.

• Given free time, I would rather be out socializing with people than sitting home watching television.

• My first response to a problem is to attempt to figure out the most practical solution.

• One of the things I like best about work is the challenge of it.

• I believe very strongly in the work ethic.

• I have a strong desire to get things done.

• When there's a difficult situation, I enjoy assuming the responsibility for correcting it.

• I frequently come up with ideas—day and night.

• I'm not satisfied with the success I already enjoy.

• I rarely miss a day of work because of illness.

• I enjoy vacations, but after four to five days I look forward to getting back to work.

• I can usually get along with six hours of sleep.

• I'm interested in meeting people and developing contacts.

• I set high standards for myself in almost everything I do.

• All in all, I consider myself a lucky person.

• I'm not afraid to rely on my instincts when I have to make an important decision.

• I can think of very few situations in which I don't have a great deal of control.

• I recover from setbacks pretty quickly. I don't dwell on them.

• I'm not afraid to admit it when I make a big mistake.

• Achieving success is very important to me.

Scoring: 85-100 indicates very high ambition. With the right skills, you're almost certain to achieve your goals. 70-84 means higher-than-average ambition, and chances of achieving goals are very good. 55-69 is about an average score. If you achieve your goal, it won't be on ambition alone. A score below 55 indicates that success isn't an important goal for you.

Source: Robert Half, author of *Success Guide for Accountants,* McGraw-Hill, New York.

Setting Goals for Success

The lack of a clear goal is the most common obstacle to success, even for people with large amounts of drive and ambition. Typically, they focus on the rewards of success, not on the route they must take to achieve it. *Remedy:*

- Whenever possible, write down your goals, forcing yourself to be specific.
- Periodically make a self-assessment. Take into account your education, age, appearance, background, skills, talents, weaknesses, preferences, willingness to take risks and languages spoken.
- Ask for feedback from others.
- Don't try to succeed at something for which you have no talent.
- Try out your goal part-time. If you dream of owning a restaurant, work in one for a while.

Targeting Success

- Visualize the results you intend to achieve and write them down. *Example:* I will increase output 10%.
- List the personal benefits that reaching the goal will confer.
- Jot down at least 10 obstacles and try to find three possible solutions for each.
- Set a target date.
- Start tackling the problems, beginning with the easiest.

Source: Audrey Cripps, Cripps Institute for the Development of Human Relations, Toronto.

Climbing to Success Without Stumbling

The behavior our parents reinforce in us when we are children always encourages us to strive for bigger and better things. We gain approval for achievement and disapproval for failure. As adults, we keep striving because our developmental makeup says "You've got to have more."

To avoid rising to your level of incompetence:

- Take your life and your job seriously. But don't take yourself seriously.
- Don't spend your life climbing and acquiring. Instead, combine accomplishment and satisfaction.
- Climb to a level that you find fulfilling, stay there for a long period, and then move forward.
- Approach promotion avoidance indirectly. One successful ploy is to display some charming eccentricities that in no way effect your work performance, but which might discourage a promotion.

Source: Dr. Laurence J. Peter, whose latest book is *Why Things Go Wrong,* or *The Peter Principle Revisited,* William Morrow & Co., New York.

Overcoming Obstacles To Success

Personality traits can be a straightaway or a dead-end on the road to success.

Don't be caught in the following common traps:

- Inability to let go. People often stick with a dead-end job out of pride, stubbornness or unwillingness to admit that they made a mistake. Sometimes the comfort of the familiar is just too seductive. *To start letting go:* Take small, safe steps at first. Start talking to friends and associates about possible new jobs. See what's available during your vacation. Shake things up at the office by suggesting some changes in your current job. Take some courses and learn new skills.

•Lack of self-esteem. This is an enormous stumbling block. But, in fact, you may be judging yourself by excessively high standards.

•Procrastination. Like alcoholism, procrastination is a subtle, insidious disease that numbs the consciousness and destroys self-esteem. *Remedy:* Catch it early, but not in a harsh, punitive, self-blaming way. Look at what you're afraid of, and examine your motives.

•Shyness. If you're shy, the obvious remedy is to choose an occupation that doesn't require a lot of public contact. But even shy salespeople have been known to succeed. As long as they're talking about product lines and business, a familiar spiel can see them through. Concentrate on getting ahead by doing a terrific job rather than by being Mr. or Ms. Charming. Or take a Dale Carnegie course. They are helpful.

•Unwillingness to look at yourself. If you're not willing to assess yourself honestly, success will probably forever elude you. People tend to avoid self-assessment because they feel they must be really hard on themselves. Realize you've probably taken the enemy into your own head—you've internalized that harsh, critical parent or teacher from your childhood. Instead, evaluate yourself as you would someone you love, like a good friend whom you'd be inclined to forgive almost anything.

Source: Tom Greening, PhD, clinical supervisor of psychology at the University of California at Los Angeles and a partner in Psychological Service Associates, Los Angeles.

Secrets of Success

Top performers in all fields have these qualities in common:

•They transcend their previous performances.

•They never get too comfortable.

•They enjoy their work as an art.

•They rehearse things mentally beforehand.

•They don't bother too much about placing blame.

•They are able to withstand uncertainty.

Source: David A. Thomas, Dean of Cornell University, Graduate School of Business.

What Successful Men Think Makes Them Successful

•Bill Blass: "I guess it is my ability to concentrate and a dedication to the best in design—first fashion, and then the best in design for other things."

•David Klein, Dav-El Limousines, New York: "Even when I was a kid in New Rochelle, New York, I had more paper routes than the rest of the kids. Then I began to run parking lots at the local country club, graduated to being a chauffeur and continued to work, work and work more. I really do love to work."

•Tom Margittai, co-owner, Four Seasons restaurant, New York: "Determined professionalism combined with high standards of quality. Also, a lot of hard work. We try to understand the psychology of our market and to be first in everything."

•Mickey Rooney: "Through the years, it has been my great faith in God, and lots and lots of energy. At last I have it all together. I guess my good health is also a factor. I've been luckier than a lot, and I have always taken a positive outlook."

•Carl Spielvogel, Backer Spielvogel Bates Worldwide: "I think getting in early and staying late and not taking the 5:15 to Greenwich is one reason [for my success]. Also, being where the business is. As Lyndon Johnson once said, "You have to press the flesh." People you do business with want to know you and to be with you socially."

•Ted Turner, head of Cable News Network and sportsman: "Every day I try to do my very best. When you wish upon a star, your dreams really do come true."

How to Be Known As an Expert

Improve your chances for promotion and attract outside job offers by displaying expertise and calling attention to yourself.

Some ways to do it:

• Write an article for a key trade journal.

• Join an association of peer professionals. Get to know your counterparts and their superiors in other companies. Run for office in the association.

• Develop a speech about your work and offer to talk to local groups and service clubs.

• Teach a course at a community college.

• Write letters to the editors of trade journals, commenting on or criticizing articles that they publish in your field.

• Have lunch with your company's public relations people. Let them know what your department is doing, and see if they know of some good speaking platforms for you.

• Use vacation time to attend conferences and seminars.

• Write to experts, complimenting them (when appropriate) on their work and their articles. Whether or not they reply, they'll be flattered and they'll probably remember your name.

Source: Errol D. Alexander, president, Profiles, Inc., Vernon, CT.

Lessons in Judgment

Good judgment is important for a successful career and personal life. But how does one develop it? There are virtually no books written on judgment and our researcher couldn't find any great articles on the subject. So—we asked six people known for their good judgment to define it and suggest strategies most people can use to improve their own judgment.

Alexandra Armstrong, financial planner...

I base logical judgments on past experiences. Whatever happened in the past is likely to repeat. What worked before is likely to work again.

Though all decisions are affected by intuition to some degree, I follow the principle *If it's logical and recurrent, go with it.* I ground my professional advice by reviewing financial trends of the past.

Example: In the summer of 1987, the price/earnings ratio of stocks was at historically high levels. In the past, this has signaled a stock market downturn. Thus our clients were prepared for the subsequent decline, although the enormity and brevity of the crash were a surprise to all of us.

Dr. Herbert Benson, cardiologist...

Judgment can't really be defined in any exact way. There has been some philosophical emphasis on decision theory, but that's very different from practical decision-making skills. Those can only be developed over time through trial and error, learning from your own experiences as well as those of others.

Good judgment really boils down to being able to weigh the relevant risks and benefits involved in a given situation and, as a result of this process, making an accurate assessment of what you should do.

When both the risks and benefits are substantial, it's important to look for ways to modify the risks without losing too many of the benefits.

One of the best ways to clarify the risks and benefits is to list them in two columns. This will help you be specific about each point and look at the decision more objectively. Before making that list, however, you've got to understand the implications of the decision.

Once I have looked at the problem objectively, I find it useful to back off and go on to something else—for a while. In our increasingly stressful world, the pace and anxiety that we live with hamper our decision-making abilities.

Being able to relax and let things rearrange in your mind is crucial to good judgment. Sometimes it just takes one night's sleep for the new perspectives—the sound perspectives—to fall into place.

Norma Kamali, clothing designer and entrepreneur...

As a designer my goal is always to create something new. I live by inspiration. What I *feel* is more important to the process than what I *think*, and a great deal of my judgment is governed by this.

Everything in my life is a totality—blending every experience and creating a spiritual connection between the outside and my inside world. I *sense* keenly everything that is going on in the world and filter it through my emotions and experiences. Then I create pictures in my head and visualize them by sketching, drawing or doodling.

I trust my intuition when making judgment calls, but I'm constantly open to improvement since I believe there is always another way to do it. I make quick decisions but then have to edit myself. Fortunately, another side of me likes to pay attention to detail. Keeping "to do" lists helps me stay disciplined and focused. I don't do this on a computer, which is too impersonal, but with pen and paper.

Bouncing back and forth from the concept to the details, zooming my mental lens in and out, is key to staying flexible, having perspective and exercising good judgment.

Dr. James Masterson, psychiatrist...

There are several important capacities that contribute to good judgment:

- The ability to perceive reality rather than living in your fantasies.
- The ability to control your impulses to act until you have figured something out.
- Having the imagination to see beyond the present to what the future holds.

But the sum of these capacities doesn't necessarily make for good judgment in all areas of life. The capacity for judgment in one arena is not always evident in another arena.

Example: Many people are very successful at work but have enormous problems in relationships because their judgment becomes severely inhibited when their emotions are involved. They act mostly on the basis of their own fantasies. The more objective they can be, the freer they are to use this capacity for judgment.

Often, bad judgment is just part of a pathological defense mechanism, as when people make self-defeating or self-destructive decisions about their lives.

Example: There are people who, because of their own fears and anxieties, pick unavailable mates to act out their fantasies. You could say their judgment is poor, but it isn't really their judgment that is operating. It's reality being denied. They never have the data to make the right judgment.

You can develop finely tuned judgment as long as you can see reality as it is—that's number one. Next—comes being able to figure out the meanings and consequences of the reality you are seeing...articulating the choices...and choosing the one that works out best.

In my profession, we tend to think that everybody who is healthy has good judgment, but I'm sure that's not true.

There is definitely an element of intuition to good judgment. We all operate on it, sometimes consciously and maybe more often subconsciously. You can hone your intuition through experimentation. Learn from what you judged —well and poorly—and put it back in the "computer" to decide how you're going to deal with the next problem. Remember where you went wrong, so that next time you will have a sense of when to back off from a course of action and reconsider what you should do.

Dr. Dagmar O'Connor, psychologist...

We use judgment in two different ways. First —when we're asked to make decisions for others. Second—when we must make decisions that directly involve ourselves.

Most of us have good judgment about an issue that involves someone else. That's because we're emotionally detached and therefore free to reason more clearly. That is also why it's smart to seek the advice of others...and why no one should serve as his/her own lawyer.

Judgment is steered by motivation to do well or badly for ourselves—to succeed or fail. Such motivations are usually formed in childhood by parental permission.

When we turn *inward* for advice or assistance, unconsciously we are searching our pasts for reference points to help us solve the problems. When we are unable to reach rational decisions, it is often because memories from our pasts are holding us back or distorting our reasoning.

This helps to explain why it is possible for someone to excel in judgment for others—but fail miserably for himself. Every day there are examples of judges—financial planners, bus drivers and parents—who consistently make wise decisions on behalf of society, clients and children but do not exercise the same good judgment for themselves. *Examples of how unresolved childhood issues can impair your judgment:*

•Personal relationships. You've ended a relationship with someone who is nice and supportive because you feel he/she is boring. You clearly want some passionate excitement with someone who is not so available. *Reason:* You probably had parents who were not emotionally available.

When you continually find yourself in abusive or dysfunctional relationships, it could mean that you were raised by parents who didn't act toward you in respectful and loving ways...and, therefore, you have learned to be attracted to people who are not respectful or loving.

If, when you were a child, your parents gave you the feeling that you didn't deserve much, you will make judgments that reaffirm that treatment. If parents teach children that they are worth a lot and will be successful, the children will then grow up to realize that in their own judgments.

Going forward, you need to present a role model of success, self-esteem and happiness for your children, because good judgment originates out of that confidence.

•Business relationships. You pick a bad business partner and confide too much in him. Everyone tells you the person isn't quite right for your needs, and the evidence confirms this, too. Yet you persist, simply because you want to be different and believe that you know better than anybody else.

You have a need to not listen to anybody's advice. This may mean that as a child you could not trust your parents—perhaps for good reason. Your parents may have been too controlling, and you are still fighting that perceived parental control in your adult life. If you consistently pick bad business partners, you should look for deeper reasons for why you want to hurt yourself. You may be reliving a parental relationship rather than succeeding at your business.

Dr. Clifford Sager, psychiatrist...

Good judgment helps you make the right decision at the right time. It can be a very small —or very important—matter. It can also be something you have time to mull over or something that must be done in a split second, such as when a car is coming toward you in the wrong lane. Some business decisions must be made almost as quickly.

Judgment is partly instinctual and partly developed through experience. As children, we learn to judge when the stove is hot. Later we must make judgments between or among a variety of alternatives, including complex decisions about other people.

The higher you go professionally, the more difficult it is to make these judgments. No matter how much information you have, you reach a point at which you must consult your instinctive judgment to make the right decision.

Often your reasons may be subliminal. Over time, you learn to discern which instincts are solid and which are based on your own associations and preconceptions.

When it comes to personal relationships, it can be more difficult to judge from instinct because we're not aware of what we're reacting to. We are often attracted to people because we want to become like them. Or we may heartily dislike someone without recognizing that it is because they share our faults—faults that we don't like and can't confront in ourselves. Part of developing good judgment is knowing your limitations—and that is important. It's best not to make judgments regarding things about which you know little.

Sources: Alexandra Armstrong, a certified financial planner and chairman, Armstrong, Welch and MacIntyre, financial advisers, 1155 Connecticut Ave. NW, Washington, DC 20036.

Herbert Benson, MD, Mind/Body Medical Institute, associate professor of medicine, Harvard Medical School and chief of the division of behavioral medicine, Deaconess Hospital, Boston.

Norma Kamali, owner and president, Norma Kamali, Inc., 11 W. 56 St,. New York 10019.

James Masterson, MD, a psychiatrist in private practice in New York, and author of *The Search for the Real Self: Unmaking the Personality Disorders of Our Age.* The Free Press, 866 Third Ave., New York 10022.

Dagmar O'Connor, PhD, psychotherapist and sex therapist in private practice in New York. She is the author of *How to Make Love to the Same Person for the Rest of Your Life and Still Love It.* Bantam Books, 1540 Broadway, New York 10036.

Clifford Sager, MD, psychiatrist and psychotherapist, 65 E. 76 St., New York 10021.

Check Your Premise

Many times we are stumped by a problem, even though what we're doing seems to be consistent and logical.

The problem in such cases is often with us —we often have the wrong premise or make faulty assumptions and fail to consider the possibility that these errors are the source of our problems.

Even in mathematics, which we consider an exact science, certain premises for a given set of assumptions are arbitrary. This means that they may as well be picked out of a hat—there's no way of proving them. People choose premises from their experiences, observations and firm beliefs, and these premises are sometimes faulty.

Example I: Euclid said the world was flat because, as far as the eye could see, it was. Since his geometry was based on a flat world, no matter how logically and consistently he worked it out, it had to be flawed.

Example II: Gorbachev believed Communism would work better if it was reformed. He believed that central planning could satisfy people's needs as well as individual free choice. And he mistakenly assumed that loosening repression would allow a slow change in Soviet society rather than the rapid dissolution of Communist rule that actually occurred. His faulty premises led to results that were the opposite of those he intended.

Premises governing human relationships are equally arbitrary. It was once assumed that women couldn't be economically independent. This was one of the premises that all social arrangements were based on. In fact, because that was assumed to be true, it made sense not to give a woman the vote because she was a dependent part of a single household and the household was thought of as having one vote, which should be cast by the breadwinner. When that premise fell away, many other things that seemed logical also changed, such as women always deferring to men in relationships.

Problems in business...

The same arbitrariness has governed many major business decisions.

Example: For many years, Detroit operated under the assumption that Americans wanted big, fast cars that could—and had to—be traded in regularly.

Faulty premise: Quality control wasn't important. The Japanese realized that quality was important and became major competitors in the American market. That false premise resulted in a huge shift of assets from one country to the other.

How false premises affect your life...

The first few times you fail with something, it may be because your technique is wrong... you haven't practiced enough...you need to clean up your act. If you fail persistently, however, you need to check your premises.

Example: The woman who is involved with her third alcoholic because she believes this one is going to go to AA as he promises.

False premise: Alcoholics need her, or someone like her, to save them. She's not seeing how dependent she is on having to take care of someone so she doesn't have to face her own problems.

People often fail when they go into business for themselves because they never check their premises.

False premise: If you invent a better mousetrap, you'll be a success. Many of the currently available great ideas have already been invented and either failed because of inherent flaws, because they're not marketable or because the skills of the business owner were poor. The process of taking a great idea and turning it into a successful business is very complex. Just having the idea is only one of the multitude of elements needed for success.

We have a strong resistance to checking our premises because life would be unbearable if we didn't come to some firm conclusions about what various commonplace things mean —clothing, certain manners, types of speech. We've learned that it's too expensive or time-consuming to check our premises, and 99% of the time things do mean what they seem to mean.

Con men take advantage of this aspect of human nature. A con man sets up a scene that conforms to your premises. He knows your reactions will not lead you to check your premises until *after* he has fleeced you.

When you should check your premise...

You should check your premises whenever things are going wrong. Even in a con situation, people usually have an intuitive feeling that something is a little off. If your intuition tells you something is fishy, check your premise. It's always worth the effort.

Helpful: Take time to think for a while if you're asked to do something that doesn't seem right. Don't let embarrassment keep you from checking someone out thoroughly.

Listen to feedback. Whenever someone criticizes you, presume he's right and your defenses are wrong. This is a tremendous learning experience. If you listen to critiques carefully, you'll find there is some truth, no matter how far-fetched. You don't have to agree with what's said, but you do have to understand where it's coming from.

Example: Someone tells you he likes your suit, but it's the wrong color for you. Instead of getting defensive, ask questions about what's wrong with the color. As a result, you might find out about color analysis and decide to see a color consultant.

False premise: If it is a well-manufactured garment and fits well, the color doesn't matter.

Important: You need to analyze not just the criticism, but the premises on which it is based. You must understand the difference between the premises of the person giving you feedback and your own.

Example: Lionel is not getting what he wants from his employees. He asks Joe, one of his workers, what the problem is and is told that he's too pushy and demanding. When Lionel takes Joe's advice, and demands less and listens more, productivity improves enormously.

False premise: The harder you push, the more you get.

Source: Martin G. Groder, MD, a Chapel Hill, North Carolina psychiatrist and business consultant. His book, *Business Games*, is available from Boardroom Classics, Greenwich, CT.

Secrets of Appreciating Life

Despite the ever-growing amount of information we have about human nature, the soul is still impossible to define in pragmatic terms and still remains an enigma.

Unlike the brain, the soul has no physical or material reality. Yet it governs our values, relatedness and personal substance. Lose touch with your soul and the effects can be debilitating...even devastating.

For example, many people who are in perfect physical health and have attained wealth and fame feel a deep sense of unease when they neglect their souls.

Not knowing how to care for your soul leaves you at a serious disadvantage, since painful experiences are unavoidable. Confronting them and learning from them are the ways to nurture the soul.

Most of us recognize that some of the more simple aspects of life are particularly satisfying.

That is why we refer to them as "food for the soul" and "music that is good for the soul."

But every aspect of life—family, love, work ...even dark aspects like jealousy, depression, and illness—can provide spiritual food for the soul if we approach them in a receptive way.

Family and the soul...

Many people today who regard themselves as self-sufficient have lost the important truth, which was taught by traditional societies, that we must honor our families.

Honoring the family helps the soul because the family is a source of religious awareness. A family forces you to realize that you did not create yourself...that you have a unique place in the world. Within your family, you can be who you really are and learn to appreciate the individuality of others.

To help family appreciation: Don't expect too much from your family. Try to appreciate each member's unique qualities. If you are miserable and feel it's because of the way you were treated by your family when you were young, try a different perspective. Ask yourself, "Where did my good qualities come from?" It's highly likely that your family had a great deal to do with them.

Love and the soul...

Many people have unrealistic expectations of love—within the family, with spouses, with friends. Love isn't perfect and eternal. It passes through different stages...and often ends.

To satisfy your soul, a loving relationship must honor the other person's soul as well. That means recognizing who the other person really is...and allowing that person to change. You must pay attention and allow the relationship to develop.

For soul-satisfying relationships: Spend time together...write letters to each other...visit friends together. When you talk to each other, don't just talk about work—talk about what's in your heart.

Work and the soul...

Work is a major part of life. Few things satisfy the soul more than a fulfilling vocation. But if the work you do conflicts with your soul—because of your sense of ethics or aesthetics—it may make you very unhappy, no matter how much you earn.

If you are in that position, look into a career change. If a change isn't immediately feasible, don't despair. Look around...for years, if necessary. And meanwhile, even though you are unhappy in your current work situation, practice other ways to care for your soul.

To help your soul if you are unhappy at work: First, acknowledge your situation. Then, make the best of it by putting more effort into areas that do satisfy your soul...family, friendships, hobbies, sports, travel, etc.

Soul and the darker side of life...

Anyone who thinks that life's only goal is happiness will be troubled. The less-pleasant parts of life cannot be avoided.

If you reflect on your unhappy experiences, you will find that they offer their own gifts... and contribute to the development of your soul. *These experiences include...*

- Jealousy, which comes with intense relationships. It teaches that relationships are demanding...and deepens your understanding of both the self and the relationship.
- Depression, which deepens the personality, leaving you better able to cope with future problems. People who have only seen the sunny side of life may be overwhelmed when something bad happens...those who have gone through depression look at the world in a more realistic, accepting way.
- Illness, which forces you to reflect on your own mortality and teaches that you are not as strong or as independent as you thought.

To benefit from troubles: When you suffer physical, social or economic setbacks, see what you can learn from the experiences. Acknowledge your human frailties...don't be afraid to ask others for help. You will gain a richer perspective on friendship and the meaning of life.

The art of life...

Modern society pursues functionality and efficiency at all costs, but the human soul craves beauty. Much of the unhappiness in today's world comes from a neglect of the beauty of life in favor of acquiring things and getting results quickly.

Since schools don't often teach the arts, your soul is starved of the imaginative diet it needs. You can make up this deficiency by striving to bring beauty into your life.

To feed your soul in everyday life: Even if you don't consider yourself artistic, you can use your imagination to enrich the way you live.

When you decorate your home, for example, don't settle for someone else's taste... even if it's advice from a high-priced interior decorator. Your home should express your feelings and imagination. Think about the location, the furnishings, and the decorations, so they satisfy you emotionally and express your soul's individuality.

By living in a way that cares for your soul faithfully every day, you can let your individual genius emerge and discover in full measure who you really are.

Source: Psychotherapist Thomas Moore, PhD, a former monk with academic degrees in theology, music and philosophy, and author of the best-seller *Care of the Soul: A Guide for Cultivating Depth and Sacredness in Everyday Life,* HarperCollins, 10 E. 53 St., New York 10022.

Key to Self-Confidence

No one is born competent. We develop competence through repeated exposure, study and practice. This requires willingness to take some risks without knowing what the outcome will be. *Also important:* Accepting the possibility of failure. Ironically, fear of failure actually creates failure. If you do not test your dreams or try to do something important to you, you are sure to fail.

Source: *On Target: Enhance Your Life and Ensure Your Success* by Jeri Sedlar, president, Sedlar Communications, New York marketing and productivity consultants. MasterMedia Limited, 17 E. 89 St., New York 10128.

The Importance of Self-Esteem

Healthy self-esteem is a basic human need. It is indispensable to psychological development...to resilience in the face of life's adversities...to our feeling of belonging in the world ...to our ability to express joy. As the world becomes more complex, competitive and challenging, self-esteem is more important than ever.

The shift from a manufacturing-based society to one based on information, and the emergence of a global economy characterized by rapid change have created growing demands on our psychological resources. Recently, the focus of my work has been to show how self-esteem principles and technology can be used to improve performance in the work place.

Self-esteem defined...

Despite the abundance of books, studies, workshops and committees devoted to the subject of self-esteem, there is little agreement about what it means. I think self-esteem has two essential components:

- Self-efficacy. Confidence in the ability to cope with life's challenges. Self-efficacy leads to a sense of control over one's life.
- Self-respect. Experiencing oneself as deserving of happiness, achievement and love. Self-respect makes possible a sense of community with others.

Self-esteem is a self-reinforcing characteristic. When we have confidence in our ability to think and act effectively, we can persevere when faced with difficult challenges. *Result:* We succeed more often than we fail. We form more nourishing relationships. We expect more of life and of ourselves.

If we lack confidence, we give up easily, fail more often and aspire to less. *Result:* We get less of what we want.

What self-esteem is not...

Self-esteem is a necessary condition of well-being. But it's not the only one. Its presence doesn't make life problem-free. Even people with high self-esteem may experience anxiety, depression or fear when overwhelmed by issues they don't know how to cope with.

I think of self-esteem as the *immune system* of consciousness. A healthy immune system doesn't guarantee you'll never become ill, but it does reduce your susceptibility to illness and can improve your odds for a speedy recovery if you do get sick.

The same is true psychologically. Those with strong self-esteem are resilient in the face of life's difficulties.

It's impossible to have too much self-esteem. People who are arrogant or boastful actually show a lack of self-esteem. Those who are truly comfortable with themselves and their achievements take pleasure in being who they are... they don't need to tell the world about it.

Becoming successful, powerful or well-liked does not automatically confer good self-esteem. In fact, talented and powerful people who doubt their own core value are usually unable to find joy in their achievements, no matter how great their external success.

Important: Self-esteem has to do with what I think of me, not what anyone else thinks of me.

The highly touted use of affirmations is also ineffective, or at best of marginal value, in raising self-esteem. Telling yourself you're capable and lovable accomplishes little if you are operating irresponsibly in key areas of your life.

Roots of self-regard...

Genetic inheritance may have a role in a person's self-esteem—it's conceivable, anyway. Parental upbringing can also play a powerful role.

Parents with strong self-esteem lay the foundation for that quality in their children. They raise them with plenty of love and acceptance, believing in their competence and setting reasonable rules and expectations.

Yet there are exceptions that we still don't understand. Some people who have these positive factors in their backgrounds become self-doubting adults, while others who survive seemingly destructive childhoods grow up with a strong sense of self-worth.

Strengthening self-esteem is not a quick or easy process. We can't do it directly. Self-esteem is a consequence of following fundamental internal practices that require an ongoing commitment to self-examination. I call these practices the *Six Pillars of Self-Esteem:*

- Living consciously. Paying attention to information and feedback about needs and goals ...facing facts that might be uncomfortable or threatening...refusing to wander through life in a self-induced mental fog.
- Self-acceptance. Being willing to experience whatever we truly think, feel or do, even if we don't always like it...facing our mistakes and learning from them.
- Self-responsibility. Establishing a sense of control over our lives by realizing we are responsible for our choices and actions at every level...the achievement of our goals...our happiness...our values.
- Self-assertiveness. The willingness to express appropriately our thoughts, values and feelings...to stand up for ourselves...to speak and act from our deepest convictions.
- Living purposefully. Setting goals and working to achieve them, rather than living at the mercy of chance and outside forces... developing self-discipline.
- Integrity. The integration of our behavior with our ideals, convictions, standards and beliefs...acting in congruence with what we believe is right.

Most of us are taught from an early age to pay far more attention to signals coming from other people than from within. We are encouraged to ignore our own needs and wants and to concentrate on living up to others' expectations.

Self-esteem requires us to listen to and respect our own sensations, insights, intuition and perspective. For some people, learning to do this may require the help of a competent therapist. For all of us, developing the pillars of self-esteem is a lifelong—and worthy—challenge.

Source: Nathaniel Branden, PhD, a clinical psychologist in private practice and founder of the Branden Institute for Self-Esteem in Los Angeles. He is the author of 11 books, including *How to Raise Your Self-Esteem,* Bantam Books, 666 Fifth Ave., New York 10103.

Unexpressed Feelings

Beware of unexpressed feelings—especially negative ones. People who do not express feelings get sick more often...stay sick longer ...and die sooner than expressive people. *Example:* Nonexpression of emotion and denial of hostility or anger are two of the factors most related to unfavorable prognosis in cancer patients. Unexpressed negative feelings feed on themselves—for instance, anger can turn against the self and emerge as depression or severe anxiety.

Source: *Lethal Lovers and Poisonous People: How to Protect Your Health from Relationships That Make You Sick* by Los Angeles psychologist Harriet Braiker, PhD. Pocket Books, 1230 Avenue of the Americas, New York 10020.

3

Putting Your Best Foot Forward

Top 10 Etiquette Rules For Adults

•Return calls and answer letters promptly. Calls should be returned within 48 hours and letters within two weeks. If you cannot respond yourself within that time, have someone else do it for you.

Telephone etiquette: When you call someone and your call-waiting signals, ignore it. You made the call, so you should give it priority. Be respectful of a person's schedule and obligations when choosing a time to call.

•RSVP within one week to all invitations. Go to an event when you have accepted...call ahead if you can't make it. If you accept an invitation and then fail to attend, call or write to apologize.

•Introduce people properly and in a flattering way. State the person's name clearly and correctly, as well as his/her title, occupation, and city of residence if somewhere other than where you are. Also give their hobbies or interests especially when they are similar to those of the person to whom you're making the introduction. And always introduce the less important or younger person to the more important or older.

•Take care to use people's titles properly. Doctors, judges, people of military rank, and elected officials should always be addressed with their titles or "the honorable." Too few of us are doing this today, and it's very bad manners.

•Be sensitive to the culture, religious laws, and diet of international friends and colleagues. Brief yourself on their country before you see them. Know their country's leading politicians, the names of their country's great museums, their universities, and what types of foods they can and cannot eat.

•Watch your table manners. This can never be stressed enough. Don't stuff food in your mouth or talk while eating. Do not leave your dirty napkin on the table when you excuse yourself during a meal. Leave it on your chair instead. Wipe your mouth frequently. When finished, move your fork and knife to the right-hand rim of the plate—and sit up straight. Ignoring these things makes you appear rather uncouth.

•Don't monopolize the guest of honor. Give equal time to every guest, regardless of how important or unimportant his/her position. This is an act of kindness as well as good manners.

•Teach your children to respect their elders. Have them stand up when your friends enter the room...say, "How do you do?"...and shake hands. Parents seem to be failing in this, perhaps because they are not around their children as much these days. But making the effort will make your children's lives much easier as adults.

•Know how and when to apologize. Always make your apology as soon as possible after the event. Some acts require only a spoken apology, others require a spoken and written apology...and some require much more.

Example: About 10 years ago, I accepted an invitation to be the guest of honor at a dinner party, and then completely forgot about it. I called several times to apologize, wrote two letters of apology, and finally sent a dozen roses. To this day, I am still apologizing for that incident.

•Write thank-you notes for gifts, favors, meals, or any act of kindness. Also write notes to encourage, congratulate, and commiserate.

Source: Letitia Baldrige, renowned expert on manners and author of 14 books, including *Letitia Baldrige's New Complete Guide to Executive Manners,* Rawson Associates, 866 Third Ave., New York 10022. The book draws upon her experiences in the business world, diplomatic life, and the Kennedy White House.

Clothing Language

To psychiatrists, grooming, clothes, makeup, and all-around physical appearance are important clues to personality and mental health. Those clues can be useful, too, to people making hiring decisions or who otherwise want to be able to size people up.

Key: Appropriateness. Clothes and appearance have to be viewed in the context of a person's position and the milieu in which he operates.

Appearance clues:

•Overly meticulous. Constricted neat, not elegant neat. (*Example:* Very narrow, tight ties. Jackets always buttoned. People who arrange trouser creases each time they sit down.) Usually good indicators of an obsessive personality. Obsessiveness may be fine for employers seeking industrious, dependable types concerned with detail. It is not for those who want someone with creative capacity.

•Careless, torn, stained clothing and lack of attention to detail. These are signs of depression. *Another trouble sign:* Somber colors such as black or maroon, worn much or most of the time.

•Incongruous clothes that seem markedly inappropriate to the age of the person wearing them. This usually indicates a lack of friends and associates through whom he would have learned what to wear.

•Clothes that are too young: Short skirts or a "little girl" look on an older woman or the "preppie" look on a man obviously too old for the style generally indicates an image problem. Such a choice of clothes suggests an inability to tune into reality.

•Identification. People who go in for prestige symbols generally are using them as a means to inflate their self-esteem and for virtually no other reason.

•Focus. Attention-getting attire, particularly on men. *Example:* Going to the office (where such dress isn't expected) in jeans and workshirt. This is usually a sign of a narcissistic personality, a type that sees the world as revolving around him and what he wants.

•Very manly styles on women. Increasingly evident in women who have left their roles as homemakers and gone back to the business world, it may well indicate discomfort about leaving home and reversing women's traditional roles. Overdoing anything in a dramatic way, whether it's "looking businesslike" or some other posture is always a sign of conflict.

•Button wearers. Whatever the message of their buttons, they have a shaky sense of self-esteem (which they try to bolster by identifying publicly with a group).

• Wearing sunglasses unnecessarily. People trust others more when they can see their eyes.

Source: Dr. Michael Levy, psychiatrist, New York.

Dressing for Success

Businesspeople's concern isn't with fashion but with function—the impact their clothes have on people. Let's face it, clothes are a power tool. Wear the right clothes and you can "sell" yourself successfully.

• Successful dress is really no more than achieving good taste and the look of the upper-middle class. The traditional styling of Savile Row dominates the world of businessmen's clothing—the understated elegance of English tailoring.

• Designers have been responsible for many positive changes in men's clothing in recent years, and some liberalization of styles, patterns and colors has taken place, but this trend is basically confined to leisure wear. Designers have had little influence on the mainstream of American business dress.

• Business styles change with glacier-like slowness, and there's no point in risking career, income and social position by gambling on fads.

• The most important element in establishing a man's authority is his physical size. Large men tend to be extremely authoritative. But they can frighten people. The large man should avoid all dark suits. *He should wear very soft colors:* Medium-range gray suits, beige suits and very light suits in the summer. The small man has the reverse problem. *The smaller man should wear high-authority clothing:* Pinstriped suits, pinstriped shirts and vests.

• Expensive ties give authority to the young. Buy the kind of tie which would obviously not be bought by a boy.

Source: John T. Molloy, corporate image researcher and consultant and author of *Dress for Success* and *The Woman's Dress for Success Book,* Warner Books, New York.

Male Body Type: A Factor in Executive Dressing

• For short men. The pinstripe contributes to an illusion of height. The vertical line formed by the classic three-button jacket will enhance the illusion, as will pockets that point inward and upward. No cuffs on trousers.

• For heavy men. Dark suits impart a lighter look. Best for men of ordinary height is a single-breasted jacket with a center vent. A double-breasted jacket is suitable for taller men—of any weight. Avoid pleats in trousers, as they add bulk. Darts are better for comfort and a well-tailored look.

• For thin men. Use pale, heavier-gauge fabrics to create a sense of bulk. Straight-legged trousers will give the legs a fuller appearance. Avoid tapered trousers, which conform to the shape of the leg.

For Men: What to Wear At the Office

Successful men dress very carefully for the office:

• Dress conservatively, in a style as similar to the style of those around you—and above you —as you can.

• Always wear a suit.

• To convey a stronger impression of authority, wear a darker suit—with a vest.

• To emphasize a financial aura, wear dark gray or blue pinstripes.

• Wear solid-color cotton shirts or conservative stripes. Avoid elaborate patterns and anything flashy, sharp or gaudy.

• The best ties are striped ("rep"), solid, dotted, "club," and "Ivy League" patterns. No flowers, foulards, or paisleys for office wear.

Source: John T. Molloy, author of *Dress for Success* and *The Woman's Dress for Success,* Warner Books, New York.

How to Dress for Success At Your Company

The key is to emulate your boss, but don't be obvious about it. *General rules:*

• Conservative-looking suit, white shirt (pale pastels if your boss and other senior managers wear them), matching tie.

• Muted colors connote trust, upper-middle-class status.

• Black, navy, pinstripe, and chalk-striped suits exude power, competence, and authority.

• Beware of loud pastels (gaudy); shades of pink (effeminate); gold or green-gray (unflattering); light blues, gray-beige (you're more likely to be liked than respected).

• *Also out:* European cuts, turtlenecks, clashing colors that hint of sloppiness or academia, sports clothes (save them for sports).

• Avoid styles or colors that threaten to become overpopular.

How to Buy Clothes that Make You Look Good

• Choosing color to "go with" your hair and eyes is a mistake. It's your skin tone that determines how a particular color looks on you.

• The more intense and dark your clothing, the larger you'll appear and the less likely to blend into the environment.

• White tends to wash out the face and yellow the teeth. Soft ivory tones are somewhat better.

• Don't rule out whole color groups—all blues or all greens. Most people can wear certain shades of most color groups. *Exceptions:* A few colors, such as orange and purple, are really not good for many people in any shade.

• Pay attention to pattern or weave. People who are short or small-boned should not wear big prints or checks. They can wear small true tweeds. Slender, smallish men and women are overwhelmed by heavy fabrics. Light wools are better for them than heavy worsteds.

• Consider aging skin in choosing colors. Wrinkled skin is minimized by softer shades. Hard, dark, intense colors maximize the evidence of aging.

• The colors surrounding you in your home or office determine the way in which the eye perceives your skin and even your features. Some colors will produce deep shadows, enlarge certain features or produce deep facial lines because of the way they interact with your skin tone.

• Don't change makeup to "go with" clothes. Makeup should be chosen according to skin tone only. Using the wrong color makeup is worse than wearing the wrong color clothing.

• Most men can't wear madras or bold plaids. When men choose sports clothes, they go wild in the other direction from the conservative clothes they wear to work. Most have had little practice in choosing dramatic colors that are suitable.

• A tan does make you look healthier, but it doesn't change the basic effect of certain colors on your skin. With a tan, wearing colors you normally look good in is important, because that's when those colors look better than ever.

Source: Adrienne Gold and Anne Herman, partners in Colorconscious, Inc., Larchmont, NY.

Dressing for Special Occasions

Unusual circumstances may call for a thoughtful adaptation of basic dress rules. Learn as much as possible about the geographical, educational and socioeconomic background of the people you'll be dealing with and tailor your wardrobe to their expectations. *Examples:*

• Appearing in court. The main problem here is establishing credibility, and the best way to appear credible is to surprise no one. For maximum effectiveness, look just as others expect you to look.

If you are appearing as a high-ranking financial officer, you'll dress differently than if you're appearing as a technical expert—even though you may be both. The higher up the management pyramid you wish to represent yourself, the more quietly opulent your dress should be.

• Keep regional/local considerations in mind. A New Yorker, for example, testifying in Texas would be well advised to tone down his dress, keeping it low-key.

• Appearing at an IRS audit. The right image for this situation combines authority with humility—respectable and respectful, but not too prosperous. *Keep it simple and conservative:* Wear one of your older suits (a well-worn Brooks Brothers would be excellent), preferably two-piece, with a plain white shirt and a conservative striped tie. Avoid jewelry and other signs of affluence.

• Television appearances. The dress standards of a TV show host are a reasonable guide. Dress less conservatively. Wear lighter colors. Leave the three-piece suit and other power symbols at home. Keep accessories simple and understated. Wear solid colors. Avoid small patterns.

• Public speaking. If you know in advance what color the background will be (or if you can choose it), wear a suit (preferably dark) that will stand out. Wear a contrasting shirt (preferably light-colored) and a solid tie.

• Job interviews. Dress for the interview, not for the job. Even if you will be a field engineer, come to the interview in a three-piece suit.

Tailor the quality of your dress to the level of the position you seek. A recent college graduate will be forgiven a $200 suit. A candidate for an $80,000 management position will not.

Source: John T. Molloy, author of *Dress for Success* and *The Woman's Dress for Success,* Warner Books, New York.

How to Prolong the Life of Your Clothes

• Hang jackets on wooden or plastic hangers that are curved to the approximate shape of the human back.

• Remove all objects from pockets.

• Leave jackets unbuttoned.

• Keep some space between garments to avoid wrinkling.

• Allow at least 24 hours between wearings.

• Use pants hangers that clamp onto trouser bottoms.

• Remove belt before hanging up pants.

Hair Care Hints

• Baby shampoos are not as mild as special-formula shampoos for dry or damaged hair. Detergents and pH levels put baby shampoos into the middle range of hair cleansers, which makes them right for normal hair.

• People with oily hair need a stronger shampoo especially made for that condition.

• Wet hair should be combed, not brushed. Hair is weakest when wet and can be easily damaged then. Use a wide-tooth comb to reduce the chance of breaking your hair.

• Twenty-five brush strokes a day is optimal for best distribution of natural oils in the hair. More brushing can cause damage.

Men's Hairstyles: The Trend isn't Trendy

Men's hairstyles today are short and genuine. Men want to look natural, not as though they just left the barbershop.

• The best stylist is nature. If we cut and comb our hair the way it wants to be cut and combed, it always looks good. If we try to imitate someone else's hairstyle, we always end up getting into trouble.

• A good barber makes the hair fit the customer's facial structure. He cuts the hair so the customer can take care of it himself. When the customer goes back to the office, his colleagues shouldn't realize that he just had a haircut. They should notice only that he looks better.

•A banker or Wall Street executive wants a conservative look. His hair doesn't come down over the tops of his ears. You shouldn't see a circle around the ear, either—just a perfect, neat haircut that tapers cleanly above the ear.

•Men in advertising can be a little more daring, with fuller, longer hair.

•The cosmetics company executive, who is in the business of making people look good, wants a little flair.

•Years ago, men who could afford it would get a toupee to cover bald spots. No more. If they do anything, they go for a transplant. But more and more, men want to look natural. They feel that if they have hair, good—if not, that's okay. As long as whatever they have is cut properly, they'll look fine. Hollywood reflects the change. Attractive middle-aged and younger stars are frankly balding: Jack Nicholson, Robert Duvall or John Malkovich.

•Eighty percent of men in their early forties cover the gray. By that time a man may have a good executive position, but he's aware that if he loses his job or wants to change jobs there's still a stigma attached to looking old.

•The man who is 50 or 60 doesn't care anymore about gray. He's been around, and he's confident about who he is. It's important to color the hair discreetly, so it looks natural. Regular touch-ups are important. Even the most professional hair-coloring jobs start to fade quickly and must be touched up.

•Beware of the former barbershop that suddenly changed its name from Joe's Barbershop to Joe's Hairstylist. The change may be in name only. The best method is to ask someone whose haircut you consistently like where he got it done.

Source: Peppe Baldo, a New York City hairstylist for bankers, brokers, lawyers, advertising executives, and other corporate and media executives.

The Secrets of A Great Shave

Treat your face to the most up-to-date equipment. It is false economy to buy anything less than the best, since the entire annual cost of shaving seldom exceeds $100. Also, blades and shaving creams are constantly being improved.

•*Shaving cream:* All types of cream (lather, brushless and aerosol in either lather or gel form) are equally efficient. Brushless shaving cream is recommended for dry skin. Buy three or four different kinds of shaving cream. Use different ones for different moods.

•*Blades:* Modern technology makes the current stainless-steel blades a real pleasure to use. *The best type:* The double-track blade.

•Proper preparation. Wash your face with soap at least twice before shaving. This helps soften the skin, saturate the beard and remove facial oils. *Best:* Shave after a warm shower.

•Shaving cream is more effective if left on the face for a few minutes prior to actual shaving. This saturation causes the facial hairs to expand by about one-third, which enhances the cutting ability of the blade.

•Except on the warmest days, preheat lather in the can or tube by immersion in hot water.

•The manufacturing process leaves a slight oil residue on the edge of the new blade. This can catch and pull the tender facial skin during the first couple of strokes. So start by trimming the sideburns, a painless way of breaking in the new blade. Always shave the upper lip and chin last. *Why:* The coarsest hairs grow here. Your skin will benefit from the extra minutes of saturation and wetness.

•When you have finished shaving, rinse the blade and shake the razor dry. Never wipe-dry a blade; this dulls the edge. When rinsing the blade, hold it low in the water stream for quicker results.

•After shaving: Save money by skipping the highly advertised aftershave lotions. Use witch hazel instead. It is odorless, less astringent, leaves no residue and is better for your skin than most of the aftershave lotions.

Clean Up

Best face-washing technique:

•Fill a sink with the hottest water your face can stand.

•Take a hard-milled soap, such as Grey Flannel (for men) or Old English Lavender (for women), and work up a rich lather.

•Work the lather into your face and throat with the tips of your fingers.

•Rinse by splashing with the sink's water, not running water. Never rinse with clear or cold water, which can dry skin or break capillaries. Hot water helps to both moisten dry skin by stimulating oil glands and dissolve excess surface oil if your face is oily.

•Blot gently (don't rub) with a towel, and let remaining moisture evaporate from your skin.

Source: James Wagenvoord, *Personal Style,* Holt, Rinehart and Winston, New York.

Messies Don't Have to Be Messy Forever

Messies are people who live with stacks of things they'll never need again—old books, last year's Christmas cards, worn-out clothes, etc. They're perfectionists who avoid making decisions for fear of making the *wrong* decision.

But so much clutter makes them inefficient. Messies save so much, they can never find the things they really *do* need.

The terrible truth: In one way or another, we're all Messies. Even people with the neatest-looking houses usually have a secret spot that has been taken over by things that really should be thrown away.

The first step in getting over the problem is to understand what makes you tick. *People hold on to things...*

...for sentimental reasons. They want to keep memories alive, and think that this means holding on to the objects associated with the memories.

...for future use. Messies keep things they think they might need one day.

...to define themselves. Many Messies surround themselves with objects from a life they think they *should* be living.

How to recover...

Once you understand *why* you're a Messie you can take control of your life by taking control of your environment.

The best way to start is by giving your house a thorough cleaning...and throwing out everything that you really don't need. *To succeed...*

•Break your cleaning project into small, manageable portions. The best strategy is now being used by the housekeeping staff at George Washington's home, Mount Vernon. *How it works:* They clean one room completely...then the next...and the next, moving in one direction around the house in a circle. When the last room is finished, the cycle starts again.

Some Messies become stalled just worrying about where to begin. *Solution:* Start at the front door. After cleaning that area, move to the first piece of furniture to the left, and so on until the whole house has been cleaned. *Exception:* Save the kitchen until the end. It's much too tough for a rookie.

Don't try to do the whole house in one day. Set a goal—an hour a day or a room a week... and stick to it. *Helpful:* Reward yourself for getting over rough spots (that awful closet, etc.) with a dinner out...or some other treat.

•Sort as you go. Get three boxes. Label them...

•Give away. Messies are frugal—they'd rather give something away than throw it out. The contents of this box must be given away within one week. *Reason:* Without a deadline, Messies will agonize over who to give things to. Do not wait to write cousin Enid to ask if her son wants the catcher's mitt.

•Throw away. Some things can't even be given away. The contents must be disposed of the same day.

•Store elsewhere. Messies are easily distracted. If they try to put something away in another room, they may turn on the TV or pick up a book...and the cleaning will end.

•Decide which items go in which box. *Ask...*

•*Does this have any monetary or sentimental value?* Messies see potential value in things. A broken toaster could be fixed, a stack of National Geographics might be worth a lot of money one day. But if there is no immediate value, the item belongs in the throw-away or give-away box.

•*Have I used it in the past year?* If the answer is *no*, get rid of it.

•*Might I find some use for this in the future?* If you have to ask this question about an item ...get rid of it. This is the sort of reasoning that got you into this mess in the first place.

How to live with a Messie...

It's not easy to live with a spouse or a child who balks at the thought of letting go of things.

Solution: Put his/her old magazines, toys and other things that you think should be thrown away into a box and write the date on it. Tell the person that the box will sit in X place (the garage, the basement, etc.) for six weeks...and that he may retrieve what he wants. At the end of six weeks, throw the box away.

If you treat the person with respect, he'll realize that you're trying to help him. And, chances are, he'll take little out of the box.

Source: Sandra Felton, a member of the National Association of Professional Organizers and founder of Messies Anonymous (MA).

Common Sense Business And Social Manners

A common error today is the failure to realize that there are at least two sets of manners—one for the business world and another for the social world. In the business world, it is not vulgar to talk about money or to brag. But the social world is just the opposite.

•In business, manners are based on rank and position, not on gender. The business lunch or dinner check, for instance, belongs to the person who initiated the invitation or the superior in the office. The gender of the person does not alter this tradition.

•Never worry about what service people (waiters, maitre d's, hotel clerks) think of you. If you use the wrong fork, it is up to the waiter or busboy to supply you with another. Don't worry about what he thinks of you.

•If you are critical of someone while at a dinner party, only to discover that the person you are belittling is the father (or close relative or friend) of the person with whom you are speaking, make a quick and complete U-turn. Add to the defamatory statement, "Of course, that's the basis of my admiration for him." Remember dinner table conversation doesn't have to be logical.

•The notion that it is unhealthy to disguise your feelings has helped lead to a decline in manners and social health. *One advantage of a little disguise:* You will have more feelings to share with intimates.

Source: Judith Martin, otherwise known as Miss Manners.

4

Communication Secrets

How to Develop the Fine Art of Negotiation

Too often we walk into a negotiation unprepared—and consequently uncertain. Whether we are going to be talking about a raise, a job, a house, the rent, summer plans, or where the kids go to school, it's unrealistic to expect to get everything we want.

That's because each person involved in a negotiation has different interests. Being well-prepared will help you understand the different interests. There is always the prospect that each side would do better by working out an agreement. The basic question is how to pursue that possibility—as a form of warfare or as joint problem solving.

Traditional haggling, in which each side argues a position and either makes concessions to reach a compromise or refuses to budge, is not the most efficient and amicable way to reach a wise agreement.

Better: Principled negotiation, or negotiation based on the merits of what's at stake, which is a straightforward negotiation method that can be used under almost any circumstances.

Checklist for principled negotiations...

Separate the people from the substantive problem. Think of preserving the relationship. Attack the problem, not the person. If the other side attacks you, as often happens, call him/her on it and ask him to return to the problem.

Focus on interests, not positions. Negotiating positions often obscure what people really want. Try to determine the true interests on both sides—usually you can find some common ground.

Generate a range of options before deciding upon one. Having a lot at stake inhibits creativity. Do not try to determine a single, correct solution. Instead, think of a wide range of possibilities that could please both sides. Look for a solution that benefits everybody.

Insist on using some legitimate standard of fairness. By choosing some objective standard

—market value, the going rate, expert opinion, precedent, what a court would decide—neither party loses face by conceding. He is merely deferring to relevant standards. Never yield to pressure, only to principle.

Develop your best alternative to a negotiated agreement. If you haven't thought through what you will do if you fail to reach an agreement, you are negotiating with your eyes closed. You may be too optimistic about your other options—other houses for sale, buyers for your used car, plumbers, jobs, etc.

The reality is that if you fail to reach an agreement, you will probably have to choose just one option.

An even greater danger lies in being too anxious to reach an agreement because you haven't considered your other options. It may be better to walk away.

Consider what kind of commitment you want. It's a mistake to think that every meeting has to result in a final decision. It's much smarter to view a meeting as an exploratory session. You can draw out what interests motivate the other side and draft promises without nailing anything down. This gives you a chance to sleep on the alternatives or consult others. If the other side comes back with new demands, you have the right to renegotiate as well.

Communicate. Without communication, there is no negotiation. But whatever you say, expect the other side to hear something different.

Solutions: Listen actively, paying close attention and occasionally interrupting to make sure you understand what is meant. Ask that ideas be repeated if there is any ambiguity or uncertainty. It's very important to understand perceptions, needs, and negotiating constraints.

Understanding is not agreeing. You can understand the other side's position—and still disagree with it. But the better you understand the other side's position, the more persuasively you can refute it.

Negotiating strategies...

•Marital roles. Learn to disagree without being disagreeable. You can disapprove of someone's behavior but still love that person. Discuss problems in a caring way. Make a joint list of issues that need to be addressed. Be firm but reasonable. Don't try to decide right away ...mull things over for a few days.

•Requesting a raise. As with all negotiations, prepare beforehand. Find out what others at your level are earning, both inside and outside your company. Be ready to explain why you deserve more—you've been coming in every Saturday to help with the workload...you've been training newcomers...you're dealing with the company's toughest customers...or you've been offered more elsewhere. Your boss needs a rationale that he can use with his boss or other employees who also want raises.

•Buying a house. Often, by exploring various options and payment schedules, an agreement can be reached that provides maximum tax advantage and financial satisfaction for both the buyer and the seller.

Example: If you want to move in before the current owners want to move out, you might allow them to store their furniture in the garage. Flexibility might be enough to make your offer more acceptable than a higher one from someone else.

•Divorce negotiation. Suppose you are a wife who doesn't trust your husband to make his agreed child-support payments. Fearing that you will have to keep going back to court to get payment, you ask your lawyer to negotiate for equity in the house instead. Your husband's lawyer says that's ridiculous. He's certain that your husband will meet his obligations. "OK," says your lawyer, "then the husband won't object to signing a contingent agreement—if he misses two payments for any reason, his ex-wife will automatically get the equity in the house and he will be off the hook for future child-support payments."

•Resisting early retirement. Your company is having financial difficulties and has to lay off thousands of people. Early retirement packages are being offered, but you really can't afford to retire yet. Instead, see what you can negotiate—offer to take part of your pay in promissory notes...if you don't need the medical coverage, offer to give it up...if health benefits kick in at 20 hours per week, offer to work only 19 hours...become a freelance contract worker.

If you can dodge the bullet for six months or a year, the company may be on track again.

Source: Roger Fisher, director of The Harvard Negotiation Project and Williston Professor of Law Emeritus, Harvard Law School, 1563 Massachusetts Ave., Cambridge 02138. He is coauthor of *Getting to Yes,* Viking Penguin, 375 Hudson St., New York 10014.

Writing it Out

Write down everything you do for one day. Be as specific as possible. *Example:* Woke up ...lay awake in bed a few minutes planning my day...went to the bathroom...took a shower ...dressed in blue sweat suit...reviewed notes for today's meeting.

Making changes in your life begins by knowing what your life already is. By recording the many things that take up your time, you can view your life clearly, without illusion or distortion.

Source: *How To Be Happier Day by Day: A Year of Mindful Actions* by Alan Epstein, PhD, co-founder, True Partners, a Marin County, California relationship counseling service. Viking, 375 Hudson St., New York 10014.

How to Read People

Much of people-reading involves making elementary, commonsense observations and then acting on them.

Observation tips:

• Don't generalize. Conventional wisdom says that if someone slumps in his chair, he's not very commanding, or if he leans forward, he's ready to make a deal. However, I've seen a lot of erect, attentive types who hung on my every word but never made a move. Any useful observation must be considered in the context of the particular situation.

• Learn the difference between posture and posturing. Look out for people who lean in toward you, who push things back on the desk at you, who sit back and strike poses, who dress pretentiously, who do strange things with lighting, or who have your chair placed lower than theirs. All those things are keys that you're dealing with a phony, someone who's more concerned with appearance than with accomplishment.

• Look at the eyes. People communicate with their eyes in situations where silence is called for. The next time you're in a meeting with people you don't know, notice the eye contact of the participants. It will tell you who's allied with whom, who is most influential, and, if you're the speaker, whether you're boring everyone to death.

• Use ego to your advantage. Most successful people are one giant ego with a couple of arms and legs attached. But a giant ego isn't necessarily a strong ego. It may be compensating for low self-esteem. Or someone who seems to have a weak ego may simply be low-key. When you know these things, you can work with them or around them.

• Make inferences from coworkers and subordinates. For example, if someone seems unwilling to commit himself to even minor details, it may be that his boss is a person whose ego demands that he make all the decisions.

• Take the fish out of water. People tend to reveal themselves in unexpected ways when outside their usual settings. For this reason I favor breakfast, lunch and dinner meetings. Even the way someone treats a waiter can be very revealing.

Source: Mark H. McCormack, author of *What They Don't Teach You at Harvard Business School: Notes From a Street-Smart Executive.*

How to Complain... Successfully

Complaining is a normal part of human life, especially among people who live together. Without complaining, our resentments fester into permanent barriers to communication. But even though they are essential, complaints have two strikes against them...

• They convey that there is something wrong with the other person's behavior, which no one likes to hear.

• They contain a command or a request—which is an indirect command—that the other person's behavior be changed.

Most adults have knee-jerk negative reactions to commands from other adults. *Result:* Rather than considering the content of the complaint, they respond with denials, defensiveness, and counteraccusations.

To complain more effectively, it's important to define the goal of your complaint. If you're simply venting your anger, it doesn't matter what you say. But if you want the other person to change his/her behavior, you should use a different technique.

The three-part message...

I use a verbal tool for complaining that works so well it seems almost magical. I call it the "three-part message": When you X...I feel Y...because Z.

The point of the three-part message is to avoid triggering the listener's resentment. It succeeds by targeting a specific, verifiable behavior and then linking that behavior to the speaker's feelings and a real-world consequence.

Example I: "When you forget to water the tomato plants, I feel angry, because the plants die."

Example II: "When you overdraw our checking account, I feel embarrassed, because our checks bounce."

Example III: "When you bring the car home with no gas, I feel anxious, because I might run out on the way to work the next morning."

The three-part message works only when you absolutely stick to the pattern. *Ground rules...*

• Part One/When you X: Cite one—and only one—specific behavior, which must be verifiable and beyond dispute. *Useful:* "When you yell at the children...." *Not useful:* "When you act like some tyrant...."

• Part Two/I feel Y: The emotion should be stated simply and without any exaggeration. *Useful:* "I feel distressed...." *Not useful:* "I feel like a second-class citizen...."

Pitfall: Drawing conclusions about your partner's feelings. *Not useful:* "I feel as if you don't respect me...."

• Part Three/because Z: Complainers must prove their right to complain...by describing a nondebatable consequence that reasonable people would want to avoid. *Useful:* "When you leave all the lights on, I feel frustrated, because our utility bills get so high." *Not useful:* "...because it means you don't care about how hard I work for my money."

The three-part message is not suited for intimate or complex issues. But if you use this to-the-point tool for your everyday problems, your partner may become more receptive to longer discussions as the need arises.

Source: Suzette Haden Elgin, PhD, founder of the Ozark Center for Language Studies in Forum, Arkansas (501-559-2273). She is the author of 23 books. Her latest book is *Genderspeak: Men, Women, and the Gentle Art of Verbal Self-Defense,* John Wiley & Sons, 605 Third Ave., New York 10158.

How to Say No to Anyone

Many of us say *yes* more often than we'd like. Whatever the reason, if you find yourself saying yes because you feel too guilty about saying *no,* here are some practical measures to help you protect yourself.

• Stall. This gives you precious time to work up an honest rationale for a total refusal. *Simply say:* "I don't know. I need time to think about it—give me an hour" (or a day, or whatever seems reasonable).

• Use humor.

• Try flattery.

• Tell white lies, if necessary.

Source: Barry Lubetkin, PhD, Institute for Behavior Therapy, New York.

How to Spot a Liar

Less than 5% of the population are natural liars...performers who lie flawlessly and make no mistakes. But research shows that the majority of people are fooled by liars. *Clues to look for:*

•The single biggest giveaway is a series of inconsistencies in the lie.

•Watch for changes in patterns of speech, especially when a person has to pause and think more often than usual to answer a simple question.

•Look for signs that the person is deviating from a usual pattern of behavior. Liars may use a monotonous tone of voice or change inflection less frequently when they lie. They may also use fewer hand and body motions than usual.

•A smile is the most common mask of a person's true feelings.

•Liars sometimes lie just for the thrill of telling a successful lie. *Giveaways:* Widening of the eyes and a trace of a smile.

•Ask questions when inconsistencies start to pop up in a story. Most people become willing prey to liars because they don't want to act suspicious or don't think they have the right to ask questions.

Source: Dr. Paul Ekman, professor of psychology, University of California, San Francisco, and author of *Telling Lies,* W.W. Norton & Co., New York.

To Rescue Yourself from Embarrassing Situations

What to do:

•Simply and quickly apologize. That gives you time to think, if nothing else. But don't overdo it. Apologizing profusely just makes the other person uncomfortable.

•Don't put yourself down by saying "I'm so clumsy" or "I can't seem to do anything right." If you go overboard, you might wind up convincing the other person that there really is something wrong with you.

•If you're habitually tactless, ask yourself if you felt enmity or anger toward the person you insulted...if something about him made you uncomfortable or envious.

•How to apologize: Don't play innocent by insisting your remark was unintentional. The other person knows you meant to hurt because that was the result. If you apologize honestly, telling the other person about your angry feelings, you're much more likely to be forgiven.

•Make a joke about your mistake. It relieves the tension of the moment and shows you're a good sport. The other person also feels less embarrassed. Sharing a good laugh about something that could have created a rift can even improve rapport.

When you get in a tough, embarrassing spot:

•If you have personality traits that make you feel awkward in certain situations, ask a friend for feedback about how you're really coming across. You might be very self-conscious about some traits, such as your shyness or a tendency to talk too much. But others most likely won't even notice.

•Change the subject when it seems that you've put your foot in your mouth.

•Agree to disagree. One of the most awkward moments for people is disagreement, especially about personal matters. Acknowledge that you have differences, but make it clear that you still like and respect that person.

•Don't relive the embarrassing moment, wishing you'd done it differently. Forget it. Don't spend the rest of the day telling everyone what a fool you made of yourself, and don't keep bringing up the incident whenever you see the person it happened with.

Source: Dr. Judith Meyerowitz, PhD, a psychotherapist in private practice in New York.

How to Start a Conversation with A Stranger

•Pay attention to the person's name when introduced. Repeat it. If it's unusual, ask about its origins.

•Look directly at the person. Lean forward a bit.

•Ask the person something about her/himself in a flattering way.

•Ask encouraging questions as the person talks about himself.

•Don't interrupt. If you have an interest in keeping the conversation going, let the other person talk about himself and his interests. Don't immediately begin talking about yourself. Be patient.

Source: James Van Fleet, author of *A Lifetime Guide to Conversation,* Prentice-Hall, Inc., Englewood Cliffs, NJ.

How to Say "No"

Say *yes* quickly. Say *no* slowly. When a letter or conversation begins with a rejection, the other person usually ignores the rest of the discussion, including the reasons for the negative decision.

The pattern to follow when saying no:

•Review the facts and reasons for the decision without revealing it.

•Build an argument in a step-by-step, fact-by-fact manner.

•Provide information to support the decision. (The goal is to have the other person acknowledge the validity of the rejection.)

•Say no politely.

Always say something good about the rejected idea, organization or person. Acknowledge the problem and the difficulty of its solution.

Source: William C. Paxson, *The Business Writing Handbook,* Bantam Books, New York.

Conversation Basics

Here are some ways to keep good conversation flowing:

•When talking with someone from a field you either don't know or don't care anything about, steer the conversation toward feelings rather than facts or details. By focusing on emotions that everyone shares, you can feel secure discussing anything.

•Make sure both people have equal power to bring up topics, change the subject and demand attention. *Avoid common conversational mistakes:*

•Bombarding the other person with questions.

•Being too quick to give advice.

•Giving too many personal details.

Sources: *Better Communication* and Gerald Goodman, associate professor of psychology, UCLA, quoted in *US News and World Report.*

Conversation Killers

Intimate talks will be more pleasant and productive if you avoid the following:

•Sentences that start with the accusatory *You* or the inclusive *Let's* or *We.* (Instead, try to begin more sentences with *I,* to make your honest feelings known.)

•Absolute statements. *Example:* "That was a stupid movie."

•"I don't know." (You probably have some inkling of an answer, even if it's only to add, "Let me think about it.")

•"I don't care." (Even a weak preference should be voiced.)

•*Ought, should, must, have to.* Instead, try *I might, I would like to* or *I want to.*

•Questions beginning with *Why,* such as "Why are you feeling that way?" *Better:* Begin with a *What,* as in "What is bothering you?"

•*Always* and *never.* More flexible phrases are *up to now* and *in the past.*

Source: Dr. Theresa Larsen Crenshaw, author of *Bedside Manners,* Pinnacle Books, New York.

How to Be a Better Conversationalist

•Don't start with your name. A name exchange gives a conversation nowhere to go. Instead, mention something in the environment that you can both talk about, such as "How's the cheesecake in this restaurant?" Then pay attention to the cues to find out whether the other person wants to talk with you. Consider tone of voice, facial expression and body language.

•Develop your descriptive power. The well-told anecdote or story will express your personality and convey warmth and charm. Many people are afraid to express their feelings when it comes to description. They stick to a dry recitation of facts instead.

•Be sensitive to the other person. Pick up on messages about how that person is feeling. Watch body language as well as listening to what's being said. Don't be one of those insensitive, endless talkers who fear that if they stop, their partner will get bored and want to leave.

•Don't use boredom as a defense. People who always claim to be bored are usually just erecting a defense against rejection. If you're at a party and don't talk to anyone because you tell yourself they're all boring, you've just insulated yourself against failure. If you feel you're boring to others, that's just another excuse for not trying and therefore not failing.

•Don't keep asking questions. Constant queries to keep a conversation going can be a crutch. The other person will finally realize that you're not really listening but are thinking up the next question. People dislike feeling interrogated and resent answering questions under those circumstances. Ask a question only when something genuinely sparks your curiosity.

Source: Arthur Reel, who teaches the art of conversation at New York City's Learning Annex and at Corporate Communications Skills, Inc., an executive training center in New York.

Learning to Listen

Here are some simple techniques to help you improve your listening ability:

•Relax and help the speaker relax, too. Give your full attention to what's being said. Stop everything else you're doing. Maintain eye contact.

•Don't let the speaker's tone of voice or manner turn you off. Nervousness or misplaced emotions often cloud the message the speaker is trying to get across.

•Prepare beforehand for the conversation. Take a few minutes to consult information pertinent to the discussion. That also helps you to quickly evaluate the speaker and the subject.

•Allow for unusual circumstances (extreme pressure or disturbing interruptions). Judge only what the speaker says, given the conditions he's faced with.

•Avoid getting sidetracked.

•Listen very closely to points you disagree with. (Poor listeners shut out or distort them.)

•Mentally collect the main points of the conversation. Occasionally, ask for clarification of one of the speaker's statements.

Bad Listening Habits

If you want to be a better listener, try to avoid:

•Thinking about something else while waiting for the speaker's next word or sentence. The mind races ahead four times faster than the normal rate of conversation.

•Listening primarily for facts rather than ideas.

•Tuning out when the talk seems to be getting too difficult.

•Prejudging, from appearance or speaking manner, that the person has nothing interesting to say.

•Paying attention to outside sights and sounds when talking with someone.

•Interrupting with a question whenever a speaker says something puzzling or unclear.

Source: John T. Samaras, University of Oklahoma.

How to Listen to A Complaint

Many people don't hear anything that doesn't fit their own assumptions. If someone comes to you with a complaint or claim, listen —just listen.

•Don't answer or explain.

•Take notes on exactly what's said.

•Try to imagine that the person is right, or at least justified.

•Put yourself in the other's place and imagine how you would feel in the same situation.

•Give yourself time to think the matter over before making any decision.

•Nobody can see all sides of an issue immediately. New facts or ideas take time to sink in.

Source: *Levinson Letter,* Cambridge, MA.

How to Get Information From Others

•Speak softly. This encourages others to take center stage where they should be if you want to learn something from them.

•Look responsive. Most people don't use nearly enough facial expression. Raising one eyebrow a little and smiling slightly makes you seem receptive. Eye contact and a calculated pause will invite the person you're talking with to elaborate.

•Give reinforcement. Comments such as "Very impressive!" or "Excellent!" can be dropped into the discussion without interrupting the flow.

•Follow up and probe. If someone fails to explain the reasons for an action that you're curious about, try a casual follow-up question.

Source: Richard A. Fear, author of *The Evaluation Interview,* published by McGraw-Hill, New York.

Hidden Meanings In What People Say

Key words tell what people are really trying to communicate. These words and phrases may be spoken repeatedly or hidden in the middle of complex sentences. But they relay the true message being delivered through all the chatter of conversations, negotiations and interviews.

What to watch out for:

•Words that jump out at you. The speaker may be mumbling, but suddenly a word (or proper name) is emphasized or spoken loudly.

•Slips of the tongue, especially when denied by the person who made them. *Example:* "We won't leave this room until we have reached a derision" (instead of decision). The speaker is mocking either you or the subject under discussion.

•Embedding. The repetitive use of words or slogans manipulated to reshape your thinking. Embedding can be insidious. *Example:* At a meeting of parties with irreconcilable differences, one side keeps repeating the word "consensus." "After we reach a consensus, we'll break for lunch." This one concept is repeated relentlessly by the speakers and members of their team until it dominates the meeting. This is a mini-version of the Big Lie.

•Hostile words and phrases. Any statement that hurts or sounds hostile is an affront, even when pawned off as a joke.

•Unstated words. These key words are those not spoken. *Prime example:* The husband or wife who can never say "I love you" to the mate.

•Metaphors. The turns of expression people choose often signal their inner thoughts. *Example:* A metaphor such as "We'll cut the opposition up into little pieces" takes healthy competition into the realm of aggression.

Source: Martin G. Groder, MD, psychiatrist and business consultant, Durham, NC.

How People Say "Yes" But Mean "No"

Here are some apparently acquiescent verbal expressions that really mean "no":

•"Yes, but..."

•"I don't know why, but..."

•"I tried that, and it doesn't help."

•"Well, to be perfectly honest with you..."

•"But it's not easy..."

- "I know, but..."
- "I don't remember."

Spot the Unspoken Thought Behind The Poker Face

Watching people's actions can bring you a lot closer to the truth than merely listening to what they say.

Here are some typical feelings and mental machinations—and their common outward expressions:

- Openness: Open hands, unbuttoned coat.
- Defensiveness: Arms crossed on chest, crossing legs, fistlike gestures, pointing index finger, "karate" chops.
- Evaluations: Hand to face, head tilted, stroking chin, peering over or playing with glasses, cleaning glasses, cleaning or filling a pipe, hand to nose.
- Suspicion: Arms crossed, sideways glance, touching/rubbing nose, rubbing eyes, buttoned coat, drawing away.
- Insecurity: Pinching flesh, chewing pen, thumb over thumb, biting fingernail, hands in pockets.
- Cooperation: Upper body in sprinter's position, open hands, sitting on edge of chair, hand-to-face gestures, unbuttoning coat.
- Confidence: Steepled hands, hands behind back, back stiffened, hands in coat pockets with thumbs out, hands on lapels of coat.
- Nervousness: Clearing throat, "whew" sound, whistling, smoking, pinching flesh, fidgeting, covering mouth, jiggling money or keys, tugging ears, wringing hands.
- Frustration: Short breaths, "tsk" sound, tightly clenched hands, wringing hands, fistlike gestures, pointing index finger, rubbing hand through hair, rubbing back of neck.
- SOS: Uneven intonation of voice, wringing of hands, poor body posture, or failure to make eye contact.

How Not to be Put On the Defensive

Criticism from fellow workers or superiors on the job can escalate if you react defensively. How to avoid this instinctive reaction:

- Paraphrase an accusation as a way of slowing down reaction time and giving the accuser a chance to retreat. *Accuser:* "How come that report isn't ready? Can't you ever get your work done on time?" *Response:* "Do you really think that I never get my work done on time?"
- Describe in a tentative fashion what appears to be the other person's psychological state. In response to a scowling superior, say: "I'm uncomfortable. I don't understand what your frown means."
- Ask for clarification. *Accuser:* "This proposal isn't what I asked you to design at all." *Response:* "Is nothing in the proposal acceptable?"
- Use a personal response to assume responsibility. *Accuser:* "This is entirely wrong." *Response:* "I guess I didn't understand. Can I review the instructions again?"

Source: Gary P. Cross, management consultant, Cross Names & Beck, Eugene, OR.

Arguments: Keeping Your Cool

- Don't fear to negotiate, even when the difference with the other person is so huge that agreement seems impossible.
- If the issue is important, you probably cannot accurately predict when and how a resolution will finally be made. The outcome may become apparent only after extensive discussions.
- Avoid the temptation to start off in a hostile manner out of anger at the other person's extreme stance.

Source: Dr. Chester L. Karrass, Karrass Seminars, Santa Monica, CA.

When to Offer a Solution To a Dispute

Let the two sides clear the air by exchanging accusations and expressing pent-up resentments over extraneous issues, not just the one now on the table. Any trained mediator waits for this venting of feelings and buildup of frustrations before exercising influence.

•The best (often the only) time to recommend an innovative solution comes when desperation peaks. Both sides know they have a problem. And both know they can't settle it without third-party help.

•To be a hero, deliver a solution where mutual goals are not being met and where all parties already recognize that there is a gap between expectations and performance.

Build Trust During A Discussion

•Begin with a positive statement, for example, "I've been looking forward to talking with you. Joe Smith said if anyone could help us, it's you."

•Avoid pulling rank.

•Don't make veiled threats.

•Don't offer a reward.

•Show yourself to be an expert.

•Associate yourself with someone the other person respects.

•Restate the other person's opinions or feelings periodically. But do not preface the restatement with "you said" or "you think." The other person may quibble over what is attributed directly.

•Share something personal about yourself if the other person is wary.

•Point out ways the information you need will help you.

•Indicate ways you can help the other person.

•Make a commitment to action, and then ask for a commitment in return.

Source: Pamela Cumming, author of *The Power Handbook,* CBI Publishing, Boston.

Choose Your Words Carefully

Avoid:

•Using popular but vague modifiers, such as "exceptional" or "efficient," without defining precisely what is meant. For example, an exceptional record can be either exceptionally good or bad. Describing something as efficiently designed does not say enough. It's better to use facts, numbers, details.

•Exaggerating. Overstating a fact is acceptable (and common) in conversation, but it destroys credibility in writing because readers take it literally.

•Generalizing. Do not use absolutes, such as: All, right, wrong, true, false, always, never. Instead, say "this is true under such-and-such conditions."

Source: William C. Paxson, author of *The Business Writing Handbook,* Bantam Books, New York.

Write as Clearly As You Think

Concentrate on simplifying your sentence structure. It's the easiest way to say what is meant and to make sure the message gets across. *Three basic rules:*

•Keep sentences short. They should be no more than 17 to 20 words. If an idea has multiple parts, use multiple sentences.

•Vary the length of sentences. The 17-20 word rule is the average. When sentences drone on at unvarying lengths, the reader's attention begins to wander.

•Vary the punctuation. Include plenty of commas, as well as a sprinkling of semicolons, to go with the necessary periods. Well-placed punctuation is a road map, leading the reader comfortably and accurately through the message.

Source: Paul Richards, author of *Sentence Control: Solving an Old Problem,* Supervisory Management, New York.

How to Measure the Clarity of Your Writing

Use the "Fog Index" to measure how clearly you write letters, memos, and reports.

• Count off a 100-word section.

• Count the number of sentences and divide 100 by that number, which gives average words per sentence.

• Count the words with more than two syllables. Add this figure to the average words per sentence.

• Multiply the total by 0.4 to get the Fog Index (indicating minimum school grade level a reader needs to comprehend it).

The lower the index, the better. A score of 11 to 12 is passable for most business writing. (The Fog Index for this item: 7.6)

Source: *Time Talk,* Grandville, MI.

How to Write A Persuasive Letter

• Grab your reader's attention by fitting in with his interests, either personal or in business. Tell him how he is going to benefit by doing as you ask.

• Give proof of what you say. The best proof is to suggest that the reader get in touch with others who have benefited from your suggestion. (Of course, you must make sure that you have people who will back you up.)

• In the next-to-last paragraph, tell the reader exactly what he must do to take advantage of the benefits you're offering.

• Close with a hook. Encourage the reader to take action by telling him about a loss of money, prestige or opportunity if he does not act at once. (A time penalty is one of the best ways to get the action you want.)

Source: James Van Fleet, author of *A Lifetime Guide to Conversation,* Prentice Hall, Inc., Englewood Cliffs, NJ.

Help Readers Understand Your Report

Readers understand a report better when they are carefully led through it. Use the right words or phrases to signal a shift of subject or emphasis:

• To get your reader to stop and consider alternatives. *Use:* However, but, by contrast, nevertheless, on the other hand, still, despite, notwithstanding.

• To expand the idea. *Use:* Actually, realistically, at the same time, unexpectedly, perhaps.

• To concede to a limitation. *Use:* Sometimes, to be sure, possibly, to some extent, conceivably.

• To make an aside. *Use:* Incidentally, digressing for a moment.

• To move ahead in the same direction. *Use:* Additionally, also, besides, moreover, furthermore.

• To make a comparison. *Use:* Similarly, in the same way.

• To strengthen an assertion. *Use:* Indeed, in fact, certainly.

• To signal importance. *Use:* Significantly, notably, remarkably.

Source: A. Weiss, author of *Write What You Mean,* AMACOM, New York.

Speeches with Impact

Only rarely is it possible to change your audience's deep-seated attitudes or beliefs. Aim no higher than getting the listeners to question their attitudes.

• Avoid alienating an audience by pressing points too hard.

• State conclusions.

• Call for action.

•When you have to speak extemporaneously, develop a theme early and stick to it.

•Use silence to underline a point.

•End a speech with a short, emotional, conviction-filled summary of the main points.

Source: Michael Klezaras Jr., director of research and planning, Roger Ailes & Associates, Inc., New York.

Public Speaking: Secrets of Success

Contrary to a lot of advice about making a speech, there is no need to memorize, rehearse, rely on extensive notes or spend weeks getting ready. The key is to keep the presentation spontaneous.

The only requirements for spontaneous speaking:

•Thorough knowledge of the subject.

•Self-confidence.

•An assured manner of delivery.

To make sure the speech does not sound rehearsed or canned:

•Don't use notes because you'll have no more than two seconds to look down, find the place in the notes and speak to the audience. You'll end up looking, reading, memorizing and reciting, but not communicating.

•Instead of notes, use one- to three-word "triggers" instead of notes. Triggers are facts or concepts designed to spark off the next train of thought. Using triggers allows you to deal easily with what is to be said. The result is that you'll gesture more, be more animated and vary your tone of voice.

•As a structure for the speech, adopt the same format that people use to communicate every day: State the purpose, support it with details, then recommend what should be done.

•Start with a 15- to 30-second grabber. The grabber explains the purpose and stimulates the audience. Work through the details by using the triggers. About five of these should suffice.

•End by telling the group something specific to do. If questions follow the talk, restate the recommended action at the conclusion.

•Stand in front of the lectern and as close to the audience as possible. This makes the talk seem more like a conversation. In a big auditorium, use a lapel microphone to avoid getting stuck at the lectern. Establish eye contact with people one at a time. Don't look at the wall.

Delivering An Important Speech

•Find out what common bonds unite the audience so that the speech can be directed to meaningful subjects.

•Remember that your audience is interested first in people, then in things, finally in ideas.

•Start by tape-recording a spontaneous flow of ideas. Don't attempt to be logical or to follow an outline. This initial tape is the raw material to prepare the final speech.

•Avoid opening with a joke. Most jokes backfire. The best grabbers are a question, personal story, famous quote, vital statistic, comparison, or contrast.

•Use questions throughout.

•Avoid unnecessary phrases such as "Now let me explain...." Or: "The point I want to make is..."

Audience attention drops off sharply after 20 to 30 minutes, so no presentation should run beyond that. If it's necessary to fill more time:

•Use slides when appropriate.

•Have a question and answer session after the speech.

Talking Effectively to Small Groups

•Meet personally as many people as possible beforehand.

• Get right to the point. The first 15 seconds is what grabs the listener. Don't start with "Thank you" and "I'm very happy to be here."

• Make eye contact with everyone in the audience at some time very early in the presentation.

• Support main points with factual information and examples.

• Repeat the main points to be sure the listeners have gotten them.

• Look for a creative conclusion—a provocative thought or action-suggesting statement.

• Never let a talk end with an answer to a question from the audience. After answering questions, always return to the main point of the presentation. The last word is important. It shouldn't be yielded to a questioner.

• Never ask the audience, "Any questions?" If there aren't any, the silence will be embarrassing. Instead, suggest, "There may be some questions." It makes a difference.

• Limit use of notes because it inhibits spontaneity. Write out key words or short phrases to jog thoughts. Alternate lines with different color ink to facilitate quick focusing on material.

• Rehearsing is usually not recommended. Unrehearsed presentations have the advantage of freshness and spontaneity which only come from thoughts uttered for the first time.

Source: Dr. Roger Flax, communications training consultant, Motivational Systems, South Orange, NJ.

Using Humor Successfully

• Avoid humor when speaking outdoors. The laughter tends to get lost, leaving people with the feeling it wasn't funny at all.

• Avoid puns, even though they may go over well in a parlor. They almost always cause the audience to groan more than laugh.

• Leave enough time for the laugh before proceeding. Audiences sometimes react slowly, especially if the humor was unexpected. To a nervous speaker, a second's delay seems like an hour.

• Be prepared to carry on smoothly and self-confidently if the audience doesn't laugh. The audience will quickly forget that the speaker laid an egg if he remains calm.

Source: Paul Preston, *Communication for Managers,* Prentice-Hall, Englewood Cliffs, NJ.

Lines to Live By

Wit surprises...*humor* illuminates. Wit is often aristocratic in its clever superiority...while humor is usually popular.

Here are just a few examples of true wit...

• *Mark Twain on his father:* "When I was a boy of 14, my father was so ignorant I could hardly stand to have him around. But when I got to be 21, I was astonished at how much he had learned in seven years."

• *Oscar Wilde:* At a dinner party, Oscar Wilde bet that he could produce a witticism about any subject that was offered.

"Queen Victoria," suggested another guest.

"Ah," said Wilde, "but she is not a subject."

One time, when James McNeill Whistler, the painter, uttered a bon mot, Oscar Wilde remarked, "I wish I'd said that."

Whistler replied, "You will, Oscar, you will."

• *George Bernard Shaw:* The actress Pat Campbell sighed to Bernard Shaw, "What a wonderful child we would have with my looks and your brains."

"But suppose," mused Shaw, "it had my looks and your brains!"

Once, when a heckler booed him after a performance, Shaw stepped to the edge of the stage, peered up at the balcony, and said, "My dear sir, I quite agree with you. But who are we among so many?"

Shaw's *Candida* opened in New York with Cornelia Otis Skinner in the title role. The critics were enraptured, and Shaw cabled the actress: "Excellent. Greatest." G. B. S.

Miss Skinner replied: "Undeserving such praise."

Shaw cabled: "I meant the play."

To which she smartly answered: "So did I."

• *Winston Churchill:* Lady Astor once hissed at Winston Churchill, "If you were my husband, I'd put poison in your coffee."

"If I were your husband, I would drink it," Churchill blandly replied.

• *Ronald Reagan:* "The Soviet Union would remain a one-party nation even if an opposition party were permitted," said Ronald Reagan, "because everyone would join that party."

• *J.B.S. Haldane:* The British scientist J. B. S. Haldane was asked what his studies had revealed to him about the nature of God. "An inordinate fondness for beetles," Haldane replied.

Source: John Train, chairman of Montrose Advisors, an investment firm, and author of *The Craft of Investing*, HarperCollins, 10 E. 53 St., New York 10022. He writes a column for the *Financial Times* and has published several books of humor.

5

Self Improvement

All About Selficide

Many people do not find satisfaction in today's world. They find life to be a flat, unreal experience. They cannot enjoy intimate relationships with others. They are not in touch with their own selves. I use the word *selficide* to describe this state of being unable to learn and grow from life's experiences.

As we age, we increasingly need to understand who we are and how to behave as responsible, caring adults. Important questions to ask yourself to see if you are on the right track...or on the road to *selficide*...

•Do you control your own behavior...or are your actions governed by a need to rebel or comply with other's rules? My patient Denise was anorexic. She ate sensibly—but whenever she reached a healthy weight, she stopped eating and lost weight again.

Her eating problem was the symptom of an internal struggle between her perception of the voice of her parents, which told her she must eat to be loved, and her desire to be herself.

She was able to solve her problem when, with encouragement, she disciplined herself not to control her eating habits. Instead she focused on doing something that she really *wanted* to do...*not* what she felt she *should* do.

•Are your thoughts, feelings and actions consistent with each other? We all know the old joke about the Boy Scout who took an hour to help an old lady across the street... because she didn't want to go. His behavior was inconsistent with his goal—to do good.

•Do you truly play a meaningful part in your own activities and dealings with others ...or are you often just there physically? Some people are so involved in regret over the past that they can't think about what they should be doing now. Others are so busy daydreaming about the future that they aren't acting now to make their dreams possible.

•Do you willingly surrender yourself to reality...or do you begrudge it? Can you ever leave a discussion without having the last word?

• Are you able to give and take...or do you insist on only one direction? Do you feel like a martyr...and let everyone know it?

• Do you accept others as they are...or do you always feel the need to judge them?

• Do you act naturally, without pretension... or are you dishonest or phony?

• Do you take joy in your experiences... not just look at life as a series of tasks to accomplish?

Example: Ned, a patient of mine, wondered why his business was always outperformed by a small rival company, so he went to check on it. He noticed that the owner of the company was an exceedingly enthusiastic individual. When Ned asked him, "You really enjoy what you do, don't you?" he replied, "Yeah, it sure beats the hell out of working!"

• Do you have an inner aesthetic sense of morality that makes it seem repellent to you to do something wrong?

• Are you willing to take risks—to try something new to satisfy your real inner desires... or are you afraid of doing anything that people don't expect of you?

• Do you exercise your creativity—the willingness to dismiss old ways or experience to be free to grow in new directions...or are you afraid to lose the security provided by always repeating the same pattern—even when you find it to be unsatisfactory?

How to avoid selficide...

People who cannot give positive answers to any of the questions are well on their way to selficide. But selficide is not the same as suicide...life always contains the possibility of growth.

If you are willing to look into yourself as you confront the issues of everyday living and examine your inner feelings, you can find new responses that better satisfy your needs and those of the people close to you.

Those new responses will develop as you embrace new experiences and adopt less fearful ways of dealing with the world. That joyful approach is not really alien to anyone's nature, because it represents a return to the way everybody starts out life.

Babies explore the world fearlessly and joyfully...they accept bumps and falls as the price of growth. They learn to walk and talk at their own pace...nobody else can make it happen faster or slower. Before babies learn to walk, they crawl...but when they learn to walk they stop crawling.

As long as they are able to act naturally, children continue to learn and grow because they are *open to new experiences*...willing to *acknowledge their true feelings*...able to *react in new ways.*

Many adults have forgotten those natural instincts.

As analyst Erich Fromm said, "We listen to every voice and to everybody but not ourselves. We are constantly exposed to the noise of opinions and ideas hammering at us from everywhere...motion pictures, newspapers, radio, idle chatter. If we had planned intentionally to prevent ourselves from ever listening to ourselves, we could have done no better."

But if we pause as we go about our daily activities and look carefully at the world around us...at the people we are with...and most of all deep into ourselves...we can find what we want from life and we can achieve it.

Source: Patrick Thomas Malone, MD, medical director of Mental Health Services at Northside Hospital in Atlanta, and a psychotherapist at the Atlanta Psychiatric Clinic. With his father, Thomas Patrick Malone, MD, PhD, he wrote *The Windows of Experience: Moving Beyond Recovery to Wholeness,* Simon & Schuster, 1230 Avenue of the Americas, New York 10020.

All About Civility

The great lack of civility in America is the major factor behind the breakdown in family life, unethical practices in business, selfishness, and dishonesty in politics.

Civility means much more than politeness. Civility is all-embracing—a general awareness by people that personal well-being cannot be separated from the well-being of the groups to which we belong...our families, our businesses, and our nation.

Lack of civility is tied to unreasonable expectations in recent decades of constant happiness and constant comfort. When real life presents us with painful experiences...when something hurts us...when we feel unfulfilled—we feel cheated. And too many of us—too often—reach for instant happiness by illegitimate means that disregard the interests of other people.

Consciousness and civility...

The route to improved civility begins with greater awareness of our shortcomings and our tendencies to manipulate others.

Greater awareness leads to a willingness to accept pain in the short term, recognizing that it is an unavoidable part of any growth process, leading to significant personal growth. Learning how to handle pain realistically is a prerequisite for warmer, more meaningful relationships over the long term. Civility does not happen automatically. You have to train yourself to be aware of your true motives, to be honest with yourself and others, and to judge yourself first.

Civility in the family...

The first training ground for civility is the family. Children learn how they are expected to behave by observing their parents' behavior, not just by listening to their words. So if you want your children to demonstrate civility now and later in life, you have to practice it yourself.

Example: Your two kids are having a disagreement and your six-year-old son slugs his little sister. Then you tell him, "Don't ever hit your sister!" and hit him.

That will deliver quite a different message than you want to give: "It's OK to hit someone else...but don't hit your sister when your mother or father is around."

With that kind of discrepancy prevalent between parental educational words and actions, it's not surprising that so many people grow up with an internal moral code that tells them, "You can do whatever you want as long as you don't get caught doing it."

Civility in business...

Successful businesses are built on cooperation. Businesses have a right to both demand and expect cooperation from their employees, because the main purpose of any business is to make a profit. But companies also have a responsibility to treat their workers fairly and honestly in the process.

Example: Some companies that vest workers with pension benefits only after a long period of employment save money by laying the workers off only a short time before they become vested.

This is uncivil. It is obviously unfair to the workers and may also hurt the company by encouraging the best employees to leave.

Better way: Set up a system that recognizes both the company's interest in dedicated, hard-working employees and the employees' interest in security and fair compensation. This will only work when both sides honestly keep their parts of the bargain.

Honest communication...

Companies, families, and all types of organizations become more civil when they encourage honest, two-way communication—straight talk and listening. That is not easy, but it can be done if you follow these principles:

- Don't expect perfection...just do your best and learn from your mistakes.
- Set aside time for communication.
- Clear your mind and listen to the other person.
- Be honest...with yourself and others.
- Judge yourself first. Look into your real motives.
- Take time to respond and think. Don't be afraid of silence.
- Be willing to be hurt—and to risk hurting others by speaking honestly. If someone is too fragile to respect your point of view, he/she cannot be a part of your community.
- Try to be as gentle as possible. Don't make any unnecessary, painful statements...yet don't be so subtle that the point is completely missed.
- Speak personally and specifically. Don't talk about "the system" or some impersonal authority. Don't generalize. Document what you say.
- Don't analyze other people's motives. Don't play psychologist.

•Speak when you are moved to speak. Don't cop out.

Bottom line: It takes hard work to get an organization to operate in a mode of civility. But those who have made the transition do not want to go back.

Source: M. Scott Peck, MD, a founder of the Foundation for Community Encouragement. He is the author of *The Road Less Traveled* and *A World Waiting to be Born*, Bantam Books, 1540 Broadway, New York 10036.

Whatever Happened To Loyalty

Loyalty is out of fashion these days. People would sooner switch than fight...not only in the marketplace, where customers rapidly switch to suppliers who offer better deals...but also in their personal, social, and political lives.

As soon as they think they might do better elsewhere, baseball players change teams ...professors leave their colleges...voters desert their parties...husbands abandon their wives, and vice versa.

Rather than trying to build better relationships where they are, people abandon their old associations and enter into new ones... which are likely to be temporary, too.

What happened to loyalty?

The breakdown of loyalty is not only a result of selfishness—it also has ideological roots.

For the past 200 years, giants of philosophy, particularly Immanuel Kant and Jeremy Bentham, have argued that people should not make decisions based on what is best for themselves but instead based on an impersonal calculation of what would be best for the entire society.

These ideas have had a powerful effect on the way many educated people think, but they certainly have not produced a society in which people act better...or even feel better. That is because the world is too complicated for people—even philosophers—to figure out what is best for humanity at large.

Result: Many people reject the old-fashioned belief that we owe loyalty to those who are close to us and helped to make us what we are. They also do not believe we owe loyalty to the nation whose benefits we enjoy. In the short run, this disregard of loyalty hurts some people. In the long run, this attitude hurts everyone.

Advantages of loyalty...

Loyalty in marriage, family life, social interactions, and politics strengthens bonds between people. It assumes that the relationships we are born into—or choose voluntarily—should continue. It encourages us to accept the other party's good faith and so includes a willingness to accept mistakes.

Under these conditions, with time to correct mistakes and a healthy degree of flexibility, relationships can become stronger. Each partner is willing to allow the other to change previous patterns of behavior without fear of immediate abandonment, so each can help the other to grow.

A one-sided, individualistic approach to life may work as long as things are going well, but it is likely to fail when problems arise. Loyalty builds strong, long-lasting mutual relationships that can help overcome temporary setbacks... it leaves both sides better off in the long term.

Loyalty in families...

Successful families are built on a web of loyalty between father, mother, and children. Today's emphasis on personal happiness over loyalty to others is a major cause of family breakdown.

The same emphasis on self that leads to divorce also corrodes the relationship between parents and children.

Example: A huge number of divorced fathers who have remarried simply abandon the children from their first marriage...therefore, a new generation fails to learn how to practice loyalty and enjoy the satisfaction it provides.

How to build loyalty...

Loyalty stands us in good stead when times are tough...but it should be established when things are still going well. *Five steps to loyalty:*

•Affirmation. Think about the good things others are doing for you. Show them how much you appreciate them...in both word and deed.

•Confrontation. Show that the relationship is important to you by pointing out how it can be improved. When you disapprove of your partner's behavior, don't be afraid to say so... but always constructively.

•Complicity. I use this term, which is translated from the French, to mean the sense that you and your partner(s) are separate from the rest of the world. You possess something nobody else has. Feel very happy about it.

•Ritual. Find ways to do things for the special people in your circle.

Example: When loved ones are coming to visit, meet them at the airport.

•Privacy. Keep the details of your shared relationship away from outsiders. How you make decisions is nobody else's business. Never complain to outsiders about your partner.

The tendency today is to think of intimate relationships in political terms. Both men and women are excessively concerned about whether their private conduct meets the standards of behavior set by their friends. Traditional men are concerned about whether they look like they are "wearing the pants in the family." Liberated women worry about whether their sisters would approve of their cooking and washing dishes. This manner of looking over one's shoulder reflects a conflict of loyalties. Loyalty to one's spouse comes into tension with loyalties to those outside the relationship. This conflict undermines trust and destroys intimacy.

Conclusion: Be loyal to your spouse and forget how your private way of doing things may look to outsiders.

The toughest challenge of personal loyalty is to stand by another when the going gets tough. Loyalty becomes important only when we are tempted to "jump ship." Fair-weather loyalty is but convenience. The next time you are tempted to leave, think, "This is the time to show my loyalty."

Source: George P. Fletcher, Beekman Professor of Law at Columbia University and author of *Loyalty: An Essay on the Morality of Relationships,* Oxford University Press, 200 Madison Ave., New York 10016.

The Importance Of Solitude

Many Americans admire the rugged individualists in novels and films who take on the system or overcome adversity single-handedly.

Yet, we don't feel comfortable with those who keep to themselves. We tend to distrust contemplation and view solitary people and pursuits with suspicion.

Opportunity: We would be better off if we engaged in positive solitude—time alone that is used thoughtfully to benefit mind and soul. Positive solitude is an important element of self-discovery and growth.

Solitude provides the opportunity to identify your most cherished goals and develop ways of achieving them. Regular reflection contributes to a sense of inner peace...and makes you feel more in control of your life.

The problems of being alone...

Positive solitude takes conscious effort, whether you live with others or alone.

•People who live with others are often so caught up in the demands of family life that they don't take time for self-reflection. Time alone feels like an expendable luxury to them. Thus, they're in danger of defining themselves through others.

These people need to make private time a priority and be creative about ways of finding it.

Examples: Evaluate work and community responsibilities, and determine which are essential—and which can be cut back. Join a babysitting co-op so someone else can look after your children one or two days a week. Plan a solitary retreat to a quiet place for a few days to reflect on what's really important to you.

People who live alone may feel left out in a world of couples and families. They may fight solitude by compulsively seeking company, filling their days with "busy-ness" that isn't very satisfying...and missing a wonderful opportunity for self-discovery and growth.

They need to challenge the belief that having a family is the only way to be happy...look for ways to nurture themselves instead of waiting for a partner to make life satisfying...and take advantage of the chance to learn more about their own values and perceptions.

I believe that living alone doesn't have to be lonely—nor should it be viewed as a way station on the path to "coupledom." Living alone can be a deeply rewarding lifestyle in its own right.

Positive solitude actually enhances relationships when people do come together. People who are not afraid of solitude can meet as strong wholes instead of incomplete halves that are desperate for fulfillment.

Turn off the TV...

One of the biggest threats to positive solitude is television. It's the easiest, but possibly least-satisfying, way to fill up your time.

Watching television does not put you in contact with other people or yourself. Instead, it bombards you with the agenda and values of the TV programmers and advertisers.

Spending a lot of time in front of the TV feeds loneliness. It encourages us to let someone else decide what's interesting, discourages us from looking inward and takes up time that could be spent developing original ideas or actively challenging or supporting the ideas of others.

Ways to use private time...

In solitude, we can explore what's most meaningful to us—free from other people's expectations. We can begin to develop a personal philosophy or life plan.

This isn't an easy task, but it's an exciting one. *Key:* Ask yourself the kinds of questions that don't have simple answers...and be prepared to return to them again and again. *Examples...*

What contribution do I want to make to the world? Focus on what's significant to you—not to your parents, spouse or boss. *Possibilities:* Create a new variety of rose...raise healthy, loving children...comfort people in distress... make music...gather and analyze information about nature or politics.

What are the gaps in my life? Are there things you'd like to understand better or have more control over? Goals you've abandoned out of fear—but still wonder about? What are some ways to address these gaps?

Tools that can help in your exploration include a journal...walking...meditation...quiet time in a natural environment. *Exercises:*

• Write for 15 minutes about a topic of your choice, without stopping or censoring yourself. You'll be surprised at the ideas that come up.

• Write about a dream you had recently, the emotions it stirred and the messages it might have. Dreams often introduce important themes we haven't yet faced consciously.

Moving outward...

Quietly thinking and writing aren't the only ways to discover meaning. In fact, planning and taking part in challenging activities can be an outgrowth of positive solitude. We can try activities that reveal new aspects of ourselves —physical, intellectual and spiritual. The key is to identify and follow those pursuits that engage you—not to please friends or family or because you've always done them. *Exercises:*

• Write down 10 or 20 activities that you used to love but haven't done for a long time. What did you most enjoy as a child or adolescent? Try some of these activities again.

• Make a list of activities you always wanted to try but never got around to. Pick one—and do it.

Planning is essential for this stage. If we don't plan, then the easiest things will happen, not the most fulfilling. We'll come home and switch on the TV instead of going to a concert or arranging a kayaking trip.

Make activity dates for yourself...pencil them into your calendar...and make sure you keep them.

Be patient...

Don't be surprised if this self-analysis feels uncomfortable at first—or if you don't make dramatic discoveries right away.

Getting to know yourself takes some time. Challenging and reexamining your assumptions do not happen in a day. But the effort will bring satisfying rewards...including a deeper understanding of your values and needs...increased confidence in your capabilities...a richer enjoyment of life...and a greater receptivity to others.

Source: Rae André, PhD, associate professor of management psychology at Northeastern University. A consultant, lecturer and workshop leader, she is the author of *Positive Solitude: A Practical Program for Mastering Loneliness and Achieving Self-Fulfillment.* HarperCollins, 10 E. 53 St., New York 10022.

To Break a Bad Habit

Make a 21-day agreement with yourself to change your behavior. It takes 21 days to form a new habit or break an old one. If you come up with excuses to break your 21-day deal with yourself, remind yourself that you only have less than 21 days to go. *Key:* If you skip one day, the whole 21-day cycle starts over again.

Source: *Choose to Live Peacefully* by Susan Smith Jones, PhD, founder, Health Unlimited, Los Angeles human potential consultants. Celestial Arts, Box 7327, Berkeley, California 94707.

Easier Learning

Make learning easier by not expecting to be perfect right away. Accept your mistakes until you learn to do things well. *Benefits:* You'll develop a solid foundation on which to build ...you'll wipe out fear of failure...the more you learn about a subject, the easier it is to learn even more.

Source: *The Secret of Getting Straight A's: Learn More in Less Time with Little Effort* by aerospace engineer Brian Marshall. Hathaway International Publications, Box 6543, Buena Park, California 90622.

Learn While You Drive

The average person drives from 12,500 to 25,000 miles each year. Translated into hours, that's one to two college semesters. *Helpful:* Use time spent behind the wheel listening to creative or self-help tapes or your favorite music. Avoid radio shows that cause you to think negatively.

Source: *101 Simple Ways to Be Good to Yourself: How to Discover Peace and Joy in Your Life* by Oklahoma City stress consultant Donna Watson, PhD. Energy Press, 5275 McCormick Mountain, Austin, Texas 78734.

Auditing Classes

You can still attend college even if you don't want a degree. Even the most prestigious, competitive colleges and universities will allow you to take two or three courses without actually applying to the school. Some let you "audit," or sit in on, classes. You pay a fee but do not have to complete exams or written assignments and, of course, you get no college credit. But auditing a course is a good way to see if you like a particular school, major or course.

Source: *College After 30: It's Never Too Late to Get the Degree You Need!* by college and university consultants Sunny and Kim Baker. Bob Adams, Inc., 260 Center St., Holbrook, Massachusetts 02343.

College Success

Students do much better in college when they form alliances with fellow students, faculty members and student advisers. *Helpful:* Enrollment in at least one small class every semester. The frequent interaction among students and between students and teacher helps counter the anonymity of large lecture classes.

Source: Five-year study by Harvard University professors, led by Richard J. Light, professor of education, reported in *The New York Times.*

Chutzpah Lessons

Probably no one knows more about chutzpah than the undefeated grand master of the art, Alan Dershowitz. His reputation as Chutzpah champion of the American legal system has been spread by his spirited defenses in famous cases like Claus von Bulow, Leona Helmsley, Rabbi Meir Kahane, Jonathan Pollard and Jim Bakker.

We asked Dershowitz, author of the best-selling book *Chutzpah,* to share his expertise...

What is chutzpah?

A polite word for it would be nerve. Chutzpah is not something you're born with...it's an acquired characteristic.

Chutzpah is a survival technique. Its goal is to level the playing field—when you are confronting someone who is more powerful than you in a situation.

Where does the word come from?

Nobody knows for sure. It's neither Yiddish nor Hebrew in origin, but is probably Aramaic, going back thousands of years. Today, its Yiddish and Hebrew meanings are different. In Yiddish it's more positive—a kind of assertiveness, a boldness, an aggressiveness. In Hebrew the meaning is more negative—arrogance and pushiness. The word has always had both positive and negative connotations, but I use it in the positive sense.

What is the value of chutzpah?

Chutzpah helps underdogs fight against bullies—people who have more power. It should never be used in a bullying way.

I believe that the reason chutzpah is considered a Jewish quality is that Jews, for centuries, have always been on the bottom, trying to fight their way up.

Is chutzpah just for Jews?

Absolutely not! You don't have to be Jewish to have chutzpah. In fact, today, in America, chutzpah is needed, and used, by several less-advantaged groups—women, Asian-Americans, African-Americans, Hispanic-Americans, etc.

You mean that any American can aspire to have chutzpah?

I have the sense that chutzpah is now the quintessential American characteristic. If you ask a native French person what Americans are like, they say we are too pushy—too aggressive...although they don't use the word chutzpah.

Mark Twain, who was able to put everybody down using his incredible wit, was one of the great *chutzapahniks* in history.

What's a chutzpahnik?

A chutzpahnik is one who possesses the quality of chutzpah.

Judge Wapner from TV's *People's Court* is the epitome of lack of chutzpah—quiet and soft-spoken. He told me that he was raised believing that chutzpah was negative and shouldn't be used. After reading my book, he realized that there was a positive meaning for it, and now he would be happy to call himself a chutzpahnik.

How do I develop chutzpah if I haven't got it?

The first rule of chutzpah is to constructively challenge authority. You have to think of yourself as equal to anybody else. You have to say over and over again in your head, *I'm just as good as they are.*

Also important: Understanding that everybody has different talents, techniques and weapons in this contest of life...and knowing where your special strengths lie. The next time someone looks at you with an aloof, smug look—because he's a foot taller than you, a million dollars richer than you, etc.—you can break through that veneer using your superior talent. That's chutzpah. That's what you have to practice.

To use chutzpah, you have to go against character. If someone is expecting you to raise your voice, for example, lower your voice.

One of the greatest acts of chutzpah of all time was author/Holocaust survivor Elie Wiesel, telling President Reagan not to go to Bitberg. He whispered to the point where Reagan had to lean over so he could hear what he was saying. Wiesel, a powerless little man, without an army, without a constituency, without a bank account, lectured the President of the United States on the immorality of the Bitberg and of going to a cemetery where the victims of the Storm Troopers were buried.

Can chutzpah be misused?

Definitely. It's often misused. I think people use it promiscuously, as a way of dealing with everything.

You shouldn't use it with working-class people—taxi drivers, waiters, etc.

And it should never, *ever,* be used in your personal life. It's too potent a weapon to be used against a loved one. It's a contest. There's a winner and a loser. In love, there should always be a tie.

I have a friend who was married to a woman whom he loved very much for many, many years. But he dealt with everything by using his chutzpah—by putting her down, by being funnier than she. My friend was a wonderful date, but a terrible husband. He had all the clever put-downs and the wonderful things that would have kept his wife laughing all the time—*on a date.* But you can't laugh 24 hours a day. There comes a time you have to have serious, direct discussions.

Can you be shy and still develop chutzpah?

Absolutely. You can develop a public personality that is very aggressive. I'm very shy at parties. I find it hard to begin a conversation with someone unless I'm spoken to first. But I am very successful using my chutzpah in my professional life.

Where did you learn chutzpah?

From my mother. But I never, never use it in relation to my mother! I learned it from watching my mother use it on other people.

My mother is a brilliant woman. I've always said, had my mother lived 30 years later, she probably would have been the first woman on the Supreme Court. She is almost 80 years old, and to this day, she's the quickest repartee of anybody I know. She could beat Jackie Mason and Alan King to the punch line every time.

Do you think that chutzpah has a future?

Without any question. My book has been very successful. I've been getting letters from people all over the country. It was even reviewed by the *Korean Times!* The sky's the limit.

Source: Renowned attorney Alan Dershowitz, Harvard Law School professor and author of *Chutzpah,* Little, Brown and Company, 205 Lexington Ave., New York 10016.

Mind Power Opportunities

There is increasing evidence that the mind has many more resources than the experts once thought.

There are hundreds of studies now that show how to use the mind more effectively—if we take the time to understand what is there for us.

Part of my interest in this area comes from the work of my grandfather, Edgar Cayce. Known as *The Sleeping Prophet,* he had an unusual mental talent: He could enter a sleep-like trance in which he accurately diagnosed the illnesses of thousands of people—whether they were in the same room or thousands of miles away.

You can train your mind to work more powerfully for you in these areas...

Healing...

The mind has a great deal of control over the immune system. Harvard psychologist Mary Jaznowski took 30 healthy students and divided them into three groups...

- One worked crossword puzzles.
- One was given relaxation training.
- One received relaxation training and visual imagery training—imagining their powerful and strong immune systems attacking weak flu and cold viruses.

Group One showed no increase in immune cells. Group Two showed a slight increase. Group Three showed a *significant* increase in immune system activity after only one hour of training.

We, too, can use the mind to teach ourselves to relax, to visualize changes in the body and to increase the probability of those changes actually occurring.

Problem-solving and creativity...

Our program teaches that if we simply pay more attention—more time and energy—to becoming aware of our mental processes, we will be much more effective. One simple way of doing this is to work with your dreams. We all dream every night. If you aren't aware of your dreams, you are missing important messages from your inner mind.

Valuable habit: Put a pencil and paper by your bed and when you wake up, write down immediately what you recall from dreams during the night. If you do this consistently, you will find answers to problems from everyday life popping up in the dream state—how to deal with a situation at work, handle specific relationships, etc.

The *pre-sleep* state is also valuable. Both Einstein and Thomas Edison got important insights while in the pre-sleep period, and both found that the mind can function more creatively then—as opposed to when it is fully awake. Suggestions made during the pre-sleep period can help you to reshape your behavior.

Example: One of my students was trying to stop smoking. He worked with pre-sleep suggestion and visualization. He made a tape for himself, describing a number of situations in which he usually enjoyed smoking—but described them without the cigarettes. Every night for four months, he played this tape just before going to sleep. Then one weekend he threw away all his cigarettes and told himself that on Monday morning he would stop smoking. It worked. Months have passed...and he hasn't resumed smoking. He had tried other techniques, but none had ever worked before.

Stress reduction...

Meditation is one of the most vital tools used in reducing mental and physical stress. But recent research suggests that beyond these effects, the regular practice of meditation can enhance creativity and increase your attention span as well.

In meditation, you quiet the body and mind, and then place the mind on a single focus for a period of minutes. Harvard psychologist Herbert Benson found that the word "one," or even a nonsense syllable, worked just as well as a mantra.

Benson showed that the body begins to change as we work with the meditation process—there is a decrease in oxygen consumption...the muscles relax and the general level of stress is reduced. In addition, I have found meditation helps to discipline and control the mind, which helps us focus our attention wherever we need to.

Intuition and ESP...

Intuitive ability is probably distributed normally in the population, just the way any other ability is—playing the piano or throwing a baseball accurately or running fast.

There are a few people who have a tremendous amount of many abilities, and a few who have almost none. Most of us are in the big bump in the middle on the bell curve. If we practice, we begin to see improvement, but we can't just sit down at the piano and play a sonata without training, as Mozart did.

Intuition can be very useful in your business life, your personal life and your health. Meditation, pre-sleep suggestion, dreams and visualization can all enhance your ability to focus the mind in an intuitive way.

Helpful: Start now asking your inner self questions... *Can I trust this person? Where did I leave my keys?* Over time, the answers will get better and more frequent.

Developing our mind's capacity doesn't take much time. People generally begin to recognize results from these exercises after a month or so.

Remember: In the Jaznowski study, results showed after only one hour of training!

Source: Charles Thomas Cayce, PhD, president of the organization founded by his grandfather, Edgar Cayce—the Association for Research and Enlightenment, Box 95, Virginia Beach, Virginia 23451.

The Secrets of Effective Thinking

The world is filled with success stories—very limited success stories...but few of us ever achieve success in even two of the following three *life dimensions...*

- Successful careers
- Satisfying work
- Rich personal lives

...and genuine "three-dimensional" success is extremely rare.

To learn more about three-dimensional success, I studied 1,200 people—lawyers, artists, blue-collar workers, teachers and students. All had successful careers, and so had achieved at least *one-dimensional* success.

My psychological tests gauged their success in the other two dimensions—job satisfaction and personal life satisfaction. *Results:*

• Fifteen percent enjoyed their work but not their personal lives—and thus had achieved two-dimensional success. *Sad:* Most thought their successful, enjoyable careers resulted from a willingness to sacrifice their personal lives. One executive I asked to rate his personal life, responded, "Personal life? What personal life?"

• Four percent enjoyed both their work and their personal lives. These people had achieved three-dimensional success. They were good at their jobs... *and* they enjoyed their work... *and* they had fulfilling personal lives. I call these people *Uncommonly Successful People* (USPs).

To learn more about three-dimensional success, I subjected these USPs to additional psychological testing. *I found that all USPs share three important traits...*

• *Inner calm* that helps them to stay focused.

• *Clear goals* and a sense of purpose that guide their lives.

• *Adventurousness* that lets them laugh at themselves and gives them the courage to take necessary risks.

Effective thinking...

That wasn't all they shared. All USPs also share an uncommon way of thinking—what I call *effective thinking.*

Effective thinking is not the same as positive thinking, although positive thinking can sometimes be effective. Effective thinking is any thought pattern that leads, directly or indirectly, to personal and professional success...to a rich and satisfying life.

Effective thinking is always result-oriented. There is an effective thought for every situation we encounter.

Note: Most USPs weren't born effective thinkers. They learned to think effectively, just as all of us can. *What's needed:*

• Finding out exactly what you want in each dimension of your life.

• Committing yourself to achieving these goals.

• Using this standard approach to effective thinking...

• *Step one:* Take notice. As you hurry through life, pause five or six times a day to take stock of your life.

Am I doing well? Am I moving toward my goal of three-dimensional success? If you can honestly answer these questions in the affirmative, no additional action is needed. Go back to what you were doing. But if the answer is no, you must pause to get back on track.

Uncommon success does not mean vast riches, nor does it mean you must enjoy every moment of your life.

Example: A meeting might not be fun, but enduring it might help land you that next promotion. Viewing such experiences as important steps along your way to uncommon success makes them easier to bear. What you *think* is entirely under your control. Don't blow minor or temporary annoyances out of proportion.

• *Step two:* Pause. If while taking notice you discover that you are not heading toward uncommon success, you must pause. This pause may last from just a few seconds to several months, while all other aspects of your life continue as before. Whatever the duration of the pause, its purpose remains the same—to break your self-defeating mind-set.

Background: All humans approach life using certain mind-sets that have been programmed into our brains by parents, friends and teachers. At times these mind-sets are helpful...but at other times they make life needlessly difficult, interfering with our journey toward uncommon success.

Example: In my seminars, I ask participants if they're familiar with Ivan Pavlov, the Russian scientist who first demonstrated the conditioned response in which an animal's assumptions begin to control his behavior—a dog fed at the ring of a bell begins to salivate as soon as the bell is rung. Invariably, several participants raise their hands. When they do, I ask who told them to do so. Of course, no one did. They assumed they should raise their hands because they had in the past. Life works the same way. We behave in certain ways and think certain thoughts because we've been trained to do so. By pausing, we learn to break old habits and view life in fresh, creative terms.

• *Step three:* Identify effective thoughts. USPs always take responsibility for their life situation, shifting away from the external to the internal.

Example: A non-USP might think, *Pressures on my job make me nervous.* But a USP in the same situation thinks, *Pressures on my job do not make me nervous. My thoughts about these pressures make me nervous.*

In this way, USPs pinpoint defective thoughts and then identify—or create—effective thoughts with which to replace them. *Aids to effective thinking:*

• Understanding anger. All anger stems from fear. Eliminate the fear, and you eliminate the anger. If you become angry, ask yourself what you fear. In most cases, fears are not justified. If you encounter an angry person, don't think, *What a terrible person!* Instead, ask yourself, *What is he/she afraid of?*

• Understanding depression. All of us experience depression at some time or another. Depression helps us cope with sadness and then provides the impetus to get us back on track. Avoiding sadness or depression actually has a negative effect. The trick is not to spend too much time being depressed.

• Understanding intimacy. No matter how many friends you have, no matter how big and loving your family, each of us, alone, is responsible for ourself. This is especially true for uncommonly successful people, who operate at the upper echelons of business and society. Accepting the inevitability of occasional loneliness makes life more pleasant.

• Understanding neediness. People prefer to have all sorts of things—love, a nice house and car, a high-paying job, etc. In reality, they need only the basics—food, shelter, and clothing. Realizing that you can make do without all your preferences helps you appreciate what you already have.

Paradox: In many cases, realizing that you don't need something makes it easier to get that something.

• Understanding resentment. Life is not always fair. Rotten people sometimes thrive, and naive people occasionally suffer. But being indignant about this unfortunate fact is useless.

Better way: Try to set right an unfairness when you can. When you cannot, mourn briefly, then get on with your life.

Once you have identified effective thoughts, all that remains is to implement them—by choosing to do so.

• *Step four:* Choose. The brain is capable of enormous tasks. Unfortunately, most people believe they have little control over their thoughts, and so are enslaved by them. As USPs already know, humans are unique among animals in that they can choose their thoughts.

In many cases, it's possible simply to choose to think of a particular effective thought to focus upon. If conscious choosing fails, however, there is an alternative...

Reverse psychology: Exaggerate whatever effective thought you are thinking until you grow weary of it. Then use this newfound sense of control to choose the effective thought. If you have insomnia, for example, try thinking thoughts that will wake you up. Once you tire of doing this, choose to think sleep-promoting thoughts.

Source: Gerald Kushel, EdD, Professor Emeritus of mental health counseling at Long Island University and president of the Institute for Effective Thinking. Lecturer and seminar leader, Dr. Kushel is the author of several books, including his most recent, *Effective Thinking for Uncommon Success,* Amacom, 135 W. 50 St., New York 10020.

New Year's Resolutions—Effective any Time Of the Year

For most people, New Year's resolutions are forgotten or abandoned soon into the year. What to do? *Stop blaming yourself.* And begin fresh with *effective* resolutions.

The problem with most New Year's resolutions is that people don't know how to make good ones.

Sworn in a haze of champagne bubbles and high expectations, New Year's resolutions sound more like a *wish* list than a *to do* list.

For more effectiveness...

• Be realistic. A *wish* has nothing to do with committing yourself to an idea and developing and following a plan. A good resolution is a goal with a starting point, a plan and a deadline.

Example: When you take a plane trip, your goal is to be on the plane before takeoff. Days before your flight, you make plans to get there on time—you calculate the travel time to the airport, pack, arrange child-care, etc. You create a *reverse calendar,* starting at your goal (the plane ride) and working back to a starting point.

Resolutions work the same way. You start with a goal...then figure out what steps you must take to accomplish it.

• Know what to do. Most resolutions involve don'ts—*Don't smoke, don't eat, don't be late.* You never get a clear picture of what it is you're supposed to *do.* By asking yourself, *What's wrong with me?* instead of, *What can I do better?* you set yourself up to fail.

Successful resolutions focus on things you can do that will build your self-esteem or make you a better person.

Examples: Breathe fresh air, eat more vegetables, leave the house earlier.

• Think small. Great expectations lead to great disappointments. *Better:* Take small steps that are easily attainable and build the momentum you need to succeed. Start with just 15 minutes a day—go for a walk, clear your desk, etc. *Key:* Be patient.

• Daydream. Think about your ideal condition one year from now—imagine that you've already achieved your goal.

Examples: If your goal is to lose weight, feel what it will be like to be thinking, eating and exercising as a thin person. If you want to stop smoking, *feel* what it will be like to breathe freely, not relying on a cigarette.

Trap: Telling yourself, *I haven't reached my goal yet, I wish I had...*or *I should be...*Such statements lead to frustration and depression.

It's also important to think about long-term goals—three to five years from now. This will let you see how accomplishing your one-year resolution—changing a bad habit or learning a new skill—will bring you one step closer to attaining your long-term goals. *Result:* You will be motivated to see each resolution through to the end because you can see how it fits into your big picture.

Alternate plan...

If you're tired of making resolutions year after year, give yourself a break. Don't make any now. Keep the same job. Don't work on the relationship with your mate. Don't change your habits. Take time to discover who you really are and how it feels.

*Then...*if you can't bear to stay where you are, you will be more motivated to make a big change later.

When to resolve and re-resolve...

There are many turning points in the year during which you can examine what you've been doing and define goals to which you're willing to commit yourself.

Best times: In addition to January 1, there's also your birthday, or the day after you've filed your tax return, the end of summer, etc.

About once a month, examine your progress and reevaluate your resolutions. As time goes by, your resolution may no longer be useful.

Example: You may find that running 40 miles per week is not satisfying your goal to run a marathon, or is in conflict with other important goals—like being able to spend more time with your family.

Key: Use your goals to help you become wiser. As you learn more, your goals may change. Apply your new knowledge to making your resolutions more realistic.

Resolutions and others...

It's usually a good idea to tell someone else about the resolutions you've made. This creates a subtle social pressure that will help you to persevere when sticking to your goals gets tough.

If you don't want to disclose your entire resolutions to anyone else, it is often useful to at least tell someone about your short-term plans. Telling your spouse that you plan to walk for 15 minutes every day, for example, will help you reach that goal.

Important: Even if you share your resolutions with others, they are still *your* resolutions. Keep them under your control and be sure they are devised for your own personal improvement.

Example: You can't resolve that your spouse will stop smoking—that decision must come from your spouse. But you can resolve to support his/her efforts to kick the habit.

Resolutions needn't all be serious. Often, we get so wrapped up in *doing* resolutions that we forget about *being* resolutions.

Resolve to give yourself plenty of guilt-free time to relax, exercise, socialize and regenerate yourself. Only when you are at peace with yourself can you be truly in control of your life.

Source: Neil Fiore, PhD, a psychologist in private practice in Berkeley, California, and author of *The Now Habit: A Strategic Program for Overcoming Procrastination and Enjoying Guilt-Free Play,* Jeremy P. Tarcher, Inc., 5850 Wilshire Blvd., Suite 200, Los Angeles 90036. His most recent book is *The Road Back to Health: Coping with the Emotional Aspects of Cancer,* Celestial Arts, Box 7327, Berkeley, California 94701.

What They Don't Teach In Even the Best Schools

Our high school and our college teachers meant well, but they drilled into us huge quantities of information that we promptly forgot...and neglected to teach us some of the most fundamental skills for living well. *Key things that they left out:*

- The purpose of life.
- The importance of forgiveness.
- The need for balance.
- How to figure out what we want.
- The usefulness of mistakes.
- How to love ourselves.

Fortunately, our education doesn't end just because we leave school. Life itself is a classroom, and our teachers are everything that happens to us—both positive and negative.

In addition, each of us has our own *Master Teacher*—that voice inside us that seems to be making calm, sure comments in the midst of mental chaos. In a sense, it's life that teaches us how to live.

Why are we here?

We can't know for sure if there's meaning to life. But it makes great practical sense to at least *assume* that there is. I believe that life's purpose has three parts:

- Doing. Human beings are busy creatures. We do far more than simple survival would require. This suggests that we thrive on doing. *All this doing leads to...*
- Learning. The more we do, the more we learn...and the more we learn, the more we do. It's a continuing cycle. *But it would quickly become tedious without the third element...*
- Enjoying. Some people complain about being on a treadmill. Others pay hundreds of dollars for the privilege of going into a gym and running on one.

Joy can exist no matter what else is going on in your life. There are lessons to be learned even from confusion and pain...and learning is enjoyable, even if the events themselves aren't.

The attitude of gratitude...

The human brain evolved to take familiar things for granted, allowing our ancestors to sit up and take notice when a saber-toothed tiger approached. That means we need to be *consciously* grateful for the good in our lives, or we may not notice it at all.

You choose your attitude at any given moment. *Ask yourself:* Do I focus on the good things in my life or the bad things?

We all have plenty of both, and the mind can only concentrate on a narrow spectrum at any one time.

It's a simple formula. If you focus on the good stuff, life is enjoyable. If you focus on the bad, life is miserable.

That doesn't mean we should never feel bad. Pain and loss happen to everyone from time to time, and sometimes feeling bad is precisely the appropriate response to a situation.

But it's more often the little, day-to-day occurrences that make or break our happiness. You can focus on the guy who cut you off in traffic on the way to work this morning...or the one who kept the store open a few minutes late just to accommodate you.

Think about all the little miracles in life. Oxygen, for example—we've never been without it.

You can have anything you want...

The Puritan ethic tells us, *It's wrong to want things. Life is nothing but sacrifice and duty, and people who have what they want are wicked.* That belief leads to frustration.

In recent decades, the popular philosophy shifted to *I want it all!* But that philosophy also leads to frustration. If you have it all, you don't have enough time to learn how to use it, much less enjoy it.

The truth: You can have *anything*...but not *everything* you want.

Sure, there are limitations, but not as many as most of us believe. It's just that you may have to give up some things you want less for things you want more.

Don't be ashamed of your desires. It's great to want noble things (world peace, good health for all), but it's okay to want mundane or *self-focused* things, too—a red sports car, great sex, etc.

Respect the whole range of your aspirations. You can't get what you want unless you know what it is. And you won't figure out what it is unless you're willing to accept it.

Love your mistakes...

One of the most destructive things we learned in school is that mistakes are bad and should be punished.

It you avoid mistakes, you avoid accomplishing anything.

Without failure there's no experimentation ...no learning...and no growth.

It's by finding out what *doesn't* work that we learn what *does*. James Joyce wrote, *Mistakes are the portals of discovery.* Make excellence, not perfection, your goal.

Forgiving is for giving...

Nursing a grievance may make us feel righteous...but it doesn't make us feel happy. Forgiving and forgetting makes you available *for giving* and *for getting*.

When you forgive someone, you give not only to that person, but to yourself. Instead of focusing on hurt, anger and betrayal, you open yourself up to love, joy and adventure.

When we judge others, we also judge ourselves for being judgmental. Deep down, we know that we're inhibiting our happiness.

Say to yourself, *I forgive (name of person) for (perceived offense). I forgive myself for judging (person) for (offense).*

It's simple. Try it.

Life is a balancing act...

Another incorrect thing that school taught: *There's always a right answer.* Life is one contradiction after another...and most contradictions are valid.

We need to be vigilant to sense when we should rest and when we should act...when we should be flexible and when we should stand firm...what we should accept and what we should change.

When in doubt, consult your Master Teacher —that quietly confident and sensitive inner voice. *Ask:* What would a Master do? Then do it.

Source: Peter McWilliams, coauthor (with educator John-Roger) of *Life 101: Everything We Wish We Had Learned About Life in School—But Didn't* and *DO IT!: Let's Get Off Our Butts*, Prelude Press, Los Angeles.

The Importance of Self-Discipline

Without discipline, we can't improve ourselves, or solve problems, or be competent, or delay gratification or assume responsibility.

Without discipline we cannot find reality and truth...we never evolve from children into productive adults.

Yet discipline is a trait that's in short supply these days, especially among young people.

M. Scott Peck, best-selling author of *The Road Less Traveled*, tells us why this is so—and what we can do about it.

Why is discipline so powerful?

Most people think that the point of life is to be happy. But life is really about self-improvement. We're not born perfect. It's our job to make ourselves as good as we can be.

As Benjamin Franklin once said, "Those things that hurt, instruct." Yet the concept that life can be difficult is alien to most people.

The only way we can improve ourselves is through discipline. Without it, we can't solve any problems. With some discipline, we can solve some problems. But with total discipline, we can solve all of our problems. Discipline makes us competent.

I used to tell my patients that psychotherapy is not about happiness, it's about personal power and competence. If you get hooked into therapy and go the whole route, I can't guarantee you'll leave one bit happier. But you will leave more competent.

The problem with competence is that there's a vacuum of it in the world. So as soon as people become more competent, either God or life gives them bigger problems to deal with.

There is, however, a certain kind of joy that comes with knowing you're worrying about the big problems and that you're no longer getting bent out of shape about the little ones.

How can people determine which problems are truly important?

Think about them. Most people don't.

I spend the first hour of each day sitting in my bedroom thinking about my priorities. *What should I be working on now? What can be put off until later?*

Important problems are ones that affect all of us.

Example: I work with many organizations, businesses and agencies on how to better integrate psychiatry, religion and spirituality. That's a big problem.

It's impossible to think about big problems if you're spending your time worrying about what you're going to watch on TV or what you're going to say to someone. Spending time on that kind of problem is a waste of energy.

Isn't it true that some people think about the little problems to put off working on the important ones?

This relates to one of the main issues of discipline—delayed gratification.

This means doing the things in life that are *un*pleasant before those that are enjoyable. If you do what you have to do first, you'll be free to enjoy yourself later.

Most people—and I'm not just talking about children—dash to what they want to do, and then feel terrible trying to get around to what they have to do.

Why do so many people, especially young people, have so much trouble delaying gratification?

Gratification is something that must be learned. We rejoice in the spontaneity of small children. But, in truth, children are all born liars, cheats, thieves and manipulators who don't know how to delay gratification.

It's hardly remarkable that many of them grow up to be adult liars, cheats, thieves and manipulators.

What's even harder to explain—but what life is all about—is that some children grow up to be disciplined, God-fearing and honest.

There are many reasons why people grow up undisciplined. Most importantly, many children lack good parenting. Parents are role models. And kids with undisciplined parents have a much harder time growing up to be disciplined.

Discipline also suffers from an image problem in our culture. We think of discipline as something that's imposed by someone else rather than as a form of self-love.

Learning discipline requires real effort. But this is what it takes for people to find the most joy and lead the most productive lives. Delaying gratification means, ultimately, enjoying things *more.*

Does a person have to be completely unselfish to be able to accept discipline?

There's no such thing as an unselfish person. I myself am totally selfish. Strictly speaking, I've never done a thing for anyone else.

When I water my flowers I don't say, *Look, flowers, what I'm doing for you...you ought to be grateful.* I do it because I like pretty flowers.

When I extend myself for my children, it's because I want to have an image of myself as a good father.

You could look at monks and nuns and think how unselfish they are. But they've decided that this is the best way to personal joy.

We need to distinguish between the path of smart selfishness and that of stupid selfishness.

Stupid selfishness is trying to avoid all pain and all problems, while smart selfishness is learning the difference between unnecessary pain and that which is an inherent part of life.

Get rid of the unnecessary pain, but meet the necessary pain head on. Work it through and learn from it.

In what ways do people fail to accept discipline?

People often look to someone else to solve their problems. This is a natural tendency. Being disciplined requires assuming responsibility. And that means saying, *This is my problem.* You can't solve a problem until you admit that you own it.

Example: Three years ago, I had a sharp disagreement with my 18-year-old son. I raked him over the coals. The next morning I found an angry letter from him outside my door. I thought about it and decided he was right. So I apologized. It wasn't easy for me, but it was very healing for my son to have his father apologize.

Lesson: You can't apologize unless you accept responsibility for being at fault.

To take responsibility, you have to value yourself. And you have to have role models. Kids who won't assume responsibility undoubtedly have parents who won't, either.

In the example with my son, one of the beauties of my apology was not just that it made peace between us and increased his self-esteem, but that it gave him a model of taking responsibility.

How do we get the discipline to accomplish what we set out to do?

It requires dedication to reality...the truth. The more clearly we see the world, the better equipped we are to make wise decisions.

But reality and truth are only things we can approach. We can't get them tied in a nice little package and put it in our briefcase.

What else does it take for people to be disciplined?

People need deadlines.

When I used to work with groups and they weren't getting anywhere, I'd impose a six-month deadline. It's amazing how a group of people who had been acting as if they had all the time in the world could get moving once they had a concrete deadline.

Death is the ultimate deadline. None of us has forever to accomplish what we want to.

Is it possible to be over-disciplined?

Yes, it certainly is.

Our parents and our culture teach us that certain things must be done in certain ways.

Result: We can become so disciplined that we're not able to stop and smell the flowers.

Example: I used to think that if I went into a fancy restaurant I had to order an appetizer, entree and dessert. But sometimes I'd be attracted to two or three appetizers. Only now that I'm in my 50s can I order two appetizers and forget the entree. It's more constructive for me to eat what I want than to please the waiter.

Lesson: You can fiddle around with discipline ...as long as you're not doing anything that's harmful.

Source: Psychiatrist M. Scott Peck, MD, author of *A Bed By the Window, A Novel of Mystery and Redemption,* Bantam Books, 666 Fifth Ave., New York 10103. His big best-seller is, of course, *The Road Less Traveled.* Much of Dr. Peck's time is spent now in management consulting. His office: Bliss Rd., New Preston, Connecticut 06777.

Secrets of Much Better Problem Solving

We run into problems every day—at home and at work, with our families and our associates. And we spend tremendous time and energy trying to solve them.

Yet at the end of the day (or the week, or the quarter), we often find ourselves no further than when we began.

Better: Breakthrough Thinking...an approach to planning and problem solving that is based on both scientific theories and years of research with effective managers and professionals.

What is Breakthrough Thinking?

Breakthrough Thinking combines Oriental vision with Western pragmatism. Rather than focusing on what's wrong with a situation, it begins by defining our *purpose* in solving it.

Breakthrough Thinking asks more than just *how* we can get something done, it also asks *what* we want to accomplish...and *why* we want to accomplish it. In the process, it saves us from wasting time and energy on the wrong problem.

Breakthrough Thinking assumes that the world is always in flux. Each solution begets a new problem. No one solution can work all the time or for all things, no matter how similar the problems may appear on the surface.

To take advantage of ever-changing conditions, Breakthrough Thinking always seeks out the *solution-after-next.* As a result, it represents a process rather than a fixed goal—a flexible plan to achieve what matters most to us.

Although there is no magic formula to Breakthrough Thinking, it rests on these basics:

•The Uniqueness Principle. Each problem is unique and requires an approach that dwells on its own contextual needs. Although no two situations are alike, most people rely on impulsive idea-borrowing to solve their problems.

Problem-solvers who accept *differences* are much more likely to be successful than those who see only similarities, and who try to shoehorn borrowed solutions into situations where they are not appropriate.

Breakthrough Thinkers don't strive to *keep up with the Jones's...*they understand that the Jones's needs are different from their own. The childless couple next door may be deliriously happy with their sporty little Mazda Miata. But if you have a large family, a Volvo station wagon will solve *your* transportation problem far better.

•The Purposes Principle. Focusing on purposes helps strip away nonessential aspects to avoid working on the wrong problem.

Example: After years of struggle to keep your lawn alive, your sprinkler breaks. The obvious solution is to buy a new sprinkler—if your exclusive goal is to have a lush, green lawn. But if you expand your own context and examine your bigger purpose first, a more satisfying range of options will present itself...

•*Broader purpose:* To maintain an attractive outdoor environment in your current location. *Possible solution:* Replace the grass with drought-resistant shrubs and ground cover.

•*Even broader:* To have a beautiful view. *Possible solution:* Move to a home (in the mountains or on the beach, for instance) where lawns and landscaping are not an issue.

•The Solution-After-Next Principle. Innovation can be stimulated and solutions made more effective by working backward from an ideal target solution.

In applying this principle, a job seeker might accept a lower salary at a growing firm with strong opportunities for advancement, rather than a higher salary in a dead-end job at a small family firm. The key question is not *What is best for me next week?* but, *What do I want to be doing five years from now?*

•The Systems Principle. Every problem is part of a larger system. Nothing exists by itself. Successful problem-solving (and problem prevention) takes into account these interrelationships between many elements and dimensions.

Example: Many people rush into a divorce because their immediate goal is to detach themselves from their spouse. They may neglect the related *outcomes* they desire from the divorce, at heavy cost later on. Without advance consideration of the property settlement, child support and social ramifications, a divorce can create more problems than it solves.

Using Breakthrough Thinking, a woman who plans to get custody of her children may decide against staying in the family's home in an isolated suburb. *Reason:* As a single mother, she may need the social support and services she can find in the city. *Possible solution:* A liquidation of the family property.

•The Limited Information Collection Principle. Knowing too much about a problem initially can prevent you from seeing some excellent alternative solutions.

Information junkies think that facts are the keys to problem-solving—and that the more facts you have, the better your solution will be. They fail to realize that facts are only *representations* of the real world, not the real world itself. And representations can be distorted, poorly interpreted, irrelevant (the wrong problem) or just plain wrong.

Even if they are accurate, a flurry of facts will obscure the primary factor in any good solution—the purpose for it.

Example: I recently bought a new car. I might have immersed myself in data about suspension systems and engine design—and gotten progressively more confused. Instead, I asked myself what I wanted from my car—Prestige? Power? The latest features? The answer, each time, was *no.* The truth is that I hate to drive, so I do as little of it as I can. My top priority is reliability, followed by economy. *My solution:* I bought an inexpensive, no-frills car.

• The People Design Principle. The people who will carry out and use a solution must work together to develop the solution.

Too many meetings are searches for blame. Because they focus on the particulars of a problem, participants take turns in pointing fingers at someone else.

Breakthrough alternative: At the beginning of the meeting, ask everyone to discuss the *purpose* of your getting together. When individuals feel free to express their needs, they become more useful (and less defensive) contributors.

• The Betterment Timeline Principle. A sequence of purpose-directed solutions will lead to a better future.

Breakthroughs often occur over a period of time, not just at one point. The easy, *foolproof* solution is usually a patch job—and it's almost always wrong. Since solutions are changes that include the seeds of *later* changes, Breakthrough Thinking demands *continual* improvement in the area of concern.

Traditional thinkers say, "If it isn't broken, don't fix it." But Breakthrough Thinkers say, "Fix it *before* it breaks."

Source: Gerald Nadler, IBM Professor of Engineering Management at the University of Southern California and a consultant to some of North America's top corporations. He is coauthor of *Breakthrough Thinking*, Prima Publishing, Box 1260GN, Rocklin, California 95677.

Everyone Can Be More Creative

One of the world's biggest myths is that there is such a thing as *creative people.*

The truth: Everyone is creative. It's just that some people know how to use their creativity, while others do not. You can experience creativity more often by using four tools...

If at first you don't succeed...

Surrender. This doesn't mean giving up. It actually means surrendering to the answer already in you, but that you're not recognizing. This is the first tool—*having faith in your own creativity.*

What's going on: Something is blocking your thought processes. It may be anxiety, concern for your self-image or your need to impress others. *Exercises:*

• Recognize that apprehension, anxiety, tension, competition and anticipation all stifle your creativity. *Helpful:* Picture yourself full of intuition, will, strength and joy.

• Apply yourself to a task. Doing something for the sheer joy of it enables you to experience your inner creativity.

Example: One of my students, a lawyer, came up with an idea for an especially difficult legal issue. After racking his brain with various lines of reasoning, he just gave in and started with the easiest section of the legal brief, hoping the rest would follow. The ideas popped up as he worked.

• Acknowledge that you don't know how things will turn out. Instead of worrying about what could happen, just go ahead and see what develops.

Destroy judgment...

The second tool is an *absence of judgment.* It's hard to pay attention to your own creativity when a little voice inside your head keeps telling you that only special people—geniuses or great artists—can create...so you can't possibly be creative.

That voice comes from our parents who said things like, *Who do you think you are?* when we tried to do something original.

To get rid of that little voice—we call it the *Voice of Judgment*, or *VOJ*—you have to pay attention to it. Watch how many times it pops up during the day and stops you from doing something you want to do.

Example: When you arrive at work, you see someone you'd like to talk to, but she's talking to someone else. You turn away because your VOJ is saying, *She'd rather talk to Tom.*

As you monitor your Voice of Judgment, you'll start to notice that the voice isn't really you at all. It comes from outside.

At that point, you'll be able to make a conscious decision not to be affected by it. You'll start to get mad at the voice for stopping you from doing what you want to do and from being all that you could be.

To get rid of your VOJ: Shout at it. Tell it to get out of your life. Make it look ridiculous by exaggerating it beyond belief. Every time you attack the VOJ you weaken it more and more.

Pay attention...

By paying attention to what's going on around you, you develop the third tool for creativity—*precise observation.* An essential part of creativity is the ability to see things *very* clearly.

If you concentrate on what you're doing, even if it's something like washing the dishes, you slow down internally. This feeds your sense of deep appreciation and lets you focus without distraction on the task at hand, a valuable tool that most of us lost in childhood.

Example: A child building a sand castle is entirely absorbed in what he's doing. He's not thinking about it, he's just creating.

There are several ways you can teach yourself to concentrate. *Exercises:*

- Set your watch to go off on the hour to remind yourself to pay attention.
- Go to the ocean and sit there for an hour and soak in the tranquility...or the powerful turbulence.
- Listen carefully to what people say.
- Make lists of things you always wanted to pay attention to but never had the time.

To be creative, you have to pay attention to your own creativity.

Exercise: Sit quietly with your eyes closed. Pay attention to your breathing until you're calm. Then remember when you had a great idea, something that solved a problem or dealt with a situation. Get absorbed in it. Think of what happened before you got the idea, how long that took, how you felt, what you sensed, what you thought. Then think about what happened afterwards, what you did about it.

The more you pay attention to your own perfect performance—the times you were creative—the greater the probability that you'll be creative in future situations. *Helpful:* Start small. Think of the many little ways in which you're creative every day.

Example: The alternate route you chose to avoid a traffic jam getting to work.

Ask dumb questions...

Creativity starts with a question, which is the basis for the fourth and final tool of creativity—*asking penetrating questions.* A creative approach to living means making your entire life a questioning process.

When you ask creative questions, you don't care what you find. You ask for the fun of it, without expectation.

Examples: Columbus asked, *Is there a sea route to India?* and discovered the new world. Picasso asked, *Is it possible to depict the human form another way?* and found Cubism. Freud asked, *Do mistakes have meaning?* and founded psychoanalysis.

Preschool children ask dumb questions about everything. And sooner or later parents and teachers give them the message that such questions aren't welcome. Their VOJ begins to build a defense against questions. Pretty soon cynicism sets in.

Exercises: Ask a dumb question or question of wonder every day to develop your curiosity naturally. Start by asking yourself, then work up to asking other people. Start small. Don't frighten yourself with, *Is there a God?* Ask, *What's a preposition?* or, *Why are you digging that hole?*

Source: Social psychologist Michael Ray, PhD, professor of creativity at Stanford Business School. He is coauthor of *Creativity in Business*, Doubleday, 666 Fifth Ave., New York 10103.

Expanding Your Thinking Power

Over the past few years, there have been important developments in our understanding of effective thinking and how to teach it.

You can improve your reasoning skills by:

• Using analogies and metaphors. Deliberately ask yourself, *What am I assuming? If art is creative, for example, does that mean business is noncreative?* This will lead you to think about the real meaning of creativity.

• Not getting bogged down in a particular line of reasoning. Deliberately step outside it. *Suggestion:* Take 10 minutes to think of the problem in a completely different way. If that doesn't work, you've lost only a little time.

• Paying more attention to the aesthetic aspects of the problem than to the pragmatic ones. If you're designing an inventory system, for example, it shouldn't only be functional but should also solve certain difficulties in keeping track of things in an easy, elegant way.

• Looking at how you're being conventional. Break that conventional set. Watch out for cliches. Avoid timeworn and obvious answers.

• Being self-conscious. It's a myth that self-consciousness is a barrier to effective thinking. Be aware of the way you do things. Do you brush aside problems, or do you take them seriously? Do you look for opportunities to think about something a little longer, or do you pass them by?

• Opening up to ideas. Don't dismiss suggestions with *That's just common sense* or *I already do that.* Common sense isn't always common practice, and if you think you already do it, you probably don't. Research on actual behavior tells us that people don't accurately perceive whether or not they follow their own advice. Typically, they don't.

• Taking a course in thinking. Look for one that requires a lot of small-group work over a 6-to-20-week period. Investigate the course carefully, including the teacher's credentials, before taking it.

Source: David N. Perkins, Ph.D., senior research associate in education, Graduate School of Education, Harvard University, author of *The Mind's Best Work,* Harvard University Press, Cambridge, MA.

Scheduling Time To Concentrate

• Time budget should include "quiet hours" when you have a chance to think without interruptions. Best time in the office is early morning before official hours begin.

• If possible, work during noon hour when interruptions are rare because most others have gone to lunch. Go out to eat at 1 p.m. or later.

• When scheduling your day, schedule the interruptions, as well. Try to restrict all calls on routine matters to a certain time of the day. If calls come in at other hours, have your secretary say you'll call them back. (Even VIPs will accept this if you establish a reputation for returning calls when promised.)

• Spend a few "office hours" at home. Use an answering machine to cover telephone calls so you won't be interrupted.

Use Your Intuition to Improve Your Thinking

Intuition, the spontaneous generation of fresh ideas for solving problems, can help you in your work and personal life. Here are some ways to use intuition and evaluate its effectiveness relative to other methods of making decisions:

Keeping a journal will enable you to discover successful intuitions. For each intuition, record at the moment it happens:

• The date and time.

• Content.

•Type (future prediction, creative insight, problem solution, etc.).

•Description (verbal, visual, a faint idea, etc.).

•Vividness.

•What you were doing and how you felt immediately before and after having it.

•Your initial reaction (skepticism, belief, etc.).

Later, add the following to your journal:

•Was the intuition a departure from custom, authority or logic?

•Was it something you wanted or didn't want to hear?

•Did it return at various times?

•Did you analyze it, try to verify it, seek other opinions?

•Were you under pressure to come up with a decision?

•Did it represent a high risk?

•How did it work out in the end?

•If you went with an intuition that was wrong, do you understand why?

•Leave room in your journal for random thoughts and observations.

•Note any patterns that you may come across.

Source: Philip Goldberg, author of *The Intuitive Edge,* Jeremy P. Tarcher, Inc., Los Angeles.

Real Problem Solving

Management's job isn't simply to predict the problems—many of them can't be predicted, no matter how well the project is planned. *What is critical:* The way managers respond to inevitable problems.

•Seeking a victim and assigning blame is the most common response to a problem—and the least effective way to solve it. *Inevitable result:* Everyone avoids blame and argues if others had done what they should have, the problem wouldn't have come up.

•Not putting the emphasis on blame creates the atmosphere for making rolling adjustments and changes in plans and specifications in any new venture. This will not take place if individuals feel that concessions will be held against them or are an admission of guilt for originating the problem.

•Don't gloss over problems and figure mistakes can be fixed up later. Solve problems when they first surface.

Source: Dr. Leonard R. Sayles, Center for Creative Leadership, Greensboro, NC.

Finding Solutions To Problems

We all have a tendency to underestimate our most serious problems and to overestimate less serious ones. Often there are serious problems that we simply refuse to face by denying that they exist.

One big mistake is waiting for a problem to solve itself. To wait is to waste time and opportunity.

•If the solution to a problem lies in getting help from some other source, don't hesitate to ask for that help.

•Insulate yourself from the negative forces and negative personalities that constantly surround you. How many times has a positive idea been slaughtered, strangled, or sunk with the words *No way?*

•Attack your problem with courage...and the possibilities with enthusiasm.

•Ask your mind and heart what your real motives are and what price you're willing to pay.

•Add up your strengths. You're stronger than you think you are.

•Adjust your mind to change.

•Accept the irrevocable negative realities.

Source: Robert H. Schuller, founding pastor of Crystal Cathedral, Garden Grove, CA, and author of 15 books, the most recent of which is *Tough Times Never Last, But Tough People Do!,* Thomas Nelson Publishers, Nashville.

Problem Solving: Some Traits that Get in the Way

Would-be problem solvers often run into trouble because they:

• Cannot tolerate the ambiguity associated with a complex problem and believe all problems must be clear-cut.

• Stick to a preconceived belief and reinterpret inconsistent data to fit it.

• Hesitate to ask questions for fear of appearing ignorant.

• Give in to unrealistic anxiety about failing without systematically doing worst-case scenarios.

Roadblocks to Creativity

• Assuming that creative means new. Borrowing and modifying the ideas of others is just as useful.

• Relying too heavily on experts or self-styled creative types, who often are blinded by traditional approaches.

• Believing that only a few gifted people can be creative.

• Confusing creativity with emotional instability. What is needed instead is the ability to let the mind wander without fear of losing control.

• Failing to promote ideas voluntarily. Not pointing out achievements to superiors (a common failing of fired executives).

• Waiting for inspiration. Concentration and fact-finding are the most solid bases for innovation.

• Getting bogged down in technology. Look for solutions that can be accomplished with existing hardware and systems.

Source: M. LeBoeuf, *Imagineering: How to Profit from Your Creative Powers,* McGraw-Hill, New York.

Fears that Stifle Creativity

• Making mistakes.
• Being seen as a fool.
• Being criticized.
• Being misused.
• Standing alone.
• Disturbing traditions.
• Breaking taboos.
• Not having the security of habit.
• Losing the love of the group.
• Truly being an individual.

Learning How To Remember

Contrary to the conventional wisdom, memory doesn't work like a muscle. You can't exercise your way to a perfect memory. But you can learn tricks and techniques that can give you a far better memory than you'd believe. *Here are the best ones:*

• *Chunking:* That's the basic technique for short-term memory improvement. *How it works:* Grouping apparently isolated facts, numbers, letters, etc., into chunks. Thus, the series 255789356892365 turns into 255 789 356 892 365.

• *Sleep and remembering:* There is some evidence to indicate that things learned just before sleep are retained better.

• *Spacing:* Don't try to memorize by swallowing the whole thing down in one gulp. Instead of a three-hour study marathon, try two 1½ hour spans. Experiment to see what time period is best for you.

• *Reciting:* Vocalizing provides a kind of feedback as you literally hear (in addition to seeing) the words. It also forces you to organize the material in a way that is natural for memory improvement.

• *Story system:* A very effective way to remember some obviously unrelated objects. Just make up a silly story, using each of the objects in the story. Thus, if you want to remember the words *paper, tire, doctor, rose, ball,* try this story:

The paper rolled a tire down the sidewalk, and it hit the doctor, knocking him into a rose bush, where he found a ball.

Source: Kenneth L. Higbee, author of *Your Memory: How It Works and How to Improve It,* Prentice-Hall, Englewood Cliffs, NJ.

Improving Your Short-Term Memory

Memory exercises are most useful for those who face special short-term tasks such as the memorization of facts for a presentation. These tasks can be accomplished through the application of a few simple techniques.

Basic steps:

• Before resorting to memorization, use such aids as shopping lists, memos, or charts.

• When you do need to memorize, do so in the kind of environment in which you function best. Learn whether you concentrate better in total silence, with background music, etc.

• Arrange for short, frequent periods of study. Memory wanes during long sessions.

• Outline what you need to learn, and carry your notes with you in a small notebook.

• Refer to your notes at every empty interval during the day—waiting in line, riding the bus, etc.

How to Remember People's Names

To remember the names of people to whom you have just been introduced, the classic system is best:

• Take an interest in the person.

• Concentrate by looking directly at him or her. Notice appearance and dress.

• If you forget the name right after hearing it, ask immediately for it to be repeated.

• Repeat the name to yourself every few minutes. Over the next few days, keep calling the name to mind.

• Gradually decrease the frequency of repetition.

Source: Alan Baddeley, author of *Your Memory: A User's Guide,* Macmillan, New York.

How to Develop Intuition

We all have intuition, though we may not be aware of it and tend to devalue it as irrational. But many of the greatest scientific and creative people in history, including Einstein and Mozart, relied heavily on intuition.

To develop intuition, the first step is to accept that it isn't a gimmick. Intuition is spontaneous. It can't be contrived or programmed. However, you can create the conditions under which it's most likely to occur:

• Promote inner calm. An agitated, tense mind creates too much mental noise for intuition to operate. Stress-management techniques help people to be more intuitive, though this isn't their stated aim.

• Relax your mind by allowing it to wander. Take a walk on the beach, watch fish swim in a fishtank, take long baths, go away for the weekend. Some people have had their best intuitions while shaving or washing the dishes.

• Don't keep working harder and harder, struggling desperately for an answer to a problem. Like having a word on the tip of your tongue, the answer will come of its own accord when you're thinking of something else. The old saw, *Sleep on it,* really works.

• Approach problems in a flexible way. Many people acquire such rigid thought patterns that they effectively inhibit intuition. Loosen up. Be prepared to go with your feelings. Improvise. Get started before you know where an idea is going.

• Avoid outlining a project before you begin. This method can extinguish the spontaneity crucial to intuition.

•Don't feel you have to defend every idea rationally. Suspend judgment long enough to keep the idea as a possibility, to let it take concrete form. No idea is too bizarre to consider.

•Try brainstorming. Do for yourself what is generally done in groups. Sit quietly and let ideas pass without evaluating them. You can analyze and evaluate them later.

Source: Philip Goldberg, author of *The Intuitive Edge,* Jeremy P. Tarcher, Inc., Los Angeles.

Remembering Faces And Names Better

There are no special gimmicks to remembering important names and faces. You need only apply a few simple techniques:

•Take every opportunity to study lists of names that are important to you. It takes time, but it's worth it.

•Look through the names carefully, taking time to study each one and recollect when, and if, you ever met the person.

•If a name looks familiar, try to recall something about the person.

•Jot a friendly note to the person thanking him for the donation or order. The act of writing the note reinforces your memory of the person.

Source: Joseph F. Anderson, vice president for communications and development, Hamilton College, Clinton, NY.

Words of Wisdom

Here are the mottoes and proverbs that helped the following celebrities get to—and stay at—the top:

Isaac Asimov, writer:

"Laugh, and the world laughs with you; Weep, and you weep alone; For the sad old earth must borrow its mirth, but has trouble enough of its own."

Helen Gurley Brown, editor, *Cosmopolitan*:

"I don't remember any motto or saying that was valuable to me when I was 'getting there,' but there is one I like now (not that it helps, but it just happens to be true.) 'There is no free lunch.'"

Midge Decter, former director, Committee for the Free World:

"The perfect is the enemy of the good."

Jean Louis Dumas-Hermes, chairman, Hermes:

"Patience and time do more than force and anger."

The late Rose Kennedy, matriarch of the Kennedy clan:

"To whom much is given, much will be required." (St. Jude)

Edward Koch, former mayor of New York City:

"Be not afraid."

Jack La Lanne, pioneer physical fitness expert:

"Pride and discipline. If you use those two words, you can't fail."

Leonard A. Lauder, president, Estee Lauder, Inc.:

"Anything can be done as long as everybody gets the credit."

Willard Scott, weatherman on NBC's "Today" show:

"If a job is once begun, do not leave 'til it is done. Be it great or be it small, do it well or not at all."

Carl Spielvogel, chairman, Backer Spielvogel Bates Worldwide:

"Do unto others as you would have others do unto you."

Gloria Steinem, founder of *Ms.* magazine and author of *Outrageous Acts and Everyday Rebellions:*

"If there's no dancing, it's not my revolution!"

Some Tough Questions

Before you can make the right decision about more job responsibility, a new venture, travel, or a big move or change, you must identify your own strengths, interests, goals, needs and priorities. *Ask:*

•To whom do I owe what? How do job-related responsibilities (to stockholders, employees, customers) rank in priority with family responsibilities? Most big jobs preclude giving equal rank to both.

•Do I feel good about my work, the people in my life, myself?

•Do I waste valuable time and energy on things that don't really matter?

•When is the last time I ___ (fill in two or three activities you enjoy for pure fun)? If it's been too long, something's wrong.

•Is the desire for "bigger, better, more" causing me to work harder without joy?

•What should I be doing differently in my work to be happier, more productive, less frustrated or bored? The answers will be an adventure in self-discovery.

Rules of Thumb

Rules of thumb are useful because they cut down on the time needed to get information and figure things out ourselves. *Some especially helpful and little-known ones:*

•Extracurricular. Don't expect any more than one third of any professional-club members to attend a meeting. Build up a large membership so enough members are around to make up for those away.

•*Horses:* To get the best price on a riding horse, the best time of year to buy is Fall.

•Walking. Without a pack, you should be able to walk 25 miles a day without serious strain. With a pack one-fourth your weight or less, 15 miles a day is reasonable on an average trail.

•Dieting. Most overeating happens at night. If you can't diet all the time, diet after dark.

•Most for your money. You can mail five sheets of average paper for 29¢.

•Holiday time. To find out how many lights a Christmas tree needs, first multiply the tree height by the tree width measured in feet. Then multiply this figure by three.

•Determining your frame size. You can determine your body frame by wrapping your thumb and index finger around your wrist. *Small frame:* Thumb extends past the index finger. *Average frame:* Thumb and index finger just meet. *Large frame:* Thumb and index finger don't meet.

•Fixing up. It takes the average person one hour to paint 1,000 square feet plus one hour for each window or door.

•Bad weather. Second gear is best for driving on ice and snow.

Source: *Rules of Thumb* by Tom Parker, Houghton Mifflin Co., Boston.

While Standing in Line

•Do isometric exercises.

•Listen to instructional tapes.

•Read a paperback.

•Watch your miniature TV set.

•Meditate.

•Meet your neighbors in line.

•Plan the week's schedule.

•Plan an upcoming trip.

•Bring along a dictionary to expand your vocabulary.

•Make a list of people you want to meet to improve your business or social life.

How to Prevent Mistakes In Decision Making

•Never make unnecessary decisions. All decisions involve risk. It can occasionally be wiser to leave well enough alone.

•Identify recurring problems. Resolve them once and for all.

•Don't develop grandiose schemes to solve simple problems. Evaluate solutions in terms of costs.

•Don't delay the decision. Moving quickly allows more time to correct the decision if it turns out wrong. And it frees you to tackle other problems.

Source: Don Caruth and Bill Middlebrook, Caruth Management Consultants, Carrollton, TX, authors of *Supervisory Management,* Saranac Lake, NY.

6

Getting Organized

Priorities

The classic crisis between work and home life for busy people with children is the school play, recital or Little League game that conflicts with an important business meeting.

Trap: Making spur-of-the-moment decisions about priorities when these conflicts arise. That almost always results in hurt feelings, poor productivity, or your own disappointment in having accomplished too little.

Solution: Longer-term time management. Budget specific amounts of time each day for certain activities—and consistently hold to the schedule you set. *Examples:*

- No business calls after 7 p.m.
- Four hours of take-home work over the weekend, and no more.
- An hour or half-hour alone with your spouse when you both get in from work—no interruptions from children, work, or neighbors.

Make those times inviolate—something that others can count on.

Helpful: Make a public announcement to family and key coworkers of the times you've scheduled. That helps "trap" you into keeping to the plan.

When you establish a record of setting and sticking to priorities, the occasional missed Little League game or dinner out won't be seen as such a catastrophe—either for family members or for yourself.

First: Choose the right priorities.

For most families, life is too full of opportunities and responsibilities to be able to do everything. To accomplish as much as possible, some low-priority activities must be eliminated. *Challenge:* Choosing *which* activities to drop. Start by asking yourself: "What must I accomplish this week...or this day, this month, this year...even if I accomplish nothing else?"

Example: For daily priorities, set aside a time each evening to list what you must do the next day. Review that list in your head in the morning as you get ready to start the new day.

Key question: "What must I absolutely get done today?" If it's a phone call or a meeting with someone that you know will be difficult but which must be done that day—don't make excuses for not following through.

Caution: Don't fall into the trap of dutifully making a long "To Do" list every day—only to end up completing less than half of it each day. "To Do" lists are useless unless you score at least a B grade every day—getting at least seven out of 10 tasks accomplished. C—five out of 10 tasks—isn't good enough. And, three out of 10 is an F.

Important: Don't get so caught up in daily schedules that your weekly, monthly and yearly priorities go unattended.

For longer-term priorities, keep a file for updating your progress weekly or monthly.

More than just getting it done...

Even a good record of task completion, however, doesn't mean you're setting priorities most effectively. For that, you must track the quality of your progress.

Key: Take time at the end of the day to analyze whether you devoted significant attention to each project you handled. Are you sure that the time and effort you spent on each task succeeded in moving it closer to completion?

General rule: To improve the quality of your work, tackle the complicated tasks first. It's too easy to persuade yourself that it makes sense to get rid of the least demanding tasks to free yourself to take on the big jobs. But it rarely works that way. This is simply a classic delaying tactic. Avoidance takes more energy than it's really worth—energy that you can direct better elsewhere.

Executives have another set of priority traps...

- Spending more and more time on big strategic decisions that are removed from the day-to-day realities of keeping the business running smoothly.
- Avoiding big decisions by spending more time on minutiae.

There's no magical way to achieve the proper balance. The most successful managers, though, are constantly aware that they are in danger of veering toward one side or the other.

They keep developing a kind of dual vision that allows them to set the short-term, day-to-day priorities that keep the company moving and improving...and to continually set longer-range, strategic priorities that steer the company toward important goals.

As you struggle to work out these priorities, explain to your staff what the priorities are and why you have set them that way.

Encourage discussion. The more those who work with you buy into your goals for improvement and positive change, the more cohesively they work and the more productive the results of their efforts.

Source: Mortimer R. Feinberg, PhD, chairman, BFS Psychological Associates, Inc., 666 Fifth Ave., New York 10103.

The Great Alan Lakein On Time Management... 20 Years Later

Those who achieve the most in this world are not those with the highest IQs...the greatest natural skills...the hardest workers...but those who make the best use of their time.

The search for better ways to use your time every day is not a recent phenomenon. Americans were grappling with the same issue back in 1973, when Alan Lakein, a leading expert on personal time management, wrote *How to Get Control of Your Time and Your Life.* This book is still a rich resource when you're looking for ways to create more time and make better use of the time you have...when you want help in deciding what you really want to do and making time for it. *His advice today...*

Time planning...

The key to using your time wisely has not changed during the past 20 years—learn how to improve your efficiency and effectiveness.

Doing things as quickly as possible—mechanical efficiency—is certainly valuable. Choosing the best task to do—and doing it the right way—that's effectiveness.

Since I wrote my book, technology has helped us boost our efficiency, but I haven't noticed a comparable improvement in effectiveness.

The mechanics of time planning have improved, thanks to a proliferation of planning books and forms that are now available from every office-supply house.

Using these aids and, more recently, computer scheduling software, we are able to account for nearly every free minute and coordinate our schedules with those of other people so that mutually acceptable meetings can be arranged.

We have become more efficient at using our time...but not necessarily more effective at doing the right thing. That depends on how you set priorities.

Setting priorities...

Setting priorities requires determination and clear thinking. To do it right, you need to make firm decisions about what you want to achieve in your lifetime as well as during the next few years, months, days...and, ultimately, right now.

As I explain in my book, only when you have a firm grasp on your priorities can you classify the tasks facing you as As, Bs and Cs. Then you have to discipline yourself to tackle the most important first—the As...and only after they are accomplished should you turn to the Bs and the Cs.

Setting priorities is more critical and more difficult than ever. In today's harried environment, you probably don't even have enough time to complete all your As.

Time management and groups...

Back in 1973, I emphasized the importance of setting your own individual priorities...making private time for yourself...avoiding pointless meetings, etc. Your personal needs are still important, but if I were writing the book for today's more complex world, I would pay more attention to the importance of teamwork.

Today, businesses—and families—realize that success depends on groups working together. The watchwords of current management philosophy are total quality management and reengineering continuous improvement. These concepts can be implemented only by group commitment to common goals and priorities.

The whole group will be able to follow priorities successfully—and the priorities will be realistic—only if they are set in a way that allows and encourages every member to participate.

That same principle is necessary to make everyone agree on the priorities shared by the whole group and the individual members.

Complexity and time pressure...

Everywhere we turn today, growing complexity is increasing the pressure on our time. Businesses are faced with new complexities... increased competition...workforce diversity. Working husbands and wives must juggle their work, homes, and families.

How can you choose priorities when you are faced with so many alternatives and they all seem to be As?

There is no simple solution. You just have to work at it. Think it through from all sides... listen to different opinions...and make a decision.

Example: You are a successful advertising copywriter who has always dreamed of writing a book. Thanks to your spouse's income, you might be able to take off some time to work on it...but your spouse wants to start working part-time in order to spend more time at home with your young child.

The only way you can arrive at a reasonable set of priorities is to discuss all sides of the question...how the decision will affect you, your spouse, and your child...and your respective employers.

Important aspects: What is most important to each of the parties...economic well-being, personal fulfillment, parental attention? How is the situation likely to change in a year or two ...or five or ten?

You are likely to come up with the best solution if everyone gives it his best try. While you are unlikely to come up with a completely consistent and mutually satisfactory set of priorities right away, don't be afraid to try out whatever seems reasonable.

If it doesn't work, you can try something else. With your hard-earned knowledge of what didn't work for you—and some thinking about why it didn't work—your next approach should do better.

Bottom line...

Setting priorities with others is more important today than ever. Investing time and effort today is the key to saving time further down the road.

Source: Alan Lakein, author of the classic time-management book, *How to Get Control of Your Time and Your Life*—more than 3,000,000 copies sold. Signet, 375 Hudson St., New York 10014.

How to Make the Most of Your Time... Without Driving Yourself Crazy

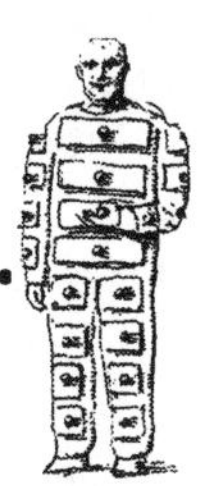

People have less free time than they did a generation ago—37% less than in 1973, according to a recent Harris survey. There is, though, more time available than you think. *Three general rules...*

• Eliminate slave-of-habit routines. *Example:* Spending 45 minutes each morning with the daily paper...when you can get the news you need with a quick scan of the front page or 10 minutes with an all-news radio station.

• Change your schedule so that you're at your best for your most important and challenging tasks. Many executives waste the start of their work day—when they may be freshest—by going through their mail. They'd do better by plunging into a tough report and saving the mail for later in the day, when they're slowing down.

• Learn to do two or three things at the same time. When you go to the bank, always bring something you need to read on the inevitable line. When you make a call and are placed on hold, switch to your speaker phone and take care of some paperwork. When your party comes on the line switch back.

Most time-saving ideas are small in scale—but those minutes add up. In most cases, a newly efficient person can save an hour a day—and that is a significant amount of time.

The morning routine...

• Pop out of bed as soon as you wake up, rather than lingering under the covers. *Incentive:* Think of the most pleasant activity on your schedule that day.

• Plan a pre-breakfast work segment—30 to 60 minutes of uninterrupted concentration in some quiet part of your home.

• Write a "to-do" list in your daily organizer book—a schedule of the high-priority tasks you need to address. Do it the night before. Less urgent tasks should be listed under "Things to Be Done This Week" and "Things for Following Weeks."

• Schedule tasks that require others' actions for early in the day. By reaching people early, you're more likely to get them to do what you need that day.

Organizing your office...

• Angle your desk away from open doorways, busy corridors or windows—all sources of distraction.

• Keep your desk neat. Clear away everything unrelated to the project at hand. *To dispose of clutter:* Eliminate dispensable items, including photos, gadgets and magazines. Put in a few inexpensive bookshelves you can get to without rising.

• Install the largest wastebasket your office can gracefully contain.

Communications...

• Use a dictation device, rather than a secretary's shorthand. *Advantages:* More speed and flexibility...simpler changes...enhanced concentration.

• Computerized electronic mail eliminates much time-wasting telephone tag. *For maximum efficiency:* Note when you'll be available for a return phone call.

• Rely on your answering machine to screen incoming calls. Your highest priority should always be the most important item on your schedule...which is rarely attending to the telephone.

The media...

Read selectively. Concentrate on one general newspaper. *Before you start reading:* Examine the general and business news indexes for stories of interest.

• If you find an item of interest in a newspaper or magazine, rip it out and read it when appropriate—and throw the rest of the publication away.

• Read for 15 to 30 minutes before bedtime. This is a good time for books that inspire or entertain.

Source: Ray Josephs, public-relations pioneer and author of the newly revised *How to Gain an Extra Hour Every Day.* Penguin USA, 375 Hudson St., New York 10014.

How to Set Your Life Goals and Attain Them Too

Everyone has dreams, but not many people know how to take the steps necessary to turn dreams into reality.

Key: Setting goals. Goals are simply changes you want to make in your life. They can be large (going to law school)...or small (making a phone call to keep up a friendship)...external (I'd like to double my salary in five years) ...or internal (I'd like to feel more comfortable with myself).

Common mistake: Confusing dreams with goals. Dreams remain in the realm of fantasy. Goals are the building blocks that make fantasies come true.

Goal-setting and life satisfaction...

Goals are necessary to give direction to our lives...but reaching them doesn't automatically make us happy.

Example: It's tempting—but unrealistic—to think, *If I lose 10 pounds, my marriage will improve, my boss will respect me, I'll communicate better and make more friends.*

Reaching goals, then setting new ones, improves the quality of our lives. But if we expect the process to make our lives perfect or problem-free, we'll be frustrated.

Trap: Focusing intently on one particular goal at the expense of other aspects of your life.

Example: If you throw all your energy into your job, you may get the promotion you want—but your health and family relationships may suffer. The overall quality of your life will not have improved.

To really make goal-setting work, you must pay attention to goals in all the major areas of life, not just one or two.

That's not as overwhelming as it sounds. We routinely juggle the many aspects of life on a daily basis—we just don't step back and think about it methodically.

Realistic approach: Set simple, easily reachable goals in some areas and tougher, longer-term goals in others...always keeping sight of the overall quality of your life.

The major life areas...

1. Self-esteem: How you feel about yourself.

Example: I'll write down three different things that I like about myself every day for a week.

2. Health and fitness: How well you take care of yourself physically.

Example: I'm going to cut back to one cup of coffee per day.

3. Communication: How clearly you express in words your identity, wants and needs.

Example: I'm going to take a workshop in assertiveness training to help me learn to say no.

4. Relationships: How you interact with the people in your life, whether family, friends or coworkers. *Included:* Developing key qualities—trust, honesty, retaining a healthy sense of individuality in the presence of others.

Example: I'll initiate a talk with my partner about where our relationship is headed.

5. Career/lifework: Experiencing challenge, satisfaction and fulfillment from the work you have chosen, be it paid or unpaid. *Included:* Job, raising children, volunteer activities.

Example: I'm going to look into training programs that can help me upgrade my job skills.

6. Finances/personal wealth: Managing your money to enrich your life.

Example: For one month, I will write down everything I buy so I'll know where my money goes.

7. Life crisis: Overcoming personal trauma through a process of healing and recovery. A *life crisis* is any event or circumstance—such as the end of a relationship, a chronic health

problem or a job loss—that interrupts the flow of your life for a period of time.

It's difficult to think about goals during a crisis, but goal-setting is an important part of recovery. Too many people grit their teeth and try to tough it out, but if they don't go through the healing and recovery process, buried emotions will come back to haunt them later. A man who is devastated by the breakup of a romance may try to cope by immediately starting to date again...but he may find that unresolved feelings of pain and betrayal make it hard for him to be open to a new relationship.

Examples: I'll find out about support groups for people with my health problem. Or...I'll read a book about coping with grief.

8. Your spiritual self: Connecting the physical and emotional aspects of your nature with spiritual awareness. Spiritual understanding has four components...

- Appreciation of nature.
- Faith or belief in a power greater than yourself.
- Faith or belief in an overall structure that gives purpose to life.
- Intuition, or sensitive perception of the world around you, that helps you feel connected to the rest of the world.

Examples: I'm going to buy a book on meditation. Or...Each day for the next two weeks, I'm going to take a walk in the woods.

Goal-setting steps...

Key elements of the most effective, achievable goals:

- Role model: An image of the person you'd like to be—or the life you'd like to have—once you achieve your goal. Your role model might be a famous person, a character in a novel or a mental vision of yourself with the qualities you hope to achieve.
- Mission: A simple statement of what you want—your motivating desire.

Example: I want to live in a house by the ocean.

- Emotional core: What the goal means to you.

Example: Having my own house would give me a sense of rootedness. Being by the ocean makes me feel centered and at peace.

- Commitment: The element that helps you distinguish between goals you set for yourself —and goals you set to please others. Ask yourself two questions:
  - *How badly do I want to achieve my goal?*
  - *Am I willing to work for it?* If you're not willing to work at a goal, you don't want it as badly as you think—and you'll be fighting yourself at every step.
- Guidelines: The action plan that will help you reach your goal. Be as specific as possible.

Example: If your goal is to lose weight, specify how much weight you will strive to lose, by what date and how you plan to lose it—the foods you'll cut back on, where and how often you'll exercise.

- Focus: Gathering information and resources.

Example: If you want to take a trip to Europe next summer, this step would include calling travel agents, pricing airfares, reading guidebooks and talking to people who have recently visited the countries that interest you.

- Timetable: A realistic and flexible target date for accomplishing each goal.
- Assessment/achievement: A review of your progress. Simple and immediate goals give you immediate feedback. For longer-term goals, assess your game plan every few weeks or months.
- Flexibility: Being able to change on a set goal. There's nothing wrong with changing a goal 30 seconds after you set it or even three years later. You may find that the steps you've been taking are ineffective and you need to adopt a new strategy. Your time frame may be too ambitious and require revision. Or changes in yourself or your life circumstances may have made the goal less valid—perhaps you need to drop it and set a new one.
- Reward: Taking time to pat yourself on the back whenever you achieve a goal, no matter how small. This will help you keep up your motivation and take pleasure in your accomplishments.

Source: Amy E. Dean, a speaker on self-help and recovery topics and the author of *Lifegoals,* Hay House, Inc., 1154 E. Dominguez St., California 90749.

Secrets of Getting Organized

- Does it often take you more than 10 minutes to unearth a particular letter, bill or other paper from your files?
- Are there papers on your desk, other than reference materials, that you haven't looked through for a week or more?
- Have you forgotten an appointment or a specific date in the past two months?
- Do your newspapers and magazines pile up unread?
- Do you frequently lose or misplace things?
- Do things pile up in corners of closets or on the floor because you can't decide where to put them?
- When you go shopping, do you find yourself running all over town, only to come home and find you have forgotten something?
- In case of a tragedy, would your spouse be able to find your valuable papers and records?
- Do you want to get organized but everything is in such a mess you don't know where to start?

If you answered "yes" to any of the above questions, you're making one or more of these mistakes...

- *Mistake:* Failure to divide a complex problem into manageable segments. *Better:* Forget about straightening up your life as a whole. Just work on the six elements in your life that need to be put in order.

Examples: Being late to work because you can't seem to get ready in the morning...losing things because you can't figure out where to put them so you can find them.

Helpful: Divide the problems on your list into smaller units. If the problem is a physical one —a disorganized wall unit or a messy closet— stand in the doorway, visually check out the entire room and list elements to work on.

If the problem is a system or process, mentally run through it and break it down.

Example: Getting up in the morning. *Breakdown:* The alarm rings too softly...you can't move quickly in the morning...you don't have time to decide what to wear.

Then, rank the problems on a list on a scale of one to 10—according to how much they irritate you.

A problem that creates serious tension is a #1...one that could wait until next year is #10. Tackle the #1s first...and so on.

Important: Work on solving only one small problem at a time.

Example: Not being able to get to work on time. *Solution:* Arrange for a wake-up service instead of depending on the alarm...lay out your clothes the night before...get up a half-hour earlier so you don't have to move so fast.

- *Mistake:* Failure to make time to organize. Set a specific time for tackling your organization problems. Write it in your appointment book as if it were a doctor's appointment.
- *Mistake:* Failure to deal with paper. There are only four things you can do with a piece of paper. I call it the TRAF system...
  - *Toss it.*
  - *Refer it (pass it along to someone else).*
  - *Act on it.*
  - *File it.*

Each piece of paper requires its own small decision. The worst mistake is picking up a piece of paper, staring at it and putting it down again because you don't know how to handle it.

To sort the papers you need: A wastebasket—and file folders marked: *Things to Do...To File ...Home...Financial.* Divide the mail according to what has interest to you and what doesn't. Toss the "no interest" pile.

Divide what you're saving into reference piles—papers you may need to refer to later—and action piles. Put the reference pile into the "To file" box or folder.

Divide the action pile into things having to do with money—bank statements, bills, financial statements—which go in the financial folder.

Anything you need to discuss with your spouse put into your home folder. Otherwise all action materials go in the "Things to do" folder.

- *Mistake:* Failure to follow up. Don't assume you'll remember what you have to do in the future. Even if you could remember, why would you want to clutter up your mind?

Simplest system: The calendar/holding file system. On your regular calendar write down what you have to do on what date. Keep a file folder labeled "holding," and if there's a document needed for a particular day, drop it in that file. That way nothing gets lost and you're always in control.

•*Mistake:* Failing to set priorities.

Use the Two-List Master List/Daily List system. *Needed:* A day-to-day appointment calendar and a notebook.

Master list: In your notebook write down every single future task that arises as it arises. Don't organize the tasks or set priorities initially.

Examples: An assignment from your boss. A reminder to call a friend.

Daily list: Each morning or evening list 10 things to do that day, compiled for the most part from items in your List notebook, follow-ups from your calendar, and one or two items from your "Things to do" file folder. *Include:* Fun things like a bike ride or a trip to the museum.

Then, rank each item on the Daily List in terms of its importance.

Mark each item #1 for high priority, #2 for medium or #3 for least urgent.

#1: Deadline items.

#2: Basic tasks.

#3: Routine tasks.

Cross each item off when you finish it. Transfer unfinished items to the next day's list.

•*Mistake:* Failure to plan ahead. If you're working on a complex project, it is extremely important to pace yourself over the weeks or months you have to complete it.

Helpful: On a single sheet, list the starting and deadline dates for *each* component. Then enter each starting and deadline date on your daily calendar. When you reach that date you can then put that job or its components on your daily list.

On a simple project, list the components and then enter each of them in your daily calendar on the appropriate date. On that date enter it on your daily list.

•*Mistake:* Failure to make use of services. Many of us were raised to feel that it's wrong to hire others to do menial tasks for us. *Necessary attitude change:* My time is worth too much to waste it doing things I loathe.

Helpful: Pickup and delivery services offered by merchants...a taxi service or private driver to take children to appointments...exercise teachers, hairstylists and others who make house calls...messenger services to deliver packages...a student to run errands...a cleaning person who'll also do the laundry.

•*Mistake:* Failure to consolidate. Return all phone calls during a specific time period rather than responding to each one as you get it.

Combine errands. When you're out grocery shopping also get your shoes and the broken lamp fixed.

Consolidate movement.

Example: Pull up the sheets, blanket and spread on one side of the bed before moving to the other.

Source: Stephanie Winston, founder and director of The Organizing Principle, a New York City-based consulting firm. The information here and more can be found in her books, *The Organized Executive* and, most recently published, *Getting Organized: The Easy Way to Put Your Life in Order,* both published by Warner Books, 666 Fifth Ave., New York 10103.

The Master List

I am a *very* organized person. As a result, I get more things done with less effort. And I make fewer mistakes.

When I work on a project, I start early and do it well. When I've finished, I never say to myself, "I could have done it better if I'd had more time." I know it's the best I was able to do...and I move on to the next project.

My secret: The Master List...

We're overwhelmed with so much information, our circuits are overloaded. We're overstimulated. Everybody is screaming for our immediate attention. Everything has become urgent.

Our projects are hanging in limbo, half done, and we can't decide what to do first. Most mistakes are self-inflicted, the result of negligence, improper planning or procedure.

To avoid these pitfalls that erode your precious time, write down all your unfinished work on a Master List.

You make lists all the time—grocery lists, lists of party guests, etc. If you make a Master List of all your current and pending projects, you'll find that it's the engine that makes your day run.

People jot down their chores, their projects, phone calls they have to return on little slips of paper. *Result:* They have 25 notes tacked to their office walls or sitting in piles on their desks.

Consolidate those notes onto one page, one that you can scan from top to bottom.

With that Master List, you know what you have to do and the time frame in which you have to do it. Without it, you're frantically trying to remember what needs to be done next.

The Master List is an inventory of all your unfinished work and ongoing projects. Go through all your papers. Ask yourself: *Is there any work that must be done by me—a phone call...a letter or report?* Write it on your Master List.

If it concerns someone else, send it on.

If it's not important, get rid of it.

The simple act of writing things down on your Master List gives you freedom—nothing will slip through the cracks, nothing will sneak up behind you and hit you on the back of the head. The more you write down, the less you have to remember.

Make a file folder for each project, and as soon as you make a note on that project, or get an idea concerning it, file it with the rest so that every folder is current and contains everything you need to know—every scrap of information—about that project.

Make an appointment with yourself...

Use your calendar to schedule appointments with yourself to complete work.

If you need to meet with a person face-to-face, you schedule an appointment. If you have work to do for that same person, why not block out an hour on your calendar and treat it just like that face-to-face meeting? Hold all calls. Close the door. Allow absolutely no interruptions.

Plan for interruptions...

I anticipate emergencies. I don't know what they'll be, but I expect them. I do this by being ahead in my work, not behind.

There are two ways you can go through life. One is by figuring that everything will go as expected. When something unexpected happens, it takes you by surprise. The other is by figuring that anything that can go wrong will go wrong.

Expect unexpected detours and distractions, so you're not thrown for a loop when they do pop up.

Deal with the disorganized...

Many of the people I work with are disorganized. Therefore, I have to be even more organized in my dealings with them—otherwise I'll never get anything done.

If you give an assignment to someone, you must assume that they are not going to do it on time. You have to take it upon yourself to follow up with them.

I try to maintain control and don't let the deadline slip through my fingers. That's where the Master List comes in again. Note the deadline on your Master List, since it's your responsibility to make sure the assigned work gets done.

When you're dealing with people who are chronically late to meetings and appointments, allow 50% more time and call to confirm how late they are running. Don't schedule appointments back-to-back. Give yourself a cushion between meetings...otherwise you're asking for trouble.

As a general rule, projects will take more time than you expect them to. If you need an hour, schedule an hour and a half.

Stay on top of your work. Expect and anticipate disorganization and lateness from others and you will take the nasty surprises out of your business day. *Result:* You'll complete twice as much work, in half the time.

Source: Jeffrey J. Mayer, one of the country's leading authorities on time-management and founder of the consulting firm Mayer Enterprises, 50 E. Bellevue Place, Suite 305, Chicago 60611. Its clients include Ameritech, Commonwealth Edison, Encyclopedia Brittanica, Sears Roebuck, Navistar and First National Bank of Chicago. He is the author of *If You Haven't Got the Time to Do it Right, When Will You Find the Time to Do it Over?* Fireside Books, 1230 Ave. of the Americas, New York 10020.

How to Conquer Clutter

Sooner or later, clutter invades nearly everyone's life. A key to clutter control is to have a place for everything. *To figure out what belongs where...*

• Organize the clutter in one complete area without stopping. Set aside a minimum of a half day—or tell yourself you won't stop until "two closets, the bathrooms or the garage" are clutter-free. *Important:* Avoid distractions.

Example: While cleaning her bedroom closet, Mary found something that belonged in the kitchen. But when she opened the kitchen cupboard she decided it needed to be organized as well—and never made it back to the bedroom closet.

Other distractions: Phone calls (take the phone off the hook)...old magazines, high school yearbooks, college term papers (do not stop to read anything)...errands (put them off until your task is complete).

• Set up large cardboard cartons. *Recommended:* One each for—elsewhere, charity and toss.

• Elsewhere. For anything that goes in another room. Do not put away items from this box until the end of the day.

• Charity. For usable items you no longer want. Do not put junk (torn clothing, broken toys that cannot be fixed, etc.) in this box—it will only tax the resources of the charity you're trying to help. Put this box into the car immediately and drop it off the next time you go out.

• Toss. For the true junk. *Suggestion:* If you're the type of person who has a problem throwing things away, have another member of the family come by once every hour and empty this box in the trash.

• Empty the target area of clutter. Sort it into the three boxes as you go. Anything not sorted into a box should be temporarily put elsewhere—the hall or on top of the bed.

What doesn't go into a box goes back to where it came from—but stored neatly. *Hint:* Group like items together and keep in "clutter containers."

Examples: Underwear goes in the same drawer with drawer dividers to keep it separated...bobby pins and hair clips are stored in a covered container, etc.

• Reward yourself for a job well done. Have a nice dinner out, take in a movie...or spend a quiet evening in your newly clutter-free home.

To help keep your clutter from getting out of control in the future...

• Take 20 minutes a day to tidy up by putting everything in the right room. Toys go in the kid's room, papers and magazines go into a reading stack, etc. Later, when you have more time, you can put things away more specifically.

Examples: Toys in the toy chest, last week's unread newspapers in the trash, etc.

• Find effective clutter storage containers. Games can be stored in a trunk that doubles as a table on top of which children can play the games.

• Make an ongoing effort to get rid of things you never use. Keep a *charity box* on hand for useable items that you no longer want. The minute the box gets full, put the items in bags and take them to your favorite charity.

Source: Stephanie Culp, founder of The Organization, a company dedicated to helping people and businesses get organized and stay organized, and author of *How to Conquer Clutter,* Writer's Digest Books, 1507 Dana Ave., Cincinnati 45207.

How to Get Your Paper Flow Under Control

Though many office workers don't agree that it's necessary to have a clean desk, few would dispute the importance of being able to quickly put their hands on information when they need it.

My principle: If you don't know you have it —or you can't find it—it's of no value to you.

Clients often tell me sob stories of missing important meetings because they misplaced the notice. Others bemoan their failure to meet loan payments or other deadlines. One entrepreneur even lost out on a promising business opportunity because he couldn't locate his passport.

Reality: Even with computers playing a bigger part in everyone's lives, there will always be plenty of paper to manage. The same principles that guide this paper management system can be applied to computers.

First—centralize...

Offices are dedicated to handling a flow of paper. But everyone needs a similar central location at home. If possible, this should be a permanent spot, available to you at all times. Avoid desks that look pretty but aren't functional.

Effective: A large butcher block top or a piece of plywood placed across two good-quality file cabinets. Since filing is a major factor in managing paper, it's ideal to have the filing system located close by.

Install adequate lighting and a comfortable chair. You want to make doing paperwork as pleasant as possible.

Key supplies: A "To Sort" tray (better to think of it this way than as an "In Box"), a large wastebasket, a nearby telephone, a rotary telephone file and a calendar.

Where to start...

Paper clutter indicates a pattern of postponed decisions. You've let those papers pile up because you failed to make an immediate decision about what to do with them. Begin now by putting today's mail, or whatever pile of papers you wish to organize, into your "To Sort" tray.

Use this spot consistently, bringing papers from everywhere to this base location. But think of it as only a temporary stopover. For most people, the goal of handling a piece of paper just once is too ambitious. But you should decide on its final resting place when it comes out of the "To Sort" tray. Sort out the tray on a regular basis.

The duty to discard...

Learning to throw out unneeded paper is the next step toward effective paper management.

People never use 80% of the paper they collect.

Your stress level will decrease as your use of the large wastebasket increases. Before the wastebasket, however, think about how to avoid even *seeing* unnecessary paper. *Examples:*

• *Get rid of 40% of your promotional mail* by writing to Mail Preference Service, Direct Marketing Association, 11 W. 42 St., Box 3861, New York 10036, and asking them to remove your name from direct mail lists. Every chance you get, instruct companies not to sell or rent your name and address.

• *Don't send for magazines you won't read.* Uncontrolled information is not a resource—*it's a burden.* Piles of old magazines or clippings—no matter how interesting or informative they may be—soon turn into dust collectors that depress you and make you feel guilty.

Better: Play a game with yourself to see how much you can throw away or recycle. *Questions to ask yourself:*

• Did I request this?

• Is this the only place this information is available?

• Is it recent enough to be useful?

• When, exactly, might I need this information? "Just in case" is not an acceptable answer.

• Are there any tax or legal reasons to keep it?

• What's the worst possible thing that could happen if I threw this away? (Most things can be reordered, found at the library, etc.)

Keep a calendar...

Using a calendar can eliminate lots of paper from your desks (home and office), dressers, mirrors, bulletin boards, and wallets.

Key: Get into the habit of extrapolating the needed information, entering it on your calendar, and then throwing away the paper—or filing it if you really must.

The most effective paper managers I know keep a master calendar that records all business and personal commitments for every member of the family. You can keep it either at home (the refrigerator door is accessible to everyone) or the office. Or, you can carry it with you.

In addition, you may need separate calendars for specific functions—a travel schedule, a meeting schedule, etc. But don't fall into the trap of having too many calendars. Coordination is an ongoing problem, especially when dates are changed. Keep key players informed.

The calendar is a tool that helps you to be realistic about time management. People who are most successful in accomplishing their goals make appointments with themselves to complete specific tasks by a certain date or to at least check on things.

I've developed some abbreviated symbols that remind me what I need to do: C (call), D (discuss), H (hold in file), LM (left message), WC (they will call me).

Note: I keep a corresponding WC file near the phone so that when people do call back I'll remember what I wanted to talk about.

If you're comfortable with a computer, you may want to use one of the many software scheduling programs now on the market. They're especially helpful when more than one person schedules your time.

Names and numbers...

Many of the little scraps of paper floating around our homes and offices contain important telephone numbers or ones that we think might become important.

Solution: Think of the one word that would prompt you to call this person—such as Atlanta...or kitchen...or speechwriter.

Then record or file the information that way and throw away the paper. I use my rotary phone file for all kinds of names and numbers, even for listing family Social Security numbers and the numbers of combination locks. Rotary phone-file cards now come in a variety of colors that you can use to flag different categories.

Action vs. reference files...

After you've eliminated as much paper as possible by using your wastebasket, calendar, a daily "To Do" list, and telephone listing, what remains will go into action files or reference files.

Action files: For papers that need immediate attention.

Reference files: For papers you know you will need at some point in the future.

Reference files can become action files or vice versa.

Example: A reference file on Europe can become an action file if you're planning a trip to Paris.

You can also have reference files and action files with the same or nearly the same heading —*Community Association* and *Community Association–1993 Dues Campaign.*

Potential action categories: Based on the next action needed, here are some of the action file categories I find useful...

- Call
- Computer entry
- Discuss
- File
- Pay
- Photocopy
- Read
- Sign
- Take to office/home
- Write

The key to reference files is not only to put papers away but to be able to find them again. File information according to *how you will use it,* not where you got it.

Ask yourself: Under what circumstances would I want this information? What word would first enter my mind?

Example: If you will need the information when you sell your house, then set up a *House—Main Street* file.

Put all papers in their most general category first—such as *Warranties and Instructions.* If that file becomes too bulky, you can break it down into *Warranties and Instructions–Kitchen Appliances, Warranties and Instructions–Autos.*

Organize your files logically—such as *Medical—Anne, Medical–John.* Group like files together.

Example: Instead of filing *Biking* under B and *Skiing* under S, you could have files named *Recreation–Biking* and *Recreation–Skiing.*

The very important master file: To remind yourself of how you filed information, keep an alphabetical master file index, with cross-references to related files. Keep the master file index right up front so when you file something, you can tell whether to put it under *Auto, Car, Chrysler,* or *Vehicle,* and you won't end up with all four.

If there's a particular piece of paper you're afraid of losing, you can list it in the index—*"Divorce decree,* see *Legal Information."*

Source: Barbara Hemphill, Hemphill & Associates, Inc., 1464 Garner Station Blvd., Raleigh, North Carolina 27603. She is president of the National Association for Professional Organizers and author of *Taming the Paper Tiger,* Kiplinger Books, 1729 H St. NW, Washington, DC 20006.

10 Ways to Get More Time in Your Life

• Slow down. Take the time to do things right...and enjoy the time you saved by not having to do them over.

• Say *no.* Just because someone requests that their concerns become important to you does not mean you must agree.

• Define your mission. Clarity comes from knowing where you are going and why you are on that path. From clarity comes vigor. From vigor comes the energy to accomplish what you want.

• Delegate. Accept that things will be done a little differently than you might have done them. Be willing to let others bring their own vision, process and reasonable autonomy to the project.

• Eliminate. Find time to address the small yet important tasks that come up each day. Otherwise they will add up, and you'll have to deal with them all at once.

• Simplify. Don't make your life more complex than it has to be. Organize your desk before you leave work or choose your clothes before going to bed, so you won't be sidetracked by these decisions the next day.

• Know when to hire help. Not every task you do yourself is a savings. Think about the do-it-yourself projects you're working on and whether they're actually the best use of your valuable time.

• Exercise/energize. Exercise gives you energy, vitality, alertness, stamina—and a longer life.

• Relax/savor. Recharge your mind and soul by closing your eyes, breathing deeply, drifting away and thinking soothing thoughts.

• Design your perfect vision. Draw a circle representing a 24-hour clock, and chart the way you now spend your time. Then, draw a second circle representing the way you would like to spend your time. This exercise will help you prioritize your time...and plan your future.

Source: Maggie Bedrosian, director, Bedrosian Communications Inc., a company that helps executives operate more effectively, 4509 Great Oak Rd., Rockville, Maryland 20853. She is the author of *Delights, Dilemmas, and Decisions: The Gift of Living Lightly.* The Positive Publisher, 1131-0 Tolland Tpke., Suite 175, Manchester, Connecticut 06040. 800-826-0529.

How to Stay Focused

We all have things in our lives that we wish would go away—marital conflicts, work stress, financial woes, problem in-laws, misbehaving kids, aging parents.

The conventional way we deal with the anxiety caused by these problems is by distracting ourselves with ordinary activities— exercising, reading the paper, watching TV, shopping, talking on the phone, socializing, doing volunteer work, visiting family members.

Although there's nothing wrong with any of these pursuits, by carrying them to extremes we turn them into dangerously addictive distractions. And we often do this without even noticing.

Why we distract ourselves...

Facing real problems by talking things out with the people involved or taking definitive action is scary. It's human nature to try to delay doing anything at all when a really painful problem arises.

Example: A dual-career couple is having marital problems, but neither partner ever talks about them. They structure their evenings at home so that while one is on the phone, the other reads the paper. They alternate using the computer. Then they go to bed, too tired to talk. *Trap:* They use their activities as an excuse for not confronting their problems.

People can fool themselves into thinking that their distractions are useful because so many of them are socially acceptable. Exercising, reading, socializing, etc., are all worthwhile...until they're overdone.

It can sometimes be hard to distinguish between a helpful activity and an addictive distraction.

Example: JoAnn talks incessantly about her romantic problems. She has fooled herself into thinking that she's doing something about them because she's constantly thinking about them. But talking to her friends on the telephone, complaining and listening to their advice only helps her *avoid* confronting the growing differences with her boyfriend.

Some distractions masquerade as very positive activities.

Example: Doing volunteer work. Although a little is great, if you start doing more than eight hours a week, it interferes with your personal life.

How it starts...

People are attracted to distractions because they're enjoyable and they relieve anxiety.

But as the time spent on a particular distraction increases, it changes from being a pleasant, anxiety-reducing, intrinsically positive experience into one that's addictive.

Example: Although following the news keeps you informed about world events, some people are so obsessed with all the bad news that they spend hours of free time reading the paper, listening to the radio and watching for more bad news on TV. It becomes their major topic of conversation.

In addition to all the time spent actually pursuing the activity, there are often many hours spent preparing for it, thinking about it, telling people about it and so on. All this helps people avoid their real problems.

Self-defense...

One way I get people to deal with their problems is to ask them to eliminate distractions. I put them on a *distraction diet.* The first step in getting rid of distractions is to find out what you're avoiding. *Ask yourself:* Is there anything I don't want to talk about?

If you're stymied and can't figure out what's bothering you, ask someone close to you what problems he/she thinks you may be hiding from.

Then look for your distractions. *Important:* Don't just look for one or two activities. Some people fill their lives with many different distractions.

If you think you don't have any problems, try giving up your distractions for a week and see what happens. It may be very illuminating.

Don't watch TV, don't read the papers, don't make unnecessary phone calls and don't exercise more than you need to keep fit. If you feel comfortable, then your distractions aren't addictive. But if you find yourself getting anxious, you'll know you're using your distractions to hide from something.

The journaling secret...

The best way to get rid of your distractions and confront your problems is through journal-writing. Write about the anxiety-provoking conflict—or situation—that you're trying to avoid.

To keep a journal, get a notebook and a soft-tipped pen, pick a quiet place and set aside some time each day when you're going to write.

Write about things that are hard for you to face, things that scare you, things that make you mad. Know that what you write is for your eyes only.

Instead of trying to express a single point of view, let each side of your personality have a full say. *Helpful:* Use multicolored pens to express the different parts of your personality.

When you've finished writing, sit quietly for a while or take a long walk by yourself. Open yourself to the babble of voices that are inside you. Let your thoughts flow. Just listen. Don't try to make judgments or come up with resolutions.

Example: If you're angry at your spouse, let yourself feel the anger without assigning blame or trying to decide what to do about your marriage.

The next step is to share your problem with someone—either a good friend or therapist. *Gained:* When you explain a problem to someone else, you clarify your own feelings and see things from a fresh point of view.

Source: Martin G. Groder, MD, a psychiatrist and business consultant, 104 S. Estes Dr., Chapel Hill, North Carolina 27514. His book, *Business Games: How to Recognize the Players and Deal With Them,* is available from Boardroom Classics, Greenwich, CT.

How to Make the Most of The Time In Your Life

Write a game plan for the rest of your life. It should include answers to the following questions:

•What things are really important in your life?

•What practical considerations have to be taken into account (earning a living, raising children, lifestyle)?

•What are your greatest personal strengths? Rank them.

•What are your most limiting shortcomings? Rank them, too.

•What are the activities you most enjoy and most dislike?

With these lists as a guide, make three sets of goals:

•Long-term—assume normal retirement age, plus 20 years.

•Mid-term—from today until retirement.

•Short-term—the next one to five years.

Long-term goals tend to be general (they should be), and short-term goals tend to be overly ambitious. A typical long-term goal is "Happiness." A typical short-term goal is "To get out of this rat race and open my own business."

Source: *Overcoming Executive Mid-Life Crisis,* John Wiley, New York.

Easy Ways to Get Organized

The most efficient people usually use systems that have two things in common—they're easy to set up, and they can be used consistently.

•Part-time employees are the key. Intelligent and motivated students will work for relatively low wages. Young mothers, too, are often looking for part-time work, and a note posted in pediatricians' waiting rooms will help them find you. Use them to prepare your tax returns, match paint swatches, address invitations to a party, collect the RSVPs, deliver collection envelopes for your favorite charity and wait in your home for the appliance repair service to arrive.

•As soon as you can each morning, make two lists of things you want to accomplish that day. The first list is activities that absolutely must get done. Reserve the second list for the wouldn't-it-be-nice-if jobs. You'll probably accomplish everything on the priority list. Consider yourself lucky if you make even a dent in the wish list.

•Find ways to get something done, no matter where you are. Carry notebooks to jot down ideas as they occur to you, or keep required reading material close at hand to review whenever a spare moment crops up.

•Don't force the issue if you're working on one thing but really want to be doing something else. Work on what you feel like doing.

•Create a master list—one place to write everything of importance that you need to remember. Include things to do, important names and phone numbers, good ideas. Use a spiral notebook instead of a pad so pages won't fall off.

Sources: Dr. Marilyn Machlowitz, author of *Workaholics: Living with Them, Working with Them,* The New American Library, New York, and Gerard R. Roche, executive recruiter.

How to Develop Good Time-Use Habits

All of us can make more of ourselves if we take the trouble to cultivate good time-use habits until they are second nature. Habits automatically steer our lives. When habits become time-thrifty, people get better use of their time for the rest of their lives, automatically.

To develop better time-use habits:

•Pick those habits that are good and drop bad ones. Make a list of times and places to substitute a new habit for an old one. It takes a month or more until a new habit is second nature.

•Concentrate on using the new technique as often as possible. Every time you use a new habit, give yourself a mental pat on the back. Otherwise, a mental kick is in order.

•Put weekly reminders to change habits on a calendar. When the reminders come up, evaluate your progress. Then list additional times and places to apply the new habit.

•Announce your intentions to develop new habits to other people. This strengthens your motivation to finish the job.

Source: Robert Moskowitz, time-management consultant, Canoga Park, CA.

Hard-Nosed Ways To Manage Time

•Concentrate on the best ways to spend time, instead of worrying about saving it.

•Keep an accurate log of activities to identify and define work patterns.

•Have only one chair (besides yours) in your office. Keeping people standing saves time.

•Each meeting should have an announced time limit.

•Have all calls screened. Make a list of who should be put through immediately.

•Arrange your office with your back to the door.

•If someone asks, "Do you have a minute?" say, "No."

•List tomorrow's priorities before leaving the office today.

•Don't rush needlessly. It takes longer to correct a mistake than to avoid making one.

Source: Merrill E. Douglass, director, Time Management Center, New York.

Avoiding the Obligation Overload

The prime cause of the overload syndrome is outside pressure to accept too many work or volunteer obligations. Another factor is the initial receptiveness of certain personality types to taking on tasks. Those people are particularly prone to guilt feelings.

Overload symptoms:

•Fear that the additional responsibilities (which suddenly seem overwhelming) won't be met.

•Inability to make decisions.

•Difficulty in communicating with family. The usual excuse is exhaustion.

•Isolation. Discarding the usual recreational outlets and exercise habits on grounds that there is no time.

What it takes to say *no:*

•A clear awareness of priorities. It's easier for a responsible person to say no if it's clear what's at stake: Obligations to family and personal health.

•The strength to accept temporary feelings of guilt.

Dealing with Details

When your mind is cluttered with details, use one of these techniques to redirect energy and improve organization:

•Take a mini-break. A short walk or a minute of relaxation and a drink of water. Or, simply breathe deeply for 30 seconds with your eyes closed (this can help concentration when you shift from one subject to another).

•Keep your schedule on paper. Resist the temptation to keep it in your head.

•Avoid interruptions. Work away from the office and keep your distance from the telephone.

•Delegate details. Rely more heavily on your secretary. Let subordinates handle routine jobs. Let them attend most of the less important meetings.

•Set time limits. If a task isn't completed within an allotted time limit, come back to it later.

Source: *International Management,* New York.

7

Finding a Job

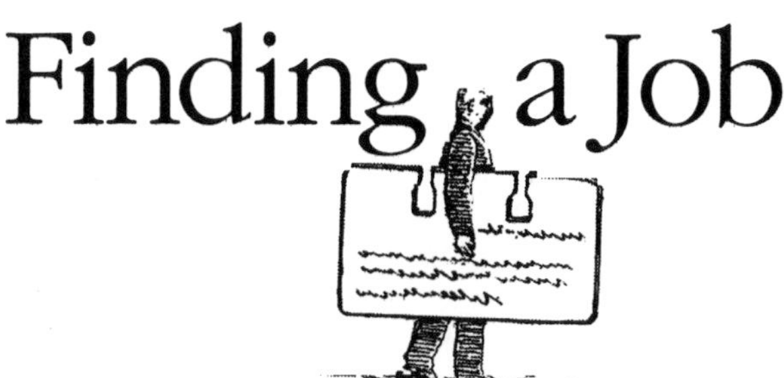

How to Make Networking Work for You

Networking is not just for executives who have fallen off the success track and need powerful contacts to help them find new jobs, assist in closing deals, etc.

Aside from helping in a career crisis, networking—continuously building contacts with people with information, expertise, and ideas from a wide spectrum of business, politics, and philosophy—is invaluable for day-to-day productivity, efficiency, and achievement.

Executives from unrelated companies face many common concerns. Sharing experiences —good and bad—on questions of compensation, incentives, labor negotiations, regulatory and legislative activities, and other topics is very helpful.

A peer outside the company may provide new information, suggest a consultant or expert, or provide an entirely fresh way for you to evaluate recommendations from your own corporate staff.

Organizing your network...

Important networking rule: Make a continuous investment of time in assessing the strengths of your own network—to identify where you are already strong and where you need to build. You can't delegate this task...you're the only one who can do it.

Tools for managing your network: A three-ring binder with loose-leaf, lined paper. *It should contain:*

- Address book.
- Business card file.
- Professional directories.
- Alumni associations and class reunion publications.
- Christmas card list.
- Membership rosters of organizations you belong to and contribute to—including groups such as the Little League, health and recreation club members.

Some people prefer to use a computer and personal organization software instead of paper and binder. There are many such programs available.

Identify your base of contacts...

Take several sheets of loose-leaf paper and give each sheet a heading from the following list:

- People in position to influence.
- People who know others.
- Coworkers and former coworkers.
- Clients and former clients.
- Suppliers.
- Colleagues and competitors.
- Family.
- Ex-family.
- Extended family.
- Neighbors/former neighbors.
- Classmates and alumni.
- Associates from organizations, charities, religious affiliations.
- Special interest groups (health, sports, bridge, etc.).

List names, addresses, and phone/fax numbers from your input sources under each category. Continue to add names and numbers as you build your network.

Once you've organized your contacts, identify gaps...and ways to fill them. Identify areas where the network can be significantly strengthened. *Key questions to ask yourself:*

- What kind of advice or information is most difficult to get?
- What group could I join that might help?
- Do I know enough senior executives in my own industry...among suppliers to my industry...in related businesses...in other areas?

Using the network...

Some of the best networkers find it difficult to use their contacts when they most need them. They're never reluctant to call a person if they have a useful piece of information or a new contact to offer. But it's hard for many successful executives to ask for help from network contacts when they really need the help and have nothing to offer in return.

It's important to remember that if you have been a giver in the past, people will respond when you need them. Call in your chips... that's part of the value of strong networks.

Example: A successful real-estate developer fell on hard times when commercial real-estate values collapsed in the late 1980s. When times were good, he had been very generous with his help to others. Now he was about to declare personal bankruptcy—and for the first time in years was looking for a job. He confided his situation to a colleague and asked him to keep his ears open for any openings. Before the day was over, the business friend's son called, explaining that his father-in-law was in a business that might be able to use the man's skills. He invited the developer to his child's christening party that weekend so that the two of them could meet. It worked. The developer was able to join the father-in-law's firm and stave off financial disaster.

Reciprocity is the glue that keeps networks together. And it's not only a career-building skill...it can be a career-saving skill. Giving without expectation works. In fact, giving is what builds your standing with a network.

Not giving back usually backfires. The network has a way of knowing when you owe too much.

Caution: A critical but frequently overlooked part of giving involves simply acknowledging advice, time, referrals, leads, or gifts from others. Gestures of appreciation are a powerful tool in the networking game.

Source: Susan RoAne, The RoAne Group, 14 Wilder St., San Francisco 94131. She is the author of the best-selling *How to Work a Room* and *The Secrets of Savvy Networking*. Both books are published by Warner Books, 1271 Ave. of the Americas, New York 10020.

First Person Interviewed Rarely Gets the Job

It shouldn't make any difference in hiring whether the candidate was interviewed first or last. But it does.

One of the major reasons that the first person interviewed is frequently not hired is that after many interviews, the interviewer tends to forget the first person. *How to avoid this trap...*

•Pay attention to your choice of interview options. You may be offered an interview on Monday, Tuesday, or Wednesday. Pick Wednesday. Or, you may be offered a choice of 9 a.m., 10 a.m., 11 a.m. or 4 p.m. If possible, opt for the last appointment.

•Don't make the mistake of deferring any interview too long. By the time you're ready to pick a mutually convenient time, the job may be filled.

•Follow up the interview by calling the hiring executive to thank him/her for his time, and if possible, add something that was not discussed at the interview.

Example: It didn't come across in our interview that I have excellent writing ability.

•Then, in a few days, mail a letter to the interviewer to serve as another reminder. It would be nice to include a newspaper or magazine clipping that you think the executive would appreciate. Polite persistence pays off.

Source: Robert Half is founder of Robert Half International, Menlo Park, California 94025, and author of *How to Get a Better Job in this Crazy World,* Plume, 375 Hudson St., New York 10014.

Businesses You Can Start for Under $500

Starting a business is not as hard as you think. You don't even need a great deal of money to launch one. Here are seven businesses that you can run out of your home with an investment of $500 or less...

•Credit-repair service. Customers usually seek this service after being rejected for a home or car loan. You would resolve their credit disputes, set up payment schedules with credit-card companies, etc.

Key: Screen potential clients. You want those you can actually help. To be eligible for your services, problem accounts must have been paid off for at least one year, preferably three or four. Guarantee clients an overall improvement in their credit.

Cost: $500 for office expenses, placement of ads in area newspapers, research of credit record-keeping and reporting laws. *Earning potential:* $100,000 a year.

•Drop shipper. You publicize, take orders for, and accept payment in full for a small manufacturer that produces consumer products such as books, garden tools, gourmet foods, etc. In effect, you are acting as a middleman.

First you negotiate a reduced price for the product with the manufacturer. When the orders come in, you forward them to the company along with half the negotiated price plus postage. The company then ships the orders with your mailing labels. You pay the balance of what you owe the company after your customers pay up.

Don't compete with established direct-mail businesses. Find a niche and work with specialized manufacturers.

Cost: $50 to $250 to publicize a product, process orders, and print labels. *Earning potential:* $3,000+ a year, part-time.

•Estate sales. Visit estate sales and study the business before soliciting clients of your own. You will need to learn how to price antiques and how to draw up a contract with clients.

Key: Letting clients know that you will take care of everything.

Cost: $200 to $300 to advertise your service in daily and shoppers' newspapers. The clients pay to advertise sales. *Earning potential:* 25% of sales.

•Mapmaker. Create colorful, informal community maps featuring advertisements for local businesses. Market each as a "community promotional piece."

Calculate costs of hiring an artist and printing. Charge businesses to appear on the map, plus $35–$40 in production costs. When the maps are printed, deliver 35 to 40 maps to each business, which they can sell for $1, recouping this cost.

Cost: $500 or less to solicit businesses. *Earning potential:* $11,000 or more per project.

•Meeting planner. Put together events, meetings, and conventions for clients.

Key: Pay attention to details. Thoroughly research hotels, restaurants, meeting facilities, and travel arrangements you make for clients. Your business will grow through word-of-mouth referrals.

Cost: $500 for office expenses, yellow pages ad. *Earning potential:* $30,000+ a year.

• Self-publisher of booklets. Research, write, and have printed—either at a copy shop or on a desktop system—informative booklets on specialty topics.

Your writing must be accurate, authoritative, and clear. *Most popular:* "How-to" booklets on money, self-help, self-improvement, special skills.

Cost: $200 to $500 for first printing, classified ads. *Earning potential:* $5,000+ a year.

• Tradespeoples' referral agency. Screen and schedule top-notch painters, carpenters, plumbers, and electricians to do everything from small repairs to major remodeling. Solicit tradespeople to list with you for free. Take 10% of the jobs you book.

Key: Familiarity with construction basics, reliability, commitment to quality.

Cost: $500 for a phone line, answering service, classified ads, flyers. *Earning potential:* $65,000 to $100,000 a year.

Source: Stephen Wagner, associate publisher and editor of *Income Opportunities* magazine and author of *Mind Your Own Business: The Best Businesses You Can Start Today for Under $500,* Bob Adams, Inc., 260 Center St., Holbrook, Massachusetts 02343.

Working the Room

The more people you know, the greater your chances for career advancement.

When you go to trade-association meetings, alumni get-togethers, or social occasions, try to have a little conversation with a number of people—mostly those you don't know.

• Introduce yourself...start with a bit of idle chatter: "This is a nice party. How long have you known the host?"

• Drop a hint about what you do: "I'm with one of the Big Six CPA firms." Then add, "What do you do?"

• If you consider it appropriate, give the person your business card. You might very well get one in exchange. If you had an interesting conversation, offer to send him/her something such as a clipping of a news item that you had just discussed. Now you have an address and perhaps a phone number, too.

Do's and don'ts...

• Don't be a leech. As soon as it appears the person you're talking to is getting restless, excuse yourself and move on.

• If you suspect that someone may be a good contact but you don't think it is appropriate to ask for an address and phone number, write down his/her full name—but not until after you walk away. You can get other information from the host.

• Don't give a sales pitch while working the room. That may be offensive to your host ...and others.

• A good way to start off is with social talk. Talk about family, friends—or play the geography game: "Oh, you're from Detroit. Do you know Charlie Smith? I think he's with one of your competitors."

• If you have unusual credentials, casually and quickly let them be known.

• Discuss interesting things—even humorous ones—that happened at work.

• If you have unusual education and business qualifications, let them be known—but keep it short.

A long time ago, I met a lawyer at a small gathering in London. We exchanged business cards. His practice was in Louisville, Kentucky, and at least once a year for 10 years, I received announcements of partnership changes, etc., from him. I thought that he was wasting his time since I would never need a lawyer in Louisville—and I was right.

But...a friend of mine, who knew our company had offices almost everywhere, asked me if I knew a lawyer in Kentucky. Guess what?

Source: Robert Half, founder of Robert Half International Inc. and Accountemps Worldwide, 2884 Sand Hill Rd., Menlo Park, California 94250.

Should You Take That New Job?

Key questions to ask your interviewer...

- What's the most common reason that people leave the company?
- What are your personal satisfactions and disappointments since you've been with the firm?
- What are the firm's overall strengths?
- When it comes to dealing with people, what are the firm's strengths—and weaknesses?
- Have you had—or do you expect—any big staff cutbacks?
- Do you generally fill openings from the outside or from within?
- What are the particular qualities my prospective boss is looking for?

Also, consider asking to meet a few current employees.

Source: Harvey B. Mackay, chairman and CEO of Mackay Envelope Corp., Minneapolis and author of *Sharkproof: Get the Job You Want, Keep the Job You Love...In Today's Frenzied Job Market.* HarperBusiness, 10 E. 53 St., New York 10022. 800-242-7737.

Landing a Job Through the Classifieds

To better your odds of landing a job through the classifieds, underline any words or phrases in the ad that relate to your qualifications. Then use similar terms to emphasize your attributes in a brief cover letter.

Source: *Careering and Re-Careering for the 1990s* by Ronald L. Krannich, PhD, Manassas, Virginia-based author of more than 20 career books. Impact Publications, 9104-N Manassas Dr., Manassas Park, Virginia 22111.

Résumé Smarts

Put your address at the bottom of a résumé for out-of-town jobs, not at the top. *Aim:* To get prospective employers to focus on you, not your location. You may fit perfectly a job that is 1,000 miles away—and be very willing to relocate at your own expense. But if your address is at the top, the company may read no further —wanting to avoid a costly relocation. *Bottom line:* For a better shot at a job, sell your credentials first, before the firm sees where you live.

Source: *The Right Job: How to Get the Job That's Right for You* by Robert Snelling, Sr., chairman, Snelling and Snelling, a Dallas-based worldwide network of franchised employment services. Penguin Books, 375 Hudson St., New York 10014.

Making the Most Of College Career Counselors

To make better use of college career counselors: Visit their facilities regularly. Get to know them while they get to know you. Find out their backgrounds, schooling, first jobs out of college. Be polite and courteous. Tell the counselor you know job hunts take time and do not expect miracles. *Best demeanor:* Serious, respectful, realistic.

Source: *How to Survive Without Your Parents' Money: Making it from College to the Real World* by Geoff Martz, author of four books for college students and recent graduates. Villard Books, 201 E. 50 St., New York 10022.

How to Turn Around Bad First Impressions

Bad first impressions aren't cast in stone. They can be neutralized. Many situations heal themselves naturally. As people get to know you, other more positive attributes will overcome the initial problem.

Or, if you don't want to leave it up to chance, there are things you can do to counteract a bad first impression:

Stop and take stock...

Before you try to correct a bad first impression that you've made, decide how serious it really is.

Most people overreact to what they perceive as a bad performance on a date, on a job interview, at a cocktail party, etc. *Ask yourself:*

•Do I have a history of tearing myself down?

•Do I analyze every little detail of my performance over and over again?

•Do I obsess about what I did wrong?

If you answer "yes" to any of these questions, you are probably being much too hard on yourself. Chances are, you did not make as bad an impression as you think you did. Try to forget about the incident.

Three types of bad impressions...

If you answer "no" to the above questions, and you think you really did make a bad impression, there are steps you can take to correct the situation. *What to do:*

•*Bad impression #1. You did something physically wrong.* Dressed inappropriately for the occasion...forgot to shave...or felt too fat, too tall, too short, etc. *Remedies:*

•Get feedback on how you look. Ask a friend for advice. Take suggestions seriously.

•Review how you prepared for the occasion. People who usually look good sometimes lose their sense of appropriateness when it comes to special occasions.

Example: Loretta, a lawyer who went to work in conservative suits, overcompensated by wearing tight, low-cut dresses on dates...and then got upset when men made passes.

•Groom yourself better. Some people consistently make bad impressions because they think others should like them no matter how they look. Recognize that the world plays by certain rules and if you want to win at the game you have to play it well.

•Feel good about yourself. Recognize that the more comfortable you are with yourself, the more likely it is that others will overlook your physical flaws.

Example: Sally blamed her nonexistent social life on her excess weight. Once she decided to accept herself the way she was, she became more relaxed and friendly...and men started to ask her out.

•*Bad impression #2. You gave inaccurate information.* Went to a meeting unprepared... pretended to know the facts when you didn't ...or made a stupid mistake. *Remedies:*

•Recognize that most people welcome the chance to correct someone. Making that mistake may not have been so terrible...some people actually do it deliberately, as a strategy to get others to open up.

•Recognize that no one condemns you for one mistake. There has to be a build-up of evidence for a really bad impression to sink in. If you make just one mistake, most people are more than willing to overlook it. Even if they don't say so...that's usually what they're thinking.

•*Bad impression #3. You said something wrong.* Came across as nasty...syrupy sweet... angry...tactless...or inappropriate in one way or another. *Remedies:*

•Give yourself credit. Recognize that if you've gotten this far in life without major trouble, your personality is probably okay.

•Ask for feedback from a friend. And review any feedback you've received from other people at other times.

•Analyze why you messed up. Maybe you need to relax, prepare better or increase your self-confidence. Perhaps you were anxious.

Example: Bobby was nervous around new people. But they often thought he didn't like them. Once he realized that a certain amount of nervousness and awkwardness was appealing, he was able to drop his aloof behavior and let others see his vulnerable side.

People are turned off by anger, belligerence or too much compliance. Nervousness is fine.

Other techniques...

Several techniques will work in any situation where you've made a bad first impression. *Included:*

•Call to explain your mistake, or do so the next time you see the person. Be appropriately self-effacing without being totally self-denigrating.

Studies have shown that unconcealed flaws evoke compassion. Embarrassment is endearing. *Especially likeable:* People who acknowledge that they made a mistake.

•Don't mention your gaffe at the time, but the next time you see the person, make a determined effort to correct it.

Assume that people will judge you not on one particular flaw but on the whole package you present over time.

Warning: Don't overcompensate.

Example: If someone gave you feedback that you were nasty, the next time you see that person watch out for acting too sweet. Or, if you gave them incorrect information the first time, don't overwhelm them with data the next.

•Use imagery to try out new ways to make a good impression.

Example: If you're anxious about a business lunch, imagine yourself at the table being confident, calm and relaxed.

•Tell yourself you don't have to be perfect. Just do the best you can.

Source: Barry Lubetkin, PhD, director of the Institute for Behavior Therapy, 137 E. 36 St., New York 10016. He is coauthor of *Bailing Out,* Prentice Hall, 15 Columbus Circle, New York 10023.

Common Mistakes That Job Hunters Make

With more people chasing fewer jobs, you can help your job hunting friends increase their odds of finding work by helping them avoid some of the most common mistakes. *Included:*

•*Mistake.* Jumping into a job search too quickly. Most executives are action-oriented people. If they find themselves out of work, their first instinct is to get on the phone and start looking for a new position. But it's never a good idea to act when emotions are in turmoil.

Better: Take at least a few days to sit back, assess the situation and analyze the options. Inform family, friends and close business associates about the situation, but limit contact with others for the time being.

•*Mistake.* Hanging out in the old office. Companies often give workers the option of remaining in their old office for a period of time after they've been dismissed. *Reason:* They can use the facilities while they look for a new position. Some people actually think that if they remain in the office their ex-boss will come to his/her senses, realize how invaluable they are and rehire them. *Reality:* Once everyone in the office learns a person has been fired, communications start to become embarrassing and awkward.

Although it's not necessary to pack up and leave by the end of the work day (unless asked to), the sooner the psychological break is made, the better.

•*Mistake.* Relying on a résumé as a door-opener. Many job-hunters spend days crafting their résumés. Then they're shocked when a mass mailing produces nothing.

Reality: People are busy. An unsolicited résumé is just a rung or two above advertising mail. A résumé is most effective when it's passed on by someone the person respects.

Think of a résumé as a short note left behind after a meeting that summarizes the qualifications already discussed in detail. Or, include one with the follow-up thank-you note that's always sent after a meeting.

•*Mistake:* Relying on recruiters. On the managerial level, employment agencies fill, at best, 10% of all available positions. Informal networking is the best way to land a new job.

This doesn't mean you shouldn't register with several agencies. But remember that finding a job depends primarily on the steps you take yourself.

•*Mistake.* Networking incorrectly. Some people think networking means calling friends and business acquaintances and asking them for a job. But the chance is remote that they'll have an appropriate position open when they get the call.

Networking is like building a spider web. Contacts are made piece by piece until a job is caught. Contacts should be used to offer ideas, suggestions and names of other executives with whom you can speak. Get in touch with them, ask for an appointment and pick their brains for ideas and additional contacts. Eventually, a solid job lead will appear.

Rule of thumb: To reach enough people, schedule an average of two networking meetings per day.

•*Mistake:* Getting in to see someone for an informal chat...and then asking for a job. This puts the person in an awkward position and lessens the odds that he'll be willing to help.

• *Mistake:* Not keeping in touch with people you've already networked with. Maintaining contact keeps the job hunter's name fresh in the person's mind.

Example: A man with a very common last name had a networking meeting with me. Several weeks later, after his name had begun to grow fuzzy in my memory, he sent a note just to say hello. That night, I came across a job lead that was perfect for him. If he hadn't written, I might not have thought of him.

Use any excuse you can think of to stay in touch.

Example: I know a woman who loves to read business magazines. While looking for a job, if she saw an article that related to a contact's company, industry or just something the two had discussed, she'd clip it and send it along with a short note.

• *Mistake:* Winging the interview. When they finally do get a job interview, many candidates go in unprepared. Learn as much as possible about the industry, the company and, if possible, the person conducting the interview.

Sources: The library, other executives in the company or industry, the business editor of the local newspaper.

Have an agenda. Know the half-dozen or so points that should be made during the meeting.

Examples: How past experience fits in with the company's needs, ideas for improving a particular division's profitability, etc.

Don't be embarrassed to go into an interview with a written list. This shows the interviewer that you've taken the time to be prepared.

• *Mistake:* Not dealing with the emotional fallout of a job hunt. No one likes to be rejected. And during the average six-month executive job search, everyone is going to be rejected more than once.

It's important to maintain a positive attitude. *Helpful:* Stay physically active. And don't keep things bottled up inside...and share your feelings with family and friends.

When to start...

The best time to start preparing for a job hunt is while you still have a job. Make it a point to make as many professional contacts as possible...and keep in touch with them. These contacts will prove invaluable if you ever find yourself out of work.

Small world: Never refuse to meet with someone who is networking. That person may one day turn out to be *very* helpful.

Source: Karl Gimber, senior vice president, Right Associates, outplacement specialists, 640 Fifth Ave., New York 10019.

Triumphing in a Job Interview

Job seekers often don't like the interviewer. But usually, they won't be working for the person who does the first interview or even some of the subsequent ones. *The goal:* To be successful enough in each interview to finally reach the person you will be working for—the one you're going to have to relate to.

But first, even if there is no "chemistry," you have to win over the lower-echelon people.

• Practice by going to as many interviews as possible.

• Practice at home. Sit before a mirror and answer stock questions ("Tell me something about yourself") into a tape recorder. Gradually, you will improve and be more at ease during real interviews, even if the stock questions don't come up.

• Be pleasant, polite and friendly—but not too friendly. Remember, you have something to sell.

• Don't eliminate the job on the basis of lower-level interviews. You might not know enough to make a choice until you move up to the next level.

• Tailor your résumé for the job you're going after and make it easier for the interviewer to pick out the highlights that apply to that particular opportunity.

• If the interviewer steers you into an area where you are weak, take charge, and steer the conversation in another direction—toward a strength.

•Make yourself as comfortable as possible at an interview. If the sun is in your eyes ask permission to move your chair or to sit somewhere else.

•Arrive on time. If it's a hard-to-reach place, do a dry run in advance. It's better to come early. You will be more relaxed that way.

•Try to avoid being the first person interviewed. Studies show that the first person has much less of a chance of getting the job. Although you can't always control this, avoid Mondays, in any case. Mondays and Fridays, the most disorganized days in an office, are also the worst for an interview.

•Don't smoke. It can't do you any good—and it can do you harm.

•Try to learn something about the interviewer, especially as you move to higher levels. You will be able to make more meaningful comments and you will be more relaxed.

•If the interviewer is getting a lot of phone calls, suggest coming back another day. He will either refuse further calls or accept your offer. Many on-the-spot decisions like these are a matter of being considerate, as you would be with a friend.

•If the interviewer stops talking, ask a specific question, such as, "Is there anything else you'd like to know about me?" Don't ramble your way into trouble.

•Somewhere near the end of the interview, tell the interviewer that you like the job, that you like the company and that you'd like to work for him/her. *Also:* Impress the interviewer with your confidence. Say, "I know I can do the job. I won't let you down. You can count on me."

•Follow up by sending a note to the interviewer. Send a note of thanks to that person's secretary, too. The secretary might mention it to the boss.

•After the interview, analyze what went wrong. Work on the assumption that something did. We're all amateurs at job interviews. If you can honestly figure out your mistakes, you won't make them again at the next interview.

Source: Robert Half, founder, Robert Half International, Inc., executive recruiters, San Francisco.

How to Handle the Silent Treatment At an Interview

A popular technique in interviewing a candidate is to clam up somewhere in the middle of the interview. This takes candidates off guard, and they sometimes get into trouble with too much loose talk and lots of nonsense.

How to keep from being derailed by the silent treatment:

•Be prepared with interesting and pertinent ideas.

•Shift the conversation to your strengths. In the event of the silent treatment, talk about these strengths as they apply to the company and to the function for which you're being interviewed.

•Sell your abilities. Instead of feeling ill at ease, consider a pause a benefit. Pick your own subject.

•Don't talk too long. After a few minutes, ask the interviewer if he wants you to continue or would like to ask you a question. If you are told to go on, do that for another several minutes and then ask again if you should continue.

•Remember, the interviewing process is a game. It's to your advantage to play it skillfully.

Source: Robert Half, founder, Robert Half International, Inc., executive recruiters, San Francisco.

Being Prepared (But Appearing Casual) At a Job Interview

•You should do about 85% of the talking in the interview. If an unskilled interviewer is doing too much talking, gracefully try to make your points. Otherwise, the interviewer will discover after you left that he knows very little about you.

•Study up on the company but don't appear too prepared. A skilled interviewer will be cautious that you are keying your replies to what you know the company wants.

•Try to find out what happened to the last person who had the job without asking a direct question. Encourage the interviewer to tell you about the job, what the best people did right and what mistakes others made, etc. The information may come out anyway.

•Don't prepare long, rehearsed answers to questions such as "Why didn't you make better grades in college?" Answer briefly and with confidence.

Source: Richard Fear.

How to Check Out Your Job Interviewer

•Find out in advance the name of your interviewer.

•Dig into his background for education, former jobs and outside interests.

•If you know his coworkers, quiz them about his personality and reputation in the company.

•Armed with this information, you may be able to maneuver the interview to your advantage. At least you'll have an idea about his priorities and interests.

Eleven Most Common Reasons Job Applicants Aren't Hired

•Too many jobs. Employers are suspicious of changes without career advancement.

•Reluctance of applicant or spouse to relocate if necessary.

•Wrong personality for the employer.

•Unrealistic salary requirements.

•Inadequate background.

•Poor employment record.

•Unresponsive, uninterested or unprepared during the interview. (Being "too aggressive" is not a serious handicap.)

•Negotiations with employer handled improperly.

•Little apparent growth potential.

•Long period of unemployment.

•Judged to be an ineffective supervisor.

Source: National Personnel Associates.

Negotiating Salary In a Job Interview

Negotiating salary is often the hardest part in a job interview.

Here are some suggestions:

•Avoid discussing salary in detail until you're close to getting an offer. If the first interviewer asks what salary you want, respond, "Salary is important, but it's not the most important thing. Why don't we develop an interest in each other and then we'll see."

•If the interviewer insists, mention your current salary and suggest using that as a guideline.

•When you are actually offered the job, you are in a much stronger bargaining position. That is the time to negotiate.

•Do not demand more than the market will bear. It's a mistake to lie about what you have been earning, especially if you're unemployed. The higher the salary, the fewer the jobs.

Source: Robert Half, founder, Robert Half International, Inc., executive recruiters, San Francisco.

How to Evaluate A Job Offer

Questions you must ask (yourself and the recruiter) to increase the chance that you land in a job that offers opportunity for promotion, mobility, power, personal growth:

•Who's in the job now?

•What is the average length of time people have stayed in the job?

•Where do they go?

•Ask to talk to people holding the same or similar jobs. Find out what other people in the company think about the job. If they think the job is dead-end, don't consider taking it. You may think you can overcome and be the "pleasant surprise." But chances are excellent that you will fail.

• Will the job give me a chance to know other people in the organization doing lots of different jobs?

• Will I represent the department (or group or section, etc.) at meetings with people from other parts of the organization?

• If the job is in the field, do I get much chance to meet with managers from headquarters? Does the job have too much autonomy? (Working on your own too much can be the kiss of death for upward movement if no one else gets to know you and your abilities.)

• Is this job in an area that solves problems for the company? The best jobs for getting power (and promotions) fast always have a sense of danger. Jobs in safe areas where everything is going well offer a slower track to promotion.

Best Days to Job Hunt

Most job seekers think Monday is the best day to look for a job because there are more jobs advertised in the papers on Sunday. But jobs advertised on Sunday actually become available the previous Wednesday.

Helpful:

• Look every day of the week.

• If you have to skip one day, Monday is the best choice. You will not be slowed down by the same hordes of competition on other days.

• The best job hunting may be when the weather is bad. Again, there are fewer competitors. Management may well believe that the bad-weather candidate is more interested in employment and will work harder with less absenteeism. However, interviewers may be depressed and executives busy filling in for absent staff when the weather is poor.

Source: Robert Half, founder, Robert Half International, Inc., executive recruiters, San Francisco.

Most Common Job Search Mistakes

• Failure to look within before looking outside. Self-assessment is the key to a successful job search. Before you begin, take the time to look inside and ask, "What have I to offer?"

• Failure to approach the job search as a multifaceted process. A good campaign mixes at least three of the following methods: Personal networking, using employment search firms, answering classified ads, doing research, conducting a direct-mail campaign and targeting (the thorough analysis of one or two companies). Do some of each, but be sure that you spend at least half of your time on personal networking. Studies show that about 70% of all jobs are filled through personal contacts. Most people know 200-500 people, though they seldom realize it. Some can be valuable to you.

• Failure to plan and organize a campaign. Map out each week ahead of time.

• Failure to keep careful records of everything you do and everyone you speak to. A month from now, you may be talking to someone whom you've spoken to before, and you might not remember what was said in the initial meeting. Information is the job seeker's most powerful tool.

• Failure to maintain the ideal job seeker's attitude: Nonjudgmental. Treat everyone with warmth and courtesy. Realize that in a job search you get back what you put in. If you're putting out positive energy, you will connect with people much more easily.

• Failure to spend enough time on the telephone. Productivity in any campaign is directly related to the number of calls you make. It is easy to fall into a campaign of sending résumés and writing letters. Spend 50% of your time on the telephone. That's the way everything happens. It's more personal. It also forces you to call people whom you know—essentially doing the networking that you might otherwise neglect. If you have a goal of meeting 10 people a week, the only way that you can do it is by using the telephone.

• Failure to maintain your vitality during a campaign. Work to keep mentally and physically fit. A good campaign is a combination of work, rest, exercise and good diet. Some people think that if six hours a day of job searching is good, 10 hours will get the job that much faster. But such people usually burn themselves out.

• Failure to prepare ahead of time for interviews. Simply go to the library and get an annual report. *Find out:* The size of the company, its products or services, and any problems in the company or in its industry. You'll be ahead of 90% of the other applicants if you know something about the company before the interview.

• Failure to maintain good grooming and personal appearance. Take care of your appearance, even when dressed informally for networking. First impressions are hard to change.

• Failure to send thank-you notes to people in the network who have helped you—and to people who have interviewed you.

• Failure to follow up...and follow up...and follow up.

Getting a job is a social process. The interaction among people is what makes jobs happen.

Source: William Ellermeyer, president of Career Management Services, Irvine, CA.

How to Win the Temp-Work Game

Temporary work has become a credible permanent career choice as the market for competent, specialized part-time help expands. Whether one views temporary work as an interim measure or enjoys the flexible lifestyle of a "professional temporary," more can be gained from the experience if the disadvantages are offset.

Here are the worst problems most temps face and how to minimize them...

• The *just-a-temp* attitude. Although temps are called in as skilled, fast-learning pinch hitters, many complain of being treated as unintelligent or unimportant. This attitude is rapidly receding as the old image of the unskilled and disinterested temp disappears.

Self-defense: Don't assume an *I'm just a temp* attitude. Temps must prove their abilities before they're taken seriously.

• Lack of benefits. Temps generally have to buy their own insurance and save toward vacations, sick leave and retirement. If the government passes a national health plan this year, some of this problem may be partially eased.

In the meantime: Shop carefully for a temporary service. Many services have begun to offer medical insurance to their regular temps, and some offer accrued vacation and sick time—but temp services with benefits are likely to pay lower wages.

• Social isolation. Those who depend on the workplace for close, long-term friendships should probably not work as temps. Temps are not treated as "one of the gang."

Self-defense: Those who want the best of both worlds can ask to be reassigned to the same companies regularly. On new assignments, seek out other temps with whom you might have lunch. Personalize your work area with flowers, or bring cookies for coworkers.

• Work isn't always available. To improve the frequency, temps can let the service know when they want to work or if they are willing to take lower-paying jobs just to be working. Call in twice a day to check on new assignments. Ask the service if it uses standbys—temps who report to the service to be available for emergency replacement calls and are paid for a minimum number of hours, whether or not they are sent out.

• Getting dumped on. Many temps find themselves the *office scapegoat*—either for piles of work no one else wants to do or for blame when regular employees make errors.

Self-defense: Don't be bullied by regular employees. Clarify your priorities with a supervisor when more than one person needs to have work done.

• Boredom. Some companies hire temps even when they have little need for them. As a result, temps may not have much to do for long periods of time.

Self-defense: Become familiar with the office equipment. Ask for more work, which always surprises and impresses employers. As a last resort, bring letters to write and other personal work so that you always look busy.

• Adaptability anxiety. Many temps experience *first-day-at-a-new-job* stress almost every week.

Self-defense: Don't become stressed. Companies that call for temps do not expect miracle workers. Be prepared to ask questions and do a professional job. If the work or workload is unreasonable, be honest. Call the temp service and say so.

• Acceptance of limited influence. Temps often see potential improvements because they are objective and have worked for many companies. But a clever temp may be resented or be seen as a threat by permanent employees.

Self-defense: Make your suggestions tactfully.

Example: Write a memo to the supervisor on the *last* day of the assignment, crediting the employees who were helpful. Add suggestions as a way of saying *thank you* for the assignment.

• Lack of growth and no clear career path. Temping tends to be a series of similar assignments that allow you limited improvement in your skills and earnings.

Self-defense: Be realistic about what can be achieved by temping.

Exception: Many temp services now function as outsourcing firms for companies with seasonal, by-the-project or right-sizing needs. They employ temps who are *already* professionals—doctors, lawyers, plant managers, executives. Many temps choose a service that promises glamorous assignments with the hope that they will be offered permanent positions.

Temporary jobs are generally *not* trial positions. But temping *is* a great way to tap into the "hidden job market"—job postings that are not advertised or sent to an employment service.

• Temp work is not accepted as work experience on résumés.

Self-defense: Temps should create résumés that detail the positions they have filled, the companies for which they have worked and their responsibilities. Prepare a positive answer in advance to the job-interview question *Why were you a temp?*

Example: "I wanted exposure to various communications industries. I've worked in publishing, advertising, public relations and television production companies. I now know I'm happiest in an advertising environment."

Source: William Lewis, president of Career Blazers, Inc., an employment and training service, 590 Fifth Ave., New York 10036. He is coauthor, with Nancy Schuman, a vice president at Career Blazers, of *The Temp Worker's Handbook.* American Management Association, 135 W. 50 St., New York 10020.

Why Job Interviewees Are So Poorly Prepared For Their Interviews

Very few people who go on a job interview are prepared because they are *afraid* to confront their weaknesses—and/or to present their strengths.

Rather than spend time taking a hard look at themselves and their careers to identify and address the flaws, they assume their personalities and enthusiasm will be sufficient.

They also assume that an interviewer has carefully read their résumés—so they don't review all of their strengths.

Result: Interviewees are surprised by interviewers' tough questions and are often unable to answer them skillfully.

Strategies for doing well in any job interview...

• Do your homework about the company. Failing to sufficiently research the company, its top executives and its business is perhaps one of the biggest mistakes job candidates make.

While many things that happen at job interviews are out of your control, you can get a clear understanding of what the company does and where it stands in its industry before your interview.

Strategies: Call the company's switchboard for the name of the person who heads the department in which you might be working. Ask your friends or business contacts about his/her reputation.

Read the trade publications that cover the company and the key people there. Find magazines and newsletters that are published weekly for cutting-edge news.

Even if they don't make reference to the key people at the company, they will give you enough information about the business so you can carry on an informed conversation. Such research will help you stand out from others interviewing for the same position.

If the publications are not at your local library, call the publishers and pay to have a half-dozen issues of each publication sent to you by overnight mail. And consider subscribing so you can stay informed.

•Rehearse your interview script. Great trial lawyers avoid asking witnesses questions to which they don't already know the answers. Such preparation keeps these lawyers from being thrown off guard by the answers. Likewise, during an interview, you should not hear a question you have not already anticipated. Of course, it's important that you not answer in a rapid-fire, know-it-all manner.

Strategy: List the obvious questions, such as *Tell me about yourself...why are you leaving your current position...why do you want to work here...what are your long-term ambitions?* Using a tape recorder, practice interviews and play them back. Keep answering the questions until you sound convincing.

•Describe your previous business relationships cautiously and creatively—especially if you had a problem boss. Attribute problems to differences in expectations or structural changes rather than personalities. Above all, don't demean anyone. Your last supervisor, for example, wasn't a *paranoid fault finder who drove you crazy*...he was a *micromanager.*

Solution: If you feel defensive about some episode in your job history, it is especially important to practice your response on tape—until you sound perfectly at ease.

•Think about the job-related questions an interviewer might throw at you. Some will ask questions to see how you perform under pressure—*what if you had to fire your best friend... what if your boss asked you to reveal inside information?* Be honest. Don't get flustered while you explain how you would handle the dilemma.

•Make it clear that you really want the job. Strangely enough, many job candidates fail to say explicitly that they want a position. People I know who do a lot of hiring say they often give the job to the person demonstrating enthusiasm for it.

Strategy: Before the interview, ask yourself if you really want the job. Spend a few minutes going over the reasons why you want it.

Then, at some point during the interview, tell the interviewer, *The job seems like a wonderful opportunity...I know I can contribute a great deal*—or words to that effect.

The key is to strike a balance between being eager and sounding desperate. After the interview, write a thank-you note to the interviewer saying you enjoyed your meeting and indicating that you hope there will be a fit for you at the company.

Important: If you make it to the final stages but don't get the job, write another gracious thank-you note stating again how much you would like to work for the company and then call to suggest the interviewer pass your name along to others in the company looking for an excellent employee. You should also drop a friendly note from time to time, praising an accomplishment or to pass along an important article. You never know where a lead or a job will come from.

Source: Adele Scheele, PhD, career strategist for organizations and individuals, 440 E. 79 St., New York 10021. She is author of several books, including *Skills for Success* (Ballantine, 201 E. 50 St., New York 10022) and, most recently, *Career Strategies for the Working Woman* (Simon & Schuster, 1230 Avenue of the Americas, New York 10020).

8

Getting Ahead On the Job

The Secrets of Career Success

After more than two decades of research on the subject of career success, I have concluded that people on the "fast track"* are made—not born.

As a group, fast-trackers are not any brighter than their slow-track colleagues. They didn't attend better colleges. And, biggest surprise of all, they don't work any harder.

The main difference: Fast-trackers advance within their companies because they know how to tap into critical resources. Slow-trackers often aren't even aware that these resources exist.

Companies don't inform people about critical resources in their orientation materials. In fact, more than 90% of what you need to know to succeed is not published anywhere.

*A career path of highly enriched professional growth opportunities.

If you want to thrive in today's competitive corporate environment, you cannot simply play by the rules and keep your nose clean. Horatio Alger is dead, and he has been replaced by a fast-track breed that has mastered the hidden code for success.

The foundation...

In virtually every case, fast-trackers are launched by bosses who invest in their subordinates' future careers.

This goes beyond training a person to do the present job well. When a boss invests in a worker, the goal is to help the person outgrow the present job and move on to increasingly responsible positions within the company.

Are you on the fast track?...

On average, the bosses studied engaged in these critical actions with 64% of their fast-trackers, but with only 27% of their slow-trackers.

You can be confident you're on the fast track if your boss...

•Provides you with special information that allows you to learn how the company really operates.

•Warns you about changes to be made within the organization.

•Assigns you challenging tasks.

•Advertises your strengths to higher management.

•Prepares you to handle more difficult assignments.

•Helps plan your long-range career.

•Gives you enough authority to complete important assignments.

•Notifies you about any promotion opportunities.

•Warns you in advance—and in confidence—about your career problems.

•Asks for your input in decisions for which only the boss is responsible.

Getting your boss to believe in you...

In deciding which of their subordinates to select for the fast track, bosses seek several qualities above all others:

•Decision-making similarity. Given the same complex problems, the boss and subordinate will make the same decision. They view the company, its markets and its constituents from similar perspectives.

•Dependability. In an emergency, the boss can count on the subordinate to complete an assignment the boss started. The subordinate rises to the occasion in times of crisis.

•Positive collaboration. The boss and subordinate have an effective working relationship. They communicate well and coordinate their efforts efficiently.

Beyond excelling in these critical areas, potential fast-trackers can boost their chances of selection and investment by:

•Learning about their organization beyond their job requirements.

•Telling their boss they want extra work.

•Making their boss look good.

•Giving their boss credit in the presence of other people.

How fast-trackers advance...

Fast-trackers engage in several activities more often than their slow-track colleagues. *To get (or stay) on the fast track:*

•Demonstrate initiative. Show the boss that you're eager to outgrow your job. Identify problem areas and act to correct them.

•Exercise leadership. Help coworkers perform their jobs more efficiently, and provide direction when necessary. Offer to take charge of special projects, such as interdepartmental task forces.

•Take risks. Let your boss know about problems in the work unit. Take stands you think are correct, even if you're bucking the tide. Admit your mistakes—and show what you've learned from them.

•Add value to your work. Go beyond your job description. Write unsolicited reports that can help your boss make improvements in your unit.

•Persist on a project. If an assignment appears to be going nowhere, try to view it in a new way.

•Seek opportunities for self-improvement. Request special training, or take on assignments that require the use of new skills. Ask your managers to define your strengths and weaknesses so that you can improve.

•Build *competence networks.* Find out who is responsible for getting things done in the organization. Then initiate relationships with these people by offering favors or providing information. *Result:* You'll compile credits with these people that can translate into critical resources down the road.

•Influence others. When coworkers come to you for help or advice, deal carefully with each person's problems.

•Resolve ambiguity. When a boss makes an ambiguous request, gather as much information as possible from other sources. Make educated assumptions (when necessary), and approach the boss for *brief* feedback regularly throughout the assignment.

•Seek wider exposure. Learn more about the company by associating with managers outside your department.

•Build up—and build on—existing skills. Keep up with technical advances in your field.

•Develop a close working relationship with the boss. This cannot be overemphasized. Volunteer favors and information. Take an interest in the boss's family and career. *To avoid being obvious or causing resentment:* Show an interest in your coworkers as well.

•Help the boss. When you help make your boss look good, the boss will be more likely to take you along as he/she advances through the organization.

Source: George B. Graen, director of the Center for International Competitiveness Studies at the University of Cincinnati. He is the author of *Unwritten Rules for Your Career,* John Wiley, Dept. 0-1006, Box 6793, Somerset, New Jersey 08875.

Behaving Like a Top Professional

You can reap a great deal of self-esteem and a wide variety of other rewards by learning how to behave like a real professional.

Essentials:

•Sense of responsibility for clients (or customers). People who are cynical about their work, who despise the people they have to deal with, demoralize themselves and generally perform badly in the long run.

•Avoid rules of thumb, quick answers and rigid thinking. Be on the lookout for exceptions—incidents where theories don't seem to fit the facts. This is an opportunity to perform creatively.

•Stay current. Take additional training and/or coursework. Force yourself to work on tough problems, do heavy business-related reading.

•Be thoughtful about trade-offs in making difficult decisions that often involve several contradictory factors.

•Approach complex problems with a general strategy plus the readiness to change as the situation unfolds or new factors develop.

•Think more about task accomplishment than about hours spent accomplishing it. Professionals aren't clock watchers. They're driven by goals that they've set for themselves. And because these are, in large part, their own goals, they're motivated to attain them.

•Be responsible for developing subordinates. You'll end up with better people, increase loyalty and motivation, and experience the pride of seeing someone you've trained advance from neophyte to polished performer.

•Understand that excellence isn't an end state. It's a process of continuously striving to meet more challenging goals, learn new things and become more adept at solving difficult problems. Suppress the temptation to take destructive shortcuts or gain selfish advantage.

Source: Dr. Leonard Sayles, Center for Creative Leadership, Greensboro, NC.

Who Gets Promoted First?

The four most important factors in determining how fast you are promoted:

•How top management feels about the person who recommended your promotion.

•Your exposure and visibility to those in higher management.

•Your background, education, work experience.

•How well you perform in your present job.

Why Managers Fail... And Succeed

People who fail in business usually have no trouble finding external reasons for their failure—economic conditions, discrimination, politics, uncooperative employees.

Although these play a part, internal factors are frequently as important.

In my psychiatric practice, I have observed that powerful unconscious issues affect work just as they do other areas of life. Our interactions are guided by a whole spectrum of beliefs and behavior styles developed over many years.

What we learned growing up influences the way we react to challenges in adulthood. Understanding and grappling with these issues can make a significant difference in job performance.

Personality style is one of the major internal factors in managerial performance. *Three lead-*

ership styles are responsible for the most serious managerial problems...

The narcissistic leader...

Characteristics: Narcissists are drawn to leadership positions by a deep need for power and prestige. They are often highly talented, hard-working and charismatic. But feelings of inferiority lead to self-aggrandizement and the need for constant, unconditional affirmation and positive feedback from others. Narcissists also tend to have a low tolerance for frustration.

Consequences: The narcissist inspires people to action, but can't always follow through. By surrounding himself/herself with yes-men —people who idealize him and reflect back exactly what he wants to hear—he is unlikely to anticipate and prepare for potential trouble spots as his ideas are executed. The narcissist's need to be in the spotlight makes it hard for him to build an effective team. He may resent and even sabotage employees whose creativity threatens to overshadow his own.

Most dangerous, the narcissist fails to encourage balance and diversity of opinion. The result can be disastrous, both to him and the company, as he inspires others to pour resources into implementing his brilliant—but unworkable—ideas.

Issues: The narcissist is likely to have grown up in an environment where nothing he did was ever quite good enough. He never developed a strong sense of self-esteem. To mask this sense of inferiority, he learned to rely on self-aggrandizement and seeks out only those people who will reassure him that he's wonderful.

The narcissist needs to develop a more complete sense of self—one that is not dependent on others' perceptions or on always being the best. He needs to recognize the value of clear, attainable goals that are reached step by gradual step. *Skills to develop...*

- Share credit. Use the words *we* and *us* rather than *I* and *me.*
- Be generous in giving praise instead of always expecting to receive it.
- Rather than relying on coworkers for affirmation, explore ways to meet that need outside work. Put time into developing family relationships and satisfying hobbies.

The authoritarian leader...

Characteristics: The authoritarian personality has an obsession with order, with being right and in control. This type of manager is poorly attuned to the emotional needs of employees. He relies on a competitive, rather than affiliative, model of work relationships.

Consequences: Though corporations and departments do need an authority figure in order to function efficiently, the authoritarian's excessive need for control can lead to numbing bureaucracy and a rule-bound, by-the-book decision-making style.

Autonomy and creativity are stifled—which can spell disaster when a crisis arises that requires quick, effective decisions.

The authoritarian manager is unlikely to build loyalty or team spirit among staff. He may appear petty and defensive...employees respond with feelings of dislike and by doing the bare minimum required of them.

Issues: Authoritarians learn this style by growing up in families where control and rules are valued...and emotions are ignored or denied. The authoritarian leader must work to become more aware of how he feels, not just what he does...and recognize that intellect and emotion can work together. Skills to develop...

- Learn to listen carefully, without interrupting or becoming defensive.
- Practice seeing things from a subordinate's point of view. You may come across more harshly than you mean to.
- Welcome criticism instead of rejecting or punishing it. Invite feedback from others.
- Share credit for positive results.

The emotionally isolated leader...

Characteristics: The emotionally isolated manager is so uncomfortable with social interaction that he becomes almost invisible—business is carried out via subordinates, other managers or committees.

This type of leader is so afraid of making a mistake that he'll avoid taking action or making a commitment—which could turn out to be the greatest mistake of all.

Consequences: Subordinates may form small groups or pairings, seeking the direction and support that is lacking from above. Since each group is likely to have its own agenda, the organization may become fragmented. This is not an environment that fosters lively, productive collaboration and interchange.

In some cases, a more socially skilled peer or subordinate will act as a kind of buffer between the manager and the rest of the organization, helping to create a responsive climate for employees. Having a gifted coworker interpret and carry out the leader's ideas may be enough. But the leader risks being left behind as the department or company grows beyond him.

Issues: Emotionally isolated leaders lack confidence in their ability to lead or even communicate with others. They are uncomfortable with the concept and enactment of power. Some dislike people and prefer the world of ideas... others are simply shy.

Many of them have been high intellectual achievers all their lives—but received little modeling or encouragement from their parents in getting along with peers. Skills to develop...

- Read about and take courses in assertiveness training to become more comfortable with collaboration, leadership and basic social skills.
- Learn to see mistakes as a way of finding out what is and isn't effective. Errors can be corrected.
- Fight inaction by recognizing that there's always more information to be gathered—but that's no reason to postpone action indefinitely. *Helpful:* Set deadlines. Resolve to stop research and to make decisions based on data gathered by that date.

Source: David W. Krueger, MD, clinical professor of psychiatry at Baylor College of Medicine and author of *Emotional Business: The Meaning and Mastery of Work, Money, and Success,* Avant Books, Slawson Communications, Inc., 165 Vallecitos de Oro, San Marcos, California 92069.

How to Turn Your Ideas Into Successful Realities

Generating significant ideas and nurturing them to reality requires stretching the mind and following six essential steps that I call the STRIKE process...

Before taking the first step toward mind expansion, loosen up your thinking power by breaking old routines and trying something new.

Change helps unleash creativity by stimulating the right side of your brain—the side that controls intuition and imagination. *Possibilities:*

- Rearrange your day's routine. Start with a bath instead of a shower. Watch a different TV program.
- Eat food you've never tasted before. Then describe the flavor in 10 words. It's harder to do than you might think.
- Try writing with your other hand for a while.
- Take movies with a camcorder as you crawl through your house on your stomach. This snake's eye view will show you a home you've never seen before.

Once the brain's right side is loose and agile, you're ready to start the STRIKE process.

"S" is for stew...

Start by thinking almost aimlessly about things you'd like to do...improvements you'd like to make...problems to solve...goals to achieve, etc.

Whether it takes two hours or two months, don't be concerned about how long you stew over the possibilities. Give your mind time to explore each area.

Helpful: Write down the main subjects and tape that list to your bathroom mirror. Seeing them next to each other helps you to evaluate them.

You'll know that the stewing phase is over when one objective begins to dominate and you're eager to go on the next step in the process.

"T" is for target...

As soon as a single objective emerges, write it down in no more than 10 words. Make sure that the statement clearly embodies the idea you want to pursue.

Example: You may have started the stewing phase with a dozen or more thoughts on how to advance your career and lifestyle. Next you may have pared these down to the desirability of a transfer to the West Coast. From that, your *target* emerges—*I want to transfer to Portland.*

You can be virtually certain that you have the right target when seeing it written down begins to generate stirrings of excitement.

"R" is for research...

You can't afford to skimp on research. Go to libraries, computer databases and public sources of information. If the goal is moving to Portland, investigate home prices, school quality, tax rates, opportunities for hobbies and other outside activities, etc.

Most overlooked source of information: People. Talk to friends with areas of expertise that you lack. Use your network to find other knowledgeable people. If Portland is the goal, don't just try to find *any* people who have lived there, but people who have moved there from *your* city.

If you have a mentor or an especially wise confidante, this is the time to ask for his/her advice. This friend might be able to see a flaw in your reasoning that you have overlooked.

There's no absolute rule for knowing how much research to do, but when a file folder is one inch thick, you've usually done enough... and are ready to go to the next step.

"I" is for ideas...

The object here is to generate ideas that will let you achieve your target goal. Start by keeping the target in mind while you conjure up words and pictures that show you how to get from where you are to where you want to be. Jot down ideas as they come to mind. Try to visualize them on paper as they unfold.

This is the point at which you'll see a big payoff from the exercises you did to loosen your mind.

"K" is for key idea...

From the ideas that you generate, pick the one you consider to be the best and the most practical. If you have new doubts, go back and do more research or consult again with your confidante. *Five essential questions...*

1. Is the idea simple?
2. Will it truly get me to my target?
3. Is it practical?
4. Can I visualize myself making the idea happen?
5. Am I passionate about it?

If you can't answer with an emphatic yes to each question, go back and mull the ideas over further.

Never choose more than one idea to act on. *Reason:* A good idea requires all your energy. Choosing more than one spreads your energy too thin.

"E" is for execute...

Now act on your idea. From your research and visualization, you'll know exactly what to do. But since it's impossible to envision every obstacle, you may indeed run into stumbling blocks. When that happens, go back and create ideas that can get around the obstacle.

Example: Mickey Schulhof, vice chairman of Sony USA in the 1970s, helped develop the idea of compact discs. But his idea initially ran into a stumbling block when he couldn't sell it to industry executives who were more interested in protecting their investment in LP (long-playing) record technology than in sound quality.

Schulhof went back to the idea phase and realized that there was another route—selling recording stars on the technology. Once top musicians became enthusiastic about CD sound, the industry took another look at the idea. The payoff for Sony and Schulhof was immense and historic.

Source: John Emmerling, chairman of the advertising agency John Emmerling Inc., 135 E. 55 St., New York 10022. He is the author of *It Only Takes One: How to Create the Right Idea and Then Make It Happen,* Simon & Schuster, 1230 Ave. of the Americas, New York 10020.

Personal File Power

All companies keep a file on each employee. It contains the employee's résumé, application form, memos for doing things above and beyond the call of duty—and memos on what the employee may have done wrong.

You should keep a personal personnel file to keep a record of your achievements—little ones and big ones—along with a copy of your latest résumé. Every time you accomplish something worthwhile, scribble a note on a piece of paper, date it, and insert it into your file. *Why this is valuable:*

•If you want to ask your boss for a raise or promotion: The best way to get the raise you want is to remind your supervisor of your achievements. If you don't write them down, you'll forget them. And if you forget, you can be sure your boss will, too.

•If you need to work up an effective résumé in a hurry: Take your old résumé and plug in your current data and significant achievements.

Source: Robert Half is the founder of Robert Half International Inc., and Accountemps Worldwide, 2884 Sand Hill Rd., Menlo Park, California 94250.

How to Read Body Language

Reading other people depends very much on developing your ability to decipher non-verbal messages. In every exchange between people, messages are sent, through words and through the underlying dynamics of the non-verbal information—what you could call *subtext*...

Subtext can reinforce and strengthen the spoken text, or it may contradict the text, canceling out any verbal promises or agreements. It is a mixture of many different elements, including...

•Each person's body language—posture, hand movements, eye contact, etc.

•How a person handles space.

•How a person uses touch.

•Tone of voice.

•How a person dresses and his/her overall appearance.

•What a person does outside a conversation that confirms or contradicts what is said during the conversation.

Identifying honesty...

What is there in the subtext of a person that tells you he's not being honest about who he really is? Or...what he really thinks? Or...what he feels? There can be any number of elements.

Most important:

•Facial expression. Maybe he smiles at inappropriate times. A real, genuinely felt emotion causes a quick smile. If someone wants to fake an emotion, he'll hold the expression too long.

A genuine smile goes up into the eyes, and involves the top of the face.

A false smile just involves the bottom of the face and is usually not as wide as a real smile.

•Physiological responses. There is no one gesture that gives away a lie. But there are a lot of little physiological responses that go with a lie—certain gestures that are used consistently by many people.

Example: When a politician is about to tell a whopper, he'll usually rub the side of his nose with his finger. In the presidential debate between Carter and Reagan, both men did this at various points—Reagan, when he said he'd accomplish all his proposals without raising taxes! We don't know why this gesture is so consistent, but it is.

It's easiest to detect these bits of non-verbal information if you know the person well and you can identify abnormal or atypical behavior. Or, if you can observe his interactions with other people and compare them to his interactions with you.

•Look for discrepancies. *Examples:* Again, a smile that appears only on the lips, not on the rest of the face...smooth words backed by nervous mannerisms.

•Know your situation. If a business deal is a bad one, you're not going to find the flaws in the way the associate is behaving. You have to examine the deal itself. Abnormal behavior is really just a tip-off that you need to look at the situation more closely. You're not going to know that this person is putting over a phony deal unless you know what a good deal is and understand the whole situation.

In the same way, you're not going to become powerful by wearing power clothes. If you're a lawyer, you're not going to become competent by wearing an expensive gray suit.

You become competent by knowing your job. Then the gray suit may help a little.

Intuition...

One term we use for this ability to read cues is *intuition*—but it's not really that magical—it's a computer in our brains adding up all the little things that are wrong in a situation, judging the subtext of the whole.

I don't believe in mysticism. And I don't believe that intuition is a leap into uncharted realms, through some telepathic power. It is the summing up of all the little things that you know about a situation, and drawing a conclusion.

Example: If your intuition tells you that you shouldn't trust your company's management team and their promises for the future, then start job hunting immediately. Chances are you're picking up lots of tiny signals that your conscious mind doesn't even see, but your inner "computer"—the brain—does.

In general, women in our society are much more intuitive than men. *Reason:* Women are raised to be more nurturing than men. As a result, they take more time to learn about other people and to really understand what motivates them.

But anyone can cultivate their intuition. *First step:* Look for the subtexts in your interactions with other people—acquaintances and strangers. When you have a funny feeling about an individual or a situation, pay attention to it. Try and figure out exactly what bothers you and why. Often you can make an intuitive leap from there.

To improve your subtext...

It is possible to learn to cultivate your appearance and manage the impression you give to other people. This is why, for example, business people and politicians hire image consultants. Or why Donald Trump works so hard for publicity. If he didn't have that aura, I don't think that the banks would have given him the leeway to get himself into such financial trouble.

But while appearance is important, giving excessive importance to appearance doesn't make sense. There are people who aren't handsome who are really wonderful, lovely people. And a fancy exterior can't make up for an inner lack of ability or talent.

Although your appearance and subtext can help you communicate who you really are to others, the best message you can send in the world is that you're someone who knows what he's talking about. Understand your talents... and learn to use them at their highest levels. The self-confidence it gives you will be the best addition to your subtext that you can possibly make.

Source: Julius Fast, author of more than 30 books on the subjects of business and psychological communication. He is most famous for his best-selling book *Body Language*. His latest book is *Subtext: Making Body Language Work in the Workplace,* Viking Penguin, 365 Hudson St., New York 10014.

Modesty Traps

Being overly modest is as bad as unabashed bragging. In either case, the people who should be aware of your accomplishments either won't learn about them (if you're too modest) or won't believe you (if you brag). *Best:* Share your accomplishments matter-of-factly, in casual conversation. For example, tell how a customer was satisfied, a crisis averted, or a problem solved. And when someone compliments you, express your appreciation.

Source: Ted Pollack, management consultant, Old Tappan, New Jersey, writing in *Production,* 6600 Clough Pike, Cincinnati 45224.

What Leaders Do Best

Leaders make the people who follow them feel secure and give them a sense of harmony.

A leader should be able to:

- Handle social occasions well.
- Use stress constructively.
- Be smooth and unruffled in tense situations.
- Rally a group to a common goal.
- Feel comfortable when faced with diverse points of view.
- Make decisions that support independent behavior by members of the group within organizational limits.

•Learn more about individuals in the group to better match their tasks to their goals and abilities.

•Review recent decisions objectively. If too many were risk-free, it could be a danger sign that the leader is failing to lead.

Power Lunching

Power lunching tactics can turn a restaurant meal into an occasion to impress your lunch partner.

Power lunching aims to impress without letting the luncheon become a tasteless display of ego and one-upmanship.

Here are some tips:

•Patronize restaurants that have a reputation for business lunches and where you're known. Select restaurants with excellent service and plenty of space between tables. Eat in restaurants that important people frequent.

•Avoid luncheon invitations to other people's private dining rooms. You lose power on their turf.

•Call the maitre d' personally to make reservations. Tell him where you want to sit and how long you expect to stay. The more details you give the maitre d', the more his staff will be in tune with your needs.

•Don't order drinks served with a paper umbrella or a lot of vegetables or fruit. Draft beer is appropriate, but bottles look tacky. The "fancy waters" are wimpy now...club soda is a power drink.

•Order food that's easy to handle. *Example:* Steak instead of lobster so that you can do a lot of talking without fumbling. *Power foods:* Black bean soup, fresh oysters and clams, brook trout, calves' liver, London broil, paella, venison and gumbo. *Wimp foods:* French onion soup, fried oysters and clams, corned beef, coquilles St. Jacques, chicken a la King, lasagna, shrimp de jonghe.

•Pay the bill with cash, if possible. Next best is a house charge. You don't have to wait for a credit card to be processed. You can quickly sign the check and leave before your guest becomes anxious to get back to the office.

•Tip 20%.

Source: *Power Lunching* by E. Melvin Pinsel and Ligita Dienhart, Turnbull & Willoughby, Chicago.

If a Rival Beats You to A Promotion By a Hair

Assuming that you and your rival are very much alike in experience, education and service with the firm, you need to find out why you lost. The reasons can affect your future with the company. *Areas to explore:*

•Your rival appeared more committed to the company. Management judged you ready to bolt for a better opportunity.

•Your rival had a sponsor higher up in the company of whom you were unaware.

•Your boss personally prefers your rival's company.

•Your boss saw your rival as less of a threat to his job.

•You are being saved for something bigger down the road, but no one thought to tell you.

•You failed at an assignment that you thought was insignificant, but your boss judged you likely to fail again.

•You have been too active politically within the company outside your department.

•You are perceived as untrustworthy by some, or they question your loyalty to your boss.

Source: Marilyn Moats Kennedy, author of *Career Knockouts: How to Battle Back*, Follett Publishing Co.

Career Booster

Volunteer to serve at a charity fund-raiser. It's the quickest way to get to know the movers and shakers in your community.

Source: *The Sir Winston Method: The Five Secrets of Speaking the Language of Leadership* by communications consultant James C. Humes, William Morrow & Co., 1350 Avenue of the Americas, New York 10019.

Better Memo Writing

Good memos use lots of white space to make points more effectively. Instead of using long sentences, indent individual items. Place bullet symbols in front of each one. Do not use numbers, which indicate priority, unless you *intend* to prioritize.

Also useful: Subheads for dealing with multiple topics. And insert dashes within an item to highlight it. Avoid parentheses—they break up the flow.

Source: *The Perfect Memo! Write Your Way to Career Success* by Patricia H. Westheimer, corporate writing trainer, La Jolla, California. Park Avenue Publications, 720 N. Park Ave.,Indianapolis 46202.

Delegation Secrets

The first step in delegating is figuring out what you should give away. *Helpful:* Delegate tasks that do not require your expertise or judgment. When in doubt, ask yourself whether an activity will get you closer to your goal...if someone else could do it just as well...if your boss would mind if you give it to someone else ...if anything really bad could happen if that person could not handle the work. Always package the delegated task so it looks like an opportunity. *Important:* Delegating work does not mean abandoning responsibility. You still should supervise work you have delegated to be sure it is done properly.

Source: *Why Good Girls Don't Get Ahead...But Gutsy Girls Do* by Kate White, editor-in-chief, *Redbook*. Warner Books, 1271 Avenue of the Americas, New York 10020.

9

Developing Good Work Habits

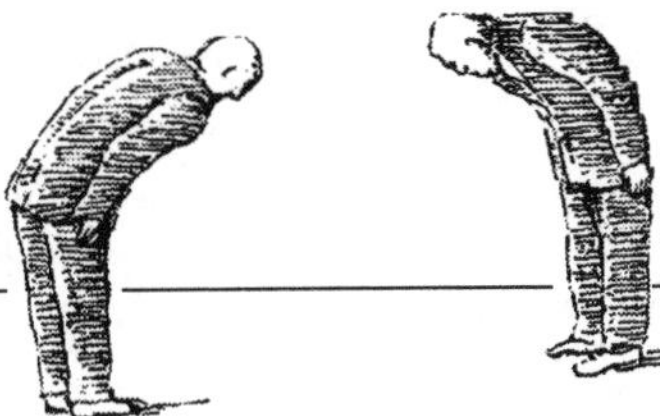

Meeting Mistake

Don't feel obligated to say something in a meeting because silence will be interpreted as ignorance. *Better:* Choose statements very carefully at the first few meetings. If what you say is well thought out and insightful, you will carry far more weight at future meetings. *Caution:* Do not use meetings to say uncomplimentary things about subordinates. This can undermine the department—and you, as its manager.

Source: *The First-Time Manager* by Loren Belker, a management trainer based in Escondido, California. Amacom, 135 W. 50 St., New York 10020.

Work and Self-Esteem

The "who/where/what we do" connection has created difficult problems for a growing number of people today who feel trapped in unsatisfying jobs. These people are afraid they won't be able to find another one...or they can't afford to lose seniority and pension rights...or they can't face the difficulty of relocating their families.

Problem: If you feel unappreciated or taken for granted or inadequately rewarded at work, it has an adverse effect on your work, your relationships with your boss and colleagues... and your own psychological and emotional well-being.

The unresolved anger that you feel in your job may spill over into your private life, with family and friends its innocent victims as you scream at the kids, kick the dog, knock down two fast martinis, etc.

Getting back on track...

Doing nothing only adds to feelings of anger, frustration and exploitation, and victimization will probably continue.

Helpful: Realize that because you have control over yourself, you have control over the situation. Then figure out what you can do to improve the situation. *Questions to ask...*

• *Am I appreciated?* The very fact that you have a job is an important sign that you are valued by your employer. If you're being paid more than people doing similar work elsewhere, that's another good sign.

• *Should I be appreciated?* If your work is marginal or if your achievement level is lower than colleagues in your unit, then it's not realistic to expect compliments and reassurances about the quality of your work.

Try to appraise your real contributions to your employer...and look for ways to bring those to management's attention.

In addition to self-appraisal, it's imperative to get frequent feedback from your boss. If your company doesn't have formal evaluations, request a meeting to discuss your job effectiveness. Work review sessions—in one form or another—should happen much more than once or twice a year, for they give you a good sense of whether you're on the right track.

Try to communicate with your boss about signs of appreciation. If he/she seems to be piling work on you or always giving you the tough tasks, you might interpret it as punishment, while your boss meant to show confidence in your ability. *It helps to talk these things out.*

Also ask colleagues what they think of your work. Assure them that you're not fishing for a compliment, but that you really need an objective appraisal.

You may find that you are far more respected than you realize—perhaps for talents or skills you didn't know you had. Team support is a two-way street. Remember to thank and congratulate coworkers when they have done something well, too.

Customers can also be a valuable source of recognition and job satisfaction. When they thank you for your promptness or effectiveness or thoughtfulness, accept the compliments graciously and tell them how much you appreciate the kind words.

But if someone *withholds* praise that you believe you deserve, do not let it cause you to lose confidence in yourself. There's nothing wrong with giving yourself a pat on the back —or a special reward.

Boredom—the bane of self-esteem...

We read frequently about the financial costs of smoking or substance abuse in the workplace, but we rarely hear about the costs of boredom.

Some of boredom's many manifestations: Indifference, anger, disillusionment, procrastination, gossiping, tardiness, absenteeism, and physical aches and pains—like headaches.

Bored individuals are not stimulated to go to work, to get there on time, to do the job promptly or well, or to remain loyal to the company. People who are bored because they feel their skills or talents aren't being adequately used often become resentful toward their employers.

Boredom is also a classic cause of stress. It is stressful to spend an eight-hour day in an unstimulating environment. It is stressful not to have the opportunity to work on challenging problems.

And, it is stressful to realize that you are not growing or developing or reaching the goals you set for yourself. We become spiritless, listless zombies whose minds are on hold.

Solutions to job boredom...

First admit that job boredom does exist and then take personal responsibility for overcoming your boredom.

Some suggestions:

• Create a log. Chart the activities that you find stimulating and those that are deadly dull. Include contextual information that might help identify whether you're truly bored or simply tired or depressed.

• Analyze your activities and look for patterns. After several weeks of keeping a log, analyze the data to see what patterns emerge. If meetings bore you but you feel stimulated while preparing for and delivering a sales presentation, it may be that you need to perform, to persuade, to be creative. Ask yourself how you can do more of this in your job.

• Reenergize your job. Balance routine, repetitive tasks with work that you find more stimulating. Wherever possible, shuffle the order, break boring patterns, and change locations. If you have a morning full of mind-deadening tasks, reward yourself by going out to lunch instead of brown-bagging it. Question whether all routine tasks are really necessary. Take occasional work breaks. Try to rotate jobs or swap responsibilities with a colleague to vary the monotony.

• Stretch—reach beyond your grasp. If you have mastered your job so that it no longer uses your full talents and abilities, ask for a new assignment or see if your job description could be broadened. *Alternative:* Transfer to a different job in another department.

• Welcome positive problems at work. Confronting and solving problems adds spice to a job. Finding solutions keeps us emotionally and intellectually alive.

• Shake it up—avoid complacency. If you've become too comfortable in your job, take a new look at it. Look for ways to improve cooperation. Set additional goals. *Bonus:* The fresh excitement new accomplishments generate.

• Do something new. Read new, relevant books. Attend a seminar, a workshop, a professional meeting, or an educational course. Create or design a new product, a new production process, a new marketing strategy, or a new information system and then try to "sell" it to management. Study Continuous Quality Improvement (CQI) to stimulate yourself by planning to do all that you do better—each time you do it.

• Develop a life outside of your job. Thoughts of how you will spend your free time away from the job can provide a mental escape from work that is boring. Pleasurable activities in private life can also provide the excitement and fulfillment that may be missing in your career—and maybe even add to it.

Coaching, reading, working on a political campaign, listening to music, volunteer work, sports and hobbies give balance and verve to your life and put you in control of your emotional well-being. Spend time with people who are energetic and enthusiastic, vital and vibrant ...and thoughtful about their life and work. *Learn from them.*

If it's impossible to eliminate boredom and reenergize your enthusiasm for the job, face the fact that it's time to move on. You've grown and changed and are now ready for new challenges...new beginnings...new dreams.

Source: John Sena, PhD, professor of English, and Stephen Strasser, PhD, associate professor, division of hospital and health services administration, both at Ohio State University. They are authors of *Work is Not a Four Letter Word*, Business One Irwin, 1818 Ridge Rd., Homewood, Illinois 60430.

How to Overcome Teamwork Blues

Teams and teamwork have become terms of worship in American business. Amazingly, though, neither works very well in most US companies. In fact, only 17% of managers and team members surveyed by Wilson Learning in 1992 said that teamwork was working well for their companies. The rest of the respondents said teamwork was mostly talk and little substance.

Probing further, Wilson Learning discovered what the companies that have succeeded in team-building have in common...

• They evaluate individuals on their effectiveness as team members. The vast majority of company performance appraisal systems still concentrate entirely on individual accomplishments—with no measures of team performance.

• They compensate managers and team members for their performance as members of teams—and for meeting defined goals.

• They reduce barriers to the free flow of important business information across functional lines in the company. Getting people to give up their urge to withhold information to bolster their status within the firm is a key factor in getting teams to function efficiently.

• They give teams clear goals and ensure that team members understand and are focused on those goals. *Too typical:* Management responds to pressure from consultants or managers who read about teams or go to seminars explaining how teams work by asserting how important it is for the company to adopt teamwork. But they fail to realize that teams are not an end in themselves. The most important factor in generating a team's effectiveness is the clarity of its objective and focus.

Mechanics of effective collaboration...

Once the company has clarified a team's goals, the team's effectiveness in meeting those goals depends on how well members work together.

Trap: Managers often stall team performance by getting too involved in working out team processes and techniques of team leadership. Instead, right from the start, management should focus on coaching team members to...

• Support themselves as individuals. This means encouraging them to advocate their own ideas and training them in ways to persuade others of their points of view. Too often, emphasis on not making waves and cooperating inhibits this essential training.

• Support others in the team. Valuing other people's styles for solving problems is essential to working well on a team. *Managing* conflict does not mean *reducing* conflict. On a team, efficiency often requires creating tension while at the same time effectively resolving conflict. Politeness alone won't suffice. Team members must learn how to air differences, tell hard truths, and ask hard questions of one another. When a team is not facing the core issues that prevent it from reaching its goal, its work will not move forward and creative solutions will not unfold.

• Support the team. Keep the goal in focus. Commit team members' energy to getting the team to work. Discourage those who try to undermine the team—or who simply refuse to "buy in" to the team spirit.

Bottom line...

Teams represent a valuable way for organizations to structure work processes. However, the key to success is getting people to work together toward common goals. Creating this collaborative environment is the challenge businesses face.

Source: Michael Leimbach, PhD, research director, Wilson Learning Corporation, developer and implementer of business training in management, quality, customer service and sales for companies around the world, 7500 Flying Cloud Dr., Eden Prairie, Minnesota 55344.

How to Increase Your Productivity

At an almost breathtaking pace, medical science is discovering new insights into human biology.

Used the right way, much of this new knowledge can help managers heighten workers' job satisfaction and increase their own productivity. *Major discoveries...*

Light and color secrets...

Researchers have found that light has a profound effect on our bodies. Though not completely understood, the reason is probably linked to the effect light has on two vital areas of the brain—the hypothalamus and the pineal gland.

Our moods, even those of color-blind people, are affected by the intensity and color of the light around us.

Examples: People brainstorm better when surrounded by bright colors. Subdued shades are usually best for negotiating. Red cars command higher prices.

Helpful: Use a consultant to help you decorate your office...and choose your wardrobe. The right color and lighting can raise output and make work more enjoyable. Wearing the right colors can also boost a sales rep's closing rate.

Where to find an expert: Most large management consulting firms can make recommendations. For color, try the Pantone Color Institute, 201-935-5501.

Also, bring more natural light into the workplace. Tests show that it has a positive impact on performance. There are lights available now that simulate natural light. For advice, consult a lighting engineer.

Sound secrets...

Women are far more sensitive to sound than men. They can also hear higher-pitch sounds. Some research suggests that women may even be subliminally sensitive to sounds beyond the conscious hearing range.

Example: Some scientists believe high-frequency tones given off by computer terminals can cause stress in women who use them. Harm may occur even though users aren't actually aware of the sound.

If your company has complaints from VDT users, consider hiring an acoustical engineer. The problem may be with the sound, not the light source.

Other research has discovered how we screen background noise from conversation that we want to hear.

Helpful: If you want someone's attention, don't talk more loudly, just move closer. Halving the distance quadruples the sound.

Smell secrets...

This may be the most exciting area of research. Science has discovered that odors have a profound effect on our moods and performance.

Examples: Exposure to apple-cinnamon may improve editing skills...fruit scents may induce women to make certain purchases...clove has a calming effect...and peppermint elevates mood and may relieve headaches.

Try scenting your office with various fragrances to find the ones that have the effect you want.

Helpful: Contact the Fragrance Foundation (212-725-2755). This organization tracks the latest research in the field and can put companies in touch with consultants.

Biorhythm secrets...

Each individual has a natural rhythm to his/her activities, but in a typical business environment we're all expected to arrive, work and eat at more or less the same times.

Helpful: Give yourself (and employees) more schedule flexibility. Experiment with having several snacks instead of one long meal. Take a midday nap if it helps rejuvenate you in the afternoon.

As far as possible within the demands of the business world, tell employees you're more interested in results than in when they're achieved.

Biorhythms are also affected by sunlight. If you must start work before sunup, take an outdoor break as early in the day as possible. It can boost your mood and productivity.

Keep a chart of your own cycles of high and low energy levels. Try to schedule meetings and other tasks accordingly.

Gender secrets...

The latest tests confirm again that women are biologically equipped to process a wider range of sensory information than men.

Women are less obsessed with beating out rivals and getting super-rich than men are. They want to succeed for the sake of personal emotional fulfillment.

Men are more prone to tunnel vision—aiming at destroying their enemies quickly. Women, by contrast, see the broader picture and strategize better for long-term success.

Despite these differences between the sexes, managers don't have to plan one set of tasks for women and another for men. Instead, be attuned to using the assets of each to the best advantage.

Example: When assembling a project team, try to include a balance of men and women. If you don't, chances are greater that the team will overlook an important strategy, side-effect, market, or other opportunity.

Age secrets...

As people grow older, their gender-hormone levels decline. In women, declining estrogen during menopause can bring on irritability and forgetfulness. In men, declining testosterone levels can cause low energy levels and loss of concentration.

If you manage people who show these symptoms, help them find support. And do the same for yourself if you're nearing 50.

Helpful: To increase productivity and job satisfaction among older workers, offer to redesign offices for them—provide softer colors, comfortably built chairs, equipment with large enough displays to be seen by someone with less than great vision.

Brain secrets...

Science is rapidly discovering that while the brain has many similarities to a computer—which stores and processes information—the brain also *interprets* information.

Not appreciating this difference has led many companies to rely too heavily on computers.

The brain works in a way that usually makes it easier to remember what we read in a book than what we see on computer screens.

Example: You probably have a good idea of where in this issue of *Facts of Life* the chapter entitled "Very Personal" appears. But you would have much less of an idea if you had scrolled through the chapters on a computer.

Recommended: Ask for advice from a neuropsychologist or neurobiologist at a local university whenever the company is developing or revising training programs. Their expertise about how people learn can be valuable in making training techniques much more effective.

Source: Edith Weiner, president, Weiner, Edrich, Brown, Inc., futurists and strategic planning consultants, 200 E. 33 St., New York 10016. She is also coauthor of the very useful and insightful new book, *Office Biology,* MasterMedia Ltd., 17 E. 89 St., New York 10128.

Business/Career Resolutions... Just in Time

Today, knowing the right way to behave in business is more than polite. It's a vital strategy for keeping clients and customers and for getting ahead.

Based on interviews with top executives, as well as an analysis of 108 surveys by human-resource professionals, here are 12 fundamental business protocol rules you should follow...

1. Cultivate new business...and maintain contact with old clients/customers...and fulfill current work assignments. Keep up with your customers throughout the year—and remember them during the holidays. Interest in others goes a long way to promote business success.

•Stanley Heilbronn, first vice president at Merrill Lynch, makes it his business to keep in touch with his clients: "If there's an article in a magazine or newspaper that I think would be of interest to them, I scribble a note right on the top—and keep the information flow to clients constant."

2. Be courteous, positive, and upbeat regardless of how you or your company is doing. Especially in these challenging economic times, customers and associates want to be around those who work even harder because times are tough. They avoid pessimists and complainers. For similar reasons, if things are going well, be humble—don't brag.

3. Accept criticism graciously. Give it carefully, preceding and following it with something positive.

•J. Douglas Phillips, senior director of corporate planning at Merck & Co.: "Look for the positive within the negative situation."

4. Sexist/racist/ethnic slurs/jokes and actions are unacceptable.

5. Say "thank you." Drop a note or send flowers, fruit, or another appropriate gift to someone who sends business your way.

•Nella Barkley, president of Crystal-Barkley Corporation, a career-consulting firm: "Make thank-you's timely and very appropriate to the occasion and the person—never pro forma. A warm, personal note or follow-up phone call with news about what happened as a result of a referral will mean much more to the recipient than a standard gift ordered by your secretary."

6. Be discreet about company business or secrets—and the intimate details of your personal life.

•Mitchell P. Davis, editor at Broadcast Interview Source, an information publisher: "People don't want to hear about your problems. They want to hear about opportunities. That's why they're in business."

7. Cultivate friendships at work and with customers. It helps to create a very pleasant workplace. It also enhances productivity, since work friends provide emotional support and comradery and network with each other. But exercise discretion in work-based friendships.

•Marsha Londe, director of corporate accounts, Shadco Advertising Specialities: "You don't have to spill your guts to make a friend."

8. Dress appropriately. Even at companies with new "dress down" codes of more casual dress, it's still important to dress to impress.

•Irene Cohen, chairman, Corporate Staffing Alternatives, Inc., a human-resource management company: "If you're in a business where letting down your guard in terms of dress code for even one day, for one hour, could make a difference with a customer, client, or applicant, don't do it. Business is too important in this economy to take this kind of risk."

9. Use proper written and spoken language. Scrutinize your memos, proposals, reports, and letters. Are you proud of the way your correspondence and written communications look and read? Are your letters too long? Show concern for others, who are also very busy, and keep written communications as brief and clear as possible. While it's usually harder to write a short, lucid letter, it's easier on the person receiving it. For the same reasons, keep your phone conversations succinct. However, include enough appropriate "chitchat" so you continue to build your business relationships. Most importantly, avoid foul language.

10. Be on time. Arriving at work on time in the morning, or turning in a report when it's due, shows you're a good time manager, a necessary trait in today's competitive workplace. It also shows you put others before yourself—another attribute of the successful businessperson—since lateness usually involves inconveniencing others.

•Lucy Hedrick, time-management consultant: "By being on time, you're saying that the person you have an appointment with is important to you."

Return phone calls within 24 hours, if possible. Try to answer letters immediately, but definitely within a week.

11. Start planning now, so next year's holiday cards, gifts, and parties are extra special.

•Mary Kent, photographer, likes to design a holiday card that can serve as a mailing piece throughout the year: "In these hard economic times, we have to think in those terms."

•Nona Aguilar, director of a money-management service for women, has figured out a special gift for her clients with substantial net worth: "They receive a letter saying that I'm paying to send an inner-city kid to the country for two weeks *in their names.*"

12. Be concerned with others. Concern for others should include customers, coworkers, superiors, and subordinates.

•Dorothy Paleologos, director, strategic planning for information technology for Aetna Insurance: "What we are selling are promises and the trust relationship that underlies those promises, and that the company is going to look after a client's best interest when it makes good on those commitments."

Source: Jan Yager, PhD, is a Stamford, Connecticut-based business-protocol and executive-communication consultant and speaker. She is the author of 10 books, most recently *Business Protocol: How to Survive & Succeed in Business,* John Wiley & Sons, 605 Third Ave., New York 10158.

How to Safeguard Your Job

When employees read about the millions of Americans who have lost their jobs in the current economy, they wonder how secure their own positions are.

They're right to wonder. If a company is concerned about financial survival, the first area to be cut is jobs.

While I believe that the worst of the employment crisis is over—that we're headed for a positive turnaround within one to two years—large and mid-sized companies are still spooked ...and still trying to cut back to "fighting weight" after the wild expansion of the 1980s.

In this climate, your job becomes more than the duties you were hired to do. It's now imperative to safeguard your job.

Even though you may be operating with smaller support staff and be busier than ever, you must take the steps now that will make you invaluable to your company—someone it can't afford to let go.

Warning signs...

When jobs in your company are in danger, you can see it...if you look. Many people close their eyes to the signals and deny reality. But denial is not a good survival skill. *Signals that your job may be on the line:*

•You or your department has been losing accounts...you're now just holding steady—rather than gaining back lost business.

•You're being left out of the communications loop. Your supervisors may have stopped including you in meetings. Or you may sense that you no longer have access to the grapevine...that informal sources of information are drying up.

•An outsider is called in—someone who looks grim and doesn't socialize. Since no company likes to fire its own people, a large organization is likely to turn over the dirty work to a consultant from outside the company...or someone from the head office, if the company is a subsidiary.

The best time to put survival strategies in place is before your job is in imminent danger. By the time you notice the warning signs, the decision to fire may already have been made.

No matter how late you develop them, the following strategies will help you build alliances with others in the industry. And if you should lose your job, these skills will help you get—and keep—a new one.

Guiding principles for job survival...

•Strengthen your relationship with your boss...and your boss's boss. Imagine that the fate of the company depends on your activities during the next few months. What would you do? Do those things now.

•Think creatively about ways to generate business. Examine past successes and build on them. Look for old projects that you can expand on or old clients you can call.

•Actively gather information. Read journal articles and conference reports. Discuss developments with others in your company—and industry. Brainstorm. Share what you're doing with your superiors.

Example: "I'd like to look into projects we've done in the last few years and see how we can piggyback on them." Or, "Here's what I've been thinking. We could have a focus group with our suppliers"..."We could continue with the project, part two"..."We could talk about a different kind of extended credit."

Bonus: If you do fall victim to "downsizing," your research will keep you up-to-date on where the opportunities are in your industry.

•Analyze the past. Examine projects that lost money, and find out where errors occurred. Look for ways to protect the company next time.

•Build morale. If you're naturally sociable, capitalize on that by organizing low-cost celebrations to boost your department's spirits.

Examples: A Labor Day picnic...a free concert in the park...a trip to a ball game to celebrate the end of a project.

•Treat your boss like a human being. For fear of appearing too eager or desperate, some employees practically ignore their bosses, except to follow orders. But at work, as in every other situation, people are your best resource. You should put as much energy into developing work relationships as you put into the technical aspects of your job.

Bosses, like everyone else, need to be appreciated. When your boss handles something difficult in a way you admire, say so. Bosses also need to be heard. So develop your listening skills.

Example: Look for an opportunity to say, "As you look ahead to the next few months, what do you see?" Ask how you can help your boss get there. Then let him/her talk for 10 minutes or so—without telling your own story or offering advice.

•Expand your network. Make sure your boss is not the only superior with whom you have a relationship. Pay attention to company reports and newsletters to find out who's doing what. Riding in the elevator or passing someone in the hall can be an opportunity to discuss what's going on.

•Improve yourself. What do you need to know in order to do your job even better? Don't wait—learn it now. If your company is exploring overseas markets, take a course in one of those country's languages. If your public speaking needs work, join Toastmasters or give presentations for your professional association. If you're dissatisfied with your appearance, get someone to go shopping with you...or use an image consultant.

•Enrich your personal life. The more stressful your job, the more you need nonprofessional, creative outlets—to lift your mood, give you a feeling of achievement, and keep your job in perspective.

Examples: Start a woodworking project... sew a quilt...join a community choir.

If the job is lost...

It's not the end of the world. Many, many people find that once they get past the initial shock, a job loss leads to opportunities they never imagined.

Make the most of the contacts and information you have been gathering. Even if every company in your industry is laying off people in your type of position, employers must still get these skills somewhere—you may be valuable to them as a consultant.

This may also be your chance to evaluate whether you'd like to change careers—or make a renewed commitment to your current career.

Source: Adele Scheele, PhD, career consultant, 225 W. 83 St., New York 10024. She is the author of *Skills for Success,* Ballantine Books, 201 E. 50 St., New York 10022.

Avoid Sabotaging Your Own Success...or Else

Why do some seemingly sensible people act in ways that harm their own interests?

They set out to succeed but somewhere along the way they either misjudge how to achieve their goals...do not want to face criticism and failure...or defeat themselves with the intention of hurting someone else. The most common types of self-defeating behavior and how to avoid them...

Deliberate miscalculation...

Most of us go through life trying to overcome the hurdles set in our way. We avoid doing things that slow us down or increase the odds of failure. Those who exhibit self-defeating behavior choose strategies that will backfire.

Poor decisions are made either because of overconfidence or because the desire for a short-term gain is stronger than the appeal of a long-term goal.

Example I: Jane wanted to study clinical psychology in graduate school. After her initial application was rejected, she decided to show the school she was really a desirable prospect by taking a few courses as a nondegree student at her own expense...a good strategy if carried out correctly. But instead of demonstrating her prowess by taking subjects in which she could easily get A's, she took the hardest courses she could find and scored only C's...dooming her graduate school hopes.

Jane miscalculated because she was overconfident. Had she estimated her strengths and weaknesses more realistically, her chance of success would have been much greater.

Example II: Gary was happily married and prosperous. For many years, he indulged his hearty appetite for eating, drinking and smoking but avoided exercise. Not surprisingly, he suffered a heart attack while only in his early 50s. When the doctor told him he had to change his lifestyle, he did so...for a time.

But after just three months, Gary decided he couldn't do without his vices. Two years later, he had another heart attack...this one fatal.

While it doesn't always lead to such unfortunate results, the same kind of poor trade-off between present benefits and future costs is found in many kinds of self-destructive behaviors—drug addiction...excessive sun exposure...overdependence on credit cards...even procrastination.

To avoid miscalculation mistakes: Evaluate your strengths and weaknesses and the long-term costs and benefits of your actions as realistically as you possibly can...and try to consider all the alternatives.

Trying to avoid the truth...

Many forms of self-defeating behavior occur because people don't want to admit their limitations. They sabotage their own success in ways like these:

- Self-handicapping. This occurs when successful people deliberately construct obstacles for themselves so they will have an excuse for failure.

Example: Whenever French chess champion Deschapelles played, he insisted on giving his opponent the advantage of removing one of Deschapelles' pawns and taking the first move.

Result: Deschapelles increased his chance of losing...but always had a good excuse if he lost.

- Substance abuse. Alcohol and/or drug abuse serves two purposes for self-destructive people. It helps them blot out their own faults and inadequacies...and gives them an external excuse for failure.

Example: A well-known musician won a coveted competition to become a national hero. But within a few years, his reputation sank as he turned to drugs and was eventually arrested after breaking into a hotel room.

Reason: Great fame at an early age creates great expectations in audiences...and great stress in performers. Drugs eased the stress Fodor felt and provided an excuse for his failure to perform adequately—but allowed him to believe in his musical ability.

To face the truth: Develop a sense of perspective on yourself, recognize your imperfections and learn to accept criticism.

The quest for revenge...

Sometimes self-defeating behavior is a misguided attempt to redress emotional wounds inflicted in childhood.

Example: Despite obvious talent, Stuart, aged 36, would break rules...steal...drink on the job...in an obvious manner that was sure to be detected. Then his supervisor would reprimand him and threaten his job.

This replicated a pattern from Stuart's childhood, when his father would beat him. After the beating, while Stuart was sobbing, his alarmed mother would scream at his father until his father withdrew into a state of depression. Thus Stuart would enjoy the sweet taste of victory over his father...even though he was in physical agony himself.

I call this self-defeating strategy "Pyrrhic revenge," after the famous "victory" of the Greek king Pyrrhus, who won a battle against the Romans but almost wiped out his whole army in the process.

Pyrrhic revenge is typically found in marriages in which one spouse suffered abuse as a child...often from an alcoholic parent. He seeks out a partner who has the same problem his parent had. He tries to correct the problem and, in doing so, cure his own childhood wounds. This usually doesn't work, so instead he ends up venting the long-repressed anger against the parent...and doesn't mind destroying himself as long as his spouse goes down, too.

To avoid self-destruction via revenge: Realize your own interests...judge whether you are acting to help yourself or to hurt someone else.

Choking under pressure...

Choking is a self-defeating behavior that occurs when people under pressure, striving to do their best, fail because they try too hard to succeed and do not perform as well as they can.

Example: Beth, an outstanding student, had to recite a speech from Shakespeare in front of her high-school class. After memorizing it perfectly, she stood up to speak...and nothing came out.

Reason: Smoothly speaking memorized lines is an automatic process. Beth wanted so intensely to succeed that her self-consciousness prevented her memory from working naturally.

The same phenomenon causes sports champions to falter in important matches and winning teams to lose championship games.

To avoid choking under pressure: Develop perspective. Remind yourself that success in life doesn't depend on just one event.

Example: If it's the last minutes of an important event or presentation, and victory or defeat depends on your next move, remember that just being there shows that you already are a success.

Source: Steven Berglas, PhD, clinical psychologist and management consultant, Harvard Medical School, Boston. He is coauthor with Roy F. Baumeister, PhD, of *Your Own Worst Enemy: Understanding the Paradox of Self-Defeating Behavior,* Basic Books, New York.

How to Win at Telephone Tag

Telephone tag, the seemingly endless cycle of calls and returned calls that are missed, is one of the more time-consuming frustrations of executive life. Beat the frustration by organizing your telephone tactics.

If the person you want to talk with isn't in, and you do want him to call you back:

- Leave a detailed message of the subject of the call.
- Note a time span when you'll definitely be available.
- Make a phone appointment—a specific time when the party can reach you.
- Tell the secretary that no reply will be an assumed consent or agreement.

If you don't want the other party to call back:

• Ask for a specific time when he/she will be available, so you can try again.

• Find out if the person can be paged.

• Request that the secretary relay the information to your secretary, keeping the bosses out of the phone process.

Source: *Execu-Time,* Box 631, Lake Forest, IL 60045.

Simple Ways to Reduce Job Stress

Job-related psychological stress takes an enormous toll on Americans. It affects one of every five workers in this country...and costs our economy billions and billions of dollars a year in absenteeism, lost productivity, and medical expenses—including expenses caused by accidents and alcoholism, both of which often originate in stress. Stress produces a remarkable variety of emotional and psychological symptoms.

Typical: Rapid heart rate and/or breathing... stammering...a sense of isolation from colleagues...headaches, stomachaches and chest pain...reduced sex drive...stomach upset, diarrhea, and other gastrointestinal problems ...chronic fatigue and insomnia...sweating... proneness to accidents...ulcers...and even drug addiction.

If you suffer from one or more of these symptoms—or if a coworker or family member remarks that you seem irritable or ill—it's time to evaluate the stress in your work life... and, if necessary, take steps to alleviate it.

The costs of chronic stress...

Untreated chronic stress leads not only to burnout, but also to heart attack, stroke, and other deadly health problems.

Workers often try to control their job stress via nonpsychological approaches—exercise, hobbies, vitamin pills, special diets, vacations, etc. While these approaches are healthful and might afford temporary relief, they eventually fail. In fact, such approaches often wind up increasing stress levels.

Example: A man who jogs every day to reduce stress feels even more anxious than usual if for some reason he must forgo jogging even for a day.

Bottom line: Stress is a psychological problem, and it can be fully controlled only by a psychological approach. I believe that the best way to do this is to recognize the 12 types of myths that cause job stress...and to systematically replace these myths with attitudes that are healthy and more realistic.

Stress-causing myths...

Myth 1. Something awful will happen if I make a mistake. *Reality:* Mistakes in the workplace may be a source of embarrassment and frustration, but rarely do they lead to anything more dire than a reprimand. The lesson sounds trite, but it's wise—don't fear mistakes, learn from them.

Myth 2. There's a right way and a wrong way to do everything. *Reality:* What's right for one person or situation is often not right for another. Mistakes are common in business, and they seldom result in tragedy. In fact, many excellent business decisions appear at first blush to be enormous blunders.

Myth 3. Being criticized is awful. *Reality:* Criticism—of oneself and of others—is central to personal growth. Being criticized is not tantamount to failing, and the process should never be viewed as something to be endured. Instead, workers should welcome criticism as a learning opportunity. *Note:* Do not accept criticism that is abusive or disrespectful.

Myth 4. I need approval from those around me. *Reality:* While you might welcome praise for a job well done, you don't really need "positive strokes" to be an effective, fulfilled worker. Expecting praise in a work environment where it is rarely forthcoming can lead to disappointment and frustration.

Myth 5. I must always be viewed as competent. *Reality:* No one is good at everything. Even if you were perfect, there is no guarantee that your coworkers would admire you. How others view you lies entirely within their control. Worrying about your image only sets the stage for anxiety and more frustration.

Myth 6. People in authority must not be challenged. *Reality:* Most superiors are willing to listen to their subordinates' complaints and criticisms—if these are presented fairly and constructively. In fact, many bosses welcome complaints because they suggest better ways to do things. If you're inclined to confront your superior, do so. Even if you don't get all you want, the act of speaking out releases emotions that might otherwise lead to anger and resentment.

Myth 7. The workplace is essentially fair and just. *Reality:* Hoping for total fairness at work is not only unrealistic, it's not even desirable. Some of the best and most productive business solutions result from controversy and argumentation, which may seem unfair at the time.

Myth 8. I must always be in control. *Reality:* The notion that you can easily meet every deadline and fill every quota is appealing, but it only sets you up for frustration and stress. Even the best routines and systems break down occasionally. Rather than worrying about control, focus upon what you're doing...and what you want out of life.

Myth 9. I must anticipate everything. *Reality:* Surprises are inevitable on the job as in other parts of life. Sensing things before they happen and gauging colleagues' "vibrations" certainly makes good sense—but remember, you are dealing with probabilities, not foregone conclusions.

Myth 10. I must have my way. *Reality:* Good salaries, beautiful offices, and prestigious positions don't come easily—in fact, they may never come. No doubt there will be setbacks along the way. Effective workers do their work conscientiously without insisting upon immediate realization of their goals. Certainly you can strive toward such goals. Just don't demand them as conditions of continued employment.

Myth 11. Workers who make mistakes must be punished. *Reality:* An effective workplace calls for effective teamwork...and teamwork is impossible when employees are continually trying to assign or escape blame.

Essential for workers: Acceptance, tolerance, patience, allowance for imperfections—in yourself as well as in others.

Myth 12. I need a shoulder to cry on. *Reality:* A compassionate coworker is often helpful in difficult times—but not essential. Workers who resent not having one only cultivate their own self-pity and dampen the morale of themselves and of people around them.

Source: Samuel H. Klarreich, PhD, vice president of Mainstream Access Corp., a Toronto-based consulting firm. He is the author of several books on stress, including *Work Without Stress: A Practical Guide to Emotional and Physical Well-Being on the Job*, Brunner Mazel Inc., 19 Union Square West, New York 10003.

Secrets of Working Much More Effectively

Being ineffective at work can lead to a downhill spiral...especially these days.

We derive a lot of our self-esteem from doing a good job and being rewarded for it. An unhappy work situation diminishes our self-esteem...and decreases our ability to work effectively.

The best way to stay effective—or become more effective—is to learn to spot the reasons for the problem.

Ineffectiveness traps...

• *Trap:* Stale technical know-how. People who haven't kept up with their basic field—whether it's engineering or sales—know less and less every year. They wind up living off their intellectual capital and eventually go bankrupt.

Fifty years ago, increased wisdom, maturity and judgment would have compensated. But today, the actual basic knowledge—the theory, practice and machinery in any field—becomes obsolete quite quickly.

Remedy: Read the latest books on relevant subjects in your field. Take refresher and training courses. Visit competitors. Read the key journals and trade magazines. Talk to the bright young stars in the company about the weird ideas that they're into...some of those ideas will become the tools of your trade in five years.

• *Trap:* Failure to maintain a network. When most people start a job, they put a lot of effort into networking. They look for mentors and take challenging and highly visible assignments.

But after many years at the same firm, their networks begin to deteriorate. Some people become so isolated that new people in the firm wonder who they are...and why anyone wants to have them around. The worst offenders are introverts, especially technical types, who don't like socializing.

Remedy: Keep up your contacts. Schedule at least one useful contact into each day. Consider this part of your work.

You can't create a network the instant that you need one. In times of reorganization or retrenchment, your network can make all the difference between whether or not you survive.

The bigger your network, the better. You never know who can help you.

• *Trap:* Inappropriate transfer. People often become ineffective after they're moved from a job that matches their talents to one that doesn't.

Example: Joette, a people person, managed a large department of a big company. After the firm reorganized, she was assigned to a technical job that she hated. Although she tried to do the new job, she became more and more frustrated and unhappy, until she was finally fired.

This is a big problem for people who are passive. They may have gotten along by going along. But that only works as long as good choices are made for them.

Remedy: Assume a tough renegotiation stance. Most companies won't force you to do an inappropriate job...but you have to stick up for yourself. *Exception:* Companies that are shy on firing may pressure people to quit by giving them jobs that they hate. Tough renegotiation makes it more likely that employees will at least get good severance and leave feeling good about themselves.

• *Trap:* Change of boss. Doing a good job under one boss doesn't mean you can work effectively with a new one.

Remedy: If the new boss is flawed—but redeemable, be a good lieutenant and work to help him/her succeed. It could give your career a big boost.

During this process however, look into lateral transfer opportunities. And think about your options outside the company.

More steps to take...

Make a careful analysis of what is going on in your job. *Ask yourself:*

• In what areas am I ineffective?

• Are my expectations too high?

• Is there enough challenge and opportunity for advancement?

• Do I have too much or too little work?

• What kind of relationship do I have with my boss and coworkers?

• Why does this job contrast so bleakly with other, more positive experiences?

• What are the ways in which this job doesn't meet my needs or that I don't measure up to it?

Once you've analyzed where the problem is, think through a strategy to increase your effectiveness.

Speak with coworkers and your boss about the dilemma. Get feedback. Your analysis of the problem may be wrong.

If you can't be open with anyone in your company, speak to people in comparable positions at other companies. Find out how they deal with the issues you're facing.

Give yourself a time limit to experiment with your strategy. *Suggested:* Six months. After the time runs out, don't sit around and get more depressed. Start looking aggressively for something else.

Source: Martin G. Groder, MD, a psychiatrist and business consultant in Chapel Hill, North Carolina. His book, *Business Games: How to Recognize the Players and Deal with Them*, is available from Boardroom Classics, 55 Railroad Ave., Greenwich, CT 06830.

Office Gift-Giving Etiquette

Giving the wrong gift can be worse than giving no gift at all—so here's how to give the right one...

•Avoid inappropriate gifts. Humor can backfire, so beware of giving a gag gift. Cash is only appropriate for tipping garage attendants, hairdressers and others in service positions—not for coworkers. Some gifts are always in poor taste—liquor...perfume and other intimate items...jewelry, neckties and other items that impose your taste.

•Don't be extravagant. While there's nothing wrong with generosity, going overboard on a gift will only make the recipient feel uncomfortable. For peers and subordinates, I recommend spending no more than $25. If you and the recipient have a special relationship or if you've worked together for many years, then it's fine to spend more.

Caution: Giving your boss a fancy gift can be interpreted as inappropriate by peers and by the boss. If you want to give him/her something, stick to a small, tasteful gift, such as well-chosen and well-presented flowers or even a simple handwritten note.

•Wrap the gift beautifully. Pretty wrapping paper makes even a modest gift seem truly special. Be sure to enclose a thoughtful note, written in ink on personal stationery. Avoid platitudes like "Thanks for your support last year." Be more specific—and creative, too.

•Present the gift in person. Mailing the gift, leaving it on a doorstep or having someone else deliver it suggests a lack of sincerity on your part. Magazine subscriptions and other items that cannot be delivered in person should be announced via a card that you hand deliver. Gifts that you receive should be acknowledged with a written thank-you note within one week.

•Keep a permanent gift record. It will help you avoid the embarrassment of presenting two coworkers with the same gift or giving the same gift twice to the same coworker. *Remember:* The gift you select today sets a precedent for future gifts. If you give your secretary an expensive gift this year, for example, don't expect him/her to be satisfied with an inexpensive trinket next year.

Source: Mary Monica Mitchell, president of *Uncommon Courtesies,* a Philadelphia-based consulting firm that teaches etiquette and international protocol to business executives. Box 40186, Philadelphia 19106.

Better Business Relationships

Good intentions don't count in a business relationship. Neither do feelings or attitudes...*unless they are reflected in overt action.* Relationships are defined by *behavior*—what each party does for and to the other.

Source: *Overcoming Resistance: A Practical Guide to Producing Change in the Workplace* by management consultant Jerald M. Jellison, PhD, based in Los Angeles. Simon & Schuster, 1230 Avenue of the Americas, New York 10020.

Leaving the Office At the Office

It's important to learn to separate your professional from your private life. Particularly today, when the business world seems more fast-paced than ever, this can be hard to do. In the now famous quote of a hard-driving executive: "Nobody ever said on his deathbed, 'I wish I had spent more time at the office.'" Bear in mind that work has its busy seasons and its peak periods. Then, and during ambitious times such as a business start-up, it may not be appropriate to think of leaving the office behind every day. But that shouldn't always be the case. Balance is the goal to work toward.

•Make a conscious effort to change your mind-set when you are not at work. Clues that your head is still at the office: You chafe because the host is slow in moving you and other guests to the dining table...You make an agenda before going out to spend the afternoon with your child and stick to the agenda even when something more interesting intrudes. These are business mind-sets inappropriate to nonoffice activities.

•Give yourself a steady stream of physical cues to help you separate your office from your private world. Don't wear a watch on weekends. If you feel time pressures even when you're at home, don't use digital clocks in the car or home. They pace off the seconds and minutes too relentlessly for many people.

•Change your clothes as soon as you get home. And if you feel naked without your dictating machine or your briefcase with you at home, experiment with feeling naked!

•Use your physical setting to help you keep work in its place. Tell yourself that you can work only at a particular place at home if you must work. Don't take papers to bed with you. Don't spread them out over the couch, the dining table and the floor.

•Relax before plunging into housework or domestic activities. Working women especially have trouble giving themselves a 10-minute break when they get home because they're inclined to feel anxious about talking with the children or starting dinner. Take the break. It can make all the difference between experiencing the rest of the evening as a pleasure or as yet another pressure.

•Rituals are a useful device for making the switch. Secretaries do this by tidying up the desk or covering the typewriter. Lyndon Johnson symbolically turned off the lights in the Oval Office when he left. For managers, some useful rituals are loosening ties or other constricting clothing, turning a calendar page or making a list of things to do for the next day. They all help make the break. The to-do list also helps curb the desire to catch up on tomorrow's tasks while you're at home.

•Resist the growing tendency to abuse the whole winding-down process by taking up activities that create problems of their own... compulsive sex...addictive exercise...overeating or overdrinking...recreational drugs. *Better:* Use the transition time as a period of discovery. Walk or drive home along a different route. Pick up something new at the newsstand instead of the usual evening paper.

...The other side of leaving the office at the office is to leave home at home. It may be productive to use lunchtimes to buy paint, but that's not helpful in keeping the two worlds separate.

Source: Dr. Marilyn Machlowitz, Machlowitz Associates, a management development firm, New York.

How to Give Productive Criticism

Although criticism is destructive if it is used to hurt, belittle, shame, insult or embarrass another person or if it is used to make someone look good or feel powerful, it can be used as a tool for positive change.

Needed: The ability to give criticism in a positive, productive manner.

To criticize constructively...

•Think strategically. Plan your criticism in advance. Take responsibility for how and what you communicate. Avoid sarcasm, blame or accusation.

Plan exactly what you want to change, and ask yourself *why?* How can you best say this so the person you're criticizing will be receptive? What solutions and goals can you offer? How can you help? What is a realistic time frame in which to expect change?

Example: A woman who works for you delivers a proposal at a meeting. But it's too long, detailed and dry.

Ineffective: "I thought you'd never finish...I almost fell asleep."

Better: "Nice job." *Then, the next day, say:* "I've been thinking...your research was so exhaustive, you may have lost a few of us early on. Next time, you might find it more effective to come to the point right away—grab our attention. Then just summarize the statistics."

•Time the criticism properly. Pay attention to the time, place and emotional state of the person you need to criticize. *Very important:* Don't criticize when other people are present.

Ineffective: "Skip the statistics and just get on with it."

Better: "I see you've done excellent research. But would you mind summarizing your statistics for those of us with limited time? Please distribute copies to the marketing people after the meeting."

•Concentrate on how the person can improve. People naturally feel more confident if it's clear that they will have a chance to improve.

Ineffective: "Your proposal was a disaster. You'll never get anywhere."

Better: "Your research gives us a firm base to build on, and your conclusions are sound. Let's develop a strategy from here."

•Protect the person's self-esteem. You want to help, not attack.

Ineffective: "You took forever to get to the point."

Better: "It's hard to cover such thorough research in a staff meeting. Next time, provide the tables in a hand-out so we can study the numbers in detail later."

•Be interactive. Allow the person you are criticizing to respond.

Ineffective: "You spent so much time on the statistics, you lost sight of the big picture. You'll never get ahead that way."

Better: "Next time, I'd like you to concentrate more on the big picture and less on the details. How else could you tighten your presentation and make it more lively?"

•Be flexible. Communicate from an advisory, teaching stance, rather than from an authoritative one, which provokes resistance. Avoid rigid *should* statements that imply your way is the only right way.

Ineffective: "You should only describe the highlights of your research."

Better: "If you think it's important to back up your conclusions in detail, let's find a way to help you do it more quickly."

•Communicate the helping spirit. Criticism is much easier to accept if the recipient thinks the critic is concerned with his/her welfare and growth.

Ineffective: "You made our whole department look silly."

Better: "Next time, I'll ask Jack in graphics to design an attractive cover for your research report, and you can distribute it before the meeting."

•Identify your criteria. Blanket criticisms do not work.

Ineffective: "No one liked your report."

Better: "Your data was useful to the marketing staff. But the sales staff gets bored in meetings that don't apply to them."

•Offer specific solutions or direction for improvement. Show the person you want to help.

Ineffective: "You need to cut your material in half."

Better: "Open with your project description and highlight the benefits. Then summarize the research."

•Come up with an incentive. What's in it for the person you're criticizing?

Ineffective: "Do it...or else."

Better: "You'll be in line for a promotion if you improve your meeting skills."

•Include the positives. Give the person something to feel good about.

Ineffective: "You didn't do anything right."

Better: "Your attention to detail has always been one of your great strengths. We know we can trust you if you tell us the research backs up your conclusions."

•Get a commitment for action. A timetable will motivate the person to act.

Ineffective: "You've simply got to improve."

Better: "When can I see a revised report?"

•Follow up. If you notice improvement, acknowledge it.

Ineffective: "Who's next?"

Better: "Thank you, that was an excellent report."

Source: Psychologist Hendrie Weisinger, PhD, a specialist in anger management and criticism. Dr. Weisinger teaches at UCLA's Anderson Graduate School of Management and conducts seminars. He is the author of *The Critical Edge*, HarperCollins, 10 E. 53 St., New York 10022.

How to Reduce Stress At Your Desk

You'll get more work done and feel better if you make your working environment comfortable. *Try these techniques:*

•Make certain that your chair is comfortable.

•Quiet your telephone's ring.

•Alter the lighting to reduce glare...or increase brightness.

•Personalize your work space with photos, prints, etc.

•Adopt at least a partial closed-door policy for your office. (If you have no way to be alone in your office, find a place elsewhere in the building where you can take breathers.)

•Avoid tight collars...they can cut blood flow to the brain and result in light-headedness and even panic attacks. Tight belts are troublesome, too.

• Establish a regular time for meals, especially lunch.

Source: Stephen Cohen, author of *The Termination Trap,* Williamson Publishing, Charlotte, VT.

Smoking Restrictions At Work

Companies can legally discriminate against smokers. More companies are doing so because it may actually head off trouble in the form of lawsuits brought by nonsmokers who demand a healthful, smoke-free work environment.

Here are some measures companies have taken:

• Total ban. Employees may smoke only in the company parking lot, and then only during work breaks and on lunch hours. And it applies to everyone, including top management, visitors and customers.

• Work station ban. Smoking is prohibited in working areas but allowed during work breaks in specified areas.

• Softer policies such as dividing the work area between smokers and nonsmokers. However, these rarely work well.

Source: Dr. William L. Weis, Albers School of Business, Seattle University, writing in *Personnel Journal.*

Recognizing Fatigue For What it is

Fighting fatigue is a concept of success-oriented people that actually makes them fatigue-prone. Fatigue is a symptom—the purpose of which is to get your attention—to tell you there's something wrong with the way you live. The main cause of fatigue is a monolithic lifestyle, in which the rational sense is used to the exclusion of the other senses, movement, and the emotions. To beat fatigue, you have to get your life back in balance.

What is fatigue?

The tiredness we feel after jogging for instance, is not fatigue. Fatigue is an absence of energy, joie de vivre, interest...It's a blunting of sensation, a shutting out of stimuli.

Behavioral clues:

• Difficulty in getting going or persevering.

• Not having the energy to do things you know you enjoy.

• Having trouble waking up or getting to sleep.

• Taking too many naps.

Most vulnerable...

People who:

• Do virtually the same thing all day, every day. The classic case is the executive who spends his work hours hunched over a desk, grabs a sandwich at lunch, takes a break only to talk to coworkers about business, and goes home to a set routine with his family each evening.

• Have lifestyles contrary to their natural inclinations. Each of us has a rhythm of activity with which we are most comfortable. If a natural doer is forced to lie on a beach in the Bahamas for two weeks, he'll come back exhausted.

Source: Mary E. Wheat, MD, an internist and counselor on fatigue at Mt. Zion Hospital and Medical Center, San Francisco.

Are You a Workaholic?

People who love their work passionately and spend long hours at it are not necessarily work-addicted. True workaholics cannot stop working even in non-work situations. They make all other activities and relationships secondary to work. While the reasons differ widely, almost all work addicts share these traits:

• Oriented to activities involving skills and skill development. Averse to activities where skill is not a factor.

• Strongly analytic. Focus on precise definitions, goals, policies, facts, lists, measurements and strategies.

• Aggressive and unable to leave things alone. An urge to manipulate and control their environment to gain a sense of satisfaction.

•Goal-oriented, product-oriented. Uninterested in the sensations of the present unless they yield products or contribute to their creation.

•Concerned with efficiency and effectiveness. Severely upset by waste and loss. Ironically, many work addicts are inefficient because they are perfectionists and refuse to delegate authority.

Source: Jay B. Rohrlick, MD, *Work and Love: The Crucial Balance,* Summit Books, New York.

Good Business Communication

•"What happened?" is the question to ask when something's gone wrong. Don't try to blame someone for the mistake right at the start. Asking "What happened?" focuses on the mistake itself, not on the person who did it, and is much more likely to lead to useful information. *Contrast:* "Who did it?" is a phrase that can turn off information flow.

•Oral orders are usually all that's needed to correct a basic mistake. If the oral order changes an existing policy, though, confirm it in writing as soon as possible to prevent future confusion.

•Tuesday is the best day for having a serious heart-to-heart discussion with an employee concerning job performance. *Friday risk:* Person broods all weekend about the conversation and comes back embittered on Monday. After the Tuesday talk, find a way by Wednesday to indicate that there's no ill will.

•Discuss serious problems with a subordinate in your office where your authority is evident. Minor matters can be handled in the subordinate's office as long as there's privacy and quiet.

•Value of a dumb question or a simple and honest "I don't know" is that you'll probably learn something you don't know now...and that you couldn't find out any other way. "It's what you learn after you know it all that really counts," said President Harry S. Truman, an expert at turning seeming modesty into great strength.

Source: James Van Fleet, former US Army officer, manager with Sears, Roebuck & Co. and US Gypsum, and consultant on the psychology of management, writing in *Lifetime Conversation Guide,* Prentice-Hall, Inc., Englewood Cliffs, NJ.

Dealing with Political Infighting

•Don't decide that one of the infighters is "right" and the other is "wrong." That encourages the winner to pick more political fights in the future, while it leaves the loser spoiling for revenge. On the other hand, deciding that neither is right and that they must compromise leaves both parties unhappy and convinced that the boss wasn't fair.

•Look for a third choice that both parties can live with, without each one feeling that he's lost or that the other one has won. The ideal "third way" incorporates all the important points of both sides. Only the irritants are omitted.

•The person who leads the way to a solution comes out stronger.

Source: *The Effective Manager,* Warren, Gorham & Lamont, Boston.

High-Level Incompetence

High-level incompetence has many faces and lurks in some heretofore unsuspected areas:

•Physical incompetence. A person who is professionally or technically competent may develop such anxiety over his work that he gets ulcers or high blood pressure. And that results in a poor attendance record. His boss and coworkers assume he's really very competent but just has health problems. In reality, he is physically incompetent to handle the strain of the job.

•Mental incompetence. This occurs when a person is moved to a level where he can no longer deal with the intellectual requirements of the job.

•Social incompetence. A person who is technically competent may be unable to get along with others. Or, problems may arise if he is promoted in an organization where a different class of social behavior is required when moving up the ladder.

•Emotional incompetence. A technically competent person may be too unstable emotionally to deal with a particular job. Creative types, who tend to be insecure, are particularly prone to this type of incompetence when promoted to administrative positions.

•Ethical incompetence. Richard Nixon is a good example. Only when the White House tapes revealed his dishonesty beyond a doubt was it clear that, in office, he had reached his level of ethical incompetence. His brand of manipulative persuasiveness, an asset in local politics, became a liability in the highest office in the land.

Source: Dr. Lawrence J. Peter, author of *The Peter Principle.*

Sexual Harassment On the Job

Sexual harassment on the job is unlawful and a violation of fair employment practices. Supervisors who allow it to occur in their offices, even though they themselves don't commit any offensive acts, can be charged.

If you think someone is sexually harassing you at work:

•Keep a diary and write a brief description of each event right after it happens. Note the time and the place, the people involved, the names of any witnesses.

•Confront the offender. Tell the person that you think the remark or action is harassment.

•Write a letter to the offender, describing the event and noting that you consider it sexual harassment. Send the letter "personal receipt requested," which means the Post Office will only deliver it to the person to whom it is addressed and give you a receipt that the person signs. Or, hand the letter to the person in the presence of a witness you can trust.

•Report the event to management and explain the actions you have taken.

As a supervisor:

•Take every complaint about sexual harassment seriously. Document the actions taken in response to a complaint.

•Write a policy statement against sexual harassment which defines it, condemns it and provides a way in which employees can bring events to management's attention.

•Don't condone a regular practice of sexually-oriented conversations and jokes in the work place. And certainly don't make such remarks to the people you supervise.

•Don't permit employees to post sexually-oriented pictures or cartoons in the workplace.

•Never tie sexual favors to job performance—not even in jest.

•Never touch an employee in a sexually-oriented manner.

Source: Howard Pardue, director of human resources, Summit Communications, Inc.

Avoid Unnecessary Overtime

Many experts feel that regular late hours at work signal inefficient, disorganized work habits, not ambition. *Ways to accomplish your work during office hours:*

•Do not linger over an office breakfast or a long lunch.

•Keep visits and phone calls to a minimum.

•Establish times when your door is shut so that you can concentrate on your work without interruptions.

•Before a late afternoon meeting, make it clear that you have to leave at a specified time. Most meetings will proceed more quickly.

•Before taking on a new job, find out if any overtime is required, aside from normal emergencies. Weigh this against the rewards of the job.

Source: *Bottom Line,* Boardroom, Inc., Greenwich, CT.

How to Reduce Work Related Stress

•Recognize the aggravating aspects of your job. Stop fighting them.

•Identify your emotional needs and accept them. Most executives are competitive, need to be liked, need to vent anger. They should have outlets for each of these needs.

•Practice listening. Listening is more relaxing than talking, and it can help you know what's really going on in the organization.

•Be sensitive to change. Recognize when it's occurring on the job and figure out what adjustments are necessary. By consciously recognizing change, you make it manageable.

•Keep alcohol consumption under control. Excessive drinking creates the illusion of dealing with stress, while in fact adding to it.

Source: Rosalind Forbes, author of *Corporate Stress,* Doubleday, Garden City, NY.

New Projects: Keep Them Exciting

New ideas have a way of exciting people, then fading away. *To maintain interest:*

•Pump in emotion and excitement by remaining personally involved.

•Organize schedules so that people working together have a sense of directed action.

•Remind everyone of the target. Make it stand out clearly as the common goal.

•Show respect for all participants by continuing to listen to their comments and ideas to improve ongoing projects.

Source: Craig S. Rice, author of *Secrets of Managing People,* Prentice-Hall, Englewood Cliffs, NJ.

What Makes Committed Employees

Committed people get a great deal of personal satisfaction from their accomplishments. They totally immerse themselves in a project and often need a brief break to recover emotionally before a new assignment.

In addition, they:

•Assess the feasibility of a task and speak up when they think the odds are bad. Uncommitted people take on anything without caring whether it is possible.

•Back up and cover for coworkers and supervisors without concern for who is responsible.

•Understand the underlying plans and objectives of a project. Know how to proceed without checking with supervisors at every point.

•Feel apprehension and anxiety at the possibility of failure. Unhesitatingly ask for help from supervisors when it seems necessary.

Source: W.C. Waddell, author of *Overcoming Murphy's Law,* AMACOM, New York.

Characteristics of A Good Helper

•Works well with colleagues.

•Is systematic. Sets priorities well.

•Gives a stable and predictable work performance.

•Accepts direction well.

•Shows up regularly and punctually.

•Detects problems in advance and refers to them when necessary.

10

Relationships

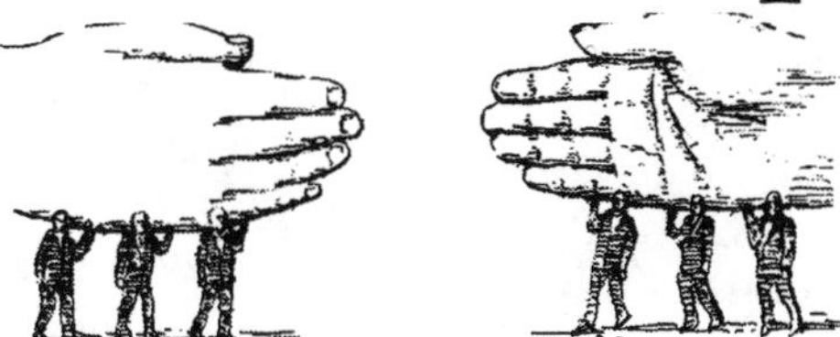

How to Get the Love that You Want

There is hope: A deep and long-lasting love and companionship in marriage *is* possible...

The secret: Couples must change from an *unconscious* marriage to a *conscious* marriage.

Almost all couples start their relationship as an unconscious marriage just by falling in love. In this state of romantic love, infatuation or "love at first sight," you feel your union is "magical"—and that your beloved is "the perfect one"... "the answer to your dreams."

What you do not realize is that this "person of your dreams" has qualities—voice tone, posture, facial expression, mood and character traits—that match an "image" in your unconscious mind of important people from your past (parents, other childhood caretakers). You actually fall in love with someone similar to those childhood caretakers.

More often we unconsciously choose mates who have similar negative rather than positive traits, that become obvious and disturbing after the "glow" of romance fades. They also have positive traits but the negative traits are more apparent.

Examples: Picking a husband who ignores you like your father, or a wife who nags like your mother.

The marriage becomes "unconscious" because both people try to recreate—in order to repair—their childhood.

They feel more or less in love depending on their unconscious anticipation of getting early needs met in the marriage.

Problems emerge when the partner, similar to the past figure, does not repair the initial hurt or give them the love they never got from their parents, leading to disillusionment, distrust or divorce.

Instead of love notes, back rubs, avid listening and time together, now each "escapes" into separate interests, friends, activities.

This unconscious repetition of the past to satisfy unmet needs—wanting from your spouse what you did not get from your parents—explains why spouses sometimes get more furious at their partners than the situation warrants.

Example: If your husband isn't at the office when you call, you panic, fearing he's having an affair or will leave you, triggering old feelings of abandonment when mother left you with a baby-sitter, or was sick and unavailable—or worse—died.

Another common problem emerging from the unconscious marriage is the power struggle, where spouses react like children toward each other or as their parents reacted toward them.

While couples may panic over such conflicts, there is a hidden gain: The end of romantic love and being numb to each other's negative traits can be the beginning of more realistic reappraisals and growing up.

This is where "Imago Relationship Therapy" comes in (imago means image). This is a synthesis and expansion of ideas and techniques from other schools—including psychoanalysis, social learning theory, transactional analysis, gestalt and systems theory—to help couples move from repetitions in an *unconscious marriage* to a constructively *conscious marriage.*

The conscious marriage brings an end to romantic attachment and power struggles. The couple makes a commitment to uncover the unconscious needs that ignited their initial attraction, to heal their wounds, and to move to a more evolved relationship based on personal wholeness and accepting and appreciating each other as separate beings. The spouse goes from being a surrogate parent to a passionate friend.

The steps to create a conscious marriage can be done alone—or with the professional help of a therapist. *Important:*

• Learn the dialogue—an essential communications skill that enables couples to heal each other's emotional wounds by...

Mirroring—repeating back what each other says about needs.

Validating—telling your partner you understand the logic of his/her needs given his/her childhood frustrations.

Empathy—experiencing your partner's feelings.

• Use the dialogue process, mutually identifying unmet needs and the corresponding specific request underlying a complaint.

Example: "You come home late" reveals "I need to feel loved" and the resulting request, "I would like you to come home by 7 p.m. on Tuesday nights."

• Identify the unmet agenda, the one from childhood that repeats in the marriage (attention, praise, comfort, independence) and how it sabotages the current relationship.

Example: "Isolators" need *"space"* out of fear of being smothered by a spouse as they were by a parent. *"Fusers,"* abandoned as children, want to merge with a spouse.

Helpful: Imagine addressing each important person in your childhood home, noting their positive and negative traits, what you liked and didn't like, wanted but didn't get. Ask then for what you want—and imagine them giving it. And—to separate yourself and your partner from parents, compare positive and negative traits, what you enjoy most, what you want and don't get.

• Develop personal wholeness—instead of seeking a mate to fill in your "holes." Find your "lost self."

Example: Because your father drank, you learned to ignore feelings of shame and sadness.

Drop the facade or "false self" that protects you from hurt. Reclaim your "disowned self" that was criticized and denied.

Example: Your mother always said you're not as smart as your brother so you don't act smart even if you are.

Change your own negative traits without projecting them onto a partner (complaining "He's bitter, not me" when *you* are really bitter) or acting them out.

• Validate and support each other's efforts.

• Communicate your needs instead of clinging to the childhood belief that your partner instinctively knows your needs. Fulfill some needs on your own.

• Meet your partner's needs more often than putting yourself first—in healing his/her wounds, you heal your own.

Example: When an emotionally unavailable man marries a woman with a similar type father, the husband heals her wound and his own by becoming more sensitive to her needs.

Stretching exercise: Do something that your partner wants that is difficult for you to do.

Make a verbal or written commitment to stop "exits"—escapes from intimacy like overworking, over-involvement with children, shopping, drinking, lying, picking fights—and to work together for a defined time. Set aside an hour of uninterrupted time together for a defined time.

Write a personal and joint relationship vision —"we are affectionate with each other," "we are loving parents," "we have fun."

Communicate better by taking turns as deliverer—who describes a thought, feeling, anger or complaint, starting with "I" ("I felt anxious today at work")—and as receiver—who paraphrases the message and asks for clarification. ("This morning you woke up wanting to stay home. Did I understand you right?").

"Re-romanticize" by sharing what pleases you now—("I feel loved when you call me from work...and when you massage my back...and when you listen when I'm upset"—what once pleased you—"I used to feel loved when you held my hand, wrote love notes, whispered sexy things in my ear.").

What would please you—("I would feel loved if you took a shower with me...watched my favorite TV show...slept in the nude.").

Do two each day for the next two months—and keep adding to the list.

Surprise each other with one new pleasure each week and one fun activity—walking, tennis, dancing, showering.

Visualize your love healing your partner—visualize your partner's love healing you.

This new conscious love will create a stable and passionate bond between the two of you, and improve physical and emotional health. This new conscious love will also help you strengthen your immune system. It will flower into broader concern for others and the environment and a spiritual union with the universe.

Source: Harville Hendrix, PhD, educator and therapist who is the founder and director of the Institute for Relationship Therapy in New York. He is the author of the best-selling book *Getting the Love You Want: A Guide for Couples*, Harper/Perennial, 10 E. 53 St., New York 10022, and *Keeping the Love You Find: A Guide for Singles*, Pocket Books, 1230 Avenue of the Americas, New York 10020.

Are You Ready for Love?

Love résumé...

Here is a way to consider—and maybe rethink—what you really want in a loving relationship and what you respond to. Think of this as a love résumé. Sometimes just the act of writing can change your thinking. Like a work résumé, it may show a tendency toward instability. Or it may show a logical progression from one "job" to the next. You can discover your own patterns in relationships.

Write a detailed report* about your three (or more) most serious relationships, including:

- A description of the person and what you did and didn't like.
- What worked and what didn't work.
- How it ended and how you got over it.
- What you think you should have done differently.
- What your partner would say worked or didn't work, and why it ended.
- Would you be attracted to such a person today?

Write a description of the person you would like to meet now, including:

- Is this person like the ones in past relationships? If not, why not?
- What sort of relationship you want (marriage, a companion for weekends, an escort, etc.)
- Characteristics you would avoid.
- Your three highest priorities.

Scoring...

Scale 1: Use a red pencil to underline the times you have written *I* or *me*. Count them, and put the score in a box.

Use a blue pencil to underline the times you have written *he, she, we, us* or *both*. Count them. Put this score in another box.

Add the numbers in both boxes. Divide the total into the number of red underlines. If the percentage is anywhere up to 35%, you're available for a relationship. From 36% to 50% means you are borderline (okay on short-term dating but unable to sustain long-term relationships). Over 50% indicates a counterfeit lover. Your concern for yourself and lack of empathy for others almost guarantee that nothing will work, no matter who the partner is.

Source: Abby Hirsch, founder and director of *The Godmothers,* a dating service.

Beyond Self

We all need to pay more attention to our roles as members of society rather than focusing on our individual rights and personal interests.

If more of us were willing to tackle our community responsibilities, we could correct many of the social ills that afflict us today.

Example: A recent study found that young Americans vigorously uphold their right to be tried before a jury of their peers...but are reluctant to serve on juries themselves.

If every citizen accepted jury duty as an opportunity to fulfill an obligation to society, it would demonstrate that our nation really wants to attack crime...not just deplore high crime rates while accepting them as an inevitable condition of modern life. Within a relatively short time, that signal would be transmitted to the entire society.

In the same way, a renewed commitment to community by more people can help improve our public schools...repair family ties...fight corruption in government...and restore faith in a political system that too often responds to special interest groups but neglects the general welfare.

The importance of strong families...

The foundations of a healthy society are adults committed to building lasting marriages, stable families and strong communities. Today, that is too often *not* the case.

Men and women show inadequate long-term commitments to their partners, children and neighbors. The whole community suffers the consequences.

In the worst cases, neglected children become juvenile delinquents who wreak havoc on themselves and society through drug addiction and violent crime. Those troubled ones who manage to survive adolescence become undesirable workers or lifelong dependents on government assistance. And even many parents who provide their children with physical care and education fail to set an example of community concern and instead raise a new generation of self-centered adults. But we can —and should—do better.

How to strengthen marriages...

- Encourage couples contemplating marriage to attend classes in conflict resolution. Every marriage has disagreements, but they are far less likely to end in divorce if the couple knows how to resolve them amicably. Premarriage programs give couples the opportunity to thrash out basic issues—how to make decisions, how to budget, etc.—before actually being faced with such problems.

Better: Require all high school students to study the subject of marriage. It will help them in all areas of adult life.

- Popularize the idea of premarital super-commitments, such as agreeing to get counseling if you have marital problems.
- Maintain open communication in your marriage. Talk about problems as they arise instead of letting them simmer. Consider renewing your vows on your anniversary to renew your commitment.

Developing children's character...

Parents need to make some tough choices that involve trading time and possibly income and job advancement for the sake of a better next generation. *Specific examples:*

- Never leave children at home alone for an inappropriate amount of time (depending on the ages of the children).
- Rearrange work schedules so at least one parent is home when the children are there.
- Look for jobs that offer some type of flextime...consider the possibility of working at home via computer.
- Before sending your young child to a day care center, investigate it carefully...pay surprise visits to see what it is really like.

As children grow older and spend more time in school, do things they may not appreciate today but will thank you for later...

- Provide a quiet setting for homework... strictly ration TV watching.
- Set a curfew on school nights.

•Don't allow children to work at a job more than 10 hours a week.

•Don't let them squander all their earnings. Require them to save for college.

Ways to improve education...

While home schooling is growing, you can only do so much...but by taking an interest in community activities, you can help your children and other people's children.

•Make the quality of schools a major factor when you decide where to live.

•Don't choose schools on hearsay...see for yourself by making surprise visits.

•Attend PTA meetings...take an active interest in school board elections.

Strengthening your community...

We don't have to live in isolation from our neighbors. We will have a better society if we take active steps to strengthen community bonds. *First steps...*

•Get to know your neighbors—join block associations...support activities that get people interacting in positive ways.

•Take an interest in local politics—support developments that encourage people to become more community-minded.

Example: Zoning changes allow people to work at home, giving them more time to devote to their families and community activities.

•Devote 5% of your time and your money to community projects you favor. Make your voice heard.

Source: Amitai Etzioni, PhD, a professor at George Washington University in Washington, DC. He is author of *The Spirit of Community: Rights, Responsibilities, and the Communitarian Agenda*, Crown Publishers, New York.

Tactful Flirting

Matchmaking is a thing of the past, so if you hope to find that special someone, you have to know how to go about it. Luckily the art of flirting can be learned.

To initiate contact with a stranger you think you would like to know better:

•Don't come on with obvious lines or a standard act. You'll be seen as crude or a phony.

•Don't get too personal. Make your conversational opener about something neutral, or you may be seen as pushy.

•Do pick up on an innocuous topic and comment on it. *Good:* "That's a lovely ring you're wearing. Is it Art Deco?" *Poor:* "You have the most beautiful hair."

•Do make eye contact—but not for too long. According to a psychological study, three seconds is optimal to indicate interest without seeming to stare.

•Don't touch the person right away. Women especially are very put off by men they consider "grabby." You might even move away to create allure.

•Do show vulnerability. People love it when you're not Mr. or Ms. Self-Confidence. If you're nervous, say so. Your candor will be appealing. *Also:* Your admission will allow the other person to admit that he or she is nervous, too. This breaks the ice, and then you both can relax.

•Do ask for help as a good conversation opener. *Example:* "I don't know this area well. Could you recommend a good restaurant around here?"

•Don't feel you have to be extraordinarily good-looking. If you have confidence in yourself as a person, the rest will follow. Whatever your type may be, it is certain to appeal to someone.

•Do be flexible. The same approach won't work with everyone. If you're sensitive and alert, you can pick up verbal and nonverbal cues and respond appropriately.

•Don't oversell yourself or feel compelled to give all your credits. Make the other person feel like the most important person in the world to you at that moment. Being interested is just as important as being interesting (if not more so). Really listen. Don't just wait until the other person finishes a sentence so you can jump in with your own opinion.

•Don't let your confidence be shattered by a rejection. It may not have anything to do with you. You may have approached someone who is married, neurotic, recovering from a devastating love affair, in a bad mood, or averse to your eye color. *The best remedy:* Try again as soon as possible.

Source: Wendy Leigh, author of *What Makes a Woman Good in Bed, What Makes a Man Good in Bed,* and *Infidelity: An American Epidemic,* William Morrow, New York.

What Men Like In Women

• Brunettes come in first with 36% of the men surveyed.

• Blondes come in second at 29%.

• Hair color is unimportant to 32% of the men surveyed.

• *Favorite eye color:* 44% select blue, 21% like brown and 20% prefer green.

• By two to one, men choose curly hair over straight.

• *The trait men first associate with a beautiful woman:* 42% say personality, 23% think of the smile, 13% say eyes and only 6% zero in on the body.

• *Favorite look:* Striking and sophisticated is first, with 32%.

• *Biggest turnoffs:* Heavy makeup, 26%; excess weight, 15%; arrogance, 14%.

Source: *Glamour.*

Talking to Women

A survey of 1,000 women revealed that they liked most to talk about (in this order):

• Family and home, including children and grandchildren.

• Good health.

• Work or job (if a working woman).

• Promotion and advancement (if employed).

• Personal growth.

• Clothes and shopping.

• Recreation.

• Travel.

• Men (especially single women).

Subjects that were least liked:

• Sports such as baseball, football, and boxing.

• Politics.

• Religion.

Source: James Van Fleet, author of *A Lifetime Guide to Conversation,* Prentice-Hall, Inc., Englewood Cliffs, NJ.

How to Talk with Men If You're a Woman

The topics men most like to talk about are strikingly similar to those women like:

• Family and home, including children and grandchildren.

• Good health.

• Work or job.

• Promotion and advancement.

• Personal growth.

• Recreation.

• Travel.

• The opposite sex (especially young single men).

• Sports.

• Politics.

Men generally dislike to talk about:

• Religion.

• Clothes, fashion, or shopping.

Source: James Van Fleet, author of *A Lifetime Guide to Conversation,* Prentice-Hall, Inc., Englewood Cliffs, NJ.

Personal Ads: A Woman's View

The personal classified ads in *The New York Review of Books, New York* magazine and *The Village Voice* are becoming an increasingly useful social medium.

Here are some tips on answering and placing ads:

• Don't lie. Even white lies do damage. Don't say you're a college professor if you really teach occasional courses in night school at several local colleges. Stretching the truth sets up unrealistic expectations, and your "date" is certain to be disappointed. Important omissions also count. If you weigh 300 pounds, it's better to say so.

• Look in the mirror. Don't say you're handsome, beautiful or very attractive if you're not. You have a better chance being honest because different people want different things.

• Don't ask for photos. When it comes to wallet-size portraits, they lie at worst. At best, they say nothing. When you like someone, that person becomes better-looking to you. And when you don't like someone, it doesn't matter how good-looking he is. Besides, some very attractive people photograph badly...and vice versa. You'll get the best sense of a person from the letter, not from the picture.

• Try humor. It always gets a better response.

• Avoid attractiveness requirements. Just on general principles don't answer any ad by a man who asks for a "very beautiful" woman or a woman with a "fabulous figure." If he's preoccupied with looks, he's superficial.

• Don't limit yourself with age requirements. Why do men in their fifties consistently ask for women in their twenties and thirties? Unless you want children, don't limit your possibilities.

• Don't brag. This unpleasant trait breeds skepticism and distaste in the reader.

• Be sincere. Nothing catches a woman's attention more surely than a sincere, straightforward, informative letter. When you answer an ad that looks inviting, let the person know why. Respond to the particulars in the ad in a warm and personal way. Talk honestly about yourself, your likes and dislikes, favorite vacations, funny anecdotes, etc. And never, never, never send a photocopy response.

• If you really liked a woman's ad but she hasn't answered your response, write again. Persistence is a virtue.

• Don't be discouraged. Chances are you won't be attracted to 99.9% of the people you meet this way. But that will also be true of singles you meet other ways. This is more efficient, however, since people are already preselected. They're singles who want to meet someone—just like you.

What You Need to Know Before Getting Married

When deciding to marry, people expect their feelings to be *completely* clear, *completely* unambiguous. *I don't really love him/her enough to marry him/her,* is a common statement.

Dagmar O'Connor, a well-known psychologist and sex therapist, dispels some of the confusion about how much you should love in order to marry.

What is the biggest mistake that people make in choosing a marriage partner?

The choice of a mate is usually based on early parental influences. *Problem:* Many of us grew up in dysfunctional homes where parents impeded rather than enhanced children's emotional growth, or treated each other with such disrespect and unkindness that they created a negative role model for adult love relationships. People raised in such environments often develop feelings of sexual attraction toward people who resemble their parents.

Example: A woman whose father verbally or physically abused her may only be attracted to abusive men. In a room full of wonderful men, she will have an attraction for the "wrong" man.

Lesson: Whom we love and how much we love them is determined by our early experiences of love interactions with our parents and siblings. If you don't love someone enough to want to marry them, listen to your feelings. If you *never* feel like committing to anybody, it may be useful to investigate your childhood through therapy.

One common reason for rejecting marriage is not feeling turned on by a partner. Yet physical attraction can also be a sign of these old dysfunctional influences and you must therefore evaluate its importance carefully.

Sexual attraction should only be a part of the package along with friendship. If the attraction isn't strong in the beginning, but the other elements are there, sexual feelings may develop as the emotional intimacy deepens, unless you have learned in childhood to separate love from sex.

Some couples who hate each other and wind up divorced have good sex all the way through their marriage—and even after the divorce. Their problem is that sex becomes a substitute for emotional intimacy.

What should you look for in a marriage partner?

A companion. Not a parent figure to fill needs that were not met in childhood. Use friends or therapists to meet those needs. For the emotionally mature person, the criteria for love are that you enjoy being with the person...you feel comfortable with him/her...and you can totally trust him. Look for qualities you'd want in a friend: Honesty, generosity, integrity, sense of humor, similar values, sensitivity and similar interests.

Why is companionship so difficult to maintain in a marriage?

Because 90% of being "in love" is the feeling that you've finally found the parent you didn't have as a child. Then if your mate refuses to act like your parental fantasy, you get furious.

Companions accept each other as separate individuals with often conflicting needs. They don't demand unconditional love or approval.

Example: When Mary has a hard day at work, she expects her husband, Joe, to be comforting and sympathetic. But sometimes Joe is too exhausted from his own day and just wants to be left alone. Mary goes into a rage and accuses him of not caring about her. If she viewed Joe as a companion rather than as a parent, she would back off, recognizing his need to be alone, and take care of her own needs by calling a friend.

It's important for couples to listen to each other, instead of each partner defending his own innocence so vehemently that the other partner's message is drowned out.

What are good reasons for rejecting someone you might marry?

If you have any reason to believe that you cannot trust this person...or if you suspect the person has destructive habits he's not willing to change.

Examples: Someone who has a problem with drugs or alcohol, is unfaithful, lies to you or has hit you a few times—even though he has promised never to do it again.

Also: Don't marry someone because of "potential." You need to accept someone the way he is. If you marry someone with potential, the person is a fantasy in your own head and the reality is bound to disappoint you.

A prospective mate might be a perfectly nice person, but have a quality you just don't think you can live with.

Example: A successful female executive dates a sweet, generous fellow who totally lacks ambition. But, she doesn't think she could accept that over the long run.

What should people who are considering a serious commitment look at in themselves?

Background patterns. Is this the first person you feel you don't love enough to commit to, or have there been several others? If so, delve deeper and investigate your difficulty loving or committing to anybody.

Trap: If you have a pattern of getting into uncomfortable or abusive relationships and you're with someone who is loving, you may find this person boring. It's important to work out your own attraction to "excitement." Excitement can at times be a way to avoid your underlying feelings.

Helpful: Ask yourself, *Who in my family does this person resemble? How does that make me feel?*

Bottom line: Any time that you feel like rejecting someone or protecting yourself, it's because your unconscious computer is talking to you. No matter what the underlying reasons are, it's important to respect that.

I don't believe that you should go against your instincts. But discovering where they are coming from can help you to make healthier decisions about your love relationships.

The most important component of a healthy love relationship is self-knowledge. Before you can decide wisely about marriage, you must learn about yourself as an individual and strive to understand your feelings.

How do you learn to trust your judgment about the opposite sex?

You make mistakes and learn from them. People who are too afraid of making mistakes don't learn much about life.

Nowadays, divorce, premarital sex and living together are permitted, so we're allowed to learn and profit from mistakes about love relationships.

Many people, unfortunately, do not learn. As a therapist, I see people who have had three or four marriages and they marry the same type of person each time—making exactly the same mistakes. They don't realize that they can only change themselves—not their partner.

What should you do if you're unsure of your decision?

I think premarital counseling is an excellent idea.

Source: Dagmar O'Connor, PhD, author of *How to Make Love to the Same Person for the Rest of Your Life and Still Love It,* Bantam Books, 666 Fifth Ave., New York 10103. She is in private practice in New York City.

Secrets of Much, Much Better Male/Female Communications

During a conversation in their car, a woman asked her husband, *Would you like to stop for ice cream?* Her husband answered, truthfully, *No,* and they kept on driving.

Later on, the man was frustrated when he realized his wife was annoyed...because she had wanted to stop. *Why didn't you say what you wanted?* he asked. *Why do you play these games with me?*

In fact, each spouse had misread the other. The wife had incorrectly taken the husband's *no* as a non-negotiable position. The husband had misconstrued his wife's questions as a request for information, rather than the start of a discussion about what *both* would like.

What's going on...

This kind of misunderstanding stems from the fundamentally different ways in which men and women speak.

Men generally engage the world as individual competitors within hierarchies of power and accomplishment. They are either one-up or one-down. Their conversations are aimed at achieving status and keeping the upper hand, as part of their struggle to preserve independence and avoid failure.

Women approach the world as individuals within a network of connections. In this world, conversations are negotiations for closeness—tools to preserve intimacy and avoid isolation.

Note: I'm not suggesting that women care nothing about status, or that men are indifferent to intimacy, but they are focused on different goals.

Both approaches are equally valid. The problems enter when we pretend that men and women express their thoughts and feelings in the same way. When we don't see the differences, we run into major misunderstanding.

Men and women who understand each other's conversational styles are better able to express themselves...and understand what others are saying.

Differences...

Men and women differ in how they express almost everything. *Examples:*

- Surviving conflict. Childhood studies show that girls attempt to reduce verbal conflict and preserve harmony among peers by compromise and consensus. Boys use appeals to rules and threats of physical violence. Boys' conflicts also tend to be more prolonged—and are often devices to create greater closeness after the argument is over.
- Coping with problems. Women often talk about problems not as a way of finding solutions, but to seek understanding and sympathy. Since men don't talk about problems unless they want advice, they're likely to frustrate women by offering advice instead of understanding.
- Asking questions. Women show concern by responding to a friend's troubles with pertinent questions. Men are more likely to change the subject out of respect for the other's need for independence. *Male assumption:* Extended discussion of a problem would make it seem more serious—and make the other man feel worse.
- Making confessions. Women are more willing to reveal emotional secrets and weaknesses, because the payoff in intimacy is worth the risk of vulnerability. Men are less likely to take the risk—particularly with other men—out of fear of landing one-down. They are more inclined to barter impersonal news about politics or sports.
- Giving feedback. Women are more inclined to ask questions when listening to someone talk.

They offer small cues like *uh-huh.* A woman who says *yeah* may mean *I'm with you...I follow,* but most men will say *yeah* only if they agree.

Men give fewer signals overall, and are more likely to respond with statements and challenges. Men also listen to women less frequently than women listen to men. *Reason:* Many men are uncomfortable listening because they don't like being passive.

•Making apologies. When women say, *I'm sorry,* it is often to establish a *connection* with the other person, as in *I'm sorry you feel bad about this—I do too.* To many men, *I'm sorry* denotes an apology, an admission of fault. To accept the apology places the accepter as one-up.

•Joking. Men are more likely to store away a set of jokes, which they can use to seize center stage in a group. *Point:* Making others laugh gives you a fleeting power over them. Women are less likely to remember jokes, but are quicker to laugh at them.

•Using body language. When women talk, they look at one another directly, with a steady gaze that supports their connection. Men normally look away from each other. *Reason:* To look directly at another man might suggest hostility—a barrier to friendly connection. A man who looks directly at a woman may imply a different kind of threat—*a flirtation.*

Source: Deborah Tannen, professor of linguistics at Georgetown University. She is the author of *You Just Don't Understand: Women and Men in Conversation,* William Morrow & Co., 105 Madison Ave., New York 10016.

Secrets of Happy Couples

The high rate of divorce, combined with the skyrocketing number of dysfunctional families, suggests that there is no such thing as a truly happy marriage...*but my interviews with couples across the country show otherwise.*

The couples I talked to had been married between seven and 55 years. More than half described themselves as very happily married. Only two or three were actually miserable.

The remaining 35 couples are hanging in there and doing all right.

The happiest couples share a number of characteristics—qualities from which we can learn. And they dispelled several popular misconceptions...

Myth: Be realistic, not idealistic.

Reality: In fact, the most happily married people idealize their spouses. Many of them say they think their husbands or wives are the greatest people in the world. That belief certainly helps bring out the best in their partners. Research has shown that people live up—or down—to our expectations.

Even after the "crazy-in-love" phase has long passed, the happy partners continue to see each other through rose-colored glasses—often more positively than others might see them.

Myth: Happy couples rarely fight.

Reality: Of course, happy couples fight—some more often than others. But happy couples fight by the rules and are able to keep conflicts from escalating.

The rules differ depending on the temperaments of the people involved. Some couples say, "We never go to bed angry." They insist on resolving issues rather than walking away from them.

Happy couples have impulse control. They are willing and able to censor themselves, even in the midst of rage, so as not to say or do the thing that would be "fatal" to the relationship.

Myth: There's no such thing as love at first sight.

Reality: Some romances blossomed slowly. But there were also many who remembered feeling a powerful attraction at their first meeting...and who are still in love with each other years later. There were also cases in which one partner fell in love immediately, while the other partner took longer to come around.

Myth: Friendship, not sex, is the key to a long-lasting relationship.

Reality: Both sex and friendship are important.

While the happiest husbands and wives say they are each other's best friends, they also have very strong sexual bonds. True, the intense infatuation—being ready to jump into bed at any opportunity—fades after a few years. But the sexual chemistry remains, even during periods when a couple isn't making love.

Example: One wife was so exhausted after having a baby that she temporarily lost interest in sex. Nevertheless, she continued to have vivid sexual dreams about her husband.

Myth: Happy couples have independent lives.

Reality: Even if they don't share all the same interests, happy couples spend a lot of time together.

This is another characteristic that has to do with temperament—some couples require less togetherness than others. But the idea that separate identities are essential is completely untrue. These couples have definitely found a shared identity. Over time, they stopped feeling *single at heart* and came to be *married at heart*. If that process doesn't happen, the marriage is in trouble.

Myth: The happiest couples raise children together.

Reality: The few childless couples I interviewed are quite happy. What seemed to be important is not whether or not a couple has children, but whether they agree that children should or should not be part of their lives together.

In fact, children are the subject couples fight about most often—more than sex, money or in-laws. Children can disrupt the unity of a couple, introducing an element of separation and continuous potential conflict.

That doesn't mean that children damage a relationship—far from it. But raising children is very difficult, with a lot to disagree about. Happy couples who are parents face and grapple with these conflicts and learn from each other.

Example: One husband was a severe disciplinarian, while his wife was very gentle with the children. This difference caused an ongoing disagreement between them. Eventually, he realized that she was able to get exactly the response she wanted from the children *without* screaming or yelling...and he began to temper his own approach.

Why couples get along...

"For a marriage to be happy, the partners need to be identical in background but opposite in personality,"one woman said.

I saw this truth borne out over and over again. If a couple shares the same background (age, religion, ethnicity, economic status), they are more likely to agree on many of the day-to-day decisions, such as how to raise the children, what vacations to take, what colors to use when decorating the house, etc.

Having opposite personalities is what provides the spark. I saw many couples in which one partner was somewhat depressive and pessimistic and the other was optimistic. They seemed to balance or compensate for each other.

I'm not suggesting that people with different backgrounds can't have good marriages. But shared reference points do make marriages work better.

Source: Catherine Johnson, PhD, author of *Lucky in Love: The Secrets of Happy Couples and How Their Marriages Thrive.* Viking Penguin, New York.

How to Improve the Quality of Time You Spend with Your Mate

Married couples today spend so much time apart that the little time spent together loses the richness it once had. They forget that the quality of time spent together is just as important as the quality in everything else.

Traps that can lower the quality of time together and what to do about them:

• Limiting conversation to terse exchanges of information. *Instead:* Speak in a way that conveys interest, involvement, a sense of love.

• Displaying affection only during full-fledged sexual interludes. *Instead:* Learn to appreciate a little physical contact, especially during very hectic or stressful periods. Don't be hesitant to touch...while shopping together,for instance, or while you're working around the house. It's important to let one another know you like each other.

• Choosing recreational activities that might prove stressful or draining, especially when work demands are heavy. *Instead:* Choose less taxing forms of entertainment at these times.

For example, watch a football game on television instead of going to a crowded, cold, noisy stadium. Talk about the game and how you feel while watching it. Take advantage of the relaxed and familiar home environment. Fix a small drink...put your arm around your spouse.

•Looking on nonwork time as a void that must be filled with more work. *Instead:* Plan and share activities from which both can benefit...redecorate a room, take tennis lessons, cook a meal together, work in the garden.

•Being afraid to talk about your deepest desires and feelings. *Instead:* Verbalize aspects of your personality that aren't apparent in daily living. Sharing sexual fantasies, for example, can be both a means of communication and a way of revitalizing a relationship.

Source: Anthony Pietropinto, MD, supervising psychiatrist, Manhattan Psychiatric Center, New York.

Successful Marrying And Remarrying

Today, with the statistical probability that two out of every three marriages will end in divorce, couples who marry or remarry need all the help they can get.

Here is some advice for a good start:

•Choose the right person for the right reasons. Too often, people make the wrong choice because they have needs they don't admit even to themselves. They know what they want, but even though the person they plan to marry doesn't fill the bill, they think he/she will change.

•Have realistic expectations about the marriage. Another person can do only so much for you. No one person can fill every need. It is important for both partners to develop their own lives and interests and not depend solely on each other.

•Learn to communicate. Get issues out on the table and talk about them. Try to reach conclusions regarding conflicts rather than let them stay unresolved.

•Respect the other person's style of communication. People express affection in different ways. Instead of expecting a spouse to react as you do, try to be sensitive to what he or she is telling you in his/her own way.

•Respect the other person's feelings about space and distance. Many people have difficulty understanding someone else's needs for privacy and time alone. Conflicts about space needs can be resolved by trial and error—and patience.

•Create a new lifestyle. Each partner comes with different concepts about customs, handling money, vacations, etc. One may be used to making a big thing about celebrating holidays and birthdays, the other, not. Combine the best elements to get a richer blend that is distinctly your own.

Source: Barbara C. Freedman, CSW, director of the Divorce and Remarriage Counseling Center, New York.

The Fine Art of Touching

Touching and being touched can solve many of our problems. You can increase your sense of general well-being and rejuvenate your relationship by learning the language of touch. *Here's how a couple should get started:*

•Have sessions in which they alternate touching each other without sexual intercourse.

•Each partner gets to initiate sessions...and to be both passive and active.

•Learn to be selfish and communicate what you like—eventually developing a nonverbal language of touch.

Helpful suggestions...

•Don't insist on separating sex and affection. Women complain that when they just want to be affectionate the man will turn it into foreplay. *Problem:* We fail to see affection and sex as a continuum. We're too used to turning ourselves off during affectionate moments because we had to as children when we kissed and hugged our parents. And now we have to as parents with our own children. But you should remember that the affectionate hug or kiss with your spouse is exactly the same physical act that turns you on during sex.

•Communicate with your body. If you can't say "I love you" with your body, there's a whole dimension lacking in your relationship. How you express yourself is an individual matter.

•Sleep in the nude to create a sense of intimacy.

•Be flexible...in terms of touch, body contacts, positions...and where you touch each other in the house.

•Don't make it a power struggle. People who have trouble touching each other often toss accusations back and forth, such as "I always touch you—how come you never touch me?" The one who's having trouble gets more resistant because he or she feels forced. *Solution:* Take it in small steps. Keep touching your partner for your own gratification, no matter what the response. Eventually your partner will stop feeling threatened and reciprocate of his or her own accord.

•Don't forget about usually untouched areas. If I don't tell my clients to touch heads and feet, they'll forget about them. Licking toes and massaging feet can be very sensual.

Source: Dagmar O'Connor, author of *How to Make Love to the Same Person for the Rest of Your Life—and Still Love It,* Doubleday & Co., Garden City, NY. Ms. O'Connor is director of the sexual therapy program at St. Luke's-Roosevelt Hospital Center in New York City.

Therapeutic Separation

Living apart temporarily can help couples on the verge of divorce resolve their differences. Most couples who try living apart temporarily remain married—and eventually resume cohabitation.

How to do it:

•Both spouses must be committed to using the time apart to work through their differences.

•During separation, keep a diary of experiences and insights.

Source: Dr. Norman Paul, psychiatrist, Lexington, MA.

Will This Marriage Survive?

Five premarital indicators that marriage will last:

•Economic stability. Neither spouse should feel they are making a great financial sacrifice or will have to overwork to maintain an unrealistically high standard of living.

•Maturity. Spouses should be able to minimize selfishness and practice selflessness comfortably.

•Commitment. A committed pair will be more able to compromise.

•Compatibility. A couple must like to do things together, enjoying each other's company.

•Parent success. Spouses who come from happy families with stable marriages have a better shot.

Source: Dr. John Curtis, Valdosta State College.

All About Adultery

Although many species of animals are monogamous...just like many human beings, they also cheat on the side—according to the latest studies from all over the US.

Helen Fisher, PhD, a leading anthropologist and expert on human sexual behavior, tells us more about why adultery is so common in so much of the animal world...

What exactly is monogamy?

It basically means one person has one spouse ...but it doesn't mean that the person has just one sex partner.

Forming pair bonds and raising children as man and wife is a hallmark of the human species, as much as language is. But we also follow the laws of nature. And the conflicting drives to form pair bonds and be adulterous is built into both animal and human nature.

Example: A male and female beaver form a pair bond and build their dam and lodge and create their territory, just the way we create our home and maintain our lawn. But naturalists have seen male beavers slip out of their lodges at night and into a neighboring female's lodge. It's the same among some birds, like chickadees, ducks and other creatures.

Is polygamy an answer?

Polygamy has been a custom in many societies...but that arrangement doesn't work, either. Co-wives fight, husbands show favoritism and the divorce rate is extremely high.

There are polygamous animals, such as horses, where one male travels with a harem of females. I would suspect that there's no jealousy in a harem-building species. But we're not a harem-building species. For the past four million years we've been monogamous.

This is why open marriages and communes have never worked. Within a few months after joining the commune, a man and a woman fall in love and want to be exclusive. It's natural.

Are men more likely to commit adultery than women?

No. In societies without a double standard, women avail themselves of extramarital sex just as often as men do.

We believe that men are more sexual than women, so our polls bear out that belief. Men like to brag about sex, women deny it. But in fact, the most recent polls show that women are just as adulterous as men are.

I wouldn't be surprised to see that in a society where women controlled the money and the power they were more adulterous than men. It's the sex that needs the other sex more that puts all its eggs in one basket.

Is adultery more acceptable now than at other times in history?

Polls say no, but the consequences today are nowhere near as harsh as they used to be. We haven't changed our negative opinion about adultery, but you're not put to death for it anymore or forced to wear the letter "A" branded on your head. Women today don't lose alimony or custody of their kids because of adultery.

We're much more relaxed about it and will probably become even more relaxed as women become less and less dependent on men economically.

Why do some people have a drive to cheat?

There are all kinds of psychological reasons —a desire for more attention, excitement, intimacy or sex—but none of those is the underlying reason.

The real reason dates back to the grasslands of Africa four million years ago where male and female hunter-gatherers formed pair bonds to raise their young.

A man who formed a pair bond with one woman and occasionally had sex with another was likely to have more children. Since the more children a man had the more likely it was that his genes would live on, by being adulterous he increased the number of genes he put into the gene pool. An adulterous ancestral man survived and passed to modern man whatever it is in the male spirit that makes men pursue extramarital affairs.

A woman, on the other hand, can't have more than one child every nine months. So it might seem as if she wouldn't have a motive for adultery. But adulterous women also had a slight reproductive edge.

If an ancestral woman took a husband and sneaked around on the side, she got extra food and extra protection. If her husband died or was injured, her lover could step in and help her raise her children. Or if she ended up with a husband with, say, lousy eyesight, she could have a child by a lover who had better genes.

Even though having children is the last thing people have in mind today when they commit adultery, from a Darwinian perspective, what occurs in an adulterer's brain is an old, unconscious pattern that drives us to look for variety.

Does adultery have to cause tremendous social upheaval?

No. That depends mostly on the individual culture.

Examples: According to Eskimo tradition, a woman is at liberty to offer sex to her mate's hunting partner or to a guest in the igloo in order to extend kinship and hospitality. And among the Kurkuru, a group of Amazon Indians, everyone in the village has between four and 12 lovers.

Americans are exquisitely prudish compared with world cultures. In a study of 139 cultures, 39% permit adultery at certain times of the year with certain relatives.

In some cultures, a man is permitted to have sex with his wife's sister, because if his wife ever dies she could legitimately become his wife. Some societies have puberty rituals with nights of sexual license.

If adultery is genetically ingrained, do we really have a choice about committing it?

Absolutely. There is something called the triumph of culture over the human spirit. Since 50% of all people are adulterous, that means 50% are not.

The most important thing the human animal does is reproduce, but we also have thousands of years of people believing in and practicing celibacy. We're genetically programmed for survival, but we will sacrifice ourselves for our country or a cause we believe in. Culture regularly triumphs over biology.

People can decide to be faithful and stick to it. But not always without a struggle. One has to appreciate that struggle and not think it's going to be easy.

Source: Helen Fisher, PhD, research associate, department of anthropology, American Museum of Natural History, New York. She is the author of *The Sex Contract: The Evolution of Human Behavior,* William Morrow, 105 Madison Ave., New York 10016.

Adultery—His and Hers

Men tend to justify their extramarital affairs by citing sexual grounds. More than half consider "sexual deprivation" a good enough reason to stray. *Gender contrast:* Women are more influenced by emotional justifications for a fling ...and 77% said they were swayed by "falling in love."

Source: Shirley Glass, PhD, a psychologist in private practice in Owings Mills, Maryland. Dr. Glass's study of more than 300 married people was published in *Journal of Sex Research,* Box 208, Mount Vernon, Iowa 52314. Quarterly.

Dividing Chores in The Two-Income Family

Family ties are strongest when both husband and wife share household responsibilities as well as contribute to economic needs. According to an ad agency survey of married men:

- 32% of the men shop for food.
- 47% cook for the family.
- 80% take care of children under 12.
- The majority said they directly influence the decisions about which brands of disposable diapers, pet food, bar soap, and toothpaste to buy.

When both spouses work, a fair division of household tasks is crucial. *One good approach:*

- Select the mutually most-hated tasks and hire someone to do as many of them as possible.
- Negotiate the remaining disliked jobs.
- Don't alternate jobs. That only leads to arguments about whose turn it is.
- Schedule quarterly or semiannual review for adjustments and tradeoffs.

Source: Nancy Lee, author of *Targeting the Top,* Doubleday & Co., New York.

How Not to Bring Up Babies

Babies may not be as delicate as many first-time parents think...but they are vulnerable to certain mistakes—some less obvious than others. *Mistakes to avoid:*

- *Mistake:* Being overly fearful of making mistakes. Conscientious adults try to avoid mistakes when interacting with children. But adults should keep this caution from turning into worry. *Reason:* It drains away the joy children bring.

Mistakes in interacting with children are inevitable—but seldom serious.

Examples: Some babies don't get enough to eat because the feeding process is rushed. Other babies get cranky because the process is prolonged. Savvy mothers minimize frustration at feeding time by paying close attention to the child's responses.

Bottom line: Even good parents make mistakes...but they learn from them.

- *Mistake:* Underestimating a baby's mind. Adults often treat babies as if they were more digestive tracts than human beings. But even at a very early age, babies feel and think. They have a very good sense of what's going on from day one.

The big difference is that babies cannot verbalize their thoughts and feelings.

For effective communication: Try to imagine what the baby thinks and how the baby feels, then act accordingly. Not all your assumptions will be on target, of course, but mistakes of this type seldom are harmful.

•*Mistake:* Exposing a baby to danger. Any activity that places a baby at risk of injury should be strictly forbidden. Even minor lapses in judgment—like leaving a baby unattended to answer the phone—can be dangerous.

•*Mistake:* Avoiding baby talk. Many adults intuitively use baby talk when addressing infants and small children. They raise the pitch of their voice, slow the rhythm, adopt a singsong melody and soften consonant sounds.

Example: "Pretty rabbit" becomes "pwitty wabbit."

Such changes are appropriate. *Reason:* Babies respond more enthusiastically to baby talk than to conventional speech.

Using baby talk does not retard the process by which a child learns to talk. Babies learn to talk by imitating speech overheard from adult conversations, not by speaking directly with adults.

•*Mistake:* Going too far when playing games. Adults who love children often go to great lengths just to elicit a smile or a laugh. Bouncing a child on your knee, playing peekaboo, hide-and-seek and games like *I'm going to get you* are great fun for adult and child.

But adults sometimes go too far. Babies—especially young ones—cannot tolerate as much intensity as adults. *Result:* Overstimulation.

Because babies cannot tell adults to tone it down a little, they resort to the only options open to them—turning away from the source of stimulation or wailing.

If a baby bursts out crying or turns away from you, take a breather. Try again later if you like, but at a lower intensity.

•*Mistake:* Feeding inappropriate foods. A toddler who can eat a cracker with no trouble can choke on a peanut. And even small quantities of alcohol can be fatal. It's shocking that so many parents allow children to sip an alcoholic drink.

•*Mistake:* Being too rigid in scheduling eating and sleeping. During the first two months of a child's life, parents should concentrate on getting the baby to eat and gain weight and to establish a regular sleep schedule.

Child-care experts often recommend feedings every four hours. Such a guideline makes sense in general terms, but individual babies are highly variable—it does not pay to be too rigid.

If a baby seems to prefer a three-hour schedule, stick to that. If a baby thrives with only one feeding every five or six hours, that's fine, too.

Similarly, experts often say that children should be able to go to sleep on their own by the age of six months. But if your six-month-old needs to be stroked or sung to sleep, so be it.

•*Mistake:* Misreading motives. Adults occasionally cause needless trouble by ascribing to children incorrect motives or emotions.

Example: Babies and young children (especially two-year-olds) are remarkably curious about their environments. They explore everything around them, including eyes, ears, noses and hair. Adults sometimes perceive such explorations as aggression and presume that the child is hostile. They may yell at or slap the child. But odds are, the child is just being curious.

Be careful when ascribing hostility or any other negative emotions to a small child—you're probably missing the mark.

•*Mistake:* Being inconsistent. The goal of discipline is to set limits to a child's behavior. Parents do this in different ways.

Some set absolute limits and mete out harsh punishment for even minor transgressions. Others adopt a relaxed approach, in which most constraints on behavior are subject to negotiation.

Children can flourish under either system, but only if parents are consistent.

Example: Spanking a child for one acting out episode and then simply discussing another similar episode only confuses the child.

Children need to know the rules.

•*Mistake:* Forcing eye contact. Adults should respect a baby's desire not only to establish, but also to break eye contact.

Breaking eye contact is the baby's way of saying, "I am overstimulated or bored." Trying to force eye contact on a child who does not want it is inappropriate.

•*Mistake:* Not keeping up with a baby's development. Babies outgrow activities and shift their interests very rapidly. Games and other modes of interaction that work well at one stage in the baby's development are inappropriate as little as one week later.

Bottom line: Always be flexible in your dealings with babies and small children.

Source: Daniel N. Stern, MD, professor of psychology at the University of Geneva and adjunct professor of psychiatry at Cornell University Medical Center, 525 E. 68 St., New York 10021. He is the author of several books on infants, most recently, *Diary of a Baby,* Basic Books, 10 E. 53 St., New York 10022.

New Parent Trap

New parents often lose support from friends and coworkers—simply because those new parents are too exhausted to maintain social ties. Mothers, who often have more friends than fathers, find it difficult to stay in touch—especially with friends from work, whom they do not see if they stay home with a baby. Fathers often work longer hours or take on extra jobs to make ends meet—and therefore have less time for friends. *Helpful:* Some investment outward —as well as inward on the new baby.

Source: *When Partners Become Parents* by University of California at Berkeley psychologists Carolyn Pape Cowan, PhD, and Philip Cowan, PhD. Basic Books, 10 E. 53 St., New York 10022.

Family Disagreements Don't Have to Be Disagreeable

Although friends, lovers—even spouses—all come and go, the families we grew up with are always with us. There is no escaping them.

Even if they live thousands of miles away or are all dead, our families are part of who we are, how we live and how we view ourselves.

Our families can be a source of extreme stress. Just because we're related doesn't mean we'll automatically get along. Unfortunately, the opposite usually applies.

Keys to family harmony...

•Plan your communications. Many people drop verbal bombs on their families, and then let their spontaneous reactions get out of hand.

Better: Make announcements at carefully chosen times. And avoid making generalizations such as *You always*...or *You never.* Stay in touch by letter and phone.

•Adjust your expectations. We expect more from family members than from others in our lives. Many people try to get their families to live up to an unrealistic TV image of domestic bliss.

Better: Instead of hoping family members will change, change the way *you* relate to them.

•Tolerate...but don't endorse. It's not necessary to like or approve of everything your relatives do. You can love them anyway.

Better: Grit your teeth and tell yourself, *Their behavior is no reflection on me.*

•Adopt a surrogate family. No matter how much we'd like them to, family members can't satisfy all our needs. Developing relationships with friends to fill the gaps will make family conflicts less important.

Examples: If your mother keeps trying to run your life, make friends with an older woman who accepts your choices. If your siblings belittle your success at work, find friends who cheer you on.

•Laugh. Much of the family chaos that drives you crazy would actually seem funny if it were happening to someone else.

Better: Pretend the incident is happening in a different family and laugh about it. You'll be more relaxed in the midst of tension—and better able to appreciate your relatives' diversity.

Cast of characters...

In all families, different members play certain roles. When you understand what those roles are, you can start to change the way they affect you...and assume some control over your reactions.

Roles aren't static—they often alternate, depending on which branch or member of the family you're dealing with. *Common family roles:*

• Dictator. Usually a parent or grandparent, this person needs to be in charge and tries to call the shots in everyone's life. Other family members live in fear of the dictator and walk on eggshells trying to please.

Most dictators are highly competent and like to see things done right. They also don't know of any other way to relate to people. They get away with their behavior because the rest of the family is too scared to stand up to them.

To deal with a dictator: Stop being a victim. Remember that you're no longer dependent on this person for survival, and set boundaries. Say *no* when necessary—politely but firmly. You'll hit major resistance at first, but if you hold your ground, eventually you'll be treated with more respect.

• Pot-stirrer. Like the dictator, the pot-stirrer loves to be at the center of attention. But unlike the dictator, he/she won't admit it.

Pot-stirrers call themselves *good communicators,* when what they're really doing is making trouble between family members by carrying gossip and inciting conflicts.

To deal with a pot-stirrer: Identify the person who's always the bringer of bad tidings. Recognize the behavior for what it is—a bid for power, not an attempt at bridge-building. Refuse to play along. Without losing your temper, say, *I don't think that's any of my business, and I don't think you should be passing this information around.* Then back off.

• Butterfly. Charming but irresponsible, the butterfly makes promises and never keeps them ...offers help but fails to deliver...disappears whenever a crisis arises.

Butterflies can't cope with real life. They want to be liked, so they agree to everything, but can't follow through because of their fears.

To deal with a butterfly: Admit to yourself that you can't count on this person. Enjoy the butterfly for what he can offer and stop expecting things he'll never be able to give.

• Free spirit. Operating under a very solid sense of values, free spirits are very secure in themselves and are not subject to feeling guilt. They balance loyalty to the family with loyalty to themselves.

To deal with a free spirit: Understand that this person is not going to change and fit into your mold. You may envy the free spirit for having the courage to do what he wants to do—and things that you may want to do as well. Reexamine your expectations for this person—you may have to lower them.

• Diplomat. This person mediates disputes instead of causing them. Always even-tempered, diplomats do the communicating that other family members should be doing themselves.

The payoff is power—the diplomat's skills are very valuable to the family. *Cost:* Burnout. Unlike the first four family types, diplomats don't cause stress to other family members—but are a danger to themselves.

If you're a diplomat: Let others fight their own battles. As hard as it may be to relinquish power, learn to say, *I'll give you my opinion, but you'll have to work it out for yourselves.*

• Scapegoat. In dysfunctional families, this unfortunate member is blamed for everyone else's problems—problems the others aren't willing to deal with themselves.

It's easier to say, *We're poor because it costs so much to send Tommy to school* than, *We're poor because Dad drinks and can't hold a job.*

Scapegoats believe the rap—whenever anything's wrong, they assume it's their fault. Like diplomats, scapegoats are more a danger to themselves than to others.

If you're a scapegoat: Build a surrogate family that accepts you as you are and gives you a lot of positive reinforcement...consider seeing a therapist...get whatever outside help you need to build your self-esteem to the point where you can say, *You're wrong—it's not my fault.*

Proceed with caution...

Change is difficult, and family members will not be happy about your efforts to disrupt old patterns. It's a good idea to warn them—lovingly—that you're going to be handling things differently from now on.

Expect some turmoil, but don't give up—eventually, your family will get used to it. In the meantime, the strength, sanity and self-esteem you regain will be worth the trouble.

Source: Denise Lang, author of *Family Harmony: Coping With Your Challenging Relatives,* Prentice Hall, 15 Columbus Circle, New York 10023.

Rules for Family Fights

Essential: Fighting fair. Every couple must develop its own rules of combat, but the following are generally sound:

•Never go for the jugular. Everyone has at least one soft, defenseless spot. A fair spouse attacks elsewhere.

•Focus on a specific topic. Don't destroy your spouse with a scorched-earth campaign. *Fair:* "I'm angry because you don't make breakfast before I go to the office." *Unfair:* "I'm angry because you're useless, and my mother was right—you're not tall enough, either."

•Don't criticize things that probably can't be changed. A physical blemish or a spouse's limited earning power is not a fair target. On the other hand, it's dangerous to stew in silence if your partner drops dirty socks on the floor or chews with mouth agape. Minor irritations fester.

•Don't leave the house during a fight. You'll be talking to yourself—your own best supporter. *Result:* A self-serving reconstruction of what happened, rather than an objective view of the situation.

•Argue only when sober. Alcohol is fuel for the irrational. Disagreements are beneficial only if you use reason.

•Keep your fights strictly verbal. A fight that turns physical intimidates rather than resolves.

•Don't discuss volatile subjects late at night. It's tempting to sum up your day at 11 o'clock. But everything seems worse when you are tired. And if you start arguing at 11, you'll be still more exhausted the next morning. *Better:* Make a date to go at it when both sides are fresh.

•Always sleep in the same room, no matter how bitter the fight. The bed is a symbol of the marital bond, and it's more difficult to stay angry with a spouse there.

•If you're getting nowhere after a long stretch of quarreling, simply stop. Don't say a word. Your spouse will have great difficulty arguing solo. You can always resume the next day.

•Don't sulk after the real fighting is over. Pride has no place here. The winner of the fight should be the one to initiate the reconciliation.

•Consider outside help. If you never seem to resolve an issue despite both parties' best efforts, use other resources...not necessarily a 10-week course or a formal session with a counselor. You might simply cultivate a couple whose marriage you admire and try to profit by their example.

•Don't give up too easily on either the fight or the relationship. A strong marriage demands risk-taking, including the risk of feeling and showing extreme anger. The intimacy of marriage is won through pain and friction as well as through pleasure.

Source: Kevin and Marilyn Ryan, coauthors of *Making a Marriage,* St. Martin's Press, New York.

How to Pick the Right School for Your Young Child

•Visit each school you're considering. Be wary of schools that try to sell themselves to you over the phone. The good ones will insist you judge their curriculum firsthand.

•Talk with the director and the staff members who will be involved with your child.

•Ask to see the school's license, insurance contract, and health and fire department inspection forms.

•Be sure the school allows only approved persons to pick up your child at the end of the school day. The school should have a strict rule that if someone who is not on the list comes for the child, the parent should be called immediately.

•Check cleanliness and hygiene.

•Review the school's educational goals. The program should be designed to develop social, emotional, intellectual, and physical skills. See the teacher's lesson plans.

•Ask how students are disciplined.

•Observe the other children. Will they be compatible with yours?

•*Ask yourself:* "Could I spend a few years of my life here?"

•If possible, make surprise visits to the school at different times of the day after your child has been enrolled. If you're denied admission to areas you wish to see, be suspicious.

When You Have to Refuse A Family Member

This is the hardest kind of refusal to deal with. You not only need the interpersonal skills to say no gracefully but you also have to rethink your real obligations to your family, so you can say no without guilt. *Suggestions:*

•Resist the hidden-bargain syndrome. Parents often operate under the assumption that since they've done all these wonderful things for their children to bring them up, the offspring owe them everything. Both young and grown children can be manipulated by this assumption. *Remedy:* Recognize that parents do nice things at least as much for their own benefit as for their children's sake.

•Recognize that a family member who acts hurt at a turndown—when it's for a legitimate reason—is torturing himself. You're not responsible for other people's reactions.

•Don't sit on guilt. As soon as you feel it, share it. Guilt pushers know better than anyone how awful it is to feel guilty. Frequently, just pointing out a guilt manipulation makes the other person back off. Once that's done, you're free to sit down and honestly discuss how making another person feel guilty hurts a relationship.

•Learn to say no to your children. Parents, more than anything, want their children to like them. But children need structure and limits in order to learn self-discipline and independence. Remind yourself that you are teaching him how to grow up rather than remain a perennial emotional infant.

Source: Barry Lubetkin, PhD, Institute for Behavior Therapy, New York.

What Makes So Many Siblings So Very Different

Any parent of more than one child—or anyone who has brothers and sisters—knows how different siblings can be.

Sometimes it's hard to believe that they come from the same family. Yet they share most of the same genes, as well as the same homes...and, of course, parents.

Judy Dunn, PhD, an expert who has studied the interactions between family members, tells us what accounts for the differences...

How is your view of child development different from the traditional approach?

Most theories about how families work assume that parents' behavior affects everybody in the family the same way. If this were true, you'd expect siblings from the same family to turn out quite similar to each other.

Yet our data show that for most psychological characteristics, the differences between siblings far exceed the similarities—and any parent will tell you the same thing.

Since Freud's day, psychologists looking at the effects of parental attitudes on children have made their comparisons *between* families. We're saying it's much more relevant to compare experiences of children within the same family.

What are some of the differences?

Kids from the same family vary widely in personality and emotional adjustment—their self-esteem, their tendency to be anxious or easygoing, the way they deal with crises.

Some children sail through unexpected events that hit the whole family, such as unemployment or their parents' divorcing, while others are badly thrown by the same events.

We do find similarities in moral, political and religious beliefs among people who have grown up together. I'm not sure why—it may be that those issues are more intellectual and less influenced by emotional dynamics.

How do kids experience the same family environment differently?

Despite our good intentions, parents tend to treat different children in different ways...in the degree of warmth and affection they show their kids, in their responsiveness, in the disciplinary measures they use.

That in itself is not so surprising when you consider not only children's inborn personality differences but also their ages—you wouldn't expect a mother to behave toward a two-year-old the same way she behaves toward a six-year-old.

In fact, parents' behavior toward children *based on age* is fairly consistent—a mother is likely to behave similarly toward a younger child at two as she did when the older child was that same age.

Some mothers absolutely love babies, and by the time the first child has turned into a contrary preschooler she'll be irritable with the child ...but very affectionate toward the new baby.

Another mother may find babies a bore and become much more responsive when her child is learning to talk.

What hasn't been acknowledged is that children as young as a year old are monitoring these differences, with extraordinary sensitivity.

Children are particularly sensitive to differences in how they're treated by their fathers. Fathers are seen as very special because the amount of time and attention they have for kids is often small. When daddy comes home from work, the children really notice who it is he relates to.

Key: We're learning that what matters to children isn't so much how well they're loved in a general sense, but how loved they are in relation to their brothers and sisters.

Couldn't some of the differences be explained by heredity?

That's one of the intriguing questions. Some personality differences appear very early in children and probably have a great deal to do with heredity.

At the same time, inborn traits may elicit different treatment from parents—a mother may find it easier to relate to an outgoing child than a shy one, or to a docile child rather than one who's always getting into trouble. We almost always find that any variation explained by heredity is magnified by the different family experience of each child.

Is this only true of early childhood?

I think it's a continuing story. The oldest children we've studied have reached early adolescence, and the findings still hold true for them.

The *kinds* of differences that matter to children may change with age.

It's also possible that peer relationships gradually become more important to adolescents than sibling relationships.

How do the interactions between the children in a family affect their development?

Siblings, of course, do have an effect on each other.

For instance, although more research needs to be done, in some families children appear more likely to develop especially well in those areas in which a sibling does *not* shine.

And if two very smart kids are growing up together, the one who thinks he is less intelligent will have lower self-esteem—even though he is very bright compared with children in other families.

What about the influence of birth order?

There's a great deal of folk wisdom about birth order.

Most people believe very strongly that first-borns are more neurotic, responsible, eager to succeed, dependent on parental approval...that

*Do this before going on to read the scoring section that follows.

youngest children are easygoing...that middle children are mediators.

Over the past five years, however, researchers have examined this issue extremely carefully, using very large samples. And they've found that birth order doesn't explain *any* of the personality differences previously thought.

Differences that used to be attributed to birth order may actually have more to do with family size, and the fact that larger families tend to be from lower educational and socio-economic levels.

What can parents do?

Unfortunately, there's no cut-and-dried rule for parents. You want to treat each child equally, yet kids of different ages have different needs.

It's important to keep an eye open for the vulnerable child—the one more likely to be shattered by a family crisis—so you can help to buffer the blow.

Key: Be aware of how closely children are picking up on any kind of competition, and try to avoid preferential treatment, while also appreciating the differences between your kids.

Making sure each child feels loved is more important than trying to figure out the rules of parenting.

Source: Judy Dunn, PhD, distinguished professor of human development at Pennsylvania State University in State College. She is the coauthor of *Separate Lives: Why Siblings are So Different,* Basic Books, 10 E. 53 St., New York 10022.

When Siblings Fight

Squabbles between siblings are inevitable. Parents can't prevent them, but they can play a constructive role.

• Ignore normal bickering. Your children will become more ingenious about settling their own disagreements.

• Avoid acting as a referee any more than you absolutely have to.

• Don't try to get to the bottom of things to affix blame. In most cases you'll never reach the unbiased "truth," anyway.

• Don't dwell on past misbehavior.

• Don't allow children to play you against your spouse. Back up each other.

• Avoid situations that are bound to cause problems. *Example:* A competitive game between a demanding eight-year-old and a six-year-old who can't stand losing.

• Help your children find varied outlets for emotions.

• Encourage children to work out their own solutions...unless the two in question are ill-matched to do so.

Source: *Raising Good Kids: A Developmental Approach to Discipline* by Louise Bates Ames, PhD, a founding member of the Gesell Institute of Human Development.

Dealing with Sibling Rivalry

• Don't blame yourself. Much sibling rivalry is unavoidable. There's no way you can blame a mother for an intense relationship with her firstborn child.

• Try to minimize a drop in attention to the first child. This change in attention is dramatic —not just because the mother is occupied with the new baby, but because she is often too tired to give the older child the kind of sensitive, playful focus he or she received in the past. (A month after a new baby was born, half the mothers in a recent study were still getting less than five hours' sleep a night.) *Helpful:* Get as much help as possible from the father, grandparents and other relatives and friends.

• Quarreling between siblings increases when the parents are under stress. Anything that alleviates marital stress will also quiet sibling rivalries.

• Keep things stable. A child's life is turned upside down when a new baby arrives. Toddlers of around two and three appreciate a stable, predictable world in which the daily schedule of events—meals, naps, outings—can be counted on. In families where the mother tries to keep the older child's life as unchanged as possible, there is less disturbance.

• Involve the older child in caring for the baby. In families where the mother draws the older child in as a helper for the new baby, there is less hostility a year later.

•Offer distractions to the older child. An older child gets demanding the moment the mother starts caring exclusively for the baby. Mothers who are prepared with projects and helping tasks head off confrontations.

•Recognize and avoid favoritism. Studies show that mothers intervene three times as much on behalf of a second child, although the second is equally likely to have been the cause of the quarrel. The first child's feeling that parents favor the second is often well-founded. Older siblings tend to hold back because they know their aggression is disapproved of, while younger ones often physically attack brothers and sisters because they feel they can get away with it.

•Be firm in consistently prohibiting physical violence. In the context of a warm, affectionate relationship, this is the most effective way to minimize sibling rivalry and to keep jealousies in check.

•Try to keep your sense of humor and your perspective when a new baby is born. Things will get better sooner than you think.

Source: Judy Dunn, author, *Siblings: Love, Envy & Understanding,* Harvard University Press, Cambridge, MA.

Understanding Sibling Rivalry

There are patterns in families that may help parents better understand how sibling rivalry is triggered.

•Where there is an intense, close relationship between the mother and a first-born daughter, the girl is usually hostile to a new baby. A year later, the children are likely to be hostile to each other.

•Firstborn boys are more likely than girls to become withdrawn after a new baby's birth. Children who withdraw (both boys and girls) are less likely to show positive interest in, and affection for, the baby.

•In families where there is a high level of confrontation between the mother and the first child before the birth of a sibling, the first child is more likely to behave in an irritating or interfering way toward the new baby.

•Where the first child has a close relationship with the father, there seems to be less hostility toward the new baby.

•A child whose parents prepare him for the birth of a new baby with explanations and reassurances does not necessarily react any better than a child who wasn't prepared. *More important:* How the parents act after the new baby is born.

•Inside the family, girls are just as physically aggressive as boys.

•Physical punishment of children by parents leads to an increase in violence between children.

•Breastfeeding the new baby can have a beneficial effect on firstborns. *Reason:* Mothers who breastfeed tend to find distractions for the older child during feeding. This turns a potentially provocative time into a loving situation where the first child is also cuddled up with the mother, getting special attention while the baby is being fed.

Source: Judy Dunn, author, *Siblings: Love, Envy & Understanding,* Harvard University Press, Cambridge, MA.

How to Build a Personal Support System

Individuals need not only a few intimate friends but also a network of friendly relationships that make anyone more effective. *To build a support system:*

•Join groups: Participate in self-help groups—not so much for the help as for the support, to get a sense of community and belonging.

•Pursue with other people some of the activities you like. A runner can join a running club, a photographer can take a photography course. This way, you weave your interests into a friendship network.

•Reciprocate acts of friendship. If someone waters your plants, you'd better be prepared to do the same for him. Reciprocity—both giving and accepting—is part of keeping any kind of friendship. People who have problems with accepting favors should remember that other people feel good doing things for them.

• Mentor friends. The younger person ordinarily seeks out the older one. However, the older person might do well to encourage such a relationship because there's something in it for him or her, too—a revitalization that comes from dealing with a younger person with ambition, enthusiasm, and a fresh education.

What Nourishes And What Poisons A Friendship

Key nourishing qualities:

• Authenticity. Inauthentic behavior is contrived and false. Authentic behavior is spontaneous and unpremeditated. Being freely and deeply oneself is important to friendship.

• Acceptance. A sound friendship permits the expression of anger, childishness and silliness. It allows us to express the various facets of our personality without fear of harsh judgment. A feeling of being valued promotes our fullest functioning with other people.

• Direct expression. Coaxing, cajoling, dropping "cute" hints, manipulating and beating around the bush are all barriers to clear communications. When people know what they want from each other, they establish clear communication and contact. They're in a position to attempt an agreement regarding their desires. They may also realize they're too different to get along and that they may be less frustrated if their relationship is more casual.

• Empathy. This involves an effort to understand another's beliefs, practices and feelings (not necessarily agreeing with them). Empathy means listening, trying to understand, and communicating this understanding to the speaker.

What poisons friendships:

• Blame. Blame shifts responsibility and also can be a way of avoiding self-examination. The antithesis of blame and defensiveness is to assume responsibility for one's own feelings. If a person is honest enough to admit his mistakes and finds he's forgiven, he can then be tolerant of his friends' foibles.

• Excess dependency. Some people have lost touch with their values and their strength and need other people to lean on. This kind of person feels unable to be alone. In the dependent friendship, growth and development are stifled rather than enhanced.

Source: Dr. Joel D. Block, clinical psychologist and author of *Friendship: How to Give it, How to Get It,* Macmillan, New York.

Making Friendships Stronger

Even the best of friendships can have their ups and downs. *How to minimize this type of stress:*

• To move closer to a friend, take him or her into your confidence. Share your thoughts and feelings. There's no guarantee that this approach will produce positive results, but the probabilities increase dramatically when you give what you want to get.

• Use compromise to resolve differences. The only other alternatives are domination by one and the consequent resentment on the part of the other or withdrawal. Compromise restores the reciprocity needed in friendship.

• Avoid a mismatch. It's foolish to pursue a friendship with someone who isn't interested in you. Friendship involves mutual feelings.

• Observe the Golden Rule. Most of us want the same things in our friendships—honesty, a sharing of good feelings and thoughts, empathy, support, fun. If you're not getting these, ask: *Do I offer the same things to others that I want for myself?*

Source: Dr. Joel D. Block, a clinical psychologist, and author of *Friendship: How to Give It, How to Get It,* Macmillan, New York.

How to Help a Friend Who Has Been A Crime Victim

The *emotional* harm caused by a crime—from a rape to a burglary—is frequently much worse than any physical damage.

Crime victims are 10 times more likely than the average person to become severely depressed—even after a decade or more.

The quality of a crime victim's support system makes a big difference in his/her recovery. *Trap:* Many well-meaning people unknowingly treat crime victims in callous or hurtful ways.

To be truly helpful, friends and family members need to understand what the person is going through.

Emotional aftereffects...

Almost every crime victim experiences rage, anger, fear, anxiety, helplessness, hopelessness, guilt, shame and humiliation—although not necessarily in this order.

Victims deal first with the emotion they can handle best. That's why some people are initially angry while others are fearful and still others are ashamed.

Crime victims feel shame because, as adults, we're supposed to be in control. When something happens that's beyond our control, it makes us feel weak and childlike. This is especially true for men. *Also common:*

- A sense of being permanently damaged. Many rape victims, for instance, may think they'll never be able to enjoy sex again.
- Inability to trust others.
- Loss of belief that the world is just.
- Intrusive, distressing recollections, dreams and flashbacks.
- Distress at exposure to events or places that symbolize or resemble an aspect of the crime.
- Denial. Avoidance of thoughts or feelings connected with the crime.
- Inability to recall an important aspect of the crime. People block out what is painful.
- Diminished ability to enjoy life.
- A sense that he is not going to live very long.
- Being overly cautious and easily startled.

Secondary victimization...

After the crime, most victims go through a *secondary victimization*—often worse than the crime itself—when they have to deal with insensitive family members, police officers, courts, hospitals, insurance agencies, etc.

Sometimes a victim will think he has recovered...only to walk into a situation that reminds him of the crime, and all the terrible memories flood back. If the crime happened in the person's home, office or a place he visits regularly, he may relive it over and over again. The aftereffects can last for years.

Although rapes and other personal attacks are particularly devastating, burglaries, auto thefts and other property crimes frequently cause emotional problems also.

Reason: We have two major barriers in our lives—the walls of our home and our skin. When either is breached we feel violated.

Others make it worse...

Crime victims need to talk about the crime. But after a week or two, friends and family often tune out. *Why:* They feel subconsciously threatened by the idea that this crime could have happened to them.

This leaves the victims isolated and their feelings unresolved. Some think that there is something wrong with them because they can't forget.

Many well-meaning friends and family members inadvertently give victims the message that they were dumb to get victimized. *Typical statements:* "What were you doing out so late at night?" "Why don't you live in a building with a doorman?"

People who do this are trying to reassure themselves that a similar crime could not happen to them—they would never walk down that street or open the door under the same circumstances.

But the victims, reliving the crime, feel ashamed. They try to figure out what they should have done differently.

How to know when victims need help...

Because most victims want to put the crimes behind them as soon as possible, emotional problems may lie dormant for months before they emerge. *Signs of trouble lying dormant:*

•Inability to concentrate. The victim finds it hard to hold a conversation, read, do paperwork ...anything. He feels like he's losing his mind.

•Behavioral changes. These can include avoiding the scene of the crime—work, school, the subway...even being out-of-doors anywhere after dark.

•Increase or decrease in oral habits. These include talking, drinking, smoking, taking drugs, having sex and eating.

•Trouble sleeping. Repeated nightmares or nightsweats are common, as are frequent wakenings.

How to help...

Encourage crime victims to get help *immediately* from a therapist or counselor trained in emotional trauma.* *Warning:* Tremendous damage can be caused by therapists who are not trained in post-traumatic stress disorder—from which crime victims suffer.

Don't tell victims to forget about the crime. Be supportive. Listen. And keep listening. *Helpful response:* "I'm sorry this happened. What can I do for you?"

Try to help in a concrete way. Offer to do the kind of things you would do if someone had a physical injury—take out the garbage, make dinner or stay overnight.

Treat victims as if they were ill or wounded, even if there's no *physical* injury. This is especially important for rape victims. Although you can't see emotional wounds, they're there just the same.

Be willing to confront your own past. Deal with any victimizations you may have encountered.

Example: Many people who have been raped in the past don't want to be with recent rape victims—it brings up bad memories.

People also shy away from victims because they remind them of traumas they've suppressed, like having been abused as a child.

Don't blame crime victims. Help them to stop blaming themselves for being responsible in any way. *Helpful questions:* "Did you mug yourself?" "Did you beat yourself up?" "Did you rob your own home?" "If you could have done it differently, you would have."

**For a referral in your area call:* National Organization for Victim Assistance, 202-232-6682...Crime Victims' Counseling Services, Inc., 718-875-5862...National Victims' Center, 817-877-3355.

Source: Psychotherapist Shelley Neiderbach, PhD, executive director of Crime Victims' Counseling Services, Box 023003, Brooklyn, New York 11202. She is the author of *Invisible Wounds: Crime Victims Speak*, Haworth Publishing Co., 10 Alice St., Binghamton, New York 13904.

What to Do When You Are Caught in the Middle Of Feuding Friends

Being in the middle of arguing friends or spouses is a very difficult position in which to find yourself.

Too often your loyalties are tested, and you're called upon to play the intermediary, act as a sounding board or perform other tough duties that you'd rather avoid.

Consolation: Being in the middle is actually a sign that you're living an interesting life filled with passionate people. *You just have to know how to deal with them.*

Roles to avoid...

•*Don't* play intermediary. Carrying information back and forth makes people feel special. But the message often gets distorted in the translation. And you may wind up the target of both parties' anger.

Just as some ancient Romans killed the bearers of bad news, intermediaries too often wind up being symbolically "killed" by one or both parties who end the friendship.

Example: Janet told Carole that Carole's husband was having an affair. Carole and her husband patched things up and saved their marriage, but Carole no longer speaks to Janet.

•*Don't* offer opinions. Even people who ask what you think don't actually want to know the truth. What they really want is to hear that you support their position.

Better way: When friends ask for your opinion, ask them what they *want* to hear—what do they wish you'd say. Once that's out in the open you can be honest.

• *Don't* be a secret-keeper. Arguing friends often tell a third party things they don't want passed on to the other person. *Purpose:* To win you over to their side. People who tell other people secrets are attempting to control them.

Self-defense: Say you don't want to hear secrets —that it would put you in a compromising position.

Sometimes, however, people get drawn into secret disclosures whether or not they want to hear them. In that case, listen...but keep it to yourself. Although it's tempting to reveal to one side what the other side thinks, *don't do it.* You may wind up losing both friends.

• *Don't* openly take sides. Even people who ask you to take sides secretly want you to remain impartial. *Reason:* If you openly take sides, you strengthen one person's position. This increases the possibility of a breakup—which neither really wants.

Trap: They may hold you responsible if their relationship collapses.

How to be truly helpful if you can't get out of the way...

Help each person reinterpret and relabel what the other's anger is all about.

Example: Lorraine and JoAnn were estranged because JoAnn thought Lorraine expected too much of her. Hurt by the rejection, Lorraine was ready to write the friendship off. Susan helped by telling JoAnn that Lorraine was a needy person who was afraid of being abandoned by her friends. And she helpfully told Lorraine that JoAnn was sensitive about her privacy and didn't want to feel smothered. *Result:* Once they saw how the other felt, the two women were able to save their friendship.

Sometimes a friend who's involved in a long, ongoing argument will insist that you're being disloyal if you don't openly take sides. *What to do:* Take the time—it may stretch on for hours —to have an honest talk about your friendship. *What to discuss:* How and why you became friends...the common elements that keep you together...why your friendship is important.

Such a straight-from-the-heart talk will show your friend that your taking sides in the argument is not crucial to your relationship and that what you have is based on a long history of caring and honesty.

Also convey that if you do take sides, it will only prolong the argument. *Reason:* The more allies they have, the longer people are willing to argue.

It also helps to counsel your friends *how* to argue. You don't need to be a therapist to teach people that it's wrong to *kitchen sink* (throw in every grievance that they've stored up for years) or *zap* (go for someone's weak spots).

What is important: Teaching people how to listen when they argue. *Best:* Encourage them to paraphrase—restate in different words—what the other person has said.

Example: If Elaine is obviously angry, rather than counterattacking, the person she's angry at could say, "I understand that you're angry at me because you think I haven't returned any invitations after you've put yourself out for me...but I'd like you to allow me to explain the reasons for my behavior."

Sometimes a friend in the middle can use a long-standing friendship with each person to remind them that they're letting their emotions run ahead of their intellect. *Also helpful:* Point out to them that most arguments aren't about important issues, they're really about ego and pride, about not wanting to lose face.

Bottom line: Even though it may feel unpleasant at the time, being in the middle of arguing friends can bring out the best in you. It gives you a chance to demonstrate your compassion and loyalty as well as negotiating and mediating skills that you may not even know you have.

And reuniting two people you care about can be quite gratifying.

Source: Psychologist Barry Lubetkin, PhD, director of the Institute for Behavior Therapy, 137 E. 36 St., New York 10016.

How to Enjoy Relationships

• Accept people as they are. Nothing kills a relationship faster than the expectation that you can change someone. It's impossible. The best you can do is to become more tolerant and flexible yourself, encourage an atmosphere for change, and then hope for the best.

• When you give, give freely. If you expect people to give the same back, measured by the cup, you'll always be disappointed. If they respond, that's great. And if they don't, that's all right, too.

• Be honest with the people you care about. Get rid of petty irritants. Don't suffer in silence until you finally explode.

• Honesty needn't be cruel. *Good rule:* Be as tactful with your spouse and children as you are with friends and distant relatives. Most people are wonderful in courtship but later get careless. Love is not a license for rudeness.

• Don't use your family as an alibi when you fall short of goals. Stop underestimating these people. They're much more flexible than most people assume. You can make your dreams real if you want them enough—and share them with the people you love. But if you never say, "Let's go to Nepal!" you'll never get there.

• It's a gamble to be vulnerable. But you never really lose because the risk itself reminds you how richly you are living.

Source: Leo Buscaglia, author of *Loving Each Other,* Holt, Rinehart and Winston, New York.

Terminating a Relationship

In terminating either a business or personal relationship, those who initiate the termination have the upper hand. They also have the bulk of the responsibility.

To walk away from the termination with a sense of moral clarity, it is essential to have made a genuine attempt to come to some degree of accommodation with the other party, whether employee or spouse. Terminators should meet with those terminated to share their dissatisfaction when they are still open to finding a solution.

Terminators should answer these questions:

• What do they need from the other party to continue the relationship?

• What support are they prepared to give the other party?

• What is an acceptable time frame for the changes to be made? A reasonable period should be allowed for making changes and adjustments. Announcing requirements for change on Friday, and then deciding on Monday that the relationship won't work, is unfair.

• What don't the terminators want?

• What aren't they prepared to give?

• How would they describe the consequences if satisfactory changes aren't made? People often resist making major changes not because they fear what's ahead but because they are unwilling to give up what they have. The same fear hinders organizational change as well as change in personal life.

Source: Gisele Richardson, president, Richardson Management Associates, management consultants, Montreal.

Changing an Enemy Into an Ally

If there's someone in your business with whom you're always at odds:

• Think of this person as someone you like, someone who can work with you.

• Create in your mind an image of the relationship restored.

• Treat this person as a valued friend and associate.

• You won't see immediate results, but over time, you'll find that this person is responding to you in a more positive way.

• *The lesson:* Be aware of your expectations of others. People are likely to deliver what you expect them to deliver.

Source: The late Dr. Norman Vincent Peale, author and lecturer, New York.

Better One-on-One Conversations

It's been said before, but the surest way to improve your one-to-one conversations is...to become a better listener. Listening skills may seem simple enough, but many people (particularly men) need to work on them.

•Live in the present moment. Resist distractions. Don't let your mind wander to your bank balance or to after-dinner plans.

•Stay alert and concentrate on what your "partner" is saying—not only the words, but the emotions behind them. Rephrase what you've heard in your own words (mentally or verbally).

•Maintain consistent eye contact.

•Lean toward the person if seated.

•Nod or smile in response.

• *To handle a long-winded anecdote or complaint:* Steer the conversation to a mutually interesting subject. Or...approach the old subject from a new angle.

•When it's your turn to talk, think about the point you want to make before you start speaking.

•Get to the point in as few steps as possible.

•Consider your audience. Make what you're saying relevant to the particular person you're addressing.

•Don't be afraid to ask a "dumb" question about a subject that's new to you.

•If your conversations seem bland, maybe you're suppressing honest disagreements. A dispute shouldn't hurt an exchange (or a friendship), as long as a certain etiquette is respected.

•Give the other person credit for something before you disagree. Never say, "How can you think something like that?" *Better:* "That's a good point, but I see it differently..." or, first point out areas of similarity: "We agree that world peace is vital—therefore..."

Sources: Mark Sherman, associate professor of psychology, and Adelaide Haas, associate professor of communications, State University of New York, New Paltz.

All About Nerds

Nerds get attention by being obnoxious. They don't pay attention to the signals other people send them.

How not to be a nerd:

•Let people finish what they are saying.

•Don't always insist that you know more than other people about the subject under discussion.

•Slow down on advice-giving.

•Open up to new ideas.

•Let yourself change your mind once in a while.

When a nerd starts to realize that much of his behavior stems from anxiety about being accepted and loved, he is well on his way to being a nerd no longer.

Source: Doe Lang, author of *The Secret of Charisma,* Wideview Books, New York.

Three A's for a Lasting Marriage

Attention—listen to your spouse and help him/her when that help is least expected. *Acknowledgment*—do not take your partner for granted. Recognize him for the little things he does to make your life easier. *Appreciation*—thank your spouse for working to make your marriage a success and say you love him for helping make you happy.

Source: Lawrence Grossman, PhD, professor of clinical psychology, Adelphi University, Garden City, New York.

Men, Women and Sex

Men and women want sex for different reasons at different points in their lives. In order to establish his own identity, a young boy separates emotionally from his mother—thus, his early relationships keep women distant. The maturing process enables men to have more loving and connected sex. Young girls are always connected with mother, and therefore, the maturing process for a woman is to learn more "separate," freer sexuality. *As teenagers:* Boys have sex for pure pleasure, while girls often are motivated by affection. *Ages 21 to 35:* Men still yearn for physical pleasure, while love remains the prime motivation for women.

After age 35: Women are now free to seek sexual pleasure, while men are more open to the love and intimacy that comes with sex.

Source: Dagmar O'Connor, PhD, psychologist and sex therapist in private practice in New York. She is author of *How to Make Love to the Same Person for the Rest of Your Life and Still Love It,* a book and video set from Dag Media Corporation, 57 W. 58 St., New York 10019.

Kids and Apologies

Apologize to your child—it's important—if you make a mistake or say something you did not mean. Keep the apology simple—*I'm sorry ...I was feeling cranky.* Kids need to know that adults, including their parents, do get angry... but that anger is not the end of the world.

Source: Nancy Samalin, founder of Parent Guidance Workshops in New York, and author of *Love and Anger: The Parental Dilemma,* Penguin Books, 375 Hudson St., New York 10014.

11

Your Home

Checklist for Move To a New House

•Arrange for the utilities (gas, electric, water, etc.) to be turned on in the new house or apartment a few days before you move in.

•Install the telephone a month before you move (or as early as is feasible).

•Enroll your child in the new local school.

•Open savings and checking accounts promptly at a bank in the new neighborhood.

•Notify companies of change of address (insurance, credit card, magazines, etc.).

•If you are moving to a new state, check to see if your auto coverage is applicable.

•Notify the IRS of the move, both at the time of the move and again when you file your income tax.

•Have pharmaceutical prescriptions renewed before moving so that adequate amounts of medication will be on hand.

•Ask the previous occupant for a list of reliable local service people (electricians, plumbers, carpenters, etc.) and good nearby stores.

•*Moving outdoor plants to a new home:* For a long move, place them in a plastic bag and cover with wet straw or weeds. If you know in autumn you'll be leaving in the spring, use a spade to cut a deep circle around a shrub or young tree to sever the roots and outline the root ball.

Cutting Utility Costs at Home

Most of us turn out the lights when we want to save energy, but there are even smarter ways to reduce your bills...

Refrigerators...

The refrigerator represents about 30% of most electric bills. To find out how well yours operates, open the door and place a dollar bill against the seal. Then close the door. If you can remove the bill easily, the seal needs replacing. Vacuuming the coils behind or below the unit can improve efficiency as well, but be sure to first unplug the refrigerator.

Insulation...

Up to 40% of home heating escapes outdoors unnecessarily because of inadequate insulation. A free energy audit by your local power company will show you how to improve insulation. *Opportunities:* Install more insulation under the roof and behind walls, and weather strip the windows or replace them entirely.

Lighting...

Compact fluorescent bulbs last at least 10 times longer than regular bulbs and use one-fourth of the electricity while producing the same amount of light. Unlike the long fluorescent bulbs found in offices, these screw into ordinary sockets. Some utilities offer compact fluorescents at a discount. Some even give them away.

Water...

Once all leaks are fixed, the largest water-waster is the toilet. At about six gallons per flush, a lot of good water—and dollars—go down the drain. Low-flush toilets only use about 1.6 gallons, but there are other ways to save water without replacing the fixture. *Simple way:* Fill two or three slim plastic bottles with dirt or gravel and place them in the toilet's water tank. This will displace the tank water so that less is used with each flush. Flow-restricters for shower heads save water, too.

Source: Susan Jaffe, a writer who has been specializing in environmental issues for well over a decade.

Environmentally Friendly Household Cleansers

Your favorite household cleansers may do a great job, but their contents are often toxic to breathe, hard on the hands and surfaces—and hazardous to the environment. In addition to being expensive, the containers in which they're sold add up to mountains of waste.

How to make environmentally friendly versions that are just as effective, but cost much less...

• Air freshener. Place a few slices of lemon, orange or grapefruit in a pot of water. Let simmer gently for an hour or more. Your house will be filled with a citrus scent.

• All-purpose liquid cleanser. Cuts grease and cleans countertops, baseboards, refrigerators and other appliances.

Combine in a plastic spray bottle: One teaspoon borax, one-half teaspoon washing soda (a stronger form of baking soda—available in supermarkets), two tablespoons white vinegar or lemon juice, one-half teaspoon vegetable-based detergent (i.e., Murphy's Oil Soap), two cups very hot water.

• Floor cleaner. Use on wood, tile or linoleum for a long-lasting shine.

Mix one-eighth cup vegetable-based detergent, one-half cup white vinegar and two gallons warm water in a plastic pail.

• Oven cleaner. Sprinkle water on the grimy spots, then cover with baking soda. Repeat the process, and let sit overnight. The grease will wipe off the next day. Use liquid soap and water to sponge away any residue.

• Overnight toilet-bowl cleaner. Pour one cup borax into the toilet bowl. Let sit overnight. Flush in the morning. Stains and rings are lifted away.

• Nonabrasive cleanser. Scours sinks and bathtubs, and leaves no gritty residue.

Combine one-quarter cup baking soda and enough vegetable-based detergent to make a creamy paste.

• Window cleaner. Combine in a plastic spray bottle...one-half teaspoon vegetable-based detergent, three tablespoons white vinegar, two cups water.

• Wood-furniture dusting and cleaning cloth. Mix one-half teaspoon olive oil and one-quarter cup white vinegar or lemon juice in a bowl. Apply to a cotton cloth. Reapply as needed.

Source: Annie Berthold-Bond, editor of *Green Alternatives,* a magazine on environmentally friendly products and services, 38 Montgomery St., Rhinebeck, New York 12572. She is the author of *Clean and Green: The Complete Guide to Nontoxic and Environmentally Safe Housekeeping,* Ceres Press, Box 87, Woodstock, New York 12498.

Smoke Detector Disposal Challenge

Most smoke detectors contain radioactive material that could, if the unit become damaged, be dangerous. *Helpful:* Pick the smoke detector up with your hand in a plastic bag. Then turn the bag inside out around the unit and seal the bag. Don't throw the detector in the trash. Don't take it to a hazardous-waste collection site—they don't accept radioactive materials. *Best:* Return the unit to the manufacturer or retailer.

Source: *Complete Trash: The Best Way to Get Rid of Practically Everything Around the House* by Norm Crampton, secretary, Institute for Solid Wastes of the American Public Works Association, M. Evans and Co., 216 E. 49 St., New York 10017.

Dust Allergy Self-Defense

House dust is the most common irritant for allergy sufferers and asthmatics. *Self-defense:*

- Dust and vacuum your home at least twice a week. Conventional vacuum cleaners can blow dust back into the room. Use a vacuum fitted with a HEPA (High-Efficiency Particulate Actuation) filter, such as Nilfisk Model GS90. *Note:* The allergic person shouldn't perform these tasks. If no one else can do the cleaning, the allergic person should wear a face mask while doing the work.
- Keep floors bare. Dust mites, the main allergen in dust, thrive in carpets.
- Cover pillows, mattresses, box springs, and furniture with plastic encasings. Mites breed in furniture and bedding, but can't get through plastic encasings. The plastic should be vacuumed once a week when the linens are changed.
- Wash linens in hot water. Warm or cold water doesn't kill mites.
- Keep the windows in your house shut. This helps to keep outdoor allergens outside. *Note:* Many trees pollinate between 2 a.m. and 4 a.m., so keep windows closed at night.
- Don't use a humidifier. It increases the mold content in the air. Use a dehumidifier for damp spaces.
- Avoid heaters that release irritating particles, such as wood-burning stoves, fireplaces.
- Use the air conditioner in warm weather. It filters out a lot of troublesome particles from the air. Clean or change the filter once a week.
- Get an air filter. Use it when it's too cool for the air conditioner. *Best:* A HEPA filter, which can remove particles that other filters can't. *Important:* When the filter is on, keep room doors and windows closed. *Cost:* About $150 and up.
- Ask your allergist about injections.

Source: Gerald L. Klein, MD, Allergy and Immunology Medical Group, 2067 W. Vista Way, Vista, California 92083. Dr. Klein is an associate clinical professor at the University of California and a member of the Board of Regents of the American College of Allergy and Immunology.

Closing Costs Vary Widely

Closing costs vary widely, from 3% to 10% of a home's purchase price. *Biggest variable:* The number of points charged. *Bottom line:* Shopping around for a no-point or low-point mortgage is an important way to keep closing costs down.

Source: *The Mortgage Book* by John Dorfman, *The Wall Street Journal* reporter and author of seven books on personal finance. Consumer Reports Books, 101 Truman Ave., Yonkers, New York 10703.

Energy Saver

Save energy by adjusting the humidity level in your home. Use a *humidifier* to add moisture to the air in winter to make your home feel warmer without turning up the heat. Use a *dehumidifier* in summer to remove moisture and make your house feel cooler without pumping up the air-conditioning.

Source: *Common Sense,* Box 215, Morrisville, Pennsylvania 19067.

Do-It-Yourself Cookbook

Use standard photo albums (the kind with clear plastic pages) to file newspapers and magazine clippings, as well as recipes written on index cards.

Source: *The Kitchen Survival Guide: A Hand-Holding Kitchen Primer with 130 Recipes to Get You Started* by cookbook author Lora Brody. William Morrow & Co., 1350 Avenue of the Americas, New York 10019.

Better Countertop Cleaning

Laminate countertops should *not* be cleaned with abrasive or chemical cleansers. They strip the high-gloss finish. Then, the only way to restore the finish is to have the countertops professionally resurfaced—at about $9 per linear foot. *Better:* Clean laminate countertops with a mild dishwashing detergent and warm water.

Source: *The Family Handyman,* 7900 International Dr., Suite 950, Minneapolis 55425.

Scratch Preventer

Prevent scratches on the kitchen floor by waxing the floor and the bottom of chair legs.

Source: *Skinflint News,* 1460 Noell Blvd., Palm Harbor, Florida 34683.

Separating Eggs

Easy way to separate eggs: Break the egg into a funnel. The white will run through, and the yolk will remain.

Source: *The Non-Consumers Digest,* Box 403, King Hill, Idaho 83633.

Better Housecleaning

Establish a halfway house for those items (clothing, books, papers, etc.) that you haven't used in years but can't bear to part with. *How it works:* Pack everything into cartons, marking the boxes with a date two years from now, and store it all away. After two years, review contents.

House Sitting Checklist

To decide what kind of sitter you need (to live in or to visit regularly, long term or short term), determine your requirements. *Typically, sitters should:*

- Make the house look lived in, so it won't be burglarized.
- Care for plants, pets and grounds.
- Make sure the pipes won't freeze.
- Guard the house and its possessions against natural disasters.

Where to find help:

- Some communities have sitting services or employment agencies that can fill the job.
- *Better:* Someone you know—the teenage child of a friend, a cleaning woman, a retired neighbor.
- Placement services at colleges.
- When interviewing, test the resourcefulness and intelligence of the candidate.
- Check references.
- If you find a writer looking for a place to stay or a person from the place you are heading to who would like to exchange houses, you might make a deal without any money changing hands.

Before you leave:

• Walk through every sequence of duties with the sitter.

• Put all duties in writing.

• List repair, supply and emergency telephone numbers and your own telephone number or instructions on how to reach you.

• Make clear that no one is to be admitted to the house or given a key without your prior consent.

Air Conditioning Secrets

Room air conditioners mounted in a window or through the wall are ideal for keeping small, comfortable havens against the worst of summer's hot spells. They can be more economical than central air conditioning because they are flexible—you cool only the rooms you are using. But even a single unit can be expensive.

To keep a room cool with minimum use of the air conditioner:

• Limit the use of the air conditioner in the "open vent" setting—it brings in hot outside air that the machine must work hard to keep cooling.

• Protect the room from the direct heat of the sun with awnings, drapes or blinds.

• Close off rooms that you are air-conditioning.

• Turn off unnecessary lights. They add extra heat (fluorescent lights are coolest).

• Turn off the unit if you will be out of the room more than 30 minutes.

• Service room air conditioners annually to keep them efficient. Replace filters, keep condensers clean and lubricate the moving parts.

• Supplement central air conditioning with a room air conditioner in the most-used room.

Source: John A. Constance, licensed engineer specializing in industrial ventilation, Newtown, PA.

Using Fans to Save on Air Conditioning

Ventilating fans can cool a whole house—or a single room—at a fraction (about 10%) of the cost of air conditioning. The trick is knowing how to use them to move in cooler air and to move hotter air out.

• Control the source of the cooler air by manipulating windows. During the day, for example, downstairs windows on the shady northern or eastern side of the house are most likely to provide cool air. All other windows should be closed and shaded from direct sun with blinds and drapes.

• At night, shut lower-floor windows for security while upstairs windows provide cool air.

• Attic fans are permanent installations above the upper floor. They are powerful enough to cool a whole house. The opening to the outside must be as large as the fan-blade frame in order to handle the air flow properly.

• Louvers, bird screening and (particularly) insect screening all reduce the exhaust capacity of a fan.

• A doorway or other opening must allow the fan to pull cool air directly up from the rest of the house.

• Direct-connected fans are quieter than belt-driven fans.

• Some attic fans have thermometers that automatically turn them off and on when the attic temperature reaches a certain degree of heat.

• Window fans have adjustable screw-on panels to fit different window sizes. Less powerful than attic fans, they serve more limited spaces.

• Box fans are portable and can be moved from room to room to cool smaller areas.

• Ventilating fans are rated by the cubic feet per minute (CFM) of air that they can exhaust. For effective cooling, engineers recommend an air-change rate of 20 per hour (the entire volume of air in the area to be cooled is changed 20 times every 60 minutes).

• To calculate the required CFM rating for a particular room, calculate its volume in cubic feet. Then multiply this figure by 20/60 (⅓). *Example:* A room 20 feet by 15 feet with an eight-foot ceiling contains 2,400 cubic feet of air.

This, multiplied by ⅓, gives a CFM rating of 800 for a proper-size fan.

•The CFM rating of an attic fan is done the same way. Total the cubic feet of the rooms and hallways you want cooled before multiplying by one third.

Source: John A. Constance, licensed engineer specializing in industrial ventilation, Newtown, PA.

How to Save Water

Whether you live in an area plagued by periodic droughts or simply want to save money on rising water bills:

•Install flow restricters in your showers and take shorter showers. (A normal showerhead sprays up to eight gallons per minute, so even a short, five-minute shower uses up to 40 gallons.)

•Get in the habit of turning off the water while shaving, brushing teeth and washing hands, except when you need to rinse.

•Put a weighted plastic container into the toilet tank to cut the normal amount of water used in flushing (approximately six gallons per flush) by as much as half. Some people use bricks to displace water in the tank, but this may damage the tank.

•Wash only full loads in your dishwasher and clothes washer. Running these machines half empty is a big water waster.

•Fix all leaks. Dripping water, even if slow, can cost you a lot of money over the course of several months.

•Use buckets of water to do outside chores like washing the car and cleaning the driveway. If you must use a hose, turn it off between rinsings—don't just let it run.

Home Energy Savers

After you've insulated your home, here are some smaller steps that can trim added amounts from your heating and electricity bills:

•Air conditioner covers. Outdoor covers not only block drafts, they also protect the machine from weather damage during the winter. Check the caulking around the outside of the machine, too. Indoor covers can be even more effective draft stoppers than outdoor ones. You can make your own from heavy plastic or buy Styrofoam-insulated ones.

•Door and window draft guards. Sand-filled fabric tubes effectively prevent uncomfortable drafts from entering around doors and windows. Easy to install and to remove.

•Light dimmers. The newest solid-state dimmers consume little energy themselves but allow reduced lighting levels and lower energy consumption. Some dimmers are installed in the wall in place of conventional switches. Others simply plug into existing sockets or are inserted into lamp cords. A dimmer can save you approximately 50% a year on a single light fixture if you dim it halfway.

•Air deflectors. Used in homes heated by forced air, these direct air from the vents away from walls and into the room. Depending on the location of your registers, significant savings can result.

•Heat reflectors. Reflectors direct radiator heat into the rooms to save energy. Very inexpensive ones can be made by covering a sheet of plywood or foam board with aluminum foil and placing it between the radiator and the wall.

•Storm window kits. You can make your own storm windows with sheets of plastic and tape. Kits are available to install them either inside or outside your existing windows. The cost ranges from as low as 85¢ to $35 per window. Removable rigid plastic storm windows in permanently installed frames are also big energy savers. Some companies will cut them to fit any window at a cost of $4–$5 per square foot. For city dwellers, they also reduce noise levels significantly. Storm windows reduce heat loss by as much as 30%, so an investment in permanent storm windows may pay off in the long run.

•Energy audits. Your local utility may offer free home energy audits. For absolutely no cost or obligation, it will inspect your home and suggest ways you can reduce your energy costs. Also, more and more utilities are acting as general contractors in making energy-efficiency changes on houses, ensuring that the work is done properly and on time.

Source: *Bottom Line/Personal,* Greenwich, CT.

Keeping Street Noise Out of Your Home

Noise intrusion is a constant and nagging problem in many buildings because of thin walls and badly insulated floors and ceilings.

How to noise-proof walls:

• Hang sound-absorbing materials, such as quilts, decorative rugs, carpets or blankets. *Note:* Cork board and heavy window draperies absorb sound within a room but do not help much with noise from outside.

• If you don't want to hang heavy materials directly on your walls, consider a frame that attaches to the wall. Insulation goes on the wall within the frame, and then a fabric is affixed to the frame.

How to noise-proof ceilings:

• Apply acoustical tile directly to the ceiling with adhesive for a quick and inexpensive fix.

• If you can undertake more extensive work, put in a dropped ceiling of acoustical tile with about six inches of insulation between the new and existing ceiling.

How to noise-proof floors:

• Install a thick plush carpet over a dense sponge rubber padding.

• *Key:* The padding must be dense, at least three-eighths of an inch thick. Your foot should not press down to the floor when you step on the padding.

When You Need an Exterminator and When You Don't

Bug problems can usually be solved without an exterminator. *Keys:* Careful prevention techniques, basic supermarket products and apartment-building cooperation.

Roaches...

Roaches are persistent pests that are the bane of apartment dwellers. The problem is not that roaches are so difficult to kill but that the effort has to be made collectively, by every tenant in a particular building. Roaches cannot be exterminated effectively from an individual apartment. If one apartment has them, they'll quickly spread throughout the building.

Most landlords hire exterminating services that visit during daytime hours when most tenants are at work. They wind up spraying just a few apartments, which is totally ineffective.

Better:

• Apartment dwellers have to get together, contact their landlord and arrange for all apartments to be exterminated at the same time. If the landlord is uncooperative, the Board of Health should be notified. If you live in a co-op, the co-op board should make arrangements for building extermination. *Best:* A superintendent or member of the building staff should perform regular exterminations, since he can get into apartments at odd hours when the tenants are not home. A professional exterminator should be called only as a backup, in case of a severe problem in a particular apartment.

• Incinerators that no longer burn garbage are a major infestation source in large buildings. Many cities, to cut down on air pollution, have ordered the compacting rather than the burning of garbage. Garbage is still thrown down the old brick chutes, which have been cracked from heat, to be compacted in the basement. Roaches breed in these cracks, fed by the wet garbage that comes down the chute, and travel to tenants' apartments. *Remedy:* Replacement of the brick chutes with smooth metal chutes which don't provide breeding places. *Also:* Compactors must be cleaned at least once a week.

• Rout roaches without poisoning your kitchen. Boric acid or crumbled bay leaves will keep your cupboards pest-free. *Another benign repellent:* Chopped cucumbers.

• Homeowners do not need regular extermination for roaches. Since a house is a separate unit, a one-time extermination should do the job.

Food stores are the major source of roach infestation in private homes. People bring roaches home with the groceries. Check your paper grocery bags for roaches before you store them.

•Ants and silverfish can be controlled by the homeowner himself, unless there is a major infestation. Don't call the exterminator for a half-dozen ants or silverfish. Try a store-bought spray first. *Exception:* Carpenter ants and grease-eating ants must be exterminated professionally.

•Clover mites come from cutting the grass. They look like little red dots. The mites land on windowsills after the lawn is mowed and then travel into the house. *Remedy:* Spray your grass with miticide before cutting.

•Spiders don't require an exterminator. Any aerosol will get rid of them.

•Termite control is a major job that needs specialized chemicals and equipment. Call an exterminator.

•Bees, wasps and hornets should be dealt with professionally. Their nests must be located and attacked after dusk, when the insects have returned to them. If the nest is not destroyed properly, damage to your home could result. *Also:* Many people are allergic to stings and don't know it until they are stung.

•Clothes moths can be eliminated by hanging a no-pest strip in your closet and keeping the door tightly closed.

•Flies can be minimized with an aerosol or sticky strip. An exterminator is of no help getting rid of flies. *Best:* Screens on all the windows and doors.

•Weevils and meal moths can be prevented by storing cereals, rice and grains in sealed containers. *Also:* Cereals are treated with bromides to repel infestation. The bromides eventually break down. Throw out old cereals.

•Wood storage and insects. Firewood kept in the house becomes a refuge and breeding ground for insects. *Risky solution:* Spraying the logs with insecticides. (When the sprayed wood burns, dangerous fumes could be emitted.) *Better:* Stack the wood (under plastic) outside and carry in only the amount needed.

Mice...

There is no 100% effective solution for exterminating mice. *Try these alternatives:*

•Trapping is effective unless you have small children or pets.

•Poison should be placed behind the stove or refrigerator where children and pets can't get at it.

•Glue boards (available in supermarkets) placed along the walls can be very effective. Mice tend to run along the walls due to poor eyesight.

Pesticides and prevention...

Many of the residual (long-lasting) sprays have been outlawed because they don't break down and disappear in the environment. The old favorites, DDT and Chlordane, are generally no longer permitted. *What to use:*

•Baygon, Diazanon and Dursban are general-purpose, toxic organo-phosphates meant for residual use in wet areas. They're recommended for all indoor insects, including roaches.

•Drione is a nontoxic silica gel, which dries up the membranes in insects. Recommended for indoor use in dry areas only, it is especially effective on roaches.

•Malathion is helpful in gardens, but it should not be used indoors.

•Pyrethrin is highly recommended, since it is made from flowers and is nontoxic. It has no residual effect, but is good for on-contact spraying of roaches and other insects. If there is a baby in the house, Pyrethrin is especially useful, since children under three months should never be exposed to toxic chemicals. Don't use it around hay-fever or asthma sufferers.

•When buying products in the store, look at the label to determine the percentage of active ingredients. Solutions vary from 5% to 15%. The stronger the solution, the better the results.

•Prevention is synonymous with sanitation. If you are not scrupulous about cleanliness, you will be wasting your money on sprays or exterminators.

•Moisture is the main attractor of insects. If you live in a moist climate, you must be especially vigilant. Coffee spills, plumbing leaks, fish tanks, pet litter and pet food all attract bugs. Clean up after your pets, and take care of leaks and spills immediately. If puddles tend to collect around your house after it rains, improve the drainage.

•Word of mouth is the best way to choose a good exterminator. Don't rely on the Yellow Pages.

•Contracts for regular service, which many exterminators try to promote, are not recommended for private homes. A one-time extermination should do the trick, but apartment dwellers must exterminate buildingwide on a regular basis.

•To remove a bat from your house at night, confine it to a single room, open the window and leave the bat alone. Chances are it will fly right out. Otherwise, during the day when the bat is torpid, flick it into a coffee can or other container. (Use gloves if you are squeamish.) Release it outdoors. Bats are really very valuable. A single brown bat can eat 3,000 mosquitoes a night. *Note:* Bats, like other mammals, can carry rabies. If you find a downed bat or you are scratched or bitten by one, call your local animal control agency and keep the animal for testing. However, very few people have contracted rabies directly from bats. *More likely source:* Skunks.

Source: Tom Heffernan, president of the Ozane Exterminating Co., Bayside, NY, and Clifton Meloan, chemist, Kansas.

Painting Trouble Areas

Often, paint peels in one section of a wall or ceiling. *Causes:*

•A leak making its way through the walls from a plumbing break or an opening to the outside.

•The plaster is giving out in that area due to age or wear and tear.

•The layers of paint may be so thick that the force of gravity, plus vibrations from outside, make the paint pop and peel in the weakest spots.

How to fix the problem:

•If it's a leak, find and correct it first.

•Otherwise, remove as much of the existing paint as you can.

•Scrape away any loose, damp or crumbling plaster.

•Spackle and smooth the area.

•Prime and paint it.

For real problem areas:

•Spackle, then paste on a thin layer of canvas. Apply it as though it were wallpaper.

•Smooth it out so it becomes part of the surface.

•Then prime and paint it.

Wrapping a Package The Right Way

•Seal a sturdy carton with six strips of two-inch-wide plastic tape (not masking or cellophane tape, which tears easily): A strip across the center of top and bottom and across each open edge on flap ends. Don't just go to the ends. Go a few inches around.

•Put an address label inside so that if the outside label is lost or defaced, the package can be opened and sent with the second label.

•Don't use brown paper or string; they only increase chance of loss if paper tears and label rips off or the string unties and gets caught in a sorting machine.

Things You Never Thought of Doing With Plastic Bags

Use plastic bags:

•As gloves when greasing a cookie sheet, cleaning the oven or changing oil in the car.

•To help preserve a plant when you are going away. Spray the leaves with water, then cover the pot with a bag secured at the top with a rubber band.

•To protect your camera, film and lenses from moisture.

•As storage bags for woolens. Add a few mothballs.

•Put meat to be tenderized inside a bag before pounding.

Cleaning Jewelry

•Gold and platinum: Use a soft brush with a mild, warm water/detergent solution.

•Turquoise, ivory, lapis and other porous gems: Mild soap and water only.

•Opals: Use barely cool distilled water (they're sensitive to cold).

•Pearls: Roll them in a soft cloth moistened with water and soap (not detergent). *To rinse:* Roll them in a cloth dipped in warm water.

•Most other gems: Add a tablespoonful of baking soda to a cup of warm water. Swish the jewelry through or rub it with a soft toothbrush. Rinse well.

Source: *Woman's Day,* New York.

Home Remedies For Plant Pests

•Red spider mites. Four tablespoons of dishwashing liquid or one-half cake of yellow soap dissolved in one gallon of water. Spray weekly until mites are gone, then monthly.

•Hardshell scale. One-fourth teaspoon olive oil, two tablespoons baking soda, one teaspoon Dove liquid soap in two gallons of water. Spray or wipe on once a week for three weeks; repeat if necessary.

•Mold on soil. One tablespoon of vinegar in two quarts of water. Water weekly with solution until mold disappears.

•Mealybugs. Wipe with cotton swabs dipped in alcohol. Spray larger plants weekly with a solution of one part alcohol to three parts water until bugs no longer hatch.

Source: Decora Interior Plantscapes, Greenwich, CT.

How to Make Flowers Last Longer

•Cut off the stems half an inch from the bottom. Make the cut at an angle so that the stem will not press against the bottom of the vase, closing off the flow of water.

•To slow water buildup (which makes petals droop), make a tiny incision at the base of the bloom.

•Fill an absolutely clean vase with fresh water.

•Add floral preservative. *One recipe:* Two squeezes of lemon juice, a quarter teaspoonful of sugar and a few drops of club soda.

•Change the water and preservative daily.

•Display the flowers out of the sun, and keep them cool at night.

•Remove leaves below the water line.

Source: T. Augello and G. Yanker, coauthors, *Shortcuts,* Bantam Books, New York.

Ten Foolproof Houseplants

These hardy species will survive almost anywhere and are a good choice for timid beginners without a lot of sunny windows.

•Aspidistra (cast-iron plant). This Victorian favorite, known as "The Spittoon Plant," survived the implied indignity in many a tavern.

•Rubber plant. Likes a dim, cool interior (like a hallway). If given sun, it grows like crazy.

•Century (Kentia) palm. A long-lived, slow-growing plant that needs uniform moisture. Give it an occasional shower.

•Philodendrons. They like medium to low light and even moisture, but will tolerate dryness and poor light.

•Dumb cane. Tolerates a dry interior and low light, but responds to better conditions. Don't let your pet chew the foliage or its tongue will swell.

•Bromeliads. Exotic and slow-growing, they like frequent misting, but are practically immune to neglect and will flower even in subdued light.

•Corn plant (dracaena). Good for hot, dry apartments.

•Snake plant. Will survive almost anything.

•Spider plant. A tough, low-light plant that makes a great trailer and endures neglect.

•Nephthytis. Will flourish in poor light and survive the forgetful waterer.

Source: Edmond O. Moulin, director of horticulture, Brooklyn Botanical Garden, Brooklyn, NY.

Poison Plants

Plant poisoning among adults has increased alarmingly in the last decade. For children under five, plants are second only to medicines as a cause of poisoning. *Prime sources:* Common houseplants, garden flowers and shrubs, as well as wild mushrooms, weeds and berries.

Among the most common poisonous plants:

•Garden flowers: Bleeding heart, daffodils, delphinium, foxglove, hens and chickens, lantana, lily of the valley, lupine, sweet pea.

•Houseplants: Caladium, dieffenbachia, philodendron.

•Garden shrubs: Azalea, mountain laurel, oleander, privet, rhododendron, yew.

•Wildflowers: Autumn crocus, buttercups, jimson weed, mayapple, moonseed berries, poison hemlock, water hemlock, wild mushrooms.

Flowers that Are Good to Eat

Many common flowers also make gourmet dishes. *Here are some suggestions:*

•Calendula (pot marigold): Add minced petals to rice, omelets, chicken soup, clam chowder or stew.

•Nasturtium: Serve leaves like watercress on sandwiches, or stuff flowers with basil- and tarragon-seasoned rice, then simmer in chicken stock and sherry.

•Squash blossom: Pick blossoms as they are opening, dip in a flour-and-egg mixture seasoned with salt, pepper and tarragon, then deep-fry until golden brown.

•Camomile: Dry the flowers on a screen in a dark place to make tea.

•Borage: Toss with salad for a cucumberlike taste, or use fresh for tea.

Source: *House & Garden*, New York.

All You Need to Know About Bird Feeders

The main thing is to mix your own seed. You can create a mix that will attract a wide variety of birds. *What birds like most:*

•Niger seed (Thistledown).

•Sunflower seeds (particularly the thin-shelled oilseed).

•White proso millet.

•Finely cracked corn.

Avoid:

•Milo and red millet, which are used as filler in commercial mixes and are not attractive to birds.

•Peanut hearts attract starlings, which you may want to avoid.

Requirements of a good feeder:

•It should keep the seed dry (mold by-products are toxic to birds).

•Be squirrel resistant (baffles above and below are good protection).

•For winter feeding of insect-eating birds (woodpeckers, chickadees, titmice and nuthatches), string up chunks of beef suet.

Source: Aelred D. Geis, Patuxent Wildlife Research Center of the US Fish and Wildlife Service, Laurel, MD.

When to Trade in Your Old Furnace

If your fuel bills seem higher than they should be, it may be time to replace your old furnace with a new one.

•Calculate whether your old oil furnace is costing you more than the price of a new one:

(1) Estimate your annual fuel bill.

(2) Divide your present furnace's efficiency rating by the efficiency rating of the new model

you're considering. (Your local utility will rate your system for a small fee or for free.)

(3) Multiply the result by your annual fuel bill to estimate the savings. A new furnace should pay back its costs in about five to seven years.

Source: *Home,* Des Moines, IA.

Painting Guidelines

Follow these simple suggestions for the effect you are looking for:

- To make a room look larger, use the same color on walls, floor and ceiling.
- Dark colors don't always make a room look smaller, though they can make a large room more intimate.
- Dark colors on all surrounding surfaces can highlight furniture and give an illusion of spaciousness.
- Cool wall colors make a room seem bigger.
- Warm colors make a room seem smaller.
- A long, narrow room can be visually widened by painting the long sides a lighter color than those at the ends.
- A ceiling slightly lighter in color than the walls appears higher...a darker one, lower.

Source: *Woman's Day,* New York.

Fiber Danger

Some organically grown fibers can be bad for the environment. *Example:* Cotton grown in some areas of the desert. Water to grow it is diverted by man-made channels. The diversion threatens dozens of species.

Source: Jason Makansi, editor, *Common Sense on Energy and Our Environment,* Box 215, Morrisville, PA 19067.

12

Buying/Renting a Home

Money for First-Time Homeowners

First-time home buyers in need of extra cash for a down payment can borrow from their 401(k) plans—without paying penalties to the IRS. You can pay back the loan over several years as long as you make equal loan repayments on at least a quarterly basis. *Drawback:* The money you use to pay the interest on the loan will be taxed twice—once as you pay interest in after-tax dollars and again when you begin withdrawing the money —including the interest you paid to yourself—after age 59½.

Source: Jonathan Pond, president of Financial Planning Information Inc., 9 Galen St., Watertown, MA 02172.

How to Buy Property with Little...or No Money Down

As hard as it is to believe, it's not only possible to buy property with no money down, it's not even that hard to do—provided you have the right fundamental information.

Note: No money down means the seller receives no down payment. It means the down payment doesn't come from your pocket.

Success strategies...

•Paying the real estate agent. If a seller uses a real estate agent on the sale, he's obligated to pay the agent's commission. *Strategy:* You, the buyer, pay the commission, but not up front. You approach the agent and offer a deal. Instead of immediate payment, suggest that the agent lend you part of the commission. In return, you offer a personal note guaranteeing to pay the money at some future date, with interest. If you make it clear that the sale depends on such an arrangement, the agent will probably go along with the plan. If he balks, be flexible. Negotiate a small monthly amount, perhaps with a balloon payment at the end. You then subtract the agent's commission from the expected down payment.

•Assuming the seller's debts. Let's say, as so often happens, that the seller is under financial pressure. *Strategy:* With the seller's cooperation, contact all his creditors and explain that you, not the seller, are going to make good on the outstanding debts. In some cases, the relieved creditors will either extend the due dates, or, if you can come up with some cash, they'll likely agree to a discount. Deduct the face amount of the debts you'll be assuming, pocketing any discounts, from the down payment.

•Prepaid rent. Sometimes you, the buyer, are in no rush to move in and the seller would like more time to find a new place to live—but you'd both like to close as soon as possible. *Strategy:* Offer to let the seller remain in the house or apartment, setting a fixed date for vacating. Then, instead of the seller paying the buyer a monthly rent, you subtract from the down payment the full amount of the rent for the entire time the seller will be living there.

•Satisfying the seller's needs. During conversations with the seller, you learn that he must buy some appliances and furniture for a home he's moving into. *Strategy:* Offer to buy those things—using credit cards or store credit to delay payment—and deduct the lump sum from the down payment.

Source: Robert G. Allen, a real estate insider and author of the bestseller *Nothing Down.* He's also publisher of the monthly newsletter *The Real Estate Advisor,* Provo, UT.

Figures to Check at Real Estate Closing

•Monthly payments.

•Per diem figures for utilities, taxes, and/or interest.

•The broker's commission.

•The rents, security deposits, and/or interest on deposits that have not as yet been transferred.

•A charge for utility bills already paid.

•A charge for loan fees already paid.

•A contractor, attorney, appraiser, or some other party to the contract who has not been paid.

Protect Mortgage Point Deduction

"Points" paid to get a mortgage loan may not be immediately tax-deductible.

Interest must actually be paid to be deductible by cash-basis taxpayers, which most individuals are. In one case, the Tax Court held that, since the points were deducted from the loan proceeds, they weren't actually paid, thus no deduction could be claimed that year. The deduction would have to be taken pro rata as the mortgage was repaid.

Problem: The typical real estate closing statement mixes up credits to the buyer and amounts actually paid.

Solution: Pay the points by single check to the lender. Don't lump the payment in with other payments.

Questions to Ask Before Signing Mortgage Papers

Because it is such a long-term contract, conditions that may seem minor when signing a mortgage loan contract can end up costing a lot of money during the life of the agreement. Some typical mortgage clauses to negotiate before signing:

•Payment of "points": Percentage of the amount of the loan paid to the lender at the start of the loan. Banks and thrift institutions have no statutory right to charge points. Their presence may reflect competitive local market conditions. And when interest rates are high, points are common. They're inevitable when rate ceilings exist. *Helpful:* Try to negotiate on points.

•Prepayment penalties: Sometimes as much as six months' interest or a percentage of the balance due on the principal at the time the loan is paid off. With mortgages running for 25 or 30 years, the chances of paying them off early are relatively high.

•"Due on encumbrance" clause: Makes the first mortgage immediately due in full if property is pledged as security on any other loan, including second mortgages. Not legal in some places and usually not enforced when it is legal. Request its deletion.

• "Due on sale" clauses: Requiring full payment of loan when property is sold.

• Escrow payment: The popular practice of requiring a prorated share of local taxes and insurance premiums with each monthly mortgage payment. The bank earns interest on the escrow funds throughout the year and only pays it out when taxes and premiums are due. Amounts to forced savings with no interest.

Have your lawyer check your state's law to see if interest on escrow-account money is required. (It is, in several states.) If not, try to eliminate escrow —pay taxes and insurance on your own.

Other alternatives to escrow...

Capitalization plan, in which monthly tax and insurance payments are credited against outstanding mortgage principal until they are paid out to the government or insurer, thus lowering amount of mortgage interest.

Lender may agree to waive escrow if borrower opens an interest-bearing savings account in the amount of the annual tax bill.

Option of closing out the withheld escrow payments when the borrower's equity reaches 40%. At that point, the bank figures, equity interest will be a powerful incentive to keep up tax payments.

Source: *The Consumer's Guide to Banks*, by Gordon L. Well, Stein & Day, Briarcliff Manor, NY.

Suggestions for Condominium Hunters

Look for a building about to undergo conversion. If you sublet an apartment in it, you get first crack at buying the apartment.

If you have trouble getting a mortgage, look for a condominium developer who has a mortgage commitment from a lender.

Rent a portion of the condominium apartment to a friend. This helps meet the monthly payments.

When Buying a New Condominium

Buying a condominium is more complicated than buying a house. *Reason:* The purchase is really for two separate pieces of property—your unit and the property held in common. Before signing any contract for a new condominium, which is harder to check out than an established condominium, buyers should study the prospectus for any of these pitfalls:

• The prospectus includes a plan of the unit you are buying, showing rooms of specific dimensions. But the plan omits closet space. *Result:* The living space you are buying is probably smaller than you think.

• The prospectus includes this clause: "The interior design shall be substantially similar." *Result:* The developer can alter both the size and design of your unit.

• The common charges set forth in the prospectus are unrealistically low. Buyers should never rely on a developer's estimate of common charges. *Instead:* They should find out the charges at similarly functioning condominiums.

• *Common charges include:* Electricity for hallways and outside areas, water, cleaning, garbage disposal, insurance for common areas, pool maintenance, groundskeeping, legal and accounting fees, reserves for future repairs.

Variation on the common-charge trap: The developer is paying common charges on unsold units. But these charges are unrealistically low. *Reason:* The developer has either underinsured or underestimated the taxes due, omitted security expenses, or failed to set up a reserve fund.

• The prospectus includes this clause: "The seller will not be obligated to pay monthly charges for unsold units." *Result:* The owners of a partially occupied condominium have to pay for all operating expenses.

• The prospectus warns about the seller's limited liability. But an unsuspecting buyer may still purchase a condominium unit on which back monthly charges are due, or even on which there's a lien for failure to pay back carrying charges.

•The prospectus makes no mention of parking spaces. *Result:* You must lease from the developer.

•The prospectus is imprecise about the total number of units to be built. *Result:* Facilities are inadequate for the number of residents.

•The prospectus includes this clause: "Transfer of ownership (of the common property from the developer to the homeowners' association) will take place 60 days after the last unit is sold." *Trap:* The developer deliberately does not sell one unit, keeps on managing the condominium, and awards sweetheart maintenance and operating contracts to his subcontractors.

•The prospectus specifies that the developer will become the property manager of the functioning condominium. But the language spelling out monthly common charges and management fees is imprecise. *Result:* The owners cannot control monthly charges and fees.

Source: Dorothy Tymon, author, *The Condominium: A Guide for the Alert Buyer,* Golden-Lee Books, Brooklyn, NY.

Condominium Emergency Reserves

Make sure the board of directors sets up a contingency reserve for emergencies. It should be at least 3% of the annual operating budget for newer buildings and 5% for older ones. *Danger:* A major assessment on very little notice when an emergency arises if no reserve is set aside.

Source: *The Condominium Community,* The Institute of Real Estate Management of the National Association of Realtors, Chicago.

Condos vs. Co-ops

When you purchase a condominium, you own real property, just like when you buy a house. You arrange for your own mortgage with the bank, pay real estate taxes directly to the local government, pay water bills individually, and have an individual deed.

When you buy a cooperative apartment, you are participating in a syndication. A corporation is formed, shares are issued, and people subscribe to the shares. The corporation raises money, takes out a mortgage, and owns the building.

Maintenance charges for a condominium are likely to cost 50% of a cooperative's charges for an equivalent building. *The reason:* The maintenance on a condominium covers only the common area upkeep. *That includes:* Labor, heating oil, repairs, and maintenance of the playground, swimming pool, and other community areas. Co-op maintenance fees cover those same items plus mortgage payments, local real estate taxes, utility and water bills.

Capital improvements: If an extensive, major repair needs to be made (such as the replacement of a roof or boiler), the board of managers of a condo cannot borrow funds from a bank, unless it receives the unanimous consent of the condo owners. *Problem:* If a dozen owners are content to live in a dilapidated building, improvements must be funded through maintenance cash flow, which may be very expensive. In a co-op, the board of directors can take out a second mortgage to fix a roof, plumbing, or other major problem. Individual co-op shareholders cannot easily obstruct the board.

Delinquency in paying maintenance fees can be handled more expediently in a co-op than in a condo. In a co-op, an owner who doesn't pay maintenance fees can be evicted almost immediately. The person is served with a dispossess and can be evicted within days. In a condominium, a lien must be placed on the apartment and then a foreclosure proceeding is brought. It could take two years to get the money, and it is a difficult legal proceeding.

Exclusionary rights: Since a co-op is considered personal property, not real property, prospective tenants may be rejected by the co-op's board of directors for any reason whatsoever except race, creed, color, or national origin. *Reality:* As long as the co-op board members don't state the reason, anyone can be excluded for any prejudice. *Problem:* A tenant may have trouble subletting a co-op if the co-op board members don't approve of the new tenant. In a condominium, each owner has the right to sell or sublet to anyone the person wants, subject only to the condo's right of first refusal, which is rarely exercised.

From the entrepreneur's point of view, a co-op can be more advantageous if the building at the time of the conversion date has a low-interest mortgage. *Reason:* When a building is converted into a condominium, it must be free and clear of all liens. In a co-op, the former financing can be kept intact.

Source: David Goldstick, senior partner, Goldstick, Weinberger, Feldman, Alperstein, Rotenberg, Grossman & Barr, Inc., 261 Madison Ave., New York 10016.

Before You Renovate An Old House

The positive aspects of renovating an old house are enticing: A sense of accomplishment, an outlet for creativity, and the possibility that it will be a good investment. However, the experience of returning a house to its former glory can be frustrating and overwhelming to anyone who attempts it for the first time without proper understanding.

The worst aspects, according to old-home buffs:

• Not knowing what you are getting into.

• Living amid the chaos of reconstruction for very long periods.

Some things to consider when buying an old home to renovate...

• Choosing the right neighborhood is the most important element on the investment side. If many homes are being renovated in your neighborhood, chances are good that your choice will be expensive. *Best:* Find a neighborhood where one or two homes have been renovated on your block and several more a few blocks away. There is a strong possibility that the neighborhood will blossom and values will rise.

• Speak to owners of similar homes in your area before you purchase. Concentrate on the steps they took.

• Get a good engineer's report about the home, and focus on foundation, plumbing, electrical, and mechanical systems. These are the most difficult to restore. Choose an engineer with considerable experience in old homes.

• If you want a modern interior and expect to gut most of the house and substitute modern fixtures, find a house that's just a shell. *Reason:* Old homes with fine architectural details such as marble mantels and restorable wainscotting cost more.

• Don't put your last penny into a down payment and take a big mortgage. The fixing-up process can be extraordinarily expensive, even if you expect to do much of the work yourself. Expenses vary nationwide, correlating most closely with labor costs in your area.

• Don't get an architect to draw up a master plan for your house immediately. It usually takes a while to know what you want out of a house. Unless you have lived in it at least six months to a year, you will probably make expensive mistakes.

• Learn how to deal with contractors. You can't do everything yourself. You must hire experienced people. Read the contract. Make sure the contractor is bonded. *Possibility:* If you are fairly handy, call in a professional to do a small portion. Watch carefully. You may be able to finish the job yourself.

• Gutting an interior can be done easily by anyone. All you need is a crowbar, sledge hammer, old clothes, and elbow grease. Most homes can be gutted in a weekend. *Keys:* Hire neighborhood teenagers to help. Find a dumpster for the plaster.

• Don't be discouraged by broken beams, crumbling interior plaster, or even a leaking roof. As long as the exterior walls and the foundation are solid, shabby interiors are secondary.

• Study local zoning laws before you make major changes. *Reason:* Removing a pipe or a wall frequently requires a building permit. However, after you get the permit, your tax assessment will be raised, probably by as much as the value of the renovation. *Important:* Be prepared to try negotiating with the tax assessor.

Most expensive changes: Changing the location of the kitchen or bathrooms. *Why:* Plumbing. Don't do it if you can possibly live with things where they are.

Way to boost resale value: Organize a walking tour of restored homes in your area. These walking tours are great sales tools.

Source: Benita Korn and Patricia Cole, directors of the Brownstone Revival Committee, Inc., 200 Madison Ave., New York 10016.

Getting a Higher Price For an Old House

An old house (built between 1920 and 1950) can be sold as easily as a new one. The right strategy and a few improvements can raise the selling price significantly.

- Invest in a complete cleaning, repainting, or wallpapering. Recarpet or have the rugs and carpets professionally cleaned.
- Get rid of cat and dog odors that you may be used to but potential buyers will notice.
- With the trend to smaller families and working couples, it may be desirable to convert and advertise a four-bedroom house as two bedrooms, library and den.
- The exterior of the house is crucial. It's the first thing a buyer sees. Clean and repair porch and remove clutter. Repaint porch furniture.
- Landscaping makes a great difference and can sell (or unsell) a house. Get expert advice on improving it.
- Good real estate agents are vital to a quick sale. There are one or two top people in every agency who will work hard to show houses and even arrange financing. Multiple listings lets these super salespeople from different agencies work for the seller.

Law When Trespassing Children are Injured

A property owner or contractor may be liable for damages if a child is hurt on the property (or by unguarded machinery), even though the child trespassed. A "No Trespassing" sign isn't enough.

Example: A swimming pool should be surrounded by an adequate fence and a locked gate.

General rule: The attractive nuisance doctrine in the law makes the property owner responsible for trespassing children who are too young to understand the dangers.

Special problem: Protection while construction work is being done or when machinery is left unguarded in a residential area (or near heavily traveled streets).

Liability for Injuries to Uninvited Guests

Courts in many states are more likely than ever to hold an owner responsible for injuries to a visitor. That's so even though the person was on the property without an invitation. The old distinction between an invitee (someone asked onto the property) and licensee (someone on the property without an invitation) is breaking down. Traditionally, invitees would be awarded higher settlements for damages.

Now courts in about one-third of the states ignore the distinction between an invitee and licensee and hold the property owner responsible for keeping the property safe for both invitees and the self-invited.

Now: Salespeople, whether they contacted the customer before their visit or not, are generally treated (by courts recognizing the distinction) as invitees.

Forming a Tenants' Organization

The most effective method of confronting a landlord about problems with rented apartments is through a tenant organization. If you are having problems with your landlord, the other tenants in your building probably are, too. If you approach the problem as a group, your chances of success improve immeasurably.

How to go about it:

• Speak with the tenants in your building and distribute flyers calling a meeting. At the meeting, elect a committee of tenants to lead the group.

• Pass out questionnaires to all tenants, asking them to list needed repairs in their apartments.

• After the questionnaires have been collected and reviewed, call the landlord and suggest a meeting with him to negotiate complaints. Many landlords will comply with this request, since the specter of all their tenants withholding rent can be a frightening prospect. Negotiation is always preferable to litigation.

• If negotiation fails, organize a rent strike. That's a procedure whereby tenants withhold rent collectively, depositing the money each month in an escrow fund or with the court until repairs are made. If your tenant organization is forced to go this route, you will need a good lawyer. Be prepared for a long court battle.

Tenant vs. Tenant

If a tenant in your building is involved in a crime or drugs or is excessively noisy, you have a number of ways to deal with the problem.

• Take out a summons, claiming harassment or assault. *Probable result:* The court will admonish the tenant to stop causing a disturbance (which may or may not have any effect).

• Sue for damages in civil court. You may win (although collecting the judgment is another story).

• Try to persuade your landlord to evict the undesirable tenant. *Best way:* Put pressure on him through your tenant organization. A landlord can't be forced to evict anyone. He has the right to rent to whomever he chooses. But if your association has a decent relationship with the landlord, he might comply, especially if the tenant is causing a dangerous condition or destroying property.

• You have the right to break your lease if you're being harassed by another tenant, but this may not be much comfort if apartments are scarce in your area.

Five Easy Ways to Cut Heating Costs

1. Clean furnaces. Home heating bills can be cut 10% or more by having the furnace cleaned and adjusted properly. If you have an oil burner, an annual inspection by a qualified technician is important.

2. Replace furnace burners. Find out if your oil burner is a *conventional* or a *retention head* burner. The latter is much more efficient. These use smaller fuel nozzles and save as much as 15% on your fuel bill.

3. Clean filters. Forced warm-air furnaces need to have their air filters cleaned and replaced at least twice each winter. A clogged filter chokes off the necessary breathing of the furnace and makes it work harder.

4. Unblock registers. When you are rearranging furniture, be sure that radiators, warm-air registers or heating units aren't blocked from proper functioning. If you prefer an arrangement that blocks heat flow, let it wait until summer when it won't affect heating efficiency.

5. Add humidity. A little extra humidity permits a lower thermostat setting without discomfort. Some furnaces will accept a humidifying system easily and inexpensively. If yours won't, use pans of water on radiators or heat registers to put a little moisture into the air.

Source: *547 Tips for Saving Energy in Your Home,* Storey Communications, Box 445, Schoolhouse Rd., Pownal, Vermont 05261.

13

Smart Money Management

Get Control of Your Finances...Now

All too many people today are wondering where all their hard-earned money is going. They feel like they're working harder than ever ...yet have nothing to show for it.

Researchers recently determined that it takes $60,000 to live the American dream. But people making $60,000 said they needed $75,000 ...people making $75,000 said they needed $100,000...people making $100,000 said they needed $150,000...and so on.

The truth is, most of us already have *enough* —we just need to shape up our spending and saving habits to what we really want and need. And that takes introspection.

What to do...

• Act now. Don't make the mistake of thinking that the future will take care of itself. Your financial future is a direct result of the decisions you make today.

Just as someone with a heart problem can avoid trouble by making lifestyle changes, changing spending habits can avert financial crises in the years ahead.

• Set goals. Every family needs goals that are tied to their values. Write them down and put a price tag on them—if necessary, get the help of your accountant or financial planner.

It's only when you spell out your goals—retiring at a certain age or income level, putting your children through college, maintaining a certain standard of living, etc.— that you can face up to the trade-offs that will have to be made.

• Analyze your spending. First identify your major spending categories.

Included: Housing, child care, groceries, debts, medical/dental treatments, transportation, insurance, work- and investment-related expenses, clothing, gifts, personal needs and entertainment.

Then gather all your cancelled checks, credit-card bills and cash-withdrawal records for the past year.

Divide the checks and credit-card receipts among the various categories. Then figure out how you spent your cash withdrawals. Don't worry about being precise. Put items you can't account for in the *personal needs* pile. Knowing where your money went will lead to better spending decisions.

•Figure out what you really need. Determine whether you spend more on *experiences* —travel, education, entertainment, etc...or on *things*—clothing, toys, collectibles, electronic gadgets, etc.

Ask yourself: Which of these provide more lasting value in my life? What could be eliminated?

Then take the money you would have spent and start saving it.

•Save at least 10% of your income. It's amazing how quickly even a small amount will grow, if you invest regularly.

Example: A 25-year-old who saves $1,000 a year and earns 8% on it will have $15,650 after 10 years. Even if he then stopped making contributions—which we don't recommend—that modest amount would grow to $157,440 by the time the investor was 65. If the 25-year-old waited until the age of 35 to start, he would never catch up with the 25-year-old, even if he made 30 years of contributions to 10 years of the 25-year-old. So act now! It's never too early to start.

•Maximize pre-tax savings. Use 401(k) plans, IRAs and Keoghs. This year you can make pre-tax 401(k) contributions of up to 16% of your pay to a maximum of $8,475. If your employer contributes, this is the opportunity of a lifetime.

Trap: Too many employees put all of their 401(k) savings into Guaranteed Investment Contracts (GICs). GICs guarantee the rate of interest and the principal.

Problem: GICs are written mostly by insurance companies...a few of which are in very shaky financial condition. The guarantee comes from the insurance companies...not your company. They also don't offer inflation protection. *Self-defense:* All long-term investors need some common stocks in their portfolios.

In deciding how much to invest in fixed-income versus equity-type investment, use your age as the maximum percentage to invest in fixed-income investments. Sometimes more should be invested in stocks or real estate, but typically not less. *Examples:*

•Forty-year-olds should put 40% of their money into fixed-income investments and 60% into stocks.

•Sixty-year olds should put 60% of their money into fixed-income investments and 40% into stocks.

•Dollar-cost average. When you invest in stocks, you can expect substantial swings in value—often 30% or more a year. But over the long term, stocks, especially small stocks, appreciate much more than bonds or Treasury bills.

You can reduce the risk of volatility and market swings by dollar-cost averaging—investing the same amount of money at regular intervals over time.

Example: If you invest $100 per month in a fund valued at $10 in the first month, $5 in the second month and $10 in the third month, you would get 10 shares the first month, 20 shares the second month and 10 shares the third month for a total of 40 shares, worth $400. But you would only pay $300...for a total return of 33% on your investment.

Dollar-cost averaging has been an effective way to reduce risk through all types of economic periods, including the Great Depression.

Example: If, starting in January 1929, a person had invested $100 a month in the Dow Jones Industrials for 64 months, he would have watched the Dow Jones Industrial Average drop 73%... yet his $6,4000 investment would have increased to $7,157 during one of the worst economic periods in history.

The key is to make regular contributions. No matter how much you save, it should be automatic. *Best:* Have the money taken out of your paycheck or bank account before you can spend it.

Increase your savings contribution as your income rises. The day you get a raise is a good time to increase your savings allotment.

Source: Glenn Pape, CPA, APFS, JD, vice president, financial-related services. The AYCO Corp., a subsidiary of American Express Co., One Wall St., Albany, New York 12205. AYCO is an independent fee-based financial counseling firm that works with corporations and individuals.

How to Cut Credit Card Costs

The effective cost of carrying a credit card balance can hit 30% annually. While various charges are almost always disclosed in fine print, credit-card terms are now so complex that they're commonly confused.

Here's a plain-English summary and advice on how to cut costs...

• Interest on unpaid balance. This has come down in recent years, to an average annual rate of 18.5%, but most consumers are effectively paying more than 20%. Those who regularly carry a balance should shop around for the lowest rate.

• Interest calculations. Banks can use several different methods to calculate interest charges. The most common is the average daily balance method including new purchases: If you start the month with a $1,000 balance and make a payment of $990, you will be charged interest on $1,000—not the $10 you still owe. The cheapest method for calculating interest is the average daily balance method, excluding new purchases, which does not include new purchases when figuring your finance charge. Only a few banks use this method.

A few issuers use the two-cycle average daily balance method, which in certain cases calculates interest on last month's and this month's balances and adds them together. This method can be very expensive for consumers who sometimes pay in full and sometimes carry a balance.

Some banks now charge interest from the date an item is purchased, rather than the date a charge is posted to one's account. This adds several days' worth of interest per month.

• Grace period. With most cards, holders have 25 days to pay a bill before interest is assessed. However, for the roughly 70% of holders who make a partial payment, and thereby have an unpaid balance each month, the grace period doesn't apply. To cut costs, send your payment as soon as you get your bill. If you pay off your balance each month, look for a card offering a full grace period.

• Cash advances. Fees range from 2% to 2.5% of a cash advance. Usually there's a minimum fee such as $2 and a maximum fee as high as $20. Few credit cards extend grace periods to cash advances. Because of these terms, cash advances are often the most costly way for consumers to borrow money.

• Additional fees. When shopping around, don't overlook additional fees that can add to the effective interest charges. For instance, fees for exceeding one's credit limit commonly run about $11 per month. Late payments entail additional fees of around $8 per month.

• Minimum payments. Many banks have low minimum payments, encouraging more people to maintain larger balances. The result, of course, has been higher credit-card costs.

Example: If you owe $2,500 and make a minimum payment of 2% per month, it would take you more than 30 years to pay off the balance and would cost $6,500 in interest charges. *Best:* Pay off your balance as fast as you can. Even paying $25 per month beyond the required minimum will help make an appreciable dent in credit-card costs.

Source: Gerri Detweiler, director, BankCard Holders of America, Suite 120, Herndon, Virginia 22070.

How Two-Paycheck Couples Can Make Their Money Work as Hard As They Do

Most working couples fail to exploit their financial clout. It gets lost in the hassle of everyday living.

A two-earner couple can raise capital much more easily than a one-earner...and capitalize on that additional borrowing power—even gamble on one of them starting a business.

What you can do...

• Take your joint earning power seriously. If you are jointly bringing home $100,000 (or $50,000), you are more than mere wage earners. Managing your money is a business.

•Start now. Two-earner couples typically talk themselves into a "tomorrow" attitude about starting to save and invest. Few take the time to compute the enormous sums they will need to buy a home, rear children, have a comfortable retirement, etc.

Guideline: Newlyweds should save at least 5% of their joint income and gradually increase the amount to 20% during peak earning years.

•Set goals. But make them flexible enough to enable you to deal with new situations—the arrival of a baby, the purchase of a home, a promotion, etc.

•Keep the lines of communication open about how to handle money. That way you can resolve differences and negotiate changes necessary to meet changed conditions. No matter how in love you are, no two people are going to agree completely about money.

Make time for making money...

Juggling job, home and family doesn't leave much time for financial management. *Helpful:* Transfer your combined knowledge of the business world to family finances. Modify the reports, forms, controls and filing systems you use at work to serve your needs at home.

•Get organized. Until you hack through the jumble, you can't tackle the real business of money management—investing.

•Set up a portion of your home as an office—with enough work space for each of you.

•Buy a filing cabinet for investment publications, articles and prospectuses, and for your bookkeeping records.

•Use in and out baskets. Pay bills when received and balance checkbooks monthly.

•Set up a "tickler" file to alert you to matters requiring action. Start with 12 file folders, one for each month, with the current month in front. Behind the current month's file, add 31-day files. File documents or projects according to the day you must start work on them, not by the deadline. At the end of each week, transfer the now-empty day files to the next month and start over.

•Open a single joint bank account. It cuts down on paperwork and administrative fees. The fewer accounts of any kind, in fact, the better...cuts down opportunities for errors.

Keep enough money in the checking account for day-to-day expenses and avoid bank charges.

Automatically transfer any excess funds to a joint money-market account with a higher interest rate. Use your money market account to pay large bills and hold savings while you decide where to invest them.

If you want to have some money separate from your spouse, pool the bulk of your incomes and put the rest in separate accounts. Do not use these accounts to pay for tax-deductible expenses unless you intend to file separate returns. You would have too many trails to follow at tax time.

•Cut back on credit cards. Carry only a few credit cards in your *individual* names. One spouse should be the "primary" cardholder on Mastercard, for instance, and the other spouse the "primary" Visa cardholder. You will save time, checks, postage and membership fees as a result.

•Keep good records. The driving force behind record keeping is taxes. You cannot intelligently spend, invest or plan without being aware of tax implications.

Sort your income and expenses in folders labeled by categories behind subject dividers. Each of you will file cancelled checks written on your separate accounts. One of you will be responsible for filing the joint accounts.

Keep current on filing. This way, you will always know where you stand. And tax time will be a snap.

At regular intervals, summarize these records, preferably on a computer. Financial software packages save time in tracking your assets and help in controlling spending—essential for successful investing.

•Staple cancelled checks and their related receipts together. Don't pay cash for tax-deductible expenses but if you must, get a receipt. Use a separate credit card for business travel and/or entertaining. There's no reason to spend time separating business from personal expenses. The monthly total will be the amount deductible.

•Delegate and rotate responsibility so that you both gain experience in all aspects of finance. In the event of disability, death, overtime or out-of-town meetings, either partner should be able to carry on. This also prevents one person from getting stuck with boring chores or losing sight of the overall financial picture.

You can divide tasks equally, then switch jobs every six months. Or one spouse can take charge completely for six months at a stretch. This latter arrangement may be the best approach if one of you is in a seasonal business or travels extensively at certain times of the year.

Consider a tradeoff if one of you is constantly traveling. The wandering spouse can assume three or four big tasks, such as preparing the tax return or studying investment prospectuses —perfect hotel reading.

Splitting authority is a great time-saver. You don't have to do everything in tandem. After a joint initial visit with an attorney, accountant or stockbroker, only one of you need go thereafter except in matters of great importance.

• Discuss financial goals and share decisions. Schedule periodic meetings to assess your financial status, confer about problems and review plans for the future. Make an appointment if you have to. Reserve a table at your favorite quiet restaurant, bring your documents and go over the scheduled topics as you would at any business dinner.

• Form an investment club with your spouse. Decide what types of investments are needed to meet your goals, then divide the work.

Example: One spouse can research and select stock funds while the other does the same for bond funds. Or you might each agree to pick one stock and one bond fund.

Compare results. Analyze why one outperformed the other and learn together.

As you get your financial affairs under control you can branch out from easy, no-fuss investments like CDs and money-market funds into more diverse and potentially more profitable ventures.

Work efficiently...

It's not enough to carve out time. You must also use it effectively.

• Batch related activities. Write all your checks on the first Sunday of the month, for example, then drop them into your tickler file by mailing date.

• Make a list of tasks that need to be done. Then work through the list, crossing off each job as it is completed. Update the list daily or weekly.

• Be decisive. Plan the research...carry it out ...see if more research is desirable...move ahead. Don't procrastinate.

Source: Mary L. Sprouse. She is the author of *Sprouse's Two-Earner Money Book,* Viking Penguin, 375 Hudson St., New York 10014.

Money Moves to Help You Get Ready for The Next Century

A tougher job market...higher taxes...an end to traditional company pensions...more litigation...bloodbaths on Wall Street. These are among the awful things in store for us as we approach the 21st century.

Are you ready? If not, here are 10 ways to prepare yourself financially for the year 2000 and beyond...

• Get ready for job insecurity. There's a growing probability of unemployment at some point in your career. And once unemployed, chances are you will stay unemployed for a longer period than you would have in the past.

Ask yourself, *What would happen if I lost my job tomorrow?* If you are prepared, you may be more assertive in demanding a better severance package. The time to demand better severance pay is when you're getting the ax, not 24 hours later.

Also consider how to survive financially if you become unemployed. There's nothing like money in the bank to prepare for unemployment.

• Pay off your debts. If you lose your job, you will be in better shape if your debts are under control. Paying off debt is also a better use for your money than leaving the cash in low-yielding bonds or certificates of deposit. How come? Being indebted has virtually no tax advantages, unless the debt is a mortgage. And the cost of borrowing money, when compared with the inflation rate, is much higher now than it has been historically.

• Get "umbrella" liability insurance. That will protect you in case you get sued. Our society is becoming more litigious. One out of 17 people gets sued each year. Umbrella liability insurance doesn't just buy you protection if you lose a suit—it also pays your legal defense costs. For $1 million of extra protection, you will pay only $100 to $200 a year.

Warning: Umbrella liability does not cover job-related lawsuits.

• Live beneath your means. There are two reasons for this:

• It gives you the latitude to pay for unexpected expenses without going into debt.

• You will free up money that can be saved for retirement. The amount you need to save for retirement is exploding—as prices rise, people live longer and company pensions are eliminated.

• Become a long-term investor. Otherwise, you could face dire consequences when it comes time to retire. Traditional company pension plans are fast disappearing. Social Security will provide only a small amount of the money needed to retire.

If you are going to live well after you leave the workforce, you need to commit a large portion of your investment portfolio to the stock market today so that you can build wealth by tapping into the handsome long-run gains generated by stocks.

But remember, those gains have a price. You must learn to live with wild swings in share prices during the short term.

• Invest internationally. In the years ahead, there will always be a bull market going on somewhere in the world, and more often than not it won't be in the US. To invest in foreign markets, buy mutual funds instead of individual stocks.

My favorite no-loads...

• *T. Rowe Price International Stock Fund* (800-638-5660) and...

• *Scudder International Fund* (800-225-2470).

• Load up on tax-advantaged investments. Taxes aren't going down, and they may well go up, so you need to protect yourself from Uncle Sam.

Consider tax-free municipal bonds, which provide better after-tax returns than corporate or government bonds, presuming you are in the 28% or higher tax bracket.

Also take full advantage of retirement savings vehicles, such as 401(k) plans, 403(b) plans and individual retirement accounts. Your money will grow tax-deferred, and your investments each year may also be tax-deductible.

• Actively manage your stock portfolio. Our parents could buy and hold good-quality stocks. That doesn't work anymore. In 1993, hardly a day went by without a sound company getting bashed on Wall Street for no good reason. The next stock to be bashed could be sitting in your portfolio. As a result, you must take a more active approach to managing your stock portfolio.

Strategy: Use mutual funds to get active management. Funds offer professional money management at a relatively low cost. They are a particularly good way to invest in foreign stocks as well as aggressive small-company stocks in the US.

• Consider sophisticated estate-planning strategies. More people are going to become subject to estate taxes. If you are married and have an estate worth more than $600,000, at a minimum you'll need a trust that will allow both husband and wife to make use of the $600,000 unified credit. In addition, people with estates that are likely to be subject to estate taxes should talk to their attorneys about putting their life insurance into irrevocable life insurance trusts.

• Learn to do it yourself. With company pensions on the wane and Social Security under attack, you can't blindly rely on a financial planner or an investment adviser for financial security. Even if you use an adviser, you still have to teach yourself about financial matters, or your finances could be mismanaged for years without your realizing what's happening.

Best of all, do it yourself. That way, you will have true control over your finances—and you will also save yourself a bundle on brokerage commissions and investment advisory fees.

Source: Jonathan D. Pond, president, Financial Planning Information Inc., 9 Galen St., Watertown, Massachusetts 02172. He is the author of *The New Century Family Money Book*, Dell Publishing, 1540 Broadway, New York 10036.

How to Stay in Control Of Your Money...Now

What should individuals expect to be charged when they retain an adviser to help them make investment decisions?

The annual fee that a financial adviser charges should not be more than 1.5% of the value of your stock investments under management. For a bond portfolio, a fair annual fee is closer to 0.75%.

Annual fees should be on a sliding scale that declines as your investment assets increase. International investing is more complex, however, and it is the only category of investments for which a higher annual fee is justified.

In addition, most money managers charge a minimum fee of about $1,000 a year. That is warranted, in my view, since a substantial amount of time goes into setting up accounts, reviewing and reporting on performance, managing paperwork and counseling clients.

Most brokerage firms offer *wrap accounts*, which combine financial planning and trading services. The money-management and brokerage commissions are grouped into a flat, annual fee of about 3%. Over time, that can be pretty steep if you don't do much trading. I think those fees will eventually come down.

What services can clients expect for these money-management fees?

At the very least, you should receive a report each quarter on how your investments are doing. Each quarter, your adviser should also give you his/her opinion about what's going on in the economy and suggest changes in your investments—if applicable—based on that outlook.

When looking for a money manager, what information can an individual get on his/her past performance...or that of a brokerage firm's wrap account?

The performance of money managers, like that of mutual funds, is monitored by independent analysts. When you're considering a money manager for equity investments, ask to be shown his/her CDA performance rating* and review it on the basis of total return—*capital gains plus reinvested dividends.* Compare it to the total return of a market index, such as the S&P 500.

If you're considering a wrap account offered by a brokerage firm, you'll be able to choose a money manager based on your financial objectives from among a group that the firm selected.

Keep in mind that how well the manager has beaten the market in the past shouldn't necessarily be the primary reason for selecting him. Equally important might be how well the manager conserves capital in bear markets or the volatility of his performance.

After you've chosen a money manager, is it unusual for him to insist on managing only a cash deposit?

Not at all. A money manager is justified in thinking that he can perform better for you if you hand over a sum of cash to manage rather than a portfolio of stocks and bonds—from, say, an inheritance. In fact, some managers will take on a new account only if it's in cash.

Reason: Since money managers report their performance to independent analysts, they don't want their records hampered by investments in a portfolio that they would not have recommended.

This means you'll either have to liquidate some of your portfolio or authorize the manager to sell securities so that he has cash to invest for you.

If someone is paying a manager to monitor an account, should any of the money be in an index fund, whose portfolio matches that of a broad-based index such as the S&P 500?

I don't think so. You're already paying the money manager to do as well—and better—than the market or an index over time.

Should investors be concerned if they don't receive a stock or bond certificate?

No. Money managers don't actually have custody of the certificates. The brokerage or bank with which they do business does.

In the near future, stock and bond certificates will probably be phased out and your holdings will increasingly appear only as computer entries. You'll just get a confirmation from the firm that handles the transaction, not a certificate.

Mutual funds do this now—sending you a regular statement showing how many shares you own, whether dividends or capital gains were reinvested, etc. Individual investors are resisting this trend, but it's inevitable.

How, then, is an investor protected when all he/she has is a statement from the broker to acknowledge what he owns?

Well, there's the brokerage industry's own insurance program, which covers up to $400,000 in securities and $100,000 in cash in each customer's account. Most firms buy additional insurance to protect their customers in case the company fails.

What kind of personal bookkeeping works best once you own a variety of investments rather than just a few bank CDs?

There are several computer software programs available that can help you keep track of your funds. I find, however, that the simplest, most effective system is a three-hole binder, loose-leaf paper, a set of tabbed dividers and a three-hole punch. You should use a tab divider for every investment account—brokerage account, trust fund, mutual funds, bank CDs, IRAs and so on.

Then, each time you receive paperwork in the mail—the original confirmation of a transaction, a dividend statement, notice of stock split, etc.—punch the holes if they aren't there already and slip it into the rings at the front of the specific section.

Mutual fund statements are cumulative, of course, so you can just take out the previous notice and put in the new one. The whole record will be right there when you do your taxes. Set it up right now for this year if you've had a lot of trouble getting your records together for last year.

Source: Alexandra Armstrong, chairman, Armstrong, Welch, MacIntyre, Inc., 1155 Connecticut Ave. NW, Washington, DC 20036.

Ten of the Most Common Mistakes in Financial Planning

Mistake: Not knowing what is enough for your financial objectives. Too many investors are caught up in the cultural bias for *more*... more for more's sake. This is akin to putting the cart before the horse and then killing the horse. Too often, in investing, the push to make more requires overreaching—taking risks that can result, in the end, in *less* rather than more. Since more is by definition never enough, financial planners are driven to accomplish the impossible. This creates anxiety for both you and your planner.

What I advocate in my professional planning practice is a radically different school of thought that I call *Enough*.

This approach puts the client into personal financial planning. It recognizes the essential truth that financial resources are only a means to achieve personal objectives. The goal is to look inward and identify your life goals and then align those goals with your personal resources.

If your retirement income needs can be met, after adjusting for inflation and tax increases, with an investment that is safely earning 6%, why take a big risk to earn 20%?

When you have *enough* you can relax and be satisfied, or you can start a new fund. But you don't have to push for more.

Mistake: Abdicating responsibility. Too many people work for 40 years (that's about 80,000 hours of making money)—but don't spend the relatively few hours needed to protect their life's earnings.

You can't abdicate that responsibility. It's OK to let a planner help you row the boat, but *you* must steer.

Once you have determined your objectives, you can use a personal financial planner to provide technical advice. Avoid planners who are transaction-oriented, such as brokers and life insurance salespersons. They're working for themselves, not you. *Fee-only* planners are a better choice, *though they're not guaranteed to be competent.*

Beware: There are 250,000 people in the US who call themselves personal financial planners but have virtually no expertise and are subject to no industry or government regulations.

Mistake: Wanting results *now*. Remember, anything worth doing is worth doing slowly. This is particularly true of investments. Going for a quick kill is a sure way to get burned. Don't convey a sense of impatience to your planner. Be satisfied to make steady progress.

Mistake: Piecemeal planning. By doing piecemeal planning you may solve one problem, but you can create two others. Planners are now pushing what's called modular planning—e.g., how to finance your child's education. But you can't plan that in isolation. What if you need to put aside $10,000 a year and you become disabled? Comprehensive planning is the only answer.

Mistake: Concentrating on finances instead of on personal goals. Much too much financial planning is based strictly on managing assets instead of on aligning your personal finances with your personal goals. Life planning must come before financial planning, not the other way around. *Enough* is a very personal thing.

Mistake: Not asking what could go wrong. Before making any investment, you should know about the downside. What could go wrong? What would be the cause of trouble? What's the probability? The seriousness? How can you prevent or minimize risk? The best surprise is no surprise.

Mistake: Neglecting to ask to see the planner's own financial plan. This should not be a secret. If he/she is going to see your personal finances, you should be able to see his. If he doesn't have a plan or won't show you, go elsewhere. People who can't plan for their own lives certainly can't help you plan for yours.

Mistake: Not distinguishing the "closer" from the "doer." There are a lot of charming professionals out there who are very good at making the sale but don't actually do the work. It may be the partner of the CPA firm who signs you up, but your account is really handled by some clerk in a position that turns over every two years, meaning that you have to keep re-educating new people. Don't pay partner fees for a partner you never see. By the same token, an hour spent with a very good (but expensive) planner may be worth more than a month of someone else's time.

Mistake: Not getting an estimate of fees and commissions up front. Don't accept an answer of, *"We won't know until we see how your account works out."* Any professional planner knows how to qualify prospects. At the very least, the planner can tell you what other investors of your general description are paying in average fees and commissions.

Note: Although there are only about 1,000 fee-only planners, you may be able to negotiate a fee-only relationship with a normally commissioned planner who's willing to strike a deal.

Mistake: Believing that the specific investment is more important than asset allocation. The term "financial planning" is used by insurance companies, brokers, investment companies, banks, partnership syndicators and others who are trying to put an independent-looking mask on what is really just a delivery system for the sale of a product. Fully 93% of portfolio value is based on investment classifications (how assets are allocated between different types of investments), *not* on the specific investment or the timing of the purchase. If you tell a planner you have, say, $100,000 to invest and the planner tells you where it should go *before* finding out about your plans, goals, other assets, etc., the planner has failed.

Source: James D. Schwartz, a fee-only personal financial planner and president of ENOUGH, Inc., Englewood, Colorado. He is the author of *ENOUGH, A Guide to Reclaiming Your American Dream*, Re/Max International, Inc., Creative Ad Fund, Box 3363, Englewood, Colorado 80155.

Better 401(k) Investing

It pays to know your options for investing your 401(k). Most company plans offer three to five choices. *Examples:* Company stock, equity mutual funds, money-market funds, and/or guaranteed investment contracts issued by insurance companies. *Helpful:* Request a prospectus from each company that manages one of these investment options and read it very carefully—with your accountant, if necessary. Contact your employer's retirement-plan manager for the name and address of each of these companies.

Source: Legg Mason, president, Legg Mason Wood Walker, Inc., investment advisers and stockbrokers, 99 Summer St., Box 1, Boston 02101.

Savings Bond Savvy

US savings bonds now pay higher annual yields than any other low-risk, liquid investment. Currently, savings bonds pay 4%, compared to tax-free money funds (3.3%), one-year CDs (3%), three-month Treasury bills (2.91%), money funds (2.6%) and money-market accounts (2.4%). *Catch:* Savings bonds must be held for at least six months before being redeemed.

Source: Norman Fosback, editor of *Income & Safety,* 3471 N. Federal Hwy., Fort Lauderdale 33306. 800-442-9000.

Student Loan Repayment Plans

Student loan repayment plans can ease the burdens of recent graduates who have low-paying jobs or none at all. *Trap:* Those who ignore lenders' collection notices can seriously damage their credit ratings. *Self-defense:* Loan holders should talk to their lenders as soon as possible if they cannot meet loan terms. Lenders contacted before payments fall behind are more likely to consider other repayment options. Possibilities include deferment—postponing repayment and perhaps stopping interest from accruing...forbearance—postponing repayment of principal while interest still accrues... consolidation—combining many loans into one...graduated repayment—smaller payments in early years, larger ones later...or some other special arrangement.

Source: Patricia McWade, dean of financial aid, Georgetown University, Washington, DC.

What to Ask a Financial Planner

The probing questions to ask:

- What's your specialty? If the planner lists specialties—say, hard assets or insurance or stocks or tax shelters—scratch him/her from your list. *What you should be looking for:* A generalist with a professional staff.
- What percentage of your income comes from fees and how much from commissions? If much of the income is generated by commissions, also scratch him.
- What are your educational background and professional experience? If he passes the background test, call his references.
- Are you affiliated with any other firm? Some planners are affiliated with an insurance company, a stockbroker, or even a marketer of tax shelters. You should eliminate them.
- Can you quantify what you can do for me? Eliminate planners who jump to that bait and start reeling off numbers.
- How much will it cost? If he immediately quotes you a package price, go on the next candidate.

Source: Connie S.P. Chen, a former financial consultant at Merrill Lynch's Personal Financial Planning Group and, for the last seven years, head of Chen Planning Consultants, New York.

No-Haggle Hassle

Car buyers who shop at one-price "no-haggle" dealerships to avoid the discomfort of negotiating may pay as much as $1,000 more for the convenience.

Reason: Prices at no-haggle dealerships are inflexible and typically higher than those that consumers could negotiate for themselves at traditional showrooms.

Source: W. James Bragg, author of *In the Driver's Seat: The New Car Buyer's Negotiating Bible.* Random House, 201 E. 50 St., New York 10022.

How to Make Your Money Work

•Earn up to 21% risk-free by paying off charge-card balances early. You may not realize that carrying a $500 balance on a bank card can cost as much as $105 per year.

•Make contributions to your IRA or Keogh Plan as early in the year as possible.

•Borrow money from your corporate profit-sharing or pension plan rather than from a bank. You may still claim the interest expense as a deduction.

•Shift income to your children with trusts or custodial accounts. The money will be taxed at their low rate.

•Increase your insurance deductibles.

•Don't rely on your accountant to find the best possible tax deductions for you. Invest in a good self-help manual.

•Prepay your mortgage. An extra $100 a month will dramatically shorten your term and total interest expenses.

Source: Dr. Paul A. Randle, professor of finance, Utah State University, writing in *Physicians Management,* New York.

Quick and Easy Ways To Save Money

•Comparison shop by phone, not by car.

•Make your own gift wrap and greeting cards.

•Use heavy-duty brown bags from the supermarket for garbage.

•Make your own liquid dishwashing soap out of leftover soap slivers (put them in a jar, cover with water and stir occasionally).

•Use toll-free numbers (call the toll-free information operator at 800-555-1212).

•Rent a room in your home to a local college student.

Source: *Parents* magazine, New York.

Stretching Due Dates On Bills

Due dates on bills can be stretched—but not far—without risk. *Typical grace periods:* Telephone companies, eight days. Gas and electric utilities, 10 days. Banks and finance companies, 10 days. Even after a late charge is imposed on an unpaid bill your credit rating should be safe for 30 days.

Source: Terry Blaney, president of Consumer Credit Counseling Service of Houston and the Gulf Coast Area.

How to Find Money You Didn't Know You Had

Few people take full advantage of the capital at their disposal. *There are a myriad of simple ways to optimize your personal financial resources:*

•Convert passbook savings accounts, savings bonds, etc. into better investments. Americans still have $300 billion sitting in low-interest passbook savings accounts when they could be so easily transferred to CDs at nearly double the yield! Review your portfolio now, particularly bonds that have recently registered nice gains. Should you still be owning what you do? People often hold investments long after they've forgotten why they originally made them.

•Borrow on life insurance (such low interest rates aren't being offered today). Many folks who bought life insurance back in the 1960s and 1970s (term insurance is more prevalent today) could borrow back the money at 3% to 6% and reinvest it in insured CDs at a higher rate.

•Pay real estate taxes directly instead of through the bank. Most banks withhold an amount on monthly mortgage payments for paying the homeowner's real estate taxes. Yet, in most towns, real estate tax bills are sent annually. The bank is earning interest on your money. *Caution:* You must make the payments on time. Banks can call in your mortgage if the taxes are delinquent, and they'd just love to do it if you are fortunate enough to have a low-interest mortgage.

•Prepay mortgage principal. Making a monthly $25 prepayment of principal from day one on a $75,000, 30-year, 13% mortgage would save $59,372, and the mortgage would be paid off in 23 years and four months. (Most mortgages allow prepayment.)

•Conduct a garage sale. Turn unwanted items into cash. (Sotheby's or another auction house will appraise a possible collectible for free.)

If you are self-employed:

•Keep good records of travel and entertainment expenses and of the business use of cars, computers and other property used for both business and personal purposes. Taxpayers who can't back up their deductions with good records will lose the deductions and may be charged negligence penalties.

•Reward yourself first. Plan for your future by putting money into your tax-deferred retirement plan now. Too many entrepreneurs wait until they're successful before taking money out of the business and risk receiving nothing.

•Park company cash in the highest yielding CDs. It's easy to compare CDs. Look at the table called Highest Money-Market Yields, now published in 23 major newspapers. The highest-yielding CDs in the country are paying 2% to 3% above the average yield. That translates into $200 to $300 a year with a $10,000 CD.

Source: William E. Donoghue, publisher of several investment newsletters, including *Donoghue's Moneyletter,* Holliston, MA.

Smart Borrowing

Even many super-successful business people find themselves short of cash at times, whether in paying a child's college tuition or in taking advantage of an irresistible investment.

Once you have decided on a sound reason and a sound plan for borrowing, you naturally want to find the best possible interest rate. There are a variety of ways to avoid the high unsecured loan rates being offered at most banks and thrifts across the country:

•Insurance policy loan: Particularly attractive if you have an old policy that provides for low interest rate loans. It is especially good if the policy has been in effect for more than seven years. *Reason:* There is a legal provision that policyholders must have paid four out of the first seven payments to get a tax-deductible loan. If the policy has been in effect for seven years, there is no question about tax deductibility. *Safety valve:* Many people fear borrowing on their life insurance policies because this reduces the coverage in case of death. *Solution:* You can use the dividends on the policy to buy additional term insurance to keep the insurance level at face value. That permits you to borrow and to maintain the death value.

•Qualified savings plan: Many corporate savings plans, including 401(k) plans, permit employees to borrow the savings that they (and their employer) have put into the plan. Typically, the borrowing rate on savings plans is lower than bank rates, although each company has its own rules. Ask your personnel office about your company's policies. *Caution:* Do not confuse this with IRAs or Keoghs. You cannot borrow against them. And although some firms permit employees to borrow against their pension funds, it isn't advisable.

•Brokerage house loan: The current big thing in the brokerage houses is cash management accounts (in their various guises)—and home equity accounts. Cash management accounts let you borrow against stocks and bonds. Home equity accounts include the value of your home as collateral against loans. Brokerage houses have the resources to appraise your home, and they permit you to borrow at a fairly good rate—the broker loan rate. *Problem:* Margin loans against stock can be called if the stock market goes down sharply and the collateral loses value.

•Second mortgage: Exercise extreme caution when using this technique. You are giving someone a lien on your home. You might lose your job, or your business might falter. It is a dangerous way to get into a bind—and you could end up losing your home.

Source: Thomas Lynch, senior vice president, Ayco/American Express, a financial consulting group that advises corporate personnel about financial and tax matters.

The Best Places to Borrow Money

There are now more ways to borrow money than ever before. By carefully shopping around, you may be able to save big dollars while establishing valuable new credit lines.

•Interest-free loans from the company have been a favored perk for key executives for years. The bookkeeping is now more complicated, but both the company and the executive may be left in the same position they were in before the new tax laws went into effect, owing little or no tax as a result of the loan.

•Preferred financing terms are often provided by banks to the employees of major commercial accounts. *Typical benefit:* Home mortgages at a half point to a full point lower than the standard mortgage rate.

•Company pension plans frequently contain provisions that allow employees to borrow against their plan accounts. Many plans allow loans to be made at a reasonable interest rate in order to help finance the purchase of a new primary residence or to meet specified emergencies. Employees can typically borrow as much as half the value of their non-forfeitable retirement benefits, up to a maximum of $50,000.

•Credit unions are usually a cheap source of funds for their members. Because they have less overhead than banks and are looking to break even rather than to make a profit, they lend at rates lower than commercial rates. *Typical:* Personal loans of up to half your salary. Many credit unions also have insurance programs.

•Home equity loans. When the original mortgage on a house has been largely paid off, and the house has gone up in value, a borrower may be able to get a loan at about two points over the prime rate. *Caution:* There are drawbacks to using your house as collateral. First, you're establishing a lien against your home. Second, there are charges involved—often a one-time fee of 2% on the credit line, plus an annual maintenance fee of $25 to $100, and perhaps a mortgage recording tax.

•Bank loans. It's important to shop around for the best terms. Remember that as a borrower you don't have to worry about the bank's solvency. You can safely take advantage of unusual terms offered by a bank that's desperate for business.

•Credit and debit cards may be the most expensive form of financing (typically charging interest rates of 18% to 20%), but they also offer the most convenient source of cash around. *Danger:* Letting charges pile up. *Rule of thumb:* Monthly loan payments, exclusive of the home mortgage, should total no more than 10% to 15% of net income.

•Merchant financing may represent a better deal than the average bank loan. *Typical case:* An auto purchase. While a local bank may offer auto loans at 12% to 13%, many auto dealers, helped out by funds from the major manufacturers, can extend credit at 8% to 9%.

Sources: David S. Rhine, partner, BDO Seidman, New York, and Israel A. Press, partner and director of personal financial management, Touche Ross Financial Services Center, New York.

Lending Money to A Friend

•No matter how friendly a loan, draw up a note stating terms and conditions.

•Be businesslike. Include a provision for reasonable interest.

•Be prepared to document the loan, so that you can take a tax deduction on any loss.

Filing a Claim for Bodily Injury

Claims against insurance companies for bodily injury can be the most complicated and negotiable type of claim, especially when based upon pain and suffering. *Be aware:*

• In a no-fault state, you are limited to out-of-pocket expenses in a nonserious injury. This includes lost wages. In a fault-governed state, you can negotiate for more.

• Don't miss damages. Start at the top of your head and go down to your toes, to include every part that's been hurt.

• Photograph your injury. In addition to medical reports, photos are the best documentation of suffering.

• Consider every aspect of your life affected by your injury. Include your career, sports, hobbies, future interests and family relationships.

• Ask the insurance company what a lawyer would ask—at least twice the actual expenses when there has been no permanent disability. Where liability is clear, the insurance company will be likely to give you what you ask, if it believes that you really had difficulties and were out of work for a few weeks. However, where there has been permanent disability, multiples of expenses do not apply. *Example:* Your medical bills for a lost eye might have been only $3,000, but a jury might award you 50 times that amount.

Source: Dan Brecher, a New York City attorney.

Before You Sign A Contract with A Health Club

• Inspect the club at the time of day you'd be most likely to attend. Check on how crowded the pool, sauna and exercise rooms are.

• Make certain all facilities that are promised are available.

• Avoid clubs that require long-term contracts.

• Once you sign a contract, if you wish to terminate, it's usually possible to avoid liability for the full term of the contract by notifying the club by registered mail, paying for services already rendered and a small cancellation fee. Check your local consumer protection agency for rules.

• *Most important:* Don't be pushed into a hasty decision by a low-price offer. Specials are usually repeated.

Financial Aid for the Mugging Victim

Financial compensation programs for mugging victims exist in more than 30 states. Compensation can cover both medical expenses and lost earnings. However, most of these programs utilize a means test that effectively eliminates all but lower-income victims. Additionally, the victim's own medical and unemployment insurance must be fully depleted before state compensation is granted.

If you are mugged, check the following:

• Workers compensation may cover you if you were mugged on the job or on your way to or from company business during your workday. It will not cover you while commuting.

• Homeowners' policies may cover financial losses suffered during a mugging.

• Federal crime insurance insures up to $10,000 against financial losses from a mugging. This program is for people who have had difficulty purchasing homeowners' insurance privately.

• Mugging insurance is now available in New York. It covers property loss, medical care and mental anguish. If successful, it may spread rapidly to other states.

• A lawsuit may be successful if you can prove that the mugging was the result of negligence.

Source: Lucy N. Friedman, executive director, Victim Services Agency, New York.

If the Dry Cleaner Loses Or Ruins a Garment

• You should be reimbursed or given a credit. Most dry cleaners are neighborhood businesses where reputation is vital. You can hurt a cleaner's reputation by giving the cleaner bad word-of-mouth. You might remind the store of this fact if there is resistance to satisfying your complaint.

• If your cleaner fails to remove a stain you were told could be removed, you still have to pay for the cleaning job.

• If your cleaner dry cleans a garment with a "do not dry clean" label, the store is responsible for ruining the garment.

• If your cleaner ruins a garment that should not be dry cleaned but lacks the "do not dry clean" label, responsibility is a matter of opinion. The cleaner may reimburse you to keep your goodwill, or you may have to complain to an outside agency.

• The amount you will be reimbursed is always up for bargaining. You will have to consider original value and depreciation, and whether you have a receipt.

• If you cannot get satisfaction from your cleaner voluntarily, most states have dry cleaners associations to arbitrate complaints. These associations go under various names in different states, so check with your local Department of Consumer Affairs. Make sure to keep all dry cleaning receipts and other relevant information to substantiate your complaint.

Social Security Number Secret

Few people know it, but the first three digits of a Social Security number are a code for the state in which the card was issued. This code, which can be used to confirm a place of birth or an employment history, is not public knowledge. However, many private detectives have the key to the code and will crack the Social Security number for a fee.

Source: Milo Speriglio, director and chief of Nick Harris Detectives, Inc., Van Nuys, CA, the second-oldest private detective agency in the US, and administrator of Nick Harris' Detective Academy.

When to Use Small Claims Court

Suing in small claims court can bring both spiritual and material satisfaction when you feel that you have been wronged. Although the monetary stakes are low—most states limit small claims settlements to no more than $1,000—the rewards can be high.

Take a case to small claims court when you:

• Have the time. Usually it takes a month for a case to be called and you'll have to spend at least a few hours in court during the hearing.

• Value justice over a monetary settlement.

• Want a public hearing of your grievance.

• Feel the money involved represents a significant sum to you.

Savings and College Financial Aid

Some people fear that if they save to finance college, they will be penalized—with more financial aid going to someone who did not save at all. *Reality:* Financial aid formulas weigh *income* more heavily than *assets.* If you have good income but no savings, you will still be expected to make a substantial contribution to college costs. *Also:* A significant amount of aid is in the form of loans—which have to be repaid. The more cash you save before college, the less debt you and your children will have afterward.

Source: Kalman A. Chany, president of Campus Consultants, Inc., a fee-based firm that assists families in maximizing financial aid eligibility, and author of *The Princeton Review Student Access Guide to Paying for College.* Random House, 201 E. 50 St., New York 10022.

Pension-Plan Savvy

Monitor your company pension plan for possible mistakes that could prove costly when you retire. First, get a summary plan description from your employer that tells how retirement benefits are calculated. It's a good idea to see the description of a prospective new employer's plan before quitting your old job and letting your old pension plan go.

Key questions: Do bonuses, overtime and commissions—or just salary—count toward retirement benefits? Are benefits at retirement based on your top-earning years...or on all years of service? How are years of service calculated if you take a pregnancy break or some other leave of absence?

Source: *Baby Boomer Retirement: 65 Simple Ways to Protect Your Future* by Don Silver, an estate-planning lawyer in Los Angeles. Adams-Hall Publishing, Box 491002-BR3, Los Angeles 90049.

14

Your Car

What to Look for When You Test Drive a Car

Before you buy a new car, take full advantage of your test drive. Make sure the dealer lets you drive the vehicle where you can give it a thorough workout...on bumpy roads...in stop-and-go traffic...and on highways, especially the entrance and exit ramps. Pay special attention to how the car matches up to your expectations for comfort, drivability, interior layout and power.

Comfort...

• Engineers call the science of fitting the car to the person "ergonomics." You'll soon see how well they did when you climb in behind the driver's seat.

• You probably won't be the only one driving the new car regularly. Don't forget that the "feel" of the car should suit your co-drivers and frequent passengers.

• *Clearance:* Can you get in and out without hitting your head?

• *Headroom:* Your hair shouldn't touch the ceiling. If it does, and you love the vehicle, consider ordering it with a sunroof. This will give you another inch or two.

• *Seat height:* Does it give you good road visibility?

• *Headrest:* Will your head, neck and back be comfortable after driving for a while?

• *Leg room:* Does the seat move far enough forward and back not only for you but for all drivers?

Drivability...

• Test drive the car at night to make sure that the headlights are powerful enough for your comfort.

• *Power:* Does the car run smoothly and accelerate adequately? *Hint:* Make sure the car you test has the engine size, transmission type, or gear ratios that you want.

• *Rear visibility:* Can you see adequately with the exterior rear-view mirrors? If they're too small, be aware that replacements don't exist.

•*Noise:* Does engine exhaust or wind noise bother you?

•*Fuel type:* Does the car need expensive high-test gas? High-performance, multi-valve, super- and turbo-charged models all do.

Interior...

•*Instrumentation:* Can you read the gauges easily?

•*Controls:* Do you hit the wiper switch and put the radio on?

•*Door handles:* Can you find them in the dark?

Bottom line...

•If you're satisfied with your test drive, don't assume the car that the dealer delivers to you will be as good.

•Check out the finish of the car you want to buy to make sure you haven't been sold a vehicle that already has been driven...or damaged in transit. Look for tell-tale signs of repainting ...like paint traces on the rubber stripping or trim, mismatched colors and misfit panels. And take a good look at the undercoating. It should look slightly weathered—not sparkling clean and still soft.

•Insist on a test drive of your new car before you accept delivery. *Also:* Never take delivery at night. You want to examine your car carefully in broad daylight. You may also want to have the car looked over by a good mechanic.

Source: David Solomon, editor, *Nutz and Boltz®*, Box 123, Butler, Maryland 21023.

Understanding Car Terms

•*Rack-and-pinion steering:* This compact system has fewer moving parts than older systems and therefore is cheaper to make. But it is not necessarily better than the standard system.

•*Unibody construction:* Everything fastens onto the body, reducing the car's weight and increasing mileage. But a minor fender-bender can create hidden damage in another part of the structure.

•*Automatic overdrive transmission:* This is a fuel-economy measure. An extra high gear slows the engine when the car is cruising at a constant speed. *Disadvantage:* The car has reduced acceleration and hill-climbing ability when in this gear.

•*Overhead camshaft engine:* This slightly improves efficiency at high speeds, which is why some race cars use it. But this difference is not significant in normal driving.

Source: Automobile Club of New York.

Making the Right Choice of Options On a New Car

The value of an optional feature depends on how, when, and where most of the driving will be done.

Important for everyone: Options that make the car safer.

•Air bags.

•Steel-belted radial tires. They hold the road better, provide better fuel economy and longer life.

•Buy accessories that relate to the character of the automobile. A very lightweight car does not require power steering or power brakes.

Important but not essential:

•Cruise control. This is a great advantage for driving long distances on a regular basis. It sets the pace and helps the driver avoid speeding tickets.

•Air conditioning. This is very important for comfort and for the subsequent resale value of the car.

•Heavy-duty suspension system. It makes the car feel taut and firm and hold the road better. There is little initial cost and little value on resale. It is important for car owners who are either going to carry heavy loads or who love to drive and are extra sensitive to the performance of the car. It's not an important feature for those whose car use is limited mainly to trips to the supermarket.

•Power seats. Extremely useful feature for drivers who go long distances regularly. Permits moving the seat back. Allows arm position to be manipulated and fine-tuned in relation to steering wheel. In some ways a safety factor because it helps ward off driver fatigue. Power seats are quite expensive.

•Adjustable seat back. Some form of this is highly recommended and should be considered because it wards off driver fatigue and thus is a safety element.

•Tilt steering wheel. This is another aid in fine-tuning the driver's relation to the car and is therefore recommended as a safety factor. It is an important feature especially for large or short people.

•Electric door locks. Key unlocks all doors simultaneously. Button locks all doors at once, including the trunk lid. It is a convenience because it makes it unnecessary to open each door from the outside in bad weather. When driving through dangerous neighborhoods, the electric lock provides immediate security with the touch of a button.

Some options have disadvantages:

•Sunroof. Redundant if the car has air conditioning. Noise and the problem of water leakage are constant irritations.

•Power windows. They are recommended for drivers who use toll highways on a regular basis. Power windows can be dangerous to both small children and pets.

Fixing your present car vs. buying a new one:

Most older cars can be refurbished—and in fact be made as good as new—for far less than the cost of a brand new car. *The key:* The break-even point of the deal.

To figure fix-up costs: Have a competent mechanic give you a detailed list of everything that's wrong and costs to fix it up. With that kind of renovation, a car should be good for another five years with no major repair expenses.

•Even if the car needed a completely new engine, it would still be cheaper to repair the old car than to buy a brand new one.

•Gas mileage is not a key consideration. Assume that a new car would get 50% better gas mileage than the older car. It would still take at least 10 years to break even on mileage alone. *Example:* Your present car gets 15 MPG, and a new car would get 30 MPG. You buy 1,000 gallons of fuel per year (15,000 miles of driving) and it costs $1.40 per gallon. Your present gas bill is $1,400 per year. The 30 MPG car would cost you $700 per year. At that rate, disregarding all the other expenses of the new car, it would take 14 years for a payback on the improved mileage.

•On the other hand, if your car is worth less than $1,000 and is rusting, rebuilding is not recommended. Severe rusting can't be fixed.

Source: Tony Assenza, former editor of *Motor Trend.*

Shopping for a Used Car

Before looking for a used car, decide the exact make, model and price you want (just as you would if you were buying a new car).

•Determine whether you want to use the car for extensive traveling, for weekends and summer travel, or just for getting to the train station and back. This helps you decide whether you want a 3- to 5-year-old car (extensive travel) or one 5 to 7 years old (suitable for weekend use and summer travel). For trips to the train station in the morning, or for equivalent use, a car that is 7 to 10 years old will do.

•Choose a popular make in its most successful and long-lasting model. Repair parts are also easier to find.

•Get the local paper with the most advertising for used merchandise. Privately owned cars are often very well maintained and are generally available at prices much lower than those being offered by dealers.

•Look for the deluxe model of the popular make you've chosen. Since it cost a lot more when it was new, there's a better chance it was well cared for.

•Establish (by shopping) the going price of your desired make and model. Then select only those cars offered at above the average price. Owners of the better-cared-for cars usually demand a premium, and it's usually worth it.

How to Check Out A Used Car

You don't have to be an expert to decide whether a used car is worth paying a mechanic to check out. *The key steps:*

• Get the name and telephone number of the previous owner if you buy the car from a dealer. If the dealer won't give you this information from the title, pass up the car. (It could be stolen.)

• Call the former owner and ask what the car's major problems were (not if it had any problems). Also, get the mileage on the car when it was sold. If the odometer now reads less, it has been tampered with. Go elsewhere.

• Inspect the car yourself. Even a superficial look can reveal some signs that will warn you off or will be worth getting repair estimates for before you settle on a price.

• Check the car for signs of fresh undercoating. There is only one incentive for a dealer to undercoat an old car—to hide rust. Check this with a knife or screwdriver (with the dealer's permission). If you find rust, forget the car.

• Rub your finger inside the tailpipe. If it comes out oily, the car is burning oil. Your mechanic should find out why.

• Kneel down by each front fender and look down the length of the car. Ripples in the metal or patches of slightly mismatched paint can indicate bodywork. If a rippled or unmatched area is more than a foot square, ask the mechanic to look at the frame carefully. (Ask the former owner how bad the wreck was.)

• Open and close all the doors. A door that has to be forced is another sign of a possible wreck.

• Check for rust around moldings, under the bumper, at the bottom of doors, in the trunk, under floor mats, and around windows. Lumps in vinyl tops are usually a sign of rust. Rust and corrosion on the radiator mean leaks.

• Check the tires. Are they all the same type? Does the spare match? If there is excessive wear on the edges of any single tire, the car is probably out of alignment.

• Check the brakes by applying strong pressure to the pedal and holding it for 30 seconds. If it continues to the floor, it needs work.

• Test drive the car, and note anything that doesn't work, from the air conditioner to the windshield wipers. Listen for knocks in the engine and grinding or humming in the gears. Check the brakes and the steering. Drive over bumpy terrain to check the shock absorbers.

Source: Remar Sutton, author of *Don't Get Taken Every Time: The Insider's Guide to Buying Your Next Car,* Penguin Books, New York.

Sensible Car Maintenance

• Average life expectancy for some vital parts of your car. *Suspension system:* 15,000 miles. *Ignition wires:* 25,000 miles. *Water pump:* 30,000 miles. *Starter:* 40,000 miles. *Brake master cylinder, carburetor and steering mechanism (ball joints):* 50,000 miles. *Fuel pump:* 75,000 miles. *Clutch, timing gear chain/belt, universal joints:* Up to 100,000 miles.

• Replace brake fluid at least once a year. This isn't a common practice, and few owner's manuals mention it, but brake fluid attracts water (from condensation and humidity in the air), often causing corrosion in the master and wheel cylinders, shortening their lives. Replacing brake fluid regularly saves the more costly replacement of cylinders.

• Cold weather probably means your tires need more air. A tire which may have lost a few pounds of pressure during the summer and fall driving season could easily become 8–10 pounds underinflated on a freezing day. This is enough to cut tire life by 25%. *Rule of thumb:* For every 10-degree drop in the ambient temperature, the air pressure in a tire decreases by one-half to one pound.

• The oil-pressure warning light on the dashboard is not a foolproof system. By the time the light flashes, the engine has been without oil long enough to harm the machinery.

• Car-scratch repair. *When the scratch hasn't penetrated to the metal:* Sand with fine sandpaper (400–600 grit) until the scratch disappears. Wipe the area clean with a soft cloth. Paint it carefully, and let the paint dry for a few days. Then apply rubbing compound according to the directions in the package. *When the scratch has penetrated to the metal:* After sanding with fine paper, apply a primer. After the primer dries, sand again with 320–400 grit sandpaper. Paint and let dry. Apply rubbing compound. Buy materials at an auto-supply store.

• Use vinegar to clean dirt from chipped exterior car surfaces. Then, when the spot is dry, restore with touch-up paint.

• Essential warmup. Idling the car doesn't warm up all the car's systems, such as lubricants, steering fluid or even all the drive train. *Better:* Keep speeds under 30 mph for the first quarter mile and not much over that for the next several miles.

• Replace radials whenever the tread is worn down to 1/16 inch from the bottom of the tire groove. At that point, the grooves are too shallow to take water away, and hydroplaning may occur at higher speeds.

• Do not "cross-switch" radials. Always exchange the left front with the left rear and right front with the right rear. Radials should never be remounted in a manner that will change the direction of rotation.

• If your car is shaking and vibrating, wheels may need aligning. Improper alignment causes excessive tire wear and increases fuel consumption.

• Wax your car at least twice a year...more often if it is exposed to salt air, road salt or industrial air or if it's parked outside. *Clue:* If water doesn't bead up on the car's surface after rain, waxing is needed.

Sources: *National Association of Fleet Administrators' Bulletin* and *The Durability Factor,* edited by Roger B. Yepsen, Jr., Rodale Press, Emmaus, PA.

Auto Service Intervals

Average recommended service intervals (in miles) under both normal and severe driving conditions, from a survey of mechanics:

• Oil & oil filter change. *Normal:* 4,155, *Severe:* 2,880.

• Replace air filter. *Normal:* 10,363, *Severe:* 5,927.

• Replace fuel filter. *Normal:* 11,597, *Severe:* 8,591.

• Replace spark plugs. *Normal:* 14,185, *Severe:* 11,298.

• Tune-up. *Normal:* 14,254, *Severe:* 11,245.

• Replace PCV valve. *Normal:* 16,202, *Severe:* 14,288.

• Flush & change coolant. *Normal:* 22,848, *Severe:* 18,049.

• Replace V-belts. *Normal:* 24,853 or when necessary, *Severe:* 20,610 or when necessary.

• Replace radiator and heater hoses. *Normal:* 29,031 or when necessary. *Severe:* 24,679 or when necessary.

• Change auto-transmission fluid. *Normal:* 25,862, *Severe:* 18,994.

• Adjust auto-transmission bands. *Normal:* 26,591, *Severe:* 19,141.

• Chassis lubrication. *Normal:* 5,550, *Severe:* 4,701.

• Repack wheel bearings. *Normal:* 21,580, *Severe:* 16,414.

• Rotate tires. *Normal:* 9,003, *Severe:* 7,929.

• Replace windshield wiper blades. *Normal:* 15,534 or when necessary, *Severe:* 11,750 or when necessary.

Source: *National Association of Fleet Administrators' Bulletin.*

Car Battery Rules

Car batteries give off explosive hydrogen gas and contain sulfuric acid. *When cleaning or working around a battery, take the following precautions:*

• Never smoke or light a match.

• Remove rings and other jewelry. The metal could cause a spark if it touches a battery terminal.

• Wear goggles to prevent acid from splashing into your eyes.

• If acid spills on your skin or on the car, flush the area with water immediately.

• Work in a well-ventilated area.

Source: *The Family Handyman,* New York.

Buying the Right Size Tire

With the exception of high-performance sports cars, the tires manufacturers install as original equipment are too narrow and too small. While they're perfectly adequate for the kind of day-to-day driving most people do, they don't offer the same performance offered by aftermarket tires. Finding the right tire depends on your needs.

- If you're a very aggressive driver, you'll want a wider, low-profile tire that puts more rubber on the road.
- If you're an average driver, who makes modest demands on his car, switching the original tires may not be a worthwhile expense. However, even an average, non-high-performance driver can gain some safety advantages in braking and wet weather adhesion by investing in uprated (wider, lower) tires.
- *The key to determining tire size for any car:* The ratio of the width of the tire to its height (called "aspect ratio").
- Most compacts these days are fitted with a 14-inch wheel and a 70 series (aspect ratio) tire.
- Some small cars still come equipped with a 13-inch wheel.
- To increase performance and traction, a driver with a 14-inch wheel and 70 series tire could move up to a 60 series tire with little or no compromise in ride.

Rule of thumb: Virtually any original equipment tire could be replaced by one size larger.

Source: Tony Assenza, former editor of *Motor Trend*.

Small Car Trap

Smaller cars are twice as deadly as larger cars. In 1991, the death rate in passenger cars with wheelbases shorter than 95 inches was 2.4 per 100,000 registered vehicles, compared to only 1.1 deaths per 100,000 in cars with wheelbases longer than 114 inches.

Source: *Fatality Facts 1993,* Insurance Institute for Highway Safety, 1005 N. Glebe Rd., Suite 800, Arlington, Virginia 22201.

Gas Trap

Taxes make up one-third the cost of a gallon of gasoline. *State with the highest taxes:* New York—45.8 cents a gallon, including 14.1 cents in federal taxes and 31.7 cents in state levies. *Lowest-tax states:* Alabama, Arizona, Kansas, Mississippi, New Hampshire and South Dakota—18 cents a gallon, including the federal portion.

Source: *Consumer's Research Magazine,* 800 Maryland Ave. NE, Washington, DC 20002.

Latest Car-Repair Scam

Beware of freon theft. Freon, used in car cooling systems, is now so expensive—between $12 and $20 per pound, with three to five pounds per car—that shady car-repair companies are stealing it while they service your car. *Tip-off:* Your car's cooling system doesn't work as well or stops working following other car repairs. *Important:* Be sure to have your car serviced by someone you trust.

Source: David Solomon, editor of *Nutz & Boltz®,* Box 123, Butler, Maryland 21023.

Highway Fatalities Down

39,235 people died in 1992 on US highways. This was the lowest number in 30 years. The fatality rate of 1.8 deaths per 100 million miles driven was the lowest number ever recorded. *Possible reasons for improvement:* Airbags... increased use of seat belts...fewer alcohol-related deaths.

Source: Statistics from the US Department of Transportation, reported in *Automotive News,* 1400 Woodbridge Ave., Detroit 48207.

Best Car Burglar Alarms

Most insurance companies will give you a discount if your car is equipped with a burglar alarm system. Generally it's 10% off the premium—each year.

Don't put stickers in the car window announcing to the world what type of burglar alarm system you have. Most experts feel that this removes the element of surprise and can even help the thief.

Cheap alarms provide little more than a false sense of security for a car owner. A good thief can foil them easily. *The features of a good alarm system:*

- Passively armed. That is, it should require nothing more of the driver than shutting off the motor and removing the ignition key, without complicated setup procedures.
- Instant "on" at all openings. That means the alarm should trigger as soon as any door, the hood, or the trunk is opened.
- Remotely disarmed by a code, instead of by means of a switch or a key. A lock can be picked. A code is impossible to break.
- Hood lock. Denying a thief access to your engine, battery, and siren is a major deterrent.
- Backup battery to prevent a thief from crawling under your car, cutting the car's main battery and killing the entire electrical system, and, therefore the alarm system.
- Motion detector. The best kinds are the electronic motion detectors that sense a car's spatial attitude at the time the alarm is armed whether it's on a hill, on uneven ground, etc. (Also least prone to false alarms.)
- *Extras:* Pressure-sensitive pads in the seats and under carpeting. Glass-breakage detectors. Paging systems and air horns.
- Wheel locks if you own expensive optional wheels.

Make Your Car Hard to Steal

- Lock your car.
- Take your keys.
- Park in well-lighted areas.
- Park in attended lots. Leave ignition key only (not trunk key) with attendant.
- Install a burglar alarm.
- Activate burglar alarm or antitheft device when parking.
- Don't put the alarm decal on your car.
- Install a secondary ignition switch.
- Park with wheels turned toward the curb.
- Remove rotor from distributor.
- Install a fuel shut-off device.
- Remove coil wire from distributor cap. (Especially useful for long-term parking at airports.)
- Close car windows when parking.
- Replace T-shaped window locks with straight ones.
- Install a steering-wheel lock, and use it.
- Install an armored collar around the steering column to cover the ignition.
- Don't hide a second set of keys in car.
- Never leave your car running when no one is in it.
- Don't let a potential buyer "test drive" alone.
- For front-wheel-drive cars, put on emergency brake and put in park.
- Back your car into your driveway. A potential thief will then be forced to tinker with ignition system in full view of neighbors.
- Lock your garage door.
- Lock your car in your garage.
- Be sure inspection sticker and license tag are current and were issued by the same state.

Source: Aetna Life and Casualty.

Flat Tire Do's and Don'ts

- Avoid use of instant tire sealants. They camouflage the slow loss of air that signals a punctured tire.

Repair a tire (rather than replace it) only when the puncture in the tread area is 1/4 inch in diameter or smaller. This puncture must be at least 15 inches away from a prior one, and tire tread depth must be more than 1/16 inch.

- Remove the tire from the wheel. A permanent repair can be made only from inside the tire. An internal inspection is a must. Driving on a flat (even a short distance at low speeds) can damage the crucial inner surface.

• After repair, have the tire and wheel assembly rebalanced. This will more than pay for itself in a smoother ride and longer tire life.

Coping with Car Trouble On the Highway

Unexpected breakdowns on the open road are frustrating and can be very dangerous.

How to avoid them:

• Practice preventive maintenance. Have your car checked before you set out on a long trip.

• *Likeliest sources of trouble:* Battery, tires, belts and engine hoses.

• Be sure you have emergency supplies, such as flashlights, flares and basic tools, and that your spare tire is inflated.

• At the first hint of trouble, move off the road, activate your emergency flashers and only then assess the problem.

• Fix the things you can yourself.

• If your car is overheating, you may be able to let it cool down and then proceed slowly to a gas station if you know one is nearby.

• If you are really stuck, wait for help. Major highways are regularly patrolled by troopers. Less traveled roads may require a Good Samaritan.

• Don't leave your car. An abandoned car is vulnerable to theft and vandalism. And in winter, you are vulnerable to the elements.

• To signal for help, raise your hood or your trunk lid as a distress signal. Hang a white handkerchief or colored scarf from it. If you have flares or reflectors, set them out (in those states where they are legal).

• Run the motor (and heater or air conditioner) only 15 minutes out of every hour, keeping a window slightly open to guard against carbon monoxide poisoning.

• If you are a woman alone, keep the car doors locked and the windows rolled up while waiting. This gives you a protected vantage point for sizing up strangers who approach the car.

• When help arrives, describe your car problem clearly so a service station can send the proper equipment. Beware of helpful strangers who are not mechanically inclined. Using battery jump cables incorrectly can cause an explosion or ruin your alternator. Improperly hitched tows can ruin your automatic transmission.

• You must stay calm and be patient. If this is too upsetting a proposition for you, consider investing in a car phone or CB radio so that you can get help sooner.

Source: Francis C. Kenel, PhD, director of traffic safety, American Automobile Association, Falls Church, VA.

Driving Small Cars Safely

In a severe crash between a large car and a small one, those in the small car are eight times more likely to be killed. *Defensive strategies:*

• Wear seat belts. A belted occupant of a small car has the same chance of surviving as the unbelted occupant of a big car in a crash between the two.

• Keep your lights on at low beam full time to increase visibility.

• Be aware that light poles and signs along the road may not break away as designed when hit by a lightweight compact car.

• Respect the inability of larger vehicles to maneuver or stop as quickly to escape a collision.

Dealing with Trucks On a Highway

To pass a truck:

• Blow your horn or blink the headlights to indicate your intentions.

• If it's raining, pass as quickly as possible to reduce road spray.

• After passing, speed up to avoid tailgating.

When following:

• Maintain a distance of 20–25 feet so the truck driver has a complete view of your vehicle.

• Be prepared for a possible truck shift to the left (even when it's signaling a right turn) as the driver makes sure he clears the right curb.

• Stay at least one or two car lengths back so as to remain in the truck driver's line of vision. This is especially important on an upgrade, where the truck may roll back a few feet.

Source: *Canadian Vehicle Leasing's Safe Driving Bulletin,* as reported in the *National Association Fleet Administrators Bulletin,* 295 Madison Ave., New York.

Driving in Hot Weather

• Inspect the auto radiator for leaks, and check the fluid level.

• Check all hoses for possible cracks or sponginess. Make sure all connections are tight and leak free.

• Test the thermostat for proper operation. If it does not operate at the proper temperature, overheating could occur.

• Inspect the fan belt for cracks and proper tension. Belt slippage is a common cause of boil overs. It also drains electrical power.

• If loss of coolant has been a problem, check for water seepage on the water pump around the engine block.

• Don't turn off the engine when the temperature warning light goes on. If stuck in traffic, shift to neutral, and race the engine moderately for 30 seconds at two-minute intervals.

• Shut off the air conditioner to avoid further overtaxing of the cooling system.

• Turn on the heater for a few minutes. It may help.

• If the radiator continues to overheat, drive the car off the road, turn off the engine and raise the hood.

• Wait at least half an hour before removing the radiator cap. Then do it very slowly and carefully, with the help of a towel or thick rag. Keep your face turned away from the radiator.

• If your car has the see-through overflow catch tank, replace any loss of coolant. Don't touch the radiator.

• If the fluid level is low, restart the engine while adding cool or warm water as the engine idles.

Source: Automobile Association of America.

Preparing for Cold Weather Driving

• *Radiator coolant:* Read the label on your antifreeze to be sure you make the right blend of water and antifreeze. The antifreeze keeps your radiator from freezing and cracking; the water, even in winter, keeps your car from overheating.

• *Battery condition:* Your car needs three to four times more starting power in winter than in summer. Have a mechanic do a complete battery draw and load test. If your battery fails, a recharge may save it for another year. Otherwise, invest in a new one.

• *Windshield washer fluid:* Frozen fluid in the washer tank is dangerous. Use a premixed commercial fluid. Check that the hoses are clear, and clean the washer nozzles out with a thin piece of wire.

• *Electrical system:* Make sure the distributor cap, points, condenser, ignition coil, spark plugs, and spark plug cables are in good shape. Borderline components that still function in summer will give out in cold weather.

• *Hoses and belts:* If they are cracking or fraying, replace them.

• *Tires:* If you have all-season tires, be sure the tread is still good enough to give you traction on slippery roads. Otherwise, put on snow tires. *Important:* If you have a front-wheel drive car, the snow tires go on the front. Store summer tires on their sides, not on the tread. (Storing on the tread causes a flat spot and an unbalanced tire.) Inflate stored tires to only 50% of their operating pressure.

• *Windshield:* Apply antifogging compound to the inside.

• *Cleaning:* Clear dead bugs off the radiator by hosing it from the inside of the engine compartment. Pick out dead leaves and debris from the fresh-air intake box of the ventilation system.

•*Stock up:* Buy flares, an aerosol wire-drying agent, a scraper and brush, chains and a military-style collapsible trench tool for emergencies. Keep a lock de-icer at home and/or at the office.

How to Brake on Ice

•Start early.

•Squeeze the brakes with a steady pressure until just before you feel them begin to lock.

•Ease up, and slowly repeat the pressure.

•Disk brakes do not respond well to pumping (the old recommendation for drum brakes). They will lock, causing you to lose control of the car.

Source: National Safety Council, Chicago, IL.

How to Get Out Of a Snow Drift

To get unstuck:

•Turn your wheels from side to side to push away the snow.

•Check to be sure that your tailpipe is clear (so carbon monoxide won't be forced into the car).

•Start the motor.

•Put the car in gear, and apply slow, steady pressure to the accelerator to allow the tires to get a grip.

•Don't spin the wheels (this just digs you in further).

•Let the car pull out straight ahead if possible.

•*Extra help:* Sprinkle kitty litter in front of the wheels for traction.

Source: National Safety Council, Chicago, IL.

Auto Dealer Ripoff

•*Car purchase padding:* A prep fee of $100 or more (whatever the dealership thinks it can get away with). The cost of preparing your car for delivery is already included in the manufacturer's sticker price.

Source: *Consumer Guide to Successful Car Shopping* by Peter Sessler, TAB Books, Blue Ridge Summit, PA.

Accidents with Aggressive Drivers

Violent and aggressive drivers are dangerous when they get into an accident. If you're in an accident with one, stay calm.

•Don't escalate any argument.

•Copy down the other driver's license number immediately.

•If you are threatened, leave at once.

•Call the police so that you won't be charged with leaving the scene of an accident...but do it from a safe distance.

•If your car is disabled, lock the doors and wait for the police to arrive.

All About Speeding Tickets

The best way to avoid speeding tickets is, of course, to avoid speeding. But all of us drive over the limit occasionally.

Here are some suggestions to help you avoid tickets:

•Know the limits. It's no illusion that police officers generally ignore cars driving just slightly over the posted speed. In fact, many departments set threshold speeds (six miles an hour above the limit in one state, for example) at which officers are to take no action. You might be able to slip by at 65 mph in a 55 mph zone, but you're unlikely to do the same at 70 mph.

•Be selective. Most speeding tickets are written during the morning and evening rush hours, when there are more motorists and more police officers on the road. Late night and very early morning are not watched nearly as carefully.

•Drive unobtrusively. Flashy cars attract attention, something to keep in mind if you drive a red Maserati. The same applies to flashy driving styles. Don't tailgate slower cars to force them aside. Don't weave in and out of traffic.

•Be vigilant. The likeliest spot to get nabbed on the highway is just beyond a blind curve or the crest of a hill, the best hiding places for patrol cars. Learn to recognize likely traps, and reduce your speed whenever appropriate.

•Remember that police officers can nab speeders from virtually any position—the rear, the front, the side, or even from aircraft. Be on the lookout at all times. An unmarked car on the side of the road with its trunk open is especially suspect. (A radar device may be inside.)

•Fight back. Radar guns can be foiled occasionally. *What to do:* Position your car close to other cars whenever possible. Police officers generally cannot match you with the speed indicated on their guns unless they have an unobstructed view of your car. In most states, motorists also can make use of radar detectors, devices designed to alert drivers to radar early enough to slow down before police officers can get a good reading. If you do a lot of driving, a detector is a sensible investment if it is legal in your area.

•Use psychology. All is not lost even if you are pulled over. Police officers feel vulnerable when stopping speeders—you could be speeding away from a murder for all they know, and consequently they are usually nervous. Put them at ease. Sit still, keep your hands in plain view (on the steering wheel is a good place). Be courteous and respectful. Above all, be honest. If you have a good excuse for going over the limit, state it. Otherwise, admit guilt and apologize. Police officers can be surprisingly lenient if you're cordial.

How to Ease Long-Distance Driving

For a safe, healthy trip when you're driving a long distance:

•Do most of your driving during daytime hours. Visual acuity is lessened at night.

•Be particularly careful to check out your car's exhaust system before leaving—a leak can send odorless but deadly gases into the car.

•To insure sufficient fresh air inside the car, leave both a front and a back window open. Tailgate windows should be kept closed. Use your air conditioner. It provides fresh air and quiet inside the car. Although it reduces gas mileage, the loss is not much more than the loss from open windows' drag.

•Use seat belts and shoulder harnesses to relieve fatigue, as well as to boost safety.

•Take 20- to 30-minute rest breaks after every one-and-a-half or two hours of driving.

•Exercise during your breaks.

•Eat frequent high-protein snacks for improved driving performance.

•Don't stare straight ahead, even if you're the only car on the road. Keep your eyes moving.

Eating on the Road

•Don't simply follow the truck drivers. Their first priority is a huge parking lot, not the best food.

•Avoid restaurants on or very near major highways and shopping centers. You're likely to do better downtown. *Good bets:* College or university towns.

•*Best authorities:* Bookstore managers, fancy kitchenware and gourmet food store's personnel. *Worst:* Tollbooth or gas-station attendants.

•Beware of large signs and quaint spellings.

•Check out the parking lot. Too many out-of-state license plates suggest a tourist trap. *Good sign:* A high proportion of foreign cars (especially European ones).

Source: *Travel & Leisure.*

How Never to Get Lost On Interstate Highways

The system to the numbering:

•One- or two-digit even-numbered highways: Major East-West routes.

•One- or two-digit odd-numbered highways: Major North-South routes.

•Three-digit figure starting with an even number: Loop route around a city.

•Three-digit figure starting with an odd number: Road that is heading to or from center city.

Safest Car Colors

Greenish-yellow is best...then cream, yellow and white. *Least-safe colors:* Red and black. *General rule:* Light-colored, single-tone cars are safer. They have significantly fewer accidents than dark cars because it is easier for other drivers to distinguish them from the surroundings.

Source: *Lemon Book: Auto Rights for New & Used Cars* by Ralph Nader and Clarence Ditlow, Moyer Bell, Ltd., Colonial Hill, Mt. Kisco, New York 10549.

Safety Tests are Misleading

Car-crash safety tests by the government give misleading results. *Why:* All cars are run into a wall at 35 mph. Lighter cars hit the wall with less momentum than heavy cars, so less damage results. But in real life, heavier cars have better safety records, especially in collisions with lighter vehicles. *Examples:* Although government tests panned the Ford Taurus, insurance records show it to be among the safest vehicles. And the Ford Escort scored well in tests, but has a poor record with insurers.

Source: *The Wall Street Journal.*

Car Engine Death Trap

Teflon engine oil additives—advertised as engine protection agents—can actually *destroy* your engine. Depending on driving conditions, these additives can either cause engine oil pressure to drop to zero, cause the engine to freeze—or have no effect at all. Safest strategy is to stay away from the Teflon products altogether.

Source: David Solomon, editor, *Nutz & Boltz®*, Box 123, Butler, Maryland 21023.

Gasoline Cancer Trap

Gas and gas fumes contain toxic chemicals that can cause cancer. *Unsettling:* Gas-station attendants have a significantly elevated risk of death from leukemia. *Consumer self-defense:* Carry old gloves in the car—wear them when you fill up at a self-service station to keep gasoline off your skin.

Keep windows closed so fumes won't accumulate in the car. Be sure to stand upwind from the pump. Choose stations equipped with vapor-recovery lines. These accordion-like bellows on the nozzles return gas vapors to an underground tank.

Source: Peter Infante, Occupational Safety and Health Administration, quoted in *Good Housekeeping,* 959 Eighth Ave., New York 10019.

Airbag Self-Defense

Airbags in cars have their own safety risks. Cars equipped with airbags require different driving techniques. Don't drape your hand or arm inside the steering wheel—you could get a broken wrist or arm if the airbag fires and traps your hand.

Airbag units are meant to be most effective for drivers sitting with their arms extended—any closer and you could suffer facial abrasions if the airbag is activated.

If you frequently rent cars with airbags, be sure you know where the horn button is on any model you drive—they're all in different locations.

Added risk for smokers: It is dangerous to have a lit cigar or cigarette in your mouth when the airbag goes off. *Important:* Even if the car you drive is airbag-equipped, always buckle up.

Source: David Solomon, editor, *Nutz & Boltz®*, Box 123, Butler, Maryland 21023.

Get More for Your Old Car

Get 25% more for your old car—on average —by selling it yourself. But beware of keeping your old car after you buy a new one—even if the dealer will not give you what you think it is worth. *Reason:* It is usually more important to lower the amount borrowed on the new car than to get the most possible for the old one. Use the trade-in value—or cash—to reduce the new car loan.

Source: *Life After Debt: How to Repair Your Credit and Get Out of Debt Once and For All* by Bob Hammond, credit consultant based in Redlands, California. Career Press, 180 Fifth Ave., Hawthorne, New Jersey 07507.28

When Buying A New Car...

If you're shopping for a new car, research the make's current national sales performance and inventory before you begin negotiating price. *Reason:* Dealers are more likely to drop a model's price dramatically when its sales are down or flat and inventory is high. This data can be found in the weekly trade publication *Automotive News*—available at most libraries.

Source: W. James Bragg, author of *In the Driver's Seat: The New-Car Buyer's Negotiating Bible.* Random House, 201 E. 50 St., New York 10022.

Look at Total Car Costs

Look at total car costs, not just the purchase price, when selecting the best car for your budget. The cost of such items as fuel, oil, tires, maintenance, insurance, financing, depreciation, licenses and registration fees, and taxes have a big impact on the total price of owning a car.

The typical total car ownership costs for different classes of cars, assuming a three-year 60,000-mile trade-in cycle:

	Cents per Mile	Monthly Fixed Cost ($)	Annual Cost ($)
Subcompact	8.65	383	6,330
Compact	8.70	425	6,834
Intermediate	9.95	458	7,480
Full-size	10.95	523	8,462
Luxury	12.25	870	12,884

Source: Larry Snyder, executive vice president, Transportation Division, Runzheimer International, management consultants, Runzheimer Park, Rochester, Wisconsin 53167.

How to Win the Car Buying Game

Car salesmen thrive on confusion. They bombard you with questions and numbers to divert your attention from simple issues.

Tactics:

• Go shopping armed with specific information. Remember that you're not there to fall in love with a car or to make a friend of the salesman. Get answers you can understand.

• Buy the latest edition of *Edmund's New Car Prices.* It lists the base costs of each car and accessories, such as air conditioning and automatic transmission.

• When you find the car you like, copy down all pricing information from the manufacturer's sticker on the window. Compare the sticker prices with those in *Edmund's* to determine the dealer's profit. This gives you real bargaining ammunition.

• Be indecisive. The salesman will think there's a car you like better down the road. That means he must give you his best shot.

• *Best times to shop:* The last day of the month, when dealers close their books and want good sales figures, and very late in the day, when the sales staff is exhausted.

• Beware of red tag sales. Dealers' profits are higher than at any other time. Customers mistakenly assume they will save money during special sales. Really, they are fantasies that draw you away from reality. Stay with black-and-white issues you can control.

•Stick with what you can afford. *This is determined by two things:* How much cash your trade-in gives you towards the down payment and how much you can pay each month.

•Tell dealers you are interested in selling your car for cash. Their figures will give you a better idea of what your car is worth than a blue book. It's best to sell your car privately.

Source: Remar Sutton, car dealer and author of *Don't Get Taken Every Time: The Insider's Guide to Buying Your Next Car,* Penguin Books, New York.

Buy a Car At Police Auction

Big-city police departments, in the course of their work, collect abandoned cars, evidence vehicles (those used in crimes) and towed-away cars that haven't been picked up. Buying a car at auctions of these vehicles can be a good deal, especially for a teenager who can do repair work.

Rules to follow:

•Inspect the autos the day before the auction. Each is listed by its make and year and is given an auction number that also appears on the windshield of the car. (You can make notes on the list of the cars that interest you and then check prevailing prices for such cars in the local newspaper want ads or in publications at the library.)

•Usually there is no ignition key, and in most cities you're not allowed to hotwire a start, either. *What you can do:* Inspect the car by opening the doors and hood and working the windows. Inspect the engine compartment for quality of maintenance and check the wires, hoses, motor oil level, transmission and brake fluid levels. Find out the mileage and determine the condition of the interior and tires.

•At the auction, fill out a form with your name and address to get a bidding number. All transactions are cash. You must pay the full price, plus tax, during the auction, not afterward. All sales are final.

•Set limits to your bidding and stick to them. No more than one-half the *Blue Book* value is recommended, and no more than one-third is safer. This way you'll come out ahead even if major repairs prove necessary.

•Collect a bill of sale acceptable to the local state motor vehicle department for registering the car when you pay. If you live out of state, check with your state automotive agency to see what other documents might be necessary to register the car in your state.

•Arrange to have the car towed away within a day or two of the auction. Even if you replace the ignition or jump-start it, the car has no license plate or insurance. It also may not run.

Auto Lemonaid

If that new car you just bought has been in the shop more than on the road, don't despair. Under state "lemon laws" you may be able to get most of your money back, or at least a more reliable car...and without the risk of heavy court costs.

• *The law:* The car is usually covered for one year or the written warranty period, whichever is shorter.

•If a defect isn't repaired in four tries, the manufacturer must replace the car or give a refund (less depreciation). The same goes if the car is out of commission for 30 days or more for any combination of defects.

•If the manufacturer has a federally approved arbitration program, you must first submit your complaint to the arbitrators. But if you aren't satisfied with their decision, you can still take the company to court.

Strategy:

•Check the state attorney general's office for details of the law. *Key point:* Whether the manufacturer (as well as the dealer) must be given a chance to solve the problem.

•Submit a list of repairs to the dealer each time you bring the car in. Keep a copy for yourself.

•Keep a detailed record of car repair dates and of periods when the car was unavailable to you.

•If the company agrees to settle but offers too little money or a car with too many miles, don't be afraid to dicker. The company doesn't want to go to court any more than you do.

Source: *Medical Economics,* Oradell, NJ.

New-Tire Do's and Don'ts

•First check your owner's manual for the correct tire size. It may also list an optional size, but tires must be the same size and construction on each axle.

•If you must mix tire constructions, the radial pair should be on the rear axle.

•If you're buying only a pair of replacement tires, put the new ones on the rear wheels for better handling.

•Buy tires according to your needs. If you are planning to sell your car soon, don't buy long-lasting radials—get a shorter-term tire, such as a bias ply or bias belted.

•Consider the new all-season tires, especially if you live in a colder climate. These radial tires combine the traction of snow tires with the quiet ride and longer tread wear of a highway tire. And twice-a-year changing is not necessary, as it is for conventional snow tires.

•Radial tires are expected to last for 40,000 miles; bias-belted tires for 30,000; and bias-ply tires for 20,000.

•Spring and fall are best for good discounts on tire prices.

•All tires sold in the US must meet Department of Transportation standards. You should always look for the DOT symbol on the sidewall of any tire sold in the US, whether foreign or domestic.

•Any tires, old or new, must be properly inflated if you expect good performance and long wear.

Source: Ed Lewis, deputy director, Tire Industry Safety Council, Washington, DC.

Cutting Down on Gas Usage

•Tuning. Poor engine tuning adds 5%–20% to fuel usage.

•Acceleration. The best mileage is at cruising speed (usually 35–45 mph). *Recommended:* A brisk, smooth acceleration to the highest gear.

•Stopping. A red light ahead? Slow down. If you can avoid stopping altogether, you will save gas. Don't follow others closely, or you'll pay for their stops in your fuel bill.

•Luggage. Every 100 pounds of needless weight costs up to .5 mpg.

•Remove ski or luggage racks (which create wind drag) when not in use.

•Speed. Driving an eight-mile commute each day at 70 mph instead of 55 mph will add more than $100 a year to fuel costs.

•Tire pressure. Inflate to the maximum listed on the sidewall.

•Radials. Cut 3–4% off the average gasoline bill.

•Hill driving. A 3% grade will add 33% to fuel usage. On the downward slope, build up momentum to carry you through the base of the next hill. Let up on the accelerator as you climb.

•Gas usage increases 2%–6% with automatic transmission: 1%–2% for each 10°F drop in temperature, 10% with heavy rain or head winds.

Source: California Energy Commission.

How to Winterize Your Car

To make your winter driving easier:

•Put snow tires on all four wheels for maximum traction. If this isn't possible, make sure to put them on the drive wheels.

•Drain and flush the cooling system on any car more than two years old. On newer cars, add antifreeze if necessary.

•*Use a concentrated windshield-washing solution:* One quart rubbing alcohol, one cup water and one tablespoonful of liquid dish-washing detergent.

•Keep your gas tank at least half full to prevent condensation that might freeze and block the fuel line.

•For better traction on rear-wheel-drive cars, place sandbags in the forward part of the trunk.

•*Keep these winter supplies where you can get at them easily:* A scraper/brush, a shovel, and a bag of sand or kitty litter.

Source: *Parents,* New York.

Your Car Radio

•Don't turn on your car stereo during the first five minutes of your drive. Use that time to listen for noises that could signal car trouble.

•Organize your stereo tapes before you leave, so you can pick them out without taking your eyes off the road.

•Keep all tapes within easy reach.

•Don't wear headphones while you drive. A safe driver must be able to hear the traffic as well as watch it.

•Wait for a straight patch of road before glancing at the stereo to adjust it.

•Read your tape cassette titles at eye level so you can see the road at the same time.

Source: *High Fidelity,* New York

Top-of-the-Line Car Stereos

For the serious music lover who spends a lot of time in a car, first-rate radio and tape systems are available—at a price. Although most factory-installed stereos are mediocre, a number of audio companies make good sound systems for cars.

Like home stereo systems, car stereos are bought in components:

•*Radio/tape decks:* Alpine, Kenwood, and Sony.

•*Speakers:* Sound to rival home units...B and W and ADS.

•*Amplifiers:* High-powered units with low distortion and good reliability are made by ADS and Alpine.

•*Essential:* Professional installation with a warranty. Proper mounting and wiring of the components affects not only the sound but also the system's longevity.

15

Insurance and Banking Savvy

How to Protect Your Money from the People Who Protect the Places That Protect Your Money

Most of us who have accounts at banks or savings and loan institutions know little about Federal Deposit Insurance Corporation (FDIC) protection.

This lack of knowledge can be costly if your bank or savings and loan goes under—for part of your money may not be insured. Answers to the most common questions about FDIC coverage...

Are all banks and savings and loans protected by the FDIC? Most banks are protected, but some private banks are not. Be sure to look for the FDIC label on your bank's door or at the tellers' windows.

Are all individual accounts covered separately by the FDIC? Up to how much? Most people know that the FDIC covers individual accounts up to $100,000. What they don't know is that an individual account is determined by adding up each account held under a common name or Social Security number.

Example: If a person has a savings account with $50,000 in it and a certificate of deposit for $60,000 at the same bank, $10,000 is uninsured.

Accounts set up under the Uniform Gifts to Minors Act are considered to be the child's account, even though the parent has control over it.

What about joint accounts? Are they fully protected? Joint accounts held by the same combination of persons at the same bank are only protected up to $100,000, regardless of whose Social Security number appears on them.

Example: A husband and wife with two joint accounts of $100,000 each are insured only up to $100,000, not $200,000.

Avoid this restriction by using both individual and joint accounts.

Example: If you have an individual savings account of $100,000 and a joint savings account with your spouse of $100,000 at the same bank, each account has full protection. Your spouse can have an individual savings account of $100,000 and receive full coverage on it as well.

Are all deposits covered by the FDIC? Mutual funds and other investments made through a bank are not protected. If you have any questions concerning FDIC insurance, call the FDIC at 800-934-3342.

Are trust accounts treated separately by the FDIC? Yes, but only if the trusts are for members of your immediate family—a spouse, child or grandchild. But, if you set up an account in trust for your father, for example, it is treated as part of your account.

Trust accounts for a spouse, child, or grandchild (including step and adopted children) enjoy separate coverage, even if you have both an individual and a joint account.

Example: If you have an individual account with $100,000, a joint account with your spouse of $100,000, and a trust account for your spouse of $100,000, the accounts are all fully insured.

Can an individual open accounts at several branches of the same bank and receive full protection for each? You cannot increase the limit of coverage by depositing funds in different branches of the same bank.

Self-defense: Diversify your funds among several banks.

Are IRAs and Keoghs fully protected? At the moment, each retirement account is treated separately from individual accounts and receives full coverage.

Example: If you have an individual account of $100,000, an IRA of $100,000 and a Keogh of $100,000 at the same bank, each account is fully insured.

Important: After December 19, 1993, IRA and Keogh accounts will be lumped together for purposes of coverage limits. But transitional rules afford some protection for existing accounts.

Self-defense: As IRA or Keogh CDs mature, roll over sufficient amounts to other institutions to maximize FDIC coverage.

Source: Cody Buck, a former executive of the FDIC and author of *The ABCs of FDIC: How to Save Your Assets From Liquidation.* CoStarr Publications, Box 2052, Coppell, Texas 75019. 800-925-3252.

ATM Self-Defense

Discarding your ATM receipt at the bank may help thieves loot your account, says bank expert Ed Mrkvicka. High-tech bandits are using video cameras to observe/record customers punching in ID numbers at teller machines. Then they match it to the account numbers on receipts left behind. Self-defense: Guard your PIN number...retain receipts to match up against monthly bank statements. If there's a withdrawal discrepancy, report it immediately to the bank.

Bank Credit Cards Are Not All Alike

Should you keep the bank credit card you have now, or apply for ones that offer greater advantages? One Visa card or MasterCard could be very different from another Visa or MasterCard.

The MasterCard and Visa organizations do not issue credit cards themselves. They provide a clearing system for charges and payments on the cards and license banks to use the Visa or MasterCard name. It is the issuing bank that determines the interest rates and fees.

A bank's name on a credit card does not necessarily mean that it is the bank actually issuing the card. Issuance of credit cards is a high-risk, low-profit business. Seldom does a small bank issue its own.

Generally, a small bank will act as an agent for an issuing bank. The agent bank puts its name on the card, but it is the issuing bank that actually extends any credit.

Aside from costs, this can be important if the cardholder encounters an error. The correction might have to be agreed upon, not by a friendly local banker, but by an unknown, larger institution, perhaps in a different state.

Visa, for example, has about 1,400 issuing banks in the US and about 10,500 agent banks.

Choosing which card to take is becoming more difficult, because some of the nation's largest banks have begun active solicitation of customers throughout the US. Individuals must be especially careful about accepting any offer that might come in the mail.

A recently discovered quirk in the federal law allows federally chartered out-of-state banks to ignore state usury laws that limit the amount of interest or fees that the issuing bank may charge on its credit cards. In Arkansas, for example, state usury laws prevent local banks from charging more than 10% interest on credit card balances. But a federally chartered out-of-state bank, in lending to Arkansas residents, may charge whatever its home state allows. Even within individual states, the terms on credit cards can vary widely.

Aside from the actual rates and fees, individuals must carefully check the fine print of their contracts. Most banks, for example, do not charge interest on balances stemming from purchases until the customer is billed for such purchases. If the bill on which the charges first appear is paid in full by the stated due date, there is no interest charge to the holder. But some banks, those in Texas, for example, begin charging interest as soon as they receive the charge slip and make payments to the merchant. Thus, interest begins accumulating even before the cardholder receives the bill. These interest charges continue until the bank receives payment from the customer.

Source: Robert A. Bennett, banking correspondent, *The New York Times*.

Unsolicited Credit Card Danger

Don't throw away a credit card you receive but didn't request. *Reason:* By not letting the issuer know that you don't want it, the card's credit line—which could be thousands of dollars—may appear on your credit report. This may prevent you from getting credit you do want in the future. *Better:* Cut up the card and return it to the issuer, along with a letter requesting that the account be closed. Send your letter by certified mail, return receipt requested, and ask for an acknowledgment from the issuer that the account has, in fact, been closed.

Source: *Everything You Need to Know About Credit* by Deborah McNaughton, founder of Professional Credit Counselors, Orange County, California. Thomas Nelson Publishers, Box 141000, Nashville 37214.

Bank Self-Defense

Not all financial products purchased from a bank are covered by the FDIC—Federal Deposit Insurance Corp.—even if the principal investment is less than $100,000. *Uninsured:* Annuities, mutual funds, insurance policies, stocks, bonds and money-market funds.

Source: Cody Buck, former FDIC executive and author of *The ABCs of FDIC: How to Save Your Assets From Liquidation*. CoStarr Publications, Box 2052, Coppell, Texas 75109.

How to Beat the Banks Before They Beat You

Since deregulation, banks vary widely in their services and in the costs of those services. In order to turn the best profit, banks depend on the fact that customers don't know what to ask for.

How you can get the most for your banking dollar:

• Deal with the smallest bank you can find. After deregulation, most large banks decided to get rid of smaller depositors. They find it cheaper to serve one corporate account than 10 individual accounts. Smaller banks, on the other hand, are more responsive to individual depositors because they need this business.

Ask about checking accounts:

• What is the minimum-balance requirement? How does the bank calculate it? Watch out for a minimum-balance calculation that uses the lowest balance for the month. A figure based on the average daily balance is best.

• Does the balance on other accounts count toward the checking-account minimum balance?

• What is the clearing policy for deposits? This is especially important if you have a NOW account.

• What is the overdraft charge? Often it is outrageous. In parts of the Midwest, for example, most banks charge $20.

• Don't buy loan insurance from the bank. Credit life or disability insurance is often routinely included on loan forms and added to the cost of your loan. Don't sign any such policy when you take out a loan. This insurance benefits the bank—not you. It covers the bank for the balance of your loan should you die or become disabled. You can get more coverage from an insurance agent for half (or even less) of what the bank charges.

• Avoid installment loans. These loans are front-end loaded: Even though your balance is declining, you're still paying interest on the original balance throughout the term of the loan. Ask for a single-payment note with simple interest and monthly payments. If you do have an installment loan, don't pay it off early—this actually adds to its real cost.

• Pay attention to interest computations. Most people compare rates and assume higher is better. Look for interest figured on a day-of-deposit-to-day-of-withdrawal basis compounded daily.

• Avoid cash machines. The farther bankers can keep you from their tellers and loan officers, the more money they'll make and the less responsive they'll be to your needs. Bankers like machines because people can't argue with them.

• Negotiate interest rates. This sounds simple, but it means combating banks' tendencies to lump loans in categories—commercial, mortgage, retail, etc. For example, banks offer a longtime depositor the same interest rate on a car loan as they do a complete newcomer. But often all it takes to get a better rate is to say, "I think my car loan should be 2% lower. I've been banking here for 15 years and I have $10,000 in my savings account."

• Forget FDIC security. Given the option of a higher interest rate investment with a secure major corporation that probably has more reserves than the FDIC, many people will still automatically opt for the bank investment because of FDIC insurance. But the FDIC has only $16 billion in reserves. That's a miniscule portion of the money it's insuring. Now that more and more banks are closing every year, the FDIC may soon find itself in big trouble.

• Ignore the banks amortization schedule for mortgages. When you make your monthly payment, especially in the early part of your mortgage, very little goes toward the principal. However, if you choose to pay a small amount extra every month, this will go toward the principal and save you an enormous amount of money.

• Don't put all your money in one certificate of deposit. Now that you can deposit as little as $1,000 for the money-market rate, split your deposits so that you get the same interest rate and more liquidity. If you put your money into a $10,000 or $20,000 CD and then find you need to take out $1,000 or $2,000, you will have to pay a horrendous penalty. Instead buy 10 or 20 $1,000 CDs.

Source: Edward F. Mrkvicka, Jr., a former bank president and author of *The Bank Book: How to Revoke Your Bank's License to Steal,* HarperCollins, New York.

Prime Rate Secret

Banks calculate their lending rate in arbitrary ways that differ from institution to institution. Your rate may be based on the prime rate set by large money center banks, but it will be calculated and applied by the bank's own formula, which will almost always be higher. *Self-protection:* Before taking out any loan, read and be sure you understand the fine print that spells out the interest rate adjustment formula. Then make comparisons from bank to bank.

Source: Edward F. Mrkvicka, Jr., president of Reliance Enterprises, a financial consulting company, Box 413, Marengo, IL 60152 and editor of *Money Insider,* a monthly newsletter.

Safe-Deposit Boxes

Guarantee that you will be able to locate all important documents quickly by renting a bank safe-deposit box. Fees are reasonable. Only two keys are made to fit the box, and you keep both of them. The box cannot be opened without your permission unless you die or you don't pay your rental fee for a whole year. In a non-payment situation, you will receive a certified or registered letter to give you one last chance to pay up. If you don't, the contents of the box will be removed in the presence of a bank official, inventoried, verified, and then stored in a safe place until you eventually claim them.

Keep in your safe-deposit box:

- Birth, marriage, and death certificates.
- Divorce or separation agreements.
- Adoption or custody papers.
- Title papers to real estate, car, etc.
- Mortgage papers.
- Contracts and legal agreements.
- Stock certificates.
- Military discharge papers.
- Copies of credit cards.
- Copies of passport (or the original and keep copies at home).
- Photographs of the inside and outside of a home to support insurance claims.

Do not put in a safe-deposit box:

- Your will. Keep it at your attorney's office, with only a copy in the safe-deposit box. *Reason:* Safe-deposit boxes are sealed at death until the IRS sees what's inside. This could prevent relatives from getting into the box right away to see if a will even exists.
- Money or other valuables on which income tax has not been paid. This is illegal and your heirs might be taxed on the money at your death anyway.

Source: Safe Deposit Department, Marine Midland Bank, NA, New York.

Protecting Your Credit Cards

- Don't be fooled by a "Good Samaritan" phone call that your stolen or lost cards have been found. It may be from a thief seeking time to run up charges. Carry cards separately from your wallet. Leave infrequently used cards at home. Make photo copies of each card you own, and keep these at home and at the office with a list of the issuers' toll-free numbers.

Source: Peter Herrick, president of the Bank of New York.

- When you check your statements each month, be on the lookout for hotels and restaurants that throw away the ticket you sign, substitute another one with inflated tips or other charges, and then forge your name on the inflated ticket. *Where it happens frequently:* Las Vegas.

Source: John Kaiser, marketing director, Summa Four Co., Merrimack, NH, quoted in *Teleconnect,* 205 W. 19 St., New York 10011.

Prevent Credit Card Rip-offs

Here's a simple trick: Pick a number and if possible—make sure that all your credit card charges end in that number. *For example:* Say you choose the number 8 and your dinner bill comes to $20.00. Instead of adding a $3.00 tip, add $3.08. When your bill comes at the end of the month, check to see if all the charges have 8 as the last digit. If they don't, compare them against your receipts and report discrepancies to the card issuer.

Beware of Low Credit Card Rates

In many cases, bank cards with the lowest rates (11%-14%) can cost much more than cards with traditional 18%-21% charges. *Reason:* A growing number of banks begin tacking on interest charges the minute a transaction is posted to their books. This interest charge accrues until the charge amount and the interest are paid in full. Even if you pay your charges off as soon as you receive the bill each month, you'll still have to pay an interest charge. *Solution:* If you pay in full whenever you use a credit card, choose a bank that charges interest only on bal-

ances that are still outstanding following the payment due date on the bill.
Source: *Money.*

How to Cut Auto Insurance

Cut auto insurance costs by:

• Raising deductibles from $100 to $500 or even $1,000. That saves 35%–60% on premiums.

• Dropping collision coverage on cars over five years old.

• Finding out whether the car qualifies for discounts on autos less likely to be stolen or less costly to repair.

• Discontinuing medical coverage if it's duplicated by your employer's health plan.

• Reconsidering extras such as coverage for towing or car rentals during repair.

Source: National Consumer Insurance Organization, as reported in *Money.*

Traps in Homeowner's Insurance

Many home buyers hastily purchase homeowner's insurance to qualify for their mortgage. *Problem:* They don't understand the choices involved in insuring a home.

Basic insurance: If a fire or other catastrophe destroys your home, you get the replacement cost, which is enough to rebuild the home to its original state, provided you carry at least 80% of the replacement cost. *What you don't get:* The market value of the home so that you can go out and buy a similar one. Land value and neighborhood are inherent in market value, yet unrelated to replacement cost.

Carry whatever percent of the home's replacement value the insurance company requires. If you don't, you will be penalized by the percentage you underinsure.

Example: You have a $100,000 house and carry only $60,000 on it. That is three-quarters of the $80,000 required. If you have $20,000 worth of damage from a fire, you will get only $15,000 or three-quarters of your damage. If you were insured for $80,000, you would get full coverage.

How to ascertain replacement cost...

Most insurance companies will inspect your house if it is worth over $100,000.

Your broker has a replacement-cost guide. This determines the cost of the average home by computing the number of rooms and square feet. It is an educated guess.

If your home was custom built, get an independent appraisal.

Replacement cost versus actual cash value: Replacement cost is only useful when you rebuild your house. If you decide to walk away and buy another house, you will only get actual cash value. *What it is:* Replacement value minus depreciation.

Example: You have a 50-year-old home worth $100,000 and $80,000 worth of insurance. You might get only $40,000 if you decide not to build, because depreciation could take away as much as 50% of the payment. (Depreciation computed by an insurance company is not related to depreciation for taxes. Depreciation is rarely in excess of 50% on a home.)

Inflation protection: Many insurance companies automatically increase coverage by whatever it costs to rebuild a home in your area under an inflation guard endorsement.

Check out: Whether inflation increases are granted annually, semiannually, or quarterly. *Problem:* If inflation is running 10%, and you have a disaster after six months, you may have insufficient coverage. *Best:* Ask for an endorsement that increases protection quarterly.

Some companies offer an endorsement which guarantees to pay the full replacement cost, even if it is higher than the amount of the policy, provided you insured to 100% of the agreed-upon replacement cost at the time the endorsement was issued and you increased coverage when required by company reevaluations, annual adjustments for inflation, or alterations to the building. Additionally, the replacement cost will be paid even if you elect not to rebuild.

Other homeowner's policy coverage...

•Contents (furniture, china, clothing, etc.): *Coverage:* 50% of the insured value of the house.

•The cost of staying in a hotel or renting a temporary apartment or house while your own home is repaired. *Coverage:* Up to 20% of insurance on the home's contents.

•Third-party liability: Protection in case anyone is injured on your property. *Or:* Someone is injured through some action of yours off your property.

•Appurtenant structures such as a garage or shed. *Coverage:* 10% of home coverage.

•Theft away from home: This covers a suitcase stolen from a hotel room. *Extended theft:* Theft from a boat or locked car. *Caution:* Coverages are limited or optional in some states.

Examine policies for restricted coverage on jewelry, furs, silverware, fine art, guns, money and securities. Schedule high-value items so that you and the insurer agree on value before there is a loss.

Seek the broadest coverage possible within your budget. Some homeowner's policies are little more than fire-insurance contracts. *Caution:* No homeowner's policy covers floods. Flood coverage must be obtained separately. The best policies, known as all-risk policies, cover nearly everything and take the burden of proof of coverage away from you. They make the insurance company prove it is excluded from the contract.

Example: A deer jumped through a picture window and destroyed the entire interior of the house. A standard policy would not cover this incident. Under an all-risk policy, the company must pay unless it can prove the incident falls within a specific exclusion.

Look for credits for higher deductibles, particularly percentage deductibles.

Example: You insure your house for $100,000. Instead of getting a $500 deductible, you can get a larger credit for a 1/2% deductible, even though it also equals $500. Realize that if the amount of the insurance is raised, your deductible will rise proportionately.

Source: Judith L. Robinson, CPCU, president of general insurance brokers H & R Phillips, 550 Fifth Ave., New York 10017.

How Much Fire Insurance Do You Need?

Most standard homeowners' policies will pay the full value of the policy only if that value is 80% or more of the replacement value of the house. If coverage is below 80%, the maximum payment is limited to the replacement value minus a depreciation charge (usually quite large) figured according to the age of the house. The burden of keeping coverage to at least 80% of replacement value rests with the homeowner. *Advice:* Increase coverage annually, to keep up with inflation.

The Most Frequently Asked Questions About Health Insurance And Life Insurance

The National Insurance Consumer Helpline (800-942-4242) operates from 8:00 a.m. to 8:00 p.m. Eastern time, Monday through Friday, as a toll-free source of answers to insurance questions.

Although people's insurance needs differ, some questions to the Helpline come up again and again.

Most frequently asked questions lately...

How do I figure out if an insurance company is reliable and solvent?

Many companies investigate and report on insurance firms' finances. The big four raters: A. M. Best (Oldwick, New Jersey)...Duff & Phelps (Chicago)... Moody's Investor Service and Standard & Poor's (both New York City). These companies' reports are available in many library reference sections.

Other information sources: Your state insurance department (it requires yearly financial reports from the companies it licenses—but it doesn't provide ratings)...the companies themselves (call or write to the home office for a copy of the most recent annual report).

Note: Since rapid changes in the economy can quickly render reports obsolete, the companies are updating them much more frequently than in the past.

What is COBRA?

COBRA is the federal continuation-of-benefits requirement for most organizations with 20 or more employees. It lets you keep group health insurance with your former company for up to 18 months (36 months for certain qualified dependents). You must pay the full price of the insurance.

Limitation: COBRA does not help if the company goes out of business, since COBRA ties you to the employer's group plan, not to a particular insurance company.

What do I do when my insurance company refuses to repay me because it says my doctor overcharged me?

Most coverage levels are based on what doctors in a particular geographic area charge for a service. Check with other doctors—if yours is out of line, ask for a fee reduction. But if other doctors also seem to charge more than the insurance company is willing to pay, appeal the reimbursement by writing a letter listing the doctors you contacted and the amounts they quoted to you.

Will I still get good medical care if my employer switches to a Health Maintenance Organization and requires me to see only HMO doctors?

HMOs help keep costs down by using internists, pediatricians and general practitioners as "gatekeepers" to determine whether or not you need to see a high-cost specialist. This does not keep you from top-quality medical care, but does represent a change in traditional ways of selecting doctors. *Advantages:* Lower out-of-pocket costs...no deductibles...no cost for regular checkups and other preventive care.

What is the basic difference among types of life insurance?

Term insurance simply protects your family for a specified—and finite—period of time. It only pays death benefits if you die during this period. At each renewal, the benefit remains the same...but your premium increases. *Whole life* insurance protects you as long as you live. Premiums do not increase year-to-year, but are averaged out over your lifetime. Whole life provides an investment—*cash value*—as well. You can cancel the policy and receive a lump-sum payment. You only pay taxes on this amount if the cash value—plus any dividends you received—exceeds the sum of premiums you have already paid.

In the past, *whole,* or *traditional,* life was the only type with a cash-value component. Today, there are others: *Modified life, limited payment life* and *single-premium* whole life. Other alternatives with cash value options: *Universal, variable* and *current assumption whole life.* An insurance agent can explain the detailed differences and help determine which type is best for you.

How do annuities work?

An annuity is basically the opposite of life insurance. Instead of being designed to pay when a covered person dies, an annuity is designed to pay benefits as long as a person *lives.* Annuities are usually set up as retirement plans. Depending on your contract, the insurance company provides you with a regular income (monthly checks) for as long as you live. Your choice would be either an *immediate annuity,* bought by retirees and payable starting now...or a deferred annuity, where you deposit money into an interest-bearing account, for your payments to start at some specified future date.

What are accelerated death benefits?

This new form of payout is already offered by more than 100 companies. It allows 25% to 100% of life-insurance benefits to be paid while the insured is still living. These *living benefits* are paid in connection with terminal or catastrophic illness or a need for long-term care or confinement to a nursing home. As living benefits are paid, however, the payments received upon the policyholder's death are correspondingly reduced.

Warning: Tax treatment of these benefits is unclear. Life insurance payments are generally not taxable, but the IRS has not yet ruled on benefits paid while the insured is still alive.

What if someone dies and their policy can't be found?

For missing policies, send a self-addressed, stamped envelope to the American Council of Life Insurance, 1001 Pennsylvania Ave. NW,

Washington, DC 20004, and ask for a *policy search form.* A search takes three months—or more—after you submit the form.

What if a policy was issued by a company that I cannot locate?

Simply call the toll-free National Insurance Consumer Helpline. Within a few weeks, you will receive a reply from the ACLI, which maintains a list of companies that have merged...changed names...or gone out of business.

Sources: Melanie K. Marsh, manager, consumer affairs, Health Insurance Association of America, and Arlene Lilly, manager, public information, American Council on Life Insurance, both in Washington, DC. The two organizations, with the Insurance Information Institute, are the principal sponsors of the National Insurance Consumer Helpline. 800-942-4242.

16

The New Investor

How to Protect Yourself from Investment Frauds

As more and more people move out of relatively simple investments, such as bank CDs and money-market accounts, and into higher yielding and more complex securities, the opportunities for misunderstanding increase. And so do the opportunities for securities fraud and deception.

When they do you wrong...

Review the record of your investment to identify any evidence of...

• Unsuitable recommendations. Securities laws require brokers and salespeople to make only those recommendations that are in line with your experience as an investor and other securities that you own.

Example: If you were looking to invest money from a maturing CD and typically invested only in CDs or money-market funds, the salesperson probably should not have encouraged you to speculate on commodities or options. And the adviser should have exercised caution in having you consider a complex tax shelter or mortgage-backed security.

• Churning. Your account should not show an excessive number of securities purchases and sales—and heavy commissions. Excessive means that the size or frequency of the transactions is out of line with the depth of your financial resources and the character of your investments.

• Unauthorized trades. There should not be any purchases or sales of securities appearing on your account statement that you do not recall personally authorizing. You have only 30 days in which to make any corrections to your account.

Misstatements and omissions...

Deception can be far more subtle and indirect, however. *This includes...*

• Important information left unsaid and never put down in written form.

- Guarantees implied.
- Risks not made clear.

If you feel sure that misstatements or material omissions of fact were what led you to make the unfortunate investment, you still have protection under securities law.

Many investors who have put money in unfamiliar fixed-income securities in the past few years, for instance, feel they have been misled about yields. The problem is that most individuals purchase bonds on the basis of a phone conversation and, as a result, tend to ask few questions.

Key questions to ask yourself about an investment in bonds...

- Were you informed that the attractive, high-yielding bond you bought with a maturity date years away was subject to a call? Were you unpleasantly surprised when the bond issuer called the bond—paying you off at face value and cutting off your income stream long before you expected anything like that could happen?
- Was the yield information made clear in the phone conversation? You want to know the yield-to-call as well as the yield-to-maturity on the bond.
- Did you purchase a municipal bond with a surprisingly high yield only to discover that it was not "rated?" Always ask your broker if the bond is rated and what the rating is.
- Does the broker have information about anything that could affect the bond's rating?

Fighting back...

The statute of limitations for securities fraud is three years from the date of the transaction or one year from the date you can prove was the first time you could have detected the fraud, whichever is later. It's in your interest to bring up possible problems promptly.

- If you believe you spot an error, request in writing that the branch manager provide an explanation. Do not rely on a phone call to your broker to get action. Brokers are often reluctant to admit errors. If the branch manager's explanation doesn't satisfy you, write directly to the firm's office of supervisory jurisdiction. Send your letter by registered mail and get a receipt. Keep a copy of both.
- If you are not immediately satisfied by the response, make it very clear that you mean business. On any call you make after it becomes clear there is going to be a problem, tell the person that you are recording the call. (Telling them you are recording the call is really a signal that you are moving toward legal action. If you record without informing the other person, the tape cannot be used as evidence.) Most answering machines allow you to record calls. If brokerage executives won't talk with you under such circumstances, conduct everything by registered mail.
- Get the name and address of your state's securities commissioner. Call the secretary of state's office in your state capital for exact information. Get the official state securities complaint form. Fill it out and send it to the broker dealer as well as to the state authorities. Request restitution and an immediate response.

What to expect: Brokers are generally willing to settle small claims promptly to avoid further problems. The smaller the sum, the easier it is to recover.

Chances are that you agreed to arbitrate disputes when you opened your brokerage account. This can be an economical and effective way to handle disputes that involve $35,000 or less. For larger sums, you probably will need to engage a good securities lawyer.

Establish the claim...

If you are unable to recoup your losses from your broker or dealer, then, to establish a loss, you must sell the investment to prove how much less it was worth than your original investment. At a minimum, you can take a tax loss and collect 31 cents on the dollar as a deduction, or use the tax loss to offset capital gains elsewhere. If there are no capital gains, then the tax loss is subject to an annual $3,000 limit.

When you begin a suit to recover a loss, you and your lawyer will seek out the "deepest pockets" among the firms or individuals who can be considered liable for misrepresenting the investment.

The Civil Liabilities section of the 1934 Securities Act states that anybody mentioned in the transaction is liable, including lawyers, accountants, bankers, investment bankers, management, even real estate appraisers or public relations firms involved in the deal.

Sources: N. Richard Fox, Jr., a former senior manager of a national brokerage firm, and Vernon K. Jacobs, CPA, former vice president and controller of a major life-insurance firm. They are two of the founders of Heartland Management Co., a fee-only investment advisory firm, 6804 W. 107 St., Overland Park, Kansas 66212. Heartland also has an audiotape on how to get out of a bad investment.

Investment Lessons

There's no shortage of financial advice on Wall Street. The problem is that much of this financial advice is conflicting and leaves individuals confused or stuck in bad investments. So what's an investor to do?

To help individuals make better decisions, financial experts George Stasen and Robert Metz give us their basic lessons of investing...

Decisions/decisions...

• "Buy low and sell high" is sound financial advice—but there are actually four decisions to make. Stock-market experts like to say that timing is everything, and most investors strive to sell at the top of a market and buy at the bottom.

This strategy is also known as the "contrary opinion"—doing the opposite of what most other investors are doing at a given time.

But moving successfully against the crowd is very difficult.

Trap: Market cycles contain many small, deceptive movements—so the buy-sell phases aren't always clear. *Here are six decisions a contrarian investor must make...*

• When the market is approaching the bottom of a cycle, sellers no longer have the stomach to buy. This creates an opportunity for bargain hunters. To determine when the market has reached this point, you can evaluate stocks using historically low valuations of revenues, earnings, and dividends. Or you can wait for an uptrend before buying.

• After you buy, don't sell immediately after the bull trend becomes obvious to everyone. Let the crowd join you as the movement upward progresses.

• When serious overvaluation is reached, go against the majority and sell. Determine this moment by setting a price objective beforehand. Or base your timing on the heat of the market. Wait for the first sign of market weakness.

• As the downward cycle advances, resist the temptation to buy back your stock at a lower price. Wait until the market approaches the bottom again before buying.

• Don't confuse portfolio activity with progress toward investment goals. A common mistake made by many investors is rapid portfolio activity. They regard time as the enemy and believe that if they wait too long, that is an invitation for something to go wrong.

It's unrealistic, however, to expect that instant profits are easy to grab. When too much attention is focused on achieving short-term goals, the real opportunity—which is long-term—is forgotten. Think of time as an ally, not as an enemy.

• Beware of the company that offers creative excuses for underachievement. Some companies have a talent for making excuses for problems. Be especially wary of companies that wrap bad news in good news. *Danger signs:*

• When shortfalls and disappointments come with good-news announcements, such as the introduction of a new product or overhead-reduction programs.

• When you find your mailbox jammed with "We love you, shareholder" letters from the company.

• When bad news is accompanied by an announcement of a management shake-up. Did the company also say what took so long for them to clean up the problem? If not, incompetents may still be in charge.

Once credibility has been destroyed, it takes a long time for a company to win it back. When management repeatedly says, "Things will be better next year," it's time to sell.

• Focus on essentials...skip the merely interesting. Experienced investors are humble. They've learned that they can't possibly know everything. Less seasoned investors, on the other hand, may feel that if they had only a few more hours to do research, their investment returns would be considerably better. Usually this is hogwash.

Save time by not seeking out the opinions of yet another expert. Formulating intelligent questions that you then go out and seek to answer is much more valuable than collecting opinions.

Focus on an industry's prospects, the strength and track record of a company, and the long-term implications of a new development.

• Good corporate news can lead to a dangerous sense of euphoria. When there's good news, companies can't wait to circulate it. Many ladle it out in advance, tipping off key stock-market analysts. The result is that these stocks often rise before the news hits the media and afterward rise only slightly—or even fall.

Reasons: Many pros "sell on the news"—or take profits as the news becomes widely known and the price rises—and companies often use good news as an opportunity to seek more equity financing.

Similarly, beware of remarkably upbeat presentations at investment conferences. Instead, wait a few weeks or a month, and you'll almost always be able to buy the stock cheaper. *Opportunity:* Look at the volume in the weeks before an "announcement." If it's high, this tells you that you may be late in getting the word.

• Study the composition of a company's board of directors. The role of a company's board of directors is to represent the interests of all stockholders. One way to determine whether the directors are representing your interests is to look at the people who make up the board.

How to tell a good board from a bad one...

• Determine how many directors come from the company and how many are from the outside. If most are from the inside, the board may not be independent enough to resist undue pressure from top management.

• Examine the credentials of the outsiders. If they are not particularly distinguished, they may have been chosen as "good buddies."

• If the board is small—fewer than five members—it's likely that outside directors were chosen for their cooperative attitude toward management preferences.

On the other hand, a large board—more than 10—is probably too unwieldy to support much independence on the part of outside directors.

• The company's proxy statement will reveal the extent of each director's stock ownership and options and interest in the future of the company. Token holdings are danger signs.

• Learn to distinguish the truly underappreciated stock from the real losers. *Key questions:* Is the stock misunderstood by Wall Street or is it more likely that management misunderstands what's happened to its market?

Don't be fooled by a company's aura or unduly impressed by its past glories. "What have you done for me lately?" is a legitimate question to ask. "What do you plan to do tomorrow?" is an even better one.

Don't jettison a stock simply because it's the biggest loser in your portfolio. That's a short-term balm that usually turns into a long-term mistake.

Sources: George Stasen, a venture-capital expert and chief operating officer of Supra Medical Corp., and Robert Metz, a financial journalist. They are coauthors of *It's a Sure Thing: A Wry Look at Investing, Investors, and the World of Wall Street,* McGraw-Hill, 1221 Avenue of the Americas, New York 10020.

The Dumb Mistakes

• *Mistake:* Following every trend put forth by the press. Sure, serious investors are supposed to know better since they deal with financial matters daily. But big investors are just as insecure as small ones, and they often give in to the many opinions of the financial press. The problem is that the press and the pundits are wrong just as often as they are right.

Don't be distracted by what you read in the papers. Keep yourself focused on your personal financial goals, and don't join every prominent economist and fund manager in second-guessing the economy and companies that momentarily falter.

• *Mistake:* Taking high-rate-of-return risks. If a broker shows you an investment returning 15% a year when comparable investments are paying 3%, there's a reason for the difference. Be suspicious if an investment seems too good to be true. Even sophisticated folks' greed occasionally overtakes their common sense—and they wind up losing money.

• *Mistake:* Not protecting the assets you already have. This often occurs when you're holding a stock whose price has declined precipitously. Say you bought at $10 a share and it has fallen to $5 a share. A common reaction is to say you'll sell when the price recovers. What you're really saying is that you expect this stock, which has fallen by 50%, to rise by 100%.

If you are so convinced that the stock is a good prospect, you should invest more in the stock. When the rationale for holding onto the stock is expressed in these terms, most people back off. The point is, be realistic. When an investment fails, sell it, forget about it... and go on to better things.

• *Mistake:* Trying to time the market—predicting each upturn and downturn, and constantly shifting from one asset class to another, such as stocks to bonds, growth companies to value companies, and so on. Even the pros are unable to do this consistently.

The only person who gets rich with market timing is your broker—by raking in commissions. Successful investors use time and patience. They set their goals and stick with them—overrunning temporary market fluctuations.

• *Mistake:* Not monitoring your holdings. You may not be doing as well as you think. Once every six months, tally up your net worth—not counting your house. Over time, that number should be rising.

You should set a specific target for how much you expect your assets to grow over the next three years and the next five years. I aim for at least 10% average growth a year. At that rate, your assets will double every seven years.

• *Mistake:* Neglecting your greatest asset... you. The rate of return on your own labor is far greater than you can get on any other investment. Think of how much income you produced between last January 1 and the end of the year. Regardless of whether you made $20,000 or $200,000, you went from no earnings at all to your total annual salary or business income. Be sure to take good care of yourself. You want to safeguard your most valuable money-making machine—you.

It's also important to invest in yourself. If your company doesn't provide a car phone, but you know it can help you conduct business, buy one yourself. If your 10-year-old knows more about computers than you do, increase your knowledge by taking a course at night school. Continuously strive for excellence...it will pay off financially.

• *Mistake:* Being afraid to invade your principal. Only the super-wealthy can afford to live on their income alone. Sure, it's great to save for a comfortable retirement, but once you've stopped working, don't forget to use some of the money you've accumulated to improve your quality of life.

Example: A 60-year-old woman with a $10 million portfolio worries about the cost of nursing-home care—until she's told that, with her assets, she could afford to hire a staff of 50 for 24-hour care for the rest of her life.

If you are worried about outliving your principal, make sure your portfolio is not 100% in fixed-income investments. Historically, they have had a low rate of return. *Better:* Fashion a diversified portfolio of stocks and bonds, which will produce a higher rate of return. That way, you can systematically withdraw some of the "growth" by selling stocks.

Your real goal should be to accumulate enough money to support you and your life partner for the rest of your lives, not to make your kids wealthy after you die.

• *Mistake:* Being embarrassed to invest small amounts of money. What's important is to establish the habit of savings, even if you're investing only $5 or $10 a month. There are several mutual-fund families that have a low minimum initial-investment requirement, and no minimum-investment requirement after that.

They know that people who get hooked on the savings habit tend to be very loyal customers. So don't be embarrassed to earmark modest sums for your portfolio. And when larger sums become available—because of a tax refund or a bonus at work, for example—siphon off at least some of that money for investments.

• *Mistake:* Being too busy making money to become financially successful. Regardless of whether you make $50,000, $100,000, or $200,000, it's important to keep track of your spending. There's no doubt that spending all you make can give you the sensation of being wealthy. Yet it's not how much you spend but how much you save that matters. The old adage, "Pay yourself first" works only if you adopt a good method for paying yourself.

Solution: Once a month, when you write a check for your rent or mortgage, get in the habit of writing another check—say, for $50 or $100—for your investments.

Once you get in the saving habit, you won't even notice a dent in your spendable income.

Source: Lawrence A. Krause, chairman of Lawrence A. Krause & Associates, Inc., a San Francisco financial-planning firm. He is the author of *The Money-Go-Round: How You Got On and How to Get Off,* Simon & Schuster, 1230 Avenue of the Americas, New York 10020.

Broker Self-Defense

Check your broker's background. Toll-free hotline—800-289-9999—will advise about criminal indictments, civil judgments, pending disciplinary proceedings and securities-dispute arbitration decisions involving your broker. *Sponsor:* National Association of Securities Dealers, Monday to Friday, 9 a.m. to 5 p.m., Eastern Time. No charge for individuals.

Surviving the Over-the-Counter Stock Market

Over-the-counter stocks, being small and often not well followed by many brokers, are especially susceptible to rumors and false reports. Stockbrokers and underwriters flourish on heavy trading and are usually themselves the source of misleading reports.

Basic wisdom: When a company sounds too good—its product will replace toothpaste—watch out!

• *Rule of thumb:* If you don't know why you own a stock—or why you're buying—or why you're selling—then you're in someone else's hands. This makes you more vulnerable to the caprices of the market.

• OTC stocks, particularly new issues, are usually short-term plays. One should never buy without having a sell target in mind.

• If the selling price is reached, even within a week of buying, stick to the sell decision unless there is some major mitigating factor you hadn't considered before.

• About 80% of all new issues will be selling below their issue price within 18 months. *Reason:* Most new issues are overpriced in relation to existing companies. But they are all destined to become just another existing company within a year.

• In evaluating a new issue, find out who the people involved are. If the underwriter is or has been the target of the Securities and Exchange Commission's investigations, this is often mentioned in the prospectus. The SEC prints a manual of all past violators. Avoid underwriters that have had lots of SEC problems. The strong companies rarely use them to go public.

• Check out the auditors of a new-issue company. (They will be named in the prospectus.) If the auditor is not well-known or is in trouble with the SEC, question the numbers in the financial reports.

• A danger in over-the-counter stocks is a key market maker who crosses buy and sell orders among its own brokerage customers so that the market price is artificial. If such a broker collapses, so will its main stocks. This illustrates the danger of buying a stock dependent on only a single market maker. To avoid such a problem, invest in stocks quoted on NASDAQ, where by definition there are at least two strong market makers, and hopefully a lot more.

• Spot companies just before they decide to go onto NASDAQ. When they do, their price inevitably rises because of the increased attention. Very often the managements will simply tell you if they have NASDAQ plans or not. *Tip-off:* If they've just hired a new financial man, it's often a sign of a move to NASDAQ.

Source: Robert J. Flaherty, editor of *The OTC Review,* Oreland, PA.

Techniques for Evaluating Over-the-Counter Stocks

• Growth potential is the single most important consideration. Earnings increases should average 10% over the past six years when acquisitions and divestitures are factored out.

• Cash, investments, accounts receivable, materials, and inventories should be twice the size of financial claims due within the next year.

• Working capital per share should be greater than the market value of the stock (an $8 stock should be backed by $10 per share in working capital).

• Long-term debt should be covered by working capital, cash, or one year's income.

• The balance sheet should show no deferred operating expenses and no unreceived income.

The criteria for final selections include:

• Ownership by at least 10 institutions reported in Standard & Poor's Stock Guide.

• Public ownership of between 500,000 and one million shares, with no more than 10% controlled by a single institution.

• Continued price increases after a dividend or split.

• Strong likelihood of moving up to a major exchange. (A good sign is strong broker and institutional support.)

Avoid companies that are expanding into unrelated fields, where they lack the required management experience and depth, and have stock selling at prices far below recent highs. This sign of loss of investor support can take months to overcome.

Source: C. Colburn Hardy, *Physician's Management.*

How to Spot a Market Decline Before it Starts

Strong market moves frequently end in one- or two-day reversal spikes. Those spikes often provide advance warning of significant market turning points. *Checkpoints that show when a market decline may be coming:*

• The market will rise sharply in the morning on very high volume running at close to 15 million shares during the first hour of trading.

• From 10:30 a.m. (Eastern time) on, the market will make little or no progress despite heavy trading throughout the day.

• By the end of the first day, almost all the morning's gains will have been lost, with the market closing clearly toward the downside. Occasionally, this process will be spread over a two-day period.

• *Steps to take:* When you see the pattern, either sell immediately or await the retest of the highs that were reached during that first morning. Such a retest often takes place within a week or two, on much lower trading volume. This may prove to be the last opportunity to sell into strength.

How Bear Market Rallies Can Fool You

Bear market rallies are often sharp. They're fueled, in part, by short sellers rushing to cover shares. However, advances in issues sold short often lack durability once short covering is completed.

Here is what you need to know about bear market rallies:

• They tend to last for no more than five or six weeks.

• Advances often end rapidly—with relatively little warning. If you are trading during a bear market, you must be ready to sell at the first sign of weakness.

• The first strong advance during a bear market frequently lulls many analysts into a false sense of security, leading them to conclude that a new bull market is underway. The majority of bear markets don't end until pessimism is widespread and until the vast majority is convinced that prices are going to continue to decline indefinitely.

•Although the stock market can remain "overbought" for considerable periods of time during bull markets, bear market rallies generally end fairly rapidly, as the market enters into "overbought" conditions.

•Price/earnings multiples for the group soar far above historical norms.

•Heavy short selling appears. Early short sellers of the stocks are driven to cover by sharp rallies. Their covering of shorts adds fuel to late rallies within the group. (Short sellers who enter the picture later, however, are likely to be amply rewarded.)

Trading tactics that work for professionals:

•Exercise extreme caution, first and foremost.

•Place close stop orders on any long and/or short positions taken.

•Enter into short sales only after these issues have shown signs of fatigue and of topping out, and then only after recent support levels have been broken.

•Wait for a clear sign that the uptrend has ended before selling out.

Spotting the Bottom Of a Bear Market

Here's how sophisticated investors recognize that a bear market is near its last phase:

•Downside breadth increases. That is, market declines become broader, including even stocks that have been strong before. More issues are making new lows.

•"Oversold" conditions (periods in which the market seems to decline precipitously) extend for longer periods of time. Technical recoveries are relatively minor.

•Pessimism spreads, but analysts and bullish advisories still discuss "bargains" and "undervalued issues."

•Stocks continue to be very sensitive to bad news. The market becomes very unforgiving of poor earnings reports and monetary difficulties.

•Trading volume remains relatively dull. Prices seem to fall under their own weight, the result of a lack of bids rather than urgent selling.

Important: The bear market isn't likely to end until pessimism broadens into outright panic, and until public and institutional selling become urgent. One of the most reliable nontechnical signals that the bear market is over is when the mass media begin to headline the fact that the stock market is hitting its bottom.

How to Make Money In Market Declines

Mistake: Most investors tend to place capital into the stock market following important market advances. This increases your risks.

Instead:

•Adopt a planned strategy of making investments in phases as the market declines. Market declines of greater than 10% are relatively unusual during bull markets and investors should look upon them as an opportunity.

•Don't take quick profits early in intermediate advances and reinvest quickly into new stocks. You miss the really good moves and simply incur additional commission costs.

•Prepare for market advances during periods of market decline. Determine which groups are best resisting market decline, and plan to purchase into such groups upon a 10% market decline. Hold for a minimum of several weeks, preferably months.

•Don't chase stocks that have already risen sharply in price, particularly when the price rise has been based upon speculative expectation.

•Try to ferret out true value—stocks in companies that feature solid balance sheets, regular earnings growth, increasing dividend payout.

•Avoid stocks with institutional followings. They tend to underperform the market.

•Study the market on days when trading is quiet. If such days show positive closing action, you can presume that the professionals are positioning themselves for market advance.

Knowing When to Wait Before Buying

Investors often think they are buying stock at a bargain price, only to see it fall further because of an overall market falloff. *Signs that such a falloff is ahead:*

• Just before the decline, the market advance becomes very selective. Gains are recorded in just a few industry groups rather than across the board.

• Speculative interest runs high in the American Stock Exchange and over-the-counter markets.

• During the first phase of the decline, the stocks that failed to participate at the end of the previous advance show the most severe declines. The strongest industry groups tend to keep rising on short-term rallies. This pattern traps unwary traders who believe that stocks are at bargain levels.

• During the second phase of the decline, most groups participate, but the previously strong groups decline only slightly.

• During the final stages, even the once strong industry groups fall sharply. Odds are that the decline will soon come to an end. Wait for evidence that all segments of the market have declined before stepping in to buy.

• As a general rule, groups that were strongest during the previous rally will advance sharply when the market starts to recover, although they may not remain in the forefront throughout the next market cycle.

• Strong market rallies often take place at quarterly intervals.

• Leaders of one quarter often do not maintain leadership in the next upward cycle.

Questions to Ask Before Buying a Stock

You'll want a yes answer to just about every one of these questions before taking a long position in a stock.

• Is the price/earnings ratio of the stock (price divided by latest 12-month earnings) well below the price/earnings ratio of the average listed issue?

• Have earnings of the company been rising at a steady rate over a period of years, preferably at a rate exceeding the rate of inflation?

• Has the company had a recent history of steadily rising dividend payouts?

• Has the stock recently risen above a clearly defined trading range that lasted for at least five weeks?

• If not, has a recent sharp decline ended with the stock trading on extremely high volume for that issue, without the price falling further?

• Have insiders of the company purchased more shares of the company than they have sold?

• Has the company recently purchased its own shares on the open market?

• Has the stock remained relatively undiscovered by the advisory services and brokerage houses? (One sign that an issue is near the end of a rise is that many advisory services suddenly begin to recommend its purchase.)

Source: Gerald Appel, president, SignAlert Corporation, money managers, Great Neck, NY.

Stocks that Benefit When Oil Prices Fall

• Airlines. Fuel prices will be lower.

• Homebuilders. Interest rates fall because lower oil prices add liquidity to the system. Lower interest rates boost home-building activity.

• Restaurants. The nondiscretionary portion of the average paycheck is 86%. With more discretionary income, people will eat out more.

• Motel chains. There will be more auto travel.

• Automobiles. Lower gasoline prices.

• Retail industry. Another area buoyed by more discretionary spending.

• Brokerage industry. People may invest some of that extra money.

• Interest-rate-sensitive stocks. As rates fall, these companies benefit.

•Japan. The yen will rise and the Japanese economy becomes healthier due to lower oil prices.

Source: Barry Sahgal, managing director of research, Ladenburg Thalmann & Co., New York.

Wise Tactics for Picking a Mutual Fund

•Analyze the advertising the mutual fund runs in the financial press. Usually it gives an excellent performance record to lure new investors.

•Consider the time frame of the fund's performance. It may be a very select period, when the fund's performance was exceptional, or a time when everyone did well in the market. During a longer period the fund may have had just a so-so performance.

•Find out what happened to the fund in down markets.

•Avoid fad funds. You can learn about new funds from many financial periodicals, from reference books such as Wiesenberger's handbook on mutual funds, or from the no-load fund directories put out by a number of organizations. Too often, when a particular industry such as gold, high technology, or international stocks gets hot, the funds jump in to grab a piece of the action. But they don't have the ultimate ability to use the money they raise, because they have bought at the top of the elevator.

•Study the discipline of the funds that interest you. This is stated in the prospectus. Some funds have a mandate to be fully invested at all times. *Trap:* In a major market slide, such as the one from 1968 through 1974, full investment (even with the strictest discipline) will not bring about good performance. It is better to find a fund that can get in and out of cash instruments. *Alternative:* Switch in and out of various funds yourself, based on the signals of a competent timer.

•Identify the risk profile of the fund. Read the prospectus to learn the price/earnings ratio and dividend yield of the average stock the fund holds. Is the average stock selling at 27 times earnings (the high end of the spectrum)? Or is it at an average or below-market multiple, as usually befits a more conservative fund? Does the firm buy volatile stocks? Find out if the fund manager is a trader or a long-term investor. And then decide whether the profile conforms to your own investment style and needs.

•Don't sign up for a family of funds with the belief that, if the stock market sinks immediately, you can switch into a money-market fund. Most funds require that money be at the institution at least 30 days before a switch is allowed.

•Mutual funds aren't banks. Although many people are used to check-writing privileges on money-market funds, they should not view equity mutual funds the same way.

•Distinguish between an investment portfolio and transactions portfolio. Don't put rent money into an equity fund. Mutual funds fall in value at times. You don't want to be forced to liquidate at a loss.

How to Read a Mutual Fund Prospectus

A mutual fund prospectus is not easy reading. The way to pry out the information needed to make a good investment decision is to focus on the following questions:

•*Does the fund's portfolio mesh with your investment goals?* Some funds have highly volatile portfolios and employ leverage or margin selling to enhance return, but at greater risk.

•*What's the fund's performance record?* Select a fund that has matched or surpassed Standard & Poor's 500 during periods of both rising and falling markets. Most prospectuses include several years' performance data. Best performers are usually funds with less than $50 million in assets.

•*What are the minimum initial and subsequent investments?* The lower the better.

•*Is there a switch privilege?* It is highly desirable to pick a fund that allows investors to switch back and forth between a firm's equity and money-market funds by phone. (Some funds charge for switching, but the charges usually don't amount to much, except for the frequent trader.)

• *Are there fees for opening and closing an account?* There is no reason to pay such fees.

• *Is it a load (i.e., sales commission) fund or a no-load?* As a group, no-load funds, those without sales commissions, perform pretty much as well as those with fees.

• *What are the limitations on how the fund can invest money?* Some funds must diversify their portfolios, while others allow management to concentrate highly on one or more industry groups. As a general rule, diversification reduces risk.

• *Does the fund have a policy of moving into cash during bear markets?* While a fund can cut losses this way, it may also delay reinvestment in equities when the market starts to rise. Long-term holders often adopt the strategy of investing in funds that have a record of increasing cash positions by selling equities before bear markets or at least at their earliest stages.

Source: *Switch Fund Advisory*, MD.

Evaluating a Mutual Fund

Before taking a position in a mutual fund, answer these questions:

• *Does the fund suit your tolerance for risk?* Certain funds are extremely volatile in price action. They suit investors with risk capital better than those who cannot afford to run the risk of a sharp decline in their capital. Secure a price history on the fund, either from the fund itself or by visiting the public library of a financial publication. Analyze the fund's historical ups and downs.

• *Does the fund have a good track record during declining markets?* Does the management make an attempt to reduce portfolio exposure during down markets or does the fund generally stay fully invested? Don't expect helpful answers to questions like these from a commissioned salesperson for the fund.

• *Has the fund's management altered policies in the past counter to your own investment objectives?* Certain funds are steadily increasing redemption charges to discourage trading. Or they're imposing restrictions that may not suit your purposes. Verify the facts in the current prospectus. Inquire if any changes are contemplated.

Fitting Your Psychology To a Mutual Fund

Techniques useful to investors for evaluating performances:

For aggressive investors:

• Each week that the market rises, divide the closing price of the mutual fund at the end of the week by the closing level of either the Standard & Poor's 500 Stock Index or the NYSE Index. Plot the results on a graph for comparison. If the fund is indeed stronger than the average during a rising market, it will show up clearly, indicating that it is suitable for an aggressive investor.

• Remember that since such funds also frequently decline more sharply than the averages during falling market periods, they may be suitable only for investors with an accurate sense of market timing.

For safety-oriented investors:

• Each week the market declines, divide the closing price of the mutual fund at the end of the week by the closing level of one of the averages. If your fund resists the downtrend more than the average stock during a falling market, the plotted results will show the fund's line declining less than that of the average.

• Don't be disappointed when mutual funds advance less than more aggressive funds during rising market periods.

For investors who want to try to beat the averages:

• At the end of each week divide the price of the mutual fund (rising or falling) by the price of one of the broad market averages, and plot the results. The result will demonstrate the relative strength curve of the fund, indicating whether it is outperforming the broad market, regardless of the price trend.

•To protect yourself, as soon as your fund's relative strength curve begins to show weakness, consider switching your holdings to a better-performing vehicle.

Selecting a Full-Service Stockbroker

Be sure that you do the interviewing. Don't let the prospective broker turn the tables and interview you. If you are reluctant to ask all these questions, select at least some of them and have the answers supplemented with a resume.

•Where did he study? What?

•How long has he been with the brokerage firm? How long has he been in the securities industry?

•What was his prior employment? Why did he leave his last place of employment?

•From where does he get his investment recommendations? His firm's research department? Company contacts? Friends in the business? His own research? A combination?

•Can he supply a certified history of his firm's and his own research recommendations?

•Does he have any client references?

•What is his theory on giving sell advice and profit taking?

•How many clients does the account executive service? (You want your telephone calls to be answered promptly.)

•How diversified is the brokerage firm? Does it have, for example, a bond department? How about an economist? An in-house market technician (essential for timing)? Money-market experts? Commodity department? Option department? Tax shelter experts?

•How many industries does his firm's research department follow? How many companies? How many senior analysts does the firm have?

•Will you get weekly, monthly or only occasional printed research reports?

•What fees, if any, will be charged for such services as securities safekeeping?

•What is the firm's commission structure? What discounts is it willing to offer?

•Can the investor talk directly to the investment-research analyst to get firsthand clarifications and updates on research reports? Must everything be funneled through the account executive?

•What is the financial condition of the brokerage firm? (You want the latest annual and quarterly financial statements.)

•How many floor brokers does the firm have at the various stock exchanges? (You want prompt order execution.)

•Is the potential broker willing to meet personally on a regular basis (monthly or quarterly, depending on portfolio size and activity) to discuss progress?

•What kind of monthly customer statements are prepared? (More and more firms now offer tabulation of monthly dividend income, portfolio valuation and annual portfolio yield estimate.)

Using Discount Brokers

Discount brokers generally charge 35% to 85% less in commissions than full-service houses. Savings are particularly good on trades involving large numbers of shares, but discounters generally don't give investment advice. Otherwise, confirmations, monthly statements, and account insurance are generally the same for discounters as they are for full-service brokerage firms.

Investors who can benefit by using discounters:

•Investors liquidating market holdings.

•Investors buying on margin. Margin rates are generally better, but this matters only if you're borrowing a substantial amount.

•Beneficiaries of estates who are moving inheritance from stocks and bonds to other kinds of investments.

•Employees whose only holdings are stocks in the companies they work for, who sell these stocks occasionally.

•Lawyers, accountants, and other professionals who believe their personal contacts and own market analyses make for better guidance than what brokers are offering.

•Retired persons or other investors with free time to do their own market research.

Who should not use discounters?

•Investors interested in commodity trading. Discount houses handle stocks, bonds, and options only.

•Investors who need mortgages, tax shelters, special bonds.

•Those with less than $2,000 to invest. Savings on discount commissions at this level do not outweigh the plus of free advice from full-service houses.

•Individuals without stock market experience.

Source: J. Bud Feuchtwanger, financial consultant, NY.

How to Place Orders With a Stockbroker

Most investors are familiar with the basic forms of execution orders which they may give to their stockbrokers. The most common are limit orders (orders to buy and/or sell at the best available price), and stop loss orders (orders to buy and/or sell at the best available price if specified price levels are crossed).

Far fewer investors are familiar with other instructions:

•Fill or kill orders. These are either executed immediately or canceled. The investor wants to buy and/or sell immediately in light of current market conditions.

•Clean-up basis. Buy an amount of stock at the asked price only if the purchase "cleans up" all available stock at that price. If the order is executed, the investor has reasonable assurance that no other heavy seller exists at the price range at which he purchased the shares. So price is unlikely to drop rapidly.

•Not held. The investor provides the floor broker with full authority to use his judgment in the execution of the order, which may mean a more advantageous price. But if the floor broker makes an error in judgment, the investor has no recourse.

•All or none. When buying or selling multiple lots, the investor requests that his entire position or none be sold at a limit price. He can often save on commissions by trading in large lots.

•Short, short exempt. If the investor holds securities or bonds which may be converted into common stock, he can sell short the amount of stock into which these convertible issues may be converted without waiting for an uptick. To do this, he places a "short, short exempt" order. *Advantages:* The market for many convertible securities is thinner than the market for the underlying common. He will often get superior executions by selling the common short and then turning the convertible security into common, which is then employed to cover the short sale.

Source: Irving Waxman, R.F. Lafferty & Co., New York.

When Not to Listen To Your Broker

The few words the average investor finds hardest to say to his broker are, "Thanks for calling, but no thanks." There are times when it is in your own best interest to be able to reject a broker's blandishments.

•When the broker's hot tip is that a certain stock is supposed to go up because of impending good news—*ask yourself:* If the "news" is so super special, how come you (and/or your broker) have been able to learn about it in the nick of time? Often insiders have been buying long before you get the hot tip. After you buy, when the news does become "public," who'll be left to buy?

•When the market is sliding. When your broker asks, "How much lower can they go?" the temptation can be very great to try to snag a bargain. *But before you do, consider:* If the stock, at that price, is such a bargain, wouldn't some big mutual funds or pension funds be trying to buy up all they could? If that's the case, how come the stock has been going down?

•Don't fall for the notion that a stock is "averaging down." It's a mistake for the broker (or investor) to calculate that if he buys more "way down there," he can get out even. Stock market professionals average up, not down.

They buy stocks that are proving themselves strong, not ones that are clearly weak.

How to Protect Yourself In Disputes with Stockbrokers

• Keep a diary of all conversations with stockbrokers that involve placing of orders, purchase recommendations, and other important matters. A detailed record adds credibilty if the dispute goes to court, arbitration, or the broker's boss.

• Note the exact time of conversation, as well as the date. The brokerage firm is liable if it fails to place an order promptly and you lose money as a result of the delay.

• If necessary, complain to the head of the brokerage firm. That's sure to get attention.

• If that doesn't get results, write a complaint letter to the SEC, which regularly examines such letters.

• If none of these work, get a new broker.

Source: Nicholas Kelne, attorney, American Association of Individual Investors, Chicago.

When Not to Pay A Stockbroker's Commission

It's not necessary to use a broker and pay a commission to make a gift of stock. Or if a sale of stock is negotiated privately.

How to transfer stock ownership to another person:

• Enter the other person's name, address and Social Security number on the back of the certificate.

• Sign the back of the certificate and have the signature guaranteed by a commercial bank.

• Send it by registered mail to the transfer agent, whose name is on the certificate.

• Allow two to six weeks for the other person to receive the new certificate. There will be no charge, although in some states the seller, or donor, has to pay a small transfer tax.

Investing in Gold

Almost all the advisers who pushed gold several years ago continue to believe every portfolio should contain some gold as a protection against inflation or economic collapse. *Here are some shrewd ways to invest:*

• Stay away from the gold futures market. Diversify holdings among gold coins, bullion, and stocks of South African gold mines.

• Pick the mines with the most marginal, high-cost production. These companies are traded internationally, and their reserves are known. As the price of gold goes up, their production becomes economic and they offer very high yields.

• Keep in mind that, as a rule, the price of mining shares moves with the price of gold, although the swings are more exaggerated. Calling the turn in the gold market is difficult because gold is a very emotional investment. The political stability of gold-mining countries is a factor to consider.

• When buying or selling, remember that gold prices are generally strong on Fridays and lower on Mondays. This is because investors are reluctant to carry short positions over weekends, when central banks sometimes make announcements that affect prices.

• Prices are also stronger toward the end of the year and weaker in summer. The supply decreases toward the end of the year because laborers on short-term contracts to South African gold mines return home to harvest crops. Demand decreases in summer, when the European gold-jewelry industry closes.

How to Choose A Prime Growth Stock

Prime growth stocks should meet all or most of the following characteristics:

•A dominant position in a growth industry.

•A long record of rising earnings and high profit margins.

•Superb management.

•A commitment to innovation and a good research program.

•The ability to pass on cost increases to the consumer.

•A strong financial position.

•Ready marketability of the stock.

•Relative immunity to consumerism and government regulation.

Source: *Preserving Capital* by John Train, Clarkson N. Potter Publishers, New York.

Before Investing in Condos or Co-ops

Despite the recent drop in housing starts, many investors are turning again to condominium and cooperative apartment houses, especially in big cities. Smart investors today can profit from errors made in the last decade. Now they know that:

•It's best to avoid investing in the development of condos or co-ops that are surrounded by rental apartments. *Best investment:* Co-ops and condos that are next to single-family housing.

•People who buy individual apartment units like buildings where apartments cost less than comparable single-family housing nearby. *Rule of thumb:* Apartments should sell for 25% less than the lowest-priced houses in the area.

•Apartment buyers also avoid units in outlying areas. For psychological reasons, people don't mind commuting 20 to 30 miles to work from a suburban house, but many dislike an apartment in a remote area.

•It's easier to overbuild the apartment market than standard housing because the cost per unit is cheaper for apartments. When there's a housing glut, a co-op or condo can have high vacancy rates for many months or even years.

•Factors that make houses cheaper will almost always make apartments difficult to sell. *Examples:* Lower interest rates. Oversupply. Changes in zoning or building codes that favor house construction.

Source: Vincent Mooney, real estate consultant on condominium building and conversion and president of Condominium Home Realtors, Tulsa, OK, and author of *Condoeconomics.*

Cashing CDs Before Maturity

•Many investors don't realize that they can also buy bank CDs through Merrill Lynch and other brokers. *Benefit:* Merrill Lynch maintains a market in CDs, so it's possible to sell them back before maturity.

Comfortable Retirement: What it Takes

Comfortable retirement requires about 50%-75% of the final working year's income.

Source: *CPA Digest,* Milwaukee.

Making Voluntary Contributions to a Company Pension Plan

Making voluntary payments to your company's pension plan, in addition to the contributions your employer already makes for you, makes tax sense.

•Make sure you make the maximum contribution to your company's 401k savings plan. *Reason:* These additional contributions will reduce your taxable income. Also, the interest earned accumulates tax free until withdrawal.

•The maximum annual contribution limit is the lesser of $9240 or your company plan's lower limit. Check with your company's benefits coordinator for more information.

Source: Martin Fleisher, an attorney in private practice who specializes in employee benefits, Springfield, MA.

How to Get the Most Out of Your IRA

Your IRA may be your most important source of retirement income. You can contribute up to $2,000 a year, as long as you're working (until the year you reach age 70½). In addition, if you leave a job, you might be able to roll over your pension or profit-sharing distributions into your IRA. As the years go by, an IRA can grow into big money.

The pros and cons of the most common ways to invest IRA money:

Banks or savings & loans...

•Usually don't charge any fees.

•Your money is insured by the federal government up to $100,000. If your IRA grows larger than this, just open a second account at a different bank.

•*A psychological advantage:* Most people are familiar with local banks and trust them. But many taxpayers feel nervous about stocks, bonds and similar investments.

•Banks offer IRAs the same accounts (except checking) as any other depositors, including passbook savings accounts, money-market accounts and CDs of varying rates and lengths.

•Penalties are charged for early withdrawal of CDs (though some banks will waive the penalty for depositors at retirement age).

•*Essential:* Keep a detailed record of maturity dates of all CDs or time deposits, so you'll know when you can withdraw the funds or switch investments.

Insurance companies...

•Insurance companies sell retirement annuities. *Most common:* Traditional fixed-rate annuity, at a specified interest rate, which guarantees a specific amount at retirement for each $1,000 contributed.

•*Advantage of fixed annuity:* You know in advance how much you'll get. And you're guaranteed an income for your lifetime (and your spouse's, if the annuity is set up that way). You can't outlive your investment.

•*Big disadvantage of fixed annuity:* No protection against inflation.

•In recent years, many insurance companies have begun offering variable annuities, invested in money markets, stocks or other investments that rise and fall with the economy and the rate of inflation.

•*Advantage of variable annuity:* They've generally worked out much better in inflationary times.

•*Disadvantages of a variable annuity:* Less certain than fixed-rate annuities and involve some risk.

•Generally, insurance companies charge fees for setting up and maintaining an IRA. There also may be a charge on contributions and withdrawals.

•These fees are tax deductible to the extent allowed by law. Pay them separately from your IRA contributions...and deduct the amount as "IRA fees" as a miscellaneous deduction on your income tax return.

Mutual funds...

•*Advantages of mutual fund IRAs:* Flexibility and diversification. Most mutual fund companies operate several funds—money market, common stock, bond funds, etc. *Important:* You can usually move your money from one fund in the family of funds to another at will, usually for little or no charge.

•*Caution:* Some funds are more speculative than others. Some are growth funds and some are income funds. (And some funds charge sales commissions.)

Brokerage houses...

•The main attraction of a brokerage house as a trustee for an IRA account is for the taxpayer who wants to manage his own IRA by setting up a self-directed account. The brokerage house is still the trustee, but you make all investment decisions—what to buy, what to sell, etc.

•*Caution:* This kind of account is for the experienced investor, who is willing to take the responsibility—and the risk.

•Brokerage houses normally charge a fee for setting up and maintaining an IRA, as well as their normal commissions on any transactions.

•The fees (but not the commissions) are deductible if separately billed and paid.

Source: Peter I. Elinsky, tax partner, KPMG Peat Marwick, CPAs, Washington, DC.

Early IRA Withdrawals

Although the Tax Reform Act clobbered the IRA deduction for many taxpayers, it created a penalty-free way to withdraw money from the account before you reach age 59½.

• *Old law:* You had to pay an additional 10% penalty tax on distributions from IRA accounts before age 59½.

• *New Law:* You won't pay the extra 10% penalty tax if you convert the account to an annuity and receive the money in a scheduled series of substantially equal payments over your life or your life expectancy.

How to Read the Economic Indicators

We hear these terms on the news all the time —*Gross Domestic Product, Consumer Price Index, Consumer Confidence Index,* etc.—yet most of us have no idea what these indicators are or how they affect the financial markets.

Here are six of the most important economic indicators, when they are released and how to invest based on their results.

Federal Reserve Board's policy...

The Federal Reserve Board directs monetary policy, which is largely influenced by the chairman, currently Alan Greenspan. He has the power to control the markets by tightening the money supply or pumping more into the system. This affects the value of money directly. *What to do:*

...whenever the chairman makes a public statement, read the key sections and study the commentary of the professional Fed watchers. The chairman's viewpoint usually takes a while to work its way through the system—but eventually it has a considerable impact.

Interest rates...

Focus on long-term bond rates and the discount rate, which is the rate the Fed charges banks to borrow money. Long-term rates change continually. The discount rate only changes when the Fed wants to make a shift in monetary policy. *What to do:*

...don't dive into the market—or bail out—at the first change in the discount rate. That alone will not alter the overall direction of the market. You can lose money by reacting too early either way.

...two or three moves in the discount rate—in either direction—constitute an unmistakable trend, and the markets will react dramatically. Know in advance how you'll respond if that second move occurs. If you're going to act at all, act fast.

...if the interest rate trend is up, rethink the asset allocation in your portfolio. Cash will likely outperform stocks and bonds. In this environment, choose a fixed-rate mortgage over an adjustable-rate mortgage, since you'll want to lock in at the low rate.

...when the trend is down, you should be buying stocks and bonds.

Gross Domestic Product (GDP)...

The GDP is the dollar value of all goods and services produced in the US. It is announced at the end of March, June, September and December, and provides a snapshot of how fast the economy is expanding or contracting. The markets typically interpret GDP growth of between 0% and 3% as anemic...3% to 5% as robust and healthy...and more than 5% as frothy and probably unsustainable. When the GDP drops for two consecutive quarters, the economy is officially in a recession. A total of three consecutive quarters in which the GDP increases is considered a growth trend. *What to do:*

...if the GDP is growing at a slow pace following a steep decline, it's a good time to buy stock or real estate. The values of both will rise as the economy gets stronger.

...if the GDP is growing at a fast pace, quality growth stocks are good investments. Just

keep in mind that with expansion comes contraction and the growth environment will not last forever.

Warning sign: If growth is 5% or more for two consecutive quarters, the Federal Reserve, which regulates the flow of money into the economy, will probably raise short-term interest rates to slow borrowing and combat inflation. Consider selling some stocks and shifting the profits into long-term bonds.

...if the GDP growth rate is declining, review your stock portfolio. *My strategy:* Hold those blue chip issues that are solid, long-term investments...and sell the rest.

Producer Price Index (PPI)...

Released around the 15th of the month, the PPI measures the rate of change in wholesale prices according to commodity, industry sector and production stage—or what it costs to manufacture goods. PPI helps show the direction of inflation—I consider three consecutive months of movement up or down a trend. *What to do:*

...when the PPI is rising slowly—0.3% or less per month—inflation is under control. Combine that with a slowly rising GDP and investors have the best of all possible worlds. Be wary of a one-time jump in the PPI—either up or down. It won't move the markets significantly. Pay careful attention to how the PPI is interpreted by the media and analysts—not just what the number is.

...if the PPI advances sharply for two consecutive months at the equivalent of a 6% annual rate (about 0.5% per month), it's costing companies a great deal to make goods. *My strategy:* Sell your stocks and bonds before the market overheats. Also, purchase big-ticket items before those wholesale prices are passed along to consumers.

...if inflation is rising and the PPI rate of change starts to slow or declines, buy stocks and bonds. Companies will be earning higher profits as it costs them less to make goods, but they can still charge consumers higher prices.

Consumer Price Index (CPI)...

Often referred to as the cost of living, the CPI measures the change in consumer prices for goods and services bought by households. It is released in the middle of every month—always one day after the PPI. *What to do:*

...if the economy is expanding moderately (a GDP of 4% or under) and the CPI is also rising at a modest rate (annual rate of about 3%), consider buying stocks or real estate...and avoid bonds because interest rates are likely to rise.

...if the CPI moves up sharply for two months and the cause of the rise is not easily explained by the economists, avoid bonds. *Attractive:* Stocks that will either profit from inflation or not get clobbered in the recession that may be looming.

...if the CPI falls by 1% or more for two months —I like stocks that pay dividends. To lock in yields before they fall, add quality corporate bonds and Treasury bonds to your portfolio.

...if the CPI rises by 4% or more over four consecutive months, expect interest rates to rise. Buy short-term CDs.

Consumer Confidence Index (CCI)...

The CCI reflects consumers' attitudes toward the economy, the job market, their own financial situations and the future. The government releases the CCI during the first 10 days of each month.

When assessing the CCI, remember that consumers account for two-thirds of all US economic activity. So how we're all feeling matters. *What to do:*

...don't react to the month-to-month ups and downs of the CCI. Rather, value it as a big-picture forecaster.

...if inflation is high and consumer confidence falls below 80—20% lower than the index's benchmark of 100—prepare for a recession.

...if inflation is low and the CCI shows signs of reviving—lower unemployment and rising auto or home sales, for example—bet on a stronger economy. Big-ticket durable goods, such as autos and appliances, may soon do very well.

Source: Jay J. Pack, vice president of Burnham Securities, Inc., 1345 Avenue of the Americas, New York 10105, and member of the New York Society of Security Analysts. He is coauthor, with Nancy Dunnan, of *Market Movers: A Complete Guide to Economic Statistics, Trends, Forces, and News Events—and What They Mean to Your Investments,* Warner Books, 1271 Avenue of the Americas, New York 10020.

17

Taxes

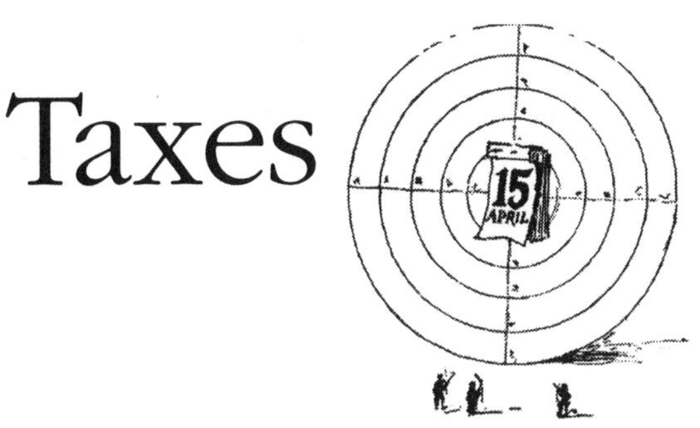

How to Get More Time To File Your Return

If you need extra time to prepare your tax return, you can get it automatically: Just file Form 4868 with your local IRS Service Center by April 15. The deadline for filing your return will be pushed back four months to August 15. If you're self-employed, the extension gives you four more months in which to make contributions to a Keogh plan (if the plan was set up by December 31 of the preceding year).

Caution: A filing extension does not extend the time for paying your tax. The instructions on Form 4868 tell you how to estimate your tax; if you don't send in a check for the estimated tax due, the extension will not be valid.

Never simply file a late return without getting an extension. The penalty for filing late without an extension is 5% of the unpaid tax per month, up to a maximum penalty of 25%. There's also a minimum penalty for not getting your tax return in within 60 days of its due date—$100 or 100% of the tax due, whichever is less. You'll also be penalized for paying your taxes late, and you'll be charged interest on the late-paid tax.

Second extensions: It is possible to get a second filing extension from the IRS by filing Form 2688. But the second extension isn't automatic. You must have a valid reason for requesting it, such as a death in the family or loss of your records. A second extension, if granted, gives you an extra two months—until October 15—to file your return.

Checklist: Before Mailing Your Return

Check to make sure you've completed everything on this list. A slipup can cause delays and inconvenience. Moreover, every time you draw attention to your return, you increase the chance of an audit. *Checklist:*

• Do your name, address, and Social Security number appear on page 1? If you used the IRS address label, be sure you have made any necessary corrections.

• Have you put your Social Security number on every page, every document, and every check to be sent to the IRS?

• Are all Form W-2s attached?

• Are all other necessary forms and schedules attached?

• Have you checked and rechecked your arithmetic?

• Is the form signed and dated? Both husband and wife must sign a joint return.

• If you owe money, is your check or money order attached to the return? Have you written your Social Security number on the check? Have you written the year and "Form 1040" on it?

• Is the return addressed to the correct IRS office?

• Have you made a copy of the return for your own records?

Big Tax Refund? You've Done Something Wrong

If you got a fat tax refund this year, don't feel too happy about it. It means you overpaid your estimated taxes or had too much withheld from your salary. In effect, you made an interest-free loan to the government, when you could have been using the money for yourself—in an interest-paying bank account.

Trap: The IRS can withhold all or part of your refund to offset a tax liability, a debt to a government agency (for instance, a student loan), or unpaid child support.

What to do: File a new Form W-4 or W-4A to reduce the amount withheld from your salary. If you pay estimated tax, reduce your quarterly payments.

Caution: Don't overdo it. You can be hit with underpayment penalties unless withholding taxes plus estimated tax payments amount to at least 90% of your total tax bill.

Tax Refunds: The Second Time Around

It's not too late to get a cash refund for past years by filing a Form 1040X with the IRS. Take the time to review old tax returns to see if you overlooked anything that may lead to getting money back.

The time limit for amending your original tax return is three years from the date you filed the original return or two years from the date you actually paid the tax, whichever is later. Early filers are treated as though they had filed on the actual due date of the return.

Caution: Filing an amended return may invite the IRS to take a second look at your original return. If there's anything on it that you think may not pass this additional IRS scrutiny, you should be wary about amending. On the other hand, if you'll get back a significantly larger refund by amending, or you know the IRS can't challenge anything on the original return, it may be worth the risk.

What you can amend...

The most common oversights that eventually lead to an additional refund:

• Filing the wrong form. Short-form filers might well have been able to file a long form and get the benefit of a lower tax bill. But you're not stuck with your original choice. Perhaps you used the short form because you were in a last-minute rush to file the return, or you thought the long form was too difficult. If you file a long form this year but filed a short form for the past two years, check your earlier returns to see if you missed anything.

No matter what your original reason for filing the short form, it is worth taking the time now to see how much you would save by filing the long form.

• Overlooking deductions. As you fill out your return this year, perhaps you will remember deductions that you should have taken in the past. If you forgot to claim an item to which you were entitled, consider amending that year's return.

• Overlooking credits. Taxpayers often forget about or miscalculate certain tax credits. *Carefully review the following on your past returns:*

- Excess Social Security tax paid.
- Child care credit.
- Earned income credit.
- Using the wrong filing status. When a married couple files separately, the overall tax bill is usually larger. If you would have saved taxes by filing jointly, you are allowed to amend your return. However, it doesn't work the other way: Once you've filed a joint return and the due date of the return has passed, you can't change the filing status to married filing separately.
- Overlooking exemptions. If you were supporting a parent who didn't live with you during the year, you may have forgotten to claim him or her as an exemption on your return.
- Neglecting to do five- or 10-year averaging on lump-sum distributions. Many taxpayers forget this special tax saver when they receive a lump sum from their retirement plan and don't expect to roll it over into another plan. If you received such a distribution, make sure you compared your tax liability with five- or 10-year averaging and without it, to see which one produced the lower tax.
- Overpaying Social Security. If you worked for more than one employer in a single year, you may have paid too much Social Security tax. The maximum you must pay changes from year to year, but you can find out the amount by looking at your old returns.
- Neglecting to check for retroactive tax changes. Sometimes the IRS, Congress, and the courts make retroactive decisions that may allow you to take a deduction for something that was disallowed in the past. Keep informed about all tax changes to see if any of them affect your past returns.

Source: John L. Withers, special consultant for IRS regulations and procedures, Deloitte & Touche, Washington Service Center, 1900 M St. NW, Washington, DC 20036.

More Facts on Amended Returns

You can file an amended return or claim a refund on Form 1040X within three years after the original return was due or two years after you actually paid the tax, whichever is later.

The time limits are absolute. If you're even one day late, your claim must be disallowed. Use Form 1040X if you file early and discover an error before April 15. You'll get faster handling.

You can use Form 1045 for claims based on carrybacks (net operating losses, certain credits). This will get you a fast refund, as the IRS must act within 90 days. But the action isn't final. The claim can be disallowed later. Time limits on these claims are figured from the year the carryback arose.

Form 1040X has space to write your income, deductions, and credits as you reported them on your original return and the changes you want to make for those amounts. *Important:* Include explanations for the changes you are making and the year you are amending on page 2. You must calculate the new tax on the corrected amount, just as you would on your regular return.

State all possible grounds. If the matter ever reaches court, you may be limited to the exact claim stated on the form. If, for example, you're not sure whether an item should be claimed as a business loss, a casualty loss, or a bad debt, state all three grounds in the alternative. You can even assert inconsistent grounds.

Where to send it: Mail the amended return to the IRS Service Center where you now live. If you moved during the year, mail it to the Service Center at your new address. Be sure to complete the information on the front of the 1040X about where your original return was processed in order to expedite your return.

Caution: When you amend your federal tax return, your state tax liability from that year may be affected, too.

It's important to assess your audit risk before you amend your return. It depends on how much you'll get back by amending, why you're amending, and the safety of your original return.

Question: Is the amount that you are getting back worth the risk for what you might possibly lose?

Safer amendments:

- Changes of very small dollar amounts, especially where the amount on the original return is very small, too.

• Mathematical changes.

Not-so-safe amendments:

• Any change that has huge tax consequences on your return.

• Tax-shelter losses.

• Losses from business activity.

• Reclassifying ordinary income to capital gain.

How Long Should Tax File Documents Be Kept?

• Normally, tax returns and supporting documents should be kept for three years from date of filing.

• If income previously has been underreported by 25% or more: Six years.

• In cases of previous failure to file or serious suspicion of criminal fraud: Indefinitely.

Suggestion: Put canceled checks and supporting documents into a manila envelope, mark with the tax year and the discard date, and put it on the top shelf of your highest closet. You'll only need this material if you're audited. Returns should be kept in an accessible file drawer.

Source: Stephanie Winston, president of The Organizing Principle, 461 Park Ave. South, New York 10016, and the author of *The Organized Executive,* Warner Books.

Frequently Overlooked Deductions

"Points" paid for mortgage on purchase or improvement of principal residence.

State unemployment and disability taxes withheld.

Expenses related to seminars attended for business purposes. Deductible items include registration fees, travel, lodging and 80% of the cost of meals.

Investment-related expenses:

• Travel expenses to check on income-producing property.

• Cost of telephone, postage, office supplies and automobile operaton (trips to and from broker).

• Books, magazines and newsletters on investment, financial, or tax matters, including appropriate daily papers (e.g., *Wall Street Journal, New York Times*).

• Insurance and storage charges for merchandise held as a speculative investment.

Out-of-pocket expenses incurred in providing charitable services. May deduct actual cost of auto usage, tolls and parking.

Out-of-pocket expenses incurred in changing jobs. Include the cost of printing résumés or traveling to an interview.

A portion of health insurance for the self-employed.

Charitable contributions made through payroll withholdings (e.g., United Way).

Deductible items on December credit card statement, even if paid in the following year, including:

• Medical expenses.

• Charitable contributions.

• Miscellaneous business expenses.

Tax reform note: Employee business expenses and miscellaneous deductions are allowed only to the extent they exceed 2% of adjusted gross income.

Source: Barry Salzberg, CPA, partner in charge of Executive Financing Counseling services with the firm of Deloitte & Touche, 1 World Trade Center, New York 10048.

Tax Return Completion Checklist

In dealings with the IRS, no news is good news. More precisely, in this case, no mail is good news.

Every time the IRS sends a letter to a taxpayer, it means that someone within the service has taken another look at the return in question. Every look taken increases the chance that "problems" will come to light (if they haven't already).

There are a number of simple steps you can take to minimize the risk of ongoing activity with your tax return.

•Before filing, make sure your return is complete. Check to see that all necessary forms and schedules are present and accounted for. This includes any and all attachments (e.g., if you donate common stock to a charitable organization, you must attach a statement of certain information regarding the gift.) Staple your return together securely. Missing pages generate correspondence.

•*Make sure the return is accurate:* Check, double-check, and recheck all arithmetic.

•Make sure your reporting is consistent with the information the IRS receives.

For example, if you have invested in IBM and General Motors stock through XYZ Brokerage, your return should list dividends paid to you by XYZ, not IBM or GM, because the IRS will receive a 1099 form from XYZ.

•Double-check to see that the return is signed by all necessary parties.

•Finally, file your return on time. By all means request an extension if you need one, but mail your return well before the expiration date.

In the event you must file at the last minute, use registered mail in order to have evidence of timely filing.

Source: Ralph C. Ganswindt, partner specializing in closely held businesses, with Arthur Andersen & Company, 777 East Wisconsin Ave., Milwaukee, WI 53201.

Answering Unreported Income Notices

The IRS mails millions of computer generated notices to taxpayers whose returns did not show dividend or interest income as it was reported to the IRS by banks and financial institutions. The notice recalculated the tax due, added interest charges...and imposed a negligence penalty.

How should taxpayers handle such notices? What can they learn from these notices that will help in preparing future returns? Here's the procedure:

First step: Study the notice carefully and define the problem. Discover precisely which item, or items, of income the IRS says you did not report. You'll find this information on a separate page of the multipage notice.

Second step: Review your copy of the return and the 1099 forms you used to fill it out. Determine whether the IRS notice is right or wrong. Never automatically write out a check for the amount the IRS says you owe. The notice could be dead wrong—many are.

Third step: Answer the notice, in writing, within the time limit given—usually 30 days. Write to the IRS Service Center at the address given in the notice.

•If the IRS is right and you did accidentally fail to report an item of income: Pay the tax and interest but ask that the negligence penalty be waived.

Sample letter:

IRS Service Center
City, State

Re: John and Sally Connell
Social Security Nos...
Form 1040-1992

Gentlemen:

In response to your notice, a copy of which is attached, you will find enclosed a check payable to the IRS in the amount of $x, consisting of tax of $y and interest of $z.

The item in question was inadvertently omitted from our return as filed under the following circumstances: (Give the reason for the accidental omission of the income.) It is contended that this constitutes reasonable cause for the inadvertent omission of this item. It is respectfully requested that the negligence penalty assessed in your notice be abated.

Sincerely yours,
John & Sally Connell

•When you did report the income or the notice is otherwise wrong:

Review the notice and your return to discover the cause of the discrepancy. One of several things may have happened. The IRS may be working with an incorrect 1099. Or the 1099 may be right and you reported the income but not as you should have.

Sample letter:

Gentlemen:

In response to your notice, a copy of which is enclosed, I am submitting the following in explanation of the alleged omission. (Examples follow.)

1. The dividend of $1,200 reported on my return as being received from General Motors should have been reported as being received from Merrill Lynch as nominee. A copy of my Schedule B is enclosed. (Circle the item where it appears on your Schedule B to show that you reported it.)

Lesson: Report dividends from stock held in street name by your broker as dividends received from the broker as nominee and not from the company. That's the way the 1099 will show them.

2. Dividend of $400 from Dreyfus Liquid Assets Fund was reported as interest income of $400 from Dreyfus. A copy of my Schedule B is enclosed. (Circle the item.)

Lesson: Most money-market funds report their income as dividends and not as interest. Report the income as it is reported to the IRS on the fund's 1099.

3. Interest of $600 from Citibank was on an account owned jointly by myself and my brother. I reported only one half of the interest—$300. A copy of my Schedule B is enclosed.

Lesson: The correct way to report interest from a joint account would be: "Interest, Citibank, $600, less amount reported by others, $300. Net amount: $300."

4. Interest of $500 from Wells Fargo Bank was reported on my return as $100, per corrected Form 1099, a copy of which is enclosed.

Lesson: Review all 1099s when you receive them. Immediately request corrected copies of any that are wrong. Report the correct information on your return. If the IRS doesn't pick up the correction, you'll have it in your files should you need it.

5. Interest of $2,140 from American National Bank was nontaxable income distributed from my IRA account and immediately reinvested in another IRA. I enclose a copy of a corrected 1099 from American National showing $0 taxable interest in this account.

How to end the letter:

If there are any further questions, please contact me.

• If you get a second notice that seems to have ignored your letter:

Gentlemen:

In response to your notice dated March 28, I received a similar notice dated February 23. I answered the first notice with the enclosed letter. It would appear that my response was not received in time to prevent the second request for payment from being issued. (Enclose photocopies of both notices and a copy of your original letter.)

Sincerely yours,
John & Sally Connell

Some Excuses that Work And Some that Don't

Taxpayers who face penalties for misfiling returns or misreporting income will do the best they can to come up with a good explanation. Some excuses work—others don't.

Excuses that work...

• Reliance on bad IRS advice from an IRS employee or an IRS publication. If the advice came from an employee, you must show that it was his job to advise taxpayers and that you gave him all the facts.

• Bad advice from a tax professional can excuse a mistake if you fully disclosed the facts to the adviser. You must also show that he was a competent professional, experienced in federal tax matters.

• Lost or unavailable records will excuse a mistake if the loss wasn't the taxpayer's fault and he makes a genuine attempt to recover or reconstruct the records.

• Incapacity of a key person can be a legitimate excuse. *Examples:* Serious illness of the taxpayer or a death in his immediate family.

Excuses that don't work...

• Pleading ignorance or misunderstanding of the law generally does not excuse a mistake. *Exception:* Where a tax expert might have made the same mistake.

•Someone else slipped up. You are personally responsible for filing your tax return correctly. You can't delegate that responsibility to anyone else. If your accountant or lawyer files late, for example, you pay the penalty.

•Personal problems don't carry much weight with the IRS. For example, don't expect to avoid a penalty by pleading severe emotional strain brought on by a divorce.

How to Get What You Need from Your Accountant

The biggest mistake people make in dealing with the professionals they hire to work on their tax returns is to drop everything in the professional's lap and walk away. To get the most from your accountant, you must take an active role in the preparation of your returns...even if you pay hundreds of dollars in preparation fees to the most prestigious firm in town. Not only must you help your accountant find everything that will save you tax dollars, but you must also understand how every figure that's reported on the return was arrived at.

•Organize the information. This saves his time and your money.

•Bring to his attention any out-of-the-ordinary deductions...job-hunting expenses, child care or dependent care, unreimbursed business travel, etc.

•Be complete. The more last-minute changes you call in after your return has been prepared, the bigger your bill will be.

•Mention changes in essential personal and financial data. If, for example, you don't tell your accountant that you're supporting aged parents, he isn't likely to know about the dependency exemptions or possible medical deductions for them, or to recommend a multiple-support agreement with your brothers and sisters.

•Discuss your audit tolerance. If you want a return that will save you top tax dollars, you must take aggressive positions on your various financial dealings. The more aggressive you are, the more likely your return will be audited. If you want to cut your audit risk, you must take a more conservative approach to the way you handle your return. You can't have it both ways.

•Assume that your return will be audited. Using a tax professional doesn't lessen that likelihood. Your accountant isn't responsible to the IRS for your return. You are. The IRS auditor will ask you how your charitable contributions were calculated, how your interest was calculated, or when depreciable assets were purchased.

•Keep worksheets detailing the calculations for each figure on your tax return.

Source: Paul N. Strassels, a former IRS tax-law specialist.

Should You File a Joint Or Separate Tax Return?

The effect of a joint tax return is to treat a married couple as one taxpayer, no matter which spouse realized the income. Filing a joint return will usually result in tax savings because the joint return rates are generally more favorable than the rates for married persons filing separately.

•Credit for child care expenses is only available on a joint return.

•Keep in mind that when a couple files a joint return, both parties are liable for the full amount of tax due, regardless of who earned the income.

But there are some advantages to filing separately:

•In community property states, all community income and deductions are reported one-half on each return. This can result in lower tax-bracket filings.

•Some married couples file separate returns so they won't have to disclose to their spouse the source and extent of their earnings.

•Filing separate returns may make sense if one of the spouses has extraordinary medical expenses. These expenses are deductible only to the extent that they exceed 7½% of the combined income of both spouses. Therefore, the smaller income on a separate return might result in a deduction that would be reduced or eliminated on a joint return because of the larger combined income.

• In certain states, the income tax saving from filing separate returns can be greater than the federal tax saving from filing a joint return.

Source: *Tax Hotline,* 55 Railroad Ave., Greenwich, CT 06830.

Before Mailing in A Tax Return

Getting the details right the first time can save the time and trouble of dealing with the IRS later. *Checklist:*

• Sign the return.

• Did your preparer sign?

• Did you answer every question on the return?

• Put your Social Security number on every page and every attachment, including your check.

• Put your tax-shelter registration number on the return.

• Make copies of your return.

• Compare your return with last year's to make sure you didn't overlook anything.

• Put the return away for a few days or a week so that you can look at it with a fresh eye before mailing it.

• Send it by certified mail so there will be no question that your return was filed on time. Mailed on time is considered to be filed on time by the IRS.

• Use a separate envelope for each return.

• Put your children's returns or estimated payments in separate envelopes.

• Attach your W-2.

• Include your check if you owe money to the IRS.

• Include any receipts and forms required to prove your charitable contributions.

• Include a check for the tax you owe if you are filing an extension request.

Top Filing Mistakes... According to the IRS

• Miscalculating medical and dental expenses. This deduction is based on your adjusted gross income—AGI. Carefully complete up to the AGI line on your 1040 before attempting to figure your medical expenses.

• Taking the wrong amount of earned income credit. Use the worksheet in the instruction booklet to avoid mistakes.

• Entering the wrong amount of tax. Use the right tax tables.

• Confusion about income tax withheld. Don't confuse this with the Social Security tax that was withheld from your pay.

• Unemployment compensation errors. Use the special formula in the IRS instruction booklet to calculate the amount of taxable unemployment.

• Mistakes in calculating child and dependent care expenses. Use Form 2441 and double-check your math.

• Errors in tax due. Believe it or not, taxpayers often err in determining the bottom line of their tax return—are they entitled to a refund or do they owe the IRS? Carefully compare the tax you owe with the amount you have paid through withholding or estimated tax payments.

• Overlooking credits. Read all IRS instructions carefully.

• Adding income incorrectly. Mistakes are frequently made by taxpayers when adding the income section of Form 1040.

Source: *IRS Publication No. 910.*

Filing Late

Reasons for getting an extension:

• You don't have all the information you need to fill out the return.

• You need time to find the cash to make a contribution to your Keogh account. (Unlike IRAs, which must be made by April 15, Keogh contributions can be made up to the extended due date of your return—as late as October 15.)

•You have a complicated transaction that you need time to ponder.

Timetable:

•First extension. April 15 is the due date for tax returns. But you can get an automatic four-month extension by filing Form 4868 by April 15. If you pay late you'll owe late-payment penalties, plus interest on the tax paid late. *Trap:* You must make estimated tax payments on Form 1040-ES by April 15. You can't get an extension of time to make quarterly estimated payments.

•Second extension. It's possible to get a second filing extension of two months. But the second extension isn't automatic; you must have a valid reason for requesting it, such as a death in the family or loss of your records. *Loophole:* It has been my experience that the closer you file to October 15 (after August 15) the less chance there is that you'll be audited. A second extension may be the way to get off the audit treadmill if you've been audited every year for the last few years.

Source: Edward L. Mendlowitz, partner, Mendlowitz Weitsen, New York.

To Avoid Late-Filing Penalties

A person who files a late tax return without getting a prior extension faces stiff penalties. It's possible to avoid these penalties, but you must convince the IRS that you had a good excuse for filing late.

Situations in which the IRS has said it may accept a late return without penalty:

•The return was postmarked on time, even if it had insufficient postage.

•The return was filed on time but in the wrong IRS district or office.

•The return was filed late because of inaccurate information received from an IRS employee.

•A filing delay was caused by the destruction of the taxpayer's records in a fire, flood or other casualty.

•An individual couldn't get proper tax forms from the IRS, in spite of asking for them at a reasonable time.

•The filer was not able to get necessary information from an IRS official, despite a personal visit to an IRS office.

•The taxpayer died, was seriously injured or was forced to be away from home for a reason that was unexpected and beyond his or her control.

•The taxpayer was ignorant of the law, in that he or she never had to file a particular kind of form or return before.

•The death or illness of an immediate family member.

•Incapacitating illness of the taxpayer himself.

•A competent and informed tax adviser told the taxpayer that a tax return was not necessary.

How to proceed: Make your request for abatement of the penalty in writing to your local IRS Service Center. Give a detailed explanation of your reason for filing late. Use the term "reasonable cause" both at the beginning and the end of the letter. To speed up the process, attach your letter to the return you are filing late. Don't wait until you get a penalty notice—that could take months.

Not-So-Safe Amendments

Filing an amended return to take a deduction for the following may result in an audit because of the high susceptibility of these items to audit:

•Travel and entertainment expenses.

•Unreimbursed business expenses.

•Casualty losses.

•Transactions with relatives.

•Charitable donations of property.

•Home office deductions.

Audit Triggers

Red flags most likely to bring on an audit:

•Deductions that are excessively high in relation to your income. A return that shows $50,000 of income and $40,000 of itemized deductions is almost certain to be pulled for an audit. Keep your deductions reasonable. But don't cheat yourself just because you're afraid of an audit. Attach an explanation to your return for an item that you believe the IRS may question. When your return gets kicked out of the computer that screens all returns for possible audit, an IRS official will read your explanation. If he's satisfied, he will probably put the return back into the processing system without sending it on to be audited.

• Undocumented charitable gifts. Attach a statement to your return showing the date of all property contributions, the fair market value, and the name of the charity. If you don't automatically supply this statement, the IRS will pull your return to look for it—increasing your chance of audit. You must now attach an independent appraisal for charitable gifts of property worth more than $5,000.

• Overstated casualty losses. Many audits are triggered because taxpayers exceeded the legal limits on casualty-loss deductions. Use the IRS worksheet, Form 4684. You can deduct only the part of your loss that exceeds 10% of your adjusted gross income. And then you deduct only the lesser of what you paid for the item or the decrease in its value as a result of the casualty.

• Overstated medical deductions. To be deductible, medical expenses must exceed 7½% of your adjusted gross income.

• Tax shelters with very large losses. These almost always trigger an audit. Avoid tax shelters unless you get professional advice. Make sure it's a legitimate shelter.

• Inclusion of Schedule C. Self-employed individuals must file a Schedule C with their tax returns. It shows all business-related income and deductions. *Warning:* It is also a red flag for an audit. Prepare it carefully, and have the records to back it up.

• Home-office deductions. These must meet stringent IRS guidelines. The office must be used regularly and exclusively for business purposes. If your family watches television there when it's not in use as an office, you lose the deduction. The office must be your principal place of business. If you have an office at the company where you are employed, you can't deduct the home office. But if you freelance in a different business at night, the office is deductible.

• Overstated business expenses. The IRS will scrutinize these deductions. Keep your travel and entertainment deductions reasonable. (And be very careful to stay within the tax law's limits for deducting your business car and computer.)

• Sloppy returns. Simple errors cause many tax returns to be kicked out of the IRS computers This means the chances for audit are greater because the return is now in human hands. *Don't make these mistakes on your return:*

• Errors in simple mathematics.

• Failure to transfer totals correctly from one page to the next.

• Use of the wrong rate tables for your filing status (single, joint, head of household, etc.).

• Failure to follow IRS instructions.

• Failure to answer all questions. A blank space where there should be an answer will wake up the computer.

• Failure to attach W-2s or other required statements.

Source: Michael L. Borsuk, tax partner and managing partner of the Long Island office of Coopers & Lybrand, Melville, NY.

Most Frequently Overlooked Job-Related Deductions

• Moving expenses incurred to get a new job, including the cost of selling your residence and getting out of your lease.

• Job-hunting expenses, including the cost of typing or printing a résumé, employment agency fees, etc.

• Professional magazines related to your job.

• Work- or business-related educational expenses that don't qualify you for a new trade or business.

• Transportation necessary for medical care. You can deduct your actual expenses or a standard mileage rate of 9¢ per mile, plus parking fees and tolls in either case.

•Traveling expenses to a second job, if you go directly from the first job to the second.

•Business gifts up to $25.

How to Avoid the 2% Floor for Miscellaneous Deductions

Miscellaneous itemized deductions include expenses directly connected with the production of investment income, such as...

1. Fees for managing investment property.
2. Legal and professional fees.
3. Fees for tax preparation and advice, investment advice and financial planning.

Problem: Most taxpayers are unable to deduct any investment expenses on Schedule A because their total miscellaneous expenses don't exceed 2% of their adjusted gross income.

Solution: Put as many expenses as possible out of reach of the 2% floor by accounting for them elsewhere on your return. *Possibilities:*

•Schedule C. Report non-wage miscellaneous income such as that earned from consulting, lecturing, or speaking engagements, on Schedule C as business income, rather than as "other income" on the 1040. The expenses you incur in producing that income are deductible on Schedule C, where they are not subject to the 2% floor.

•Schedule E. Expenses of earning rent, royalties, or other income that is reportable on Schedule E are deductible on Schedule E, where they are not subject to the 2% floor.

•Adjust the cost of assets. Add the expenses of acquiring a capital asset to the asset's cost. This will reduce the amount of capital gain you must report when you eventually sell. While this approach doesn't give you a current deduction for the expense, it does reduce the tax you pay on the gain.

•Bunch payment of expenses so that you get two years' worth into one year and exceed the 2% floor in at least one year.

Source: Richard Lager, national director of tax practice, Grant Thornton, CPAs 1850 M St. NW, Washington, DC 20036.

Most Frequently Overlooked Real Estate Deductions

•Points, also called loan origination fees, paid for obtaining a mortgage on your principal residence. They must be a customary practice in your area.

•Mortgage prepayment penalties.

•Real estate taxes. If you sold your home during the year, don't forget the portion you paid while you still owned the house.

•Your proportion of co-op or condo real estate taxes.

If You Can't Pay Your Taxes

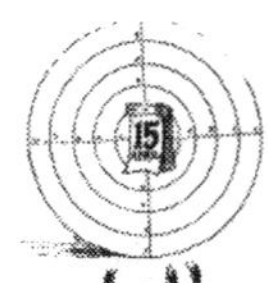

Most creditors must have a court order before they can seize your property. All that's required of the IRS is that it present you with a bill for unpaid tax and wait 10 days. After that, if you still haven't paid, it can seize your bank accounts, garnish your wages, and even sell your house. Fortunately, the IRS seizes property only as a last resort in the collection process. Before invoking its enforcement powers, the IRS generally gives financially strapped taxpayers a chance to try to work out a payment agreement.

Here's how to proceed when there's no cash to pay the bill:

•File a tax return. The worst thing you can do when you owe the IRS money is not file a tax return. Owing money to the IRS that you simply can't pay is not a crime. The IRS can't put you in jail for not having the money. But it is a crime not to file a tax return—a crime for which you can go to jail. By filing, you also avoid the big penalties for late filing. If you don't get your return in on time (or don't have a valid extension), you'll incur a late-filing penalty of 5% a month (or any fraction of a month), up to a maximum of 25% of the tax you owe.

• Pay what you can when you file your return. Keep to a minimum your penalties for late payment and interest on the tax you owe. *Trap:* If you file for an extension, you must send the IRS 90% of the tax you expect to owe or they'll charge you late-payment penalties. And if you lie on the extension form and say you expect to owe no tax, you can be charged with perjury.

• Six to eight weeks after you've filed, you'll get a bill for the unpaid balance. The bill will include interest and penalties. Don't ignore it. If you're still short of money, arrange a meeting at your local IRS office to work out an installment-payment arrangement.

• Be prepared to submit a financial statement showing that you don't have assets that can be liquidated to pay your tax. Don't expect the IRS to give you extra time to pay if you have certificates of deposit in the bank that you simply don't want to cash in early.

• Go easy on the hard-luck stories when asking for an installment arrangement. The IRS has heard them all. Concentrate on negotiating, in a businesslike manner, a series of monthly payments that you'll be able to manage.

• When you give the IRS an analysis of your monthly income and expenses, show that there's money left over for tax payments. If you come up broke each month, the IRS will be less inclined to agree to installment payments. Where will you find the money to make the payments?

• The IRS likes to see a tax bill paid up in a year or less. If you can figure out a way to pay the debt in less than a year, you have a better shot at getting an installment agreement than if you say you need five years to pay.

• File all your delinquent tax returns before you negotiate an installment agreement. Establish all your tax liabilities, and have them all covered by the agreement. *Trap:* If you agree to a payment plan for one year and then get a bill for other years' back taxes, you'll be in default on the agreement. The IRS will then demand payment in full.

• Never miss a payment without first talking to a revenue officer. You're technically in default of the agreement when you miss just one payment. And when you're in default, you have to start over again, trying to negotiate a new agreement.

• If you can't make a payment: Meet with a revenue officer. Explain the unusual circumstances that make it impossible for you to pay and hope that the officer will alter the terms of your agreement.

Source: Randy Bruce Blaustein, Esq., partner, Blaustein & Greenberg, New York, and author of *How to Do Business With the IRS*, Prentice-Hall, Inc., Englewood Cliffs, NJ.

Negotiation Tactics

• Provide only the information requested. *For an office audit:* Take with you only the documentation relating to the requested items.

• If the agent requests support for other items, suggest, diplomatically, that since this would require yet another meeting, perhaps such information could be mailed in.

• Involve a supervisor only if necessary. If you've reached an impasse—because of an honest disagreement or a personality conflict—enlist the agent's help by asking, "Would you discuss this with your supervisor?" Communicate through—not around—the agent.

• Avoid a change of agents, if possible. You'll avoid the double audit that results from starting afresh.

• Know your appeal rights, and let the agent know that you do. Use this knowledge to achieve agreements. Agents like to close cases "agreed."

• Sign an agreement form only if you truly agree with all the proposed adjustments. Never allow yourself to cave in to pressure. If unsure, ask for time to consider and to consult your tax adviser.

Dealing Personally With the IRS

Taxpayers sometimes choose to deal personally with the IRS on routine matters. Here are some pointers to help you deal productively with the Service:

• Be prepared. It's to your advantage to organize and summarize all requested information. Have an adding machine tape to show how you calculated each questioned deduction. This will expedite the review and let the reviewer know you're in control.

• Be honest. Don't try to disguise a problem area, such as lack of certain types of documentation. Never risk arousing IRS suspicion. *Best:* Explain the problem in terms of what proof you have. If that's not sufficient, then ask if you can gather additional proof to satisfy the IRS.

• Be businesslike. Use good-sense rules of courtesy and tact in all your dealings with the IRS.

• Be prudent. Limit your involvement to nontechnical, routine matters. Don't get in over your head. Do only what, and as much as, you feel comfortable doing. *Alarm bells:* Uncertainty, anxiety, frustration and anger are the signs that professional help is needed.

• Office audits held at a local IRS office—are typically used to determine if income and deductions claimed are properly supported by documentation. They are usually limited to several items, and are not likely to involve technical or legal issues.

• Field audits—held at the taxpayer's business and/or residence are generally used to scrutinize a variety of IRS concerns—in many cases related to business returns—often involving technical or legal issues. Discuss how best to handle such an audit with your tax adviser. In most cases, it's wise to have your adviser represent you at the audit.

Source: Roy B. Harrill, tax partner in charge of firm-wide practice for IRS procedures and administration, Arthur Andersen & Co., Chicago.

Keeping it Simple

When you mail your tax return to the IRS each year, do not include any other tax filings that you may owe the IRS that are not directly related to your return. In one recent case, a taxpayer included an important nonreturn filing with his return to save postage—and the IRS said it never got it. A court eventually ruled for the taxpayer, after describing an IRS computer log of filed documents as an incomprehensible maze of figures without any legend. But it is much safer to keep things simple for the IRS by sending evey filing in a separate envelope, requesting a certified mail delivery receipt for each filing you send.

Filing Safety

When you mail your tax return to the IRS this April 15 be sure you correctly fill out the certified mail receipt you will keep as proof of filing. When a taxpayer miscopied two digits of an envelope number onto a receipt and the numbers didn't match, the court rejected the receipt as proof of filing.

More Time to Claim a Refund

When a tax is paid through several partial payments, the full amount of the tax is deemed paid when the very last payment is made, according to a recent court decision. This is especially important if you later decide you are entitled to a refund of the tax. Why: You can claim a refund of the full tax within a statute-of-limitations period computed from the date of the last payment—even if the limitations period has expired as to earlier installment payments.

Levy Lifted When Notice Mismailed

An individual argued that an IRS levy was invalid because the notice of levy had been sent to the wrong address. The IRS said that the notice had been properly sent to the address shown on the individual's tax return, but he objected that he had since moved. Court: The address on the tax return is the proper mailing address when it is the IRS's last known address for a taxpayer, even if the taxpayer has moved. But here the taxpayer had told the IRS of his move, and the IRS had sent letters on other matters to his new address. Thus, the notice hadn't been sent to the last known address, and was invalid.

Extension Save

Paul E. Harper requested a filing extension for his tax return. On it he estimated that he owed no further taxes for the year, and he made no payment when he filed it. When it turned out that he still owed more than $90,000 in taxes for the year, the IRS retroactively revoked the extension and imposed late filing penalties. Court: Mr. Harper had relied upon an accountant to prepare the extension, and the accountant had underestimated the tax still due because full business records for the year weren't yet available—which was why the extension had been requested. The extension had been filed in good faith, so it was valid.

Invalid Alterations

The IRS asked Joseph Monti for extra time to examine his return, so he proposed terms for an extension. The IRS changed the terms in its favor, then sent an extension to Mr. Monti with a cover letter saying it had been prepared as per your request. Mr. Monti signed the form and returned. The IRS then found a typographical error in the expiration date of the extension and corrected it, giving itself even more time for the audit. Court: The IRS's behavior in altering the extension without informing Mr. Monti was inexplicable. The extension was invalid and the audit deadline had passed, so Mr. Monti was free from the potential tax.

18

Staying Healthy

About Your Immune System

The immune system can be compromised by many things—from an ordinary cold to deadly cancers. That's the bad news.

The good news is that your immune defenses regularly repair themselves, and there are simple measures you can take to assist them when they have been breached.

Basically, your immune system is a thriving swarm of billions of white blood cells, all with just two goals...

- Recognize germ invaders.
- Respond to the threat.

When bacteria enter your body—for instance, through that razor nick you got yesterday—specialized cells called neutrophils rush to the scene to virtually devour the marauders. Other cells soon come by to clean up any bacterial fragments.

Against viruses—which are more insidious than bacterial infections because they sneak into our cells and commandeer them for their own evil purposes—your immune system dispatches antibodies to tackle the attacking aliens.

More important, your immune system has memory cells that look at the viral perpetrators and remember those particular villains for the rest of your life. When antibodies recognize and defeat a virus, your system has established an immunity.

Vaccines and medications may be thought of, in a sense, as backups that assist a person when the immune system is overloaded.

There are a lot of microscopic threats out there. But, don't worry. We have plenty of memory cells—enough to recall every virus, bacteria, or toxin that is in existence.

Why it fails...

Without an immune system, even the mildest infection would be lethal. Under normal circumstances, our immune system serves us admirably. When it does malfunction, it is usually for one good reason or another...

•Stress. Chronic, unrelieved stress is probably the most severe threat to your immune system. Along with depression, grief, and anxiety, stress can trigger chemical changes, stimulating the release of neuropeptides, which adversely affect the operation of your immune system.

•Exertion extremes. Moderate exercise is necessary for basic health, of course, and that includes maintaining a healthy immune system. But, too much exertion—for instance, marathon running, mountain climbing in arctic conditions, or other such strenuous activities—has been shown to temporarily depress immune system functions.

•Malnutrition. The relationship between nutrition and the immune system is still a puzzle. We do know, though, that those with poor diets are more susceptible to illness and infections, increasing the burden on their immune systems.

•Rapid and excessive weight loss, through quirky diets or periods of starvation, also drastically reduces your immune system's effectiveness.

It is natural to want to keep your immune system operating at its peak efficiency. Remember, though, that it has gotten you this far without much attention. As with a smoothly running computer, tinkering with your immune system can do more harm than good.

Routine maintenance...

•Keep stress at a reasonable level. Stress reduction is critical for your immune system to function well. If you're not addressing this common problem, make it a health-care priority.

•Vaccinations. These are key to preventing "sneak attacks" on your immune system. Follow the vaccination schedule your child's pediatrician recommends. You may be due for a tetanus booster yourself. When traveling internationally, seek medical advice on specific vaccinations you may need.

•Follow a balanced diet. Sustaining a fit immune system is another good reason for healthy eating. But, avoid the temptation to "boost" immunity defenses through fad diets or the currently popular vitamin or mineral therapy. Such self-treatment can have serious consequences. Large doses of iron, for example, can cause dangerous digestive tract problems. And, while vitamin A is crucial to combat infections, massive supplemental doses can actually suppress vital immune functions.

•Follow your physician's advice exactly when you are ill. Take *all* medication prescribed, especially antibiotics, which we tend to discontinue using immediately after symptoms disappear.

Give your immune system time to fight your illness and recover afterward. Finally, realize that we often have unrealistic expectations for our health. A few colds a year is not a sign that something is wrong with your lifestyle. Being sick occasionally is just a part of being alive. Thanks to your immune system, so is getting well.

•Stay happy. Just as depression and anxiety can adversely affect all aspects of your health, a happy and optimistic outlook will contribute to a healthier immune system. Recent studies show that this may not be entirely psychological, but may have a neurological basis as well.

Source: David S. McKinsey, MD, codirector of epidemiology and infectious diseases at the Research Medical Center, 2316 E. Meyer, Kansas City, Missouri 64132.

Diseases Humans Get from Pets

The same household pets that raise our spirits can also transmit diseases—some serious and potentially deadly—to us. *The most common of these diseases are...*

•Cat-scratch fever. This usually mild infection—caused by a bacterium found on the claws of cats—produces swelling and inflammation in the area around the scratch. It usually goes away without treatment.

To avoid trouble: Clean cat scratches carefully. Your doctor will probably prescribe a course of antibiotics to clear up persistent symptoms.

•Lyme disease. This tick-borne bacterial infection can be carried by dogs, cats, horses, etc. and passed to their owners. It is easily cured with antibiotics—*if it's detected early.*

Late detection can result in severe—and permanent—neurological problems and arthritis.

To avoid trouble: Keep pet dogs and cats as tick-free as possible. Check your body for ticks after each venture into tick-infested areas. See a doctor immediately if you develop fever and a bull's-eye rash around a bite.

• Plague. Although this potentially deadly infection is rare, an Arizona man recently died of pneumonic plague. He caught it by breathing the same air of an infected cat that he pulled from a crawlspace.

There are actually three kinds of plague, depending on which part of the body is infected...*pneumonic plague* affects the lungs, *bubonic* the lymph nodes and *septicemic* the bloodstream. Bubonic plague and septicemic plague are usually spread by the bites of fleas from cats and rodents, but pneumonic plague is often spread through the air.

To avoid trouble: See a doctor at once if you develop a high and persistent fever in conjunction with badly swollen lymph glands—or with difficulties in breathing.

• Psittacosis. Caused by a bacterium found in the droppings of parrots, parakeets, pigeons and turkeys, this illness produces coughing, shortness of breath, fever, and other pneumonia-like symptoms.

To avoid trouble: Bird owners who develop these symptoms should see a doctor. Persistent symptoms can usually be cleared up with a course of antibiotics.

• Rabies. The disease remains a real threat. Rabies is frequently transmitted to humans when pets, bitten by infected wild animals, bite their owners.

To avoid trouble: Make sure your pet is fully immunized, especially if rabid wild animals have been spotted in your area. Alert your local health department of any domestic or wild animal that behaves oddly, attacks without provocation, or foams at the mouth.

Helpful: If a person is bitten by an animal not known to have been immunized against rabies, the animal must be captured and tested for rabies. Otherwise, the bite victim must undergo the standard four-shot series of immunizations.

• Rocky Mountain Spotted Fever. Like Lyme disease, this ailment is tick-borne and is easily cured with antibiotics. But Rocky Mountain Spotted Fever is sometimes fatal.

To avoid trouble: Again, keep dogs and cats tick-free, and check yourself after venturing into the outdoors. See a doctor immediately if you develop a fever and body rash in conjunction with headaches and muscle pain.

• Toxoplasmosis. Spread by microscopic parasites found in cat feces, this relatively uncommon disease produces, in most cases, a mild flu-like illness that clears up without treatment.

Exception: Toxoplasmosis that develops during pregnancy. It can cause *spontaneous* miscarriage or serious health problems in the newborn, including jaundice, seizures, high fevers—even birth defects and mental retardation.

For a safe pregnancy: Wash your hands carefully after handling cat litter. If swollen glands or a fever develops, see your doctor and have your blood tested for toxoplasmosis.

Source: Evan Bell, MD, an infectious disease specialist in private practice in New York City, where he is affiliated with Lenox Hill Hospital.

Genetic Predisposition to Heart Disease or Cancer

If there is a history of heart disease or cancer in your family, there's a straightforward way to cut your risk by up to 90%, no matter how strong your genetic predisposition to these killers.

Like many American families, my family was hard hit by heart disease.

My father was just 12 years old when his father died of a heart attack...and I was only 22 when the same fate befell my dad. By the time I reached my mid-30s, I too seemed headed for an early death. I was overweight, I had Type II diabetes and my cholesterol level was elevated. According to the statistics of the Framingham heart study, my risk of a heart attack was 175% of normal. ("Normal" in our society is a 75% chance of having a heart attack in one's lifetime.)

I decided to try to cut my disease risk by adopting the 30%-fat diet recommended by the American Heart Association. *Problem:* The diet had little effect on my excess weight, diabetes and cholesterol levels.

Reversing the inevitable...

At this point, I immersed myself in scientific literature and developed an alternative approach to this problem. I cut my fat intake all the way down to 10% of calories and adopted a program of regular exercise and stress control. In a few months I lost 45 pounds, my diabetes vanished and my cholesterol level fell so low that my risk of heart attack wasn't just normal, it was below that of someone with no family history of heart disease. My risk of heart disease fell 97%.

Bonus: I felt more relaxed and energetic than I had in years.

Here are the most common questions people ask me...

What exactly is involved with your "10% solution"? Several things. First, regular aerobic exercise. I recommend working out at least four times a week, for at least 45 minutes each time. Next, stress control. Learn to strike a balance between self, friends, family, and work. Stop smoking. Get plenty of sleep. *Note:* I don't mean to gloss over these nondietary recommendations because they're all-important. But the issue of fat intake is more critical—and more often misunderstood.

What's it like to eat a 10%-fat diet? Most people think it must be terribly Spartan. In fact, while you will have to eliminate certain foods from your diet, you can continue to enjoy many of the foods you currently eat. The key is learning the subtle art of food substitution.

Illustration: A meal of broiled chicken, peas in a cream sauce, baked potato with sour cream and a dish of ice cream contains a whopping 55 grams of fat. But a similar meal of baked skinless chicken, steamed peas, baked potato with nonfat sour cream, and a dish of nonfat frozen yogurt contains only nine grams. Once you get used to low-fat eating, this meal is just as satisfying—and much more healthful.

But I love fatty foods. I don't think I have the willpower to eat as you recommend. What can I do? Oddly enough, while it's quite hard to eat a little less fat, it's actually quite easy to eat a lot less.

Reason: If you cut back only to, say, 20% or 30% fat, your appetite for rich, fatty foods never goes away. Consequently, every meal becomes a test of your willpower. But after five to six weeks on a 10%-fat diet, your taste buds actually begin to change. Fatty foods you once enjoyed will begin to taste too greasy while foods that once seemed impossibly bland will become tastier. *Bonus:* Because you'll be eating so little fat, you'll easily lose excess weight—while never feeling hungry or deprived.

Are any foods prohibited? I divide foods into three categories—those to eat as often as you like, those to eat occasionally and those to avoid.

Emphasize...

- Breads made without oils, butter or margarine and any other whole grains or grain products.
- Pasta made without oil or eggs.
- Cereals free of fat, salt, or sugar.
- Fruits, fruit juices, and vegetables (except avocados and olives, which are too fatty).
- Peas, beans, lentils, and other legumes.
- Nonfat dairy products.
- Tofu and other soy products.
- Egg whites.
- Lean meats, preferably fish or fowl. Up to 4 ounces daily of fish, clams, oysters or mussels or white meat of chicken or turkey (without skin). If you want red meat, choose round steak, flank steak, or other lean cuts.

Eat occasionally...

- Sugar, sucrose, molasses, and other sweeteners.
- Breads and cereals made with added fat.
- Pastas made with eggs.
- Low-sodium soy sauce.
- Low-fat dairy products (one-percent fat).
- Olive or canola oil...use very sparingly.
- Caffeinated drinks...no more than two cups daily.
- Lobster, crab, and shrimp. They contain too much cholesterol to be eaten regularly.
- Smoked or charbroiled foods. They contain a potent carcinogen.

Never eat...

- Fatty meats, including organs, cold cuts, and most cuts of beef and pork. Poultry skin is pure fat.
- Meat fat, butter, hydrogenated vegetable oils, lard, and margarine.

• Nondairy creamers and other sources of tropical oils like palm or coconut.

• Mayonnaise.

• Polyunsaturated fat, including corn oil and most vegetable oils.

• Whole dairy products, including cream, whole milk, and sour cream.

• Nuts (except chestnuts, which may be eaten regularly).

• Salt or salty foods.

• Egg yolks.

• Fried foods.

How can I tell how much fat I'm getting? At first you'll need to keep a food diary. Jot down the calorie and fat content of each food you eat. At the end of each day, calculate the all-important fat percentage.

Procedure: Multiply your total daily intake of fat (in grams) by nine (the number of calories in each fat gram), then divide this number by your total daily calories. If this number is above 10%, you must find ways to cut out more fat. After several weeks, you'll be able to judge your fat intake without using the diary.

How about polyunsaturated fats? Margarine, corn oil, and other sources of polyunsaturated fat have long been touted as safe alternatives to saturated fats. In fact, they are far less healthful than once thought—and may be more harmful than saturated fats.

Recent finding: Polyunsaturated fat not only raises levels of LDL (bad) cholesterol, but also reduces levels of HDL (good) cholesterol. And now it looks as if polyunsaturated fat promotes the growth of cancer cells.

Cancer rates in the US began to rise just about the time polyunsaturated fats began to replace saturated fats in the American diet. *To be safe:* Limit your intake of all fats—saturated and polyunsaturated fats in particular.

Are there any immediate benefits to eating less fat? Absolutely. Each time you eat a fatty meal, your red blood cells become "sticky." They clump together, moving slowly through the circulatory system and clogging up capillaries. This deprives your brain of oxygen, resulting in grogginess. But when you stop eating such meals, your red cells return to normal, and your capillaries open up. *Result:* You feel calmer and more energetic, you sleep better and your complexion improves. And at the same time a subtler but even more important change is taking place within your body. The fatty plaques inside your arteries shrink and your immune system grows stronger.

Doesn't a vegetable-rich diet raise your intake of pesticide residues? No. The pesticide content of fruits and vegetables is well below that of meat—which comes from animals raised on pesticide-sprayed crops. But to minimize your intake of potential toxins, buy organic produce.

Source: Raymond Kurzweil, chairman of Kurzweil Applied Intelligence, a Waltham, Massachusetts–based computer manufacturer. He is the author of *The 10% Solution for a Healthy Life: How to Eliminate Virtually All Risk of Heart Disease and Cancer,* Crown Publishers, 201 E. 50 St., New York 10022.

What a Good Dermatologist Does

Dermatologic emergencies are rarer than other types of medical emergencies, but as anyone who's ever suffered a sudden rash or allergic reaction knows, they're not unheard of.

For this reason, a good dermatologist is accessible 24-hours-a-day, seven days a week—preferably via a professional answering service (answering machines are sometimes unreliable). *Rule:* After-hours calls should be returned within four hours.

Of course, accessibility isn't the only mark of a good dermatologist. *Other considerations:*

• Proper delegation of work. As a cost-cutting measure, some dermatologists are now leaving much of their routine office work to nurses or assistants. *Problem:* Assistants may lack the training to perform these procedures safely and effectively.

I believe nurses can safely take patient histories, check blood pressure, change dressings and perform the most basic procedures, such as opening pimples and administering ultraviolet treatments.

The bulk of work, however, including chemical peels and collagen injections, should be performed by the dermatologist. You're paying for a dermatologist's expertise...don't let yourself be exploited.

•Institutional affiliation. Besides being certified by the American Board of Dermatology, first-rate dermatologists are affiliated with a medical school or major hospital—or both. Such institutional affiliations confirm that the dermatologist is a skilled practitioner, up-to-date on the latest methods of diagnosis and treatment. It also indicates that he/she is in good standing within the medical community.

Bonus: If necessary, patients of a hospital-affiliated dermatologist can often get admitted to the hospital faster and with fewer headaches than patients of an unaffiliated practitioner.

•Medical philosophy. By the time certain forms of skin cancer are detected, it is often too late—they've spread and become fatal. Therefore, it's absolutely essential that dermatologists stress preventive care.

However, simply urging patients to wear sunscreen or avoid the sun is not enough. A top-notch dermatologist listens to patients' questions, then explains all aspects of prevention—how the sun damages the skin, for example, and how best to use protective clothing and sunscreen.

As an extra precaution, your dermatologist should offer a total surface examination of your skin. Such an exam, performed periodically, catches melanoma and other dangerous lesions in their earliest stages—when treatment is still effective.

Cost: $115 to $125 (often included in the price of a routine office visit). *Note:* Surface exams should be performed annually on adults with especially fair skin, every three years or so on those with darker skin. Your dermatologist should suggest what's most appropriate for you.

•Cost-consciousness. Like most doctors, dermatologists receive free drug samples from pharmaceutical salespeople. A thoughtful practitioner passes these samples along to patients, saving patients the needless expense and aggravation of filling their own prescriptions.

Source: Neal B. Schultz, MD, a dermatologist in private practice in New York City. Dr. Schultz is on staff at Mt. Sinai Hospital and Lenox Hill Hospital in New York City.

New and Healthier Way Of Looking at Life

Heart disease, cancer, AIDS, and other life-threatening illnesses bring pain and suffering, to be sure. But they can also serve as a "wake-up" call, bringing a new and healthier way of looking at life...of distinguishing that which truly matters in life from mere distractions.

Of course, it's best to learn these invaluable lessons before you're diagnosed with a life-threatening illness...

•Don't be afraid to show your vulnerabilities. Almost all of us were raised to be strong in the face of adversity, to put on a "brave front" no matter what. *Problem:* Acting one way when we're feeling another way saps our vitality, leaving us vulnerable to depression and illness and resentful of the world. We wind up with few friends and little support to help us through life's inevitable crises.

Better way: Admit your frailties. If you feel you need help, ask for it—and be willing to help others.

Exercise: Next time someone asks how you're doing, admit your true feelings. If you feel fine, say so. But if you feel lousy, admit it. Being honest might be hard at first, but it paves the way to honest, caring communication. That's essential for good health and happiness.

•Relinquish your need to be in control. As a young doctor, I thought the key to life was to get things done. My daily routine involved jotting down and then ticking off entries on "to-do" lists. When I failed to get everything done, I got nervous and frustrated.

As I grew older and got in closer touch with my feelings, I came to realize that life is inherently disorderly. Now I know that living well means forgetting about rigid schedules. It means learning to find happiness, fulfillment, and tranquility in the face of disorder.

Lesson: Stop trying to control all situations. Don't be a slave to your intellect. Make plans, but don't be upset by redirection. Something good may come of this redirection.

•Learn how to say "no." Our parents and teachers taught us that it's rude to say "no" to others. So when people ask for favors or tell us how to behave, we give in to their wishes.

Danger: Saying "yes" when you'd rather say "no" may be good manners, but it's destructive to our health. Doing so keeps us in unfulfilling jobs and makes us bitter. It leads us to do things we detest, and it distracts us from the things we cherish. We wind up resentful and possibly ill.

Better way: Stand up for yourself. If you don't want to mow the lawn, pursue a particular career, etc.—don't do it. I'm not asking you to be selfish or needlessly rude. I'm merely asking you to have enough self-esteem to stand up for yourself, to pursue life on your own terms, to realize that you can say "no" when someone asks you to change your plans.

• Confront your fears. People in crisis often seek peace of mind by burying or denying their fears. But real peace of mind comes only when we confront our fears head-on.

What to do: First, define exactly what it is you're afraid of. Don't say, "I'm afraid of dying." Be specific.

• Are you afraid of pain?

• Or what a medical treatment might do to you?

• Or that no one will take care of you?

Once you've pinned down your exact fear, find a metaphor for it. I tell patients to imagine their fear as a tiny baby crying in a crib. I tell them to pick up the baby, caress him/her and see what happens. This exercise shows people that they're distinct from their fears and suggests that they, and not their fears, are in control. Learning to control fear is very reassuring.

• Live in the moment. If you spend all your time ruing the past or fearing the future, you'll have a hard time deriving any pleasure from the present. To fight this tendency, remind yourself that death could come at any moment. Don't let that thought frighten you. Just try to assimilate it into your psyche. Once you do, you'll be freer to enjoy a blue sky or a poem or the presence of a loved one. *Ultimate goal:* To approach life with a childlike sense of awe and wonder.

• Identify your true feelings. Ask a child what he wants to do, and you'll get 40 answers.

Ask an adult, and the response will likely be, "I don't know. What do you want to do?" Adults have a hard time knowing what to do—for an afternoon or a lifetime—because they're so out of touch with their feelings that they've lost track of what really matters to them.

People without emotions live almost like automatons. Helen Keller used to ask, "If you had three days to see, what would you choose to see in those days? Your answer to this question will teach you about what you truly love in your life."

• Define pain and suffering in positive terms. When I ask my lecture audiences if they think life is fair, they usually answer with a resounding, "No!" But I believe that life is fair. All of us experience difficulties, problems, pain, and losses. But while some people give in to self-pity, others retain their vitality and optimism—even in the face of terminal illness.

Lesson: We should not only avoid suffering, we should respond to it in a constructive manner.

Strategy: Redefine whatever pain you're feeling as labor pains. Just as the anticipation and joy of bringing a new baby into the world can help to ease a mother's suffering during childbirth, other types of pain will seem less awful if you view them as integral to the process of birth you're undergoing.

Examples: The pain of chemotherapy leads to the birth of a person who is cancer-free... the pain of divorce leads to the birth of a happy single person.

• Refuse to be a victim. To some extent, we're all prisoners. Some of us are prisoners in the literal sense. Others, suffering from some debilitating ailment, are prisoners of our own bodies. Still others are imprisoned by emotional scars from a difficult childhood or a violent crime. No matter what form your prison takes, you don't have to feel or behave like a victim.

Example: Franklin Roosevelt could have pitied himself after polio left him wheelchair-bound. Instead, he became president of the United States.

Bottom line: No matter what befalls you, retain the ability to choose what sort of life to lead.

Source: Bernard S. Siegel, MD, a noted lecturer on healing and the founder of Exceptional Cancer Patients (ECaP), a nonprofit support group for people with cancer, AIDS, or other life-threatening illnesses. A retired surgeon formerly on the staff of Yale University School of Medicine, Dr. Siegel is the author of three books, including *How to Live Between Office Visits: A Guide to Life, Love, and Health*, HarperCollins, 10 E. 53 St., New York 10022.

Cholesterol Testing

Cholesterol testing can usually wait until men reach age 35 and women age 45. Adults found to have elevated cholesterol at younger ages will obtain almost all the benefits of cholesterol-lowering therapy by waiting until middle age to start treatment.

Earlier treatment could actually do harm if dietary control did not succeed and patients started lifelong regimens of medications that could have side effects.

Source: Research led by Stephen Hulley, MD, MPH, epidemiologist, University of California at San Francisco.

20 Simple Ways To Stay Healthy

Despite media scares about health dangers —in our environment and in our food—most of the major factors that determine our chances for a long and healthy life are within our control. *Twenty keys to good health:*

1. Don't smoke. Cigarette smoking is the leading cause of premature disease and death in this country, causing nearly 500,000 deaths each year in the US.

2. Don't smoke. Ninety percent of cases of lung cancer—the number-one cause of cancer deaths in America—are caused by cigarette smoking.

3. Don't smoke. Cigarette smoking is the leading cause of *preventable* cases of cancer of the esophagus, pancreas, throat, bladder and cervix.

4. Don't smoke. Smoking is one of the top-three modifiable causes of heart disease. The other two are high blood pressure and elevated blood cholesterol.

5. Don't smoke. Cigarettes are the leading cause of emphysema and other chronic lung diseases.

6. Never drink and drive. Driving under the influence of alcohol is the top cause of traffic accidents. An estimated 25,000 Americans die each year from vehicular accidents related to alcohol. Don't drive under the influence...and don't ride in a car driven by someone who has been drinking.

7. If you drink, use alcohol responsibly. A large portion of *non-vehicular* accidents are also related to alcohol consumption. Drinking interferes with your ability to swim, ski, use power tools, drive a boat or perform other activities.

Long term excessive use of alcohol can cause serious health problems, including cirrhosis and other liver diseases, disorders of the heart and nervous system and throat cancer.

Complete abstinence from drinking isn't necessary for good health. The key is moderation.

8. Wear your seat belt every time you drive. The National Highway Safety Administration says conscientious use of seat belts could reduce traffic deaths by 50% and injuries by 65%. Other experts estimate even higher.

Air bags are no substitute for seat belt use. Seat belts protect you in all collisions...but air bags only work in frontal collisions—only 20% of all crashes.

9. Put a working battery in your smoke detector. Fires are the second most common cause of accidental death in the home, claiming more than 5,000 lives every year. If everyone used smoke detectors, the death toll would be reduced by 40% or more.

Following manufacturer's instructions, test your smoke detector regularly to make sure that it's working. Replace worn-out batteries promptly. And remember to put the batteries back in after you remove them for any reason—such as after setting off a false alarm while cooking.

10. Beware of the effects of too much sunlight. Overexposure to sunlight is the leading

cause of deadly melanoma as well as superficial skin cancer...not to mention premature wrinkling of the skin. If you're going to be in the sun, wear sunscreen with an SPF of at least 15 and reapply it every few hours. Try to stay out of the sun between 11:00 a.m. and 3:00 p.m., when it's strongest. And never, ever let yourself get sunburned.

11. Wear a helmet when you ride a bike—and make sure your child wears one too. Strapping a child into a carrier seat won't protect his/her head.

12. Practice safe sex. Safe sexual practices help you protect yourself against a variety of sexually transmitted diseases. *Best protection:* Abstain from sex outside a mutually faithful relationship with a partner whom you know is not infected.

13. Don't use cocaine. Cocaine use interferes with your ability to work and function, and can have deadly effects on the cardiovascular system. *Hidden danger:* You can't know the quality of what you're buying on the street, even from a trusted supplier. You risk your life with even one use.

14. Avoid obesity. Being more than 20% over your ideal weight increases the risk or severity of many medical problems...heart disease, high blood pressure, diabetes, arthritis, gallbladder disease, respiratory ailments, pregnancy problems, complications after surgery, etc.

15. Eat a variety of foods in moderation. Although obesity can be harmful, unwise dieting can also be dangerous. Some of the currently popular formula-based diets are safe, but others provide too few calories for good health. Many so-called diet aids—starch blokers, spirulina, glucomannan, body wraps, etc.—have never been shown to be of any benefit.

Losing weight and keeping it off requires you learn to live *with* food...not without it. Eat plenty of grains, fruits and vegetables, and cut way down on fats. Don't expect overnight results. And whether or not you're overweight, meet your nutritional needs by keeping in mind the guidelines: *Variety, moderation and balance.*

16. Exercise daily. Exercise reduces the risk of coronary disease, lessens tension...and helps control weight.

Important: If you have health problems, are at risk for heart disease, or aren't used to exercising regularly, consult a physician before beginning an exercise program. Avoid injury by starting slowly and increasing your activity level *gradually.*

17. Get your blood pressure and cholesterol checked regularly. High blood pressure and high cholesterol levels greatly increase your risk of heart disease, the number-one killer in this country. Have your blood pressure checked at least once a year, twice a year if you're over 40 and more often if you're at risk for heart disease. Have your blood cholesterol and lipoprotein levels (the so-called *good HDL* and *bad LDL)* checked at least once every five years. If your blood pressure, total cholesterol or cholesterol-to-HDL level is elevated, follow your doctor's advice about how to reduce it.

18. Have regular screening exams for cancer ...including a Pap test, breast examination, prostate exam and tests for colon cancer. Early detection frequently means the difference between beating cancer and dying from it.

19. Be skeptical of medical fads and scares. They often turn out to be groundless...and lead to *unhealthy,* or at the very least, irrational behavior.

Example: The panic over Alar. Two years ago, people were panicked by perfectly nutritious apples over an issue that turned out to have no basis in science.

Example II: The oat bran fad. Oat bran is wholesome, but it's no magic bullet. Expecting too much from it could cause you to eat an unbalanced diet—which would *not* be good for your health.

20. Pay attention to the real risks. Like everything else in life, good health involves setting priorities. We're surrounded by health information and can't humanly follow all the advice we read. There's much more to life than worrying about health. Learn to separate the real dangers from the hypothetical ones so you can avoid the major, proven risks...and still enjoy life.

Source: Elizabeth M. Whelan, ScD, MPH, president of the American Council on Science and Health, 1995 Broadway, New York 10023. Dr. Whelan is the author of 21 books on health-related subjects, including *Toxic Terror,* Jameson Books, 722 Columbus St., Ottawa, Illinois 61350.

Secret of Good Health: An Ongoing Relationship With Your Doctor

People who seek out a doctor only after a significant medical problem surfaces are missing a very important point about good medical care—that is, a congenial, ongoing relationship with your primary doctor affords several key benefits. *Most important...*

• Quick answers to medical questions. Such a relationship gives you someone to call in case of a medical emergency, or, important, too, if a simple problem or question arises. It's psychologically easier to call a doctor to discuss a problem if he/she already knows you. And a doctor familiar with your medical history gives sound medical advice—and gives it fast—with greater confidence than a doctor who comes to your case "cold."

• Individualized treatment. Any competent doctor knows the importance of taking a good medical history. But only a doctor familiar with your social and behavioral patterns as well as the specifics of your medical chart can individualize treatments for you. Individualized treatment means not only avoiding unpleasant or needlessly aggressive treatments, but also getting treatments that are more effective and convenient.

Example I: Because of the slight risk of barotrauma (pressure-related injury) to the ear, patients with ear congestion are usually told to avoid air travel. But a doctor familiar with a patient might be able to help a sufferer take the slight risk and take steps to enable him/her to fly, including possibly a short course of powerful anti-inflammatory steroids.

Example II: Some people with basically normal blood pressure are vulnerable to "white coat" hypertension. This condition, in which the anxiety of visiting the doctor causes a transient rise in blood pressure, is essentially harmless. A doctor who knows a particular patient is susceptible can easily make arrangements for testing to be done in a nonclinical setting. But a doctor unaware of this susceptibility might needlessly prescribe antihypertensive drugs.

• Reduced anxiety. One of the most important things that a doctor does for his/her patients is reassure them when medical problems strike. A doctor who has seen you through previous medical problems will be reassuring when new problems arise. Visiting a "new" doctor typically produces a great deal of anxiety—even in the absence of a serious medical problem.

• Fewer missed diagnoses. A doctor who has treated you for years is better able to spot subtle, yet often significant, changes in your appearance and health. What's appropriate for one patient might suggest a serious problem in another—even if these results fall within "normal" ranges.

Examples: A patient whose white blood cell count has for years hovered around 4,500 cells per deciliter suddenly turns up with a count of 9,000. Because 9,000 is within "normal" range, a doctor new to this patient might give a clean bill of health. But a doctor who knew the cell count was out of line with previous counts would suspect trouble—perhaps leukemia—and could order additional tests to find the problem. Conversely, a patient with a chronically enlarged pupil who suffers head trauma would quickly wind up getting a CAT scan or some other anxiety-provoking diagnostic test...unless the doctor knew the enlarged pupil was a preexisting and harmless condition.

• More effective counseling. A doctor who knows you is more effective at persuading you to make good decisions regarding your diet, use of alcohol, tobacco and other drugs, and ways to cope with anxiety. Also, such a doctor is more helpful in times of personal upheaval, such as the loss of a job or the dissolution of an important relationship.

• Earlier intervention. Many family physicians are now making available to their patients quick, convenient medical tests—blood-pressure tests, throat cultures, pap smears, mammography and screenings for colon and testicular cancer. Patients in close contact with a primary physician are more apt to have problems diagnosed—and treated—at the earliest possible moment.

Source: Bruce Yaffe, MD, an eminent internist and gastroenterologist in private practice in New York City.

The Language of Health

With medical costs rising astronomically and no relief in sight, it's increasingly important for Americans to reduce their dependence on outside experts—and take at least some control of their own health care.

One of the best tools for doing so is also one of the most basic—language.

The language of health...

There are many ways that language can be used to affect our health—both for good and bad. *Included:*

• Messages that we give ourselves. Whether we're aware of it or not, most of us talk to ourselves continuously.

Pessimistic, helpless messages *(I feel terrible, and there's not a thing I can do about it)* tell the body to give up.

Positive messages *(I can stand this discomfort, and I will feel good again)* help the body to fight illness.

• How we respond to others. Chronic exposure to hostility is a risk factor in many diseases—and the primary factor in heart disease.

We can't always avoid hostility and conflict, but we can learn to use language to deflect a verbal attack and spare ourselves mental and physical strain.

• Metaphors we use. Visualization can be an effective healing tool in dealing with illness.

Example: Patients are advised to imagine the disease as an army of enemy invaders, and the immune system as a good army destroying the invading forces.

But warlike images are only helpful to people comfortable with military themes. For others, violent imagery may work *against* healing by equating illness with violence and slaughter.

As an alternative, focus on *fixing* rather than killing.

Examples: Think of your immune system as a gardening crew pulling up weeds...or a road crew fixing potholes in the street...or a piano tuner restoring harmony to an out-of-tune instrument.

• Doctor/patient relationships. When doctors and patients don't communicate well with each other, patients wind up with poor health care.

A pain-phobic society...

What we tell ourselves about pain has a profound impact on our well-being. TV commercials bombard us with the notion that pain is terrible—that no one should ever hurt even a little. But pain is a normal part of life.

That doesn't mean that discomfort should be ignored. If running makes your shins hurt, *rest* ...don't push on for another mile.

Pain alerts us to our limitations, and chronic discomfort *may* be an indicator of a physical condition that requires medical attention.

People who panic every time they're in pain end up spending a lot of money needlessly on doctors and drugs, without appreciable benefits. In fact, their fears—and the drugs' side effects—may make them feel even worse.

Coping with pain...

If you're plagued with chronic or acute pain, instead of telling yourself, *I can't bear this,* substitute the thought, *I can stand this pain for 15 minutes.*

Then spend that 15 minutes doing something you enjoy—gardening, playing music, absorbing yourself in a challenging project at work. At the end of 15 minutes, you're likely to find that the pain is gone.

If not, say, *I can stand this pain for another 15 minutes.* You'll notice that the pain ebbs and flows. This attitude enables you to go on with your life, instead of focusing your life around the pain.

Another way to cope with pain is to keep a journal. Describe what the pain feels like and what sets it off. Give it a name. Compare it with something else that has a similar distinguishing feature.

Example: My pain is like an earthquake—sudden and unpredictable.

As you start to define your pain and give it boundaries, you will see it less as an overwhelming force that's controlling you, and more as an object...which you can control.

Deflecting attack...

We can relieve ourselves of a great deal of stress by learning not to get hooked into other people's hostility.

Verbal attacks aren't always easy to recognize. Someone can be smiling, or using words like *sweetheart* and *darling,* and still be sending a hostile message. *Key:* Verbal hostility has a characteristic melody in which many words are emphatically stressed.

Examples: "*Why* do you *always* think *only of yourself?*" Or, "I'm *only* thinking about what's *best for you.*"

There are several ways to deflect verbal hostility...

• Remember that nobody can fight alone. If you refuse to fight, even the most hostile verbal attacker will give up.

• When in doubt about how to handle an attack, try the boring baroque defense. Treat the attack as if it were a serious, rational question or statement, and talk the other person into a coma.

The idea is to answer in such excruciating detail that the attacker has no fun at all. *Example:*

Attacker: "*Why* can't you ever stick to your *diet?*"

Boring baroque defense: "You know, that's an interesting question. I think it has to do with when I was a kid in Wisconsin, and our family...no, maybe it was when we were living in Illinois. Yes, it must be Illinois, because that's when my uncle was working for the Post Office, and...."

This technique won't work if you let sarcasm creep into your voice. You must keep your tone serious.

How to talk to doctors...

It's easy to become resentful when dealing with doctors, especially if the doctor is brusque, uses jargon or acts condescending. Unfortunately, in our society, inequality is built into the doctor-patient relationship.

Acting resentful, however, will not help you achieve your health goals. The doctor is as trapped in the system as you are, and communicates in doctor-speak because he/she has been taught to.

Your doctor is a channel through which you get access to medicine, surgery and other treatments that affect your health. Annoying your doctor makes about as much sense as annoying your computer or arguing with a traffic light.

To get what you need, learn to interact with your doctor effectively...

• Before your appointment, make a list of things you want the doctor to know and any questions you need answered. Don't leave the meeting until those subjects have been covered to your satisfaction—even if you have to repeat your questions several times.

• Remember that a meeting with a doctor is not a social conversation. Don't worry about being entertaining or bouncing the conversational ball back and forth.

• Keep each question or statement to 18 seconds at most. Research shows that's the longest period of time doctors allow patients to talk before interrupting them.

• Don't try to talk like a doctor. If you've been feeling short of breath, say so—don't say you have *dyspnea*. Using medical jargon may be taken as a challenge—the doctor may try to top you by using even more technical language, and you won't get your questions answered.

Your goal isn't to impress the doctor, it's to get the information and care that you need.

Source: Linguist Suzette Haden Elgin, PhD, who teaches communications skills to health-care professionals nationwide. She is the author of a series of books on verbal self-defense, most recently *Staying Well with the Gentle Art of Verbal Self-Defense,* Prentice Hall Business and Professional Publishing, Route 9W, Englewood Cliffs, New Jersey 07632.

Women Should Go to the Bathroom More Often

There is no rule on how frequently a person should go to the bathroom. *What is important:* Following the calls of nature and going when you have to.

Unfortunately, many women *don't* listen when it comes to moving their bowels. *Trap:* Women—much more so than men—are uncomfortable in unfamiliar places, and suppress their body's signals.

If suppressed too often, the colon becomes less sensitive to stimulation and grows too full, making it difficult to expel. This is worsened by hard stools, caused by not drinking enough water, not eating enough fiber, being inactive ...and by one's natural cycle (women tend to be constipated premenstrually).

Common, unfounded fears: Too much water will make me gain weight...too much fiber will make me feel bloated.

Danger: Chronic constipation increases the risk of diverticulosis—small herniations in the colon that can cause bleeding from the rectum and may require surgery. This condition can lead to diverticulitis—inflammation of these herniations that can obstruct the colon or lead to serious abdominal infection. *Added danger:* Chronic laxative abuse impairs colon function. Avoid stimulant laxatives, including natural herb-types.

Bottom line: Eat a high-fiber diet, drink plenty of water, exercise and go when you have to. See your doctor if you notice an abrupt change in bowel habits to rule out other medical causes.

Source: Bruce Yaffe, MD, an internist who specializes in gastroenterology. Dr. Yaffe is in private practice at 121 E. 84 St., New York 10028.

Keep Your Own Medical Records

Keep your own medical records. *Reasons:* Few of us see only one doctor, so it is unlikely that anyone has your complete medical history ...most people change doctors several times—it may be difficult to obtain copies of your past doctors' records...doctors' records may be incomplete—they may have only scant detail on health problems, may not include drug reactions and probably don't include over-the-counter (OTC) treatments, vitamins or prescription refills. *Helpful:* Set up a notebook with sections for family medical history...personal medical history...doctor visits (including dental and eye care)...outpatient procedures...hospital records ...laboratory test results...prescription and OTC medication...immunizations.

Source: Charles B. Inlander, president of The People's Medical Society, 462 Walnut St., Allentown, Pennsylvania 18102. 800-624-8773. The organization publishes *Your Complete Medical Record,* a system for maintaining an individual's health history.

Dental Floss Update

There's a great new dental floss from the *Gore-tex* people. *Glide* floss is thinner than most flosses currently on the market...and much, much stronger than any of them. It really does glide over teeth—and doesn't shred, like other flosses. At $3.50 for a 15-meter package, it's about three times more expensive than others. But for people with "tight teeth," this floss is best.

Source: Alan Winter, DDS, periodontist in private practice, 30 E. 60 St., Suite 302, New York 10022.

Stroke Stoppers

Cut the risk of stroke by 30% or more by lowering blood pressure and stopping smoking. *Important:* Exercising regularly, even if only modestly, and treating any irregular heartbeat cuts risk.

Source: Roundup of medical experts, reported in *Men's Health,* 33 E. Minor St., Emmaus, Pennsylvania 18098.

Myopia Warning

Close-up visual activity—like playing video games or reading—can bring on *myopia.* Extensive reading and game-playing seem to make nearsightedness likelier. *Reason:* Unknown. *Likely:* Nearsightedness has a strong genetic component that may be triggered or worsened by close-up activity.

Source: Hilda Capó, MD, assistant professor of clinical ophthalmology, Bascom Palmer Eye Institute, University of Miami School of Medicine.

Aspirin Miracle

A remarkable, inexpensive key to better health is probably right in your medicine cabinet. It's called acetylsalicylic acid—better known as aspirin.

Research suggests that one aspirin tablet, taken every other day, helps reduce risk of heart attack, certain kinds of stroke, cancer of the gastrointestinal tract and possibly Alzheimer's disease, among other serious ailments. All this for $1.83 per year—less than a penny a day.

Caution: Aspirin is not a substitute for healthy habits like eating a balanced diet, exercising regularly or not smoking, nor should it be taken regularly without your doctor's approval.

About aspirin...

Aspirin's active ingredient, *salicin,* occurs naturally in the willow tree. Willow leaves and bark have been used to relieve pain and inflammation at least since the time of Hippocrates.

Aspirin was first made commercially in Germany at the turn of the century. If it had first been synthesized today instead of a century ago, odds are it would be available only by prescription. *Reason:* Aspirin is far more complex and powerful than many people realize.

Inexpensive generic aspirin is just as effective as more costly brands. In fact, there's less difference than you might imagine. Although there are many brand names of aspirin for sale in the US, all the salicin found in these aspirin formulations is made by just six companies.

How aspirin works...

No one knows exactly how aspirin works. It seems to interfere with the production of *prostaglandins,* hormones made by the body in response to injury. Aspirin seems to reduce the pain and swelling caused by prostaglandins.

Prostaglandins are also involved in blood-clotting. By blocking prostaglandin synthesis, aspirin acts as an anticoagulant. That probably accounts for its effectiveness against heart attack and stroke.

Aspirin also seems to prevent atherosclerosis, the buildup of fatty deposits in the arteries. However, it cannot *reverse* atherosclerosis.

Aspirin and heart attack...

In the 1950s, doctors first observed that patients who took aspirin for pain while recovering from a heart attack were less likely to have a second attack.

Supporting data on aspirin's preventive value come from the Physicians' Health Study, a five-year study of more than 22,000 male doctors between the ages of 40 and 84.

Half of the subjects took a standard five-grain aspirin tablet every other day. *Result:* Subjects older than 50 who took aspirin were 44% less likely to suffer a heart attack than were similar men given a placebo (sugar pill).

If the group who took aspirin had also been eating well and getting moderate exercise, even fewer might have had heart attacks.

Researchers looked only at men. However, a subsequent study of female nurses suggests that aspirin also helps prevent heart attacks in women.

Another study found that coronary care unit patients given aspirin immediately after a heart attack were about 25% more likely to survive the attack than patients who did not receive aspirin.

Evidence also suggests that an aspirin a day lowers the risk of a second attack.

And stroke...

Most strokes occur as a result of atherosclerosis. When arteries are narrowed, even a tiny blood clot can block blood flow to the brain, thereby depriving the tissue of oxygen.

Aspirin apparently fights stroke by preventing atherosclerosis and thinning the blood, which helps prevent blood clots.

One warning sign of impending stroke—sometimes the only warning—is a *transient ischemic attack* (TIA). This temporary deficiency of blood in the brain is caused by a blockage of blood flow or by a piece of arterial plaque or a blood clot that lodges in a blood vessel inside the brain. *Symptoms:* Weakness, numbness, dizziness, blurred vision, difficulty in speaking.

A study by Dr. James C. Grottar (published in the January 28, 1988, issue of the *New England Journal of Medicine*) showed that taking aspirin after a TIA cuts the risk of stroke by 25% to 30%. Although aspirin is often prescribed for TIA, it is not usually appropriate for anyone with high blood pressure or an increased risk of hemorrhage.

And colon cancer...

Cancers of the colon and rectum account for roughly one out of five cancer deaths in the US.

In 1991, the *Journal of the National Cancer Institute* reported that people who took aspirin or other nonsteroidal anti-inflammatory drugs at least four days a week for three months *halved* their risk of colorectal cancer. The results held for men and women across a broad range of ages.

A recent Emory University study suggested that taking one aspirin a week significantly reduces the risk of these cancers. Another study found a 50% reduction in the colon cancer death rate among daily aspirin takers.

But another study of older subjects (average age 73) showed that frequent aspirin users face a *heightened* risk of kidney and colon cancer, as well as of heart attack. More research is needed. But—at least for younger patients, the preliminary findings are promising.

And Alzheimer's disease...

A University of British Columbia scientist recently observed during autopsies of arthritis patients—who tend to take a great deal of aspirin—that their brains showed fewer than expected signs of Alzheimer's disease.

This observation certainly doesn't prove that aspirin prevents Alzheimer's. However, it does suggest an important avenue for future research.

And more...

Though aspirin isn't very helpful in relieving migraine pain, it may help prevent migraines. Preliminary research suggests that migraine sufferers who take aspirin regularly may be able to reduce their headaches by as much as 20%.

Aspirin seems to stimulate the production of *interferon* and *interleukin-2*—immunity-boosting proteins produced inside the body. This may explain why aspirin may prevent certain kinds of cancer...and suggests that it could be used in the fight against other immune disorders.

Finally, some evidence suggests that aspirin helps prevent cataracts, diabetes and gallstones. As with other possible uses of aspirin, these potential uses of aspirin require further study.

Aspirin precautions...

• *If you're thinking about starting an aspirin regimen, check with your doctor first.* This is especially important if you're taking anticoagulants...if you have diabetes, gout or arthritis...or if you are taking any other over-the-counter or prescription drug.

Caution: Aspirin should generally be avoided by anyone with asthma...ulcers or other chronic stomach problems...or an allergy to aspirin.

• *If you're pregnant or nursing an infant, take aspirin only with a doctor's consent. Danger:* Aspirin taken during the last three months of pregnancy can injure the fetus or cause birth complications.

• *If regular aspirin irritates your stomach, ask your doctor about buffered or coated aspirin.* Also, tell your doctor if you experience ringing in the ears or hearing loss while taking aspirin.

• Drink with caution when taking aspirin. Aspirin boosts the concentration of alcohol in the blood. If you want to drive safely after a party, for instance, you may need to drink even less or wait longer than you normally would.

• *Children should not be given aspirin without a doctor's approval. Reason:* Aspirin has been linked to Reye's syndrome, a rare but potentially fatal brain disorder.

Source: Robert S. Persky, coauthor of *Penny Wonder Drug: What the Label on Your Aspirin Bottle Doesn't Tell You,* The Consultant Press, Ltd., 163 Amsterdam Ave., #201, New York 10023.

Coffee Hazards

Although a cup or two of coffee a day is safe for most people, there are exceptions...

• People who have a genetic susceptibility to the effects of caffeine. *Example:* Some people experience heart palpitations after drinking only a single cup.

• People with high blood pressure or heart disease. Coffee exacerbates symptoms in these people.

• Women who are pregnant or trying to conceive. As little as one cup of coffee a day reduces a woman's ability to conceive by 50%, according to one recent study. Some studies suggest that women who drink coffee during pregnancy are more likely to have miscarriages and low-birth-weight babies, but this finding remains a topic of debate among researchers.

Trap: In men, coffee apparently boosts the mobility of sperm cells...although recent evidence suggests that it increases the incidence of abnormal sperm—which may lead to miscarriage.

Heavy consumption...

Drinking more than two cups a day can cause even more serious problems...

• Ovarian cancer. One study showed that it's twice as common among women who drink two or more cups of coffee a day as among women who drink only one cup a day.

• Digestive disorders. Nausea, bloating, gas, heartburn and ulcers have all been linked to excessive coffee drinking. The caffeine, oils and acids in coffee irritate the stomach lining. *Surprising:* Most of the irritants are formed during the roasting of the beans, so switching to decaf won't help.

Most troublesome: Drinking coffee on an empty stomach. In some people, the increase in stomach acid causes an almost immediate stomachache.

• Headaches. Heavy coffee consumption causes alternating constriction and dilation of blood vessels. This then leads to so-called "rebound" headaches that can occur on a daily basis.

• Breast cysts. Women who drink four or more cups a day are twice as likely to suffer from fibrocystic breasts as other women, one recent study found. Another study found that women whose daily consumption of tea is greater than four and one-half cups are 10 times more likely to suffer from premenstrual syndrome (PMS) than other women. (Tea has about half as much caffeine per cup as coffee.)

Helpful: Eliminating, or at least reducing, coffee intake a week or two before your period.

To cut back or quit...

Cutting coffee consumption all at once can lead to severe headaches and other symptoms of withdrawal. Try cutting back gradually...

• Switch to decaffeinated coffee for every other cup you drink. Gradually increase your consumption of decaf until your caffeine consumption is negligible. *Warning:* Conventional decaf is processed using the solvent methylene chloride—a known carcinogen. To protect yourself, choose water-processed (Swiss-process) decaf, which is made with a natural compound. Or choose another hot beverage, such as herbal tea or a grain-based coffee substitute.

• Cut back by one cup every three or four days—until you're drinking only the amount you want.

Life with less coffee...

Learn to live and enjoy life with less coffee. Exercise—a short run, yoga or stretching—can provide that burst of energy you used to get from coffee. And if you've been using coffee to relax, consider a massage, a hot bath or a stroll through your favorite park. They can be just as relaxing and more fun.

Source: Bonnie Edwards, RN, BSN (Bachelor of Science and Nursing), University of California, San Francisco. She is the author of *America's Favorite Drug: Coffee and Your Health,* Odonian Press, Box 7776, Berkeley, California 94707.

Women Get Less Preventive Care

Women get less preventive care than they should—often because doctors do not give them enough information, or because preventive exams are not covered by insurance. *Troubling survey:* In the past year, 35% of women surveyed had not had a Pap smear...33% had not had a clinical breast exam...36% had not had a pelvic exam...39% had not had a complete physical...44% of those 50 and older had not had a mammogram.

Source: Survey of 2,525 women by the marketing and research firm Louis Harris & Associates, 630 Fifth Ave., New York 10011.

The Yeast Trap

New evidence suggests that many puzzling, chronic health problems resistant to treatment —from infections and allergies to the aches and exhaustion of chronic fatigue syndrome—are yeast-related.

One type of yeast is regularly found on the body's mucous membranes, especially the intestinal tract and vagina. When we talk about this kind of yeast, we usually mean Candida albicans, by far the predominant type found in the body.

In a healthy man or woman, candida (pronounced *can-did-a*) is kept under control by so-called "friendly" bacteria living in the intestinal tract. But several factors can upset the yeast-to-bacteria balance—especially long-term use of broad-spectrum antibiotics. When this happens, yeasts grow out of control—leading to unpleasant symptoms.

Based on my critical review of continuing research, I believe there are three possible mechanisms for yeast's troublesome effects...

- Just as some people are allergic to pollens or mildew, some may be allergic to candida.
- Candida may produce certain toxins that are harmless in small amounts, but that in larger quantities weaken the immune system... leaving the body vulnerable to disease.
- Yeast overgrowth in the intestinal tract (candidiasis) may lead to changes in the intestine. In turn, these changes can cause the body to absorb and react to allergens in food.

The connection between yeast and health problems is highly controversial. Beginning with Dr. C. Orian Truss's article in the late '70s, a number of reports have linked yeast to illness, but the mainstream medical community remains skeptical.

Yet, my experience in treating hundreds of chronically ill patients, as well as similar experiences of a number of colleagues, suggests that a diet designed to curb yeast growth—along with certain antifungal medications—helps alleviate many symptoms that have proven resistant to other forms of treatment.

Do you have a yeast problem?

There is no simple diagnostic test for a yeast-related problem. For this reason, patients must undergo a thorough physical exam to rule out other possible causes of their symptoms. *Next step:* A complete medical history.

You may have a yeast problem if you...

...have used antibiotics repeatedly over a long period of time, such as for control of acne or recurrent infections.

...have taken corticosteroids. One known side effect of nasal cortisone spray is candidiasis of the nose.

...have used birth control pills. Women on the Pill are far more prone than others to vaginal yeast infection.

...eat a high-sugar diet. A recent study at St. Jude Research Hospital in Memphis found that mice eating large quantities of the sugar glucose had 200 times as much candida in their intestinal tracts as did other mice.

...experience frequent digestive problems, such as abdominal pain, bloating, constipation or diarrhea.

...have a history of vaginal or urinary infections. Women develop yeast-related health problems far more often than men for a number of reasons. These include anatomical differences and hormonal changes associated with the menstrual cycle that promote yeast growth.

...have symptoms involving many parts of the body—for which usual examinations have not found a cause.

Treating a suspected yeast problem...

The cornerstone of treatment is a sugar-free diet. Yeasts in the digestive tract feed on sugar —and multiply. Some patients show remarkable improvement from dietary changes alone. Others need additional help—in the form of over-the-counter anti-yeast preparations sold in health food stores...and, for more serious cases, from prescription antifungal medications.

The yeast control diet...

- Eliminate sugar and other simple carbohydrates, such as honey and corn syrup.
- Avoid foods containing yeast or molds, such as cheese, vinegar, wine, beer and other fermented beverages, and pickled or smoked meats. Although breads are probably safe, try eliminating yeast-leavened breads for a few weeks.

Note: Yeast-containing foods should be avoided not because intestinal yeast feeds on food yeast—it doesn't. But most people with candida related problems are sensitive to yeast in foods and can have negative physical reactions. As the candida problem improves, the sensitivity may subside...and yeast can again be included in your diet.

•Strengthen your immune system by boosting your intake of vegetables, minimally processed whole grains and other wholesome foods. Eat lean rather than fatty meats, and cut back on other sources of fat. Avoid potentially harmful additives, including artificial colors and flavors.

Some physicians recommend eliminating fruits from the diet, because fruits are quickly converted to simple sugars inside the body. I believe fruits are safe—unless your yeast-related symptoms are severe. However, I do recommend avoiding commercially prepared fruit juices, which may be contaminated with mold.

Follow this recommended diet for at least three weeks. If your symptoms subside, resume eating forbidden foods one by one. If your symptoms flare up again after you add one of the forbidden foods, stop eating that food for good.

Good news: After they show significant improvement, most people find that they can follow a less rigid diet—and can occasionally consume a bit of sugar.

Over-the-counter remedies...

Many preparations sold in health-food stores can be a useful adjunct to the yeast-control diet...

•*Citrus seed extract,* an antimicrobial substance made from tropical plants. Because the extract can irritate mucous membranes, it should be generously diluted with water before drinking.

•*Caprylic acid,* a saturated fatty acid available in tablet form. It helps keep yeast from reproducing.

Note: Some patients develop digestive problems or notice a slight worsening of yeast-related symptoms during the first week on this medication. If these don't go away within a few days, stop the medication and check with your doctor.

•*Lactobacillus acidophilus,* a friendly bacterium that helps restore the normal balance of intestinal flora. It is present in yogurt, especially homemade varieties. Store-bought yogurt that contains active cultures will be labeled to that effect. Be sure to buy only unsweetened varieties. Acidophilus is also available as a nutritional supplement.

•*Garlic.* This herb is known to stimulate the immune system...and at an international medical conference several years ago, researchers reported that garlic also seems to fight candida. Persons wary of the taste of cooked garlic—or its effect on the breath—should consider aged garlic extract (Kyolic), a deodorized supplement. It is widely available in local health food stores.

Antifungal medications...

When a yeast-related symptom fails to respond to diet or supplements, prescription medication often helps—although the drug may take up to a year to have any effect in severe cases. *Drug options:*

•Nystatin (Mycostatin or Nilstat). In more than 30 years of use, this oral medication has demonstrated no toxic side effects. It knocks out candida in the intestines. It is not absorbed by the bloodstream, however, so it is ineffective against particularly severe cases of candidiasis.

•Fluconazole (Diflucan). This safe, highly effective anti-yeast medication has been available in the US for about three years. Unlike nystatin, fluconazole is absorbed into the bloodstream.

•Itraconazole (Sporanox). This medication, a chemical "cousin" of fluconazole, was approved for use in the US earlier this year. Although it appears to be quite safe, a related drug, ketoconazole (Nizoral) has been linked to liver damage.

For more information on yeast-related health problems, send a self-addressed, business-sized envelope with 64 cents postage to the International Health Foundation, Inc., Box 3494-HC, Jackson, Tennessee 38303.

Source: William G. Crook, MD, a fellow of the American College of Allergy and Immunology, the American Academy of Environmental Medicine and the American Academy of Pediatrics. He is the author of *The Yeast Connection* and *Chronic Fatigue Syndrome and the Yeast Connection*, both published by Professional Books, Inc., Box 3246, Jackson, Tennessee 38303.

Depression—How to Spot It, How to Beat It

Many Americans share a tragic misconception about depression—that people who are depressed could "snap out of it," if they wanted to. As a result, more than 30 million Americans troubled by emotional illness never get the help they need.

The result is devastating. Sufferers feel hopeless, inadequate and unable to cope with daily life. Their self-esteem is shattered—and so are their ties with family and friends. What's more, depression is often lethal. Up to 30% of people with serious mood disorders kill themselves.

Feeling "blue" from time to time is a normal part of life—we all experience the sadness of failed relationships, the loss of loved ones, etc. Periods of sadness that are mild and short-lived do not require medical help.

Understanding...

But if enjoyable activities, the passing of time and confiding in friends, family or even psychotherapists fail to alleviate emotional pain, you may be suffering from a biological form of depression. Such disorders, triggered by chemical changes in the brain, call for medical treatment. They cannot be cured by talking to a therapist or reading a self-help book.

While the causes of depression are not fully understood, new technology has provided insight. Scientists believe that depressed people have decreased amounts of certain mood-regulating chemicals called neurotransmitters.

In most cases, depressive illness caused by such chemical imbalances is inherited. *Evidence:* Children of depressed parents have a 20% to 25% risk of having a mood disorder. Children of nondepressed parents have a 5% risk.

Warning signs of depression...

If you have felt sad or down in the dumps in recent weeks, or if you've lost interest in many or all of your normal activities, you may be suffering from depression. *Warning signs:*

- Poor appetite or overeating
- Insomnia
- Sleeping more than usual
- Chronic low energy or fatigue
- Restlessness, feeling less active or talkative than usual, feeling "slowed down"
- Avoidance of other people
- Reduced interest in sex and other pleasurable activities
- Inability to derive pleasure from presents, praise, job promotions, etc.
- Feelings of inadequacy, low self-esteem or an increased level of self-criticism
- Reduced levels of accomplishment at work, school or home
- Feeling less able to cope with routine responsibilities
- Poor concentration, having trouble making decisions

If you're experiencing four or more of these, consult a doctor immediately.

Kinds of emotional illness...

The most common type of depression is unipolar illness, in which the person's mood is either normal or depressed. *Other common types:*

- Dysthymia. This condition is marked by a chronic mild state of depression. Sufferers of dysthymia experience little pleasure and are chronically fatigued and unresponsive. Sadly, many people suffering from dysthymia mistake their illness for a low-key personality...and never get the help they need.
- Manic depression. Patients whose periods of depression alternate with periods of euphoria are suffering from manic depression (bipolar disorder). During the "high" periods, manic-depressives may also have an inflated sense of self-esteem...a decreased need to sleep...a tendency to monopolize conversations...the feeling that their thoughts are racing...increased activity...impulsive behavior (including buying sprees, promiscuity, rash business decisions).

Though manic episodes sometimes occur when a person has never been depressed, they are frequently followed by severe depression. *Danger:* Manic-depressives often do not realize that they're ill, even though the problem may be obvious to family and friends. As with all forms of biological depression, manic depression calls for immediate treatment.

• Cyclothymia. A variant of manic depression, this disorder is characterized by less pronounced ups and downs. Like manic-depressives, cyclothymics are often unaware of their problem and must be encouraged to seek help.

Diagnosis and treatment...

First, have a complete physical exam to rule out any medical disorders. Certain ailments including thyroid disease and anemia can produce various symptoms that mimic depression.

If the exam suggests no underlying medical problem, ask for a referral to a psychopharmacologist—a psychiatrist who is trained in biological psychiatry. *Caution:* Nonphysician therapists, such as psychologists and social workers, lack medical training and cannot prescribe medication...and may be less adept at distinguishing between *biological* and *psychological* forms of depression.

When a biological form of depression is diagnosed, antidepressants should almost always be used as the first line of treatment. They completely relieve or lessen symptoms in more than 80% of people with severe emotional illness... and they are not addictive, nor do they make people "high." Once medications have brought the depression under control, however, psychotherapy often proves helpful—especially to patients embarrassed or demoralized by their illness.

Antidepressants...

Among the oldest and most effective antidepressants are the so-called tricyclics and monoamine oxidase inhibitors (MAOIs). These drugs are often very effective, but they must be used with caution.

Tricyclics have a wide range of side effects, including dry mouth, constipation, blurred vision and sexual difficulties. MAOIs must never be taken in combination with foods containing high levels of tyramine—such as aged cheese. Doing so causes a potentially dangerous rise in blood pressure. Other side effects include low blood pressure, sleep disturbances, weight gain and sexual difficulties.

Although these medications are still valuable in the treatment of depression, newer classes of drugs, including fluoxetine (Prozac), sertraline (Zoloft) and paroxetine (Paxil), are often superior. These new medications have few side effects, although some people who take the drugs complain of drowsiness or anxiety. *Note:* Despite one recent report claiming that Prozac caused some patients to attempt suicide, follow-up studies have not confirmed this finding.

For manic depression, the clear treatment of choice is lithium. Common minor side effects include diarrhea, a metallic taste in the mouth, increased frequency of urination, hand tremor and weight gain.

For seriously depressed or suicidal patients who do not respond to antidepressants, electroconvulsive therapy (ECT) is often a lifesaver. In this procedure, electrical current is applied to the brain via electrodes.

Sad: Many patients who stand to benefit from ECT refuse it altogether—because they consider it a brutal form of treatment. Today, however, patients receive a general anesthetic and a muscle relaxant prior to the application of current, so there's no emotional or physical trauma. Side effects—including slight confusion for several hours after treatment and occasionally memory loss—generally fade with time.

How to find the right help...

If your family doctor cannot recommend a good psychiatrist, contact the nearest medical school or teaching hospital. Many have a special treatment clinic for depression. Local branches of the American Psychiatric Association will provide names of psychiatrists in your area, but they cannot evaluate the psychiatrist's training in biological psychiatry.

The National Foundation for Depressive Illness (800-248-4344) gives referrals to psychiatrists interested in pharmacological treatment of mood disorders. Finally, additional information can be obtained from the National Depressive and Manic-Depressive Association (312-642-0049).

Source: Donald F. Klein, MD, professor of psychiatry at the Columbia University College of Physicians and Surgeons and director of research at the New York State Psychiatric Institute, both in New York City. Dr. Klein is coauthor of *Understanding Depression: A Complete Guide to its Diagnosis and Treatment,* Oxford University Press, 200 Madison Ave., New York 10016. 800-451-7556.

Uncommon Advice for Avoiding Common Colds

As a healer and scientist, I've developed my own highly effective system for defending myself against the common cold. *Result:* I don't get colds anymore. And my students rarely do.

To avoid getting colds, I've figured out what I usually do just *before* I get one. I then avoid those situations—or take action as soon as possible to keep a cold from developing.

Common causes...

• Overwork...and other sources of stress. When things get tough, make an effort to take *extra* good care of yourself. Go to bed earlier than you usually do...take time out for a nap after you eat lunch...meditate, which calms the mind, lowers stress level and recharges your energy.

Helpful exercise: Sit or lie down, and slowly inhale. As you inhale, imagine your body filling with the color red...relax...breathe out.

Do this three times. Then repeat, in turn, with orange, yellow, green, indigo and white. These are the colors of the *chakras*—the energy centers in the body's *auric field*.*

If you have trouble meditating, a good alternative is dancing to your favorite music...and it's wonderful exercise for your whole body.

• Poor diet. Eating a well-balanced diet is a simple—yet vital—way to keep the immune system strong. And take a daily multivitamin/mineral supplement. *Also:* Don't postpone meals—eat when it's time to eat.

If you slip, as we all do, and binge on high-fat, high-sugar foods, be sure to eat *very* well for the next few days. *Important:* Lightly cooked vegetables and salads, grains and low-fat proteins, especially fish.

• Exposure to somebody who has a cold. Go home and gargle with salt water. Take extra vitamin C. Wash your hands.

• Exposure to cold, damp weather. Many people fail to dress properly when the weather starts to turn chilly. *Be realistic.* Be more aware of the weather—dress appropriately. If you do get a chill, warm yourself immediately. *Helpful:* A hot bath.

More self-defense...

• Exercise. Regular physical exercise enhances the body's immune system tremendously.

• Don't work under fluorescent lights. They have a negative impact on the human energy field.

• Get sun for 10 to 20 minutes a day. The sun charges the auric field.

• Drink a gallon of clean water every day. It washes out waste material and toxins that are left in the system as a result of the healing process. Don't load up on fruit juice—it's full of sugar. If you want fruit, *eat* it.

• Avoid cold, dry air. This is especially damaging if you have a sore throat or laryngitis. Use a steam vaporizer at night.

• Eliminate negative thoughts. Negative thoughts create an imbalance in the auric field. If the imbalance lasts for a long enough period of time, you can become ill. To erase negative thoughts, figure out what's causing them...and take action to eliminate the problem. Don't just put the blame for your negative thoughts on others and attempt to live with the problem.

At the first sign of a cold...

• Stop eating all wheat and dairy foods. They generate mucus.

• Increase vitamin C intake. I take 2,000 mg of vitamin C every two hours, up to 10,000 mg a day, for two days. *Warning:* Too much vitamin C can cause pain in the joints...and diarrhea. Tolerance levels vary greatly by individual—fine-tune your intake to figure out exactly what yours is.

• Take deodorized garlic pills. It clears mucus out of the digestive tract amazingly fast...and, because it is deodorized, you won't taste or smell like garlic. Sold over-the-counter at drug and health food stores.

Source: Barbara Brennan, a faith healer, physicist and psychotherapist. The Barbara Brennan School of Healing trains people to become professional healers. She is author of *Hands of Light*, available from her school, Box 2005, East Hampton, New York 11937, 516-329-0951.

*The auric field is the field of bioenergy that runs through and around the body. The more powerfully charged, balanced and clear it is, the stronger your immune system is and the less susceptible you are to illness.

Staying Healthy

In recent years, most Americans have launched what amounts to a health revolution. *What we know now:* We have a great deal of control over our own health. There are steps we can take that will enhance the way we feel, both physically and emotionally.*

Studies have shown us that most medical problems are related to lifestyle. *As a result, we're:*

•Smoking less. There has been a significant drop in smoking among adults (although not among teens). *Reason:* Cigarettes have unequivocally been linked with lung cancer as well as heart disease (the country's number-one killer).

•Drinking less. There has been a dramatic decrease in the consumption of alcohol in recent years. We now know that alcohol, if it is consumed at all, should be drunk in moderation.

And even the *definition* of moderation has changed. Where it used to mean two drinks a day, we now recognize that the threshold may well be lower. Each person must determine on his/her own how drinking affects his health and appearance.

•Exercising more. More and more people have started a program of regular exercise. *Gained:* A decrease in the risk of heart disease and an increase in life expectancy.

•Eating well. Most Americans have made positive changes in their eating habits. We are limiting our intake of certain foods—especially fatty items—and *adding* certain foods—especially fruits and vegetables—to our diet to help prevent cancer and other diseases.

The next step...

Despite our new awareness, one very important health factor—*stress*—is still being overlooked by many people.

When we're alarmed or anxious, our heart speeds up and our cholesterol and sugar levels rise. *Possible results:* Heart attacks...backaches ...stomach problems...increased sensitivity to pain. Stress can also be a precursor to the abuse of alcohol and drugs...even food.

*This doesn't mean that it's your fault if you get sick. Taking things that far causes needless emotional damage. And it doesn't mean that people who become ill should ignore proven treatments and try to *will* themselves back to health. They can't.

Stress can be caused by everything from the loss of a job to traffic noise. Although you can't escape stress in today's world, you can learn how to handle it.

How to cope with stress...

Studies have shown conclusively that people who have socially involved lives have far fewer health problems and live longer than people who are isolated.

Note: This does *not* mean that single people are in trouble. It's not so much whether we live with others (although married couples usually report better health) as whether we interact with people regularly and feel like we belong.

The most helpful contacts are regular activities that occur at least once a week—church, club meetings, card games, discussion groups, etc. *Even better:* Volunteer work.

The Institute for the Advancement of Health recently conducted a study that found that people who volunteer regularly—at least once a week for two hours—are 10 times more likely to be in good health than people who don't. Benefits range from an increase in their overall sense of well-being to a decrease in stress-related problems.

The most important component in volunteering is getting involved with the people you're helping. Just writing a check is not enough.

Example: A woman with multiple sclerosis volunteered on a telephone hotline. Although she usually had problems just picking things up, she found that while she was counseling others she could drink a glass of water without much trouble. Volunteering obviously didn't cure her ...but it did help her feel and function better.

Although we don't know exactly why social contact is so beneficial, we suspect it may be due to a *buffering* effect. The support and concern of others helps to ease life's pressures. The old wisdom that sharing one's burdens helps to lighten them appears to hold true.

Volunteering links us to people in a very special way. It decreases our awareness of our problems. And, at the same time, it increases our sense of commitment, challenge, joy and self-esteem—positive emotions that help ward off stress.

Completing the cycle...

Up until now, the health revolution has been inwardly focused. But changing how we eat, drink, smoke and exercise is only part of the picture. It's time to focus outward as well. You can't stay well in a stressful world unless you're involved with people. And, although nothing can guarantee perfect health, helping others is a major step in the right direction.

Source: Allan Luks, executive director of Big Brothers/Sisters of New York, 223 E. 30 St., New York 10016. He is the former executive director of the Institute for the Advancement of Health.

To Protect Your Immune System

Your immune system is made up of white blood cells. To give optimal protection, these cells should be working 24-hours-a-day. They're directly affected by the quality of food you eat,* the way you behave, and the nature of your thoughts.

Dangers to the immune system:

- Excessive sugar.
- Inadequate protein.
- Inadequate zinc, iron, or manganese.
- Inadequate Vitamin C or Vitamin E.
- Diet and psychology are intimately related. Be especially cautious during times of stress, bereavement, sorrow, and trauma. They often translate into suppression of the immune function.
- Monitor magnesium intake. Most people don't get enough magnesium in their diets. And a magnesium deficiency can create anxiety symptoms. The minimum amount necessary is usually 300 to 500 milligrams a day. Under conditions of high stress, you would need more magnesium (since it's utilized very rapidly at such times). *Best sources:* Green leafy vegetables, lean meat, whole grains.
- Exercise enhances the function of your immune system by reducing stress.

*The amount of nutrients you need is best determined on an individual basis. To find out how much you need, consult a physician who specializes in disease prevention. Also useful: *Nutrition Against Disease* by Dr. Roger Williams, Bantam Books, New York.

- Examine your expectations about health. Do you expect, and accept, a couple of bouts with colds or flu each year? Instead, focus on strengthening your immune system. Sickness a couple of times a year is inevitable only if your immune system has been compromised.

Source: Jeffrey Bland, Linus Pauling Institute of Science and Medicine, Palo Alto, CA and author of *Nutraerobics,* Harper & Row, New York.

Dr. Dean Ornish Clears Up the Confusion Over Cholesterol

Despite all that's been said and written about cholesterol in recent years, many Americans remain understandably confused on the topic. While most of us know that too much cholesterol in the bloodstream can cause heart disease, many people remain unclear on certain subtle but very important issues...

What's a healthy cholesterol level? For years, the American Heart Association and the National Institutes of Health have recommended an optimal total serum cholesterol level of less than 200 milligrams per deciliter.

But we now know that roughly one-third of all heart attacks occur in individuals with cholesterol readings between 150 and 200. In fact, only when cholesterol falls to 150 or lower does heart disease cease to be a meaningful risk.

Unfortunate: The average American has a cholesterol level around 220... and the average American develops heart disease.

What about "good" and "bad" cholesterol? Total serum cholesterol is made up of two different compounds—low-density lipoprotein (LDL) cholesterol...and high-density lipoprotein (HDL) cholesterol.

- LDL (bad) cholesterol forms fatty plaques inside your coronary arteries, which can lead to heart attack.
- HDL (good) cholesterol is what the body uses to remove excess LDL from the bloodstream.

Doctors sometimes use the ratio of total cholesterol to HDL as another means of gauging heart disease risk.

Example: Someone with a total cholesterol count of 200 and an HDL level of 50 has a ratio of 200/50 or 4:1. In general, a ratio of 3.5 (200/57 is 3.5:1) or lower puts you at minimal risk for heart disease. The lower the ratio, the lower the risk—at least for people eating a traditional fatty, cholesterol rich diet.

Exception: Vegetarians and others on a very low-fat, low-cholesterol diet with less than 10% fat and virtually no cholesterol. Because they consume less fat and cholesterol and thus have less LDL in their blood, their bodies don't need to make as much HDL. Consequently, they may have high ratios yet they have a reduced risk of heart disease.

What causes high cholesterol? The single biggest factor is simply eating too much saturated fat and cholesterol. In fact, in the traditional American diet, roughly 40% of calories come from fat...and foods rich in fat are often rich in cholesterol. In countries where people eat much less cholesterol and less fat and where cholesterol averages around 130, heart disease is very rare.

Eating too much fat causes not only heart disease, but also has been linked with cancers of the breast, prostate, and colon, as well as stroke, diabetes, osteoporosis and, of course, obesity.

There is a genetic variability in how efficiently or inefficiently your body can metabolize, or get rid of, dietary saturated fat and cholesterol. On one end of the spectrum, some people are so efficient that they can eat almost anything and not get heart disease. On the other end of the spectrum are people who may get heart disease no matter what they eat. Ninety-five percent of people are somewhere in the middle. If your cholesterol level is less than 150, then either you're not eating very much fat and cholesterol or your body is very efficient at getting rid of it. Either way, your risk is low.

If it's above 150, begin by moderately reducing the amount of fat and cholesterol in your diet. If that's enough to bring it down below 150, that may be all you need to do, at least as far as your heart is concerned. If not, then continue to reduce the fat and cholesterol in your diet until your cholesterol stays below 150...or you are following a low-fat vegetarian reversal diet.

Which foods contain cholesterol? All foods derived from animals, including meats, poultry, fish, and dairy products. Meat is also high in iron, which oxidizes cholesterol into a form that more quickly clogs arteries. Skim milk has almost no fat and virtually no cholesterol. "Low-fat" milk is not really very low in fat. Foods derived solely from plants contain no cholesterol.

Caution: Some plant foods, including avocados, nuts, seeds and oils, are rich in saturated fat.

Just because a food is "cholesterol-free" doesn't mean it's good for your heart. All oils are 100% fat, and all oils contain at least some saturated fat, which your liver converts into cholesterol.

How often should I have my cholesterol checked? About once every two years, starting as early as age two. *To insure a reliable reading:* Find a testing lab certified by the Lipid Research Clinics. Use the same laboratory each time. Be sure to fast for at least 12 hours prior to your test.

How can I get my cholesterol under control? Exercise—it raises HDL cholesterol.

Stress raises LDL cholesterol, as does eating a high-fat, cholesterol-rich diet.

So the best way to raise HDL and lower LDL is to get regular exercise, avoid smoking, practice meditation or other stress management techniques and eat a healthful diet.

If you have heart disease: Eliminate all animal products except egg whites and nonfat dairy products...and all high-fat vegetable products, including oils, nuts, seeds, avocados, chocolate and other cocoa products, olives and coconut. In most cases this "reversal" diet not only keeps heart disease from progressing, but also reverses its course.

Eat more vegetables, fish, and skinless chicken. Use skim milk instead of whole milk. Use as little cooking oil as possible. Avoid oil-based salad dressing. If after eight weeks your cholesterol remains high, go on the "reversal" diet.

What about cholesterol-lowering drugs? I prescribe cholesterol-lowering drugs for people with heart disease who make only moderate changes in diet and lifestyle. Why? Several studies have shown that people with heart disease who only follow the American Heart Association guidelines tend to show worsening of their disease. People who follow the reversal diet—or who take cholesterol-lowering drugs—often can stop or reverse heart disease. Diet is preferable, because you avoid the high costs and side effects (both known and unknown) of drugs.

Source: Dean Ornish, MD, assistant clinical professor of medicine and an attending physician at the School of Medicine, University of California, San Francisco and at California Pacific Medical Center. He is the author of *Dr. Dean Ornish's Program for Reversing Heart Disease.* Ballantine Books, 201 E. 50 St., New York 10022.

Eight Rules for Staying Healthy

Some people work too hard at making themselves healthy. Actually, the human body is an intricate organism with feedback mechanisms to maintain itself in a healthy state. *Eight ways to help your body do its best:*

•Eat a well-balanced diet. For most people, diet should be high in fiber content.

•Maintain a comfortable weight. Being too thin is not healthier than maintaining your normal weight.

•Do not take vitamin supplements if your diet is proper.

•Learn to cope with stress. The best ways to achieve this are through relaxation exercises, biofeedback courses or, if necessary, psychotherapy.

•Exercise all muscle groups daily without excessive strain.

•Avoid sleep medications. If anxiety or depression causes poor sleep patterns, come to grips with the underlying problems.

•Establish good rapport with a physician you can trust.

•Listen closely to your body. Good health is a combination of using common sense and allowing the body to heal itself. By avoiding all the good things in life, you will not live longer. It will only seem longer.

Source: Dr. Bruce Yaffe, fellow in gastroenterology and liver diseases, Lenox Hill Hospital, New York.

Health Hints

•Before buying vitamins: Check Vitamin A and D dosages. Safe limits are 10,000 International Units for A, 400 for D. Signs of overdosage: Irritability, fever, bone pain (Vitamin A); lethargy, loss of appetite, kidney stones, or kidney failure (Vitamin D).

•Don't take Vitamin C and aspirin together. Studies at Southern Illinois University indicate that combined heavy doses produce excessive stomach irritation which could lead to ulcers (especially for those with a history of stomach problems).

•Eye care: Use eyedrops sparingly, especially commercial brands. They relieve redness by constricting blood vessels so eyes will look whiter. If used frequently, varicose veins can develop and eyes will become permanently reddened.

•The best cold medicine may be no medicine at all. No capsule or pill can cure a cold or the flu and may actually prolong the discomfort and hinder the body's own inherent ability to fight off the virus. *Best advice:* Rest and drink fluids.

Source: *Harvard Medical Health Letter,* Cambridge, MA.

Making a Plan For Wellness

Passing an annual physical exam was once enough to satisfy most people about their health. But today an increasing number strive beyond that— for optimal health or the condition of "wellness." *How to set up a wellness plan for yourself:*

•Try to clarify your most important reasons for living and write them down in a clear and concise fashion.

•With these in mind, identify the health goals that bolster your chances of living longer and healthier. *Be specific:* Do not plan to lose weight but to lose 20 pounds in six months. *Other possible goals:* Lowering blood pressure by a specific amount, accomplishing a dramatic feat, such as riding the Snake River rapids or completing a marathon.

• List supportive actions for each goal. *Example:* Joining a fitness club, training for long-distance running.

• Also identify the barriers to each goal and how they can be overcome.

• List the payoffs for each goal, whether they are new energy at the office or more fun at the beach.

• Before starting the program, list friends you can rely on for bicycle rides, tennis or other activities in the plan. Virtually no one can hope to stay on a wellness plan without support from friends.

• Once the plan is under way, set realistic quarterly benchmarks to track your achievements. A log or diary is usually helpful.

Source: *14 Days to a Wellness Lifestyle,* Donald B. Ardell, Whatever Publishing, Inc., Mill Valley, CA.

The Major Threats To Your Life

The biggest, most deadly risks today are smoking and drinking.

• Smoking's association with lung cancer is well-known, but perhaps more startling is the fact that the habit doubles your risk of death from coronary heart disease (which accounts for 40% of all deaths these days).

• The deleterious effects of alcohol are less well-known. Even though wine consumption lowers your risk of heart disease, the overall impact of drinking is that three drinks before dinner regularly doubles your risk of premature death. The major causes of alcohol-related deaths are auto accidents, cirrhosis, suicide, gastrointestinal diseases.

Source: John Irquhart, MD, a former professor of physiology and bioengineering and coauthor (with Klaus Heilman, MD) of *Risk Watch: The Odds of Life,* Facts on File Publications, New York.

Life's Real Risks

Although we live in an era of low risk, with people living longer and healthier lives than ever before, we nevertheless seem to feel more at risk than we used to. Not all of our fears are well founded.

Here are some common myths many of us believe—and the realities:

• *Myth:* People were healthier and life was safer in "the good old days." *Reality:* Your chance of premature death 50-75 years ago was much higher than it is today.

• *Myth:* Pollution is a serious risk that never existed in the past. *Reality:* Pollution has shown no statistical sign of being a serious risk. If pollution were a big risk, you might expect a rise in certain cancers in the general population, like cancer of the bladder, since many substances that go into the body come out in concentrated form in urine. This hasn't happened.

• *Myth:* Death or injury by criminal violence has increased greatly. *Reality:* Life in London in the 18th century, Tom Jones vintage, included cutthroats and cutpurses just like today. Although murder is on the rise in our cities today, much of it is confined either to people who know each other or to young males in the lower socio-economic brackets.

• Myth: We're having a cancer epidemic. *Reality:* The opposite is true. We're having an epidemic of one kind of cancer—lung cancer caused by cigarette smoking. If lung cancer is removed from the statistics, fewer people than ever are dying from cancer. The perception of an increase in cancer is due to the increased longevity of the population. Cancer is an age-related disease: The longer you live, the more likely you are to get it.

• *Myth:* The risk of dying in an auto accident is greater today than 50-75 years ago. *Reality:* In England, although there are 10 times as many cars on the road as 50 years ago, and 30% more people, the same number of people are killed in cars today as in the 1930s. US statistics are similar. This is because people drive better, roads are better, cars are safer and medical care is better.

• *Myth:* We shouldn't use nuclear energy to produce power because the risk of an accident is too great. *Reality:* More people die in mining accidents every year than in nuclear power plants. The actual problems of nuclear power are minimal compared with the environmental damage from fossil-fuel generation (including destruction of the land by strip mining, of the seashore by oil drilling and of the forests by acid rain).

Source: John Urquhart, MD, a former professor of physiology and bioengineering and coauthor (with Klaus Heilman, MD) of *Risk Watch: The Odds of Life,* Facts on File Publications, New York.

Building Your Stress Resistance

• Change your expectations. The difference between expectations and perception of reality is the measure of how much stress you will experience. *Example:* If you begin the day with an attitude of "the world is changing, finances are fluctuating, nothing stays the same," and you perceive that to be so, you'll experience very little stress. If, instead, you assume that tomorrow will be the same as today and that things will go as you planned, you'll experience a lot of stress if your expectations aren't met. Either the environment or your own performance will displease you. *Remedy:* Be more realistic about your expectations and pay attention to your perceptions of reality.

• You won't be able to deal with stress if you feel that your past performances have been inadequate. You'll just assume that you'll fail again. *Remedy:* Find out the average or expected performance for any given job and gear yourself to that. People under stress tend to feel extremely anxious and afraid. These feelings often come across to others as anger rather than fear. If people see you as hostile (even though it is not really so), it may adversely affect any evaluation of your performance.

• Seek a socially cohesive work situation. In England during World War II, there was less illness and higher performance among Londoners who weathered the bombings than before, or after, the war. Great social cohesiveness was provided by an external enemy. That same kind of cohesiveness occurs in any organization geared toward a strong goal.

• Do relaxation exercises. The purpose is to get the focus on a nonlogical part of the body. It's the constant logical planning and rumination that keep stress going. *Best:* Approaches that focus on breathing. Proper breathing triggers other parts of the body to relax. The body is born with the innate ability to counter stress. These exercises allow you to activate that mechanism, and eventually you'll be able to call upon it at will.

• Make time to do something relaxing. Take some time away from your desk to window-shop or do something "silly." Eat lunch out of the office. Plan something pleasurable each week, and then follow through. *Caution:* If you eat while under stress, you'll have a 50% higher cholesterol level after the meal than if you were relaxed.

• Physical exercise helps only if you do it right. For instance, if jogging is just another chore that you don't enjoy, but you squeeze it into a heavy schedule because you feel you should, it only puts an extra load on your heart. Exercise while under stress can be dangerous. But if you see the trees and smell the air and feel high and good after running, you're doing it right. Exercise that makes you feel good is as helpful as any relaxation technique.

Source: Dr. Kenneth Greenspan, psychiatrist and Director of the Center for Stress and Pain-related Disorders, Columbia Presbyterian Hospital, New York City.

Attitudes that Combat Stress

In today's fast-moving, success-oriented world, it seems as though one must be able to withstand a very high stress level in order to get ahead and stay ahead. Many ambitious people put themselves under a crushing stress burden for years, eventually paying the price in heart disease, ulcers and so on.

But there are busy, high-achieving people who are seemingly immune to stress.

You can be one of them:

• Seek out and enjoy change. See it as a challenge. This is extremely important. How we view a stressful event determines how our bodies and minds react. If an event is seen as a threat and we feel victimized, the actual physiology of the body changes to meet the threat. If we see change as a challenge, with potential for growth and excitement, the body's response is entirely different.

• Don't be overly self-critical. Perfectionists —a very stress-vulnerable group—are always condemning themselves for not having coped well enough in the past. When a new challenge comes along, they view it as just another threat to their self-esteem.

• Identify with your work. When your work seems an extension of your personality it ceases to be an alien threat. Work-related stress then becomes less dangerous because it's for something you've chosen.

• Have a sense of control over your life. If you participate in the planning of a project and handle your part in its execution you will have a sense of control and get a sense of completion when the job is complete. This is why top managers are under less stress than middle managers.

Source: Dr. Kenneth Greenspan, psychiatrist and Director of the Center for Stress and Pain-related Disorders, Columbia Presbyterian Hospital, New York City.

Executives' Ranking Sources of Stress

What bothers executives most:

• Failure of subordinates to accept or carry out responsibilities: 92% of those responding to a survey listed this as their most serious problem.

• Inability to get critical information: 78%.

• Firing someone: 48%.

• Incompetent coworkers: 47%.

• Owner or board of directors challenging recommendations: 33%.

• Subordinates who question decisions: 5%.

• Conducting performance reviews: 3%.

Source: The Atlanta Consulting Group, Atlanta, GA.

The Best Ways To Control Stress

• Work at something you enjoy (not always easy to do, but a goal to strive for).

• Express your feelings freely.

• Relax (another tough order for some people).

• Identify and prepare for events or situations likely to be stressful.

• Talk to relatives, close friends or others about personal matters. Don't be afraid to call on them for help.

• Participate in group activities (such as church and community organizations) or hobbies that you enjoy.

Source: National Health Information Clearinghouse, Washington, DC.

Thorough Check-Up For Men

A man's thorough physical includes these procedures:

• Blood pressure test (most important).

• Eye and eye pressure exam.

• Check of lymph nodes and thyroid for swelling.

• Stethoscopic exam of heart and lungs.

• Stress tests (particularly for vigorous exercisers).

• Examination of the aorta.

• Testicle examination.

• Reading of pulse in legs.

• Proctoscopic exam of rectum and lower large intestine.

• Prostate examination.

• Stool sample for blood.

• Superficial neurological exam (reflexes and muscle strength).

•Laboratory test: Blood sugar, cholesterol, uric acid, complete blood screening (every three years), triglyceride, kidney function and calcium.

Source: *M* magazine.

What to Ask Your Plastic Surgeon

No matter how many questions you have or how trivial you feel they are...ask!

•Realistically, what will be done? Not what can be done, or what you can hope for, but what you can expect.

•What will happen if you don't get the result the doctor promises? How will he remedy that situation? Will you have to pay for the unsatisfactory job? Will he do a corrective procedure at no cost? *Crucial:* Preoperative and postoperative pictures taken by the same photographer. Only with photos can you prove that you didn't get the promised result.

•What is the chance of real damage, and if it happens, what might the extent of it be? Plastic surgeons aren't gods. They are physicians who have had extensive training in delicate repair of skin—but nobody can break the integrity of normal skin without leaving a mark. If you have a big growth in the middle of your cheek, you can't expect the doctor to cut it out without leaving a mark. *Other areas of concern:* The chances of infection and other complications.

•Where will the surgery be done? Although many reputable plastic surgeons operate out of their own offices, surgery done in a hospital inevitably offers more quality control. There's much less room for nonprofessionalism in a hospital, where nurses and operating room teams are provided by the institution and there is peer review of a surgeon's work. *Generally safest bet:* A doctor who is university affiliated and teaches in a hospital or medical school.

•May I see your book of "before and after" pictures? You may want to speak to a surgeon's other patients, but since this might violate confidentiality, he may only be willing to show you before and after pictures. If he offers you a whole book of good results, you can feel confident.

•Can the surgery be done in stages? *Why that can be important:* A male model had facial moles treated with liquid nitrogen. His skin darkened, and there were brown spots and scars. The surgeon hadn't done a trial on one mole, but had treated them all at one session. *Suggestion:* If you have many of the same defects, have one corrected first to see if you like the result.

•Is there a less serious procedure that will produce a similar result? Collagen injections available today can sometimes eliminate both wrinkles and acne scars. Suction lipectomy can remove fat pockets. Look into such lesser procedures before undergoing full-scale surgery.

•How much will it cost?

•How much time will it take?

•How long will I be out of work or away from home?

What to Look for On Eye Checkups

You should have a professional eye examination by an ophthalmologist or optometrist every two years, even if there has been no noticeable change in your vision since your last visit.

The examination should include:

•Full medical history, including details on previous or existing eye disease or injury in yourself and your family (first visit).

•Measurement of visual acuity, with and without corrective lenses.

•Tests for color blindness and stereopsis (binocular vision).

•Examination of the eyes' ability to track a moving object (usually with a tiny flashlight).

•Examination of the pupils' ability to constrict and dilate in response to changes in illumination and viewing distance.

•Screening for defects in the visual field (peripheral vision). This important test could indicate the presence of tumors, brain damage or a detached retina.

• Microscopic examination of the external portions of the eye, as well as the lens, optic nerve, retina and other interior structures. (Your eyes will be dilated for this step.)

• Screening for glaucoma.

Source: Richard L. Abbott, MD, associate clinical professor, department of ophthalmology, Pacific Presbyterian Medical Center, San Francisco.

A Skilled Eye Examination Checks More than Vision

By looking carefully into the eyes, a skilled physician can detect clues to literally hundreds of different systemic illnesses. The eyes can act as an early warning system for diseases that may not otherwise be apparent:

• High blood pressure: Changes in the eyes can include blood vessel spasm or narrowing and microscopic hemorrhages within the retina. Swelling of the optic nerve in the back of the eye indicates severe high blood pressure that requires emergency treatment.

• Diabetes: A patient might experience blurriness of vision and sudden sightedness. This change occurs because high blood sugar affects the water content of the lenses, causing them to swell. Distance vision improves and near vision deteriorates. Once the sugar problem is corrected, vision often returns to normal. Examination of the retina can reveal vascular changes, some of which respond to laser therapy. This could prevent visual disability in the future.

• Heart valve infection: This is most characteristic in patients who have run a low-grade fever over a period of time and may have a history of childhood heart disease or rheumatic fever. *How it happens:* From a wound or infection somewhere else in the body, the bloodstream is temporarily seeded with certain bacteria that can settle on a heart valve, especially if it was previously damaged. The bacteria slowly grow like vegetation on the valve. The symptoms can be very subtle, including headaches, sweating and low-grade fever. Occasionally little infected blood clots with bacteria on them travel to the eyes. Called *Roth spots,* these might be the only clue to a heart-valve problem that could be cured with intensive antibiotic therapy.

• Strokes: Episodes of amaurosis fugax (temporary blindness) can be evidence of an impending stroke or an indication of atherosclerosis of the carotid artery (the large artery in the neck).

• Brain tumors and other neurological problems. Some can come to light as a result of vision problems, such as loss of peripheral vision.

• Thyroid disease. This can cause swelling and increased prominence of the eyes. Sometimes only one eye seems to bulge, or there may be a too-wide stare or an eyelid lag.

• Inflammatory diseases. Rheumatoid arthritis and certain back diseases occasionally cause the eyes to be red and very dry, sandy, and scratchy.

• Hereditary defects. On occasion, metabolic disorders can be seen in the eyes. It may be possible to examine an entire family to see who is at risk for a particular genetic disease.

• Infectious diseases. Long-term syphilis and other abnormalities in the bloodstream may affect the eyes.

• Don't be frightened if the ophthalmologist recommends a medical checkup. Very often there are minor or unimportant findings that require confirmation of your general health.

Source: B. David Gorman, MD, adjunct ophthalmologist and coordinator of resident education at Lenox Hill Hospital.

How to Buy Contact Lenses Wisely

As contact lenses become more sophisticated, the options for wearers seem endless and the differences confusing. Before buying lenses, take into account your budget, your lifestyle and the degree of vision correction you need.

Regardless of the type of lenses you end up with (hard, gas-permeable, soft, or extended-wear), follow these guidelines:

•Select a professional eye-care specialist you trust and who comes well recommended.

•Be wary of discount commercial eye-care establishments. They deal in quantity, not quality, and emphasize product, not service.

•Be aware that physical changes can take place in the eyes as a result of wearing contacts. Your eye-care professional should carefully monitor such changes and adjust for them, if necessary.

•Ask about a service (or insurance) contract that offers replacement lenses at reduced fees. This is usually worth the modest price, as you may well lose a lens every year or so.

•Follow the cleaning/disinfecting procedures recommended by your eye-care professional. If you take shortcuts, you could shorten the life of your lenses and/or damage your eyes.

•Although you may wear your lenses every day, keep an updated pair of glasses to wear in emergencies.

Source: Robert Snyder, OD, an optometrist in private practice, Beach Haven, NJ.

How to Take Your Temperature

•Take your temperature first thing in the morning for the most accurate reading.

•Wait 30 minutes after eating, drinking, smoking, or exercising so your mouth will be neither cooled down nor heated up.

•Shake down the thermometer to below normal—mercury rises from the last reading.

•Relax.

•Hold the thermometer under the back of your tongue for four minutes.

•Don't move your tongue, breathe through your mouth or talk.

•When using a rectal thermometer on an infant, lubricate it with water-soluble jelly and hold the baby's legs so a quick movement won't dislodge it or break the glass.

•Leave the thermometer in at least two minutes. Don't use the new disposable thermometers. They're not very accurate. *Better:* The old-fashioned kind.

Testicular Cancer

Without prompt treatment, 29% of men who have testicular cancer will die from it. But virtually all could be cured if treated within a month of the onset of symptoms. *To lower your chances of being a victim:*

•Give yourself a testicular self-exam once a month. The exam takes only three minutes. The best time to do this is after a warm bath or shower, when the scrotum is most relaxed.

•Technique: Examine the testicles separately, using fingers of both hands. Put your thumbs on top of the testicle and your index and middle fingers underneath. Roll the testicle gently. (If it hurts, you're applying too much pressure.)

•Be aware that a normal testicle is firm, oval and free of lumps; behind it you'll feel the epididymis (sperm storage duct), which is spongier.

•If you feel a small, hard, usually painless lump or swelling on the front or side of the testicle, you could have a problem. When in the slightest doubt, see a doctor.

Source: *Prevention,* Emmaus, PA.

Skin Cancer Alert

Malignant melanoma, a form of skin cancer, has doubled in incidence in the past 10 years. If the cancer is caught and excised in the earlier stages of development, the patient can be cured. But if the malignancy goes too deep, the cancer invades the body, and neither radiation treatment nor chemotherapy is effective.

•Malignant melanoma can develop independently as a dark tumor in the skin or it can come from a potentially malignant lesion, the "dysplastic atypical mole."

•People with dysplastic moles should be checked by a dermatologist at least every six months.

Characteristics of malignant melanoma and dysplastic moles:

•Bigger in size than a pencil-eraser head.

•A mixture of colors in the same mole.

•Asymmetrical shape.

•Bumpy texture.

• Irregular or notched borders.

• Development of malignant melanoma is directly related to the sun. It is more common in fair-skinned, blue-eyed people, who are more sensitive to the sun. Many victims of malignant melanoma had a severe, blistering sunburn in childhood or adolescence, and areas such as the back that get weekend sunburns are often affected. Malignant melanoma and dysplastic moles also tend to run in families.

• *Myth:* A mole that suffers trauma (such as a cut during shaving) or sprouts hair will become cancerous.

Source: Harold T. Eisenman, MD, a dermatologist and dermatopathologist in private practice in West Orange, NJ.

Adult Acne: Myths and Realities

Pimples, breakouts, blemishes, zits. There are almost as many words for acne as there are myths about it.

To promptly dispel one such myth—acne is *not* a problem only for teenagers. In fact, more and more adults are seeking help for this embarrassing skin condition.

More acne myths...

Myth: Acne is caused by poor hygiene. In fact, the process that leads to breakouts takes place well beneath the skin's surface. It has nothing to do with dirt.

Acne occurs when oil (sebum) from the skin's sebaceous glands mixes with dead cells and clogs ducts in hair follicles. These oily plugs —called *comedones*—are the whiteheads and blackheads that can lead to tender swellings called cysts deep within the skin.

Myth: Pimples are caused by chocolate or greasy food. There's no evidence that any particular food causes acne...nor that acne is caused by psychological stress or too much—or too little—sex.

In reality, we still don't have a very clear idea of what causes acne. We suspect, however, that several factors are involved...

• Heredity. Acne seems to be inherited. If one identical twin has acne, there's more than a 95% chance that the other twin will have it, too. Also, 80% of acne sufferers have siblings with acne...and 60% have at least one parent who had acne while growing up.

• Oily skin. Acne is most common in people with oily skin. However, it also occurs in those whose skin is normal or even dry...and some people with very oily skin have no acne.

• Hormones. The sebaceous glands of acne sufferers may be oversensitive to androgens (male hormones)—which are produced by both males and females. Female hormones (estrogens) decrease sebum production. But even small amounts of androgens can counteract large amounts of estrogen.

• Blocked follicles. In a person with normal skin, cells lining hair follicles flake off periodically and are carried to the surface of the skin by sebum. But in people with acne, these dead cells block the follicles and form comedones. *Result:* Stagnant sebum that accumulates beneath the comedones is metabolized by skin-dwelling bacteria, releasing substances that inflame the skin.

Myth: Scrubbing the skin helps get rid of acne. Vigorous cleansing with washcloths, soaps or cleansers can cause additional pimples by damaging already weakened follicles.

Better: Wash gently with soap and water. Pick a detergent (nonsoap) skin cleanser that's oil-free. (Oils can clog pores and promote comedones.) Or find a soap that contains the drying agent benzoyl peroxide. It kills acne-causing bacteria and dries oily, acne-prone skin.

Caution: Benzoyl peroxide can cause excessive dryness or peeling. About 3% of users develop an allergic rash.

Myth: Taking vitamin A or applying vitamin E to the skin helps acne. Vitamin A is useless against acne—because acne is not caused by a vitamin deficiency. In large doses, vitamin A is toxic. But some vitamin A-like drugs called *retinoids* (including tretinoin and isotretinoin) are helpful.

Since acne is often associated with oily skin, applying vitamin E or any other kind of oil is the last thing you want to do.

Many acne sufferers find that their skin improves when they bask in ultraviolet (UV) light from the sun or a sunlamp. *Problem:* Such exposure causes wrinkles, discoloration, benign skin growths and even skin cancer.

For this reason, dermatologists generally treat acne not with UV light but with drying agents, antibiotics and other drugs.

Myth: Squeezing blemishes is harmless. In fact, this can easily break the walls of affected follicles and spread inflammation. It may also cause permanent scarring.

Instead of performing this form of "self-surgery," keep your skin clean, apply warm compresses to large pimples or cysts and use appropriate medication prescribed by a dermatologist.

Prescription therapies...

Dermatologists have a variety of effective acne treatments to offer, including topical agents and antibiotics. *Most effective:*

• Tretinoin (Retin-A). For mild to moderately severe acne. Tretinoin dries the skin, clearing up existing blemishes and helping prevent new ones. Common side effects include skin irritation and increased sensitivity to sunlight.

To minimize these possible problems, ask your doctor about using lower-strength tretinoin ...and about limiting your exposure to sun and drying agents like benzoyl peroxide.

• Antibiotics. For mild to moderately severe acne. Topical antibiotics (lotions or creams) work by penetrating follicles to kill blemish-causing bacteria. Side effects include dryness, peeling and itching—but these are typically caused by alcohol in the lotion, not the antibiotics.

For deep pimples or cysts, antibiotic pills are often more effective. Side effects include stomach and intestinal upset.

Oral antibiotics sometimes cause vaginal yeast infections. *Reason:* Just as antibiotics kill bacteria on the skin, they kill vaginal bacteria. These are what normally keep yeast under control.

Self-defense: Ask your doctor about adjusting the dose of antibiotic or switching to another one. In some cases, eating yogurt containing *lactobacillus* bacteria helps keep yeast under control.

• Isotretinoin (Accutane). The strongest treatment available for severe cystic acne. Isotretinoin works by shrinking overactive oil glands. *Side effects:* Dry skin, chapped lips, dryness inside the nose and eye irritation. Some patients experience pain in their bones, muscles and joints.

Isotretinoin may also raise cholesterol levels and affect the liver. If taken during pregnancy, it can cause birth defects. For these reasons, isotretinoin is appropriate only for people with very severe acne that has not responded to other treatments. Patients must be closely monitored during isotretinoin therapy, which typically lasts 20 weeks.

• Hormone therapy. Because estrogen seems to help alleviate acne, women with severe acne are sometimes treated with birth-control pills, which contain estrogen. Side effects may include nausea, weight gain and breast tenderness.

• Acne surgery. Various surgical methods are used to remove blackheads and whiteheads and open up pimples and cysts.

Beware: To avoid scarring, only a doctor or a trained medical assistant should perform these removal procedures.

What to do about scars...

There is no perfect solution for acne scars. Before opting for any procedure, be sure you understand what results to expect, possible complications and cost...

• Dermabrasion. Best for soft, scooped-out scars, this technique removes the upper layers of skin with a rotating steel brush. Skin remains red and sensitive for several months. Antibiotic salves are often applied to prevent infection.

Complications may include blotchy skin, tiny white pimples called *milia*—and more scarring.

• Excision. There are several surgical techniques to improve "ice-pick" scars. These procedures result in new, less obvious types of scars. In some cases, skin discoloration occurs.

• Fillers. Some scars can be minimized via injections of collagen (a protein derived from cows) or of fibrin (a substance derived from human blood). Both substances may cause allergic reactions. Improvement lasts only about a year.

Silicone is a long-lasting filler, but it doesn't have FDA approval. Only a limited number of physicians can use it—on an experimental basis.

Acne rosacea...

People with acne rosacea have a defect in the small blood vessels. Initially, their skin may simply look ruddy instead of pimply.

But left untreated, rosacea causes visible veins, acne blemishes and thickening of the skin. The nose can become coarse and distorted by bumps.

Patients with rosacea must avoid aggravating factors like hot liquids, spicy foods and alcohol. Sunlight, extremes of temperature and stress also provoke the condition.

Treatments include topical antibiotics and corticosteroids. The newest medication is metronidazole gel, which decreases acne and improves the red rash.

Source: Richard A. Walzer, MD, special lecturer at Columbia University Medical School and consultant in dermatology at Columbia-Presbyterian Hospital, New York City. He is the author of *Treating Acne: A Guide for Teens and Adults*, Consumer Reports Books, 101 Truman Ave., Yonkers, New York 10703.

19

Healthy Healing

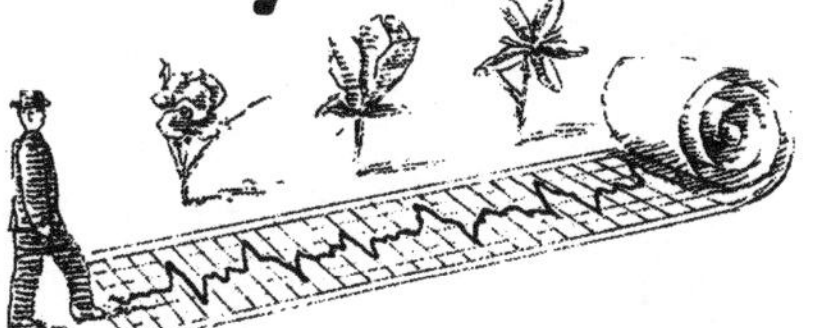

Faster Healing

Heal faster—by increasing your intake of zinc. Cuts, scrapes, blisters, and minor burns heal about one-third faster in those who take a minimum of 15 mg. of zinc daily. Fast healing decreases the chances of infection, scarring and stiffness. *Best:* A multiple vitamin-mineral supplement containing zinc rather than plain zinc tablets, which sometimes cause heartburn or indigestion.

Source: *Prime Time: A Doctor's Guide to Staying Younger Longer* by John E. Eichenlaub, MD. Prentice-Hall, Route 9W, Sylvan Ave., Englewood Cliffs, New Jersey 07632.

10 Common Health Problems

Many common diseases can be treated quite easily. Others take more effort. There are some we can't do anything about—but that go away by themselves. Even though doctors can't cure every disease, there's no harm in seeing a doctor when you aren't feeling right. At the very least, your physician can help you understand what's going on in your body, and advise you on relieving the discomforts.

Colds and flu...

These are caused by viruses, and nothing a doctor gives you will cure them. The infection will run its course by itself—usually within a few days though sometimes it takes several weeks.

Cold clues: If you have congestion, a cough and/or a sore throat, you probably have a cold.

Flu clues: If you have a fever and your muscles feel weak and tired, it's probably flu.

Antibiotics are completely ineffective against viral infections—though patients continue to demand them.

The best we can do is treat the symptoms. Aspirin, acetaminophen, or ibuprofen can relieve pain and fever. *For cough medicines, decon-*

gestants, and throat treatments: Those containing dextromethorphan are most effective.

Bed rest will not make the cold go away any faster, but it might make you feel better in the meantime.

Bladder infections...

Bladder infections affect far more women than men. Because the urethra is shorter in women than in men, germs that live around the anus and vaginal area can travel up to the bladder fairly easily.

Antibiotics generally clear up most bladder infections within a week.

Some people believe baths encourage the spread of germs into the bladder. This has never been proven, but it can't hurt to take showers instead of baths until the infection clears up.

Cranberry juice is a popular folk remedy. It makes the urine more acidic—a hostile environment for germs. But, you have to drink a large amount of juice (a quart or two a day) for it to be effective.

It's hard to find pure cranberry juice—look for it in health food stores. The kind you buy at the supermarket is mostly water and sugar and won't do a thing.

Irritable bowel syndrome...

Irritable bowel syndrome (IBS) is considered the most common digestive complaint. When the intestinal muscles don't function as smoothly as they should, patients may experience constipation, diarrhea, cramps, and bloating, or some combination of the above.

No one really knows what causes IBS...and there's no sure cure. *Helpful:*

- Adding fiber to the diet can be beneficial. Eat lots of fruits and vegetables.
- If you know you're sensitive to certain foods—such as caffeine, other acidic foods, seeds, etc.—avoid them.
- Get plenty of exercise.

Also helpful: Low doses of antidepressants. We're not sure why—it may be that they alter nerves in the brain that regulate muscle function.

Lower back pain...

The back is very poorly designed for walking upright. The muscles are too small and weak to support the weight of the upper body, and the disks are easily injured. Ordinary wear-and-tear makes a certain amount of back pain almost inevitable with age.

If you experience acute pain, rest the back as you would any injured area. Applying heat and taking ibuprofen usually helps ease the pain. Most acute backaches subside within a few weeks.

If your problem is chronic, be aggressive. Most doctors don't know much about back pain, so look for one who specializes in backs—and who *doesn't* rush to recommend surgery. Minor complaints can often be helped by exercise programs and physical therapy to strengthen the back.

Psoriasis...

Psoriasis is a condition in which the skin grows more rapidly than normal, causing patches to turn red and flake off.

We don't know what causes psoriasis. Once the condition has erupted, however, any injury or irritation to the skin is likely to result in an outbreak. So psoriasis sufferers should avoid getting sunburned, and wear gloves when doing the dishes or if working with harsh chemicals.

Doctors commonly prescribe cortisone creams, which work by discouraging skin cells from multiplying. But long-term use of cortisone is a bad idea—it will make the skin thin and delicate.

Exposure to ultraviolet light is another fairly common treatment, but it increases the risk of skin cancer.

Best treatment: Tar, applied topically. Tar is a very old remedy. The current bottled solutions are not nearly as messy or smelly as the older kind of solutions. If the sufferer's doctor doesn't know about tar treatment, find a doctor who does.

Panic attacks...

It's very common for patients to complain of pounding heart, dry mouth, sweating, difficulty breathing, and feelings of intense anxiety or fright—for no obvious reason.

Some people are awakened in the night by these attacks—others may experience them in the middle of a meeting. They seem to be most common among young adults.

We don't understand much about panic attacks, except that they're usually harmless.

Symptoms are caused by the release of adrenaline, and they subside when the body runs out of adrenaline...usually after 20 or 30 minutes. They're generally not a sign of heart disease. And they don't usually occur often. If the attacks are chronic and interfere with everyday functioning, several medications can help. Check with your doctor.

Impotence...

Not so long ago, impotence was thought to be a psychological problem, and patients were sent to psychiatrists for long, expensive treatments. Now we know that there are many physical causes as well—and that most cases respond to treatment fairly quickly.

Drugs are a common physical cause. Marijuana, alcohol, even smoking can interfere with sexual performance.

Impotence is also a frequent side effect of high blood pressure medication. If you take drugs for high blood pressure, ask your doctor about adjusting the dosage. There are so many different medications that you should be able to find one that doesn't cause this side effect.

Impotence is also associated with diabetes—but only as a long-term complication associated with damage to nerves or arteries.

Psychological causes include boredom, depression and anxiety.

It's rarely necessary to embark on a long, involved course of psychotherapy in order to cure impotence. Often, just understanding that these emotions can contribute to the condition —and that it's temporary—is enough to provide relief. For stubborn cases, sex therapy may be helpful.

Migraine headaches...

Unlike some other kinds of headaches, migraines are *vascular.* Blood vessels in the scalp become highly sensitive, and heartbeats stretch the arterial walls, creating a throbbing pain.

Migraine attacks tend to start during the teen years and decrease as a person gets older. They usually disappear by middle age.

Unless your symptoms are truly peculiar, don't invest a lot of time and money in tests—they probably won't show anything. Fortunately, migraines are treatable. Several drug families—including antidepressants and antihistamines—can be helpful.

Helpful: Standard pain medications, such as acetaminophen or Darvon, will relieve mild pain.

Better: Drugs that stiffen the arteries. Caffeine does this—a few cups of coffee for a minor attack may be effective.

For severe migraine, ergotamine is effective and prescribed by many doctors to be taken at the first sign of a migraine. It can be taken as a pill, suppository, or inhalant, and is sometimes combined with caffeine.

Nausea is a common side effect, so if the pill form makes you nauseous, ask your doctor about experimenting with the other forms.

Insomnia...

The best treatment for insomnia may be to put it in perspective. Very few insomniacs spend a lot of time feeling sleepy during the day. They may be sluggish in the morning, but once they get going they don't feel too bad.

Upsetting: Lying awake in the middle of the night, trying to sleep and feeling frustrated because you can't.

Sleeping pills don't cure insomnia—they just induce poor-quality sleep. And they can be addictive.

Try to view insomnia as simply irritating—not dangerous. If you can't sleep, don't drive yourself crazy about it. Turn on the light and read.

Note: Insomnia can be a symptom of depression. If that's the case, then the underlying problem should be addressed.

Warts...

Warts are viral and contagious—you can catch them from going barefoot in a public place, using someone else's comb or from scratching and spreading your own warts. However, they may not appear until up to a year after exposure.

Though unattractive, warts are not dangerous. They're more common in children than adults—it's possible that we build up resistance as we age.

The vast majority of warts go away by themselves within a year or two. Treatments include freezing with liquid nitrogen, corroding with acid, and burning or electrocoagulation. I prefer liquid nitrogen—it's simple, effective and not very painful.

Source: Family practitioner Michael Oppenheim, MD, who practices in Los Angeles. He is the author of *A Doctor's Guide to the Best Medical Care* and *The Complete Book of Better Digestion*, both published by Rodale Press, 33 E. Minor St., Emmaus, Pennsylvania 18098.

Natural Remedies For a Stuffy Nose

Chinese ephedra—Ephedra sinica—is an ancient medicinal herb used as a bronchodilator and a stimulant. The source of ephedrine—predecessor of pseudoephedrine, the active ingredient in Sudafed—this dried herb comes in pill form, or works well when you drink it as tea. *Caution:* No more than one cup every four hours. *Also helpful:* Bioflavonoids—available at vitamin and health food stores. Take one or two capsules...stuffiness should clear up in about 20 minutes.

Important: Check with your doctor before using. Ephedra is not for use by those with hyperthyroidism or prostate disease.

Source: Marvin Schweitzer, ND, is a naturopath with the Center for Healing Arts, in Orange, Connecticut.

Music Can Help Heal the Brain

A prescription for music therapy is becoming more common as scientists prove how combinations of sounds affect brain and body.

Humans have long used the rhythm and tempo of music to make repetitive tasks easier. Stanford University experimenters recorded electrical patterns from the elbows of women 18 to 35-years-old performing tasks. They found music really did improve synchronization of nerves and muscle signals.

Music is being studied intensively today for its physiological effects. It has been shown to be beneficial for muscular development, physical coordination, a sense of timing, mental concentration, memory skills, visual and hearing development, and stress control. The cerebellum, at the base of the brain, is devoted to the regulation of the sort of movement we use when playing an instrument or dancing to music. Current research suggests one of the cerebellum's fundamental functions may be to help us learn and remember movements.

Dr. Jon Eisenson, a Stanford University Medical Center professor emeritus of hearing and speech science, has long advocated music for stroke and brain-trauma patients unable to speak.

Many beneficial physical effects can be derived from listening and moving to music. In fact, merely listening to music has been found to lower blood pressure and reduce sweating and respiratory rates.

Music can also change moods. Just think of how rock concert patrons behave—or how you feel when you hear a song associated with a past love.

Source: Arthur Winter, MD, FICS, director of The New Jersey Neurological Institute. He is a coauthor, with his wife, Ruth Winter, of *Build Your Brain Power*, St. Martin's Press, 175 Fifth Ave., New York 10010.

Healthier Blood Pressure Levels

Blood pressure is more likely to remain at healthy levels in people who eat a diet that is rich in beans, rice and other sources of vegetable protein...higher than usual in polyunsaturated fat...and low in saturated fat and cholesterol.

Source: Kiang Liu, PhD, professor of preventive medicine, Northwestern University Medical School, Chicago. His study of more than 1,800 men, ages 40 to 55, was reported in *Internal Medicine News and Cardiology News*, 12230 Wilkins Ave., Rockville, Maryland 20852.

Drill-less Dentistry

Drill-less dentistry is now offered by some dentists. A new process called *kinetic cavity preparation* "sandblasts" away decay with a high-speed stream of tiny particles. *Eliminated:* Heat, vibration, noise, smell and friction—and 80% of pain. There's less need for anesthesia. This new process can be faster, too.

Source: Ronald Goldstein, DDS, clinical professor, school of dentistry, Medical College of Georgia, Augusta. He maintains a private practice in Atlanta.

Your Dentist and Your Medical History

Your medical history should be known by your dentist as well as your doctor. Without this knowledge, dentists may fail to take the precautions necessary to prevent complications in treating "medically compromised" persons—those with heart trouble, infectious disease or certain other medical problems. *Also:* A dentist who knows your medical history will be better able to treat and/or arrange for medical care in case of an emergency.

Source: Barbara J. Steinberg, DDS, professor of medicine and assistant director of the division of dental medicine, Medical College of Pennsylvania, Philadelphia. Her recommendation appeared in the *Journal of the American Dental Association,* 211 E. Chicago Ave., Chicago 60611.

Best Cold Medicines

For teens/adults: Combination antihistamine decongestants. They reduce nasal congestion, postnasal drip, coughing—and also reduce cold symptoms involving the ears. These medicines don't appear to be helpful for young children.

Source: William Feldman, MD, head of division of general pediatrics, Hospital for Sick Children, Toronto. His study, which reviewed 106 studies on colds, was published in the *Journal of the American Medical Association,* 515 N. State St., Chicago 60610.

How to Warm Cold Hands Caused by Stress

Cold hands are often a sign of stress if you are indoors and there is no reason for them to be chilled. Biofeedback research indicates that techniques to warm hands can also reduce the stress load. *What works:*

- Close your eyes and imagine yourself holding and playing with something soft and warm.
- Touch your cheeks, which are usually warm, and imagine the warmth flowing into your fingers.
- Interlock fingers, squeeze gently for one second, release for one second.

Repeat sequence several times.

Source: Robert Hall, president, Futurehealth, Inc., Bensalem, PA.

Headache Relief Without Drugs

Relief from incapacitating tension, vascular and migraine headaches is possible without drugs, using a self-administered form of acupuncture know as acupressure.

The technique:

- Exert very heavy thumbnail pressure (painful pressure) successively on nerves lying just below the surface of the skin at key points in the hands and wrists. As with acupuncture, no one's sure why it works.

Pressure points to try:

- The triangle of flesh between the thumb and index finger on the back of your hands (thumb side of bone, near middle of the second metacarpal in the index finger).
- Just above the protruding bone on the thumb side of your wrist.

How to Treat Fever

•Take aspirin or acetaminophen only when your temperature is over 102° and you're uncomfortable.

•Dress lightly enough so that body heat can escape.

•Sponge with tepid water, not alcohol (the vapors can be dangerous).

•Take a bath and wash your hair if you feel like it—the evaporating water may lower your temperature.

•Drink eight to twelve glasses of liquid a day to avoid dehydration.

Fever: When to Call the Doctor

Call the doctor for a fever when:

•A child's temperature goes above 102° or an adult's over 101°.

•The fever persists for more than 24 hours with no obvious cause.

•The fever lasts for more than 72 hours, even if there's an obvious cause.

•An infant under three months old has any temperature elevation.

•There is a serious disease involved.

•In short, call the doctor when you feel really sick (even if you haven't got a fever).

What to Do About Colds

Doctors cannot cure a cold. But sufferers can help themselves by keeping in mind what is known about the ailment. *Essentials:*

•Chills don't cause colds, but they encourage existing viruses to multiply.

•Colds spread most effectively by direct contact and are most contagious in their early stages before the symptoms are even noticeable.

•The body's process of curing a cold requires about the same energy as hard physical labor. Keep vigorous exercise to a minimum so your energy goes toward fighting the cold.

•Taking vitamin C may help. Advocates suggest one to three grams a day at the outset of a cold and 500 milligrams daily throughout its duration.

•Avoid stress during a cold. It reduces antibody production in the nose and mouth.

•Don't numb pain by drinking alcohol.

Source: *Executive Fitness Newsletter,* Emmaus, PA.

The Office Cold is a Myth

People pick up relatively few cold viruses from their associates at work. An office may have many people nursing colds, but chances are few of them have the same virus strain. The majority of colds are caught at home. And the main carriers are children, who are exposed to the most viruses through close association and direct physical contact with their playmates. Parents then catch the cold from the sick child.

•Shaking hands with someone who has a cold and then rubbing your eyes can be riskier than standing directly in front of a sneezing person. Current research indicates that most colds are probably spread by direct physical contact. The viruses grow in the nose and eyes (but not the mouth). When infected people wipe or blow their noses sloppily, some of the cold virus can get onto their hands. Outside the body, the virus can survive as long as a day. *Result:* Unless washed off, it spreads to toys, furniture, drinking cups and other people's hands.

Colds are contagious, beginning with the onset of symptoms until the symptoms vanish. *Worst period:* The first two to three days.

•Use a tissue or handkerchief when covering coughs and sneezes. Bare hands pick up the virus and spread the cold.

•Wash your hands frequently when around people who have colds, especially after touching things they have handled.

•Keep hands away from nose and eyes immediately after contact with a person with cold symptoms.

•Do not rely on household sprays to disinfect objects. Their value is unproven.

Source: Jack Gwaltney, Jr., MD, professor of internal medicine, University of Virginia Medical School.

A Cough: Getting Rid of it the Old-Fashioned Way

Skeptics of cough medications say home remedies may be more effective and less risky. *Try these:*

•Chicken soup.

•Fruit juices.

•Vaporizers and humidifiers.

•A drop of honey on the back of the tongue.

Sources: Dr. Sidney Wolfe, MD, and others, quoted in *Executive.*

Back Strain and Driving

The probability of spinal disk problems is three times greater for those who spend a big part of their work lives driving. *To reduce the strain on your back:*

•Keep your head and shoulders erect while driving. Place a 1½-inch-thick pillow, or a wicker back support, at the small of the back. Keep the back pressed against it.

•Change driving position often.

Take frequent breaks to stretch your legs and do one or two of these exercises:

•Grab your wrists, and raise your arms to shoulder height. Try to pull your arms apart for a count of six. Repeat three times.

•Hold your forehead, then push your head against your hand. Repeat for each side of the head. Do slowly three times.

•Lace your fingers behind your head and press back against them. Do slowly three times.

•Using the car to steady you, do at least four deep-knee bends when you stop for a rest.

Source: Shirley Linde, author of *How to Beat a Bad Back,* Rawson, Wade Publishers, New York.

Using Your Mind To Fight Cancer

Your beliefs can be powerful allies against cancer. The body produces billions of cells and routinely identifies and kills cancerous ones. Once the major cancer-removal job is done by surgery and chemotherapy, your body can take over. But you must free up energy to mobilize your body to fight cancer.

•Express your feelings. Patients who express anger and sadness survive the longest. Expressing your feelings reduces stress and releases energy. Suppressing feelings uses up valuable energy that should be mobilized to fight the cancer. *Example:* In a study at Johns Hopkins, patients with metastatic breast cancer who survived more than a year were those who expressed their depression, anxiety, and sense of alienation. They were also judged by their doctors as being poorly adjusted to the disease and as having negative attitudes toward their doctors.

•Avoid blame, guilt, and self-criticism. You are not being punished for wrongdoing. The question *Why me?* should be replaced with *What can I do about it now?*

•Seek support. Discuss your situation with a therapist, family member, or support group. *Important:* Talk with a former cancer patient who has been pronounced cured or has survived for years with the disease. This can be a powerful combatant of negative feelings.

•Take positive steps to help yourself. Recognize that your life has changed, probably forever, and that your old ways of coping are no longer viable and may even be implicated in your illness. *What must change:* Gratification from compulsive goal-seeking. The cancer patient must start to develop a sense of self-worth that comes from within rather than from outside goals such as success, money, or sexual conquests.

•Learn to say no. Every moment is precious. Why waste it on trivia or worrying about whether an extra phone call will bother your doctor.

•Speak the unspeakable. The relatives and friends of cancer patients often feel certain subjects are taboo. This leads patients to suppress their feelings in order to protect their loved ones. But when patients and the people they're close to talk openly about their feelings, it can be an enormous relief and source of strength.

•Participate in choosing your treatment to reduce the stress of feeling like a passive victim. You may feel emotionally and physically debilitated by the side effects of chemotherapy and slip into thinking that you have to take these drugs for your doctor. Remind yourself that you are taking the drugs because they are powerful allies of your body.

•You must choose a doctor you feel has some concern for you as a human being and who takes your values and life goals into consideration when medical decisions are made. Your doctor should give you information about treatment plans and alternatives and be open to negotiating alternatives with you rather than assuming a "take it or leave it" attitude.

Source: Neil A. Fiore, PhD, a psychologist who works for the University of California and has a private practice in Berkeley. He has worked with many cancer patients, and is the author of *The Road Back to Health: Coping With the Emotional Side of Cancer,* Bantam Books, New York.

Antibiotics: Handle with Care

Say you have a scratchy throat, aching muscles and a mild headache. If you're like millions of Americans, you'll reach for an antibiotic in your medicine cabinet or ask your doctor to prescribe one.

Better think again. Overused and vastly misunderstood, these so-called miracle drugs may do you more harm than good, especially if taken when they are not needed.

Antibiotics are designed to fight *bacterial* infections. But too often, we take them casually and for the wrong reasons—for *viral* infections such as a cold or flu.

Sometimes we use antibiotics prescribed for a previous illness to treat a current one...or we may even take antibiotics prescribed for a friend.

Or we may discontinue antibiotics too soon, before they've had a chance to do their job. Unfortunately, such careless, naive and inappropriate use not only is ineffective but also can pave the way for more serious illnesses later on.

Breeding trouble...

Even when taken under the *best* of conditions—when we have a clearly identified bacterial infection and use a drug designed to fight it —antibiotics don't always work.

Reason: Some bacteria manage to survive despite the antibiotic. With the more vulnerable bacteria knocked out, *drug-resistant* survivors are free to multiply and cause a new infection that cannot be cured by the antibiotic.

To make matters worse, some bacteria defend themselves by *developing* resistance to antibiotics after repeated exposure. This renders the same antibiotic far less potent the next time around.

Indeed, bacteria have evolved many ingenious—and very tricky—ways to elude the effects of antibiotics.

Some simply expel any antibiotic that gets inside their cell membrane. Some destroy or chemically alter the antibiotic so that it is no longer active. Others mutate to become less sensitive to the effects of the drug.

Bottom line: Using antibiotics too often or for prolonged periods of time promotes buildup of drug-resistant bacteria among the protective bacteria colonizing our skin and intestinal tract. If we should someday need an antibiotic to fight a truly serious infection, it may be far less effective in doing its job, leaving us possibly without effective treatment when we really need it.

Unfortunately, turning to another antibiotic may not help. Bacteria resistant to one drug are often resistant to other drugs—a property known as "multiple drug resistance."

Classic case: A South American businessman who had been using antibiotics for sore throats, colds and other minor viral complaints developed acute leukemia along with a serious intestinal infection. The doctors successfully treated his leukemia. Ironically, however, the common *E. coli* bacteria causing his infection proved resistant to *eight* different antibiotics. The bacteria spread to several of his internal organs. He died several weeks later.

Because of his abuse of antibiotics, this man had transformed ordinarily harmless bacteria into bacteria that were resistant to several drugs ...and which eventually killed him.

Deadlier diseases...

Paradoxically, taking too little of an antibiotic can be just as hazardous as taking too much. Consider tuberculosis, for example, a bacterial disease that was once all but eradicated—but which recently has been making a major comeback throughout urban America.

One reason TB has returned is that many TB patients take their medication sporadically—or stop taking it too soon. Such erratic habits spawn drug-resistant strains of TB bacilli. Then these haphazardly treated and still-infected individuals spread the same drug-resistant bacteria to others.

Result: What was once an easily curable disease has become a formidable—and growing—threat to public health. Antibiotic misuse has also brought about new, drug-resistant strains of gonorrhea, strep throat, urinary tract infections, childhood ear infections, pneumonia, meningitis and salmonella.

Getting to the source...

Doctors also play a part in the widespread mishandling of antibiotics and the consequent emergence of drug-resistant bacteria.

Patients typically demand antibiotics, thinking they will relieve the symptoms of a cold or flu or other viral conditions invulnerable to antibiotics. And some doctors give in to these demands—even though they may be well aware that prescribing antibiotics in such cases is useless. Some prescribe antibiotics too freely without clear evidence of a bacterial infection.

Often it is relatively easy to distinguish a viral from a bacterial infection—just by the symptoms on physical examination. The definitive way to tell the difference is to perform tests, called bacterial cultures, of the affected body site, such as the throat. Using this information, the doctor can determine the likelihood of a bacterial infection and the need for an antibiotic.

Another problem: Too many times doctors rely on "broad-spectrum" antibiotics to hit every possible cause of the infection. Unfortunately, such antibiotics generate more bacterial resistance than the narrow-spectrum drugs.

Other drawbacks...

Antibiotics can cause gastrointestinal problems and allergic reactions. Prolonged use can lead to yeast infections and to toxicity in critical internal organs.

Another common side effect of antibiotics is the overgrowth of certain undesirable bacterial flora, including those that produce dangerous toxins.

Example: Diarrhea caused by excessive growth of intestinal bacteria may follow treatment with certain broad-spectrum antibiotics. Candida and other yeasts are resistant to antibiotics. If present, they can easily overgrow an area where the protective bacteria have been eliminated by antibiotics.

Being safe and smart...

Used prudently and with caution, of course, antibiotics play a critical and often life-saving therapeutic role. They can even help *prevent* infections under certain vulnerable conditions.

Example: For surgical patients and individuals with diseased heart valves or heart murmurs, antibiotics are highly effective at preventing potentially life-threatening bacterial infections.

To use antibiotics wisely and well:

- Be discriminating before taking antibiotics. Do not demand that your doctor prescribe them.
- Take an antibiotic only after your doctor has prescribed one for your current condition.
- Follow directions carefully. Take antibiotics only at the correct dosage and for the prescribed time period.
- Never take an antibiotic prescribed for someone else.
- Never save antibiotics for future use or give them to others. Discard unused prescriptions. *Caution:* Antibiotics tend to lose their potency over time, so old pills may be medically useless ...and possibly dangerous.

Example: The popular antibiotic tetracycline undergoes a chemical change that renders it toxic to the liver.

Source: Stuart B. Levy, MD, professor of medicine and molecular biology/microbiology, Tufts University School of Medicine, Boston. He is the author of *The Antibiotic Paradox: How Miracle Drugs Are Destroying the Miracle*, Plenum Publishing, 233 Spring St., New York 10013.

20

Nutrition

Food Oddities/ Food Realities

While there's little doubt that a diet that's high in fat and cholesterol is linked to heart disease, such a diet is by no means the sole culprit. In fact, it's quite clear that the primary causes of heart disease are your genes, obesity, smoking, uncontrolled high blood pressure or diabetes, and a sedentary lifestyle. Yet many Americans are now adopting extreme diets in a misguided attempt to protect their health. Extreme diets not only fail to eliminate risk, but in some cases they can raise the risk—of heart disease and of several other ailments. *Here's why...*

Case study #1...

A middle-aged man's triglyceride and cholesterol levels remained high even though he had been on a radical low-fat/low-cholesterol diet for eight years. He was worried—and rightly so—that unless his levels were brought under control, he would eventually suffer a fatal heart attack, like several other members of his family.

A battery of tests revealed that this man's ultra-low-fat diet had thrown his metabolism completely out of whack. In fact, he was eating so little fat that his body was behaving as if it were starving. *Result:* His liver was producing more, rather than less, bad cholesterol, and his triglycerides were out of control.

To reverse the problem, I recommended that this man—who had been living mostly on steamed vegetables and skinless chicken—eat more fat. He did so reluctantly, but eventually it brought the fat in his diet from roughly 10% of his total calories to 25%. His triglyceride and bad-cholesterol levels fell to a much safer level. His risk of heart disease is now dramatically reduced—all as a result of raising his fat intake.

While adding fat to the diet is not the answer for everyone, it can help those whose fat intake is dangerously low.

Case study #2...

A woman in her thirties was experiencing many vague, troubling symptoms, including anxiety, dizziness and a feeling of pressure inside her chest. Her previous doctor had prescribed nitroglycerine for her chest pressure, and—believing her other symptoms to be psychosomatic—had given her sedatives. He also had recommended psychiatric care.

That doctor's diagnosis was incorrect. I traced this woman's emotional problems to a bad case of hypoglycemia, caused by a poor diet, and to multiple allergies, including severe reactions to mold, pollen and certain foods. Once these allergies were treated, her symptoms disappeared. She is now full of energy, anxiety-free, and the chest pressure has vanished and she no longer feels the need to carry nitroglycerine pills.

Allergies can produce all sorts of symptoms beyond a runny nose, itching, hives, etc. Mysterious symptoms call for thorough allergy testing by an experienced allergist.

Case study #3...

A middle-aged business executive came in to see me after his boss told him he needed help controlling his extreme emotional volatility.

Even though he had a history of severe allergies, he did not suspect that allergies were to blame for his emotional problems. He thought he might need to see a psychotherapist. Yet, as it turned out, he was allergic to food additives and to a mold found in certain foods.

Once he changed his diet and began regular allergy treatments, his emotional explosions disappeared.

He got a promotion, his marriage improved ...and he stopped coming to see me. Two years later he called to say that he was again having emotional problems. When I asked how his allergy treatments were going, he confessed that he had stopped them. He resumed treatment, and his symptoms again disappeared.

Case study #4...

A nine-year-old boy was suffering from severe Attention Deficit Disorder (ADD), plus some apparently unrelated symptoms including a skin rash and indigestion.

His ADD was so severe that he was scheduled to be transferred from his regular class to a special-education class—and his parents were distraught at the prospect. I discovered that his "mental" problem was actually the result of a hypersensitivity to sugar. Once sugar was eliminated from his diet, he calmed down immediately. Not only was he able to stay in his regular class, but he is also now an outstanding student.

Self-defense...

Though the specifics of these cases vary widely, I recommend for all my patients the same basic medical advice for preventing illness. *Key points:*

• Maintain your total fat intake to roughly 25% of calories. That's leaner than the traditional American diet, which is roughly 40% fat, but more fatty than the 10%-to-15%-fat diet recommended by many health gurus. Avoid fried foods and fatty cuts of meat—hamburger, sausage, etc. Limit your intake of both saturated fats (butter, tallow, lard and tropical oils) and polyunsaturated fats (corn oil, safflower oil, margarine, etc.). Concentrate on monounsaturated fats such as olive oil and canola (rapeseed) oil. They're far less likely to act as oxidants in the body, and thus are less likely to promote formation of atherosclerosis and heart disease.

• Exercise regularly. Twenty to 30 minutes at least three times a week is ideal.

Caution: Working out at extremely high intensity promotes formation of free radicals, substances that promote oxidation in the body and thus lead to premature aging and heart disease.

• Don't smoke. Period.

• Drink alcohol sparingly, *if at all.* Consume at least six eight-ounce glasses of water a day.

• Take supplemental vitamins and minerals. For maximum protection against oxidants, take vitamin E (400 international units a day), vitamin C (1,000 milligrams, twice daily) and beta-carotene (25,000 international units daily) ...but check with your doctor first.

• Consume 1,500 mg. of calcium a day to help ward off osteoporosis and colon cancer. A cup of low-fat yogurt contains roughly 400 mg...a cup of whole milk/291 mg...a cup of skim milk/302 mg.

Source: Thomas Brunoski, MD, a physician in private practice in Westport, Connecticut. Dr. Brunoski specializes in the treatment of medical problems with nutritional and allergy therapy rather than medication.

Food Danger

The bacteria that cause food poisoning are frequently tasteless, colorless, and odorless. *Self-defense:* Keep refrigerator temperature at 40°F and freezer at 0°F. *Also:* Don't eat foods you feel might be unsafe. Refrigerator life for raw fish is, at most, two days...fruit/one week...leftovers/three to four days...raw meat and poultry/two to three days.

Source: *American Institute for Cancer Research Newsletter,* 1759 R St. NW, Washington, DC 20069. Four issues/year.

Breakfast Cereal Trap

Most people buy dry cereal because it's convenient...but prices keep going up and a large family can finish a $4 box in one sitting. *Better:* Buy only if the price is less than eight cents per ounce (it can run as high as 20 cents per ounce —that's 40 cents per serving). Low-cost options (five to eight cents per serving): Cooked oatmeal...cornmeal mush...cooked rice (serve like oatmeal—with milk and sugar)...homemade pancakes, waffles, granola, muffins... eggs and toast.

Source: Amy Dacyczyn, editor of *The Tightwad Gazette,* RR 1, Box 3570, Leeds, Maine 04263.

How to Protect Yourself When Buying Seafood/ When Eating Seafood

Seafood and fish are an excellent protein source that is low in saturated fat, light on calories, and high in vitamins, minerals, and the omega-3 fatty acids that help reduce the risk of heart disease.

But there *are* risks. More than 80% of the seafood eaten in the US has not been inspected for chemical or microbial contaminants. Fortunately, there are things that you can do to enjoy maximum health and minimum risk...

- Avoid chemical contaminants. When you buy fish, choose younger, smaller ones, since they've accumulated fewer contaminants. Low-fat, offshore species like cod, haddock, and pollack are especially good choices. Always trim the skin, belly flap, and dark meat along the top or center, especially when it comes to fatty fish such as bluefish. Don't use the fatty parts to make sauce. Don't eat the green "tomalley" in lobsters or the "mustard" in crabs.

- Avoid natural toxins. When traveling in tropical climates, avoid reef fish such as amberjack, grouper, goatfish, or barracuda, which are more likely to be contaminated. Buy only seafood that has been kept continuously chilled, especially mahi-mahi, tuna, and bluefish, which produce an odorless toxin when they spoil.

- Avoid disease-causing microbes. Bite for bite, raw or undercooked shellfish is the *riskiest* food you can eat.

Self-defense: Don't eat shellfish whose shells remain closed after cooking. Do not eat raw fish or shellfish if you are over 60, HIV-positive, pregnant, have cancer or liver disease, or are vulnerable to infection. Cook all fish and shellfish thoroughly. Raw clams, oysters, and mussels should be steamed for six minutes.

- Don't buy fresh fish that has dull, sunken eyes, or fish that smells "fishy." Do not buy ready-to-eat seafood that is displayed too close to raw seafood.

Source: Lisa Y. Lefferts, an environmental health consultant in Hyattsville, Maryland, who specializes in food-safety, environmental policy and risk-assessment.

Nutritional Supplements

Over-the-counter nutritional supplements—popular among bodybuilders and fitness buffs —often contain ingredients whose effects on the human body are poorly understood...and they may be toxic. *Particularly suspect:* Supplements containing ingredients derived from the testicles, hypothalamus glands, adrenal glands or pituitary glands of animals. However, because different supplement manufacturers use different names for the same ingredient, and because Food and Drug Administration regulations allow supplements to contain untested ingredients, it's often hard to tell what's safe and what's potentially dangerous. *Generally safe in moderation—with doctor's OK:* Conventional vitamin and mineral tablets.

Source: Rossanne M. Philen, MD, a medical epidemiologist at the Centers for Disease Control and Prevention in Atlanta.

Margarine Health Risks

Women who eat the equivalent of four or more teaspoons a day have a 50% increased risk of developing heart disease. And women eating other forms of solid and semisolid vegetable fat—equal to six or more spoons of margarine daily—have a 70% increased risk. These types of vegetable fats are found in cookies, cakes and fried fast-foods.

Source: Eight-year study of more than 88,000 women, aged 34 to 59, led by Walter Willett, DrPH, professor and chairman, department of nutrition, Harvard School of Public Health, Boston.

Odor and Weight Loss

Sniffing your favorite food odors helps weight loss. In a recent study, dieting patients inhaled a common food additive that smells like corn chips whenever they felt hungry. They had 10 times the weight-loss of those who didn't. *Reason:* The olfactory bulb, the part of the brain that processes aromas, is linked directly to the part of the brain that controls hunger. Strong odors of any favored food may diminish hunger. *Dieting strategy:* Sniff food deeply before eating...eat hot food (smells are enhanced by heat)...chew thoroughly to get more aroma molecules to the olfactory bulb.

Source: Alan R. Hirsch, MD, neurological director for the Smell and Taste Treatment and Research Foundation, Chicago. 800-458-2783.

Fat Facts

Some poultry is fattier than others—and some parts are fattier than some cuts of beef. If you are on a low-fat diet, you should know...

- Chicken has 1½ times the fat of turkey.
- Skinless chicken thighs have almost twice the fat of skinless drumsticks.
- A 4-oz. skinless chicken thigh has more saturated fat than 4 oz. of thoroughly trimmed, select-grade round steak, sirloin—or even pork tenderloin.
- Chicken wings are fattier than drumsticks —backs are even fattier than thighs.

Self-defense: Stick to breast (white) meat... eat ground chicken and turkey only if made from breast meat—with no skin. Beware the "other white meat"—pork. Typical trimmed cuts of pork are one-third fattier than skinless chicken—and twice as fatty as skinless turkey.

Source: Bonnie Liebman, director of nutrition, Center for Science in the Public Interest, 1875 Connecticut Ave. NW, Washington, DC 20009.

Muffin Madness

The average muffin contains 800 to 900 calories—which can be 50% *or more* of the required daily caloric intake. *Problem:* Most muffins—even bran and sugar-free ones—*aren't good for you.* Breakfast should be 300 to 400 calories. Replacing a muffin with a low-fat option—even with no other dietary changes—can help you lose weight. *Weight-loss guidelines:* A man needs 12 calories per pound of body weight to sustain his daily needs (*Example:* 2,160 calories for a 180-pound man)...a woman needs 11 calories per pound. To lose weight, eat less than that number by making low-calorie substitutions for high-calorie foods and begin an exercise program. *Important:* Check with your doctor before beginning any weight-loss program.

Source: Jeffrey Fisher, MD, a cardiologist in private practice, 311 E. 72 St., New York 10021, and clinical associate professor of medicine, New York Hospital-Cornell Medical Center.

The Truth About Chinese Food

Chinese food can contain surprisingly high amounts of fat. One dinner-size take-out order of kung pao chicken (chicken and peanuts in hot pepper sauce) has 76 grams of fat—more than the 60 or so grams the average person should eat in an entire day. *Self-defense:* Order steamed or stir-fried vegetables or Szechuan shrimp—they contain one-fourth the fat of kung pao chicken. Eat a cup of rice for each cup of entrée...mix entrées with steamed vegetables...before eating, lift individual food pieces onto the rice, leaving behind excess sauce, egg and nuts. Then eat directly from the rice bowl.

Source: Jayne Hurley, RD, associate nutritionist, Center for Science in the Public Interest, Washington, DC. She is coauthor of a study of Chinese food published in *Nutrition Action Healthletter,* 1875 Connecticut Ave. NW, Washington, DC 20009.

Your Grandmother Was Right

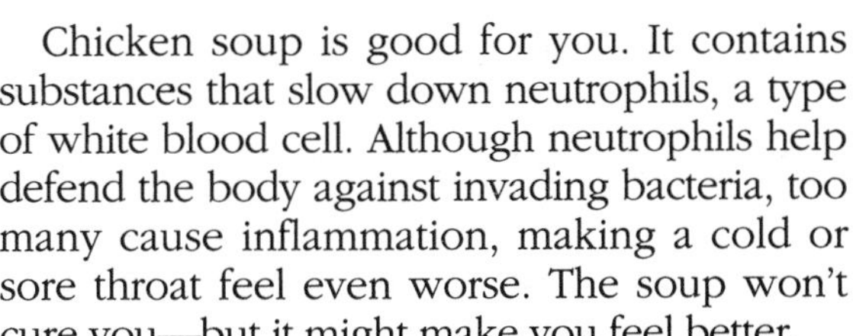

Chicken soup is good for you. It contains substances that slow down neutrophils, a type of white blood cell. Although neutrophils help defend the body against invading bacteria, too many cause inflammation, making a cold or sore throat feel even worse. The soup won't cure you—but it might make you feel better.

Source: Stephen Rennard, MD, chief of pulmonary and critical-care medicine, University of Nebraska Medical Center, Omaha. His study of chicken soup was presented at a meeting of the American Thoracic Society and reported in *New Choices,* 28 W. 23 St., New York 10010.

How to De-Fat Your Favorite Recipes

Choosing low-fat prepared foods in the supermarket is as easy as reading labels. Preparing a heart healthy meal from scratch, however, is an entirely different matter.

If you'd like to reduce the fat content of your favorite recipes, remember the three r's—reduce, remove and replace.

- Reduce fat by spraying pots with a thin film of cooking oil instead of dumping in a tablespoon of oil...or use nonstick cookware, for which no oil is needed.
- Remove skin from poultry and all visible fat from meat.
- Replace...

...whole milk or cream with skim milk, evaporated skim milk, low-fat yogurt or homemade mock sour cream (made with eight parts cottage cheese, one part skim milk and lemon juice to taste).

...regular cream cheese with light cream cheese or homemade mock cream cheese (made with two parts each of ricotta cheese and dry-curd cottage cheese and one part low-fat yogurt).

...high-fat cheeses with skim, reduced-fat or light varieties of American, Swiss, mozzarella or Monterey Jack cheese.

...bacon with Canadian bacon or lean ham.

...one whole egg with two egg whites...or ¼ cup egg substitute...or one egg white combined with one teaspoon of vegetable oil.

...one ounce of baking chocolate with a mixture of three tablespoons of powdered cocoa and one tablespoon of vegetable oil.

...sour cream with plain low-fat yogurt or reduced-fat sour cream.

...oil for sautéing or in sauces with beef, chicken or vegetable broth.

Source: Linda Hachfeld, MPH, RD, a registered dietitian in Mankato, Minnesota. She is the author of *Cooking a la Heart,* Appletree Press, 151 Good Counsel Dr., Suite 125, Mankato, Minnesota 56001.

Sweets Trap

Candy, soda and other sweets, if consumed in large quantities over time, can contribute to high triglyceride levels, a risk factor for heart disease. *Problem:* Most sweet snacks contain large amounts of sucrose, a simple sugar that is converted to triglyceride in the blood. In an average daily diet of 2,000 calories, no more than 200 should come from simple sugars. In a typical chocolate bar, 108 of the 254 calories are from simple sugar. Normal triglyceride levels run from 40 to 250 milligrams per deciliter of blood. Levels above 500 are considered high. Consult your physician if you are unsure of your triglyceride level.

Source: Steven Zeisel, MD, PhD, chairman, nutrition department, University of North Carolina, Chapel Hill.

Lean Cuisines

You can stay on your diet even while dining at your favorite restaurants. *Here's how to order to avoid excess fat, sugar, cholesterol or salt:*

• Italian: Pasta dishes with marinara (meatless) sauce. Baked or broiled chicken or veal. Pizza with mushrooms, bell peppers, and tomatoes (but ask them to go light on the cheese). Minestrone.

• French: Grilled swordfish. Chicken breast with wild mushrooms. Steamed vegetable plate. Salade nicoise (with dressing on the side). Poached salmon. Raspberries.

• Mexican: Chicken taco in a steamed corn tortilla. Tostadas (light on the avocado, sour cream on the side). Red snapper Vera Cruz. Avoid fried rice or beans.

• Chinese: Broccoli, scallops, and mushrooms sautéed with ginger and garlic. Stir-fried bean curd or chicken. Steamed fish and rice. Ask for preparation without MSG or soy sauce.

Source: Dr. Cleaves Bennett, author of *Control Your High Blood Pressure Without Drugs,* and Chris Newport, a Paris-trained nutritionist and chef, cited in *Los Angeles.*

The Healthy Gourmet

• Cut fat in your favorite recipes by 25% to 50%. *Example:* If the recipe suggests one cup of oil, try ¾ cup. If that works, try ⅔ cup the next time. In many casseroles and soups try eliminating butter or margarine completely.

• Instead of sautéing vegetables in oil or butter, add several tablespoonfuls of water or broth and steam them in a covered pot.

• Compensate for lost fat flavor by adding spices and herbs.

• Use skim or low-fat milk instead of whole milk...evaporated skim milk instead of cream.

• In sauces that call for cheese, stick to grated Parmesan or Romano (about 25 calories per tablespoonful).

• Rather than starting sauces with a fatty "roux," add cold milk or fruit juice to the flour or cornstarch.

• Substitute veal, skinless poultry, or flank or round steak for fat-marbled cuts of beef.

• Slice meats thinly and add more vegetables to the meal.

Source: *Tufts University Diet & Nutrition Letter,* NY.

How to Reduce the Fat in Your Food

• Sauté vegetables in a few tablespoonfuls of soup stock rather than in fat.

• Sauté and fry foods less often. Steam, broil, bake, and poach instead.

• For salads and cooking, use corn, safflower or olive oil—sparingly.

• Substitute egg whites or tofu for egg yolks.

• Use low-fat yogurt instead of sour cream or mayonnaise.

• Try low-fat cheeses such as part-skim mozzarella in recipes.

• Use ground turkey or crumbled tofu in place of ground beef.

• Thicken cream-style corn with a mashed potato or uncooked oatmeal.

• Replace nut butters with bean spread for sandwiches and snack dips.

Source: *Medical Self-Care,* Inverness, CA.

All Calories Aren't Equal

Dieters myth: A calorie is a calorie is a calorie. *Reality:* Fat calories are more fattening than carbohydrate calories. A single fat calorie has a greater chance of being converted into body fat than a single carbohydrate calorie.

• *Reason:* The body burns up 25 of every 100 carbohydrate calories converting them into fat—net gain, 75 calories. But it burns up only 3 calories of every 100 fat calories—net gain, 97 calories.

Source: Dr. Jean-Pierre Flatt, of the University of Massachusetts Medical School.

How to Read Nutrition Labels

Cutting down on cholesterol, sugar and salt requires a close reading of nutritional labels.

A simplified guide to understanding the fine print:

• *Ingredients:* They are listed in descending order, according to their weight.

• *Sugar:* Whether it's called sugar, dextrose, sucrose, corn sweetener, corn syrup, invert sugar, honey, or molasses, the food has little nutritive value if it's among the first three ingredients. When listed as a minor ingredient, a combination of two or more sugars may mean a hefty sugar count.

• *Cholesterol:* Avoid coconut and palm oil. They are more saturated than animal fats. Non-specified vegetable oils frequently mean palm or coconut. When purchasing margarine, choose the brand with liquid vegetable oil as the primary ingredient. It contains less saturated fat.

• *Salt:* While sodium levels are not shown on many ingredient lists, look for brands that list sodium by milligrams. *Rule of thumb:* No one should consume much over 4,000 milligrams of sodium daily. Those on restricted diets should have considerably less than that amount.

8 Ounces of Milk

Types of milk vary in taste, fat content and nutritional value. *Here's the breakdown:*

• *Buttermilk:* 90 calories, two grams of fat. Easily digested, since active bacteria break down the milk sugars.

• *Dry nonfat milk:* 80 calories, less than one gram of fat. As nutritious as whole milk, but with a flat taste.

• *Low-fat (2%) milk:* 120 to 140 calories, five grams of fat. A good choice when fat restriction is important but calories are secondary.

• *Skim (nonfat) milk:* 80 calories, less than one gram of fat. Best for dieters and those on a strict low-fat diet.

• *Whole milk:* 150 to 180 calories, eight grams of fat. Best only for children under two years old.

Source: *Berkeley Wellness Letter,* published by the University of California, Des Moines, IA.

How to Get Along Without Cream And Mayonnaise

Fat is the enemy of both the heart and the waistline. Learn to substitute yogurt and other low-fat milk products. They are tasty as well as healthy.

Yogurt...

• Thicken commercial yogurt. Line a sieve with a paper coffee filter and place it over a bowl. Pour in the yogurt and let it drain until it is the consistency you want...that of light, heavy or sour cream.

• Use the drained yogurt as a base for any dip that originally called for sour cream. (If the yogurt seems too thick, beat a little of the drained whey back into it.)

• In cooking or baking, replace each cup of cream or sour cream with ¾ cup of drained yogurt mixed with 1 tablespoonful of cornstarch. The yogurt should be at room temperature.

•In dishes such as beef Stroganoff, where the yogurt-cornstarch mixture replaces sour cream, fold it gently into the beef at the last minute...and let it just heat through.

Basic Recipes...

•*Light mayonnaise:* Mix ⅓ cup thickened yogurt into ⅔ cup mayonnaise.

•*Light salad dressing:* Mix ⅔ cup slightly thickened yogurt into ⅓ cup mayonnaise.

•*Mock sour cream dressing*:* Mix 1 cup drained low-fat yogurt with 2 tablespoonfuls of wine vinegar. Add a dash of sugar (or substitute), a bit of garlic powder, and ¼ cup vegetable oil. Mix and chill.

Other good substitutions...

•Replace the cream in cream soups with buttermilk, which is satisfyingly rich, yet low in calories. To eliminate any hint of buttermilk's slightly acidic taste, add a liberal amount of mild curry powder.

•Mix 1 cup skim milk with ½ cup dry skim milk. Add to soup to thicken it. This works with all cream soups, including vichyssoise.

**The Low-Cholesterol Food Processor Cookbook* by Suzanne S. Jones, Doubleday, Garden City, NY.

Just When You Thought It Was Safe to Eat Salt...

The vast majority of foods sold in stores are laden with salt. Since we've eaten these foods for most of our lives, we're conditioned to expect the taste of heavily salted foods.

To cut down on salt intake:

•Reduce salt gradually. When people are abruptly placed on a very low-sodium diet, they develop cravings for salt that cause them to revert to their former eating habits. But a gradual reduction of salt will change your taste for salt...so much so that food salted to its previous level will taste unpleasant. *Time:* Allow up to three months to adjust to a salt-free diet.

•Keep daily records of the amount of sodium you eat. This is now relatively easy because federal law requires most grocery store foods to be labeled for sodium content. A pocket calculator is sometimes useful as you shop, but don't think you'll have to keep count for the rest of your life. After a couple of months, separating high- from low-sodium foods will be almost automatic.

•Substitute other flavor enhancers, especially herbs and spices.

•If you have children, start now to condition their taste by not feeding them salty foods. For the first time, low-sodium baby food is now on the market.

Source: Dr. Cleaves M. Bennett, clinical professor, University of California at Los Angeles, and author of *Control Your High Blood Pressure Without Drugs,* Doubleday, New York.

Tasty, Low-Salt, Low-Fat Cooking

If your doctor puts you on a no-salt, modified fat, cholesterol and sugar diet, with limited alcohol consumption, you might feel as though you're in a gastronomic straitjacket. However, the benefits are enormous—no more edema, a reduction in blood pressure, considerable weight loss and a feeling of well-being—and you can increase your food intake without increasing your weight.

Basics of the diet...

Do use:

•Low-sodium cheeses.

•Seltzer.

•Trimmed meat.

•Stews and pan drippings skimmed of all fat.

•Fish, poultry without skin, veal and lamb.

Don't use:

•Eggs, except those used in food preparation.

•Sugar. Drinks made with sweet liqueurs. Soft drinks.

•Canned or packaged foods.

•Sodas with high salt content.

•Rich and/or salty products—bacon, gravies, shellfish, organ meats, most desserts except fruit and fruit ices.

Tricks to fool the taste...

•The sweet-and-sour principle. A touch (sometimes as little as half a teaspoonful) of sugar and a dash of vinegar can add the sweet-and-sour flavor needed to fool the palate.

•Garlic. Essential in salad dressings and tomato sauces. Use it with rosemary to transform broiled chicken, broiled fish or roast lamb.

•Fine or coarse black pepper. When broiling and roasting meats and chicken, use as much as a tablespoonful for a welcome flavor. Use a moderate amount in soups, stews and casseroles (the pungent nature of pepper will not diminish in these as it will with broiling and roasting).

•Crushed hot red pepper flakes. A good flavor distraction or flavor addition. Not for every palate.

•Curry powder. Use judiciously and without a large number of other spices. Combine it only with a bay leaf, green pepper, garlic or black pepper. Add smaller amounts for rice, more for poultry or meat.

•Chili powder. Similar to curry, but you might want to add more cumin, oregano or garlic. Also try paprika, ground coriander, ground hot chilis. They're good with almost any dish made with tomatoes.

•Homemade hot-mustard paste. Dry mustard and water does wonders for salad dressing and grilled foods.

•Freshly grated horseradish. Goes well with fish or plain yogurt.

•Bottled green peppercorns. A welcome touch for bland foods.

•Plain boiled or steamed rice, cold yogurt relish, chutneys and other sweet relishes are a good foil for spicy dishes.

Cooking techniques...

•Charcoal broiling helps compensate for lack of salt.

•Steaming is preferable for fish and better than boiling for vegetables.

•No-salt soups are difficult to make palatable. *Solution:* A stockpot going on the back of the stove, to which you add bones, cooking liquid, vegetables. The more concentrated the broth, the greater the depth of flavor. Use only the freshest, ripest vegetables.

Source: Craig Claiborne, food critic.

"Good" Foods that Can Be Bad for You

•Blood-sugar-sensitive types who experience a temporary lift from sugar followed by fatigue should be cautious about fruit juice intake. Six ounces of apple juice contain the equivalent of more than five teaspoonfuls of sugar—40% more sugar than a chocolate bar. *Recommended:* Eat a whole apple or orange instead of drinking juice. The fiber dilutes the sugar impact. *Alternative:* Eat cheese, nuts or other protein with juice.

•Nondairy cream substitutes, often used by those on low-fat diets, usually contain coconut oil, which has a higher fat content than most dairy products.

•Decaffeinated coffee can lead to significant stomach acid secretion, causing heartburn and indigestion in many persons. Caffeine was assumed to be the culprit. A new study shows that decaffeinated coffee is even worse. The effect is seen in doses as small as a half cup of decaffeinated coffee. People experiencing ulcer symptoms, heartburn and dyspepsia should avoid decaffeinated as well as regular coffee.

•Most commercial products billed as alternatives to salt are based on potassium chloride. *Problem:* Although potassium chloride does enhance flavor, it leaves a slightly bitter or metallic taste. And excessive potassium may be as bad for your health as too much salt. *Alternatives to the alternatives:* Mrs. Dash, a commercial blend of 14 herbs and spices; Lite Salt, a half-sodium, half-potassium blend. Or try adding parsley.

•One of the few proven substances that can bring on flare-ups of acne is iodine. Excessive, long-term intake of iodine (a natural ingredient of many foods) can bring on acne in anyone, but for people who are already prone to the condition, iodine is especially damaging. Excess is excreted through the oil glands of the skin, a process that irritates the pores and causes eruptions and inflammation. *Major sources of iodine in the diet:* Iodized table salt, kelp, beef liver, asparagus, turkey, and vitamin and mineral supplements.

•Chronic diarrhea, gas and other stomach complaints are often linked to lactose intolerance, the inability to digest milk. One of every four adults suffers from this problem. Their bodies don't make enough lactase, the enzyme that breaks down milk sugar in the intestinal tract. *Among the offending foods:* Milk, ice cream, chocolate, soft cheese, some yogurts, and sherbet. Lactose is also used as a filler in gum, candies and many canned goods.

• People on low-sodium diets should check out tap water as a source of salt intake. Some local water systems have eight times the amount of sodium (20 milligrams per quart) that people with heart problems or hypertension should use.

• Health-food candy is really no better for you than traditional sweets. *Comparison:* Health-food candy often contains about the same number of calories. The fat content is often as high or higher. Bars made of carob are caffeine free, but the amount of caffeine in chocolate is negligible. And the natural sugars in health bars have no nutritional advantage over refined sugars.

Sources: *Journal of the American Medical Association,* Chicago; *Dr. Fulton's Step-By-Step Program for Clearing Acne,* by J. E. Fulton, Jr., MD, and E. Black, Harper & Row, New York; *The Sodium Content of Your Food,* Consumer Information Center, Co.

Best Whole-Grain Breakfast Cereals

Whole-grained breakfast cereals are a rich source of protein, vitamins, minerals and fiber. *Bonus:* They have relatively low percentages of cholesterol, fat and calories. *Added bonus:* Often the cheapest cereals are the best nutritionally.

What to look for:

• Cereals in which the first listed ingredient is a whole grain—whole-grain wheat, oats (rolled or flour), whole corn kernels or bran.

• Cereals with three or more grams of protein per serving.

• Avoid cereals with sugar or other sweeteners (honey, corn syrup, fructose) as a main ingredient. *Guide:* Four grams of sugar equals one teaspoonful.

• *Also avoid:* Cereals with dried fruits. They are concentrated sources of sugar. *Better:* Add your own fruits.

Drugs vs. Nutrition

Don't overlook the interaction of medication and nutrition.

• Chronic aspirin users can suffer microscopic bleeding of the gastrointestinal tract, a condition that also causes loss of iron. Aspirin can also increase requirements for vitamin C and folic acid.

• Laxatives may deplete vitamin D.

• Antacids can lead to a phosphate deficiency.

• Diuretics prescribed for hypertension can promote the loss of potassium.

• In all these cases, vitamin and mineral supplements may be the solution.

Avoiding the Lure Of Megavitamins

When it comes to vitamins, the old advice is still the best: There is no reason to take more than the recommended dietary allowance (RDA) of any vitamin, except for relatively rare individuals who cannot absorb or utilize vitamins adequately. If you want nutrition "insurance," take a regular multivitamin capsule containing only the RDA of vitamins.

A megadose is 10 or more times the RDA. This is the level at which toxic effects begin to show up in adults.

Some of the medical problems adults may experience as a result of prolonged, excessive intake are:

• Vitamin A. Dry, cracked skin. Severe headaches. Severe loss of appetite. Irritability. Bone and joint pains. Menstrual difficulties. Enlarged liver and spleen.

•Vitamin D. Loss of appetite. Excessive urination. Nausea and weakness. Weight loss. Hypertension. Anemia. Irreversible kidney failure that can lead to death.

•Vitamin E. Research on E's toxic effects is sketchy, but the findings suggest some problems: Headaches, nausea, fatigue and giddiness, blurred vision, chapped lips and mouth inflammation, low blood sugar, increased tendency to bleed, and reduced sexual function. Ironically, one of the claims of vitamin E proponents is that it heightens sexual potency.

•The B vitamins. Each B has its own characteristics and problems. Too much B-6 can lead to liver damage. Too much B-1 can destroy B-12.

•Vitamin C. Kidney problems and diarrhea. Adverse effects on growing bones. Rebound scurvy (a condition that can occur when a person taking large doses suddenly stops). Symptoms are swollen, bleeding gums, loosening of teeth, roughening of skin, muscle pain.

Vitamin C is the vitamin most often used to excess. Some of the symptoms of toxic effect from Vitamin C megadoses:

•Menstrual bleeding in pregnant women and various problems for their newborn infants.

•Destruction of Vitamin B-12, to the point that B-12 deficiency may become a problem.

•False negative test for blood in stool, which can prevent diagnosis of colon cancer.

•False urine test for sugar, which can spell trouble for diabetics.

•An increase in the uric acid level and the precipitation of gout in individuals predisposed to the ailment.

Source: Dr. Victor Herbert, author of *Nutrition Cultism: Facts and Fictions,* George F. Stickley Co., Philadelphia.

Candy Bar Myth

Many people think that candy bars are a good "quick energy" source. Not true, in reality, the high amount of fat in chocolate slows absorption of the candy bar. The tired person looking for a pick-me-up should opt for fruit or a bagel.

Source: Bonnie Liebman, director of nutrition, Center for Science in the Public Interest, Washington, DC.

Foods that Can Give You a Headache

MSG is not the only culprit. Look out for tyramine-containing foods like:

•Aged cheese.
•Chicken livers.
•Chocolate.
•Pickled herring.
•Beer.
•Champagne.
•Red wine.
•Sherry.
•Ice cream. A brief, but intense pain in the throat, head or face sometimes results from biting into ice cream. The pain is a physiological response of the warm tissues of the mouth to the sudden cold. The pain is sometimes felt throughout the head because cranial nerve branches in the area spread the pain impulse along a broad path. *Prevention:* Allow small amounts of ice cream to melt in the mouth before eating successive large bites.

Sources: Joel R. Saper, MD, and Kenneth R. Magee MD, coauthors of *Freedom from Headaches.*

Lower Cholesterol Naturally

Corn bran lowers cholesterol naturally. Men with high cholesterol who supplemented their low-fat diet with 20 grams of corn per day bran saw sharp decreases in their levels of total cholesterol, triglycerides and very low-density lipoproteins (VLDL). Levels of LDL and HDL did not change significantly.

Source: Jan M. Shane, PhD, RD, associate professor of human nutrition, Illinois State University, Normal.

Nondairy Creamer Warning

Nondairy creamers are often made of coconut or palm oil, which are high in saturated fat. They contain at least as many calories as light cream. *Better choice:* Milk with 1% or 0.5% fat. It has a similar consistency and flavor as half-and-half...but only a fraction of the fat.

Source: Kim Galeaz, RD, American Dietetic Association, 216 W. Jackson Blvd., Suite 800, Chicago 60606.

The Truth About Carnitine Supplements

Carnitine supplements marketed as "fat burners" and "energy enhancers" do *not* enhance athletic performance. These amino acid supplements—increasingly popular in recent years—had been thought to boost stamina and promote weight loss. *Reality:* A recent study found that even high doses of the supplements had no effect on performance.

Source: Matthew Vukovich, PhD, assistant professor of exercise science, Wichita State University, Wichita, Kansas.

21

Fitness

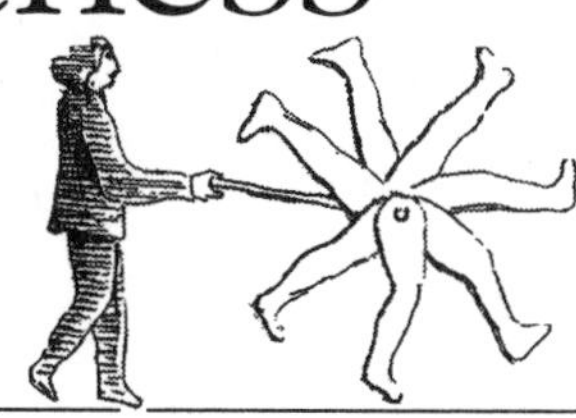

Vitamins and Workouts

Supplements of vitamins C and E significantly reduce muscle damage that can occur during heavy physical training.

Result: Athletes taking vitamin supplements can potentially train longer and harder—and recover faster—than athletes who do not use the supplements. *Unexpected bonus:* The vitamin supplements also helped keep male athletes' testosterone levels—and sex drives—at normal levels.

Source: Research led by Ian Gilliam, lecturer, Phillip Institute of Technology, Canberra, Australia, reported in *The Medical Post,* 777 Bay St., Toronto, Ontario M5W 1A7.

Headphones and Jogging Danger

Noise triggers a release of adrenaline, which constricts the blood supply to the ears and diverts it to the arms, legs, and heart. Aerobic exercise also diverts blood from the ears to those muscles. *Result:* The one-two punch of loud music and less blood destroys cilia in the ear canal...doubling risk of hearing loss.

Source: Audiologist Richard Navarro, PhD, quoted in *Men's Health Advisor 1992,* edited by Michael Lafavore, editor, *Men's Health* magazine, 33 E. Minor St., Emmaus, Pennsylvania 18098.

Walking vs. Running

Running and walking are equally effective forms of exercise. Both improve your muscle tone and cardiovascular system...and help you burn calories. *Advantages of walking:* Easier on joints...better for those starting a fitness program—especially older or overweight people.

Advantage of running: Provides a better cardiovascular workout for those already fit.

Caution: If you have a family history of heart disease or have been inactive, ask your doctor before starting to run.

Source: Mark Anderson, PhD, PT, ATC, professor of physical therapy at the University of Oklahoma Health Sciences Center.

Benefits of Exercise

Once-a-week exercise lowers the risk of adult-onset (type II) diabetes by as much as 23%. *Furthermore:* Vigorous exercise from two to four times a week reduces a person's risk of developing diabetes by 38%...at five times or more per week, the risk is cut by 42%.

Danger of inactivity: Lack of exercise contributes to as many as one of four cases of type II diabetes.

Source: Study of more than 21,000 male physicians, aged 40 to 84, reported in *The Johns Hopkins Medical Letter, Health After 50,* 5 Water Oak, Fernandina Beach, Florida 32034.

Better Jogging

Rest one or two days a week for a balanced training program. The body must have time to replenish the *glycogen* (blood sugar) lost during training. Weak muscles—drained of energy—are more prone to injuries. If trained hard without resting, the body cannot regenerate the muscle filaments, which can cause damage in the long term.

Source: David L. Costill, PhD, director, Human Performance Laboratory, Ball State University, Muncie, Indiana, writing in *Runner's World,* 33 E. Minor St., Emmaus, Pennsylvania 18098.

Healthy Walking

Brisk walks strengthen your immune system—but too-strenuous workouts can lower immunity to colds and flu. Exercising near your maximum capacity for just 45 minutes—or more—produces a six-hour "window" of vulnerability afterward. *Better:* Exercise at a moderate level—the equivalent of a brisk walk —if not training for competition.

Source: David Nieman, DrPH, professor of health, department of health and exercise science, Appalachian State University, Boone, North Carolina.

The Best Exercise Videos

Exercise videotapes are not all alike. A videotape that one person finds highly motivating may prove discouraging—even dangerous—to another.

For a safe and satisfying workout, match the tape to your specific needs*...

- Best for beginning exercisers: *Jingo,* by Debbie and Carlos Rosas. This easy-to-follow video blends non-impact aerobics—no jumping—with elements drawn from dance and martial arts. 60 minutes.

Available from Niawave, Box 712, Portland, Oregon 97207.

- Best for dancers: *The Hip Hop Solution,* by Victoria Jackson. This innovative video affords a good workout and teaches dance steps made famous by pop musicians. 30 minutes.
- Best for "step" enthusiasts: *Step Aerobic and Abdominal Workout,* by Jane Fonda. By far, the best video for users of the popular "step" apparatus. No tricky choreography, just a high-intensity workout. 57 minutes.
- Best for die-hard exercisers: *Firm Arms and Abs* and *Lean Legs and Buns,* both by Karen Voight. Demanding videos for already-fit people who want to boost muscle tone. Users must provide their own dumbbells, ankle weights and weight-lifting bench. 47 minutes/51 minutes.
- Best for stress relief: *Yogarobics,* by Larry Lane. Blends gentle exercise with soothing relaxation techniques. 53 minutes.
- Best for overweight people: *Sweatin' to the Oldies,* by Richard Simmons. The first of a four-tape series, this is a fast-paced, effective weight-

*Unless otherwise noted, all videotapes are available through videotape stores. A good mail-order source for exercise tapes is Collage Video Specialties, 5390 Main St. NE, Minneapolis 55421. 800-433-6769.

loss program presented with humor, compassion and—most important—a high-energy band playing hit songs. 43 minutes.

•Best for pregnant women: *Pregnancy Program*, by Kathy Smith. Safe workouts for all stages of pregnancy and the postpartum period. Mixes low-impact aerobics with exercises for flexibility and good posture. 95 minutes.

•Best for kids: *Hip Hop Animal Rock*, by Gilda Marx. Uses animated animals to teach kids proper exercise techniques. Suitable for ages five through 12. 30 minutes.

•Best for persons over age 50: *Positive Moves*, by Angela Lansbury. Great motivation plus gentle strength and stretching exercises from the famous actress. Also includes general tips for active living and recipes. 46 minutes.

•Best for back pain sufferers: *Back Health*, by Joanie Greggains. Pain-free routine for toning muscles in the back, buttocks and legs. Includes tips on pain prevention. 38 minutes.

•Best for disabled people: Exercise tapes for paraplegics, quadriplegics, amputees and persons with cerebral palsy are available from Disabled Sports USA, Rockville, Maryland. 301-217-0960. 30 minutes each.

Source: Peg Jordan, RN, author of several books on fitness and editor-in-chief of *American Fitness*, 15250 Ventura Blvd., Sherman Oaks, California 91403.

Mistakes Hikers Make And How to Avoid Them

When it's done right, hiking is a serene, soul-warming pursuit—an opportunity to see nature with fresh eyes and to rediscover the joy of one's own company.

When it's done wrong, however, hiking can be miserable, frustrating, painful...even injurious.

What makes the difference is preparation, equipment, trail smarts and common sense.

You don't need a vast amount of technical knowledge, equipment or experience to enjoy hiking. *But you do need to avoid these common errors:*

•*Mistake:* Buying equipment without doing your homework. Not all packs, sleeping bags, boots, tents and stoves are created equal. For reliable product reviews, check the annual spring ratings issue of *Backpacker* magazine.

•*Mistake:* Hitting the trail without a dress rehearsal. Lace up and load up before you take your first hike.

Load your pack, then adjust the straps and belts for a comfortable fit. Find uneven terrain where you can test your pack and boots. A paved road, no matter how steeply inclined, will not tell you what you need to know.

•*Mistake:* Buying unsuitable boots. For most beginners, lightweight fabric boots are preferable to leather ones.

The fabric boots (which are comparable to tough nylon sneakers) are more comfortable, and don't require a break-in period. They also have less negative impact on the trail, since they don't drag so much soil.

Leather boots, however, are more durable and provide more support, and are more sensible for cold-weather hiking.

To buy the right size: Try the boots on while you are wearing two thick pairs of socks. *Reason:* When hiking, your feet will swell by a half-size...and the extra pair of socks simulates that.

•*Mistake:* Using inadequate blister prevention. Hikers are most likely to develop blisters from boot-rub on their heels.

Prevention: If you are prone to getting blisters on a specific part of your foot, put a piece of moleskin on it prior to hiking. Carry some moleskin with you.

•*Mistake:* Carrying too much weight. Beginners should limit themselves to a maximum of 25% of their body weight. That means a 160-pound hiker should pack no more than 40 pounds.

To lighten your load: Buy a nylon mummy sleeping bag, rather than a heavier cotton bag. Carry food that is boxed or bagged rather than canned.

•*Mistake:* Packing unnecessary items. You won't have any need for a hatchet or bowie knife (a pocket knife will serve as well)...an oversized, high-powered flashlight (keep it small)

...or several changes of clothes (one change should suffice for any hike up to 10 days).

• *Mistake:* Hiking in too large a group. Large groups damage the trail ecologically. *Best:* No more than eight people.

• *Mistake:* Backtracking needlessly. Many hikers dislike covering the same ground twice to get back to their car.

Solution: Split your group into two parties. Drop one party off at one end of the hike, then park the car at the other end. The car key is exchanged when the two parties pass on the trail. *Note:* This method also works with two cars...the parties trade keys when they pass.

• *Mistake:* Failing to limber up. By investing a few minutes in stretching your hamstrings, calves, feet, shoulders and back muscles, you can do much to avoid muscle strains down the trail.

• *Mistake:* Moving too fast. Most hikers will be comfortable with an average pace of two miles per hour.

At three miles per hour (the pace favored by some hiking clubs), many hikers will experience premature fatigue. They will also risk a wide range of injuries, from blisters and sore feet to knee problems and sprained ankles.

• *Mistake:* Competing within your group. A hike should be a cooperative venture. To keep the group together, set the pace by your slowest member. You may also need to shift some heavy gear from someone who's lagging to someone who's shooting far ahead.

• *Mistake:* Forgetting to rest enough. I recommend a 10-minute rest every hour, and a break of 30 to 60 minutes every three hours. There is no absolute formula...when you are tired, stop.

• *Mistake:* Being inflexible. Always consider the possibility that you may not reach your goals. Someone in your party might get hurt...bad weather might slow you down. Plan a bail-out route or a shorter schedule—just in case.

Source: Cindy Ross, a contributing editor to *Backpacker* magazine, and the author of *A Woman's Journey on the Appalachian Trail,* Appalachian Trail Conference, Box 807, Harper's Ferry, West Virginia 25425, and *Journey on the Crest: Walking 2600 Miles from Mexico to Canada,* The Mountaineers, 306 Second Ave. W., Seattle 98119.

Better Pre-Race Warm-Up

Arrive early enough to prepare yourself mentally for the task ahead...jog easily for about a half hour or so, using visual imagery to picture yourself running the race you've planned... leave time to stretch and make one last bathroom stop...stay active after your warm-up jog to keep your heart rate up...about five minutes before the gun, take six to eight short runs of about 100 yards each, gradually working your way up to just under race pace.

Source: *Running & FitNews,* 4405 East-West Hwy., Suite 405, Bethesda, Maryland 20814.

Bike Smarts

Maintain the right tire pressure...lubricate the chain frequently...rotate tires every 1,000 miles ...always carry a spare tube when planning to ride in the rain—flats happen more often in bad weather, when patches are hard to apply. *Useful:* Write your name, address and phone number on a piece of masking tape, and stick it to the fork's steerer tube—so that if the bike is stolen, you have a better chance of getting it back.

Source: *600 Tips for Better Bicycling,* by the editors of *Bicycling.* Rodale Press, 33 E. Minor St., Emmaus, Pennsylvania 18098.

High-Top Hoopla

High-top athletic shoes offer no more protection against ankle sprains than low-tops. *Survey:* 600 college basketball players were given either low-tops, standard high-tops or high-tops with inflatable air chambers. Of the 15 sprains that occurred during one season, seven were in players wearing standard high-tops, four in players wearing low-tops and four in players wearing inflatable high-tops.

Source: Jeffrey L. Tanji, MD, family physician and a researcher at the University of California, Davis, School of Medicine. His survey was published in the *American Journal of Sports Medicine,* 230 Calvary St., Waltham, Massachusetts 02154.

Safer Hiking

Hiking fans—take along a first-aid kit containing topical antibiotics and 1% hydrocortisone cream...bandages, gauze dressing and athletic tape...saline eye irrigators...sunblock for skin and lips...pain reliever...decongestant...antacid ...diarrhea medication. *Recent survey:* Illness or injury affected 82% of people who backpacked along the Appalachian Trail.

Source: David Josephs, MD, practicing physician, Indian Health Service, Crownpoint, New Mexico. His study of 180 backpackers was published in *The Journal of Family Practice,* 25 Van Zant St., Norwalk, Connecticut 06856.

How to Stay Fit While You Sit

Exercises to do at your desk to keep mentally alert, tone sagging muscles and relieve muscle strain:

- Tummy slimmer. Sit erect, hands on knees. Exhale, pulling abdominal muscles in as far as possible. Relax. Inhale. Exhale as you draw in stomach again. Repeat 10 to 20 times.
- Head circles. Drop head forward, chin on chest, shoulders relaxed. Slowly move head in large circle. Reverse direction. Do 5 to 6 times each side.
- Torso twist. Raise elbows to shoulder level. Slowly twist around as far right as possible, then reverse. Do 10 to 12 turns each way.
- Heel and toe lift. Lean forward, hands on knees. Lift both heels off floor, strongly contracting calf muscles. Lower heels, lift toes high toward shins. Do 10 to 15 complete movements.

Source: Doug MacLennon, The Fitness Institute, Willowdale, Ontario.

Exercising When You Don't Have Time

- While you talk on the phone, do leg raises, arm exercises or isometrics.
- Park your car far from the building and walk.
- Do things the hard way (walk the long way to the office, take six trips carrying things upstairs instead of saving items for one trip, shovel snow instead of using the snow blower).
- Exercise while watching TV (run in place, skip rope, use an exercise machine or do yoga, isometrics or toe-touching).

Source: Stephanie Bernardo, author of *The Ultimate Checklist,* Doubleday, New York.

Moving Gradually into A Fitness Program

- Before launching any fitness program, have a complete physical examination, including an electrocardiogram. Your doctor should schedule a stress test to check on the heart's capacity.
- Don't let your new enthusiasm for getting fit make you too competitive. If you try to get back to the level of achievement you reached as a college athlete, you risk severe injury to ankles, knees, and hips.
- Don't jump into a racquet sport or a basketball league. Instead, prepare your body with a six-month program of walking, stretching and perhaps light jogging and weight training.
- Choose a sport you like as a primary activity and a complementary activity to go along with it. A swimmer might walk or jog two days a week. A runner could work with weights.

Source: Everett L. Smith, director of the Biogerontology Laboratory, Department of Preventive Medicine, University of Wisconsin, Madison.

Working Up to Rigorous Exercise

It takes middle-aged men and women six months of regular exercise (fast walking, light jogging, weight training, etc.) to work up to rigorous exercise. Even then, they should move gradually into each workout. *The steps to follow:*

- Walk or jog in place for two or three minutes.
- Do 10 minutes of stretching.

•When you move into your sport, take the first five minutes at a slow pace (a relaxed volley in tennis, for example) until you break into a light sweat.

•For the first few months, aim for 40% to 60% of your maximum heart rate. After six months, go for 70%. After nine months, shoot for 85%.*

•Take 10 minutes to cool down with slow jogging and more stretching.

•Recognize when you've done too much (if it aches to take a step the next day).

*To calculate these goals, subtract your resting heart rate from your maximum rate—220 minus your age—and multiply by the desired percentage. Then add your resting rate to get your goal. *Example:* A 45-year-old man has a maximum heart rate of 175 and a resting rate of 60. To perform at 70% of maximum, he should reach a rate of 140.

Source: Everett L. Smith, director of the Biogerontology Laboratory, Department of Preventive Medicine, University of Wisconsin, Madison.

Swimming: The Best Exercise of All

Swimming helps the entire musculature of the body, particularly the upper torso. It tones muscles (but does not build them). *Greatest benefit:* To the cardiovascular system.

•*Best strokes for a workout:* Crawl, butterfly, and back strokes are the most strenuous.

•*Less taxing:* The side, breast, and elementary breast strokes.

•The elementary back stroke is best for survival. The face is clear of the water for easy breathing, and the limited muscle use saves energy.

•The side stroke is traditional for lifesaving. It can be performed with one arm, which leaves the other free to tow someone. It is very relaxing—and effective.

•*To build up the legs:* Hold a kickboard while swimming. This forces propulsion by the legs alone. Or swim with the flippers favored by divers. Their surface increases the resistance to the water, making the legs work harder.

Source: James Steen, swimming coach at Kenyon College, Gambier, OH.

Aerobic Ratings of Sports

•*Best for cardiovascular fitness:* Stationary bicycling, uphill hiking, ice hockey, rope jumping, rowing, running, and cross-country skiing.

•*Moderately effective:* Basketball, outdoor bicycling, calisthenics, handball, field hockey, racquetball, downhill skiing, soccer, squash, swimming, singles tennis, and walking.

•*Nonaerobic:* Baseball, bowling, football, golf, softball, volleyball.

Source: Dr. Franklin Payne, Jr., Medical College of Georgia, Augusta, GA.

Walk for Good Health

Exercise doesn't have to be strenuous or punishing to be effective. Despite its economy of muscle use, walking is considered by most experts to be one of the best exercises. *Benefits:*

•Preventative and remedy for respiratory, heart, and circulation disorders.

•Weight control. Walking won't take off pounds, but it keeps weight at a desirable level. (Particularly effective in keeping excess pounds from coming back, once they have been dieted off.)

•Aids digestion, elimination, and sleep.

•Antidote to physical and psychological tensions.

Best daily routine:

•Time. Whenever it can be fitted into daily routine. (A mile takes only 20 minutes.) People doing sedentary office work usually average a mile and a half in a normal day. Stretch that by choosing to walk down the hall to a colleague instead of picking up the interoffice phone.

•Place. Wherever it's pleasant and convenient to daily tasks. Walk at least part way to work. If a commuter, walk to the train. Walk, not to the nearest, but to the second or third bus or subway stop from the house. Get off a stop or two from the usual one. Park the car 10 blocks farther away. Walk 10 blocks to and from lunch. Walk after dinner, before sitting down to a book, TV or work.

•Clothes. Comfortable and seasonal, light rather than heavy. Avoid thin-soled shoes when walking city pavements. It may be desirable to use metatarsal pads or cushioned soles. (The impact on concrete weakens metatarsal arches and causes callouses.)

•Length. Walk modest distances at first. In the city, the number of streets tells you how far you've gone. But in the country, you can walk farther than you realize. *Consequences:* Fatigue on the return trip. *Instead:* Use a good pedometer.

•Walking for exercise should feel different from other kinds of walking. Set out at a good pace. Use the longest stride that's comfortable. Let arms swing and muscles stretch. Strike a rhythm and keep to it.

•Don't saunter. It's tiring. Walking at a good pace allows the momentum of each stride to carry over into the next.

•Lengthen the customary stride by swinging the foot a little farther ahead than usual. Lengthening the stride speeds the walking pace and also loosens tense muscles, puts other neglected muscles to work and provides continuous momentum that puts less weight on feet.

•Most comfortable pace: Three miles per hour. It generally suits the average male and is the US Army pace for long hikes. With the right shoes and unconfining clothes, most women will be comfortable at that pace, too.

Source: Aaron Sussman and Ruth Goode, authors of *The Magic of Walking,* Simon and Schuster, New York.

Easy Exercises to Strengthen Your Back

Strengthening the back and stomach muscles is the best protection against a back injury. If you have back trouble, consult your doctor before starting this, or any, exercise program.

•Flexed-knee sit-ups. Lie on your back, with knees bent and arms at your side. Sit up slowly by rolling forward, starting with the head.

•Bent-knee leg lifts. In the same position as the sit-ups, bring one knee as close as you can to your chest, while extending the other leg. Alternate the legs.

•Knee-chest leg lifts. Work from the bent-knee sit-up position, but put a small pillow under your head. Use your hands to bring both knees up to the chest, tighten the stomach muscles and hold that position for a count of 10.

•Back flattening. Lie on your back, flex the knees, and put your arms above your head. Tighten your stomach and buttock muscles and press the lower back hard against the floor. Hold this position for a count of 10, relax and repeat.

•Don't overdo the exercises. Soreness is a sign to cut back.

•Never do these exercises with the legs straight.

Source: *American Journal of Nursing,* New York.

Realities of Exercise Equipment

The sophisticated machinery that has turned old-fashioned gyms into today's health clubs is designed to offer continuous resistance during each of the movement exercises you use it for.

•Using machines is a much faster, more efficient way to build muscle strength than using weights.

•Doing all the exercises for all the muscle groups on a regular basis does not make you perfectly fit.

Strength and fitness are not equivalent. Although muscle strength is a component of fitness, you also need flexibility and heart-lung capacity. Stretching exercises make you flexible, and aerobic exercises such as running and bike riding build up your heart muscle and your lung capacity.

•Strengthening exercises do not turn fat into muscle. It doesn't work that way. People who are overweight need to follow a calorie-restricted diet and do aerobic exercises, which trigger the body to use up fat. Working out on machines only builds up muscle under the fat layer. However, combining a weight-loss program with strengthening exercises can improve body tone as the weight comes off.

•The machines are safe if you learn the proper technique for using each machine, including proper breathing, before you are allowed on the equipment alone. On the Nautilus, for example, all the straps must be secured before you start. If one is broken or missing, don't use the machine. Poor form on the machines can lead to serious injuries. So can using the wrong weight settings.

•*Good rule of thumb:* Use a weight setting that lets you do 8–12 repetitions comfortably. If you must struggle to get beyond five, the setting is too heavy. If you complete 10 without feeling any fatigue at all, it is too light. You will have to experiment with each machine to get the right setting. Then, from time to time, you can adjust the weights upward. But be cautious. Pushing yourself too hard not only invites injury, it also discourages you from sticking to the program on a regular basis.

How to Pick a Stationary Bicycle

A good in-home stationary bicycle should be made from sturdy steel (not lightweight aluminum).

Check that it has:

•A comfortable, adjustable-height seat.

•Smoothly rotating pedals.

•A selector for several degrees of pedal speed and resistance (simulated "uphill" pedaling that makes your heart work harder).

•A heavyweight flywheel, which creates a smoother and more durable drive system.

Sophisticated electronic gadgets, such as "calories-burned" or "workload" meters are frills.

To choose the right cycle: Visit a large sporting goods store and try a variety of models. The one that works you hard and still feels comfortable is right for you.

Source: Eastside Sports Medicine Center, New York.

How to Use a Stationary Bicycle

To ride without pain or injury:

•Check with your doctor, especially if you have any heart, knee, or leg problems.

•Raise the seat on your cycle high enough so that in the downward position your foot just reaches the pedal with your knee slightly bent. This is the proper mechanical position for cycling.

•Always warm up and cool down with your bicycle set on a low resistance level. After a three- to five-minute warmup, set a constant pedal speed and increase the resistance to the level of difficulty at which you want to work. Cool down with a lower resistance setting, again for three to five minutes.

•When you begin a stationary bicycle program, work at 60% of your predicted maximum heart rate. If your heart is beating faster, then you are overdoing it. As you become more fit, you can work at up to 80% of your predicted maximum heart rate. But remember to keep the increase slow and gradual.

•Start cycling in 10-minute sessions. Then increase to 15, then 20, and then 25 or more minutes per session. Gradual increases over a period of weeks help prevent injury to muscles and joints. Once you build up your physical strength, pedal for as long as you feel comfortable.

Source: Eastside Sports Medicine Center, New York.

To Get into Shape For Skiing

Being physically fit makes skiing more fun and helps prevent soreness and injuries. *What to focus on:*

•Muscle tone and flexibility. Stretching exercises keep your muscles long and pliable. They also warm muscles up for strenuous sports and help relax them afterward. Always stretch slowly. Hold the extended position for 20 to 30 seconds. Don't bounce.

•Do sit-ups with your knees bent to strengthen abdominal muscles (they can take stress off the back).

•Practice any active sport, from swimming to tennis, for three one-hour sessions a week.

•Jogging builds up the muscles of the lower torso and legs. Running downhill strengthens the front thigh muscles, essential to skiing. Running on uneven terrain promotes strong and flexible ankles. Biking builds strong legs and improves balance.

How to Improve Your Tennis

Here are some secrets that help tennis pros on the court:

•Psych yourself up for a big point by triggering the adrenaline response. *Here's how:* Open your eyes wide and fix them on a nearby object. Breathe deeply and forcefully. Think of yourself as a powerful, aggressive individual. Exhort yourself with phrases like "Fight!" Try to raise goose bumps on your skin—they signal a high point.

•To switch from one type of playing surface to another, practice easing the transition. If you're moving to fast cement from slow clay, for example, practice charging the net before the switch. If it's the other way around, spend extra time on your groundstrokes.

To play well against a superior player:

•Suspend all expectations. Avoid thinking about the situation. Watch the ball, not the opponent.

•Play your game. Don't try to impress your opponent with difficult shots you normally never try.

•Hit the ball deep and down the middle. The more chances for your opponent to return your shot, the more chances for him to err.

•Concentrate on your serve. No matter how outgunned you may be, you can stay in the match if you hold your serve.

Source: *Tennis* and *World Tennis.*

Martial Arts Schools Teach More than Martial Arts

The martial arts offer more than a simple exercise program. They build both physical and mental strengths. Students learn the skills to extricate themselves from dangerous situations and, if necessary, to defend themselves.

Styles and systems...

•Tai Chi Chuan uses slow, graceful movements.

•Karate employs powerful, focused techniques.

•Judo and aikido make use of joint locks and throws.

Finding the right school...

•To get a list of schools, talk with friends and check out the ads in your local Yellow Pages.

•Visit the schools to observe a few classes before you sign up.

•Clarify your goals before you make a choice —do you want mainly a physical fitness and self-defense program, or are you interested in the mental/spiritual aspects?

What to consider...

•A balanced approach to both the mental aspects (such as concentration and focus) and the physical aspects of the particular martial art.

•The temper of the fighting classes, if the school has them. Make certain that care is taken to minimize injuries. Fighting is a part of most martial arts, and you should be comfortable with the school's fighting program.

•Thoughtful answers to your questions. If the school is evasive in its explanations, it is probably not a good bet.

•Instructors create the training environment of the school. Make certain they suit you. Some people like a "marine sergeant," while others might prefer a more temperate teacher.

•Students should be brought into the regimen slowly in a progressive process. Only as a student gets used to one style should new techniques be added to his repertory.

• Make sure the school accommodates different levels of athletic ability and different ages. Inflexible standards may only frustrate you.

• Attitudes of students. Do they encourage and help each other? Or are they bullying? The attitude of the instructor is passed on to his students.

• Facilities. Is there room to practice in between classes? Does the school have exercise equipment such as weights and jump ropes? Are the locker rooms big enough for the number of students? Are there showers?

• Schedule. If you will have a hard time getting to the workouts, you probably won't go often enough.

Source: Ken Glickman, third degree black belt and coordinator of Educational Services, Greenwich Institute for American Education, Greenwich, CT.

Exercises that Can Harm You

The most important benefit of exercise is that, properly done, it increases longevity. But exercises that promote a single aspect of the body, such as form, stamina, coordination, speed, or strength, generally have a negative impact. *Especially dangerous are:*

• Muscle-building exercises. They can harm joints and connective tissues. Weight lifters are not known for longevity.

• Skill-producing activities. Ballet, handball, and squash require arduous training and stop-start patterns. Both are negatives for long life.

• Marathon sports. Jogging, swimming, cycling, and strenuous walking can work the body to the point of exhaustion. This is dangerous because stress and injury occur more easily during body fatigue.

• Speed-oriented activities. Those that require lots of oxygen, such as sprinting or speed swimming, can be fatal, especially for those who have not trained extensively for them.

Source: Dan Georgakas, author of *The Methuselah Factors: The Secrets of the World's Longest-Lived Peoples,* Simon & Schuster, New York.

Fitness Facts

• *Easy fitness plan:* Walk at least one mile a day at three miles per hour. Your body will thrive—and without the injury risk of running, the knee strain of bicycling, or the inconvenience of swimming. *Optimal plan:* Walk a mile twice a day at four-miles-per-hour.

Source: Dr. Henry A. Solomon, a New York cardiologist, in *Signature.*

• For every week you've laid off because of illness or vacation, allow one week to return to your full exercise program.

Source: Michael L. Pollock, director of cardiac rehabilitation and sports medicine, Universal Services Rehabilitation and Development, Inc., Houston, TX, in *Mademoiselle.*

Unexpected Health Club Hazard

Number and motility of sperm cells are decreased for up to six weeks after a dip in a hot tub.

• *Shocking:* Only one hour of soaking in water 102.4 degrees or hotter (most health clubs keep tubs at 104 degrees) causes immediate harm to sperm.

• *Fertility low point:* Four weeks after bath, when sperm that were immature upon bathing mature.

• *Remedy:* Patience...sperm life span is 75 days, so all damaged sperm are replaced within that time frame.

Source: Dr. Richard Paulson of the University of Southern California School of Medicine.

Winter Sports Pointers

• Ice skating is an underrated exercise that works all your muscles. It's also easy to learn ...most people can glide around the rink after three or four sessions.

• *Skier's hazard:* Sunburned corneas, caused by the sun's ultraviolet rays. (Snow reflects 85% of those rays, compared with 10% from water and 5% from grass.) *Helpful:* Goggles or wraparound glasses made of impact-resistant polycarbonate.

Source: Dr. Paul Vinger, a Boston ophthalmologist and eye/medical consultant to the US Olympic Committee, in *Executive Fitness Newsletter.*

Home Exercise Machine Dos and Don'ts

• Treadmill. *Don't* grip or lean on handrails ...*do* keep arms moving while walking...*don't* lean too far forward while walking up an incline...*do* maintain good posture.

• Stairmaster. *Don't* lean all your weight on the handrails...*do* rest your hands on top of the machine for stability...*don't* let pedals hit the top or bottom of the machine's range... *don't* take "baby steps," using only a small portion of your own natural range of motion.

• Stationary bicycle. *Don't* hyperextend your legs on the downstroke...*do* adjust the seat so you maintain a slight bend at the knee.

• Rowing machine. *Don't* pull by lifting with your back...*do* use your legs to push your body away from your feet.

• Cross-country ski machine. *Don't* let your feet slide in front of the stomach pad...*do* lift your heels on the back stroke...*do* always keep knees slightly bent.

Source: Chris Vincent, MA, fitness consultant at the Athletic Club Illinois Center, Chicago.

Few Teenage Girls Exercise

Only 25% of female high school students exercise vigorously on a regular basis—compared with 50% of boys the same age.

Source: Gregg Health, Dsc, MPh, division of surveillance and epidemiology, Centers for Disease Control and Prevention, Atlanta.

Swimming Pool Danger

Lap swimmers might be inhaling high doses of chloroform, a carcinogen formed when chlorine reacts with water pollutants. *Evidence:* In a study conducted recently in an indoor swimming pool in Quebec, breath samples taken from men before, during and after an hour-long daily swim showed that chloroform concentrations rose from 52.6 parts per billion (ppb) before the swim to 100 to 1,093 ppb afterward. Researchers are now assessing the possible health risks associated with chloroform inhalation. It may be necessary to modify current water treatment practices in swimming pools.

Source: Benoît Lévesque, MD, medical adviser in environmental health, Centre de Santé Publique de Quebec, Ste.-Foy, Canada. His study was published in *Environmental Health Perspectives,* US Department of Health & Human Services, 1233 Research Triangle Park, North Carolina 27709.

A Stitch in Time...

To relieve a stitch—a cramp in the side—that occurs while running, try grunting loudly as each foot strikes the ground. A forceful grunt relaxes the diaphragm, relieving the muscle tension that may be causing the pain.

Source: Owen Anderson, PhD, editor, *Running Research News,* Box 27041, Lansing, Michigan 48909.

High Humidity Dangers

High humidity can lead to heat exhaustion or other serious problems even if it's not particularly hot. *Self-defense:* Drink six to eight ounces of water every 15 to 30 minutes—more if you are working hard or exercising vigorously. Do not take salt tablets. *Also:* Use oil-free sunscreens. Oil-based sunscreens can clog pores, slowing perspiration even further.

Source: *University of Texas Lifetime Health Letter,* 7000 Fannin, Houston 77030.

22

Better Sleep

The Straight Story On Sleep

•There's nothing particularly natural or inevitable about daytime sleepiness. Americans have developed an unhealthy tolerance of daytime sleepiness and fatigue.

•Both drowsiness and fatigue during the daytime hours are usually the result of sleep disorders of which sufferers often aren't aware. There are also chronic sleep disturbances of which the sleeper may not be aware. *Example:* Loud noises from aircraft or a nearby highway that disturb sleep regularly even though people don't always waken.

•Contrary to common notions, the inability to get a refreshing night's sleep is rarely caused by stress or anxiety. For people younger than 15 or older than 50, the main cause is usually a physical one. In older people, the most common problem is apnea, a disorder that causes them to stop breathing periodically during sleep. *Other frequent problems:* Asthma and chronic disease.

•A cool bedroom is not necessarily better for sleeping than a warm one. No temperature (within a normal range) has been proved better than another for sleep.

•Some people who have insomnia do sleep, and much more than they think they do. *The real test of sleeping well:* Whether you feel fully alert the next day, not the number of hours you've slept. If you sleep just five hours and you don't feel tired the next day, you don't have a sleep disorder.

•Heavy snoring followed by daytime sleepiness is virtually a sure sign of apnea. In this condition, episodes of impaired breathing or failure to breathe at all causes the apnea sufferer to wake up many times a night. *Most vulnerable to sleep apnea:* Middle-aged males (particularly those who are overweight) and people with large adenoids, a deviated septum or polyps. Some apnea sufferers are so used to their condition that they're not aware of their wakening, only of their daytime fatigue.

•A cigarette before bedtime is likely to keep you awake (in addition to creating a fire hazard). Nicotine is a stimulant to the central nervous system.

•The position in which you lie when going to sleep is not important. *Fact:* Everybody moves around many times during sleep.

•A couple of stiff drinks every night will not help you sleep. Stiff drinks before bedtime will more likely cause you to wake up in the middle of the night, when they wear off. Small quantities of alcohol (one drink) may help on a particularly difficult night, however.

•Drink a glass of milk and eat a light snack before going to bed. *Reason:* Hunger can disturb sleep. Avoid rich or spicy foods or stimulants such as coffee, tea, cola, drinks, or sweets. (Sugar is a stimulant.) Eating the wrong foods before bedtime may not actually keep you from falling asleep, but it will often wake you within a few hours.

•Check to see if there are noises that may be disturbing your sleep without your being aware of them. Mute the sounds by putting up heavy curtains or by using earplugs.

•Avoid too much mental stimulation in the period before you go to sleep. Don't discuss family problems or finances, and don't take up unfinished work problems before bedtime. *Instead:* Do some light reading or watch a television show that relaxes you.

•If you wake up in the middle of the night and can't get back to sleep right away, don't lie there. Get up, put the light on and use the time, perhaps to read. Lying in bed and trying to sleep without success only makes you more tense.

•Avoid strenuous physical exercise within a few hours of bedtime. It can cause excessive stimulation and stress, which can disturb sleep. Exercise can benefit sleep if taken in the afternoon or early evening. Morning exercise is of no great help in inducing a good night's sleep.

Source: Dr. William C. Dement, director, Sleep Disorders Center, Stanford University School of Medicine.

Good Sleep Demystified

People spend almost one third of their lives asleep. The primary sleep disorder is insomnia. That's difficulty falling asleep, trouble remaining asleep or early-morning awakening. *Causes:*

•Depression is often the cause of early awakening.

•Sexual stresses lead to nighttime insomnia.

•Boredom.

•Some medications, such as drugs for asthma and heart and blood-pressure pills, cause poor sleep.

•More than moderate alcohol intake usually disturbs the sleep cycle.

Ways to promote better sleep:

•Follow a good physical fitness program.

•Sleep in a quiet, dark, well-humidified room and in a comfortable bed.

•Avoid late-night physical or mental stress, snacks, coffee, cola, or drug stimulants.

•Do relaxing exercises or biofeedback exercises.

•Don't take sleeping pills.

Source: Dr. Bruce Yaffe, fellow in gastroenterology and liver disease, Lenox Hill Hospital, New York.

Improve the Quality Of Your Sleep

•Researchers cannot easily determine how much sleep is optimum for a specific person. They have determined that, on average, people need seven or eight hours of sleep a day.

•Keep a diary of sleeping patterns for at least 10-14 days. If you feel productive and alert, the average sleep time during that period is probably the amount you need.

•Establish a regular bedtime and wakeup schedule. Stick to it, even on weekends and holidays.

•Avoid trying to make up for loss of sleep one night by sleeping more the next. Sleep deprivation of two to four hours does not severely affect performance. Having the normal amount of sleep the next night compensates for the loss without changing the regular sleep pattern. And that has long-term benefits.

•Relax before bedtime. *Good ways to unwind:* Take a bath, read, have a weak nightcap or snack (milk is ideal for many people), engage in sex. Avoid late-night exercise, work, arguments and activities that cause tension.

•Knowing the reason for insomnia is the only way to start overcoming it. If the cause is not quickly obvious, see a doctor. Many emotional and physical disorders express themselves as sleep disturbances.

•Avoid sleeping pills. On a long-term basis, they are useless and sometimes dangerous. And when taken infrequently, they may produce a drug hangover the next day.

•Avoid naps in the middle of the day to compensate for lack of sleep the previous night. Take them only if you do it regularly and feel refreshed, instead of groggy, after a nap. *Test:* If you dream during a catnap, it is likely to delay sleep that evening or to cause insomnia.

•Don't attempt to reduce the total amount of sleep you need. Carefully researched evidence from monitoring subjects in sleep laboratories indicates these schemes are not only ineffective but unhealthful. The daily biological cycle cannot be changed by gradually cutting back sleep over a period of months. Older persons apparently need slightly less sleep, but even here the exact difference is not yet known.

Source: Dr. Charles P. Pollak, codirector, Sleep/Wake Disorders Center, Montefiore Hospital, New York.

Insomnia Trap

Many drugs can interfere with your sleep, including nasal decongestants, diuretics, cancer and blood pressure medications, some gastric ulcer drugs, such as Tagamet and Zantac, and several antidepressants—Marplan, Nardil, Parnate, Prozac and Wellbutrin. *Helpful:* If you suspect one of these drugs is interfering with your sleep, ask your doctor about changing medications or doses...and about taking the drug early in the day.

Source: Philip M. Becker, MD, director, Sleep/Wake Disorders Center, Dallas.

How to Become An Ex-Insomniac

•Condition your sleep environment. Learn to associate your bed and your bedroom with sleep.

•Pay attention to bedroom conditions, such as light, heat, noise. Shut off telephones if necessary. Keep temperature cool (around 68°). Make sure your mattress and your sleep clothing are comfortable.

•If you don't fall asleep right away, get up, leave the bedroom, and go do something else. Don't lie awake thinking about it or you'll begin to associate your bed and your bedroom with trying to get to sleep.

•Stick to a regular bedtime schedule. Go to bed at the same time every night—weekdays and weekends. Don't expect to catch up on missed sleep on the weekends. You can't do it. Trying simply disrupts your biological rhythms.

•Exercise early in the day. Late in the evening it's too stimulating.

•Sexual activity, within a comfortable relationship where no tension or anxiety exists, is helpful in inducing sleep.

•If you think widely advertised insomnia cures like vibrating beds, prerecorded cassette tapes, and sleep masks will relax you, try them.

•Don't take nonprescription, over-the-counter sleeping pills. Studies have shown "sugar pills" to be just as effective.

•If you have a particular emotional or physical upset, see your doctor.

•If sedatives are prescribed, use for no more than a week or two. Expect that the first night or two after stopping the pills will be very disturbed sleep. That's perfectly normal.

Source: Dr. Frank Zorick, clinical director of the sleep disorder center at Cincinnati Veterans Administration Hospital and the University of Cincinnati.

Sleep Can Be Disturbed By...

Only about one third of people wake up refreshed. While many sleep problems for the other two thirds are caused by anxiety, these factors can also reduce the quality of sleep:

• Alcohol. Can affect both dream and deepest-sleep stage. *Best:* Make your drink with dinner the last of the evening.

• Room temperature. A cold room does not make you sleep better. *Ideal:* 60–65°.

• Exercise. Aches and pains from strenuous exercise can keep you awake.

• Sex. Unless it is both physically and mentally rewarding, it can inhibit sleep.

• Caffeine. Effects linger 6 to 7 hours.

• Smoking. Nicotine is a strong central-nervous-system stimulant. Heavy smokers who quit usually sleep dramatically better within days.

• Irregular schedule. The body functions on a regular rhythm.

Source: *Executive Fitness Newsletter,* Emmaus, PA.

How to Fall Back Asleep

Agony: Awakening in the middle of the night and not being able to fall back to sleep. *Prime cause:* Advancing age. People over 50 tend to middle-of-the-night insomnia. Those under 50 often have difficulty falling asleep.

How to cope:

• Don't become angry when you find yourself awake at 3 a.m. Anger only excites you, preventing sleep. Fix your mind on a single relaxing image. *Example:* Visualize a flickering candle.

• If you are still awake after 30 minutes, go to another room. Watch an old movie on TV, or read a book or magazine.

• When you feel sleepy, return to bed. If sleep still eludes you, go back to the other room and read some more.

Preventive steps:

• Eliminate daytime naps if they have been a habit.

• Do not go to bed too early. This only increases the chances of middle-of-the-night insomnia.

• Set your alarm an hour earlier than usual. This makes you more tired for the following night. Advance the alarm by 15-minute increments until you are sleeping through the night. Then slowly extend your sleep period until you are back on a normal schedule.

Source: *A Good Night's Sleep* by Jerrold S. Maxmen, Contemporary Books, Chicago.

How to Stop Snoring

• Put a brick or two under the legs at the head of your bed. Elevating your head will keep the airway open.

• Don't use extra pillows. They'll only kink the airway.

• Avoid all depressants a few hours before bed. Take no alcohol, tranquilizers, sleeping pills or antihistamines late in the day.

• Lose weight. Three of four snorers are at least 20% over their ideal weight.

• Wear a cervical collar. It keeps the chin up and the windpipe open.

• Wear a "snore ball." Cut a small, solid-rubber ball in half. Using two patches of Velcro, attach the flat side of the half-sphere to the back of your pajama top. If done right, it should keep you off your back—the position for virtually all snoring.

Source: *Prevention,* Emmaus, PA.

To Eliminate Fatigue

• Analyze your lifestyle. Write down what you do every day. Be sure to include the amount of physical exercise you get and the kinds of demands (emotional and otherwise) that are made on you. Include your time with people and your time working alone. Document the times when you feel fatigued. Is it at work or at home? Is it better or worse around other people? Correlate your fatigue diary with your activity record, and look for patterns.

• Try some small changes in your work style. If your job puts you under constant pressure, take minibreaks to do some gentle stretches. If you spend a lot of time with other people, make some private time for yourself. If you do paperwork alone, schedule some social breaks.

•Pay attention to diet, and eat regularly. A breakfast of complex carbohydrates such as whole-grained toast and protein will keep you going until lunch. People who skip meals or have an erratic eating pattern are more fatigue prone.

•Stick to a regular, moderate exercise regimen—not weekend overexertion. The best exercise is walking. Besides being healthful and safe, it also gives you time alone to notice the outside world and reflect on your inner life. Aerobic exercise stimulates the brain to produce endorphins, the body's natural painkillers and antidepressants.

•Look within yourself. Do you like your job, friends, home life? Could you admit it to yourself if you didn't? If for the next two weeks you could do anything you wanted, what would it be? Is there a way of incorporating that fantasy into real life? What's the biggest price you have to pay for your current lifestyle?

•Once you identify problems, see what you can do about them. For example, if you like your job but hate the long commute, maybe you can stagger your hours to work fewer days a week—or move closer to the office.

•Get a physical checkup. Although there is no physical basis for fatigue in 99% of the people who visit doctors complaining of it, occasionally a health problem is a factor. The most common medical cause of fatigue is mild low thyroid, which occurs more commonly in women.

Source: Mary E. Wheat, MD, an internist at Mt. Zion Hospital and Medical Center, San Francisco.

How to Buy a Mattress

The quality of sleep makes the quantity less important. To enable you to relax, your mattress must provide proper support for your body, yet be resilient enough for comfort.

Basic considerations:

•Mattress prices. Depend on the materials, quality of construction, size, number of layers of upholstery and the store's markup. (May be lower in small neighborhood stores.) Queen-size innerspring sets cost \$325–\$800, sometimes discounted to \$225–\$500. A high-density queen-size foam mattress costs about \$300.

•Construction. Innerspring or foam rubber are the basic types. Top-quality innerspring mattresses have covered metal coils, cushioning material and an insulator between the coils to prevent them from protruding. Foam mattresses are made of a solid block of urethane, high-resiliency foam or laminated layers of varying density sandwiched together (preferably 5–6 inches thick).

How to shop for a mattress:

•Sit on the edge of the bed. The mattress should support you without feeling flimsy, and it should spring back into shape when you get up. A reinforced border increases durability.

•Lie down. (If the bed is to be used by a couple, both partners should test it lying down.) Check several different firmnesses to choose the one you're most comfortable with.

•Roll from side to side and then to the center. The mattress should not sway, jiggle or sag in the middle. If you hear creaking springs, don't buy it.

•Examine the covering. The best is sturdy ticking with a pattern woven in, not printed on.

•Check for handles on the sides for easy turning, small metal vents to disperse heat and allow air to circulate inside, and plastic corner guards.

•Don't forget about the boxspring which bears up to 80% of the sleeper's weight. When you need a new mattress, both the mattress and spring should be replaced to ensure that the support system is specifically designed for the mattress.

Buy a sleep set made by a manufacturer with a good reputation and sold by a reputable dealer. Be very wary of advertised bargains.

Drug-Free Remedy For Insomnia

An epsom salt bath relaxes the muscles and calms the mind. Use two to three cups of Epsom salt, and make sure the bath water is as close to skin temperature as possible. *Also helpful:* Light a candle, burn some incense or play soft music to enhance the feeling of relaxation. Be sure to go straight to bed once the bath is over.

Source: Jane Guiltinan, ND, a naturopath and chief medical officer at Bastyr University Natural Health Clinic, Seattle.

Surgery for Sleep Apnea

Surgery for sleep apnea is usually unnecessary...and may be falsely reassuring. More than four of every five people who suffer from apnea (repeated interruptions of breathing, often caused by excessively lax tissue in the throat) can be helped by *continuous positive airway pressure* (CPAP). *How it works:* A CPAP mask, attached to a fan-driven pressure generator, blows air through the nose into the sleeper's throat, preventing the airway from collapsing. CPAP is only for apnea—not for simple snoring. *Apnea symptoms:* Daytime sleepiness...nighttime heartburn...frequent nighttime awakening.

Source: Daniel Wagner, MD, neurologist, Sleep-Wake Disorder Center, New York Hospital-Cornell University Medical Center, New York City.

23

Coping with Emergencies

It Pays to Prepare For Emergencies

Emergencies, of course, come without warning. But that doesn't mean you can't be prepared when they do arrive. *Steps to take now:*

•Familiarize yourself with the emergency rooms in your area. Look into freestanding urgent-care clinics as well as hospital emergency rooms. Ask your doctor which facility is best for which type of emergency—and chart his/her recommendations on a family bulletin board.

Know where the entrance and parking area are for each emergency facility recommended by your doctor. Go for a visit. Park in a visitor's space and go in and look around. If the admissions clerk is not busy, ask how things work in an emergency.

Call your county health department. Find out the rating of each local emergency room. Level 1 facilities offer only basic emergency care... Level 2 offer more advanced care...and Level 3 are comprehensive trauma centers capable of handling the most severe, life-threatening emergencies. *Caution:* If you go to a Level 3 center for a minor cut, you may have to wait in line behind people with more serious injuries.

•*Always carry in your wallet...*

•Health insurance card.

•Insurance company phone number.

•Your blood type, although it will be tested for verification anyway.

•A list of all medications you take regularly.

•Your doctor's name, address and phone number.

•A brief description—written and signed by your doctor—of any health condition that might affect emergency care.

•The name and phone number of any pharmacy where your medication history is on file—ideally one that is open 24-hours-a-day.

•*Keep handy in your home—and tell everyone the location of...*

•A comprehensive first-aid manual, such as the one published by the Red Cross and sold in bookstores. Be sure that it's up-to-date.

•Instructions for doing the Heimlich maneuver.

•A blood pressure cuff.

•Literature on emergency treatment for any disease or condition relevant to anyone who lives or works regularly in your house—heart disease, epilepsy, asthma, etc.

•*Always wear a bracelet or pendant describing any serious medical condition... Examples:* Diabetes or severe allergies.

•*Learn...*

•Basic first aid.

•Cardiopulmonary resuscitation (CPR) for adults and children—especially if you have a pool.

•The Heimlich maneuver.

•How to take blood pressure—even if no one in your family is hypertensive.

•*Tape to your telephones the numbers for...*

•Your family doctor and any medical specialists used by your family. List the specialty beside the name and number, just in case the caller doesn't know, for example, that Dr. Jones is a cardiologist.

•Family dentist, orthodontist, endodontist, periodontist, etc.

•Police and ambulance. Call ahead to inquire about the normal response time for each.

•Private ambulance.

•Fire department—for first aid as well as fires, in case neither your doctor nor your first-aid squad can be reached.

•Poison-control center. Ask your hospital about the location of the nearest one.

•Emergency room.

•Family veterinarian and animal hospital.

•Neighbors who could be called at any hour, especially those who have a car.

•*Read...*

•All parts of your health insurance policy pertaining to emergency care. Make sure you know how soon after an emergency you must notify the insurance company...and whether your policy offers better coverage at certain hospitals.

•Your first-aid manual.

•*For an elderly or infirm person...*

•Sign him/her up with an emergency response system.

•Provide him with a portable telephone. Make sure he keeps the telephone charged and nearby at all times—especially if he is wheelchair-bound.

•Arrange with someone—neighbor, friend or commercial elder-care service representative—to check on the person each day.

Source: Neil Shulman, MD, associate professor of medicine, Emory University School of Medicine, Atlanta. He is the publisher of *Better Health Care for Less*, 2272 Vistamount Dr., Decatur, GA 30333. Dr. Shulman is coauthor of *Better Health Care for Less*, Hippocrene Books, 171 Madison Ave., New York 10016. He also wrote the novel *Doc Hollywood*, which was made into a movie.

Dealing with a Medical Emergency

In a medical emergency, emotions can run high. Knowing how to get someone to the hospital quickly and efficiently can not only calm the patient, it may even save his life.

Call your local municipal emergency number for a public ambulance. The response time is usually quicker than for a private ambulance.

•Answer all the dispatcher's questions as completely as possible. The answers determine the priority of your call. A broken leg, for example, may not get assistance as quickly as a heart attack.

•Tell the dispatcher exactly what condition the patient is in, as clearly and calmly as possible. Simply saying "I think he is having a heart attack" is not enough. Try to be specific about all the symptoms you have observed.

•Don't hang up until the dispatcher does. Let him decide when he has enough information.

•Give the dispatcher your phone number even if he doesn't ask for it. If something happens to delay the ambulance, he may need to reach you.

•Give careful directions that include your street address, prominent landmarks and any other information that will help the ambulance crew find your location quickly.

•Tell the dispatcher that you will have someone wait outside, put the porch light on, or hang a bed sheet out the window so the driver can see where you are right away.

• Stay with the victim or at least keep him in sight.

• Gather all relevant information, such as insurance numbers, medical history, medications currently being taken (the actual bottle of pills is even better) and anything else that concerns the patient's condition.

• You can usually ride in the ambulance with the patient, unless the patient needs emergency procedures en route.

• In that case, get the name and address of the hospital and the care unit where the patient will be admitted, to go there on your own. (Don't speed or run lights.)

• At the hospital, find out who is caring for the patient. Let the floor nurse know that you are there. Offer to expedite the admitting office paperwork.

Source: Brian Maguire, director of training, BRAVO (Bay Ridge Ambulance Volunteer Organization), NY.

The Well-Stocked Medicine Cabinet

What you *shouldn't* have in your medicine cabinet is as important as what you put in it.

General guideline: Check with your doctor before purchasing any over-the-counter medication...or if your symptoms persist longer than a few days.

What to include...

• Pain, fever and anti-inflammatory medicines. *Examples:* Acetaminophen (Tylenol, Datril and Panadol). It reduces pain and fever without damaging the intestinal tract. However, it is not an anti-inflammatory—it will not reduce swelling.

Aspirin and ibuprofen (Advil, Nuprin and Medipren) relieve pain and inflammation... aspirin also relieves fever. *Warning:* At high doses, both can lead to internal bleeding and wearing away of the stomach lining. *At greatest risk:* The elderly.

Aspirin is also associated with ulcers and *tinnitus* (ringing in the ears)...ibuprofen with kidney toxicity. *Self-defense:* Always take aspirin or ibuprofen with food or liquid antacids, and never exceed the recommended dosage—no more than eight regular-strength tablets a day.

• *First-aid materials:* Hydrogen peroxide for cleaning wounds (*not* alcohol, which is drying and more irritating), antibiotic creams, cotton swabs, gauze pads, surgical tape, adhesive bandages, blunt scissors and tweezers.

• *Skin protectors:* Petroleum jelly or mild moisturizers for dry skin...over-the-counter vaginal cream for mild yeast infections...hydrocortisone cream (no more than 0.5% strength) for poison ivy or other rashes.

Caution: Do not use hydrocortisone on face or genitals without consulting a doctor. And don't use it on fungal infections, such as athlete's foot or jock itch—it will make the problem worse.

• Syrup of ipecac...to induce vomiting after ingesting a poison.

Caution: Call a poison control center before administering—vomiting makes certain kinds of toxins more destructive.

What to use less of...

• Over-the-counter cold remedies. These fight symptoms but don't cure colds. And by drying out mucous membranes, they can hamper the body's natural defenses, slowing recovery.

Antihistamines can be sedating—don't drive or operate machinery while using them.

Decongestants can constrict blood vessels and increase heart rate, making them dangerous for people with heart problems or hypertension. Talk to your doctor before taking them.

Cough medicines may contain alcohol, as well as added decongestants and antibiotics. Read the label carefully and don't exceed recommended dosages.

What to leave out...

• Diet pills. These are completely ineffective over the long-term—they work only as long as you take them. They can be addictive. And they are very, very dangerous for people with heart problems—especially *undiagnosed* heart problems—or high blood pressure.

• Decongestant nose drops. These create a rebound effect—when you stop using them, you become as congested as before...if not more. *Better:* Steroid nasal sprays, available by prescription only.

Source: Robert L. Perkel, MD, clinical associate professor of family medicine at Thomas Jefferson University, Philadelphia 19107.

Car Emergency Equipment

- Flashlight with fresh batteries.
- Flares or warning reflectors.
- Extra washer fluid.
- First aid kit.
- Drinking water and high-energy food.
- Booster cables.
- Extra fan belt and alternator belt.
- Fully inflated spare tire.
- Tool kit (including jack, lug wrench, screwdrivers, pliers, adjustable wrench and electrical tape).

Extras for winter driving:

- Tire chains and traction mats.
- Ice scraper.
- Warm clothing or blankets.
- Square-bladed shovel.
- Extra antifreeze.

When to Go to the Emergency Room

A hospital is advisable when *any* of these symptoms are present—and you can't see your doctor:

- Suspicious abdominal pain. Most pain in this area stems from a temporary digestive problem and will subside by itself. But if the pain is accompanied by fever, extreme tenderness or sensitivity to jarring (it hurts more when you hop), emergency treatment is called for. The same advice holds for any extreme, writhing pain.
- Visible blood in vomit or the stool. These symptoms generally point to a dangerous condition.
- Any condition that steadily becomes worse.
- Respiratory symptoms that suggest pneumonia. Although most pneumonias are caused by viruses and are self-limiting, the bacterial varieties can progress rapidly and are life-threatening. *Danger signs:* Difficulty breathing or shortness of breath, yellow-green sputum and a high fever—more than 102°F—with shaking and chills.

Your best guide in self-diagnosis is common sense. It can also be helpful to ask the opinion of a family member or friend.

Source: Mickey Eisenberg, MD, director of emergency medical services at the University of Washington Medical Center, Emergency Department, 1959 NE Pacific St., Seattle 98195.

How to Beat Hospital Emergency Room Traffic Jams

The first rule for coping with the crowded, and often chaotic, conditions prevailing at many hospital emergency rooms is to seek treatment elsewhere whenever appropriate.

Severe chest or head pain, uncontrolled bleeding, loss of consciousness or breathing difficulties do call for a visit to the ER.

However, many cuts and other seemingly serious problems can often be treated safely—and with far less delay—right in a doctor's private office.

Smart strategy: Discuss with your physician before an emergency arises precisely which emergencies he/she can treat...and which call for the services of an emergency room.

Important: Know whom to contact if your physician is out of town when trouble strikes.

Key emergency room strategies...

- Know the emergency rooms in your area. Some ERs offer only "plain vanilla" service—suturing cuts, setting fractures, treating heart attacks and the like.

Others, such as trauma centers, burn centers and head treatment centers, have the specialized staff and equipment required to treat more difficult cases.

You won't always be able to pick your emergency room—there may be only one in your community, for instance, or you might be away from home when illness or injury strikes.

For times when there is a choice, however, try to pinpoint in advance the one, or ones, best suited to meet the special needs of your family members. If you have children, for instance, pick an emergency room that is capable of dealing with pediatric cases. If a family member is mentally ill, find an emergency room that has psychiatric backup. Discuss local emergency rooms with your family doctor, and with friends and family members. Do your own research, too—phone the various emergency rooms directly. In most cases, a staff doctor or nurse will discuss with you the specifics of the facility.

• Know how to call an ambulance. Although dialing 911 now works in most areas, some communities still require patients to direct-dial the ambulance dispatcher. If you're unfamiliar with the procedure in your area, consult with your family doctor—and the emergency rooms of your choice. Knowing the exact procedure often saves precious minutes that spell the difference between life and death. *Note:* Public ambulance services seldom let patients choose which hospital they'll be taken to. However, it's usually no problem to be transferred—by private ambulance, if necessary—to the emergency room of your choice after you've gotten initial treatment at the first emergency room and if you are not critically ill or unstable.

• Know your medical history. Unlike your family doctor, who is well acquainted with your medical history, emergency room personnel have only a few minutes—if that—to find out all they need to know regarding your health. Any difficulty in taking your history delays your treatment and opens the door to potentially deadly mistakes—such as giving penicillin to someone allergic to it.

To be safe: Prepare a list detailing your allergies, chronic ailments and what medications you take, as well as the name and phone number of your family doctor and the particulars of your health insurance policy. Take this list along with you, if possible, when you head for the emergency room. If you can, also bring along recent electrocardiograms, medical test results, etc. *Alternative:* A medical information card or—better because it is more obvious to rushed emergency room personnel—a Medic-Alert medical information bracelet. The bracelet contains all vital information and allows emergency room physicians to obtain much more medical information by calling into a computer bank that stores that information. For information on purchasing a bracelet, call 800-ID-ALERT.

• Alert your family doctor as soon as possible after an emergency. If you don't have time to phone before leaving for the hospital, phone as soon as possible after you arrive. Whether your physician comes to the emergency room and speaks to the staff in person or communicates with them by phone or fax, your doctor's guidance will greatly facilitate your treatment.

• Bring along a friend or family member. Having someone to talk to while you await treatment not only comforts you and helps you pass the time in the emergency room, but also gives you an "advocate" to press for better or more prompt treatment. An advocate also helps convey to emergency room personnel important information regarding your condition.

• Stand up for yourself when necessary. Emergency room patients often are troubled because they have to wait so long before being treated. Emergency rooms do not operate upon a first-come, first-served basis. Instead, all patients are evaluated using a rigid triage process —those judged sickest or most gravely injured are treated before those whose illnesses or injuries are less severe regardless of who arrived first. Attempting to "jump ahead" of others awaiting treatment is futile. Of course, triage nurses do sometimes make mistakes—serious ones. If you feel that you need immediate attention—or if your condition significantly worsens as you await treatment—speak up...fast!

Source: Stephan G. Lynn, MD, FACEP, director, department of emergency medicine, St. Luke's/Roosevelt Hospital Center, New York.

Heart Attack Self-Defense

Before using CPR, call 911—if an adult is having a heart attack. Doctors used to recommend that trained rescuers give one minute of cardiopulmonary resuscitation before calling the emergency number. *New finding:* Survival and recovery rates are better if 911 is called first. *Important exception:* For children under age eight, a trained rescuer should use proper techniques *before* calling 911. All untrained rescuers should call 911 immediately.

Source: Emergency Cardiac Care Committee and subcommittee, American Heart Association, guidelines for cardiopulmonary resuscitation and emergency cardiac care, reported in *Journal of American Medical Association*, 515 N. State St., Chicago 60610.

If You're All Alone And Choking

A choking person can save himself by falling so that a table or chair hits his diaphragm, thrusting it up against the lungs. It is the forced expulsion of air from the lungs that blows out the obstruction.

Source: Henry J. Heimlich, MD, originator of the "Heimlich maneuver" (whereby a second person saves the choker).

Home Emergencies

Vital information about the house should be known by everyone in the family in case of emergency. *Key items:*

•The location of the fuse box or circuit-breaker panel.

•Placement of the main shutoff valves for the water and gas lines.

•The location of the septic tank or the line to the main sewer.

•Records of the brands, ages and model numbers of the stove, refrigerator, freezer, dishwasher, furnace, washer and dryer.

Source: *Woman's Day,* New York.

Frostbite Remedies

If you can't get indoors, breathe warm air onto the affected area or get it near warm skin. *Example:* Keep frostbitten hands under clothing and under the armpits. *Important:* Do not massage frostbitten skin. Rubbing can worsen skin damage even in mild cases of frostbite.

Source: *Johns Hopkins Health After 50,* 550 North Broadway, Suite 1100, Johns Hopkins, Baltimore, MD 21205.

Poison First Aid Basics

This year alone, three million people in the US will be the victims of accidental poisoning. More than 400,000 will become ill...and more than 500 will die.

Depending on the amount taken, many medicines—prescribed or over-the-counter—can be toxic. And accidental poisoning can occur anywhere—at home, on the job, etc.

If you suspect that someone has been poisoned...

•Check the person's physical appearance. If he/she shows signs of illness, call 911 or your local emergency number immediately.

If he is not breathing, administer rescue breathing and, if necessary, cardiopulmonary resuscitation (CPR). If you do not know these procedures, find someone who does...or follow the phone directions of trained medical personnel.

•Try to determine what substance the person has ingested and in what amount. This will help medical personnel to determine the appropriate course of treatment, if necessary.

•Contact your regional poison-control center. The number can be found on the inside cover of your phone book.

Using information that you provide, the poison center will determine the danger posed to the patient and tell you what to do.

Warning: Do not administer an antidote unless directed to by a poison center or a physician. Administered in incorrect dosages, some antidotes can have serious side effects.

Source: Scott Phillips, MD, an expert in clinical toxicology at Rocky Mountain Poison Center, Denver.

How to Treat a Cut

When you first cut yourself, decide quickly if you need to see a doctor.

You do need medical help if...

•The cut is deep—or bleeds a lot.

•You've cut an artery. You'll know because bright red blood will spurt out.

First aid: Apply pressure on the side of the wound nearer the heart.

•You've cut a large vein—at the wrist or higher and at the ankle or higher. (A toe or finger is not critical.) *Dark* blood flows steadily from a vein.

First aid: Apply pressure on the side of the wound away from the heart.

When in doubt about what you have cut...

Apply pressure directly on the wound—*and seek medical attention promptly.*

•You've cut yourself on something dirty. If you have not had a booster within the last year, a tetanus shot is advisable.

•You've cut a hand or foot and can't move your fingers or toes.

•You've sliced off a finger, toe or even a flap of skin. These can often be reattached. Wash and transport the piece in anything that's clean. A handkerchief that has been ironed is always good to use.

For less serious cuts...

•Clean the cut. Use an antiseptic, such as peroxide, or tap water.

•Cover it with a clean bandage—and remove bandage when a scab forms.

•Replace soggy dressings.

•Avoid picking scabs.

•Monitor the healing process. Watch for signs of infection. *See a doctor if:*

A cut that hurt at first, stops hurting and then becomes painful again...Streaky red lines arise, leading away from the wound...You feel tender lumps either near or far away from the cut—your lymph nodes may be swelling...A pus-filled abscess forms...A fever develops.

Source: Jack Rudick, MD, professor of surgery, Mount Sinai School of Medicine, New York.

Better Burn Advice

Nothing hurts quite the same way that a burn does. Even the smallest of burns—from a spatter of grease or the touch of a hot iron—can smart for hours or even days. Although millions of Americans suffer burns each year, most burns (more than 90%) are relatively minor...

•*First-degree burns* affect the skin's top layer, causing redness, pain but *no* blistering. They can be treated at home and heal within hours.

•*Second-degree burns* also affect some underlying skin and can cause redness, blistering, sensitivity to air and more severe pain that may not subside for several days (many sunburns are classified as second-degree burns). These burns frequently require a visit to a hospital for treatment.

Most minor burns are caused by grabbing hot objects without realizing how hot they are or spilling hot drinks or boiling water.

And most of these burns involve the hand.

Important: Hand burns must be treated more aggressively than burns on most other parts of the body. *Reason:* The hands contain many delicate muscles and tendons in a relatively small area. If not treated quickly, permanent damage can result.

Treating minor burns...

•*Run cool water over the burn.* This will ease the pain and even reverse some damage.

•*Apply salves liberally.* Several over-the-counter products, including petroleum jelly, shark-liver oil and aloe vera gel can be used to temporarily ease the stinging.

•*Monitor the burn very closely.* If it shows any signs of infection, be sure to see your doctor immediately. *Caution:* Burns are very susceptible to secondary infections. *Helpful:* Over-the-counter antibiotic products.

Things to avoid...

•Ice. Although ice can make a burn feel better, a burn packed in ice or immersed in ice water can make the injury worse. *Warning:* You can get a burn from grabbing very *cold* as well as very hot objects.

•Butter. The salt in the butter will aggravate a burn.

Second-degree burns...

Second-degree burns should be treated by a doctor...who will:

• *Cleanse and treat the burn.* It will be washed in soapy water and then rinsed with a saline solution. Fluid may be removed from unbroken blisters, and the skin left in place to provide a natural cover.

Many emergency departments use drugs containing 0.5% silver nitrate solution or a 1% silver sufadiazine cream. They may also be prescribed for home use. These thick creams and gels are applied over the burn, which is then wrapped in a sterile dressing.

New: Duoderm (Squibb), a sterile air-tight dressing, is used for several weeks until the body begins to generate new skin.

• *Help you cope with the pain.* Analgesics may be prescribed.

• *Know your tetanus status.* People who suffer second-degree burns require current tetanus immunization. If you haven't had a tetanus shot in five years, you will be given one.

Severe burns...

Immediate hospitalization in a facility with a burn-care unit is needed to treat severe burns.

• *Third-degree burns* adversely affect the skin's full thickness. The burned area has a white leathery appearance. Although you may not suffer from blisters or even pain (because of destroyed nerve endings), these burns are actually very dangerous.

• *Fourth-degree burns* affect the skin's full thickness *and* underlying tissues, including muscles, tendons and bones. The burned area has a blackened appearance.

Treating severe burns...

Skin-grafting procedures may be necessary. Such procedures are performed by a surgeon or plastic surgeon or burn-care specialist who takes live skin from one part of the body and moves it to another part to replace cells that have been destroyed and won't regenerate. In cases where large amounts of skin are needed, it may be removed from a donor's cadaver.

Note: A great deal of promising research is now being conducted in the area of skin-grafting. *Artificial skin,* for instance, may soon be put to use in the treatment of severe burns and minimize disfigurement.

Source: Steven Chernow, MD, medical director of the emergency department of University Hospital of Boston University.

First Aid for Chemical Burns

Chemical burns to the eye usually don't cause permanent damage if rinsing starts within 15 seconds. After that, chances of recovery decline rapidly. Any innocuous water fluid can be used. Continue flushing for at least 20 minutes.

Source: John Paul Wohlen, Bradley Corp., Menomonee Falls, WI, writing in *Plant Engineering.*

Summer Safety Advice

Warm weather brings a variety of fun-filled activities including family cookouts and visits to the beach...but it also brings a range of potential health hazards...

• Animal bites. Observe extreme caution when approaching unfamiliar animals and insist that your children do likewise. Use cold water to separate fighting dogs or cats—never your hands.

Bite treatment: Superficial bites from a pet call only for washing with hot, soapy water. Pet bites that draw blood, however, as well as any bite from a wild animal, require immediate medical attention—you may need antibiotics to prevent infection.

Rabies defense: Capture or kill the biting animal, if possible, and have the local health department check it for rabies. If the animal proves rabid, or if for some reason the animal cannot be tested, you must undergo a course of rabies prophylaxis—a series of five shots administered over a one-month period. Contrary to popular belief, these shots are given in the arm, not the abdomen.

Good news: Rabies is extremely rare among cats, dogs, squirrels and rodents—although skunks, bats, raccoons, foxes and cattle are sometimes infected.

•Bee stings. Avoid bright colors, perfumes, soft drinks and sugary foods while in bee territory. Instead, douse yourself with bug repellent and don white or khaki clothing, long sleeves and pants, sturdy shoes and insect netting.

Persons allergic to bee venom should carry an epinephrine injector while outdoors...and should avoid lawn-mowing, flower-picking and other activities that are likely to put them in proximity to bees.

If you're bitten: Gently remove the stinger from your skin. Use ice packs and cold compresses to minimize swelling.

•Drowning. The third-leading cause of accidental death in the United States, drowning claims more than 4,500 victims a year.

To reduce risk: Swim, snorkel and scuba dive only with a partner...wear a Coast Guard approved life preserver whenever you're on a dock or aboard a boat...never dive into water of unknown depth.

If you become fatigued while swimming, float face-down—lifting your head only to breathe—until your strength returns or help arrives. Most people can float quite easily simply by filling their lungs with air.

•Head injuries. Motorcyclists, bicyclists, skateboarders and roller skaters should at all times wear helmets approved by the Snell Memorial Foundation. Skateboard only on driveways, empty lots, parks and other traffic-free areas. Roller skate on public roads in light traffic only if you are sufficiently skilled to move smoothly and predictably.

•Heat exhaustion and heat stroke. Strenuous exercise in hot, humid weather can cause fatigue, confusion, unconsciousness and even death.

At greatest risk: Athletes, laborers, children, the elderly and persons taking antihypertensives, antipsychotics, antidepressants and certain other prescription drugs.

To avoid trouble: Consume plenty of water or electrolyte drinks (such as Gatorade), and take frequent breaks. If you begin to experience symptoms, get out of the heat immediately. Remove all clothing, then apply cool water or ice to the skin. If symptoms persist, go immediately to the emergency room. If you are with someone who has lost consciousness, call an ambulance or get that person to an emergency room.

•Lawn mower accidents. There are more than 60,000 lawn mower accidents a year.

Self-defense: Protect yourself and your family by clearing away rocks, branches and other obstacles before mowing...wearing protective glasses, sturdy shoes and earplugs...and keeping small children indoors. Never give children mower rides—the risk of falling under the blades is too great.

•Lightning. Each year, lightning causes more than 100 deaths.

To avoid being struck: During rainstorms, avoid golf courses and other large, open areas ...isolated trees, towers and other tall structures ...wading in puddles or swimming...and holding or touching anything metallic. Quickly get inside or into a car. If nearby shelter is unavailable, head for a heavily forested area.

Last resort: Crouch.

If you are struck, seek immediate medical attention. If someone nearby has been struck, immediately call for emergency medical help. Lightning causes not only severe burns, but also cataracts and potentially fatal electrical disturbances in the heart.

•Playground injuries. Last year alone, more than 250,000 children sustained playground injuries. Inspect playground facilities carefully beforehand. *Common dangers:*

- •Swing sets.
- •Monkey bars and other equipment situated less than six feet from fences and other obstructions.
- •Equipment loosely anchored in the ground.
- •Equipment not surrounded by rubber mats, wood chips, sand or other energy-absorbing materials.
- •Improper spacing of rungs and steps. (Less than nine inches separation, and children's heads can be trapped.)
- •Swing seats made of wood or metal rather than rubber, canvas or another soft material.
- •Fine, chalky sand found in some sandboxes. It may contain asbestos-like fibers that some believe cause respiratory problems. Children should play only in sandboxes containing coarse sand.

•Sunburn. Red, blistered skin is only one result. Less conspicuous but far more ominous is the fact that even one severe sunburn boosts your lifetime risk of melanoma and other forms of skin cancer by 10%. Gradual tanning is safer, but it too can lead to cancer—and should be avoided.

Sun-taming tools: Broad-brimmed hats, UV-absorptive sunglasses and sunscreen rated at least SPF 15. Stay out of the sun between 11 a.m. and 3 p.m., the hours of greatest sunlight intensity. *Note:* The effects of sunburn cannot be undone. However, cold compresses combined with aspirin or ibuprofen will ease discomfort as your skin recovers.

•Tick bites. Insect repellent is one obvious precaution, but it also makes sense to wear light-colored clothing (dark colors hide ticks), a long sleeved shirt and long pants tucked into your socks.

Upon returning indoors, conduct a thorough head-to-toe body search. If you find a tick, gently pull it off using your fingers or tweezers. Removing a tick using a hot match or nail polish only boosts the odds that the tick's head will be left in your skin, where it can cause infection.

Warning: Anyone bitten by a tick should be extremely wary of Lyme disease and Rocky Mountain spotted fever, two serious tick-borne illnesses. See a doctor at the earliest hint of telltale symptoms—fever, headache, muscular aches or a skin rash (especially a circular rash around the bite). Both illnesses are curable if caught early. Left untreated, however, they lead to several potentially lasting ailments, including double vision, arthritis, irregular heartbeat—even death.

Source: Kelley Hails, MD, former clinical instructor of medicine, Michigan State University College of Human Medicine, East Lansing. Dr. Hails specializes in emergency medicine.

What to Do If Someone Faints

Old-time fainting remedies are dangerous. Placing a fainter's head between his legs could cause brain damage. Most smelling salts contain ammonium hydroxide, which can cause chemical burns of the nose and lungs. *Better:* Lay the fainter on his back. Then raise his legs. Gently massage the calves to return blood to central circulation. Wait about 20 minutes and then raise the person in stages.

Source: *RN.*

Taking a Spill

Relax and give in to your fall. Try to slide as you touch the ground. Drop any packages right away. If you tumble forward, put open hands out to break the impact and protect your face. When falling backward, try to sit as you go down, to protect your spine. If you catch a foot in a hole, drop to the side that's caught.

After the fall: Breathe deeply and get up very slowly—so you won't get dizzy and fall again.

Source: *Woman's Day*, New York.

First Aid: Diabetic Coma

Thousands of people die each year because they fall into diabetic comas and do not get the right treatment promptly.

Trap: Most diabetics' family members, friends and coworkers do not know how to properly react during such a crisis.

What to watch for: Just as there are two types of diabetes, there are two types of diabetic comas:

Hyperglycemic coma...

Patients lack enough insulin to digest sugar. *Result:* They become hyperglycemic (have excess blood sugar).

Warning sign: The inability to keep down fluids.

Times of greatest risk: When diabetics are ill, their insulin requirements rise.

Timing: These comas come on gradually over anywhere from several hours to several days.

What to do: Rush the person to the emergency room. Only professionals can administer the intravenous fluids, insulin and salts needed to correct the problem.

Hypoglycemic coma...

Patients produce excess insulin and digest sugar too fast. *Result:* They become hypoglycemic (have low blood sugar).

Warning signs: Fight or flight symptoms—anxiety, tremors and agitation. People entering these comas may act inappropriately, as if drunk.

Times of greatest risk: When patients take too much insulin...or take the right amount but miss a meal...or exercise too hard.

Timing: These comas can occur very quickly, without warning. *Note:* If your child is diabetic, be sure his teachers know that comas like this may arise.

What to do: If the person is still alert and conscious, feed him carbohydrates or protein. *Best:* Six ounces of juice or skim milk. Avoid giving the person extra table sugar or excess concentrated sweets—they force blood sugar too high. This treatment can be repeated in 20 minutes if the person fails to respond adequately.

If the person cannot ingest food, get immediate medical help. If this is not possible give him a glucagon injection. All families of insulin-dependent diabetic patients should have a glucagon kit and know how to use it.

Source: James R. Gavin III, MD, PhD, William K. Warren Professor for Diabetes Studies, department of medicine, Oklahoma University Health Sciences Center, St. Francis Medical Research Institute, Oklahoma City, OK 73104.

Dental Emergencies

Toothaches, broken or knocked-out teeth, fractured jaws and other dental emergencies require immediate attention.

How to minimize pain and maximize treatment until you reach the dentist...

• Bleeding. Slight bleeding is common following a tooth extraction. If the bleeding persists longer than an hour, try pressing gauze or an ice cube against the area for 20 minutes. If that fails to stanch the flow, apply a wet tea bag. *Note:* Profuse bleeding typically requires sutures.

• Broken tooth, filling or crown. Control pain with an over-the-counter analgesic—then get to the dentist as soon as possible. Be sure to take along the piece of tooth, filling or crown.

• Gum boils. These painful, pimple-like swellings form when pus from an abscess works its way to the surface. Since they are usually a sign of a serious infection or gum disease, always consult your dentist promptly if one appears. *Helpful:* Rinse your mouth with warm salt water to keep the pus draining.

• Knocked-out (avulsed) tooth. Often these can be successfully reimplanted—if you get to the dentist promptly and if the tooth is handled delicately. *What to do:* Gently rinse the tooth in water or milk, taking care not to detach any attached soft tissue. Place the tooth in water or milk, and take it with you to the dentist or the nearest emergency room.

• Mouth sores. To reduce discomfort, apply a paste of baking soda. *Also helpful:* Over-the-counter analgesics and topical anesthetics (Anbesol, Orajel, Campho-Phenique, etc.).

• Toothache. Most toothaches result from an inflamed or dying nerve, and invariably get worse until the tooth has been treated. Take an over-the-counter analgesic, and treat the inflamed area with a few drops of oil of clove. *Avoid:* Aspirin and hot packs applied directly to the gum.

Source: Jack Klatell, DDS, chairman of the department of dentistry, Mount Sinai School of Medicine, New York. Dr. Klatell is coauthor of *The Mount Sinai Medical Center Family Guide to Dental Health*, Macmillan Publishing Co., 866 Third Ave., New York 10022.

Big Help in Little Emergencies

• To remove a sticky bandage without pain, first soak a cotton ball in baby oil and douse the bandage with it. The oil significantly reduces the bandage's adhesion.

Source: *Parents*, New York.

• A quick, handy ice pack in an emergency is a bag of frozen vegetables (like peas or corn niblets). The bag is clean, water-tight and pliable enough to fit almost any part of the body. (It is, of course, only a stopgap substitution.)

Source: *Harvard Medical School Health Letter*, Cambridge, MA.

• To remove a ring from a swollen finger, use a few feet of string. Slip a few inches under and through the ring toward the wrist. Then wind the long end of the string tightly down the finger toward the tip, with the loops touching one another. (In most cases this will not be painful.) Finally, take the short end of the string and pull on it toward the fingertip. As the coil unwinds, the ring is pulled along until it falls off.

Source: *Emergency Medicine*, New York.

• Muscle trick to relieve cramps and spasms: Contract the muscles in the muscle group opposite the one that is cramped. This confuses the troubled muscle, making it relax. (*Example:* If your calf cramps, tighten the muscles in the front of your lower leg to relieve the discomfort.)

Source: *American Health.*

• Treating burns with butter or greasy ointments is dangerous. Neither is sterile and either can make subsequent treatment by a doctor more difficult. *Better:* Flush a burn with cold water or immerse it in cold water for up to 30 minutes. *Alternative:* Apply cold compresses. Cover with clean bandages. Never puncture a blister. For serious burns, seek a doctor at once.

Source: Gustavo Colon, MD, associate professor of plastic surgery, Tulane University Medical School, quoted in *Vogue*, New York.

24

Self-Defense

How to Tell When Someone is Lying

Detecting a lie isn't easy...even for experienced law-enforcement professionals. They spend many hours studying videotapes to understand the psychology of liars as well as the physical and emotional signs that give them away.

My research, however, has uncovered a variety of telltale clues that often can help you determine when someone is trying to deceive you.

What is a lie?

It's important to remember that not every untrue statement is necessarily a lie. Some are innocent mistakes, some are attempts to be polite...and some are purposeful and to be expected.

Example: At a magic show, the audience knows the magician is trying to fool them. The magician knows that they know it, so his/her untrue statements are not lies.

When I use the word "lie," I mean a deliberate attempt to mislead someone without making that person aware of it.

Lies are also usually at the other person's expense. They may be outright false statements... or a concealment of something the liar is obligated to tell.

Example: A job applicant who omits information that he is required to disclose, such as a previous job.

Why we believe lies...

Sometimes people deliberately overlook obvious lies because they want to believe what they're being told. This is especially true when the misinformation confirms the listener's way of doing things.

Straining to accept a lie may be a short-term way to avoid admitting that you have been fooled, but you may not be able to avoid the truth in the long term. So it is important to know when you're being told a lie—and how to overcome the psychological factors that cause you to accept the misinformation.

How to spot a liar...

A person who is lying is likely to give himself away through a variety of clues related to one or more of the emotional effects that lying produces.

• Fear of being caught. A liar who is afraid of being caught may signal that fear verbally and/or physically. Watch out for words that are evasive, indirect and halting—and a voice that is strained and/or higher pitched than normal.

These signs are not definite proof of lying. They are best when you can compare the "suspicious" indicator with what is normal behavior for the suspected liar.

• Unconscious gestures. Psychologists recognize three kinds of gestures that change in different ways when someone is nervous...as a liar often is. But detecting them is not easy. I have found that it takes at least eight solid hours of training exercises with videotapes for the average person to acquire the necessary sensitivity. The basic clues...

• Emblems. These are deliberate gestures whose meanings everyone understands, such as shrugging your shoulders to show you don't know. Someone telling a lie may give it away by unconsciously signaling via an incomplete emblem...like shrugging only one shoulder. Not everyone makes these slips. They are subtle—therefore, hard to notice.

• Illustrators are body movements that accompany speech...like the way people move their hands when asked to describe a spiral staircase.

Lies are likely to be accompanied by fewer than normal illustrators because the liar has to think more about his invented story than someone who is telling the truth.

• Manipulators are fidgeting gestures—like scratching or twisting hair—that become more common when someone is nervous. But everyone is aware of the stereotype that guilty people look nervous, so any liar with normal intelligence will try not to fidget. Therefore, fidgeting is usually not a very good indicator of lying.

• Facial clues. A lie-catcher needs to become sensitive to the two messages sent by the face—the false expression that the person wants to give...and the true expression that he cannot hide.

• Squelched impressions, when his concealed emotion starts to emerge and he quickly covers it with a false smile.

• Micro-expressions, when the true feeling flashes on his/her face for an instant. While micro-expressions are easy to miss, you can train yourself to catch them.

• Inability to control muscles. This occurs when certain facial muscles used in natural expressions of emotion cannot be controlled because the emotion is not felt. That is why a genuine smile, not a fake one, crinkles the eyes.

Caution: Truly skilled liars—or those who have come to believe their own lies—may not give any of these clues because, like actors, they are able to truly feel the emotion they are trying to express to you.

Bottom line...

There is no infallible way to detect lies, because all liars are different.

Source: Paul Ekman, PhD, professor of psychology at the University of California, San Francisco. He is the author of *Telling Lies: Clues to Deceit in the Marketplace, Politics and Marriage*, W.W. Norton and Company, 500 Fifth Ave., New York 10110.

What to Do if There's a Burglar in the House

Outdoor lighting, alarm systems, timers that automatically turn on and off household lights, and other precautions all help protect your home from burglary.

Just as important as taking steps to keep burglars outside is planning what to do if someone makes it inside. *Most important:*

• Create a "safe haven." Inside every home should be a specially equipped room where occupants can retreat in case of an attack or intrusion. This room—ideally a bathroom or bedroom—should have a window or some other means of escape...a solid-core door with a one-inch deadbolt that latches from the inside...a telephone...and a list of emergency phone numbers. If your home is equipped with an alarm system, install a panic button inside your safe room.

•Develop an escape plan. Know the fastest way out of your house from every room. Periodically rehearse your escape. Make sure windows, doors, and other escape routes can quickly be opened from the inside.

•Don't go to investigate. Confronting a burglar face-to-face can turn a simple burglary into an assault or even murder.

More prudent: Leave the investigation to the police. If you arrive home and find evidence of a break-in, *don't go inside.* The intruder might still be there. Leave the premises immediately and call the police.

If the burglary takes place while you're inside, lock a door between yourself and the intruder—ideally that of your safe haven—and telephone the police. If you cannot reach a phone, open a window and yell for help.

If it's possible to escape without risking an encounter with the burglar, then do so. Call the police from a neighbor's house.

•Remain calm. If you come face-to-face with an intruder inside your home, try not to panic. The more level-headed you are, the more likely you'll be able to think of a way to defuse the situation...and the less threatening you'll appear to the burglar.

If you don't provoke him, odds are he/she won't harm you. Most burglars just want to get out of the house once they've been detected. Don't attack or attempt to hold him until the police arrive. Just give him a wide berth so he can escape.

Most important: Fight only if attacked. Then use any weapon at hand—a knife, scissors, a heavy object, a canister of irritating chemical spray, etc. A gun is useful only if you know how—and are willing—to fire it at the intruder. If you wield a gun tentatively, he might take it away and use it against *you.*

Source: Richard L. Bloom, founder of the Crime Deterrent Institute, Houston. A frequent lecturer on crime prevention and victims' rights, Bloom is the author of *Victims: A Survival Guide for the Age of Crime*, Guardian Press, 10924 Grant Rd. #225, Houston 77070. 800-771-8191.

Antacid Warning

Eating too many calcium-containing antacid tablets can damage the brain and the heart. A 53-year-old man with mild kidney trouble who consumed 20 to 25 antacid tablets a day suffered both a stroke and a heart attack. *Cause:* Too much calcium in his blood from the antacids. *Self-defense:* Get dosage instructions from your doctor before taking antacid tablets.

Source: Jeffrey Frank, MD, director of neuromedical/neurosurgical intensive care, The Cleveland Clinic Foundation.

How to Avoid Becoming a Victim Of a Violent Crime

From purse-snatching and car-jacking to assaults, rapes, and kidnappings, violent crime has become a frightening fact of everyday life. While there's little you can do to control the rise of these crimes, there are ways to limit your chances of becoming a victim.

In your car...

•Car-jacking self-defense. Unlike professional car thieves, who have no wish to encounter car owners, car-jackers are out for a thrill—and violence for them is thrilling. Tell yourself *now* that if someone tries to pull you from your car or demands your keys, you will behave passively and give them the car. When the event occurs, you should instinctively give up the vehicle rather than panic and fight back.

•Keep doors locked while driving. Close windows in slow traffic and at red lights. When coming to a stop, leave enough room between you and the car in front. This will allow you to maneuver around the vehicle if necessary.

•Pay attention to your surroundings. Car-jackers almost always approach on foot. Avoid self-absorbed distractions, such as combing your hair, fumbling with cassette tapes, etc.

•Park under a street light or as close as possible to the mall or well-lit buildings and stores.

Avoid parking next to potential hiding places, such as dumpsters, woods, etc.

•Scan parking lots before approaching your car. Try to walk with other people, or ask a doorman or security guard for an escort.

•Have your key ready in your hand as you approach your vehicle. Look inside the car and around the outside before getting in. *Caution:* On some new cars, all doors will unlock when the driver's door is unlocked—a dangerous feature if someone is hiding outside the passenger door. If you do sense danger, retreat to a place of safety and call the police immediately. Do not confront an intruder.

On the street...

•Carry purses and briefcases close to the body—but be able to release them if necessary. *Avoid:* Shoulder straps across the body, straps wrapped around the wrist. People have been dragged by the straps and injured in purse-snatchings. If someone tries to take your wallet or purse, let it go. *Useful:* "Fanny pack" belts and pouches seem to be an unattractive target for street thieves.

•On the bus or subway, do not sit next to an exit door or place briefcases or purchases on an empty seat. Robbers tend to grab valuables as they are leaving and while doors are closing.

•If you are held up, do not resist. Most armed robbers only want your money. *Problem:* Many will turn to violence if they are alarmed or disobeyed. Surrender your valuables quickly.

At home...

•Keep doors and windows locked, especially after you turn in for the night. Keep curtains drawn after dark. Most home intruders are opportunists.

•Install deadbolt locks with reinforced strike plates on front and back doors. A few dollars will purchase a reinforced strike plate that secures the door frame to the first wall stud. Locks like these are also deterrents.

•Secure sliding glass doors by placing a broomstick or piece of wood along the interior track and by blocking the dead space in the upper channel that allows the door to be lifted off the track.

•Consider installing an alarm system. Ground-floor windows can be equipped with an alarmed jamming stick for $30 to $40.

•Never confront a burglar. If you come home to a door that's ajar or has been tampered with, leave the scene immediately and call the police. If you wake up to find an intruder in your bedroom, pretend to be asleep until he leaves.

•Don't depend on your dog to alert you. Most people command their dogs to *stop* barking when a stranger arrives. Many a dog has slept through a burglary or been seduced by a doggie treat.

•Do not open the door to strangers. If you have to hire an unfamiliar repairman, ask someone to be with you at home or plan to be on the phone when he arrives...or pretend there is someone else at home. If a repairman or stranger arrives at your door unannounced, do not let him/her in. Lock the door and call his office for verification.

•If you think you hear a prowler, call the police. Don't assume it's just the wind, that the police are too busy, or that they might get mad if no one is there. It is always better to feel foolish than to be a victim.

•Unless you are well-trained, do not keep a gun in the house. People who are untrained with firearms are more likely to have them stolen or taken away from them by intruders, who may have arrived unarmed. If you do keep a gun in the house, the gun and ammunition should be stored separately.

Caution: According to law, in order to shoot an intruder on your property, you must be "in fear for your life." This does not mean in fear of losing your TV and jewelry.

•Know your neighbors. Neighborhood watch programs and "telephone trees" to alert neighbors of strangers in the area are very effective.

At work...

•Know your neighbors. Set up a building-wide security policy to identify visitors. "Business watch" programs for merchants in shopping areas are highly effective, too.

•Team up in pairs to use public rest rooms or locked rest rooms located in public hallways. Avoid using remote stairwells alone.

•Keep the office's doors locked when working late, on weekends, or early in the morning.

•Do not get on an elevator with someone who makes you feel uncomfortable or unsafe.

•When traveling on business, ask a bellhop to accompany you to your hotel room and to check it before you enter. Avoid ground-floor rooms. Make sure that the phone is working and that security numbers are provided. Never open the door to someone you're not expecting. If someone knocks unannounced, call the lobby for verification.

At play...

•Exercise with a partner, or take along a dog or stick while jogging. Avoid isolated parks and paths. Wear glasses if you normally need them, and do not use a stereo headset. Avoid loose clothes that are easy to grab.

•At parks, beaches, or other recreation areas, know where the ranger or lifeguard stations are located. Leave expensive cameras, jewelry, and credit cards at home or locked in the trunk of the car. Do not use recreation areas after hours.

In all situations...

•Make direct eye contact with people around you. This sends a message of confidence, an effective deterrent to violent crime. Criminals seek passive, distracted victims, who make easy targets.

•Trust your instincts. Humans are extremely instinctive. *Important:* Tune into the messages. Some of the most common statements police officers hear following a crime are, "I had a feeling I shouldn't have walked to my car," "The guy gave me the creeps, but..."

Bottom line: If a situation makes you nervous, avoid it. Learn to respect your instincts and act on them.

Source: Patricia Harman, a crime-prevention officer with the Prince William County, Virginia, police force. Harman, who conducts lectures nationally on personal safety, is the author of *The Danger Zone: How You Can Protect Yourself from Rape, Robbery, and Assault,* Parkside Publishing, 205 W. Touhy Ave., Park Ridge, IL 60068. 800-221-6364.

The Most Commonly Asked Legal Questions

Sooner or later, you'll probably need the advice of a lawyer. What are you most likely to ask about and how can these legal problems be resolved? Here are the top eight...

When and how can I use small claims court? This is a quick, inexpensive way to solve minor legal problems (typically around $1,000). You don't even need a lawyer.

Step 1: Look in your local telephone directory under "Courts," "City of..." for Small Claims Court, Justice Court, Magistrate's Court, or Court of Common Appeals. You must sue in the county where the defendant lives or conducts business. Check the county clerk to make sure it's the right court, and to get the proper legal name for the company you're suing.

Step 2: When you arrive at court for the first time, a clerk will give you a complaint form to fill out. *Cost:* Between $2 and $10. It asks for your name and address, the defendant's name and address, a brief description of why you're suing and the damages claimed. *Note:* Small claims courts only award money. They cannot order actions.

Step 3: The clerk will assign you a hearing date (usually in about two weeks) and notify the defendant by mail. Often the sessions are held in the early evening.

Step 4: Before your hearing, gather evidence—contracts, photographs, accident reports, witnesses—and organize how you will present your case. A written outline helps. Be sure to get to court on time.

Step 5: If the judge is overloaded, you may be asked to submit your dispute to arbitration—to an impartial third party...often an attorney. That may make sense, but you should know that an arbitrator's decision is final. You won't be able to appeal it to a judge or a higher court. If the defendant fails to appear, you will be sent before an arbitrator who will listen to your testimony and award you appropriate damages (usually including repayment of your filing fee and interest). If the defendant, after being notified by mail, fails to pay up, call the court clerk and ask how to use law-enforcement personnel to collect your judgment.

Is there a statute of limitations on medical malpractice? Yes. As with other causes of action, claims of medical malpractice must be initiated within a given period of time, which differs from state to state. In New York, in the absence of qualifying circumstances, a medical malpractice suit must be initiated within 30 months of the act. However, New York and most other states grant children under age 18 who are the victims of malpractice an extension of time within which to sue. Ask your local bar association for the name of an attorney who can tell you exactly what the law is in your state given your particular circumstances.

What can I do if my landlord refuses to make repairs...or paint? A lease is a contract entitling the landlord to receive rent if he/she provides you with certain guarantees, including a "warranty of habitability" that the place is safe and livable. This means the plumbing should work, etc. Repairs must be made within a "reasonable" period of time, which, of course, varies depending on whether it's a dangerous gas leak or merely a broken dishwasher.

Recourse: Most towns have special housing courts where tenants can file complaints without a lawyer. You could also send the landlord a letter by certified mail warning him that if repairs are not made immediately you will hire a contractor yourself and deduct the cost from your monthly rent.

Under very damning circumstances—if, for example, he has a policy of refusing repairs in order to drive tenants out—you could withhold rent. However, this carries with it the risk of eviction. Don't do it without first consulting a lawyer.

The terms for painting are usually specified in the lease. If the landlord stalls, you can go to the special housing court or to small claims court to have your rent reduced or to get the money needed to hire a painter yourself.

Do I need a lawyer when I'm buying a house? Yes. Buying a house is an extremely complex undertaking and you should be represented by counsel who will look out for your best interests. Is the title good? Does the seller have a faulty deed? Are there any outstanding claims against the property? Does the house satisfy zoning ordinances? Many of these questions are matters of subtle legal interpretation, and you will want written guarantees that fully protect you.

What happens if my credit card or ATM card is stolen? Under the Consumer Credit Protection Act consumers are liable for only $50 if a credit card is stolen, and even that may be waived under some circumstances. However, a different standard applies to automated teller machine cards. Under the federal Electronic Fund Transfer Act, your liability is limited to $50 if you notify the bank within two business days. Thereafter, your liability jumps to $500.

If an unauthorized transfer appears on your bank statement and you don't report it within 60 days of the mailing date you risk losing everything in your account plus any credit line. Report any lost or stolen card to the bank immediately by phone and in writing.

Protection: Don't carry your ATM password in your wallet, and avoid obvious numbers like your birth date and the first four digits of your Social Security number.

Am I legally entitled to see my personnel file at work? You might be, depending on the kind of job you have and the state in which you work. Virtually all employees of the federal government have access, and union contracts provide this same privilege to many workers in the private sector.

Otherwise, your rights depend on the laws of the state where you work. California's Labor Code mandates access to all records "which are used or have been used to determine that employee's qualifications for employment, promotion, additional compensation, termination, or other disciplinary action." Letters of reference and records relating to the investigation of possible criminal offenses are exempt.

Many states have similar statutes, and Oregon requires employers to keep personnel records available to employees for at least 60 days after termination of employment. Contact your State Department of Labor to find out what the law allows.

What can I do about a noisy neighbor? Depending on the specific complaint, your neighbor's actions may constitute a violation of civil or criminal law. Playing loud music late at night amounts to disorderly conduct, for which you can call the police. Civil steps can also be taken under the "nuisance" law, which provides that people have the right to reasonable comfort in their homes. Acts that might be perfectly proper under some circumstances become unlawful if they interfere with your enjoyment of this right.

Example: Your neighbor can use a chain saw, but not at midnight. He has the right to mow his lawn, but maybe not at 6 a.m. on a Sunday morning since he could do it at another time that wouldn't interfere with others' one day to sleep in late.

Do I have a case when I wait for a delivery person who never comes? Yes. This is a breach of contract. If you take a half day off work, for example, and the couch isn't delivered as promised, the store has violated its part of the contract. Call and ask for a new delivery time at your convenience. Most stores can deliver at night, for example, although they don't advertise that. Failing satisfaction, demand that the cost of additional time off from work be deducted from your bill. If all else fails, take the case to small claims court.

Source: Thomas Hauser, lawyer and author of *The Family Legal Companion,* Allworth Press, New York.

Crime Victims

Crime victims who remain calm stay safer. If you are calm, an enraged assailant is more likely to calm down too, and you can prevent any undue harm. *To keep yourself calm:* Breathe slowly and deeply...say the word "relax" over and over in your head...view the mugger as a person instead of an evil criminal—this image is much less intimidating. *To keep the assailant calm:* Be respectful—listen closely to what he says...never argue...give up any possessions he asks for.

Source: Arnold Howard, a black belt in karate in Mesquite, Texas, teaches self-defense nationwide.

Fabric Danger

Formaldehyde resin used to keep no-iron linens, permanent-press clothing, and polyester/cotton fabrics wrinkle-free emits formaldehyde fumes for the life of the fabric—which could be years. *Symptoms of formaldehyde vapor inhalation:* Tiredness, headaches, coughing, watery eyes, respiratory problems. *Self-defense:* Buy only natural fibers, which are generally not treated with formaldehyde. *Also:* Avoid fabrics with labels reading "easy care 100% cotton" or "no-iron cotton," which could mean formaldehyde finishes.

Source: *The Nontoxic Home and Office: Protecting Yourself and Your Family from Everyday Toxics and Health Hazards* by consumer advocate Debra Lynn Dadd, Jeremy P. Tarcher, Inc., Los Angeles.

Beware of Telemarketers

Beware of telemarketers who ask for your checking account number rather than your credit card number. With a checking account number, they can print a "demand draft," which permits them to withdraw your money. Your bank probably won't notice that your signature is missing because drafts look like checks and are processed quickly.

Source: Gerri Detweiler, a consumer credit consultant in Arlington, Virginia. She is author of *The Ultimate Credit Handbook,* Good Advice Press, Elizaville, New York.

How to Get Rid Of Nightmares

A nightmare, technically, is a frightening dream that wakes you up. If you don't wake up, it's a bad dream. Nightmares' contents are no different than the contents of normal dreams, according to my research. *What is different:* How you react to your dreams.

How we respond to our dreams is affected in great part by how we feel both physically and emotionally. You can get rid of your nightmares by getting rid of things that can cause you to react badly to your dreams. *These include:*

• *Medications.* Certain drugs can increase the incidence of nightmares. Beta blockers (for hypertension and irregular heartbeat), tricyclic antidepressants, sleeping pills, nasal sprays.

Solution: Ask your doctor about changing prescribed medications.

• *Stress.* Feeling on edge increases your susceptibility to nightmares.

Solution: Use stress-reduction and relaxation techniques...and exercise.

• *Illnesses.* Any illness can make you feel bad. And feeling bad can cause nightmares. Sometimes, a nightmare can warn you of a medical problem that hasn't even been diagnosed yet.

Solution: For minor illnesses, the nightmares will go away as you get better. If other nightmare-causing factors are ruled out, see your doctor for evaluation.

• *Miscellaneous problems.* For many, nightmares have no obvious cause.

Solution: Figure out what's causing the nightmares by making a connection between the nightmare and real life. *To make the connection:* Think metaphorically.

Example: A nightmare about being assaulted may be a metaphor for feeling threatened or intimidated by your boss, or a friend or relative.

Alternate solution: Confront a recurrent nightmare by imagining how you want it resolved before you go to sleep.

Examples: A person who dreams that he's being followed by a stranger can imagine that the person is simply a friend who wants to say hello...a child who dreams that a monster is chasing him can imagine turning to the monster and saying, "You can't scare me anymore. Go away."

Source: Milton Kramer, MD, director, Sleep Disorder Center, Bethesda Oak Hospital, Cincinnati.

Lead Poisoning From Pewter

Eating or drinking from pewter can cause lead poisoning. Even though pewter sold in the United States is supposed to be safe, don't bet your life on it. Although the US has regulated lead content in pewter manufacturing since 1867, it is difficult to establish an item's age or country of origin.

And pewter products that contain no lead may be soldered with it. *Bottom line:* Any pewter should remain suspect until it has been tested for lead leaching. *Home test:* The Frandon Red Alert Kit, 800-332-7723.

Source: Richard Wedeen, MD, nephrologist and author of *Poison in the Pot: The Legacy of Lead.*

Computer News That You Can Use

Protect computer systems by using modems that will connect with an outside call only if the call comes from an authorized phone number. A hacker trying to gain access to the system won't be at such a number, and so won't be able to succeed.

Source: Eric Paulak, editor, *411,* 11300 Rockville Pike, Rockville, MD 20852.

How to Prevent Cellular Phone Fraud

Even companies that make minimal use of cellular phones are vulnerable to being ripped off by the growing number of cellular hackers.

Achilles' heel: The phone's electronic serial number (ESN)—embedded on a computer chip inside the phone...and its mobile ID number (MIN)—the telephone number assigned by the cellular phone company.

These numbers can be detected and decoded by criminals equipped with special devices that pick up cellular phone signals and record the two key numbers. These can then be used for illegal cellular service, ending up on the company's bill. They can also be picked up from office files or computers. *Self-defense:*

- Instruct the cellular carrier to block all international calls—unless you absolutely must use your cellular phone for overseas calling.
- Keep all cellular phone records locked.
- Don't keep ESNs and associated MINs on a computer. If a hacker wants your numbers, chances are he'll know his way around computer files as well as he does around the cellular airwaves.
- Don't divulge ESNs and associated MINs to anyone except the person responsible for dealing with the cellular company. The numbers should be in as few hands as possible to maintain maximum security.
- Ask for the most detailed form of billing available from the carrier—so you can carefully scrutinize calling records.

Source: Dick Sharman, The Guidry Group, telecommunications consultants, 1400 Woodloch Forest Dr., Woodlands, Texas 77380, quoted in *411*, 11300 Rockville Pike, Rockville, MD 20852.

Diamond Savvy

Beware of a diamond that has been set so that the pavilion (bottom) of the stone is blocked from view or enclosed in metal. A closed back is often a sign that something is being hidden. *Examples:* The stone may be a rhinestone (glass with a foil back)...a lower quality diamond with a coating to improve its color...a single-cut diamond made to appear like an expensive brilliant-cut diamond.

Source: *The Diamond Ring Buying Guide* by Renée Newman, International Jewelry Publications, Box 13334, Los Angeles 90013.

New Gold Card Scam

A caller says you have been pre-approved for a gold card and he/she just needs a little information to send the card to you. He asks for Social Security, checking account and credit card numbers and your mother's birth name. You never get the card. The caller gets information to tap into your bank accounts and credit lines. *Self-defense:* By law, credit card issuers must have your written approval to send you a card. Tell any caller to send you an application by mail. Or just hang up.

Source: John Barker, National Consumers League, 815 15 St. NW, Washington, DC 20005. 202-639-8140.

The Angry Victim Syndrome

Some victims are strong-willed people who get angry when they can't control others.

These people, whom I call *angry victims,* want others to live up to their often unreasonable expectations...and then feel angry when people inevitably disappoint them.

In order to change, angry victims have to realize that the problem lies within themselves, and that controlling others is not the solution.

Who's an angry victim...

Angry victims, most of whom are women, swing between two poles—the desire to control...and the desire to please.

Example: When Laura disagreed with her husband, she would first suppress her anger in order to please him. Eventually, however, she would swing to the control pole and fly into a rage. But then, she would start to worry about losing him ...and backpedal, apologizing profusely for getting so angry. *Result:* He became confused and the relationship ultimately suffered.

Angry victims constantly flip back and forth in their emotions because they're not comfortable in either mode. They're afraid that if they exert too much control, people will become distant and angry with them.

At the same time, they're afraid that if they try too hard to please, people will take advantage of them.

Whichever pole they gravitate to, they're *afraid* of something...and sure to lose no matter what they do. *Result:* Angry victims live in a state of constant fear.

Since pain hurts more if you're already fearful and tense, angry victims are often stunned by the depth of the feelings generated by a minor disappointment. A normal domestic problem can seem like a tragedy.

Example: Len's wife, Nora, got tied up at the office one night. She came home late and forgot to call. Len felt rejected and flew into a rage.

Although angry victims expect a lot from their friends and loved ones, most have a limited tolerance for the expectations and desires of others. This allows them to blame others for their problems.

Example: Sue, who hadn't had a serious relationship in years, finally met a man who appeared to be perfect for her...but two months later, she was complaining about him. For one thing, he dropped in whenever he wanted to, which she thought was rude and demanding. After some counseling, Sue realized that she hadn't had a relationship for so long because she didn't want to put up with anyone else's schedules. The problem was hers, not his.

Are you an angry victim?

There are three aspects to the angry victim syndrome:

- Fear of abandonment.
- Fear of engulfment.
- Need to control.

If you suspect you're an angry victim, give yourself these tests:

- Abandonment test. Fantasize that everyone in your life calls you on the same day and says they never want to talk to you again. How much rejection would it take—one person, two people, 10 people—for you to feel devastated?

If even one rejection would be extremely hurtful, you're probably trying too hard to please people.

- Engulfment test. Fantasize that everyone in your life calls you on the same day and invites you out to dinner. How many offers would it take to make you uncomfortable?

Again, the fewer people it would take, the more likely it is that you're afraid of being overwhelmed with a lot of love and attention.

- Control test. Think back to minor disappointments, when people who you depended on did something that you thought was wrong. What was your reaction to those incidents? Did you laugh or cry or get angry?

If you got angry or frustrated, you probably have a control problem. And the sooner you felt that way, the bigger the problem.

How to stop being an angry victim...

If the above test shows that you could be an angry victim, follow these steps:

- Go easy on yourself. Most angry victims are extremely self-critical. Don't beat yourself up because you've discovered the problem—understanding that you have a problem should be the first step toward overcoming it.
- Realize that your expectations are not unnatural. They come from our bedrock fears about the world—that we're not going to be loved and cared for...that we can't control what happens to us.

Instead of rejecting these fears, be aware of them and be honest about them...with other people as well as with yourself.

- Let others know how you feel. Talking things over with people you're close to is the best way to work out your angry-victim problems.

Example: Jody was upset because her friend Tina never seemed to have enough time for her. She fought the desire to get angry and told Tina how she felt. Tina explained that her idea of friendship was having a lot of casual friends to see occasionally for lunch. Although the two couldn't be close friends, the conversation helped Jody break out of her angry-victim cycle.

- Recognize when you're out of balance. Work to stay in the *golden zone*—where you feel adequately loved yet adequately free to do what you want and reasonably in control of your life.

This is a very hard balance to maintain, and you won't get there by pushing yourself. *Better:* Respect and acknowledge your needs for love, freedom and control.

Source: Martin G. Groder, MD, a psychiatrist and business consultant in Chapel Hill, NC. His book, *Business Games: How to Recognize the Players and Deal With Them,* is available from Boardroom Classics, 55 Railroad Ave., Greenwich, CT 06830.

Better than an Unlisted Number

Have the phone company publish the number under your wife's maiden name...or your dog's name...or some other easily remembered "made-up" name. This will also keep strangers from getting your phone number, and it costs you nothing. Unlisting costs a few dollars a month. *Added benefit:* You'll be able to identify some sales calls immediately ("Hello, Mr. Fido...").

Source: Herbert J. Teison, publisher, *Travel Smart,* 40 Beechdale Rd., Dobbs Ferry, NY 10522.

High-Heel Danger

High-heeled shoes shift most of the wearer's weight to the front of the foot. *Result:* Calluses ...hammertoes...blisters...Achilles' tendinitis... Morton's neuroma (an inflammation of the nerve between the third and fourth toes). Shoes with narrow, pointed toes can cause ingrown toenails ...corns...bunions.

Help for feet: If you must wear high heels—elevate tired feet...soak them in a warm water bath...massage them gently.

Source: *University of Texas Lifetime Health Letter,* 7000 Fannin St., Houston 77030.

Instant Revenge Against Obscene Phone Caller

Electronic voice boxes are available with a preprogrammed joke script by comics such as Henny Youngman and Jackie Mason. Hold it up to the phone, press a button and have the last laugh.

Warning Signs Burglars Fear

If a burglar sees warning signs, no matter how outlandish, on your house, he will think twice before breaking in. These signs should be handwritten, in large, clear print, on six-inch by eight-inch cards posted above each doorknob. Don't put them on the street or in your yard where passersby can see them. You don't want to give a burglar a reason to case your place and find out they are not true. Make up your own wording. Just be sure the signs look fresh and new. *Some suggestions:*

• "Danger: Extremely vicious, barkless German Dobermans." In his nervous frame of mind, a burglar probably isn't going to wonder if there is such a thing. He won't want to take the chance.

• "Knock all you want. We don't answer the door." Most burglars check to see if anyone's home before breaking in. About 95% of those questioned said they'd pass up a house with that sign.

• "Carpenter: Please do not enter through this door. My son's three rattlesnakes have gotten out of the cage, and we've closed them off in this room until he returns. Sorry for this inconvenience."

• "Attack dogs trained and sold here." Again, 95% of those questioned said they'd pass up a house with that sign. Have one engraved, and post it on your front door (so it can't be seen from the street).

• Leave extremely large bones and two-foot wide dog dishes near all entrances. A person up to no good will think a very large dog lives there.

How Burglars Say They Break In

Some burglar-survey results:

• 75% were more likely to go through windows than doors. (Sliding glass doors are easier to open than wooden ones.) *Remedy:* Storm windows. No one surveyed would bother with them at all.

•85% cased out a house before hitting it. *Important:* If you see a stranger hanging around, call the police.

•Only 20% picked locks or tried to pick them. It takes too much skill. There are so many faster ways into a house.

•63% cut the phone lines before entering. *Remedy:* A sign saying that the police will be notified automatically if the phone lines are cut.

•65% said that a large, unfriendly dog would scare them away. *Most frightening:* Dobermans.

•80% looked in garage windows to see if a homeowner's car was there. *Remedy:* Cover your garage windows.

•50% said that neighborhood security guards didn't deter them.

•72% made their entrance from the back.

•56% continued to burglarize if they were already inside when they realized people were home sleeping.

Choosing the Right Lock

There are two major components to a truly thief-resistant lock system: Strong, tamper-proof basic hardware and a key that is impossible to duplicate without your knowledge and permission.

Assuming that the main access door to your house or apartment is structurally sound and hinged on the outside, the standard mechanism for keeping it securely closed is an interlocking deadbolt latch. What makes the latch burglar-proof is the outside lock that controls it and the plate that protects the lock.

• *Current best cylinder and plate:* The Abloy disklock. Instead of pins, which can be picked, it has rotating disks like the tumblers on a bank vault door.

• *Next best locks:* The Fichet, Medeco, Bodyguard and Miwa systems.

Add-on security devices:

Steel gates for windows near fire escapes or at ground level (gates must be approved by the fire department).

Source: Neal Geffner, vice president, Abbey Locksmiths, New York.

Choosing a Locksmith

•Go to the locksmiths' shops to size them up.

•Make sure the store is devoted exclusively to the locksmith business and isn't just doing locksmithing on the side.

•Ask to see the locksmith's license if it's not displayed. There are a lot of unlicensed people doing business illegally.

• *Best:* Locksmiths who belong to an association. They are keeping up with the latest developments. Look for a sticker in the window indicating membership in a local or national locksmiths' association.

A Secure Door

•If you're buying a door, buy a metal flush door without panels and get an equally strong frame to match it. *Cost:* About $500. *What makes a good frame:* A hollow metal construction, same as the door.

•On a metal door, use a Segal lock on the inside and a Medeco on the outside with a Medeco Bodyguard cylinder guard plate. If it's a tubular lock, get Medeco's D-11. It gives you the option of a key on the inside, and you don't need a guard plate.

•If your door has panels on it, put a piece of sheet steel on it. If the panels are glass, replace them with Lexon, an unbreakable plastic.

•If you have a wooden door, get what the industry calls a police lock. This is a brace lock with a bar that goes from the lock into the floor about 30 inches away from the base of the door. Also, get a police lock if your door frame is weak. It keeps the door from giving because of the brace in the floor. Even the best regular locks won't protect you if the whole frame gives.

•Jimmy bars: Don't bother with them. They're psychological protection only. If you have a metal door, a good lock is sufficient protection. Use a jimmy bar on a metal door only if the door has been damaged through a forcible break-in and is separated from the frame. The bar will straighten out the door and hide some of the light shining through. On a wooden door, a jimmy bar can actually help a burglar by giving him leverage. He can put a crowbar up against it, dig into the wood and break through the door.

•If your door opens out instead of in, get a double bar lock—one that extends horizontally on each side. With a door that opens out, the hinges are often exposed on the outside, allowing a burglar to remove the door from its hinges. With a double bar lock, he can't pull the door out.

Source: Sal Schillizzi of All-Over Locksmiths, Inc., New York, a national safecracking champion.

Buying a Burglar Alarm

Home alarm systems, once mainly for the rich, are coming into widespread use because locks aren't deterring burglars. Recent FBI figures show that 82% of the time, illegal entry is gained through home doors, most often the front door.

Burglars just break open the door with their shoulders. Faced with a deadbolt or double lock, the burglar will use a heavy tool to take out the frame.

•What to look for in an alarm: One that sounds off (not a silent alarm), so that the burglar is aware of it and alarm central (a security company office or the local police) is alerted.

•Select a system with sensors on vulnerable doors and windows. Good systems need a complex electrical tie-in in the basement, as well as a control panel installed away from prying eyes and little children. Good systems can also switch on lights and TV sets and alert alarm central by automatic telephone dialing or a radio signal.

•Have a secondary line of defense. This can be a few thin electronic pressure pads under rugs in high traffic areas or strategically placed photoelectric cells.

•Choose a reputable, well-tested system. The brand names are American District Telegraph (ADT), Honeywell, Silent Knight and ADEMCO.

•Be aware of the danger of continual false alarms. The police may ticket you if the family is to blame.

•Don't forget to test your alarm system regularly.

•Don't be lulled into a false sense of security.

•Continue to take all necessary precautions with locks and garage doors.

Best Places in Your House to Hide Valuables

Even if you have a safe, you still need a good hiding place for the safe key or combination. It should not be hidden anywhere near the safe. And, if you don't have a safe, you should hide your jewelry and other valuables where they won't be found.

•Don't hide things in any piece of furniture with drawers. Drawers are the first place burglars ransack.

•Don't hide anything in the bedroom. Thieves tend to be most thorough in checking out bedrooms. Find hiding places in the attic, basement or kitchen. In 90% of burglaries, the kitchen is untouched.

•Don't be paranoid. If you have thought up a good location, relax. A burglar can't read your mind.

Try hiding things in the following spots:

•Inside the phony wall switches and generic label cans sold by mail-order houses.

•In a book, if you have a large book collection. So you don't forget which book you chose, use the title to remind you (for example, *The Golden Treasury of Science Fiction*). Or, buy a hollowed-out book for this purpose.

• Inside zippered couch cushions.

• In the back of a console TV or stereo speakers (thieves usually steal only receivers, not speakers) or in the type of speakers that look like books.

• Under the dirt in a plant. Put non-paper valuables in a plastic bag and bury them.

• Under the carpet (for small, flat things).

• In between stacks of pots in the kitchen, or wrapped up and labeled as food in the refrigerator or freezer.

• Inside an old, out-of-order appliance in the basement.

• In a pile of scrap wood beneath the workbench.

• In the middle of a sack of grass seed.

Source: Linda Cain, author of *How to Hide Your Valuables,* Beehive Communications, Medfield, MA.

What to Do if You Come Home During a Burglary

• If you walk in on a burglar by accident, ask an innocent question.

Example: "Oh, you're the guy who's supposed to pick up the package, aren't you?" If, at this point, the burglar tries to run away, it's smart to step aside.

• Resist the temptation to yell or otherwise bring on a confrontation. Go as quickly and quietly as possible to a neighbor's and call the police from there.

• Avoid walking into your home while a thief is there by leaving a $20 bill conspicuously placed, near the door. If the bill is gone when you return home, someone else may be there. Leave at once and call the police.

Source: Margaret Kenda, *Crime Prevention For Business Owners,* AMACOM, NY and *How to Protect Yourself From Crime,* Avon Books, NY.

Safe Food Storage

• Yellow bananas can be held at the just-ripe stage in the refrigerator for up to six days. Although the peel might discolor slightly, the fruit retains both its flavor and nutrition. Ripen green bananas at room temperature first. Mashed banana pulp can be frozen.

• Nuts in the shell keep at room temperature for only a short time. Put them in a cool, dry place for prolonged storage. Shelled nuts remain fresh for several months when sealed in containers and refrigerated. For storage of up to a year, place either shelled or unshelled nuts in a tightly closed container in the freezer.

Storage times for frozen meats vary significantly. *Recommended holding time in months:*

• Beef roast or steak, 12.
• Ground beef, 6.
• Lamb, 12.
• Pork roasts and chops, 8-12.
• Bacon and ham, 1-2.
• Veal cutlets and chops, 6.
• Veal roasts, 8-10.
• Chicken and turkey, 12.
• Duck and goose, 6.
• Shellfish, not over 6.
• Cooked meat and poultry, 1.

Keep an accurate thermometer in your refrigerator or freezer. *Optimal refrigerator temperature:* 40°F for food to be kept more than three or four days. *For the freezer:* 0° is necessary for long-term storage. *Note:* Some parts of the freezer may be colder than other parts. Use the thermometer to determine which areas are safe for keeping foods long-term.

Freezing leftovers:

• Raw egg whites: Freeze them in ice cube trays.

• Hard cheeses: Grate them first.

• Soup stock: Divide it into portions.

• Stale bread: Turn it into crumbs in the blender.

• Pancakes, french toast and waffles: Freeze and reheat in the toaster oven at 375°.

• Whipped cream: Drop into small mounds on a cookie sheet to freeze and then store the mounds in a plastic bag.

• Citrus juices: Freeze in an ice cube tray.

•Freezing fish: Make a protective dip by stirring one tablespoonful of unflavored gelatin into ¼ cup lemon juice and 1¾ cups cold water. Heat over a low flame, stirring constantly, until gelatin dissolves and mixture is clear. Cool to room temperature. Dip the fish into this solution and drain. Wrap individual fish pieces in heavy-duty freezer wrap. Then place them in heavy-duty freezer bags. Use within two months.

•If you do your own food canning, preserve only enough food to eat within one year. After that time, quality deteriorates.

Sources: Tom Grady and Amy Rood, coauthors, *The Household Handbook,* Meadowbrook Press, Deephaven, MN, and Joan Cone, author of *Fish and Game Cooking,* EPM Publications, McLean, VA.

Keeping Food from Becoming Tainted

When in doubt, throw it out. This is the general rule concerning food you think may have become spoiled. This includes frozen food that has thawed too long or dishes that haven't been properly handled. *Example:* Cheesecake left on a counter to cool overnight can easily go bad.

Other tips for storing and handling food:

•Keep food at temperatures below 45°F or above 160°F.

•Always keep in mind that food left away from heat or cold for two to three hours is probably unsuitable for eating. This is particularly true of foods that are moist, high in protein and low in acid.

•Refrigerate leftovers as soon as possible. Don't let them sit at room temperature for more than two hours.

•Reheat food in wide, shallow pans rather than deep, narrow ones. Place foods in a preheated oven, not one that's warming up.

•When refrigerating large quantities of dishes such as stews, spaghetti sauce or chili, pour them into large, shallow containers. The point is to expose the greatest mass to the preserving effects of the cold refrigerator.

•If possible, thaw frozen foods by placing them in the refrigerator. If thawing must be done quickly, immerse the food in cold water or use a microwave oven.

To Avoid Food Poisoning

•Never let food cool to room temperature before putting it in the refrigerator. Slow cooling encourages the growth of bacteria.

•Do not thaw frozen foods for hours at room temperature. Allow them to thaw slowly in the refrigerator, or, wrap them in plastic and soak in cold water.

•Bacteria in raw poultry, fish or meat could contaminate your cutting board. Scrub the board after each use.

•Do not use cans that bulge or that contain off-color or unusual-smelling food. *Dangerous:* Tasting the contents to see whether they are bad.

•Lead poisoning can result from storing food in open cans. The solder that seals the tinned-steel can leaches into the contents. *Most hazardous:* Acidic foods, especially juices. They interact quickly with metal.

•Although cooking spoiled food destroys bacteria, it does not remove the poisons the bacteria produced.

Source: *Modern Maturity.*

What to Do If You're Mugged

Getting mugged these days is a real and personal threat, not something that happens just to other people. Fortunately, most muggings are simple robberies in which neither the criminal nor the victim is hurt. However, the possibility of violence is always there.

Suggestions:

•Cooperate. Assume the mugger is armed. No matter how strong or fit you are, you are no match for a gun or knife. Remember that your personal safety is far more important than your valuables or your pride.

•Follow the mugger's instructions to the letter. Try not to move too quickly or too slowly—either could upset him.

•Stay as calm as possible, and encourage companions to do the same.

•Give the mugger whatever he asks for. Don't argue. But if something is of great sentimental value to you, give it to him, and only then say, "This watch was given to me by my grandfather. It means a lot to me. I'd be very grateful if you'd let me keep it."

•When he has all he wants of your valuables, ask him what he wants you to do while he gets away—stay where you are, lie face down, whatever. If he dismisses you, leave the scene immediately, and don't look back. Don't call the police until you are in a safe place.

Some important don'ts:

•Don't reach for your wallet in a back pocket without explaining first what you plan to do. The mugger might think you are reaching for a gun.

•Don't give him dirty looks or make judgmental remarks.

•Don't threaten him with hostile comments.

•Don't be a wiseguy or a joker. Even smiling is a dangerous idea. He may think you are laughing at him.

•Don't try any tricks like carrying a second empty wallet to give to a mugger. This could make him angry. Some experts even recommend that you carry at least $50 with you at all times to keep from upsetting a mugger.

Source: Ken Glickman, third degree black belt and coordinator of Educational Services, Greenwich Institute for American Education, Greenwich, CT.

Toilet Seat Danger

You can catch diarrhea, intestinal bugs, and hepatitis from toilet seats. *Trap:* When toilets are flushed, a fine mist of water that could contain contagious fecal bacteria rises and lands on toilet seats and flush handles. *Best defense:* Clean your toilet three times a week with disinfectant...avoid using public rest rooms—especially the most popular middle stall...stand before flushing.

Source: Dr. Charles Gerba, University of Arizona.

Wash Away Poison Ivy

Poison ivy can be nipped in the bud if you wash the resin off your skin within 10 minutes of exposure.

Source: *The Pharmacist's Prescription: Your Complete Guide to the Over-the-Counter Remedies That Work Best* by F. James Grogan, Pharm. D., Rawson Associates, New York.

Tap Water Danger Signals

Check the color of your water to find clues to its quality.

Green stains in your sink or toilet are a sign of higher-than-normal levels of copper which may cause kidney problems. Brown stains may mean that there are high levels of iron in your water.

25

Breaking Bad Habits

Smoking: The Sobering Facts

By now, most Americans are well aware that smoking causes lung cancer.

But tobacco is a far bigger villain than most of us could ever imagine. Cigarettes, pipes, cigars, snuff, and chewing tobacco kill more than 434,000 Americans each year—accounting for almost one out of five premature deaths in this country.

Lung cancer is just the first in a long and harrowing litany of tobacco-related problems.

Other tobacco dangers...

- Addictiveness. While some people have likened the addictive potential of nicotine to that of heroin, the good news is that tens of millions of people have been *trying* to quit smoking.
- Back pain. Smoking is probably a major risk factor in recovery from back pain (the leading cause of worker disability in the US) because poor oxygen levels of those who smoke prevent lumbar disks from being adequately oxygenated.
- Bladder cancer. Smoking causes 40% of all cases of bladder cancer, accounting for more than 4,000 new cases annually.
- Breast cancer. Women who smoke are 75% more likely to develop breast cancer than are nonsmoking women.
- Cervical cancer. Up to one-third of all cases of cervical cancer—7,000 new cases a year—are directly attributable to smoking. Women who smoke are four times more likely to develop the disease than are nonsmoking women.
- Childhood respiratory ailments. Youngsters exposed to parents' tobacco smoke have six times as many respiratory infections as kids of nonsmoking parents. Smokers' children also face an increased risk of cough, chronic bronchitis, and pneumonia.
- Diabetes. Smoking decreases the body's absorption of insulin. *Also:* Smoking exacerbates the damage of small blood vessels in the eyes, ears, and feet of diabetics.

•Drug interactions. Smokers need higher than normal dosages of certain drugs, including theophylline (asthma medication), heparin (used to prevent blood clotting), propranolol (used for angina and high blood pressure), and medications for depression and anxiety.

•Ear infections. Children of smokers face an increased risk of otitis media (middle ear infection).

•Emphysema. Smoking accounts for up to 85% of all deaths attributable to emphysema (chronic obstructive pulmonary disease).

•Esophageal cancer. Smoking accounts for 80% of all cases of esophageal cancer, which each year kills 15,000 Americans.

•Fires. Smoking is the leading cause of fires in homes, hotels and hospitals. The toll is astronomical in terms of suffering and of economic loss.

•Gastrointestinal cancer. Preliminary research indicates that smoking at least doubles the risk of cancer of the stomach and duodenum—the portion of the small intestine just downstream from the stomach.

•Heart disease. Smokers are up to four times more likely to develop cardiovascular disease than nonsmokers. *Mechanism:* Carbon monoxide and other poison gases in tobacco smoke replace oxygen in the blood cells, promote coronary spasm and cause accumulation of clot-producing platelets.

•Infertility. Couples in which at least one member smokes are more than three times more likely to have trouble conceiving than nonsmoking couples.

Explanation: Tobacco smoke interferes with the implantation of a fertilized egg within the uterus. It reduces the number and quality of sperm cells in a man's ejaculate and raises the number of abnormal sperm cells...and increases a man's risk of penile cancer. Women who smoke are more likely to miscarry or deliver prematurely than nonsmoking women. Some scientists now theorize that toxins in the bloodstream of pregnant smokers pass through the placenta to the fetus, sowing the seeds for future cancers.

•Kidney cancer. Smoking causes 40% of all cases of kidney cancer.

•Laryngeal cancer. Smokers who smoke more than 25 cigarettes a day are 25 to 30 times more likely to develop cancer of the larynx than nonsmokers.

•Leukemia. In addition to tobacco smoke condensate, better known as tar, tobacco smoke contains several powerful carcinogens, including the organic chemical benzene and a radioactive form of the element polonium, both of which are known to cause leukemia.

•Low birth weight. Women who smoke as few as five cigarettes daily during pregnancy face a significantly greater risk of giving birth to an unnaturally small, lightweight infant.

•Mouth cancer. Tobacco causes the vast majority of all cancers of the mouth, lips, cheek, tongue, salivary glands and even tonsils. Men who smoke, dip snuff or chew tobacco face a 27-fold risk of these cancers. Women smokers —because they have tended to use less tobacco—face a six-fold risk.

•Nutrition. People who smoke tend to have poorer nutrition than do nonsmokers. People who smoke also have lower levels of HDL (good cholesterol).

•Occupational lung cancer. Although a nonsmoker's risk of lung cancer increases six times due to prolonged occupational exposure to asbestos, that risk jumps to 92 times in an asbestos worker who smokes.

•Osteoporosis. Women who smoke experience menopause on an average of five to 10 years earlier than nonsmokers, causing a decline in estrogen production—and thinning bones—at an earlier age.

•Pharyngeal (throat) cancer. Last year cancer of the pharynx killed 3,650 Americans—and the vast majority of these deaths resulted directly from smoking.

•Premature aging. Constant exposure to tobacco smoke prematurely wrinkles the facial skin and yellows the teeth and fingernails.

•Recovery from injury or surgery. Smokers have delayed wound and bone healing. They also have a greater risk of complications from surgery, including pneumonia (due to weaker lungs) as well as a longer hospital stay.

•Stroke. Smoking doubles the risk of stroke among men and women. *Special danger:* In women who smoke and use oral contraceptives, the risk of stroke is 10-fold.

•Tooth loss. Use of snuff or chewing tobacco causes gum recession and tooth abrasion, two frequent contributors to tooth loss.

Source: Alan Blum, MD, family physician, department of family medicine, Baylor College of Medicine, Houston. Dr. Blum is the founder and president of Doctors Ought to Care (DOC), c/o department of family medicine, Baylor College of Medicine, 5510 Greenbriar, Houston 77005, an anti-smoking group long-recognized for its service to public health.

Kicking the Cigarette Habit

Tactics for giving up cigarettes vary according to the underlying motivation for smoking. *Keys to the right strategy:*

•Habitual smokers reach for a cigarette in response to such cues as talking on the phone or drinking. *First step:* Make the cigarettes difficult to reach, or put them in a hard-to-open package.

•Positive-effect smokers actually enjoy smoking. *First step:* Find an equally enjoyable activity that can't be done while smoking.

•Negative-effect smokers smoke because of nervousness or depression. *First step:* Professional advice on the basic problem.

•Physically addicted smokers should quit cold turkey. The reactions to quitting are always unpleasant. But the worst of them will be over in a week.

Source: *Executive Fitness Newsletter,* Emmaus, PA.

Learning Not to Smoke

Will-power has less to do with kicking the cigarette habit than acquiring the skills to stop smoking. One widely successful treatment uses a gradual, self-directed learning program.

First, plan to stop smoking during a relatively stable period in your work and social life. Understand your smoking habits by keeping a simple diary that records how many cigarettes you smoke daily and how badly you want each one. Score the craving on a scale of one (automatic, boredom) to four (powerful desire). Firm up your commitment by enlisting a nonsmoking buddy to call up and encourage you several times a week.

Phase out the cigarettes in three stages...

1. *Taper.* Heavy smokers should reduce to 12 to 15 cigarettes daily. If that's your present level, then reduce to eight or nine a day. Use a smoke suppression drill, a mental learning process, each time you have an urge to smoke. Begin by focusing on the craving; then immediately associate it with a negative effect of smoking, such as filthy lung passages, clogged, fatty arteries, or skin wrinkled and aged by carbon monoxide and nicotine. *Next:* Relax and imagine a peaceful scene. Follow up with a pleasant image associated with nonsmoking (smooth skin or greater vitality).

2. *How to withdraw.* One week before your scheduled quitting date, smoke only four cigarettes a day. Smoke two cigarettes in a 15-minute period. Wait at least an hour, and then smoke the other two. While gulping down the cigarettes, concentrate on the negative sensations: Scratchy throat and lungs, foul breath. Keep up negative thoughts for at least five minutes after finishing the last cigarette.

3. *Quit.* When a smoking urge arises, conjure up the negative image, relax, and follow it with a pleasing fantasy. Also, call your non-smoking buddy for moral support.

Note: Never label yourself a failure. If you have a relapse, return to the tapering phase, and try the procedure again.

Source: *The American Way of Life Need Not Be Hazardous to Your Health* by John Farquhar, MD, W.W. Norton & Co., New York.

Prescription Drug Addiction

For every person addicted to heroin in the US, there are 10 hooked on prescription drugs. And withdrawal can be as painful as from any in the illicit-drug world.

Why addiction happens: The doctor prescribes a psychoactive drug (one that affects the mind or behavior) to relieve a physical ailment. By altering your moods, psychoactive drugs can affect your ability to make judgments and decisions. Some drugs mask the symptoms of serious ailments or can impair your physical activity. These drugs have their place among useful medications (generally for short-term relief), but they do not cure physical ailments.

Most commonly abused psychoactive drugs: Codeine, Valium, Librium, Demerol, Dalmane, and Nembutol. *Worse:* Mixing drugs or combining a drug with alcohol.

- If your physician is reluctant to make a specific diagnosis or refuses to explain the effects of drugs, find another doctor.
- Question every prescription you're given: Will it cure the ailment or will it just relieve the symptoms?
- Before accepting a drug for an emotional problem, seek another solution: a vacation, exercise, counseling.
- If the problem is physical, ask why this drug is being prescribed rather than another treatment.

Source: *Executive Fitness Newsletter,* Emmaus, PA.

26

Psychology

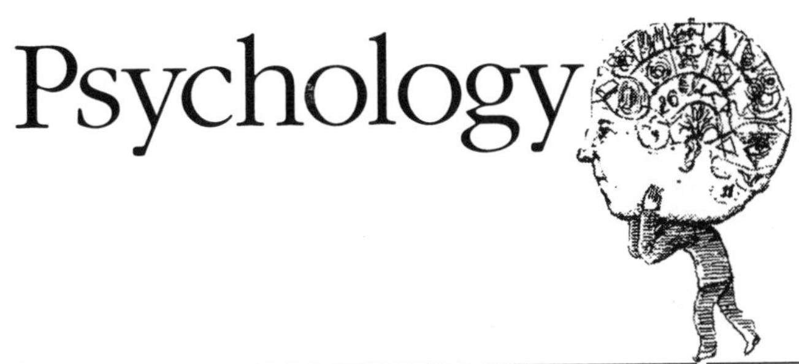

The Power of Positive Relationships

People who build constructive relationships with their personal friends and family members gain important benefits...

- They are healthier.
- They live longer.
- They succeed in most of their activities.

A Duke University study of 1,300 patients who had suffered coronary attacks showed that those patients who were socially isolated ...unmarried, with no confidants...had a death rate three times as high as those with stronger social ties. *How positive relationships help...*

- Sociable people take better care of themselves. People who value their friendships with others are more likely to stop smoking...continue to take required medications...go to the doctor more often when they're ill. That's because even when they are tempted to let things slide, their friends get after them.

Example: In a support group for women with breast cancer observed by Dr. David Spiegel of Stanford University, when one woman mentioned new pains, the other women in the group convinced her to report it immediately to the doctor even though she was inclined to wait until her next appointment.

- Sociable people are physically healthier. Researchers have found that social ties have physiological effects that make people healthier. Sociable people feel less depressed...notice fewer aches and pains...have lower levels of stress-related hormones.

Psychologist James Pennebaker found that when people discussed stressful events with others, even with strangers, their blood pressure declined.

Building better relationships...

Obviously, it's in everyone's self-interest to build good relationships with others...and fortunately it's a skill that can be learned even if it doesn't come naturally.

If you want to form more positive relationships but have always found it difficult because of your personality, your best strategy is to begin by changing your behavior, not your attitudes. *Strategies that can help you improve your relationships...*

•Practice listening. At least once a day, when someone is talking to you, force yourself to let that person finish what he/she is saying. Even if you find it hard to pay attention, don't interrupt or disconnect...at least look attentive.

It may be difficult at first, but gradually you will learn that other people may have something worthwhile to say, you can learn something from them...and when you show them that you recognize that, you'll get through to them better, as well.

You will gradually come to appreciate where other people are coming from, become *more tolerant,* and find relationships with others easier to make and more enjoyable.

•Get involved with community affairs or volunteer work. If you don't already have satisfying personal relationships, one good way to make connections is to participate in community-service activities. Research studies have found that men who volunteered had greater longevity and reported better health than their non-volunteer counterparts.

Volunteering to help other individuals or groups is not only an excellent way to learn specific caring behaviors, it also enlarges your capacity for empathy with others and helps reduce your social isolation.

Helpful...

Seek out opportunities for about two hours a week of one-on-one helping...try to help strangers...look for problem areas where you can feel empathy with those you are helping...look for a supportive formal organization so you can feel part of a team...find a service that uses a skill you possess...and when you are volunteering, forget about the benefits you are giving or receiving—concentrate on enjoying the feeling of closeness with the person you're helping.

•Have a confidant. The best source of personal support is an intimate relationship with at least one person. A spouse or best friend with whom you share your inner life can help you carry out your duties...act as a sounding board to help you make important decisions...and comfort you when you are feeling down.

If you already have a confidant, cultivate the relationship to forge even closer ties. If you don't, try to find someone suitable.

•Get a pet. If you're initially uncomfortable with people...or live in socially isolated circumstances...positive relationships with animals can produce dramatic health benefits. A University of Maryland study of coronary patients showed that only 6% of the pet owners died within a year...compared with 28% of those without pets.

Source: Redford Williams, MD, director of behavioral research at Duke University. He is coauthor of *Anger Kills: Seventeen Strategies for Controlling the Hostility that Can Harm Your Health,* Times Books, 20 E. 50 St., New York 10022.

Secrets of Stress-Resistant People

Most people in America live incredibly hectic lives. We push ourselves to manage successful careers, families and relationships.

We're constantly pushing for more...and more...and more.

Result: Most of us are up to our necks in stress—and that stress is climbing.

Raymond B. Flannery, Jr., PhD, tells us more about stress and how to better cope with it...

What exactly is stress?

Stress is the physical and psychological distress that we experience when our day-to-day problems exceed our abilities to solve them.

While most of us think of stress in emotional terms, it also causes dramatic physiological changes. It floods the body with adrenaline, speeds up the heartbeat, deactivates the immune system and focuses our thinking.

When we are in genuine danger—facing an automobile accident or being attacked by a vicious dog, for instance—stress-induced physiological changes can be lifesavers.

But when stress becomes chronic, persisting even without the threat of physical danger, it serves only to damage our physical and emotional health.

Stress forces the body to go into overdrive, sapping our energies, making our lives joyless and sending us to early graves.

Is life more stressful today than in years past?

Probably so. Life was hard prior to 1900, but stress as we know it did not become a particular problem until the past few decades.

In fact, stress wasn't a problem for earlier generations precisely because life was so hard. Our ancestors worked long hours at hard physical labor just so that they could procure adequate food and shelter. They were physically exhausted at day's end.

Now, thanks to the ready availability of most consumer goods and the proliferation of telephones, TVs and countless other labor-saving devices, we can choose to work fewer hours and have more leisure time. Yet today's faster pace of life leaves us frantic.

Result: We've stopped focusing on the truly important things in life—good relationships with the people that we love, for example—and stress ourselves trying to acquire and make use of everything that's in sight.

It's ironic that although America has the greatest array of consumer goods in the history of the world, instead of making our lives easier, these goods have imprisoned us.

How do labor-saving devices cause stress?

These devices encourage us to think we can and should do more, to cram more living and greater productivity into each day.

The telephone affords us instant access to people all over the world. TV distributes vast amounts of information at the speed of light. Computers let one person do the work of many.

Although these breakthroughs can be helpful, they may actually increase our stress levels. *Reasons:*

- We have to work hard to earn the money to buy such devices, and more work means more stress.
- Once we own these devices, we feel we must put them to best use. As a result, we spend time using them even when we don't really need to.
- Such devices have to be maintained, and that takes even more time and money.

Lesson: Before you buy anything new, make sure it really will make your life better.

What are the signs of excessive stress?

The earliest signs include a loss of a sense of well-being—malaise, boredom, reluctance to get up each morning and face another day.

Next come emotional problems, including anxiety, depression, edginess and aggression. Some people experience a decline in the libido.

Eventually, physical symptoms emerge. These include headaches, ulcers and cardiovascular disease.

People under severe stress try to do several things at once. They go through life running when they should be walking. *Result:* Many of these people wind up in the hospital with injuries sustained in easily avoidable accidents.

What is the primary cause of stress?

The pervasive cultural misconception is that it is possible for a person to *have it all*—a happy family, a high-paying job, a nice home, good vacations, etc.—*all at the same time.*

In fact, there's no way for any of us to have everything, at least not all at once. Getting what you want in one aspect of life necessitates sacrifices in others.

Bottom line: Each of us must learn what is truly important to us, and devote less energy worrying about or striving for trivial things.

Are you talking about materialism?

I'm talking about *excessive* materialism. Although there's nothing wrong with hard work, we should also make it a point not to work or think about work when we're not on the job.

Just look at the way Americans relax. We listen to the radio, watch television, cook food in the microwave, ride the exercise bike and more—*all at the same time.*

We no longer know how to relax. As a result, we're sleeping less and exercising less than we should, eating the wrong foods and hurting ourselves in various other ways. Sometimes it's okay to do nothing.

But can people really be happy in our society now without having it all?

Yes. Most people think that they know what they need to be happy, and they spend their whole lives going after it. In fact, it's a rare person who really does know.

Many people who attain the material success that they've been striving for soon become disillusioned with its trappings. Often they go back to school or start a new career. That makes sense.

That's something that all of us should remember.

What should I focus on if having it all may be harmful?

Try to obey the central tenet of most religions—*concern for other people.* This not only helps them, it also gives you a better perspective on your problems.

Life is short. Day-to-day snafus that drive us crazy are meaningless if you consider the plight of others. One hundred years from now, who will care if you were stuck in traffic?

How can I become stress-resistant?

I advise several things. *Included:*

- Assume control of your life. Learn to distinguish avoidable sources of stress from unavoidable ones...and focus only on what you can avoid.

If something is a continual source of stress in your life, try to resolve it. If doing something is impossible, accept it.

- Make a long-term commitment to something or someone. Long-term goals make short-term problems and sacrifices easier to bear.

Bonus: People with something to live for are happier and healthier, whether the commitment is to raise good children, get a college degree or write a book.

- Take better care of yourself physically. Cut your intake of caffeine, nicotine and other stimulants, but do so gradually to avoid headaches and other withdrawal symptoms.

Devote time each day to meditation or some other form of genuine relaxation. Do aerobic exercise at least three times a week. *Caution:* If you're 35 or older, consult a doctor before beginning a rigorous exercise program.

- Develop an extended network of friends and family. The more people you know and care for, the greater your resources of emotional and financial support in times of trouble.

Just how effective are these steps?

Very effective.

The notion of becoming stress-resistant is not nonsense. The process takes several months, but it really does work.

I have successfully taught these skills to business and professional men and women, and their health and well-being have improved remarkably.

What mistakes do people make in trying to reduce stress?

The biggest problem is failing to identify the real source of the stress. There's no way to reduce your stress level if you're trying to solve the wrong problem.

Example: An administrative assistant in a law firm got into intense arguments almost every day with her boss. One night, she came home especially jittery, and burned dinner. When her husband asked if he could help, she lashed out at him and went to the bedroom to sulk. Although this vented her anger, it didn't address the real problem—her stressful work situation. Only after she recognized the true source of her stress was she able to learn how to control it.

Is it possible to have too little stress?

Yes. Each of us operates best with a specific level of visual and auditory stimulation. Too much stimulation, and we become cranky and hostile. Too little, and we get bored.

Important: Determine just how much stress you need to be happy and productive, then strive to attain that amount—no more and no less.

Source: Raymond B. Flannery, Jr., PhD, assistant professor of psychology, department of psychiatry, Harvard Medical School, Cambridge Hospital, 1493 Cambridge St., Cambridge, MA 02139. He is the author of *Becoming Stress-Resistant,* Continuum, 370 Lexington Ave., New York 10017.

How to Get Over Shyness

Most people think of shyness as a minor problem...but many people are so shy that they don't fully live their lives. By hiding from interactions that make them uncomfortable, they become increasingly lonely and unhappy.

People who are shy suffer from low self-esteem. Because they have no reserve of self-confidence, they see any rejection or social slip—no matter how small—as an indictment of their worth as a person. Over time, these rejections set the stage for a lifetime of shyness.

The truth about shyness...

•*Myth:* That far more women than men are shy. *Truth:* At least as many men—possibly more—say they are shy.

•*Myth:* That shy people are born shy. *Truth:* Many shy people report they weren't shy at all until adolescence. At that point, they became self-conscious—often about their looks—and had problems establishing their identity.

•*Myth:* That shy people are aloof and unfriendly. *Truth:* Most actually crave companionship.

•*Myth:* That loners are shy. *Truth:* People can be reclusive without being shy. They simply choose to be alone.

How to overcome shyness...

•Make a list of social interactions that are difficult for you. Start with the easiest.

Example: Asking a clerk at the store if there is a shirt in your size.

Continue working on your list until you come to the interaction that you find most difficult.

Example: Going to a business party where you don't know anyone.

•Take small steps to overcome the problems on your list. Start with the first—the easiest.

Example: If you're shy with store clerks, practice going into stores and asking simple questions—*What time do you close...does this come in red...is this item on sale?*

Concentrate on short interactions. That way, if you're overcome by shyness, you can back off quickly...and try again and again.

Goal: After repeated practice, you will be able to perform this interaction without feeling shy.

•Move on to the next challenge. Achieving each step will build self-confidence. Don't push yourself. If you try to take on too much too soon, you risk negative reinforcement.

Example: A person tries to overcome his/her shyness by forcing himself to go to a party...has a horrible time...and is very reluctant to try again.

Also helpful...

•Join a therapy group for shy people. This is one of the best treatments because you get the support of others and have a laboratory in which you can take risks in a supportive environment.

•Make a list of major accomplishments. Pull it out and review it just before you go into a social situation. This will defuse your shyness by reminding you of the things you are good at.

•Give yourself permission to be shy in some situations. By accepting your shyness under some circumstances, you decrease your anxiety and you're more likely to enjoy yourself.

Helpful self-statement: I'm going to be shy at dinner tonight...and it's okay.

•Don't assume that others are judging you. Tell yourself that you refuse to give them the power to do so.

Helpful self-statement: I'm going to be myself, no matter what.

•Focus on others. Listen carefully and intently to what they're saying. It's impossible to be self-conscious while you're concentrating on someone else.

Source: Psychologist Christopher J. McCullough, PhD, author of *Managing Your Anxiety*, Jeremy P. Tarcher, Inc., 5858 Wilshire Blvd., Los Angeles 90036.

How to Make It in the Needy...Numbing 1990s

Almost 20 years ago, I wrote that anyone who wanted to succeed could do so. That remains true today...but it is both more difficult and more important to succeed now than it was then.

Today, management at all levels is less tolerant of those who fail to produce...and less generous to those who are merely competent. Corporations are eager to trim workers who do not excel, and company loyalty is not enough to ensure survival.

Even if you do your job well, success is not an automatic consequence. It results from a systematic approach that makes sure you get things done and that others see you as successful. To achieve these two results, you must cultivate a number of specific qualities—energy, competitiveness, realism, memory and communication.

Energy...

Success requires a great deal of energy. This does not mean a capacity for long hours of hard work. It means enthusiasm to get things done—combined with the ability to do them right.

•Structuring your time. If you are not a hard worker by nature, structure your time to encourage achievement by following two rules:

•Break up your workload into small, manageable parts.

•Reward yourself as you complete each task.

As you reach each goal, you will develop a sense of accomplishment that will encourage you to continue.

Example: My energy level used to dissipate within two hours of my arrival at the office each morning. I found myself trying to deal with a deluge of phone calls, letters to answer and people waiting to see me.

Solution: I decided to spend my first hour each morning doing nothing but answering mail. By completing this limited but essential chore, I was able to start my day with an "achieving" frame of mind. Then, I rewarded myself with a short coffee break and was ready to go on to successfully tackle the more ambitious tasks of the day.

•Focus on the important tasks. You won't get very far if you stick to small tasks, but it is tempting to put off an important job that will take a few hours or days of hard work.

A simple trick to tackling large projects: Promise yourself a period of relaxation after you complete the necessary hard work. That will help you put in the extra effort to finish the job as quickly as possible and show how much you can accomplish when you work at a high level of efficiency.

•Eat and sleep well. You won't have much energy in the afternoon if you have a heavy midday meal, so stick to a light lunch. If you get drowsy in the middle of the afternoon, don't be embarrassed to take a short nap...as long as everyone is aware of how busy you were in the morning and how energetic you are after your nap.

•Look energetic. Promote an image of success, both to others and yourself, by always appearing energetic. Always move briskly... don't slouch—stand straight, with head up, stomach in, chest out...and never keep your hands in your pockets.

Competitiveness...

To get ahead, you must be willing to compete with others and eager to accept responsibility.

Sometimes, competition leads to direct confrontation. Make sure that it is no more brutal than it has to be and that you keep the advantage. *Rules of direct confrontation:*

•Don't sit opposite your opponent—it sharpens the conflict. Try to sit side-by-side. To keep your resolve, look at his/her mouth, not eyes.

•Strike the first blow...capture the advantage by stating your case rapidly and terminate the initial confrontation as soon as possible.

•Take responsibility for your position. Otherwise, you will get bogged down in a pointless discussion of your personal opinion. Successful people carry out decisions after they have been made...they don't agonize after the fact.

You also must accept responsibility without being asked. This means taking on vital tasks that others avoid because the tasks are perceived to be too trivial or tedious. Within a short time, you will acquire knowledge and skills that nobody else has, and more important responsibilities will begin flowing to you.

Hint: Pay careful attention to routine memos that everyone else ignores. You will find many problems as you search for solutions. If you suggest and volunteer to implement improvements, your reputation for success will grow.

Realism...

To succeed, you must see the world as it is ...not as you think it should be. *Some important examples:*

•Be realistic about other people. You can't trust everyone, and those whom you can trust may not always perform the way you want them to.

•Be realistic about yourself. Recognize your good points...but be aware of your faults.

•Study your past failures. You may find a way to transform them into successes.

Important: Realism must be balanced by an ability to fantasize. Dreams of success will motivate you to achieve them in reality.

Memory...

You are unlikely to succeed unless you can remember what you have to do and who you should know.

•Use the best memory aid. *Lists.* Don't try to memorize every fact you need to know—simply write them down.

•Remember people's names. Get them correct from the start. When you are introduced to someone, repeat his name several times during the first conversation and make sure of the spelling. At the earliest opportunity, write down the name together with other useful memory-jogging information, such as the person's occupation and where you met.

Hint: If you run into someone whose name escapes you, a graceful solution is to announce your own name. The other person will usually reciprocate.

Communication...

Successful people know how to let others know who they are and what they want. Good verbal communication requires you to speak and write clearly in positive terms.

Hint: Try to postpone areas of disagreement until you have demonstrated how much agreement you share.

Use body language to get attention.

Example: At meetings, don't sit forward with your elbows on the table. Sit back to listen. When ready to speak, straighten out, move forward and put your arms on the table. You will get everyone's attention.

•Speak in public successfully. Speak in short sentences...touch on a variety of points...be unambiguous...summarize at the end. And always finish sooner than the audience expects.

Source: Michael Korda, editor-in-chief of Simon & Schuster. He is author of four nonfiction best-sellers, including *Success! How Every Man and Woman Can Achieve It,* Ballantine, 201 E. 50 St., New York 10022, and five novels, including *The Immortals,* Simon & Schuster, 1230 Avenue of the Americas, New York 10020.

How to Handle The Bullies in Our Lives

Bullies are those who, by using threats of physical or emotional force, try to get others to follow their will. *There are two types...*

Malignant bullies are the worst. Fortunately, they are less-often encountered. These tyrants deliberately aim to cause harm and should be avoided if possible.

Nonmalignant bullies are much more frequently part of our lives. At one time, all of us have had to deal with a boss, a spouse, a parent, a child, a relative, a friend, etc., who acts in a bullying way.

It is unpleasant to deal with these bullies, but it is possible to defuse the encounters if you understand the psychology that motivates them and use your understanding to counter their tactics.

Bullies are anxious people...

Bullies act the way they do in order to relieve their own anxieties. When faced with problems that they perceive as urgent, bullies use threats and bluster to transfer their anxieties to someone whom they hope will handle the problem.

Nonmalignant bullies do not care if their tactics harm their chosen victims. Causing harm is incidental to their main objective—relieving their own anxieties. To make these bullies change their tactics, you must adopt a strategy that will...

•Convince them that their bullying will not succeed, and...

•Demonstrate a better way to deal with the underlying anxieties.

Two unsuccessful strategies...

Many fail to deal well with bullies because their self-defense strategies don't meet *both* objectives. Common approaches that fail are love and power. *Reasons...*

Love. The victim recognizes that the bully is motivated by anxiety and tries to relieve that anxiety by being kind, helpful and caring. *Result:* The bully's anxiety is relieved...but he/she has found a willing partner who can be victimized every time a new problem arises.

Example: When a wife caters to a domineering husband's unreasonable demands, she is responding with love to bullying. But the bully—her husband—is accepting her behavior as tribute, not love.

Power. The bully's chosen victim refuses to submit and replies in kind. *Result:* A continuing power struggle. The bully will change his tactics after a while. But with his anxiety unresolved or even increased, he will seek revenge in indirect ways.

How to handle bullies...

Achieving the two objectives of a successful anti-bullying strategy requires *detachment,* so you can analyze the source of the bully's anxiety, and *calm confrontation,* so that the bully realizes you will not submit to threats but are willing to negotiate.

Example: Clerks who work at department store complaint desks deal every day with irate customers who often threaten them. The clerks are trained not to take the situations personally. They understand that the customers are trying to bully them because of their own anxieties that the store will not exchange the unwanted items or give refunds. The complaint desk clerks explain the store policy and make it clear that threats will not help.

Result: The threatening customer may still be angry, but he calms down and discusses his claim rationally...or goes away.

The same combination of detachment and calm confrontation is the way to deal with the bullies you know personally.

Exception: Bullies who won't go away. If detachment, constraint and calm confrontation have no effect, confront the pattern when the bully is not anxious. Discuss and support new ways to plan, budget and anticipate in order to reduce anxiety.

If that is not enough, consider the ultimate confrontation: *I do not want to be bullied again. Please stop it. If you won't or can't, then I would like to realign our relationship.*

Bullying at work...

Example: Your boss repeatedly seeks to humiliate you publicly and threatens to fire you whenever he/she is anxious about a project on which you are working.

One day your boss starts screaming at you in the hall about the progress report you handed in last week. It set a revised project-completion date two weeks later than you had estimated earlier. He calls you an incompetent idiot who may not be with the company much longer if you can't meet the original deadline. *Wrong reactions:*

• Thinking of your financial position, you cringe and tell your boss that it might be possible to finish the project sooner than you thought.

• You decide this marks the day you have taken enough abuse and announce in colorful terms in front of the whole office that the delay is due to the blustering bully's typical failure to provide the additional worker he had promised.

Neither of these emotional reactions to your boss's unreasonable threats will serve you well. Whenever you are faced with a bully, you have to determine the framework.

Strategy: Tell your boss calmly, but firmly, that you are willing to discuss the project with him but in a more private setting.

When you meet for the discussion, apologize for any actual errors that you have made... but not for the failure to achieve an impossibly perfect level of performance. State realistically what you think can be done to meet his goals ...and if he continues to threaten you, call his bluff.

Firmly but politely, tell your boss, "If you really want to fire me, that's your choice. But if you want me to help on this project, we have to get down to business immediately."

Bullying in family situations...

• Within the family, bullying in place of negotiation or calm discussion often stems from a lack of understanding of normal development patterns. Parents and teenagers...adult children and older parents...husbands and wives...do not understand each others' needs, and they often resort to threats to try to get what they want.

Example: A teenager who is anxious because his/her parents won't give him something that he wants may try to bully them emotionally. He may threaten to drop out of school...to take drugs...even to run away.

Strategy: Be tough, but reasonable. Ask him, "Do you want to talk over what is bothering you, or are you just going to bluster? If you don't want to talk now, go away for a while and come back whenever you're ready to discuss your problem."

Example: An aged parent, unable to take adequate care of him/herself, may not consider entering a nursing home because of his anxiety about the physical, emotional or financial aspects of the new accommodations. He uses emotional bullying tactics against well-intentioned adult children who suggest the idea.

Strategy: The adult children should defer making any choices until they have discussed the situation with professionals and explored all possible living arrangements.

If it is clear that the parent's current living arrangement poses serious risks to his life or health, the children should state their case firmly but politely...and take the appropriate action, difficult as it may be.

•Husbands/wives in roughly equal power relationships often end up in situations in which they bully each other.

Example: George and Mary are a middle-aged couple with one late-born young child, George, Jr. Both have many independent interests that they want to pursue outside the house in their limited spare time. Each one feels the other should stay home to watch Junior. Their constant arguments on the subject often end when one says, "I'm leaving now," and goes out. That is bullying...because one party insists on an outcome to which the other has not agreed.

Strategy: Next time this situation occurs, the victim of the bullying should state calmly, "You are welcome to leave now...but when you come back we are going to discuss this problem and determine a mutually agreeable solution."

George and Mary have to budget their free time until they agree on how to divide responsibility for Junior. Neither will find the result to his/her complete liking, but it will have been achieved by mutual thinking—the opposite of bullying.

Source: Martin G. Groder, MD, a psychiatrist in private practice and a business consultant, 104 S. Estes Dr., Suite 304, Chapel Hill, NC 27514. His book, *Business Games*, is available from Boardroom Classics, 55 Railroad Ave., Greenwich, CT 06830.

Hints for a Happier Life

Give yourself permission to be happy...act on a spontaneous impulse now and then, and do something fun...pick one or two things you want to accomplish each day and then celebrate those accomplishments...learn to think like a child—inquisitive, curious, flexible... choose to forgive those who have hurt you in the past...each day, make a difference in one person's life by being encouraging, uplifting and inspiring.

Source: *Downscaling: Simplify and Enrich Your Lifestyle* by Dave and Kathy Babbit, publishers of *Downscaling 46510*, Moody Press, 150 W. Chicago Ave., Chicago 60610.

Stress Reducers

Put troubles into a broader perspective. Step outside yourself, and ask who will know or care about the problem in five years—or even 50 years. Use delays creatively—in a waiting room or on a delayed train or plane, read, write or reflect on your life. Practice gratitude—and spend a day being thankful for your life.

Source: *Kicking Your Stress Habits: A Do-it-Yourself Guide for Coping with Stress* by Donald Tubesing, PhD, psychologist, Duluth, MN. Whole Person Assoc. Inc., Box 3151, Duluth 55803.

Simple Secrets of Being Healthier and Happier

Did you know that loosening your necktie or collar will improve your vision?

Indeed, according to Cornell University researchers, tightly knotted ties interfere with blood flow to the brain and eyes. So, computer operators, pilots, surgeons and other professionals who must pay close attention to visual detail should avoid confining neckwear. If you must wear a tie, make sure your shirt has plenty of neck room and leave the top button on your collar unfastened. Make the knot loose enough that you can slip a finger between your collar and neck.

Other ways to feel healthier, smarter and safer...

•Exercise in the morning. A recent study showed that 75% of morning exercisers were likely to still be at it one year later, compared with 50% of those who worked out at midday and 25% of the evening exercisers.

Explanation: As the day progresses, people are more apt to think of excuses for avoiding exercise.

• Minimize your exposure to pesticides. They have been linked to birth defects, nerve damage and cancer...yet pesticide use has doubled over the last 20 years. *Self-defense:* Wash fruits and vegetables in hot, soapy water —and rinse thoroughly. Buy US-grown produce whenever possible—imported produce is more apt to contain pesticide residues. Be especially careful when cleaning strawberries, peaches, cherries and apples.

• If you eat bacon, cook it in a microwave. Bacon cooked in a microwave contains lower levels of cancer-causing compounds called nitrites than bacon that is pan-fried or baked. Drain away as much fat as possible—bacon drippings contain twice the level of nitrites as the meat itself.

Vitamin C helps counter the cancer-causing effect of nitrosamines (which are formed when nitrites combine with amino acids in the stomach). People who eat bacon, ham, pepperoni, bologna or other nitrite-preserved meats should be sure to include oranges, tomatoes and other vitamin C-rich foods in their diet.

• Cure hiccups with sugar. Swallowing a teaspoon of sugar almost always does the trick. In a recent study published in the *New England Journal of Medicine,* sugar worked in 19 out of 20 people—some of whom had been hiccuping for as long as six weeks!

Other effective remedies: Grasping your tongue with your thumb and index finger and gently pulling it forward...swallowing a small amount of cracked ice...massaging the back of the roof of the mouth with a cotton swab...and eating dry bread slowly.

Caution: Hiccups that recur frequently or persist for more than a few minutes may be a tip-off to other health problems, including heart disease. Consult a doctor for such hiccups.

• Don't suppress a cough. Coughing is the body's way of clearing mucus and other debris from the lungs.

• To avoid motion sickness, close your eyes. Motion sickness occurs when your eyes and the motion-sensing system of the inner ear receive conflicting signals—the inner ear says you're moving in one direction while your eyes say you're going in another. Keeping eyes closed helps reduce the conflict.

If you're prone to motion sickness in cars, offer to drive. Like closing your eyes, keeping your eyes focused straight ahead on the road helps reduce queasiness. *Also helpful:* Air from the air conditioner or an open window directed toward your face.

• Don't aggravate a strained back. Many people use heat immediately after a minor back injury. But heat increases circulation to the area, causing increased swelling and inflammation. *Better:* To reduce swelling and pain in the first few days following a back strain, use cold compresses made of crushed ice wrapped in a towel. Keep the pack on for 20 minutes, then leave it off for 20. Repeat this cycle for two to three hours a day for three to four days. Only after this interval should heat be applied.

Caution: For severe or persistent back pain, consult a doctor.

• Eat fresh fruit. Fruit juice doesn't give you as much fiber—or vitamins and minerals—as whole fruit. Dietary fiber promotes regularity and helps regulate digestion of carbohydrates. The sugar in fruit is absorbed more slowly than the same sugar in fruit juice. The longer absorption time makes fruit more filling, a boon if you're watching your weight. This keeps your blood sugar levels stable, leaving you feeling more energetic.

• Don't drink tea if your blood is iron-poor. Tea contains tannins, compounds that inhibit iron absorption. (Herbal tea is okay.) *To raise iron levels:* Eat more green, leafy vegetables, lean red meat, poultry, fish, wheat germ, oysters, fruit and iron-fortified cereal. Foods rich in vitamin C help your body absorb iron from other foods.

• Stop snoring—with a tennis ball. Sewn into the back of your (or your mate's) pajama top, it discourages sleeping on the back, a major trigger of snoring. *Also helpful:* Using blocks to raise the head of your bed...or using pillows to elevate the snorer's head.

• Use a cookie jar to lose weight. But—instead of cookies, fill the jar with slips of paper reminding you to do some calorie-burning activity, like going for a walk or gardening.

•Make exercise a game. If you're a swimmer, for example, see how long it takes you to "swim the English Channel." If you swim in a standard 75-foot pool, you'll have to do 1,478 laps to go the 21 miles from Dover to Calais. For stair-climbers, reaching the 29,028-foot summit of Mt. Everest takes 49,762 stairs. Be creative in whatever form of exercise you pursue, and you'll be more apt to stick with it.

•Be careful when shoveling snow. To avoid back injury or heart attack, keep knees bent and both feet firmly planted...push the snow aside instead of lifting it up...protect head and hands from the cold and avoid caffeine or alcohol before going outdoors.

•Develop a "cancer-resistant" personality. Although this finding remains controversial, cancer seems to be more prevalent among people who take a hopeless, helpless view of life, suppress their feelings, allow anger to build and have long-standing unresolved conflicts with loved ones.

A lifetime of built-up emotions may cause a release of hormones that interferes with the body's natural defenses against disease. To reduce the risk, actively try to solve problems within your control. Don't hold grudges.

Researchers have found that people who survive cancer or live longer with the disease tend to be feisty, demanding and emotionally expressive.

Source: Don R. Powell, PhD, president and founder of the American Institute for Preventive Medicine, Farmington Hills, Michigan. A licensed psychologist, he is the winner of numerous awards for his work in the health field and is the author of *365 Health Hints*, Simon & Schuster, 1230 Avenue of the Americas, New York 10020. The book was written in consultation with physicians, dietitians, exercise physiologists and other health-care professionals.

How to Fight the Blahs

•Count your blessings.

•See a funny movie or TV show.

•Read a joke book.

•Go for a long, brisk walk.

•Spend a weekend in a deluxe hotel with breakfast in bed.

•Listen to beautiful music.

•Read a very good and engrossing novel.

•Exercise a lot.

•Rent a convertible and ride with the wind around you.

•Go to the airport and watch the planes land and take off.

•Buy a new and exciting game for your video machine.

•Look at old family albums.

•Sing songs around the piano with friends.

•Get a haircut.

•Go for a swim.

•Buy a dog or cat to keep you company.

•Get some new tapes or records.

•Buy something you have always wanted.

•Fix up your house.

•Go to an art museum.

•Meditate.

•Clean out your closets or bureau drawers.

•List your assets and accomplishments.

•Call a special friend who always makes you feel happy.

•Take a deep, warm, bubbly bath.

•Eat a large piece of chocolate cake.

•Blast the stereo and sing along at the top of your lungs.

•Spend some time at a religious retreat.

Fighting Holiday Blues

Visits to psychiatrists and physicians jump 25% or more during the holiday season that lasts from Thanksgiving to New Year's. *The most common underlying causes of distress:* Holiday depression, boredom and burnout. *Specifically:*

•A longing for happier holidays (real or imagined) in days past.

•Loneliness. This is especially true for those in a new location or those who have recently lost a loved one or gone through a divorce.

•The feeling that holidays should be a happy time, that family life should be perfect, and that presents will bring your heart's desires.

•For those whose health is frail, a primitive fear of not getting through the cold, dark winter.

The best ways to combat the blues:

•Don't expect too much. Unrealistic anticipation only breeds disappointment. As expectations are reduced, every pleasant surprise becomes a bonus.

•Be selective about the festivities you attend. Enjoy the fellowship more than the alcohol.

•Try not to be alone. But spend your time with people who are comfortable and easy to be around.

•When the holidays seem too grim, take a trip or try some totally new experience. Perhaps volunteer work in a hospital, where the emphasis will be on bringing cheer to others.

•Skip those Christmas-shopping crowds by ordering your gifts by mail and visiting small, local shops or those in out-of-the-way places.

•Keep holiday entertaining simple. If traditions become too much of a burden, try something offbeat (for example, decorating with cut flowers instead of ornate evergreens). Or, go out. Above all, don't try to give huge, exhausting affairs.

•Unless you love to receive cards from others, save the bother and expense of sending them yourself.

The Simple Secret of Sabotaging Self-Sabotage

If we routinely fall short of our goals... and/or make decisions that interfere with our personal, professional or financial growth... and/or feel inadequate to meet the challenges in our daily lives—we may be victims of our own *self-defeating behaviors.*

Self-defeating behaviors are responses that originally protected us and helped us to cope with life...but which now work against us.

Example: A child who is subjected to excessive criticism learns to keep a low profile—to avoid notice or possible derision. Such a child is apt to mature into a painfully shy adult, incapable of making friends or achieving career goals.

By coming to understand these negative patterns and the purposes they once served, we can learn to replace our destructive behaviors with constructive ones.

Variety of self-defeating behaviors...

The average person in our culture regularly indulges in a dozen or so self-defeating behaviors.

These range from serious threats to health, such as smoking or drug abuse...to more subtle forms of self-sabotage like perfectionism, procrastination, hostility, compulsive worry or shyness.

Displaying a self-defeating behavior does not mean you're "sick." It simply means that you're still being controlled by negative external forces that have been *internalized*—family members, church, school, etc. These institutions are too often sources of criticism, prejudice, unrealistically high expectations and even abuse.

We may have been victims of these environmental influences earlier in our lives. But as adults, we victimize *ourselves*—by continuing to behave in ways that are no longer helpful.

Dangerous patterns...

Because these destructive patterns are learned and reinforced *unconsciously,* it's sometimes hard to spot the danger they pose. Two powerful forces keep these destructive patterns alive...

•A promise of protection. For example, you might think to yourself, *If I worry all the time, I'll be prepared when disaster strikes.*

•Fear. This is often expressed as an almost superstitious thought—*If I stop worrying, disaster will surely strike.*

Unfortunately, the behavior doesn't deliver on the promise...and people wind up being ruled by the fear.

Example: Chronic worry undermines both your health and your enjoyment of life. When bad things do happen, you're too tied up in knots to deal with them effectively.

Five steps for changing self-defeating behavior...

Step 1: Identify the behavior. We'll continue to use the example of compulsive worry.

Step 2: Identify the situations that trigger the behavior. You may feel as if you fret *constantly.* But give the matter some thought and you may notice that you worry only under certain circumstances—for example, when you're trying to fall asleep...when your child comes home late from school...when a major project is due at work.

Step 3: Observe how you build the behavior. Self-defeating behaviors aren't floating around in space waiting to attack us. We create them by following a specific pattern of thoughts and behaviors. Breaking down the parts of this sequence can help us to regain control.

There's always a split-second between the triggering situation and the moment we begin to construct the behavior.

In this instant we *choose* to think a self-defeating thought...focus on that thought...and begin behaving so as to reinforce the thought.

Example: You come home early from work and are enjoying the afternoon paper. *Trigger:* You glance up at the clock and notice that your 13-year-old daughter is 15 minutes late. A split second later you think that something terrible may have happened to her.

You may also hear an inner voice saying, *If I continue to enjoy myself, and something awful does happen to her, it will be my fault.*

Panic sets in, and you imagine all of the horrible possibilities—*What if she's been mugged ...kidnapped...hit by a car?*

Finally, you cement the behavior by *disowning* it—you find a way to shift the responsibility for your reaction to a source outside yourself. *If only she would call when she's going to be late, I wouldn't feel this way.*

It's nearly impossible to change this pattern once it's been set in motion—one step follows automatically on the heels of another. But—by repeatedly observing the sequence of mental events, you can learn to break this pattern of behavior in the future.

What once happened automatically will gradually become a conscious process—and will therefore lose much of its power.

Key: In the split second before you build the self-defeating behavior, you'll begin to ask yourself, *What can I do instead?*

Step 4: Find a healthy replacement behavior. Simply trying to stop the self-defeating behavior is a recipe for certain failure—you cannot replace something with nothing. Instead, you must *substitute* another, more constructive action. *Examples:*

- Engage in gardening, weight-lifting or another physical activity that leaves you no mental energy for worrying.
- Force yourself to repeat to yourself reassuring, rather than catastrophic, statements.
- Calm yourself with deep breathing exercises.
- Call an upbeat friend.
- Organize a messy drawer.
- Read.
- Take a nap.
- Plan your weekend.

Where to find replacement behaviors:

- Your past. What did you do before negative experiences led you to create the self-defeating behavior?
- Role models. What would one of your "heroes" do in a similar situation?
- Your body. What would feel good physically in this situation?
- Your wiser self. Often, we already have the answers we need—if we can only trust ourselves.
- Feedback from others. Ask friends and other people you trust for suggestions.

Step 5: Practice replacing the old behavior with the new, healthier one. At first you'll need to be vigilant. It will feel unnatural not to slip into the old pattern.

But if you persist, you'll reprogram your unconscious mind...and the new, self-enhancing behavior will become as automatic as the self-defeating behavior once was.

Source: Robert E. Hardy, EdD, a licensed psychologist affiliated with Personnel Decisions, Inc., a Minneapolis-based international consulting firm that applies the principles of behavioral science to building successful organizations. He is coauthor, with Milton R. Cudney, of *Self-Defeating Behaviors,* Harper/San Francisco, 10 E. 53 St., New York 10022.

Traumatic Events Don't Have to Be Traumatic

Sooner or later we all suffer a traumatic life event—the death of a loved one, a divorce, a job loss, a serious illness. When it happens, the rules for staying healthy and happy all change. People who suffer a trauma have to replace the resources—both internal and external—that they have lost. They must reinvent their lives.

What is traumatic...

Trauma is often caused by the loss of anyone who is very important to us—a spouse, a parent, a friend, etc.

Although the loss of a relationship is the most common cause of trauma, it can also result from a loss of *productivity*...whether it's a job or an endeavor—raising children, volunteering, following creative interests, etc.

The loss of a productive outlet causes a change in our identity or role. And this makes us question who we are.

Many people think trauma is something that strikes from the outside. But traumatic problems—midlife depression, for instance—can arise from within, as well.

How not to cope...

Most people who experience a trauma feel out of control. They think their whole world is falling apart and they don't know what to do about it. It's like having a nervous breakdown. *Common no-win reaction:*

• Feeling like a victim. Victims sit back and say, *Look at what life has done to me.* They blame their problems on other people or organizations, and then expect to be rescued. Victims don't want to take responsibility for recovering.

• Becoming aggressive. You can sue the company that fired you or the hospital where a relative died. But in the end you'll get little satisfaction, and you're doing nothing to rebuild your life. Aggressors think they're acting in their own best interest. But once again, they're focusing on external forces.

Better ways...

The best way to recover is to focus internally. You need to concentrate on yourself for a while. A major life crisis is a time to turn inward and challenge yourself to recover. Appraise your situation realistically. Face the fact that you are in trouble and look for ways to make even this experience useful.

Example: A man who is in the midst of a painful divorce should ask himself what he can do to develop new relationships and be a better partner.

Different kinds of trauma require different kinds of action...

• Death of a loved one. When someone close to us dies, we confront our own mortality. We wonder why we are alive.

Helpful: Use this as an opportunity to evaluate what you are contributing to society. Look for ways to make your life better and more productive.

• Major illness. Although cancer and other illnesses are terrible traumas, there is much we can learn from them.

Helpful: Realize that this illness may even help you in some ways.

Example: People who have had heart attacks often start eating right and exercising for the first time in their lives. *Result:* They wind up healthier than ever.

• Breakup of a relationship. Although it's difficult to do, we all have to admit that there is no one relationship that can take care of us forever ...we can't rely on any other person to do the things we need to do for ourselves.

Helpful: Ask yourself how you contributed to the problem—perhaps you were too needy. Look for ways you can act differently in the future. *Important:* Many people who make a healthy adjustment after a relationship fails start loving themselves for the first time.

• Job loss. People who lose a job immediately start redoing their résumés, reading the classified ads, networking, etc. But your first task should be to get over the trauma by taking care of yourself—eat well, exercise, get enough rest.

Helpful: Realize that it may take a year or more to find the right job and rebuild your life. Nothing good is going to happen in a hurry. See the job loss as an opportunity to get out of a rut and do something different—something you've always dreamed of doing.

Source: Kathryn D. Cramer, PhD, president of Heath Psychology Consultants, 206A N. Clay St., St. Louis 63122. She is the author of *Staying on Top When Your World Turns Upside Down,* Viking Press, 375 Hudson St., New York 10014.

How to Cope with This Age of Diminished Expectations

With all the talk about excessive taxes and budget deficits, people in the US have come to accept a faltering economy as almost inevitable.

Result: We have greatly diminished expectations for the future of our economy...and our own standard of living.

Where people used to expect a robust economy with steady economic growth, nowadays we're satisfied just to keep our heads above water.

If this current economic drift continues, the US is destined to become a second-rate economic power by 2000. *Precedent:* Great Britain, once the world's mightiest empire, has seen its power, its wealth and its citizens' relative standard of living suffer steep and apparently permanent declines.

Meet the enemy...

Many people think there is something fundamentally wrong with our government—with politicians, in particular. I disagree. Politicians are not a special breed of people, greedy and dishonest. They're just caught between what they think is right and what will play well in the hometown newspaper.

The real problem is not with the politicians, but with the voters. Most people in the US are unwilling to suffer the kinds of changes that need to be made to save our economy.

Example: Some of our cities and even some states are facing bankruptcy because the voters refuse to accept new taxes. Yet they expect government services to continue at the same level.

Imaginary problems...

Many people spend much too much time worrying about things that do not matter. *Examples:*

- Inflation. Although rising prices cannot be ignored, at its current level, inflation has no impact on the growth of the economy. Pushing for zero inflation is dangerous. It's an impossible, inappropriate goal.
- The trade deficit. Our foreign debt is increasing at a rate so slow that it will not cause any significant problem for our economy in the foreseeable future.
- The budget deficit. Although the deficit was a problem a couple of years ago, recent legislation has dramatically cut government spending. In fact, the automatic spending limitations imposed by the Gramm-Rudman Act are so severe that they are now wreaking havoc on public services.
- Excessive taxes. Many people blame our declining standard of living on a too-high tax burden. Not so.
- Tax rates in the US are lower than those in other developed countries. The real problem is unfair distribution of the tax burden.

Incomes exploded during the 1980s, but only for people at the top of the economic ladder. Those lower rungs saw a decline in their standard of living because the income tax burden is unfairly shouldered by those in the lower brackets. I don't advocate soaking the rich, but the well-to-do could easily survive higher tax rates.

- Bloated bureaucracy? Many people think their tax dollars are wasted on an army of unproductive bureaucrats who do little but shuffle paper. This is a misconception. *Reality:* The federal bureaucracy is not bloated. In fact, the combined salaries of all non-military federal employees amount to no more than 5% of the US budget.

What's really wrong...

While most people are worrying about the imaginary problems, the real problems are being ignored. *Included:*

- Our crumbling educational system. At one time our kids were the best educated. Now they're among the worst. We've obviously fallen behind Germany and Japan, and also behind Spain and other nations of comparatively modest means.

Poor education produces poor workers... which means reduced productivity, which translates into less money to spend on education—a vicious cycle.

Self-defense: Agitating for better education is the single most powerful weapon against a faltering economy.

• Our crumbling infrastructure. Visitors from abroad have asked me, *If the US is such a great country, why are the roads and cities in such terrible shape?* And they're right to question.

Roads, bridges, communications networks, railroads and other systems essential to fast, efficient movement of goods and information—the national infrastructure—are in a sorry state. And they're getting worse. The decline of our nation's infrastructure is the most obvious damage done to our economy by the tax cuts of the 1980s.

Self-defense: Support higher taxes. A nation that's unwilling to pay for the maintenance of its infrastructure cannot grow and prosper.

Source: Paul Krugman, PhD, professor of economics, Massachusetts Institute of Technology. A former consultant for the International Monetary Fund, the World Bank, the United Nations and the State Department, Dr. Krugman is the author of several books, including *The Age of Diminished Expectations: US Economic Policy in the 1990s,* MIT Press, 55 S. Hayward St., Cambridge, MA 02142.

How to Survive Turmoil

Our response to a disaster is highly correlated to the way we handle life issues in general. Some of us deal with them well, while others get depressed and self-blaming.

The best response is what I call *reasonable vigilance,* a recognition and acceptance of the randomness of events. This attitude is one we should all try to adopt, since disasters of all sizes are an inevitable part of life.

Typical responses...

Self-blame is probably the single most virulent and negative psychological response to disasters. Some people blame themselves even when their home is destroyed by a runaway truck. *Trap:* A refusal to accept the senselessness of events. We personalize disaster—so no matter how unpredictable the occurrence, we think it's somehow connected to us.

Example: The Wall Street executives, traders and brokers that I work with responded to the 1987 stock market crash with crushing guilt. They felt terrible that they hadn't sold before the crash. They thought they had let their clients down. Many had information that they should have told, information that they didn't act on. This intensified their guilt.

A loss of trust in the system can also result. Some traders and investors who lost a lot of money began to think that the system was unreliable, and they were terrified to trade. This can generalize to other people or systems until the person develops a pervasive lack of trust. Relationships with others can be seriously affected.

Example: A trader who lost several hundred thousand dollars became highly irritable, fearful, depressed and mistrustful—and his sex life died.

The adaptive response...

An adaptive response means understanding that the world is basically unfair and metes out bad and good luck independently of what you hope and pray for, dream of or desire. It means living your life with reasonable vigilance—*not* with constant caution. Reasonable vigilance includes accepting a certain amount of risk as part of being human.

People need to review the demands, shoulds and ought-tos by which they live. These always surface when disaster strikes and make recovery more lengthy and painful.

Typical: I should have made better financial decisions. I shouldn't have built my house on a hill that might have a mud slide. *What people forget:* When they made the original decision, they probably had all the data available at the time. It's not that the decision was foolhardy or reached prematurely.

Helpful: When disaster strikes, take an inventory of how you made the decision that got you into trouble—buying an unstable stock or building a house in a dangerous location. It will lower your anxiety to realize you couldn't have anticipated the disaster.

Key: Reasonable judgment. If you built a house along a shore that is flooded every year, or refused to set a bail-out figure on an investment, you may be riding more on ego than on good sense. You may not be able to acknowledge that you're human—fallible—and that there's a time to admit your mistakes and get out.

To bounce back...

Draw a time line from the time you were one-year-old until the present, dividing it into years and months. Then plot disasters you've experienced and the residue from them. *What you'll see:* Each disaster is an infinitesimal pimple on your lifeline. Even a real tragedy, such as a premature death in the family, still dominates only a certain part of your life, not all of it.

Try projection imagery. Imagine yourself a year down the road being free of guilt, shame or depression. See yourself being able to talk and even joke about the disaster. Projection imagery will give you a sense of hope.

Remind yourself that time *does* heal all wounds. Don't expect things to right themselves immediately. Depression, fear and guilt are all appropriate and typical responses to disaster. You have to work through these feelings before you can accept and reconstruct your life.

Don't get down on yourself for feeling bad. It's natural to be upset when something terrible happens. And don't let others try to talk you out of it.

Example: A woman bought a car that turned out to be a lemon. Although others tried to minimize her loss because she had not lost a fortune, she had only a small income and had used *all* her savings for the car.

If your disaster is economic, recognize that there are Indians living along the Amazon who are probably happier than the richest man in the world. Some people are so ego-driven that they'll run back into a fire to snatch their favorite antique, or commit suicide over a lost fortune.

Most important element: Perspective. As long as no one close to you has been seriously hurt or died, you really haven't lost much at all.

Source: Psychologist Barry Lubetkin, PhD, director of the Institute for Behavior Therapy, 137 E. 36 St., New York 10016.

How to Forgive And Forget

To forgive another is the greatest favor you can do—for yourself. It's the only way to release yourself from the clutches of an unfair past. Beyond that, it opens the possibility of reconciliation, often a gift in itself.

What to do:

•Take the initiative. Don't wait for the other person to apologize. (That cedes control to the one who hurt you in the first place.)

•If the forgiven person wants to re-enter your life, it is fair to demand truthfulness. He or she should be made to understand, to feel the hurt you've felt. Then you should expect a sincere promise that you won't be hurt that way again.

•Be patient. If the hurt is deep, you can't forgive in a single instant.

•Forgive "retail," not "wholesale." It is almost impossible to forgive someone for being a bad person. Instead, focus on the particular act that hurt you. (It might help to write it down.)

•Don't expect too much. To forgive doesn't mean you must renew a once close relationship.

•Discard your self-righteousness. A victim is not a saint. You, too, will need forgiveness some day.

•Separate anger from hate. *To dissolve your hate:* Face your emotion and accept it as natural. Then discuss it, either with the object of your hatred (if you can do so without escalating the hatred) or with a trusted third party.

•Forgive yourself. This may be the hardest act of all. Candor is critical. Admit your fault. Relax your struggle to be perfect. Then be concrete and specific about what is bothering you. Your deed was evil. You are not.

• *To make self-forgiveness easier:* Prime the pump of self-love. Do something unexpected (possibly unappreciated) for a person you care about. By acting freely, you'll find it easier to think freely.

Source: Lewis B. Smedes, author of *Forgive & Forget,* HarperCollins, New York.

Disarming Difficult People

To deal with infuriating people, what counts is your response, not what they do. If you don't confront them, you end up making a negative judgment on yourself. *Familiar types:*

•The person who keeps repeating negative remarks about you made by others.

•The person who keeps referring to everything he has done for you.

•Those who insist you act in a certain way: "Isn't my daughter Frannie wonderful?" (demanding applause). Or, those who tell a joke or story and wait for you to laugh on cue.

How to handle such people:

•Avoid recriminations.

•Don't attribute bad motives or bad character.

•But make the point that you have as much right to your response—or lack of response—as the speaker does to his. You'll put a stop to the annoyance, and in most cases you'll also improve the friendship.

•Understand that if this doesn't work and you lose a friend, that's better than to be in a state of constant, impotent fury.

Source: Dr. George Weinberg, author of *Self Creation,* Avon Books, New York.

Stop Driving Yourself Crazy

Driving can make your pulse race and your blood pressure soar. About 40% of Connecticut's one million commuters, for instance, are troubled by stress while on the road, according to a recent survey by that state's Department of Transportation. Although you can't do anything about the traffic, you can keep it from getting to you.

Self-defense...

•Join a car pool or take public transportation to work. The conversation and companionship will take your mind off the commute, even when it's your turn to drive. When you're a passenger, you have the freedom to work, read —or sleep.

•When you drive alone, visualize your car as a refuge, not a battleground. Use this as getaway time to recharge your batteries and relieve the pressures of the day.

•Listen to soothing music. Play your favorite tapes. If you listen to the radio, do so without constantly switching stations. If you don't want to hear a particular song or commercial, just lower the volume.

•Buckle up. Somewhere in your subconscious you know it's safer—and therefore less stressful—when you drive with a seat belt. *Also:* Be a safe driver. Don't tailgate, make quick lane changes, run yellow and red lights, etc. You'll not only feel safer, you'll *be* safer.

•Give yourself extra time to reach your destination. Eliminate the need to rush. And remember, everyone is sometimes late...people will understand.

•Don't be a traffic judge and jury. If another driver does something stupid, stay calm. *Don't let it bother you.*

•Don't fight the traffic. Give in. Go with the flow. You can't prevent the flooding or the jackknifed tractor-trailer and anxiety about it isn't worth it.

•Believe that you are the master of your own behavior. *Exercises:* Drive using your brakes as infrequently as possible. Keep several car lengths between you and the car in front of you.

•Know when *not* to drive. Never, ever drive after drinking alcohol or taking antihistamines or other drugs that can impair your performance.

Source: Psychiatrist Martin Brenner, MD, an authority on driver stress and freeway violence and a recovering Road Warrior. His *Stress Care Driving Program* was developed for the Connecticut Department of Transportation.

How Not to Be a Victim of Negativity

We've all had the experience of feeling uneasy or uncomfortable in certain places or with certain people, often without knowing why.

Although we usually blame these feelings on ourselves, much of the time they are being transmitted to us by others.

What this means: Knowing how to defend yourself against invisible emotional assaults is even more important than knowing how to defend yourself physically.

Negative emotions...

It's a difficult concept for many westerners to grasp...but everything in the world is made up of energy, even our emotions. And because most of us aren't aware of this, many people become psychic sponges for the negative emotional energy of others.

Example: You have lunch with a friend who's getting divorced and is very depressed. Although you feel great when you sit down, by the time the check arrives you're in a funk that lasts the rest of the afternoon. *What happened:* You absorbed some of your friend's negative energy.

Some people find it impossible to defend themselves against emotional energy. These very sensitive people never develop strong egos or boundaries. Not knowing where they end and others begin, they indiscriminately absorb whatever's around them.

Babies aren't born with any defenses, physical or emotional. They must develop over time. *Result:* We all take on the family neurosis—self-denial, not expressing your feelings, internalizing your anger, etc.—at a very early age.

Enlist your psychic defenses...*

• Identify your area of vulnerability. Most people are especially susceptible to at least one kind of negative emotional energy—anger, sadness, fear or physical illness. *Ask yourself:* Which of those emotions brings back a strong reaction that I remember from childhood?

Example: I grew up in a family where every single person was physically ill in one way or another. That's probably why I became a healer. *Trap:* If I'm not careful, I pick up the pains of my clients.

• Set up your defenses. This involves developing your psychic sight, learning to see clearly everything that is around you.

Example: Keep your psychic antennae up at work instead of shutting them down. Try to figure out who's feeling good and who isn't. See what kind of energy—good or bad—is coming from your boss.

*Psychic self-defense does *not* mean shutting off your emotions and becoming invulnerable. *Goal:* To keep your heart open from a position of strength. People who try to close themselves off emotionally draw negativity to them like a magnet.

• Protect yourself from encountering negative energy. Before you go to work, for instance, visualize your office filled with blue light. Blue is the color of peace and is a potent pain reliever.

Example: I know a nurse who performs this exercise every morning before going to work in a ward for premature infants. *Result:* When she gets to work, all the babies are calm. On mornings when she forgets to do this exercise, she finds chaos. She says it never fails.

You can use this technique for any event that's making you anxious.

• Release negative energy that you've picked up from others. Close your eyes and take a couple of deep breaths. Clear your mind and relax each part of your body as much as you can. Look inside yourself to see if you can find where that person's negativity has affected you. Then eliminate that negativity.

Example: If you had a fight with your boss, visualize him yelling at you. Notice what happens in your body—see where you feel tense, angry or frightened—and relax each part of your body where you feel that negativity. Then imagine a circle of light around you that acts as a shield. See your boss's anger bouncing off of it. *Say to yourself:* "This anger isn't mine. I let it go. I can protect myself and take a stand in the face of anyone's anger."

• Repair the energy of the environment. If, for instance, you want to repair the energy in your office after a scene with the boss, open a window and literally air the place out. Visualize the fresh air and sunlight coming in and cleaning the environment of angry feelings.

• Forgive. Forgiving people who have hurt or frightened you releases their power over you. *Reason:* When you feel anger and hatred towards someone, you—not they—get stuck with all the negativity.

This doesn't mean condoning something terrible that someone has done. It means saying, *I can let this go...I'm not going to let you harm me further.*

More psychic self-defense...

• Pay attention to your intuition. Ignoring it is an easy way to get into trouble.

Example: One afternoon, I had a strong feeling that I should move my car to a different parking area. I was in a rush and ignored my feelings—and when I got back to the car, I found it had been broken into.

• Take a healing break. After an upsetting emotional encounter where you've absorbed a lot of negativity, spend a few minutes in the sun. The sun is a great healer. At the end of the day, take a shower. Water is a cleanser and gives off healthy negative ions.

Exercising is another wonderful way to help heal yourself. Going to the gym, taking a shower and then putting on clean clothes makes you feel refreshed because you've counteracted all the day's negative energy.

• Be aware of what you eat. Food is a balancer of energy.

People who overeat are often tremendous psychic sponges who are trying to protect themselves by making themselves numb. Because food closes down the psychic channels, eating builds a boundary between them and the world.

Source: Elizabeth K. Stratton, MS, who has a private practice as a counselor and healer in New York and teaches workshops in psychic self-defense and holistic healing techniques around the country. She's on the faculty of the Esalen Institute, the New York Open Center and Omega Institute.

The Mind-Body Relationship

• Mental abilities don't deteriorate with age, contrary to popular belief. Wisdom—the ability to use past experience to judge a problem for which there is no correct answer—grows at least through a person's sixties. And the ability to grasp new relationships slows down, but can remain strong. *Helpful mental exercise:* Challenging reading, adult education courses, games.

Source: *University of California Wellness Letter.*

An understimulated brain will often attempt to counter boredom by causing back pain, obesity, hypertension and even cancer. *Most susceptible:* Once-active people who feel they've seen it all. *Helpful:* Seek out the new and fresh in the ordinary—even a new way to brush your teeth.

Source: Dr. Augustin de la Pena, University of Texas Medical School, in *New Age Journal.*

• An energy slump (postprandial dip) affects many people between 2 p.m. and 4 p.m. Although it often follows lunch, it doesn't seem to be caused by eating or digesting. *To combat the dip:* Run a physical errand, rather than doing purely mental work.

Convert Worry Into Productivity

Reduce worrying by disassociating it from common worry-inducing situations. Techniques from Penn State psychology researcher Thomas Borkovec:

• Set aside a half-hour worry period each day.

• When you start to worry, put it off until the worry period.

• Replace worrisome thoughts with task-oriented thoughts.

• Use the worry period to think intensively about current concerns.

All About Happiness

Sometimes happiness seems like a terribly elusive goal. We tend to forget that it doesn't come as a result of getting something we don't have, but rather of recognizing and appreciating what we do have. *Some steps on the pathway to happiness:*

• When you think about time, keep to the present. Those who are excessively future-oriented often score very high in despair, anxiety, helplessness and unhappiness. As much as practical, focus on the here and now.

• Don't dwell on past injustices. You'll be unpopular company. No one wants to hear about how you got a raw deal in your divorce or how your boss doesn't appreciate you.

•Develop the habit of noticing things. An active mind is never bored. Make a resolution to notice new things each day—about nature, people, or anything else that interests you. Ask questions. Don't assume you know all the answers or that showing curiosity will be considered prying. Most people love to talk about themselves or their interests.

•Don't wear too many hats. Focus on one thing at a time. Set time aside for your family, yourself, your golf game, etc.—for having fun.

•Drop your bucket where you are. Take advantage of what you already have. There are already interesting, stimulating adventures waiting in your own backyard. Get to know your own children, for example.

Source: Dr. Frederick Koenig, professor of social psychology, Tulane University, New Orleans.

Benefits of a Personal Philosophy

Developing a personal philosophy of life is crucial for meeting crises to be faced day by day. (And those crises can get more complicated as one grows older.) *The virtues are:*

•It provides a guideline for living.

•It sounds an alarm when one's behavior is inconsistent with one's beliefs.

•It supports the ability to make a rational explanation of life's events, including the most disruptive or seemingly senseless ones.

What's required in a personal philosophy:

•It must be comprehensive. Ideally, it will provide an ability to meet all life's normal crises in a balanced way.

•It requires one's full commitment. Personal philosophy can't be taken on and off like a coat. It has to provide a sense of worth.

Meeting the Challenge Of Personal Growth

•Personal growth is a positive commitment that is aided by in-depth reading and conversations with those who have done it. Search out people who are skilled in a field in which you wish to advance. Learn about the dedication required and the attitudes that will help to make your effort fruitful.

•Never forget the level of application demanded. *Depressing cycle:* Beginners start out wildly enthusiastic, eager to master a chosen endeavor, such as playing the violin or unraveling the secrets of Zen. But they have been oversold on self-development without effort, and they quickly become discouraged at the first patch of difficulty. Do experimental trials before making the total commitment. Try a class, session, interview, or book. Be certain you are ready to give yourself to the project.

•Persevere when the spirit is weak. Many creative people develop mental blocks from the fear of defeat or failure. The term "writer's block," for example, describes a creative person who has temporarily lost the courage to take the risks that writing entails. A negative attitude is a defense employed by people hoping to avoid the pain of failure by rejecting their chances of success.

•You are more likely to be courageous when you have a positive mind-set. And, it will be easier to find purpose and the strength to accomplish the objective.

•Knowing your limits and accepting yourself. That is also part of realizing your potential.

Source: Martin G. Groder, MD, a practicing psychiatrist, business consultant and author of *Business Games: How to Recognize the Players and Deal with Them,* Boardroom Books, 55 Railroad Ave., Greenwich, CT 06830.

Becoming a More Complete Person

Many executives neglect personal growth in favor of career.

Penalties for failing to develop other interests:

•Produces a feeling that life has gone stale.

•Lowers the ability to love or take interest in family and community.

•Leads to despair. You pretend that you don't mind being so job-oriented, but you do.

Rewards of extending your interests:

• You drop some psychological defenses and use that energy to enjoy life more fully.

• You lose the anxiety, confusion, and identity crises of youth. You appreciate the joys that being older brings.

Source: Richard C. Hodgson, in *Business Quarterly,* published by the School of Business Administration, University of Western Ontario, London, Ontario.

How to Enjoy Yourself By Yourself

The problem most people have with doing things by themselves is a holdover from when they were teenagers—being alone meant nobody loved you. Remember that being alone doesn't mean rejection. A lot of people who are with someone would rather be alone.

To avoid loneliness or boredom when you're alone, try these activities:

• Go out to eat. Make a reservation at a nice restaurant, dress well and tell yourself: "I'm going to ask for a good table and enjoy myself!" Once you get there, you might ask another interesting-looking person eating alone to join you.

• Go to the movies. Many people avoid going to the movies alone when they're in their hometown. One advantage is that no one is constantly whispering comments to you, asking questions about the movie or stealing your popcorn.

• Look in stores. Shopping just for the fun of it is another thing busy people don't often do. Look around. There's always something to learn about products and merchandising.

• Take a tour. Pretend you're a tourist, and see your town through others' eyes. *Best:* Walking tours. You see a lot and get exercise.

• Meander by yourself. Discovering an unfamiliar place is fun. And doing it at your own pace is wonderfully relaxing.

Growing-Up Realities

• Negative events in infancy do not irreversibly damage the mental health of the adult. Some repair is possible if the environment becomes more benevolent.

• The behavior of an infant does not provide a good preview of the young adult. A one-year-old's tantrums don't foreshadow teenage delinquency, for example. Many infantile qualities disappear as their usefulness is outgrown. Adult behavior becomes more predictable after the age of five than it was before.

• Human beings are not saddled with a fixed "intelligence" or "temperament" in every situation. These qualities are related to context and can vary in different circumstances.

• A biological mother's physical affection is not basic to a child's healthy emotional growth. More important is consistent nurturing from primary caregivers, related or not, female or male. The key is a child's belief in his own value in the eyes of the caregivers.

Source: Dr. Jerome Kagan.

Stopping Unwanted Thoughts

The average person has more than 200 negative thoughts a day—worries, jealousies, insecurities, cravings for forbidden things, etc. (Depressed people have as many as 600.) You can't eliminate all the troublesome things that go through your mind, but you can certainly reduce the number of negative thoughts. *Here's how:*

• When a negative thought begins to surface in your mind, pause. Just stop what you are doing for a few seconds. Don't say anything—talk reinforces the bad feeling.

• Take five deep, slow breaths. By taking in more oxygen, you flush out your system and lower your level of anxiety. If you do this correctly, you will approach a meditative state.

• Concentrate on a pleasant, relaxing scene—a walk on a breezy beach, for example. Take two to three minutes for a minor trouble, up to 10 minutes for a serious upset.

•Use this technique continuously until the upsetting thoughts begin to decrease. Then practice it intermittently.

Source: Elior Kinarthy, PhD, professor of psychology, Rio Hondo College, Whittier, CA.

The Tough Job Of Setting Your Personal Priorities

How you already allocate your own time is the best indicator of what's important to you. It tells you what your priorities really are. Anxiety about personal time management comes from confronting what you are doing with what you think you should be doing.

•Confront your real needs and time values and be honest about what you see.

•Resist the temptation to be sucked into other people's needs. Face the risks inherent in not answering some phone calls, not answering certain letters, not jumping when someone asks you to do something.

•Beware of the open door policy at the office. People who report to you need something more important than ready access.

•Be honest about how you feel about meetings. Many executives complain about them as time-wasters but actually call many meetings themselves because they enjoy chairing them, being the center of attention and putting other people's ideas down.

•Consider cutting down on dictated formal letters. Dictation is inefficient but ego-satisfying. Most memos and letters can be answered by a handwritten note or comment across the original. And people appreciate the quick turnaround much more than the perfectly typed memo or letter.

Source: Charles E. Dwyer, Wharton School, University of Pennsylvania, Philadelphia.

Fitting Priorities Into Categories

Even some of the most efficient managers sometimes lose ground because they don't accurately weigh the relative importance of their activities. To prevent this problem in your life, categorize activities carefully according to priority, and revise the categories daily.

•Category A. Important and urgent.

•Category B. Important but not urgent.

•Category C. Urgent but not important work. This category is usually the big trap because the crisis nature of the activity makes it seem more important than it is.

•Category D. Neither urgent nor important. For example, cleaning drawers, straightening files.

•Activities will vary in urgency as time passes, so it is important to revise the priority list each day.

•Tackle the A and B priorities, and then the C tasks, if you have the time. If you never get to the D jobs, what has been lost?

Source: Milton R. Stohl, president, Milton R. Stohl Associates, Farmington Woods, CT.

Selfishness is Not Necessarily a Sin

The whole notion of sacrificial relationships is wrong, whether you are sacrificing yourself to other people or vice versa. What's essential to relationships is exchange.

Selfishness, or honoring the self, means:

•Be aware of yourself and the world.

•Think independently and have the courage of your own perceptions.

•Know what you feel and accept your right to experience such feelings...fear, anger or other emotions we often consider negative.

•Accept who you are, without self-castigation or pretense.

•Speak and act from your innermost convictions and feelings.

•Refuse to accept unearned guilt. Attempt to correct the guilt that you have earned.

•Commit yourself to your right to exist. Acknowledge that your life does not belong to others and that you were not put on earth to live up to someone else's expectations.

•Be in love with your own life and with your own possibilities for growth, joy and the process of discovering your human potential.

Source: Dr. Nathaniel Branden, a Los Angeles psychologist and author of *Honoring the Self,* Jeremy P. Tarcher, Inc., Los Angeles.

Avoiding Needless Personal Sacrifices

A fair number of men and women remain workhorses for their entire lives to avoid the stigma of selfishness. *Example:* A middle-aged man who is bored with his career may want to switch to another career that will give him personal fulfillment. If the change involves a drop in family income, he is often accused of being "selfish."

The steps to change involve having the courage to face up to the following:

•Human relationships should be based on an exchange of values, not of sacrifices. Here a market analogy is apt (without implying that human relationships are meant to be materialistic):

If you want something someone else has, you must offer value in exchange that will be perceived as roughly equal, appealing to the self-interest of whomever you wish to trade with. *Formula for respect:* Never ask anyone to act against his or her self-interest.

•Other human beings are not put on earth to satisfy your needs, wishes or expectations. You are not put on earth to live up to someone else's needs, wishes or expectations.

•What we call our fear of being selfish is really our fear of disapproval or our fear of being condemned for perfectly honest and legitimate forms of self-assertion.

•When we do sacrifice ourselves to others, we hate them for it and make them pay for it in all sorts of indirect and underhanded ways.

Source: Dr. Nathaniel Branden, a Los Angeles psychologist and author of *Honoring the Self,* Jeremy P. Tarcher, Inc., Los Angeles.

How to Get Out of a Rut

No matter how old you are or what kind of rut you're in, there is a way out.

•Accept that no one is going to do anything for you. It is your responsibility, and yours alone, to change your own life.

•Start thinking constructively about what you want rather than moaning about what you don't have.

•*If you're upset about your career, stop complaining and ask yourself:* What do I really want to do? Where do I want to do it? With whom? Under what circumstances? What are my skills? (Include not only business experience but also hobbies, interpersonal skills and non-job-related skills.)

•*Ask yourself:* What are my short-term goals? Long-term goals? Think long and hard and in great detail about what would make you happy. Don't be afraid to fantasize or hatch grandiose schemes. You may be able to make at least parts of your fantasy come true.

•Give yourself an imaginary $10 million and think about what you would do with it. Be specific. Then use your brain to see how much of your fantasy you can turn into reality. *Sample fantasy:* To live on a South Sea island and spend all my time sunbathing, fishing and picking coconuts. It may not be possible to move to the South Seas and loll about all day, but if you're living in a cold climate and really love the tropics, you might be able to get a job in Florida and spend all the spare time that you choose sunbathing and fishing.

•Change your job without leaving the company. Negotiate a move to another state. Redesign your job so you can focus on your strengths and hand over other tasks.

Source: The late John C. Crystal, founder of John C. Crystal Center, New York, which offers intensive courses in creative life/career planning.

Breaking an Undesirable Habit

•Before trying to break a habit, take at least a few days to observe it in action.

•Then try to stop completely instead of tapering off. Performing the act reinforces it, while abstaining strengthens the habit of not doing it.

•Don't fret over lapses. It takes time to establish new patterns.

•Be aware that you cannot change just any habit. Work hardest to change those that both annoy others and violate your own standards. You can improve yourself only if the changes sought are in accord with your own moral and ethical standards.

Source: Dr. George Weinberg, author of *Self Creation,* Avon Books, New York.

Rid Yourself of Nervous Gestures

Audio-video cameras are an excellent way to check yourself for nervous physical gestures that can interfere with your ability to communicate effectively. Record a conversation with another person or the draft of a talk you are about to deliver. *Look for:*

•Repetitive phrases such as "you know."

•Cracking your knuckles.

•Rubbing your nose.

•Pulling your ear.

•Adjusting your glasses.

•Stroking a mustache.

•Jingling change in a pocket.

•Leaning too heavily on the lectern.

•Pacing back and forth all the time.

•Shifting weight from one foot to the other.

•Using a chart pointer excessively.

Source: James K. Van Fleet, author of *Lifetime Conversation Guide,* published by Prentice-Hall, Inc., Englewood Cliffs, NJ.

If You Want a Drastic Change in Your Life

•Start your own business. This does not have to be a total gamble. *Overlooked clue to success:* Research not only your venture but yourself. Too many people go into businesses they are personally unsuited for. *Example:* The couple who dreams of running a little hotel in the mountains won't make a go of it if they're shy, retiring types.

•Start communicating openly with your family. This hardly sounds like a prescription for drastic change. However, lack of communication is the primary reason for a marital rut. It can be an exciting, startling and totally new experience to find out what your spouse and children really think.

•Consider going to a weekend marriage workshop, sometimes called a "marriage encounter." This is a group of couples with an experienced leader. Spouses are taught how to be open with each other. It can be more effective than marriage counseling, which is often the last stop before the divorce.

Source: The late John C. Crystal, founder of the John C. Crystal Center, NY. The Center offers intensive courses in creative life/career planning.

How to Plan a Major Change in Your Life

The change that's needed to execute any major personal plan: Willingness to accept less than 100% perfection. *Set the parameters of performance:* The ideal level and the acceptable level. Then aim for performance within that range. That's easier said than done.

Between the recognition of what has to be done and the courage to change, you must do some hard work.

•Sit down with an accounting spread sheet and, on the vertical axis, write down all the things you want to do in your personal life. On a separate list, write down all the things you want to do in the business.

• Spend two to three days working out this list.

• Think audaciously, creatively, freely. *For instance:* I want 2,000 people working for me. *Or:* I want to run a $1 billion company. *Or:* I want to be married to Michelle Pfeiffer.

• After the list is made, mark the items, A, B or C, using this ranking:

A: Top priority—the things that need to be done tomorrow (or at least sometime in the future).

B: The things impacting today.

C: Lowest priority—the things that I should have done yesterday, but didn't.

• *Rationale:* You have to change the tempo of what you do. And you must do it on paper. You can't change what happened yesterday—so it gets lowest priority. The only thing you can really affect is what happens tomorrow. That's where to put all the energy and skill.

• Ask yourself, of everything listed, what tasks can be done by someone else.

• On the horizontal axis, assign the tasks.

• Work out some sensible (not grandiose) time schedule for meeting all the goals you really plan to meet.

How to Push for Change

To improve the likelihood that a recommendation for a change will be accepted:

• Demonstrate a thorough knowledge of the status quo, including essential figures.

• Make claims for improvement absolutely accurate. Quantify them whenever possible.

• Do not play down the real costs of change.

• Investigate the less obvious effects a change could have in some areas, in order to head off a quick rejection because of the side effects.

• Find someone to play devil's advocate and test the validity of the proposal before presenting it.

• Bring copies of supporting data to the proposal meeting.

Source: *Purchasing,* Boston, MA.

Focusing on Your Strengths

Some evening at home, go into your bedroom and close the door. Tell the family you need some time alone.

• Take off your clothes and stand in front of the mirror. You'll feel absurd. Everyone does.

• Talk to yourself. You'll feel even more absurd. Everyone does.

• Ask yourself what you like about what you see. Most people are very hard on themselves. I'm too fat. Too gray. Too many wrinkles. You have to get over that—and you only can do that if you stick to it. *Keep talking:* My arms are strong. My legs aren't too bad. My back is straight.

• The lesson, both personal and professional: Don't focus on improving the flaws. Accept the flaws and identify the strengths that you have to work with.

• In business, too, achieving the goals you want to achieve is a process. The process is using the company's strength—and your own.

Coping with Disappointment

We have become addicted to the notion that personal change is a simple, painless matter. TV and the movies always present a dramatic crisis and then a resolution. Advertising tries to convince us that this car or that perfume will make us powerful or sexy. Even psychology has contributed by spreading the fiction that a book or weekend seminar will profoundly and quickly transform our lives. But true change doesn't happen overnight. It takes time, commitment, energy, and courage.

Disappointment styles...

There are four basic disappointment styles. Once you identify your patterns, you can start to deal with the problems they cause you.

• Acquiescent. She (it's most often a she) responds not from her inner needs but from a desire to please. Disappointment results from the impossible attempt to meet all the demands, real or imagined, of others.

• Deprived. This type was deeply disappointed in early life and has developed a defensive posture based on always expecting the worst. *Typical premises:* "Life is pain" and "You never get what you want."

• Romantic. This is a variation of deprived. Romantics were emotionally deprived in childhood and so became attached to unrealistic fantasies of being rescued by love. But since they feel undeserving of intimacy, they sabotage relationships and then cling to the anguish long after a relationship has ended. They are constantly disappointed as each successive lover ultimately fails to fulfill their ultra-romantic expectations.

• Self-important. These individuals view themselves as special and therefore different from others. They expect the world to recognize their superiority and to treat them accordingly. Having been raised by families that convinced them they were favored beings, they are disappointed when the rest of the world doesn't treat them the same way.

To prevent disappointment...

• Maintain flexible expectations. Flexibility allows you to plan for the future in a realistic manner while maintaining your excitement and enthusiasm. *The key:* When you find your expectations aren't being met, change them.

• Put more into "assessment" and less into "wish." Every expectation is a combination of an assessment (what you've determined will probably happen) and a wish (what you want to happen). Often our wishes exceed our assessments, and our expectations are therefore unrealistic. But you can change your attitudes to avoid future disappointment. *How to go about it:* Know what you expect from your family, job, friendships, etc. Then make sure your expectations are realistic. *Ask yourself:* Has this expectation ever been met before? What were the conditions under which it was met? Do I have control over those conditions?

• Have fewer expectations. The ability to live in the present without preconceived notions of how life should be is a great gift. If you can accept life in the here and now, enjoying whatever comes your way, you'll experience much less disappointment and much more fulfillment.

Source: David Brandt, PhD, a clinical psychologist and author of *Is That All There Is? Overcoming Disappointment in an Age of Diminished Expectations,* Pocket Books, NY.

Recovering from a Disappointment

Some steps that will help you to recover from disappointment:

Acknowledge the pain and allow yourself feelings of loss and dispossession.

• Take a step back to gain perspective. No single hoped for event is necessary to your survival. Remember some of your past disappointments and realize that life went on—that you achieved satisfaction without fulfillment of those particular expectations.

• See the positive side. Disappointment is a lesson in reality. It tells us what's possible and what isn't. It may tell you to give up a certain set of expectations or to change your behavior in order to make what you expect actually happen.

Coping with a Major Loss

The death of a loved one, the loss of a job, separation or divorce, all involve change and loss. A sense of loss accompanies all major changes in life, even when the change is positive, such as a job promotion, marriage or a job transfer.

Stages by which people respond to a major loss:

• Shock or denial.
• Fear and paralysis.
• Anger, at others or at oneself.
• Sadness and depression.
• Acceptance and reformulation of goals.

All the stages are important to the process of adaptation:

• The omission of any single stage can result in depression or incomplete adjustment because the energy needed to cope with the present remains bound up in the past.

•The longer people have to rehearse a new situation and work through feelings about it, the less stress there will be and the less time it will take to adapt. For example, research among widows shows that those whose husbands died after a long illness, such as cancer, had a much less difficult time making the transition to widowhood than those whose husbands died unexpectedly, in a car crash, for example.

Learning from Failure

Sooner or later, everyone who is ambitious will experience a failure. Many don't recognize, however, that failure is necessary. You can't succeed without struggle. But if you're able to learn from what went wrong, you can do it right the next time.

•Evaluate honestly what stands between you and success, both in the outside world and within yourself.

•Find a mentor who will be open with you about his or her own struggles with such blind spots.

•Read biographies of people who overcame their own fears to become successful.

Taking Criticism

•Don't read more into the criticism than the speaker intends.

•Don't be deaf to positive comments.

•Separate legitimate from inaccurate criticism.

•Don't argue about the critic's feelings rather than the facts of the situation.

•Delay a direct response until you have figured out whether the critic is trying to come off better by putting you down.

•Make sure the critic knows enough to make an intelligent observation about the subject. Then, pick your response to fit the circumstances.

Source: Dr. Jack E. Hulbert, North Carolina Agricultural and Technical State University, Greensboro, NC, and Dr. Barbara Pletcher, director, National Association for Professional Saleswomen.

How to Save Face While Encouraging Criticism

While most people agree that dissent and discussion are vital, many bristle when their own ideas are challenged or criticized. How to be open and avoid ego damage:

•Ask for specific ways to strengthen or improve an idea rather than for a general opinion.

•Meet in individual sessions rather than in a group. Opposition is easier in private.

•Solicit reactions to only one part of the proposal at a time.

•Ask for written criticism. It can be less traumatic and can be put aside for a calmer moment.

Source: *Personal Report for the Executive,* Research Institute of America, New York.

How to Profit From Criticism

You can improve yourself by encouraging friends to criticize you, and learning how to take criticism. Your critics may not always be right. But if you don't get the truth from others, you may never find out.

•Let your critic finish what he has to say before you answer.

•Don't go into the reasons for your actions or behavior. This is really just a way of excusing them.

•Don't jest. It is insulting to the critic.

•Show that you have understood (whether or not you agree) by briefly repeating the criticism in your own words.

•Let your critic know that you understand how your behavior has caused inconvenience or made him feel.

•Don't open yourself to criticism for what you are—only for what you do. You are not responsible for anything but your actions. It is by changing these that you can change yourself.

Source: Dr. George Weinberg, author of *Self Creation,* Avon Books, New York.

Big Drains on Personal Energy

Unwillingness to face up to emotions leads to fatigue. Normal energies are expended in the effort to repress sadness or anger. *Some common instances:*

•Grieving that hasn't been attended to. Surprising, but typical examples, are getting a new job and moving to a new city. The event can be exhilarating. But, the new situation still implies some loss. This holds true for promotions or getting married—which mean saying goodbye to certain freedoms, contacts, options. People who don't deal with the negative aspects of even the most positive changes are vulnerable to psychological fatigue. Some of their energies remain bound up in the past.

•Situations of acknowledged loss, i.e., the death of a loved one or the fact that the children have grown up and left home, or having to face the fact of limited potential (executive's sudden realization that he'll never fulfill career objectives).

Recognizing Psychological Fatigue

As a rule, if a person has been overworking for some time and then takes three or four days off and sleeps adequately, he should be refreshed.

But often rest is not the answer. People whose tiredness is psychological need stimulation. The more rest such a person gets, the more tired he becomes.

Who's prone to psychological fatigue:

•People who are unwilling to ask for what they want or who keep waiting for people to guess.

•People who refuse to say what they don't want. Nothing saps energy and produces fatigue as much as unacknowledged resentment.

•If chronic tiredness persists and the doctor says there's no physical cause, acknowledge the problem is a psychological one.

•Explore the feelings engendered by work or by important relationships.

•Figure out what unmet needs and wants you have in these areas.

•Determine which expectations are realistic and which aren't, and how to go about resolving that draining aspect of your life.

Source: Gisele Richardson, management consultant, Richardson Management Associates, Montreal.

Tension-Reducing Techniques

Basic rules for tense individuals:

•Wake up early to avoid hurrying and getting keyed up before leaving the house.

•Take a short walk after lunch. Do it any time that tension is high. (Just say, "I'll be back in five minutes," and go.)

•Have a daily quiet hour. No phone calls or visitors.

•Plan social engagements to allow for a short relaxation period between the end of the business day and the start of the evening's activities.

•Always be prepared for those tense moments during the day and, when they come, concentrate on breathing slowly and deeply.

Source: *Personal Health.*

Reducing Pain-Producing Jaw Tension

Five exercises to ease discomfort:

•Start by opening the mouth wide, then closing it. Do this repeatedly and as rapidly as possible.

•Continue the same motions, but now place the palm of your hand beneath the chin when opening the mouth, and above it when closing. This offers a slight resistance.

•Repeat the same two steps with a sideways motion of the lower jaw, first doing it freely and then doing it against the resistance of the palm of the hand.

•Go through the same steps with a motion that protrudes the jaw.

•Chew a piece of gum alternately on each side of the mouth, then in the center of the mouth. Do each exercise for three to five minutes.

Source: Patricia Brown, RN, *American Journal of Nursing,* New York.

How Nine Celebrities Handle Anxiety

Many successful people have developed their own special ways of dealing with anxiety with a significant emphasis on physical activity. Their approaches may be worth a try for you.

•Yogi Berra, baseball great:

"I spend lots of time on the golf course, often with my son, who is also a ball player. And I like to play racquetball."

•Jane Brody, *New York Times* science writer and author of the bestselling *Jane Brody's Nutrition Book* and *New York Times Guide to Personal Health:*

"I find the best way to avoid anxiety is to exercise. I drop everything and do something physical—jog, swim, whatever. I clear the slate and calm down. When I come back, things don't seem so bad. Another thing—I keep a continuing calendar and try not to let too many things pile up at once. And I have also learned the fine art of saying "No."

•Joyce Brothers, psychologist and TV personality:

"Whenever I get anxious, I swim. (Studies indicate that 15 minutes of strenuous exercise have a more tranquilizing effect than strong drugs.) Another good way to fight stress and anxiety is take a long, brisk walk."

•Dr. Frank Field, CBS science editor:

"The key word, for me, is 'awareness.' Once I am aware of my anxiety, I stand back and look at it. If someone tells me that I am shouting, I try to do something about it—not just deny it. I get swept up with so many things that often I am unaware that I am becoming anxious. So then I take control of myself."

•Eileen Ford, Ford Model agency:

"I do yoga deep breathing. The tension just flows from my body."

•Roger Horchow, founder of The Horchow Collection:

"I don't have much anxiety in my life. When I do, I guess it is when I eat too much. But mostly, I try to work harder to eliminate what is bothering me...try to accomplish more and deal with the source."

•Reggie Jackson, baseball great:

"My best cure for anxiety is working on my collection of old cars. I also enjoy building cars, and I find that doing physical work can relieve stress for me. Reading the Bible also puts my mind at ease and gives me spiritual comfort."

•Ann Landers, syndicated columnist:

"My work is not anxiety-producing, but occasionally, if there is a hitch, I get into a hot bath, take the phone off the hook and count my blessings. I have a great deal to be thankful for, and I know it."

•Dr. Ruth Westheimer, prominent sexologist:

"When I get anxious, I say, 'Ruth Westheimer, get hold of yourself.' The important thing is to recognize your anxiety. Sometimes this makes it go away. If it were a really serious anxiety, I would go for professional help."

Depression Myths And Realities

Common as it is, depression is shrouded in popular misconceptions. Whether short-term and mild or more serious and longer-lasting, those feelings of low self-esteem, aimlessness and purposelessness afflict many people periodically. You'll be able to cope with depression better if you understand the major fallacies about it.

• If you're feeling depressed, the cause must be psychological. *Fact:* Not necessarily. Many psychiatrists consider much emotional distress to be caused by genetically inherited body chemistry. Also, a variety of physical illnesses, such as viral infections, can cause low psychological moods.

• People who lack ego strength and character are more likely to get depressed than those with strong personalities. *Fact:* If anything, it's the strongest characters who are most subject to feelings of depression and low periods. Strong personalities have very high standards of success and morality and suffer most from a loss of self-esteem.

• Men and women are equally susceptible to depression. *Fact:* Women are more likely, by a ratio of two to one, to develop feelings of depression. On the other hand, men tend to have more serious depressions and a higher rate of suicide.

• Depression will affect you psychologically but not physically. *Fact:* Prolonged and serious periods of depression can result in weight loss, sleeplessness and other stress that can make the sufferer vulnerable to serious physical problems, such as heart attack and multiple sclerosis.

• Falling in love will lift you out of depression. *Fact:* People who are feeling low and emotionally distressed are too internally preoccupied to be either very interested or successful in handling relationships. Feelings of depression also cause a decrease in the sexual impulse.

• Help for depression can come only from long-term psychotherapy. *Fact:* There are ways of combating depression effectively that don't require long-term therapy. Antidepressant drug therapy may help in several weeks. People who are having a mild, short-term depression may profit from seeing a therapist or a counselor several times. However, serious and disabling depression that lasts for months does call for continuing professional treatment.

• Tranquilizers will help you combat feelings of depression. *Fact:* Valium and alcohol are both depressants themselves, as are all tranquilizers. The only medications that work are antidepressant drugs, which must be carefully prescribed.

• The cause of your depression is usually obvious. *Fact:* The cause that seems most obvious is most often not the real one. *Reason:* Depression has to do with unconscious conflict. For example, one of the frequent causes of depression is repressed hostility. When that hostility is acknowledged, the depression usually lifts.

• You always know when you are depressed. *Fact:* There are common forms of depression in which people do not know how they feel. Such people express their depression in other ways. Obese people and alcoholics often may not feel depressed, but their obesity or drinking are the equivalent. People who feel their depression have an advantage because they, at least, have a chance to do something about it.

• There are usually some after-effects from depression. *Fact:* It's possible, after a period of feeling depressed, to jump right back to where you were with no residuals. Depression does not change the psyche.

Source: Michael Levy, MD, psychiatrist, New York.

How to Cope With Depression

• Avoid isolation. Talk with someone who can provide counsel.

• If a period of depression lasts for more than a few weeks, or if your ability to function is impaired, more professional help is needed.

• Recognize that your outlook during a low period is going to be pessimistic and distorted. In such a period, your judgments of yourself, of your situation and of other people are not based on reality.

• Difficult as it may be, try to be active, do things and see people. People who are most successful at coping with feelings of depression are those who fight them.

Source: Michael Levy, MD, psychiatrist, New York.

New Treatment for Manic-Depression

Two drugs long used to treat epilepsy—*divalproex sodium* (Depakote) and *carbamazepine* (Tegretol)—control manic episodes without the weight gain, grogginess and memory impairment often caused by lithium, the standard treatment. New treatments for manic-depression are needed because about one-third of individuals with manic-depression fail to respond to lithium...and 60% who take it regularly will have another manic episode.

Source: Charles L. Bowden, MD, professor of psychiatry, University of Texas, San Antonio. His three-week study of Depakote use in 179 manic patients was published in the *Journal of the American Medical Association*, 515 N. State St., Chicago 60610.

How to Treat Compulsive Shopping

Compulsive shopping that cannot be controlled with the help of psychotherapy and/or support groups can usually be controlled with antidepressant drugs, including *fluoxetine* (Prozac) and *fluvoxamine* (Luvox). In a recent study, compulsive shoppers given fluvoxamine experienced a marked decrease in their urge to shop and in their time spent shopping.

Source: Donald Black, MD, associate professor of psychiatry, University of Iowa College of Medicine, Iowa City. For information on support groups in your area, contact Debtors Anonymous, Box 400, Grand Central Station, New York 10063.

27

Very Personal

Surprising Cause Of Impotence

Impotence is caused in 10% to 15% of all cases by injury during intercourse. Weight-induced pressure or abnormal bending of the erection can cause chronic impotence by damaging the lining of the erection chamber. The most common situation in which such injuries occur is when the female is on top.

Source: Research led by Irwin Goldstein, MD, Boston University Medical Center.

PID Danger

Bacterial vaginosis (BV), which affects up to one in four women, raises a woman's risk for pelvic inflammatory disease (PID) and infertility. *Problem:* BV is frequently misdiagnosed as yeast infection—and the two conditions require different treatments. *BV symptoms:* A foul or "fishy" vaginal odor and a milky discharge that can stain undergarments. Your doctor can administer a vaginal pH test and a microscopic examination for "clue" cells.

Source: James McGregor, MD, professor of obstetrics and gynecology at the University of Colorado.

Unreliable Birth Control

Breast-feeding is unreliable as a means of birth control, even though the ovaries do remain unresponsive to fertility-stimulating hormones for some time after the birth of a child. *Recent finding:* Nursing mothers do take longer to resume normal ovulation after childbirth than do mothers who bottle-feed, but the effectiveness and duration of this contraceptive effect vary greatly. Some women become fertile again in as little as 90 days after childbirth, while others remain infertile for as long as a year. *Rule of thumb:* The effect lasts longest when a nursing mother continues to nurse her baby at night as well as during the day...and when she delays the introduction of solid foods in her baby's diet. But because of the risk of unwanted pregnancy, it's safer to rely on other methods of birth control. *Flip side:* Breast-feeding mothers who do want to conceive may experience problems doing so.

Sources: Susan K. Schulman, MD, a pediatrician in private practice in New York City, and Audrey Rosner, CPNP, coauthors of a report on post-partum fertility.

All About the Virtues of Being Open...Very Open

True intimacy is the key to personal, emotional, and physical health and interpersonal fulfillment.

True intimacy is achieved when two people travel beyond conventional romance and explore each other's emotions, experiencing the deepest level of trust, openness, and sharing. They feel a flame in their spirits, a celebration of self and each other, a movement toward wholeness, and a lust for life.

Genetic predisposition and cultural norms do play a role in how close we allow ourselves to get to others. It starts at the beginning of life, in the bond that unites mother and child and serves as a model of giving and receiving care.

Everyone can experience true intimacy—if they're able to overcome the barriers that prevent them from freely expressing themselves.

The basics of intimacy...

True intimacy is a two-way street. It requires that two people be able to express the following:

• Trust. You must be able to rely on the other person to live up to his/her word so you can be open without the fear of being betrayed.

• Empathy. This requires putting yourself in someone else's shoes, to know and anticipate what the other person is feeling.

• Enthusiasm and courage. Both are needed to shatter illusions, strip defenses, break through stereotypes, confront fears, and explore emotional boundaries together until our insides "touch."

• Sharing each other's worlds. You must be able to maintain a solid sense of self. While you are fully engaged with the other person, you do not give up your separate life.

Sex and intimacy...

The spiritual connectedness and awakenings triggered by true intimacy can be achieved in a relationship without sex—between friends and family members. But sex within an intimate relationship can unite mind, spirit, and body to an explosive energy release. When no limits are placed on the physical interactions, touch and nonverbal communication can express deep levels of pleasure and intimacy.

The goal is to be with someone who expresses an equal interest and commitment to the journey toward true intimacy. Most people, however, are not so fortunate. Types of people who fight true intimacy...

• The macho but insecure man who tells a woman he loves her in order to seduce her into a sexual relationship.

• The workaholic who says he/she wants to be in love but constantly breaks dates to work.

• The martyr who appears to fall madly in love but constantly with "the wrong people." People who profess they want but cannot find anyone capable of true intimacy have an intimacy problem themselves.

• The avoiders, or those who engage in transitory relationships or make superficial commitments. They do not seek or encourage strong emotional ties. These include loners, control freaks, abusers, misanthropes, self-absorbed narcissists, and romanticists endlessly seeking the perfect romance.

• Intimacy junkies, who are so concerned about being emotionally close to others that it interferes with their ability to accomplish responsibilities. When deprived of the "rush" of such closeness, they get depressed and are further unable to function.

This problem can lead to an endless cycle of starting and ending relationships, an inability to make commitments, chronic infidelity, and destructively inappropriate choices of partners.

Fears...and realities...

The goal to achieving true intimacy is to acknowledge your fears...and analyze your misperceptions. See your fears as repressed excitement, and mobilize this energy to be intimate. Make an effort to get over the most common fears...

- Fear of being judged.
- Fear of abandonment, rejection, or loss.
- Fear of conflict.
- Fear of being hurt.

At the same time, you must also move beyond the common misperceptions about intimacy...

- *Misperception:* A long-term relationship with true intimacy gets boring. *Truth:* It is quite the opposite. There is no limit to learning about oneself and each other. Face guilt, shame, laziness, and other feelings underlying boredom. Keep digging deeper into each other's archeology of self. See boredom as an opportunity into which risk, engagement, action, and communion can enter.
- *Misperception:* Intimacy is a loss of freedom. *Truth:* Fear of intimacy is a prison of the self where no one can touch you. More intense intimacy frees you to discover yourself.
- *Misperception:* People who resist intimacy are tough. *Truth:* These people are missing joy and deep down can be very lonely, disengaged, and alienated.

Overcoming the hurdles...

- Explore and self-analyze your feelings. The deeper you know and feel for yourself, the deeper you are able to enter the lives of others. Understand the past that defines present patterns of intimacy.

Example: The woman who witnessed her father's constant betrayal of her mother grows up mistrusting all men.

- Be open and honest. Disappointment over past relationships and other issues cause you to close up emotionally.

Example: A 40-year-old man in danger of losing his job and being unable to send his child to college becomes fearful of sharing his concerns with his wife, so he shuts her out.

- Develop self-esteem and independence. In order to feel confident about sharing oneself, and prevent being either suffocating or suffocated in a relationship, one must develop a secure sense of self. Repeat affirmations and focus on successes.
- Unfreeze your emotions. The deeper you feel, the more you can enter another's life.

Exercise: Imagine lying on a rug before a fire with your partner. He/she whispers "I love you" in your ear. Feel the tenderness flowing.

- Recover your "personal mythology." Identify the negative stereotypes that you grew up with...and recognize the truth about who you are and what relationships and life are all about. Identify these stories so that you can recognize the difference between living a lie and experiencing a more honest and fulfilling relationship.

Limits to intimacy...

It's important to remember that in real life, the perfect balance needed for true intimacy is difficult to achieve—or sustain. Each person can be rocked anywhere along the way by insecurities, illness, distractions, stress, etc. In addition, people can naturally have different goals, careers, or levels of sophistication, maturity, or commitment. Frequently, there is discouragement or depression over these barriers to true intimacy.

Solution: Appreciate and adjust to differences as best as possible, but expect fluctuations in intimacy levels. Work toward the greatest potential of sharing, but allow for supplemental relationships with friends.

Source: Sam Keen, PhD, author and philosopher who practices in northern California. Keen is the author of several books, including the best-selling *Fire in the Belly and Inward Bound: Exploring the Geography of Your Emotions*, Bantam Books, 1540 Broadway, New York 10036.

Is it Possible for Men To Get Breast Cancer?

Men can get breast cancer—although the disease is far more common in women. About one out of nine women develop breast cancer, compared with about one out of 1,000 men. *At highest risk:* Men who have male or female blood relatives with the disease.

Source: A study led by Karin Rosenblatt, University of Washington School of Public Health and Community Medicine, Seattle.

Old Condom Danger

Old condoms rupture far more frequently than new ones. *Study:* 262 couples were asked to test about 5,000 condoms over a four-month period. *Result:* Less than 5% of brand-new condoms ruptured during intercourse. But condoms a year or two old broke about 10% of the time... and seven-year-old condoms broke about 19% of the time.

Source: Research by Markus Steiner, BA, contraceptive use and epidemiology division, Family Health International, Research Triangle Park, North Carolina.

College Students' Hepatitis B Problem

Incidence of this sexually transmitted disease has increased 77% in the past 10 years among college-aged adults. It is 100 times more contagious than the human immunodeficiency virus (HIV), which causes AIDS. Symptoms range from mild nausea and vomiting... to more dangerous liver disease and death. *Important:* Hepatitis B vaccinations for all college students—especially those who have had more than one sex partner in six months... engage in unprotected sex...or have had other sexually transmitted diseases.

Source: MarJeanne Collins, MD, chair, American College Health Association's Vaccine Preventable Diseases Task Force, Baltimore.

Cycling and Sex

Male bicyclists who ride up to 100 miles a week may become impotent. Repeated thrusting down on the pedals pounds the groin against the seat, damaging the critical arteries and nerves. *Initial symptoms:* Buttock numbness and difficulty getting an erection for a day or two. *Trap:* Damage may be irreversible and may not be apparent for years. *Self-defense:* Padded bike seat and shorts...rise off the seat occasionally, especially when sprinting...a correct size bike—you shouldn't have to shift your body on the downstroke.

Source: Harin Padma-Nathan, assistant professor of urology, University of South Carolina School of Medicine, quoted in *American Health,* 80 Fifth Ave., New York 10011.

Most Preferred Time for Sex

The most preferred time for sex is between the hours of 8 p.m. and midnight. *Second favorite time:* Before breakfast on the weekends.

Source: Survey of 3,144 men and women, reported in *New Woman,* 215 Lexington Ave., New York 10016.

Decreased Sperm Count Can Be Reversible

Decreased sperm count and motility—common in heavy smokers—may be reversible. *Key:* Vitamin C. Male smokers who received 200 or 1,000 milligrams of ascorbic acid daily for four weeks produced more healthy sperm than did heavy smokers who did not take the supplements. The larger dose produced a greater improvement.

Source: Earl Dawson, PhD, associate professor of obstetrics and gynecology, University of Texas Medical Branch, Galveston. His study of 75 male smokers was published in *Fertility and Sterility,* 1209 Montgomery Highway, Birmingham, AL 35216.

Women and HIV

HIV infection is often overlooked in women who visit hospital emergency rooms for routine care. *Recent study:* Only 18% of HIV-infected women were diagnosed as having the virus (compared with 40% of men).

Source: Ellie E. Schoenbaum, MD, department of epidemiology and social medicine, Montefiore Medical Center, Bronx, New York. Her study of more than 850 men and women treated in a New York City emergency room was published in the *American Journal of Public Health*, 1015 15 St. NW, Washington, DC 20005.

More Men Declining Sex

More men are declining sex. Men see sex as another area in which to perform, while women see it as a form of relaxation. *Other reasons:* Preoccupation with work or school...fatigue... stress...illness...depression...anxiety...fear of pregnancy...dislike of birth control...lack of exercise or too much exercise. *Self-defense:* Better communication...women's willingness to be sympathetic to partners' problems.

Source: Janet Wolfe, PhD, New York City psychologist and author of *What to Do When He Has a Headache*, Penguin Books, 375 Hudson St., New York 10014.

Why People Have Extramarital Affairs

Common hidden motives for having an affair:

•Unwillingness to confront the possibility of a breakup. Outside excitement takes the partner's mind off the real problem, which may be a lack of intimacy, respect, or sexual satisfaction in the marriage.

•Need for emotional support and courage to break up a weak marriage. Rather than risk being left alone emotionally, the partner looks for a new attachment in the form of an extramarital affair before walking out on the old one.

•Fear of intimacy. Some people find that commitment and intimacy provoke anxiety. The only way they believe they can tolerate marriage bonds is by savoring the feeling of freedom that affairs give them.

•Need to show resentment or anger toward the spouse indirectly.

Source: Dr. Helen Singer Kaplan, psychiatrist, head of the Human Sexuality Teaching Program, New York Hospital–The Cornell University Medical College, New York.

Sex Therapy

It isn't easy for couples who have sexual problems to seek professional help. *The most common problems:* Lack of interest. Trouble with erections and orgasms. Pain, real or imaginary.

When to consider therapy:

•When the problem becomes so great it jeopardizes the relationship.

•When preoccupation with the problem becomes so overwhelming that work suffers and enjoyment of life wanes.

•Especially dangerous: Trying to avoid the problem by drinking, abstaining from sex or turning to extramarital partners.

To find a reputable therapist:

•Ask your physician or county medical society for a recommendation.

•Review the directory of The American Association of Sex Educators, Counselors and Therapists. It sets education and training standards.

•Look for a therapist with degrees in a behavioral science (psychology, psychiatry) as well as training in sex therapy. Although sex therapy focuses primarily on sexual problems, a knowledge of psychology is essential because sexuality is so connected with total personality and life events.

•If a sex therapist doesn't ask at the first visit if you've had a medical exam, or refer you for one, find another therapist.

Most Common Sexual Concerns

Among men:

•Premature ejaculation. It is easier than you think to control the timing of ejaculation. You have to find the point at which you can no longer stop yourself from ejaculating. During masturbation, practice ways in which you can decrease or increase feelings of arousal. Discover which fantasies or behavior triggers your excitement and what diminishes it, and learn how to focus on the latter, in order to postpone ejaculation. But don't use the old-fashioned trick of thinking about baseball scores or work, which can be destructive to sexuality. Instead, focus on any minimally sensual thought, which at least keeps you in the realm of being sensual (but not at the peak of excitement).

• Sexual deviations and fetishes. Men are very much concerned with what they consider unnatural desires, such as the wish to be spanked by women or to wear women's clothes. These desires arise from deep psychological needs, such as the need to be punished for feeling sexual or a wish to be "close to Mommy" by dressing like her. If these kinds of problems are causing disruptions in your life, seek professional counseling.

• A desire for more sexual aggressiveness from female partners. A great many men wish that their wives or lovers would take the sexual initiative and behave less passively.

Unusual Infertility Cure

Weight gain may cure infertility in some women. Women below their medically ideal weight may experience reproductive-cycle shutdowns which make pregnancy less likely or impossible. Eighty-five percent of women studied who had been unable to conceive for four years became pregnant after gaining an average of eight pounds through a well-balanced diet—and without the use of hormones, drugs or surgery.

Source: G. William Bates, MD, professor of obstetrics and gynecology, Medical University of South Carolina, Charleston.

The Physical and Psychological Roots Of Impotence

Many factors can cause impotence. Contrary to the opinion that has prevailed since Masters and Johnson did their research, not all impotence is caused by psychological problems. New research shows that a variety of physical problems can cause impotence and that these are treatable. Included are hormonal problems and vascular and neurological conditions.

Impotence may be caused by medical or organic factors if:

• Medications are being taken to lower blood pressure, or if antidepressants, tranquilizers, antihistamines, or decongestants are being taken.

• A man drinks heavily. Alcohol has very strong negative effects on sexual function, including possible long-term problems such as reduced production of the male hormone, decreased sperm production, and reduced sex drive.

• There is a major illness, especially diabetes, thyroid disease, or arteriosclerosis. Illness doesn't dictate erection problems but should be considered as a possible cause.

• The man has lost sexual desire (as well as capacity).

Impotence is likely caused by psychological factors if:

• A man has firm erections under some circumstances (waking at night or in the morning, during masturbation, etc.). This indicates that the physical mechanism is in good working order and that the difficulty probably stems from emotional factors.

• Firm erections are lost just before or after entry. The odds here greatly favor an emotional cause.

• The problem started suddenly, over a period of a month or less. Most likely this is an emotionally caused impotence, since physical problems affect sexual function more gradually. There are exceptions, however. Emotional causes are not always sudden in their effect. And medical causes can surface quickly, especially if a drug is prescribed.

•The problem started after a very stressful emotional experience (the death of a spouse, the loss of a job, a divorce, rejection by a partner).

•Penis size. A very common concern, disguised with euphemisms such as "I have a handicap." (*Translation:* I think my penis is too small.) The solution is to understand that psychologically the small penis is not a deterrent to sexual pleasure. It is important to find out what penis size means to you or your partner and the ways it affects your desire and pleasure.

Among women...

•Not having orgasms. The first part of the solution is to learn not to focus on the missing orgasm—if it is missing. Studies show that at least half the women who think they don't have orgasms in fact do have them, but they're looking for some ideal of an orgasm that they've heard about. Genuinely nonorgasmic women can often overcome this problem by learning to achieve orgasm via masturbation. After acquiring the capacity to accept the sexual pleasure she has learned to give herself, a woman can usually go on to the next step, the pleasure of orgasm with a male partner.

•Conflict over the way they're treated in relationships with men. Men are much more concerned with sexual performance and physical fears than are women. Women care far more about the psychological and emotional aspects of relationships than do men. Many women still settle for "half a loaf" in a relationship. The first step out of this trap is to reject the false security of relationships that offer very little satisfaction.

•Problems integrating the role of parent and lover. It isn't only men who suffer from the madonna-prostitute complex (separating women into categories such as the "pure madonna" and the "sexy enticer"). Women also suffer from this syndrome. The most common example is the woman who has a child and thus comes to feel she isn't sexy and shouldn't feel sexy because she is now a mother. She may avoid sex on the grounds of fatigue, a problem with the baby or concern over money.

Among both sexes...

•Whether it's healthy to get involved in a sexual relationship with someone much older or much younger. There usually isn't a great deal wrong with this sort of thing, even though such pairings are often a holdover from incestuous childhood desires. When such desires are acted out by two adults, it can be taken as psychological information, but nothing else.

Sources: Dr. Judith Kuriansky, clinical psychologist and sex therapist, New York; Saul H. Rosenthal, MD, editor of *Sex Over Forty*.

Intimate Relations

•Couples rate talking to each other about their own relationship as the #1 topic to avoid ...especially couples in the "romantic potential" stage (in between a platonic friendship and an intimate relationship).

•Most couples are afraid of revealing their differing levels of involvement. The partner who is more committed fears scaring the other away, while the less committed may fear hurting the other person.

Sources: Study by Leslie Baxter, Lewis and Clark College, and William Wilmot, University of Montana.

•Affection expressed physically but not necessarily sexually is important to a love relationship. Nonsexual physical affection nurtures feelings of caring and tenderness and opens new avenues of communication. The newfound closeness can give your sex life, as well as your relationship, new vigor.

Source: Dr. Bernard Zilbergeld, clinical psychologist and coauthor of *Male Sexuality*, Bantam Books, New York.

•Men today welcome a woman's sexual initiative, contrary to the macho myths of the past that have put men in charge of initiating sex. Most men prefer to take turns taking the lead because they enjoy feeling desirable and giving sexual decision-making power over to their partners at least some of the time.

Source: Donald L. Mosher, PhD, professor of psychology, University of Connecticut, Hartford.

•Foreplay works best if a woman takes more responsibility for her own arousal. *Problem:* Many women believe it's the man's duty to arouse them. *What works:* Being honest about needs and desires...not worrying about the kids, jobs, etc...being specific about technique.

Source: Judith E. Steinhart, sex therapist, in *Medical Aspects of Human Sexuality,* Secaucus, NJ.

Sexual Side Effects of Mood Altering Drugs

•Librium and Valium have quite opposite effects on different individuals. For some, these drugs reduce inhibitions and increase sexual desire. In other cases, they decrease libido.

•Depression itself often causes a lack of interest in sex. Antidepressant drugs sometimes increase libido and sometimes decrease it. Other sexual side effects vary widely and are not well recorded. Possible problems include impotence, testicular swelling, breast enlargement and milk secretion, impaired ejaculation in men and delayed orgasm in women.

•Many medications used to treat psychosis have adverse sexual side effects that have not been fully documented. Among the symptoms are impotence, difficulty in ejaculation, irregular menstruation, abnormal lactation, increased and decreased sexual desire and even false positive pregnancy tests.

•Sleeping pills reduce the desire for sex. As administered in therapy, barbiturates often diminish sexual inhibitions, which raises sexual enjoyment. But chronic use of sleeping pills causes difficulty in reaching orgasm. *More dangers:* Men can become impotent, and women may suffer menstrual problems.

Sources: Joe Graedon, pharmacologist and author of *The People's Pharmacy* and *The People's Pharmacy-2,* Avon Books, New York, and Dorothy DeMoya, RN, and Dr. Armando DeMoya, MD, both of Georgetown University, writing in *RN,* Oradell, NJ.

28

The Savvy Consumer

How to Make the Most Of Coupon Clipping

By clipping coupons and mailing in hundreds of rebates, Sue Diffily has saved $3,700 on her supermarket bill during the past three years. *Her cost-cutting, income-stretching secrets...*

Setting aside time...

At my clipping peak five years ago, when all of my three children were still at home and my food bill was $500 a month, I saved $75 every two weeks by using coupons and rebates. While today my food bill is lower, I still devote 17 hours each month to coupon clipping and rebates:

•Three hours for coupon clipping and sale hunting.

•Eight hours for filing the coupons.

•Four hours filling out paperwork on rebate offers.

•Two hours meeting with my coupon club, where I swap coupons and rebates.

This tally excludes the eight hours a month I spend shopping, since I would do that anyway.

Payoff: About $9 an hour in income, after taxes and expenses. It's a job for which I make my own hours and answer only to myself.

Rating the sources...

•Supermarket flyers are a great source of store coupons and company rebate forms. They are distributed through the mail or at the stores themselves. You can also find valuable rebates in the flyers of supermarkets at which you don't ordinarily shop. Many contain rebate offers from national companies—such as Pillsbury or General Mills—which are valid regardless of where you purchase the items.

•Daily newspapers—especially Wednesday and Sunday supplements—and women's and parenting magazines, such as *Parents, Good Housekeeping, McCall's, Ladies' Home Journal,* etc., often have coupon sections.

•Coupon club. Although it's not essential to join a club to profit from coupon clipping, it can't hurt. I joined one about 10 years ago by responding to an ad in my local supermarket. Today, six of us meet for two hours once a month to pool nearly 1,000 unwanted coupons and rebate offers. Anyone in the club is welcome to take as many coupons as he/she would like. But a simple rule applies to the rebate forms—which may be worth several dollars apiece or much more—when you take one, you replace it with another.

•Family and friends. They can be a great resource. If you put the word out, you'll be deluged with coupons they've clipped for you.

Organizing your files...

•Coupons. I keep my coupons in an expandable, accordion folder. Some people file them alphabetically by brand. This is great if you can keep track of every brand. However, I find this too difficult.

I prefer to organize my coupons by product category—breakfast products, meat and poultry, dairy and oils, beverages, desserts, cleaning products—which is how I shop.

Every two weeks, before I go shopping, I comb my file and pull out any coupons that are due to expire that month as well as any others I think I'll use. I also check the newspapers to see which products are on sale at my favorite supermarket. When I shop, I take along a shoe box filled with coupons.

•Rebates. Until recently, most rebate offers required that you mail a box top or side in with the rebate form. To save these items required a fair amount of space—for me, that meant three boxes, each of which was 1-foot-by-2-feet-by-1½-feet deep.

But lately, companies ask only for the product's bar code or proof-of-purchase seal, which is much less bulky. For every product I buy, I simply tear off the front of the product package, put it in a large resealable bag, and slip in the proofs-of-purchase and bar codes as I accumulate them. This helps me know immediately which products they're for, in case a rebate is offered.

To keep track of my rebates, I keep a notebook. I divide the pages into columns for the company, the particular item, the date I mailed the form, the amount of the offer, and the date I received the rebate. It usually takes between one and three months to receive a rebate.

In the event of a long delay, I call the company's 800 number. In most cases, the rebate check arrives soon after my call—often with some free coupons thrown in.

Some people spend their rebates as soon as they get them. To stay motivated, I have set up a separate bank account. Whenever I've collected $10, I make a deposit.

Saving more...

I don't clip every coupon—and I don't use every coupon I clip. I only purchase items that I know my family will use. If I overbought just to cash in my coupons, I'd be losing money on the deal. My other strategies...

•Watch for sales. By waiting until prices are marked down, you effectively increase the value of a coupon.

•Don't get locked into brand loyalty. I'll buy a store brand if the price is right and I have a good coupon. Often, one brand turns out to be just as good as any other brand, and if I don't like the store brand, I avoid it in the future.

•When you find a good deal, stock up. My family used to laugh when I'd come home with 20 bars of soap or a dozen bottles of cooking oil that I bought on sale with a coupon for each. But I knew we would use them eventually. In the long run, these big purchases make great financial sense.

•Look for "double plays" and "triple plays." These can save you two or three times what you would have saved with just a coupon.

Double play: This purchase involves a combination of a sale and a coupon or rebate.

Example: While I like a particular brand of lipstick, it normally costs about $6, which I feel is a bit steep. But when the company ran a "buy-one-get-one-free" sale, I got four for a total of $12. With a rebate form I obtained at my local beauty aids store, I got back $2.50 per stick. *My net cost:* 50 cents per stick.

Triple play: This is a purchase involving a sale, a coupon and a rebate. By capitalizing on all three, you could wind up paying virtually nothing for an item.

Example: My favorite detergent normally costs $3.99 for a 64-ounce box. I'll accumulate a number of $1 coupons for that brand—and then use them all when it goes on sale for $1.99. *My net cost:* 99 cents per box. But if I then use a typical rebate—$2 back for two proofs-of-purchase—I get the detergent free.

Triple plays and organization are the keys to couponing and refunding.

Source: Sue Diffily, a homemaker and former second-grade teacher who lives in Smithtown, New York. She lectures locally on coupon clipping.

Appliances: Repair or Replace?

Appliance repair people are becoming scarcer by the year, and the cost of service calls has gone through the roof. Consumers face a difficult decision over whether to repair appliances or opt for new ones. A survey of appliance marketers and repair people disclosed what life expectancy appliances have and how to determine whether they are worth fixing.

• Televisions. The big, old American sets (like Zenith and RCA) frequently lasted ten years. Today, most sets last from five to eight years.

After that, the set will start needing a new high-voltage transformer, a new picture tube, and a new tuner. It's best to replace the television at that point.

Television repair. It costs from $250 to $300 to repair or replace the picture tube of a color television (including parts and labor). It costs more to replace the tube of a 13-inch or 19-inch color television than of a 23-inch set.

Reason: Most color replacement tubes are rebuilt from old tubes. And there are more 23-inch tubes around to salvage because that size used to be more popular.

The most expensive television set to repair is the Sony. Repair people find it the most difficult to work on, and its parts are hard to get. Picture tube replacement can cost $400.

• Air conditioners. They should have a life expectancy of ten to twelve years.

Two problems may arise at that time: The compressor fails or the Freon leaks. If Freon leaks, don't expect a repair person to fix it permanently.

• Refrigerators. They have the same time span and problems as air conditioners.

• Dishwashers and washing machines. They last ten to twelve years.

Longest-lasting items: Stoves, vacuum cleaners.

Rule of thumb...

When repairs cost 50% of the price of a replacement, it's time to get rid of the appliance.

If you are going to repair...

Try to deal with authorized service centers. They have a better knowledge of individual brands. Furthermore, you can be sure with an authorized service center that you are getting the right parts.

When buying a new unit...

The best buys on appliances can usually be had at discount appliance stores or through buying co-ops. The discount stores advertise loss leaders to get you into the store. Go with the advertised special.

Alternative...

Rebuilt appliances. They come with complete warranties and are generally below the discount house's prices.

Better Shopping

Department store fluorescent lighting often distorts colors. *Result:* You may not be able to tell the true color of clothing, lipstick or other merchandise you've purchased until you get it home. *Self-defense:* If what you buy doesn't live up to your expectations, take it back and demand a refund—the store's poor lighting isn't your fault.

Source: *Live Better for Less*, 21 E. Chestnut St., Chicago, IL 60611.

How Amy Dacyczyn Avoids Overspending At the Supermarket

Although most people go to the supermarket with a budget in mind, they usually spend much more money than they had planned to spend. But by using a variety of strategies, I spend only $180 a month to feed our family of eight.

The first step to saving money at the supermarket is to overcome your most common excuses for why your bill is so high...

The big myths...

• *Myth:* Never shop with your kids. *Reality:* If you can't say no to your children, you have a parenting problem, not a shopping problem.

• *Myth:* Shop the aisles in reverse order to avoid temptation. *Reality:* If you can't resist temptation, you have a problem with self-discipline, not budgeting.

• *Myth:* Menus must be planned in advance to save at the supermarket. *Reality:* Don't plan meals more than one day in advance, or you're likely to spend more at the supermarket.

Example: If you scheduled pork chops and they're too expensive, you'll probably buy them anyway. *Better:* Stock up on foods that are purchased at a good price. Then prepare meals with the foods you have already bought. There should be pork chops that you bought on sale in your freezer.

Supermarket strategies...

Once you've overcome the myths, you're ready to put serious money-saving strategies into place. *My favorites...*

• Work on your attitude. Saving money on groceries depends on a consistent attitude toward shopping—every time you shop. It is essential that you enter the supermarket fully conscious and determined about what you will—or will not—buy.

If you are prone to impulse shopping, you must decide to take control of your shopping habits.

Helpful: Practice. Try the strategies listed below, and learn more about what it costs for your family to eat the food you normally buy. Before you know it, nothing on earth could induce you to spend your hard-earned cash on a hamburger mix or sugar-coated cereal.

• Shop with a list. Make a list of specific groceries that you will buy at certain prices...but be flexible. What's on your list may not be on sale, but you may find a great deal on something that's not on your list.

Key: Be steadfast about what you will not buy. Certain products, such as toaster pastries, are too expensive at any price.

• Keep a price book. This strategy helps to save me more time and money than anything else I do.

In fact, comparison shopping is essential, since most people's memory for prices is not as good as they think it is. It's easy to figure out the cheapest can of green beans in one store, but most of us shop at more than one location—supermarkets, wholesale clubs, farmers' markets, natural food stores, discount stores—and foods come in different-sized packages.

To keep track of prices, I carry a small loose-leaf notebook that fits in my purse. On each page, I have listed the prices I've encountered for a specific product, with abbreviations for the store name, brand, item size, price and unit price. The pages are arranged alphabetically by product for easy reference.

Try shopping at a different good value store each week, so that you visit them all within a month. You will soon find patterns emerging.

Example: Cheese is usually a good buy at the wholesale club and seldom on sale at the supermarket.

Added benefit: You'll soon find that not every advertised sale is really a sale. Prices at the same store for the same item may vary from week to week by as much as a third.

Rule of thumb: The items at the front and back of the sale flyers are usually the best deals, though there may be a few on the inside pages.

•Buy groceries in bulk. This does not necessarily mean you have to buy huge quantities. It simply means you must buy enough of each item at its lowest price to provide for your family from sale to sale—or to last until your next trip to the wholesale club. Buying in bulk can save the average family at least $50 a month.

Helpful: Not all food has to be stored in the kitchen. If you were offered $50 a month to rent the space under your bed, would you do it? Use a closet or a shelf in the garage for that bargain case of peanut butter.

For maximum savings: Invest in an extra freezer. For example, the largest Sears model costs less than $6 a month to run. Even apartment dwellers can often arrange to keep locked freezers in the basements of their buildings.

•Determine which products are the least expensive, and how to buy them as inexpensively as possible.

Examples: I calculate which meats are the least expensive based on portion size, and I watch for sales. I generally choose from the lower end of cuts—with occasional treats. I also calculate the cost per gallon of fruit juice, whether it is frozen, bottled or canned.

My family drinks apple, orange or grape juice ...or lemonade made from sugar, water and lemon juice concentrate. We don't buy processed blends of fruit juices, which are always more expensive than other juices. We do buy store brands.

Stay away from: Single serving packages, snack packs, lunch sizes...almost anything disposable, except toilet paper and tissues.

Examples: Diapers, paper plates, napkins, tablecloths.

•Set limits on what you are willing to pay for staple food items. Gradually, you will determine realistic upper limits for the items you routinely buy. Stick to your limits.

Example: In my area of the country, I will pay no more than 69 cents a pound for meat on the bone—or $1.20 a pound or less for boneless.

•Buy food in its "original" form. Avoid convenience and processed foods. Pop your own popcorn. Make your own breading for chicken and pork. Buy regular oatmeal rather than processed cereal or "instant" oatmeal.

Source: Amy Dacyczyn, author of *The Tightwad Gazette*, Villard Books, a book of cost-cutting strategies that have appeared in her newsletter of the same name. Rural Route 1, Box 3570, Leeds, ME 04263.

To Make Wool Garments Last Longer...

Brush wool clothes frequently...rest wool for at least 24 hours before wearing again... refresh it by hanging in a steamy bathroom... use sturdy hangers. Remove spots and stains promptly. *To remove:*

...alcohol or food—place a towel under the area. Sprinkle soda water over it and rub gently toward the center of the spot.

...coffee or tea—sponge with glycerine. If none is available, use warm water.

...grease—sponge with dry-cleaning solvent or spot cleaner.

...ink—immerse in cold water.

...mud—once dry, brush and sponge from back of the garment with soapy water.

...lipstick—rub white bread over the area with a firm, gentle motion.

Source: The Wool Bureau, Inc., 330 Madison Ave., New York 10017.

Supersavers

•When food shopping, weigh produce priced by the bunch, such as carrots, celery, broccoli, onions, and fruit. Buy the heaviest and get extra pounds free.

•Drink water. It takes 15,000 eight-ounce glasses of tap water to equal the cost of a six-pack of soda.

•Freeze your credit card—literally. Freeze in a plastic bag partially filled with water (it will not damage the magnetic strip). In an emergency, thaw.

• Furnish a college student's dorm or apartment with "finds" from garage sales.

• If you have a chronic illness, schedule telephone home visits with your doctor in place of regular office visits. This is a new option you should explore with your doctor.

• Veterans and senior citizens can qualify for an exemption on property taxes. Your local tax office has information on the amount to which you are entitled.

• Make your own stationery. Press small flowers and leaves in a thick phone book. Later glue the dried flowers on paper for an elegant look.

• Enlist your children's help to lower the utility bill. Post last month's bill and let them share any money saved in the future.

• Put summer grass clippings, autumn leaves, and vegetable scraps in a "compost pile." Next spring there will be free mulch and fertilizer for the garden.

• Get a shoe "tune-up." Have the uppers conditioned, attach neoprene protective soles, and apply a sealant to uppers that allows wear in any kind of weather with minimal damage.

• When the supermarket sells out of the loss-leader items, always ask for rain checks and buy at rock-bottom prices when items are back in stock.

• Do your own wallpapering after viewing a do-it-yourself video. Purchase wallpaper at a discount store for additional savings.

• Save on your food budget. Contact the County Cooperative Extension Agent and receive information on gardening in your locale.

Source: Jackie Iglehart, editor of *The Penny Pincher* newsletter, Box 809-BL, Kings Park, NY 11754. 516-724-1868.

Beware of Paying Full Price

Never pay full price unless you are sure you have exhausted all other options. Decide if you must have something new, or can buy it used. If you need an item urgently, improvise—try borrowing it instead of rushing out to buy it.

Source: *The Tightwad Gazette: Promoting Thrift as a Viable Alternative Lifestyle* by Amy Dacyczyn, founder, *The Tightwad Gazette* newsletter, Villard Books, 201 E. 50 St., New York 10022.

Limited-Edition Collectibles Trap

Very few coins, plates, and artworks touted as rarities make good investments. They are manufactured on assembly lines and sold at high prices by professional direct-marketing firms. Within a couple of years, you can find these items at secondhand stores for a fraction of their original prices.

Source: *Scrooge Investing* by Mark Skousen, PhD, adjunct professor of economics, Dearborn Financial Publishing, Inc., 520 N. Dearborn St., Chicago 60610.

Filing Savvy

File all receipts for returned merchandise with receipts. When you get your credit card statement, make sure you were credited for the returned item. *If no credit appears:* Contact your credit card company at the 800 number on your bill.

Source: *How to Return Just About Anything* by Patricia Forst, Longwood, Florida-based lecturer on consumer satisfaction, Thomas Nelson Publishers, Box 141000, Nashville, TN 37214.

Avoid Service Contracts

Manufacturers' service contracts are almost never a good buy. Salespeople push them because they carry high sales commissions. But the contracts very rarely pay back their costs—and are usually not renewable when a product has reached the end of its typical useful life—when it might start to need major repairs. *Better than a service contract:* Pre-purchase research to find reliable, high-quality products.

Source: *100 Ways to Avoid Common Legal Pitfalls Without a Lawyer* by Stephen Christianson, Esq., a Virginia-based lawyer specializing in civil litigation, Citadel Press, 600 Madison Ave., New York 10022.

Better Clothes Buying

To gauge the true cost of a piece of clothing, calculate the price-per-wear. *Example:* A $200 pair of shoes, worn twice a week for a year, costs about $2 per wear. But a $25 pair, worn for only two special occasions, costs $12.50 per wear—not a bargain. An item's versatility and durability can be more important than its purchase price.

Source: *Out of the Rat Race,* Gregory Communications Group, Box 95341, Seattle 98145.

Pay Special Attention at The Checkout Counter

Group special sale items together when unloading the grocery cart, along with anything missing a price tag or a tag that may be wrong. Pay special attention when these items are rung up—they are the most likely to be rung incorrectly, even in stores using scanners. *Self-defense:* Watch closely as all items are rung up —and check your receipt at home.

Source: *Money,* Rockefeller Center, New York 10020.

Lightbulb Savvy

Compact fluorescent bulbs screw into standard lightbulb sockets and give off light that looks like that from incandescent bulbs...but last more than 10 times as long and use only one-quarter the energy. *Cost per 60-watt bulb:* About $20, plus $10 of electricity over its lifetime. Ten traditional bulbs would cost less (about $10) but use $45 of electricity. *Best places to use:* Where lights are left on at least two hours per day. *Caution:* The fluorescent bulbs won't fit all lamps or covered fixtures.

Source: *You Can Change America* by The Earth Works Group, dedicated to facilitating change at a grassroots level, Earthworks Press, 1400 Shattuck Ave., Box 25, Berkeley, CA 94709.

Better Shopping

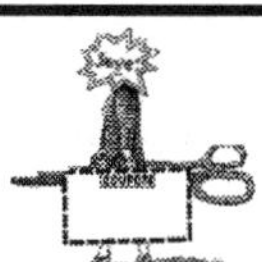

Plan ahead. Do extensive research to find out just what you need. Plan finances so you can pay as much cash as possible.

Source: *The Tightwad Gazette: Promoting Thrift as a Viable Alternative Lifestyle* by Amy Dacyczyn, founder, *The Tightwad Gazette* newsletter, Villard Books, 201 E. 50 St., New York 10022.

Better Lawn Mowers

Cordless, rechargeable electrics need no oil, gas, starter ropes or tune-ups—and are much quieter than gas-powered mowers. Electrics use far less energy—around $5.50 a year, about the same amount as a toaster. And they generate practically no pollution. Using a gas mower for one hour creates as much pollution as driving a car 50 miles. *Cost:* $350 to $550—about the same as high-end gas mowers.

Source: Joel Makower, editor, *The Green Consumer Letter,* 1526 Connecticut Ave. NW, Washington, DC 20036.

No-Haggle Trap

Car buyers who shop at one-price "no-haggle" dealerships to avoid the discomfort of negotiating may pay as much as $1,000 more for the convenience. *Reason:* Prices at no-haggle dealerships are inflexible and typically higher than those that consumers could negotiate for themselves at traditional showrooms.

Source: W. James Bragg, author of *In the Driver's Seat: The New Car Buyer's Negotiating Bible,* Random House, 201 E. 50 St., New York 10022.

Generic Drug Savings

To save money on drugs, ask your doctor for a generic version of the prescription (at a savings of up to 70%)...comparison shop at pharmacies ...consider mail-order (for discounts of up to 40%). *Major mail-order pharmacies:* Action Mail Order/800-452-1976...Family Pharmaceuticals (Medi-Mail)/800-922-3444...Medi-Mail/800-331-1458.

Source: *Money,* Rockefeller Center, New York 10020.

Multiple-Deposit Leases

When leasing a car, ask the finance company for a "multiple-deposit lease." It will allow you to leave a larger deposit in exchange for a lower interest rate. *Result:* Reduced expenses over time. *Example:* You're told that the minimum deposit for a three-year lease on a $30,000 car is $500, and your monthly payments will be $520. If you leave $4,000 instead, your payments would be $460—or a total savings of $2,160. That's more than 54% return on your investment, since the $4,000 deposit is returned to you at the end of the lease.

Source: Art Spinella, vice president and general manager of CNW Marketing/Research, a Bandon, Oregon firm that tracks car-leasing trends.

Supersavers #2

•Prolong the life of shoes by using an unfinished cedar shoe tree ($10 to $20 per pair). Cedar slowly withdraws moisture from leather, leaving the shoes pliant and looking like new.

•Use a clothesline or drying rack instead of a dryer and save $0.50 to $1 on each load of laundry.

•Water lawns and gardens in the early morning to reduce evaporation and prevent fungus. Just before sunrise is best.

•Shop "high-and-low" at the supermarket. The most expensive items are stocked at eye level. Bend over—or stand on tiptoe—to reach for cheaper items.

•Make your own baby food. Puree home-cooked foods in a food processor, and freeze individual portions in an ice tray. Store food cubes in a plastic bag.

•Buy ready-to-use pizza dough from a pizza shop, add your own toppings and bake at 450 degrees for about 20 minutes.

•Rotate and keep tires properly inflated. Everyone knows tires last longer that way—and you get better gas mileage—but only a small percentage of people follow through.

•Save energy by using a toaster oven for small items. It heats the house less in summer and doesn't need to preheat.

•Decrease excessive use of water and prevent septic system overflow by installing an ultra-low flush toilet, which will cut indoor water usage by 25%. Toilets are the biggest indoor water-wasters.

•Grow your own fruit and save space by planting dwarf fruit trees, which grow to one-third the size of regular fruit trees and produce two-thirds the amount of fruit.

•Assemble a 72-hour emergency kit. Be prepared for hurricanes, earthquakes, tornadoes, etc. A good source for these items is Emergency Essentials, a mail-order company in Orem, Utah. For a free catalog, call 800-999-1863.

•Grow a variety of vegetables in a small space by interplanting—planting seeds of one type of vegetable in between seeds of another. A few good combinations are tomatoes/basil, beans/corn/squash/carrots, and peppers/carrots/onions. For a free list of these combinations, send a self-addressed, stamped, business-sized envelope to *The Penny Pincher.*

Source: Jackie Iglehart, editor of *The Penny Pincher,* Box 809-BL, Kings Park, NY 11754.

How to Be a Bargain Shopper

The biggest problem most shoppers have with bargaining is a feeling that nice people don't do it. Before you can negotiate, you have to get over this attitude. Some ammunition:

•Bargaining will not turn you into a social outcast. All a shopkeeper sees when you walk in is dollar signs. If you are willing to spend, he will probably be willing to make a deal.

•Bargaining is a business transaction. You are not trying to cheat the merchant or get something for nothing. You are trying to agree on a fair price. You expect to negotiate for a house or a car—why not for a refrigerator or a winter coat?

•You have a right to bargain, particularly in small stores that don't discount. Department stores, which won't bargain as a rule, mark up prices 100%-150% to cover high overhead costs. Small stores should charge lower prices because their costs are less.

The savvy approach:

•Set yourself a price limit for a particular item before you approach the storekeeper.

•Be prepared to walk out if he doesn't meet your limit. (You can always change your mind later.)

•Make him believe you really won't buy unless he comes down.

•Be discreet in your negotiations. If other customers can overhear your dickering, the shop owner must stay firm.

•Be respectful of the merchandise. Don't manhandle the goods that you inspect.

•Address the salesperson in a polite, friendly manner. Assume that he will want to do his best for you because he is such a nice, helpful person.

•Shop at off hours. You will have more luck if business is slow.

•Look for unmarked merchandise. If there is no price tag, you are invited to bargain.

Tactics that work:

•Negotiate with cash. In a store that takes credit cards, request a discount for paying in cash. (Charging entails overhead costs that the store must absorb.)

•Buy in quantity. A customer who is committed to a number of purchases has more bargaining power. When everything is picked out, approach the owner and suggest a total price about 20% less than the actual total.

•If you are buying more than one of an item, offer to pay full price on the first one if the owner will give you a break on the other. Or, ask to have an extra, probably small-ticket, item thrown in.

•Look for flawed merchandise. This is the only acceptable bargaining point in department stores, but it also can save you money in small shops. If there's a spot, a split seam or a missing button, estimate what it would cost to have the garment fixed commercially, and ask for a discount based on that figure.

•Adapt your haggling to the realities of the situation. A true discount house has a low profit margin and depends on volume to make its money. Don't ask for more than 5% off in such a store. A boutique that charges what the traffic will bear has more leeway. Start by asking for 25% off, and dicker from there.

•Buy at the end of the season, when new stock is being put out. Offer to buy older goods —at a discount.

•*Neighborhood stores:* Push the local television or appliance dealer to give you a break so you can keep your service business in the community.

Source: Sharon Dunn Greene, coauthor of *The Lower East Side Shopping Guide,* Brooklyn, NY.

What Goes on Sale When

A month-by-month schedule for dedicated bargain hunters:

January...

•After-Christmas sales.
•Appliances.
•Baby carriages.
•Books.
•Carpets and rugs.
•China and glassware.
•Christmas cards.
•Costume jewelry.
•Furniture.
•Furs.
•Lingerie.
•Men's overcoats.
•Pocketbooks.

- Preinventory sales.
- Shoes.
- Toys.
- White goods (sheets, towels, etc.).

February...
- Air conditioners.
- Art supplies.
- Bedding.
- Cars (used).
- Curtains.
- Furniture.
- Glassware and china.
- Housewares.
- Lamps.
- Men's apparel.
- Radios, TV sets and CD players.
- Silverware.
- Sportswear and equipment.
- Storm windows.
- Toys.

March...
- Boys' and girls' shoes.
- Garden supplies.
- Housewares.
- Ice skates.
- Infants' clothing.
- Laundry equipment.
- Luggage.
- Ski equipment.

April...
- Fabrics.
- Hosiery.
- Lingerie.
- Painting supplies.
- Women's shoes.

May...
- Handbags.
- Housecoats.
- Household linens.
- Jewelry.
- Luggage.
- Mothers' Day specials.
- Outdoor furniture.
- Rugs.
- Shoes.
- Sportswear.
- Tires and auto accessories.
- TV sets.

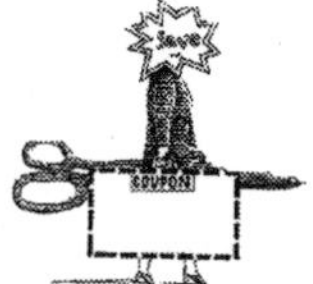

June...
- Bedding.
- Boys' clothing.
- Fabrics.
- Fathers' Day specials.
- Floor coverings.
- Lingerie, sleepwear and hosiery.
- Men's clothing.
- Women's shoes.

July...
- Air conditioners and other appliances.
- Bathing suits.
- Children's clothes.
- Electronic equipment.
- Fuel.
- Furniture.
- Handbags.
- Lingerie and sleepwear.
- Luggage.
- Men's shirts.
- Men's shoes.
- Rugs.
- Sportswear.
- Summer clothes.
- Summer sports equipment.

August...
- Back-to-school specials.
- Bathing suits.
- Carpeting.
- Cosmetics.
- Curtains and drapes.
- Electric fans and air conditioners.
- Furniture.
- Furs.
- Men's coats.
- Silver.
- Tires.
- White goods.
- Women's coats.

September...
- Bicycles.
- Cars (outgoing models).
- China and glassware.
- Fabrics.
- Fall fashions.
- Garden equipment.
- Hardware.
- Lamps.
- Paints.

October...

- Cars (outgoing models).
- China and glassware.
- Fall/winter clothing.
- Fishing equipment.
- Furniture.
- Lingerie and hosiery.
- Major appliances.
- School supplies.
- Silver.
- Storewide clearances.
- Women's coats.

November...

- Blankets and quilts.
- Boys' suits and coats.
- Cars (used).
- Lingerie.
- Major appliances.
- Men's suits and coats.
- Shoes.
- White goods.
- Winter clothing.

December...

- After-Christmas cards, gifts, toys.
- Blankets and quilts.
- Cars (used).
- Children's clothes.
- Christmas promotions.
- Coats and hats.
- Men's furnishings.
- Resort and cruise wear.
- Shoes.

How to Choose the Right Checkout Line

Successful people play to win. They know the rules, devise plans of attack and follow their plans with discipline, whether it's on the job, in the stock market—or just doing the grocery shopping. *To spend less time in the supermarket...*

- Look for the fastest cashier. Individual speeds can vary by hundreds of rings per hour.
- Look for a line with a bagger. A checker/bagger team will move a line up to 100% faster than a checker working alone. When the supermarket uses optical scanning equipment, the bagger increases line speed by more than 100%. *Note:* Two baggers in the same line are barely more helpful than one.
- Count the shopping carts in each line. If all else were equal, the line with the fewest carts would be the quickest. But...there are other factors to consider. *Look for...*

A) Carts that contain many identical items. Two dozen cans of dog food can be checked out faster than a dozen different items. They don't have to be individually scanned or rung into the register.

B) Carts that contain a lot of items. Because each new customer requires a basic amount of set-up time, it's better to stand behind one customer who has 50 items than behind two customers who have 10 items each.

C) Carts that contain a lot of produce. Each item has to be weighed.

D) People with bottles to return. This can take a lot of time.

E) People who look like they're going to cash a check. This too can take a lot of time. *Most likely check-cashers:* Women who clutch a purse.

Source: David Feldman, author of *How to Win at Just About Everything,* Morrow Quill, William Morrow & Co., 105 Madison Ave., New York 10016.

A Good Desk Chair

A good desk chair can add as much as 40 minutes to your workday because you won't develop fatigue-induced problems...back strain, leg cramps, etc. *Important:* Don't sit for longer than 60 minutes at a time or you will tire your body.

What to look for in a chair:

- *Seat:* Made of porous material to let body heat dissipate. Opt for a hard one, slightly contoured to the buttocks (soft cushions roll up around and put pressure on joints).
- *Front of seat:* Rounded or padded so it doesn't cut off circulation in your legs.
- *Backrest:* Extends the width of the chair. Conforms to your spine, and supports the lower

and middle back. Straight at the shoulder level to prevent neck strain. Small of the back should fit snugly into the chair back.

• *Height:* Your feet should rest flat on the floor. Otherwise circulation to your feet is slowed. This also takes some of your body weight off your lower back. Be sure height is adjustable.

• *Arm supports:* Firm, softly padded, at least two inches wide.

• *Swivel ability:* This enables you to face your work at all times. You'll avoid eyestrain from moving your eyes back and forth.

• Look for back- and position-adjustable chairs that let you move forward, tilt backward, sit upright for posture changes that rest and relax you if you're sitting for hours at a time.

Source: *Do it at Your Desk: An Office Worker's Guide to Fitness and Health,* Tilden Press, Washington, DC.

Recognizing Quality In Clothes

To take advantage of sales, discount designer stores or consignment shops, look for the details that signal first-class workmanship, label or no label.

• Stripes and plaids that are carefully matched at the seams.

• Finished seam edges on fabrics that fray easily (linen, etc.).

• Generous seams of one-half inch or more.

• Buttons made of mother-of-pearl, wood or brass.

• Neat, well-spaced buttonholes that fit the buttons tightly.

• Felt backing on wool collars to retain the shape.

• Ample, even hems.

• Straight, even stitching in colors that match the fabric.

• Good-quality linings that are not attached all around. (Loose linings wear better.)

Source: Viki Audette, author of *Dress Better for Less,* Meadowbrook Press, Deephaven, MI.

How to Care for Leather Clothes

Leather and suede garments need the same careful treatment as furs. Otherwise, you may lose them.

• Buy leather garments a little bigger than you need, because they can never be enlarged. This is particularly important in women's trousers.

• Be aware that leather and suede may shrink in cleaning.

• Avoid wearing your leather garment in the rain. If the garment does become wet, dry it away from heat.

• Use a dry sponge on leather occasionally to remove the surface dust.

• Wear a scarf inside your neck to prevent oil stains from your skin.

• Don't store the garment in a plastic bag. Put dust covers over the shoulders.

• Never put perfume on a suede or leather garment. Even putting it on the lining is risky.

• Don't pin jewelry or flowers on leather garments. Pinholes do not come out.

• Store leathers as you do furs, in a cool spot. Better yet, store your leathers at the same time you store your furs.

Source: Ralph Sherman, president of Leathercraft Process, New York.

What Dry Cleaners Don't Tell You

The dry cleaning process is not mysterious but it is highly technical. After marking and sorting your clothes on the basis of color and material type, the cleaner puts them into a dry cleaning machine. This operates like a washing machine except that it uses special solvents instead of water. After the clothes have gone through the dryer, the operator removes stains from them.

A good dry cleaner will use just the right chemical to remove a stain without damaging the fabric. Pressing correctly is next—also a matter of skill. With some fabrics, the garment is put on a form and steamed from the inside to preserve the finish. After pressing, the clothing is bagged.

What to look for:

•Suits should be put on shoulder shapers.

•Fancy dresses and gowns should be on torso dummies.

•Blouses and shirts should be stuffed with tissue paper at the shoulders.

•Except for pants and plain skirts, each piece should be bagged separately.

Taking precautions:

•Examine your clothes before leaving them with the cleaner. Point out stains and ask whether or not you can expect their removal. For best results, tell the cleaner what caused the stain.

•Don't try to remove stains yourself. You may only make them worse. Bring stained clothing to the cleaner as soon as possible. Old stains are harder to remove.

•Bring in together all parts of a suit to be cleaned. Colors may undergo subtle change in the dry cleaning process.

•Check all pockets and remove everything. A pen left in a pocket can ruin the garment.

•Read care labels carefully. Many clothes cannot be dry cleaned at all. Do not dry clean clothing with printed lettering or with rubber, nylon or plastic parts. If in doubt, ask your dry cleaner.

•Make sure your dry cleaner is insured if you intend to store a large amount of clothing during the winter or summer months.

•Don't wash clothes and then bring them to the cleaner's for pressing. The saving is minimal.

•Ask if the dry cleaner will make minor repairs as part of the cleaning cost. Many cleaners offer such service free.

•Don't request same-day service unless absolutely necessary. Rushed cleaners do a sloppy job.

•"French cleaning" means special handling for a fragile garment. The term used to be applied to all dry cleaning, since the process originated in France. Now it indicates shorter dry-cleaning cycles or even hand cleaning. *Best:* Alert your dry cleaner to the term "French cleaning" on the label.

How to Buy Sunglasses

•Be sure they are large enough.

•Make sure no light enters around the edges.

•For best performance, select frames that curve back toward the temple.

•If you choose plastic lenses, remember that they scratch easily. So clean them with a soft cloth, not a silicone tissue.

•If your main concern is preventing glare, buy greenish grays, neutral grays and browns.

•Avoid other colors, which absorb wavelengths and can upset color balance.

•Always try on sunglasses before buying. The world should appear in true colors, but not as bright.

•If you plan to wear sunglasses near water much of the time, get polarized lenses, which block glare reflected off the water. You can have an old pair of prescription lenses tinted to a desired polarized density.

•*Best all-round sunglass choice:* Sunsensor lenses that adjust from dark to light.

Picking the Right Running Shoes

Running shoes do not need to be broken in. They should feel good the moment you try them on. *Look for:*

•A heel counter that holds your heel in place and keeps it from rolling in and out.

•Flexibility in the forefoot area so the shoe bends easily with your foot. (If the shoe is stiff, your leg and foot muscles will have to work too hard.)

•An arch support to keep the foot stable and minimize rolling inside.

•A fairly wide base for stability and balance. The bottom of the heel, for example, should be as wide as the top of the shoe.

•Cushioning that compresses easily. (Several different materials are used now.) The midsole area absorbs the most shock and should have the greatest amount of padding. However, the heel (which, particularly for women, should be three-quarters of an inch higher than the sole) needs padding, too. Too much causes fatigue, and too little causes bruising.

•Start with the manufacturers' least costly shoes first. Try them on. Then keep trying up the price range until you find the one that feels best. Try on running shoes with the same kind of thick socks you will be wearing with them.

•Adequate toe room (at least one-half inch of clearance). Running shoes, particularly in women's sizes, run small, and women often need a half-size or whole-size larger running shoe than street shoe.

Source: Gary Muhrcke, proprietor of the Super Runner's Shop, New York.

How to Buy Ski Boots

First rule: If a boot is not comfortable in the store, it will be worse on the slopes.

•Toes should be able to wiggle while the heel, instep and ball of the foot are effectively, but not painfully, immobilized.

•Buy in a shop with an experienced shop technician who can expand the shell and modify the footbed and heel wedge.

•Check forward flex. When you bend your foot, you should feel no pressure points on your shin or upper ankle.

•Look for a high boot with a soft forward flex. Low, stiff boots concentrate loads just above the ankle, which can be painful for the occasional skier.

Choosing a Long-Distance Telephone Service

Guidelines to help make the decision easier:

•Choose a service that offers the cheapest rates for your calling pattern. (Analyze your last year's telephone bills to see where you called, when you called, and how long you talked to each location.) If you are a heavy long-distance phoner, a company's minimum monthly charge won't hurt you. If you make few long-distance calls, however, the minimum charge might be more than your average telephone bill.

•Some companies also have minimum monthly usage requirements and/or volume discounts. Again, choose according to your needs. If you make only a few short calls a month you'll be hard pressed to justify the minimum. If you have high long-distance bills, a volume discount may offer big savings.

•Consider whether a company charges by distance or according to its service abilities in the areas you call most frequently. If you tend to call distant or hard-to-reach places, a "cheap" service with fewer connections may end up costing you more.

•Rounding off the number of minutes per call can add as much as 10% to your phone bill, especially if you make a lot of shorter calls. Check to see if the company you are considering rounds to the minute or to the tenth of a minute.

•Test each long-distance carrier that you consider for line clarity and ease of connection. There is still a big difference among services.

Source: Robert Krughoff, author of *The Complete Guide to Lower Phone Costs,* Consumers' Checkbook, Washington, DC.

How to Change Your Mind After Buying from Door-to-Door Salespeople

Impulse buys made from door-to-door salespeople or at houseware parties need not be binding. Under Federal Trade Commission rules, you have three business days to reconsider at-home purchases of $25 or more.

What to do:

•When you buy something from a door-to-door salesperson, always ask for two copies of a dated cancellation form that shows the date of sale and a dated contract with the seller's name and address. The contract should specify your right to cancel.

•If you wish to cancel, sign and date one copy of the cancellation form and keep the second copy. Send the cancellation to the company by registered mail (receipt requested).

•You can expect sellers to act within 10 days. *Their obligations:* To return any signed papers, down payment and trade-in. To arrange for pickup or shipping of any goods. (Sellers pay shipping.)

•You must make the merchandise available for pickup. If no pickup is made within 20 days of your dated cancellation notice, the goods are yours.

•If you agree to ship the goods back and then fail to do so, or if you fail to make the goods available for pickup, you may be held to the original contract.

•Be aware that the same rules apply at a hotel, restaurant or any other location off the seller's normal business premises. They do not apply to sales by mail or phone, or sales of real estate, insurance, securities or emergency home repairs.

How to Buy a Good Man's Shirt

When choosing a man's shirt, look for these signs of quality:

•Soft tissue-paper packaging (no cardboard).

•A well-set collar finished with small, flat stitches.

•16-18 threads per inch in a moderately priced shirt and 22-26 threads per inch in a very good shirt.

•Cross-stitched pearl or bone buttons.

•Smooth, supple collar fusing (proving that it has not been glued to the material inside and will not flop after laundering.

•Removable collar tabs.

Source: *Personal Style* by James Wagenvoord, Holt, Rinehart & Winston, New York.

Buying a Cellular Phone

Before you buy a cellular phone, be aware that:

•They are now connected to brain cancer in some studies.

•Phone bills are expensive because you're billed for incoming as well as outgoing calls. And—an access charge is tacked on to your monthly bill.

•Insurance costs may go up because few basic auto policies now cover the theft of cellular phones from cars. Figure on $50 a year per vehicle for additional insurance.

•Some equipment is being marketed by companies that may not be in business in the future as the competition gets tougher.

•The phone is worth the expense whenever (1) Making calls from your car actually frees you for more productive activities at the office, or (2) You can prove that the calls really result in an increase in company business.

What to look for today when you buy a cellular phone:

•A speaker-phone model so you can talk without holding the handset, a valuable feature because it lets you keep both hands on the wheel except when you're dialing.

•A system that hooks into the company switchboard. Then office calls can be forwarded directly to you by the switchboard operator.

•An electronic lock that lets you dial a code number to stop calls from being made to or from the phone.

•A switch that enables you to talk on both frequencies that cellular transmitters use in cities when they're available. Phones with only one frequency occasionally lose quality when the car passes through an area where there's interference with the radio waves that carry the conversation.

•A manufacturer that's been in existence for several years and isn't known to have financial problems.

Source: Fritz Ringling, vice president of communications research, Gartner Group, Stamford, CT.

Supersavers #3

• Wax-paper liners from cereal boxes can be saved. They are high quality and perfect for placing between meats before freezing, lining cake pans or rolling out pie dough.

• Lipsticks. Rather than discarding them when the tips flatten, extend their use by applying with small paint brushes.

• Prepared foods at the supermarket are more costly than buying raw ingredients and cooking them yourself, but they can be a less-costly alternative to eating out.

• Phone services. Cancel any add-on services that you don't use, such as call-forwarding, call-waiting, speed-dialing, etc.

• Permanent flowers. Don't replace dusty silk-flower arrangements. Clean them by washing under running water. They dry beautifully and look like new.

• Cloth napkins, which you can launder, are much cheaper to use than paper ones. *Save more:* Buy no-iron tablecloths at garage sales, cut into 18-inch squares and hem the edges.

• Nonfat dry milk is an effective substitute for pricey coffee creamers.

• Hospitalized friends. When mailing a card to a friend in the hospital, use his/her home address for the return address. If he has left the hospital when the card arrives, it will be "returned" to him. You will save a stamp, and he will be sure to receive your card or note.

• Plastic hangers that come with socks can be used as hangers for doll clothes.

• Make your own brown sugar. Mix one cup of white sugar with one tablespoon of molasses (two tablespoons for dark brown sugar). Store in a jar or plastic bag.

• A narrated videotaped record of your home and furnishings can be made in case your home or property suffers damage. Update the video every two years—or when changes are made. Keep the tape in a safe place, and keep a second copy off the premises—in a safe-deposit box, or with a friend or with family.

• Don't cover presentable floors with wall-to-wall carpeting. Save by buying a remnant and having the edges bound. Leave 12" to 18" of floor exposed. For a room that is 12' x 14', go with a remnant that is 10' x 12' or 9' x 11'. When the remnant begins to wear, turn it 180 degrees. Get twice the life at less than half the price.

Source: Jackie Iglehart, editor of *The Penny Pincher,* Box 809-BL, Kings Park, NY 11754. 516-724-1868.

How to Buy Shoes That Really Fit

Shoes should provide a lot of cushioning. The running shoe is the most physiologic shoe made. Soft and malleable, it provides cushioning and a little bit of support.

• If you're a woman and you wear a high-heeled, thin-soled shoe, have a thin rubber sole cemented onto the bottom to cushion the ball of the foot.

• Fit shoes with your hands, not with your feet. There should be an index finger's breadth between the tip of the toes and the front of the shoe.

• Tell the salesperson to start with a half-size larger than you usually wear and work down. The shoe shouldn't be pushed out of shape when you stand. The leather should not be drawn taut.

• An ideal heel height for a woman is 1½-2 inches. This is not a magic number, simply the most comfortable. If a man wore a 1½-inch heel, he'd be more comfortable than in the traditional ¾-inch heel.

• If you have flat feet, look for low-heeled shoes that feel balanced. They should not throw your weight forward on the balls of your feet or gap at the arches.

• Buy shoes in the late afternoon when your feet have had a full day's workout and are slightly spread. Shoes that you try on first thing in the morning may be too tight by evening and uncomfortable for all-day wear.

Source: John F. Waller, Jr., MD, chief of the foot and ankle section, Lenox Hill Hospital, New York.

29

Funtime

Have More Fun At Disney World

•Plan what you want to do before you go. The less time you spend waiting in lines and the more you are able to see, the more value you get for your money. Call in advance to see if any rides are closed for repair.

Also...

•Get going early. The theme parks open about one-half hour earlier than the "official" opening time. The same four rides you can enjoy in one hour early in the day could take up to three hours after 11:30 a.m. *Recommended:* Arrive 50 minutes before the official opening time, an hour and a half on major holidays.

•Avoid major holidays. Disney World is busiest from Christmas Day through New Year's Day, the week of Washington's Birthday and during spring break and Easter weeks.

Least busy times: After Thanksgiving weekend until Christmas, September until the weekend before Thanksgiving, January 4th through the first half of February, the week after Easter until early June.

Lightest days: Friday, Sunday.

•Buy tickets in advance by mail from Disney World or a Disney store. Do not buy tickets at non-Disney hotels, because you'll have to pay up to 10% more.

*Admissions options:** 1 Park/1 Day, about $40 for an adult. 4-Day Value Pass, about $132. 4-Day Park Hopper, about $146. 5-Day Pass, about $198. Annual Passport, $243. Florida-resident Pass, $222.

Best bets: For one- or two-day visits, one day tickets. For longer visits, the 4- and 5-Day Passes. If you do not plan to visit the smaller attractions, don't pay for the Super Pass.

•Save the Magic Kingdom for last, especially if you are traveling with children who may not appreciate the more serious parks. Its rides and attractions are highly rewarding for kids and

*Admission prices are subject to change without notice. For more information, call 407-824-4321.

adults. *Recommended:* See EPCOT first, then MGM, then the Magic Kingdom. Allow a full day for each park.

•Consider a non-Disney World hotel. Some hotels near the Main Gate entrance on US 192 are closer to MGM and the Magic Kingdom than many on-site hotels. Staying off-site can cut your lodging costs by 40% to 60%. Savings on food off-site, especially breakfast and lunch, can be tremendous.

Trade-off: Luxury, convenience. The Disney hotels are much nicer than off-site hotels, and provide certain advantages.

Examples: Child-care options, preferential treatment at the theme parks, transportation independence for teenage children. Most of the expensive Disney hotels provide transportation to the various Disney parks. You do not need a car unless you want to visit attractions outside of Disney.

Best bets: Stay on-site during busy seasons. Join the Magic Kingdom Club ($65 for two years) for Disney hotel and admissions discounts. During the off-season, there is little impact on convenience staying off-site, and off-site may be more convenient if you plan to visit Universal Studios or other area attractions.

•Evaluate travel packages carefully. Choose a package with features you'll use. Compare package prices with what you would pay booking the trip yourself. If you don't intend to rent a car, choose a package that includes transportation from the airport. Cab fare to Disney World can run up to $42 one way.

•Limit on-site snacks. It is easy to spend $40 a day on popcorn, ice cream, etc. *Helpful:* Bring snacks, and set an itinerary before entering the park: *We're going to go like crazy until 11:30, have a snack break, then go to a show and then sit down and have lunch.*

•Watch out for souvenir-madness. Even the most jaded visitors to Disney World find themselves wanting a Mickey T-shirt. Prepare your kids to stay within a budget and set limits for yourself, too.

•Remember that you will be in Florida. Bring sunscreen, sunglasses, hats, cool, comfortable shoes, aspirin, etc. Drink plenty of fluids. If you suffer from motion sickness, stay off the wilder rides.

Source: Bob Sehlinger, author of *The Unofficial Guide to Walt Disney World & EPCOT,* Prentice-Hall Travel, New York.

Cut Costs in Las Vegas And Atlantic City

You don't have to be a high roller to enjoy free meals, rooms and drinks in Las Vegas or Atlantic City. *Here's how:*

•Garage parking. Available to even non-gamblers. Have the parking ticket validated at the casino cage.

•Drinks. Served to anyone at a table or slot machine. Most hotels will also buy a round when you finish playing. Order from a casino waitress or ask the pit boss for a "chit" to be used at any hotel bar.

•*Breakfast or coffee-shop lunch:* Bet $5 to $10 per hand for one hour. Ask the dealer or pit boss for a "meal ticket."

See the pit boss for the following...

•*Line pass:* $5 to $10 per hand for an hour. Allows entrance to the casino show via the shorter VIP line.

•*Free show pass:* $50 to $200 per hand (depending on the performer) for four hours.

•*Room discounts:* $25 per hand for four hours. The "casino rate" averages 50% and ranges up to 100% off the regular room rate.

•*Room, food, drinks and a show:* $100 per hand for four hours per day, for three days.

•*Airfare, mini-suite, food, drinks:* $200 per hand, four hours per day, for three days.

•*First-class airfare, suite, food, drinks:* $500 to $1,000 per hand, at least four hours a day for three days.

Other ways to cut corners...

Join a casino slot club. Members earn points equal to about 1% of what they wager in the slot machines. Points can be redeemed for cash or room and food credits. *Membership:* Free.

Have your play "rated"—or tracked—by the casino. Up to 40% of what rated players are expected to lose (even if they don't) is rebated in room, food and beverage credits. Contact the pit boss.

Sit down at a game just before a table is scheduled to close, usually between 2:00 and 4:00 a.m. The pit boss will be generous with comps to get you to leave.

Source: Max Rubin, author of *Comp City: A Guide to Free Las Vegas Vacations*, Huntington Press, Las Vegas, NV.

Videotaping Basics

To hold the camera as steady as possible, keep your feet apart with your weight evenly distributed between them...tuck elbows into your body for support...for a smooth, side-to-side pan, keep the bottom half of your body still and pivot the upper half, "rolling" your body over a solid support, such as a wall...in windy conditions, find a firm support—wall, railing, car trunk—to lean against.

Source: *John Hedgecoe's Complete Guide to Video* by John Hedgecoe, professor of photography, Royal College of Art, London, Sterling Publishing Co., New York.

Rules to Keep a Friendly Poker Game Friendly

Neighborhood poker—exemplified by the guys on *The Odd Couple*—is more than just a game. It's a friendship around a table. And friendship thrives in a comfortable atmosphere where friends show each other consideration. *Bottom line:* Poker should be fun. To set the scene:

Make it comfortable...

•The room. It should be big enough for a table and at least seven chairs, with plenty of room to gèt up and leave the table without bumping other players. *Important:* A window that opens at the top...if there's cigarette and cigar smoke, it has to go somewhere. Provide large ashtrays or your floor will suffer.

•TV. Good for players who drop out of the game...and for everyone when there's a major sports event. It doesn't matter where the TV sits, but keep the sound low—it can be turned up for the exciting moments.

•Music. It's up to the individual group whether to have music...and what kind of music. Play the radio, so that no one has to hop up to change tapes, etc.

•Table. A round table is preferred, but any shape will do. Use a tablecloth to make a smooth, cushioned surface. Chips bounce when tossed on a bare table top.

•Chairs. Use strong, metal folding chairs... wood is not strong enough. Comfort is not a concern in poker games. If you're winning, you'll be very comfortable.

•Cards. Use high-quality cards. Cheap cards crease and bend easily—a card with a folded corner will be a marked card for the rest of the evening.

Use two decks at a time, each with a different color backing. While one deck is being dealt, the other can be reshuffled by the player who dealt the previous hand. Hold on to decks from previous weeks in case you need an emergency replacement deck.

•Chips. Have at least three colors—one for each of the minimum and maximum bets, and one for double the maximum. Clay chips handle better than plastic. They're available from gambling supply houses—check your *Yellow Pages.*

•Food. Chips, pretzels, popcorn and nuts are the old standbys. Select food that can be eaten with one hand, leaving the other free to hold cards.

Later in the evening something more substantial will be necessary. Cold cuts or pizza work well. Both can sit for a while and remain edible, require few utensils and don't make a mess. Use paper plates, and keep plastic bags handy for garbage. *Mistake:* Chinese food. It's too messy.

Food should be supplied by the host...but paid for by all. Arrive at a set donation or take a cut from each pot.

•Disaster control. Keep plenty of paper towels and a portable vacuum cleaner handy.

•Clean-up philosophy. Nobody leaves until the garbage is bagged, ashtrays are emptied and the immediate area is made neat.

Playing etiquette...

•Know what you are going to deal when the deck comes to you. Poker has a rhythm. Being indecisive breaks it.

•Turn all your cards face down to indicate you're out of a hand. Or toss them to the dealer or into the pot so they're out of the way. Take care that no one sees your cards. What one player knows, all should know.

•Clean up condensation from beverage bottles and cans. Wet cards ruin the game.

•Be honest. You only have to be caught once to be marked forever.

•Bring enough money to play for at least half the night. The worst thing you can do is quit early and leave only four players. *Rule of thumb:* Bring enough money to buy three full stacks of chips.

•If you must leave early, make it known in advance. This gives the other players a chance to find someone else.

•If you drink beer...bring beer. Once it comes into the house, though, it's community property. *Note:* If you want to drink or eat something different than what is being served, bring it.

•Keep your up cards fully exposed in a stud game so everyone can see them. Players who try to cover up their cards in a stud game are not trusted.

•Announce your ante. Say something like "I'm in" loud enough so that others hear you. Then, if the pot comes up short, you'll have witnesses.

Don't give another player advice on betting, even if asked. Your advice could sabotage a bluffer, or simply be bad advice.

•Once you've dropped out, don't look at another player's hand without permission. And don't react to what you've seen.

•Don't look at another player's hand if you've seen someone else's. Your expression could give something away. *Worse:* Giving advice to either of the player's whose cards you've seen. Your advice would be based on knowledge of two or three hands (including your own)—knowledge not available to other players.

•Don't call out what cards or possibilities another player has showing. Only the dealer has this right. This is all the more true when you've dropped out.

•Never help another player figure out what he/she has. A player must call his own hand.

•Don't feel sorry for a loser and hold the bet down. It's humiliating for the loser. Play to win big. It's not malicious—it's the game.

•Don't feel sorry for a novice. It's sink or swim. And you could find yourself in the position of carrying a bad player.

•Don't show your complete winning hand if you win the pot by default. You may have been bluffing and that's information no one paid to see...and you don't want anyone to know. Only by calling your final bet do players pay for the privilege of seeing your hand.

•Never play poker with someone whose nickname is a city. If he's good enough to be the best in town, he's good enough to beat anyone in your neighborhood.

Source: Stewart Wolpin, author of *The Rules of Neighborhood Poker According to Hoyle*, New Chapter Press, 381 Park Ave. South, New York 10016.

Dog-Training Basics

•Keep lessons short. Four half-hour lessons will be more productive than one full hour.

•Give lessons at the same time and place each day, in an area where there are no distractions.

•Don't attempt to teach just after the dog has eaten a full meal.

•Keep lessons consistent and interesting.

•Make sure you've got the dog's attention before giving a command.

•Limit commands to one or two words. Use the same tone of voice all the time.

•Praise or blame the dog during an act, not afterward, so it knows what it has done right—or wrong.

•Wait until the dog learns one lesson before moving on.

•Command with firmness and authority, yet with kindness and patience. Do not show displeasure if the dog makes a mistake—stop if you find yourself losing patience.

•Always finish with a game.

Source: *The Howell Book of Dog Care* by Tim Hawcroft, veterinary surgeon in private practice in Sydney, Australia. Howell Book House, 866 Third Ave., New York 10022. 800-257-5755.

Better Kitten Buying

Buy from a busy household with children. *Less desirable:* Kittens from pet stores or rescue shelters, where infectious diseases are common. *Traits to look for:* Interest when you play with a moving object...a glossy coat...clean, dry eyes and ears. *Minimum age:* eight to 10 weeks. *Warning signs:* Nasal discharge or sneezing...diarrhea...black dust in the coat (a sign of fleas).

Source: *A Miscellany of Cat Owners' Wisdom* by Kay White, Running Press, 125 S. 22 St., Philadelphia 19103.

Mistakes People Make Training Their Dogs

Dogs that misbehave are usually not to blame ...their owners are. With the proper training, almost any dog will be obedient. *Common dog-owner mistakes:*

•*Mistake:* Choosing the wrong breed in the first place. Different breeds have vastly different temperaments. Make sure to match the breed with your family's needs and situation.

Examples: Border collies, English setters and most other English breeds are usually easygoing, making them appropriate for families with children. Pit bulls, rottweilers and Middle European breeds, such as dobermans, are usually aggressive and not appropriate for families and children.

•*Mistake:* Start training too late. Dog owners often wait until a puppy is six months old to start obedience training—far too late. Bad habits learned during the first months of a dog's life are hard to break later on.

The best time to start training is as soon as the puppy leaves the litter—at 49 days (seven weeks). Between 7 and 13 weeks, the training should be very low-key. Put the puppy on a light leash or string. Show it how to sit, stay and come. But do not reprimand the puppy if it fails. *Note:* If you can teach your dog the sit, stay, come commands, you can teach it anything within the realm of its learning.

After 13 weeks, training can begin in earnest, with firm-voiced reprimands for incorrect behavior.

•*Mistake:* Failing to socialize the dog. Dogs should be introduced to everything they will normally encounter in their lifetimes as soon as possible—start at no later than eight weeks of age. They need to learn how to react to other dogs, cats, adults, children, noises, cars, etc.

Owners who fail to socialize their dogs early on often wind up with overly aggressive or overly timid animals. Dogs that fail to get socialization training by 11 weeks often prove difficult to train later on. Those that make it to 13 weeks with no socialization are impossible to train.

•*Mistake:* Being inconsistent. Dogs don't understand spoken language as humans do. They merely learn to associate a specific command—a particular word, whistle or some other signal—with a particular response.

Spoken commands should be short and must always be given in precisely the same manner. Inconsistent commands confuse dogs.

Example: A dog who learns to respond to the command *Sit,* cannot be expected to respond to *Come on, boy, sit down. I said sit.*

•*Mistake:* Failing to reprimand effectively or to consider the dog's age. Dog owners often scold their puppies for misbehavior. But puppies—unlike older dogs—really don't understand scoldings. They must be reprimanded in a different manner.

Be patient when you train a small puppy—it's only in kindergarten. If it does something wrong, patiently start the lesson over with encouraging words.

Then later loom over the adult dog to make it feel threatened. This makes you the dominant animal—the leader of the pack.

• *Mistake:* Using corporal punishment incorrectly. Never strike a dog with your hand—it makes it fear your hand—or with a newspaper. And never hit a dog in the face.

Using a strap or a leash, strike the dog lightly, a few times on the flank. Don't hurt your dog—just help it to understand that its behavior displeases you and show it in your voice. After the dog encounters the strap the first time, chances are it will respond merely to the threat.

• *Mistake:* Using food as a reward. Giving dogs treats is fine, but never train a dog using food as a reward. Doing so exercises its stomach ...not its brain.

Reward good behavior during training with a friendly word or a good pat. Save treats until after the training is completed for the day.

• *Mistake:* Overestimating a dog's attention span. Puppies 8 to 12 weeks of age learn fastest when given repeated, but short, training sessions—two minutes of training three times a day.

Don't continue a session if the dog is uninterested or fatigued. *Clue:* Watch the dog's tail. When it stops wagging...stop training.

Source: Dog expert Richard A. Wolters. He has published nine books about dogs, including *Family Dog*, Dutton, New York.

Stereo Savvy

When placing all components of a stereo system in a single cabinet, put the amplifier on the top shelf. That's because the amplifier produces heat that will rise and could damage the other components if allowed to build up in a confined space. Be sure there are at least two inches of space between the top of the amplifier and the top of the cabinet. Consider drilling a few small holes in the back of the cabinet and leaving the front doors open to assure adequate air circulation while the equipment is in use.

Source: Joseph Giovanelli, contributing editor, *Audio* magazine, New York.

Gambling Odds

No betting system will change the house odds at games that consist of "independent plays," such as craps, roulette and slots. The fact that 10 straight passes have been made at the craps table has no impact on the odds that another pass will be made. The length of time since a slot machine last paid off has no impact on when it will next pay off. Odds change in a game with "memory," such as blackjack, in which the cards that have already been dealt limit the cards that remain. Sports betting has independent plays, but the odds are different on each event.

Source: Wally DeShield, PhD in mathematics, writing in *Blackjack Confidential*, 513 Salsbury Road, Cherry Hill, NJ 08034.

Top 10 Skiing Resorts

What makes one ski resort more exciting than all the rest? According to our insider, it's the destination's diversity...thrilling trails, cushy lodges and lots of after-ski activities. *The following are his North American favorites...*

• Lake Louise, Alberta. Wilderness views of the Canadian Rockies. Fifty-two trails, a beautiful 515-room chateau abutting an alpine lake.

• Snowbird, Utah. One hour from Salt Lake City. Forty feet of snow each winter, plenty of difficult trails and a first-class spa.

• Snowmass, Colorado. Wide-open cruising terrain. Sixteen lifts (five of them high speed), 72 trails. Lodge lets you ski from your room to the lift.

Bonus: Trendy Aspen is only 10 minutes away by frequent, free shuttle bus.

• Steamboat, Colorado. Located above a quaint Western town, great mix of tree skiing and wide-open cruising trails. Has 108 trails and 20 lifts. Hot-springs-fed pools for bathing, horse-drawn sleigh rides.

• Stowe, Vermont. New England's tallest peak. Forty-five trails, modern lifts, improved snowmaking, great food and views. Cross-country skiing and night skiing. Twelve lifts (two high speed) and 90 trails.

•Sunday River, Maine. Super-efficient lifts, snowmaking and grooming, plus all-ability terrain and lodging that allows you to ski to and from your door.

•Taos, New Mexico. One of the finest ski schools. Seventy-two trails, 10 lifts, abundant powder and sun 300 days a year.

•Telluride, Colorado. An expert's paradise, located above an old silver-mining town nestled in a spectacular canyon. A modern ski lodging development.

•Vail, Colorado. Largest single ski mountain in the US. Twenty-five lifts (eight of them high speed), 4,014 acres of terrain, 121 trails, and lots of powder, thanks to the high altitude. And, there are horse-drawn sleigh rides—including evening trips to local restaurants.

•Whistler/Blackcomb, British Columbia. Two mountains, 28 lifts, 6,900 acres of terrain, a mile of vertical descent that allows skiers to take their time winding down their choice of 200 trails. Has an enchanting base village with more than 100 shops.

Source: An industry insider who has visited more than 120 North American ski centers during the past 22 years.

How to Choose a Kennel

When you need to board your pet for any length of time, visit the kennel with your dog a week or two before you leave him there. *Plan to spend some real time looking for:*

•Operators who own the kennel. They will have a real stake in your satisfaction.

•A staff that shows sincere concern for the pet's welfare, not willingness to do whatever you tell them.

•Kennels and runs that are well designed. A combination of two feet of concrete with four feet of fencing above it is desirable so that timid dogs can hide from their neighbors. *More important:* No dog can urinate into another dog's run. (Urine and feces spread disease.)

•A security fence around the entire establishment (in case a dog escapes from its run).

•Kennels that are neat and clean. Kennel helpers are picking up waste, hosing down runs, exercising the dogs, etc.

•Beds that will not harbor parasites. Fiberglass is good. Wood is bad. Dogs with parasites should be dip-treated before boarding.

•A requirement of confirmation of your dog's shots, either by a recent inoculation certificate or contact with your veterinarian.

Questions you should ask...

•What is the kennel owner's background? Ask about his/her experience in breeding and handling. Such experience helps the kennel owner notice when an animal is not feeling or moving well.

•What kind of food is used? A good kennel is flexible and serves nearly anything. Some even cook to order.

•What will you do if my pet won't eat? If a dog does not eat for two days, the kennel should try a variety of foods until it finds one that works.

•What kind of medical and behavioral history is taken? A thorough history includes more than a record of shots and your vet's name and phone number. You should be asked about your pet's temperament, behavior, sociability, likes and dislikes.

•Who will administer my dog's medication? Only the owner or the kennel manager should administer medicine, and careful records should be kept.

•What happens if my dog gets sick or there's a medical emergency? The kennel owners should call your veterinarian first, then bring your dog to your vet—or, if that's not possible, to a local veterinarian. If it's an emergency, your pet should be taken immediately to the kennel's attending veterinarian. Check the professional credentials of the kennel's attending veterinarian with your own vet.

•How often will my dog be walked? Dogs should be walked at least twice a day, in addition to exercising in their kennel runs.

Will my dog be played with, and how often? Your pet should be played with and petted at least twice a day. Some toys should be allowed.

Source: Michael and Phyllis Scharf, owners and operators of Pomona Park Kennels, Pomona, NY.

Planning Your Leisure Time

If you're like most people, there are lots of activities you'd like to do in your leisure time, but you never seem to get around to them. The solution is to plan—not so much that you feel like you're "on the job," but not so little that you fail to accomplish whatever is important to you, whether that means learning French or going dancing. *Recommended:*

•Create a "to do" list for your spare time just as you might for your workday. You probably don't want every hour accounted for, but you should at least list what you most want to do with each leisure evening or weekend.

•Allot some specific times on a regular basis when you will pursue the leisure activities that are most important to you. A scheduled time will help ensure the successful fulfillment of your plan.

•If it's culture you're after, consider getting at least one subscription series to eliminate some of the paperwork and phone calling that often accompany even leisure-time plans. (You will also avoid wasting time in line!)

•Set up regular social contacts, like monthly Saturday dinner with specific friends, so you spend less time coordinating your meetings and more time enjoying them.

•If you use too much of your recreation time for household chores, try delegating those tasks to professional help or family members. Or do it more efficiently and less frequently.

•If you often work in your leisure hours, consider that you may be more efficient if you plan, and carry out, pleasurable activities that energize you (and prevent work burnout).

•To keep your leisure-time plans active (not reactive to other people's demands on you), make appointments with yourself. You will be less inclined to give up your plans if someone else asks you to do something, since you have a previous commitment to yourself.

•Just as a "quiet hour" of uninterrupted time at the office increases your work efficiency, a "quiet" leisure hour enhances your nonwork time. On a fixed schedule, if possible, take some time each evening and weekend to meditate, listen to music, reflect, or just plain old "unwind."

•How can you find more hours for recreation? By setting your alarm clock only half an hour earlier on weekends you'll gain four hours a month. Become more efficient at work, so you can leave earlier (and not have to take work home as often). To find the time to read that mystery novel, try switching from showers to baths, and read in the tub.

Source: J. L. Barkas, PhD, author of *Creative Time Management*, Prentice-Hall, Englewood Cliffs, NJ.

47 Inexpensive Ways To Have a Good Time

Having fun can't be calculated in dollars and cents. Sometimes the less money you spend, the more you enjoy yourself. *Here are some inexpensive ways to have fun:*

•Explore the beach and collect seashells.

•Visit the zoo and feed the monkeys.

•Go to a free concert in the park.

•Pack a picnic and drive to an attractive spot for lunch.

•Go skiing at your local park or a nearby mountain.

•Window-shop at your favorite stores.

•Eat early-bird-special dinners at local restaurants. Then go home and see a movie on TV.

•Hug each other more.

•Dress up with your favorite person and enjoy a formal dinner at home with fine food and wine.

•Go camping or backpacking.

•Go gallery-hopping. See the latest art exhibits.

•Enjoy your public library. Go to the reading room and catch up on the new magazines.

•Go for a drive on the back roads to just enjoy the scenery.

•Visit friends in a nearby city. (Arrive around lunchtime.)

•Eat dinner at home. Then go out for dessert and coffee.

•Instead of eating dinner out, eat lunch out over the weekends. It's less expensive.

•Seek out discount tickets and twofers for local entertainment.

•Take in the local museum's cultural events, including low-priced lectures and concerts.

•Invite friends in for drinks when a good movie is on TV.

•Take an afternoon walk in the park.

•Row a boat on the lake.

•Have a beer-and-pizza party for friends.

•Go back to the old family board games.

•Raise exotic plants or unusual herbs in a window box.

•Learn to paint or sculpt.

•Learn calligraphy.

•Take a long-distance bus ride.

•Go out to the airport and watch the planes.

•Visit the local amusement park and try the rides.

•Have friends over for a bring-your-own-specialty dinner.

•Become a do-it-yourselfer.

•Take an aerobic exercise course.

•Join a local political club.

•Go shopping for something really extravagant. Keep the sales slip and return the item the next day.

•Play cards for pennies, not dollars.

•Go to the races and place $2 bets.

•Explore your own city as a tourist would.

•Learn to be a gourmet cook.

•Treat yourself to breakfast in bed.

•Hold a family reunion.

•Attend religious services.

•Learn a foreign language.

•Join a local chorale or dramatic club.

•Watch local sports teams practice.

•Play golf or tennis at local parks or courses.

•Read everything in your area of interest at the library.

•Buy books. Get many hours of pleasure (and useful information) for still relatively few dollars.

To Celebrate a Really Special Occasion

•Take over a whole performance of a play or concert for your special guests. During the course of the event, have a prominent individual step out of character and tell the audience about you and your special day.

•Have a song written especially for the occasion.

•Run a tennis or golf party, with a name professional hired to give lessons to all.

•Hire a boat and bring along a large group for a cruise and buffet supper.

•Arrange a block party.

•Rent a hay wagon and a big barn for a square dance.

•Hire the museum or the lobby of a key office building in the downtown area for a huge buffet supper and dance.

•Hire a well-known singer to entertain at a party.

•Have a cookout on the beach, with the guests digging for related buried treasures.

•Take over a country inn for a day, and run a big house party.

•Fly a group of friends to a special place for a holiday.

The Six Best Champagnes

•Taittinger Comtes de Champagne—vintage only. A rosé champagne that should go far to overcome Americans' prejudice toward this celestial brew. Taittinger also makes a fine blanc de blancs and a nonvintage brut.

•Dom Perignon—vintage only. Probably the most widely acclaimed champagne and deservedly so. Elegant and light, with delicate bubbles. The producer also makes, under its Moet et Chandon name, a vintage rosé champagne, a vintage champagne, a nonvintage champagne, and a nonvintage brut.

•Perrier-Jouet Fleur de Champagne—vintage only. This house produces champagne of the highest quality in a particularly popular style. The wine is austere, yet tasteful. It is also extremely dry without being harsh or acidic. Perrier-Jouet is introducing a rosé champagne.

•Louis Roederer Cristal—vintage only. Cristal's magic lies in its plays with opposites: Elegant yet robust, rich taste without weightiness. Roederer also produces a sparkling rosé, a vintage champagne, and a nonvintage brut.

•Bollinger Vieilles Vignes—vintage only. This is the rarest of all fancy champagnes. Its vines have existed since before phylloxera (a plant louse) killed most French grapevines in the middle 1800s. The wine is robust and rich flavored. Bollinger also makes a vintage champagne and a nonvintage brut.

•Dom Ruinart Blanc de Blancs—vintage only. Produced by Dom Perignon in Reims rather than in Epernay, it is a sleeper. It is held in low profile so as not to compete strongly with its illustrious co-product but is every bit as good. The wine is light (not thin), complex, very alive, yet velvety.

Source: Grace M. Scotto, veteran of the wine business and former owner, D. Scotto Wines, Brooklyn, NY.

Networking: Constructive, Fun Get-Togethers

Do you often wonder how to get to know someone you've met in passing without seeming too pushy? Would you be interested in finding out about current issues from people who are actually involved in them? It is possible to do all of the above, and in addition expand your business and social contacts and have a great time, without spending a lot of money. *Here are some suggestions from three veteran networkers:*

Networking dinners...

•Have dinners for 13 to 15 people on Tuesday, Wednesday or Thursday at 6:30 so people can come straight from work and leave at a reasonable hour.

•Don't worry about the mix. There's a surprising commonality that develops among people of all ages and professions. Avoid inviting co-workers, couples or business partners. Candor diminishes when a guest comes with someone he sees all the time. Guests who spark conversation especially well: Journalists, headhunters, celebrities.

•Use a modest typewritten or telephoned invitation. Send the invitations at least two weeks in advance.

•It's up to you, as the host or hostess, to get conversation started. Give informative introductions for each guest, mentioning at least three things people can ask questions about.

•A cozy, circular table keeps one conversation rolling rather than several private ones.

•The food needn't be fancy—only good, and plentiful, with lots of wine so tongues loosen. Chinese food works well because everyone seems to like it.

•Don't worry about inviting equal numbers of men and women. People are being matched for dinner, not for life.

Networking salons...

•Encourage guests to drop off their business cards as they enter. This serves as a conversation-opener and theme. Since business networking is the purpose, it is socially acceptable to go up to someone and ask, "What do you do?"

•People should be encouraged to exchange business cards. The cards you collect may become one basis for invitation lists.

•Hold salons on a regular basis, from 6 p.m. to 9 p.m. on Wednesday or Thursday. For example, every week it becomes a different, exciting mini-event with new people.

•People, not food, are the focus. You might have a simple but beautiful vegetable spread. The wine might be donated as a promotion.

Issue discussion groups...

•Finding people to invite is not hard. And it gets easier as time goes on.

•Send out a list of topics six months in advance to those who've come to previous groups, and they often recommend others. At this point, many people know about the groups and call to ask about upcoming evenings.

•The key to success is active participation. Encourage guests to do homework, read relevant articles and bring copies with them.

•To begin, each person introduces himself or herself briefly, explaining why he's interested in the topic, and then presents an interesting fact unrelated to the main topic for a 15-second presentation.

•The groups should be held after dinner hour. Each guest might bring something for dessert. Eat after the discussion to give people an opportunity to socialize.

•Get ideas for topics from articles that you file based on what you predict will be newsworthy in six months. Try to plan evenings around upcoming events. Topics tend to grow out of each other.

Source: Machlowitz, Rubin & Yaffe.

How to Taste a Wine

Careful tasting allows you to evaluate and appreciate a wine's quality and value. It also helps you identify the components that make a wine pleasurable to you.

Proper wine tasting is performed in systematic steps that involve three senses...sight, smell, and taste.

Sight:

•Study the wine's color by tilting a glass of it away from yourself and toward a white surface. The color is your first indication of its quality. Be aware that a white wine gets darker and richer in color as it ages, while a red wine becomes lighter. So a lighter-colored red is older and presumably better than a very dark one.

Smell:

•Swirl the wine in your glass by moving the stem while leaving the base of the glass on the table. This lets the wine's esters accumulate in your glass.

•As soon as you stop swirling the wine, bring the glass to your nose (actually put your nose into the glass) and inhale. What does the wine smell like? Fruity? Woody? Your sense of smell affects your taste buds, giving them a hint of what is to come.

Taste:

•Sip the wine, being conscious of three stages in the tasting process:

The attack is the dominant taste in the wine, the one your taste buds respond to first. (If a wine is very sweet, for example, that will be the first taste impression.)

The evolution involves the other taste components that you become aware of after the attack. Notice the more subtle flavors such as bitterness and acidity.

For the finish, evaluate how long the flavor remains in your mouth after you swallow. What is the aftertaste? Is the wine memorable? And do you like it?

Source: Mary Ewing Mulligan, director of education, International Wine Center, New York.

Naming Your Poison: The Hangover Potential Of Various Alcohols

Part of the reason you may feel bad after drinking stems from the congener content of the booze you consume. Congeners are toxic chemicals formed during fermentation. The higher their content in the beverages you drink, the worse you will feel.

Here's how various types of alcohol stack up:

• *Vodka:* Lowest congener content.

• *Gin:* Next lowest.

•*Blended scotch:* Four times the congener content of gin.

•*Brandy, rum and pure malt scotch:* Six times as much as blended scotch.

•*Bourbon:* Eight times as much as blended scotch.

How to Reduce Hangover Discomfort

•Retard the absorption of alcohol by eating before and during drinking, especially foods containing fatty proteins, such as cheeses and milk.

•Use water as a mixer. Carbonation speeds the absorption of alcohol.

•If you get a hangover anyway, remember that the only known cure is rest, aspirin and time. The endless list of other remedies—ranging from cucumber juice and salt to a Bloody Mary—have more to do with drinking mythology than with medical fact.

•Despite the preceding caveat, believe in a cure if you want to. Psychologists have found that believing something helps may actually do so.

Alternatives to Alcohol

Fruit juices for adults come in wine-type bottles, are alcohol- and caffeine-free, and cost relatively little. Essentially sophisticated ciders and grape juices, these grown-up drinks come in sparkling and plain versions that range in taste from crisp to sweet.

Sparkling juices...

- Grand Cru Cider
- Martinelli's Gold Medal Sparkling Cider.
- Challand French Sparkling Apple Juice.
- Ecusson Sparkling White Cider.
- Ecusson Sparkling Red Grape Juice.
- Meiers Sparkling Catawba.
- Meiers Pink Sparkling Catawba.
- Meiers Cold Duck.

Still juices...

- Grapillon French Grape Juice (white or red).
- Meiers Pink Catawba Grape Juice.
- Meiers Catawba Grape Juice.
- Lehr's Black Currant Beverage.
- Lehr's Pure White Grape Juice.
- Lehr's Pure Red Grape Juice.

Surviving Weekend Guests

Weekend guests can be a drag. They leave the lights on, show up late for breakfast and expect to be waited on. This is a checklist for the clever host or hostess who graciously but firmly takes charge and doesn't let guests become a nuisance.

•Be a benevolent dictator. The host or hostess has the right not to be put upon. If someone is cadging an invitation when you'd rather be alone, suggest another time. Set the dinner hour at a time that's most convenient for you.

•If you live without servants, tell guests what you want them to do—pack the picnic lunch, bring in firewood. You'll resent them if they're having fun and you're not.

•Don't let food preparation become a chore. Plan ahead to have options if you decide to spend the afternoon on the boat instead of in the kitchen. Have a dish you can pull out of the freezer, or a fish or chicken that will cook by itself in the oven or crockpot and maybe yield leftovers for other meals.

•Involve guests in preparation and cleanup. If guests volunteer to bring a house gift, ask for food. If guests have special diets that vary radically from your own, give them the responsibility for supplying and preparing their own food.

•Give guests a kitchen tour and coffee-making instructions so they can fend for themselves when they wake up.

•Present your own fixed responsibilities and activities. Don't be embarrassed to do something without your guests.

•Present optional activities for everyone. Mention anything you expect them to participate in. Discuss availability of transportation facilities and other amenities.

•Set up a way to communicate changes in schedules and important information (a corkboard for messages, an answering machine, etc.).

•Encourage independence. Supply maps, guidebooks, extra keys. And provide alarm clocks, local newspapers, extra bicycles.

Putting Off Unwanted Guests

Favorite ploys of city dwellers who don't want to put up all the out-of-town relatives and friends who invite themselves: "We'd love to have you, but..."

- The apartment is being painted.
- We will be out of town ourselves.
- The house is full of flu.
- My mother-in-law is visiting.
- The elevator is out of order.
- The furnace is broken and we have no heat or hot water (winter version).
- The air conditioning is out, and you know how hot and humid it gets here (summer version).

How to Make a Party A Work of Art

- Serve only one kind of hors d'oeuvre on each serving tray. Guests shouldn't have to stop their conversations to make decisions about food.
- Don't overload hors d'oeuvres on your trays. Space them elegantly, and garnish the trays with attractive combinations of flowers, vegetables, greenery, or laces and ribbons.
- Small bouquets of flowers and greenery tied with a satin ribbon make a convenient decoration that can easily be removed and replaced in the kitchen as trays are returned to be refilled.
- A layer of curly green parsley makes a good bed for hors d'oeuvres such as stuffed grape leaves, which have a hard time standing up by themselves. Parsley also makes a good bed for somewhat greasy hors d'oeuvres.
- Don't limit yourself to conventional equipment. Woven baskets, wood trays, colored glassware, lacquered trays, an unusual set of pudding molds—anything beautiful can be put to use for serving hors d'oeuvres.
- Heavy glassware is a good idea at an outdoor party. Unusual glasses (such as colored Depression glass) make drinks interesting, as do offbeat combinations of glassware and drinks (using long-stemmed wine glasses for mixed drinks, for instance).
- Lights should be soft but not dim. Abundant candlelight or tiny electric spots can be very effective.

Surviving the Cocktail Party Game

You can't avoid cocktail parties? How can you survive them? *Five tips:*

- If possible, attend with someone sociable and loquacious who will stand at your side and banter with passers-by as you think about tomorrow's headlines.
- Pick one interesting person, someone who seems to be eyeing the clock as longingly as you, and spend the next half hour getting to know that person as though you two were alone in the world. If you choose well, time will fly.
- Act as you would if the party were in your honor. Introduce yourself to everyone, and ask them about themselves head-on. People will be profoundly grateful for your initiative. They don't call you overbearing—they call you charming.
- Tell the host you have an injured leg. Then commandeer a comfortable chair and let people come to you. (They'll be glad for an excuse to sit down.) If no one does, find an oversized art book to browse through, or indulge in a few fantasies.
- Help the host. You'd be amazed at how overwhelmed a party giver can be and how many small tasks need doing—even with hired help. You can pass the hors d'oeuvres, hang up coats, refresh the ice buckets and generally free the host for socializing. What's in it for you? A chance to move around (some call it "working the room"), the gratitude of your host and a nice feeling of usefulness.

Source: Letty Cottin Pogrebin, writer and editor.

Hot Tub Etiquette

- Take a towel.
- If it's daytime and the tub is outdoors, you might want sunglasses.
- If you're ambivalent about dress (or undress), take your cue from the host or hostess. It's like avoiding the awkwardness of using the

wrong fork at a dinner party. Nudity works best with everyone doing the same thing, too.

•Nonchalance is absolutely de rigueur—a combination of Japanese politeness and California cool is recommended.

•Sustain the mood by maintaining eye contact with members of the opposite sex, especially when they are getting in and out of the tub.

•If you think it's getting too hot, speak up. Better still, get out.

Great Party Themes

•A Raj ball with decor, food, music, and costumes out of India.

•A Venetian masked ball, where the guests dress formally and vie for the best and most elaborate masks.

•A night in Montmartre, with red, white and French blue decorations, wine, can-can dancers, and costumes from the Paris Left Bank.

•A Sunset Boulevard party: Decor and costumes are Hollywood, 1930s and 1940s vintage.

•A Kentucky Derby party around a TV set, with mint juleps and a betting pool.

•A speakeasy party: A password gets you in, the men wear wing collars, the liquor is drunk from cups, and hoods carry violin cases.

•A Wild West party: Dress is cowboys and cowgirls, and the room looks like an old saloon.

•An Old Customs House party: The invitations are in the form of passports, and guests wear costumes from their country of origin.

•A patriotic party: Guests wear red, white and blue, and there must be fireworks.

•A Mexican party with strolling musicians, waterfalls and Mexican food and drink.

•A Moroccan dinner where guests sit on low pillows, eat roast lamb and couscous with their fingers and watch belly dancers.

•A bal blanc with balalaikas for music, an ice-palace decor, Russian food and vodka.

•A New Orleans jazz party with hot music and Creole food.

•A Viennese waltz party: The music reflects the theme and guests dress appropriately.

•A physical-fitness party: Hold it in a health club, and let guests work out, then eat a healthful meal.

•Celebrity look-alike party: Guests dress as famous people from the past or present and try to guess each other's identities.

Source: Sheelagh Dunn, associate, Gustavus Ober Associates, New York 10021, a public relations firm that specializes in business parties.

Parties on Cruise Ships

If you want to impress your friends, invite them to the ship for a bon voyage party. It can be quite elegant but remain inexpensive.

•Make all the arrangements through the shipping company.

•The ship will usually supply setups, soda and hors d'oeuvres at a very modest price.

•Expect to bring your own liquor when the ship is in port, but you can easily buy a few bottles from a local liquor store and take them aboard.

•The steward can serve drinks and other items to your guests in your cabin.

•If your crowd is large enough, ask for a section of one of the public rooms.

•Play expansive host by holding nightly parties while cruising, and it won't be too costly. The ship's staff will help you with parties in your room or in a public room at a fraction of the cost of a party in a hotel ashore. You also usually get the service of waiters and bartenders at no cost (but you provide the tips).

Overcoming Dinner Party Jitters

•Define the goals of this dinner party. The main purpose may be to establish a professional connection or to bring together two people likely to be attracted to each other.

•Eliminate anxieties by verbalizing them. Ask your spouse or a close friend to listen while you describe your worst fears. Once verbalized, the actual possibilities will appear less of a problem than when they were vague apprehensions.

•Specify that the invitation is for dinner. It's not enough to say that you are having a get-together at 7:30.

•Let people know about dress—casual, nice but not formal, formal but not black tie.

•While phoning, mention one or two of the other guests, what they do and, if possible, what they are interested in. If a guest is bringing a friend, don't hesitate to ask something about the friend.

•Do not serve a dish you have never prepared before. Guests will enjoy what you prepare best.

•Have everything ready at least an hour before the party. Take a relaxing warm bath or shower. Allow extra time to dress and make up, and give yourself an additional 20 minutes to sit quietly.

•Arrange to be free from the kitchen when the first two or three guests arrive. They need the host's help to start up conversation.

•*For the single host:* Reduce last-minute anxieties by inviting a close friend to come over early, test the food and look over the arrangements.

Source: *Situational Anxiety* by Herbert J. Freudenberger and Gail North, coauthors, Anchor Press, Doubleday & Co., Garden City, NY.

Party Size

The kind of entertaining you do depends on the length of your guest list and the dimensions of your house.

•For 10 or fewer people, a sit-down dinner is appropriate.

•For 25, a buffet is usually better.

•An open house—usually 1-4 p.m. or 3-6 p.m.—can accommodate more people. If your rooms for entertaining hold 90 to 100 people for a party, you can invite as many as 250 to an open house. *Trick:* Stagger the hours you put on the invitations.

•To entertain several disparate groups—family, business associates and/or social friends—consider giving separate parties on succeeding nights. It takes stamina, but it does save effort and expense. You buy one order of flowers and greens for decorating the house. You assemble serving dishes and extra glasses (borrowed or rented) just once. You arrange furniture one time only. And you can consolidate food, ice, and liquor orders, which, in bulk, can save money. Extra food from the first party can be served at the second.

•Remove some furniture—occasional chairs and large tables—to give you space and keep guests moving. Clear out a den or downstairs bedroom, and set up a food table or bar to attract guests to that room, too. If you have a pair of sofas facing each other in front of a fireplace, open them out so guests can easily walk around them. Use a bedroom or other out-of-the-way place for coats. (You can rent collapsible coat racks, hangers included.)

•Set up different foods at different parts of the party area. If you have open bars, put different drink makings at each set-up. A group drinking a variety of cocktails will not be able to congregate for refills in the same place.

•To avoid bottlenecks: Don't put a bar or buffet table in a narrow hall, for example, or at the back of a tiny room.

•To make the most of a small space, have waiters to take drink orders and a bartender to fill the orders in the kitchen or pantry. Waiters can also pass the hors d'oeuvres in tight quarters, saving the clustering at a food table.

•Count on seven hors d'oeuvres or canapes per person. Stick to finger foods. You'll want a variety of 8 to 10 canapes, but pass each separately, starting with the cold foods and bringing out the hot dishes later.

•For long parties where a turnover of guests is likely, arrange two cycles of passing food, so the later guests get the same fresh selections as the earlier guests.

•Figure that a 40-pound bag of ice will provide enough cubes for 50 people. Get more if you are also chilling wine.

•Use a bathtub to keep the ice in. (No matter what kind of holder you devise for ice, the container will sweat and you'll have a puddle.)

A bathtub full of ice and chilling champagne can be a festive sight by itself. Or, you can decant from the tub to smaller ice chests for each bar. If the nearest bathtub is too far from the party area, buy a plastic garbage can to hold the major supply.

Source: John Clancy, chef, teacher, restaurateur and author of several cookbooks.

Hiring Help for a Party

•The ideal ratio is one tray carrier for every 10 guests.

•Two or three extra kitchen workers are sufficient.

•One extra person can tend bar for up to 30 to 40 guests.

•In the kitchen, set out a prototype of each hors d'oeuvre, and expect your helpers to make exact replicas.

•Servers should be neat and pleasant and should avoid conversing with guests.

•Serving people are responsible for maintenance—keeping the party attractive. Provide lots of ashtrays (if you permit smoking), and make sure servers are told to empty them frequently.

•Avoid hors d'oeuvres that lead to messy leftovers (for example, shrimp tails or skewered foods) if you don't have enough people to clean up after your guests.

•If you expect a caterer, empty the refrigerator and clear all kitchen surfaces. In an office, make sure all desks are cleared. Food should be prepared well in advance and, when possible, frozen.

•Stock wine and liquor a day or two ahead of time.

•Flowers and decorations should be in place two hours before the party.

Source: Martha Stewart, the coauthor of *Entertaining* and author of *Quick Cook* and *Martha Stewart's Hors d'Oeuvres*, all published by Clarkson-Potter, a division of Crown Books, New York.

How to Enjoy Holiday Entertaining

Although everyone is supposed to look forward to the holidays, they can be a season of great strain, especially for those who are entertaining. *To minimize the strain:*

•Include nonfamily in your invitations. *Reason:* Everyone is then on "party manners." Snide comments, teasing or rivalries are held back. This is not the time for letting it all hang out.

•Accept help. Encourage your family and friends not only to make their favorite or best dish but to be totally responsible for it—heating or freezing or unmolding and serving. Meals then become a participatory event, rather than one or two people doing all the work and the rest feeling guilty or, worse still, awkwardly attempting to help. (The one who hates to cook can supply the wine or champagne.)

•Let the table itself set a mood of fun, not formality. Use place cards wisely and make them amusing with motifs appropriate for each guest, rather than names. Or, let one of the younger children make them with a sketch of each guest or hand lettering. Set them out with forethought. Make sure a particularly squirmy youngster is nowhere near an aunt known for her fussy table manners. If there are to be helpers, seat them so they can get up and down with ease. Put the famous spiller where the disaster can be readily cleaned up. If the light is uneven, seat the older people in the brightest section.

•Put everyone around a table. It creates a warmer, more shared meal than does a buffet, and it's amazing how tables can expand. *Hint:* Use desk or rental chairs, which are much slimmer than dining chairs. (Avoid benches for older folks.)

•Borrowing and lending furniture, such as tables, can help you to find room for everyone. It doesn't matter if the setup is not symmetrical or everything doesn't match. A ping-pong table covered with pretty new sheets can provide plenty of room, or you can have tables jutting into hallways or living rooms.

•Have some after-dinner games ready. Ping-pong, backgammon, chess and cards are among the favorites. You may want to buy the latest "in" game or a new word game.

•Bringing out old family albums can be fun.

•Gift exchanging is really a potential hazard. Children, especially, can grump all day if something they expected hasn't been forthcoming. Grandparents often ask what is wanted, but they may be unable to do the actual buying. Do it for them. A check is not a fun package to open. If you want to be sure no one overspends, set a limit. Or set a theme. Or rule out gifts altogether, except for the children.

Source: Florence Janovic, writer and marketing consultant.

Planning a Big Family Reunion

Because a reunion brings together people of all ages, it presents special challenges. *To make your party more enjoyable for everyone:*

•Infants and toddlers. Parents will appreciate a place to change diapers and a quiet room for naps and nursing. Let them know if you can provide high chairs, cribs, safety gates or playpens. *Toys:* A box of safe kitchen equipment. *Food suggestions:* Mild cheese, bananas, crackers, fresh bread or rolls.

•Preschool children. Set aside a playroom. *Best toys:* Balloons, bubbles and crayons. Pay an older cousin or neighborhood teen to baby-sit.

•School-age children. A den or basement room and board games, felt pens and coloring books will keep them happy. Put them in charge of setting and decorating a children's dining table.

•Teenagers. Most teenagers find family reunions boring. For those who have to come, provide a room with a stereo, video games, and radio. Teenagers may be shy around relatives they don't know. When they come out of hiding, give them tasks that encourage their involvement with others, such as helping out grandparents.

•Older folks. They need comfortable chairs where they can hear and see what's going on without being in the way. Some may also need easy access to a bathroom and a place to rest or go to bed early. *Food considerations:* Ask if anyone needs a low-salt, low-cholesterol or special diabetic diet. Spicy foods are probably out.

•Make travel arrangements for those who can't drive so they don't worry about inconveniencing others.

•Now that you've seen to individual needs, how do you bring everyone together? *Common denominator:* Family ties. Make an updated family tree and display it in a prominent place. If you have an instant camera, take pictures as people arrive and mount them on the appropriate branch of the tree. *Special:* Ask everyone to bring contributions to a family museum. *Suitable objects:* Old photographs, family letters, heirlooms, written family histories, old family recipes. After dinner, gather around the fire and exchange family anecdotes. You may wish to record them.

Source: *Unplug the Christmas Machine: How to Give Your Family the Simple Joys of Christmas* by Jo Robinson and Jean Staeheli, co-authors, Morrow, New York.

Self-Indulgent Ideas For New Year's Eve

•Get away to a country inn and enjoy a peaceful respite away from home with your spouse.

•Have a white-tie party in your home, complete with champagne, caviar, an elegant menu, your stored wedding-present silver serving dishes and crystal and your fanciest table linens.

•Rent a batch of old movies for good friends to share throughout the night. Serve beer, popcorn and pretzels.

•Plan a dinner for people you haven't seen in at least five years and catch up on old times.

•Charter a yacht for a lavish but intimate supper-dance.

•Hire an artist to document your New Year's party with sketches.

•Run an ethnic party—French, Italian, etc.—with appropriate food, wine, music, and dress.

•Go to a ski resort for the weekend to enjoy the bracing air, good athletic activities and grog.

•Run a masked ball, complete with fancy dress costumes and prizes for the best. Have plenty of room for dancing and include at least one waltz.

•Have a wine-tasting party for a group of appreciative friends. Or, design a meal around special vintages from your own cellar that you want to share with some fellow wine lovers.

•Have a country party with a caller and musicians for square-dancing.

•Take a group to Atlantic City or Las Vegas and gamble the evening away.

•Organize a literary evening. Let each person recite or read from his or her favorite works. Or pick a favorite play and do a reading, with each guest taking a role.

•Invite close business associates for dinner to discuss the coming trends for the next 12 months—in business and in national and international politics.

Holiday Shopping

Those wonderful but tiring gift-buying chores can be relatively painless with organization.

•Know what you're looking for. Browse through mail-order catalogs and department store catalogs before you go out.

•Shop during the early morning or at dinnertime, when stores are least crowded.

•Shop by yourself. One person travels more efficiently than two.

•Wear comfortable shoes.

•If it will be a long tour with lengthy stops at several stores, leave your heavy winter coat in the car.

•Write the names of recipients on the sales slips and save them. They may come in handy for exchanges.

•Keep a list of what you give to whom, so you won't buy duplicate presents next year.

Guidelines for Christmas Tipping

•Newspaper deliverer: $5 to $10.

•Garbagemen: $5 to $10 each if it is legal in your community; a bottle of liquor or fancy foodstuffs are an alternative.

•Mailmen: While it is technically illegal to tip the postman, many people give $5 to $10 to their regular carrier.

•Deliverymen: $10 per person for those who come regularly to your house, like the dry cleaner, the milkman or even your United Parcel Service man, if you get a lot of packages.

•Baby-sitter: A record or a book for a regular teenage sitter; a bottle of perfume or $10 to $15 for an adult.

*For apartment dwellers:**

•Superintendent: $25 to $50.

•Doorman: $15 to $25.

•Elevator operator: $15 to $25.

•Concierge: $20 to $25.

•Handyman: $20.

•Porter: $15.

•Garage attendant: $15 to $20.

Outside the home:

•Restaurants where you are a regular customer: Maitre d', $20 to $40. Bartender, $10 to $15. Captain, waiter, busboy: Divide the average cost of a meal among the three of them.

•Beauty salon or barber shop: Give the owner-operator a bottle of wine or a basket of fruit. For employees who regularly attend you, $15 to $25.

•Butcher: $10 to $15 for regular good service.

•Tailor or seamstress: $10 or wine or perfume.

*If your building establishes a pool for tips that is divided among employees, you need only give an additional amount to those service people who have gone way beyond the call of duty for you this year.

How to Get Attention For Your Favorite Charity Event

- Hire skywriters to spread the message.
- Take a full-page advertisement in the local newspaper or advertise over a local cable TV station.
- Commission an artist to design a lithograph for the event.
- Have the mayor declare a special day and read a message from City Hall.
- Get a letter of congratulations from the President of the United States...or from the Governor of your state...or Senator...or Congressman.
- Run a special supplement of the event in your local Sunday newspaper.
- Videotape the event as news and offer it to your local TV station.
- Have special funny money printed with your face and message on it to give out as a token of the special event.
- Hire a marching band and have a parade.
- Arrange for displays of the event in the windows of local stores.
- Have cases of wine imprinted with a private label to mark the event.
- Have a special sandwich or dish named in honor of the event on the menu at a major restaurant.
- Have an automobile or train named in honor of the event.
- Hire the huge local stadium or concert hall.
- Have a street renamed for the day.
- Float specially designed and painted balloons all over town with the message you want to relay.
- Underwrite a special event—tennis, golf, marathon, polo, etc.
- Have the post office issue a stamp in your name. If this is not possible, print stamps designed by a major artist and have them affixed to all correspondence.
- Have a race horse named in honor of the event.

How to Really Appreciate Movies

If you really want to appreciate movies, stray a little from the heavily beaten track. There are a number of good critics in small or specialized magazines who can alert you to fine—and unusual—new films, as well as notable revivals.

Movie buffs typically go through three stages in their appreciation of films:

- First, they find movies awe-inspiring magic.
- Second, they begin to realize those are actors up there and that all kinds of technology are involved. In this stage, which some people never leave, they become "fans." Many fans don't care about movies—they're just interested in following their favorite actors.
- Third, they realize movies aren't magic, that it may be a miracle they ever get made, but that they're a human achievement that also happens to be marvelous. At this stage they can start to look at movies critically.

To get the maximum enjoyment from movies:

- Watch a lot of them. Make a special effort to see foreign films. You'll begin to see what's original and fresh and what's stereotyped.
- Learn about movie forms and genres and the unique visual language of cinema.
- Read, follow other art forms. Read about psychology, politics, history and other branches of knowledge.
- Avoid the rush. Don't dash off to see the latest blockbuster. It'll be around a while. See a film more likely to close soon, even though it was well-reviewed.
- Watch movies on cable TV and on cassettes. Both these forms have done a lot to make film scholarship possible and good movies accessible.
- Go to foreign films. More than a few are worth seeing, but most people aren't interested in them anymore. In the past, the "ooh-la-la" factor drew viewers. But now that American films are no longer censored, foreign films have lost their cachet.

Source: Andrew Sarris, film critic for New York's *Village Voice*, a professor of cinema at Columbia University, and author of *The American Cinema: Directors and Directions*, Octagon Press, New York, and *Politics and Cinema*, Columbia University Press, Irvington, NY.

Traps in Casino Gambling

Casino gambling can be high-risk entertainment, if you're not careful. *Avoid these common casino mistakes:*

•Making "flat bets"—wagering the same amount each time. Since the odds are against you, your progress will soon resemble a sales chart in a recession...peaks and valleys, but down in the long run.

•Trying to get even by chasing losses with meal money...or the next month's rent. It's a big mistake to dig into your pocket after your stake is gone. You can't outspend the casinos.

•Flitting from craps to baccarat to the slots. It's better to stick with one game until you're comfortable.

•Taking too many long-shot bets (such as "proposition" bets in craps). They generally offer the worst odds.

•Staying at a "cold" table too long. If a new dealer is giving you terrible cards, or there's a loudmouth across the table, or you don't like the smell of your neighbor's cigar, move on. The problem may be purely psychological, but it can throw off your game nonetheless.

•Accepting complimentary alcohol. When you drink too much you start making irrational "hunch" bets, and you get frivolous with your money.

•Playing when tired. The casino may stay open till 4 a.m., but you don't have to close the casino. Stick to your normal weekend hours.

•Getting caught up in the casino mentality. When everyone refers to $5 as a "nickel" and $25 as a "quarter," it's easy to treat money like plastic. Never forget that it's real money. Stick to your basic units and progressions.

•Viewing the dealer as a shark who's out to get you. At worst, the dealer is a mechanical device. At best, he can be your ally. *Example:* In a hot craps game, he may remind you when to take a bet down. To keep him on your side, don't forget to tip. (Dealers make two thirds of their income from tips.) *Tactic:* It's more effective to bet $1 for the dealer (giving him a stake in your game) than to give him $10 when you leave.

•Celebrating prematurely. Be happy when you win, but don't brag about it. You don't want to advertise that you're carrying a lot of money. And...don't play with a huge pile of chips in front of you. If you hit it big, convert to larger denominations, and put them in your pocket. (For safety, use the casino's valet parking. With a validated ticket it will cost you only a tip, and it's far better than walking three blocks to your car.)

•Forgetting what you came for. Take in a floor show and enjoy a good meal. If you lose at the tables, write it off as entertainment. If you're not a professional, that's the whole point of visiting a casino...to have a good time.

Source: Lee Pantano, a professional gambler, teacher, consultant, and editor of *Gamblegram*, Atlantic Highlands, NJ.

Winning at Poker

Not so many years ago, every poker book told you the same thing: Play tight (fold bad hands). This is still good advice, as far as it goes. *But there are other tactics to keep in mind:*

•Be selective but aggressive. Ideally, you should end a hand by either folding or raising. Avoid calling bets with vulnerable hands, such as two pair.

•To own the table psychologically, so that other players are glancing at you every time they make a bet, be friendly, but at the same time confusing and unpredictable.

•Never gloat. You want your opponents to enjoy trying to beat you.

•In a low-to-moderate-limit game, you can win without mathematical genius or brilliant originality. Most of your profit will come from your opponents' mistakes. *Their chief error:* Calling for too many pots with mediocre hands.

•Bluffing is a poor strategy in a low-stakes game. Unsophisticated opponents won't even understand your intended deception. Second, they're likely to call you anyway, a habit you want to encourage. Try a strategic bluff just once, early in the session, as an "advertisement."

•Discipline is especially crucial in a low-limit game, when you need more hands to make up losses.

•Decide in advance how you will react in each of various situations. Never play a hand out of impatience or on a "hunch." Play it for a good reason.

•Monitor yourself carefully. If you make a mistake, admit it to yourself and get back on track. Don't let one bad play erode your entire system.

•Don't look for immediate revenge after an opponent burns you on a big pot. If you force the action, you're apt to get burned again.

•Stay later when you're ahead and leave early when behind. When you're losing, you lose psychological control of the game, too. Opponents try to bluff you out of pots and are less likely to call your good hands.

•Watch for and learn to read opponents' "tells"—the mannerisms they fall into that tend to give away whether their hands are good or bad. *In general, follow the rule of opposites:* Players usually act weak when their hands are strong, and they commonly act strong when their hands are weak.

•Look for reasons to fold just as eagerly as you look for reasons to call.

Source: Mike Caro, a gambling teacher and columnist for *Gambling Times* and, according to world poker champion Doyle Brunson, the best draw poker player alive. He is also the author of *Caro on Gambling*, published by Gambling Times, Hollywood, CA.

Successful Poker: Reading Your Opponents

Bluffers generally:

•Breathe shallowly or hold their breath.

•Stare at their hands—or at you as you prepare to bet.

•Reach for chips out of turn.

•Bet with an authoritative pronouncement.

•Fling chips into the pot with an outstretched forearm.

•Show unusual friendliness toward opponents.

Players with powerful hands:

•Share a hand with a bystander (especially a spouse).

•Shake noticeably while making a bet. (This reflects a release of tension. Most players show obvious outward nervousness only when they feel they're in little danger.)

•Talk easily and naturally.

•Behave in an unusually gruff manner toward opponents.

•Lean forward in their seat.

•Bet with a sigh, shrug, or negative tone of voice.

•Ask, "How much is it to me?" or request another clarification.

•Glance quickly at the player's chips after receiving a (good) card.

Source: Mike Caro, author of *Mike Caro's Book of Tells—The Body Language of Poker*, published by Gambling Times, Hollywood, CA.

Darts: Tips from a Champ

•Start off with a set of three brass darts with a one-piece plastic shaft and flight. Brass darts are big and easy to handle. They're also the most durable. As you throw more, the dart will feel lighter.

•As your game improves, you'll want to buy tungsten darts. The darts are heavier, narrower, and a little harder to control.

•Buy a pressed bristle board. When you remove a dart from this material, it doesn't leave an indentation. Cork or wood boards are cheaper, but they'll disintegrate with heavy play.

•To play well, you need eye-hand coordination, good concentration and good balance. Keep your head still so that your eyes stay on the target.

•When throwing darts, use your forearm, not your entire body. (It's like hammering a nail.)

•Stay loose and fluid on the follow-through movement after the dart leaves your hand. If you jerk your arm back, the dart won't reach the board.

•Most newcomers to the game overthrow to the left of the target. You can start by aiming a little to the right, but that's not a long-term cure. You must see the pattern of your throw and move accordingly on the toe line.

• *Strategy:* The two most important targets are the triple 20 and the outer double ring.

• *Basic courtesy:* Shake hands before and after play.

• Take your darts out of the board promptly.

• Be quiet when someone else is shooting.

Source: Nick Marzigliano, singles champion of the Brooklyn (NY) Dart League.

Contest Winners: Secrets of Success

Cash, vacations, houses, cars, electronic equipment, cameras and much, much more are the dream prizes that keep millions of Americans doggedly filling out entry blanks for contests. More than $100 million worth of prize money and goods are dispensed annually through an estimated 500 promotional competitions and drawings.

Dedicated hobbyists know that there is an advantage of a planned approach to overcome the heavy odds against each entrant.

Here are some winning strategies:

• Use your talents. If you can write, cook or take photographs, put your energy into entering contests rather than sweepstakes. Contests take skill, so fewer people are likely to compete...improving your chances. Photography contests have the fewest average entries.

• Follow the rules precisely. If the instructions say to print your name, don't write it in longhand. If a three-inch by five-inch piece of paper is called for, measure your entry exactly. The slightest variation can disqualify you.

• Enter often. Always be on the lookout for new sweepstakes and contests to enter. *Sources:* Magazines, newspapers, radio, television, store shelves and bulletin boards, product packaging.

• Make multiple entries. The more entries you send in, the more you tip the odds in your favor.

• *For large sweepstakes:* Spread out your entries over the length of the contest—one a week for five weeks, for example. When the volume of entries is big enough, they will be delivered to the judges in a number of different sacks. The theory is that judges will pick from each sack, and your chances go up if you have an entry in each of several different mailbags.

• Keep informed. Join a local contest club or subscribe to a contest newsletter. Either source will help you to learn contest traps and problems—and solutions. They'll alert you, too, to new competitions.

• Be selective. You must pay taxes on items that you win, so be sure the prizes are appropriate for you. If you don't live near the water, winning an expensive boat could be a headache. (Some contests offer cash equivalents, but not all do.)

• If you do win, check with your CPA or tax lawyer immediately. You must report the fair market value of items that you win, whether you keep them, sell them or give them away. This can be tricky. Also, if you win, you can deduct the expenses of postage, stationery, etc. that you have used to enter this and other sweepstakes and contests in the same year. These costs are not deductible if you don't win.

• Most contests and sweepstakes ask you to enclose some proof of purchase or a plain piece of paper with a product name or number written on it. Many people assume that a real proof of purchase will improve their chances of winning. *Fact:* In a recent survey, more than half the winners of major prizes reported that they had not bought the sponsor's product.

Source: Roger Tyndall, coeditor with his wife, Carolyn, of the newsletter *Contest Newsletter*, Fern Beach, FL.

Reluctant Vacationers

Not everyone loves to get away from it all on a vacation. Some people really prefer to work. But families need vacations, and so do workaholics occasionally.

How to take yourself away from the office successfully:

• Make vacations somewhat similar to your year-round life, so that they offer continuity as well as contrast. If you enjoy a daily swim at the gym, be sure to pick a vacation stop with a pool. If you never step into art museums at home, don't feel you have to drag yourself to them when you're away.

•Leave your calculator, beeper, dictating device and briefcase at home.

•Avoid finishing lots of work at the last minute. It can leave you feeling frantic.

•Don't drive your staff crazy by leaving lots of lists and memos or calling continually. Limit yourself to two calls the first day and one a day thereafter.

•Take enough time off to recharge your energy. Two weeks may feel too long, but three days is too short.

Source: Dr. Marilyn Machlowitz, a New York organizational psychologist and consultant.

Don't Let Your Vacation Home Cut into Your Leisure Time

The most desirable thing to look for in a weekend house is ease of maintenance.

•Get rid of rugs in the summer.

•Ask the landlord to remove his accumulations of dustcatching peacock feathers and other decorator touches.

Keep your own importations to a minimum.

•Cut down on weekend cleaning chores and outdoor work with hired help.

•Consider expanding leisure time by commuting with the laundry. That's cumbersome, but better than hours in a laundromat on a sunny afternoon.

•Cultivate the fine art of list-making. Shopping and menu planning can be almost painless if the list is done right.

•If you're planning a Saturday dinner party, don't rely on the local supermarket for the perfect roast unless you've ordered (and confirmed) in advance. The accompanying wines might be better purchased at home, too, unless you're sure of your local supplier.

•Don't forget to take the same precautions as you would for a trip—extra reading glasses and copies of prescriptions might save you an unwanted journey home.

Fishing a New Lake

If you know where to start looking, you can fish any lake successfully.

Where bass congregate:

•Near trees that have recently fallen into the water.

•*In hot weather:* Under lily pads, especially in the only shallow spots around.

•*In consistently mild weather:* In backwater ponds and coves off the main lake. *Best:* Good weed or brush cover, with a creek running in.

•*Any time at all:* In sunken moss beds near the shore.

Source: *Outdoor Life.*

Portrait Photography Secrets

People are the most popular subject for photography. There are ways to turn snapshots of family and friends into memorable portraits. *Techniques:*

•Get close. Too much landscape overwhelms the subject.

•Keep the head high in the frame as you compose the shot. Particularly from a distance, centering the head leaves too much blank background and cuts off the body arbitrarily.

•Avoid straight rows of heads in group shots. It's better to have some subjects stand and others sit in a two-level setting.

•Pose subjects in natural situations, doing what they like to do—petting the cat, playing the piano, etc.

•Simplify backgrounds. Try using a large aperture (small f-stop number) to throw the background out of focus and highlight the subject.

•Beware of harsh shadows. The human eye accommodates greater contrast of light to dark than does a photographic system. Either shadows or highlights will be lost in the picture, usually the shadowed area.

For outdoor portraits:

•Avoid the midday sun. This light produces harsh shadows and makes people squint. Hazy sun, often found in the morning, is good. Cloudy days give a lovely, soft effect.

•Use fill light to cut shadows. A flash can be used outdoors, but it is hard to compute correctly. *Best fill-light method:* Ask someone to hold a large white card or white cloth near the subject to bounce the natural light into the shadowed area.

•Use backlight. When the sun is behind the subject (but out of the picture), the face receives a soft light. With a simple camera, the cloudy setting is correct. If your camera has a light meter, take a reading close to the subject or, from a distance, increase the exposure one or two stops from what the meter indicates.

•Beware of dappled shade. The effect created in the photograph will be disturbing.

For indoor portraits:

•Use window light. A bright window out of direct sun is a good choice. However, if there is high contrast between the window light and the rest of the room, use filter-light techniques to diminish the shadow.

•Use flashbulbs. A unit with a tilting head lets you light the subject by bouncing the flash off the ceiling, creating a wonderful diffuse top lighting. (This won't work with high, dark or colored ceilings.)

•Mix direct light and bounce flash. An easy way to put twinkle in the eyes and lighten shadows when using bounce light is to add a little direct light. With the flash head pointed up, a small white card attached to the back of the flash will send light straight on to the subject.

•Keep a group an even distance from the flash. Otherwise, the people in the back row will be dim, while those in front may even be over exposed.

Making New Year's Eve A Family or Neighborhood Affair

•Invite close relatives to spend the evening reminiscing and becoming a family again. Organize a slide show of old family photographs or show home movies to break the ice.

•If you are a runner, do an evening five miles with running friends and then see the new year in with a pasta feast. (New Yorkers can run in or watch a mini-marathon in Central Park, with fireworks at the finish line at midnight. Check for similar events in other cities.)

•Rent the local high-school auditorium and sponsor a band concert for the community. Or organize your own band with fellow musicians.

•Have a bake-in in your kitchen, with prizes for the best chocolate desserts.

•Have a multigenerational party for your whole family and friends of all ages.

•Spend New Year's Eve taking down holiday decorations, finishing your thank-you notes for holiday gifts, and otherwise cleaning the slate for the coming year.

•With your mate, make a list of do's and don'ts and resolutions for the new year.

•Organize a neighborhood "progressive dinner" with a different course in each house. Watch the time so you get to the last stop and the champagne by midnight.

•Rent a skating rink—ice or roller—for a big, many-family party with an instructor or two to get the fainthearted going smoothly.

How to Solve Caterer Problems Before They Arise

•The ideal way to select a caterer is to attend one of his or her parties.

•If that's not possible, ask for recommendations from your most trusted and sophisticated friends and acquaintances.

•Another source of information is gourmet magazines. Local publications often write articles about caterers, too.

•Many caterers provide pamphlets or sample menus, but these are a poor substitute for a solid personal recommendation.

•Try, if at all possible, to sample the food each caterer offers. Keep in mind, however, the kind of party you are planning. Someone who prepares exquisite nouvelle cuisine may not be the best person to cater a large outdoor barbecue.

•When you have the names of a few reputable caterers, meet with each, preferably where the party will take place. Many hosts are distressed by caterers' tendency to "take over" —to dictate all arrangements and ignore the host's concerns. Know your own feelings about this and try to gauge the caterer's willingness to accommodate you.

•Never hire anyone who has a specific number of parties in her repertory and simply "does" party number six at your home. Even if the caterer is to take total control, you want her to approach your party as a unique situation.

•Ask at the beginning of the discussion whether the caterer herself will be present at the actual function. If she plans to send an assistant, meet that person and make sure you have confidence in her abilities.

•Be sure also to discuss clean-up arrangements with the caterer.

•Although most caterers actually only prepare the food and hire the service themselves, they can certainly make arrangements (and take responsibility for them) with liquor stores, florists, musicians, etc. They can also recommend people whom you can contact directly (possibly helping you to cut corners economically). Or, you can come up with your own choices.

•Never hire independent help to serve your caterer's food. After the quality of the food itself, service is probably the most important ingredient in a successful party. Your caterer should work with people she knows and trusts.

•The caterer should draw up a contract that spells out every cost and makes the caterer's list of duties clear.

•You will probably be asked to make a down payment for up to half the total cost.

•The caterer's price is all-inclusive; you are free to tip the staff if you should wish to, but you need not feel obliged to do so.

•The caterer will expect to find the scene of the party clean and ready for her to get started. Your equipment (serving trays, etc.) should be at its sparkling best.

•Now you should stand back and let her do her job. Don't make any last minute additions to the menu or suddenly rearrange the floor plan.

Source: Germaine and Marcel Chandelier, owners and managers of Germaine's, Long Island City, NY.

How to Make Slot Machines Pay Off

•*Key to successful play:* A basic understanding of slot mechanics. In Las Vegas, dollar slot machines return on average 88¢–98¢ per dollar invested. (At the high end, they compare favorably with the odds offered by craps, roulette or any other game.)

These are long-term returns over six hours or six months...depending on the machine. The short-term return for a given player will vary tremendously—but not randomly. Every machine has a pay cycle and a down cycle. During its pay cycle, the machine will give back far more than you put in. It might stay "hot" for a hundred pulls or more, spilling out jackpot after jackpot. (At one machine, I hit a triple-bar jackpot—a $150 to $1 payoff—three times in a row.) But during a machine's cold cycle, you can easily drop $100 in less than an hour.

Finding pay-cycle machines...

•Observe before you play. If you see a player empty $100 or more into a machine (whether or not he hits a few small jackpots along the way) and walk away with nothing, step up and try your luck. There's a good chance the machine is near the end of a down cycle and entering a pay cycle.

•If you play a machine "blind," without prior observation, feel the coins in the tray after your first win. If the money is warm, it's probably been sitting in the machine for a time without a jackpot. *Point:* A down cycle may be ending. If the money is cool, move on.

•Ask a change clerk to steer you to a hot machine...with the unwritten understanding that you'll tip him/her 10% of your winnings on that machine. (Casinos tolerate this because it doesn't affect their overall take.)

•Play machines near casino entrances and exits. The house programs these slots to pay off the best, because their jackpots will attract the most attention. *Also hot:* Any machines near blackjack or other gaming tables. The casino hopes to lure to these machines wives who are watching their husbands play the other games. *Colder:* Machines isolated against the rear wall (and especially in the corners), where jackpots have less advertising value.

•Watch for empty coin racks—coin holders next to each machine used by players to stack coins for play or to hold winnings—and play the machine immediately to the left of one. An empty rack means the previous player busted. (When a player hits a jackpot, the rack is used to cart away the coins.) The more empty racks near a machine, the closer it is to a pay cycle.

•After I gave an extravagant tip, a casino mechanic once told me to look for three-reel machines with a cherry sitting in the middle reel. While worthless in itself, he said, the cherry was a sign that better times were coming. Since then, I've found that 75% of middle cherry machines return at least a small jackpot within five to six pulls. They're also good bets for a pay cycle.

•Your odds are best on single-line, dollar slots. Multiple-line machines offer a greater chance of hitting any jackpot, but the payoffs are much smaller. *Also:* For top value, play the maximum number of coins for each pull.

•"Progressive" slots, where the jackpot can build to $1 million or more, can be wildly profitable, but only if they're within their programmed payoff range.

Example: At the Sands in Las Vegas, a clerk told me (after a big tip) that one progressive machine always paid off when the jackpot reached between $48,000 and $64,000. I found it one night at $59,000 and pumped in $300 before I had to leave town. The next morning, the clerk called to tell me that the machine had been hit at 10 a.m., when its jackpot reached $62,000.

•If you ever see a new machine being uncrated, jump on it. Play it until it bursts. Casinos program new slots to pay particularly well for the first two days so they'll draw more business later.

Source: Dick Phillips, author of *Winning Systems on Slots,* Box 12336, Beaumont, TX 77706.

Secrets of Doing Crossword Puzzles Much Faster

In order to successfully complete a crossword puzzle, follow these helpful hints...

•Start with the fill-in-the-blank clues. These are usually the easiest and the least ambiguous.

•Next, try to fill in an across answer in the top row or a down answer on the left side. You can then proceed to answers that start with a known letter...and they're always easier to solve than answers where the known letter is in the middle.

•In a thematic puzzle, the longest blanks on the grid always relate to the theme.

•When the clue is expressed in the plural, the answer is probably plural. Most clues that are expressed in the past have answers ending in -ed. Most clues that are expressed in the superlative have answers ending in -est.

•Remember that e and s are the most popular word-ending letters. Also, puzzles use a disproportionate number of common letters and very few rare letters, such as q, z, x, j, etc.

•When you are missing one or two letters in a word, scan the alphabet. Plug in all possible letters or combinations...one is bound to work.

Source: David Feldman, author of *How to Win at Just About Everything,* Morrow Quill, William Morrow & Co., 105 Madison Ave., New York 10016.

The Pleasures of Organic Gardening

There really is no need to use chemicals and gasoline-powered machines when gardening or tending to your lawn. Organic methods are just as successful and use only fertilizers and pest controls found in nature. *Advantages:*

•Creates a healthier environment by rebuilding the top soil, protecting ground water and using less energy.

•Produces homegrown, organic (chemical-free) vegetables—fresher and cheaper than the ones you can buy in natural-foods stores or supermarkets.

Organic fertilizers...

While synthetic fertilizers feed the crop, they deplete the soil, then make future crops dependent on continued applications. Organic fertilizers feed the plants and nourish the soil.

All plants need...

•Nitrogen for lush foliage.

Best organic sources: Homemade or bagged compost—decomposed plants or animal wastes rich in nitrogen and other trace minerals. Add up to two inches to each garden bed yearly. *For fast results:* Use blood meal and dried blood (by-products of slaughterhouses), or cottonseed meal (ground from seeds of the cotton plant).

•Phosphorus for flower and seed production.

Best organic source: Colloidal phosphate, a rock powder, also rich in lime and trace minerals. *For fast results:* Try bone meal—it's effective, but more expensive.

•Potash (Potassium) for strong roots and solid branches.

Best organic sources: Granite dust (a rock powder) and greensand (a mineral-rich deep sea deposit). *For fast results:* Try wood ashes left from a wood stove or fireplace.

Important: Soil conditions in your garden—and the specific needs of plants you want to grow—should determine your choice of fertilizer. Your local garden center or the US Department of Agriculture's cooperative extension service can test your soil and recommend the best organic fertilizer for your needs.

Organic pest and weed control...

•*Insecticidal soaps:* Spray every three to five days for about three weeks to eliminate most pests on specific plants or plant groupings.

•*Fabric coverings:* Sheets of very thin-woven polyester or thin-spun polypropylene, sold as "floating" row covers or super-light insect barriers. Use only for vegetable gardens—not for ornamental plants...make sure plants have enough water—high temperatures under the fabric can make them dry...and remove covers over squashes, melons and cucumbers when the flowers start to bloom—in time for pollination.

•*Beneficial insects:* Bugs that kill harmful insects that eat your vegetables or plants. They can be purchased at local garden centers or by mail order.*

•*Mulching:* Cover the earth around each plant or row to deter weeds and conserve water with shredded bark mulch, wood chips, cocoa or buckwheat hulls. (Also use straw and shredded leaves for vegetable plants—but not for ornamentals.) Old mulch decomposes and can be worked into the soil. New mulch is spread after planting.

*Mail-order companies that sell these insects include: Gardens Alive!, 5100 Schenley Pl., Lawrenceburg, IN 47025, 812-537-8650...Gardener's Supply Co., 128 Intervale Rd., Burlington, VT 05401, 802-863-1700.

Source: Bonnie Wodin, Golden Yarrow Landscaping, Heath, Massachusetts 01346, designs custom gardens and landscapes. She also lectures frequently on horticulture and landscaping.

For Very Special Occasions

Here are some very classy, exclusive hotels frequented by those who know the right places to stay when they travel. Make reservations a few months in advance.

•*Malliouhana Hotel in Anguilla, the Caribbean.* On a small little-known island with few tourists. This new hotel is the ultimate in luxury. Suites and private villas are available, some the size of private homes. Tennis courts, boating and all water sports, including scuba instruction, attracts a jet-set crowd of all ages.

•*Baden-Baden in Schwarzwald, Germany.* In the elegant style of a 19th-century spa. Extensive grounds, impeccable service, an excellent restaurant and hot springs where you can "take the waters." Attracts an old world, conservative crowd.

•*Hotel Los Monteros in Marbella, Spain.* On one of the Mediterranean coast's most fashionable stretches. Wide range of sports, spacious rooms and tropical gardens. Has a 1920s charm reminiscent of the Gatsby era. Ask for a room with an ocean view. Attracts all types, from young families to older couples.

• *Hotel San Pietro in Positano, Italy.* Picturesquely perched on top of a cliff, with all 55 double rooms overlooking rocky coast and sea. Scenic beaches. Secluded and elegant, it attracts a young to middle-aged highly sophisticated crowd. Open March 14 through November 3.

• *Mount Kenya Safari Club in Nairobi, Kenya.* A distinguished private retreat located halfway up Mt. Kenya. 100 acres of rolling lawns, waterfalls, gardens, a heated pool, sauna, three dining rooms, and safari excursions for both photography and hunting. Special events such as African barbecues and tribal dances. Dress is formal, with jacket and tie required for dinner. Guests tend to be families, couples and ultra-exclusive tours and groups.

• *Lake Palace in Udaipur, India.* Originally an 18th-century royal residence. Located on an island in the Middle of Lake Pichola, it has air-conditioned rooms, exotic suites, water sports, a marble-inlaid pool, and a restaurant serving Continental and Indian cuisine. Guests are all ages but tend to be very sophisticated.

• *Hotel de Paris in Monaco.* A superior hotel. Has an underground passage to the Casino and Le Club. Palatial rooms and facilities. Spa, sauna, two restaurants and a cabaret. Old money stays here. Frank Sinatra is a regular, and the Prince of Monaco often comes for tea.

• *Voile d'Or Hotel in St-Jean-Cap-Ferrat, France.* Overlooks the harbor. Its spacious, French provincial-style rooms all have balconies and marble baths. A favorite honeymoon spot, the atmosphere breathes intimate elegance. Gourmet cuisine. Open February to October.

• *Splendido Hotel in Portofino, Italy.* A super-deluxe classic hotel on high ground overlooking the sea. Charming rooms, suites, gardens, a seawater pool, sauna and health spa. Attracts all types and ages, including many business-people. Open March 29 to October 29.

Source: Francesca Baldeschi, manager, Ports of Call Travel Consultants, Inc., New York.

Plan for Very Special Trips

If you're the type who finds the sameness of Holiday Inns comforting or prefers to have dinner at McDonald's—in Paris—this checklist isn't for you. But if you love country inns, a pot of coffee brewing in your room, four-poster beds, claw-legged bathtubs, lunch beside a swan pond, discovering the best wine cellar in Vermont or the trail that isn't on a map, then you might want to plan your vacations differently.

• Consult the guidebooks and travel agent last.

• Year round, collect information on all kinds of interesting vacation possibilities.

• Keep geographical files labeled Caribbean, West Coast, The South, New England, Europe, Israel, Japan, and Exotic Places, for example. You can make your own headings and add new folders when the catch-all category gets too full to be manageable.

• Subdivide your files into subject files labeled Ski Vacations, Tennis Vacations, Club Med Locations, Charming Inns/Elegant Small Hotels, Houses for Rent or Exchange and Great Restaurants in Other Places (to distinguish it from your home town restaurant file).

• File articles from airline magazines, newsletters and the travel section of your newspaper.

• Interview friends: When you agree with your friends' taste in food, furnishings, theater or painting, chances are you can trust their vacation advice.

• Talk with neighbors, clients, friends at work.

• Think of exchanging visits with friends you meet on vacation.

• Save picture postcards from active travelers.

• Eavesdrop in an airport or restaurant, on the bus or train to work. If you hear a total stranger describe a perfect meal she had in Kansas City, or a rustic lodge in the Adirondacks with a gorgeous view of the sunset, jot it down. Check out the details later. (That's where guidebooks and travel agents come in handy.)

• Books, movies, magazines. In vacation terms, life can imitate art. You'll want to visit Big Sur if you've read Henry Miller.

Best Uncrowded Resorts In Mexico

For the cheapest prices and probably the most exciting vacations, stay away from well-known, overcrowded resorts like Acapulco and Taxco.

Travelers who know Mexico well say they especially like:

• *Ixtapa,* 150 miles north of Acapulco on the Pacific. Warm, dry and uncrowded, the resort has one of the most luxurious hotels in Mexico, the Ixtapa Camino Real.

• *Merida,* the capital of Yucatan, is old, exotic and cheap. The elegant Montejo Palace costs much more than other hotels. Merida is the takeoff point for excursions to nearby Mayan ruins, where hotels are similarly priced.

• *Oaxaca* is near the site of some of the most beautiful pre-Columbian ruins. A 16th-century convent has been converted into El Presidente hotel.

• *Vera Cruz,* not touted by Mexico's tourist officials, is a picturesque old city on the Gulf of Mexico with some of the best food in the country. The six-hour drive from 7,200-foot-high Mexico City to sea-level Vera Cruz is spectacular. The beachside Mocambo Hotel is reasonably priced.

Offbeat Three-Day Weekends

For an extra-long weekend you will never forget:

• Ballooning. A great way to see the countryside. In most of the US, ballooning trips are available within 100 miles of major cities. You can also take a trip that includes gourmet picnics in France and Austria or wild-game-watching in Kenya.

• Spas. Most spa resorts include massage, aerobics, swimming and succulent diet cuisine, and many feature beauty facilities for facials, pedicures, etc. Spas can be found in Florida, California, Arizona, Texas, New York, New Jersey and Illinois. *A favorite:* World of Palmaire, Pompano Beach, Florida.

• Iceland. Not too far a flight from most northeastern cities, Iceland offers swimming in naturally heated bubbling springs and quick flights to the smaller islands (which the US astronauts used to simulate the lunar surface). Reykjavik, the capital, features great Scandinavian restaurants and shops.

• Tennis ranches. Besides excellent tennis facilities, these ranches usually provide horseback riding and swimming.

• Snowmobiling. Many national parks have snowmobile trails and rental arrangements and lodging is available in cabins or lodges at low, off-season rates.

• Cruise to nowhere. Going (or actually not going) from various East and West Coast cities on a cruise ship can be great fun. All normal shipboard cruise facilities are available for a luxurious weekend.

• Dude ranches. Most prevalent in the West and Southwest. Smaller private ranches and farms that take in guests are homier than the bigger ones. Families are especially welcome. An inexpensive get-away-from-it-all including riding lessons and home cooking.

• Biking tours. You can travel in the Berkshires, the Smokies, or any beautiful countryside.

Source: Carole M. Phillips, CTC, of Certified Travel Consultants, New York.

How to Select A Puppy

The main thing is to buy from a breeder rather than a pet shop. Don't buy a puppy on impulse. *Consider the following points:*

• It's best to see both the pup's parents or their photographs at the breeder (chief reason to buy there rather than at pet store). Not only will you see what the puppy will look like as an adult, you will also be able to judge its genetic inheritance by the health of its parents.

•Buy a puppy at 6 to 12 weeks of age. That's when they make the best adjustment to a new home.

Try these quick and easy visual tests:

•Shine a pocket flashlight at the pup.

•Show it a mirror.

•Roll a ball toward it.

•Wave a sheet of white paper.

•Drag an object along on a string.

Similarly, here are some hearing tests (to be done out of the puppy's sight):

•Blow a police whistle.

•Honk a car horn.

•Clap hands.

•Blow a kazoo or noisemaker.

•Body sensitivity is important in training. Gently pinch the puppy's ear between the ball of the thumb and the forefinger. Then push down its hindquarters, forcing it to sit. A puppy that doesn't react has little body sensitivity and won't feel corrections. A puppy that whines, cowers or runs away is so sensitive that it will fear corrections and be difficult to train.

•Temperament can be tested by seeing the puppy's attitude toward strangers. Jump right in front of the puppy. It should show neither fear nor anger. Surprise followed by friendliness is a good reaction.

Training Your Puppy

Some suggestions:

•Don't encourage a puppy to chew on facsimiles of valued objects. You can't expect it to tell an old shoe from a new one.

•Never place your hand or finger in a puppy's mouth when playing. That biting might seem cute today, but you won't enjoy it a year from now.

•Allow the puppy to climb and jump on you only when you're seated on the floor. If you let it jump on you when you're in a chair, you're teaching it to sit on furniture.

•Never encourage a puppy to bark on command. This can lead to excessive barking and a dog that "talks back."

•Puppies become bored and anxious easily. If you leave your puppy alone too long and too often, you must expect destructive behavior.

•Praise the puppy when it's good. Treat bad behavior with a stern *No* and a shaking or a harsh noisemaker. Physical abuse will teach a dog only fear.

What to Feed Your Dog

Commercial dog foods usually contain parts of an animal that a dog would never eat in the wild. Sometimes these foods include diseased animal parts rejected for human consumption. *To provide your pet a good diet:*

•Feed it table scraps, including meat, vegetables, grains, fruit and even salad.

•Avoid sugars and other sweets, except as treats.

•For variety, mix scraps with a little commercial food. (Buy only products that contain no additives.)

•Give your dog trimmings, tripe, spleen, kidney or liver served raw or partially cooked. (The entrails of a freshly killed animal are the first thing a wild dog eats.)

•Always supplement the diet with minerals and multivitamins, especially vitamins C and E.

Source: Wendell O. Belfield, DVM, author of *How to Have a Healthier Dog,* Doubleday, New York.

Appreciating Autumn

The fall is a season of holidays and rituals. In addition to the harvest, we celebrate Hallowe'en and Thanksgiving. And several religions also celebrate their New Year at this time of year.

Many of our celebrations have ancient roots. Merlin Stone, an historian who specializes in ancient religions, has this to say...

What makes autumn such a special time?

Although autumn is joyous because of the harvest, Hallowe'en and Thanksgiving, it can also be somewhat sad because of the approach of winter. Many people start to feel melancholy as the days grow shorter.

In many religions, fall is a time of judgment. For instance, the Jewish holiday of Yom Kippur is a day of atonement and judgment. The Jewish New Year, Rosh Hashana, also arrives in the fall.

Isn't it unusual, having a new year in the fall?

Although the Jewish New Year is now one of the few that comes in the fall, it wasn't always so.

The pagan new year was once in the fall. The Akkadians, an ancient Semitic people, also celebrated their new year in the fall.

Are there any other similarities between these holidays?

In the Sumerian religion, the new year marked the annual judgment of the people according to the laws of the goddess Nanshe, who dates back at least 5,000 years.

Although we think of pagan religions as being without ethics or morals, Nanshe raised very tough questions on judgment day. She stood in front of the people and asked: *Did you comfort the orphans? Care for the elderly and ill? Give shelter to the homeless? Give food to the hungry?*

Many of these ethical precepts were absorbed into Jewish law and Christianity. *Similar:* The Christian notion of St. Peter standing at the pearly gates looking in his book to see what kind of lives people led before he lets them enter heaven.

Also related to autumn being the time of judgment is the Greek goddess of justice, Themis. She is depicted with the scales of justice in her hand, the astrological sign of Libra, which occurs in late September and early October.

How does our holiday of Thanksgiving relate to ancient celebrations?

All over the world, whenever the harvest is brought in, it's a time of dancing, feasting and general joy to celebrate the abundance of food.

Even the ancient Greeks celebrated this event. Thesmophoria, the Greek harvest festival, and the rituals at Eleusis are in the ancient Greek month of Boedromion, in the fall.

The Greeks, in fact, had a wonderful myth that explained the seasons...

Demeter, the goddess of grain and the inventor of agriculture, had a little girl, Persephone, who one fall day was kidnapped by Hades, the god of the underworld. Persephone protested by refusing to eat while in captivity, but she accidentally ate four pomegranate seeds.

Demeter was furious at Zeus for allowing his brother Hades to kidnap her daughter. She refused to let anything grow until Persephone was returned. Persephone was held underground for the entire winter, and was returned to her mother in spring.

Every year, however, she has to go back to the underworld for at least four months because she ate the four pomegranate seeds. This is why we have at least four months of the year when nothing grows.

Where did Hallowe'en originate?

Hallowe'en comes after the harvest, when the earth is quiet. It's a time when pagan cultures believed the veil between life and death was the thinnest, allowing the living to communicate with the dead. The story of Persephone being taken to the underworld may also be related to this theme.

Today, Christians celebrate All Souls Day on the first day of November with prayers for those who have passed on.

The Jewish New Year celebration includes lighting candles for and remembering the dead. And many other cultures have or had similar observances.

In Scandinavia they used to celebrate the Alfablot, or elfblood, a rite where the goddess Hel raised the souls of the dead.

The Celts celebrated Samhain, which was basically the same as our Hallowe'en, as the start of the New Year. It is still celebrated by some people.

The Mexican Day of the Dead comes around the same time. Traditions include picnics in the cemeteries, lighting skull-shaped candles and leaving food for the dead.

Our non-religious Hallowe'en rituals—trick-or-treating, trying to frighten each other and dressing in scary costumes—are also quite ancient. The tradition of skeletons and ghosts on Hallowe'en comes from the sense that this is the best time of year to communicate with the dead.

How do you think we should celebrate the fall today?

Fall is a good time to remember the past and those who have gone before us. It's a great time to make resolutions. I suspect it was when our ancestors resolved to do things differently.

And fall is for making up for wrongs. During the Jewish New Year, people are supposed to think about whom they've wronged during the year and make amends. This can fend off fall depression and help you feel better about your relationships and yourself.

Go out and see the leaves change. Although green leaves are around all summer, the colored leaves fall quickly, reminding us of the temporary nature of beauty and of our own mortality.

I like to read O. Henry's short story *The Last Leaf.* Although it's basically melancholy, it also provides a bright ray of hope.

The story is about a little girl who becomes ill in the fall, and grows obsessed with the notion that she will die when the last leaf falls from the tree by her window. But a friend, an artist who visits her regularly, secretly paints a golden leaf on the wall behind the tree. It stays there all winter...and the little girl does not die.

Source: Merlin Stone, author of *When God Was a Woman,* Harcourt Brace Jovanovich, Orlando, FL.

You Can Communicate With Your Cat

We all know people who treat their pets as if they were human. Silly as it may seem, scientific research has proven time and again that animals and humans really *can* communicate.

With dogs, it's easy. They're social animals who are eager to communicate with just about anyone.

Cats, however, are another story. To communicate with a cat, you have to show respect and speak to him/her *on his own terms.* Only then will your cat open up to you.

A cat's-eye view of the world...

The first step in talking to your cat is to see the world as your cat sees it.

As far as your cat is concerned, he is an independent, solitary creature who sets his own rules. He has no owner. If anything, your cat thinks of you as his property. If you do something your cat likes, he will reward you. On the other hand, if you do something to upset him, *you* will be reprimanded.

How to talk to your cat...

• Observe your cat's behavior patterns. Cats tend to sit in certain places to sun or rest. To talk to your cat, you want to meet him on his own terms while he's relaxing.

• Let your cat rub against you when you enter the room. This is how he claims you. If you don't let your cat do this, he may become angry. He certainly won't talk to you.

• Rub your head against your cat's head. This is the way cats greet each other—they understand it quite well.

• Bring a gift. Cats love toys that move...or you can drag a stuffed toy mouse across the floor. If you really want to get in good with your cat, give him a paper bag or box to climb in.

• Speak softly and warmly. If your cat does not appear to be listening, establish eye contact. But don't stare too intently—that's considered aggressive.

If your cat still ignores you, and you really want him to listen, imitate the harsh, hissing sound cats make when they fight. This will get any cat's attention immediately.

How to listen to your cat...

• Listen to your cat's meows. Each type of meow has a different meaning. You don't have to meow back, but it will help the two of you to bond. Watch what your cat is doing at the time of his meow to help you figure out what it means.

Example: If your cat meows at the door, he obviously wants to go out. If he meows when you're eating, he wants to be fed.

Consider yourself on good terms with your cat when he purrs. Purring is the cat equivalent of a human smile. Your cat is pleased with you and with what's going on around him.

• Watch your cat's tail and eyes. Cats show their feelings by moving their tails in different ways and by the size of their pupils.

A tail straight up is the sign of a happy cat. A slightly bent tail means your actions are in question—he's not so sure about you. A lowered, swishing tail in a standing or crouching cat means you're going to get swatted if you don't stop what you're doing.

In the absence of extreme lighting conditions, large pupils indicate pleasure...narrow pupils, anger.

• Watch your cat's ears. Ears that are back mean displeasure, while ears that are up mean everything is fine and your cat is relaxed.

Source: Jean Craighead George, author of *How to Talk to Your Cat*, Warner Books, 666 Fifth Ave., New York 10103. She has been "owned by" approximately 172 cats of all ages over a 12-year period. She is also a nature writer who has written more than 56 books, many of them for children.

30

Travel Smarts

Health Hazards of Flying

Although crashing is the most obvious and dramatic threat faced by airline passengers, the risk of going down is so small as to be almost negligible. *More realistic threats:*

• Dry/oxygen-deficient air. Air inside an airliner cabin contains only 2% to 20% of normal relative humidity—and about 25% less oxygen —than air on the ground. Cabin air is about as thin as the air atop a peak 6,000 to 8,000 feet high.

For most passengers, dry, oxygen-poor air presents no particular problems beyond dry skin and thirst. But for those afflicted with certain chronic cardiovascular and respiratory ailments—especially heart disease, asthma and bronchitis—cabin air can be life-threatening. *To avoid trouble...*

• Drink at least one glass of bottled water for each hour you're aloft.

• Avoid alcohol, coffee, tea, colas and other beverages with a diuretic effect.

• Sit with your legs elevated to prevent blood clots in your lower legs—a real possibility if flight-induced dehydration is severe enough to cause your blood to pool and thicken.

• If you begin to feel breathless or faint while flying, ask a flight attendant for oxygen. Federal law requires airliners to keep oxygen tanks on board for just such an emergency. If your breathing difficulty persists, ask if there's a doctor on board.

• Reduced air pressure. As an airliner climbs to its cruising altitude, air pressure inside the cabin falls. Most passengers recognize this phenomenon by the familiar "popping" effect that occurs when air that's inside the ears is squeezed out. Unfortunately, not all the effects of reduced air pressure are as benign. *Dangers:*

• Severe intestinal gas, toothache and—far worse—sudden hemorrhaging of stomach ulcers, ovarian cysts, or surgical incisions.

• Reduced air pressure can also cause the bends in scuba divers who fly too soon after diving. And, a boy wearing a plaster cast developed gangrene when air trapped beneath the cast expanded and cut off circulation in his arm.

To avoid trouble: Wear loose-fitting pants while flying, and avoid beans and other gas-producing foods for several hours before take-off. If you suspect you have any loose fillings, have them repaired before your departure. If you've been diagnosed with ulcers or ovarian cysts, or if you've recently had surgery, consult a doctor before flying.

Do not fly with a plaster cast. Never fly within 12 hours of scuba diving (24 hours if you've dived below 30 feet or have been diving for several days).

• Contaminated air. Long notorious for poor ventilation and stale air, airline cabins have gotten even stuffier in recent years.

In the interest of cost-cutting, cabin air on most flights is now being recirculated for 12 minutes at a time.

In the past, cabin air was recirculated for only three minutes at a time before fresh air was pumped in.

Result: Cabin air is depleted of oxygen and laden with disease-causing germs, carbon dioxide, carbon monoxide and other contaminants—especially on flights where smoking is permitted.

Stale, contaminated air can cause coughing, shortness of breath and headaches, as well as eye infections, colds, the flu and even lung cancer.

To avoid trouble: Use a saline nasal spray to keep your nostrils clean and moist (the greater the moisture in your nostrils, the more effective they are at filtering contaminants from the air). On smoking flights, sit as far as possible from smokers.

• Radiation. Modern airliners fly in the upper reaches of the atmosphere, where cosmic and solar radiation are particularly intense. The longer and more frequent your flights, the greater your exposure. In most cases, this extra exposure causes no apparent problems. Under certain conditions, however, it can cause birth defects, infertility, and cancer.

To play it safe: Pregnant women should avoid flying during the first trimester, when rapidly dividing cells in the fetus are especially vulnerable to radiation.

Persons who spend more than 11 hours a week on an airplane should monitor their radiation exposure with a radiation film badge (dosimeter) worn at all times while aloft.

Frequent flyers should have regular check-ups by a doctor who specializes in aviation medicine.

For a list of flight doctors in your area, contact the Aerospace Medical Association at 703-739-2240 in Arlington, Virginia.

Source: Farrol S. Kahn, founder of the Aviation Health Institute in Oxford, England, and author of *Why Flying Endangers Your Health: Hidden Health Hazards of Air Travel*, Aurora Press, Box 573, Santa Fe, NM 87504.

Better Car-Rental Rates

Quote the advertised discount directly from the company's ad when calling the reservation number. *Problem:* Reservation agents often will not volunteer the best available price up front. *Helpful:* Mention the promotion's discount code, usually listed in small print beneath the boldly displayed rate, or in the description of the terms and conditions of the rental.

Source: Ed Perkins, editor, *Consumer Reports Travel Letter*, 101 Truman Ave., Yonkers, NY 10703.

Airfare-Bargain Traps

Airfare "bargains" are often not what they seem. *Example:* One airline recently offered a discount on companion tickets, but the base fare rate was higher than normal. *Self-defense:* Find a smart travel agent with access to reservation computers that can track prices...and delay buying a ticket until 14 days before your flight, *except during holiday periods*. For holiday travel, book early to be sure of getting a seat. Insist that your travel agent continue to inform you about all deals that become available to your destination.

Source: Herbert J. Teison, editor, *Travel Smart*, 40 Beechdale Rd., Dobbs Ferry, NY 10522.

Cheaper Travel

Ask about visitor transit-system passes. Many public transit systems in major cities sell passes that permit unlimited or extensive travel on buses, subways, trains and trolleys. Some are issued by the day, others cover multiple days or a week.

The price is more than one daily round-trip but can add up to significant savings—and you won't have to fumble for exact change each time you ride. For information, write, call, or visit the city tourist-information office.

Source: *Consumer Reports Travel Letter,* 101 Truman Ave., Yonkers, NY 10703.

Secrets of a Much More Comfortable Flight

Airline travel may be fast, but it is not always comfortable. Too often, travelers, especially those seated in coach, are crammed into confining seats, fed factory-produced meals and confronted with delays or lost luggage. Flights can be made more bearable, however, if you know how to work the system.

Getting a good seat...

Most travelers don't want to sit in the middle seat of a row. But if you're late checking in for a crowded flight, you're almost certain of getting one. *Problem:* Airlines automatically assign aisle and window seats first, even if the two passengers in a row are traveling together.

You can improve your chances of getting an end seat by asking the agent at the check-in counter to search the passenger list for two travelers with the same last name in the same row. Request the middle seat in that row. Chances are the other two passengers are related and will want to sit together, leaving you either the window or aisle seat.

Storing luggage...

Finding room for your carry-on luggage is always challenging. It is best, however, not to wait until you arrive at your seat to store your bags. Instead, put them in the first overhead compartment after you pass through the first-class cabin.

These compartments will likely be empty, since they are for the last passengers that board. In addition, you won't have to carry your bags to your seat as you enter or to the front as you exit the plane.

Better baggage handling...

Bags that have first-class or priority tags attached are usually first to come off the plane into the baggage claim area. Even if you're traveling in coach, you can benefit from this quick service by getting one of these tags.

Sometimes the airlines will give you a first-class tag if you ask for it. If not, try to find an old one from any airline. You can even make one up in advance by having a brightly colored card stamped with the word "priority" and laminated at a local printer. This will attract the attention of the baggage handlers.

Getting an upgrade...

Just because you have enough frequent-flier miles to qualify for a better seat doesn't always mean you'll get one, especially if the flight is crowded.

In fact, you may actually stand a better chance of getting one if the flight is overbooked. In this situation, airlines commonly offer free tickets to passengers turning in their tickets. If you hear this announced, immediately notify the check-in personnel that you're still interested in upgrading.

Reason: A surprising number of first-class travelers give up their seats for free tickets, opening up space in the forward cabin.

A more comfortable flight...

Strong sunlight is a common problem that travelers face when flying during the day. It often forces you to travel with the shade down. To avoid the sunny side when traveling eastbound, request an A, B, or C seat. When traveling westbound, request a seat on the other side of the cabin.

Source: Randy Petersen, who travels up to 400,000 miles a year and is editor of *InsideFlier,* a magazine for frequent fliers, 4715-C Town Center Dr., Colorado Springs 80916.

Developing Film

When having film developed, attach a label with your name and address to the container itself in case the envelope is lost.

Source: Professional photofinishers quoted in *The New York Times.*

Cutting Costs When Traveling to Europe

The costs of traveling to Europe can be cut without sacrificing comfort. All it takes is a willingness to ask questions and a basic knowledge of how the travel industry works. Using this strategy, which for example might involve traveling off-season, can trim 25% to 50% off the price of hotels, airfares, and car rentals.

Airfares...

There are big advantages to going through a strong travel agent. Many have tremendous buying power that allows them to pass along cut rates to their regular clients.

Or, consider a tour package. It is a great way to trim 25% or more off the cost of hotels and airfares.

Or, check for deals on airfares in your Sunday paper. Important: Don't bother calling on Monday. The deals are probably already booked up by then. *Better:* Call past fare promoters on Thursday before they send in their ads to the Sunday papers.

Hotels...

• Stay away from the center of town. Hotels away from the tourist centers are 15% to 40% cheaper than downtown hotels. Most major cities offer great public transportation so it isn't difficult to get around. Consider staying in small towns surrounding major cities. These usually have easy, inexpensive access to the more expensive tourist centers.

• Negotiate. Americans usually aren't comfortable bargaining about price. But it is a way of life in Europe. Most hotels, in fact, are willing to negotiate their rates, especially if you're planning to stay for at least three days. So long as there isn't a convention in town, you might get a break of 20% to 50%.

• Ask for the corporate rate. Virtually all hotels cut prices by at least 20% for business travelers.

Transportation...

Europe's special railway passes generally pay off if you're traveling far or at a fast pace. Buying individual tickets may be best for intercity or side trips.

Train travel may be best for a side trip. In most cases, purchase a second-class ticket. The cost is about a third less than first-class and the ride is still comfortable. Only in Italy, Spain, and Portugal, where second-class coaches get crowded, is it worth paying the premium.

Car rentals in Europe are always expensive. High local taxes is one reason. Some countries, however, traditionally offer lower rates. Good deals are usually found in Spain, Luxembourg, Ireland, and England. Also, check local rental companies. Sometimes they offer better rates than the big international firms. And always try to rent for a week on an unlimited mileage basis. The per-day charge is generally exorbitantly higher.

More money-savers...

• Entry fees for museums can be pretty high. Many major cities, such as Paris, sell museum cards that offer unlimited entry into its major museums for one low price. Some museums also set aside one day a week when admission is free.

• Tax refunds. European countries charge a value added tax of about 15% for most items. Visitors can get this back. The quickest way is to use a credit card. Ask for payment and VAT refund slips at the same time. If the store refuses, ask for specific details on VAT refunds for the country.

• Theater. In London, the discount ticket booth in Leicester Square sells tickets when available at half price. Many theater box offices also sell tickets at a discount that have been returned just before show time.

Source: John Whitman, who has logged more than two million miles exploring how to travel on a budget. He is the author of *The Best European Travel Tips*, published by Meadowbrook Press, available from the author, Box 202, Long Lake, MN 55356.

Jet Lag Smarts

To minimize jet lag, schedule important activities for when you will likely have the most energy. *High-energy times:* Evenings after jetting east...the next morning after jetting west.

Source: *Jet Smart* by Diana Fairchild, former flight attendant, Flyana Rhyme, Inc., Box 300, Makawao, Maui, HI 96768.

Traffic Tickets

1. Keep talking. The longer an officer chats with you before writing a ticket, the better your chances of getting off with only a warning. To buy yourself as much time as possible, pull your car off the shoulder as far as you can so the officer can talk to you without fear of becoming roadkill.

2. Know his place. Using a policeman's correct rank will make it seem that you're somehow involved with law enforcement or the military. Check his sleeve; if it has three or more stripes, call him "Sergeant" or "Sarge." If it has one or two stripes, call him "Corporal." If you see no stripes and he's a state cop, call him "Trooper." If he has no stripes and he's driving a county sheriff car, call him "Deputy." If you're not sure, call him "Officer."

3. Don't make a scene. The less an officer remembers about you and the stop, the better your lawyer's chances of getting you off the hook. Most tickets get reduced, or won by the defendant in court, because the cop doesn't remember the specifics of the stop.

Source: Sgt. James M. Eagan, retired New York State Trooper, author, *A Speeder's Guide to Avoiding Tickets.*

Nonsmoking Seats

Nonsmoking seats are *not guaranteed* on overseas flights on non-US airlines. US carriers must provide a nonsmoking seat to every passenger who asks for one, except standbys. International carriers usually set aside a limited number of nonsmoking seats on a first-come, first-serve basis. Policies keep changing—ask your travel agent before booking.

Source: *Condé Nast Traveler,* 360 Madison Ave., New York 10017.

Headphones In-Flight

Wear headphones in-flight—even if you're not listening to music. With headphones on, you're less likely to be disturbed by a talkative seatmate.

Source: *Office On the Go: Tools, Tips and Techniques for Every Business Traveler* by Scottsdale, Arizona computer consultant Kim Baker, Prentice-Hall, Route 9W, Englewood Cliffs, NJ 07632.

Easier Air Travel

A single airline flight number does not mean it is a nonstop flight—or even that you won't have to change planes to get to your destination. Airlines often label connecting flights as if they were on a single plane. Changing planes entails hassle and increases the risk of lost or delayed luggage. *Self-defense:* When making reservations, ask the agent if the flight requires you to change planes—most will not volunteer such information. If it does, ask if there's another, equally convenient flight available that lets you stay on the same plane throughout.

Source: *Consumer Reports Travel Letter,* 101 Truman Ave., Yonkers, NY 10703.

Flying Comfort

Door rows: Most wide-body jets have mid-cabin doors, and the seats right behind them have extra leg room due to the aisle to the door. *Exit rows:* Most narrow-body jets have mid-body emergency exits—with aisles that provide extra leg room. *Bulkhead rows:* If you have a seat right next to a cabin divider, nobody in front of you will be able to recline a seat into you.

Source: Ed Perkins, editor, *Consumer Reports Travel Letter*, 101 Truman Ave., Yonkers, NY 10703.

Safety Away from Home

Bring a smoke detector when you travel. This will protect against any hotel that—in violation of state laws—does not have smoke detectors in rooms...or has smoke detectors that have dead batteries. *Also helpful:* A portable burglar alarm that trips when someone tries to enter your room.

Source: *Office on the Go: Tools, Tips and Techniques for Every Business Traveler* by Kim Baker, Scottsdale, Arizona computer expert and consultant. Prentice-Hall, Route 9W, Sylvan Ave., Englewood Cliffs, NJ 07632.

Travel Advisories

Travel warnings from the State Department advise travelers about countries that are dangerous for Americans to visit. A warning means conditions are potentially threatening to American travelers—and the US cannot help them in emergencies. Warnings are updated every six months—but more often if events warrant. *For copies of warnings:* Send a self-addressed, stamped, business-sized envelope to Bureau of Consular Affairs, Room 4811 NS, Department of State, Washington, DC 20520. To check on a specific country: Call 202-647-5225, Monday through Friday, 9 a.m. to 5 p.m., Eastern Time.

Always Carry Your License

Always carry your driver's license when driving a car. *Risky:* Assuming that you have 24 hours to produce your driver's license after you are stopped for a driving violation. *Problem:* If you don't have your driver's license, you probably don't have any other identification either ...so you could be brought to jail. There's more flexibility with car registrations. It's generally OK to have a *photocopy* of your registration in your car and keep the original at home—or in your wallet. Most states accept a photocopy to prove ownership—call your state motor vehicle department to be sure. If your car is stolen and the thief is stopped by the police, the police will be suspicious when the name on the registration is different from that of the driver.

Source: Jim Eagan is a retired New York State police supervisor and author of *A Speeder's Guide to Avoiding Tickets*, Avon Books, 1350 Avenue of the Americas, New York 10019.

How to Get More Out Of Your Travel

- Take along a small tape recorder when you travel. This is easier than jotting notes or trying to find the time to keep a diary.
- Interview people you meet along the way. Ask them all about their lives, occupations and backgrounds. This will preserve the facts and actual voices of interesting people you meet.
- Tape guided tours. Guides give out lots of information that is forgotten during the excitement of a tour but can be enjoyed later.

How to Make the Most Of Your Time in Unfamiliar Towns

- Be a part-time tourist. An hour or two between appointments gives you enough time to check out the local aquarium, museum, library, antique district, park or waterfront. Major tourist attractions are often located near enough to a city's business district for you to mix meetings with pleasure conveniently.
- Have a great meal. Do some advance research, and equip yourself with a list of the best restaurants in each city on your itinerary. Then, when your free time coincides with a mealtime,

invest instead in a delightful hour of gourmet adventure.

•Look up old friends. Perhaps you can share that gourmet meal with a college friend you haven't seen in years, or surprise an uncle or cousin with a call or visit.

•Take pictures. If you're into photography, you know that a new environment frequently yields new visions and special scenes and subjects. Keep your eyes open and your camera ready.

•Go gift shopping. On autumn trips, carry a list of holiday gift ideas for friends and family. Use even a spare 15 minutes to pop in on the local boutiques and specialty shops. Charge and send your purchases, and when you get home they'll be there, all ready for your December giving.

•Bring busywork. When you're too tired to kill time on the move—or it's raining or the neighborhood is threatening or everything is closed—you should have something to do in your hotel room other than watch TV and order room service. Try catching up on a pile of periodicals or going through seed catalogues.

Source: Letty Cottin Pogrebin, author of five books including *Family Politics,* McGraw-Hill, New York.

Making the Most Of Travel Time

Some people claim that they can work on airplanes, trains or boats, but you may not be one of them. If you, too, are unable to concentrate while traveling:

•Go to sleep. Traveling is a natural soporific. Catching up on your sleep will give you an edge when you arrive.

•Find someone to talk with. Walk around and see if anyone who looks interesting has a copy of the Official Airlines Guide (which frequent travelers carry) or other travel guides. Start talking about travel, and you'll learn a few things.

•Clean out your wallet or briefcase. This is something you always mean to do but never get around to.

•Write letters. They don't take much concentration.

Killing Time Creatively At Airports

•Make phone calls. Check into your office, pick up a dozen phone messages and return eight calls before being driven from the public phone by the furious stares of others waiting to use it.

•Write letters or pay bills. Bring notepaper, envelopes, bills and your checkbook. Use your briefcase as a desk.

•Shop for the unexpected. Airport gift shops are notoriously glitzy. And at first glance, the merchandise in every gift shop looks alike except for the city etched into the beer mugs. But you may well find a Pierre Cardin belt at a bargain price in Cleveland, live lobsters in Boston and sourdough bread in San Francisco.

•Read indulgently. Buy a spy novel if you usually lean toward business books. Pick up a foreign magazine and test your French. Indulge in a crossword puzzle magazine or cartoon book. Read the local papers.

•Get a haircut or shoeshine. Men have the edge here. Although airport barber shops sometimes advertise "unisex," I've never seen a woman in any of them. Bootblacks will gladly shine a woman's shoes.

•Jog. With throngs of people running to catch their planes, no one will know you are just jogging along the concourses to kill time. Leave your coat and carry-on bag under someone's watchful eye while you run.

•People-watch. This is a surprisingly diverting pastime, especially for hyperactive types who don't often stop to observe the world around them.

•Eavesdrop. Airports are great places to tune in on some fascinating conversations—one as melodramatic as a soap opera dialogue, another as funny as a Mel Brooks sketch.

•Think. If you're uninspired by the above alternatives, you can simply stare out at the landing field, letting your mind go blank. Or you can give yourself a specific problem to mull over. Sometimes the brain does a better job of thinking at rest than it does under pressure.

Source: Letty Cottin Pogrebin, author of five books including *Family Politics,* McGraw-Hill, New York.

Saving Time and Money at Hotels

•When you arrive at a hotel, check your bags. Then go to the pay telephone in the lobby and call the hotel. Ask to have your reservation confirmed, give them your charge card number and go on your way. You'll sidestep convention check-in lines.

•To avoid the long check-out line after the convention, go down to the desk very early in the morning, before official checkout time, and check out. You won't have to turn in your room key, and you can still use your room until official checkout time (usually around 1 p.m.).

•Don't stay glued to your hotel room if you're waiting for a call. If you ask, the hotel operator will transfer your calls to another room, interrupt the call you're on for a more important one or hold any calls while you run out for a soda.

•Save money by not paying for things you didn't order. Don't charge anything to your hotel room. It's too confusing when you're checking out to verify the list of room charges. And it's only too easy for the hotel to make a mistake. If you don't charge anything at all, you'll know that extra items on your bill can't be yours. How to do it: Use your telephone credit card for calls, and pay cash for room service, laundry, etc. Use your credit card for food.

•Don't depend only on the hotel for services such as typing, film developing, etc. Call the local convention bureau. It's specifically set up to help out-of-town businesspeople, and every city has one.

Source: Dr. Barbara A. Pletcher, executive director of the National Association for Professional Saleswomen, is author of *Travel Sense,* Ace Books, New York.

Don't Be a Victim of Hotel Overbooking

It's not always the hotel's fault. Sometimes guests overstay. (Hawaii is the only state that allows hotels to compel guests to leave on time.) But hotels generally accept more reservations than they have rooms, betting that some reservation-holders won't show. Sometimes they bet wrong.

To keep from being a loser:

•Plan trips sufficiently in advance to get written confirmation of reservations. That gives you something extra to argue with should you need it. If there's no time for a written confirmation, try to get a confirmation number when the reservation is made.

•Get "guaranteed" reservations with a credit card. This does obligate you to pay for the room even if you can't make it. However, it reduces the incentive a hotel clerk has to sell your room to somebody else. American Express has an "assured reservations" program. Under it, the hotel that "walks" you has to pay for the first night's lodging in a comparable hotel room nearby, for a long-distance call to inform the office or family where you will be, and for transportation to the substitute hotel. Several chains have a similar policy.

•Arrive early in the afternoon, when last night's guests have checked out, but before the bulk of new arrivals.

•Take your case to a higher-up—probably the assistant manager on duty—since it's unlikely that the desk clerk will find a room after telling you he has none. The assistant manager might be persuaded to "find" one of the rooms that inevitably are set aside by luxury hotels for emergencies such as the arrival of a VIP. Make a loud fuss, some people suggest. This often works, since hotels try to avoid drawing public attention to their overbooking practices.

•If neither raving and ranting nor quiet persuasion moves the assistant manager, insist that he call other comparable hotels to get you a room, and at the same or lower price. The better hotels will usually do their best.

How to Save on Air Travel

•Fly between 9 p.m. and 7 p.m. Most airlines have cheaper night flights, especially on long distances.

•Plan business trips so that the schedule qualifies the business traveler for vacation excursion fares (discounts up to 50%).

•Fly out-of-the-way carriers looking for new business.

•Make sales or service trips, or tours of branch offices, using the unlimited mileage tickets offered by some airlines.

Source: Harold Seligman, president, Management Alternatives, Stamford, CT.

Getting a Good Airplane Seat

Getting the seat you prefer on an airplane has become an increasing problem.

•If you're assigned to a seat you don't like, go back to the desk when all the prereserved seats are released (usually about 15 minutes before flight time). Prime seats for passengers who didn't show up are available then.

•If you discover on the plane that you don't like your seat, don't wait until the plane takes off to find a better one. Look around the plane, and the second before they close the door, head for the empty seat of your choice. Don't wait until the seat-belt sign goes on.

•Prereserve a single seat on a nonjumbo where the seats are three across and you'll increase the odds of getting an empty seat next to you.

•Ask for a window or aisle seat in a row where the window or aisle is already reserved by a single. The middle seat between two singles is least likely to fill up.

Know When Not to Fly

Avoid flying if you have had:

•A heart attack within four weeks of takeoff.

•Surgery within two weeks.

•A deep-diving session within 24 hours.

Don't fly at all if you have:

•Severe lung problems.

•Uncontrolled hypertension.

•Epilepsy not well controlled.

•Severe anemia.

•A pregnancy beyond 240 days or threatened by miscarriage.

Source: *Pocket Flight Guide/Frequent Flyer Package.*

Your Ears and Air Travel

•Avoid flying with a cold or other respiratory infection. A cold greatly increases the chances of your suffering discomfort, additional fluid buildup, severe pain or even rupture.

•Take decongestants. If you must fly with a cold, or if you regularly suffer discomfort or pain on descent, decongestants can give real relief. For maximum effect, time them to coincide with the descent (which begins half an hour to an hour before landing). Use both oral decongestants and a spray for best results. *Suggested timing:* Take quick-acting oral decongestants two to three hours before landing or slow-release tablets six to eight hours in advance. Use nasal spray one hour before landing. *Caution:* If you have hypertension or a heart condition, check with your cardiologist about taking decongestants.

•Don't smoke or drink. Smoking irritates the nasal area, and alcohol dilates the blood vessels, causing the tissues to swell.

•Try the Valsalva maneuver. While holding your nose closed, try to blow through it as though you were blowing your nose. This will blow air through the ears. Do this gently and repeatedly as the plane descends. *Warning:* Don't use this method if you have a cold, as you'll be blowing infection back into the middle ear. Use the tried-and-true routines of yawning and swallowing instead. They can be quite effective if the problem is not too severe. Chew gum and suck candy. *Aim:* To activate the swallowing mechanism in order to open the eustachian tubes.

•If your ears are stuffed after landing, follow the same routine. Keep on with decongestants and gentle Valsalvas. Temporary hearing loss and stuffiness may persist for three to four weeks. If the symptoms are really annoying, a doctor can lance the drum to drain the fluid. If pain persists for more than a day, see a doctor.

•See a doctor before flying if you have a bad cold, especially if you have a history of ear pain when flying. If you absolutely must fly, the doctor can open the eardrum and insert a small ventilation tube that will allow the pressure to equalize. The tube should eject by itself in a few weeks...or you can go back to your doctor.

Source: Neville W. Carmical, MD, attending otolaryngologist, St.Luke's-Roosevelt Hospital Center, New York.

Coping with High Altitudes

One out of three travelers at altitudes of 7,000 feet above sea level (Vail, Colorado, for example) experiences some symptoms of altitude sickness. By 10,000 feet (Breckenridge, Colorado), everyone is affected. *Common complaints:* Headaches, nausea, weakness, lack of coordination and insomnia.

To minimize the effects:

•Take it easy the first two or three days. Get plenty of rest and don't schedule vigorous activities.

•Eat a little less than usual. Avoid hard-to-digest foods such as red meat and fats. Carbohydrates are good.

•Drink more liquids than usual. (Breathing harder in dry air causes you to lose water vapor.)

•Avoid alcohol, smoking and tranquilizers. Their effects are compounded at high altitudes.

Flyer's Health Secrets

•Taking your mind off the motion can help your body restore equilibrium without drugs. *How to do it:* Close your eyes, or concentrate on a spot in front of you, and hold your head as steady as possible. Then focus your attention on your breathing or on alternately tensing and relaxing your muscles. Continue to concentrate until the nausea has vanished.

•The low air pressure in an airplane's interior can aggravate some medical problems unless precautions are taken. Gas trapped in the colon can expand, causing severe discomfort or cramps. People with heart or lung diseases should check with their doctor in advance to discuss requesting supplemental oxygen.

•Don't fly with a serious sinus problem. If a sinus is blocked, the trapped air inside expands and can lead to serious infection. Improve drainage prior to ascent and descent with decongestants or nose drops.

•The arid atmosphere of pressurized cabins encourages evaporation from the skin's surface, drying the skin. *Remedies:* Avoid beverages that contain alcohol or caffeine (they both have a diuretic action). Drink plenty of water during the trip and afterward.

Getting to and from the airport:

•Arrive early to avoid stress.

•Schedule an appointment at the airport. If you're in a strange city, try to get your last appointment of the day to meet you there a few hours before your plane leaves. Why should you be the one to do all the running?

•Join an airport club. Most airlines have them. Choose the one that belongs to the principal carrier flying from your city. Then you can relax in comfort while you wait for your flight. *Benefits:* Special services to members, such as a separate check-in desk.

Source: *Healthwise* and Commission on Emergency Medical Services, American Medical Association, Chicago.

Car Rental Tips

Car-rental competition is hotter than ever, especially among the small intracity and intrastate firms. *What to keep tabs on:*

•Does the price include fuel? Very few still do. Dry rate means the customer buys the gas. Find out where gas is cheapest. Fill up there, too, before dropping the car off.

• Special restrictions or charges for one-way rentals.

• Special weekend or weekly rates.

• When luggage space is important, make sure you're getting a large enough vehicle. (A compact or intermediate model may still be suitable.)

• Extra charge if a larger car is substituted. There shouldn't be one if the rental firm does the switching.

• Special corporate discount. Comparison shopping on this could hold surprises.

• Special fly/drive packages offered by airlines.

• The rental firm's policy in case of car trouble.

• In case of an accident, does the contract include primary liability coverage? (In California and Florida, only secondary coverage is required.)

Source: *Medical Economics,* Oradell, NJ.

How to Avoid Vacation Time-Sharing Traps

Some owners of time-shares in beach-and ski-area condominiums are becoming disenchanted. *Reasons:* They find that committing themselves to the same dates at the same resort every year is too restricting. Or they find they overpaid.

To avoid problems:

• Locate one of the companies that act as brokers for swapping time-shares for owners of resort properties in different areas.

• Don't pay more than 10 times the going rate for a good hotel or apartment rental in the same area at the same time of year.

• Get in early on a new complex. Builders usually sell the first few apartments for less.

• Choose a one- or two-bedroom unit. Smaller or larger ones are harder to swap or sell.

• Deal with experienced developers who have already worked out maintenance and management problems.

• Pick a time in the peak season. It will be more negotiable.

• Look for properties that are protected by zoning or geography. Vail, Colorado, for example, has a moratorium on further time-share development.

• Beware of resorts that are hard to reach or are too far off the beaten track. Your time-shares will be harder to rent, swap or sell.

If Your Tour is a Disappointment

To get your money back:

• Go back to the travel agency or sponsor who promoted it with your evidence of a breach of contract.

• Keep all brochures or detailed itinerary that constitutes your contract.

• Keep evidence that the promises were not kept. *Example:* Out-of-pocket receipts, pictures you took of your hotel or room, etc.

• If you come to an impasse on the terms of the tour agreement, check with the American Society of Travel Agents in New York, for an explanation of standardized industry terms (first class, deluxe, etc.).

• *Last resort:* File a complaint with either small claims court or civil court. *Advantage with either:* You don't have to retain a lawyer. Judgments are made quickly.

• *Final action:* Class-action suits have been successful in cases where it's unclear who is at fault. Sometimes it's your only hope for recovering anything from wholesalers and suppliers that are hard to reach.

• *Warning:* If your complaint is with a travel agency that went out of business while you were on tour (such things do happen), your recovery chances are virtually nil against that business, no matter how far you take your case.

Source: Patricia Simko, Assistant Attorney General, New York State Bureau of Consumer Frauds, New York.

How to Get a Passport Faster

If you seek a passport at the height of the tourist season, you'll inevitably face a long wait. But whenever you go for your passport, you can ease the delay by doing the following:

•Go to the passport office in person.

•*Bring:* Your airline ticket, two passport pictures, proof of citizenship (an old passport, voter registration or birth certificate), a piece of identification with your photo on it and the fee.

•Give the passport office a good reason why you are rushed.

If your passport is lost or stolen when you're traveling abroad, here's what to do:

•Immediately notify the local police and the US embassy or consulate. An overnight replacement is sometimes possible in an emergency.

•To hasten this process, know your passport number.

•*Next best:* Have a valid identification document with you. A photostat of your passport is best.

Source: *Travel Smart.*

If You Lose Your Passport Or Credit Cards Overseas

•If your passport is lost or stolen, contact the nearest US embassy or consulate immediately. A consul will interview you.

•If he is satisfied of your US citizenship and identity, a new passport can be quickly issued. Most Americans are able to satisfy the consular officer on the basis of a personal interview and presentation of identification that was not stolen or lost with the passport.

•In some cases, the consul may find it necessary to wire the Department of State to verify that you had been issued a previous passport.

•The consul will be able to refer you to local offices of the major credit cards and travelers checks to report losses.

•If you lose all your money, the embassy will assist you in having funds transferred from a friend or relative in the US through State Department channels.

•The embassy will *not* lend you money.

Currency-Exchange Strategies

Even though the dollar has been strong, a sudden drop could leave you vulnerable while overseas. *To protect yourself:*

•Take about 40% of your travelers checks in commission-free foreign currency and the rest in dollars.

•Prepay your foreign hotel in its own currency to lock in the current rate.

•If you fly first class, business class, or on the Concorde, find out if you can pay for the return trip in foreign currency.

•When shopping overseas, ask for prices in the local currency. Then request a discount if you intend to pay that way.

What to Do If You're Arrested Overseas

In a sample year, 3,000 Americans were arrested in 97 foreign countries for offenses ranging from narcotics and disorderly conduct to murder. *If arrested, here's what you should do:*

•Don't panic. Keep your wits about you.

•Ask to contact the US embassy. Be polite but persistent in making this request.

When a consular officer comes to see you in jail, here's what he or she can do for you:

•Provide you with a list of local attorneys.

•Call an attorney for you if you are unable to make a call.

•Notify relatives or friends at home.

•Make sure your basic health and safety needs are being met.

•Make sure you're not being discriminated against because you're an American.

•Do not expect the embassy to get you out of jail. You are subject to the laws of the country you're visiting.

Source: John P. Caulfield, Bureau of Consular Affairs, US Department of State, Washington, DC.

Index

A

B

C

D

E

F

G

H

I

J

K

L

M

N

O

P

Q

R

S

T

U

V

W

Y

Z

W9-AYE-039
I D H
OONEY
1918
CHAMPION
KATHY ROONEY
ARTHUR J. ROONEY
PITTSBURGH STEELERS
"THE PREZ"
ARTHUR J. ROONEY
PITTSBURGH STEELERS
HOF 1964
ART ROONEY
the Chief
©KARCHNER·2007
RUANAIDH (RU-AH-NEE) IS GAELIC FOR ROONEY

May. 2009

Dear Mom,

Happy Mother's Day!

Love,

Christine

Ruanaidh

By Art Rooney Jr.
with Roy McHugh

The story of Art Rooney and his clan

www.artrooneyjr.com

Third Printing: August, 2008
Third Edition

Manufactured in the United States of America
ISBN No. Hard Cover: 978-0-9814760-2-5
ISBN No. Soft Cover: 978-0-9814760-3-2

Printed by Geyer Printing Company, Inc.
Fifty-Five 38th Street
Pittsburgh, PA 15201

Typography by Cold-Comp
91 Green Glen Drive
Pittsburgh, PA 15227

Cover design by Kathy Rooney; illustrations by Merv Corning

For my parents, Art and Kathleen (Kass) Rooney

For my wife, Kathleen (Kay) Rooney

For all of my relatives who crossed the high seas to America
and worked in the steel mills and coal mines

*"... If a book must be written about me, wait 30 years ...
for I touched all the bases."*
- Art Rooney (The Chief)

*"Sorry, Dad, I could only wait 18 years
because I'm getting to be an old fogey myself."*
- Art Rooney, Jr.

Ruanaidh
(Rooney)

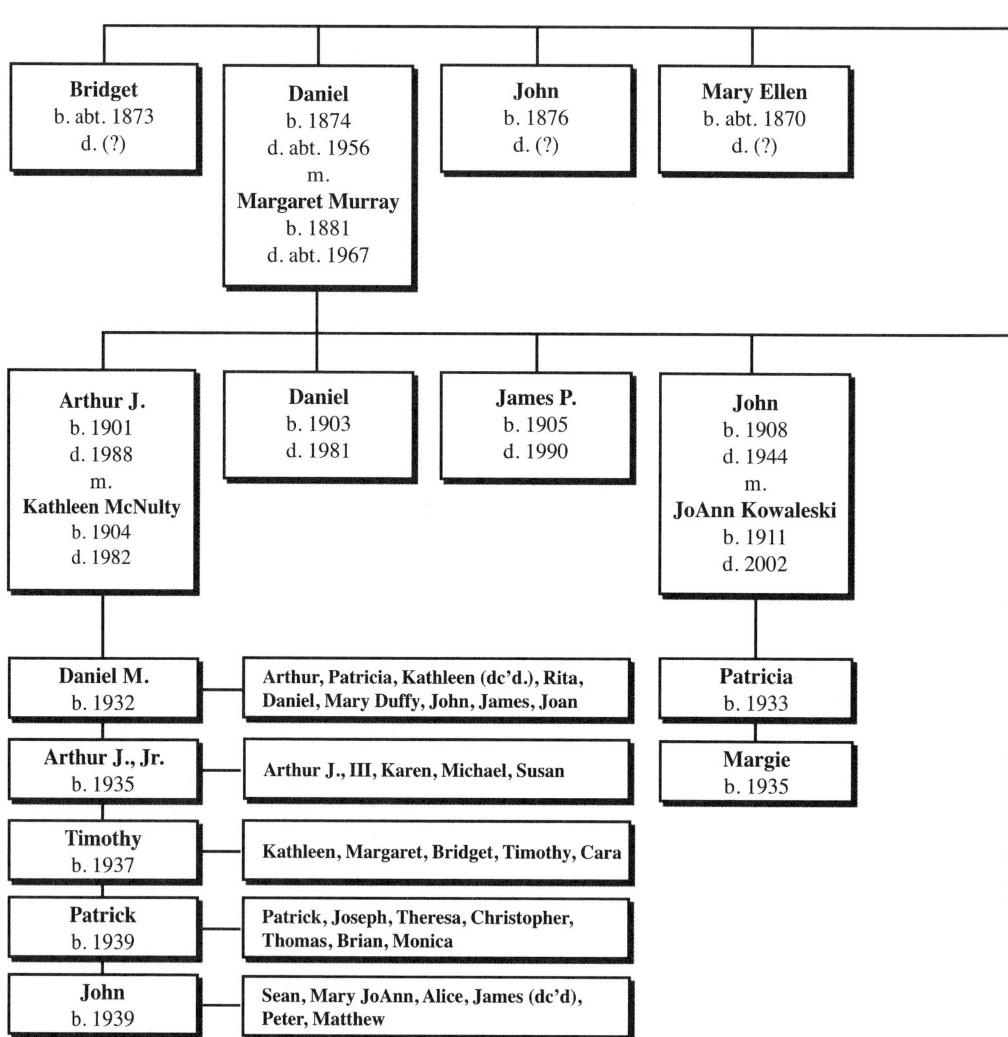

Bridget
b. abt. 1873
d. (?)
Daniel
b. 1874
d. abt. 1956
m.
Margaret Murray
b. 1881
d. abt. 1967
John
b. 1876
d. (?)
Mary Ellen
b. abt. 1870
d. (?)
Arthur J.
b. 1901
d. 1988
m.
Kathleen McNulty
b. 1904
d. 1982
Daniel
b. 1903
d. 1981
James P.
b. 1905
d. 1990
John
b. 1908
d. 1944
m.
JoAnn Kowaleski
b. 1911
d. 2002
Daniel M.
b. 1932
Arthur, Patricia, Kathleen (dc'd.), Rita, Daniel, Mary Duffy, John, James, Joan
Arthur J., Jr.
b. 1935
Arthur J., III, Karen, Michael, Susan
Timothy
b. 1937
Kathleen, Margaret, Bridget, Timothy, Cara
Patrick
b. 1939
Patrick, Joseph, Theresa, Christopher, Thomas, Brian, Monica
John
b. 1939
Sean, Mary JoAnn, Alice, James (dc'd), Peter, Matthew
Patricia
b. 1933
Margie
b. 1935

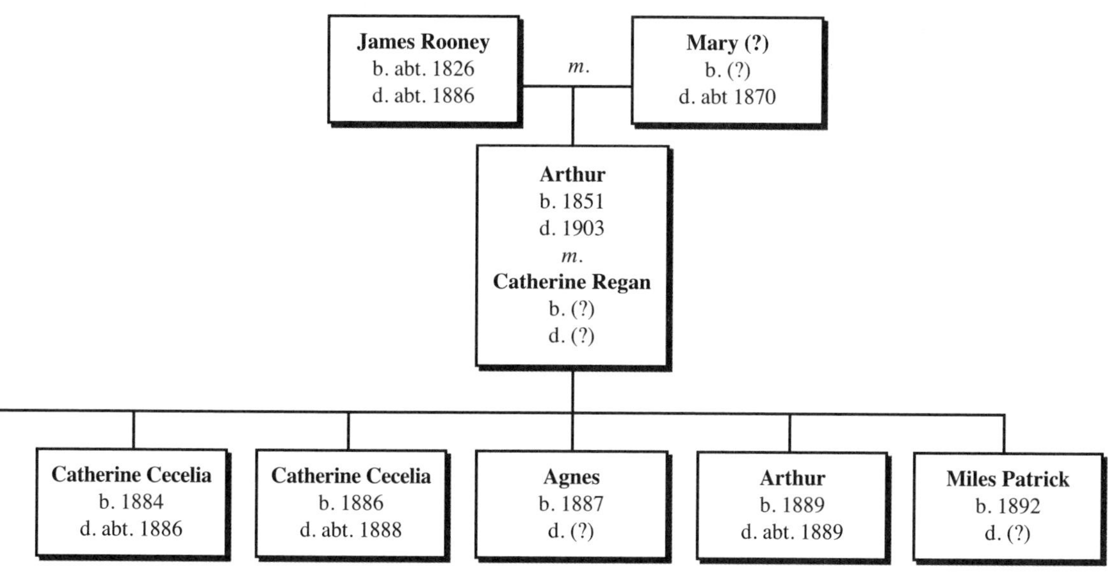

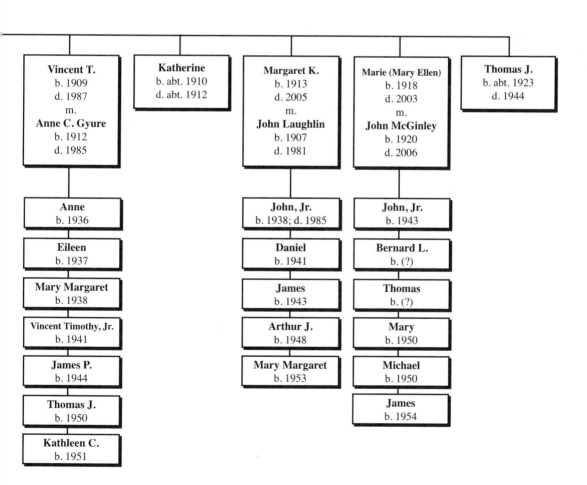

Vincent T.
b. 1909
d. 1987
m.
Anne C. Gyure
b. 1912
d. 1985

Anne
b. 1936

Eileen
b. 1937

Mary Margaret
b. 1938

Vincent Timothy, Jr.
b. 1941

James P.
b. 1944

Thomas J.
b. 1950

Kathleen C.
b. 1951

Katherine
b. abt. 1910
d. abt. 1912

Margaret K.
b. 1913
d. 2005
m.
John Laughlin
b. 1907
d. 1981

John, Jr.
b. 1938; d. 1985

Daniel
b. 1941

James
b. 1943

Arthur J.
b. 1948

Mary Margaret
b. 1953

Marie (Mary Ellen)
b. 1918
d. 2003
m.
John McGinley
b. 1920
d. 2006

John, Jr.
b. 1943

Bernard L.
b. (?)

Thomas
b. (?)

Mary
b. 1950

Michael
b. 1950

James
b. 1954

Thomas J.
b. abt. 1923
d. 1944

Acknowledgements

Contributing Artists

Merv Corning, The Preeminent Sports Artist
Dan DeBonis
George Gaadt, *www.gaadtstudio.com*
Dino Guarino, *www.dinoguarino.com*
Denny Karchner, *www.karchnerwesternart.com*
Kathy Rooney, Art Director & Cover Design, *www.krooney.net*

Support

Tula Corning (Mrs.) supplied encouragement and allowed use of Merv's art work.
Mike Fabus, Steelers Photographer, photographs
Clark Gardner, Transportation
Dee Herrod, Our secretary and #1 reason this book is a reality after 12 years.
Keith Maiden, Geyer Printing
Maureen Maier, Finance
Jim O'Brien, Self-Publishing Advisor
Joe Polk, Web Design
Mike Rooney, Interactive Telecommunications
Rob Ruck & Maggie Patterson, for sharing research from their Art Rooney book.
The Pittsburgh Steelers, for the players who gave permission to use their images.

Readers

Tom Atkins, Actor, "The Chief"
Jack Butler, #80
Larry Deer, Teammate at North Catholic High School
Sean Doherty, R.I.P.
Dr. Robert Friday, PH.D.
Carl Hughes, former *Pittsburgh Press* Sports Columnist
Kay Rooney, Invaluable support.
Kathy Rooney, Art Direction
John Troan, Editorial Assistance
Rev. Raymond Utz, Cousin
Jeff Weber, Statistics

Art Rooney and his Hope Harvey players at the Hope Fire Station, North Side

(Drawing by Kathy Rooney)

Roy McHugh

The spare elegance of supreme craftsmanship marked Roy McHugh's column writing for the *Pittsburgh Press* in the second half of the 20th century. McHugh is a native of Iowa and graduate of Coe College, where he cultivated a love of both sports and language. McHugh became both sports editor and columnist-at-large during the "City of Champions" era in Pittsburgh's distinguished sports history. None of the heroes of that era were any more distinguished than the quiet, meticulous columnist who chronicled their triumphs and foibles. He traveled with Muhammad Ali, contributed with distinction to national magazines, and his humanity and insight was indispensable to the dozens of American journalists who've examined the life and death of Roberto Clemente, Art Rooney, Sr., Billy Conn, and many more.

– Gene Collier, Sports Columnist
Pittsburgh Post-Gazette

Contents

Part One: The First Hundred Years

Part Two: Bit Player 1956-1965

Part Three: A Seat at the Table 1965-1969

Part Four: A New Broom 1970-1973

Part Five: Full Speed Ahead
1974-1980

Part Six: Winding Down

Preface

The idea for this book was Mort Sharnik's. A versatile and knowledgeable *Sports Illustrated* writer, Mort was doing research for a story about my father and his football team, the Steelers, the day I met him. This was in 1968, when the Steelers were still occupying outgrown quarters in the Roosevelt Hotel. I took Mort into the Sylvan Room restaurant, and there we found my Uncle Jim having coffee. His droll observations and unique way of speaking in a confidential undertone fascinated Mort. From the Sylvan Room, Mort came with me to the small, drab, windowless office from which I directed the Steelers' scouting organization, and Dr. Art Sekay, the team dentist, paid us a visit. Blunt and outspoken, he made as vivid an impression on Mort as Uncle Jim had. Later in an adjoining office, we encountered two old friends of my dad's from the North Side. Dago Sam Leone was an animated story teller, steadfast horse player, and amiable eccentric, Patsy Scanlon a battered ex-prizefighter whose flower store in the downtown business district was a front for his bookmaking operation. Their off-the-cuff reminiscences kept Mort entertained for most of the next hour.

As soon as we were by ourselves, he said, "Art, you have to write these things down for posterity, or at any rate for your children and grandchildren. Get the whole cast of characters down on paper."

I considered this good advice, but I didn't act on it. Mort kept after me. He kept after me for more than twenty years before I started to write.

Gradually it became an obsession. I attempted, as Mort had urged me, to put everything down. It would be the story, through my own eyes, of Art Rooney and his clan, the chronicle of his life and times. Off and on, with no clear notion of where I was going, I recorded memories pretty much as they occurred to me. I wrote in longhand, filling several dozen voluminous journals. My prose style, two friends who looked at samples of it told me, was stream-of-consciousness. "You write like James Joyce," they said, not intending it as flattery. They meant that in Joyce's great novel "Ulysses" there were countless digressions, and that I digress, too. We write alike in the sense that an elementary-school football team and the Super Bowl champions might both line up in the T-formation.

If any publisher was ever to see my manuscript, it needed editing, and Roy McHugh, a former *Pittsburgh Press* columnist, offered to help. "I'm not touchy about having my words changed," I told him, "so rewrite with a free hand." He preserved as much of my raconteur's voice – a blend of North Side Irish and Pittsburghese – as he could. The stories are mine, or as I heard them, but my collaborator's newspaper background and familiarity with the subject matter enabled him, in certain cases, to add details. The judgments I make and the content of the personal portraits I include are mine alone.

We pulled together several different narrative threads. There is family legend in the text, and some anecdotal history of the old North Side. There are race-track stories and football stories. It's a memoir, so a lot of it's about me. I write of the players and coaches I knew, of scouting trips and scouts, of the drafts I prepared for and the arguments they triggered.

I reconstruct long-ago conversations as I remember them or as others remembered them. Direct quotes make for easier reading, and I quote people directly when I can, but I am not about to pretend that every quote in the book is one hundred percent verbatim. That would be an impossibility, so in places where no harm would result I take some creative license. Let me state for the record, however, that my powers of recall are above average and nowhere have I intentionally changed the substance of what anybody said.

It is customary for an author to thank the people who've read and commented on parts of the manuscript, or all of it, and I do so. I did not seek permission to name them. The computer know-how of my secretary, Dee Herrod, was indispensable. One final acknowledgement: My good fortune in being Art Rooney's son is the only reason I ever could have thought of getting a project like this under way and the only reason I could finish it.

Daniel Rooney

Part One: The First Hundred Years

Margaret Murray Rooney

Chapter 1

Forebears

From the seacoast manufacturing town of Newry, in Northern Ireland, James and Mary Rooney, steerage passengers on a sailing ship, crossed the Atlantic Ocean to Canada during the Irish potato famine near the end of the 1840s. The young married couple settled in Montreal, where James Rooney, who had worked with hot metal in a Newry iron forge, became a millwright and where Arthur Rooney, an only child, was born in 1851. Over the course of the next fifty years, Arthur Rooney had a son named Daniel and Daniel Rooney had a son named Arthur. This Arthur Rooney was my father, the focus of these memoirs.

I'm indebted to his official biographers, Rob Ruck and Maggie Patterson, for what little I know about the personal history of my nineteenth-century forebears. When the first Arthur Rooney was 21, his parents returned to the British Isles, taking him along – not to Ireland, but to Wales, where the iron industry was flourishing. In a town called Ebbw Vale, father and son landed jobs in a mill. Ebbw Vale (pronounce it "Ebba") is a place of special importance to the Rooneys. It was where Arthur met and married an Irish girl named Catherine Regan and where Daniel Rooney, my grandfather, was born.

Not that Roman Catholics like the Rooneys were popular in Ebbw Vale. When they marched off to Mass, Dan Rooney in later life would recollect, their Protestant neighbors bombarded them with stones. Imminent hard times compounded the family's miseries. During a phase-out of iron production – the age of steel had begun – James and Arthur Rooney lost their jobs. Then, not long afterward, Mary Rooney died, and, for Arthur Rooney, that was enough. Back to Canada he sailed in 1876 with a family that now included one more son and a daughter. James Rooney, who had taken another wife, remained in Ebbw Vale.

Arthur Rooney's trail for the next few years is hard to follow. By 1879 he had somehow made his way to Youngstown, Ohio, and was working again at the occupation he had learned in Wales, puddling iron. Rooney folklore has it that he walked across the border and into the United States alone and without a passport. How, then, did he manage to reassemble his family? On that point, there is no information.

As a puddler and then a roller, Arthur Rooney worked ten, sometimes twelve, hours a day. He worked in debilitating heat at a job that took know-how, endurance, and strength. Puddlers and rollers supervised their own crews, crews of as many as a dozen men. By the standards of the times, they were highly paid – the aristocrats of the working class, Ruck and Patterson call them. And yet for all their specialized skills, they were no more immune than common laborers to the ups and downs of the economy. When in one town the economy tanked, Arthur Rooney would move on, and in 1884 his wanderings brought him to Pittsburgh.

He was 33. There were now four children, with two more to come. For extra money, Arthur and Catherine Rooney took in boarders. They lived on the South Side and bought property there, a lot and a house costing seven thousand dollars. They owned a smaller plot of land in Mansfield, now Carnegie. They were frugal and persevering. They believed that a penny saved was a penny earned. And they were prospering.

But then a major depression hit. Once more Arthur Rooney was jobless. His union, the Amalgamated Association of Iron, Steel, and Tin Workers, had gone on strike, and there was violence in the offing. Henry Clay Frick, the manager of Andrew Carnegie's Homestead steel works, hired Pinkerton detectives to protect the scabs who took the place of the strikers. Arriving by barge at four o'clock in the morning on July 6, 1892, three hundred armed Pinkertons attempted an amphibious landing at the mill site on the Monongahela River. The strikers resisted with rifles, revolvers, and sticks of dynamite. Ten union men and three Pinkertons lost their lives. Outnumbered, the Pinkertons surrendered, but Governor Robert E. Pattison called out the state militia. Eight thousand strong, they kept the mill open, and the strikers eventually gave in. Henry Clay Frick had broken the union.

Arthur Rooney's role in all this can only be guessed at. Between 1892 and 1896 he worked at a series of low-paying menial jobs. He sold his Mansfield property and his house on the South Side. In this second transaction, there was more than meets the eye. Michael Concannon, his daughter Bridget's husband, bought the house from Arthur for the original purchase price, seven thousand dollars, and transferred the deed to Catherine, Arthur's wife. My interpretation is that he thus shielded Arthur from his creditors.

Somehow or other, Arthur was sufficiently well off by 1896 to buy a saloon on the South Side – to be specific, on East Carson Street. (Even that far back, there was no better place to open a saloon.) His new business seemed depression-proof, for in good times or bad, men drank. But, with housing scarce – housing for immigrant steelworkers – the Rooneys continued to take in boarders. There were five altogether and they lived in a single room. They worked in shifts and they slept in shifts, making way for one another in what beds were provided or maybe even doubling up.

Four of the Rooneys' children, all but the three oldest, were still at home. Catherine Rooney did the cooking and the housework. She did the laundry, hand-scrubbing her boarders' filthy work clothes. In the daytime during the summer months, Catherine and two of her daughters fetched laundry water, cooking water, and drinking water from the polluted Mon River. They carried it to the house, several hundred yards distant, in buckets. The mills, Ruck and Patterson tell us, made such prodigal use of water during their peak hours that none was available for the taps of the South Side's resident population.

Such details are illuminating, but not much else is chronicled about these first of the Rooneys to settle in Pittsburgh. Arthur, according to Ruck and Patterson, was wiry and probably muscular. We know that he had a red beard; we know that he rode a white horse, on which he sometimes led the St. Patrick's Day parade in downtown Pittsburgh; we know that he had a nickname – Cap, its derivation obscure. Besides the beard, the horse, and the nickname, he had a shotgun, and he used it, the story goes, in a confrontation on a bridge. In the words of my uncle John, one of Arthur Rooney's grandsons, he met his adversary, "a notorious scoundrel," in the dead of night. Shots rang out. There were flashes from the guns. "Only Grandfather Rooney walked off the bridge," Uncle John would intone.

Could the "notorious scoundrel" have been a Pinkerton detective? Recall that Arthur belonged to the Amalgamated Association of Iron, Steel, and Tin Workers. One of his sons, I have heard, kept a shotgun he described to younger relatives as an heirloom, explaining, "We used this to shoot the Pinks." Was it the weapon that felled the notorious scoundrel? We'll never know.

In Uncle John's version of what happened, Western Pennsylvania was too hot for Arthur after the gun fight. Whether his enemy on the bridge lived or died, Uncle John could not say; what he did say was that, one step ahead of whatever retribution may have been coming, Arthur Rooney left the country, taking temporary refuge in Ireland. Ruck and Patterson point out that no confirmation exists for this tale. Believe it or don't; the choice is yours.

The Salt of the Earth

Arthur Rooney died in 1903 of either typhoid fever or pneumonia. He may have been 51 or he may have been 52 – for that time and place a normal lifespan. Although my knowledge of Red Beard is sketchy and for the most part undocumented, I saw his signature once on the deed to his Carson Street property. What I remembered about it was the calligraphy. His hand was unsure and he wrote in an old-fashioned script. I had the feeling that his name was the only thing he could write. His wife Catherine signed with an X. As the years went by, his sons and daughters came to believe that the property they inherited was worth a great deal of money. There were squabbles over what to do with it until Dan – my grandfather – put an end to the rhetoric by selling this piece of land for a sum he divided with the others.

It amounted to very little.

In 1903, Dan Rooney was 29. He had worked a year or two in the mills, had been a cook on a riverboat (Pittsburgh to Cincinnati and back), and, like his father before him, had opened a saloon of his own. It was in Coulter, or Coultersville, a Monongahela Valley coal patch near McKeesport. And it was there that he had married a coal miner's daughter, Margaret Murray, called Maggie – red-haired, pretty, and petite.

In their saloon, which was also a boarding house, the same as old Arthur's, Maggie did most of the work. She cooked and baked, specializing in bread – crusty on the outside, soft and white on the inside. She picked wild berries for her homemade jellies and jam. She scrubbed and cleaned for the boarders; she prepared ham sandwiches for the saloon clientele.

In a room above the bar on January 27, 1901, Arthur Joseph Rooney, my father, came into the world. Shortly afterward, Maggie's mother, who was 43, gave birth to a daughter. How unusual was it, I ask, to acquire both a son and a sister just hours apart?

Around Coultersville, alas, the coal was now all but mined out, so the Rooneys picked up and moved to Monaca. Dan and Maggie again became the owners of a boarding house and saloon, naming it the Colonial Hotel for a nearby steel mill, and in 1903, also in a room above the bar, their second son, Dan Junior, was born.

1903 must have been the year that Dan Rooney, Sr., got into trouble of some kind. The details are to this day obscure. At any rate, suddenly and mysteriously, he sold his hotel and left Monaca, sustaining himself with part of the $16,000 sales price and leaving the remainder with Maggie. His hideout, I'm guessing, was in St. Louis, or near there. I say that because my father, years later, recalled a trip to the 1904 St. Louis World's Fair with his mother and baby brother for a family reunion.

Maggie and the kids were making their home then with Catherine, Dan's mother, in a boarding house she ran in the Beaver Valley town of Crescent City, where Maggie helped with the work and gave birth in 1905 to a third son, James Patrick. The date of her husband's return is unclear, but by 1906 or 1907 the Rooneys were together once more. They lived in a rented house in the heavily Irish Pittsburgh neighborhood of Homewood. Dan Senior, struggling to pay off his debts, clerked in a paint store. Soon there were two more sons to feed and clothe – John, born in 1908, and Vincent, born in 1910. A daughter named Katherine, born in 1911, died at the age of two.

The big turning point for the Rooneys came when Maggie's parents, Mike and Mary Ann Murray, bought a three-story wood and brick building at the corner of Corey Street and General Robinson Street on Pittsburgh's North Side for six thousand dollars and sold it for the same amount to their daughter, who had learned to scrimp and save. The year was 1913. On the first floor of this building, Dan Senior, going back to the trade he knew best, opened a "bar and café." On the second and third floors were the living quarters.

In a very short time, there was still another addition to the family – a daughter named Margaret for her mother. Then along came Marie, born in 1914, and, belatedly, one last son, Thomas Joseph, born in 1919. By 1920, the rooms above the bar and café were crowded to the eaves. There was the ten-member immediate family; there was Helen Ward, an adopted daughter; there were Maggie's two sisters, Gertrude and Stella Murray. Besides these permanent residents, there were other assorted relatives, coming and going, and always a few castaways of the most helpless and pitiable kind – the orphaned children of friends.

Hygienic conditions in the early years of the twentieth century created a steady flow of orphans. And the Rooneys – Dan and Maggie – were willing when called upon to give them safe harbor.

These forebears of ours, my aunt Margaret used to say, invoking a phrase from the Bible (Matthew 5:13), were "the salt of the earth."

Maggie Rooney was notable for her strength and determination, Dan for his clear-eyed probity. "He was free of guile," a friend named George Quinlan once said, "and he called a spade a spade."

Of the men in Maggie's family – the Murrays – there were some who dug coal and others, like Maggie's father, who tested for gas, going deep into the mines' lower passages. A Murray who preferred the wide open spaces enlisted in the Army and fought in the Indian wars of the Western frontier. Wild Indians, he may have thought, were not as dangerous as coal mines. Decades after they had left Coultersville, an old-timer from the area described the Murrays as "gentlemen, all of them," and the Rooneys as "a pack of hooligans."

If the first Arthur Rooney ever worked in a mine, it was probably in Wales. His son Dan might have known, but Dan recollected next to nothing of Wales and seldom mentioned the place. Being interviewed once for an insurance policy, he was asked where he was born. "Wales," he said reluctantly. The insurance man put down his pen. "Dan," he said, "you've been telling people in Pittsburgh all these years that you're Irish. You're not. You're a Welshman."

"Look," said Dan patiently. "If you had a cat, and the cat had kittens in an oven, would you call the kittens biscuits?"

The insurance man dropped the subject.

Rooted

The First Ward on the North Side – everybody omitted the numerical designation and called it simply "The Ward" – was where Dan Rooney at last put down roots. His sons and daughters and grandchildren called him Pop. In the family quarters above the saloon, my father – AJR from now on – shared a room in the attic with his brother Dan Junior. Waking up on a cold winter morning, they would often find snow on their blankets, snow that had blown in through cracks in the walls. On the grandstand roof at neighboring Exposition Park, which had been the Pittsburgh Pirates' home field until 1909, there were ornamental steeples. One day a hard wind blew a steeple off the roof and it fell through a window into the barroom.

At least twice a year the Allegheny River would flood, sending residents of The Ward to their high and dry second stories to be rescued by skiff or rowboat. One time during a flood, AJR and his brother Dan were rowing across the site of Exposition Park in a canoe. A kid named Squawker Mullen was with them, a kid who could never sit still. When Squawker tried to move from one end of the canoe to the other, it overturned, dumping the three boys into the water. They started swimming for the unsubmerged part of the grandstand on the third-base side of the field. Squawker and Dan made it easily; AJR was wearing boots and an overcoat and only saved himself from drowning with a last desperate lunge.

There were no public swimming pools when AJR was a boy. Everybody swam in the rivers. On the banks, there were roped-off areas with bath houses – makeshift structures where people could take a shower. Swimmers who crossed from shore to shore – they did it to show off – were playing dice with their lives. Boat and barge traffic was heavy and the current was swift. Every summer, AJR often recalled, a friend or acquaintance would drown.

No women were allowed in the Rooneys' bar. Typically on Saturday night a fight would break out, with Pop in the middle of it, restoring peace. Afterward, he would drag himself upstairs and change from his torn, bloody shirt into a fresh one. The troublemakers, he always said, were the crazy Irish from Galway. "Go over there some day," Pop urged his sons, "and find out what makes them tick." To Pop, it remained a dark mystery.

When Pop was new to the North Side, people warned him about the neighborhood bully, a man they predicted would tear up the barroom and scare away all the respectable drinkers. Resolutely, Pop went into training. He shadow-boxed; he lifted weights. At last the bully appeared – and at the sight of him Pop could only laugh. "Why, you greasy bum!" he shouted, using his epithet for unsavory characters. "I've thrown you out of my other bars, and I'll do it again." The greasy bum saved him the trouble. He left without further encouragement, and the First Ward from then on regarded Pop as a man to be reckoned with.

Uncle Jim liked to talk about Pop's night watchman – a big, mean German police dog. Jim described the animal as "nobody's friend." Even the Rooney kids were careful to be in the house before Pop closed the barroom and turned the dog loose. This, of course, pleased their mother. "Anything important," she always said, "can be done before midnight, and should be. After that hour, you're up to no good."

In search of a more upscale environment for the family, Pop bought a house in Manchester, and there he came down with smallpox. The house was quarantined; Pop's bed was moved to the attic; his mother Catherine nursed him back to health. Obeying doctor's orders – up to a point – she burned all his clothes except a fine pair of woolen long johns, which she took to the back yard and soaked in boiling water. For the rest of his life, Pop's nose was heavily scarred by the pox.

The Rooneys and the Murrays, it seemed to me, were different in temperament. Rooneys tended to be outgoing and flamboyant, Murrays much less so. No one could be as outgoing as AJR, and yet in my opinion, anyway, he was more like his mother Maggie than his father. For one thing, she believed very deeply in the Roman Catholic religion, and so did AJR. He told me that once when his mother was seriously ill, he prayed for her recovery in St. Peter's Church from 6 o'clock in the morning until 7:30 or 8 at night. He was 15 years old, I think he said.

Maggie Rooney hoped fervently that AJR would be in the church choir, and from her household funds she gave him the price of a tryout – fifty cents. The trouble was that he lacked a qualification thought to be necessary: he couldn't sing. When the choirmaster conveyed this to him, AJR replied that he was not going to quit. He'd be letting his mother down and wasting her fifty cents. There was only one thing for the choirmaster to do – pay hush money. He returned the fifty cents, AJR faced the fact that he was no John McCormack, and the choir got back on key.

The performance art in which AJR excelled was not music, but sports. He was spending most of his time now at a playground in the neighborhood, punting and passing a football or in baseball season learning to hit and field. He had a natural aptitude for sports of all kinds, and sports were to be his main occupation from boyhood into maturity.

The pattern of his life had taken shape.

Fun And Games

AJR worked at sports with more determination and energy than any of the other boys from The Ward. Dan and Jim were good at sports, too, John and Vince less so. Tom, the youngest brother, born when his parents were past 40, belonged to a different era. When Tom was growing up, the family lived on Perrysville Avenue. They were still North Siders, but in those days suburban North Siders.

Baseball games between AJR's team and teams from other neighborhoods frequently turned into free-for-alls. In one such altercation, AJR and his friends got the worst of it. They were the visiting team, but a return game was scheduled in The Ward, and their opponents had the audacity to show up, or it may have been more like simplemindedness. As they trooped onto the field, AJR – perched on a fence post like Cecil B. DeMille directing a battle scene in a movie – singled out the dirtiest fighters among them. He would shout, "There's one!" or "Get that guy!" – the cue for his teammates to attack in a group. They sent the enemy home badly mauled.

AJR was one of the baseball players from The Ward who had dinner one night with Harry K. Thaw. In 1906, Harry K. Thaw, the demented heir to a Pittsburgh industrial fortune, had murdered the architect Stanford White at his table in the rooftop restaurant of Madison Square Garden, the New York landmark building White had designed. It seems that White had seduced Thaw's wife, an artist's model from Tarentum named Evelyn Nesbit, when she was single. At his trial, Thaw pleaded insanity, escaping prison but not confinement to a mental institution. Now he was back home on North Lincoln Avenue, where Pittsburgh's earliest millionaires lived. His mother, still believing he could lead a normal life, had grasped at the idea that an evening's conversation with some healthy teenage athletes might be good for him. She could not have been more mistaken. Before, during, and after dinner, AJR reported, Thaw sat mute, inter-acting with no one.

As the Rooney boys outgrew their adolescence, they became interested in such gambling games as craps. A pair of dice and a blanket were all that was needed to play, and the blanket was optional. Dan, by common consent, ordinarily served as the pit boss. If the dice went off the blanket, Dan made the call.

One day an outsider organized a game. By the standards of The Ward, big money was at stake. Dan, who'd been hurt playing football, came hobbling around on crutches just to observe, and a state of tension quickly developed. The outsider, as it happened, was a "greasy bum" – in the parlance of the Rooneys a "bad guy." AJR had a way of distinguishing between bad guys and tough guys. A tough guy, he said, wasn't necessarily a bad guy. You could be a bad guy or a tough guy or both. This particular bad guy was both. He immediately let Dan know that it was "his" game – that he was making the calls. And, no matter how obviously wrong they were, the calls favored himself every time. Finally Dan said something. The "greasy bum" continued to cheat. Again Dan spoke up.

"What are you going to do about it? You're on crutches," the bum said scornfully.

So Dan let one of his crutches fall to the ground and used the other crutch to beat the hell out of the guy.

According to family friend George Quinlan, Dan could be "a one-man riot." No one in The Ward was more feared, but his brother Jim got to thinking he could handle Dan. It was arranged that they were to settle the issue at Phipps Playground. At the appointed hour, a good-sized crowd was on hand. Jim, approaching the area cleared for combat, with enthusiastic backers egging him on, began to lose confidence. The sight of Dan calmly waiting unnerved him completely. He turned around and bolted for home.

It was Dan Senior – Pop – who encouraged the boys to fight. "Do you know what he got them for Christmas?" asked Quinlan. "Boxing gloves and a punching bag. And, boy, could they punch and, boy, could they fight – even Duke, who never weighed more than 120 pounds." Duke was Vince, the No. 5 son.

AJR boxed in the amateurs. He was runner-up twice – in different weight divisions – for the National AAU championship and won an international tournament in Canada. AJR sometimes said that he qualified for the 1920 Olympic team but passed up his chance to compete in the Antwerp games in order to play baseball at Georgetown University. In researching their book, Rob Ruck and Maggie Patterson found that, though the Olympic regional trials were held in Pittsburgh, AJR did not participate. He had beaten two fighters on the team that went to Antwerp, Sammy Mosberg and Frank Cassidy, and this may have accounted for the confusion in his mind.

KR

Art Rooney, Boxer
(Drawing by Kathy Rooney)

Mosberg, a New Yorker, was the gold medalist in Antwerp at 135 pounds. After he returned to the United States, AJR beat him again. My brother Tim suggests that the real reason AJR did not enter the trials was for fear of raising questions about his amateur status. Since the age of 15, he'd been playing semi-pro baseball for money. No such reservations kept him out of the 1921 national amateur tournament in Boston. In 1920 he had been the runner-up as a lightweight. This time he boxed as a welterweight and lost again in the title bout. Dan, a light-heavyweight, got to the semi-finals before losing.

Traveling carnivals had house fighters back then, hired professionals who would take on all comers from the audience. For every round a challenger lasted, the carnival paid him either a dollar, three dollars, or five dollars, depending on the owner's generosity. AJR's problem, and Dan's too, was making certain the house fighter lasted. "Those carnival guys could handle a farmer, all right, but they were very ordinary fighters," AJR told Myron Cope in an interview taped when he was 69 years old. Once when Squawker Mullen, a national amateur champion at 110 pounds, was getting the worst of it from a carnival guy, Dan, Squawker's second, "reached up over the ropes," said AJR, "and hit the fellow – nailed him like you'd nail a bird in the air." It started a "hey rube" – carnival terminology for a riot – and there was no more boxing that night after the tent came down.

One of the carnival boxers the Rooney brothers took on was KO Circus. KO's manager – a bit of a thief – paid him off in one-dollar bills. KO had a poor grasp of currency values and thought that five one-dollar bills were obviously worth more than one ten-dollar bill. The manager – I forget his name – parted grudgingly with one-dollar bills, ten-dollar bills, or bills of any other denomination. A dollar was all he offered to challengers from the audience for each round they lasted with KO. For AJR and Dan, keeping KO on his feet for three rounds, the maximum number permitted, hardly seemed worth the effort, but they worked at it doggedly. They returned to the carnival night after night and the dollar bills added up. KO's manager couldn't stand the sight of them.

And then, to his chagrin, they started showing up with Jim. Like AJR and Dan, Jim could punch. George Quinlan always said he could punch from any angle. "I saw him stretch a guy once when he was flat on his back," Quinlan declared. "The other guy had Jim down and had fallen on top of him, and Jim reached up and knocked him out."

With KO, Jim took it easy – his brothers had warned him not to spoil a good thing. The Rooneys were now costing KO's manager nine dollars a day instead of six. Clearly something had to be done. And cutting his losses, he decided, was the answer. In search of help, he went to Dan Senior and made him a proposition. "I'll give you six bucks a day for your boys to split up if they promise to stay away from the carnival," he said, adding, "It was bad enough when Art and Dan were going three rounds with KO every night, but now they've got Jim doing it, too. I'm paying those kids NOT to fight."

That being the case, he was willing to pay them a little bit less for not even pretending to fight, but easy money in small amounts never satisfied AJR. If his fists were to be his fortune, he'd turn professional. He joined a stable of boxers under the management of an Australian – barnstormers going through Pittsburgh. They were fighting their way across America; when they reached the West Coast they would all board a ship for Australia.

AJR didn't get far. Despite having won all his fights on the tour, he'd begun to suspect that the ring as a career was not for him. He could see himself twenty years in the future – a washed-up ex-pug with cauliflower ears, scar tissue, and brain damage. By most accounts, including his own, he fought like a bulldog, wading into his opponent and taking a lot of punches. He won on sheer persistence, wearing the other guy down. He was game; he was tough; he was strong; he packed a wallop. But others before him who'd been game, tough and strong, and could hit hard, were walking around on their heels.

Before the barnstormers reached the West Coast, a woman on the tour, the wife of the best Australian fighter, took him aside. "You come from a good family," she said. "You're educated. There'll be opportunities for you in life. Go home."

AJR listened. He took the next train back to Pittsburgh still undefeated, neither better off nor worse off than he'd been on the day he left, and without regrets.

Among themselves, the Rooneys boxed for recreation, and AJR, with his advantage in years and experience, punched the others around at will. Sometimes, though, there were sweet, heady moments of revenge. Once in later life, when AJR was standing with his hands in his pockets and a cigar in his mouth, he said to Vince, who had had several beers, "Why don't you go home? You're drunk." Vince wound up and slugged AJR, knocking him down. By the time he got up, Vince was running for his life, a block away.

AJR won his matches with Dan until Dan got to be nearly six feet tall and substantially outweighed AJR, who was maybe 5 feet 8. After that, according to George Quinlan, Dan started "lathering" AJR, who said to him finally, "Dan, it's disgraceful, two brothers fighting like this. We've got to stop." And Dan said, "I'm just now beginning to enjoy it."

Dan licked a street fighter called the toughest and meanest in The Ward. This guy was so strong the "detention boxes" used by the police to hold unruly prisoners until the paddy wagon arrived couldn't contain him. Arrested one night for drunkenness and placed in the nearest box, he knocked it over and broke the door open, but he was no match for Dan.

It surprised people to learn that Dan was religious. One time after a baseball game, a few of Dan's teammates informed him that they intended to visit a whorehouse in Steubenville, notorious for its red-light district. Dan, full of evangelical fervor, tried to talk them out of it. "You'll be committing a mortal sin," he uselessly warned them.

"That was when I knew he was going to be a priest," said the man who told me the story.

Learning The Ropes

AJR, meanwhile, was developing political skills. In Pop's saloon, he got acquainted with the ward bosses who gathered there and started running errands for them. AJR had street smarts. At first he could get small things done and then he could get bigger things done. In some ways he was strangely naive. As an old man, he said that in his younger days he'd had no idea that it was breaking the law to vote more than once in an election.

Many people in the early 1900s voted for the last person to "duke" them – which is to say give them money – as they entered the polling place. This was a time when there weren't any welfare checks, when there weren't any Social Security checks. If you needed help, you got it from your relatives, or the church, or the ward chairman. Cars and drivers were scarce, so in case of a death in the family the politicians supplied them. Thanks to the politicians, the bereaved had a ride to the cemetery.

AJR not only rounded up drivers but did some driving himself, making friends. He took care to remain on extra good terms with the family of Kathleen McNulty, his future wife, in part because the McNultys owned an automobile agency and were willing to let him have cars.

Among his regular drivers was a small-time gambler called Cocky O'Malley. As a sideline, O'Malley sold pedigreed dogs to people who wanted pets. He had an eye affliction of some kind, but could recognize quality in dogs. If he spied a valuable pooch on the way to the graveyard – dogs at that time still ran loose – he would stop, pick it up, toss it into the back seat with the mourners, and drive on. This callousness in matters pertaining to mortuary etiquette was by no means exceptional in the drivers recruited by AJR. Once the burial service was over, they would break all speed limits in their haste to be on time for the party that followed every funeral, knowing how freely the liquor would flow.

The police in The Ward respected AJR for his political clout and athletic ability, which was helpful to him sometimes when trouble occurred. On Federal Street one cloudy afternoon, he stopped to show concern for a friend who was seated on the sidewalk and holding his ankle. Two strangers were standing over him, a man and a woman, the woman tightly clutching a folded umbrella. AJR asked what had happened. His friend explained that he and the other guy had been fighting. In the midst of the fracas he'd fallen down, and he suspected his ankle was broken. AJR looked inquiringly at the other guy, who ordered him to mind his own business. "Or I'll take care of you the same way," he added.

Cheerfully, AJR invited him to try. They squared off, and at this point, lifting her umbrella, the woman brought it down on AJR's head.

"Don't do that again," he said.

And she did it again.

AJR accepted no abuse from anyone of either sex. "Well, you've had your last warning," he said. Feinting a punch at the man, he "crossed over," as he put it, "and hit the broad right on the button." Down she went. He then belted out her boyfriend.

Moments later a Black Maria pulled up and the cops jumped out. Recognizing AJR, one of them said, "Art, what's going on here?"

"These two beat up my pal," he answered, indicating the pair he had flattened. The cops threw them into the paddy wagon and gave the man with the broken leg a ride to the hospital.

Not every policeman knew that AJR rated special treatment. Once when his big new car ran out of gas on the Sixth Street Bridge, a traffic cop berated him for failing to keep an eye on the gauge.

"Maybe you could do better," AJR suggested.

"I sure could, you dumb hick," the cop said.

AJR got out of his car. "Then do it," he said, and walked across the bridge to the North Side and home.

That night he received a telephone call. The police had delivered the car, unticketed and filled with gas, to his father's saloon.

He was getting to be a man of some importance.

Oddballs

Grandma Rooney – Maggie – had a sister whose name was Stella. My mother described her as "very pretty, with fine features, a nice figure, and red hair." In the personal column of a Pittsburgh newspaper, a man with the Anglicized name of Jackson announced that he was looking for a bride, and Stella responded to his ad. The man was Slavic; he was a Communist, or perhaps a Socialist; he did not believe in a deity.

Atheism was hard for an Irish-Catholic girl like Stella Murray to swallow, but she and Jackson were married. They had children. Jackson was opposed to Catholic baptism or to any other kind of baptism, so Stella made secret arrangements with a priest. At one baptism, my Uncle Dan was the godfather. The baby, christened Anne, grew up to be a well-known stage and screen actress.

Anne Jackson's father had a great deal to say about the "pie-in-the-sky" Catholic religion, all of it negative. Returning from a family funeral one day, he ridiculed Christian burial. This was too much for Pop Rooney, who proceeded to give him hell – holy hell, Pop may have thought. "I am what I am and you are what you are, so keep your big mouth shut," Pop shouted. There are differing accounts as to what happened next. Either Jackson took a punch at Pop or Pop took a punch at Jackson. In any case, if it was Pop who threw the punch – and I believe that to be true – he had nothing but sore knuckles to show for it. In this scenario, Jackson, it seems, was in the front seat of an automobile while they were yammering at each other and Pop was standing just outside. And, unaccountably, Pop failed to notice until after he delivered the punch that Jackson had rolled up the window.

Eventually, the Jacksons all moved to New York City, where Anne got her start in the theater. Grandma Rooney, who never said anything negative about anybody, made her brother-in-law the only exception, pronouncing him "a bad one." My mother gave Jackson higher marks. She said he was kind and considerate, but my mother did not really know him.

Another relative my elders always talked about was Pop's brother Jack, a man who had money enough to sponsor amateur baseball teams. Well past middle age, he was still unmarried. He took a liking to AJR, the best baseball player in the family, and it seemed a foregone conclusion that AJR would be provided for in Jack's will. But Jack met a woman named Bobbie Smith, previously married and twenty years younger than he was, and she allowed him to sweep her off her feet. Jack proposed; they went to the altar. Not long after the wedding, Jack broke his neck in a fall down some steps. The injury was fatal, and Bobbie, of course, inherited his money.

I met Bobbie once. It was in Kaufmann's or Horne's, where I had gone with my mother to shop. A woman said hello to us and my mother said hello and they exchanged a few pleasantries. When the woman went on her way my mother said to me, "That was Bobbie Smith, who was married to Uncle Jack." The Bobbie I met in the department store that day had a bubbling, agreeable personality.

Pop's most colorful, headstrong, and irresponsible brother was Uncle Myles. Margaret Laughlin, his niece, said that whenever she saw Myles he was smiling. There were others more familiar with his serious side. One of AJR's political-minded friends told him that Myles had been a "slugger" – an enforcer of party discipline – at election time. He would punch people out if they voted the wrong way. According to family folklore, Uncle Myles mixed it up with a heavyweight champion, Jim Jeffries, during World War I. This was after Jeffries had retired undefeated and then lost a comeback fight to Jack Johnson. Myles was in the service and Jeffries was touring the Army camps. For the entertainment of the troops, he would spar with their unit's best fighter or with anyone intrepid enough to climb through the ropes. In exhibition matches, there is very little actual fighting as a rule, but Uncle Myles, the story goes, fearlessly tore into Jeffries and turned their sparring session into something that was more like a war. Anyway, that is how my father and my uncles told the tale.

Myles was a bit of a daredevil. To win a bet, he would jump off any bridge in Pittsburgh. On one of his descents he appeared to be heading for the skiff that always took him ashore. The skiff's oarsmen leaped into the water, but Myles came down with a splash, not a thunk, and lived to collect the wager he had made. How it affected his rapport with the crew of the skiff I don't know.

After the Eighteenth Amendment became law, Pop Rooney was forced to close his saloon and put his unsold liquor into a bonded warehouse. The only legal customers for it were outside the United States, and to market the stuff would take time. This gave Myles an idea. He was working then as a mail carrier and he knew that some old-model Post Office trucks were for sale. Myles bought two of them. Their colors had been changed and their insignia painted over, but Myles could use a paintbrush himself. In twenty-four hours they looked like mail trucks again, and Myles carried out his scam. He would drive to the warehouse, pick up all the booze a truck would hold – for shipment overseas, as he explained – and then return in the second truck for another load. Finding his own buyers in Allegheny County was never difficult. Perhaps inevitably, the Prohibition agents caught up with him, and Myles served time in the slammer.

He came to a sad end, partly because of his weakness for women and partly because of an unfortunate misjudgment. I happened to be in Belle Vernon once on a ticket promotion job for AJR's professional football team, the Steelers, when a friend of Uncle Jim, a man called Possum, said to me, "I know your cousin who lives here." I told him I did not have any relatives in Belle Vernon. "Well, this lady," he said, "claims to be the illegitimate daughter of a Rooney named Myles." I could only say, "I believe it." At any rate, some time after Myles got out of jail and was working in a roadhouse, a certain Joe the Barber came to see him. He accused Myles of trifling with his wife and pulled a gun. Myles took it away from him, but then made the mistake of giving it back, "You're too gutless to use it," he said. They were the last words Myles ever spoke. Gutless Joe the Barber shot and killed him.

Joe went to prison for the deed and served fifteen years before coming up for parole. Pop Rooney testified at his hearing. "Let him go," Pop said to the parole board. "He's paid his debt, and, anyway, Myles provoked him."

Myles had a son named Art (for his grandfather, the original, red-bearded Art Rooney.) The kid became an excellent football player, one of the best halfbacks in the late 1930s at North Carolina State University. On my scouting trips to Raleigh thirty years later I would sometimes be asked if I were the same Art Rooney. Apparently the other Art, in addition to being quite a football player, was pretty good with his fists. I met a shoe salesman in Palm Beach who told me that "little Art Rooney" had belted out his (the shoe salesman's) brother when they were North Carolina State classmates. Art was a World War II Army officer and made the service his career, retiring with the rank of lieutenant colonel. He was married, but had no children I ever heard of. One thing he did have, like many another Irishman, was a serious drinking problem.

The McNultys

My knowledge of the McNultys is limited. The McNultys all seemed to lead conventional lives. They were Irish for the most part, but with Scottish and German blood in the mix. My mother, Kathleen McNulty, who married AJR in 1931, belonged to the third generation.

I have a single vague memory of being alone at the bedside of my grandfather, John McNulty, in the last few days of his life. He was calling for his daughter Harriet. "Go fetch her, Artie," he begged me. I was too young to know what death was, but old enough to realize that this was no ordinary request, and I hurried to deliver the message.

One of John McNulty's relatives, a man named Free, was a city councilman. McNulty himself owned a cooperage on Herr's Island in the Allegheny River and had a permit from the city to scavenge for old or damaged barrels in a dump (today we would call it a landfill). He cleaned and repaired the barrels and then sold them. Almost every business used barrels for shipping and storage back then. Later, during Prohibition, Pop Rooney used McNulty barrels to ship out his illegal booze.

My maternal grandmother, Bridget, was a Devlin. I never knew her. She died at 38, of cancer. Radiation treatment was in its infancy then, and in my grandmother's case, according to her daughter Alice, misused. Some of the male Devlins were railroaders, and another Devlin – Chris, who went to Penn State University – was a linebacker on the football team and afterward played for the Cincinnati Bengals. No Rooney ever played beyond the college level.

A Devlin who worked on the railroad was in charge of returning wrecked trains to the track. After finishing a job, he would send his office a wire: "Off again ... on again ... gone again. Devlin."

Because their names were so similar, my mother and Henry McAnulty, a Holy Ghost priest and former Air Force general who was president of Duquesne University in the 1970s, believed, or pretended to believe, that they were distantly related. Father McAnulty was a man of wit, charm, and intelligence.

Like the Rooneys, the McNultys were North Siders and attended St. Peter's Church. St. Peter's had a tough old pastor who would call out from the sacristy when his assistants were giving longwinded sermons, "Come on – get it over with!" He accused them of endlessly repeating themselves.

The McNultys lived on Lacock Street in a neighborhood more upscale than The Ward. By saying yes to AJR, their daughter Kathleen, the McNultys thought, had "married down". Old John McNulty had always done well financially, but when wooden barrels gave way to steel drums he was slow to make the changeover and lost everything – his stable, his horses, and his business. Meanwhile, the Russian immigrants who had worked for him saw that steel drums were the future, went into business for themselves, and, according to Alice McNulty, my mother's sister, became rich.

The McNultys often spoke of their missed opportunities. "Any fool can make money," my mother would say. "It takes a wise man to keep it." My mother had a million of these sayings and she used every one.

Aside from his lack of business acumen, there was still another reason why John McNulty went broke. After the death of his wife he got into booze and lost his competitive spirit. When things were going good, he had helped his brother George start the first Buick dealership in Western Pennsylvania; now that it was John who needed help, George put him to work as a night watchman in the Buick garage. For my mother and her sisters, this was heartbreaking.

The North Side Buick Company, by the way, was in business for many years under the ownership of the McDonoughs, who were cousins of the McNultys.

My parents often talked about the great flu epidemic of 1918. It seems to me that my mother lost a sister, a young girl named Elizabeth; if I had listened more closely I would not be in doubt. Other families were wiped out completely. The dead would be laid out at home, my mother said, and in almost every house there would be a casket. When the Diocese of Pittsburgh called for its young male parishioners to help with the work in the cemeteries, AJR, Dan, and Jim became volunteer gravediggers. It was a time they would never forget.

Chapter 2

School Days

AJR and his brothers learned the three Rs at St. Peter's parochial school, but got their secondary educations at Duquesne Prep – Holy Ghost Academy when AJR first enrolled and later called University School. Even in the dead of winter, they made the long daily trek from the North Side to the Bluff – and back – on foot.

At University School, AJR played football, basketball, and baseball. In 1917, his junior year, the football team had a 7-1-1 record, and according to the school paper its success was in large measure due to the "wriggling, squirming, and serpentine runs" of "Halfback Rooney." This same Halfback Rooney, wrote the anonymous author of the piece, "stands head and shoulders above his companions."

Due to the influenza epidemic of 1918, even high school journalists were preoccupied with matters of more importance than football games, and Halfback Rooney's accomplishments in his senior year are lost to us now. We know that at the end of the season two or three colleges offered him athletic scholarships. And we know that these offers were not accepted. His mother, the dominant early influence in AJR's life, had ideas of her own for the oldest Rooney boy. She thought he should go to work, which as she understood it meant working with your hands. A man who worked was a coal miner, like AJR's grandfather on his mother's side, or a steelworker, like Pop Rooney's brother-in-law, Mike Concannon.

Uncle Mike Concannon, a foreman in one of the mills, pulled a few strings to get a job there for AJR. It was not the kind of job that AJR himself would have chosen. The work was hard, it was boring, it was dirty, and it made you sweat. On his first day, at lunch-time, he put a question to Uncle Mike. "How much money do you make?" Mike told him. AJR was not impressed. At the suggestion that in, oh, about fifteen years he, too, might be a foreman earning a foreman's wages, AJR had heard all he needed to hear. He was playing summer baseball, for a semi-pro team, and making more money than Mike Concannon made. With a thank-you-very-much, he picked up his lunch bucket and went home, never to return. Nor did he bother to collect the half day's pay that was coming to him. In his old age he reckoned that, with interest, the steel company owed him a sizable sum.

Unquestionably, the few long hours he spent that day in the mill were life-shaping for AJR. His mother's notion of work, it was now clear, differed radically from his own. He saw that manual labor was the deadest of dead ends. He would get where he intended to go by using his wits.

And a college education was to be the first step. He considered Notre Dame, having heard from the new football coach, a Norwegian immigrant by the name of Knute Rockne. Years later, when AJR off-handedly mentioned this to his sons, we took it with a small grain of salt. Knute Rockne by then had entered mythology. Everybody knew all the fables about winning one for the Gipper, about the Four Horsemen outlined – in Grantland Rice's imagination – against a blue-gray October sky. But a Rockne-Rooney connection? Long after Rockne's death, and shortly after AJR's, we came across proof. A footnote in a book, a biography of Rockne, revealed that in his files there indeed was a letter to AJR, or a copy of one. Would he be interested, Rockne had asked, in playing football at Notre Dame?

Penn State wanted him, too – badly enough to offer a share of the program concession on game days. The NCAA had been in existence since 1910, but essentially it had no policing powers. There were rules and regulations, but not many. In the end, though, AJR opted for Indiana Normal, now called Indiana University of Pennsylvania.

One reason may have been that he had a girlfriend there, a girl with an Irish name I don't remember. In due time they went their separate ways. Years passed. And then, unexpectedly, when AJR was famous as the owner of the four-time Super Bowl champions, the woman wrote to him. She was proud to have been his classmate, she said. Of equal importance in her life, she continued, was one other distinction she could claim. Indiana Normal had been a two-year teachers' college in her day and his, and she had taught after graduation in the local Indiana school system, where her students included a shaggy-haired, drawling home-town boy named Jimmy Stewart.

It's about even money that AJR had to be told who Jimmy Stewart was. In the 1970s friends of his in Los Angeles – Hollywood Park race-track people – introduced him to Cary Grant. Making conversation with Grant, AJR casually asked, "Do you work at Hollywood Park?" Later on when someone explained that Grant sort of worked in the movies, AJR said, "Well, if he doesn't make cowboy pictures I wouldn't know him."

Jimmy Stewart made cowboy pictures, but not the kind that AJR normally would have seen.

At Indiana, AJR played football, of course. His old associate George Quinlan described him as "a little-bitty halfback who could run like hell." Trained down to the lightweight limit, AJR was a 135-pound boxer. For football he must have weighed more – 145 pounds at the least. In the days before behemoths roamed the earth, college football players no bigger than that were commonplace. In any case, AJR was not a runt. Fully mature, he had a frame that could carry 160 pounds of mostly muscle.

At Indiana, lacking enough credits for his high-school diploma, AJR took the college preparatory course but competed on the varsity teams in football, basketball, baseball, and track while continuing to box. (After winning a tournament somewhere, he returned with two black eyes to a hero's welcome; the entire Indiana student body was waiting to greet him at the railroad station.) In all four team sports, Indiana scheduled other normal schools and the freshman teams from Pitt, Penn State, Carnegie Tech, Syracuse, and West Virginia. Dividing time between halfback and quarterback, AJR was named by the Indiana yearbook as "the individual star" of a team that won state normal championships in 1919 and 1920.

In 1920 he was also – and this is hard to believe – the individual star of the Duquesne University team. Old newspaper files contain stories that recount AJR's exploits on behalf of both schools. If it occurred to the writers of these stories that there was anything unusual about this, they kept such reflections to themselves. Perhaps there was no eligibility issue, Rob Ruck and Maggie Patterson conjecture, because at Indiana AJR was a prep student. Moreover, "questions of eligibility were not frequently raised at the time." It was the age of the tramp athlete, that much is certain.

No football player made of flesh and blood, not even AJR, could have been in two places at once, but Duquesne and Indiana did not normally play their games on the same day of the week.

Once when both teams did play on the same date — October 23, 1920 — the starting times must have differed by several hours. In any case, Ruck and Patterson tell us, AJR played for Duquesne against St. Mary's of Emmitsburg, Maryland, and for Indiana against the Penn State freshmen. Exhausted, apparently, from his earlier efforts, he could not keep Indiana from losing to Penn State by the score of 54-0.

Just as he afterward said, AJR went from Indiana to Georgetown for baseball, but also to be the boxing instructor at Georgetown Prep, where lessons in the manly art were compulsory. Besides his work with the preps, he boxed for the university team and won medals. To his lasting disappointment, he played little baseball. The coach, a man named John O'Reilly, had a veteran team returning. His lineup was set before the season ever started, and AJR sat on the bench. It was his first and only experience with failure in baseball. He was a left-handed batting, right-handed throwing outfielder whose arm did not completely measure up but who covered a lot of ground, took extra bases and stole them almost at will, and could hit.

Whatever John O'Reilly may have thought, the Boston Red Sox considered him a major-league prospect. He signed a contract with the Red Sox calling for $250 a month and could have gone to their spring-training camp. In the end, he decided to stay at home. "Playing around here," he explained, "I could make two hundred and fifty dollars in a couple of weeks." By June he had dropped out of Georgetown and in the free and easy spirit of the times was playing left field for Duquesne University. Dan, his growing baby brother, caught and batted cleanup for Duquesne Prep. Both played that summer for a touring independent team called the Pittsburgh Collegians. In previous summers, AJR had played for as many as three and four independent teams at the same time.

He was back at Duquesne in the fall, a starting halfback on the football team. His brother Dan was the Dukes' quarterback. In their opening game, a 7-7 tie with Marietta, AJR injured his shoulder and was out for the season.

Enrolled in a pre-law course, he cut most of his classes. When he bothered to show up, he argued with the professor, who suggested that they meet in private.

"You're being disruptive," the pedagogue said when they got together. "You remind me of a gandy dancer," he added.

"What's a gandy dancer?" AJR asked.

"He's the boss of a crew that works on the railroad tracks with sledgehammers. When the gandy dancer yells 'Yup' the guys with the sledgehammers drive in the spikes that hold the rails in place."

The professor then asked if AJR was in college to improve his mind and acquire knowledge or to make himself more attractive to employers.

"Either way it's OK," the professor said, "but you don't need a college degree if the only reason you're here is to get ahead. You are loaded with leadership qualities. The only thing you must learn is how to use them."

AJR took the advice to heart. He left Duquesne soon afterwards without a degree. And, just as the professor foretold, he didn't need one to be a success.

'Nobody to Fool Around With'

Tradition required that the first son born to Dan and Margaret Rooney be named for the father's father and the second son for the father himself. It's either an Irish tradition or a Rooney tradition, I'm not sure which. In any case that is how AJR and the oldest of his five brothers got their names.

Something about Dan Junior — old Dan's second son — lifted him above even AJR. Seeing them together, I felt that AJR may have held Dan in awe. Why? Not for his enviable prowess as an athlete; not for his intellect, as smart as I knew Dan to be; not for his political astuteness — he had none. No, the reason, it seemed to me, was that Dan had put aside everything else in life for the Catholic Church, which greatly impressed AJR.

Thanks to their upbringing they were both deeply religious. It was what separated them from their friends and from Jim, Red, and Duke. Faith was a gift, AJR used to say, but I knew it was more than that. You could not have faith without wanting to, without working at it.

In the fall of 1998, when both were long gone, their sister Margaret spent some time as a patient in Allegheny General Hospital. One day her nephew, Jack McGinley, Jr., stopped by to say hello. They talked for a few minutes, sitting by the window in her room. Aunt Margaret glanced out at the cityscape below and said, "Jack, we're right above the street where my brother Dan was pinched."

Jack was stunned. "Your brother Dan? The priest? Arrested?"

"Well," said Aunt Margaret, "he hadn't been ordained yet. He was still in the seminary, or about to go into the seminary. He had a summer job driving a beer truck, but it was during Prohibition and beer wasn't legal."

Technically, the cop did not arrest Dan. He listened to whatever explanation Dan may have come up with and accepted it. Anywhere on the North Side, the name Rooney carried weight with the police.

For all his piety, Dan was a tough customer in his youth – very much similar to AJR. They had spent countless hours on the playground in The Ward, wearing out most of their friends. They could box and they could fight rough and tumble. Dan was the more serious of the two – "nobody to fool around with." He had a temper, which he tried to keep in check. Once on a Steeler road trip my roommate was Uncle Jim, who'd been drinking and acting up. The morning after, he was sleeping it off. Somebody sent for Dan – Father Silas, to use his Franciscan name – and we met by accident in the lobby of the hotel. "Take me to Jim's room," he said. I tried to think of an excuse. "Look," he went on, in his usual matter-of-fact tone, "I have to have you with me or there's no telling what I might do."

All of the stories about him, I realized at that moment, were true.

AJR used to say that Dan had more knockouts than Jack Dempsey. At least once he mixed pugilism with football. Dan played fullback at St. Bonaventure University, and on this particular Saturday a guard by the name of Dave Packard kept failing to block his man, who would tackle Dan for a loss. Dan ordered Packard to start doing his job, but the missed blocks continued. Finally Dan called out from the huddle; "Man injured!" The St. Bonaventure trainer ran onto the field just as Dan hit Packard on the chin. In his billfold for years afterward, Packard carried a newspaper clipping about the only player in the history of football ever to be knocked out in a huddle.

Art Rooney, Baseball
(Drawing by Kathy Rooney)

Another time, in Frostburg, Maryland, the Rooney brothers took on a baseball team, or as much of a team as they could get their hands on. Dan and AJR played for the Wheeling Stogies in the Mid-Atlantic League, and Frostburg's bench jockeys started taunting them with anti-Catholic jibes. Dan attacked them ferociously, with AJR pitching in. They broke up the game, but that was not the end of it. The same Frostburg players wandered into the restaurant where the Stogies were eating that night, and the Rooneys went after them again.

Frostburg's city council reacted swiftly, sending an ultimatum to the owners of the Wheeling team. The next time the Stogies played in Frostburg they were to leave their catcher, Dan Rooney, and their center fielder, Art Rooney, at home. By official decree, the Rooney brothers could never set foot in Frostburg again for as long as they lived.

During their one season with Wheeling, 1925, AJR led the Mid-Atlantic League in runs scored, hits, and stolen bases and was runnerup for the batting title with a .369 average. Dan hit .359. Both had dead arms or they might have ended up in the major leagues. AJR made a swing around the National League with the Chicago Cubs, but never got into a game. A team in the Southern League offered him a contract for a salary he considered inadequate. Turning it down, he said to the manager, "I can make more money at the race track." As young as he was at the time, there were few better handicappers than AJR.

Off and on, the brothers played sandlot baseball for the Pittsburgh Collegians and the North Side Board of Trade. AJR played for a team in Michigan, Dan for a team in Cumberland, Maryland.

Dan even played in Panama for a while. Pitching to him high and inside was not prudent. Once when Smoky Joe Williams of the Homestead Grays hit Dan on the head with a fastball, Dan chased him out of the ballpark.

Dan played football at Duquesne University as well as at St. Bonaventure, and by the time he got to Olean he had probably used up his eligibility. Moreover, he had played professional baseball. These facts may explain why he was Mike Rooney, not Dan Rooney, at St. Bonaventure. When the Bonnies took the field for a game with Cornell, one of Cornell's assistant coaches looked at Dan closely and said, "Hey – I played minor-league baseball with that guy five years ago!" Repeated to the officials, his words put an end to Dan's football career.

He continued to play pool, and he was good at it, good enough to recognize a hustle when he saw one. During his years at Duquesne, he had a partner, a Fast Eddie Felson called Scarface who could blow away everybody in The Ward. Dan was his backer, or manager. Dan put up the money, Scarface reeled in the suckers. Sometimes they went on the road together. Less often, it would be Scarface alone. He was in Canton, Youngstown, or maybe New Castle when a stranger came to Pittsburgh and took up where Scarface had left off. Nobody could beat him. To make matters worse, the guy was obnoxious. The situation cried out for Scarface, but not even Dan knew where to find him.

And then, by happenstance, everyone thought, Scarface called a friend of the Rooney brothers, Sam Leone, from Akron. Sam told him, "You're needed here," and spread the word through The Ward that Scarface was on his way. Dan, in the role of backer, set up a match between Scarface and the stranger at the fanciest pool palace on Federal Street. The betting was hot and heavy. Special stands were brought in for the crowd. All of The Ward's money was on Scarface.

Dan got there late, delayed by urgent, unfinished classwork at Duquesne. To his consternation, he learned that Scarface was off his game – missing easy shots, leaving the table open for the other guy. Sam Leone couldn't understand it. "We're going to lose all our dough," he said to Dan, who did understand – immediately.

"Time out!" he called. He quietly took Scarface aside. He said, "You leave on a trip. This guy shows up and busts everybody out. You finally call Sam. And now you're missing shots you should make with your eyes closed." They were standing next to a window. "If this bum beats you," Dan said, "right through the glass you go – head first."

Scarface never missed another shot. He ran the table three times and there were no bankruptcies that night in The Ward. But Dan would have nothing more to do with him.

Visiting old friends at St. Bonaventure in his mid-seventies, he stayed at the Marriott Hotel in Buffalo. Off the lobby, in the game room, was a regulation pool table. He picked up a stick, leaned over the rail, and hesitated. He was wearing thick glasses. After a moment he looked up, put the stick down, and said, "I can't see the balls."

He studied for the priesthood at Catholic University in Washington, D. C. On the campus, the seminarians wore cassocks, and once when Dan was in a group that approached some students hanging out at a recreation area, he heard somebody say, "Here come the girls." Dan went back to his dormitory, changed into street clothes, and returned to the recreation area. 'Now do I look like a girl?" he said, and proceeded to give two of the wise guys a thrashing.

He was devoted to the Lord but quick to use his fists – characteristics that may seem incompatible. It was not until I had known him for years that I came to appreciate how kind he could be and how concerned for the welfare of others.

Chapter 3

Jimmy Coyne

James Joseph Coyne was an immigrant from Galway. Immigrants from Galway customarily settled in Oakland, and those who did not become firemen or policemen went to work for the Pittsburgh Traction Company. On streetcars back then the motorman was at one end of the car and the conductor, wearing a change belt, took fares at the other end. Jimmy Coyne got a job as a motorman. "I'm on the wrong end," he complained to his friends.

There was room on the right end in politics. Coyne worked as a sandhog, a teamster, and a mill hand before catching on with a construction firm owned by William Flinn, the Republican Party's city and county chairman. Flinn promoted Coyne to superintendent, helped him buy a saloon on Bates Street in Oakland, and made him Republican chairman of the Fourth Ward.

Rob Ruck and Maggie Patterson describe Coyne as a hulking, florid-faced man with small gray eyes, a fondness for cigars, and considerable personal magnetism. In the 1920s, long after William Flinn's death, he aligned himself with the most powerful Republican in Western Pennsylvania, William Larimer Mellon. With Mellon behind him, he won election to the State Legislature and then the State Senate and became a mighty dispenser of patronage.

On the side, he made a fortune in real estate.

AJR was his North Side lieutenant. Coyne bought property all over town and constantly urged AJR to do likewise. "Buy land, Art," he would say. "They're not making any more of it." Uninterested, AJR dragged his feet. "What do I know about real estate?" he asked. All because of a gambling debt, he ended up with thirty acres anyway.

The man who owed him the money couldn't pay. "Forget it," said AJR.

"Forget it, nothing – I'm not a deadbeat," the man replied. Almost as a favor, AJR accepted the deed to an undeveloped plot in the North Hills.

Over three or four decades, the land increased in value, and he sold it for what he said was "a nice piece of change." Speculating in the commodities market, he lost every nickel of it.

Politically liberal, AJR was more like a Democrat than a Republican. He believed, and so did Coyne, in putting his supporters on the city or county payroll, but on the North Side the patronage king was a political foe, a Republican state senator named Eisenstadt. So popular was Eisenstadt in Germantown that the infamous "Suicide Bridge" over East Street had been given his name. Everybody, of course, kept calling it the Suicide Bridge, but no matter. Not even Jimmy Coyne was powerful enough to control him.

So Coyne and AJR got their heads together. They could make trouble for Eisenstadt in the primary election, they thought, by persuading the owner of a prosperous bakery to run. He had friends, money, and a good reputation, and though his chances of winning seemed remote, he turned out to be a vigorous campaigner. Voters who considered Eisenstadt arrogant, a sizable minority, were switching their allegiance to the baker.

Election day drew near. The baker appeared to be gaining ground. And then with no explanation he suddenly dropped out of the race. Eisenstadt, unopposed, won his easiest victory, thus assuring himself of another term. In general elections back then, Republicans always beat Democrats.

Meanwhile, people wondered why the baker had quit. To AJR it was incomprehensible. And then one evening as he strolled past the North Side Market House, a chauffeur-driven limousine pulled up beside him. The man being driven – Eisenstadt – asked AJR to get in. Making small talk, they slowly circled the block. They circled it again and again until Eisenstadt at last told the driver to stop. He had taken up enough of AJR's time. They said good night, and AJR, still in the dark as to what it all meant, opened the car door and stepped down onto the curb. "By the way," called out Eisenstadt, having waited until the very last minute. "The next time you and Jimmy Coyne try to teach me a lesson; don't ask a baker who sells his doughnuts to the Pennsylvania Railroad to do it."

With those words the pieces of the puzzle fell into place. Eisenstadt, AJR remembered, was on the Pennsylvania Railroad's Board of Trustees. AJR and his teacher, Jimmy Coyne, had met their match.

In the Republican pecking order, Coyne answered only to William Larimer Mellon, one of the Mellon banking and industrial overlords, and William Larimer Mellon answered only to his uncle, Andrew Mellon, secretary of the treasury under Presidents Harding, Coolidge, and Hoover (1921-1932). AJR liked to relate a story that illustrated graphically how the table of organization worked. In a small inner room adjacent to Coyne's main office, the senator was presiding in a high-handed way at a meeting of GOP ward bosses, as AJR described the incident, when a secretary interrupted to say that he had a telephone call.

He dismissed her with an impatient gesture. "Tell whoever it is to call me later."

In less than one minute, the secretary was back. "This call," she said, "is very important."

Coyne made no attempt to hide his annoyance. "Didn't you hear me? I'm busy. Tell whoever it is to call me later. I don't care if it's the Pope himself on the line."

The secretary hesitated. Then she said quietly, "It's Mister Andrew Mellon."

Coyne was a big lumbering fellow, but he bolted out of his chair like a sixteen-year-old, recalled AJR. The side pocket of his trousers caught on the arm of the chair and ripped loose, exposing his underwear. Without pausing, Coyne rushed to the door and headed straight for the telephone.

"Everybody, including Jimmy Coyne, has a higher-up to report to," AJR would pontificate.

Politician, real estate tycoon, and country squire, Coyne was a man of many facets. He owned a hardscrabble farm and a pickup truck. Aware of his status as a rich and influential Pennsylvania state senator, he made up his mind to buy a Cadillac. He drove the pickup truck to the agency and traded it in. He was now the possessor of wheels that reflected his material worth, and he prepared to drive the Cadillac home. At this point the salesman spoke up. In the back of the truck, which now belonged to the Cadillac people, was a calf.

"We'll have it delivered to your farm," the salesman said.

Not necessary, Coyne informed him. Taking purposeful strides, he went to the rear of the truck, lifted out the calf, carried it to his shiny new car, and plopped it down in the middle of the plush back seat.

"Pig-shit Irish," someone murmured. Someone usually did when Jimmy Coyne was being himself, but never in the presence of AJR, who loved and admired the old Hibernian.

Aviator

Everybody on the North Side called Sam Leone "Dago Sam." The ethnic slur did not seem to bother him – not if whoever used it was a friend. Sam was a small-time gambler, well-liked and a good story teller. He could get himself into jams, but his friends helped him out of them. He lived by his wits – God knows how.

Milton Jaffe, called "Big Nose," was Sam's opposite – a very shrewd gambler with wits as sharp as a razor. Milton had "offices" on lower Federal Street in The Ward. Before he knew AJR, he had heard "positive things" about him, mostly from Sam. So Milton told Sam he'd like to meet AJR, and Sam "brought him around." When AJR showed up wearing a letter sweater from Duquesne, or maybe Indiana Normal, Milton dismissed him as "just another jock," or whatever athletes were called in the early years of the twentieth century. In that, Milton admitted later, he was greatly mistaken.

As Milton and others came to realize, AJR could do almost anything. One of his early interests was aviation, this at a time that was not too far distant from the Wright brothers' flight at Kitty Hawk. A friend who had played for the Pittsburgh Pirates was into flying and prevailed on AJR to take lessons. Seeing that AJR had the instincts to be a good pilot, he urged him to study navigation and aeronautical engineering in a course he taught at Carnegie Tech.

AJR was dubious. "I couldn't pass that stuff," he said. The friend advised him to show up for all the classes, take notes, and keep quiet. AJR did as he was told. But he worried. He said the star of the class, a guy who answered all the questions, made him feel like a dolt. Relax, his friend told him. Though smart as a whip and not a bad kid, the guy had no judgment as a flyer, whereas AJR was a natural in the cockpit.

At final examination time, the smart kid passed with a high score. AJR's friend counseled him to sit through the test and hand in a blank sheet of paper with his name on it. Again AJR did as he was told, and the ex-Pirate – his name escapes me – gave him a passing grade.

Now came the hands-on flying. The student who had answered all the questions crash-landed and was lucky to walk away from the wreck of his plane. He did not get a license to fly; AJR did.

His career as a pilot had its spectacular moments. On a landing one time, he bounced off the runway and over some trees and onto the Oakmont golf course. Reputedly, he flew under every one of Pittsburgh's many bridges.

Marriage to Kathleen McNulty grounded him – permanently. Flying, said his bride, was too dangerous. As the head of a family – and since husband and wife were both Irish Catholic the family was bound to be a large one – he could take no more chances in the air.

Bridegroom

AJR was 29 and Kathleen McNulty 25 when they were married – the first time. "Kass," as AJR called his wife, used to say that she had a rival, namely Imogene Coca, the gifted comedienne who became a television star in the 1950s. In the late 1920s, in partnership with Milton Jaffe, AJR owned The Showboat, a floating casino on the Allegheny River, and Imogene Coca's act was part of the entertainment.

Pittsburgh during Prohibition was a wide-open town – a "paradise," in fact, for entrepreneurs like AJR and Milton Jaffe and for scufflers like George Quinlan, who ran a wildcat brewery in Millvale. "You had to pay the police, but not the Mafia," Quinlan explained. His point of view was the same as AJR's: drinking and gambling were "illegal but not illicit."

Getting back to Imogene Coca, she was crazy about poodles. Where Imogene went, her poodles went, and when Imogene played The Showboat it was AJR's job to exercise them. "Good thing you didn't marry that woman," the woman he did marry told him. "You'd have had poodles instead of children."

The way it turned out, AJR was married twice – both times to Kass. A civil ceremony in New York City preceded their marriage at St. Peter's Church. That is my understanding, at any rate; nobody ever talked about it except Kass's three sisters, Aunt Alice, Aunt Harriet, and Aunt Mary Miller, and their conversations on the subject were private. Although the rest of us sometimes eavesdropped, we did not ask questions.

Anyway, it seems that by 1930 AJR was something of a public figure – a shy public figure. Getting married would result in unwanted attention, and Kass's wishes apparently dovetailed with his. Conscientious Catholic that he was, he went to the pastor of St. Peter's, a Father O'Shay, and notified him of their plan to elope. Father O'Shay was not pleased, but AJR had made up his mind.

He chose as his best man George Engel, a fight manager. Engel had managed Frank Klaus and Harry Greb, middleweight champions from Pittsburgh, and had worked with Gene Tunney, the heavyweight champion who took the title from Jack Dempsey. During the honeymoon, Engel and the newlyweds stayed at the same hotel. AJR made his living in those days as a gambler, and, as gamblers will, he carried a lot of cash, thousands of dollars, which he deposited in a pillowcase upon going to bed. One morning as he and Kass were having breakfast with Engel in the hotel dining room he reached for his money to pay the check and became aware that it was still in the pillowcase. Honeymooners and best man jumped up from the table and hurried to the bridal suite. They were not in time. The bed had already been stripped. AJR said with a shrug, "Forget about it. I'll send for more cash. Either that or we'll just go home." At this point Engel took over.

Careful not to show undue concern, he went to the head housekeeper. An inexpensive "brooch" of considerable sentimental value – a gift from Mrs. Rooney's "Aunt Minnie" – had been lost, Engel lied. Could she give him the name of the maid who had cleaned the room? And where did the soiled linen go before it was sent to the laundry?

Engel, remember, was a fight manager, and it is second nature with fight managers to regard everybody as a thief. "If you let those people know you're looking for a bankroll," he cautioned AJR and Kass, "they'll be in competition with you. They'll find it before we do and keep it."

From the housekeeper Engel learned that the dirty sheets and pillowcases were dropped down a chute to the basement. If he hurried, she said, he could get there before the pillowcase with the "brooch" in it was gone. Engel hurried, and so did the newlyweds. Laundry workers directed them to the proper chute and after digging through piles of rumpled bedclothes they found the right pillowcase, its contents still undisturbed.

I have to admit that the first time I heard this story I was baffled. How could AJR have been so absent-minded? To leave all that money in a pillowcase in a hotel room wasn't like him. Not until much later did the realization come to me that he and Kass must have had a big night.

The honeymoon indeed was exciting, Kass acknowledged, and the excitement had begun with their arrival at the Pennsylvania Railroad Station. Waiting to pick them up, in a bullet-proof armored car belonging to Owney Madden, a big-time Irish mobster, was Madden's lieutenant, Bill Duffy. The car had embrasures in it, Kass noticed – gun embrasures. No doubt the couple spent time at the Cotton Club in Harlem, where Prohibition was just a rumor. Madden owned it.

Kass couldn't help but be impressed. Did she also wonder, "What am I getting myself into?"

Owney Madden, an Irishman born in England, committed his first murder at the age of 17 and had racked up several more by the time he was 23. Crime reporters called him "the little banty rooster from hell." For his fifth or sixth murder, the shooting of a gangland rival named Patsy Doyle, he served his first prison term, eight years in Sing Sing – where he met Bill Duffy.

The stretch in the slammer reformed Madden a little. Turned loose in 1923, he abruptly stopped killing people and took up the profession of rum-running. When Prohibition ended, in 1933, he was wealthy enough to retire. He spent his last thirty years in the Arkansas resort town of Hot Springs, married to the postmaster's daughter and living next door to the police chief. Notable for the easy-going ways of its law-enforcement officers, Hot Springs was a mecca for horseplayers (it had a race track), card players (there were half a dozen casinos), pool sharks, and criminals on the lam.

The connection between Owney Madden and AJR is unclear. AJR was a man who "knew" people. Someone's name might come up, and he would say, "Oh, I know that guy," which could mean that they were friends or could mean that they were nothing more than speaking acquaintances. How well he knew Madden, and what he thought of him, I have no idea. It wasn't something you asked about. Certainly he and Madden did not do business together. My guess would be that they met through Bill Duffy and that AJR knew Duffy because Duffy managed fighters.

One fighter Duffy managed, with Owney Madden a presence behind the scenes, was the awkward Italian giant Primo Carnera. By arranging a long series of tank jobs, Duffy and Madden steered their 6-foot-7, 270-pound man mountain to the heavyweight championship. Carnera held the title from June 1933 to June 1934, and during that time he boxed an exhibition match in the St. Peter's school yard to raise money for North Side families being squeezed by the Depression. Duffy brought him to Pittsburgh, against his will, as a favor to AJR. Carnera had balked when Duffy told him he'd be boxing in a school yard. He growled that he wouldn't do it, whereupon Duffy – or maybe Madden – slapped him across the face. Such was their power to exploit this hapless pituitary case, for alongside Carnera they were pygmies. Carnera did come to Pittsburgh and seems to have had a good time. Dago Sam Leone took charge of him after the exhibition bout, and they socialized the night away in various North Side Italian-American haunts, with Carnera the admired guest of honor.

Carnera wasn't much of a fighter. In what was probably his first honest fight, he lost the title to Max Baer, and in his next honest fight he took a merciless beating from Joe Louis. Duffy and Madden, having no further use for Carnera, went on their way, which in Duffy's case was downhill. He served time for tax evasion and ended up broke. Carnera was penniless, too, but later made some money as a wrestling attraction. He wrestled once in Pittsburgh and paid a visit to AJR at his office in the Fort Pitt Hotel, where they reminisced like old friends about the time Carnera boxed at St. Peter's School.

AJR's honeymoon lasted a whole year. Traveling by train, the carefree couple went from New York to Hot Springs – Owney Madden had not yet taken up residence there – and from Hot Springs to San Diego, accompanied by an entourage. AJR owned race horses by then, just a few, and hired a special freight car to transport them. There were men to run errands and men to provide security. When the honeymooners stopped to visit race tracks along the way, there were men to place bets and collect winnings. The men were young, tough, and athletic. And AJR was a good captain. His subordinates ate well and slept comfortably. Too comfortably at times. They were called on to attend early Mass – AJR continued to practice his religion – and to clock the horses in their morning workouts, and getting them out of bed was never easy.

San Diego in 1930 was a quiet seaport city and naval base. The Rooney contingent stayed at the El Cortez Hotel downtown. Just across the Mexican border in Tijuana was the Agua Caliente race track. Connected to San Diego by a highway called "The Road to Hell," Tijuana was known as "Sin City." It reminded AJR of the old Wild West, he always said. "Anything went." Kass said the same thing differently: "It was 'Out of my way or a leg off.'"

In "Seabiscuit," her best-selling book about a race horse, Laura Hillenbrand tells what the Tijuana of the 1920s and '30s was like. It offered "unlimited indulgence." It had the longest bar in the world, 241 feet, jammed from end to end by Americans sick and tired of the Eighteenth Amendment. Tijuana was wide open, "every hour, every day." There were quickie divorces and quickie marriages. "Single men were steered into one of the many brothels, a cottage industry in Tijuana."

But the town's greatest tourist attraction, Laura Hillenbrand writes, was its race track. California had outlawed betting on horses in 1916 after a series of scandals involving bookmakers. Tijuana promptly opened a track which at once became a haven for American racing stables and race fans. It didn't look like much – one jockey compared it to an outhouse – and yet it had the first movable starting gates and the first photo-finish camera. Hillenbrand: "The racing was lawless and wild and the Americans loved it." In 1929 a flood washed the track away, and a new three-million-dollar park – Agua Caliente – came into existence "just down the road."

AJR and his coterie made frequent visits to Agua Caliente. At times another pair of honeymooners, Pirate third baseman Pie Traynor and his bride Eve, joined the party. Once when Pie and Eve were with the group and they were late returning, the customs people informed them that the border was closed for the night. AJR told the others not to worry. He led the way down the fence to a dark, quiet spot where illegal immigrants crossed over. One by one they squeezed through an opening and eventually found a taxi that took them to San Diego.

On a trip into Mexico by touring car, AJR observed that one of his sidekicks, Harp Vaughan, was toting a shotgun.

"What's that for?" AJR demanded.

"To protect ourselves. We're carrying a lot of money," Harp said.

"Take that thing apart," ordered AJR.

Harp took the shotgun apart. There was never any doubt as to who was the boss.

"Now give me the pieces," said AJR.

And piece by piece as they motored along, he threw them out of the car.

He said, "Harp, if you have a gun, you'll use a gun. Use your brains or your fists instead. From now on, think ahead of the play." (This was Dad's way of telling someone, "Think before you act.")

Years went by. AJR owned a football team, the Pittsburgh Steelers. There was a game in San Diego between the Steelers and the Chargers, and, for old time's sake, Kass made the trip from Pittsburgh with her husband. They drove around the city, looking for familiar places. The old hotel was still standing, but so dilapidated that no NFL team would stay there. They revisited Agua Caliente, where somebody called out their names. Two ancient horse players, befriended in the old days by AJR, had spotted and instantly recognized them.

This was half a century after the honeymoon, which continued into 1931. When it was over, finally, and the lovebirds returned to Pittsburgh, tongues were still wagging. Everybody in St. Peter's parish knew they had "run away," knew they'd been married by a justice of the peace in New York. Father O'Shay, family legend has it, summoned them to the rectory for chastisement. They had given a bad example, and so on and so on. A second marriage, this one in the church, followed soon afterward. AJR got off with a light penance. Poor Kass did not fare so well. As her sisters told the story, she was forced to kneel in prayer at the altar rail all through Sunday Mass.

It's the woman who pays. But I know that if old Father O'Shay had lived his life twice, and had spent every minute in service to the Lord, he would still not have been as good and faithful a Catholic as my mother was.

Ship Ahoy

Back from the West Coast, AJR and Kass moved into an upstairs apartment on Western Avenue. They would never again leave the North Side. In the second year of their marriage, Daniel Milton Rooney was born.

"Milton" is not a typically Irish name. The new parents conferred it on the first of their five sons as a special mark of esteem for AJR's business partner, Milton Jaffe, who was Jewish.

Milton Jaffe had kept The Showboat afloat while AJR was on his honeymoon, and now the partnership was fully restored. Milton had know-how and pizzazz. AJR had know-how, pizzazz, and, most important of all, political connections. You could gamble and drink at The Showboat, and both forms of entertainment were illegal. It was therefore essential to be on good terms with the politicians and by extension the police.

The Showboat catered to a respectable clientele. The food was good and the gambling honest. Few men in Pittsburgh or anywhere else were more familiar with games of chance than Milton Jaffe, an expert card player and craps shooter. AJR once told me that even in his old age, when Milton was still in Las Vegas running the Stardust Casino, he could beat Jimmy the Greek at cards. But, then, Jimmy the Greek, added AJR, was more of a P.R. man than a gambler. Milton Jaffe believed in a fair shake for the customers, as did AJR. On the other hand, they were quick to spot professional cheaters and knew how to deal with them. The Showboat's stated policy – stated off the record, by AJR – was: "Treat everybody as you would like to be treated yourself, but never let kindness be mistaken for weakness."

It was Milton who booked the acts, the best obtainable. Decades after The Showboat's demise, AJR and some family members were dining at Moore's Restaurant in New York City. Seeing Groucho Marx just a table away, AJR was in doubt as to whether he should speak. Groucho had played The Showboat, but appeared not to recognize him. After two or three minutes, AJR broke the ice. "Do you remember Milton Jaffe, from Pittsburgh?" he asked. With a smile, Groucho answered, "Do you guys still have that riverboat?"

Allegheny County in the 1920s and '30s was not a Mafia stronghold. The nearest power base of the mob, a term under which AJR lumped racketeers in general, was New Kensington. Two brothers from New Kensington, goes a story that may or may not be fictitious, called on Milton Jaffe at The Showboat one day and introduced themselves as his new partners. Milton advised them to check that out with AJR, on the other side of the main deck, and his response when they did so was to throw them into the river.

A more credible story has AJR telling a couple of strong-arm guys who came on board packing heat that they'd be overmatched. "I've got three hundred guys of my own with guns – and badges and blue suits. The Pittsburgh Police Department," he said.

Dago Sam Leone had his own unique method of handling gunslingers. AJR was at a table with him once in a restaurant on the North Side when two men brandishing pistols burst through the door. "Sit still!" one of them shouted at AJR. "We're after Sam – not you." But Sam was too fast on the draw. Before they could fire a shot he started throwing things at them – salt and pepper shakers, a sugar bowl, cups and saucers, plates, water glasses, knives and forks. The gunmen when last seen were running down Federal Street, fast.

Like Inspector Renault, in "Casablanca," any Pittsburgh law-enforcement officer would have been SHOCKED to discover that gambling was allowed on The Showboat and SHOCKED at the news that there were other, less conspicuous gambling operations in town – false-front places, hidden away. Aunt Margaret Laughlin told of an evening when her brother "Arthur" – she never called him Art – took a carload of Rooneys to dinner. He parked near a building that to Margaret looked like a warehouse, and they followed him to the door. A peephole opened; somebody scrutinized them. The peephole closed and they went inside. At the top of some stairs, they passed through an area where card players, dice players, and roulette players were crowded around an assortment of tables. Beyond it was an elegant dining room. Efficient waiters served them an excellent meal. AJR paid the bill and they left, never to return or to speak of the occasion again. The most vivid impression Aunt Margaret retained was that "everybody there seemed to know Arthur."

No doorman stood guard at The Showboat. It was easy to find and easy to board. Access for those who arrived late at the wharf was by speedboat. There were two of them, both high-powered. One day John and Vince Rooney, in need of a little excitement, commandeered these fast, lively boats. They raced them down the river and flew right over a flood-control dam, still at full throttle. John and Vince, by some miracle, escaped serious injury. The speedboats were totally destroyed.

Flood-control dams in the 1930s did not prevent annual floods, and a big one, carrying heavy debris, left The Showboat damaged beyond repair. By mutual agreement, AJR and Milton ended their partnership, disappointing no one at police headquarters. Times were changing by then; sooner or later, The Showboat would have been drydocked. Instead, it remained half-sunken in the Allegheny River, a blight on the waterfront, for years.

Chapter 4

She Rattled and Rolled

North Side people were either Irish or German. The Germans, for the most part, worked in the trades. They considered themselves somehow more "substantial" than the Irish in The Ward. They drank a lot of beer but were not addicted to booze, the curse of the Irish. Instead of getting drunk, they'd get depressed and commit suicide. North Siders would say on a dark, gloomy day, "Hide all the clotheslines in Germantown." One German who hanged himself was a man we knew. "The Dutch Act," everyone called it.

According to my mother, intermarriage between the Germans and the Irish was all to the good. German genes gave the Irish stability; Irish genes gave the Germans light-heartedness. My mother believed that Germans were very law-abiding. The police, she pointed out, kept busier in The Ward than in Germantown. However, H.J. Heinz lived in Germantown, and a North Side fireman boasted that back around 1900 he made a citizen's arrest of the ketchup and pickle king for driving his horse and buggy at a reckless rate of speed.

Stella Guier drove horses and wagons recklessly and could even drive wagons that were powered by nothing but gravity. Stella Guier was a teamster in the days when women stayed at home, did the housework, and looked after their kids. AJR remembered her well. He said she looked like a man and dressed like a man. He said she could outwork, outdrink, outswear, and outfight any teamster in Pittsburgh.

Whooping it up with the boys one night, in a bar at the foot of Galveston Avenue and Reedsdale Street, Stella repeated a claim she had made before. She said that in a wagon with no horses hitched up to it she could drive all the way down Galveston Avenue and onto the Manchester Bridge, which crossed the Allegheny River between the North Side and the Point. And she could do it, she said, without ever using her brakes.

This time the boys offered to bet. They knew that what Stella proposed was insane. She would literally be taking her life in her hands.

Galveston Avenue cut through Monument Hill, the North Side's answer to Mount Washington. It was not as steep or as high as Mount Washington, but steep enough and high enough to make the trip down Galveston Avenue an adventure. Even as late as the 1940s and '50s, many automobiles with brakes that failed to hold would plow into parked cars at the curbside as drivers tried desperately to halt their descent.

AJR was a witness to Stella's ride. Hundreds of spectators were there – almost everybody in The Ward – and a big majority of them had not come to cheer Stella but to see her get killed. As AJR gently put it, Stella was not a woman with countless friends.

To provide traction for horses pulling heavy loads uphill, Galveston Avenue was paved with Belgian blocks – cobblestones brought to this country from Europe as ballast in the holds of ships. With Stella hanging onto the tiller, the long, heavy pole to which the horses would have been yoked, the wagon bumped and bounced on its descent. Its steel-rimmed wheels made a deafening racket and sparks flew up from the cobblestones as if all hell had erupted. Stella leaned forward in the driver's seat, wrestling with the tiller. She was steering her horseless wagon with her hands, a feat that looked next to impossible.

But Stella managed it. She rattled and rolled to the bottom of the hill, from where momentum took the wagon onto the bridge. That night in the saloon, collecting her bets, Stella remained in character.

"Any teamster worth his salt could have done it, but not you bastards," she crowed, "because you're all too yellow!"

The Irish

The North Side Irish seem to have been an unruly lot. On the other hand, they could also be generous and likable.

Pop and Maggie Rooney, as I have said, were glad to make room in their house for down-and-out relatives and friends. Some of these transients stayed for weeks or months, with never a complaint from their hosts.

The Irish faced problems matter-of-factly and with a dash of good humor. They were proud of their nationality and strong in their Catholic faith. True, they had weaknesses – in particular a fondness for drink.

It was inbred, I think, a habit they brought from the old country. On my first trip to Ireland I stayed at a hotel in Limerick. Everywhere in the lobby there were empty glasses and bottles.

Whether or not the cause is genetic, the Irish have difficulty with booze. Before his death at 87, AJR had not touched a drop in years. "There are three types of people who can't drink," he told his sons. "The Indians, the Irish, and everyone else."

AJR's father always had a bar, and AJR's business kept him around bars, but experience taught him that alcohol is an evil. Instead of succumbing to his environment, he put it to use.

Pop's saloon was a schoolroom for AJR. He learned about politics there. He learned about human nature. As a boy, he ran errands for the ward bosses. As a young man, he made himself useful to them by driving their constituents to churches, to wakes, and to funerals. He learned how to get things done and he learned how to make things happen.

In many ways he was puritanical; in other ways, liberal. There were God's rules and man's rules, and he knew which was which.

Unlike some of his brothers, he did not have trouble with booze. Unlike many of his friends, and in common with Dan, the brother who became a Franciscan missionary, he did not have trouble with sins of the flesh.

The Little Mayor

It would not be much of an exaggeration to say that everybody on the North Side had a nickname. There were nicknames that the cultural sensibilities of today would not abide – nicknames like Dago Sam and Nigger Smitty and Big Nose Milton. On the North Side of the 1920s an ethnic or racial slur was nothing to get excited about, and physical characteristics were fair game for ridicule. A nickname like Nigger Smitty would be unthinkable today – so toxic it could not be uttered by any decent person. In what was called "polite society" when AJR was growing up, blasphemy and obscenity were the forbidden areas of speech. Words having to do with race or ethnicity rolled off the tongue almost casually. What was shocking back then was the kind of language now heard in theaters and on the air, language routinely printed in books and magazines and sometimes even newspapers – four-letter Anglo Saxon words. The revolution in attitudes that began in the 1960s changed everything. Smitty, by the way, was not black. And his name wasn't Smith; it was Schultz, or something similar. He was a white man, said to be Jewish, who came to Pittsburgh from Cleveland. He was before my time, just a little, and I have never heard anyone describe his appearance.

Somehow, nicknames for the Irish – the Vaughan brothers answered to "Big Harp" and "Little Harp" – did not offend. Sticks and stones, the Irish figured. Better to be a harp or a mick than anything else.

There were nicknames based on personal idiosyncrasies. Game Boy, for instance. Was he game in the sense of being courageous and persistent or was he someone who liked to gamble, who liked the action? I never knew Game Boy. I did know St. Francis, an ex-pug. In the ring, he was Buck Crouse, and he fought the best middleweights of his day, including Harry Greb and George Chip, who were champions. Too many punches to the head scrambled his brain. After hanging up the gloves, he changed his identity. He stopped being Buck Crouse and was now, he explained, St. Francis of Assisi.

Unlike the original St. Francis, he continued to put a value on worldly goods. Once when AJR gave him a ten-dollar bill and told him to light candles at St. Peter's Church for a seriously ill mutual friend, St. Francis spent the money on himself. Instead of lighting candles he lit kerosene lamps, which he assured AJR would make a stronger impression on the Lord.

Growing up, I never heard AJR called by any name but Mister Rooney or Art. Later, in recognition of his title – president of the Steelers – his friends in the media nicknamed him "Prez." Later still, "Prez" gave way to "the Chief." It seems that my brothers John and Pat, the twins, detected a close similarity between AJR and a television character known as the Chief. The television Chief, a newspaper editor, was bossy and demanding but at the same time big-hearted. So John and Pat started calling their dad "the Chief," and soon the football players were doing it. Then the coaches, front-office people, newspapermen, and broadcasters got in on the act, and of course the football fans, too – at first just in Western Pennsylvania, but everywhere in the country when the Steelers were piling up Super Bowl victories.

Back in the 1920s and '30s, as the unelected, unofficial political boss of the North Side, AJR had a nickname less familiar to the general public – "The Little Mayor." He never acknowledged it, and he disavowed the label of "boss." "If I'm the boss," he would say, "the North Side is in trouble." Actually, not a week went by when North Side residents by the dozen were not in trouble, and most of them came for help to The Mayor. Some people asked for money. Others wanted jobs for their kids. Some had aged parents they were trying to place in a retirement home, or mentally ill relatives they were trying to place in a hospital. Others had relatives on trial for felonies, or relatives already in prison but coming up for parole. AJR was much in demand as a character witness.

Whatever the request, he did what he could, never more successfully than in the case of the grocer's son who fell for a floozie.

He was young, inexperienced, naive – and, on the evidence, not very smart. The girl thought his people were rich. Everyone knew her game except the kid, who was blinded by love. Either he failed to see, or preferred not to see, that as soon as she got her hands on his money she would dump him for somebody else. His successor, in fact, was waiting in the wings.

When at last he wised up, he went looking for the girl and her dude. He was Italian, the hot-blooded kind, and he had a gun. He found them in West Park, holding hands. In an uncontrollable jealous rage, oblivious to the fact that there were witnesses, he shot them dead.

The district attorney charged him with first degree murder. He went to jail, and his parents, who were anything but rich, spent all their money paying lawyers' bills. In desperation, they turned to AJR. The expense of a trial, they confided, would put them in hock; they expected to lose their store.

AJR gave the problem his full attention. He liked both parents; he liked the kid. So did Kass. The kid had delivered their groceries. Tell me everything you know about the shooting, AJR said to the parents.

It had happened the way the papers reported it, they answered. Their son had no alibi. On the advice of his lawyer, they added, he was going to plead guilty.

"No, he isn't," said AJR. "Never! Let me work on this."

Wasting no time, AJR talked to the judge. He talked to the parish priest. The parish priest talked to the judge. In the end, there was no plea of guilty. Like another North Sider in the same kind of fix – remember Harry K. Thaw? – the kid pleaded temporary insanity. Also like Thaw, he did not go to prison but was sent for a short time to a mental institution. The court then released him into AJR's custody.

Eventually the kid married. His wife was a nice Italian girl. They had children. The parents kept their grocery store and left it to the kid when they died. AJR and Kass continued to trade there, receiving good service, gratitude, and nothing else, which was exactly how they wanted it.

A former cellmate of the kid's, a convicted murderer who received a life sentence, brooded on the inequities of the criminal justice system. "I had the wrong lawyer," he complained. "I should have had Art Rooney. Here's a kid who shot down two people in front of witnesses, screaming, 'Take that – if I had more bullets I'd put them into you!' and he gets off with an insanity plea. Nobody saw me do anything – I was framed – and I'm in prison for life."

AJR, as everyone in the know understood, was not called The Little Mayor for nothing.

Curly

George Quinlan used to talk about Curly Lacock. He said that Curly Lacock weighed 300 pounds, that his mother was a prostitute, and that she gave birth to Curly in a whorehouse on Lacock Street and named him Edward Lacock.

By occupation, Curly was an ironworker. In spite of his great bulk, he could ride an iron beam into the sky. On the side, he ran a whorehouse, a wildcat brewery, and a bingo game.

The bingo game was in Millvale, in a big unused stable built for brewery horses. The Catholic church in Millvale also ran a bingo game. In those days – the 1920s – bingo operators gave baskets of food, rather than money, as prizes. If the church in Millvale gave a basket with one ham in it, Curly would give a basket with two hams. When Father McSwigan, the pastor, had had enough of this, he went to the police, who raided Curly's whorehouse, brewery, and bingo game and shut them all down.

Curly was distraught. Using Quinlan as an intermediary, he pleaded his case with AJR. He believed that AJR could prevail upon Father McSwigan to go back to the police and get the charges dropped. Curly said to Quinlan, "I don't care about the brewery and the bingo game, but please ask Art to save my whorehouse."

Quinlan liked Curly, so he delivered the message to AJR. The conversation that resulted was a short one. AJR heard Quinlan out and then he exploded.

"Are you crazy?" he said. "How can I ask a priest keep a whorehouse in business?"

A painter in Millvale, a friend of Curly's, dropped dead. Curly and Quinlan and AJR got three hundred dollars together and gave it to the widow for funeral expenses. A day or two later, Curly asked the woman where her husband was laid out.

"Nowhere," she said. "I sold the body to a clinic for fifty dollars."

Curly said, "Give me my money back."

As described by George Quinlan, he was one of the North side characters who made up the environment in which AJR and his brothers learned to cope with the world's vicissitudes.

The Legend

He was known simply as Pittsburgh Phil. A gambler and horse player whose name has entered legend, he flourished from the mid-1870s to about 1915. Pittsburgh Phil Smith came from the North Side but worked the race tracks and casinos in every part of the country. Although we never knew him, my brothers and I held him in awe. There were Rooney kin who knew Smith kin, and AJR was said to be the reincarnation of Pittsburgh Phil.

Both were special; what made them so was that both took up residence in the perilous world of big-time gambling and were not destroyed by it. Even in strongly Presbyterian turn-of-the-century Western Pennsylvania, Pittsburgh Phil was considered a man of consequence.

He is buried in one of those upscale cemeteries on Brighton Road, his marker a statue of himself. He is holding a newspaper – the Racing Form, Kass always said.

Uncle Jim used to claim that after a good day at the track he would take his marked Racing Form to Phil's grave and respectfully drop it off.

Chapter 5

With Arthur

Uncle Jim reminded me of Victor McLaglen, the actor who played the title role in John Ford's classic movie "The Informer" and won an Academy Award. Like McLaglen in so many of his screen appearances, Jim was a lovable, larger-than-life, drunken-Irishman character. With his sense of timing and his deep, resonant voice, he could have been an actor himself. He was tall – a little over six feet – and distinguished looking. Roy Blount, a *Sports Illustrated* writer who spent the 1973 football season with AJR's Steelers and recorded his impressions in a book called "About Three Bricks Shy of a Load," said of Uncle Jim that he talked in "a series of asides." He talked at such times in clearly audible stage whispers, from the corner of his mouth. There was no eye contact. You had the feeling that everything Jim said was "on the Q.T.," as he put it.

Jim fancied dark blue suits, the kind that bankers wore. One shoe was built up to compensate for a short leg, the result of a serious automobile accident. Still in his twenties, Jim was making trips to New York City to see a showgirl named Polly Lux. Now and then he traveled with friends, and there came a time when the friend at the wheel, driving in snow and ice, smashed up his car on a lonely mountain road in central Pennsylvania. Forever after, Jim walked with a limp.

Everybody liked Jim. Everybody liked him for his constant good humor and his gently sardonic wit. When people who assumed that he worked for a living, but saw no evidence of it, were rude enough to ask what he did, he would answer confidentially, "I'm with Arthur." Being "with Arthur" could mean almost anything. It could mean that he was Arthur's "main man" (without portfolio) – lobbying politicians, taking care of payoffs, "setting things up." Or it could mean that Arthur paid him a salary for doing nothing, which was closer to the truth. Either way, Jim was always around, saying little. He could be wise, flippant, caustic, kindly, street-smart, trusting – but never responsible. Or sober.

Instead of attending Duquesne Prep, as his older brothers had, Jim went to Allegheny High School. Duquesne Prep was for boys only. More than a few women have told me over the years that they were Jim's one and only at Allegheny High. I didn't doubt them. Marriage, however, was not in his plans. He preferred to live at home with Mom and Pop. Jim's younger sisters, Margaret and Marie, said their mom thought of Jim as her reason for staying alive. When he was drunk, she would say he was sick.

Jim could play football, and the legendary coach Jock Sutherland recruited him for Pitt. Sutherland made it a practice to stockpile excess talent at Bellefonte Academy, a sort of football finishing school in the middle of the state, and he sent Jim there for seasoning. When Jim entered Pitt, he would be bigger, stronger, older, and more mature.

There were rich men's sons at Bellefonte and there were immigrants' sons – the coal miners and steelworkers Sutherland was stashing away, raw material for future Pitt juggernauts. Meanwhile, they were making the Bellefonte Academy team a fearsome opponent for the college freshman teams on its schedule. Bellefonte beat one freshman team so badly, Jim said, that the president of the university – it may have been Cornell – told the headmaster of the prep school that never again would such a hardened bunch of mercenaries be allowed within sight of the campus. They were tough and unpolished, these young manual laborers reeled in by Sutherland from the mines and the mills, but higher education brought out their potential. In later years, if you went down the list, you'd find there were doctors, dentists, lawyers, and businessmen among them.

John Bain Sutherland was a big, rawboned immigrant Scot who came to this country at the age of 18 and worked at any job he could find. He was walking a police beat in Sewickley when a YMCA director advised him to go to college. Courses at Oberlin Academy, in Ohio, readied him for Pitt. At Pitt. Sutherland majored in dentistry and there he discovered football. Biographers always note that he played in the first game he ever saw. Pitt lost only once in Sutherland's first year and not at all in the next three. He was an All-American guard as a senior.

His coach was Pop Warner, who had coached Jim Thorpe at the Carlisle Indian School and was one of football's accredited masterminds. Pop Warner invented the single wing, a power-blood-and-guts formation that Sutherland made his trademark. He used it at Lafayette, in his first coaching job, and when Warner left Pitt for Stanford, and Sutherland succeeded him, the transition was seamless. Actually, Sutherland's single wing put even more stress on the power-blood-and guts aspect. If you bled, his players said, he would tell you to "get back out there" and bleed some more.

Sutherland's pre-season training camp near Windber in the Allegheny Mountains was cut off from civilization and fenced in by barbed wire. The team slept in Army tents on bags filled with straw. To keep everybody dehydrated during practice, Jock put oatmeal in the water bucket. Too much water, the coaches in those days believed, made a football player sluggish. Pitt's twice-a-day practice sessions – three hours in the morning and three in the afternoon – were brutal. In the rigid Sutherland system, everything had to be done in precisely the same way every time. Running backs always took exactly three steps, no more and no less, before cutting to the hole. From the never-ending repetitions Jock demanded, they wore out the turf, Jim said, tracing a deep rut.

In the single wing, the primary running back was the tailback – Jim's position. Jim was big and fast, and he made some long runs for the undefeated 1929 team. What he did best of all, though, was punt. Jim could kick a football tremendous distances. One of his punts in a game against Duke traveled seventy yards. Five times that day, he punted out of bounds inside the 12-yard line.

On the train trip to California for the Rose Bowl game in Pasadena with Southern California, Jim's luggage consisted of a shaving kit and a pocket full of twenty-dollar bills. There were stops along the way for publicity photos, and he would take the opportunity to buy shirts, ties, socks, and underwear at the nearest clothing store. That way, he could travel unencumbered and still have a daily change of haberdashery. To get rid of the things he'd been wearing, he would stuff them into a toilet for the porter to gather up. Forty-eight hours out of Pittsburgh, a teammate, Luby DiMeolo, noticed what Jim was doing. On the spot, he became a scavenger, retrieving Jim's good-as-new discards day after day and packing them into his luggage. When the train reached Los Angeles, Luby had to buy an extra bag.

Traveling with the team at Jock Sutherland's invitation was Yutzie Pasquarelli, proprietor of the newsstand at the corner of Forbes and Atwood in Oakland. A Pitt student himself in the 1920s, he had irritated his economics professor by falling asleep every morning in class.

"Mr. Pasquarelli," the instructor said to him one day, "why can't you keep your eyes open when I'm lecturing?"

Because he stayed up all night selling papers, Yutzie explained.

"How much do you make at that job?" the professor asked.

"Around a hundred and twenty-five dollars a week."

The professor thought about that for a minute and then finally said, "Do you know what my teaching job pays, Mr. Pasquarelli? *Thirty* dollars a week. My advice to you, sir, is: drop out of school and sell newspapers full-time."

So ended Yutzie's exposure to higher learning.

He had gone to Pitt initially in the hope of playing football. Three factors worked against this ambition: he was short, fat, and slow. Humanely, Jock Sutherland kept him out of scrimmages. Appearances to the contrary, Sutherland had a heart and a conscience. In his gruff way, he was fond of Yutzie, who solidified himself further with the coach by making interest-free loans to Pitt football players. Pitt football players were chronically hard-up (all except Jim), and Sutherland, to show his appreciation, reserved a place on the Pitt bench for Yutzie at home games and road games alike, including the one in Pasadena.

AJR now requested Yutzie's help on a matter concerning Jim. He had given Jim money for the train ride, but, knowing his spendthrift habits, had held back five hundred dollars. This was cash Jim would need for the team's five days at the game site. Notoriously, the other Pitt players would be dependent on Jim's largesse. Almost to a man, they were from families that lived hand-to-mouth. Entrusting the five hundred to Yutzie, AJR outlined an installment plan for passing it on to Jim. Yutzie was to let Jim have one hundred dollars a day, and no more than that. It was good thinking on AJR's part, and, up to a point, Jim went along with the system. He accepted his allowance for the first day and spent every cent of it. On the second day, feeling deprived of what was rightfully his, he demanded all the rest of the money.

For a minute or so, Yutzie stood firm. "Your brother said one hundred dollars a day."

Jim said, "Yutzie, if you don't give me the rest of that dough I'm going to have to slug you."

"And if I do give you the rest of it," pleaded Yutzie, "your brother will slug me."

Face to face with Jim and separated from AJR by four thousand miles, Yutzie did the sensible thing. He handed Jim four hundred dollars.

For the record, AJR refrained from slugging him. Also for the record, Jim was broke at the end of the second day.

The Pitt players elected their captain every fall at a pre-season meeting in the Pittsburgh Athletic Association. Only seniors could vote. In the 1920s, the Pittsburgh Athletic Association was a bastion of the city's WASP ruling class. Sutherland himself lived there, his home for twenty-five years a single room. He took a very keen interest in the voting for captain, never more so than in Jim's senior year. On the day of the election, Sutherland sent for Jim and asked him to "help make sure" that the players chose an Anglo-Saxon Protestant as their leader. It would be best for the team and best for the university, he said. Jim replied that he would do what he could, but reminded Sutherland that most of the players had Italian, Slavic, or Irish names and were Catholic. (Jim never failed to address Sutherland as "Doctor." Although he had not practiced dentistry since getting his D.D.S., Sutherland insisted upon the title. He was "Jock" to the sportswriters, but only in print. Face to face, they dutifully called him "Doctor.")

Regardless of any promises, Jim had no intention of complying with Sutherland's request. In balloting uninfluenced by Jim or anyone else, the man with the most votes was the very Italian, very Catholic Luby DiMeolo. To appreciate how much this meant is rather difficult now, but in Luby's day it was no small honor. Keep in mind that the city did not have a professional team and that, in any case, pro football was still just a fledgling sport. The only real football was college football, and though Carnegie Tech and Duquesne had their moments, the only college football team in Pittsburgh, the only one at least in the public perception, was Pitt. And when Pitt elected a captain – his identity always revealed at a banquet the same night – every football fan paid attention.

On this occasion, as on all such occasions, the banquet, of course, was at the PAA. Alumni and various bigwigs were present. The men wore tuxedoes, the women their finest evening gowns. Waiting for the team to appear, the band leader called for "Hail to Pitt," and the diners applauded in rhythm. Behind closed doors where the players were secluded, Luby DiMeolo climbed into a huge silver hollowed-out football. Somebody closed the lid, and designated bearers picked up the contraption, Luby now hidden from view. Ceremoniously, they carried it into the banquet hall.

"Then they opened the top," Jim said, "and there sat Luby, with his dark skin and curly hair ... like he just got off a banana boat."

It was a memory Jim cherished to the end of his days.

The Senator

Jock Sutherland asked Jim to help out at spring practice when Jim was a senior, his eligibility used up. Jim coached the punters. "Got a hundred dollars for it," he said, managing to convey, by his tone of voice, a mixture of disdain and amusement. The good Doctor's reputation was that of a tightwad. No doubt he paid his assistants the going rate, but to Jim a hundred dollars was chump change.

Jimmy Coyne now induced him to run for the State Legislature. There was no need to campaign; if you were Jimmy Coyne's man you couldn't lose, and Jim's friends barely waited for the votes to be counted before they started calling him "Senator." Misnomer though it was, the title suited him. He had the looks and deportment of a senator. The fact that he actually served in the House of Representatives seemed irrelevant.

Jim went to Harrisburg unversed in the ways of politicians. The first piece of advice he received was, "Make sure there's a transom over the door in your room at the hotel so they can throw in the money." Jim knew all the rascals and he knew the reformers and he got along best with the rascals.

According to George Quinlan, Jim made two speeches as a legislator. Commenting on Vice President Marshall's assertion that what America needed was a good five-cent cigar, Jim said, "My constituents don't care about nickel cigars. What they want is a good five-cent glass of beer."

"His other speech," Quinlan said, "was when a guy got up and started preaching about honesty in government. Jim got up and said, 'Honesty is the best policy after you get yours.'"

Jim probably did say that his constituents wanted a -five-cent glass of beer. The Volstead Act was still in effect and Jim was asking the legislature to petition the United States Congress for an amendment, an amendment that would legalize four percent beer. The rest of Quinlan's story may well be apocryphal. Jim was capable of having said that honesty is the best policy after you get yours, but on the floor of the General Assembly? I think that is doubtful.

Quinlan was Jim's closest confidant. "Any bill Coyne gave him," Quinlan said, "Jim would go up and present it. He wouldn't even read it. One time he presented a bill to put school boards back in politics. The next day he woke up, and about two hundred schoolteachers were marching around with signs that said, 'Down with Senator Rooney.'"

There is one obvious misstatement here. The signs could not have misidentified Jim. Schoolteachers are better informed than that. Really they are. For another thing, there is reason to believe that Jim was nowhere near Harrisburg on the morning of the demonstration. A colleague had warned him to get out of town, and the likelihood is that he was visiting Polly Lux in New York.

Jim's proposed legislation – to make school boards elective with a salary of five thousand dollars a year for each member – was roundly assailed by newspaper editorial writers as an attempt to increase the patronage power of local and state politicians. Abandoned by Coyne, who denied being the source of the idea, Jim stopped pushing for the bill, and it never became law. Nor did a bill he introduced calling for tax money to support parochial schools. AJR said that Jim made a speech predicting a march on the state capitol by thousands of Catholic schoolchildren, all waving American flags. Nothing of the kind ever happened, and financial help for parochial schools has continued to be a lost cause.

In calling for the repeal of the Pennsylvania Blue Laws, Jim was on safer ground. By 1933, Sunday football and Sunday baseball were no longer illegal. And Jim, swept out in a great tide of anti-Republican feeling, was no longer in politics.

Cracks in the Coyne machine began appearing in 1931, when the puppet he had installed as mayor of Pittsburgh, Charles Kline, was convicted of malfeasance in office. Given a six-month suspended sentence, Kline resigned in disgrace. Coyne himself ran for county commissioner and lost. In the same election, at Coyne's behest, Jim ran for City Council and lost. Coyne's motivation was simple: there were now more patronage jobs in the county and the city than in Harrisburg.

But the course of events was against him. The Great Depression had peaked, hitting Pittsburgh and the steel industry with devastating effect. Men without jobs sold apples on street corners. Soup kitchens fed the hungry. The homeless built Shantytowns and Hoovervilles. Father James Cox of St. Patrick's parish in the Strip District led a march of the unemployed on Washington, D. C.

In Allegheny County, as in most other parts of America, blame for the Depression had settled on the Republican Party. The few Democrats in the county were led by David L. Lawrence, who was not so much a rival of Coyne as his friend and collaborator. Coyne tossed him patronage jobs that might otherwise have gone to Republicans. But Lawrence could see what was coming: the Republicans were the party of the past, the Democrats the party of the future. He therefore dissolved his marriage of convenience with Coyne. In the 1932 presidential election, a Democratic landslide, Franklin D. Roosevelt carried Allegheny County by 37,000 votes, a substantial margin. And in the Seventh Legislative District, the Democrat running on FDR's coattails beat Jim, temporarily ending his political career. He was 27 years old.

In 1933, Dave Lawrence's candidate for mayor, William McNair, easily defeated the Republican hand-picked by Coyne. Three years later, Coyne lost his Senate seat, and he was finished. For the rest of the century, no Republican could be elected to any political office in Pittsburgh or to any important office in Allegheny County. Almost alone among Jimmy Coyne's followers, AJR remained steadfast. Davey Lawrence urged him to change parties, as countless others were doing, but though AJR had the highest regard for Lawrence, and though they often were seen together at prize fights, football games, and Kentucky Derbies, he was not a turncoat.

Nor was Jim, for whatever it may have been worth. He ran again for the legislature in 1934 and won, but retired at the end of his two-year term. Politics meant little to Jim. His priorities were booze and wild times.

Of Jim's many girlfriends, the most interesting was Polly Lux. They had known each other since she lived on the North Side, and there were those who believed that Jim had serious intentions.

"Polly Lux" was a stage name. For show-business purposes, her real name, Eastern European in origin, was apparently too ethnic. She was blond and she was beautiful and she made it all the way to the Ziegfeld Follies.

Jim spent weekends with Polly in New York from time to time. Like Imogene Coca, Polly owned a poodle. And Polly's poodle, like Imogene's, had to be taken for walks. This, of course, was where Jim came in. Hadn't AJR tended to Imogene Coca's little dog? Anyway, the story is that one day when Jim was in Polly's apartment she told him to walk the dog and went into another room. Jim – the story is – took the dog to a window and dropped it onto the sidewalk, eight floors below. Returning, Polly said, "Where's my dog?" And Jim said, "He went for a walk by himself."

That's a story I have heard about people other than Jim, a story I think may be closer to myth than to fact.

Jim was lucky to be alive after the automobile accident that crippled him on March 22, 1933. Driven by a man called Ticky Tock Toth, the car in which he was riding had skidded on the icy road and slammed into a brick wall. For days Jim remained in a coma. His skull was fractured. His chest was crushed. He had a dislocated hip and a broken knee. Another passenger, fight manager Al Kane, died of similar injuries. The driver, Ticky Tock, escaped with a brain concussion and "lacerations." While Jim was in the hospital, Polly Lux came from New York to see him. All he would say to her was that he wanted his Mom. Jim could never stand pain. Polly distanced herself from him after that. In the end, she married an exiled Polish baron and lived in Florida.

Jim was not exactly heartbroken. Once his romances were over, he never seemed to give them a thought. I remember mentioning to him the name of an old girlfriend whose sister I had met. "Ah, yes," Jim said in his W. C. Fieldsian manner. "A nice girl ... Killed by a truck, ya know."

That was that. Jim wasted no time on sentiment.

Plain Speaking

As one last favor to Jimmy Coyne, who still had control of a hamstrung Republican Party, AJR agreed to run for an Allegheny County row office – register of wills – in 1936.

So discredited were the Republicans that his chances of winning looked infinitesimal. They could not, however, be completely written off, and for the candidate who ended up with the job a nice little windfall seemed possible.

In those days the register of wills received a modest percentage of each estate that was processed. Ordinarily it amounted to very little, but in this particular election year the outlook was more promising. Andrew Mellon, the owner or part owner of a bank and trust company, an oil company, a gas and coke company, an aluminum company, and a coal company – the list may be incomplete – was extremely old and frail. If he went to his reward without dawdling, the register of wills could expect to cash in.

So, after his own fashion, AJR gave it a try.

"Oh, what a campaigner he was," said George Quinlan. "He never asked anybody to vote for him and he never asked anybody for a contribution."

According to Quinlan, this was how AJR ran:

"We'd get full of beer" – AJR had not yet sworn off – "and then we'd start out, four or five of us. One night we started in Wilkinsburg. There were twenty-five people at the meeting and twenty-four of them were anti-Irish, anti-Catholic little old ladies. Wilkinsburg was a strait-laced Protestant town with nineteen churches and no saloons. Rooney got up, and do you know what he talked about? The great ability and character of the people he met in horse racing. He didn't get too many votes from that crowd."

One afternoon the campaigners pulled up at a picnic grounds, unannounced. A polka band was playing; people were dancing. At a concession stand, AJR bought some beer and some food for the crowd. Then he and his friends joined the merrymaking. AJR, circulating among the bystanders, charmed one and all and let it be known that he was running for register of wills.

"In what county?" someone asked.

"Allegheny."

"Well, gee," the questioner said. "I'd like to vote for you, but I can't. None of us can."

"Why not?"

"All of us live here in Houston. And Houston is not in Allegheny County. It's in Washington County. Where you aren't on the ballot."

AJR lost the election, done in by a forthright campaign speech which the saloonkeeper Owney McManus, his campaign manager, had warned him not to make.. "I don't know what a register of wills is supposed to do," he told a large crowd at the Syria Mosque in Oakland, assembled to hear all the candidates deliver their last pitch for votes, "and I don't even know where the office is. But if you elect me, I promise to hire people who can run the place, the very best people I can find."

The speech was in some ways a success. Everybody in the audience, and everybody who read about it, laughed. The newspapers played the story big, praising AJR on the editorial page for his candor, and even Time magazine picked up on it. The election, however, went to his opponent. In politics, as Uncle Jim supposedly said, honesty isn't always the best policy.

It was AJR's last hurrah. He was never again a candidate for anything. In fact, when Tip O'Neill, the Massachusetts Democrat who was speaker of the House of Representatives at the time, asked if he would like to be ambassador to Ireland, AJR demurred. O'Neill offered to recommend him for the appointment. Jimmy Carter was president, and the Democrats were handing out plums.

But AJR wasn't interested. "I'm too old," he said. "And not rich enough. And besides," he added, remembering his ties to Jimmy Coyne, "I'm a Republican."

Sandlot Tycoon

When AJR was in his twenties he owned, coached, and sometimes played halfback for a semi-pro football team that underwent a series of name changes. In the beginning it was known as the Hope-Harveys. Hope, as AJR once explained, was the name of the firehouse in The Ward where the players put on their uniforms and showered, and Harvey was the name of the team's doctor. Later, acquiring a sponsor, the Hope-Harveys became the Majestic Radios. Later still, in 1930, when Uncle Jim ran (so to speak) for the State Legislature, AJR re-named them the J. P. Rooneys to publicize his brother's campaign, which consisted, as I have said, of waiting for the votes to be counted.

Uncle Jim had played for the Majestic Radios, using an assumed name to protect his eligibility at Pitt, and even during his term in the legislature he played for the J. P. Rooneys. He was a triple-threat halfback who could run, pass, and kick.

AJR's playing career had by this time come to an end. He seldom spoke of it except to recall that in a game with the Canton Bulldogs he was instrumental in the Hope-Harveys' defeat. He tried a field goal; somebody blocked it; Jim Thorpe, who was ten years past his prime, picked up the ball and ran for the winning touchdown.

With AJR and Dan in the backfield, the Hope-Harveys were usually the best sandlot team for miles around. In a 1926 article, the *Pittsburgh Post* referred to AJR as "the Red Grange of the independents." Dan was even "more dominant," a straight-ahead runner with breakaway speed and a kicker in the mold of Uncle Jim.

In AJR's opinion, the Hope-Harveys, the Majestics, and the J. P. Rooneys were on a par with the teams of the National Football League. The pay was about the same – very little. If there were fences and gates, the home team charged an admission price. Otherwise, management fell back on the time-honored expedient of passing the hat. The personnel was a mixture of players like Jim – former college stars – and ordinary neighborhood guys who worked all day at their jobs and practiced football in the evening.

Game day was Sunday. Under the Pennsylvania Blue Laws, organized sports and other occasions of sin were prohibited on Sunday, but friendly constables could be induced – nobody ever used the word "bribed" – to look the other way. So the games went on, sometimes doubly disrupting the peace of the Sabbath. Often if the home team was losing, its supporters would circle the field and wait for a provocation from anyone who looked unfamiliar. Then fists would start flying, the

KR

Hope Harvey Player
(Drawing by Kathy Rooney)

players would join in, and the game would end in a riot, which canceled all bets. Without an official conclusion, the home team technically hadn't lost.

A game at Exposition Park between the Hope-Harveys and West View ended earlier than usual – in the first quarter. Hope-Harvey blocked a punt, and a fight broke out. "Pretty soon the crowd was all over the field," recalled AJR, "and the fight turned into a riot." Playing tackle for the Hope-Harveys that day, for a promised seventy-five dollars, was ex-Notre Damer Joe Bach, an assistant coach at Duquesne University. He saw that the game wasn't going to be finished and went home. "The next day," said AJR, "I sent a guy over to pay Joe his seventy-five dollars. He wouldn't take it. 'Go ahead,' the guy told him. 'The Hope-Harveys never finish any of their games.'"

Always in the crowd there were hoodlums and petty thieves. On train trips to road games – that was how everybody traveled back then – the hoods would be in one car, the team in another. The Majestics, or it may have been the J. P. Rooneys, went by train once to Johnstown for a game, and the mayor of the city came to watch. A man named Eddie McCloskey, he was famous at the time for having marched on Washington with Father Cox's Army. Father James R. Cox was the pastor of St. Patrick's Church in the Strip. In January of 1932, disillusioned with the Hoover administration's handling of the economic crisis, he led an army of the unemployed, three or four thousand to start with, many more as the march proceeded, from Pittsburgh to the national capitol. When they passed through Johnstown, McCloskey joined them. McCloskey and AJR were good friends. They met on the field after the football game and did not part company until the Majestics (or the Rooneys) entrained for Pittsburgh, together with their fans.

Returning home, McCloskey discovered that his wallet was missing. "My pocket has been picked," he said to his wife, "but don't worry. Art Rooney will take care of this for me."

He telephoned the station master at a stop between Johnstown and Pittsburgh. There the train was sidetracked while AJR called the mayor. At the end of their conversation, he knew what to do.

Back on the train, he conferred with a few of his henchmen. "This game in Johnstown," he reminded them, "is a real big payday for us. I'd hate to blow it. Not only that, but when somebody picks the mayor's pocket it makes us look bad. So find the guy who did this. He'll be in the club car, playing cards."

Faster than you can say Oliver Twist, the search party flushed out the thief. He was where AJR had said he would be – in the club car, playing cards. He gave up the wallet without an argument. Not a dollar was missing. He apologized for failing to realize that the mayor was AJR's friend. If he'd had any notion, it never would have happened, he said. He hoped that AJR understood.

All's well that ends well. AJR called the mayor from Pittsburgh that night. When the mayor hung up, he said to his wife, "I told you I'd get that wallet back. It couldn't have been safer in my pocket."

As a matter of fact, it hadn't been nearly as safe.

Enfranchised

Given advance information that the Blue Laws would be changed to allow professional athletic contests on Sunday, AJR paid $2,500 for a National Football League franchise in time to arrange a schedule of games for the 1933 season.

If $2,500 seems like a piddling sum, bear in mind that the economics of sports were far different back then. "The pro game," as AJR put it, reminiscing some forty years later, "wasn't even a hop, skip and jump from semi-pro ball, maybe just a hop. For a hundred dollars a game, you could hire a good player. You didn't make a lot of money, but you didn't lose a lot, either."

Originally – or unoriginally – he called his new team the Pirates. There was a baseball team in Pittsburgh called the Pirates, but nobody hollered "trademark infringement." Former Pitt, Duquesne, and Carnegie Tech players, including some who had worked in the coal mines and steel mills, packed the eighteen-man roster. The quarterback was Harp Vaughan, using Hope-Harvey and Majestic Radio plays. Harp took the field with a bandanna tied to his head; it rippled in the wind when he ran. Even for the NFL of the 1930s, that was sandlot stuff. Uncle Jim would have been in the backfield, too, if not for the automobile accident that left him a permanent cripple.

For the team's first coach, AJR wanted Earle "Greasy" Neale, from Parkersburg, West Virginia. Neale, who had played college football (at West Virginia Wesleyan), professional football (with the

Canton Bulldogs), and major-league baseball (for the Cincinnati Reds), was on the verge of signing a contract with the new Pittsburgh team when an Ivy League college offered him a job as an assistant. That this would be a better career move, fantastic as it may seem to us now, was obvious. The Ivy League had prestige; the NFL was still a shoestring operation. Willingly, AJR released him from their agreement.

Neale would have been an excellent choice for the Pirates. He did eventually coach in the NFL, winning a division championship and two league championships with the Philadelphia Eagles. Like AJR, he is now in the Hall of Fame. The coach AJR ended up with, Forrest "Jap" Douds, is not. Douds played tackle for the Pirates, as he had for some good Washington & Jefferson teams. If Uncle Jim's opinion carried any weight, that must have been the extent of his contribution. "Between you and me," Jim said in one of his confidential asides after the 1933 team had passed into history, "he was no coach."

Actually, the Pirates' record of three victories, six defeats and two ties in Douds' only season wasn't at all bad for an expansion team, but AJR, convinced as he was that the Hope-Harveys or Majestic Radios were the equal of most NFL teams, had higher expectations. It may be that he underestimated the difficulty. I don't think he was wrong in believing that Western Pennsylvania football players were as tough and tenacious as they come.

The first game the Pirates ever played was on a Wednesday night at Forbes Field. They lost to the New York Giants, 23-2, and AJR wrote in his diary, "Our fans" – the paid attendance was 13,483 – "didn't get their money's worth." Two days before the team's first scheduled home game on a Sunday; AJR received a telephone call from Mayor William McNair. "Some preacher," the mayor said, was constantly reminding him that Pittsburgh's City Council had not yet ratified the amendment to the Blue Laws. Legally, therefore, the game at Forbes Field between the Pirates and the Brooklyn Dodgers could not be played.

AJR was flabbergasted. "Mayor," he said, "I never heard of this thing, ratification."

Neither had McNair, it turned out. He advised AJR to see the public safety director, a man named Harmar Denny. Typically the politician, Denny washed his hands of the affair. "I'm going away this weekend," he decided on the spur of the moment.

AJR said, "Good. You go away." He then took his problem to the chief of police, Fran McQuade. McQuade heard him out and asked for two tickets to the game.

Over the next forty-eight hours, the preacher and his followers pressed on relentlessly in their efforts to keep holy the Sabbath day, but they were spinning their wheels. They could not find Denny, who was out of town. They could not find McQuade, who had gone into hiding. Sunday came, and right up to kickoff time they looked for him everywhere except in the one place he knew they would never think of looking – Forbes Field.

The Pirates played poorly, losing by a score of 32-0. AJR's reaction is not to be found in his diary.

'Arthur, What Can I Do for You?'

What everybody remembered about Mayor Charles Kline was not the forty-seven counts of malfeasance that ended his political career, but the fact that in the middle of the Depression he bought, with public funds, an outrageously expensive Oriental carpet for his office in City Hall. Any mention of Kline as the years went by reminded AJR of the carpet.

"And they're still using it," he would say.

AJR had no dealings with Kline but on one occasion went to see his executive assistant about Pittsburgh's interpretation of the Blue Laws. A tough, prudish, anti-Catholic Protestant, this untitled deputy mayor kept AJR waiting for an unreasonable length of time and then re-scheduled the interview.

Before their next appointment, AJR happened to be talking with the biggest numbers operator in Mount Oliver and asked him how things were going. "OK," was the answer, "but this guy down at City Hall is putting the squeeze on me."

And who would that be? inquired AJR.

None other, replied the numbers writer, than Mayor Charles Kline's executive assistant.

"He's a creep," the numbers guy continued. "A creep, a phony, and a hypocrite. He's a deacon in his church, and his hands are in every racket in town."

Not long afterward, AJR's meeting with the administrator in question took place.

Predictably, the man was cold and condescending. In ways that were subtle and not so subtle, he put down the Catholic Church. AJR did not respond, but merely stated his business and listened to what the executive assistant said. The executive assistant then dismissed him.

AJR got up and went to the door. He opened it a little before turning to say, "Oh, I knew there was something else. I saw your old friend [Joe Blow] from Mount Oliver. He told me to give you a big hello."

The executive assistant straightened up in his chair. "Arthur!" he said. There was warmth in his voice. Always before, it had been "Mister Rooney." "Wait just a minute. Come back and sit down. So we share a good common friend?"

It was certainly no secret to the executive assistant that AJR had remarkably close contacts among newspapermen. With a well-placed word, he could generate unpleasant headlines.

"Arthur, what can I do for you?" the executive assistant asked.

As a result of the conversation that followed, twenty-eight young men from the North Side, for the most part Irish Catholics, went to work in the Fire Department or the Police Department, and one of those twenty-eight eventually became the city's fire chief.

Chapter 6

Growing Pains I

In their first three seasons, AJR's Pirates had three different coaches. Jap Douds made way for Luby DiMeolo in 1934 and Luby DiMeolo made way for Joe Bach in 1935.

Douds, after stepping down as coach, continued to be a starting tackle for two more years. The other tackle, Ray Kemp, disappears from the roster after 1933. Ray Kemp was not the first black player in the NFL – several others preceded him – but after Kemp's one season a de facto color line existed in both the college and professional games for too many years.

AJR was familiar with Ray Kemp because Kemp had played for his semi-pro teams and also at Duquesne University. The discrimination blacks met with back then did not come exclusively from whites. Kemp told a story, perhaps with humorous intent, about making a good hit on a running back who happened to be a full-blooded Indian. Aware that in a white man's world, Indians, for the most part, were treated no better than blacks, Kemp reached out a brotherly hand to help him regain his feet. The Indian pushed it away.

"I don't want any help from a black bastard," he said.

In 1934 Kemp did not return, and there were no more black players in professional football until 1946. It was all such a waste of talent and so unfair to a lot of good people.

Luby DiMeolo asked his former Pitt teammate, Uncle Jim, to be the backfield coach of the Pirates. Still convalescing from the automobile accident that shortened one leg, Jim was of little assistance, and the Pirates had an unsuccessful season, winning only two games. Under Luby, the team lacked discipline. He was too much one of the boys.

One afternoon in the Pirate offices at the Fort Pitt Hotel, Luby fell to arguing with AJR about a hypothetical question: in a fight between a boxer and a football player, who would prevail?

"The boxer," said AJR.

"The football player," insisted Luby.

Boxer and football player, AJR could have taken either role. It appears in this instance that he thought of himself as a boxer. Luby had only played football. "There's a way we can settle this," said AJR, and he sent for a pair of boxing gloves. Luby, a tender-hearted fellow, began to dwell on the possibility of doing his opponent serious harm.

"I'm too big and strong for you," he protested.

"Maybe," said AJR. "I'll take my chances."

The gloves arrived. They pushed the office furniture up against the wall and squared off – and Luby's size and strength were mostly wasted. AJR, much the quicker of the two, and by far the more skillful, handled him easily.

After leaving the Pirates, Luby found his calling: he became a U. S. marshal. His friendship with the Rooney family continued for as long as he lived.

Joe Bach, Luby's successor, was one of Notre Dame's Seven Mules, the linemen who blocked for the celebrated Four Horsemen in the Notre Dame-Army game of 1924, but were not, unlike the Four Horsemen, outlined against the blue-gray October sky depicted by Grantland Rice in the *New York Herald-Tribune* and did not, unlike the Four Horsemen, derive their nickname from Rice. The Seven Mules nicknamed themselves. Center Adam Walsh, who played with a broken hand, was the only Mule visible to Rice. In his lyrical game story, he mentioned no others.

AJR had sized up Joe Bach as "a take-charge guy and a top organizer." Certainly Bach took charge of the Pirates. In his second season, 1936, they had the Eastern Division championship in their grasp, but then December came, bringing disaster. They lost their last two games, which were both on the road because AJR had rejiggered the schedule as a favor to another owner, sacrificing a home date..

Consequently, Joe Bach blamed him for the Pirates' sorry finish. AJR, for his part, believed the coaching was at fault. Sure, the Pirates had shown improvement. Their 6-6 record was a big step forward. Even so, it was galling to watch them fall apart. And though AJR acknowledged that Bach had done a better job than his predecessors, take-charge guys can be irritating at times. The trouble was that Bach took charge, or tried to take charge, in areas where AJR thought that he, as the employer, was in charge. Taking charge was second nature to Bach. "If you were playing cards," said AJR, "he'd grab the deck and deal."

Tensions between them came to the surface after a 13-3 defeat at the hands of George Preston Marshall's Boston Redskins, forerunners of the Washington Redskins, in the next-to-the-last game of the season. On the train ride home, Bach complained that AJR had scheduled too many exhibition games during the regular season. They argued; owner and coach came to blows. And they fought, witnesses said, from one end of Massachusetts to the other.

Luby DiMeolo had been no competition for AJR. Joe Bach was a handful. He was almost as big as Luby and just as strong, and apparently he knew how to fight. AJR held his own – perhaps he more than held his own – but there was no satisfaction in it for him.

He had duked it out, for different reasons, with two of his first three coaches. In The Ward, that was normal behavior; that was the way differences were resolved, by duking it out. And he was still only 35, still with rough edges, still in his physical prime and full of enormous energy.

AJR respected Joe Bach, but there was no way, he thought, that Bach could stay on as coach. So after a season-ending loss to the Giants in New York, AJR let him go – and quickly regretted it. "If I'd been a little more patient," he said, looking back, "we'd have had a winner for years and years. Joe took care of details, and not many pro coaches were doing that in the 1930s."

Let the record show that AJR made amends. When Father Silas was the athletic director at St. Bonaventure University and needed a coach, AJR suggested Bach, who got the job. And when, in 1952, St. Bonaventure dropped football, AJR rehired him to coach the team that was now called the Steelers.

Saratoga

It was not too surprising that AJR, growing up in The Ward, became a horse player. Horse parlors and bookie joints were easy to find in The Ward, and horse players congregated at Pop Rooney's saloon. Pop played the horses himself, at the track in Cleveland, where he and his friends had to go because racing in Pennsylvania was forbidden by law. AJR would be with them, enhancing his education.

The Ward was a raffish, sports-centered neighborhood. Exposition Park, where the baseball team called the Pirates played its home games for many years, was just across the street from Pop's bar. There were fight shows there, too, and carnivals and football games.

One of the characters in The Ward, a woman named Nettie Gordon, was said to preside over forty-one "sporting houses," as they were called. "Oh, she made a ton of money," said George Quinlan after Nettie's demise, "and the politicians got most of it."

Maggie – Grandma Rooney – knew nothing of Nettie Gordon except that her hats, elaborate feathered constructions, were "funny looking." "But she's a very nice lady," Maggie announced, evoking a burst of laughter from Uncle John. He said, "Mom! She's a madam! She runs sporting houses!"

AJR's sister, Margaret Laughlin, often repeated a story about Nettie. "I'll never forget the day after Pop's brother Myles was shot – I mean died," she would say. "He was laid out at the Perrysville Avenue house. There were so many well-wishers. But do you know what happened? Aunt Annie, Pop's sister, had five dollars taken from her purse. The last person there who could afford to lose money. Aunt Annie was as poor as a church mouse. It was some crowd of mourners. Little Tommy" – the youngest of AJR's brothers – "had some change in a milk bottle. Pennies and nickels. He was saving up to buy roller skates. And somebody stole the change out of that milk bottle.

"Anyway, this very big floral wreath is delivered to the house. On the ribbon, it's printed, 'For Myles ... with love ... from Nettie Gordon.'

"The *notorious* Nettie Gordon, some would have said. But Mom" – Maggie Rooney – "never hesitated. She put Nettie's wreath in front of the casket. A few minutes later, one of Pop's sisters, she was married to a man named Brooks, moved it *behind* the casket. Then somebody put it in front again. And then it went back behind the casket. Back and forth, back and forth. What was the right thing to do? Obviously, Myles and Nettie had been pretty good friends. But there were members of the family who didn't think it ought to be advertised."

AJR believed that the kind of recreational facilities Nettie ran served a worthwhile purpose. They were safety valves, he thought, protecting decent young women from the kind of sexual aggression which has come to be known as "date rape." This idea goes back to the Middle Ages, when the Roman Catholic Church endorsed it. Prostitution, in the view of the Church, was the lesser of two evils. Later the Church reversed itself. AJR, who would argue the point with Catholic priests, resisted their attempts to change his mind.

None of Pop Rooney's sons worked in the family saloon. All were athletes. All attended college. All went through life without ever punching a time clock. AJR was born to play the horses, and he quickly surpassed in expertise his teachers from The Ward, the touts and bookies and racing-form readers who recognized his precociousness and took him under their wing. Betting on horses paid for his piece of The Showboat and financed his marriage and honeymoon. Then in 1936, in two days at two tracks in New York, he made a killing that people talked about for years.

Talked about and wrote about. Joseph Madden, a New York saloonkeeper with literary aspirations, was the first to record the details. They appeared in his book of memoirs, "Set 'Em Up." Under the caption "Rooney's Ride," John Lardner re-told the story in his *Newsweek* column. Other accounts followed, all describing how AJR picked as many as eleven straight winners in that two-day spree and won an indeterminate amount of money which may have totaled upwards of $380,000. Roy Blount, in his book about the Steelers and the Rooneys, said it was "probably the greatest individual performance in the history of American horse-playing." Nobody since has disagreed.

Rooney's Ride to Riches began on a Saturday afternoon at the Empire City track in Yonkers, which forty years later, when AJR bought it, was a harness racing track. .According to Joseph Madden, who had changed his name from Penzo for business reasons – his bar clientele was largely Irish – AJR came to Empire City with $300 in his kick and ran it up to $21,000. Buck Crouse, the punch-drunk ex-fighter, was with him. When the races were over, they adjourned to Madden's saloon and steak house and set out from there for Saratoga, upstate, with Madden at the wheel of his beat-up jalopy. En route, it had "four bad coughing spells," Lardner wrote. "Mr. Rooney and Mr. Crouse," he added, "got out and pushed."

There was no racing on Sunday at Saratoga, but on Monday AJR continued to pick the right horses and won an additional sum which can only be guessed at. On an 8-to-1 shot in the fifth or sixth race, he was able to get down just $10,000 of the $15,000 he wanted to bet. (In those days, bookmakers took your action; there were no parimutuel machines.) The race was a photo finish involving four horses. Madden, who said he had "bet a few clams" himself, "nearly died waiting for the picture." AJR, unconcerned, went off to the men's room. When Madden rushed in to tell him their horse had won, he was talking football with the attendant.

Madden and Lardner wrote that AJR cleared $256,000 at Saratoga that day. AJR told me it was more, but did not say precisely how much more. A friend of his, the director of racing at our Yonkers track, put the figure at $380,000. Other estimates are higher. Whatever he won, and the officials at Saratoga offered him a Brink's armored truck to carry the money back to New York City, he won it at a time when working men were supporting wives and children on as little as twenty dollars a week.

Those two memorable days in 1936 were the foundation of AJR's fortune. When he returned home, he said to either his brother Vince or to Kass – or maybe to both – "We'll never have to worry about money again."

The story is, and I'm sure it's true, that AJR gave $10,000 of his winnings to Father Silas, who needed a roof for the mission house in China, where the Franciscans had sent him to do missionary work. Another tale – that AJR paid for his NFL franchise out of the Empire City/Saratoga money – doesn't compute. The football team had been his for three years. However, his take from that weekend paid a lot of bills and helped keep the team afloat.

One mild summer evening before the start of the hot weather, AJR took me to a movie called "Saratoga Trunk" at the Kenyon Theater on Federal Street. Afterward, walking home, we passed the Planetarium and St. Peter's School. At East Ohio Street we waited for the light to change. (AJR preached constantly against jaywalking.) As we stood on the curb, he fell to reminiscing, stimulated perhaps by the movie. He talked about Saratoga, which had been a nineteenth-century spa. "Bluebloods" from New York City went there for the waters, he said. In that small country town, hotels, casinos, and a race track were built. Decades later, the casinos had gone out of business, the hotels, though still grand, were aging – in AJR's room a coil of rope on the floor was the fire escape – and the mineral springs had lost their attraction, but still the bluebloods came in the racing season, rubbing elbows now with the proletariat.

"In my day at Saratoga," said AJR, "horse racing was king." On the Saturday he picked all those long shots, a premonition came over him. "I just felt I was going to win," he said as we walked through West Park. It had happened before and would happen again, this feeling of invincibility, but never with such forcefulness. Maybe, after all, the Irish really do have visions. I thought of Gary Cooper in the movie at the Kenyon, merely acting out a part my father had lived.

When the parimutuel system replaced bookmakers, AJR cut back on the scale of his betting. If you placed a bet with a bookie at, say, 3-to-1 odds, those were the odds he paid off on. In parimutuel betting, the odds continually change on the basis of where the money is going. Also, the state and the track take their cuts. Parimutuels, it seemed to AJR, threw the percentages way out of whack. Winning $256,000 or $380,000 in a single day would no longer be possible.

So instead of just betting on horses he took to breeding them and racing them. He bought a stud farm in Maryland and named it Shamrock Farm, which later became Shamrock Farms.. It was there that I saw something unusual one day – AJR on horseback. As much as he knew about horses, I don't think he ever had ridden one. But on this particular day, he slowly climbed onto the saddle of an old lead pony the kids used to ride. He had a cigar in the corner of his mouth and was wearing a suit, a topcoat, and a hat. He looked very serious and uncomfortable. As you might expect, the ride didn't last long. I assumed at the time, and still do, that it was something he wanted to say he had done, and for no better reason, if there is a better reason, than his own satisfaction.

'Holy God, You're a Priest!'

Upon being ordained, Uncle Dan became Father Silas, O.F.M. The original Silas was an early Christian missionary who accompanied St. Paul on his travels.

Father Silas Rooney, wearing his Roman collar, attended a baseball game at Griffith Stadium, the home of the Washington Senators. The team's manager and shortstop, Joe Cronin, had played in the Middle Atlantic League for Johnstown when Dan played for Wheeling, and from his field-level box seat the new Franciscan missionary waved a greeting. Cronin tipped his cap. At the end of the inning, on his way to the dugout, he stopped and said:

"Father, I don't know you, but you put me in mind of a tough Irishman who played in the Middle Atlantic League. His name was Dan Rooney."

"I'm Dan Rooney," came the reply.

"Holy God!" Cronin exclaimed. "You're a priest!"

The Franciscans sent Dan – Father Silas from now on – to China. He spent the early-to-late 1930s in a small provincial town, propagating the faith and running an orphanage. In view of the Chinese attitude toward unwanted female children, the orphans were sometimes the lucky ones.

Crossing a foot bridge one day, Father Silas observed a man with a bag over his shoulder. The bag was moving. Father Silas flagged him down and discovered that inside the bag there were two baby girls – twins. The man intended to drop them into the river, which was how the Chinese disposed of excess baby girls. Father Silas paid him off – he demanded a small sum of money – and took the girls to the orphanage.

Years later, during the time when AJR's Steelers had their pre-season training camp at St. Bonaventure University and Father Silas was St. Bonaventure's athletic director, a newspaper photographer posed a young rookie quarterback with two Franciscan nuns for a publicity shot. The quarterback was Johnny Unitas, a detail worth mentioning for one reason: Unitas went on to a Hall-of-Fame career with the Baltimore Colts after Coach Walt Kiesling of the Steelers declared him expendable – "too dumb" to succeed in the National Football League. The nuns – theological students at St. Bonaventure – were the sisters Father Silas had saved from a watery grave.

He protected both the orphanage girls and the town girls from the predatory warlords who ruled China's countryside. Passing through, the warlords and their men would be looking for virgins to rape. So Father Silas dispatched the virgins and maybe some non-virgins as well – he didn't discriminate – to a hiding place in the hills.

Along with the warlords, the villagers had to deal with the Japanese, who overran parts of China starting in 1938. At one of our family reunions, my brother Dan's son Jim told me of meeting a very old Chinese woman in Colombia, where he was working as a volunteer with an organization similar to the Peace Corps. She had made it out of China during the Japanese occupation, she told him. Before her escape, she added, an American missionary priest had hidden her from Japanese soldiers with rape on their minds.

"My Uncle Dan was a priest in China when the Japanese came," said Jim.

"Oh?" the woman answered. "What did you say his name was?"

"Father Silas."

"That was him!" said the woman excitedly.

No surprise.

In all of those years there was famine in China. Father Silas made his rounds on a broken-down race horse, donated to the mission by some philanthropist, and it was fated to end up in a dozen or more cooking pots.

The horse was an old plug, barely able to move. But one day something startled it. Bolting, it galloped down the principal street of a village. Father Silas could do nothing. He pulled at the reins, but the nag kept going. And then in full stride it suddenly dropped dead.

A throng of peasants voracious as buzzards instantly descended on the corpse. All of them seemed to have butcher knives, and they were fighting one another to get at the choicest cuts. Father Silas jumped to his feet and called for order. The peasants backed off. Taking charge, he organized a lottery. Numbers were drawn, civility maintained, and everybody went home with fresh meat.

In addition to famine, there was plague. Father Silas stopped a man who was poised to jump into the river. "I have nothing to live for," he said. "The plague has killed all of my children, and the famine has destroyed all my crops. All I have left is my wife, and I've never liked her."

Father Silas took the man to the orphanage and gave him a job. In time, he was baptized a Catholic. When others in the town were joining the Communist Party, this man would have none of it. Father Silas had shown him what faith was, and how could the Communists offer more?

Eight years in China left their mark on Father Silas. He fell once, into the river – the river that took the lives of infant children and suicidal men – and a microbe got into his ear. From then on he was partially deaf. After the Japanese invasion, the Franciscans sent him home. He returned with what the medical men called malaria; I know it was amyotrophic lateral sclerosis – Lou Gehrig's Disease – and eventually it killed him.

In public Father Silas rarely talked about China. A story he told at a banquet in McKeesport was uncharacteristically humorous. It involved Jake Mintz, the Rooney-McGinley Boxing Club's matchmaker, and it may or may not have been apocryphal. You must understand to appreciate the punch line that Mintz had a bashed-in nose, the result of his own years in the ring. On this night in McKeesport, with Mintz among those at the speakers' table, Father Silas told of entering a Chinese village where no Occidental before him ever had ventured. Two men were staring at him. "My God, isn't he ugly?" one of them said. They spoke a dialect Father Silas understood, and he could not let it pass.

In their own language, he said to the men, "You should see Jake Mintz."

Chapter 7

Stand-Patter

AJR never left the North Side. He lived for the rest of his life in the first house he bought – an eleven-room, two-story red brick Victorian at 940 North Lincoln Avenue that cost him five thousand dollars.

The year was 1939. Kass always called their house the smallest on the street. Perhaps at one time it was. North Lincoln Avenue had been a Millionaire's Row when fortunes were being made in the steel industry, but then as smoke from the mills sent the people who lived there to such clean-air havens as Oakland, the East End, and Sewickley, a transformation occurred. Working-class Irish and Germans moved in; they partitioned the mansions, tore down the stables, and opened mom-and-pop stores and saloons. But neighborhoods age and deteriorate. In time, the Irish and the Germans departed, and North Lincoln Avenue became heavily black.

AJR refused to join the exodus. Black or white, rich or poor, the North Side was still the North Side, and good enough for him. He was scornful of people who "put on the dog." To "put on the dog" meant to show off your money. I asked him about it once – where did the expression come from? Well, he said, when you see a woman wearing expensive clothes and parading around with a fluffy French poodle on a leash, that's the stereotype. She's putting on the dog.

"Acting like Johnny O'Donnell" was something else the Chief could not abide. Johnny O'Donnell was a North Side bricklayer who got a job buying bricks for the construction of a sewer system. He was making good money, and it went to his head. He bought a new car, a big black Cadillac, and hired a chauffeur. Dressed in full uniform, the chauffeur would drive him to work every day, and then Johnny O'Donnell would step into his coveralls, step out of the Cadillac, and go down into the sewer to oversee the laying of the bricks. So anyone guilty of ostentation, which AJR had no use for, was "acting like Johnny O'Donnell" – which was pretty hard to distinguish from putting on the dog.

North Lincoln Avenue suited Kass. She was not one to put on the dog, or to act like Johnny O'Donnell. The size of the house, she thought, was just about right. There was room for her sister Alice and their niece Trish, but not for the vagabond relatives so common back then in large extended families. Times were hard and the government unresponsive; a house could become a hotel. Aunt Alice spent her life at 940 because AJR was absent so much at night and on weekends. It had bothered Kass, being left alone, when they lived in a rented apartment, and she said so. "Look," replied AJR, "you weren't a kid when you agreed to marry me. You knew how I made my living."

The solution to the problem was Alice. At first she would come for just a night or two when AJR was out of town, and then she was coming more often, and finally when Grandfather McNulty died – Alice had been his primary caretaker – it seemed logical for her to move in and stay.

This was a rather Irish thing to do, the unmarried aunt living in and helping out with the children. "Why didn't she marry, a pretty girl like Alice?" people would ask. Because, for one thing, a lot of Irish old maids are hard to please. They don't just say yes to the first proposal – or the second, sometimes, or the third. Then, too, there is always one daughter who stays at home with the parent left alone. In the McNulty family, it happened to be Alice.

So Alice moved in, and a routine developed. Alice would be up in the morning with the kids and make a good breakfast. Then she would fix lunch, leaving Kass plenty of time to prepare the big dinner, always with a homemade dessert.

The sisters were lively story-tellers, quick to express opinions about everything that happened, and they could swear like troopers when the occasion demanded it. Alice seemed always to be calling someone a "simple son of a bitch," giving scandal, it may be, to AJR, who never was known to use even the mildest of expletives, never so much as a "hell" or a "damn." What must have pleased him, on the other hand, was the sisters' daily habit of going to Mass. These were women who lived good religious lives and placed the welfare of the family above their own.

In the early, pre-Alice days, the household included a full-time maid. Not long before he died, AJR told a story about the maid. It was a story I never had heard, and if not for the fact that AJR was 86 years old, an age when inhibitions tend to fade, I don't think we'd have heard it at all, because sex was involved. When it came to sex, the Rooneys were puritanical, AJR very much so. One day, as he related it, he suddenly told Kass, "Get rid of that maid."

Kass was nonplussed. She said, "Of course I won't get rid of the maid. The girl's a hard worker and she's good with the kids."

"I said, 'Get rid of that maid,'" repeated AJR. "Just take my word for it."

Again Kass objected. Again AJR insisted that the maid had to go.

Days went by, and nothing happened, except that AJR lost his patience.

"Kass, I told you to get rid of that girl," he said, raising his voice. "Fire her! Do you need a ton of bricks to fall on you?"

Apparently Kass did. The message, for some reason, was not getting through.

"She wants to go to bed with me!" AJR shouted, putting it into words at last. As for himself, he added, so that nothing would remain in doubt, he desired to go to bed with no one but Kass.

When she emerged from beneath the ton of bricks, Kass fired the maid. And at 940 North Lincoln Avenue, there was no further cause for domestic unease.

New Year's with Owney

New Year's Eve was like any other night as far as AJR and Kass were concerned. Curiosity once prompted me to ask why they never went out. Because the last two times they did go out, replied Kass, it was with Owney McManus and his girlfriend.

Owney McManus had a restaurant and bar on Fourth Avenue, Downtown, where the sports crowd gathered. The security system was activated by voice. When a dubious character walked in, the bartender called out, "Paul Waner at bat." If Owney said, "Pitch to him," the customer got a drink. "Walk him" was the signal for an invitation to leave.

Owney McManus was a hotheaded little guy who had boxed professionally at 118 pounds. For Billy Conn's major fights in New York – the one with Melio Bettina for the light-heavyweight championship and the two with heavyweight champion Joe Louis – Owney would charter a private car or two on a train and sell tickets. "The Ham and Cabbage Special," everyone called it, which was just a name. No ham and cabbage or anything else edible was served.

After closing his bar at two in the morning, Owney would sit down with a few favored customers and give vent to his animosities, which were numerous. To Havey Boyle, sports editor of the *Post-Gazette*, this relaxation time was "the Hour of Hate." Owney despised Franklin D. Roosevelt and he was outspokenly anti-Semitic. "One night," said George Quinlan, "I'm sitting at a table with Owney and Havey Boyle, and Owney got started on the Hebes. I said, 'Here, I'm giving Havey a ten-dollar bill, and you put up a ten-dollar bill, and for every lousy Hebe you name, I'll name a lousier Irishman.' He started off with Jake Mintz. I said, 'Splash Gallagher.' He said, 'You win.' Then Owney named another Jew he didn't like, and I named an Irishman he hated. Same result – 'You win.' See, Owney had a million enemies out in the Strip, which was all Irish then, and I knew who they were. After the fifth name, he took a punch at me, and I punched back and hit the wall and broke my right hand."

In any situation involving Owney, as you can see, there was always the likelihood of trouble.

AJR must have known that, but on a New Year's Eve after Prohibition ended he and Kass double-dated with Owney and a girl named Marie. The death of Owney's wife had left him alone with their son, Owney Junior. They lived above the restaurant – not the best environment for a child. Owney Junior was a quiet, sensitive boy, the temperamental opposite of his father. He attended Catholic boarding schools, earned a law degree at Pitt (AJR hired him to represent the Steelers), and, like his mother, died young. Marie, Kass thought, resented Owney Junior – "wasn't nice to him," as she put it. This is why Kass didn't care for Marie, but AJR and Owney Senior were friends, and so the couples from time to time socialized.

Owney and Marie liked to drink. AJR, up to the age of about 45, drank moderately. Then he quit – cold turkey. The only time I ever saw him not completely sober was on a day he had lingered too long at the Ligonier Golf Club's nineteenth hole. Driving home, he went off the road. (I should say here that AJR was an excellent golfer. He took up the game to prove he could beat Milton Jaffe, who'd been playing for some time. Without a lesson or a practice swing, he did beat Milton Jaffe. He then made a bet that before the summer was over he could beat the club pro, and that happened too. AJR was good at any game he ever tried. But as though the time had come to get rid of another bad habit, he stopped playing golf as suddenly as he had given up alcohol.) Once he was on the wagon, he delivered stern temperance lectures to his sons. None of us ever dared to lift so much as a wine glass in his presence. If Kass took a drink he remained silent – one way of showing displeasure, perhaps.

The New Year's Eve parties with Owney and his girlfriend pre-dated all this. On the first one Kass told me about, the two couples met at the Wildwood Golf Club, where AJR was a member. Probably there were drinks before dinner. Most certainly there were drinks after dinner, coming slower now for AJR and Kass, but faster for Owney and Marie. The drinks of course loosened their tongues. Owney said something that Marie didn't like, or Marie said something that Owney didn't like, and it started a fight. Quickly they were shouting obscenities at each other. Except for the combatants, the room fell silent. The New Year's Eve hum came to a stop; laughter and conversation died away. All eyes were focused on Owney and Marie, shouting at each other, on Kass, who was red with embarrassment, and on AJR, poker-faced as always. Owney's Christmas present for Marie had been a "friendship ring," a half-hearted tender of devotion, and now he demanded it back.

"Like hell you'll get it back!" yelled Marie.

Owney made a lunge for her hand. Marie, too fast for him, ran to the ladies' room. Owney galloped after her, never pausing at the door. He rushed on through, and then there were screams, muffled noises from within, and women emerging in states of disarray. Behind them came Owney, clutching his friendship ring.

A reception committee awaited him – the husbands of the women who had exited in fright. They had a few choice words for Owney, none being "Happy New Year." When somebody gave him a shove, Owney started swinging. After that, said Kass, "it was real mayhem."

To AJR, she said, "Never again," a resolution he persuaded her not to keep.

On New Year's Eve of the following year, they were celebrating once more with Owney and Marie (the friendship ring back on her finger), but at the Highland Country Club, not Wildwood. This time the party included Havey Boyle and his wife. Nothing went amiss until Owney, smoking a cigarette, spilled the ashes on Mrs. Boyle's dress. The dress was chiffon. It caught fire. Women started screaming. Men jumped around, accomplishing nothing. At last to save Mrs. Boyle from incineration, her rescuers tore off her dress.

"And that," said Kass, "is why we never went out again on New Year's Eve."

An Army of Midgets

AJR was always driving to Miami, sometimes with Kass, sometimes with Kass and the kids, sometimes with race-track friends, and sometimes alone. The family would stay in a large rented house and the friends in a room above the garage.

Sometimes Uncle Jim would make the trip. Once when Kass was in the car with Uncle Jim and two of the kids, she remarked that she needed change for a fifty-dollar bill. They were passing a bar called Mother Kelly's, and Jim said, "Stop here." He took the fifty inside and was gone for what seemed to Kass like a very long time. Reappearing, he handed her twenty-five dollars. "Jim, where's the rest of the money?" she asked. In all innocence he answered, "I couldn't go in there without setting up the house, could I?"

That was Jim. He thought of fifty-dollar bills as tip money. At The Showboat one night, Jim said to George Quinlan, "Give me a couple hundred." Quinlan produced four fifties, and Jim gave one to the hat-check girl. "And he wasn't wearing a hat," Quinlan said. Puzzled, he asked Jim, "Why did you do that?"

"She looked like a nice kid," Jim explained.

If AJR had horses that were running at Hialeah, he would drive from Pittsburgh to Miami non-stop and go directly to the race track. On one such trip he had a passenger with him. They arrived at the track in time for the first race, and AJR plunged on the daily double. When the second race tapped him out, he said to the other guy, "Come on," and led the way to the parking lot. They got into the car, and he drove back to Pittsburgh – non-stop.

In a hurry or not, AJR drove at breakneck speed. On one of his solo trips to Miami, a Georgia state trooper chased him the length of the state, or close to it, over the two-lane highways of the 1930s. Unaware he was being followed, AJR steadily put distance between them. He crossed into Florida, where no Georgia law enforcement agency could touch him, and was drinking coffee at the counter of a roadside restaurant when the trooper walked in. "Who has the car with the Pennsylvania license?" he demanded. "I do," said AJR. The trooper sat down next to him and said, "I just wanted to meet the guy who outran me."

Within minutes, AJR had learned that the trooper was Irish and a Catholic, one of only three in the ranks of the Georgia state police, and from that moment on they were kindred spirits.

When the Hialeah season was over, AJR and his companions would rent a boat and a crew in the Keys and go deep-sea fishing. They went to a place one winter where the crew members were "Conchs" – pronounced "Conks" – the part-Indian, part-English, part-Spanish, part-Negro descendants of early settlers and pirates who intermarried or interbred with the natives. Uncle Jim said they married their cousins and didn't have any sense. As AJR described them, the ones who went out with the fishermen were short, black-haired guys with dark complexions. He would have occasion before the day was over to learn something else about Conchs: they were tough, vicious, unrelenting fighters.

Besides Uncle Jim, AJR's fellow anglers, all from Pittsburgh, included Billy Conn, a future light-heavyweight boxing champion; Milton Jaffe, Conn's business manager; Walt Kiesling, the coach of the Steelers; Ed Karpowich, one of Kiesling's players; and the North Side character called Nigger Smitty. Kiesling, Karpowich, and Uncle Jim were men of imposing size. Billy Conn and AJR had the unmistakable self-confident look that accompanies success in the ring. And Smitty, you somehow sensed, was a guy who could hold his own in a free-for-all. None of which meant a thing to the Conchs.

The day began peacefully enough. All morning long the fish were biting. Afternoon came, and the boat headed back to port with a sizable catch. One of the Conchs cut up a piece of the bait and threw it overboard to the seagulls. Fighting for the scraps, the birds went wild. They would snatch them out of the air with their beaks or their claws. AJR and his friends were so impressed and entertained that they cut up the fish they had caught and tossed every piece to the gulls. They got a kick out of seeing them work for this unexpected meal. The Conchs, meanwhile, were seething with anger.

By the terms of an unwritten contract, all the fish that were caught belonged to the crew. No one, unfortunately, had explained this to AJR or Milton. When the boat reached the dock, the Conchs began calling to other Conchs at work around the waterfront. AJR and Milton, still not foreseeing any trouble, paid for the cruise and threw in a generous tip, but the Conchs became increasingly hostile, increasingly belligerent. They jabbered at the fishermen in pidgin English. No! They didn't want their tip. "Never let anyone confuse kindness with weakness," AJR used to say, and the Conchs were confusing kindness with weakness.

Exactly what they did want was not at all clear, but Karpowich, the burly football player, thought it might be a fight. Probably just to see what would happen, he picked up the nearest Conch and pitched him into the water.

Instantly, a hey rube broke out. Smitty, I like to think, may have actually shouted, "Hey rube!" – the battle cry of carnival workers when they went into combat with local yokels, as in the old days they frequently did. Smitty had been a "carnie" himself, and his experience served him well against the Conchs. He rabbit-punched, he used his knees, and he gouged a few eyes – techniques that had been effective in previous hey rubes. Above all else, he protected his back.

Karpowich, alas, did not protect his back. A Conch sneaked up behind him with a grappling hook and brought it down on his head. Karp from then on was out of commission, a serious loss to the Pittsburgh forces. He'd been flinging the Conchs around and pitching them off the dock as if they were babies.

Next, Uncle Jim went down. The Conchs were armed with fish knives, and Jim took a thrust between the ribs. That left AJR, Kiesling, and Smitty to hold off the enemy on their own. Billy Conn was with them, yes, and Conn was a great Marquis of Queensberry fighter, but hey rubes were bare-knuckle affairs. Conn was "terrified," Uncle Jim recalled, of hurting his hands, a boxer's most indispensable asset. All through the battle, he held them under his armpits. "Billy showed excellent footwork," said AJR later, striving to give Conn his due. In every other respect, Billy's usefulness to the Pittsburgh cause was limited. Milton Jaffe, a lifelong pacifist, was of no use at all. He did a marvelous job, noted AJR, of keeping space between himself and the action.

One-sided already, the odds became prohibitive when Conch reinforcements from the fishing village joined the melee. "We were up against an army of midgets," said AJR afterward. "They wouldn't stop coming and there were lots of them. Everywhere you looked, you saw blood. There were guys in the water and guys sprawled out on the ground."

In the nick of time, the sheriff and his deputies arrived. They got the outnumbered Pittsburghers safely into their cars. "Now, take off," the sheriff advised them. "These Conchs have killed people. You're lucky to be alive."

Uncle Jim and Karp recovered from their wounds in a hospital. Jim had somehow lost a jacket during the fight, and AJR resolved to go back and retrieve it, this time with an army of his own – Pittsburgh friends eager to take revenge for Jim and Karp on "those nasty little wharf rats."

But first the sheriff found out. He spoke to AJR on the telephone. "You have a jacket you'd like to pick up? That's a bad idea," he said. "I have it here in my office, and I'll drive up to Miami with it myself. Stay away from this part of the Keys. Don't come back down here – EVER."

AJR thought it over, and decided to let bygones be bygones.

Penn-Mint

Kass always said that AJR made a ton of money during the Great Depression. Not all of it came from the killing at Saratoga, which put him on Easy Street in 1936. Nor did the football team become profitable until television so greatly enhanced the NFL's sources of revenue. "Maybe you made five thousand dollars a season or maybe you lost a few thousand," AJR reminisced when Myron Cope interviewed him in 1970 for a book called "The Game That Was."

AJR did well at the race track and not all that badly in the slot-machine business. On a train trip from Pittsburgh to Chicago, Kass said, he met a man named Dan Odom, who had worked for a carnival or a circus but now was a broker of slot machines. Odom knew AJR by reputation and offered to supply him with as many slot machines as he could place.

"If you can set things up politically," Odom said, "I can guarantee you a million dollars a year."

In venues open to the public, slot machines were illegal, but the authorities allowed them, or were willing at any rate to tolerate them, in social clubs like the Elks, the Moose, or the American Legion, and in the private clubs exempt from the Pennsylvania Blue Laws. AJR had all the right political connections, and Kass always said that he did make a million dollars a year. Maybe so, but Kass was something of a romanticist, and in her marvelous stories about the old days it is not inconceivable that she indulged in poetic license now and again. Whatever AJR's take actually was, he believed that when times were tough people would find money to gamble, "looking for a way to improve their luck."

Under pressure from the reformers and the newspapers, the state passed a law requiring slot machines to pay off in candy – rolls of mints – rather than coins. There was a way, of course, to get around that. The mints could be used like chips in a poker game. If you won, you turned them in for cash.

AJR named his slot machine company Penn-Mint and put Uncle Jim in charge, which was not a judicious move. When Jim had money at his disposal, he would either give it away or drink it away. One of Jim's duties as company president was to deliver the machines to the clubs. At first he transported them in a hearse, which AJR thought was unwise. Jim then obtained a big black truck and was driving it around with no identification on the panels until AJR happened to notice.

"Jim," he shouted, "get a sign on that truck! I don't care if it reads 'Merry Christmas' or 'Happy New Year,' but get a sign on that truck."

Jim got a sign on the truck: "Penn-Mint."

In his various enterprises, AJR avoided any connection with the mob, as he called the Mafia. There were certain kinds of favors you could prudently do for a mob guy, he used to say. And then he would add, "But never, never let a mob guy do a favor for you." In any event, he did not long remain in the slot-machine business. A conversation with Mayor Dave Lawrence hastened his early departure.

"Do you think this business of yours is legal?" asked the mayor.

"Of course it is not," replied AJR.

"Then you'd better do something about it," said Lawrence.

Nothing more had to be explained.

AJR left an estate valued at two hundred million dollars. He was at one time the head of ten corporations that owned or controlled the Steelers, Yonkers Raceway, the William Penn Racing Association at Liberty Bell, Green Mountain Race Track in Vermont, and the Palm Beach Kennel Club, a dog-racing track in Florida. He owned the Shamrock Farms and bred race horses there. During the 1920s and '30s he invested heavily in the stock market, but came out a loser. He was leery of putting his cash into real estate. "I don't know about anything, only horses," he told Roy Blount. "And football. Sports. I didn't know you could go to the bank and borrow money. I thought you had to have it in your pocket."

He lived just as simply as he ran his various enterprises. His suits — he always wore one — were not expensive. The only car he ever drove was a Buick. Cadillacs and Lincolns were for showoffs. When his sons moved away from the North Side and bought houses in ritzier neighborhoods they were "putting on the dog." He permitted himself one extravagance: he smoked good cigars, constantly. Toward the end of his life he merely chewed them. A friend with the mind of an accountant once estimated that AJR had spent more money on cigars than on the college educations of his sons.

I could give you examples by the dozen of AJR's generosity. Uncle Jim practiced philanthropy on a first-come, first-served basis, shoveling out money — as long as he had money — to bartenders, hat-check girls, elevator operators, doormen, and anybody else who happened to be within reach. AJR was more discriminating, and he continued to give beyond the grave.

A provision in his will earmarked one million dollars for charitable contributions to be made by each of his five sons. Broken down, that was two hundred thousand apiece. From my share, on the last day of 1996, I sent a check for fifteen thousand dollars with my son Art III to the Little Sisters of the Poor, and the head nun told him a story. At regular intervals, she said, AJR would come into the convent and empty his pockets. Large wads of cash would fall out. The nuns of course surmised that he had had a good day at the race track.

"So we prayed that his luck would continue," Sister Madeline went on. "We felt that some of it, anyway, was coming from a source up above."

Chapter 8

Local Talent

During the 1930s AJR's team in the National Football League had a Western Pennsylvania component. Besides Harp Vaughan, there was Ray Kemp, who played at Duquesne University. There was Armand Niccolai, who also played at Duquesne. There was John (Bull) Karcis, who played at Carnegie Tech. There was Mose Kelsch, who went directly from the Pittsburgh sandlots to the NFL. There was Ed Karpowich, who played at Catholic University.

Ray Kemp, as I have said, was one of the pioneer black players in the NFL. Explaining to me once why his first season with the Pirates, 1933, turned out to be his last, he said that AJR was color blind but went along with the wishes of the other owners, who were not. In the spirit of the times, they wanted an all-white NFL, and from 1934 until 1946 that is exactly what they had. Pigmentation-wise, the contrast between then and now is enormous and speaks for itself.

I don't know how well Kemp could play. What I do know is that he *looked* like someone who could play: he had the physique. Tackles in the present era weigh 300 pounds and up. Kemp wasn't nearly that big – in the 1930s, nobody was. He was big, though, for his day, and big enough to have played in any decade before weight training, steroids, nutritional advances, and evolution changed the standards by which football coaches measure size.

Bull Karcis was the fullback on the Carnegie Tech team that won from Notre Dame in 1928. According to the *Pittsburgh Post-Gazette*, he was "as unstoppable [that day] as Niagara Falls." Although somewhat less unstoppable in the NFL, he prolonged his career until 1943, logging four years with the Brooklyn Dodgers, three with the Pirates (1936-38), and three with the New York Giants. After World War II, he coached and taught mathematics at North Catholic High School. In Bull's final season, my brother Dan played quarterback on the varsity, and I played tackle on the freshman team. Karcis was not the freshman team's coach, but both teams used his playbook. Whether he thought that North Side kids were dumb or that any play is a good one if you execute it properly, his offense was as simple as two plus two.

At the start of each season, Karcis would remind his players at a squad meeting that they represented a Catholic institution and should watch their language. Karcis was not a Catholic himself but decided to take instruction in the faith. Not long afterward, the Brothers of Mary fired him. What effect this had on his conversion to Rome I never learned.

Karcis was built like a barrel. His wife had a set of mammary glands that won her the nickname of "Iron Tits." (Kids can be cruel.) Delivering a package to the coach's door one day, a North Catholic player glanced through the window and saw the two of them – Bull and his wife – fencing. They had the face masks on and the protective clothes and were going at it with foils. For the rest of the football season their friendly little duel was the talk of the dressing room.

Mose Kelsch was a tough old semi-pro who did not wear a helmet (the rules were different then) or need one. He had a big, bald head that attracted more attention than Harp Vaughan's bandanna. Mose Kelsch and Harp Vaughan were backfield teammates in 1933, Mose's only year with the team.

Mose lived on the North Side and was said to have played football at Christian College. There's a Christian Brothers College in Tennessee. Christian College, my researchers tell me, is as mythical a place as Brigadoon. But here's a fact that may add to the confusion: Mose's first, or Christian, name was Christian.

In the 1930s AJR was the same age as some of his players, and he made it a practice to socialize with them. There were card games, there were trips to the race track. Two of his best friends on the team, Ed Karpowich and Armand Niccolai, were both from the Mon Valley. When they played for the Pirates they rented rooms or an apartment in an old brick mansion on Ridge Avenue, not far from North Lincoln, a remnant of the days when the North Side was teeming with the rich and the powerful. They called the house they lived in El Rancho Grande.

Karp and Nick were good guys. Because they spent a lot of time at our house, I knew them when I was a kid. Karp was a two-way end, Niccolai a tackle. Nick played for AJR from 1934 to 1942 and later coached football at Monessen High School, where his wife just happened to be the principal. The Niccolais often sat with the Rooneys in the owner's box at Three Rivers Stadium, and, looking back, I see that I missed an opportunity. Instead of pumping Nick for stories about the old days, I was satisfied with conventional small talk.

I recall that he volunteered a story about a game the Pirates moved from Pittsburgh to New Orleans when they were having attendance problems one year. Nick was the team captain, and for some reason he missed the train. Mortified, he at once headed South in his car. It was late November or early December; there was snow and ice on the roads, which were nothing like modern freeways; twice he was pulled out of ditches. Driving night and day, he got there in time for the kickoff —and played what was probably his worst game of the season, he said.

Vagabond Halfback

On a fall afternoon in 1933, John Victor McNally, who played football under the name of Johnny Blood for the Green Bay Packers, came to practice drunk. Attempting a punt, he missed the ball completely and fell on the seat of his pants. The Packers' coach, Curly Lambeau, traded him to Pittsburgh before the start of the next season.

After one year with the Pirates he was back in Green Bay, but Pittsburgh had not seen the last of him. In 1937, AJR decided – quixotically – that Blood was the man to succeed Joe Bach as the Pirates' coach.

His credentials for the job were obscure. Tall, gaunt, and lithe, with heavy black eyebrows and thick black hair, Blood was an exotic free spirit. The way he acquired his football name reflected his attitude toward life, which was whimsical. Having played three years at St. John's University in Minnesota, he went to work as a stereotyper for a Minneapolis newspaper. Along with a friend who was also a stereotyper, he agreed to play football on Sundays for a semi-pro team, the East Twenty-Sixth Street Liberties. Both felt they might have some college eligibility left and realized they would need false names. On the way to the field, riding McNally's motorcycle, they passed a theater marquee advertising "Blood and Sand," a bullfighting film starring Rudolph Valentino. So when the Liberties' coach asked them what names they intended to use, McNally said, "I'm Blood and this guy is Sand."

Blood/McNally became known as the Vagabond Halfback. From St. John's he had gone to Notre Dame but never played a down for the football team. Suspended for breaking curfew once too often, he left academia for the stereotyper's job and left newspaper work for a Hall-of-Fame career in the NFL. There were teams called the Milwaukee Badgers, Duluth Eskimos, and Pottsville Maroons back then, and he played for all three before moving on to Green Bay. With Blood making long runs from scrimmage and catching passes for a record number of touchdowns, the Packers proceeded to win three straight championships. It was for his deeds off the field, however, that Blood is remembered in folklore.

The Packers, like Notre Dame, enforced a curfew. Locked into his sixth-floor hotel room on the night before a game on the road – with Blood, extreme measures were necessary – he opened a window, climbed out onto the fire escape, and jumped to the ledge of a teammate's window several feet away. All it took from there was a tap on a pane of glass to set him free.

On another occasion, Blood missed a 10 a.m. train with the rest of the Packers aboard. Accompanied by the young woman with whom he had spent the night, he got into his touring car, beat the train to the nearest railroad crossing, and stopped it by parking on the tracks.

Blood coached the Pirates for two seasons and part of a third, during which AJR became gradually aware that "you couldn't depend on John a whole lot." Not that they failed to get along. "Art liked Irishmen," Blood was to reminisce, "but I think I disappointed him. He pressed me to go to confession to make me a better Roman Catholic. Let's just say I came under that heading but spell it a little differently. I was a roamin' Catholic."

He was also, as it happened, a roamin' football coach. One Sunday when the Pirates were playing the Philadelphia Eagles in Pittsburgh, he was absent without leave in Chicago, watching his old team the Packers play the Bears. To a reporter he explained that the Pirates had an open date. Just then the public-address announcer was heard from: "Scores of other games ... Philadelphia 16, Pittsburgh 7."

"On most teams," said AJR, "the coach worries about the players. On our team, the players worry about the coach."

Blood's skills had greatly deteriorated and his blazing speed was by now just a memory, but in certain situations he would put himself into a game. If the Pirates reached their opponent's 20-yard line, he insisted on going in to call the plays. Against the New York Giants one Sunday, he did that two or three times, and two or three times the Pirates' offense lost its momentum. Near the end of the game they were back in scoring position, and here came Blood once again. The captain of the team conferred with the referee.

"What happens," he said, "if I don't accept a substitute?"

The referee said, "In that case, we won't accept him, either."

So the captain sent his coach back to the bench, and the Pirates scored the game-winning touchdown.

On another day, in a punting situation, Blood went in for the team's regular kicker, Johnny Gildea. AJR, sitting on the bench – owners did that in the 1930s – shouted, "No! No! No!" It was too late. Blood was waiting for the center snap. AJR turned to Max Fiske, a second-string halfback, and said, "I don't care if he kicks the ball sixty yards and it goes out on the two-yard line. He should let Gildea punt." With the words scarcely out of his mouth, Blood kicked the ball sixty yards – out of bounds on the two-yard line. AJR turned to Fiske again and said, "What do you do with a guy like that?"

Blood saved him the trouble of deciding. After a 2-9 season in 1938 and three straight defeats at the start of the 1939 season he resigned, and Walt Kiesling, an all-pro guard the Pirates had picked up when his all-pro days were gone beyond recall, succeeded him. Kiesling began enforcing curfew and bed checks and the Pirates managed to win a game and tie one while losing the other six.

"The players all loved John," said AJR of the departed Blood. Unfortunately, their performance on the field did not reflect it.

All through my teens I had heard so many stories about Johnny Blood, stories having to do with his eccentric behavior, that when AJR told us he was coming to dinner one night I guess I expected a sideshow. Would he do something bizarre – maybe dance on the table while we ate? To my surprise, a distinguished looking man with courtly manners, graying hair, and piercing black eyes knocked at our door. He was wearing a smartly tailored conservative dark suit. He walked with a soft tread, like a cat. Blood greeted Kass with a peck on the cheek, and the evening passed uneventfully.

Over the years I encountered him several other times when he was more like the Johnny Blood of legend. AJR's sixty-fifth birthday party was a big affair at the Hilton Hotel. Tom Landry and Tex Schramm came from Dallas, Toots Shor from New York, and Johnny Blood from Minneapolis. Bishop John Wright, soon to become a cardinal, was the principal speaker. Blood looked much the same as on the night he had been our dinner guest. His hair was completely gray but still abundant, and he looked as distinguished as ever. He might have been a senator, a judge, or an aging matinee idol. Called on to address the audience, he did not go all the way to the podium, stopping instead where Bishop Wright was seated. In a deep, dramatic voice, he said, "Your Excellency. Would you kindly stand?" Puzzled, Bishop Wright got to his feet. "Ladies and gentlemen," continued Blood. "This," he said, resting a hand on the bishop's shoulder, "is a saint." He paused a few moments for effect. "I," he went on, "am a sinner." The crowd roared with delight, and Blood resumed his trip to the podium.

I saw him again at an NFL meeting in Honolulu. He was there with his (second) wife, and wherever he went in the Royal Hawaiian Hotel he carried a large palm branch in one hand, even on the dance floor. Before the night was over he had an orchid behind each ear and orchids festooning his hair.

Blood fancied himself as a philosopher and a theorist. Ruminating about the Great Depression, he put his thoughts down on paper and developed them into a book (never published) called "Spend Yourself Rich." The essence of it was that depressions are caused by a scarcity of consumers; the way to terminate one, then, is to encourage consumption. He wrote that everybody, no matter how poor, has money, if only a dollar or two, and so by not holding back we can spend ourselves rich.

His ideas impressed someone at St. John's University, and Blood taught economics there while at the same time coaching the football team. When he was 50, he resigned to take a graduate course at the University of Minnesota, later confessing that he didn't know why. Having inherited money, he could do just about as he pleased, and in 1976 he embarked on a campaign to draft Supreme Court Justice Byron White for president.

Nothing came of it. Only AJR ever drafted Byron White, and that was in 1938, when White was an All-American halfback called Whizzer (a nickname he detested) at the University of Colorado. He was also a Phi Beta Kappa who planned on going to Oxford as a Rhodes Scholar. AJR offered him a salary of $15,800, outlandish by the standards of the day, to sign with the Pirates.

No football player had ever before earned that kind of money, and the other owners were aghast. They said that AJR was destroying the salary scale. "All I'm trying to do is bring a little class to the game," he responded. Still White was dragging his feet. According to AJR, it was Blood, through his persistence, who prevailed on the Whizzer to put off going to Oxford for a year.

White took the $15,800 (in his later years AJR said he'd forgotten what the eight hundred was for) and led the league in rushing. Returning from Oxford in 1940, he led the league in rushing again, but this time for the Detroit Lions, who lost him to the Navy during World War II and subsequently to the legal profession.

White was no charmer. His face, with its high cheekbones, appeared to be made of granite. Being interviewed and photographed was distasteful to him. "You know, I've been exhibited like a freak ever since I signed with the Pirates," he complained in his rookie year to a sportswriter. Johnny Blood liked him, but White was never one of the boys. "He's cold as ice. You can freeze sitting next to him," said George Quinlan, who managed the Pirates' training camp when White was with the team. Big Ed Karpowich made $100 a game. In perverse ways, he liked to call attention to the difference between his own small salary and White's. "Come on," he would say to the serious-minded rookie, "I'll get you a two-dollar broad."

"Whizzer didn't go for that," Quinlan recalled.

The Pirates lost money during White's year with the team, and he offered to return some of his salary. AJR refused to hear of it. He said that White worked harder than anybody else the Pirates had. He said it was no accident that White led the league in rushing, because this was a player who worked and fought for every yard. White worked for, and richly deserved, every honor he achieved, and there were many, culminating in his appointment to the U.S.Supreme Court by President John F. Kennedy.

His friendship with Johnny Blood endured for as long as Blood lived. A strange relationship, I thought, but they did have something in common. Each in his own way, Johnny Blood and Whizzer White were unforgettable members of the Pirate/Steeler family.

Name Change

In 1940 the Pirates became the Steelers. AJR had grown tired of their copycat name and held a contest to pick a new one. The *Pittsburgh Post-Gazette* cooperated with him, inviting its readers to send in suggestions.

Thirty years later, AJR told Myron Cope that the winner of the contest was the girlfriend of the Pirates' business manager, Joe Carr. With a touch of wryness, he added, "There were people who said, 'That contest don't look like it was on the level.'"

Actually, there were multiple winners, Joe Carr's girlfriend (who later became his wife) being one of them. When Joe Santoni, the owner of a restaurant in Carnegie, died in 2003, the headline over his obituary in the *Post-Gazette* was: "Restaurateur who named Steelers." Santoni's sister, Norma Fayer, recalled that his prize was a pair of season tickets. That same year, as I was about to enter a church in Palm Beach, Florida, to attend Mass one Sunday, a nun introduced herself to me. "I'm from Pittsburgh," she said, "and I'm a celebrity up there. I named the Steelers." Apparently all of the winners, and there were twenty or more others, either forgot or chose to forget that the distinction of re-naming the team was a shared one. For *her* prize, the nun received a war bond, she told me.

In one respect, the Steelers were no different from the Pirates. They continued to lose. Their record in 1940 under Walt Kiesling was 2-7-2. Over the eleven-game season, the team with the new identity scored a total of 60 points.

AJR was discouraged. In his eight years as owner he had lost about $100,000. Impulsively, he sold the team to Alexis Thompson, a rich young Bostonian, and quickly regretted it. A few months later, he bought a piece of Bert Bell's team, the Philadelphia Eagles. Next, he persuaded Thompson and Bell to trade franchises. Thompson took over the Eagles and Bell took over the Steelers, with AJR and Barney McGinley as his partners. Each owned a third of the stock. Barney McGinley, as it happened, was AJR's partner in the Rooney-McGinley Boxing Club as well. They promoted almost every big fight in Pittsburgh between the mid-1930s and the early 1950s.

AJR's genius, I've always said, resided in the fact that he was able to stay in business through thick and thin.

At the start of the 1941 season Bert Bell was the Steelers' coach. Scion of a Main Line family in Philadelphia, Bell had played and coached at the University of Pennsylvania. He had coached the Eagles as well, but not before serving as publicity director, ticket manager, and general manager.

Responding no better to Bell than to any of the coaches before him, the Steelers proceeded to lose their first two games, and he voluntarily stepped down. The owners now made an incomprehensible decision. They brought in, as head coach, Aldo (Buff) Donelli, who happened to be coaching, and would continue to coach, the Duquesne University team. How could he do this? By coaching the Steelers in the morning and the Dukes in the afternoon. On Saturdays he would be with the Dukes and on Sundays with the Steelers.

Buff was a local guy from Bridgeville, one of the coal-mining towns in a soccer hotbed populated largely by European immigrants and their offspring. Soccer, in fact, was Donelli's best sport. Football coaches had not yet learned to convert soccer players into placekickers, or Buff would have excelled at that specialty. As it was, he played center and fullback on some of Elmer Layden's fine Duquesne teams in the late 1920s. Another Donelli, Buff's brother Allan, played halfback for the Steelers in 1941 and 1942. In the 1950s a third brother went to work as the team's trainer but suddenly got religion and became a full-time drum beater for the Seventh Day Adventists.

Football in those days was all blocking and tackling.. Buff put some pizzazz into the game. He was not the inventor of the box formation, the spinner series, or the wing-T, but he refined those systems and added something to them. His offense involved a lot of quick and clever ball handling. Blocks were set up by quickness and deception, with all eleven men participating at either the point of attack or farther downfield. And, more than most other coaches did at the time, he emphasized passing. My two high school coaches and my coach at St. Vincent had played for Buff at Duquesne, and all three of them adopted his methods.

AJR, for his part, felt that Buff was a bit too full of himself. Buff met with the press at Owney McManus's restaurant every week, and AJR said that he once used a blackboard to show how the British generals under Sir Harold Alexander should be maneuvering their tanks against Erwin Rommel's German army in the deserts of North Africa..

Buff's 1936 Duquesne team had upset Pitt and had beaten Mississippi State in the Orange Bowl (on a 72-yard pass play) and his 1939 team was undefeated. His 1941 team also went undefeated, but the Steelers under Buff lost five games in a row. In their sixth game with Buff as the coach they were scheduled to play the Eagles in Philadelphia; Duquesne that weekend had a game on the West Coast with St. Mary's. Unable to be in two places at the same time, Buff chose the trip to California. At that point Elmer Layden, the NFL commissioner and Buff's old coach at Duquesne, intervened. An edict was handed down from league headquarters, and Buff's dual role came to an end, leaving the Steelers once more without a coach.

Walt Kiesling, as usual, moved up from the ranks of the assistant coaches to take command. The Steelers went to Philly and tied the Eagles, and then they won a game – from Jock Sutherland's Brooklyn Dodgers, an unexpected show of strength that cost the Dodgers an Eastern Division title. Two defeats followed as the Steelers reverted to form, and another dismal season was over.

Duquesne dropped football after the United States entered the war, and when peace came Donelli did not return. He coached for a while at Boston U. and then in the Ivy League at Columbia. On a scouting trip to Boston College in the early 1970s, just before Chuck Noll turned the Steelers into a championship team, I met Buff by chance. He was not any longer in coaching. As we talked, though, he casually suggested, "Have your dad call me ... I can help him."

I reported this to AJR. Although he made no reply, I could tell from his body language and the expression on his face that he did not feel the need for Buff's assistance. If the British Army got by without it, so could Chuck Noll, he may have thought.

Chapter 9

Big Harp

There were two Harp Vaughans – Big Harp Vaughan and Little Harp Vaughan. Big Harp's first name was John. He was actually not very big –5 feet 9 or 10 at the most – but he was bigger than his brother, Little Harp, and so their friends started calling him Big Harp. They called him other things, too, that were not as complimentary.

Big Harp's background was similar to AJR's. In fact, I think they were distant relatives. Harp may not have lived in The Ward, but he came from the North Side. He was good at sports. He took an interest in politics. And he was not without Irish charm. Those were the similarities. But AJR was the genuine article and Harp an inferior copy. He was a guy, you might say, who could never quite get to the next level.

It bothers me to take such a negative view of Harp, because on the surface at any rate we were friends. He officiated football games at St. Vincent College when I played on the team there, and often he would drive me home to Pittsburgh. During one of our games, Harp called a penalty on a kid from another team who seemed to know who he was. When Harp dropped the flag, the kid said, "Gee, Mister Vaughan, I'm a Catholic too." It made him angry at the time, Harp said, but he appreciated the humor as well.

Harp was a state legislator from the late 1930s to the early 1940s. Jimmy Coyne, I suppose, had quite a bit to do with Harp's election, but after Coyne lost his Senate berth and his power to hand pick candidates, Harp kept going back to Harrisburg. In the 1960s, he held a political office that was little more than a sinecure – boxing commissioner for Western Pennsylvania. Defying Governor Raymond Shafer, who was in Nelson Rockefeller's camp, Harp supported Richard Nixon for president at the 1968 Republican national convention. Nixon, as it turned out, won both the nomination and the election, but Shafer was still governor and he lost no time in appointing a new boxing commissioner.

Harp's career as a state legislator had ended when he lost to a superior politician, Tom Foerster. Foerster, like Harp, was born on the North Side. Unlike Harp, he had issues to run on. Subsequently, he served for many years as the Democratic chairman of the county commission. Harp complained to me once that Tom supplanted him by using dirty tricks. I said, "Harp, you're mad because you didn't think of doing those things yourself."

I know I was out of line, and yet my assessment of Harp still seems accurate.

As the years went by, AJR gradually distanced himself from Harp. Whatever bond had existed between them was not the enduring kind.

Coal Heaver

John Miller, Aunt Mary McNulty's husband, was a short, tough, violent drinking man with a large beer belly. To underestimate him, though, would not have been wise. He owned a couple of coal trucks and stopped working only long enough to drink, go to the movies, eat, and sleep. Cultural activities, including sports, held no interest for him. John's brother Clarence, his partner in the coal business, drove one of the trucks. They shoveled and hauled and delivered coal from early in the morning until supper time.

John and Aunt Mary – Kass's sister – lived in an upstairs apartment on Cedar Avenue, not far from North Lincoln. On the way home from work, John would stop somewhere for drinks. After eating, he would take in a movie by himself – the only kind of popular entertainment he liked – or go off to bed.

On days when the coal business was slow, he made a few dollars by picking up scrap iron in and around the mill towns and selling it to junk dealers. This source of income dried up after the residents found out that they could pick up the stuff and sell it themselves. The Depression had not yet lifted, and unless you were rich you watched every penny. To make ends meet, the Millers scrimped and saved.

John was a bad drunk. With his snoot full of "boilermakers" – whisky and beer, in that order – he would take out all of his malice on Aunt Mary, who could always set him off with a word or two.

Miller nursed a hatred for AJR. In neighborhood bars, he denounced his wife's relative by marriage as a tinhorn gambler, "the Little Mayor of Pittsburgh." When AJR got wind of this, he made a habit of dropping in at John's usual hangouts. He would settle down with a beer at an out-of-the-way corner table and hope to catch John unawares, mouthing off. AJR figured to be more than John could handle in a bar fight, but it would not have been easy. Once when John came home looking pretty well beaten up, Aunt Mary screamed that his jacket was covered with blood. "It's from the other guy," John said. But when he stripped to his shirt he found a knife wound in his side. "Son of a bitch!" he exclaimed. "That bastard!" Galvanized into action, he flew out the door. "Where are you going?" Aunt Mary called after him. "Down to the bar," he shouted over his shoulder. "I'm gonna get that dirty bum!"

On one occasion he bit off more than he could chew. This was when Aunt Alice lived on Cedar Avenue in the apartment below John and Mary's. Arriving home from a visit to a bar, John *was* yelling and screaming and cursing his wife as he mounted the stairs. Aunt Alice came into the hall with a vase and threw it at John. Unhurt, he stumbled up a few more steps. So Alice went after him with a broom, and *whack!* She broke it over his head. Meanwhile, Alice was swearing a blue streak. Together, the vase and broom and her vocabulary succeeded in bringing John to his senses, at least temporarily.

Too much food, too much work, and too much booze were the death of John Miller. After a stroke that laid him low he survived for several years as an invalid. By that time the Millers had moved to a well-kept-up house on East Street, in the "suburban" part of the North Side.

John and Mary had a son called Jack, who went to North Catholic High School, studied engineering at Pitt, and became a man of high moral values. Eventually he was head of the Pittsburgh Water Commission. Jack's son, also called Jack, turned out equally well, ending up in the planning division of the Western Pennsylvania History and Landmarks Foundation.

After John's bad stroke he could never drink or work again. He sold the coal trucks and all of the tools that went with that job. He spent his time hobbling around his garden and house, doing what he could to stay busy. Television by then was delivering movies right to his living room. Without the booze he was greatly mellowed. At last Aunt Mary had some peace in her life.

All in all, the original John Miller, product of Depression that he was, did quite well for his family, but seemed to regard himself as just an unsuccessful rival of AJR.

Max

Aunt Harriet married Max Fiske, a halfback from DePaul University in Chicago who played in 1936, 1938, and 1939 for the Pirates and in 1937 for the Chicago Cardinals. Max was a good-looking, very personable guy with some wit and a gift of gab. He was not, unfortunately, an ideal husband, and Harriet was not a devoted wife.

A truly beautiful girl, she could hold her own with Max when it came to expressing herself cleverly. Her beauty, alas – this and the fact that her brother-in-law owned the football team – gave her a sense of entitlement. She did not take responsibility well and neither did Max.

To be fair, it was not an auspicious time for two rather young, undisciplined people to be starting a new life together. The Depression was not yet over; a world war was impending. After Max went into the Army, leaving Harriet at loose ends, the marriage disintegrated.

Almost as soon as Max got out of uniform they divorced. With football out of the question, he returned to Chicago, his home town, and opened a couple of bars. Harriet stayed in Pittsburgh, too busy gadding about to care for her young daughter, Patricia. Kass and Alice stepped in, and Trish became a member of the Rooney family at 940 North Lincoln Avenue.

Max Fiske had brothers who were good amateur athletes and successful in later life. Max himself was another Art Rooney wannabe. He tried to operate shrewdly on the edges of the law but without knowing how.

AJR eventually lost respect for Max. From time to time he would be in Chicago for a football game or a championship fight, always with friends, and frequently Max would join them for dinner. On one occasion, with a train to catch, AJR and his crew were running late. He tossed the check to Max, telling him, "Sign my name to this and put on a tip." Max may have thought he was being treated like a flunky. At any rate, the tip he put on was one hundred dollars – more money, at the time, than the waiter who had served them could expect to take home in a week. Attributing this grandstand play to spitefulness or ignorance, AJR had no use for Max from then on.

With Harriet in mind, he would say to his granddaughters, "Never marry a football player." There were football players who'd have done the family proud, but what he knew of Max Fiske had left a sour note.

Car Salesman

Kass's brother, John McNulty, was a little wiry guy whose hair had turned steel gray prematurely while at the same time retreating from the front of his head. Uncle John wore glasses; he had an artificial eye as the result of a boyhood accident. George McNulty, John's uncle, owned the North Side Buick Company and gave him a job as a car salesman. He was a sporty dresser and had a pleasing personality, but also a couple of hangups.

An addiction to booze was one of them. The other went back to the injury affecting his eye. A surgeon took it out while his mother, Bridget Devlin McNulty, held him in her arms. From then on as far as his mother was concerned he could do no wrong. Until her death at 38 she spoiled him terribly, and then his three older sisters babied him for the rest of his life.

The McNulty family was upper middle class before the bottom fell out of the wooden barrel business, and John McNulty, Sr. lost everything he had. "Johnny," he would tell his son mournfully, "when you have a good day at work you never want it to end. You could work all night long." But the good days by then were coming less often, and in time they stopped coming altogether.

As the years went by for John Junior at North Side Buick, there were more bad days than good. AJR directed customers his way, but Dortha, John's wife, was no helpmate, and he was taking their problems to work. His relatives the McDonoughs, who ran the place, gradually lost patience with him and did not attempt to conceal it. John's sisters and many of his customers – he was a popular salesman – resented this. Something else came into play. Through an inheritance, John owned stock in the company – which mattered not a bit to the McDonoughs. Only the fact that he was George McNulty's nephew kept him from being fired.

AJR never took John seriously, but saved him one day from a beating. Outside the apartment building on Western Avenue where AJR lived with Kass in the early years of their marriage, John had words with a big, mean truck driver. The guy was pushing John around, daring him to retaliate, when AJR intervened. On the ground floor of the building was a division office of Anheuser-Busch, fronted by a plate-glass window. AJR sent the truck driver crashing through it, head over heels. From that moment on, Uncle John held my dad in considerable awe. I was afraid of him myself and could understand why others might be.

John told another story that contributed to the mystique building up around the man who would one day be known as the Chief. For a trip from Pittsburgh to Miami, or, more specifically, to Hialeah race track, AJR had engaged John and two others – "rough-looking guys," John called them – as drivers. Actually, John was the driver and the rough-looking guys may have been bodyguards, because AJR always carried large amounts of cash on his person. Anyway, somewhere on the outskirts of Washington, D.C., his big Buick Roadmaster broke down. John was able to get it to a General Motors garage, and AJR asked the manager how long the repairs would take.

"Couple of days at least. Gotta get a new part."

"Couple of days?" AJR didn't like that. "I don't have a couple of days." He was hell-bent on getting to Hialeah.

They were standing in the showroom, and he glanced around quickly. Indicating another Buick, the latest model, he said to the manager, "How much for that car over there?"

The manager stated a price.

"How much with my car as a trade-in?"

The manager stated a somewhat lower price.

"I'll take it," said AJR. Then to John and the tough guys, he said, "Come on, let's get going."

Eventually, John and Dortha were divorced. John died young – in his mid-fifties – of an alcohol-related illness. Dortha, who was a registered nurse, went to work for the Allegheny County Health Department. She retired with a pension and moved to Florida.

John and Dortha had a son and two daughters. The son, John McNulty III, worked for a long time at our race tracks in Florida, New York, and Vermont. Late in life, he made the admirable decision to give up his racing connections and start an entirely new career as a counselor of mentally and emotionally disturbed children in Vermont.

John McNulty II was a good guy who could not overcome his weaknesses. Those who suffered most from the way John and Dortha's story unfolded were their three children and his sisters, Kass, Alice, and Mary.

The Pittsburgh Kid

I was never much interested in boxing. When I was in high school, playing football at North Catholic, George Engel tried to teach me the rudiments. Engel was one of the fight game's top managers. He said that I looked like the great nineteenth-century heavyweight champion, John L. Sullivan. We were all up in Ligonier for the summer, and George had some time to spare. He showed me how to move my feet and hold up my hands. But I wasn't into it, and he picked that up pretty quickly. You have to have the temperament for boxing, I guess. It was something I failed to inherit from AJR.

From the mid-1930s into the early 1950s, AJR and Barney McGinley promoted almost every big fight involving Pittsburgh champions like Billy Conn, Fritzie Zivic, Billy Soose, and Sammy Angott at Forbes Field, at Hickey Park in Millvale, or in places like Duquesne Gardens, across the street from St. Paul's Cathedral in Oakland, and Motor Square Garden on Baum Boulevard in East Liberty. In 1951 The Rooney-McGinley Club promoted the heavyweight championship fight in which Jersey Joe Walcott took the title from Ezzard Charles, knocking him out in the seventh round with a single left hook.

Before teaming up with AJR, Barney McGinley had owned a saloon and a horse room in Braddock. Barney was the silent partner, a genial white-haired man. AJR considered him a standup guy he could call on to help meet the football team's payroll. As it happened, there was never any need for Barney's cash.

Ray Foutts, who had managed middleweight champion Teddy Yarosz of Monaca, was the boxing club's first matchmaker. When he returned to his home town, East Liverpool, Ohio, Jake Mintz succeeded him. Excitable and terrier-like, Mintz had been a fighter himself, with a misshapen nose to prove it. His record in the flyweight division was perfect – three fights and three knockout defeats. As matchmaker, he shared an office in the Fort Pitt Hotel, the football team's headquarters, with Bert Bell, whose voice was so loud, and so continually at full volume, that when Mintz had to make a telephone call he would crawl under the desk they both used.

When Mintz left the organization to become the manager of Ezzard Charles, Barney McGinley's son Jack took over the matchmaking. In time, as AJR and the senior McGinley became more and more preoccupied with football, they left the boxing end of the business entirely in Jack's hands. It was Jack who made all the arrangements for the Walcott-Charles fight at Forbes Field. The crowd, more than 28,000, was a record for boxing in Pittsburgh, and still is.

Jack McGinley was a decorated veteran of World War II. After graduation from Pitt, married now to Marie Rooney, AJR's sister, he enlisted in the Navy and became the engineering officer on an LST (landing ship/tank) with the rank of lieutenant junior grade. In the North African and Italian campaigns, he was cited for heroism. And then in the hours before dawn on the morning of June 6, 1944, – D-Day – his LST shoved off for Omaha Beach with 216 men in half a dozen amphibious landing-craft vehicles. In addition, they had a load of "ducks" – floatable tanks – with troops in them. Seven miles offshore was as close as they could get. Later McGinley recalled, "It was too jammed up. We had to let the troops out."

Whether their passengers made it to the beach they never knew. The LST returned to England and boarded more troops on the night of June 8th. In the middle of the English Channel, headed for Normandy again, they took a hit and then another from a German torpedo boat and sank. It was 3 a.m.

"God only knows how many people we lost. Hundreds," McGinley said. He was tossed about in the water for the next three hours. "We had life belts," he said, "and six of us held onto one of those little rubber doughnuts. As we were leaving the ship, one fellow had said, 'We'd better take this along.'" It saved their lives. Around daybreak, a British destroyer picked up the lucky half-dozen.

Meanwhile, AJR had heard from a friend in the Navy Department that McGinley's ship had been lost with all aboard. "Get ready to break the news to the family," he was told, but then came word of the rescue. I never knew about that until I heard it from Judge Barney McGinley, Jack's son.

At the end of the war, Jack was a full lieutenant. Back home in Pittsburgh, he went to work in the family's sports conglomerate, doing whatever had to be done. His most important job was to learn the boxing business, and in just a few years he was one of the most respected promoters in the country, known by all who had dealings with him as a man of the highest character and integrity.

AJR's favorite fighter was Billy Conn. At the age of 21 he took the light-heavyweight championship from Melio Bettina in New York. After winning their return match at Forbes Field in a fight the Rooney-McGinley Club did not promote (Conn's manager, Johnny Ray, was feuding with Ray Foutts), he started looking for bigger game. Because "that's where the money is," as he said, he relinquished his light-heavyweight title and moved up into the heavyweight class.

In less than a year he had beaten all the other contenders and was ready to fight the champion, Joe Louis. As a final tune-up, he took on a nobody named Buddy Knox for the Rooney-McGinley Club. He won by a knockout, which was only to be expected, but a crowd of 27,000 came to see the fight at Forbes Field.

Conn was the original "Pittsburgh Kid" – black-haired, handsome, devil-may-care. He had fallen in love with beautiful Mary Louise Smith, the teenage daughter of Greenfield Jimmy Smith, a tough former major-league baseball player. Once when Jimmy Smith was a utility infielder with John McGraw's New York Giants, he challenged a whole bench full of Brooklyn Dodgers, shouting, "All right, you sons of bitches, I'll fight you one at a time or in groups of five." Jimmy was barely 5 feet 9, but nobody in the Brooklyn dugout moved a muscle.

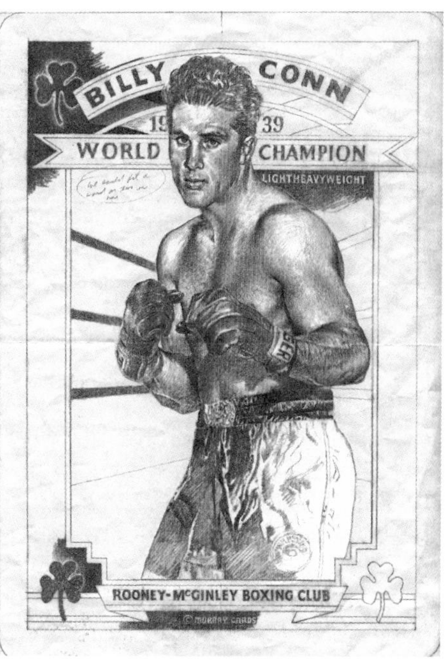

Billy Conn
(Drawing by Merv Corning)

Though he had introduced his daughter to Conn, Jimmy disapproved of him – disapproved of any fighter – as a son-in-law. To get her away from Billy, he sent Mary Louise off to Rosemont College, in Philadelphia. That didn't keep them from sneaking up to Brookville, in northern Pennsylvania, the day after the Knox fight, to take out a marriage license. But Jimmy Smith heard about it and stopped the young lovers from getting the knot tied at St. Philomena's in Squirrel Hill by storming into the residence of the bishop himself and telling him what would happen if Mary Louise ever married a pug.

Billy had another major distraction while training for his fight with Louis. Maggie, his beloved one hundred percent Irish mother, was dying of cancer. Fight night came – June 18, 1941 – and Billy went into the ring at the Polo Grounds in New York weighing 169 pounds. Louis weighed 201. This was seen as an embarrassment to the promotion. In the first place, no one was giving Billy a chance. With such a difference in the weights, it looked all the more like a mismatch. So the crowd of 54,487 was informed by the ring announcer that Conn weighed 174 and Louis weighed 199 ½.

Public interest in this fight, especially in Pittsburgh, was phenomenal. Owney McManus's Ham and Cabbage Special disgorged hundreds of Conn's admirers, wearing leprechaun hats, at Grand Central Station. They were waving paper shamrocks and sucking on clay pipes. At Forbes Field that night the Pirates were playing the New York Giants. Before the start of the fourth inning the umpires called time. Both teams retired to their dugouts, and for most of the next hour everybody listened to the amplified radio broadcast of the fight.

All over America people listened. Conn started slowly, as he usually did, and nervously. Skipping around the ring as Louis plodded after him, he slipped and fell. Both feet went out from under him. But after trading punches a few times, and taking Louis's best shots with no apparent ill effects, Billy gained confidence. He was quicker than Louis, quicker with his hands and quicker on his feet, and was beating him to the punch, moving in and landing fast combinations and then disengaging. By the eleventh round Conn seemed to be coming on strong. In the twelfth, he staggered Louis with a left hook. Going back to his corner, he lifted his right hand to acknowledge the cheers of the crowd.

"I've got him," he said to Johnny Ray. "I'm going to knock him out."

"Box," Ray advised him. "Stay away."

"No, I've got him," said Conn. When he answered the bell for the thirteenth, Ray called after him, "OK, then. You're on your own."

After fiddling around for half a minute, Conn tore into Louis. He threw a seventeen-punch combination, and more than half of the punches found their mark. But suddenly over a missed left hook Louis drove a murderous right. Conn was hurt, and Louis leaped to the attack. He landed twenty-five punches without a return and Conn went down. He wobbled to his feet a split second too late. Arthur Donovan, the referee, had counted him out.

In Conn's dressing room, the reporters waited for his tears to dry before one of them asked, "Billy, why did you go out there and slug with Louis in the thirteenth round? You were winning the fight." Conn's answer has gone down in ring lore. Smiling, he said, "What's the use of being Irish if you can't be dumb?"

Mary Louise had listened to the fight with her aunt at the Waldorf Hotel, or, rather, had listened to her aunt's account of it between rounds. She spent the rest of the time in the bathroom, shutting herself off from Don Dunphy's dramatic blow-by-blow description on the radio. When Billy had showered and dressed, he walked with Johnny Ray from the Polo Grounds to the Waldorf, a distance of five miles, recognized here and there on his passage through Harlem by exuberant Joe Louis fans who called out words of condolence. At the Waldorf, Mary Louise opened the door of the suite for him. Standing there alone, he told her, "I did my best." The tears were back in his eyes. "Billy," she said, "it's all right."

Billy's mother died on June 28th, ten days after the fight. She died in the large brick house he had bought for her with his ring earnings, a house on Fifth Avenue in Shadyside, where rich people lived. On Billy's last visit to Maggie's bedside, she had persuaded him against his own wishes to go ahead with a recuperative trip to the Jersey shore. "I'll see you when I get back," he promised.

"No, son," answered Maggie. "The next time I see you will be in Paradise."

Billy got the news of her death by telephone. On the day after the funeral Billy and Mary Louise eloped, having found a priest in Philadelphia who feared neither bishops nor Greenfield Jimmy Smith and was willing to marry them. Mary Louise had just turned 18.

Shortly after Pearl Harbor, both Conn and Louis went into the Army. Their return bout was scheduled for the following June, and the Army allowed them time off to train. It would be a big-money fight for everybody concerned, including the military's United Services Organization, or USO, which was guaranteed a cut of the gate receipts. In May, Conn came home on furlough for the christening of his first son, Timmy. AJR was the godfather. In the company of Milton Jaffe, Conn's business manager, he approached Jimmy Smith and talked him into patching things up with Billy and Mary Louise. Timmy was baptized at St. Philomena's Church on a Sunday, with Jimmy present, and then the guests all gathered at his house in Mount Lebanon for a party.

Jimmy and Billy were polite to each other – at first. Late in the afternoon, they got into a mild argument over the regularity of Billy's church attendance. Jimmy told him he'd better start going to Mass more often. They were with AJR and some others in the kitchen, and Billy was sitting on the stove. He said something back; Jimmy threatened to punch him. Long afterward, AJR told the writer Frank Deford, "I can still see Billy coming off that stove."

AJR and the rest of the men jumped in to break up the fight, but not before Billy had broken his left hand on Jimmy's head, and Milton Jaffe, caught in the middle of the scuffling, had broken an ankle in a fall down the steps to the basement. There were scratches and bruises all over Billy's face; Jimmy Smith was unmarked. When Joe Louis would see Billy after both had retired from the ring and were good friends, he never failed to ask him, "Has your father-in-law beaten you up lately?"

Conn's broken hand put the return bout on hold until after the war. As was all too evident, neither Conn nor Louis had been in a real fight since 1941. Louis looked slow, but he could still punch. Conn's skills had disappeared completely. In the sorriest exhibition of his career, he lost by an eighth-round knockout.

Today that fight is largely forgotten. So is the fact that Conn fought eleven world champions twenty times and won from them all except Louis. He's remembered for one thing. In the biggest fight of his life, he was too Irish and too headstrong to be satisfied just with winning it. "I'm going to knock him out," he told Johnny Ray, and instead he was knocked out himself.

Patsy

Like David L. Lawrence, Patsy Scanlon came from the Point, that triangular wedge of land where two rivers converge to form a third. During the early years of the twentieth century the Point was heavily Irish. In Stefan Lorant's Pittsburgh book, there's a photograph of the Point the way it looked around 1900. What you see is a slum, a wretched clutter of warehouses, freight sheds, and low-roofed buildings that squat side by side, blackened with soot. There were planing mills and grog shops and a boiler works. There were "unsightly, rickety tenements."

Uncle Jim recalled that, as kids, he and his brothers and friends would "go over to the Point and visit Patsy's mother. She'd give us tea and Irish cake." Irish cake was bread – heavy, coarse white bread with raisins in it. "The houses they lived in!" Jim said. "No carpets on the floor. No bathrooms. No hot water. There'd be a big wooden barrel under the rainspout. On winter mornings, to get a pan of water to cook in, first you had to break the ice."

Such neighborhoods were spawning grounds of fighters and politicians. Patsy Scanlon became a fighter, a good one, although never quite a champion. A gnome-like figure with a meandering nose, he had a sharp left hook, but his right was "nigh useless," as a Pittsburgh sportswriter called Jim Jab put it. Scanlon's biggest fights were with bantamweight champions Pete Herman in 1919 and Kid Williams in 1921.

The Herman fight was one-sided. Jim Jab depicted Scanlon as "a plaything in Herman's hands." Herman handed Scanlon "the worst beating doled out in moons," Jim Jab wrote. "Patrick's face," he continued, "was a sight. One lamp was just peeping out, the other was mussed." When the tenth round ended, "old friends could hardly recognize him."

Scanlon and Harry Greb were stablemates and sparring partners. Someone else Scanlon boxed with was AJR. Woogie Harris, a numbers writer from the Hill, saw them spar one time, and he told George Quinlan, a long time afterward, "Art was a bulldog. He fought like Henry Armstrong, always boring in. But Patsy batted the hell out of him. He hasn't hit Patsy yet." This must have been before 1921, when AJR was an amateur, one of the best in the country but still just a kid, and Patsy was at his peak, fighting all the best men in his weight class.

When Patsy Scanlon retired from the ring, he opened a flower shop and a bookie joint, both on the same premises. I knew him later on. He was still running a book, but working out of a saloon near the Roosevelt Hotel. His once red hair was receding and had turned to pure white. He had a red complexion – beet red at times, which was due, I suppose, to the pickling effect of John Barleycorn.

At least when I was around, Patsy never talked a great deal. He appeared to be very well liked and was said to have a sense of humor.

Dad once invited Patsy, Dago Sam, Owney McManus, and Tom Bodkin, a former boxing promoter and referee who later became a theatrical agent in New York, to 940 North Lincoln Avenue for a dinner party. Mom that night was impeccably groomed and she received these guests as though they were big-shot owners from the National Football League. (That was one of the reasons people loved her; she treated everybody the same.)

Tom Bodkin had had some exposure to the good life, and even Owney McManus could play the part of a gentleman, but Patsy and Dago Sam were uncomfortable, Patsy more so than Sam, who didn't really give a damn. In any case, both had trouble deciding what fork to use and where to place the napkin when dinner was finished.

On that one memorable night, Kathleen McNulty Rooney's grand old home looked like the stage setting for a Damon Runyon Alumni reunion.

Chapter 10

Big Kies

Off and on, Walt Kiesling was AJR's head coach from 1939 until the late 1950s. The Chief had other head coaches during that time span but except for a number of years after World War II, during the Jock Sutherland-John Michelosen era, he kept his good friend Kies on the payroll as an assistant.

Kies was a quiet, somber-looking German from the upper Middle West, 6 feet 4 inches tall with a large frame. Usually he weighed more than 300 pounds. By his early thirties, he had a full, round face and a bald head.

Like Johnny Blood, Kies played college football at a small Catholic school in Minnesota – in his case, St. Thomas. He was in the NFL, as player and coach, for thirty-four years, starting out with the old Duluth Eskimos. From Duluth he went to another of the teams that shortly became extinct, the Pottsville Maroons. His all-pro years (1929-33) were with the Chicago Cardinals. In 1934 he moved across town to play for the Bears, who were undefeated that year but lost the championship playoff to the New York Giants on an ice-covered field at the Polo Grounds. For better traction, the Giants put on tennis shoes at half-time and scored twenty-seven points in the fourth quarter to win going away, 33-13.

Kies was so quick that despite his size he played guard rather than tackle, pulling out to lead the interference. Before football took up all of his time, he had been a baseball player, and a good one. His ungainly looks were deceptive. When navigating wooden steps he went about it carefully, for fear they'd collapse under his weight, but to see him dance was a revelation. He was agile and light on his feet and he could do all the ethnic dances, such as the polka.

Jack Butler, the Steelers' all-pro defensive back, described a post-game incident in the bar of a hotel on the West Coast, where the players and coaches were killing time before they were due to catch a train. Kies had been drinking beer, and now nature called, but he was seated at a table in back, cut off from the men's room by tables that were pushed close together. Squeezing through would be impossible, and in order to clear a path for him the other members of the traveling party would have to vacate their chairs. "Don't worry about it," Kies said. He stepped up onto his own chair and then up onto his table. All of these tables – Butler didn't say how many there were – had plate-glass tops. Very nimbly, this 6-foot-4, 300-pound old football player tiptoed from one table to the next all the way to the end of the row. His audience just sat there and gaped, expecting him at any minute to crash through the glass.

AJR considered him as much of a crony as a coach. Kies liked to play cards and he liked to play the horses. He would come to 940 North Lincoln Avenue every morning to pick up the boss and drive him to work. He'd arrive when we were having breakfast in the kitchen and accept an invitation to sit down and drink a cup of coffee. One day he sat in one of those cast-iron and plastic S-shaped chairs, and it collapsed, dumping him on the floor amid the wreckage. Everybody laughed – except Kies. The next morning he sat in what he took to be a different chair but was actually the same one, restored to some semblance of its former appearance by the twins. And it happened again. Down went the chair, with Kies again riding it to the floor. The hilarity, of course, was even greater than before. After that, Kies drank his coffee standing up.

Kies was very bright but had some strange ideas about football players, which I'll get into later on. His brightness was most apparent at the card table. According to AJR, at any point in the game he could remember what cards had been played and thus seemed to know exactly what cards were left in everybody's hand.

At the race track, he made some decent side money by betting on the horses that AJR had picked. In fact, to AJR's annoyance, he would sneak a big bet with a bookie, telling no one. Pretty certain of where Kies's information had come from, the bookies would bet on the horse themselves, diminishing the payoff. After Big Kies died, somebody found a shoe box full of money under his bed – money he apparently had won at the race track and at cards.

The contents of the box went to his wife, a nice, kind woman who cooked the good German food that Kies liked. On social occasions, she would not say no to a cocktail, and it loosened her up.

She told Kass one time that her husband would win more games if AJR would spend more money on better players. This happened to be true, but it was also true that there wasn't any money to spend – the Steelers in those days operated at close to the break-even level – and Mrs. Kiesling's suggestion was not well received by Kass.

Anyway, Kies was head coach in the wartime year of 1942, and the Steelers had their first winning season, finishing second in the Eastern Division with a 7-4 record. Their success was largely due to the all-around ability of the player they had made the NFL's No. 1 draft pick that year – Bill Dudley, an All-American halfback from the University of Virginia. He led the league in rushing with 696 yards – 129 more than Whizzer White had gained in 1938 – scored six touchdowns, passed for two more, and was an extraordinary defensive back. His selection as Rookie of the Year followed automatically.

I will have more to say about Kiesling, and more about Dudley, later on.

Chaplain

"St. Francis Church in New York," said George Quinlan, "was on Thirty-Fourth Street, right off Seventh Avenue. They had what was called an Actors' Mass at 2:30 Sunday morning. So on this one Sunday there was a little disturbance in the vestibule. A short, bald-headed guy was telling jokes to some people gathered around him. Everybody was laughing. A priest goes into the vestibule and takes the bald-headed guy by the arm and ushers him out onto Thirty-Fourth Street and says, 'Now get going.' On Monday a housekeeper came to the priest's room and said, 'There's a man here to see you.' It was the little bald-headed guy. He said to the priest, 'You know something, Father? You damn near broke my arm.' And he gave the priest a five-thousand dollar check. The bald-headed guy was Jimmy Durante. The priest was Father Silas Rooney."

When Father Silas went to China to be a missionary, he was big, strong, and athletic. He came back to America weighing 125 pounds and ravaged by the onset of Lou Gehrig's disease. A few years at St. Francis, his next assignment, apparently did wonders for him.

The Franciscans had ordered their missionaries to leave China when the Japanese invaded that country in the late 1930s. A Japanese cruise ship took the priests to Hawaii, and Father Silas became friendly with one of the stewards. He said the steward called his attention to the removable cabin walls. They were removable, the man explained, so that the cruise ship could be turned into a troop ship. The Japs were preparing even then for war with the United States.

Not long after Pearl Harbor, Father Silas went into the Army as a chaplain. After D-Day, he served with the troops that were fighting the Germans, but first he spent some time at a staging area in England. There was a recreation room, where one day he picked up a pool stick and got into a game with some high-ranking officers, including a general or two. The ease with which he ran the table excited a few captains and lieutenants; its effect on the generals, colonels, and majors was different.

"Where did you learn to play like that?" one of the generals asked. "There must be something in your past you don't talk about."

Father Silas was in the Battle of the Bulge. During the siege, he was pinned down in a bunker with two other chaplains. Panicking, one of them made a break for it. He was gone before the others could stop him, running across open ground while the shells and the bullets were coming. The next day the Americans found his body. Father Silas said the German soldiers who shot him must have been practicing Christians. The chaplain's corpse was laid out on a bench, with his hands crossed on his chest and the uniform cap over his face.

Before a battle, said Father Silas, the troops would give the chaplains their money to take care of. If a soldier was killed, it would be up to the chaplain to get that money to his family back home. This, said Father Silas, was one of the most difficult parts of his job.

After the Americans crossed into Germany, Father Silas was with an outfit located near a Catholic orphanage. One day he got hold of a jeep and loaded it with C-rations for the children and the nuns. As he was about to take off for the orphanage, an officer caught sight of him.

"Just where are you going with that?" he demanded.

Father Silas explained what the purpose was.

The officer said, "Leave that jeep where it is. You don't have any authority to give food to the enemy."

Father Silas was upset but obeyed orders. The officer outranked him. Forty-five minutes later, a truck full of food pulled into his area. The officer who had halted his jeep came up to him and said, "If we're going to help those orphans, let's do it right."

Years after the war, Father Silas showed up at Three Rivers Stadium with a copy of an old insurance policy. It was not for a large amount. Grandma Rooney had taken it out when he was in Europe. He could now cash it in, and he was misty-eyed.

"God bless her," he said.

Civilian

On December 11, 1941, four days after Pearl Harbor, Hitler's German Reich, as an ally of Japan, declared war on the United States. AJR was in a German restaurant in New York with Walt Kiesling the previous night and spoke to some German sailors at a nearby table who appeared to be having a good time. "They seemed like such nice guys," AJR remembered thinking. The next day in the papers he read that these same German sailors had scuttled their ship in the harbor. I was just a kid at the time, and I asked AJR what it meant to scuttle a ship.

"To pull the plug and sink it." he said.

AJR had been too young for World War I, and now he was 40 years old, but he went to the Navy recruiting office in Pittsburgh and volunteered. As a married man with children, the officer in charge informed him, he would need his wife's signature on the enlistment papers. So AJR came home with the documents, and Kass reluctantly signed. When he took them back to the recruiting office, the Navy man was extremely cordial. He watched while AJR put his own name on the papers and then a remarkable change in his manner took place.

"Well, big shot," he said, "now you're in the Navy, and you'll do what *we* tell you to do," etc., etc. He was waving the papers in AJR's face.

There were other volunteers waiting to sign; no one, including AJR, had been given the oath. "Are we officially in the Navy before we're sworn in?" AJR asked the recruiting officer.

"No," said the recruiter, "but that will be taken care of as soon as I get the rest of these guys signed up."

Without another word, AJR yanked his papers out of the officer's hands. He tore them to pieces, dropped the pieces on the floor, and walked out, ignoring the Navy man's cries of "Hey, wait a minute!"

Kass said that even though she never had met that sailor, she couldn't thank him enough.

As the fighting in the Pacific and in Europe heated up, AJR gave blood at the Red Cross so many times he was finally told not to come back. And he arranged for the Steelers to play a game with the profits all going to the USO. (I remember a USO canteen near the Pennsylvania Railroad Station for military men passing through Pittsburgh.)

Gasoline rationing was now in effect, but AJR had a way of getting around the regulations and continued to travel extensively. I know he had friends who owned gas stations. One place, near Ligonier, had a garden hose rigged up to a gasoline pump for favored customers. In my youthful naiveté, I couldn't figure out why the attendant was putting a water hose into our gasoline tank.

There were shortages of almost everything, but I don't recall doing without necessities. Up to a point, AJR felt that government rules were for other people to obey. There were government rules and there were God's rules, and AJR followed God's rules. He was lucky and smart and never got into trouble.

On the highway he picked up hitchhikers in uniform and would take these passengers to wherever they were headed, within reason. He hoped, as he said to Kass, that someone would do the same for his brother Tom, who was in the Marines.

Late one night with the temperature in the teens, he picked up a young Navy yeoman at the New Stanton exit on the Pennsylvania Turnpike. As the yeoman later described it, he'd been waiting thirty minutes in a razor-sharp wind, and his ears were frosting over. When a pair of headlights approached, he frantically waved his arms, only to watch the big sedan roar by.

"But whoa!" the sailor went on. "About a hundred yards beyond me, the car braked to a stop and began backing up – on the Turnpike, a real no-no. As it reached me, a door swung open and a voice boomed out, 'Hop in." A man in the back seat extended his hand and said, "Hi. I'm Art Rooney.'"

The sailor was momentarily flustered. He said, "Oh." Huddled in his Navy peacoat, glad to be out of the cold, he was silent for a moment. Then he said, "I'm afraid to tell you who I am."

"Why would you say that?" AJR wanted to know.

"Because I work for the *Pittsburgh Press*. And when you ran for register of wills, our paper creamed you." (As a matter of fact, the *Press* had declared AJR to be "utterly without qualifications for the office" and "the hand-picked tool of James J. Coyne.")

AJR laughed. "Best thing the *Press* ever did," he said. "I never had any business being in politics."

The sailor was John Troan. In another twenty-five years he would be editor-in-chief of the *Press*, a Steeler season-ticket holder, and one of AJR's many friends.

He said that AJR was returning to Pittsburgh from the Army-Navy football game in Baltimore (the price of admission was the purchase of a war bond). He himself was trying to get home from his Navy base near Baltimore. Of course Troan said something like, "Drop me off anywhere that's convenient for you," and of course AJR had the driver – Harp Vaughan? Walt Kiesling? – deliver him to his front door.

"Good luck," said AJR as they parted, "and look me up when the war is over."

However he did it, wherever he was, AJR could always find gasoline. On a solo trip South, deep in the boondocks of Georgia, he was flagged down for speeding and hauled off to the rustic police station. It was in a clapboard house with woods on all sides. The speed trap had netted several others, among them a young guy in a sailor suit, and they were being told they could pay their fines on the spot or wait for the judge to appear.

"How long will that be?" asked the serviceman.

"Three days."

"Three days? In three days, I report back to my ship. How much is the fine?"

"Fifty dollars."

The young sailor was in shock. He said, "But fifty dollars is all the money I have."

"Pay the fine or wait for the judge," said the cop.

AJR stepped up. He pulled a hundred-dollar bill out of his pocket. "I'm pleading guilty and that sailor is pleading guilty," he told the cop. "Here's a hundred bucks for our fines." He turned to the sailor. "Let's get out of here, kid," he said, and, together, they took off.

Randomly, in ways of his own choosing, AJR contributed to the war effort.

Red

AJR's brother John was called Red for good reason – his full head of strawberry blond hair. Red was about 5 feet 11 with a medium build. He had been an athlete at Duquesne Prep, although not of the same caliber as AJR, Dan, and Jim. However, the Rooney Reds, one of AJR's semi-pro football teams, were named for John, I am sure.

He took a pre-med course at Duquesne University but was working for AJR in the Steeler ticket office when he volunteered for the Army – or was drafted; I'm not sure which – nine months before Pearl Harbor. AJR would say, without elaborating, that Red "screwed up" at some point during the time that he served – four and a half years. When Aunt Margaret heard him talking this way, she stoutly defended Red. "He fought in all the big battles in western Europe. And he was hurt real bad in an ammunition dump explosion," she told me.

Red's job as a toxic gas handler in a chemical warfare outfit that fought in the North African campaign, as well as in Sicily, Italy, France, and Germany, was to issue high-explosive shells for 4.2 chemical mortars. The risks, more than likely, were enormous. Red earned six Bronze Stars and a medal called an Invasion Indian Arrowhead before the ammunition-dump explosion somewhere in Germany.

It is hard to separate fact from fiction where Red was concerned, but Aunt Margaret and the Chief agreed on one thing: after Red returned from the war, he was never the same man.

There were war veterans back then who suffered from what was called "shell shock." Bruce Catton, in one of his marvelous Civil War books, wrote of veterans who could only sit and stare. The war in Vietnam gave us a different term for this malady: "post-traumatic stress disorder."

Having graduated from Duquesne in 1933, Red could have gone to medical school under the post-war GI Bill but decided against it. In the kitchen at 940 North Lincoln Avenue one night, Kass tried to change his mind. Red wasn't listening. "It's too late for that," he insisted. "It's time to get on with my life."

Getting on with his life was a process lubricated by alcohol. Red was a good-looking, likable, gregarious sort of guy. He could tell a good story, extracting all the drama. I've written how the first of our ancestors to be born in North America left a "scoundrel" for dead on one of Pittsburgh's many bridges, and the words I used came from Red. "A shot rang out in the night," he would say, "and only Grandfather Rooney walked off the bridge."

Could Red have been a doctor? He was smart enough. "Red had a lot on the ball," a friend of his said, "but he wanted to be like his brother Art – a hot-shot gambler." What he lacked was the temperament and the aptitude.

He did have an air of refinement. While I was being tutored by a straitlaced old spinster called Miss Hall in AJR's offices at the Fort Pitt Hotel. Red would come in and exchange a few words with her in French. She considered him superior in looks and intelligence to the horse players, card players, and newspapermen who frequented the Fort Pitt. I heard Miss Hall tell Kass how much she admired Red. In fact, she once asked if he would like to meet her niece. "No, thanks," he replied. "I've had enough woman trouble as it is."

Which was true. Red had been married and divorced. There were two children, Margie and Patty, and both grew up to be fine young ladies. As a result, Kass said, of Red's interest in medicine, Margie became a nurse. Both girls left Pittsburgh for greener, sunnier pastures in California.

AJR put Red to work at the Steelers' pre-season camp in Cambridge Springs doing odd jobs, and he may have looked upon this as demeaning. At any rate, one of the football players – Ralph Calcagni – died of a ruptured appendix, and Red put the blame on the "brutal" training methods of Jock Sutherland, the new coach. Using this as an excuse, he immediately left camp. Back in Pittsburgh, he told family members that in Cambridge Springs the players were "dropping like flies." He said there was too much hard physical contact; the drills were too exhausting; the practice sessions lasted too long.

For all his potential, he ended up driving a Yellow Cab. On a raw winter day when I was still just a kid, Red saw me playing near the North Side Carnegie Library. Noticing that my hands were bare, he stopped his cab, called me over, and handed me a dollar. "Artie, you look cold," he said. "Take this and buy yourself a pair of gloves."

Red died at 42, another nice guy who wasted his life. The cause of death, as Jack McGinley put it, was "too much booze and too little self-esteem." Something else that contributed, at least in my opinion, was post-traumatic stress disorder, which we did not yet understand.

The Day Art Rooney Cried

Born to Irish Catholic parents who accepted the strictures of the Church against birth control, my Uncle Tom, the last of Dan and Maggie Rooney's eight children, was young enough to be AJR's son. If you were Catholic you took all the kids that God sent you.

So Tom Rooney was a gift of God, but with some deviltry in his makeup – a "wild thing," Kass said, who would "fight at the drop of a hat." Tom had red hair and fair skin. He was of medium height – maybe 5 feet 10 – but compactly built. Rip Scherer described him to me as "one of the best high school football players I've ever seen." They were teammates at North Catholic, where Tom was a halfback and Rip a freshman fullback. In years to come, Rip coached AJR's sons at North.

Uncle Tom always seemed to be somewhere nearby when you needed him. I have a boyhood memory of being locked in the bathroom at 940 North Lincoln Avenue. The door could not be opened from either the inside or the outside. I was getting desperate when here comes Tom, crawling through the window. He had found a ladder that would reach the second floor. On my part after that, there was hero worship for Tom.

When my brother Dan was 10 he came home one day with a story about a "flasher" accosting kids around the North Side park area called Monument Hill. He said the man who exposed himself was wearing a dark blue or gray business suit. Uncle Tom happened to be in the house, and he ordered Dan into the family car. Wasting no time, they drove to Monument Hill. The dark-suited man was still there.

"Is that him?" asked Tom.

"That's him."

Tom jumped out of the car, grabbed the pervert by the scruff of his neck, and gave him a tooth-rattling shake. "Keep away from those kids, you son of a bitch!" Tom shouted. "If I ever see you around here again, you're dead!"

And it was no idle threat.

When Tom was a kid he went to St. Peter's School through the eighth grade and then to Duquesne Prep, where he skipped so many classes that AJR got involved. His motivational tool was sarcasm. In a snowstorm one morning, Tom set out for the Bluff on foot, battling heavy drifts all the way. Anything to escape his oldest brother's withering tongue. Except for the headmaster, he found the place deserted. "Rooney," the headmaster said, "you don't show up when the weather is good. Today it's terrible outside – nothing is moving – and here you are. Well, you can turn right around and go home – we've canceled all classes."

On the theory that a change of environment might be helpful in some fashion, Pop and Maggie removed Tom from Duquesne Prep and sent him to North Catholic. I'm not sure how it turned out. In any event, with the European powers at war, AJR perceived that sooner or later the United States would be drawn in, and he believed he could use his political pull to get Tom appointed to the Naval Academy. The stumbling block was Tom's academic record at North, but AJR knew what to do about it. Bullis Prep, in New Jersey, made a specialty of preparing athletes with weak grades for higher education, in particular the higher education the Naval Academy offered. Thanks to AJR, Bullis Prep was the next stop for Tom. He may have lasted a semester before dropping out.

The one option left to him, AJR thought, was the military service. "It's better than being a bum," he would say. As though in agreement, Tom enlisted in the Marine Corps. Afterwards, AJR regretted having pushed him in that direction.

Once when his mother was ill, Tom all but threatened to go AWOL in persuading the company commander to grant him an emergency leave. He was home for a few days looking fit. I can still see him passing a football around at the family cottage in Ligonier ... the red hair, the fair complexion. He was wearing a Navy blue turtleneck sweater that AJR had bought in Canada. AJR told him to keep the sweater, but Tom said no, it was not regulation equipment. His wardrobe had to be one hundred percent government issue.

He said that never in his civilian days had he imagined he could get through anything as demanding, both physically and psychologically, as boot camp at Parris Island, in South Carolina. What he talked about more than the rigorous training, though, was how the non-commissioned officers exploited the personal fears and hang-ups of the recruits. If they discovered that someone had a snake phobia, or a spider phobia, there would be snakes or spiders that night in his bed. But Parris Island was child's play, the veterans back from the Pacific all said, compared to the experience of combat against the Japs.

Tom's leave was soon over, and we never saw him again.

He fought in three major battles. Writing home after the first or second, he said that if he was fortunate enough to get out alive he would seriously consider the priesthood. I'm sure he meant it. "There aren't any atheists in foxholes" was a saying that came out of the war. But in July of 1944 when the Marines recaptured Guam, an island the Japs had held for two and a half years, Tom was killed.

Weeks passed before the family received the news. First, Tom's letters stopped coming. Then a Marine friend of Tom's, in a letter to Aunt Harriet, wrote: "Too bad about Tommy. He was a great guy." His use of the past tense prompted AJR to get in touch with some people he knew in the Navy Department, and they confirmed that Tom was a casualty of the invasion.

"I'll never forget that day," said George Quinlan. "It was the only time I ever saw Art Rooney cry."

Tom's mother was a long time recovering. His remains were sent back from Guam after the war and he was buried in the North Side Catholic Cemetery. In January of 2002, I met a pharmacist named Carl Wincalowicz who had been a Seabee. He said that for fifty-five years he had wanted to speak with somebody from the Rooney family but always held back out of reticence. Learning that Rip Scherer had kept in touch with me emboldened him. He had known Rip and Tom at North Catholic High School, and through Rip, we got together. This was the story he told: When his Seabee outfit went to Guam, once the island was secured, he had recognized a sailor from Pittsburgh. The sailor was a Fogarty, a brother of Fran, the Steelers' accountant. He told Carl where Tom was buried – up on a nearby hill – and at the cemetery, among the rows of white crosses, Carl found the one with Tom's name on it. Breaking a rule, he took a picture of the grave, and for all these years he had wanted a Rooney to have it. The moment was rather touching, as he talked of Tom, North Catholic, and the photograph.

Another time after the war – this must have been in the 1980s – I met a friend of the family who had preceded Tom into the Marines. He was driving a truck for a bakery. Tearfully, he told me that after Tom's death Grandma Rooney had refused to see him or speak to him. He said she believed that what had influenced Tom to become a Marine was the sight of this friend in his handsome green uniform. If she knew that AJR had encouraged Tom to enlist, it was something she never mentioned.

Down through the years, AJR and Kass would sometimes come across veterans of the war who had been in Tom's outfit. Tom may have thought he had a religious vocation, but their stories portrayed him as still very much a wild kid. He'd been a sergeant or a corporal but was busted to private, it seems, for "borrowing" a jeep while on liberty. Unofficially, the top brass in the Corps did not disapprove of such behavior. High-spirited Marines were the kind who excelled in combat.

There were conflicting accounts of how Tom lost his life: "killed in the water when his company stormed the beach" ... "using a flame thrower that exploded in his face." No one will ever know. On the day of the invasion, one story went, Tom was among the first to board the landing craft from the ship. Another Marine, about to climb down the netting, caught Tom's eye and gave him a thumbs-up. Smiling, Tom returned the gesture. And then quickly, with a twist of the wrist, he converted thumbs-up to thumbs-down.

During the late summer of 1944 when there was no word from Tom, something very strange and very Irish happened. Two owls appeared at our cottage in Ligonier one night. Hooting ceaselessly, they perched on a utility pole outside the second-floor bedroom occupied by AJR and Kass. They did not fly away until AJR and the kids tossed rocks and shined flashlights at them. The next night they returned and again were driven off, a routine that went on for at least a month, and then at last they stopped coming. It was not long afterward that the Navy Department confirmed Tom's death. Kass and Aunt Alice always felt that the first appearance of the owls corresponded to the date on which Tom was killed.

One more reminiscence: On a Memorial Day evening a long time after the war, my family was gathered for dinner. One of the young people at the table asked what Memorial Day signified. When the explanation was given, another young one asked, "Did anyone here ever know anyone who was killed in a war?"

I picked up my glass and quietly said, "Here's to Uncle Tommy Rooney, United States Marine Corps, 24 years old ... killed on Guam during World War II."

Home Front

With World War II, the Depression years came to an end and Western Pennsylvania's economy turned around. Pittsburgh always had been a dark, forbidding place; as the raw materials of war rolled out of the steel mills and manufacturing plants, it became even darker. Smoke and smog hung in the air, but the night-time glow of the open hearths lit up the riversides, and there was action Downtown until dawn.

The restaurants and clubs were always packed. Broadway plays and revivals came to the sold-out Nixon Theater. On a Friday or Saturday after 6 p.m., you couldn't buy a ticket to a movie. Owney McManus, who ran a thriving bar on Fourth Avenue, said the paddy wagons were full every night with petty wise-guy hoodlums from Donora, Brownsville, Ambridge, and the other surrounding mill towns. Everybody out of uniform had work; everybody out of uniform had money.

There were men the Army and Navy didn't want. Men in their thirties and forties. Men with wives and kids like AJR (who was over the age limit as well). Four-Fs like gimpy-legged Uncle Jim and one-eyed Uncle John McNulty and sickly Uncle Vince (who lived to be 75). Men with defense-related jobs like Uncle John Laughlin. And men besides these who paid off someone in politics to avoid the draft.

All things considered, the Rooneys did more than their share. Father Silas was an Army chaplain in France. Uncle John was a soldier in the ranks. Uncle Tom, a Marine, died in combat. Aunt Marie's husband, Jack McGinley, had a ship blown out from under him in the English Channel. Not to mention Aunt Harriet, with a husband *and* a boyfriend in the service.

I saw the war from the perspective of a child. When the Japanese bombed Pearl Harbor I was six years old. When the Enola Gay dropped its load on Hiroshima I was ten. My brothers John, Pat, and Tim were even younger. At the cottage in Ligonier and in the back yard at 940 North Lincoln Avenue we played war games, launching attacks on one another from our fox holes. AJR brought us war toys, a scarce commodity. He kept the family supplied with the necessities of life and kept the Steelers from going out of business.

Many government functions were suspended for the duration. I knew that something called the "infrastructure" was falling apart. Bridges, ramps, and roads crumbled. Beating the enemy – the Germans and Japs – came first. In a crowded North Side bakery a woman hoped out loud that the war would go on forever: it had given her money to spend. The saleslady picked up a pie and threw it right into her face.

Jeeps and tanks, instead of new cars, rumbled off the assembly lines in Detroit. Cars, which were irreplaceable, had to last just as long as the war did, but AJR could beat the system. We were never without a car that looked and ran like new, and always there was plenty of gas. In the summer we drove to Ligonier. Or Kass would take the kids to North Park, with a stop for ice cream at the North Hills Dairy on McKnight Road.

The way to get around in the city was by streetcar. Everything that could move was on the tracks, including old wooden relics that may once have been pulled by horses. At Pennsylvania Station, railroad trains were constantly arriving or leaving. Sternwheeler riverboats paddled up and down the Allegheny, the Mon, and the Ohio.

I remember the sounds of the streetcars on a summer night, and the sounds coming into my second-floor bedroom, the one I shared with Tim, in the morning – the bells clanging, the steel wheels grinding against the tracks, the screech of the cars as they turned onto Western Avenue. In those long-ago days before air-conditioning, we slept with the windows wide open. Later, with my brother Dan married and gone, I had the back bedroom to myself, but the streetcar sounds and the whistles of the trains – the Pennsylvania's main line to Chicago ran through West Park – were my constant companions. In the late 1940s, when the houses on Millionaires' Row were coming down, I heard the whistles and horns of the riverboats, too.

Everyone had a relative in the service. You could put a star in the window for every family member in the military – gold stars for those who had died. Grandma Rooney had a gold star for Tom in her window. The radio was the great communicator. We would all sit around and listen to the "stories," and then the old folks would tune in the war news, which Gabriel Heatter knew how to dramatize. Walter Winchell mixed war news with gossip. Milton and Ruth Jaffe spent time in New York, and Ruth would return with all the scandal about the stars of stage and screen.

Rural West Virginians came here to get jobs in the war-related industries, and many of them lived on the North Side, in the nineteenth-century mansions partitioned off as rooming houses. Behind the Tiffany-glass windows they lived as they had in their mountain shacks. They tore the handcrafted woodwork from the walls and drove nails into the plaster for coat hooks. North Lincoln and Ridge avenues would never be the same again.

The last house to go on our part of the street belonged to a member of the Mellon-related Scaife family. He hired a watchman who lived in the basement and kept an eye out for intruders. Thanks to Kass, 940 North Lincoln remained in pristine condition. Anxious to keep up appearances, she poured a lot of money into the house. More than once during those years the doorbell would ring, and relatives of the original owners, introducing themselves, would tell Kass how grateful they were that she had not let the place deteriorate. One woman became very emotional, calling our house "an island in a sea of disaster."

Pop Rooney's bar was just a memory by then, but some of the old First Ward people – the McCabes, the Yuhaszes, and the Mareks – still lived in the neighborhood. They were solid citizens. For other North Siders, the war was the end of the line. There were no drugs then, but lots of booze, and lots of people who'd rather drink than take the jobs to be had for the asking.

Our neighborhood was primarily white. The First Ward School was still there. St. Peter's School was nearby, at the summit of Arch Street. It was nonetheless an unforgiving location. For every family like the McCabes, who eventually got out, there were more that sank into the muck. If you were young, all you had was one chance. You couldn't sow your wild oats and then make a second new start, or a third, or a fourth. If you flunked out of school, it was either the Army or a crummy job. The kids we hung out with were athletes, mostly. Football players and basketball players finished high school; the most skilled among them had scholarship offers from colleges and universities.

Our friend Mike Kearns lived with his mother and sister in the billiard room of a big old house on Ridge Avenue, a block from North Lincoln, broken up now into "apartments." In these gray brick and red brick Georgian and English Manor landmarks, the tenants were the poorest of the poor. Down the hall from the Kearnses, another family, a mother and several children, occupied the original pantry – sharing it, Mike said, with the chickens the woman kept for their eggs.

Mike was a bright kid, one of the brightest among the thousand or more boys at North Catholic High School, a football, basketball, and baseball star and the "end man" in the yearly minstrel show. Kent State offered him a football scholarship. After two years of college, he went into the Army – we were fighting now in Korea – and in the Army he did very well. He returned to civilian life, married, and became a devoted drunk.

With eight kids to support, all he could ever handle was a routine job making Clark bars and Teaberry gum at the Clark Candy Company, where many North Siders without his ability ended up. The marriage, strained to the utmost, didn't last, but neither did Mike's boozing. He gave up drinking after twenty years, remarried, and contributed something to society, helping other reformed drunks in Alcoholics Anonymous.

Mike's sister had a master's degree from Pitt and went into social work, specializing in children's psychology. With five kids of her own – three boys and two girls – she divorced a husband who drank. Soon afterward, she married a well-to-do Seattle lawyer, a North Sider she had known in high school. She moved to the West Coast, continued her work in psychology, and gave birth to another daughter.

Mike and Mary Jane were North Siders with talent and a mother who cared. They survived. Hundreds of others couldn't make it through the trash heap, lacking the toughness to overcome their environment. Of course the Kearnses were not the only exceptions. One North Sider I knew became a general in the Air Force. Richie McCabe became a good defensive back for the Steelers and a coach in the NFL.

AJR took these kids for what they were. Some of them he helped – the unlucky ones, the children from a family of drunks. A saloon owner's son, he hated booze and spent frequent odd moments in the last forty years of his life preaching temperance sermons to his own sons and to three of his brothers.

Mongrels

In the middle of the Depression, AJR had scraped up $2,500 to buy an NFL franchise. He kept it going through continued hard times. Now, just as the team was beginning to show promise, the Second World War subordinated all other activities, including professional sports, to the task of defeating Germany and Japan.

By 1943, the armed services had started drafting married men with children. Only 4-Fs, defense workers, and middle-aged has-beens were left to play football. The Cleveland Rams suspended operations, and the Steelers, at the suggestion of Commissioner Elmer Layden, merged with the Philadelphia Eagles to form a team officially known as Phil-Pitt but which the sportswriters called the Steagles. By going along with this idea, AJR showed his pioneering spirit and his genius for toughing it out.

The Steagles played two of their five home games in Pittsburgh and three in Philadelphia. Watching the team practice, AJR remarked to one of the sportswriters, "The name is different and the colors are different, but when you get down to it they're the same old Steelers." It was a phrase that haunted him for years after the war, appearing repeatedly in the newspapers as losing season followed losing season: "S.O.S. – Same old Steelers."

"I should have kept my mouth shut," AJR said to me more than once.

The Steagles had two head coaches, Walt Kiesling and Philadelphia's man, Greasy Neal, who despised each other and argued constantly. Players holding jobs in war plants worked by day and practiced with the team at night, from 6 to 9. Bill Dudley was in the Pacific as an Army bomber pilot. The center, Ray Graves, had one ear. A guard, Ed Michaels, had two ears but was almost deaf. Tony Bova, the team's best pass catcher, was almost blind. Jack Hinkle, a halfback, had washed out of the Air Corps, classified as "unfit for service" because of ulcers. Bill Hewitt, 34, was back in the game after four years of retirement to play end.

Before the war, people did not have money to spend on football tickets. Now there was money enough, but the manpower shortage had depleted the talent available to the teams, and crowds were still sparse. I remember that when I watched the Steagles practice one evening I was more impressed with a column of soldiers drilling in the sunset than with the football players.

Despite the animosity that existed between Kiesling and Neale, the Steagles ended the season with a decent 5-4-1 record. Frank (Bucko) Kilroy, a 240-pound rookie tackle who was still going to Temple University as a student in the Navy College Training Program, said that Kiesling and Neale could not have been less alike as coaches. Neale stressed offense, Kiesling defense. Neale was humorous, confident, and upbeat. Kiesling was serious – even, at times, glum.

For years after the war, Kilroy played for the Eagles and took pride in his reputation as one of the meanest, toughest linemen ever to wear a uniform. His off-the-field persona was different. Irish, red-haired, and full of blarney, he expressed great admiration for AJR and Bert Bell and was always very friendly toward me, a young kid. When I was grown, just in talking with Bucko, I learned a lot about what to look for as a scout.

In the mid-to-late 1970s we were trying to get a team picture from every year since the beginning and soon had them all with one exception. Missing was a photo of the 1943 Steagles. At last one turned up – standing out from all the rest because the players were not in uniform. They wore business suits. Something else about it was eye-catching as well. There were not enough men for a backup at every position. The total, as I recall it, was twenty. On game days, they must have picked up extra players to round out a squad.

In 1944 the Eagles resumed operating on their own, and the Steelers merged with the weak Chicago Cardinals, owned by AJR's good friend Charley Bidwill. Named the Card-Pitts, this team was so bad the sportswriters took to calling it the Carpets. The Carpets were coached by Kiesling and Phil (Moxie) Handler. They lost every game, ten in all, and every game was one-sided.

After a 34-7 defeat at the hands of the Bears, Kiesling and Handler fined three of their players for showing "indifference" on the field. One of the three was Johnny Grigas, a fullback from Holy Cross. Grigas that year scored nine of the Card-Pitts' sixteen touchdowns and led the team in rushing. Going into the final game of the season, in fact, he led the whole league in rushing.

That final game, a rematch with the Bears, was at Forbes Field, where two high school teams had played the day before in the rain, creating a lot of mud. Overnight the temperature fell, and the mud changed to hard, icy ridges. AJR recalled that they were "sticking out of the ground like spikes." Grigas suited up and went out on the field before the game. He looked at the ridges and tested them with his foot. They felt like concrete. So Grigas returned to the dressing room and put on his street clothes again. He called a cab. When the next train left for Boston, Grigas was on it – bound for home. The Bears beat the Card-Pitts by 42 points. Meanwhile, Bill Paschal of the New York Giants, playing on a weekend pass from the Army, ran for enough yardage that day to win the rushing title. Grigas finished second.

Phil Handler fitted right in with AJR and his crowd. During the season he got a letter from a high school coach who wanted a copy of his playbook. When AJR heard about it, he told Phil, "That guy must be nuts – we haven't won a game."

Phil had something in common with AJR, a fondness for betting on race horses. Years after the Card-Pitts were history I saw Phil at the College All-Stars' practice field the week of their annual game with the NFL champions, later discontinued. He was scouting the All-Stars for the Bears. I hardly knew Phil, but when I walked up beside him he turned and shook hands. Then he said matter-of-factly, "Tell your dad to give me a call when he has a horse running." With that, he turned back to the field and watched the rest of practice without ever saying another word to me. Somehow Phil reminded me of an old uncle I did not spend much time with but who recognized and acknowledged me when we met.

There was always a bond, I felt, between the Steelers and our partners in those wartime mergers, especially Mr. Bidwill's team. Charley's sons, Billy and Stormy, ran the Cardinals after his death, and after a falling-out between them, Billy alone was in charge. I valued them both as friends

World War II ended in August of 1945, the year the Steelers regained their name and their identity. Walt Kiesling was gone, not to return until 1954, and Jim Leonard, a Villanova guy, became the new head coach.

Earlier in the decade, Jim had been an assistant under Kies. Some of the good pre-war players were filtering back, but not quite soon enough. The Steelers ended up with a 2-8 record. Bill Dudley was available for the last four games and led the team in scoring with three touchdowns.

Jim Leonard and AJR were very fond of each other. I recall a family trip through the New Jersey countryside in the 1950s. We were on our way to a seashore resort, with a stop at the Monmouth race track, but made a detour to look for Jim, who had an asparagus farm in the vicinity. AJR wasn't sure where it was, so we covered a lot of ground on our search. Leonard by then was out of football and spending most of his time in the asparagus fields. Suddenly AJR caught sight of a man on a tractor. He tooted his horn. Climbing down from the tractor, Jim Leonard came over to the side of the road, a big smile on his face. He shook hands with all of us, and then AJR drew him aside for a private conversation that lasted about fifteen minutes.

I saw Jim again at one of our games in the 1970s and for the last time ever at AJR's funeral in 1988. Jim was an old man, but still tall and robust looking. He lived for another five or six years.

'Me?'

Chuck Cherundolo was all man. You'd have sworn he was 6 feet 6 instead of 6 feet 2 and weighed 320 pounds instead of 250. His classic Italian face looked like something carved out of marble by a Renaissance sculptor, and he had what is known as a foghorn voice. The way he walked and the way he talked reminded people of John Wayne, only with Cherundolo there wasn't any play-acting. Chuck was the real article. A child of the Depression from the tough hard-coal region of northeastern Pennsylvania, he had played college football – linebacker and center – at Penn State.

In the NFL, Cherundolo started out with the Cleveland Rams and Philadelphia Eagles, but ended his career with the rugged Steeler teams of the years just before and just after the Second World War. The Navy took him in 1943, and he was thus never stigmatized as a Steagle or Card-Pitt.

On shore leave one time and due to ship out unexpectedly, he found himself with two full bottles of high-grade whiskey he hadn't gotten around to finishing off. He might have smuggled it on board, but did not. Cherundolo was an officer, the kind who toed the line. In the lobby of the hotel where he was staying he noticed two young Navy enlisted men. They looked thirsty. "Hey, swabbies, would you like a drink?" he bellowed. The sailors seemed to take it as an order and responded with meek yes sirs.

"Come on, then," Cherundolo said, leading them to the elevator. Up to his room they went, the swabbies showing signs of uneasiness. Roughly, Cherundolo handed them the bottles. "The only reason you're getting this stuff," he said, "is that I'm shipping out right away, and I'd rather give it to you guys than waste it on officers. Now, scram." He had left the door open, but the two sailors paused before leaving. A change had come over them. They thanked Cherundolo for the bottles with unusual effusiveness and continued to thank him as they went on their way.

Cherundolo stood watching their backs, nonplussed. What had been going on in the minds of those guys? And then all of a sudden he saw the light. "Why, those little farts," he said to himself. "They came up here thinking I was queer. Me! A queer! ME!"

He told the story about the sailors in pre-season training camp one year. "Well, Chuck," a teammate said after the laughs had died away, "you never know." Cherundolo chased him out of the room.

Captain of the team, Cherundolo led the Steelers in their daily calisthenics. With his big voice, he bullied, cajoled, and encouraged, booming out the cadence, keeping an eye on the shirkers, putting hecklers in their place. "If you're gonna soar with the eagles, you can't hoot with the owls," he would roar.

Unlike some of the other players, he always had time for the water boys. Often he shot baskets with them after practice or meetings. Though his appearance belied it, he was agile and quick, and he knew enough basketball to offer the kids helpful little tips.

After the 1948 season, Cherundolo joined the coaching staff. Head coaches came and went; Cherundolo stayed on into the 1950s. He coached and scouted elsewhere for something like fifteen more years and meanwhile went into business for himself. On the roof of his bar and grill on Route 51 at the south end of the Liberty Tubes was a big neon sign in the shape of a football. Cherundolo served beer and sandwiches mostly and he entertained his customers with unscheduled showings of Steeler highlight films.

When my son Mike attended Washington & Jefferson College, he wrote a paper on AJR for one of his English courses. In doing research, he asked Cherundolo for some reminiscences. The old war horse answered in writing and ended his long account with the sentence: "I was lucky to have played in Pittsburgh for the Steelers and Art Rooney, one of the finest men I ever knew."

Chapter 11

On the Road

AJR knew all the roads and shortcuts between Pittsburgh and New York and between Pittsburgh and Philadelphia. He was a very fast driver on those two-lane highways, but he was also very sure of himself. "The best driver I ever drove with," he would say, "was me."

The narrow, dangerous mountain roads never gave him the slightest pause. He would shoot past other cars, and on the Pennsylvania Turnpike, which opened in 1940, he would even pass cars in the tunnels when there were still just two lanes, with traffic moving both ways.

When he drove he would smoke big Cuban cigars and spit the ends, chewed to mush, out the window. The tobacco juice would be blown back into the car and onto the faces of the passengers in the back seat, who were usually his sons. We sat there choking in cigar smoke and listening to static on the radio. In his ceaseless efforts to get the news or the baseball scores or the race results, AJR would be fiddling with the station selector.

Kass and his friends had gone through this experience before we did, and a generation later his grandkids had to endure it. The grandkids, more resourceful than the sons, would open the back windows a crack, make a funnel out of a newspaper – there were always newspapers in the back seat – stick one end of the funnel into the crack, and breathe through it.

On Route 30 once, Johnny Blood was with AJR, who asked him to drive for a while as they were coming out of the Allegheny Mountains toward Pittsburgh. It was three o'clock in the morning. They changed places, and AJR said to Blood, "I'm going to take a nap. Wake me up when we get to Greensburg." Some time later, jostled out of his sleep, he looked around and said, "Where are we?"

"Zelienople," answered Blood.

Zelienople is northwest of Pittsburgh. Greensburg is east of Pittsburgh.

"Why didn't you wake me in Greensburg?" asked AJR.

"I didn't see it," Blood said. "We went through some little towns, but nothing as big as Greensburg."

AJR reflected on that for a minute. Then he said, "To get where we are, we had to go through Pittsburgh, and Pittsburgh's not exactly a small town."

"It's not exactly a big town, either," said Blood, "or I'd have waked you up for sure."

Blood had a reputation for eccentricity. It was well deserved.

'Ever Been Arrested?'

There's a theory called six degrees of separation. Simply put — too simply, perhaps — it holds that everybody knows six people who each know six other people who each know six other people and so on and so on until you reach the sixth degree and have a chain that connects everybody in the world to everybody else. It sounds pretty dubious, but AJR always knew someone who knew someone who knew someone, and it helped ease his way through life. To illustrate:

On the primitive roads of the 1940s, he and Harp Vaughan were driving to Buffalo when a rainstorm blew in from Lake Erie. Dad's big old touring car skidded into a ditch and there was nothing they could do to extricate it. Somehow they located a farmer. He came with a team of horses and got them headed toward Buffalo again. It was close to 3 a.m. when they pulled up in front of their hotel. The desk clerk eyed them suspiciously — bedraggled, mud-spattered strangers climbing out of a battered, mud-spattered car.

"What can I do for you?" he asked.

"We called for a reservation," said AJR.

"Your names?"

"Rooney and Vaughan — from Pittsburgh. We had car trouble. All that rain. Needed help getting out of a ditch. Farmer pulled us out with his horses."

"Just a minute," said the clerk.

He went into a back room and called the police. "Looks like we've got a couple of hoodlums over here. They're trying to check in. I think they might be on the lam." The tourists had not moved an inch when two cops walked into the lobby.

"Who are you guys?" the cops demanded. "Can you show identification?" AJR reached into his back pocket. Empty. His side pockets. Empty. The pocket on the inside of his suit. Empty. His exertions in the ditch had dislodged his wallet.

"Ever been arrested?" asked one of the cops. "Ever been in jail?"

Quickly, AJR answered, "I haven't, but he has," indicating Harp with a nod and a gesture.

Turning from the cops to AJR and back to the cops, Harp looked perplexed, and a little hurt.

"Uh ... yeah. That's right," he said. "But only one night."

"You fellows will have to come with us," the cop said, but AJR said, "Wait a minute. Do you know Charley Murray, the football writer at the Buffalo News?"

"Sure. We've seen him around."

"Well, call Charley Murray. He'll vouch for us."

So at 3:15 in the morning, Charley Murray, sound asleep at home, was getting a telephone call from a policeman. "I know Rooney," he said. "Vaughan? I'm not sure."

"Will you come down to the hotel and identify Mister Rooney?"

Charley Murray got out of bed, put on some clothes, drove into town, and identified Mr. Rooney, which was good enough for the cops and the hotel clerk. The six degrees of separation factor had saved Harp Vaughan a trip to the police station, but one thing bothered him.

"Why did you tell that cop I'd been arrested?" he asked AJR in the elevator on the way to their room.

"I was afraid you'd tell him you hadn't been," said AJR. "And then we really would have been in trouble."

Footnote: Many years later AJR was a pallbearer at Charley Murray's funeral. Coming out of the church, he remembered something important. A horse of his was running that day at Bowie and he wanted to get a bet down — a big one. He looked around and spotted Ken Stilley, a football coach he knew very well. He caught Stilley's eye, beckoned him over, and said in an undertone, "Do me a favor. Take this end of the casket. I have to get out of here and call my bookie. Please fill in for me. Charley was our friend. He'd understand."

That was what Stilley thought, too.

Rooneyspeak

AJR and his brothers – Jim and Father Silas in particular – had their own distinctive way of talking. Much of what they said was in the form of pronouncements. They spoke as though laying down the law. They were making statements that could not be contradicted.

They would stress certain vowels or consonants, stretching them out. "Hey ... you-u-u ... big-g-g ... bum-m-m" could be a form of greeting or a protest of some kind. When AJR was annoyed with someone, he might exclaim, "Say-ie-ie ... you-u-u ... big ... sa-a-p ... star-r-t ... using ... your ... hea-a-d!" Another way to express this was "Think ... ahead ... of the ... pla-a-y!" "Wha-a-t ... a ... piec-c-c-e ... of w-wor-r-k ... he-e-e ... is!" defined an absent third party who was also a yegg or a bum.

The nearest approximation to Rooneyspeak I can think of would be the elongated syllables used for comic effect by W. C. Fields.

I never heard AJR swear either casually or in anger. He might call somebody a "bum," or a "stiff," or a "greaser," or a "rube." John and Pat, the twins, were called saps so often they looked up the word in the dictionary. The definition they found was "a dumb or stupid person who can only dig ditches" – or so they said.

AJR and his brothers had deep, challenging voices when they talked in this very assertive manner. With Uncle Jim, talking was an art form. While getting the words out, he could snicker or laugh in the same breath. I never heard these inflections in the speech of Pop Rooney or the boys' two sisters.

Another thing I noticed about AJR, Jim, and Father Silas was the way they used figures of speech. Eating, for example, was "putting on the feed bag." If you tipped a waiter, you "duked" him. And so on.

A locution that originated with Pop Rooney is still used by some of his grandchildren. When the need comes to urinate, you "go to see a man about a horse."

Think Ahead of the Play

AJR had some catchy little phrases he would lay on his sons: "Don't kid the kidder" ... "Don't be a sap" ... "You are brand new" ... "He's come a long way" ... "Kidding on the square" ... and one that he picked up in sports, "Think ahead of the play." This one may have been handed down by his long-time mentor Dick Guy, a sportswriter and manager of sandlot and minor-league baseball teams.

Dick was one of the "main gazzumboes" of the Middle Atlantic League when AJR and Uncle Dan played for the Wheeling Stogies. AJR seemed to love him. It was interesting to find out from Rob Ruck and Maggie Patterson's research that Dick Guy and others like him would use the sports pages to inform the sandlot players that there was a game on such and such a date, naming a time for them to gather at the pickup spot. The managers and promoters used the newspapers as a bulletin board. Knowing enough to look in the sports section for the information on when and where to assemble would be "thinking ahead of the play." Dick must have repeated that to youngsters like AJR and Uncle Dan again and again.

When brother Pat was putting a lot of time in on baseball, Dad would have Dick Guy work him out at Monument Hill Field. By this time Dick was up in years; he reminded me of Coleridge's Ancient Mariner. Pat would pitch, John would catch, and the rest of us would shag balls, with Dick looking on. I think he felt we were rich kids fooling around rather than dedicated athletes like Dad and Uncle Dan.

Dick was a big part of Dad's formative years. I heard many stories about him – how he could give the players "holy hell," how they tried to avoid his ire. Before every game, Dick counted the balls and bats, and afterwards he counted them again. One time when some balls were missing, the player in charge of the "poke" – the canvas bag they were kept in – told Dick that AJR was in charge of it. Dick chuckled a bit and said nothing. AJR was starting to show the leadership qualities that distinguished him later on, and, recognizing this, Dick always treated him deferentially.

"Thinking ahead of the play" carried over from the playing fields to all of your endeavors in life. "Kidding on the square" had its counterpart in Mary Poppins singing "a spoonful of sugar makes the medicine go down." It was telling the truth in such a way as not to hurt the feelings of a friend or a child. Often Dad would say, "Well, I told him what I thought was right, but I kind of kidded him on the square as I did it."

I don't doubt that Dick Guy had kidding on the square down pat, but he looked like such a stern old bird to me.

"He's come a long way" could either be sarcasm or a true compliment. Some of Dad's acquaintances who found redemption of a sort deserved it as a compliment. But if you said "He's come a long way" about a phony who had a hand in everyone's pocket it was a warning: "Watch out for this yegg. He couldn't have changed all that much."

I heard these little phrases until AJR's dying day.

Dress Code

AJR and his cronies all seemed to dress the same way. I don't remember seeing Dad in anything but a dark blue or gray suit. Perhaps he had a brown suit in his wardrobe; if so, he'd forgotten about it.

At banquets and other formal affairs he wore his dark blue suit with a snap-on black tie. On trips, he would carry the tie in his pocket, referring to it as his "tux." Until his later years, when he was often the guest of honor at testimonial dinners, he never owned a black suit, much less a tuxedo.

I remember once when I was still a young boy – it must have been in the early 1950s – that the Knights of Columbus made him a grand knight, requiring the purchase of tails, a white tie, and a plumed hat. The sword he had to carry was a gift from the K.C.'s. A cobblestone alley called Maolis Way separated their headquarters, one of the old North Side mansions, from our house on North Lincoln Avenue. On the night of the big affair, AJR got into this "get-up," as he called it, sneaked across the alley, and went through the back door of the K.C. building. At the end of the evening, he returned by the same route.

He put the sword away in the closet where he had hidden a snub-nosed pistol, but my brothers and I found it one day. We took it out of the scabbard and engaged in a series of duels. One of us would have the sword and the other the scabbard. We dueled all over the second floor of our house, and it was only by a miracle that nobody lost an eye.

When Dad was a young man he always wore a cap. In middle age he wore a fedora. In old age he went back to the cap, having developed a fondness for caps from Ireland. He said you could get into and out of automobiles and taxicabs without knocking your cap off, but not so with a hat. During the time that he wore a hat – the 1930s, '40s and '50s – a newspaperman from San Francisco wrote that nobody wore a hat with more flair than Art Rooney. Seldom did Dad buy a new one and almost never did he have his old one cleaned and blocked. The well-worn gray fedora he favored resembled a John Wayne hat with its wide turned-up brim. He wore it at a bit of a rakish angle. In spite of his efforts to keep from calling attention to himself, the cigars, his suits, and the big dark overcoat he wore all marked him as a character. In his seventies he began wearing a sport jacket, slacks, and a raincoat.

Kass tried to dress well but modestly. Her good friend Ruth Jaffe steered her to the most fashionable women's clothing stores in Squirrel Hill and Shadyside, and AJR gave her money to spend. She had a dignified figure which she chose not to show off. Once when she and my wife Kay were going to a formal dinner party, both in low-cut evening gowns, Kass stood in front of a mirror and pulled at the upper part of her dress to cover the cleavage. She sighed and said to Kay, "God! I look like a whore."

Kay thought that was hilarious. Actually, their dresses were demure for the styles of the late 1970s.

Aunt Alice inherited her sister's old clothes, which were never very old, and so she, too, was always well dressed.

I was with Mom one time when she took Dad to Larrimor's, a fancy clothing store Downtown, to buy him an overcoat as a gift of some kind. Mr. Schlesinger, the manager, brought out the best coats he had – cashmere ... wool ... cashmere *and* wool. AJR selected one that he liked and asked Mr. Schlesinger, "How much?"

"Three hundred and fifty dollars" was the answer.

AJR said, "We're looking for an overcoat, not a used car." My father was anything but a clothes horse.

Mom often dressed us kids in football shirts and slacks. We were dressed this way one night to have dinner with Mom and Dad at Poli's Restaurant in Squirrel Hill. But Dad said, "Take those shirts off the kids. I don't want it to look like I'm advertising our business." Mom's feelings were hurt. She felt that she had dressed us in perfect good taste.

Because he spent so much time in automobiles, AJR's suits were always wrinkled. In the summer months he wore broadcloth dress shirts. From early fall until late spring he favored long-sleeved cashmere polo shirts or golf shirts. Such shirts are not meant to be worn with neckties, but for weddings and funerals AJR put on a necktie.

Black dress shoes, well worn but never down at the heels, completed his ensemble. He was punctual about replacing the heels, and he would reinforce the toes with metal plates. When he walked down the aisle in church, complained Kass, his shoes made an unholy noise.

Dad never wore trench coats. If you constantly smoked cigars, as he did, you were apt to burn a hole in a trench coat. Raincoats were more resistant to that sort of thing. His habit of leaving raincoats in restaurants was unbreakable, so whenever he bought a new one he kept an embossed plastic card with his name on it in one of the pockets.

Even in old age he walked with the bounce and swagger of an athlete. He walked each day for his health, conscious of the figure he cut, though ready at all times to deny it. As boastful as he was about his modesty, he knew he had style.

We knew he knew it, too, but we never said so. To the end we were mindful of the rule that he himself always lived by: "Don't kid the kidder."

Lighting Up

Dad, Milton Jaffe, Uncle Jim, and a lot of their friends smoked fine Cuban cigars. AJR would chew tobacco or just the end of his cigar. He would tear out a sheet from a newspaper or the Racing Form and toss it into a waste-paper basket in order to be able to spit.

He continued to chew right up to the end of his life, tapering off as he aged. The cigars, of course, had become his trademark. Cigarettes, he once told me, were for girls.

To get his cigars going, Dad used matches in preference to a lighter. He kept them in his home office, which also served as the downstairs sitting room. One day my brothers and I discovered these matches, with the predictable result that we somehow set the contents of the waste-paper basket on fire and might have easily burned down the house.

All over Dad's study there were humidors, filled for the most part with the best Cuban cigars. First he would smoke a Cuban cigar and then a Marsh Wheeling or a tobey from one of the old cigar makers still doing business in Pittsburgh or Philadelphia. He liked to chew and spit out the Cuban cigars and the tobeys. He said the Marsh Wheelings tasted good but were not satisfactory chewers.

Oddly, he was a bit of a pyromaniac. After removing the cellophane wrapper from a cigar, he would twist it up and set it ablaze. His fireplace would be an ash tray. When the flames rose high, he would remove the paper ring from his cigar and toss it into the inferno. If the fire got out of hand, Mom would come rushing in from the kitchen and put it out with a wet tea towel.

There were ash trays all over the den and all over Dad's office in the Roosevelt Hotel. Many of these receptacles were gifts – fine Waterford crystal ash trays from Ireland, ash trays he brought back from the Kentucky Derby (all told, he went to about fifty Kentucky Derbies), ash trays from the Shrine of St. Anne de Beaupre in Quebec.

On the shelves above his big reclining chair were humidors made of glass or expensive wood. Next to the chair, on the floor, was a brass spittoon. More than once, the spittoon caught fire. Mary Roseboro, our white-uniformed maid, would come into the den each morning with long rubber gloves on and take the ash-laden thing to the basement for a thorough cleaning. She would polish the brass until it looked like new – a labor of love, for Mary idolized AJR. Among ourselves we would say that no one could be paid enough for this kind of work.

People sent chocolate candy, as well as ash trays and humidors, to AJR. Wearing pajamas and his cashmere robe, with fleece-lined slippers on his feet and a cashmere blanket around his shoulders, he would settle himself into his reclining chair and reach for his cigars or a chocolate or the telephone, all conveniently placed on the table at his side. Finished with the cigar, he would go outdoors and toss away the stub. Cigar stubs were "dead Indians" in his lexicon. It never troubled him to be seen outdoors in his nightclothes. He would go for the paper dressed like that, or even just to catch a breath of air, lingering to talk if a neighbor passed by.

I never saw him work on his checkbook. Fran Fogarty, the football team's accountant, kept it in balance. The bills that came to the house were paid in cash – the old horse player's way.

AJR read the New York papers and the Pittsburgh papers, the Daily Racing Form, and the Morning Telegraph. He read magazines. And of course he read his prayer book, bound in red leather and dog-eared from constant use. He never read fiction or biography or history. If he wasn't reading he was talking on the telephone. If he wasn't on the telephone he was saying the rosary. He had glass rosary beads, gold rosary beads, wooden rosary beads, plastic rosary beads. He was a man who lived his religion

His humility, although he made a great display of it, was real. Even so, he enjoyed the celebrity that came to him after the Steelers' Super Bowl years. When he was going to be on television, we would gather in his den or in the kitchen if the show had been taped ahead of time. As soon as it began he would hold up his hand, which meant: "Silence." He was always a good performer on television, confident and unflappable. Never did I know him to make a fool of himself. There would be times when his role in a panel discussion or something like that seemed inconsequential. Hardly worth the bother, we would think, but it was not wise to say so. Always, we remembered the maxim he liked to repeat: "Don't kid the kidder." Because kidders are always thin-skinned, went the unspoken corollary.

Chapter 12

Papa Bear

The National Football League goes back to 1920, and if you start at the beginning you start with George Halas, the founding father.

At the University of Illinois, where he studied civil engineering, Halas had been an end on the football team and an outfielder on the baseball team. He was good enough at baseball to play for the New York Yankees in 1919, but the Yanks sent him down to the minors and from then on football came first. When A. E. Staley, a starch manufacturer from Decatur, Illinois, asked him to organize a company team in 1920, Halas got in touch with representatives of ten other independent teams in five states. They met in an automobile showroom in Canton, Ohio, and talked into existence the American Professional Football Association, forerunner of the NFL.

In 1921 the Decatur starch factory went out of business, so Halas moved the Staleys to Chicago, his home town, and renamed them the Bears. He owned the team, coached it, and for ten seasons played end. In his forty years as coach, the Bears won eight championships.

Halas was a tough-looking Czech, reputed to be close with a buck. AJR knew how to charm sportswriters; Halas did not. One columnist wrote that he possessed all the warmth of broken bones. It may be true that he was tight and it is certainly true that he was tough, but in my opinion, anyway, he kept a lot of people who were not super producers on the payroll, and I can personally vouch for his kindness and courtesy.

After our second or third Super Bowl, when I was the Steelers' personnel director, he invited my wife Kathleen and me to have dinner with him. Assuming he meant to include the rest of the family – AJR, Kass, Dan and his wife Pat, etc. – I volunteered to notify them. The invitation, he replied, was for Kay and me – no one else. The only others present were his daughter Virginia and his son-in-law, Ed McCaskey. At the end of the evening, he asked me to pull my chair closer to his. "Kathleen," he said, calling to my wife, "you come over here, too. I want you to hear this." He then turned to me. "Arthur," he said, "you have done the best job of scouting and putting together a great football team that I have seen." From there he proceeded to ask my advice on some personnel problems his team was having. Because my head was swimming, I don't think I answered him sensibly.

So much for mean old tough-guy George Halas.

AJR liked to tell about the time back in the early days of the NFL that he agreed to change the date and location of a game with the Bears as a way of doing Halas a favor. The new site was to be a medium-sized midwestern city, and to sweeten the deal for AJR, Halas promised him five hundred dollars "off the top." Owing to bad weather, lack of interest, or both, the game drew a pitifully small crowd. The reaction of Halas, said AJR, was bitter disappointment. When they divided the meager box-office receipts, AJR put his share in a satchel and started out the door. At that point, it occurred to him that Halas had withheld the extra five hundred dollars, which would be the difference, as things turned out, between taking a loss on the game and breaking even. He stopped and asked where it was. Halas denied having made such a deal. AJR said, "You know that's a lie. Come on, George, come across with the dough."

Halas wasn't lying, he was stalling. He glared at AJR and said, "I'll fight you for the five hundred bucks."

AJR said, "George, I don't want to fight. I just want the money."

Grudgingly, Halas coughed it up. For the second time, AJR turned to leave, and for the second time he paused in the doorway.

"Thanks, George," he said, "but don't be so sure you'd have won that fight."

Considering the status of pro football and the cost-of-living index at the time, five hundred dollars was quite a substantial sum. In not too many years it would look like chicken feed. I was present one day in 1962 when AJR said to Halas, "George, I've had an offer to play a pre-season game in Europe, but we need an opponent. It's a big payday. Would you be interested?"

"No, Arthur," replied Halas, "and neither should you. You have a good ball club this year. Don't take a chance on messing it up with a trip like that. Something bad could happen."

These were the days before fast, reliable air travel. AJR had been ready to pack his bags. Halas talked him out of it. So there was no big payday, but the Steelers that year won nine of their fourteen games. Halas had been one hundred percent right.

He was "Papa Bear" by then, the league's presiding guru. At a meeting I attended, a resolution was passed to change the football used by the NFL. Halas spoke out against it, and everybody listened. He said that in the 1930s a sporting-goods salesman promoting a new ball gave the owners a demonstration. Placing it endwise between two lead pencils, he made the ball spin. He made it spin for several minutes, and the owners were impressed. "Let's adopt it," some of them said. A ball that would spin between lead pencils would make passing easier, which would open up the game and add to the excitement. But a few less impulsive voices were raised, Halas went on. "This ball looks good," one owner suggested, "but why don't we try it out in the exhibition games before we commit ourselves?"

"So we did," Halas said, "And nobody – not even the best passers – could get a good spiral on this ball that would spin between lead pencils."

Case closed.

Halas was such a presence in the NFL that as rival coaches would have it he intimidated the officials. Jack Butler, a great defensive back for the Steelers, believed that to be true. He told of watching a Chicago Bear put a flagrantly illegal block on Pittsburgh's Ernie Stautner, a Hall-of-Fame tackle who played in nine Pro Bowls, and of watching the official toss a flag. Out on the field at a dead run came Halas, screaming and waving his arms. There was no way, said Butler, that the official could pick up the flag, but he knew what to do. "He called the penalty on Stautner – unsportsmanlike conduct for causing the other player to throw the illegal block."

The advantage his reputation gave him was not lost on Halas. Don Joyce, a scout who had been a tackle for several NFL teams, told me that when he played for the Baltimore Colts he knocked a Chicago player flat one Sunday directly in front of Halas on the bench. Instantly, Halas was in his face, pounding on his shoulder pads and pulling at his shirt. To the Chicago fans it appeared that he was tongue-lashing Joyce for a needlessly vicious hit. Not so, Joyce said. "He was yelling, 'Joyce, I love you! You're the type of guy I want for the Bears! I'm going to make a trade for you!'"

There were those who found none of this amusing, who thought that Halas threw his weight around too freely. One man seemed bent on doing him serious harm. This was Mickey McBride, the owner of the Cleveland Browns and no stranger to violence. Before the Browns came into the league in 1950, McBride had been running the taxicab business in Cleveland. He took an immediate dislike to Halas, resentful of his high-handed ways.

"How can you put up with that guy?" he said to AJR, and in the next breath was telling him of a plan he intended to carry out.

"When a bully is pushing you around, you can't go after his working stiffs. You go after the main culprit," he said. In this case, the main culprit was Halas. A game was coming up between the Browns and the Bears in Chicago, and McBride had arranged to have a dozen or so members of the private army he deployed against union organizers – real thugs who specialized in breaking arms and jaws – planted behind the Chicago bench at ground level. At the first sign of rough play on the part of the Bears, McBride would give a signal and his goons would pour out of the stands. The police, McBride thought, would stop most of them short of the bench, but two or three would be able to reach Halas. "And they'll work him over good," McBride said.

It wasn't easy for AJR to convince his friend McBride that this type of activity had no place whatever in professional football.

Halas had a son named George Junior. Everybody knew him as Muggsy. During games, he sat on the Bears' bench, frequently jumping up to shout and swear at the officials and the players. Imitating his father, he carried on to such an extent that Halas at length banished him to the stands.

Muggsy was always in evidence at meetings of the scouting service called Blesto, an acronym for Bears-Lions-Eagles-Steelers Talent Organization. Once when a disagreement could not be quickly resolved, Muggsy wanted to end the meeting and re-convene the next morning and the others wanted to work things out before adjourning. Muggsy refused to give in, so Russ Thomas of the Detroit Lions suggested that we settle the matter by flipping a coin. Muggsy objected to that too, but was voted down. So Thomas went ahead and flipped a coin, and Muggsy put on a display of hand speed and throwing accuracy that astonished us. He snatched the coin out of the air and hurled it cleanly through a crack of no more than two or three inches between the slightly raised window and the window sill.

Halas Senior and AJR outlived all their contemporaries. At NFL meetings, they would take their meals together. Very often Ed McCaskey would join them. In the 1970s and '80s Ed became a great friend of the Rooney family. He would pal around with AJR at the meetings, joining him for breakfast and lunch and to smoke cigars.

When my mother passed away, Halas came to Pittsburgh to pay his respects. He'd had a hip replacement and was very feeble but stood at the side of the grave for the last rites of the church. Not long afterward, Halas himself was dead, and the entire Rooney family attended his funeral in Chicago.

Laundryman

When George Preston Marshall owned the Boston Redskins he hired a full-blooded Indian, Lone Star Dietz, as coach. On the first day of practice the players lined up for the team picture in war paint and feathered headdresses. If any Indians took offense, Lone Star Dietz was not among them.

Marshall brought showmanship into the NFL. Deciding that Boston wasn't ready for showmanship, he moved his team to Washington, D.C., where he owned a laundry business, and entertained the fans with halftime shows and a marching band. Slingin' Sammy Baugh, the pinpoint passer from Texas Christian University, was the Redskins' No. 1 draft choice that year – 1937 – and Marshall instructed him to appear at his introductory press conference with a cowboy hat on his head and high-heeled boots on his feet. Never having worn either, Baugh had to purchase those items before leaving Texas.

Even though Marshall came from Grafton, West Virginia, there was nothing of the hillbilly in his makeup. He was a tall, well-barbered, well-tailored, gray-haired man who carried himself with an air of authority – at times with an air of condescension – and whose gravelly speaking voice commanded instant attention. He was married to Corrine Griffith, a leading lady in the films. Once when AJR was their dinner guest, Mrs. Marshall objected to his cigar smoking and later accused him of spitting tobacco juice into her fish pond with fatal consequences to the fish. Actually, AJR had deposited both his cigar butts and expectorations in a much more convenient receptacle – the pots holding her plants.

Marshall had a friend who arranged for the team to be met by a brass band on its arrival in Washington from Boston. Corrine Griffith had objected to that, too, so Marshall buttonholed the fellow and told him to knock it off. Insulted, he brought his entire band to the Marshalls' hotel suite late that night and gave the persnickety Mrs. Marshall a serenade she did not greatly appreciate.

Marshall made every effort to please Corrine. To start with, he toned down his lifestyle. Where once he had been a ladies' man, he suddenly became monogamous. It may or may not have been Corinne who persuaded him that the Far West was a good place for his pre-season training camp. Whoever was responsible, it worked out rather well. The Redskins pitched camp in Washington – the state – but played two of their exhibition games in Los Angeles and made money. Remember, there were no NFL teams on the West Coast back then. At Corrine's invitation, her pal Fred Astaire met with the Washington players and showed them his regimen of exercises to prevent sprained ankles – something they could all tell their grandchildren.

Marshall was more than just a ringmaster. He suggested and lobbied for many important structural changes in the NFL. A set schedule, two divisions with a championship playoff, moving the goal posts to the goal line (when field-goal kicking exponentially improved, they were moved again to the rear of the end zone), a slimmed-down football to facilitate passing – all of these things were the Washington owner's ideas.

In Baugh's first season the Redskins won the Eastern Division title and the playoff for the league championship, defeating the Chicago Bears. Three years later the same teams met again in the playoff. During the regular season the Redskins had won a 7-3 game from the Bears, and when the Chicago players complained about the officiating, Marshall called them "front-runners," "quitters," and "crybabies." In the championship game, using the brand new T-formation installed by Clark Shaughnessy, the infuriated Bears made him eat his words. The final score – Bears 73, Redskins 0 – still looks like a misprint.

There was still another title game between the Bears and the Redskins – in 1942, with the country at war. On the blackboard in the Washington dressing room, Coach Ray Flaherty, who would be going into the Navy the following week, wrote "73-0" in large numerals. The Redskins responded with a 14-6 victory.

The Redskins won two more division titles for Marshall but lost to the Bears again and to the Cleveland Browns in the playoffs for the championship. In 1949 Marshall decided that his coach, Turk Edwards, was too indecisive. Declaring that the Redskins needed a forceful military leader, someone who had helped win the war, he transferred Edwards to the front office and hired a retired admiral, John Whelchel, to succeed him as coach. A former coach at the Naval Academy, Whelchel was a fish out of water in the NFL. One Redskin who played for him told me that in a game the team was losing by forty points at the start of the fourth quarter, Whelchel went to Sammy Baugh, who'd been benched, and said to him, "Sam, you better get back in there before this thing gets out of hand."

Whelchel walked off the practice field one day after Marshall started telling him how to coach. He was quitting, he said, but agreed to return for one last game. The Redskins won and carried Whelchel to the locker room on their shoulders.

Throughout the 1940s there were two George Marshalls in Washington. The owner of the Redskins insisted on being known as George *Preston* Marshall to distinguish himself from George Catlett Marshall, Army chief of staff during the war and afterwards secretary of state. The story is often told of the clash between George Preston Marshall and the War Department on Sunday, December 7, 1941. The Redskins were playing the Philadelphia Eagles at Griffith Stadium in Washington – named for Clark Griffith, owner of the Washington baseball team, and not for Corrine – and AJR was in Marshall's box. A low-ranking Navy officer came in and said the Navy would like permission to make an announcement over the public-address system. Marshall refused, stating emphatically that *no one* could make an announcement over his system. The Navy man left, and Marshall said to AJR and the others that if you let one outfit in Washington get away with that kind of thing, then all the rest would be making demands. A few minutes later a much higher-ranking officer confronted him. He informed Marshall sternly that the Japanese had just bombed Pearl Harbor and that the public-address system would be commandeered in the interest of national defense. "There will be no discussion about this," he said. Then came a series of announcements – first, that all Navy personnel would immediately report to their bases; next, that all *military* personnel would report; then all State Department and embassy people, and so on and so on.

I don't believe Marshall was a racist, but he had put together a radio network that broadcast his team's games in the Deep South, and clearly for that reason he was slow to allow the signing of black players. At last the pressure of public opinion in the North compelled him to draft one – halfback Ernie Davis, the Heisman Trophy winner from Syracuse. He immediately traded Davis to the Cleveland Browns for another black player, Bobby Mitchell, an all-pro running back and receiver. Bobby told me that he was seated next to Marshall at a banquet one night when the band started playing "Dixie." Marshall nudged him, he said with a smile, and whispered, "Sing, Bobby, sing." Just to humor Marshall, Bobby lip-synched the words.

In the Redskins' front office, Marshall installed an antique wooden Indian. It remained there for years and years. At last the office staff complained that it was gathering dust and taking up space. Declaring the thing had "sentimental value" for him, Marshall "bought" it from the ball club at a bargain-basement price and moved it into his own private office. Some time later, in need of walking-around money, he had a friendly antique dealer over-appraise the Indian and sold it back to the team for much more money than it was worth. According to his lawyer, Leo DeOrsey, this got to be a routine.

A misunderstanding occurred once between Marshall and AJR over the railroad fare of a player who'd been traded from the Redskins to the Steelers. They were arguing back and forth on the telephone over fifty dollars at the most, although neither would think twice about handing out a tip for that amount. Marshall kept repeating, "Arthur, send me the dough." Finally AJR said he would do just that, whereupon Marshall hung up, feeling triumphant. As good as his word, AJR dispatched Fran Fogarty, the Steelers' accountant, to the Ritz Bakery with an order for fifty individual pieces of raw dough. Fogarty had them wrapped in gold foil and sent to Mr. Marshall in Washington.

In all the years that he knew Fogarty, and conferred with him on business matters, Marshall never learned to pronounce his name. "He'd call me Mr. Flaherty ... Mr. Flogarty ... Mr. Foglerty ... everything but Fogarty," Fran said, and he didn't exaggerate. I was with my father in the lobby of the Hotel Drake in New York one time when Marshall walked over to us and said, "Arthur, you have a good man in that Fran Flaherty."

Marshall behaved more like royalty than like a simple laundryman from Grafton, West Virginia. I saw him once at a morning NFL meeting in a silk robe or dressing gown, a pair of silk pajamas, and bedroom slippers. At other times he would wear a suit with his pajama shirt underneath. Once in the dining room of the Kenilworth Hotel in Florida, he spoke to a man whose face was familiar. "Aren't you a doctor?" Marshall asked. The man said he was, adding that they had recently met. Marshall then remarked that he was feeling a bit rundown. "Be a good fellow," he said to the M.D., "and have your nurse send a large bottle of Vitamin B-12 to my room." To my astonishment, the doctor agreed.

As the years went by, Marshall's health began to fail, and he wasted away before our eyes. I attended a scrimmage one day at Dickinson College, in Carlisle, Pennsylvania, where the Redskins trained. It was well under way when a large black limo pulled up to the edge of the field: Marshall and his entourage. He emerged from the car and waved to the spectators. Then he got back in, watched for a while, and left. Just an appearance. No doubt it took every bit of his waning strength.

At the next NFL meeting he walked into a conference, very muddled. He would stand up, say something eloquent, maybe even powerful, and then almost fall back into his seat. He was resilient, though. That winter at a meeting in New York City, my brother Tim and I saw him getting onto the elevator in the hotel. With him, on each arm, was a tall, lovely, well-dressed showgirl; they were young enough to be his granddaughters. As the elevator door closed, Marshall had a grin on his face.

His marriage to Corrine Griffith had ended some time earlier, so he was now a free agent where the ladies were concerned and attempting to be as flamboyant as ever. That same year during the football season, Tim and I left the press box in RFK Stadium, where the Redskins were playing the Steelers, to get a hot dog. An elevator door close to where we were standing slid open and there in a wheelchair, with a blanket over his knees, was Mr. Marshall, now a true invalid. Tim looked at me; I looked at him. Tim then put into words what I was thinking. He said, "Those two showgirls in New York last winter were too much for the old guy."

Marshall owned a house in Miami, where the NFL's next meeting took place, and all of his old friends, advised to do so by Commissioner Pete Rozelle, went to see him. In effect, they were saying good-bye. One of the other old-timers told AJR that George would much prefer to be caught in bed with a beautiful woman and shot in the head by her irate husband than wither away as he did. Perhaps so.

Blueblood

AJR liked to say that Bert Bell was a blueblood. He said it with facetious intent, but Bert actually did come from an old French family of aristocratic origins. His middle name, in fact, was Bienville. The Bienville-Bells had money, lived on Philadelphia's Main Line, and saw to it that Bert received a good education.

But if Bert was a blueblood, he never acted like one. Far from conforming to any High Society model, he resembled AJR in his personality and outlook on life. There were people who thought the two partners were relatives, or came from the same neighborhood. Both were open and accessible. Both wore old, rumpled, dark-colored suits and wide-brimmed fedoras. Both had a passion for football and the NFL. More truly than George Halas, George Preston Marshall, or the Maras – Tim and his two sons, Jack and Wellington – Bert was a Damon Runyon type.

He smoked cigarettes and had a loud, gravelly voice. When he co-owned the Steelers with AJR and Barney McGinley, he slept on a cot in the office he shared with Jake Mintz, the Rooney-McGinley Boxing Club's matchmaker. Given the opportunity, he would never stop talking football. I remember a time in a New York restaurant when Bert talked football through dinner, dessert, and coffee, and then on into the night, with the waiters, bartenders, and busboys all listening.

By the 1940s, Bert's family was no longer rich, and Bert himself, by living beyond his means, had run short of cash. His wife, the former Frances Upton, had been a Ziegfeld Follies girl. "Why fool around with a broken-down jock?" her show-business friends wanted to know. "You can do a lot better than that," they advised her. Hollywood beckoned, and Frances signed a movie contract for one thousand dollars a week, but soon she was back in New York, unsuited by her Catholic upbringing for the free-and- easy ways of Tinseltown. (The sexual mores of Broadway must have seemed puritanical out there.) Hurrying home, she married Bert, converted him to her faith, and became the mother of three fine kids.

AJR told a story that illustrates the influence of his conversion on Bert. An NFL meeting ran late, so Bert sent out for sandwiches. It was discovered when the time came to eat them that the only kind he had ordered was cheese. "Why aren't there any meat sandwiches?" demanded George Preston Marshall. "George," Bert reminded him, "it's Friday." For Catholics back then, Friday was a day of abstinence. "Do you think the whole world is Catholic?" roared Marshall. "Get some meat sandwiches in here!"

When Elmer Layden's contract as NFL commissioner expired in 1946, AJR and other insiders campaigned successfully for Bert to succeed him. Bert, AJR, and Barney McGinley had been equal partners in the ownership of the Steelers. A realignment now took place. Bert sold his stock to AJR, making him once again the team's majority owner. In the long run, this move had tremendous financial importance for the Rooney family. In 1946, the franchise was not worth a great deal, but its value increased significantly over the years. I hope the transfer of stock was put through with Barney McGinley's agreement and understanding.

As one of the owners, Bert had been frugal to a fault. He kept a sharp eye on expenditures, even making sure that nobody wasted any postage stamps. In Hershey, where the team had its pre-season training camp, he would stand at the head of the cafeteria line and take food off the players' trays, saying, "You are now on a diet." He slept, as I have said, in his office, on a cot. Joe Carr, the ticket manager, claimed that Bert would have the cot brought out on his visits to Pittsburgh as commissioner.

The commissioner's job was one that he took with the utmost seriousness and sense of responsibility. On the eve of the 1946 championship game in New York between the Bears and the Giants, there were rumors of a fix. Supposedly Frank Filchock and Merle Hapes of the Giants were involved. Jack Sell, who covered the Steelers for the *Pittsburgh Post-Gazette*, told me that he and some others had been out to dinner with AJR the night before the game and found Bert Bell in AJR's suite when they returned to the hotel. "He was in a terrible state," Sell said. "He told Art there'd be hell to pay, and that the scandal would ruin the NFL." AJR remained calm, Sell said, assuring Bert that "everything would be OK."

The investigation that was going on cleared Filchock, but not Hapes. For failing to report a contact by gamblers, the NFL suspended him. Filchock played against the Bears, and played well, but Chicago won, 24-14.

Bert went through another stressful period during the war between the NFL and the upstart All-America Football Conference. Attempting to outbid the rival league for players, almost every NFL team lost money. When peace came in 1950, the NFL assimilated the Cleveland Browns, the San Francisco Forty-Niners, and the Baltimore Colts of the AAFC. At the end of the season the Baltimore team, insolvent, gave up its franchise, but Bell, in a speech to the city's Advertising Club, said he would keep the Colts in the league if the fans would buy fifteen thousand season tickets and a new owner turned up.

The fifteen thousand tickets were sold within six weeks, and Bert himself hand-picked the new owner – Carroll Rosenbloom, a business executive from Philadelphia. Bert had coached him at Penn, and now they were personal friends. While he was at it, Bert selected a general manager for the Colts, Donald Kellett, and a head coach, Keith Molesworth.

As part of the deal, the understanding was that Bert would become a minority owner of the Colts when he retired as commissioner. It never happened. In 1959, still the commissioner, Bert died of a heart attack at a game in Philadelphia between the Eagles and the Steelers. He was 64.

Some time before that, he did get jobs with the Colts for his sons, Bert Junior and Upton. After Bert Senior's death, they remained with the team until 1969 or 1970, when Bert Junior left to work for a gambling casino in Atlantic City and Upton became general manager of the New England Patriots. Quickly let go, he went into radio as the host of a long-running sports talk show in Boston.

I once addressed Upton by his baptismal name, George. "Hey, Art," he said, "don't call me by that fruity name – call me by my real name, Upton." So from then on, Upton it was.

With Bert gone, AJR and some of the other old-timers made sure that Frances, the widow, and Janie, her daughter, were well taken care of. It was only proper. These were the days before pensions and bonuses, and Bert Bell had been as instrumental as anyone in keeping the NFL afloat through the war-time years and the years of competition with the AAFC. Pete Rozelle, the commissioner who followed him, gets all the credit for the television policy that has meant so much to the NFL, but Bert played a part in the early negotiations.

Jane Bell, by the way, went into the television business and became a successful producer.

Chapter 13

Lessons in Living

Mom and Dad sent all five of their sons to grade school in Oakland, at Mount Mercy Academy. It was part of Mom's plan to control our environment – Mount Mercy during the school year and Ligonier in the summer. But we were still North Side kids and could not avoid picking up some street smarts.

Our instructions from AJR were: travel in groups; keep moving; don't speak to strangers; don't act like big shots; don't attract attention. Even though there were close calls, we survived.

Walking across the Manchester Bridge from Downtown one day, I was with friends of my own age – 10 or 11. We encountered two roughnecks of 14 or so. They grabbed one of our smaller kids and, each holding a leg, dangled him from the bridge above the river. The rest of us ran. We could hear the big guys laughing and the friend we abandoned screaming bloody murder. None of us tried to help. We were anything but heroes. I ran to the end of the bridge and jumped over the railing onto a huge pile of loose, ground-up coal. There I felt safe; what I never gave a thought to was the possibility of starting a slide. I could have been suffocated.

We took the streetcar to and from school. Streetcars all over town were operated by old men. North Side kids would climb up in back of the car and ride hanging on. There were special cars for the North Catholic High School kids, who would crowd them to capacity and make the car sway by shifting their weight. Fearful it would overturn, the operator would often jump off. In response to threats from the traction company – "We'll cut off service to North Catholic" – the Marianist Brothers had to keep the kids from getting on in packs.

During World War II the site later occupied by Three Rivers Stadium was a junk yard. There were huge piles of scrap iron and slag and other raw materials and, most impressive to us kids, dozens of captured German tanks, delivered by rail and by barge. From time to time some friend of ours would find a German helmet or a Luger gun in all the debris. The scavengers included grown-ups as well. One man, I remember, gave a beautiful German pistol in a black leather holster to AJR, who let us handle it briefly before he put it away. A nice souvenir, he said, but too dangerous for kids; there were bullets that came with it. He presented the gun later to a policeman he knew.

For protection from burglars, AJR kept a snub-nosed revolver in the house. One day we found it, hidden in his underwear drawer. In another drawer we came across the bullets. We took the bullets, but not the gun, to Mount Mercy. The nuns had a fit, and at home we got a lecture we did not soon forget.

AJR believed in corporal punishment but could terrorize you just as easily with a yell or even a look. He could be very sarcastic – make you feel like a dog. Kass, for the most part, kept him in check. She never laid a hand on us herself. One day our youngest, John the twin, sneaked off to the junk pile with a kid called Johnny Blue Coat because his family was so poor he wore the same old blue rag of a coat until it seemed to be nothing but tatters. How the two of them ever made it through security John didn't say. At any rate a patrol car came along and the cops saw them wandering close to the river bank. It was spring, and the water was rising dangerously. The escapade earned John a beating from Dad. I never knew what happened to Johnny Blue Coat.

When I was seven or eight years old I wrote my name in red fingernail polish on the door of a car that belonged to a neighbor. That night he paid us a visit. The evidence against me was still on the car door – a big red ART. Frightened, I told a lie. I said that I had written the "A" but that other kids had added the "R" and the "T." I said they had egged me on; that much, at least, was the truth. AJR must have seen I was scared stiff – he let me off with nothing more than a reprimand. Just his disapproval was so intimidating I never again defaced anyone's property. Looking back, I wish I'd been brave enough to confess that I deserved all the blame.

After finishing five grades at Mount Mercy, all of us attended St. Peter's. We went back and forth on foot, and AJR was adamant about the route he wanted us to take. We liked to cross Western Avenue at the bridge over the main line of the Pennsylvania Railroad near a sharp curve where traffic came through very fast. AJR insisted that we walk up to Sherman Avenue and cross at the light. To see that we obeyed orders, he would follow us. I was never afraid to cross the street at the bridge but always afraid to cross Dad.

When he was with us we watched our manners. Once I was sent from the dinner table for burping. This happened also to my brothers. In restaurants he was especially vigilant. One time all of us made a dive for the bread and the French fries. We had to put everything back and start over, taking turns.

I never heard him tell a lie or repeat an off-color story. Girl talk was taboo. His one-time business partner, Milton Jaffe, had a brother named George who owned and operated the Casino burlesque house on Diamond Street, later Forbes Avenue, Downtown. This place of course was off-limits to all five of us, but I went there once to pick up a package. While I was waiting in the lobby I peeked at the dancers on the stage. Nothing too evil seemed to be going on. In fact, the girls were no more scantily clad than the Wild West floozies in the cowboy pictures at the Barry Theater a few blocks away. I was maybe 12 years old. My curiosity satisfied, I never went back.

Dad, Mom, and the Sisters of Mercy warned us to stay away from the Art Cinema, which specialized in "dirty movies" – actually foreign films and "art" films. I remember going there once with Uncle Jim to fetch a pal of his called "Fish," who was standing at the box office, talking with the ticket seller. Neither Jim nor Fish seemed to think of this place as a den of iniquity, but Jim used to tell us that pornography softened the brain.

"Dirty" magazines, he said, were for old men like Pop Rooney's friend, Mr. Curley. Just why he singled out Mr. Curley I never knew. Mr. Curley would come to the Steelers' training camp for a week, and all he ever did was take walks, eat in the dining hall with the players, and go to Mass. My belief is that Mr. Curley got a bum rap from Jim.

The twins, Pat and John, said they "ducked" into the Art Cinema once and were terribly embarrassed when the father of a schoolmate spotted them. Later they began to wonder what *he* was doing there and realized that his embarrassment must have exceeded their own.

At home we said the rosary together every night. Daily Mass was not uncommon. You got there early and stayed until it was over. AJR always sat in the same place at St. Peter's – on the left side not far from the altar. We went to novenas all over Pittsburgh. Our favorite was at a church in the Lower Hill called St. Benedict the Moor. If AJR was out of town, Kass and Aunt Alice would take us. I remember a big fat Italian guy who sang all the hymns off-key: "Tantum Ergo," "Holy God, We Praise Thy Name," "Oh, Blessed Mother Mary ..." He was always there and he knew every word.

Farther up the Hill was a small church presided over by Father Charles Owen Rice, who lived to be well past 90. Uncle Jim called him a Commie. Dad would just say he was "different." Father Jim Campbell, AJR's dear friend, liked Father Rice, which was good enough for Dad. Father Rice was Irish, a fine speaker and writer, a man of great spunk and learning. He was known as "the labor priest" for his activity on behalf of the steelworkers' union. But AJR said he was "different." The other priests would play cards with Dad; Father Rice never did. A priest named Francis Rooney – no relation – let me see a letter Dad wrote in which he said that priests were his heroes. The ones he brought home were OK with Kass, but she admitted they made her ass tired, as she put it – always around to be waited on.

AJR's hatred of coarse language was amusing to Kass. She'd tell him he wouldn't say "shit" if he fell in it. Kass always had a putdown for AJR. Once when her gaze lingered on him reprovingly for some reason, he asked what she was looking at. "Can't a cat look at a king?" she replied. Another time he complained that she was using the tea bags only once. "What do you want me to do?" she demanded. "Dry them and use them for snuff?" Kass was more than a match for the Chief ... unlike her sons.

The Great White Way

The big respectable movie palaces Downtown were Loew's Penn (later Heinz Hall), the Stanley Warner (later the Benedum Center), the Harris, and the Fulton. All had large seating capacities and all were grand places to see a film.

During World War II and shortly afterward there was money around, and for movies like "Red River," starring John Wayne, the theaters would be packed. I heard one old film distributor say that if you opened a can of sardines, a line to see you do it would form.

Actually, the entertainment was much better than that. Along with the movie, you could take in a vaudeville show. I remember that the non-talking Marx brother, Harpo, did a solo act before a Tarzan picture at the Stanley one week. When the movie came on, Harpo returned to the stage with a spear and used it to stick Johnny Weissmuller's pet elephant in the bum (our word back then for posteriors.)

The Barry, "catty-corner" from the Stanley on Sixth Street, had the class B action movies we liked. In a psychology course I took at St. Vincent, we were taught that you could tell something about children and adolescents by the way they reacted to the characters in movies. If they identified with the good guys, that was salutary. If they identified with the bad guys, it was cause for concern.

The Washington lawyer Edward Bennett Williams had a problem son who worked for AJR at the Shamrock Farm in Maryland one summer. Dad thought the kid was pretty normal until they spent an evening together watching television. He said the kid not only cheered for the bad guys all the time but also got violent about it. At least the Rooney brothers always cheered for the good guys.

We had a kid in our neighborhood who made the Williams kid look like an altar boy. Father Flanagan of Boys Town said there was no such thing as a bad boy, but he never met Skippy Guzik. Skippy always, I mean always, identified with the bad guy, and he laced his conversation with the foulest obscenities. One day when Tim and I were with him, Skippy made a crack about Mom. We jumped him right away, and though he got in some good licks, we fought clean. We would fight for a while, take a rest, and start in again. During one of the rest periods, Skippy pretended to drop some papers on the ground. He casually bent over to pick them up and instead grabbed a rock, which he threw in our general direction. It missed us both, and from then on Tim forgot about fighting clean. A good-sized branch from a tree – a branch the size of a club – was lying within reach. Tim armed himself with it and chased Skippy Guzik from one end of North Lincoln Avenue to the other.

Tim never fought clean again in his life, I don't think.

As for Skippy, he ended up doing time for rape and armed robbery. Detective Jack Stack described him as one of the worst kids who ever came out of the North Side or anywhere in Pittsburgh. After serving his sentence, he joined the American Nazi Party, got into another scrape, and went back to jail.

Oh, yes ... that business of dropping the papers on the ground and picking up a rock was something he learned from an old Boston Blackie movie.

We called the movies "the show," as in "Mom, can we go to the show?" And most of the shows we went to were the ones on the North Side. The two best were the Kenyon, on Federal Street, and the Garden, across West Park on North Avenue. The upper part of Federal Street was full of bars, drunks, panhandlers, and perverts, but there were always big crowds at the movies, the entertainment of the masses.

At St. Peter's Church, we had to take a pledge that we would not go to movies that were blacklisted by the Catholic Legion of Decency. I think for Irish Catholics the only real sins were sins of the flesh. If you avoided booze and sex, you'd go to heaven. On Federal Street, there was plenty of booze, and on the screen at the Kenyon and Garden no shortage of sex.

I remember how the nuns at St. Peter's warned us against movies like "Forever Amber" and "The Outlaw." Years later I saw "The Outlaw" on television; it was tame in comparison to the films of the '70s, the '80s, and the '90s. Nowadays, in fact, the television commercials are more explicit than the worst of those wartime movies.

(Speaking of "The Outlaw," condemned by the Legion of Decency because Jane Russell's cleavage was deemed an occasion of sin, I met her husband, Bob Waterfield, Hall-of-Fame quarterback for the Los Angeles Rams, on a scouting trip. He was quiet and polite. Scouting friends who met the seductive Miss Russell reported her to be a very nice lady involved in church and charity work.)

The Kenyon was the place where Chris McCormick, who weighed 350 pounds, had two seats in back remodeled into one seat. He paid for the carpenter work himself, and this giant single seat was reserved for McCormick alone.

On Friday nights the Kenyon would have a double feature for kids – a cowboy or war movie and maybe a Tarzan movie or a movie starring a dog. There would also be trailers (previews), a newsreel, and a cartoon or two. An off-duty cop would be present to keep order. Management needed extra help because some of the eighth-grade kids from St. Peter's or the public schools would be too much for the ushers to handle. My eighth-grade classmate Charley Pruett sat next to a man who put a hand on his leg one night. Charley was big for his age. He threw the guy into the aisle and gave him a pretty good thrashing. When he was finished, he took hold of the pervert by one foot and dragged him up the aisle to the lobby. "This queer," he said to the manager, "attacked me." The manager must have wondered just who had done the attacking.

The Garden, although not as upscale as the Kenyon, had an orchestra pit and vaudeville acts. In time it became a venue for Triple X-rated movies – the kind that could not have been even imagined by the nuns at St. Peter's who worried about Jane Russell's cleavage.

Seamy Side

There were two other movie houses in our neighborhood – the William Penn and the Novelty. The William Penn, a theater that belonged to the Harris family, who were pioneer motion-picture exhibitors, was on Federal Street near the Allegheny River. The William Penn was not the "dive" the Novelty was, but the admission price was the same – ten cents. Both places had third- and fourth-run films. For your dime you could see a double feature, a short subject, two cartoons, a newsreel, and lots of previews. And the Novelty would throw in a candy bar now and then.

When you went to the William Penn or the Novelty you descended to the lower end of the social ladder. Couples came in to make out, drunks to sleep off hangovers, and of course there was always a sprinkling of perverts in the crowd. Rats would be crawling underfoot, nibbling at spilled potato chips. Lice would get into your clothes and ringworm onto your scalp.

Bald-headed men were targets for smart-aleck kids like Jimmy Scanlon. Jimmy's game was to creep up behind a bald guy and slap him on top of the head. He had another favorite trick – blowing air into a paper bag and then slamming his fist into it, which created a loud bang. Once when he exploded a paper bag around the time that the war ended a man in the row ahead of him jumped up screaming. "I just got out of combat! Knock that shit off!"

Sometimes, instead of going to the rest rooms the kids would pee on the floor. As a result, both theaters smelled like a urinal. The movies were pure escape stuff, but the live, unrehearsed floor show was better entertainment if you were looking for certain kinds of realism.

AJR made sure by bringing us up in that environment that his kids saw the seamy side of Pittsburgh and did not enter adulthood with fancy ideas. Too busy becoming or being Art Rooney, he was never around much himself. He was lucky to have a wife like Kass, who was lucky to have a sister like Alice McNulty. Kass and Aunt Alice lived their lives for us kids. In turn, they were lucky to have the Mercy nuns at St. Peter's School teaching us values, because the North Side was the Barbary Coast.

When he was not out of town, AJR would usually be attending a sports event somewhere, most often a Pirate game at Forbes Field. Often he took us with him to these events. He sponsored a sandlot baseball team and a sandlot football team. He called the football team the Rooney Ninety-Eights in recognition of the fact that 98 was the number on every uniform. All the kids wanted to wear it because Don Hutson of the Green Bay Packers wore that number, and Hutson was the greatest pass catcher in football. The team bus was an old pickup truck or dump truck supplied by one of AJR's friends in the construction business.

The Rooney kids traveled to events at Forbes Field or Pitt Stadium or Duquesne Gardens in a broken-down station wagon, hauling as many of their friends as the back seat would accommodate. It had a door that would not stay closed unless we sealed it with heavy-duty tape. My brother Dan, who had just turned 16, did the driving. On the way home from Oakland he'd take a shortcut past Pitt Stadium and up Herron Hill, and one day AJR was with us. When we came to the steepest part of the grade, Dan pulled into a driveway, backed out onto the street, and proceeded up the hill in reverse. AJR thought he had gone nuts. "What are you doing?" he shouted. Patiently, Dan explained that the station wagon was so feeble and worn out it could not get to the top in forward gear.

At least we had wheels, which was more than our North Side pals ever did. Because of sports, our home life, and the family rosary, we came out of the North Side undamaged. Except for Father Silas, AJR's brothers were not so fortunate.

Rough and Tumble

The multimillionaires who lived on the North Side in the nineteenth century left one enduring legacy – the parks. These industrial barons wanted fresh milk and cream on their tables and had set aside acres and acres of grazing land for their cattle. It survived in the form of a park system ringed by stately old mansions that did not fall to the wreckers' ball until the 1950s.

The East Park swimming pool was adjacent to a bath house where the First Ward and Federal Street poor – strangers to indoor plumbing – could shower for five cents. When black kids started using the pool, the whites of the neighborhood took to calling it the Ink Well.

In the age-old tradition of Irish Catholic prudery, I thought it was something scandalous that mothers nursed their babies on the park benches. AJR viewed the parks as gathering places for bums, perverts, and Communists, but stopped short of declaring them off-limits.

By edict of the Parks Department, the grass was off-limits. That did not deter us from playing pickup football and softball games until the park police came by in their squad cars. Then we'd scatter, heading for home through the alleys and hidden walkways we knew. The cops were simply doing their job but did not get much sympathy from the residents of the neighborhood, whose attitude was: Let the kids play; it keeps them out of trouble.

One of the bigger kids in the neighborhood was Varney, nicknamed "Flat Foot Floogie" because of his slow, awkward gait. The cops had an easy time running him down, and then he would squeal on the rest of us. Once as my brothers and I were congratulating ourselves on getting home free, the cops pulled up behind us with Varney in the back seat. AJR came out of the house and conferred with them. They immediately turned Varney loose, and that was the end of it.

In West Park, up past the bronze deer and the railroad footbridge, we could play football or a game we called "rough and tumble" on a field that was all coal cinders – soft soot, actually, deposited there by the trains. "Rough and tumble" had other names, such as "fumbles." It was played like this: to start with, somebody tossed a football into the air, and the kids all jumped for it. The one who came down with the ball would run for his life through the soot. None of us wore football equipment except for an occasional pair of shoulder pads or hip pads or cleated shoes with high tops. There was fierce competition for the ball – and the privilege of being thoroughly mauled – and no interference from the cops.

I think I have said before that the Pennsylvania Railroad cut a huge path through these parks. In the early 1900s, business took precedence over ecology, and the Pennsylvania Railroad was the big boy of Pennsylvania politics. I have heard it argued that the laying of the tracks through the park system was the first nail in the coffin of Allegheny City, as the North Side was called until about 1908.

During World War II the Signal Corps took over West Park as a training ground for its short-wave radio operators. You would see them moving around with their hand-cranked generators – exciting stuff for the neighborhood kids. And then one day the trainees disappeared, all reassigned to regular Army camps.

Over by man-made Lake Elizabeth, there were wonderful old monuments dating back to the Civil War. They fell into disrepair and began to crumble. Next, the kids started climbing all over them. An arm from a statue would come off, and then a nose or an ear. When the neighborhood's racial makeup changed in the late 1950s the statues were deliberately vandalized. Beheadings would leave only the trunk and the legs and finally just the feet, immovably cemented to the base. Thus did ancient Rome fall to the barbarian tribes.

Through the years of deterioration, AJR and Kass remained steadfast North Siders. They were there to stay. For Kass, 940 North Lincoln Avenue had become a beautiful cage.

If the area we played in was a soot field, the swimming pool was even worse. In the old days, when Allegheny City was an independent municipality, there were swans and ducks on Lake Elizabeth, small wooded islands in the middle, and a boat house on the shore. By the 1940s the trees and bushes and flower beds were gone and the lake was a vast swimming pool, thickly coated with railroad soot. The Rooney kids never swam there. We had the pool at the Wildwood Golf Club and later a pool near the cottage in Ligonier. Away from the North Side, we were not apt to get polio. Money may not be everything, but it comes in handy at times.

I remember an aluminum collection for the war effort. After V-J Day, much of it went into the lake. Filled with old pots and pans and other kinds of junk and topped off with soil, the lake was now a playground on which football games were allowed. Almost always, they ended up in fights. As the years went by, it got worse: big kids crowded out little kids; teen-agers crowded out the big kids; young adults crowded out the teen-agers. Once on Thanksgiving, the Parks Department sponsored a turkey chase. Instead of chasing the turkey, the kids staged a free-for-all, piling on top of one another, but at last Charley Pruett broke free from the mob. He snatched up the turkey by its neck and kept running, too fast to be caught.

In the 1950s the city fathers tried to restore these parks to their original grandeur. Although nothing could be done about the railroad, it no longer sprayed us with soot: diesel fuel had replaced coal. The lake was dug out and the islands reappeared, trees, bushes, and flowers included. Footbridges were built, ducks put back on the water. However, the area by now was 90 percent black, and quickly the ducks vanished. At least the blacks, if they were guilty, took the ducks home for a family feast. White vandals would have killed the ducks and left them to rot.

Pete Lybock

My mom was a very saintly woman. She went to Mass each day. She said a lot of rosaries. She made novenas. She visited shrines.

When she was peeved at Dad, however, or when she was aggravated, her language was hardly fit to repeat. She could swear, as I have said, like a trooper. In the years since she left us, I have come to believe that there are other saints in heaven who could swear up a blue streak too.

Once I heard Mom calling Dad "a cheap Pete Lybock bastard."

Dad was anything but cheap, but Mom had her own way of gauging such things. What I wondered about, though, was Pete Lybock. I'd never heard of Pete Lybock. Who could this Pete Lybock be?

I put the question to Aunt Alice.

Pete Lybock, she said, was a well-known North Side miser. He lived on Ohio Street, or maybe East Street, in the heavily German part of the North Side. Wearing ragged second-hand clothes, he went around with his pushcart and picked up all kinds of junk – empty bottles and cans, small pieces of scrap iron, everything of any possible use. Junk dealers higher up on the economic ladder would buy this stuff, and he pinched every penny he got his hands on.

"When he opened his purse," Alice said, "the moths would fly out."

Pete lived alone, and he lived in squalor. As he aged and became more reclusive, the neighbors began to worry about him. It was feared that he would freeze to death in the wintertime, or that his gas stove would leak and asphyxiate him. Was he getting enough to eat? people asked.

Somebody must have notified the public health authorities. In any case, investigators came knocking at his door. Pete wanted nothing to do with them. As far as he was concerned, they were trespassers. When he put up a fight they overpowered him, forced their way in, and found hiding places all over the house where Pete had thousands of dollars stashed away. Acting on a tip, they dug up the back yard, where still more cash was buried in tin cans.

The authorities now faced the problem of what to do about Pete. Had he broken any laws? No – unless it's a crime to be distrustful of banks. Was he in need of supervision or help? It didn't appear so. For an old guy with no one to look after him, Pete was in pretty good physical condition. He fed and clothed himself, after a fashion. He wasn't harming anybody.

All that could be done was to take Pete's money, put it in a trust, and allow him to get on with his life.

He did not die for many more years. When the end came, the do-gooders returned. Again they found thousands of dollars hidden away. As before, they dug up the back yard and found buried treasure. Pete hadn't changed.

For a long time after the funeral, said Aunt Alice, the neighbors would come to Pete's back yard with their shovels, hoping to turn up an overlooked tin can or two. If anyone struck it rich, she didn't tell me.

None of Alice's nephews ever had seen the old junk dealer, but "cheap Pete Lybock bastard" was an epithet we never forgot. When my brother John was living near Philadelphia, he met a guy named Lybock at his golf course one day.

"You wouldn't be from Pittsburgh, would you?" asked John.

"No," the guy said, "but my family was."

"Did you have a relative named Pete?"

"Yes, a distant relative – a great-uncle. I didn't think anybody in Philadelphia would have known about old Pete," Lybock said. "I guess you're from Pittsburgh yourself – from the North Side of Pittsburgh."

"That's right, I'm from the North Side of Pittsburgh," answered John. "And in our family your Uncle Pete was a legend!"

Commies, Perverts, and Bums

Question: How do you get to the North Side?
Answer: Drink wine.

North Side jokes were common currency in the 1950s and '60s. Allegheny Center, the Allegheny County Community College, and Three Rivers Stadium rose up on the North Side in the 1970s, but winos still populated Federal Street. West Park got the overflow. In AJR's demonology a special place was reserved for the urban planners who laid out the parks – gathering places, AJR used to say, for "Communists, perverts, and bums."

I don't know about Communists, but there were perverts and bums to be found in the Garden Theater, which had made the overnight transition from family motion-picture house to den of iniquity, showing porn films seven days a week. Next door was the notorious Apache Grill. Over on Woods Run, a bar with the ironic misnomer Cuddles attracted under-age drinkers, my cousin John McNulty among them.

When Cousin John was 15 he showed up at Cuddles with a friend the same age. They had one fake I.D. card between them. First John and then his friend presented it to the bartender. "Hey, this is something!" the bartender said. "These two guys were born on the same day." And with the same name, he might have added, but didn't. Smiling, he took their orders – beer, I suppose – and set the glasses on the bar with a hearty "Drink up!"

Cuddles' best customer was the owner of the place, who passed out one night while tending bar. With no one tending the cash register, the patrons became his guests. They helped themselves to all the booze in the place, starting with the very best stuff. They broke into the food lockers and gorged themselves. Fights broke out over the choicest take-home items, the hams. When Mr. Cuddles came to, nothing was left.

Industrial Manchester, just down the hill from North Lincoln Avenue, was a neighborhood undergoing change – in other words, a slum. Over in the Woods Run section of the North Side, people were still using outdoor privies. Teen-age boys hung out on every corner, sitting on stoops, sitting on car fenders, sitting on mail boxes – and waiting for the next street fight to begin. The Work House – "Work House" being a nineteenth-century euphemism for slammer– overlooked the Ohio River. Jokesters like Baldy Regan and Mike Kearns said there were fewer crooks behind bars in the Work House than outside its doors walking the streets.

And it may have been literally true. So many murders took place in the vicinity of Cuddles that the cops finally shut the place down, describing it officially as a public nuisance.

After that, was the North Side a haven of peace and quiet? Not exactly. But AJR was determined never to leave. Nine forty North Lincoln remained a shining jewel in a dung heap.

Mrs. Kearns

Mike Kearns's mother was a fine-looking, dignified woman, fastidious in her choice of words. She referred to her son as "Michael," never Mike, and once in my hearing, when Mike and I were children, accused him of "playing truant." I had to ask what it meant.

As I have said, the three Kearnses – mother, son, and daughter – lived on Ridge Avenue in what once had been the billiard room of a decaying old mansion converted into a rooming house after the rich people who built it had moved away.

When Mike was eight months old, his father, looking for work, had gone by himself to Chicago and never returned. The mother, left on her own, struggled to make ends meet. Despite the elegance of her speech, Mrs. Kearns lacked a formal education and was forced to take the meanest of jobs. At home, she did the housework, easing the burden when possible in ways that were sometimes ingenious.

I am thinking in particular of her garbage-disposal system. For the upper-floor tenants especially, garbage disposal was a problem in these big old rooming houses because of the great distance between the apartments and the trash cans in the alley. So Mrs. Kearns would wrap her garbage in neat, attractive packages tied with a ribbon or a string and leave them on streetcars. Invariably, they were picked up by other passengers, carried home like discovered treasure, and opened with high expectations. This arrangement worked to perfection until a cop came knocking at the door to the

Kearnses' billiard-room abode. At the station house, Mike, who was 13 at the time, gallantly took the rap for his mom, claiming to have planted the packages, but there remained the little matter of a ten-dollar fine. Somehow, Mrs. Kearns was able to pay.

In her old age, Mrs. Kearns had a well-off friend – a Mrs. McCarthy. When they were both past 80, Mrs. McCarthy acquired a brand new set of upper front teeth. Mrs. Kearns wore false uppers too, but a welfare dentist had made and installed them. They looked bad and felt bad. Time went by, and Mrs. McCarthy died. The first to discover the body was Mrs. Kearns. Since the day Mrs. McCarthy obtained her new teeth, Mrs. Kearns had admired them. What could be the harm, she thought, in switching dentures with the corpse? Mrs. McCarthy, after all, would have no further use for those teeth. The thought was the mother to the deed.

It was Mike's daughter who noticed something different about Mrs. Kearns. "Daddy," she said to Mike, "Grandma's mouth looks all swollen." Ever the dutiful son, Mike checked it out. He said he knew at a glance what had happened.

"Mom," he told his mother, "if you did what I think you did, you should be ashamed of yourself. Furthermore, the teeth don't even fit."

Mrs. Kearns put Mike in his place. "You're talking to the one who changed your diapers," she said. "Anyway, I feel entitled to those teeth. Mrs. McCarthy would want me to have them."

Some years later, Mrs. Kearns passed on. At her wake, the funeral director took Mike aside and said, "We did our best to make your mother look good, but we had a lot of trouble with that upper plate. The dentist who made those teeth for her should be put in jail!"

Chapter 14

Betting Man

In my childhood, the scene at the Fort Pitt Hotel, where AJR ran his football, boxing, and race-track businesses from a ground-floor office, was always the same: guys at a table playing cards and guys just sitting around, all of them listening to somebody on the telephone, perhaps Uncle Red, call a horse race in progress at an out-of-the-state track. Racing in Pennsylvania had not yet been legalized.

There was nothing about racing that AJR didn't know. He knew the terminology, he knew how to bet, and he understood the nuances of the parimutuel system. Before there were parimutuels he had mastered the art of betting with bookmakers. He studied the Racing Form and the Morning Telegraph for countless hours in hotel rooms.

At the track he would bet from twenty dollars to fifty dollars a race, which he considered chicken feed. But if one of his horses or a good friend's horse was going to the post, and he liked the horse's chances, he would sometimes bet thousands on it to win.

There were times when he wanted to bet at the track and bet on the same race by telephone. Often the telephone – invariably a pay phone – would be two or three miles away and he would send Uncle Jim with a driver. In order to get there quickly, Jim would first make friends with the cops who patrolled the road.

Phones were very important to AJR and his people. He could not have them tied up. When his sons started using the phone, extended conversations were forbidden. "Go to a pay phone," he would order us if we talked too long. Once when he tried to call Mom, the line was busy. He tried again. Same result. So AJR had a telegram delivered to 940 North Lincoln Avenue, asking her to get off the line.

You could not call a bookmaker from a race track, or weren't supposed to. There were ways of getting calls out to horse rooms around the country, to be sure, but the tracks all did what they could to discourage this sort of thing. Calls from the track's business office were recorded. This was before the invention of the cell phone. John the twin told me that where cell phones are concerned the tracks have had to throw in the towel; there is no way to police them.

Always there were people who wanted to tap in on AJR's expertise. They would follow him around at the track, hoping to overhear a scrap of dialogue, or hoping to see him make a bet. They would follow his friends around. As a defense against eavesdroppers, AJR would separate himself from the people who were with him. Going to the track, they would be on the same bus or train, but never seated together. They took pains to avoid speaking with one another. Some would watch the races from the grandstand, others from the clubhouse. They might even be in different parts of the grandstand or clubhouse. There were prearranged signals to deliver information picked up from a trainer or some other source. Displaying a handkerchief, opening a newspaper, adjusting or removing a hat might mean: don't bet.

When he was plunging or taking advantage of a tip, AJR liked to bet at the last minute, so that the tote board would not reflect a suspiciously large amount of "smart money" showing up on a particular horse. For the man he entrusted to get the bet down, that could be nerve-wracking. As post time neared, the line at the ticket window might be long. It might be moving slowly because a timid or inexperienced bettor was suddenly gripped by indecision.

AJR, who had nerves of steel, could time the placing of a bet to perfection. He knew how to make himself invisible. And he was always very careful to maintain a good image at his work place – i.e., the race track.

'Is Mr. Goldfarb There?'

AJR's routine on visits to Monmouth Park was always the same:

Check in at the hotel, the Berkeley Carteret in Asbury Park.

Eat dinner.

Return to hotel room with Racing Form, Morning Telegraph, and one of the local newspapers.

Tear the local paper into small pieces and use them to cover the bottom of the waste basket.

Remove shirt.

Bite off a cigar end and chew it.

Study Monmouth Park entries for following day in Racing Form and Telegraph, meanwhile spitting cigar juice into waste basket.

Pick out four or five horses to bet on – a job that required hours of deep concentration – and circle their numbers heavily with a lead pencil the size of a cigar.

Go to bed.

Up and at 'em early enough for 5 a.m. arrival at track.

Clock the horses in their morning workouts.

Eat breakfast in track kitchen.

Return to hotel, stopping on the way to attend Mass.

Clean up and get dressed for the day.

Call Steeler office in Pittsburgh to stay abreast of what's going on.

Return to race track; eat lunch.

Talk with trainers, friends, and other horse people, absorbing information – information that might or might not affect the plan of action decided upon the previous night.

It would be post time by then – as freighted a moment, for AJR, as the kickoff at the start of any Steeler game. Over the next few hours, all of his expertise, all of his preparation, would come into play, with thousands of dollars at stake.

One night about forty-five minutes before AJR turned in, a loud, alcoholic party got under way in the room adjoining his at the Berkeley Carteret. AJR expected it to taper off, but the commotion only increased. There were probably no more than three to five men in the room, he judged, but they were making enough noise for a biker's convention, shouting and laughing uproariously. Occasionally a fight would break out; sounds of cursing and scuffling would come from the room. On one thing the men all agreed. They did not like Jews, and said so in voices that penetrated the walls.

At one o'clock, AJR called the front desk and asked the night manager to send the house detective to his floor. The noise next door continued without abatement.

At half past three – his wake-up call was at four – the party ended. Finally there was silence, but for AJR it had come too late to think of sleep. He got up and put on his clothes.

The revelers, he knew, had not left the room. In all probability, they were lying stupefied on the beds and the sofa. He began calling them on the phone. Every time someone answered, he would ask for "Mr. Goldfarb," or "Mr. Bernstein," or "Mr.Rosenberg." At last one of the drunks took the receiver off the hook. AJR turned on his radio and placed it right next to the door between the rooms. He had the volume as high as it would go. With the radio blaring, he pounded on the door for several minutes.

It was time to leave for the track now, and he pounded on the door in the hallway. Whoever opened it would be greeted with his best right hook. No one did. At the front desk, he spoke to the manager, who said he was sorry the house detective's threats had gone unheeded; both he and the detective had assumed there would be no further trouble. He would not charge AJR for his room. AJR walked away from him. Before going out to his car, he gave the switchboard girl ten dollars and instructed her to call the bums who'd been making all the racket every fifteen minutes. She should ask for Mr. Cohen or Mr. Levine or Mr. Silverman.

When he was back from the race track, he stopped at the switchboard again. What effect had the calls had? he asked the operator. Enough, after an hour or so, to get the phone off the hook, she said. AJR went up to his room, stopping in the corridor to pound on the door to the room where the drunks were sleeping it off. No one answered. The radio in his room was still blasting away, and he turned it off. He pounded on the connecting door. Still no answer. He picked up his phone book and threw it against the door. He kept throwing it against the door until the binding came off and it fell apart. He did the same thing with the book containing the yellow pages. The only other missile he could find was the Gideon Bible. Sturdier than the phone book, it lasted a good long time. After slamming it against the door, he would shout, "Hey, Mr. Rubenstein," or "Hey, Mr. Shapiro," or "Hey, Mr. Horowitz."

Suddenly his phone rang. In a tired, thick voice, someone said, "I'm calling from next door. You win. All of us over here apologize. Now will you please let us get some sleep?"

AJR accepted this offer of surrender and started thinking once more about the horses he would bet on that day.

Metamorphosis

Kass, though she could swear like a trooper, was never obscene and limited her profanity to damns and goddams. Her vocabulary of invective included S.O.B., bastard, dirty bastard, old bastard, and goddam old bastard. It was truly amazing that Mom, and Aunt Alice also, could cuss like that and at the same time be so devout, attending Mass every day, saying tons of rosaries, making novenas, and praying the pages out of their prayer books.

They were not Bible quoters, and neither was Dad. In fact, we did not get a lot of preaching from Mom or Aunt Alice or from Dad until almost the end of his days. They all for the most part taught by example. Looking back on it, they were really impressive people. They had lived through world wars, the flu epidemic, and the Great Depression. The McNulty girls' mother had died when she was only 38 and Old Man McNulty lost his worldly possessions a piece at a time. As Aunt Alice put it, what all of this did was make them stronger — and stronger in their faith.

AJR came from a rough, tough environment and also grew stronger in his faith. He would give you a lot of hell for small infractions, such as keeping late hours, but was with you to the hilt when there were major problems, or so I was told by my brothers. I was always pretty dull and domesticated and did not often get into scrapes. Perhaps for this reason, AJR tried to interest me in the priesthood, but that would be years down the road.

The Second World War was over, and Pop and Grandma Rooney had lost their red-headed youngest boy in the fighting. Still, life went on. Pop was retired, but AJR — and Social Security — kept the old folks comfortably fixed. They could count on AJR for everything they would ever need. That did not suit Pop entirely. Pounding on the wall with his cane, he would say, "It's time for me to go back to work." Unhappily, there was nothing he could do. Uncle Jim had no desire to work and never did, even though Pittsburgh's economy was thriving.

The city had once seemed almost beyond repair. I remember hearing Bill Walsh, a center for the Steelers from 1949 to 1954, say that his parents — Easterners — always bypassed Pittsburgh on their way to see him play at Notre Dame, driving on old Route 40 through Washington, PA. Pittsburgh's dirt and smoke were too much for them. I know it is not a myth that on overcast winter days the street lights would be burning at high noon or that businessmen changed their shirts at lunchtime. But David Lawrence, the politician, and Richard Mellon, the financier, had brought together the forces of government and industry to clean up the rivers and the air. A Renaissance, as they called it, was under way.

As Pittsburgh changed, so did AJR's reputation. The public no longer thought of him as a colorful gambler. He was now the owner of the Steelers and a "sportsman" and becoming known, in addition, as a giving and sharing kind of guy, free with his time and his money and able to make people believe in his sincerity. After spending a few minutes with AJR, strangers instinctively felt that he was their friend, and always had been.

He was a legendary big tipper, and so was his old pal Milton Jaffe. Neither, of course, was as profligate as Jim, who thought of money as something to get rid of as soon as possible. AJR knew the value of a buck, but believed in what the nuns used to teach: "Bread cast upon the water is twice returned."

All of these people – the Rooneys, the McNultys, Milton Jaffe, and I include Dago Sam – had a ripe sense of humor, and it helped them get over the bumps we encounter in life. One thing North Siders always clung to was hope. You could be down and out one day and hit a number the next. You could win a lot of dough at the race track. When Uncle John McNulty was going through a particularly bad period, Uncle Jim told him cheerfully, "Johnny, it can't continue like this. Your luck is bound to change. And when it does change, I hope you are at the race track – and I hope I am with you."

Daily life on the North Side was somewhere between a Eugene O'Neill play on the sad side and a John Ford movie on the bright side.

For the Rooney family, old St. Peter's Church was a pivotal location. St. Peter's was the center of our lives. Situated on the threshold of beautiful West Park, it was built when Allegheny City teemed with power and money. In our time, coal smoke from the trains of the Pennsylvania Railroad had blackened the magnificent stones of the church, but the stained-glass windows and fine interior woodwork had remained as good as new.

The Sisters of Mercy ran the school. They had taught Mom and Dad and now they were teaching a second generation of Rooneys. These dedicated ladies in the long black gowns were not above handing out corporal punishment. On days when the whole class was disruptive, we lined up obediently to have our fingers slapped with a ruler, boys and girls alike. There were girls who considered this harsh and unnecessary, but the boys put on a show of indifference. If you were yelled at or hit, and told AJR, you'd be yelled at again and maybe hit again, too. "Don't give those holy women any trouble. They have offered up their lives to God and are trying to help you," he would say.

It was easy to forget that under the long black gowns the sisters were still just women, with all the problems of women. Reined in by strict rules, they could not leave the convent except in pairs or in groups; they could not shed their cowls or their starched white breastplates; they could not let their hair grow long; they could not drive a car.

When Pope John XXIII opened the windows of the church for air, loosening the grip of the vows they had taken, little wonder that some of them bolted. They had tasted freedom and liked it.

Retreat

Often Dad would go to the retreats at St. Paul's Monastery on the South Side and often he would take someone with him. His friend Havey Boyle, sports editor of the *Pittsburgh Post-Gazette*, was a talented writer with a drinking problem – among other weaknesses. Dad liked Havey a lot and thought a retreat at St. Paul's would do him some good.

The idea was not well received. Havey demurred, offered excuses, dragged his feet. But AJR was persistent and Havey at last gave in.

Retreats lasted two days at St. Paul's. They began with an assembly at which the priest in charge spoke of the subjects he would be covering. Afterward, the men who were there to listen, pray, meditate, and confess retired to their cell-like rooms.

Ten minutes had not passed before Havey, with his suitcase packed, came to AJR's room. "Arthur," he said without preamble, "I have always considered you my friend but now I know I was mistaken. You are not a true friend at all."

AJR was shocked.

"What do you mean, Havey? Why would you say that?" he asked.

"For this reason: That priest who just spoke to us was talking about the sins he was going to deal with. He named them – every one. And they were sins I've committed over and over. And all the time he was talking, he looked right at me.

"Now, who knows me better than you do, Arthur? You know all the things I've done wrong in my life. So how did that priest find out? Arthur, you must have told him. After all, you're the one who brought me here. You went to that priest and you ratted on me."

I am unable to say whether AJR could talk Havey Boyle into going through with the retreat. But whenever he repeated the story as I have told it, his eyes would light up.

Masses, Rosaries, Novenas

At a memorial Mass in St. Peter's Church on the anniversary of Aunt Alice McNulty's death, my son Art asked me to take a good look at the stained-glass windows. "Look at the names of the saints on them," he said. "They're our family names."

Sure enough. The names on the windows were Joseph, Peter, John, Matthew, Patrick, Bridget, Francis, Anthony, Michael the Archangel ... The children, grandchildren, and great-grandchildren of AJR and Kass, who went to Mass in that church for so many years, had been given all of those names. Though it's a stretch, I am tempted to add Catherine, for Kathleen.

I can't emphasize too much the importance of the Catholic Church in the lives of Dad, Mom, and Aunt Alice. As I have written before, novenas, the rosary, and daily Mass attendance were routine. Another thing the three of them were into was holy oil and holy water from the shrine of St. Anne in Quebec. Cuts and scratches could be healed with those sacred liquids and recovery from an operation could be hastened.

This belief was passed on to others in the family. My brother Pat, while he was living in Philadelphia, underwent back surgery. He was lying face-down on his hospital bed, groggy from the anesthesia, when John and his wife JoAnn came into the room. Immediately, JoAnn reached into her purse and pulled out a bottle of St. Anne's holy oil. Then she yanked up Pat's hospital gown, exposing his rear end as well as the recent incision in his back. With the holy oil she anointed the entire area. "This is just what you need to get better, Pat," she said. Pat, who was pretty much out of it, kept his thoughts to himself. My wife Kay, however, whispered to me, "Aren't you afraid that oil on an unhealed cut might cause an infection?" I shook my head. "Don't you have any faith?" I demanded. "Yes," Kay said, "but don't push it."

We made novenas for everything – novenas to St. Anne to find a good wife, novenas to St. Anthony to find a lost valuable, novenas to St. Joseph the carpenter to find a job, novenas to St. Cecilia for better eyesight, and of course novenas to St. Jude asking help for hopeless cases.

We prayed to them all, and we had a lot to pray for. Mom and Aunt Alice prayed very hard for the Steelers. On Sundays when the team had a home game, Mom took her statue of the Blessed Mother into the back yard. Mary's presence out there, she felt, would guarantee fair weather – and fair weather would bring a good crowd.

When the Rooney boys played for North Catholic High School, Mom and Aunt Alice prayed for the Trojans. When I played at St. Vincent College they prayed for the Bearcats. They prayed for the success of those teams – and the Steelers, of course – but also that no one would get hurt. Where Tim was concerned, it didn't seem to help. In a game between North Catholic and Scott High of Braddock he was knocked unconscious while making a tackle on the kickoff. Then at Kiski Prep he took a punishing blow to the testicles.

Would he be able to have children? we wondered. Who is the patron saint of virility and potency?

Following North Catholic all over Western Pennsylvania, Mom and Aunt Alice found their way to football stadiums in tough little mill towns and mining towns like Ambridge, Aliquippa, Windber, and Masontown. They were troopers. Dad came, too, if he could get away. We never minded when he couldn't; we'd be spared his words of criticism and his even more damning silences.

Mom and Aunt Alice were looking on from the stands at St. Vincent when I came off the field with a bloody mouth and a missing tooth. Simultaneously, they dived into their purses for rosary beads. My own prayers were mostly for the Steelers. I remember a promise to give up cigars if we won our first Super Bowl. God allowed us to beat the Vikings and I kept my vow – for thirty days.

Chapter 15

The Great Stoneface

Over fifteen seasons, the Pitt teams coached by Jock Sutherland won 111 games, lost 20 and tied 12. Three of those twenty defeats came in the Rose Bowl. Pitt lost in Pasadena to Stanford (by one point) and Southern California twice (the scores were embarrassing) before the 1936 team routed Washington. Sutherland's undefeated 1937 team was a consensus national champion; his '36, '34, '31, and '29 teams all were declared national champions by at least one of the mathematicians who had worked out the various complicated rating systems that existed back then (remember Dick Dunkel?). Uncle Jim, you may recall, was on the 1929 team that won all nine of its regular-season games but lost to USC in the Rose Bowl by thirty-three points.

With the appointment in the mid-1930s of John C. Bowman as Pitt's chancellor, friction began to develop between Sutherland and the administration. In its simplest terms, the reason for their strained relations was a difference of opinion about football's importance in the overall scheme of things. To Sutherland, it seemed that the administration was ashamed of his success. Starting in 1932, Sutherland won so often from Notre Dame – five times in six games, with the Irish held scoreless in four of them – that Notre Dame dropped Pitt from its schedule. Then Wisconsin backed out of a two-year commitment and there were troubling allegations of "professionalism." Most Pitt players worked five hours a week at campus jobs for forty-eight dollars a month. Others simply picked up their stipends. Pitt had no dormitories or training table, so the players needed money for room and board. How was this worse, a few realists asked, than the popular alternative of under-the-table payments?

But Chancellor Bowman, uncomfortable with the whole situation, ordered cutbacks in recruiting, scholarships, and practice time. At the Pitt-Washington Rose Bowl game, Sutherland clashed openly with Athletic Director Don Harrison, a former English teacher. The issue was spending money. Each Washington player had one hundred dollars from university funds, each Pitt player seventeen dollars from the pockets of Sutherland and his staff. Confronting Harrison at the post-game dinner-dance, Sutherland accused him of "penny-pinching." Within a few months, Harrison was no longer the athletic director, but his successor, Whitey Hagan, a Pitt tailback under Sutherland in the 1920s and later one of his assistant coaches, enforced all of Bowman's restrictions as relentlessly as Harrison had. When the 1937 team voted not to accept the Rose Bowl invitation that arrived as a matter of course, and Sutherland heard about it at second hand, he felt stripped of authority. After coaching one more season, he resigned.

This was in March 1939. For days on end the story was front-page news. The *Pittsburgh Press* ran a cartoon in which Sutherland towered over the Cathedral of Learning, Pitt's 36-story classroom skyscraper. So now a real big-name coach was providentially available to the highest bidder, and AJR made his move.

Johnny Blood had coached the 1938 Pirates (two years away from becoming the Steelers), but AJR knew that he would soon have to find a replacement. The replacement he had in mind was Sutherland, who agreed to a secret late-night meeting at the Fort Pitt Hotel. Sutherland wanted no publicity. But a desk clerk leaked the story to sportswriter Jack Sell, and it appeared the next day in the *Post-Gazette*.

Sutherland was incensed. Blaming AJR, he cut off negotiations.

The offer from AJR was one of several he refused. To keep his hand in, he coached an assemblage of college "all-stars," culled for the most part from his 1938 Pitt team, against the NFL champion New York Giants in a pre-season charity game promoted by the *New York Herald-Tribune*, and the professionals won, 10-0, poking holes in the argument that major-college football was superior to the NFL brand.

Before the 1940 season, Dan Topping, the owner of the Brooklyn team in the NFL, a rich man married to Sonja Henie, the ice skater/movie star, went after Sutherland. Where AJR had failed,

Topping succeeded. Sutherland coached the Dodgers in the last two seasons before America got into the Second World War – missing out on a division title in 1941, as I have written, when Brooklyn lost to the Steelers, who did not win another game that year and whose record was the worst in the league.

Not long after Pearl Harbor, Sutherland volunteered for the Navy. While he was doing his bit for the war effort as a lieutenant commander in charge of physical-fitness centers, the Brooklyn Dodgers went out of business. And with America once more at peace, AJR made a second, more adroitly handled attempt to interest Jock in the Steelers.

He signed him to a contract for fifteen thousand dollars a year and twenty-five percent of the profits. In the Steelers' entire history there seldom had been any profits, but Sutherland's name was magic. He had kept his own list of Pitt's season-ticket holders and to each of them he wrote a personal note, promising great things from his new team. His old team, Pitt, had been going downhill. Exactly how many Pitt fans changed their allegiance is hard to say, but for 1946 the Steelers sold twenty-two thousand season tickets. In 1946 and 1947 every game at Forbes Field was played before a capacity crowd. Cash customers, for once, outnumbered the deadheads, and Sutherland gave them something to watch. Under his iron hand, a team long noted for succeeding only at failure began to win – just half of its games in 1946 (which stood for improvement), but enough the next season to tie for first place in the NFL East.

John Bain Sutherland was a formal, aloof disciplinarian who did not inspire universal love. A lifelong bachelor (though fond of the ladies), he lived in one room at the Pittsburgh Athletic Association. He allowed no summer to pass without a visit to his aged mother in Scotland. Nobody called him "Jock" except the sportswriters – and they called him that only in print. Chet Smith, sports editor of the *Pittsburgh Press*, gave him a nickname – The Great Stoneface. But even AJR addressed him as "Doctor."

He had a reputation for tight-fistedness which may or may not have been deserved. Jack McGinley recalled that Sutherland came to the Steelers' office in the Union Trust Building at the end of the 1946 season to examine the books. Having walked all the way from the PAA in Oakland, as he usually did, he came through the door wearing an overcoat and a hat, neither of which he removed. "Is Arthur satisfied with these figures?" he said to McGinley. "Yes," answered Jack. "Is Bernard satisfied?" Sutherland asked, referring to Jack's father, Barney McGinley. Again the answer was yes. "Then so am I," Sutherland said. "Just send me my check." And without another word he turned and walked out.

By 1946 almost every team in football was using the T-formation. Sutherland stayed with the old single wing he had coached for twenty-five years. To build up the Steelers' confidence he scheduled pre-season games with minor-league teams like the Richmond Rebels, the Erie Vets, and the Roanoke whatevers. They were low-scoring games which the Steelers just barely won. Nick Skorich, one of the linemen, said their offense consisted of five plays. Sutherland worked the team so hard that Frank Wydo, a tackle, claimed to be worn out by the time the regular season began. Before the last play of a game with the Erie Vets, Wydo said, he told the quarterback, "Call something simple. I'm too tired to block anyone."

At the Steelers' 1947 training camp in Cambridge Springs, Sutherland instructed the trainer, Doc Sweeney, to put Mother's Oats in the water buckets. I was a water boy that year, and I tried this concoction one day. It was like drinking puke. Once after practice when a few of the players started to pour the gooey stuff over their heads to cool off, Sweeney and his assistant, Jack Lee, yelled at me in their Boston accents to "get those buckets away from those guys." So I tipped the buckets over, and the unappetizing mess spilled out on the ground. Val Jansante, an end, was standing there with a thick oatmeal paste in his hair and all over his face – glop that resembled vomit. He gave me a look I still remember and said with pure venom, "Kid, you're a mean little prick."

The players despised Sutherland's blocking sled, constructed of heavy wooden beams and equipped with large springs. The recoil of the springs made it almost immovable and sometimes knocked players to the ground. Their name for the sled was "Big Bertha." Two of them tried to set it on fire with lighter fluid one night, bungling the attempt.

Meanwhile, candidates to make the roster were leaving camp in droves. They would slip away at night after the lights in the Alliance College dormitories went out. As the exodus increased, Jock's assistant coaches stood guard by the doors. They appealed to the players' pride, but continued to torture them on the practice field. Most of these players were World War II veterans and not quitters. I heard a guy who had been in combat say that he ran harder for Jock than he did when the Germans were chasing him.

One player who liked all the hitting was Chuck Mehelich, a rock-solid defensive end from Duquesne. He was about 6 feet 1, all muscle and bone, and he couldn't have weighed much more than 190 pounds. Mehelich was born tough. If you played for Jock you started hitting as soon as you stepped on the practice field and you never stopped, and this was what Mehelich liked best. He could tackle with leverage and strike the rising blow. He made teeth rattle. "When Number 55" – Mehelich – "hit you," said Steve Van Buren, the Philadelphia Eagles' Hall-of-Fame runner, "you stayed hit."

Mehelich's teammates knew what that meant. Sutherland had a drill in which the defender lined up about seven to ten yards from the ball carrier, with no room for more than a single fake, or "juke." The good backs could get the defender off-balance with their juke, lower a shoulder, and run right through him. But what Mehelich did, he told me, was watch the ball carrier's belt. "They can fake with their head and shoulders and maybe even their hips, but not with their belly," he said.

With his eye on the belt buckle, Mehelich terrorized these guys. When it was their turn to go against him, the runners would cringe. One time Sutherland caught Steve Lach, an all-Southern Conference halfback from Duke, pretending to tie his shoe so that somebody else would move ahead of him in the line and face the hard hitter from Western Pennsylvania. As he dropped to one knee, Jock called out, "That's all right, Steve, we'll wait for you."

Mehelich had a successful pro career. Steve Lach didn't last very long.

Jock's scrimmages were ferocious. One player, unaware that his coach was a dentist, thought he could skip practice by claiming to have a toothache. Sutherland took him into an office, turned up the lights, and did some probing. "Is it that tooth?" "No, Doctor." "This one?" "No, Doctor – the one next to it, I think." Jock told the guy he'd be able to practice.

The trainer, Doc Sweeney, a tough, smart New England Irishman, had worked with Jock in Brooklyn. I remember watching him sew up all kinds of wounds, mostly to the chin or the hands. He would dose the cut with alcohol or iodine and put in the stitches right away. It was a little bit like a Civil War field hospital, but no bad infections resulted.

Jock's single-wing formation called for power, strength, and toughness, plus execution, execution, and even better execution. Offensive linemen had to pull out and block, which demanded quickness. Guards like Nick Skorich and Red Moore were not big, but they were tough, strong, and smart. In Jock's style of rock 'em, sock 'em football, there were injuries and there was pain, but his players developed great stamina. They were at their best in the fourth quarter, when the guys on the other side had started to wilt. "You might beat the Steelers on the scoreboard," a player from an opposing team once told me, "but they'd give you such a physical beating that you'd lose your next game."

Here's a story I heard from Jim Parmer, a fullback for the Philadelphia Eagles. He said the Eagles played the Steelers in the last game of the season one year and he was staying on the field with the defensive unit because Ebert Van Buren – Steve's brother and a regular linebacker – was hurt. Ebert sat on the bench wearing his helmet and a field cape which came down to the top of his football shoes while Parmer exhausted himself in his double-duty role. Parmer told me that in the second half he walked over to Ebert and said, "How about spelling me off? I'm dead tired." Ebert just smiled. He opened his cape, and Parmer saw that he was dressed in a white shirt, necktie, and blue serge suit with the pant cuffs tucked into his football socks.

"No way I'm going in there against those guys," Ebert said. "When this game is over I'm heading straight to the railroad station. And next week I'll be duck hunting, not lying in some hospital."

In Ebert Van Buren's three years with the Eagles they never closed the season with the Steelers, so it must have been another player in another season who wore the field cape over his street clothes and said that to Jim, but whatever their source was, the words summed up a prevailing attitude.

'He Never Changes'

Sutherland-coached teams owed their success to execution and conditioning, everybody said. Jock's message to his troops was always the same: One, keep it simple. Two, don't make mistakes. Three, wear down the opposition.

The star of the show was the left halfback, or tailback. He would take a direct snap from center and run inside or outside or maybe even pass now and then – mostly then. The fullback was primarily a blocker, although sometimes he would take the ball into the line. The quarterback was by necessity a big guy – a pulling guard in the backfield with brains enough to call the plays. On occasion the left halfback or right halfback would throw him a pass. Almost everybody played both ways. On defense, the halfbacks would be defensive backs; the fullback, quarterback, and offensive guards would be linebackers. In a system like this, it was easy to see the importance of conditioning.

Sutherland had his faults as a coach, and one of those faults was inflexibility. In Sutherland's system the tailback was required to take three steps before cutting. Not one step or two steps, but three – no more and no less. Bullet Bill Dudley, who had uncanny vision, quickness, and body control, liked to improvise. No matter how many steps he had taken, he liked to cut when an opening presented itself.

To Sutherland, this was heresy. He demanded adherence to his system the way the Pope hands down Roman Catholic dogma. If you did not run the play exactly as he had drawn it up, it was like not being properly baptized, married, or ordained. There's a story that Sutherland's unwillingness to bend – to allow the slightest departure from his blueprint – was why Dudley left town.

In a practice scrimmage, the story goes, Dudley took one step or two steps or four steps before cutting, but went through the designated hole and ran sixty-five yards for a touchdown. Sutherland, looking grim, called for the play to be repeated.

"We're going to keep doing this," he said, "until we get it right."

Dudley responded, "How was it for distance?"

Never happened. "It's just a story," Dudley would say whenever somebody asked. "You didn't talk to Doctor Sutherland like that."

There was no single cause for the personality clash between Dudley and Sutherland, just a steady accumulation of incidents.

In the Steelers' seventh game, a 14-7 win over Washington, Dudley cracked a rib or two, and for the rest of the year – some said at Jock's insistence – he played hurt. After beating Washington, the Steelers were 4-2-1. Of the four games that remained, they lost three. And Dudley was fed up.

As stubborn in his own way as Jock was, he threatened to quit football unless the Steelers traded him. He was AJR's favorite player; he had led the league in rushing, punt returns, and interceptions; he was voted its MVP. But AJR, feeling he must back up his coach, peddled Dudley to Detroit for two very ordinary backs and a number one draft choice.

Jack McGinley was present when Sutherland spoke to Dudley for the last time. The way Jack remembered it, Sutherland said, "Bill, I've coached great players, and you're a great player. But I don't have to have great players." In 1947, with Johnny Clement, a good but not great player, at tailback, the Steelers finished with an 8-4 record, the best in their fourteen-year history.

There were high hopes for the future – high expectations, actually. The Steelers' 5-5-1 finish in 1946 had been hailed by the public as a great leap forward. After the 2-8 record in 1945 and the Card-Pitts' 0-10 season, it was. But in 1942, with the last of the players who later went into the service, the Steelers were 7-4 and even the 1943 Steagles had won more games than they lost. Pittsburgh, however, looked upon Sutherland as a savior. No matter how exciting Dudley could be – and something good or spectacular happened whenever he got his hands on the ball – it was Sutherland who energized the fans. By now he had reached the status of a deity. If the great Bill Dudley was unable to follow protocol, he must go.

And so Dudley went. He played six more seasons in the NFL, three with Detroit and three with the Redskins.

Johnny Clement was called Zero because that was the number on his black and gold jersey. He had played in college at Southern Methodist and spent one season with the Chicago Cardinals before going into the Army Air Force. Like Dudley, he flew a lot of combat missions. After his football days he became a commercial pilot and died in a plane crash.

As I have said, the tailback position in the single wing created stars, and Clement played so well in 1947 that the Steelers did not miss Dudley. In that respect, Johnny Zero took Jock off the hook. He followed the offensive scheme with no deviations, and that made the coaches happy. Statistically, Clement had an excellent season. He finished second to Steve Van Buren of the Eagles in rushing, passed for more than one thousand yards, and accounted for eleven touchdowns.

While doing all this, he took a beating. Injured, he missed the Eastern Division playoff game with the Eagles, a 21-0 defeat. With Clement's backup, Gonzales Morales, hurt too, the Steelers had no offense.

For still another reason, it was not a good way to end the season, which no one knew would be Sutherland's last. Demanding to be paid for their extra week of practice, the players had gone on strike a few days before the game. They returned in twenty-four hours, without the extra pay, but Sutherland was outraged. The performance of his team against the Eagles, before a disappointed full house at Forbes Field, was in keeping with the atmosphere in the locker room.

Johnny Clement played one more season with the Steelers and one in the All-America Conference. I remember him as a kindly fellow with a soft Southwestern accent. At training camp he sometimes went fishing with the kids who carried water and helped the equipment manager.

As for Dudley, when his football career was over he sold insurance — a lot of it — and served in the Virginia state legislature.

Dudley played well for the Lions and Redskins, but never had a better season than his last with the Steelers, 1946. Even by the standards of the 1940s he was undersized. "Don't tell me I'm too small," he would say. "Tell me I'm not good enough." Nobody ever did that.

What Dudley lacked in size he made up for in toughness. He wore the old leather helmet with no faceguard, and in one game he came to the sideline with nothing recognizable as a nose. He went to the trainer's room, had some tape put on, and resumed playing.

Dudley was not fast but had a low center of gravity, which gave him uncanny balance. His other attributes were strength, quickness, soft hands for pass catching and punt receiving — his ability to put on a sudden burst of speed made him a threat to return any punt for a touchdown — and remarkable vision.

He was the master of the cutback. With Dudley the ball carrier, off-tackle plays would become reverses or inside plays; inside plays would end up as sweeps. This was the sort of thing that drove Jock Sutherland wild, but Dudley followed his instincts.

As a passer, he had no arm, yet the ball seemed to go where he intended it to go. If his receivers were covered, he would take off and run. He was also a fine defensive back — some said the best they ever saw. Coach Steve Owens of the Giants warned his quarterbacks that if they threw into Dudley's area they'd be fined. Dudley had great ability to run with the ball after an interception.

Kicking field goals and extra points, he used a pendulum stroke. He stood just behind the spot where the holder would place the ball, with his left foot planted and his right foot back, held in readiness. When the ball was centered and placed he would swing his leg into it without taking a step. That is why I call him a pendulum kicker. He had limited range — about thirty-five yards from the line of scrimmage — but in those days the goal posts were right on the goal line and he was seldom inaccurate.

"Could Dudley play today?" was a question I still heard in the 1990s. As a free safety and punt-return man, I think so. With his quickness, his ability to see the whole field, his sure hands, his moxie, and his toughness, Dudley would have earned his keep.

My brother Dan and I were standing on the sideline at a Steeler game one fall when Dudley got loose for a 65-yard touchdown run on a punt return. We cheered him every step of the way and were told by AJR to control our enthusiasm. AJR held Dudley in the same high esteem that we did, but on this particular day he happened to be playing for the Redskins..

Year after year he returned to the University of Virginia every spring to play in the annual alumni game. Old bones are brittle; in mortal fear of an injury, officials took to hiding his uniform. He coached for a while but preferred the insurance business. Settling down, he married a former Miss Virginia, who converted him in his old age to Catholicism. I was present at the ceremony and observed how happy his wife was. Afterward, Bill told me that AJR and Bert Bell would have been just as pleased.

I had a long conversation with Dudley in April of 1998 and it proceeded quite pleasantly until I asked him about Sutherland. To my surprise, his language immediately grew heated, not to say violent.

He told me that in 1946 Sutherland was losing his mind. As an example, he cited a play in the game against the Redskins. "We were supposed to go off-tackle down by the Washington goal line," he said. "The offensive guard – I think it was Nick Skorich – gave me a signal from the line of scrimmage with his hand: 'Run off of me instead of to the outside.' I did that. Nick made a hole, and I dragged a tackler through it for the winning touchdown. If I had gone to the outside, they'd have nailed me. There was nothing there." Dudley was getting more and more worked up. I am leaving out all of his F-words. "When we watched the game film," he said, "Jock stopped the projector on my touchdown run. He said, 'Bill, what play was called?' 'Off-tackle.' 'Well,' Jock said, 'you went to the inside.' I told him, 'Watch the play again, and you'll see Skorich wave his hand. That was his signal for me to go inside. Hell, we scored! We won the game!'"

Sutherland wanted the Steelers to win, but he wanted them to do it his way. That same season, 1946, the Chicago Cardinals were making a goal-line stand against the Steelers. With the ball on the one-yard line on fourth down, the Cardinals' safety, Marshall Goldberg – who had played for Sutherland at Pitt – told his teammates exactly what to look for. "He never changes," Goldberg said. The Steelers ran the play Goldberg knew they would, and he stopped it for no gain.

If Sutherland hadn't died after his second year in the NFL, would he have switched to the T-formation? Could he have coached the new, much more open type of game? AJR believed so, convinced that Jock was a realist ... a pragmatist. Like everybody else in football, he would have been forced to adjust. Sure, the hard-headed old Scotsman was set in his ways. But the college players coming into the league were schooled in the T, accustomed to the T, enamored of the T. Recognizing this, Sutherland would have done what was necessary.

There were those who agreed with that line of reasoning and those who did not. There were those who thought they knew what Goldberg knew: "He never changes." The question must remain unanswered, but here is one last thing to consider. It's a show-business truism I often invoke: an actor who plays a part too long will find it's the only part he can play. The mask becomes the face.

End Game

On March 22, 1948, one day after his fifty-ninth birthday, Jock Sutherland drove to Coatesville, in eastern Pennsylvania, for a coaching clinic. From there he proceeded south to observe spring football practice at Wake Forest and Duke, reporting to the Steelers' Grant Street offices by telephone. After that, silence. There were no further calls.

Shortly after daylight on the morning of April 7th a man got out of a 1947 Cadillac which was up to its hubcaps in a Western Kentucky swamp. He had been in the car all night. He took a suitcase from the trunk and carried it the short distance to a narrow country road. Muddied and confused, he started walking.

He was wearing a topcoat, a hat, a business suit, and a necktie. A milk-truck driver, making his early rounds, pulled up and offered him a lift. In these wet, dismal lowlands not far south of the Ohio River and not far east of the Mississippi, a stranger on foot toting a suitcase attracted attention.

Except in one particular, the man's conversation did not make sense. To the milk-truck driver, to the owner of a garage in Bandana, Kentucky (population 100), and to John Shelby, the county sheriff, he kept repeating, "I'm Jock Sutherland."

With none of them did the name ring a bell.

In response to the sheriff's questions, Sutherland wasn't able to say where he had been. Shelby asked him to empty his wallet. It contained hotel receipts showing he had gone from North Carolina to Atlanta to New Orleans, plus $329 in cash.

"You shouldn't be carrying all that money around," Shelby cautioned him. "Somebody might take it away from you."

The effect of the words was instantaneous. For a moment – no longer – Jock Sutherland's true self re-emerged. He was 6 feet 3, still a powerful wrestler given to impromptu matches on carpets and lawns with anyone big and brave enough to test him, and he put equal value on his money and his life. He said, "It wouldn't be as easy as you think."

It was his last coherent statement. Doctors at a hospital in Cairo, Illinois, across the Ohio River from Kentucky, diagnosed his problem as amnesia. Or mental exhaustion. Or a nervous breakdown. They were not sure which.

By now Sutherland's identity had been established. Back in Pittsburgh there were big black front-page headlines. It became known that for months the coach had complained of "excruciating headaches." Anxious friends flew to Cairo in a private plane belonging to Thomas E. Millsop, the president of Weirton Steel, and brought Sutherland home. Late that night at West Penn Hospital, surgeons discovered an inoperable brain tumor. The next morning – Sunday, April 11th – Sutherland died.

Mourners by the thousand filed past his open casket in Calvary Episcopal Church. Several eulogists said that football in Pittsburgh had "lost its heart and soul."

And Bill Dudley called Sutherland "the best coach I've ever had."

Chapter 16

Meeting Al Smith

AJR would take Kass and his friends to the Union Fishing Club on the North Side and to the Lotus Club on the South Side. As private clubs, they could keep selling liquor after midnight and on Sunday, when commercial establishments were shut down by the law.

Kass said that one night in the Union Fishing Club a customer sidled up to her and said that, as proof of his devotion, he would "kill" for AJR. She answered, "I hardly think that will be necessary." Such twisted loyalty frightened her, Kass said.

AJR needed no one to fight his battles. There was the time in the Union Fishing Club, Kass went on, that a "tough guy" – somebody he disliked – accidentally bumped into her chair. It was "no big deal," she insisted. But AJR jumped up, Kass said, and "beat the tar" out of the guy.

"He's no good," AJR later explained.

After football games on Sunday, we went to the Lotus Club as a family. The change in the Blue Laws put the Lotus Club out of business eventually, but for as long as it remained open AJR continued to go there. It wasn't much for atmosphere. Everyone praised the steaks and chops, but all I ever ordered was a sandwich and most of the time it came with stale bread. Yet AJR would invite football people to the Lotus Club, and when I'd see them years later on scouting trips they would ask about the place and speak of it fondly.

I never could figure that out.

Once after a game between the Steelers and the New York Giants, the two coaches, Jock Sutherland and Steve Owen, got their snoots full at the Lotus Club. They began to argue about blocking and tackling techniques and before very long were down on the floor, demonstrating. Both were big, strong guys and former linemen and they were slamming into each other. Jack Sell, the *Post-Gazette* sportswriter, said the roughhousing became so intense that it almost turned into a fist fight.

Fights in restaurants and bars were not unusual. AJR's most memorable fight brought him to the attention of the first Irish-Catholic – actually, Irish-Italian-Catholic – ever to run for president.

It happened at Luchow's, a fine German restaurant in New York City. AJR had spent the afternoon at a race track – Jamaica, perhaps, or Aqueduct or Belmont – and planned to eat by himself and afterward drive back to Pittsburgh.

Pulling up at the curb – pulling up onto the sidewalk, in fact – he gave the parking attendant a very large tip to watch his car, but locked it and kept the keys. In the glove compartment was $10,000.

When AJR went to Luchow's alone, he ate at the bar. The bar was informal and by custom off-limits to women. So that night all the drinkers and diners were men, and one of them stood out from the rest. He was being totally and purposely obnoxious.

AJR had seen him at Luchow's before. He used his size and intimidating presence to bully people. Usually he was drunk. On *this* occasion he was drunk. Spotting AJR, he made an insulting remark.

"Hey," said AJR, "I'm your friend. Have a drink." He ordered a doubleheader for the guy. Down it went in a single gulp. Then the hectoring resumed. AJR was taking a lot of lip.

He said, "Look, we're pals. Have another drink." A second doubleheader arrived and went the way of the first.

AJR's table was ready by now. He sat down to eat, and once again the pest was in his face.

Still playing for time, AJR said, "You need one more drink." One more was exactly right, because the third doubleheader incapacitated the guy. He tossed it off and slumped against the bar with his head down. AJR finished eating and called for the check.

He then walked over to the guy, said, "You're ready now," and flattened him.

As AJR was leaving the room, a man with a very prominent nose and thin white hair, parted in the middle, detached himself from the group he was with. "Young fellow," he said to AJR, "I've been watching you all night. I saw you setting up that bum. Good work. It was beautiful." He held out his hand. "I'm Al Smith."

Alfred Emmanuel Smith had been the governor of New York and in 1928 the Democratic candidate for president. (His campaign was a lost cause. He was a Catholic, he was wet – opposed, that is, to the Eighteenth Amendment – and he came from immigrant stock. The Republican, Herbert Hoover, swept the country.)

AJR told the Al Smith story three or four times in my hearing and never changed it. There are stories that improve with each telling. This one remained forever the same.

Duke

AJR and his brother Vince, called Duke, never could get along. In almost every large family there are siblings who have trouble connecting with each other, and this was true of the Rooneys.

The clash of personalities between AJR and Duke had its origin in their natures. Like three or four other Rooneys, Duke overindulged in drink on occasion, and AJR made it clear that he disapproved. His role as the family's alpha male was important to him. So for this reason, among several, Duke plainly thought that his brother was too controlling.

And Duke didn't like to be controlled. Thus when he worked for a time in the Steeler organization he was often at odds with his boss. After one misunderstanding he borrowed AJR's car and took off for Texas. When his money ran out, AJR flew down to wherever Duke was stranded and brought him home.

The smallest of the Rooney brothers, Duke was a pretty good amateur boxer. He followed Dan – Father Silas – to St. Bonaventure University but dropped out before earning a degree. AJR's political pull helped him to get a job with the Sanitation Authority and he was doing well there until his health failed. Upon hearing from Kathy, Duke's daughter, that a stroke had put her father in the hospital, AJR broke into tears. Down deep, his estrangement from Duke, which persisted right up to the end, was something he always regretted. At Duke's wake, he posted himself near the casket and remained there for every minute of the viewing.

Long after Duke was gone, my son Mike spent some time as AJR's unofficial chauffeur. "He reminds me of my brothers, who were *all* good regular guys," the Chief told me. In a roundabout way, he was extending to Vince the affection he felt for Red, Jim, Father Silas, and Tom.

I never found Uncle Vince to be anything less than a pleasant companion. He could tell a good story with humor and skill. All of us, including AJR, had the highest regard for Anne, Vince's wife. She worked as a volunteer at Divine Providence Hospital, and once when AJR had me drive him there to visit a friend we stopped at the information desk to ask for the room number. The person who gave it to us was Anne. We conversed for a few minute, and then on our way to the elevator AJR took my arm and said, "Do you see that woman back there?" He meant Anne. Obediently, I glanced over my shoulder for another look. "She's a living saint," he continued.

When AJR promoted you to the status of living saint, that was the ultimate tribute.

Duke and Anne were the parents of seven children, and they all grew up to be successful in life. One of the three sons, Vincent Timothy, played football at California University of Pennsylvania and became a scout in the NFL, first for the Steelers, when I was personnel director, then with the Detroit Lions and later the New York Giants.

If your children are your legacy, there is much to be said in my Uncle Vince's favor.

Dago Sam

Dago Sam Leone was Dad's oldest friend. He was very Italian, so Italian he must have come from the tip of the boot, or maybe even Sicily. He would speak of Italians he did not resemble as "American-looking."

Sam was the Latin Lover type, still rather handsome in middle age even though he wore Coke-bottle glasses with wire rims that made his eyeballs look like balloons. He had dark olive skin and the remnants of what he said was once an excellent physique. When bragging about this, he called attention to his "very flat breasts," as he described them.

By his own account, he was irresistible to women. But Sam never married. He told me once that, long-term, he wanted nothing to do with women who were not like our moms, his and mine. As far as other kinds of women were concerned, you never knew what to expect. He said that in a gambling house one night the wife of a close friend sidled up next to him and placed a note in his hand. The note expressed her desire to have sexual relations with him. Sam was shocked and disgusted, he said.

Despite his rather low position on the social scale, he could behave with unusual refinement. I am certain he kept his distance from the Mafia. Perhaps the most arresting thing about him was the way he spoke. He used his hands a lot, but told side-splitting stories without ever changing his expression. He had a high-pitched voice that got higher and higher the longer the story went on. He seemed to be grabbing you by the lapels and screaming, "What do you think of *that*?"

Like Uncle Jim, he sometimes would talk in a series of asides. When Jim and Sam were together it was like something from "Guys and Dolls." Actually, the characters in that Damon Runyon play could only hope to be as funny as these two. I had coffee one time with Jackie Gleason and went away thinking I had never met anyone funnier, but Dago Sam, in his own way, was Gleason's equal.

I can't do justice to the stories he told by paraphrasing them. You had to see and hear him to appreciate the humor.

One story involved an old friend, a carnival guy he hadn't seen for a while. They bumped into each other in a cigar store that was really a bookie joint. Sam wanted to know what the carnie guy was doing in Pittsburgh. He answered, "Sam, I've got the greatest job you ever heard of. The money is good, it's easy, and it's fun.'"

Now Sam was interested. Maybe he could get a piece of the action. Before saying anything else, the carnie guy suggested that they step outside, where no one would be likely to eavesdrop. When they were by themselves, he told Sam that he worked for a Christian evangelist, a faith healer whose prayer services in churches all over town and in places like the North Side Public Library attracted huge crowds. She cured her devoted followers of every disease known to medical science. "Cancer and carbuncles. Blood clots and bunions. Warts and welts," wrote the author of a *Pittsburgh Magazine* article. From near and far, the afflicted came. The evangelist stood before them on a platform and dealt with their illnesses as, one by one, they approached her. "I rebuke your cancer in the name of JEE-sus!" she would say.

The carnie guy's role, as he explained it, was to have some curable ailment. Deafness, for example. Invoking JEE-sus, the healer would give him the power to hear. Or he'd be a cripple, carried to her platform on a stretcher. "Stand up," she would order him. "Now you can walk. You are healed." And the carnie guy would do as she instructed him. He would get up and walk.

Dago Sam rejoiced in his friend's good fortune, but decided it wasn't his kind of scam, one reason being that he was too well known on the North Side to get away with such outright fakery.

Uncle Jim had plans of his own concerning Sam. If you converted a heathen to Catholicism, Jim believed, that was your ticket to heaven. So he worked on Sam like a missionary and took all the credit when Sam was baptized. I hope for Jim's sake he had the right information about the ticket-to-heaven business.

Sam told me before I was old enough to realize it myself that Jim drank too much, and not for social purposes. According to Sam, you had to pace yourself when you drank. Jim, he said, drank too quickly. He drank to get pie-eyed. Sam thought this was a shame.

Sam was also well aware of Jim's other great weakness, his attitude toward money. Once as they were going into a saloon, Jim borrowed ten dollars from Sam. Then even before they ordered a drink he handed the ten to the bartender. As a tip.

Sam said, "What did you do that for?"

"To ensure good treatment," answered Jim.

Sam went into the Army when the United States entered the First World War and discovered right away that he wasn't cut out for soldiering. At the camp in the South where he took his basic training, an officer asked if there was anyone in the outfit who knew something about horses. Looking for an escape from close-order drill, Sam stepped forward. The fact that he often bet on horses made him feel more than qualified. Of course, except at the race track, he had never actually been close to a horse. Unconcerned about that, the Army packed him off to a cavalry regiment – where his job was to clean out the stables. The worst part of it was that they assigned him to the stables where the mules were kept. Sam was eloquent in describing the foul toilet habits of mules.

Then came another opportunity. The Army sent out a call for soldiers who could speak and understand Italian. In World War I, the Italians were America's allies, but communication was a problem. Sam volunteered and was happy to turn in his shovel and broom. The North Side Italian language differed greatly from the mother tongue, and Sam's vocabulary had severe limitations, but he managed to get by as an interpreter and enjoy what was left of the war.

As unpleasant as his time in the cavalry had been, Sam kept on playing the horses. Back in civilian life, he would sometimes take the bus to Waterford Park in West Virginia. The bus company offered a round-trip package that included transportation from Downtown, admission to the track, and a program. One hot day, Sam made the trip wearing slacks and a golf shirt but no underwear. He bet on the Daily Double and his horses finished first in both races. The parimutuel ticket was in the pocket of his shirt, but before cashing it in, Sam took a detour to the men's room. He was carrying, in his pants pocket, ten dollars – just enough money to continue betting until the bus left for Pittsburgh.

In the men's room, however, Sam got into an altercation with somebody. How it started I do not recall, but one thing led to another and the altercation developed into a scuffle. The other guy took hold of Sam's golf shirt and ripped it right off his back. Just as suddenly as it began, the fight now came to an end, but Sam was left standing bare-chested and with rags for a shirt. Even worse, the pocket had been torn off and was nowhere to be seen. And the pocket contained the parimutuel ticket. Sam looked all over the men's room for his pocket. He got down on his hands and knees, poking around under the wash basins and toilet bowls, and he could find no trace of either pocket or ticket.

So now he was desperate. Times were different then. No matter how flat his pectorals might be, a man without a shirt or an undershirt could easily end up in jail. Sam appealed to a black guy who shined shoes in the men's room and had helped him look for the ticket. "Sell me your shirt." The guy probably lived near the track, Sam figured. He'd be able to sneak home in his undershirt, if need be, whereas Sam – half-naked – faced a bus ride from Waterford Park to Pittsburgh and then a walk through Downtown across the Sixth Street Bridge to the North Side.

He haggled with the guy, who gave in at last and agreed to sell his shirt, but set the price at ten dollars. So there went Sam's betting money. All he had now was his ticket for the bus, which would not leave the track until the last race was over. Busted, he spent the rest of the afternoon in total boredom – and wearing a shirt that made him look like a Federal Street wino.

Actually, Sam never dressed in high style. His clothes were old and baggy, in conformance with the way he lived. When AJR or Uncle Jim were not buying, he ate in lunchrooms – greasy spoons. He depended for an income on small-time card games and crap games, but that source dried up as his eyes began to fail. There came a day when Sam was in the crime news, arrested for running numbers. AJR said to him, "Sam, I didn't know that about you. How long have you been a numbers guy?"

Almost shrieking, Sam protested, "I'm not! I'm not! I was standing in a store on General Robinson Street and a guy puts these papers in my hand. He says, 'Hold these.' And then he takes off – out the side door. And a plainclothes cop is coming in the front door. He grabs me right away, and the stiff won't believe what I'm telling him."

For a guy with a reputation as a sharpie, and whose best friends were the real thing, Sam seemed to be on the receiving end of many a bad deal. In defiance of professional ethics, a dentist named Baum advertised an easy-payment plan. Sam needed work on his teeth, and Dr. Baum sold him a complete new set of uppers, a bridge, and maybe a couple of crowns. Now Sam could smile again, but he did not feel like smiling when Dr. Baum sent him the bill. It was clear that once more Sam had been taken.

He yelled and screamed – and refused to pay. Weeks went by, and then the upper plate started giving him trouble. Something was wrong with the fit; all Sam knew was that it hurt when he chewed. He returned to Dr. Baum. To his surprise, the dentist greeted him cordially. Removing the plate, Baum said he would have to examine it. Meanwhile, Sam should go sit in the waiting room. An hour later he was still cooling his heels. His patience running thin, he demanded an explanation. What was taking so long? Calmly, the dentist told him that he would not get his plate back until he paid every penny he owed.

"Try eating without teeth for a while," Baum said.

Sam did try, but found it was difficult, if not impossible. In the end he came across with the ransom money.

He lived to an advanced age, hanging around the Steeler offices in the Roosevelt Hotel and later Three Rivers Stadium and outlasting most of his contemporaries. The faces of AJR's friends, of the coaches and scouts and trainers kept changing. Sam the entertainer was a constant presence.

His stories amused every new audience, but the burden of the years was increasing. He worried about medical care. One winter day on his way to Three Rivers he was unable to make it through the snow. Stadium security rescued him. AJR learned that Sam could be admitted to a Veterans Administration hospital. Nothing doing, said Sam. He would stay on the North Side. He died a lonely old man, subsisting as best he could on Social Security and his World War I pension.

Chapter 17

Cum Posey

Our "colored" maid, Mary Roseboro, was about 25 years old when she first came to work at 940 North Lincoln Avenue in the 1940s. Mary may have had some American Indian in her. She was tall, with high cheekbones and a reddish-brown complexion. I never heard Mary raise her voice or complain. She was a kind, loyal Christian woman devoted to her church – ladylike but not at all prim. In fact, she had a good sense of humor.

She arrived every morning and went home every evening in a jitney. To the best of my knowledge, she never married. She had a boyfriend, she told Kass, but apparently did not regard him as husband material.

After Mary had been with us for many years, Kass gave her permission to bring an old friend who was senile to 940 North Lincoln. While Mary did her chores, this patient, elderly woman sat in the basement. From time to time, Mary would go down there to visit with her.

We knew that in Mary Roseboro someone out of the ordinary had come our way. She blended in; we considered her one of us; our problems were her problems. She was part of the chemistry, in short, that made 940 North Lincoln a special place.

Mary outlived Kass, AJR, and Aunt Alice. When she died at 75, the Rooneys who were left attended her wake in the Hill District. Talking with the funeral director, Evan Baker, Jr., I received confirmation of a story I had heard from AJR.

It concerned a friend from his days as an athlete, Cum Posey. Cum – short for Cumberland – was a light-skinned black man who had played baseball and basketball at Penn State and also at Duquesne. He could easily pass for white and often did, it was said. But after leaving college in 1911, he joined a black semi-pro baseball team, the Homestead Grays, becoming their manager. first baseman, and eventually their owner.

Cum was a tireless promoter. Recruiting talent from New York and Chicago, he was able to pay monthly salaries by 1922. The Grays drew good crowds against semi-pro white teams in the mill towns of Western Pennsylvania, and by 1925 they were playing home games at Forbes Field (although forbidden by management to use the locker rooms and showers). Eventually, Posey helped organize the professional National Negro League in 1928.

In 1930, he discovered and signed Josh Gibson, a 19-year-old catcher out of Allegheny Vocational School on the North Side. It was not too long before scouts, other players, and sportswriters were calling him the best catcher, black or white, in all baseball. Gibson hit prodigious home runs and hit lots of them – nobody knows exactly how many because the Negro Leagues took a casual approach to record-keeping. In any case, when Gus Greenlee, the Hill District numbers king, acquired a team called the Pittsburgh Crawfords in 1932, he raided Posey's lineup, making off with two future Hall of Famers, Gibson and Oscar Charleston, a first baseman.

Through the rest of the 1930s and the early 1940s, Gibson jumped back and forth between the Crawfords and the Grays as the two rival owners engaged in a bidding war for his services. Greenlee, with his numbers money, had the advantage. He built the Crawfords a 6,000-seat lighted stadium on Bedford Avenue in the Hill District. Both teams had a serious problem making ends meet, and this was where AJR came into the picture.

The Grays, like the white teams, went South for spring training. To economize, they traveled in two ancient Buicks, ate fat, greasy take-out food, and rented rooms where they could find them in the colored section of town. Posey still couldn't manage to pay for it all, so AJR made up the difference. For fifteen years – until the end of segregation in baseball put the Negro Leagues out of business – he advanced his friend "loans." As repayment, Posey once offered him part ownership of the Grays. "Forget it," said AJR. "You have your team and I have mine." Live and let live.

The undertaker Evan Baker substantiated this. He said that AJR was "a true saint." And he told me a story I had not previously heard.

It seems that Posey once had a political club that held regular meetings. Before one such gathering he confided to AJR that there was not enough money on hand for beer and sandwiches. AJR took care of both needs, calling the Bubbles and Sherman restaurant for the food and the Duquesne Brewery for a truckload of beer.

So many of the things our dad related to us had the flavor of half-truths or legends, but I learned over the years never to doubt.

Dan Hamill

AJR had a great friend named Dan Hamill, who owned the Pittsburgh Paper Products Company. Dan was a bachelor and the epitome of a Catholic gentleman. Two of his nephews and many of his friends were priests, and, like Dad, he gave a lot of money to the Church.

He was also a bit of a prude. Once he told AJR that he had found a wonderful place to eat supper – well off the beaten path on Evergreen Road, not far from North Park. It was in an old house up on a hill. So they went there together, and Dan was surprised that many of the patrons and many of the waiters spoke or nodded to the Chief.

He said, "Art, a lot of people seem to know you here."

Dad said, "Yep ... they do."

"How is that?" inquired Dan.

"Well," said AJR, "there's a gambling joint upstairs. This is a roadhouse."

That information did not upset Mr. Hamill, but a few minutes later Dad said to him: "Have you noticed all the pretty girls around here?"

Dan replied that he had.

"I've been in the gambling joint upstairs a lot of times," Dad continued "but never to the other part of the place."

"And what would that be?" asked Dan.

"Why, a notch joint," Dad told him. A notch joint was a house of ill repute.

Dan couldn't eat another bite, and he never went back to this restaurant he had liked so much. Nor did he ever allow the fact to slip out that he had taken Art Rooney to a "notch joint."

Another restaurant he crossed off his list was Klein's, one of the best places Downtown for fish. Dan would go there on Friday and order the clam chowder. There was no other clam chowder like it, he thought. After finishing a big bowl on a Friday during Lent, he happily discussed its merits with the cook.

"How do you make such good clam chowder?" he asked. "What is your secret?"

"Well," said the cook, "the ingredients are pretty much the same as the ingredients in all clam chowder. The difference with mine" – becoming confidential, he lowered his voice – "is that, for the starter, I use pork broth."

Dan's face turned white. "But it's Friday," he reminded the cook.

"Mr. Hamill," said the cook with a smile, "what you don't know won't hurt you."

Klein's that day lost a regular customer.

Like AJR in his later years, Dan was a total abstainer. There's a story about a request he made to a friend, a successful engineer named John Laboon, on a fishing trip. The weather was hot, and he asked Laboon to hand him a bottle of Coke. Laboon took a bottle from the cooler and surreptitiously spiked it with whiskey. One sip was enough to convince Dan he'd been tricked. With fire in his eyes, he sent the bottle flying toward Laboon's head, just missing the target. He was ready to slug it out until the rest of the fishermen pacified him.

Dan kept in shape by playing handball, often with AJR. One time in making a shot, he accidentally elbowed Dad, raking the side of his face. Although his eye was blacked and his mouth gashed, Dad thought nothing of it, having taken harder knocks in the boxing and football arenas, but Dan's remorseful apologies gave him a wicked idea. For the next few days, when people inquired about his bruises, he would say with a straight face, "Dan Hamill hit me," and leave it at that.

One of Dan's idiosyncrasies was walking backwards, even up a hill, for exercise. We thought this was strange, but in modern fitness centers people do many strange things. Dan may have been ahead of his time.

Possibly because he was lean, Dan looked tall. He had a silver-gray, almost white head of hair and sharp features. Going to the races with AJR was his only known vice. I doubt if Dan Hamill ever committed a bad deed, spoke a bad word, or entertained a bad thought in his life. He was squeaky clean.

His association with AJR was so close that the directors of St. Paul's orphanage asked them to be co-sponsors of an entire confirmation class one year. I like to think that the boys in that class remembered the occasion all of their lives. Far-fetched? Maybe not. At the Shamrock Hotel in Houston some time ago the bellhop who handled my luggage refused to accept a tip. I asked him why. Well, he'd been an orphan in the school at Hershey, Pennsylvania, he said; AJR and Bert Bell had visited the place a number of times (no doubt writing checks before they left), and he wanted to show his gratitude in some small way. I am sure that my dad and Mr. Hamill wrote a few checks for St. Paul's.

Unquestionably, Dan made money in the stock market as well as in the paper business. Before investing, he would get in touch with a firm's chief executive officer and pump him for information not found in the annual report. I understand that in 1929 he anticipated the crash. By the time the market collapsed he was out of it.

One year he was ordered to appear in the Downtown office of the Internal Revenue Service with all his books. "Why can't you come to *my* office?" he asked. "Because things just aren't done that way," he was told.

Don't be too sure, Dan thought. He called the Federal Bureau of Investigation and explained the situation to an old friend – J. Edgar Hoover by name. Soon afterward he heard from the IRS agent who had spoken to him earlier. "One of our men will be over to conduct your audit," the agent said. The next call Dan got was from Hoover, asking if everything had worked out all right.

Until television made professional football both popular and profitable, there were times when AJR needed help to meet the payroll. On one such occasion he went to Dan Hamill. In return for financial assistance from Dan, he offered him a piece of the team. "Also, I'll make you an officer of the company," Dad said.

Hamill answered with no hesitation. He said, "I'll lend you the money [$25,000], but I want no part of the ball club. The ball club's for you and your family. Pay me back when you can."

Dan Hamill was not a relative of ours, but the Rooney kids thought of him as a kindly, beloved old uncle.

Down on the Farm

In 1948, AJR's horse trainer, Jimmy McGee, talked him into buying a dairy farm in western Maryland, near Winfield. There would be no cows on the farm, and no milking machines. Instead, it was AJR's intention to breed and raise thoroughbred race horses. He converted the dairy farm into a stud farm.

On the side, Jimmy McGee had some roosters, which he entered in illegal cockfights. On visits to the farm many years later, AJR would ask the manager, Jim Steele, if any of the chickens running around the place were descendants of Jimmy McGee's contraband gamecocks.

McGee was the first manager, long before Steele, and a poor one. He thought that race-track guys could do the farm work, a colossal mistake. As a result of his hiring practices the work simply didn't get done. Everywhere you looked there were empty whiskey bottles, evidence enough that the men had other priorities.

McGee's prize stud was a stallion named British Buddy. He produced some big, strong, beautiful horses that were not especially fast. AJR was more successful at winning bets than at building up a stable – I was with him one day at a track in New York when he won an even hundred grand betting on a horse of his named for Pat Livingston, the *Pittsburgh Press* football writer – but he knew how to hold down overhead and managed to stay in business.

Jimmy McGee's real name, I understand, was Gray. He knew the horse business and he knew how to get a thoroughbred ready for a race. He also had a touch of the rogue in him. For a short while, he was a real good matchup with AJR. He made the mistake, however, of thinking that AJR needed him more than he needed AJR, and when Kass overheard him say that he had "big plans for Mr. Rooney – if Mr. Rooney's money holds out," his days at Shamrock Farm were numbered. Kass was not a meddling wife, but for that very reason her opinions carried a great deal of weight with the Chief.

The best money winners in Dad's stable were Air Patrol and Little Harp. These horses and several others of his he would send to the good Eastern tracks – Pimlico, Laurel, Bowie, Havre de Grace. The scrubs ran in claiming races at Charlestown and Shenandoah Downs. AJR knew horse flesh. No trainer could fool him by saying a horse was a good one when it was not.

Unlike John Galbreath, the owner of the Pirates, AJR never had a horse he could enter in the Triple Crown races or the big handicap races. There was a time in the 1950s, though, when it might have happened. A former trainer of his, a little fellow named Carl Hanford, was working for the stable owned by the DuPonts of Delaware. One day in a telephone call, he informed AJR that the matriarch of the family was ready to sell "a real nice horse" – a gelding – that for reasons of her own she didn't like.

"Mister Rooney," Hanford said, "I talked her into giving it one more race. If it doesn't win, I'll have to get rid of it. I think you should buy that horse, Mister Rooney. It's going to be something special."

"Sounds good, Carl. Anything you say," replied AJR, willing to accept the trainer's judgment.

But the horse won its test race, and Mrs. DuPont decided not to sell.

The horse was Kelso. Over a long career it won thirty-nine major stake races and purses adding up to nearly two million dollars.

I think there's a good chance that AJR had money riding on Kelso in most of these races – big money, if I know how he operated, and I do. Winning money on a horse like Kelso was more important to him than owning such an animal. Let the bluebloods in the racing business talk about improving the breed (not that Kelso improved the breed; turned into a eunuch by the veterinarian, all he could do was win races). Let the bluebloods pose for the television cameras with their Derby horses and garlands of roses, or their Preakness champions and fake black-eyed Susans. The engraved cups and the silver plates meant nothing to AJR. Kass, visiting the homes of his trainers, would notice on the mantel the trophies won by Air Patrol and Little Harp at events like the Atlantic City Stakes.

"Those things would look good in *our* house," she said once to AJR.

"Come off it, Kass," he told her. "What do we need with that stuff? For those people, it's different. Racing's their life! What I'm in it for is the money." He was in it, too, for the respect of the bookies, the turf writers, the trainers, the jockeys ... even the warm-up boys and hot walkers. "Yep, I like horses. But I like people more," I heard him say.

One of the people he liked was a "layoff guy" named Danny Shea. A layoff guy doesn't book bets, he places them. My wife Kay and I met Danny Shea on our honeymoon. All three of us were staying at the old Monmouth Hotel in Spring Lake, New Jersey. Mr. Shea, I perceived, was rather smitten with the beautiful red-haired math teacher who had married me. In an out-of-the-way spot in the lobby one day, he caught sight of us counting our money. He called me aside. "Artie," he said, "I know you're on your honeymoon, so I know you're probably having a cash crunch. To see you through this happy time, I can let you and Kay have a thousand dollars." When I assured Mr. Shea that we were merely taking inventory, he said there was no expiration date on his offer. If we ever needed help, I must let him know. I told this to Kay, and she was touched.

Years later I was able to find a place on the Steelers' training-camp roster for Mr. Shea's nephew, who had played at a small college in Connecticut. It puzzled AJR and I suppose the coaches as well that I would interest myself personally in a kid who had no real chance of making the team.

Despite the way he talked, AJR was openly on the lookout for a horse that could win the big races. The man he expected to find him such a colt, Tom Barry, had trained the Irish-bred Belmont Stakes winner, Cavan, and trained the horses the Chief entered in races at the major tracks. Nothing came of Barry's search for a horse that would put the Shamrock Stable in racing's top echelon except a strengthening of his friendship with AJR.

Barry himself was from Ireland, and he spoke in a soft Irish brogue. On the day that Kay and I met Danny Shea at the Monmouth Hotel, we met Tom Barry at the Monmouth Park race track. He won us over immediately by telling Kay that she was even more beautiful than she was reputed to be. His Hibernian charm so thoroughly disarmed her that by the end of the day she was confiding in him. She knew next to nothing about horse racing, she admitted. It was nevertheless very clear to her what AJR had to do if he was ever to make a splash as a stable owner. "Buy a great horse and get a good jockey to kick that great horse in the rear end."

She hadn't mentioned the need for a great or good trainer, but Barry was not offended. He chuckled and said, "Young lady, you have sized things up exactly right."

The first step in Kay's formula – buying the great horse – was the step that AJR could never negotiate. His contract jockey, a handsome little devil named Bobby Martin, could have ridden a great horse. My brothers Tim, John, and Pat looked upon jockeys as interesting characters. They were all about the size of pre-teen kids – little full-grown men who reminded me in that way of ponies. All seemed to have girlfriends and wives up to a foot or so taller than they were and without exception good-looking. There was a big, virile Steeler football player who lost his own wife to one of these pocket-sized Romeos. The dapper Bobby Martin, after leaving the Shamrock Stable, came to a bad end. Uncle Jim used to tell me, "That kid has larceny in his heart" – prophetic words. As a result of some shady business I never quite understood, he was barred from racing for life.

The Shamrock Farm was a no-frills place. It neither made nor lost money. AJR thought the land was as good as any in America, but his buildings – I have to be honest about this – were firetraps, including the farm house where all of us stayed. Again, AJR's strength was in betting on horses, not breeding them. He left the administration of the farm to his accountant, Fran Fogarty. A distant relative, Fogarty had been a hockey player at Duquesne University. During World War II, he escaped from a Nazi prison camp and worked with the French underground. He ran the Steeler front office day to day and negotiated contracts with the players, who did not then have agents. At Shamrock Farm, he audited the books, taking no guff from the trainers and hired hands. No one, but no one, put anything over on Mr. Fogarty.

After AJR's death, the farm became my brother Tim's responsibility. It was never a very opulent place – more like the kind of subsistence farm you would find in parts of Ireland. But for as long as he lived, AJR took pleasure in driving down there to relax. He liked to spend time with the mares and the foals and the yearlings. There were moments, I think, when he needed to get away from his football coaches. The horses were more restful; they couldn't talk back.

Chapter 18

Sutherland Clone

Almost by right of succession, John Michelosen took over as head coach of the Steelers after Jock Sutherland's death in 1948. He was Sutherland's protégé, dedicated to preserving all that the older man stood for. He believed in Sutherland's blood-and-guts philosophy, believed in his Spartan training methods, believed with all his heart in the single wing.

Recruited out of Ambridge, in the Beaver Valley, during the Great Depression, Michelosen had played on Sutherland-coached Pitt teams that in 1934, 1935, and 1936 lost only two games and won for the first time in the Rose Bowl. As a senior, he was the captain, becoming more and more Sutherland's clone. Once, the story is, when Pitt was protecting a lead against Notre Dame, running out the clock in the final minutes, a halfback broke loose and went all the way, twenty-one yards. Now Pitt would have to kick off – and give up the ball. Michelosen, the quarterback, collared the offending touchdown maker. "Dammit," he snapped, "the Doctor won't like this!"

Sutherland, for his part, considered Michelosen an extension of himself. He put him to work in 1938 as Pitt's assistant backfield coach, and when the blowup came, when Sutherland resigned as a protest against de-emphasis, they walked out together. Where Sutherland went as coach from then on – to the Brooklyn Dodgers in 1940, to the Steelers in 1946 – Michelosen went as second in command.

Johnny Michelosen was a man of honor, dignity, and character. But his uncritical devotion to Sutherland robbed him of individuality and in the end brought about his undoing. AJR had made him, at 31, the youngest head coach in the NFL. He was still the youngest coach when AJR let him go – not necessarily because of his undistinguished four-year record (4-8, 6-5-1, 6-6, and 4-7-1), but because of his refusal to abandon the single wing. He could not betray his teacher, Dr. Sutherland.

By the end of the 1940s the single wing was passé, and AJR knew it. Jock Sutherland had been special, but now he belonged in the history books. Pittsburgh's fans wanted to win, and they were seeing the Cleveland Browns twice a year. Paul Brown, Cleveland's coach, was revolutionizing the game. His best-known innovation – the messenger boy system of alternating two guards at the same position – enabled him to call every play, but he innovated in other ways too, and most of his innovations became standard procedure throughout the league.

It was Brown who developed the draw play, Brown who first used the fullback as both a blocker and a safety valve on pass plays, Brown who first saw the possibilities of the sideline spot pass as a means of gaining ground and at the same time stopping the clock, Brown who stationed his punter fifteen yards behind the line of scrimmage instead of ten, getting back the difference – and then some – at the other end of the field, Brown who hooked up the coaches in the press box and the coaches on the field by telephone. His players were quick and clever. They threw the ball all over the place. The Steelers would control the ball five to eight minutes to get a score; the Browns would come back, complete three passes, and kick a forty-yard field goal in two minutes.

The Browns were up to date. So were the other good teams, and every one of them, Pittsburgh fans noticed, was using the T formation. So why couldn't the Steelers? Of course it was more than just the T that went into winning. There was defense; there was talent. Get the best players and don't mess them up. To the fans, it looked as simple as that.

As rigid in his thinking as Sutherland had been, Michelosen couldn't bring himself to take the first step – junking the single wing. After all, it was Sutherland's formation. On the practice field, he paced back and forth with his head bowed, looking for answers in the grass.

For all their similarities, they were not much alike. Sutherland had great presence – intimidating presence. Michelosen did not. Sutherland was in some ways a hypocrite. Uncle Jim recalled from his Pitt days that on train trips Sutherland would carry a satchel into his stateroom. The players all knew what was in it – Scotch, in small bottles, and a small brass hammer. As Sutherland and his cronies finished each bottle, he would hammer it into fragments and flush them down the toilet. Michelosen, though secretive, never went to such lengths. He did not really have a façade.

Dismissed by the Steelers, Michelosen returned to Pitt as defensive coordinator under Red Dawson. When Dawson developed heart trouble in the middle of the 1954 season and quit, Tom

Hamilton, the athletic director, installed himself as head coach, but Michelosen did the actual work, and in 1955 he became the head coach officially. He kept the split-T formation Pitt had been using, having figured out a way to incorporate single-wing blocking. Some years later he went to a pro-style offense with an end split wide. Two of his teams played in bowl games and his 1963 team, overlooked by the bowls, had a 9-1 record. Meanwhile, a new chancellor, Edward H. Litchfield, was busily raising academic standards, and at last the time came when Michelosen no longer could recruit. By 1966 he was unemployed.

The San Francisco Forty-Niners hired him as a scout and later on made him their personnel director. Freed from the burden of living up to Jock Sutherland, he was finally able to relax and be himself. I saw him often then and enjoyed his company. Perhaps without the legacy Sutherland left him, he'd have been a better and happier coach.

Bach Is Back

In Shakespeare we learn what happens to actors. They strut and fret their hour upon the stage and then they disappear. The same thing was true of the Steelers' tailbacks. Bill Dudley's successor, Johnny Clement, had one good season, 1947, and one bad season, 1948, when he rushed for only 261 yards, and his hour came to an end. In 1949 the tailback was Joe Geri, a rookie from the University of Georgia.

Georgia's recruiters had dug him up in the hard-coal region of eastern Pennsylvania, but he arrived at the Steelers' training camp with a Southern accent. He ran, he passed, he kicked extra points, and he punted. At 5 feet 10 and 180 pounds Geri was just a little guy, and the battering he took wore him down, which explains why the 1949 Steelers lost five of their last seven games.

Even so, his statistics were respectable. In the single wing, the tailback is always the star. The following year he was better still. He rushed for 704 yards. Neither Clement nor Dudley nor Whizzer White ever had gained that many yards in one season. Disconcertingly, the Steelers' won-and-lost record did not improve. It was 6-6. Now the only single-wing team in the NFL, the Steelers were spinning their wheels.

AJR could not persuade his coach, Michelosen, to modernize the offense. Then in 1951 Joe Geri's production as the primary ball carrier fell off drastically. Michelosen responded by letting the other halfback, Ray Evans, do the passing, with indifferent success. The Steelers had a third-year player named Jim Finks who held all the passing records at Tulsa University. Michelosen used him as a defensive back.

Going into the last week of the season, the Steelers were 3-7-1. "Put Finks on offense" was the cry that went up from the fans. Michelosen kept him on defense. But injuries to Geri and his backup, Chuck Ortmann, knocked them out of the season-ending game with Washington, and Finks moved over to tailback (there was nobody else who could play the position). On a snow-covered field – not the kind running backs like – he completed thirteen of the twenty passes he threw, giving the Steelers enough offense for a 20-10 win.

AJR had seen as much of the single wing as he could take. Catching up with popular demand, he sent Michelosen packing. And then in answer to no demand whatsoever, he hired as Michelosen's successor Joe Bach, the coach he had fought with and fired in 1936.

By now they were fast friends. Bach's return to the Steelers, in fact, was viewed by the press and public as an act of nepotism once removed. Bach had been coaching at St. Bonaventure, Father Dan's school, but was out of a job, there being no team to coach after Father Dan, the athletic director, took a budgetary ax to the football program. Had AJR, possibly at the request of his brother, taken pity on Bach? Did he feel that he owed him a soft place to land? That seemed to be the perception.

The reality, I think, was different. Sportswriters are trained to be skeptics. What they failed to understand was the depth of AJR's respect for Joe Bach. "That bullheaded Dutchman is the best organizer I've ever had," he was quoted as saying. Bach was a take-charge guy, and in the 1930s AJR had not been ready for that type of coach. It seemed to him that Bach was taking charge of the whole organization. They clashed over that, and went at each other with their fists. Since then, both men had matured. Bach was less officious now, less insistent on having his way, and AJR had learned to make allowances.

It was clear to him now that a coach can't be one of the boys. Certainly Jock Sutherland had never been one of the boys. But where Sutherland simply laid down the law, Bach was a rah-rah guy. At Notre Dame he had listened to Knute Rockne's impassioned half-time speeches. Returning to the Steelers, he brought with him a watered-down version of Rockne's upbeat, inspirational approach. It was something the team needed after the negativity of the Michelosen years.

More important still, Bach was a strong advocate of adopting the T-formation. One of the assistants he hired was Gus Dorais, whose name is forever associated with the forward pass, which was legalized in 1906. It was called the *forward* pass to distinguish it from the lateral pass. Until Dorais started throwing to the aforementioned Rockne when they were Notre Dame teammates in 1913, football coaches regarded the forward pass with contempt. No one had ever heard of Notre Dame, a little backwater college in northern Indiana, but then the Irish came East and beat an astonished Army team, 35-13. They did it with Rockne, a short, stocky end, catching pass after pass from Dorais, a small, light quarterback.

Coached by Jesse Harper, Notre Dame lined up in the T, football's original formation, but shifted left or right into a box formation. Other teams were junking the T for the punt, short kick, single-wing, and double-wing formations. When Rockne succeeded Harper, he continued to use the shift, but also ran some plays without shifting. Dorais was on Rockne's staff and probably used the same offense in his years as a head coach at Gonzage (1920-'24) and Detroit (1925 –'42).

Not until 1940 did the T as we came to know it appear, worked out in its modern form by the Chicago Bears' coaches under George Halas. Clark Shaughnessy, an "advisor" to Halas, took the T to Stanford that year and rode it to an undefeated season. The Bears, in the meantime, were winning the NFL championship, and coaches everywhere (except in Pittsburgh) saw the T-formation as the new magic formula.

If Dorais was of any help to Bach, it must have been minimal. He was 60 years old, or close to it, and showing his age. He hadn't coached in some time. He was window dressing for the Steelers – living history, a well-liked old-timer who could talk about football's early days with the newspapermen.

Bach put Jim Finks at quarterback in the T, but the team did not immediately adjust, losing its first four games. As Finks gained confidence, so did everybody else. The Steelers won five of their next eight; they beat the New York Giants by a 63-7 score, getting off to a good start when Lynn Chandnois returned the opening kickoff ninety-one yards for a touchdown. All told that season, Finks threw twenty touchdown passes, including nine to Elbie Nickel.

Joe Geri played very little (his position had become obsolete) and in 1953 was traded to the Chicago Cardinals. With that team, his performance was so disappointing that Charley Bidwill, the Cardinals' owner, called AJR to say that he planned on having Geri tailed by a private detective. Mr. Bidwill suspected him of involvement in some kind of betting ring. AJR said, "No, Charley, he's not a bad guy, just a drunk."

In his last couple of years with the Steelers, Geri had taken up carousing and skirt chasing. I remember an incident at training camp. Joe saw me running laps and held up a hand. I stopped, and he said, "Artie, you run like a girl." Then he corrected my form. "Swing your arms like this. Bend your knees like that." He watched me do a few more laps, giving advice. I was now his pal. Two days later he took me aside on the practice field and called my attention to a good-looking girl among the spectators. He said, "Do me a favor, kid. Go over there and ask her if she'd like to have a date with Joe Geri."

I was too much the product of my home training to oblige.

After one season with the Cardinals, Geri reformed. He went into coaching and became a born-again Christian. At Chattanooga State in Tennessee, where he was wrestling coach and assistant football coach, he enforced a strict set of rules. No smoking. No drinking, No swearing. Like the private detective Bidwill wanted to hire, he would follow suspected miscreants in his car. He would count the cigarette butts they tossed out the window. Geri lasted twenty years at Chattanooga, so he must have been pleasing his bosses.

Back to Joe Bach. The Steelers under Michelosen had been accused of leaving their game on the practice field. He worked the players at least as hard as Sutherland had. Joe Bach's attitude was: Do the drills and be done with it. Joe had mellowed since his first time around with the Steelers.

He also had developed some physical problems – diabetes, for one thing. At first, AJR was not aware of it. When he saw what the effects were, he began to have doubts. In asking Bach to return, had he made a mistake? Maybe yes, maybe no. In appointing Walt Kiesling the No. 1 assistant to Bach, he most certainly made a mistake.

Poison Gas

I never have said that Kiesling turned the coaching staff against Bach. There was no need to. If the assistant coaches looked to Kies as their leader, rather than Bach, they did so without his collusion. But Kiesling was supposed to be Bach's right-hand man. He might have shown him the loyalty a head coach is entitled to expect. He did not. Nor did anyone else.

By the time AJR re-hired him, diabetes had changed Bach in ways that were plain to see. The take-charge guy became docile and compliant. Instead of calling the tune, he deferred to Kies and the other assistants, costing him their respect. They ridiculed Joe behind his back.

Kiesling was smart and experienced. He was also inclined to disparage any football man who knew less, in his opinion, than he did, an overcrowded category with Bach at its head. In truth, Bach was losing his grip. The game, it was clear, had passed him by, and Kiesling made certain that the whole Steeler family, from the owner right down to the trainers and equipment men, got the picture.

On the practice field, Bach would watch a drill for several minutes, demonstrate or explain something, and walk away. As soon as he was out of earshot – no great distance because Joe was getting deaf – Kies would say to the players, "Don't listen to that donkey."

He poisoned the team's attitude toward Bach, and the infection went deep. During a game in Bach's second season I was standing on the sideline next to Lynn Chandnois when one of our guys made a boneheaded play. "Saint Bonaventure!" Chandnois muttered disdainfully. St. Bonaventure was where Bach had been coaching, and to Chandnois it epitomized the bush leagues.

The Steelers opened the 1953 season as dark-horse contenders, but Jim Finks was playing hurt. A knee injury hobbled him from the start, and his passing suffered. His completion rate was so poor that Bach had him splitting time with the undistinguished Bill Mackrides. Of course Finks was not the whole Steeler team. Elbie Nickel was still a top receiver – whoever put the ball up, he could catch it. Chandnois excelled as a runner and kick returner. Jack Butler intercepted nine passes, turning three of those interceptions into touchdowns. It wasn't enough. The Steelers finished the season with a 6-6 record.

And the backstabbing continued at training camp the next year. My brothers and I, who were always around the team, might have passed the word along to AJR. What we told him instead was that Pittsburgh needed a coach like Paul Brown. Actually, AJR knew what was happening all along. At one point, he advised Bach to fire Kies. Bach refused. AJR, in keeping with the hands-off policy he adhered to, did not insist. Effectively, Bach's decision meant that he himself would leave and Kies would stay.

The end came for Bach at a squad meeting. Two days earlier the Steelers had lost a pre-season game, and he was showing the film. Within minutes one of the players ... there is no other way to say this ... farted. He farted explosively. A burst of laughter interrupted Bach's spiel. Bach was hard of hearing, remember, and the outbreak of levity puzzled him. As he started to speak again, another player erupted. Then a third. And a fourth. An epidemic of flatulence swept the room.

Players and assistant coaches were laughing and screaming, bent over double in their chairs. At last Bach realized what was happening. He turned on the lights and called out in his best Knute Rockne voice, "That's it!" The hilarity, but not the odor, died away. "Grow up! You're supposed to be college men," Bach snapped, shutting off the projector. The meeting was over; giggling and babbling, the players went back to their dormitory.

Unnoticed by all, AJR had come into the room at the height of the commotion. Standing in the back, he had seen and heard everything, and he understood now that Bach had lost control of the team.

On the following Sunday, the Steelers played another pre-season game, which resulted in another defeat. The game was at Forbes Field. Walking home with some of my brothers and friends, I saw AJR as he drove across the Sixth Street Bridge. He blew his horn at us. He looked grim, and not without cause. He was on his way, we found out, to do something distasteful – fire a head coach.

Again, there is no other way to put this: Joe Bach was farted out of the league. He might still have survived the farcical aborted squad meeting except for an earlier incident. In one of the first pre-season games, a player had gone out of bounds and careened into Bach near the bench, knocking him over. Bach was not seriously hurt, but the team doctor insisted on a precautionary checkup at a hospital. Only then did AJR learn that his coach was a diabetic. Whether Bach himself had known is unclear. At any rate, the doctors told AJR that diabetes could be a mood-altering disease, giving him more of an insight into Bach's loss of assertiveness and his consequent failure to lead.

AJR made him an offer. He could stay with the team as personnel director and head scout. At the time, 1954, personnel directors were a rare new species in the NFL. The Steelers, up to then, never had seen the need for one. A personnel director's work was a part-time occupation for front-office people with other responsibilities. Assistant coaches did all the scouting, most of which took place when the colleges were holding spring practice. AJR now was prepared to put Bach in charge of the scouting operation. There was also an implied guarantee. Barring the unforeseen, Bach could remain with the Steelers for the rest of his life.

Bach said that first he must talk with his wife. AJR asked him not to. "Take the job now and tell your wife later," he said. No, Bach replied. He and his wife had promised each other years before that they would always do things together. AJR could not dissuade him. He talked with his wife and called back the next day. He said that *they* had decided he would not stay with the team.

AJR, looking for a reason, concluded that Mrs. Bach's pride must have been hurt.

Bach never coached again. It took some difficult string-pulling, but AJR got him a job that Mrs. Bach's pride allowed him to accept. Recommended by Mayor Lawrence (at AJR's urging), he went to work for the state as a labor mediator and arbitrator.

He served the state well and seemed perfectly content, but you could tell that deep down he missed football. In the late 1960s an opportunity came along. Jack Butler by then was director of the Blesto Group, and he hired his old coach as a part-time scout. The irony here was inescapable. Bach had refused an opportunity to be a director of scouts, a job that would have paid him a good salary, and now he jumped at the chance to do the same kind of work at the lowest level and for very little money. Go figure.

Bach had two important qualifications to be a scout. First, he was well organized. Second, he was well connected. A scout needs friends who are college coaches, and Bach knew more coaches than he could count.

I saw him one Saturday up in north central Pennsylvania, where Lock Haven State College is located. Lock Haven was playing one of the Negro colleges, and we were there, as I recall, because the Negro team had a kid worth looking at. It was small-time football in a small-time setting, but Bach could not have been happier.

He had some age on him. My intention was to stay in Lock Haven overnight and rest up for the trip back to Pittsburgh, but Bach put me to shame by saying that *he* intended to drive back right after the game. He was looking forward to a Steeler game the next day and to a social affair preceding it. I thought, well, if an old-timer like Joe can drive all night, so can I. And I did. Bach drove back, I drove back, and on Sunday we both watched the Steelers.

On Monday Bach attended the Curbstone Coaches luncheon at the Roosevelt Hotel. He was there to receive an award for his contributions to football. When the speeches were over and the crowd was departing, he lingered on the dais to chat with Joe Tucker, who did the play-by-play for the Steelers' radio broadcasts. Suddenly he fell to the floor.

"Joe! Joe!" Tucker cried. "Are you all right?" There was no reply. Joe Bach had died of a heart attack.

'Get a Football'

Before Bert Bell replaced him as the NFL's commissioner, Elmer Layden brushed off the upstart All-America Conference with a curt piece of advice: "Get a football." The new league founded by the *Chicago Tribune's* sports editor, Arch Ward, did get a football. Its equipment was the same as the NFL's and its rules were the same. But there was one important difference neither Layden nor his employers foresaw: the All-America Conference had no color barrier.

Not so the NFL. Although AJR never mentioned this to me, the NFL practiced de facto segregation. Since 1934, when the old established owners forced AJR to drop Ray Kemp from his team, no blacks had played in the NFL. Giving Kemp his release was painful for AJR, but after only one year as a member of the club he did not yet belong to the in-group.

The All-America Conference came into being in 1946. World War II had ended and the culture was changing. In 1947 the earth seemed to shake because the Brooklyn Dodgers signed a black man, Jackie Robinson, to a major-league baseball contract. The year before, without fanfare, the Cleveland Browns of the All-America Conference had signed two black players, Marion Motley and Bill Willis.

Quickly, an NFL team, the Los Angeles Rams, added Kenny Washington and Woody Strode to its roster. The Browns' pair and the Rams' pair were the vanguard. By the time the leagues merged, in 1950, blacks were still few but no longer a rarity in football. Coaches began to realize that a great, untapped pool of talent existed. The Steelers, under Jock Sutherland and John Michelosen, had remained one hundred percent white, but when Joe Bach took over in 1952 he announced that his players would be judged on their ability, not their race.

And the word got around. Black players were showing up at pre-season camp in Olean uninvited. Bach at first made an honest attempt to give everybody a fair tryout, but there wasn't enough time, there wasn't enough space in the dormitory. He reverted to a policy of turning the walk-ons away.

I was 17 that year, a camp functionary. What I noticed about the black guys was that they were built well, moved with more fluidity than many of the whites, and were quick. The white players would tell me, "Yeah, yeah, they look good, but they don't have the smarts."

There were coaches who talked that way, too. For some time to come, an element in football clung to the idea that blacks did not have what were called the intangibles. In 1955 the Steelers drafted Willie McClung, who was black. An assistant coach informed me that Willie would absolutely never be good enough to make it. How could he tell? By Willie's walk. Willie did not have the stride of a football player.

Plodding, shuffling, or pussyfooting into his guard position, Willie McClung held his own in three full seasons with the Steelers, two with the Browns, and two with the Lions.

From Uncle Jim came a different appraisal of blacks. I heard him say that without them no football team would again be able to win. The statement at the time seemed radical. Could he have known there would be a day when all the best running backs, all the best defensive backs, most of the good wide receivers and defensive linemen, and most of the first-round draft choices were black?

The first black player drafted by Bach – the first to make the team – was Jack Spinks, a fullback. Spinks had played college football at Alcorn State in Mississippi. He had the ideal build for a football player and he could run. When somebody asked one of the coaches about Spinks, the coach answered as follows: "He doesn't even own a suit jacket to wear on road trips." Uncle Jim stood up and took off his own jacket, saying, "Here – he can have mine if that's all he needs to make the team."

Spinks made the team, but there were whites who continued to resent him. At practice one day, he took a swing pass or screen pass and ran right over the defensive back, a white player from one of the segregated colleges in the South, shaking him up both physically and emotionally. The defensive back called Spinks a lot of racial names and threw a football at him – hard – from point-blank range. Spinks returned to the huddle without a word.

After practice, AJR, who either had witnessed the incident or heard about it, took Spinks aside and said, "Jack, the guy who threw that football at you is a good kid, but the next time anything like that happens I want you to punch him out."

Spinks had a solid career in the NFL. He ended up playing guard for the New York Giants' 1956 championship team. By the mid-1960s, blacks were becoming established in the league. We had one who dated white girls. This surprised some of the players. However, he was not ostracized.

Willie Asbury, as he was listed on our draft chart, was a running back from Kent State. When he arrived at training camp I welcomed him, using his first name, or what I thought was his first name, as we talked. Noticing that he appeared to be uncomfortable with the way our conversation was going, I asked, "Is it Willie or Bill?" Swiftly, he answered, "Bill. It's Bill," and from then on he was more at ease. "Willie," I had suddenly realized, was a stereotypical black name. Asbury led the Steelers in rushing that year – 1966.

One of the blacks on the squad in 1952 was Willie Robinson, a North Side kid who had played for the Rooney Reds and then for Lincoln University of Pennsylvania. When his days as a Rooney Red were finished he was watching them play a Mount Lebanon team sponsored by Bob Prince, the broadcaster of Pirate games. Accompanied by his Steeler coach, Jock Sutherland, AJR was in the crowd. To his surprise – to the surprise of everybody, in fact – the "cake eaters" from suburban Mount Lebanon were pushing the tough North Siders all over the field. Suddenly one of the bigger Rooney Reds took off for the dressing room. He did not return. In his place – and wearing his uniform – here came Willie Robinson.

Whether Willie turned the tide I don't remember. What I do remember is that his dash to the rescue had Jock Sutherland, The Great Stoneface, roaring with laughter.

Willie Robinson was a speedster, as sleek and finely honed as a thoroughbred race horse. He took a realistic view of his opportunity with the Steelers. "The only thing these coaches know about Lincoln," he said, referring to his alma mater, "is that he was president."

It was true that the coaches were not too high on Willie. AJR allowed his coaches to coach, but before the first pre-season game he asked Joe Bach to let Willie run back a kickoff. The game was with Green Bay, and AJR went to Gene Ronzani, a former Steeler assistant who was coaching the Packers, and told him about Willie. "He's a kid from my neighborhood," AJR explained. "He isn't going to make the team. He won't be in there after the kickoff, and I'd like to see him get his hands on the ball. Could you kick it into his area?"

"Art," said Ronzani, "it's a pre-season game. I'll do better than that. I'll make sure he gets the ball and takes it all the way for a touchdown, if that's what you want."

AJR was appalled. "No! No!" he protested. "We can't do that. We have the integrity of the game to think about." Then he noticed Ronzani's broad grin. The offer had been meant as a joke.

Ronzani did tell his kicker to get the ball to Willie instead of to Ray Mathews, the other return man. The kick went into the end zone. Willie caught the ball and started up the field. Ray Mathews was screaming at him. "Down it, Willie! Down it! Come back!" But Willie was out to the one-or two-yard line. He skidded to a stop and backpedaled. Now he was back in the end zone, and the Green Bay coverage guys were all around him. The instant a Packer laid a hand on Willie, Green Bay had an automatic safety.

In the locker room afterward, Willie said, "Well, I wrote my own ticket home." He wasn't wrong. He drifted out of football and had to live with the nickname "Wrong Way Willie" for a while.

There were truly gifted athletes in the black schools back then, and most of them were pretty good guys. With some extra coaching and seasoning, many black players who were cut before the season started could have been standout contributors. The coaches at the black schools were competent but spread too thin. They could not give the players a lot of individual attention. So when the kids from these black schools and even the smaller white schools came to the NFL they needed special tutoring. They were not going to get it for several more years.

Pragmatism

In the late 1950s Tom Gallery, sports director of the National Broadcasting Company, made a deal with the Steelers and the Baltimore Colts to televise some of each team's home games on Saturday nights. It guaranteed them more money than other teams were getting from their regional broadcasts, but Carroll Rosenbloom, the owner of the Colts, refused to accept a fifty-fifty split.

He would take nothing less than two-thirds, he insisted. The Colts, having recently won a championship, were much the more attractive team to viewers and advertisers, went his argument. A team like the Steelers, whose ragamuffin status was beginning to look permanent, had to be content with the leavings.

Ed Kiely of the front office and my brother Dan, negotiating for AJR, were steamed. In no uncertain terms they let their adversary know what they thought of his arrogance. AJR, however, reined them in. As much as he liked their spunk, he could see that if Rosenbloom did not get his way the deal might collapse. With his gambler's mentality, he had worked the numbers: one-third would be better than nothing at all and still an improvement on the fee for a regional telecast. He could afford to pay better players – a Bobby Layne, a Big Daddy Lipscomb. Pride, he used to say, can be important, "but don't cut off your nose to spite your face."

The lesson was not lost on Dan, his heir apparent. Kiely and Fran Fogarty had some decision-making power, but Dan now surpassed them in authority. No playboy, no dumbbell, Dan kept his eye on the ball. "Out of my way or a leg off" was more than just a saying with Dan.

As for Rosenbloom, when reports that he was involved in serious unsavory activities began to circulate, the NFL appointed AJR a committee of one to investigate them. He learned that the accusations were undoubtedly true, but could pin nothing down. Hearsay evidence wasn't good enough. For example, a man in Las Vegas told AJR of having burned down Rosenbloom's house. He said that Rosenbloom had hired him to do it and used the insurance money to pay off gambling debts. AJR believed the man completely, but how could he ask the NFL to convict one of its own on the unsupported word of a professional arsonist?

Meeting with Rosenbloom in a hotel room somewhere, AJR laid out the case against him. Rosenbloom, he said, promptly fell to his knees and swore on the lives of his wife and children that all of these charges were false. For AJR, that was enough. As far as he was concerned, a man who would swear on the lives of his wife and children had to be telling the truth, and he pursued the investigation no further.

"But do you know what?" he would add when Rosenbloom's affairs were just a memory. "One year later, one year after swearing on the life of his wife, he divorced her."

In time, Rosenbloom became suspiciously curious about the Rooney family's race-track business, and AJR warned his sons not to answer any questions. "That Rosenbloom," he would say. "Lots of charm. Knows how to sweet-talk. But he'd hijack a deal in a minute."

Officially, Rosenbloom's death in the surf off the coast of South Florida was an accidental drowning, but rumors persisted that "frogmen" hired by the mob had pulled him down into the water and held him there. As with the stories about his gambling, there was only the most insubstantial proof.

Chapter 19

Boyz 'n the Hood

North Side kids thought it was great sport to give wrong directions to motorists who had lost their way. "Keep going for three blocks and then turn right and when you come to the first light, turn left." By the time the driver did that, he'd be nowhere near his hoped-for destination. I remember an old radio show called "Fibber McGee and Molly'." One of Molly's signature lines after hearing a tall one from Fibber would be "'T'ain't funny, McGee." Nor was there anything funny about playing tricks on unsuspecting strangers. Small wonder people felt that North Side kids were nothing more than hoodlums.

Certainly there were high-class North Siders like Ray Utz, a distant cousin of mine who became a priest; like Larry McCabe, who got a Ph. D. and spent his adult life as a teacher; and like Mike Hayden, an Air Force general who was head of the CIA during the Bush 43 administration. On the other hand, there were also plenty of hooligans, and a lot of them ended up in the pokey.

Many North Side kids believed that the way to settle an argument was with your fists or by letting loose with a barrage of filthy language. It was not until I got to St. Vincent College that I learned the difference between vulgarity and profanity. One of my football teammates asked old Father John, a Benedictine monk from Hungary, for the loan of his car. Father John answered, "I will not loan you my car. I know what you want it for. All you American boys think about is fucking." We were shocked at the use of this forbidden (to us) power word by a pious monastic. "Well, boys," he said, taking note of our reaction, "I see you're ashamed for me. But the word I have used is merely vulgar. We should be able to express ourselves without vulgarity, yes. Now, you boys, I know, take the name of the Lord in vain. *That* is a sin. To call somebody a "fucking S.O.B." is not a sin. To say it in anger may be a sin, but the words themselves are not sinful. I have heard you boys say 'God damn you' to one another, and that is the sin of taking the Lord's name in vain."

Without a Father John to set parameters for them, North Side kids used vulgar language and profane language indiscriminately, and often it led to a hey rube. There was a fight between two of our schoolmates at St. Peter's that ended in a death. One of the grade school's best football players was involved; he went to the juvenile detention house in Morganza for all of his junior high school and high school years. Another boy who had a peripheral role in the fight was given a lesser sentence.

When my brother Tim played freshman football at North Catholic, the Morganza team was on its schedule. Tim said that the North kids expected the Morganza kids to disregard the rules against unnecessary roughness, so they decided to hit first and hit hard. From the opening kickoff to the final gun, Tim said, they punched, kicked, elbowed, and bit. Surprisingly, the reform-school players did not retaliate. Because as football players they were disorganized, grabbing and leaning instead of blocking and tackling, the game was one-sided in North's favor. "When it was over," said Tim, "we felt kind of sorry for them."

Later, the North kids learned that the Morganza players had been warned by their overseers that if they tried any rough stuff against decent Catholic kids from Pittsburgh they would pay for it. Also, the North kids found out, the work requirements at Morganza were so strict that the football team had little or no time to practice.

"All in all," Tim said, "it was a hollow victory for us."

The Rooney brothers' overseer was AJR. "Idle hands are the tools of the devil," so we were always kept busy with chores around the house – shining all of Dad's shoes, for example. Once, as a punishment, the good Brothers of Mary at North Catholic had two of our football teammates clean and shine the shoes of the marching band. Humiliated (football players feel vastly superior to band members), our friends saved face by using brown shoe polish on black shoes and by mismating the shoes – pairing a size nine with a size twelve and so on. We wouldn't have dared to try that with AJR's shoes.

At 940 North Lincoln Avenue, there was an old tin garage, a storage place for junk, in the back yard. By order of AJR, it was taken down. A permanent rubbish bin would replace it, but meanwhile, to prepare the ground for the pouring of concrete, a lot of earth had to be moved.

AJR decreed that his sons and any friends they could recruit would do the manual labor. The McCabe brothers, Richie and Jumbo; the Hart brothers, Billy and Jack; and Babe Hugo volunteered. AJR supplied us with picks, shovels, and a long steel instrument that looked like a spear, and we went to work. Before we could start, we had to carry some trash cans out of the way, and all hell broke loose.

Hordes of rats jumped out of the cans. They scurried for safety, but not as fast as we scurried ourselves. Our yells and the screeching of the rats brought Kass out of the house. She told us to forget about moving the dirt, she'd get an adult to do it. Our pride hurt, we shouted her down and started excavating. Soon we hit a tunnel, and out of it poured rats—big rats, little rats, medium-sized rats. We scattered, some of us heading for the back porch, others climbing up on the fence.

Once the rats had dispersed, Richie McCabe was the first to pick up a shovel and go back to work. He was soon followed by Jackie Hart. The rest of us followed his lead a bit later. When we got to the next tunnel and the next pack of rats came streaming out, we didn't run. We fought them, flailing at the rats with our shovels and picks. There were stones in the back yard, and we used them as heavy artillery. Digging again, we unearthed more tunnels, all full of rats. We were ready for them and won every battle. What it all added up to was more damn fun than we'd had the entire summer.

Rat hunts from then on became a part of our lives. The North Side, it seemed, was infested with rats. We would arm ourselves with clubs and broken pavement bricks and start down an alley at dusk. Someone would bring along a flashlight. In back of the big old rooming houses or the overcrowded one-family houses or the houses where the black families lived, the garbage was piled high. The bravest kid in the gang would shake the trash can; a rat would jump out and the brickbat barrage would begin.

Other rats would tumble out after the first one. The kid who shook the can was the bravest one in the gang because the hurlers of brickbats did not have perfect control. He was putting himself in harm's way. When a rat lay wounded, some kid with a club would beat it to death. Put these tough North Side kids on an uninhabited island and you'd have a re-enactment of what happened in "The Lord of the Flies" – everybody reverting to primitive savagery.

The rat hunts ended with the coming of television. AJR won our first black and white set, which had a screen about the size of a dinner plate, in a raffle. The neighborhood kids would flock to our house when their favorite shows came on – "Captain Video," studio wrestling, the Friday Night Fights. By the time the poorer families had television, everybody was mesmerized by it. We did get outdoors to play softball, touch football, and basketball.

In the softball games, AJR would do some pitching and take a turn at bat. Like Wee Willie Keeler, who said the secret of his success was to "hit 'em where they ain't," he could place a ball anywhere he wanted to. He would run to first base, but no farther. It was fun to have him actively taking part, but then pretty soon he'd be coaching us – or, rather, preaching to us on how to play the game.

When we played touch football, everybody demanded to be the quarterback or a receiver. Nobody wanted to block. The games started out as "touch" and invariably ended up with the players on defense tackling. The footballs and equipment – oversized but coveted – came from the Steelers. When we put on the helmets and pads, we meant business. We were going to hit. Actually, it was all mostly grab-ass, lean, and react, with lots of piling-on.

I am sure that sports– along with a good family life – helped to keep the Rooney kids and perhaps a few others out of trouble.

Hepburn

Whenever a new kid moved into the neighborhood, we initiated him into our gang. For this purpose, we had an old Steeler training table which we kept in the basement at 940 North Lincoln Avenue. The newcomer, shirtless, would lie on the table face down, with a few kids on both sides holding his arms and legs. By twisting his neck, he could see us heating a sharp table knife with a cigarette lighter.

As he watched, he became more and more apprehensive. He knew that something was about to happen. But what?

On another table, out of his sight, rested a piece of ice and a piece of bacon. Suddenly, when the knife was red hot, one of us would plunge it into the bacon, creating a sizzle and a smell – the smell of burning flesh? – while at the same time, somebody else would slap the piece of ice on the initiate's bare back. To the human senses, for a moment or two, extreme heat and extreme cold feel alike. The initiate would think he'd been stabbed.

At this point, everybody would laugh, ending the game.

But there was one kid, Hepburn by name, who could not quite appreciate the joke. Instead of joining in the merriment, Hepburn went berserk. He threw off the guys who had him pinioned as if they were rag dolls. No one could pacify him. He was turning the basement into a rumpus room when Aunt Alice McNulty flew down the steps. Taking immediate control, she chased us outdoors, where Hepburn, much calmer now, was made to see that we had meant him no harm.

Hepburn was 17 years old at the outbreak of the Korean War and his parents allowed him to enlist. Home on furlough, he came to our house in his Army uniform. He was toting the kind of knife used to kill people. Later in the week, the police picked him up for carrying a revolver. He told them he needed extra firepower in case his Army rifle failed him, and the cops took his word for it. We never saw Hepburn again. I hope he made it back from Korea.

To keep us off the streets of the North Side in the summer, Mom and Dad carted us off to the family cottage in the mountains near Ligonier. Defeating their purpose, we brought the streets with us.

World War II movies were popular back then, and a weapon called the flame thrower intrigued us. My brother Dan constructed a home-made flame thrower by filling an insect pump with lighter fluid and shooting the spray over a candle, which ignited it. After that he experimented with a bicycle pump, gasoline, and matches, and then with a fire extinguisher, which was close to the real thing. Whoever lighted the match was risking third-degree burns, but our contraptions usually worked. We set the woods near our cottage on fire before the protests of the neighbors forced us into tamer pursuits.

There was just one minor casualty from all this. Fooling with the lighter fluid, Tim burned a hand. I ask myself how we survived, and the only answer I can think of is divine intervention.

Doomed

In the summer of the twins' graduation from St. Peter's School a note came to AJR at the Steelers' office Downtown. It was neither handwritten nor typed, but put together with letters and words cut from newspapers and magazines and pasted on plain white paper. Unsigned, it demanded X amount of money to be delivered to a certain place at a certain time. If AJR did not comply, the note warned, his sons Pat and John were "DOOMED."

On or about the same date, the Heinz family – pickle and ketchup and baby food makers – received a similar communication. If a certain sum was not paid, its scion, young John Heinz, a future United States senator, would be done away with.

Dad and Mom took the threat seriously. They had a vivid recollection of the Lindbergh baby's kidnapping in 1934. Dad, according to Mom, put on a good front but was visibly shaken. He got in touch with the FBI. and then packed off the twins to our summer cottage in Ligonier, where they could be kept under family surveillance.

In July he sent them to the Steelers' training camp at St. Bonaventure. There were exhibition games scheduled that year in Shreveport, Louisiana, and Des Moines, Iowa. Dad took the twins along on the train rides with two of the older camp kids, Jack Hart and Richie McCabe, assigned to watch over them. Coaches, players, trainers, equipment men, and even the newspaper reporters helped out.

This was the summer an anonymous letter writer threatened *to* shoot the great Pirate home-run hitter, Ralph Kiner. As AJR's guest at Forbes Field for another pre-season game, he sat on the Steelers' bench, not far from the twins. "My God, look at that!" someone said "All three of them together! Perfect targets for a sniper!" Perfect targets to be sure, but the day went by without gunfire.

In the fall the twins enrolled at North Catholic. Rooney males all played football and they went out for the freshman team. Attempting to be inconspicuous about it, two plainclothesmen from the city police department shadowed them all day at school and looked on from the sidelines at football practice. Because the twins, wearing helmets and pads and dirty gray uniforms, were hard to distinguish from their teammates, some confusion arose. Another problem was that Tim and I practiced with the varsity squad, which used the same field, and there were times when the gumshoes seemed to be watching the wrong set of brothers.

Furthermore, they attracted suspicion. Here were these two big strangers who never missed football practice, rain or shine. Were they the would-be kidnappers, waiting for their chance? That was one school of thought. Another had them sized up as perverts.

The football coaches, until I explained what was going on, leaned toward the opinion that they were scouts for a rival team. To aggravate matters, one twin, John, lost interest in football and quit. You had to love the game to practice on Gardner Field, which was just oil-coated dirt under ordinary conditions and a slithery quagmire when it rained. And there were the smells – the disagreeable mix of odors from the rendering plants, the Heinz pickle factory, and an old abandoned brewery at the foot of North Catholic's perch on Troy Hill. So John turned in his equipment, and now with the twins split up for a part of each day, the bodyguards' work was twice as difficult.

The twins went to school and back home again on the jam-packed trolleys that served North Catholic, changing cars at the North Side Market hub, and the bodyguards would lose them in the crush. At a meeting with AJR and their boss, they complained that the job was too much for them. One even argued that if they themselves couldn't keep up with John and Pat, there was no chance the kidnappers could do it. In the end, the four parties worked out a compromise: the cops would continue to monitor the twins, but not as closely or obtrusively as before.

A month or two after the meeting, the FBI cracked the case. Its agents arranged a "sting" in West Park – a drop-off of the ransom money in the muzzle of the Civil War cannon near the statue of a soldier. An FBI agent and a Pittsburgh policeman hid out in the park on the appointed day and kept watch. Other agents and cops, men and women, blended into the normal flow of West Park pedestrian traffic. One pair was pushing a baby carriage (with no baby in it). Another couple sat on a bench and romanced – sweethearts lost to the world. An FBI man with a brush and trash can picked up litter. Two retired cops posed as an elderly couple out for a stroll.

The minutes went by and nothing happened. People came and went, making their usual daily rounds. The cops waited and watched, eyes fixed on the cannon. They saw two young girls approach it and stop. The agent in charge was exasperated. Why didn't they move on? If there was action, they'd be in the middle of it. Still the girls lingered, earnestly conversing.

"Damn! Someone get them away from the cannon!" the agent muttered. But now what was this? One girl walked up to the cannon and reached an arm into the muzzle. She pulled out the bait – a package that may or may not have contained money. And the FBI had the culprits. One girl was 12 and the other 13.

They were taken into custody and given psychological testing. They said the idea for sending threats to two prominent families came to them from something they had read. The older of the two was confined to a mental hospital for a period of time and then released. Neither the Rooney family nor the Heinz family ever knew what eventually became of her. The other girl's fate has also remained a mystery. To Mom and Dad, none of this mattered. All they wanted to do was forget the whole bothersome affair.

Man of Iron

My coach at North Catholic, Chuck Mehelich, was a taskmaster – after all, he had played for Jock Sutherland when Sutherland coached the Steelers. Mehelich was as tough as they come. In a game between the Steelers and Detroit, I saw him go down the field on kickoff coverage and put a thunderous hit on Leon Hart, who went from Turtle Creek to Notre Dame and won the Heisman Trophy. Considered the prototypical tight end, even though he also played defense, he was six inches taller and seventy-five pounds heavier than Mehelich, but a stretcher was needed to get him off the field. I intend to discuss this seismic event in fuller detail later on.

In addition to being tough, Mehelich was also inclined to be testy. The Steelers' center, Frank Sinkovitz, who also played linebacker, liked to encourage his teammates by patting them on the rump, which irritated Mehelich. During one game he warned Sinkovitz. "Don't do that to me again." A couple of plays later, Sinkovitz did it again. "Stop!" Mehelich growled. Still later, Sinkovitz patted him a third time. Wasting no more words, Mehelich uncorked a right-hand uppercut that missed contact with Sinkovitz's face mask – I don't know how – but not with his jaw. Sinkovitz played no more football that day.

Mehelich played so hard that by the end of his sixth season he was physically beaten down. The head coaching job at North Catholic was open, and AJR went to bat for him. No other endorsement was necessary. But lacking experience or the foresight to prepare himself – it would have been better if he had served an apprenticeship somewhere – Mehelich wasn't ready to coach.

There were times when he forgot that he was dealing with high school kids. Demonstrating some of the basics of defensive line play, he knocked our little nose guard, Jack Embersits, unconscious. (There were no lasting ill effects. After North Catholic, Embersits attended Yale, captained its 1952 football team, and returned as a graduate to be vice president for management operations and an officer of the Yale Corporation.)

Mehelich overdid the theatrics, I thought. Between halves of a game we were losing he called us quitters. At the climactic moment of his rant, worked up into a frenzy, he drove his fist through the blackboard in the locker room.

Sometimes in practice he scrimmaged with us, and one day, to our consternation, a third-string defensive end who liked to hit as well as Mehelich did, but had no other qualifications for the game, turned the tables on him. He blindsided Mehelich, knocking him head over heels.

Prizefighters will tell you it's the punch you didn't see that knocks you out. So blindsiding, I guess, doesn't count. The guy who really cut Mehelich down to size was not the blindsider, but our center, Larry Deer. Many years later he recalled his greatest day as a football player.

"It was near the end of the season," he said. "We were going through a tackling drill down on one corner of the field. The tackling dummy had two legs on it, simulating a runner, and must have weighed close to seventy pounds. Chuck liked to stand behind the dummy with his arms wrapped around it, and the tackler would get a ten-yard running start. At the moment of impact, Chuck would throw the dummy into him. On this particular day, as we were lining up to take turns, a red film seemed to cover my eyes. All the bullshit of that year gripped me in an uncontrollable rage. Going in low on the dummy, I hit it like a runaway freight train and put Chuck down on his ass."

Deer remembered that Mehelich got up, patted him on the back, and said, "Nice hit." There were two other things Deer remembered: the agonizing pain in his shoulder and a feeling of immense gratification.

If Mehelich lost status as a result of Larry's hit, my brother Tim unwittingly put him back on his pedestal. Mehelich gave a class in physical education, and Tim saw to it one day that several carpet tacks were placed on his chair. When Mehelich entered the room and prepared to sit, there was great anticipation. Suspecting nothing, he plopped himself down in such a way that penetration by the tacks was unavoidable. The tacks could not have failed to do their work.

Amazingly, though, Mehelich gave no sign of discomfort. He didn't jump. He didn't cry out. He didn't wince. He didn't change his expression.

From then on the students called him Iron Ass. They were totally and irreversibly in awe.

Baldy Regan

North Catholic High School, at the top of Troy Hill, was a streetcar ride from the part of the North Side where I lived. All the kids I knew, and many I did not know, boarded that trolley every morning, and one of the kids I did not know always sat next to me. He was cheerful, gabby, and undersized, and it got so I looked forward to seeing him. On the way up he would borrow his carfare from me – ten cents – never failing to repay it after lunch. Had he borrowed a dime in the meanwhile from somebody else? I never asked.

Nor did I ask him to tell me his name. This was at the start of our freshman year, and a lot of us were strangers to one another. Almost from the first day, though, everybody seemed to know my seat companion, and vice versa.

When the call went out for freshman football, we reported for practice at Gardner Field. I looked around on the first day and saw the kid who always borrowed a dime. He was there on the second day, too. The coaches never bothered to cut the squad. Three days of conditioning drills – calisthenics and wind sprints – took care of that. A lot of self-proclaimed tough guys quit of their own accord. My little friend, though, kept returning. When we ran the wind sprints, I noticed, he limped. It appeared to be a struggle for him, but he never dropped out.

On the fourth day, we were issued our hand-me-down uniforms and my friend was among the survivors. He had made the team. But then one night as we were riding home on the streetcar he told me that instead of playing he was going to be the student manager. The coaches, he said, had suggested it. He'd had polio, it seems, which accounted for the limp. No doubt for reasons having to do with liability insurance, a history of polio disqualified a kid from any contact sport.

We continued to ride the streetcar together. Meanwhile, I'd been hearing a lot of talk about a freshman called Baldy Regan. It was Baldy this and Baldy that. Baldy said this and Baldy did the other thing. Was there a kid in our class who was losing his hair? Nobody fit the description. I was too vain to ask questions. It would make me look like a know-nothing, I thought, but my curiosity got the better of my conceit. I put the question to a friend:

"Who is this Baldy Regan?"

He stared at me without answering. I asked him again. "Who is this Baldy Regan, anyway?"

"Are you kidding?" he said

"No! There isn't a bald-headed kid in the whole school. How would I know who Baldy Regan is?" My friend was still looking at me as if I had a screw loose. He said, "You sit with him every morning on the streetcar."

I was flabbergasted.

The mystery cleared up, I waited a few days, and then asked Baldy about the origin of his nickname. When he was in grade school, he said, his mother, to save money on haircuts, had made him tell the barber to shave his head.

So he was Baldy for the rest of his life, never Bernard (the name his parents gave him), and he always had hair, although his forehead receded as he aged. He did not remain small and thin.

As a North Catholic upperclassman, he was big enough to play on the baseball and basketball teams. Baseball and basketball players were allowed to have gimpy legs. What counted was ability, and he could throw and hit a baseball so well that he played with grown men in a twilight league. In basketball, he was good enough to make the first team.

He never gave up his job as the football team's manager, running and fetching for the coaches until graduation. He could get things and he could get things done. He was well-liked and smart and he passed all his courses, with help from a sympathetic teacher or two. Academics did not seem to interest him. He kept his grades just high enough to be eligible for baseball, basketball, and extracurricular activities.

Baldy's substitute for an older big brother was Mike Kearns, another North Side kid who lived on the edge of poverty and excelled at sports. Mike played football at North Catholic, and Baldy never missed a home game. Smuggled onto the team bus in the duffel bag Mike used for his pads, helmet, and uniform, Baldy saw some road games as well. The success of this arrangement depended on Baldy's small size. In later life, he added to his dimensions both lengthwise (to about 5 feet 10) and breadth- wise (in his fifties he must have weighed about 220 pounds).

Mike Kearns had been the end man, and therefore the star, of the minstrel shows at North Catholic. Minstrel shows in that long-ago time were still not seen as racist. To be the end man brought status and prestige. To be the end man and also a top athlete, as Mike was, made you the cock of the walk. Baldy, in a sense, outdid even Mike. In his senior year, he was the end man, the best baseball player, a good enough basketball player, and class president. His sports and theatrical achievements Baldy took in stride; being elected class president overwhelmed him. "Wow!" he exclaimed when the ballots had been counted. "Only in America!"

It was the first time I ever had heard him say that, but "Only in America" became his mantra, repeated on many occasions as a sort of all-purpose observation.

At the graduation ceremony each year, the tradition was for the senior class president to address the assembled students, teachers, administrators, and parents. Uncertain whether Baldy could handle such an assignment, a member of the faculty offered to pick a surrogate speaker. It would be Baldy's decision. If he did not feel up to making a speech, the teacher would ask someone else. Baldy wanted to know what I thought about that. No doubt he asked others as well. I told him I thought the faculty guy's suggestion was out of line. I said he had done a good job as president. He'd been in charge of the senior prom, which had gone off without a hitch. He'd been the end man in the minstrel show. Reciting lines in a stage production was just like giving a speech. "You can do it, Baldy," I said.

Baldy did it. His performance was smooth and free of gaffes and went over big with the audience.

When Baldy and I were seniors we made a trip to Shamrock Farm with AJR and my brother Tim. It was late in winter, when the hills and the fields were brown and the trees stripped of leaves, and there would be nothing much to do, but I could sense Baldy's excitement. He'd be the guest of Mr. Rooney, the owner of the Pittsburgh Steelers, and that was sufficient. As for AJR, he'd be taking Baldy's measure while giving no indication of it – not by so much as a word, a blink, a change of expression. That was his way with everybody he met. He'd be watching every move of this hot-shot kid he heard us talking up, and before the weekend was over he would know something important about him.

Baldy got the usual tour. We looked at the horses, and that was it. When we were back from the barns we watched television. AJR was the boss and decided what programs we could see. If he was talking on the telephone, the farmer and his wife, the caretakers of the place, controlled the set.

So that Baldy would not think we had brought him all the way from Pittsburgh to watch kiddy TV shows with the farmer's children or cooking shows with the farmer's wife, Tim and I suggested a walk. There were interesting things in the barns that we hadn't inspected – old tractors, a box of dynamite.

I don't remember what the dynamite was for, but we merely looked at it, removing and replacing the lid of the box with great care.

We took a second look at the horses. The colts and the stallions could be temperamental, so we gave them a wide berth, and almost all of the mares were in foal, or already had one. To my regret, it was not the breeding season. Watching the mares and the stallions get it on would have been an unforgettable experience for Baldy. We were left with nothing to hold our attention for long but an ancient lead pony from the race track. It belonged to one of Dad's trainers, who was boarding it at the farm.

All lead ponies were called Bill, or Billy. This one was in his stall, peacefully munching hay. We stood watching for a minute, and Baldy then asked if we could take the nag for a ride. I knew that Billy was at the farm for rest; I thought he might be injured or sick; so I said there probably weren't any saddles around, but Tim blurted out that he had seen one in a room near the stalls.

When we approached old Bill with the saddle and the reins, he gave us a sidelong look, showing the whites of his eyes. This was not a good sign, I had heard. He began to stamp his feet. Another bad sign. I could see that old Billy was nervous. He had been around horsemen all his life – people who knew what they were doing. And he was sure we were not that kind. Tim and I had taken riding lessons. We had ridden old nags on all the dirt roads of the Ligonier Valley. We had learned how to saddle up and how to put on a halter and reins. We could tell the front end of a horse from the rear, but that just about summed it up.

Old Bill made an effort to stay in the barn. He dug his hoofs into the ground, refusing to be led. Tim and I pulled at the reins. Baldy got in back and started to push. "Get away from there," we yelled at him. "Those horses can kick." Baldy just laughed. He was feeling giddy. All three of us were.

I was bigger and older than the others, so I said I would ride Billy first. It took me three tries, with Tim holding the reins at Billy's mouth, to get my foot in the stirrup. Billy then started to prance. I was hopping around on one foot, while Baldy and Tim laughed their heads off, before I could finally make it onto the horse's back.

Keeping a tight rein on Billy, which he fought, I galloped him up and down the road and across the meadow. I was never really able to hold him in check, but I didn't fall off (my football conditioning may have helped). When I returned, Tim and Baldy gave me a cheer. "Piece of cake," I said. "Nothing to it."

Now it was Tim's turn. Tim had the same trouble in mounting that I did, but, taking Billy up and down the road and across the meadow, he looked much better in the saddle. Maybe Billy was tiring or getting used to us and would not be too difficult for Baldy, who never had been on a horse in his life.

His approach, to say the least, was original. To avoid being dragged around the paddock with one foot in a stirrup and the other on the ground, as Tim and I had been, he got up on the paddock fence and declared he would mount from there. If we could bring the horse close enough, he would jump right onto the saddle,

We told him he was crazy. "You'll get hurt."

"No I won't. Bring him over here. I'll show you."

Baldy was as fearless as a rodeo rider. He made the leap onto Billy's back, somehow got hold of the reins, and jammed his feet into the stirrups. Then he was off. Heading out over the meadow, Billy never ran so fast. Baldy had on a white knit stocking cap, and soon it was all we could see of him, the cap bobbing up and down as Billy traversed hill and dale. We could hear Baldy's cries of either terror or elation.

Then they stopped. At the same time, we lost sight of the white knit cap. Had there been a spill? Had Baldy been thrown?

He was gone a long time. When he reappeared, it was not from the same direction in which he had started. We heard Baldy's cries before we saw him. Billy was still galloping. Baldy was still bobbing up and down, perpendicular one moment – sitting straight up – and horizontal the next – parallel from head to waist with the horse's neck. He did not have command. And yet, in a strange way, he did.

AJR, the farmer, the farmer's wife, and their kids were now on the back porch of the farm house, spellbound. Clotheslines were stretched across the farmer's back yard, and Billy headed for them. Baldy now demonstrated his athleticism. Just before reaching each clothesline, he ducked his head, bending over as far as he could. He had to do this three times. Next, Billy ran straight at the stone wall surrounding a little ice house. None of us were laughing, yelling, or cheering – not Tim, not me, not Dad, not the farmer and his wife, and not their kids. Billy dashed up to the wall and all of a sudden put on the brakes. He came to a dead stop – and Baldy did not pitch forward into the wall. A moment later he was off Bill's back and onto his own two feet.

"Wow! Only in America!" he shouted.

The farmer had Billy by the reins. "This horse ain't been ridden all winter," he said. "All of yez are lucky ya didn't get kilt."

On the way back to Pittsburgh we stopped at the Catholic church for a visit and at a hotel in Frederick, the nearest big town, for dinner. The hotel was old and elegant. College girls waited on tables. Our girl brought each of us a finger bowl filled with warm water, a slice of lemon floating at the top. While AJR asked her his usual question – "Where are you from?" – Tim and I, without being obvious about it, watched Baldy. He looked at his finger bowl and then did exactly what we thought he would do. He picked up a spoon and took a sip of the water.

When we were able to stop laughing we explained that the water was not for drinking. "Wise guys," he muttered, forgoing his customary "Only in America."

AJR had been watching Baldy from a different perspective than ours. "He's a fine guy," Dad said to us later. "Good little athlete. President of his class, isn't he?"

I said, "Yes, but he's real poor and there aren't any athletic scholarships for kids as small as he is."

Dad said, "Maybe something can be done."

He knew a Polish politician connected with Alliance College in Cambridge Springs, where the Steelers had gone for pre-season practice in the 1940s. The politician awarded a scholarship to Alliance every year. "I have a great kid," AJR told him, citing Baldy's qualifications, "but he's Irish, not Polish."

"Don't worry about it. He's in," the politician said.

Thus did our short trip to the farm pay off for Baldy in triplicate. He rode a horse for the first time. He learned about finger bowls. And now he'd be going to college.

He lasted just two semesters at Alliance, an extracurricular success, as always, but a failure in the classroom. He was into all kinds of activities and made a name for himself as the star of a one-man comedy hour on Alliance's campus radio station. He represented the college in a Golden Gloves boxing tournament in Erie and did all right. When a Polish jet pilot defected, stealing his fighter plane, and flying over the Steel Curtain to the West, the Cold War hero accepted an invitation to visit Alliance and spent more time with Baldy, it seemed, than with anybody else. Only in America. They shot enough pool at the student union to remind everybody of Fast Eddie Felson and Minnesota Fats, Baldy teaching the pilot English words and the pilot improving Baldy's Polish. In short, Baldy replicated his North Catholic High school career. It was a shame that he had to go to class.

He sold shoes for a while, and athletic equipment, and then through political influence (the district attorney, Ed Boyle, went to bat for him) he landed a patronage job as a county detective. Emerging from a take-out place in the Hill district with a box of fried chicken one day, he encountered three black men.

"Hand over that chicken," said the one in the middle.

"Brother," replied Baldy, "why should I do that?"

"Three reasons," the guy said, indicating himself and his two sidekicks. "Me, him, and him."

Baldy pulled out his service revolver, which he wore tucked into his waistband. He said, "Well, here are six reasons you can't make me give you that chicken."

The would-be poultry thief looked at the gun and shook his head. "Man," he conceded, "six beats three every time."

By the late 1970s, Baldy was a justice of the peace. During the week before Christmas every year, in his courtroom on the North Side, he gave a party that lasted from early afternoon into the evening hours. Judges, magistrates, lawyers, and doctors, City Council members, state legislators, captains of industry, newspaper reporters, and television personalities, Catholic priests and Protestant ministers, bank presidents, police inspectors, saloon keepers, high school teachers and college professors, working men and office girls, taxi drivers and jitney drivers came. Steeler football players came. Baldy, who never drank, remained sober. Once he performed a wedding, putting on his Benjamin Franklin glasses to read from the Bible. Always, he would break out the champagne (Chateau Luzerne), serving it in tall plastic cups from the Iron City brewery. The Santa Claus in full regalia would be David Barnett. "Wait a minute," he objected when Baldy first nominated him for the role. "I'm not the type." David Barnett was black. "Don't worry about the color scheme," said Baldy, settling the issue.

In the 1980s, his friends on City Council urged him to run for an open slot. He was elected, but not re-elected. His great popularity had peaked. Baldy, however, could be satisfied looking on from the sidelines. There was the time during his years as a magistrate when the lord mayor of Dublin came to Pittsburgh. Behind a police escort on motorcycles, he arrived at City Hall, where a big crowd had gathered to welcome him. Baldy, of course, was there. He turned to Jack Lynch, the county controller, and said, "Isn't it wonderful how everybody loves the Irish?"

"Baldy," said Lynch, "you know the lord mayor is Jewish, don't you?"

"Jewish? The lord mayor of Dublin?"

"That's correct."

For a minute Baldy was speechless. Then he smiled and said, "Only in America."

Chapter 20

The Survivor

In their first two decades the Steelers had some very good players, some moderately good players, and some fair players, but nothing to back them up. AJR, minimizing the importance of reserve strength, did not like to pay a lot for guys who sat on the bench. It requires supernatural luck to get through a season without injuries, and when the regulars are hurt the guys on the bench take their place.

There was no such thing as a taxi squad to draw from. The Steelers would start the season with thirty-three players and end it with twenty-six, twenty-seven, or twenty-eight. Guys who were playing both ways would be covering kicks. After all, reasoned AJR, that is what they were hired to do – play. If some of them got "nicked," so be it. Welcome to the ranks of the walking wounded.

Remarkably, when I came across these players twenty or thirty or forty years later, they all expressed affection for AJR, the Steelers, and the NFL. I think they put more into football than they ever took out of it, but that was not their attitude at all.

My opinion is that with better substitutes and some sort of taxi squad the Steelers of the '30s and '40s might have had more seven-win seasons and fewer three-win or two-win seasons. However, AJR's goal was survival, and he knew how to achieve it.

Other owners who had big ideas about winning and selling out their stadiums came and went. AJR, the Maras, and the Bidwills outlasted them all. They were proof that strong, dedicated individual owners could succeed where corporations and unwieldy partnerships fail. Only death released the hold of George Preston Marshall on the Washington Redskins. Tim Mara, Charley Bidwill, George Halas, and AJR established dynasties.

All of these founders had a passion for the game. They were pioneers with the vision to see what professional football might become and with the good sense to put restraints on free enterprise. By instituting the draft of college players, which gave the small-market teams equal access to this renewable source of talent and ready-made stars, and by consenting to an equal division of the television money that began to pour in after the mid-1950s – by, in other words, sharing the wealth – they increased it for one and all, the haves and the have-nots alike.

To survive, to make it through the lean years, AJR paid a price. The football fans in his own home town were not shy about blaming him for the Steelers' inability to win championships, or in most seasons even to challenge for one. In the public perception, he was cheap and he was dumb. Frugal he may have been – he had to be. He was anything but dumb. The Steelers of the 1930s were Depression babies. With smoke and mirrors, he weathered the hard times and then the manpower shortage of World War II.

The closest he came to bailing out was in 1940, when he sold the team to Alexis Thompson for $160,000 and engineered a deal whereby he still owned a third of it while Thompson ended up with the Philadelphia Eagles. As I have written, the transaction involved a switch of franchises between Thompson and the Eagles' owner, Bert Bell, and the need for AJR to share a certain amount of decision-making power with Bell and Barney McGinley. Five years later, when Bell replaced Elmer Layden as NFL commissioner, AJR had the resources to acquire most of Bell's stock and become majority owner once again.

Out of necessity he played it close to the vest. As generous as he was with the Church and with people down on their luck, he did not throw money around, the way Uncle Jim would have done, although there were times ...

Jamestown, New York, boasted a famous furniture maker patronized only by the rich. Condescendingly, this man escorted Kass, AJR, and Aunt Alice on a tour of his factory. "No point in your even looking at the dining-room pieces," he said. "They would be far too expensive for you. President Eisenhower has a complete set at his farm in Gettysburg, the gift of a wealthy admirer. But, as I say, there's no point in showing it to you."

"Let's look at it anyway," suggested AJR.

With his nose in the air, the man led these plebeians from Pittsburgh to the dining-room section. The set like the one that went to the Eisenhower farm was French Provincial – a table that seated eighteen or twenty people, twelve matching chairs elegantly upholstered in blue damask fabric, a mammoth breakfront for crystal, a long serving table, a pair of girondeles (lightly-carved "leaves" that stood two feet high) and a small buffet. The wood was an unusual blending of gray and brown. Kass could only agree that the pieces were dazzling. She gazed at the set lovingly and then turned to leave. But AJR, with a few words to their guide, stopped her in her tracks.

"We'll take it," he said.

Kay, my wife, called it the most beautiful set she ever saw. Dinner at 940 North Lincoln Avenue, with Kass's crystal glasses and figurines on the breakfront, her sterling silver tea set on the serving table, and a crystal chandelier fit for royalty over our heads, was from then on a special event.

Accidentally on Purpose

As far as his sons were concerned, AJR was a "sportsman" – the man who owned the Steelers, the man who promoted boxing matches, the man who owned the Shamrock breeding farm in Maryland and raced horses. We never thought of him as a gambler.

Oh, we knew that he made money by betting on horses. Otherwise, we'd have had to be blind and deaf. All I'm saying is that we disconnected ourselves from this part of his life. The Rooneys of North Lincoln Avenue were "pro football people." Both Mom and Dad encouraged us to think of ourselves that way. Either accidentally or "accidentally on purpose," as Mom would say, they shielded us from the gambling aspects of AJR's profession. Football was what the Rooneys were about. It monopolized our attention. Whether the Steelers won or lost was vitally important to us. The boxing matches at Hickey Park, Forbes Field, and the old Duquesne Gardens were not. The horses – the horses and the farm – existed in our minds as trappings, as accessories. They were things that belonged to us because AJR was a sportsman and had nothing at all to do with gambling.

We saw the horses on the farm; while we were kids, we never saw them race. Horse racing in Pennsylvania was illegal. The nearest track – Waterford Downs – was in West Virginia. Sometimes Dad raced his horses there. More often, he took them to places like Pimlico, Laurel, Bowie, or Aqueduct – hundreds of miles away. The Steelers were here in Pittsburgh, under our noses. We saw them play. We read about their games in the Pittsburgh newspapers. Every Monday there were stories and pictures. There were stories during the week. The papers' horse-racing coverage was limited. Pittsburgh reporters might go to the Kentucky Derby or the Preakness or the Belmont, but AJR's horses never raced in those events. To read about a Shamrock Farm horse you waded through the long, gray columns of agate type that appeared in a far corner of the sports section every day, captioned "Race Entries" and "Race Results."

When we were old enough to go to the track – you had to be over 16 – we made infrequent visits with AJR, and our interest was faintly stirred. We asked questions like "When are you going to get a top stakes horse?" John Galbreath, the owner of the Pirates, seemed not to have any other kind. In the 1960s two of his horses, Chateaugay and Proud Clarion, won the Kentucky Derby. Roberto, named for Roberto Clemente, the Hall-of-Fame Pirate outfielder, won the equally prestigious English Derby. AJR's best horse was Little Harp, named for a sandlot football player from the First Ward.

"Listen," he would tell us, "Little Harp has won more money than all of those fancy horses put together." We were not yet sophisticated enough to understand what he meant. Tim may have been, but not me. I knew that John Galbreath's horses raced for big purses. I knew that Little Harp raced for extremely modest purses. So how could this be?

Later on, it came to me. It wasn't the purses Little Harp won, but the bets Dad made on him that paid for a lot of our amenities.

I was slowly learning to add two and two.

New Digs

From the mid 1950s until Three Rivers Stadium went up on the North Side in 1970 the Steelers had their offices in the Roosevelt Hotel.

In some ways it resembled the Fort Pitt Hotel, where the Rooney-McGinley Boxing Club had shared the football team's headquarters. Both the Roosevelt and Fort Pitt were piles of red brick, undistinguished as architecture. The Fort Pitt, the older of the two, was a "railroad hotel," located near the Pennsylvania Station at the northeast corner of the Golden Triangle. It went back to the days before the Wright brothers lifted off at Kitty Hawk – back to the days when people dismissed the automobile as a plaything. There were marble floors and overstuffed chairs in the lobby, a coffee shop, and two attractive dining rooms. The boom in rail transportation during World War II extended the Fort Pitt's life span, but decline had already set in. When AJR moved to the Roosevelt, the Fort Pitt was a fleabag, long overdue for the wrecking ball.

There had been a partial move to the Union Trust Building on Grant Street some time earlier. In 1946, with the hiring of Jock Sutherland, AJR felt that changes must follow. He knew that his new head coach, a man of austere bearing, would be grotesquely out of place in the digs at the Fort Pitt among the fight managers, horse players, flunkies, and hangers-on who walked in and out through windows a step above the pavement – windows that were eight feet high. So with encouragement from Sutherland he split the football and boxing ends of the business, renting rooms for himself and the coaches in the tastefully ornate Union Trust.

His own private office was at ground-floor level, unobtrusively tucked away behind the ticket office. A meeting room and Sutherland's office, which he shared with his assistant coaches, were eight stories higher, inaccessible by design to the low-life element that frequented the Fort Pitt. But AJR's more respectable friends – among them Pie Traynor, the Hall-of-Fame Pirate third baseman now launched on a second career, sportscasting – also stopped coming around. Meeting Traynor on the street one day, AJR let him know that he was missed.

He said, "Where have you been, Pie? We never see you any more."

Traynor's answer became a staple for collectors of Steeler folklore. "You're too high up over there," he said. "I'm afraid I'll forget I'm not at the Fort Pitt and step out the window."

After Sutherland's death in 1948, AJR stayed on at the Union Trust for another four years. At the end of that time the boxing club turned up its toes. Free fights on television had destroyed boxing's customer base, and Uncle Jack McGinley, the club's promoter, matchmaker, treasurer, bookkeeper, and publicity man, was making a nice income with his partner Fritz Wilson in their Miller Beer distributorship. Accordingly, with no further reason to keep two offices open, AJR said goodbye to the Fort Pitt and skipped across town to the Roosevelt, on Liberty Avenue.

The Roosevelt, like the Fort Pitt, had seen better days but was ideally situated near the restaurant and theater district a few minutes' walk from the Sixth Street Bridge, the span that connected downtown Pittsburgh with the old First Ward. Among the glories of the Roosevelt was the Sylvan Room, moderately famous for its roast ribs of beef. The bellhops tended to be wise guys but could make themselves useful if properly tipped. Bag carriers like Wally, a personage of sorts in his tiny domain, were human surveillance cameras. They knew all the dirt about big shots and nobodies alike – knew all and told all. AJR inflated the bellhops' self-esteem by remembering their names. Quite often he remembered the names of their wives and children. If they needed help to get a relative into a nursing home, a hospital, or any other kind of institution, AJR was their man.

As they did at the Fort Pitt, the Steelers had offices with an entrance off the lobby. The Roosevelt's lobby and the Fort Pitt's lobby came from the same mold. They were big, dark, and high-ceilinged. AJR's private office in the Roosevelt was a windowless room with two adjoining desks, one for himself and one for Fran Fogarty. Neither desk lacked for telephones. AJR had three and Fogarty two, plus an adding machine.

Inconveniently, the command center Dad occupied was right next door to the men's room, and it was not uncommon for guests of the hotel to walk in unzipping their flies. The moment could be embarrassing for everybody concerned if AJR was talking business with a visitor he wanted to impress or with a newly-drafted football player from a large and prestigious university. Showing his best face (as he used to say), AJR would smile and make an effort to put such intruders at ease. Fogarty, when he was present, played bad cop to AJR's good cop. "Next door!" he would bellow. "Next door!"

Lunch in the Sylvan Room was always a prolonged affair. AJR, of course, would know the names of the waitresses, where they had gone to school, and what church they attended. The waitresses were apt to be from Irish or Italian Catholic parishes, but he quizzed the few Protestants among them with the same fatherly solicitude. Dragging in the name of someone's minister, he would show off his aptitude for finding a connection: "Played baseball against that fellow before he went to the seminary."

The waitresses were mostly middle-aged. AJR was "Mister Rooney" to them, a mark of unusual respect. The rest of us they addressed by our first names. If a waitress whose name was Peggy knew the customer well, she rarely bothered to take his order. "Fran," she would say to Fogarty, setting a plate of food down in front of him, "this is our special today. I know you'll like it." Or, conversely, "Fran, our special don't look too good today, so I brought you this." Like it or not, you ate it. If there were no empty tables, Peggy might seat you with a stranger. "This here's Mister Smith – he's one of our regulars," she would say.

For an evening news feature on KDKA, the television personality Marie Torre posed as a Sylvan Room waitress one day with a cameraman shooting unnoticed from a sort of shelf, or platform, high up on the wall at the far end of the room. A tall, big-boned woman, striking in appearance, she attempted to disguise herself with the aid of a hairdresser and makeup artist. The point of all this, a promotional stunt for KDKA, was to see how many people would recognize her.

I came to lunch that day with AJR, and as slow as I am on the uptake I immediately spotted the cameraman. We sat with Bill Burns, the KDKA news anchor, and he gave me the high sign: *Don't tip off your father.* To AJR, the name and renown of Marie Torre meant nothing, I am sure. Characteristically, he treated her with matter-of-fact politeness, as though she were Peggy or any other waitress. After twenty minutes or so, Burns and I spilled the beans – we let Dad in on Miss Torre's true identity. Without missing a beat, he called her to the table and said, "I have to tell you something – you could make your living at this, you're so good."

Unaccountably, I didn't notice whether AJR left a tip.

Bill Burns was about 6-1 or 6-2, a good-looking black-haired guy with a little wayward curl that fell down over his forehead. Women of all ages doted on him and men were not resentful, a tribute to his masculinity. Wounded in combat during World War II, he wore a brace on one leg and walked with a limp.

It was interesting to have lunch with Burns. One day a well-groomed matron came to our table, leaned over swiftly, and kissed him on the cheek. Then she apologized. Burns maintained his considerable aplomb. I expressed surprise at what had happened, and he said, "Oh, that was nothing." He told me that a woman came up behind him one time and started pulling at his hair with both hands. When he managed to get disentangled, the woman said to him, "I could have sworn you were wearing a wig."

Burns never joined us before 1 p.m. Two hours later he would still be drinking coffee with AJR and whoever else might have lingered – Jack Butler; my brother Tim, who worked in a nearby brokerage house; extroverted Mossie Murphy, assistant to Alex DiCroce, the man in charge of the restaurant. And many more. There were usually two tables – AJR's and another for late-comers. If Mossie Murphy arrived late, he would crash the Chief's table. Mossie liked to sit at the right hand.

One day when the gathering included prominent politicians and civic leaders, a large, ferocious-looking rat crawled out of its hole, scurried across the floor, and disappeared. Those of us consigned to the second table let out a cheer. "Rat!" we shouted. "Rat!" Alex DiCroce was indignant. There had NOT been a rat, he insisted. The rest of us argued; Alex stuck to his guns. At the high table – AJR's – the conversation had come to a halt. When our yammering ceased, and all was peaceful again, the rat came back for a curtain call. "Alex ... look!" we hollered. "Rat!" But in a flash it was gone, and Alex, defiant, said there was simply no way – simply no way – a rat could gain admittance to his ever-immaculate Sylvan Room. It was Tim, finally, who compelled him to face the truth. "Alex, you must be blind," he said. "That rat was as big as a kangaroo." Backtracking, Alex began to make concessions. He allowed that, well, they were tearing down a lot of old buildings near the Roosevelt. And rats do migrate. Rats were always looking for warmth and water. And food, someone suggested. Maybe they'd heard about "ribs at the Roosevelt," the sales pitch Alex used in his newspaper ads.

Just for the record, Alex got in the last word. "I can promise you," he said, "that the situation will be taken care of."

Although he did not have the title of manager until the 1960s or later, Alex seemed to run the whole place. He lived at the hotel with his family for many years. There were others, some of them football players, who lived at the hotel during periods of domestic turmoil. It was also a landing place for newcomers to the team. Fran Fogarty would book them into the Roosevelt and Alex DiCroce would see that they were made to feel at home. Downtown hotels still practiced de facto segregation, but the Roosevelt was an exception, at least where our players were concerned. White or black, most of them left after finding an apartment or a house; others were content to stay put. Dedicated hell-raisers could be counted on to get out quickly. They wanted distance between themselves and the front-office people.

Because anyone at all – a judge, a prelate, the mayor, the head of a corporation – might be coming to see him at the Roosevelt, AJR insisted on a dress code for his sons: jacket and tie, white shirt, shoes shined. And we were to keep our hair neatly trimmed. "Judge," he would say (or "Mayor" or "Bishop So-and-so"), "this is my boy Artie." I was always his boy Artie, never his son Art. Taking note of my girth, he would sometimes tell me to eat less or exercise more. What I hated about this was that his lectures came with the judge or the bishop or the mayor for an audience.

Again there were less distinguished visitors, too – the old Fort Pitt crowd, or its remnants. Patsy Scanlon showed up part of the time, Dago Sam Leone most of the time – more often, in fact, than Uncle Jim, who was still on the payroll for being "with Arthur," his duties as mysterious as ever.

John and Pat, the twins, had well-defined duties. Every Monday night and Thursday night during the football season they manned the Roosevelt Hotel ticket office, which faced the street. Monday and Thursday were the nights the department stores remained open, and AJR professed to believe that hordes of shoppers would be looking for Steeler tickets, never mind how pathetic the team was. His real objective, the twins felt, was to keep them away from their girlfriends.

With little else to do on the nights they sold tickets – there were precious few buyers – John and Pat sought diversion in an offshoot of baseball called whiffle ball. By rearranging the furniture in the executive suite, they were able to lay out a diamond. The player pool, consisting of themselves, various bellhops, any North Catholic classmates who happened to wander by, and walk-ons rounded up in the lobby, was sufficient now and then to put infielders and outfielders behind the pitcher and to have a batter always waiting to hit. At the ticket counter, meanwhile, wearing a Steeler shirt and a Steeler visor cap, stood a football-headed manikin rigged up from a coat rack. If Ed Kiely, the P.R. guy, or Fran Fogarty came around, the manikin and the whiffle ball players evaporated.

At some time during the twins' second season on the job it became apparent to AJR and to Fogarty that a night-time ticket office was uneconomical. Bad enough that the tickets weren't moving. John and Pat drew salaries, but their pay of four bucks a night for the two of them was the least significant expense; the trouble as Fogarty saw it was that the ticket sellers had to eat, and that these particular ticket sellers were running up a tab in the Sylvan Room.

As a cost-cutting measure, the night-time ticket office was closed. John and Pat were free once again to upgrade their social life. And the Roosevelt Hotel was a quieter place after dark, a portent of things to come. In the late 1970s, under the federal government's rental subsidy program, a real-estate company bought the rundown old hostelry and converted it into a high rise for senior citizens.

Chapter 21

Disciplinarian

Father Silas was always away when I was a kid. He spent eight years as a missionary in China, four in the Army as a military chaplain during World War II, and then eight years as athletic director at St. Bonaventure.

From time to time, though, he would be in Pittsburgh and might unexpectedly turn up at 940 North Lincoln Avenue. One night after dinner I was leading my three younger brothers in the rosary. We said the rosary every night at AJR's insistence. If he and Kass were not present, Dan, the oldest brother, led. If all three were out of the house, as on this occasion, the job fell to me.

I took it seriously, and on this particular night I felt that Tim was not showing sufficient respect for the prayers. I told him so. He took exception. We dropped our rosary beads and went after each other. I was having the best of it when he picked up a desk lamp and bounced it off my head. There was a fair amount of blood on me. As I made a lunge for him, the doorbell sounded. It was Father Silas, and we were instantly transformed into perfect gentlemen.

He was not taken in. Looking directly at me, but addressing all four of us, he said, "What are you guys up to?"

Together, we answered, "Saying the family rosary."

Slowly and cynically, Father Silas repeated, "Yes ... you are ... saying the family rosary."

We knew we'd been reprimanded. Father Silas had a temper, and we were fortunate that he had kept it under control.

One year when the Steelers were training at St. Bonaventure, a priest named Father McKean was draining the swimming pool. To his annoyance, the ball boys kept driving over the hose he was using. Many of these ball boys and assistant equipment men were Father Silas's nephews. Recklessly, Father McKean asked him to keep his "stupid, retarded relatives" out of the way. Father Silas hauled off and knocked his fellow Franciscan out cold. Years and years later, when Father Silas was dying at the Franciscans' retirement home in St. Petersburg, Florida, Father McKean spent a lot of time at his bedside.

Priestly garb was no protection if Father Silas thought a line had been crossed. Long after he no longer was with us, I happened to be at a Carmelite church in Niagara Falls, Canada. The pastor, a Father Jason Rooney – no relation – said he had taken a summer course at St. Bonaventure when Father Silas was there, and he proceeded to tell me a story. He and another priest, Father Rooney went on, were playing golf on the university's private course one day. "And we were taking a few divots," he said. "Father Silas came by on his tractor and saw that we weren't replacing them. He stopped and gave us holy hell."

Father Silas was a "good guy," Father Rooney said, "but tough. He wouldn't put up with any nonsense." Father Rooney remembered hearing that one of the football or basketball coaches made the mistake of giving Father Silas some lip one day and that Father Silas reached across a desk and belted him out. There were several other versions of this story. In one, Father Silas punched out a big football player for getting involved in some kind of trouble on the campus.

Could it be that he hit both a coach and a player? I know because he told me so that when he was father superior at St. Anthony's Mission in Boston in the late 1950s or early 1960s he in some way manhandled an alcoholic priest who was stationed there, injuring the man's ribs. Father Silas felt a lot of remorse about this.

Hard taskmaster or not, he was popular with his coaches. Ken Stilley, an assistant to Joe Bach at St. Bonaventure, said that Father Silas would show up at the end of their nightly meetings with beer for the whole staff, hidden discreetly under his cassock.

There were priests at St. Bonaventure who criticized him for eliminating football and building up the basketball program. Basketball required fewer scholarships and cost much less for uniforms, equipment, travel, and coaches' salaries.

"What are we going to do with our time on weekends in the fall?" one priest demanded.

"Do what you were ordained to do – hear confessions and say Mass," Father Silas told him, closing off further discussion.

He was not an easy man to oppose.

Summer Vacation

The summer following Jack Butler's rookie season AJR invited him to Shamrock Farm. Going over, Jack drove AJR's Buick; Tim and I, along with our dad, were passengers. We spent a night at the farm and drove to the Jersey shore the next morning, checking into a hotel. Jack, Tim, and I took a dip in the ocean, and then all four of us went to the race track, Monmouth Park. Jack placed some bets for AJR and put a few bucks of his own on the same horses. He won a little money. At the races the next day, after our morning swim, he was not so lucky. AJR told him, "I'm glad you lost. If you'd had two good days in a row, you'd think this was easy and get hooked."

After the races were over on the second day, we returned to the farm, stopping to eat at one of AJR's favorite restaurants. He liked a place that served good fish and steaks and was not too fancy. Usually there would be pictures of race horses on the walls. The owner was almost always an old racetrack guy or a former athlete and he always made a fuss over AJR.

Back at the farm, AJR took Jack and me to the country store and bought us work clothes. All I needed were gloves, because I knew what was up and had work clothes in my luggage. AJR outfitted Jack with a straw hat, a pair of blue jeans, and some cotton shirts. Jack was mystified until AJR said, "You two can help bring in the hay." Addressing Jack, he added, 'This will get you in shape for the football season. I'll be back next week to pick you up."

For six endless days, Jack and I pitched hay with the farm hands. I was on the football team at North Catholic and though I welcomed the chance to build a few muscles the work exhausted me. Jack, who was older and stronger, handled it rather easily. As perplexed as he must have been – this had started out, after all, as a pleasure trip – not once did I hear him complain. We went to bed early and were up with the birds. The farm boys worked swiftly and efficiently, hardly seeming to expend any effort. I did my best to keep up with them, and with Jack, but I thought I was going to die.

On the seventh day, AJR reappeared, bringing Tim. When he left, I was with him in the car. Jack, to his surprise, remained at the farm with Tim and worked for another ten days. Returning once more, AJR picked them up and drove from the farm to our cottage in Ligonier, where, earlier, he had dropped me off. It was a Saturday night. On Sunday morning, after Mass, Mom fixed a huge breakfast for us, and Jack cleaned up everything on his plate, and then some. At first he was quiet and reserved, but once he saw that Mom was a true friendly soul they got to talking. He told her the farm had been "an experience" – boring at times but good conditioning for the football season.

Now he expected to be taken home. Instead, AJR drove him back to the farm with Tim for ten more days in the hay loft.

Forever after, when Jack went on trips with the Rooney boys and AJR, which happened often, he was careful to make certain that he knew in advance what the agenda would be.

For Tim and me, there were periodic visits to race tracks, most frequently Monmouth Park. New Jersey state laws prohibit race tracks from admitting minors, but Tim and I were big for our ages and nobody ever asked questions. In Boston once, however, we had to climb a fence. AJR was waiting for us on the other side.

AJR ran his horses at Monmouth as long as the season lasted and kept a stable there. We'd go to see the horses in the morning and have lunch in the track kitchen. Before the races started, AJR would drive to the clubhouse parking lot, leaving Tim and me in the stable area. If he was betting on the daily double or even had a horse in the third or fourth race we didn't mind. If, on the other hand, there was a horse he wanted to bet on in one of the later races, it could be a long afternoon. We'd watch the trainers ready their thoroughbreds for saddling; we'd go to the little grandstand overlooking the backstretch and watch the horses come flying by; we'd watch them being rubbed and washed down and walked to cool off after running.

Eventually all this would get tiresome and we'd wander into areas that, for unauthorized personnel, were off-limits.

"What are you kids doing here?" a security guard might ask.

We'd say that our father owned the Shamrock Stable and we were looking for him. "Well, get back where you belong," the guard would tell us. "And stay there."

When at last I arrived, a few years before Tim, at the magic age of 18, I was free to watch the races from the clubhouse or grandstand, and one of the many things I noticed was the number of pretty girls in the crowd. Always they seemed to be with an older, prosperous-looking man.

I said to Uncle Jim once, "Gee, a lot of these guys bring their daughters or granddaughters to the track."

He corrected me. "No, no. Never let them hear you say 'daughter' or 'granddaughter.' No. Those young, pretty girls are their nieces."

And then he laughed.

The Natural

Jack Butler spent his high school years at a Carmelite seminary in Niagara Falls, Ontario, and never had played football except in the way that kids do when he enrolled at St. Bonaventure University, no longer a candidate for the priesthood.

One of his several brothers was a priest, representation enough for the Butler family, he thought. The Butlers were from Pittsburgh and well known to AJR. Jack's father had been an all-around athlete and a sandlot teammate of the two oldest Rooney brothers. Father Dan, now the athletic director at St. Bonaventure, guessed that Jack might have inherited the senior Butler's aptitude for football and urged him to try out for the team.

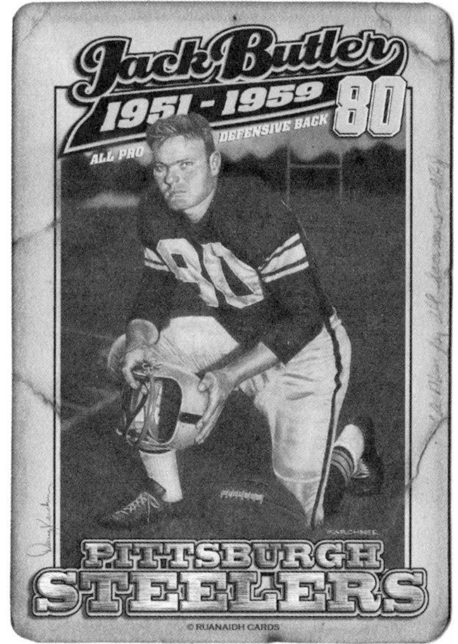

Jack Butler
(Drawing by Denny Karchner)

Well, why not? Asked by the coach what position he played, Butler was stuck for an answer, so he improvised. "Offensive guard," he said, prompted by the recollection that his roommate in the dormitory had claimed to be an offensive guard.

Practice started, and Jack worked hard at trying to block full-sized defensive tackles. "Wait a minute," said the line coach. "You're too small to be a guard, but you're tough and you're fast. What you look like to me is an end."

Butler played end for four years, both on offense and defense, and was outstanding. As so often happened if you played for St. Bonaventure, hardly anyone noticed. In the 1951 NFL draft he was overlooked entirely. Father Dan, knowing what the scouts did not, buttonholed AJR. "Give this kid a tryout," he said. One other team offered Butler a tryout, but he was from Pittsburgh, after all, and the Steelers took precedence.

At pre-season training camp, assistant coach Bob Davis observed that the newcomer was getting lost in the shuffle. Davis mentioned this to a visitor – one of Jack's brothers. Rookies, he said, had to assert themselves; they couldn't be shy. From that moment on, Butler was first in line for all the drills.

Cut-down day arrived, and either Jack or an end from Pitt would make the team. Head coach John Michelosen liked the Pitt man, perhaps out of loyalty to the old school tie, but fate took a hand in the guise of the Korean War. The Pitt man, it turned out, was prime material for the military draft. Butler, as the sole support of his widowed mother, had a deferment. Two of her other grown sons were married, with children, and one, as I have noted, was a priest. In this case, a draft worked to Jack Butler's advantage.

He made the team as a defensive back, not an end, although in special situations his coaches lined him up at wide receiver. The Steelers threw to Butler when they badly needed a score. Of the seven passes he caught in nine seasons, four went for touchdowns, and two of the four were game-winners. Jim Finks, who played quarterback from 1949 to 1955, declared he'd have been a better one with Butler catching his passes all the time.

Jack's soft hands were more useful, the coaches believed, on defense. To put his career total of fifty-two interceptions into perspective, NFL teams were still playing twelve-game schedules. In the history of the league, only two defensive backs up to then had been more prolific. They are Emlen Tunnell and Night Train Lane, Hall of Famers both. Butler should be in the Hall, too, but as I write this he is not.

And it's a shame. Let the record show that he played in four Pro Bowls and in one of those games was the MVP; that in a publication called "The First 50 Years of the NFL," Butler and Lane are named "the two best defensive backs of the 1950s;" that on the NFL's seventy-fifth anniversary, Butler and Tunnell were named the two best defensive backs of the 1950s; that on the all-time Steeler team picked in the fiftieth year of the team's existence, Butler and Mel Blount were the cornerbacks; that Pro Football Weekly, in 1998, included Butler among "the top one hundred players in NFL history."

Emlen Tunnell pronounced him "a defensive genius." Blessed with keen vision, he knew the whereabouts of every man on the field. While Butler was with the Steelers, Chuck Noll played for the Browns. Receivers, Noll said, hated to turn their backs on Butler. He was a vicious tackler with perfect timing. No sooner did the pass reach the receiver than Butler was there, jarring it out of his hands. Only great leapers – R. C. Owens comes to mind – could outjump him, and Butler would hit them so hard that from then on self-protection was paramount in their thinking, which precluded getting up in the air.

Self-protection to Butler was not important. By the end of each season, as others went down with injuries, he was filling in on special teams to cover kicks. He played with such abandon that a serious knee injury shortened his career.

Butler coached for a while in the NFL, with the Buffalo and Steeler organizations, and later became a scout. He was head of the Blesto group for more than thirty years, evaluating, over all that time, thousands of college players for the Bears, Lions, Eagles, Steelers, and Vikings. Great athletes who succeed in the administrative end of their sport are rare. Jack Butler was one of the few.

Chapter 22

Taskmaster

Ed Kiely, the Steelers' publicity director, would run bets for AJR at the race track. His orders were to hide out in the grandstand until it was nearly post time for a certain race and then go to the parimutuel windows as unobtrusively as possible. He would be carrying Dad's money in tens, twenties, fifties, and hundreds and take it to two or three different windows to conceal the fact that a single bettor was getting down big on one particular horse. I had done this for Dad myself, and it could be nerve-wracking. To blow your cover was simply not an option.

By watching the tote board, AJR could track the "smart" money – tell where it was going. Two-to-one shots didn't interest him. Rarely did he bet on a horse unless the odds were at least five to one. He might wait until the last minute and then toss his runner a bill. "Number eight horse to win," I can hear him saying. A man named Clark Gardner, an accountant who worked at our track in Yonkers, told me once that when AJR gave him twenty dollars to bet, a scant ninety seconds before the mutuel windows closed, he resolved to book it himself if he ran out of time. It could have cost Mr. Gardner a month's pay, but nobody ever wanted to displease AJR.

Ed Kiely had a habit of asking his boss questions, which required the most delicate judgment. There was a right time, a right place, and a right approach. If you asked a question undiplomatically you were going to be abruptly cut off. Kiely told my son Art that one day he was asking why AJR bet in such and such a way instead of some other way. AJR seemed exasperated, according to Ed. At last he said, "I don't know why I bet the way I bet. Why do you ask so many questions? I just do it!"

Ed persisted. He said that betting on horses was something he hadn't known about and he was trying to educate himself. Softening, AJR said, "Well, Ed, I've been at this so long I have a feel for it. But I'll tell you one thing. When I'm ahead of the game and playing with the track's money instead of my own, that's when I take more chances."

I left the probing questions to Kiely. Neither Dan, John, Pat, nor I dared to show any interest in wagering. We knew this about AJR: he didn't want his sons to be gamblers. Tim had thicker skin than the rest of us. He did ask questions, and the information he dragged out of AJR about everything connected with horse racing was useful to him later on, in his career as a breeder and track owner.

AJR could only teach by example. It was by example that he taught his five sons religion, morals, and character. He went to Mass every day. He made novenas. He went on retreats. We said the family rosary. He never told dirty jokes (though he could tell funny stories about his experiences, he was not very good at telling any kind of joke, tending to smother the punch line with laughter.)

Giving us baseball or boxing or field-goal kicking instructions, he was always impatient and brusque. If he had us fielding ground balls, and somebody ducked away from a hot one, he would say, "Get in front of it! Stop it with your glove!" After that, he would hit the ball harder and harder until he drove everybody off the field. Then if you went into the house, crying, Mom would come out and scream at Dad, calling him "a mean old bastard." He would shrug and tell her disgustedly that none of us could have lasted in The Ward.

When we boxed, it was much the same. He would put the gloves on and show us how to block with our shoulders or tuck our chins into our chests; meanwhile, he'd be throwing some pretty good punches without meaning to. We did our best to be somewhere else whenever it was time for a boxing lesson.

None of us developed into superior athletes, but all of us made the high school football and baseball teams. For Dad, this was insufficient. He would tell us how great he and his brother Dan were and how "near-great" Uncle Jim was.

He did not have much to say about Red and Duke as athletes. Tom, killed in the Second World War, belonged to a special category. Heroism on the battlefield transcended all other varieties.

After getting her fill of this, Mom would sometimes tell AJR he couldn't possibly have been a great athlete. "Why, you're a midget!" she would scoff.

Dad would then point to the evidence, his scrapbook of newspaper clippings. I wish I knew where it was. George Quinlan told somebody that one day when Dad was reading it, Mom said to him, "Why don't you burn that thing?" and he took her advice. From other sources, I have learned enough over the years to believe Dad was giving us the unadorned facts.

Out of His League

In his own world, AJR was a guy who knew the ropes, but as a handyman he could never have made it. At fixing things, or doing odd jobs around the house, he was useless. His working life had consisted of half a day in a steel mill. In those three or four hours, he had seen enough to realize that there were better and easier ways to earn a living.

At Ligonier one summer the heads of all the families in our vacation complex decided to build a wall and put in some steps near the part of the creek that was used as a swimming hole, and AJR, despite his unfitness for manual labor, felt called on to help.

He was making enough money at the race track to hire a construction crew and a bulldozer and finance the improvements himself, but this was a matter of pride. The other men who owned cottages were going to roll up their sleeves and get the banks of the creek shored up, so AJR, in a bathing suit and a pair of old shoes — and wearing his hat, a brown or gray fedora — joined the work gang .

Well, you never saw anyone who was more out of place. Men like our neighbor Mr. Duhon seemed to know by instinct where each rock and stone belonged and how to apply the cement. AJR did not have a clue. The athletic ability he possessed was in this case utterly wasted. He carried and lifted; he held things; he looked thankful when the work was completed.

Mom and the rest of us were happy, too. It was Dad's brain, not the sweat of his brow, that put the bread on our table and the clothes on our backs and the roof over our heads, not to mention the amenities and indeed the luxuries we enjoyed.

Easter Parade

After Mass on Holy Thursday every year, the whole family would pile into AJR's big old Buick Roadmaster for our annual trek to the Blue Grass country. The itinerary was always the same: an overnight stop in Cincinnati and then a tour of the thoroughbred horse farms around Lexington, Kentucky, the next morning. AJR would take a look at the yearlings his trainer had picked out and decide how many to buy for his Shamrock racing stable. It was important to be back in Pittsburgh for Mass on Easter Sunday; the return trip, therefore, might begin as early as Friday evening or on Saturday morning at the latest.

Seven people overloaded the Buick, so when Dan reached the age of 16 and could legally drive, we would split into two groups, with Dan at the wheel of the football team's station wagon, spelled now and then by his friend Billy Hart.

It was more fun to ride with Dan than with Dad and Mom. The radio would be playing and we'd wait for a tune called "The Saber Dance." Then we'd lower all the windows and Dan or Billy would step on the gas. At Easter time the air was usually cold and it would blow through the car ferociously. The cold air, the fast music, and the high rate of speed left us exhilarated.

Later, we'd catch hell from Dad for driving too fast, but our instructions were to stay fairly close behind the Buick so as not to get lost, and nobody drove faster than he did.

We were also ordered to say the rosary in the car. After all, it was Holy Week. Holy Week or any week, we were always expected to say the rosary on motor trips. On the way South we'd make stops at nine different churches. It had to be nine, just as there were nine First Fridays. Breaking the string was unthinkable. There was some kind of heavenly reward involved, but its nature is unclear to me now. I know we believed that if Catholics everywhere went to Mass and received Communion on the first Saturday of nine consecutive months, the Soviet Union would renounce Communism and convert to Christianity. When the government fell and the churches reopened in the 1990s I began to think that, hey, all those prayers must have worked. For certain the Rooney family by itself observed enough First Saturdays to ensure the salvation of a good-sized Russian city.

In hotels on these trips, our parents did their best to keep us from running wild. They remembered an experience in a Washington, D.C., hotel when the water bags we had thrown from the windows, aimed at passing targets on the sidewalk, brought an unhappy house detective to our floor. After that, we settled for pillow fights and simple rampaging from one connecting room to another.

If breakfast in the hotel restaurant got out of hand, AJR could silence us with a word and a look, the word a muffled roar. None of us ever wanted to be yelled at more than once by AJR. The ever-present likelihood of bringing down his wrath on our heads was one of several reasons we fought for a place in the station wagon.

By the 1950s all five Rooney boys were driving, and AJR was using us as chauffeurs. He subjected our driving skills and judgment to a drumbeat of criticism. We were either going too fast or too slow. "You know I want to get there for the first race," he would say. Or: "You know I want to get there for the kickoff." If, on the other hand, his driver had an agenda, safety considerations took precedence over making good time. "Hey, slow down," he kept saying to John the twin when John was taking him back to Pittsburgh from the St. Bonaventure training camp in Olean. He knew that John was in a hurry to keep a date that night with his girlfriend, JoAnn Wallace. It wasn't worth risking their lives for, AJR kept reminding him.

When we could turn over the driving chores to someone like Peezer Klingensmith we were always elated. Peezer Klingensmith had been a friend of Uncle Tom, the Marine who lost his life in combat during the Second World War. Temporarily out of a job – he was disputing an insurance claim with the railroad that employed him – he went to AJR for advice. "You can be my driver," AJR told him. "I need someone to take me to camp. The rest of the time, you can help our equipment manager." (Football season was about to begin, and the Steelers were back in Olean.) "Great," Peezer said." When do I start?" The answer – "Now" – startled him. He had barely enough time to go home and pack a gym bag before they were in the car.

It was late afternoon. Peezer drove out to Route 19 and headed north. "Wait a minute," AJR told him. "We're going to stop at the farm first." The Shamrock Farm was in Maryland, so Peezer turned east. They arrived after dark, ate dinner and went to bed, and were up at 5:30 the next morning so that AJR could attend early Mass before breakfast. After a tour of the farm, Peezer again started north. "What are you doing?" demanded AJR. There'd be a stop, he explained, at Laurel race track, farther east. He had a horse in the first race and wanted to get there early to talk with the trainer.

All the way to Laurel, AJR read the Racing Form, listened to the sports news on the radio, and filled the car with cigar smoke. From time to time, he issued directions "Hey, you missed the turn. Go back and take the first right." Peezer would have to slam on the brakes. A little later he would hear: "Stay on this road for ten miles and then make the first left. It's a shortcut. Save us a good ten minutes." They'd be on unpaved or badly paved farm-to-market back roads.

At the track, AJR entrusted Peezer with the task of getting his bets down. Exactly two minutes before post-time he was to bet part of the money at one window and the rest at another window. Peezer, who didn't even know what "post-time" meant, was in a state of high anxiety, aggravated by unmet needs. Because AJR was keeping him on the run he hadn't eaten since breakfast, nor been able to visit a men's room.

Peezer thought the day would never end. When at last the afternoon did, and he pointed the car toward Olean, he was ordered to take another detour. There was racing that night at Yonkers, "which is on our way," declared AJR disingenuously. "If you step on it, we can make the first race." It was hot, and AJR's Buicks were never air-conditioned. Feeling suffocated, Peezer stepped on it, speeding toward Yonkers through the twilight.

They missed the first two races but not the rest of the card, and then they were back on the road. "We'd better look for a place to stop," said AJR. It was getting on toward 11 o'clock. But each time they approached a motel, and Peezer took his foot off the accelerator, AJR would tell him, "No, not here – keep going." After a gasoline stop – it was now past midnight – AJR decided that pressing on would be the best thing to do. "I'll drive for a while. You grab some shut-eye," he said. He did drive – fast – over narrow country roads, and they pulled into Olean at 3:30.

The manager of the training camp found sleeping space for them in a dormitory. Breakfast was at 7:30. By 8 o'clock, Peezer was in the equipment room, helping Jack Lee. His stomach began to ache. He grew dizzy. At noon, Jack drove him to the hospital in Olean. Dehydration was the diagnosis, brought on by exhaustion and stress.

Soon after Peezer had recovered, he came to terms with the railroad and went back to his regular job. "I love your dad," he told me, "but I'm glad I'm not driving for him any more."

Chapter 23

Miss Hall

In the early 1950s I had my own special tutor, Miss Hall. Our classroom was an office in AJR's ground-floor suite at the Fort Pitt Hotel. Earlier, we had met at the Ursuline Academy, where Miss Hall lived, and later there were sessions at her next home, the Convent of the Little Sisters of the Poor near St. Peter's Church. In the years just before I enrolled at St. Vincent College, she would come to 940 North Lincoln Avenue.

Sometimes she worked with my brothers and me together, but at the Fort Pitt Hotel it was usually one on one. The Fort Pitt Hotel, an ancient pile of bricks, stood rather forlornly at the northeast corner of the Golden Triangle, within walking distance of the farmers' market in the Strip District. AJR's offices were accessible to the public by way of the lobby; for habitués, the summertime entrance was an eight-foot-high window, its sill at the level of the street. In those days before air-conditioning, the window was always open during business hours from June to September. The hangers-on who came for the card games or race results simply stepped right in from the sidewalk and took the same route when they left, saving themselves a trip through the lobby.

If the card players were using the office where Miss Hall gave me my lessons, Fran Fogarty, AJR's accountant, would move them into another room. Margaret Hall was a fastidious schoolmarm, and I think the Damon Runyon types who foregathered at the Fort Pitt were unsettling to her at first. In time she became accustomed to them. With Uncle Red, Uncle Jim, and Fran Fogarty, she was never ill at ease.

During football season, or when the Rooney-McGinley Boxing Club was putting on an important fight, Miss Hall and I adjourned to the lobby, taking our books. There were comfortable armchairs in the lobby, and we could always find vacant ones side by side. It was actually more peaceful in the lobby, because AJR's cronies were constantly invading our usual space to get to the toilet or use the pay phone on the wall. AJR had had the pay phone installed as an economy measure. Too many people were making long-distance calls to their bookmakers or girlfriends on the phone in his private office. Calling from our classroom, they would lower their voices out of deference to Miss Hall, and though every word was audible she pretended not to hear.

In the time she spent at the Fort Pitt, a side of life opened up to her that must have been entirely new. Thus she advanced her own education along with mine. Miss Hall had been tutoring Rooneys and McNultys for years, going all the way back to the girlhood of Aunt Alice. A Bryn Mawr graduate, she attempted to whet our interest in the symphony and the theater but without making noticeable headway.

I remember she angered my mother by declaring the North Side to be no fit environment for growing boys. "You've already lost Tim," she told Kass. Dan by then was a freshman at Duquesne and the rest of us were going to high school, so we had probably reached a point beyond redemption.

Miss Hall was from Oil City, where her forebears had made money in – you guessed it – the oil business. She was extremely well-traveled. When she was paid for our lessons, she would pull up her skirt and tuck the bills away in a purse attached to her petticoat. Since the petticoat nearly reached her ankles, it was not a display of immodesty. She had learned to protect her money like this while traveling in Europe, she said. She encouraged us to see the world ourselves and to read good books.

Broaden your horizons, she was saying. How much of Miss Hall rubbed off is for others to judge.

A Done Deal

On matters of importance, I deferred to my dad without an argument. After graduation from North Catholic in 1953 I had a hard time deciding on a college to attend. I was a decent student, if far from outstanding. I had been a first-string tackle on the football team. In four years, I never had missed a day of school. For that I received an award. For never having earned a bad-conduct demerit I received a pat on the back. The University of Dayton had accepted me, but I dragged my feet. Inevitably, AJR grew impatient. One late-summer day when we were still at the cottage in Ligonier, he said to me, "Jump in the car. We're going over to Latrobe. I want you to take a look at Saint Vincent." Latrobe was only nine miles away. I was quite familiar with St. Vincent and said so, but AJR was the boss. He knew the football coach, Al DeLuca; we could talk. There was no point in resisting.

DeLuca seemed glad to see me. I was a big kid for my age and at least I had the general conformation of a football player. Also, North Catholic was in the upper tier of high school teams back then. He asked if I had applied at St. Vincent. I told him no, but I'd been accepted at Dayton. AJR glared at me. DeLuca said, "I'll get you over to the registrar's office," and ordered one of his players to show me the way. It seemed to be all cut and dried. The registrar, a tall white-haired man in a black cassock – a Benedictine monk – greeted me from behind a counter.

"Are you Art Rooney's kid?" he asked.

"Yes, Father."

"Where did you go to high school?"

"North Catholic, Father."

"Just a minute," he said, and went to a telephone. He dialed a number he apparently knew by heart and spoke to somebody in a low, inaudible voice. After just a few minutes he looked up and pointed a finger at me.

"You're in," he announced.

And I was.

Getting in had been easy, thanks to AJR. Surviving the next four years, and getting out with a bachelor's degree in history, I would be on my own.

'OK for Ginger Ale'

Phil Musick, a talented sportswriter for the *Pittsburgh Press* and later the *Pittsburgh Post-Gazette*, described the Steelers as "shot-and-a-beer guys" and the Dallas Cowboys as "sippers of daiquiris." The term "shot and a beer" was familiar to me, but I never had heard of the sweet rum drink called a daiquiri. Now that I have added the word to my vocabulary, I'm not sure it was the beverage of choice for the Cowboys, but that is neither here nor there.

Although I came from a family of saloon keepers and bartenders, I was slow to pick up the terminology of the trade. Having taken to heart my father's lectures on the evils of booze, I had tasted the stuff only on special occasions: Easter, Thanksgiving, Christmas, New Year's, and the birthday of a family member. Kass, who followed her own rules for alcohol consumption, irrespective of what AJR may have thought, felt that a sip of wine or beer on such holidays (champagne was a particular favorite) would act as a sort of inoculation for the five Rooney sons. "Just a sip, you understand, so it won't be a mystery to you." In mystery, there is allure, Kass believed. With some of her boys, and they know who they are, her prescription did not have the desired effect, but it worked for me.

It was with a sense of invulnerability, then, that in my freshman year at St. Vincent, I swaggered into a bar one night with two of my football teammates. Latrobe was more of a steel town than a college town, and the place we chose to patronize reminded me a little of Grandpa Rooney's saloon on the North Side. The customers all seemed to be loud-talking, tough-acting mill hands. Somewhat preppy in style, the clothes I was wearing made me a marked man. My St. Vincent friends, Tuck and Jimmy B., were dressed like everybody else. Still, no one paid me any mind. It may be that my physical dimensions – I was 6 feet 1 and weighed about 210 pounds – discouraged sarcastic comments.

The three of us did our best to be unobtrusive. We took our places at the long shellacked bar of blond mahogany and waited to be asked what we would have.

"Draft," said Jimmy B. The bartender looked at Tuck. "Shot and a beer, draft." My turn.

"Let's see your driver's license," the bartender snapped.

I did not immediately catch on. "Driver's license?" Why would the guy be interested in my driver's license?

"Yeah, your driver's license. Your I.D."

Tuck spoke up. "You're being carded," he informed me.

"Carded?" The word meant nothing to me. "I'd just like to have a ginger ale."

"Doesn't matter," the bartender said. "Show me some ID." He was a partly bald, slovenly looking fellow in a dirty white shirt. Tucker suggested I show him my driver's license. The bartender glanced at it. "OK for ginger ale," he said. He wasn't hostile, I decided, just worn down, like a quarterback who's been sacked a dozen times.

Jimmy B. was quietly putting away his beer. Both he and Tuck were very much at ease, blending right in with the mill hunks. Watching Tuck swallow his shot of whiskey and chase it with three or four gulps of beer, I felt like a tenderfoot. I was "brand new." With my ginger ale, I tried to imitate Jimmy B.'s way of sipping his beer. He had emptied his glass and was tipping it gently up and down, which captured the attention of the bartender. "Same," Jimmy said, keeping his voice low. The bartender looked over at Tuck. "Yeah," Tuck said, "same here."

Feeling left out, I blurted, "I'm OK." The bartender seemed not to hear. In an instant, he put a draft down in front of Jimmy and a shot and a beer at Tuck's place. Tuck took the shot of whiskey in his hand, looked at me, and said, "Boilermaker." He poured the whiskey into his beer and drained the whole glass in a few gulps, just as he had done before.

I started talking with Jimmy about the St. Vincent football program. Looking back, I think we must have been sorry excuses for football players, but we were young and hopeful and convinced that we had what it takes. I wondered if the bartender was listening to us.

Tucker patted the side of his glass, and the guy in the filthy white shirt brought him another shot and another beer. For Jimmy, he drew another draft. He now looked at me. I said, "I'll have another ginger ale, please."

This time Tucker not only poured his whiskey into his beer, but tossed in the shot glass too. "Depth charge," he announced, and gulped it all down – all except the shot glass.

Quickly, Jimmy and I finished our drinks and then we left. I still didn't know what a daiquiri was, but Tucker had expanded my vocabulary. I could now define 'boilermaker" and "depth charge." I had learned what it means to be a shot-and-a-beer guy. And I knew that drinking ginger ale in a steelworkers' bar doesn't quite make the right impression.

Chapter 24

Kiesling Again

After firing Joe Bach before the start of the regular season in 1954, AJR named Walt Kiesling head coach for the third time.

Before Bach's tenure he had sent Kies to study the T formation under the man who brought it back and modernized it, Clark Shaughnessy. Kies learned the fundamentals – he was a good football man – but imagination is a quality that doesn't rub off.

The Steelers under Kies were the same team they always had been. Like Jock Sutherland and John Michelosen before him, Kies was a grind-it-out guy. His approach was simplicity itself: establish the running game, control the ball, and play tenacious defense.

In 1942, when he coached the Steelers to their first winning season, this had worked. In 1954 and again in 1955 his teams won four of their first five games, but tapered off at the end of the season and had losing records. In 1956, with Jim Finks retired and little Ted Marchibroda from St. Bonaventure at quarterback, the Steelers were neither very much better nor very much worse, just not quite good enough, once more, to win as many games as they lost.

As was usual with Steeler teams in the 1950s, there were inadequate replacements for the starters. Kies had no other choice but to use his best players on kickoffs and punts. Selected offensive players would double up on defense; selected defensive players would double up on offense.

Kies was a man's man, popular with the assistant coaches and front-office people but not with the players – not, at any rate, until after they had finished their careers. Kies and Lynn Chandnois hated each other; the feeling between Kies and Jim Finks was something a bit closer to dislike.

Lynn Chandnois was an All-American halfback from Michigan State with size, speed, and strength. He could catch the ball and he could run. But Kies, the assistant coaches, and even some of his teammates were convinced that he lacked toughness. Kies thought that Chandnois would try only hard enough to get by, which may have been true. It was also true that his natural ability enabled him to do things that most other players were incapable of.

In back-to-back games one year, Chandnois returned kickoffs for touchdowns. After his second long runback, Kies said to AJR with a shake of the head, "Can you imagine that lucky bum – going all the way on kickoffs TWICE?" Gently, AJR told him, "Kies, when you do it once it might be luck. When you do it twice, it's talent."

Before a pre-season game in Oregon, Jim Finks got so upset with Kies that he walked out of camp. Their dispute was smoothed over, but Finks went on referring to Kies as "Krauthead."

One player Kies regarded with complete admiration was Fran Rogel, a tough little fullback from Braddock who had been with the Steelers since his graduation from Penn State in 1950. On the first offensive play in every game, following orders from Kies, the Steeler quarterback, whoever it might be, sent Rogel bucking into the line for one or two yards. The predictability of the thing became a joke. "Hi diddle diddle, Rogel up the middle!" chanted the fans, but they weren't amused.

The derision in the stands and in the newspapers got under AJR's hide. So did the taunts of Bob Drum, a 6-foot-3, 260-pound sportswriter for the *Pittsburgh Press*. Sitting at AJR's side in AJR's private box, and smoking AJR's cigars, Drum was the loudest critic of all.

Finally AJR resolved to break one of his rules. He called Kies on the telephone and demanded his presence at the Steelers' business office in the Roosevelt Hotel. Kies protested that he couldn't miss practice. "Just work it out," said AJR brusquely. When Kies found his way to the office, AJR waved him into a chair and said, "Now, I'm going to put in a play that I want you to call the first time we get the ball in next Sunday's game." Kies jumped to his feet as though lifting off from the top of a red-hot stove. Before he could speak, AJR said, "Sit down!" Seeing that AJR meant business, Kies complied. His boss then delivered the next hammer blow.

He said, "Kies, you are going to have the quarterback fake a handoff to Rogel up the middle and then throw a pass – a long pass – to an end." Kies opened his mouth to object, but AJR silenced him. "Kies," he went on, "you are going to do it!!!" The discussion, Kies knew, was over

At Forbes Field the following Sunday, on the first play of the Steelers' first possession, Jack Scarbath, playing quarterback, faked to Rogel and threw a bomb to Goose McClairen, a tall rookie end from an all-black school in Florida, Bethune-Cookman. Massed to stop Rogel, the New York Giants had left McClairen wide open. He gathered in the ball and crossed the goal line untouched. The crowd was on its feet, roaring with disbelief and delight. Up in his private box, AJR turned to Bob Drum with a what-have-you-got-to-say-now look.

But a penalty flag was on the ground. A Steeler end – the other one – had jumped offside. Touchdown nullified. The hubbub in the stands died away. And Drum, seizing on his moment of triumph, bellowed in AJR's ear, "Kies told him to do that! He told him to go offside! You can't control your own coach!"

AJR never called another play. From then on, as long as Kiesling coached the team, it was hi diddle diddle, Rogel up the middle on the first Steeler offensive play of every game.

Gary Glick the Bonus Pick

For a little over a decade after the Second World War, an NFL team determined by lot drafted a "bonus pick" every year, giving that team its choice of the best college football player – or college senior, anyway – in the country. In 1956, for the first and only time, the bonus pick went to the Steelers. Pretty much by common consent, the best college football player that year was Lenny Moore, a halfback from Penn State. Coach Walt Kiesling passed him up for an unknown defensive back, Gary Glick of Colorado A. & M.

Nobody in Pittsburgh ever had heard of Gary Glick and there was little awareness of Colorado A. & M. In time, Colorado A. & M. would change its name to Colorado State and play in a 30,000-seat stadium, but in the 1950s the football team played its home games before crowds of a few thousand in wooden bleacher seats.

Understandably, therefore, the coming of Glick to Pittsburgh met with widespread ridicule. Sportswriter Bob Drum mockingly called him "Gary Stick the Bonus Pick." Instead of drafting the best player, the Steelers had drafted a player to fill a certain position – a position where they felt they needed help. The fans did not appreciate this kind of thinking. Their reaction was: "Same old Steelers – taking a guy they could get for small change."

Lenny Moore, drafted by the Baltimore Colts, played on three championship teams and ended up in the Hall of Fame. Gary Glick turned out to be a serviceable, if unspectacular, safety. He was strong and steady and tough; he had decent movement, decent speed; he intercepted some passes and made some big plays. But the fans and the media wanted a game-breaker, which Gary Glick was not. After four years with the Steelers, he played an additional four seasons in Baltimore, Washington, and San Diego.

Gary Glick had long since departed when some media people, scouts, and coaches were sitting in the beer room at the Steelers' training camp in Latrobe, cooling off on a hot summer day. Sportswriter Jack Sell was making fun of the team's draft picks and harking back, as he always did, to Gary Glick. Don Joyce, a scout who had played for the Baltimore Colts, listened quietly. At last he said, "Well, Jack, I don't know how Gary played in Pittsburgh. I don't know about that bonus pick stuff. I do know this: He didn't ask to be drafted by Pittsburgh. He was tough and he played well in Baltimore. He helped us win. And he was a heck of a good guy. The Gary Glick you are talking about is not the Gary Glick I played with – a good player on a good team."

There wasn't another peep out of Sell.

'Foxy'

There are four things I can tell you about Fred Miller of the Miller Brewing Company.

1. He was a proud Notre Dame alumnus.
2. He was therefore interested in Notre Dame football.
3. He was rich.
4. He had Pittsburgh ties (the Miller beer distributors in Pittsburgh were his good friends Fritz Wilson, also a Notre Dame alumnus, and Jack McGinley).

Fritz Wilson recruited Western Pennsylvania high school players for the Notre Dame football coaches and generally kept in touch with ex-Notre Damers like Bill Walsh, drafted by the Steelers in 1949. After the 1954 season Walsh left the team to become an assistant coach at Notre Dame and after the 1955 season Jim Finks left the team to become an assistant coach at Notre Dame. Did Fred Miller and Fritz Wilson have anything to do with this? More than likely. To augment their Notre Dame salaries, Fred Miller gave the two Steelers part-time jobs with his brewery.

"He took the heart out of our team," said AJR. Walsh was an outstanding center and Finks ran the Steelers' offense.

Of course the loss of Finks was the more disturbing. In the T formation the quarterback makes everything work, and Finks had developed into a good one. His three years as a defensive back while John Michelosen was coaching the single wing undoubtedly tried his patience. But when his chance came, in the last NFL game Michelosen ever coached, the one in which Finks stepped into a tailback position denuded by injuries, he was ready. Operating out of the shotgun formation, he passed the Steelers to a 20-10 come-from-behind upset of the Washington Redskins.

Finks preferred baseball to football and played in the minor leagues until his career stalled. From the time he joined the Steelers as a rookie, sportswriters, camp followers, trainers, equipment men, and ball boys – everybody, in fact, but Michelosen – could see that his talents were made to order for the T. On Joe Bach's part, there was no hesitation in making him the quarterback. He was smart and had excellent vision. He could set up well and his experience as a defensive back helped him to read defenses. His arm was quite strong enough for the medium and medium-deep routes, but his forte was the accurate touch pass, thrown with an easy overarm baseball delivery. He was nimble enough to elude rushes and he ran with determination enough to pick up first downs. Though not a very big man – a shade over six feet tall and built on the scale of a dancer, a clothes model, a bullfighter – he was able to take hits. He played with cuts, bruises, broken bones, and even a skull fracture.

His personality resembled a politician's. He was temperamental – sometimes even childish, as when he walked off the field in Oregon – but also ingratiating. Everybody liked him and he in turn liked everybody, or seemed to. His teammates had a nickname for him – "Foxy."

I saw him show up the Steelers' No. 1 draft choice one time in a way that was oddly inoffensive. In 1955 the Heisman Trophy winner from Notre Dame, halfback Johnny Lattner, reported to the Steelers after the College All-Star game. Lattner was a great guy, but not a great NFL player. On his first day in camp, Walt Kiesling had him running "dummy" drills, in which there isn't any contact. He was following his blockers through the line and swinging the ball carelessly in one hand. Observing on the defensive side, Finks reached out quickly as Lattner ran by him and knocked the ball loose. It was neatly done and embarrassing to Lattner, but Finks, smiling at him, converted the incident into a friendly little lesson: Kid, he was saying, hang onto the ball.

Neither Walsh nor Finks remained long at Notre Dame. Walsh spent his life as a good assistant coach in the NFL, while Finks went into the management end of football. He was personnel director and later general manager of a team in the Canadian League, and then the Minnesota Vikings hired him as their general manager. He built the great Viking teams of the 1970s and did the same thing in Chicago with the Bears. After Pete Rozelle died, there was talk that Finks might succeed him as NFL commissioner, but the job went to Paul Tagliabue.

Finks was general manager of the New Orleans Saints when he died in his mid-sixties of cancer. For his work with the Vikings and Bears, he's in the NFL Hall of Fame at Canton, Ohio, elected posthumously.

Johnny U

In the 1957 college draft, the Steelers picked Len Dawson, a quarterback from Purdue, over the intimidating Syracuse running back, Jim Brown. Dawson, Coach Walt Kiesling announced, was "the quarterback of the future."

As it turned out Dawson was something less than that, but he did have a future in football. Kiesling himself did not. Before the start of the season, AJR replaced him with Buddy Parker, who had unexpectedly walked out on the Detroit Lions. Dawson, never more than an understudy to Bobby Layne with the Steelers, took the Kansas City Chiefs to the Super Bowl twice (in Super Bowl I, they lost to the Green Bay Packers; in Super Bowl IV they beat the Minnesota Vikings). Jim Brown, drafted by Cleveland, was a ground-gaining machine, the NFL's leading rusher in eight of his nine seasons.

Passing up Brown to take Dawson was a misjudgment much remarked on, but quickly forgotten in Pittsburgh. The gaffe for which Kiesling will always be remembered, little noticed at the time outside the Rooney family, had occurred two years earlier.

There are coaches who know how to build successful teams and there are coaches who don't. And there's an easy way to assess this. Chuck Noll – more about him later – told me what it is. If the coach of a team that is losing has cut a lot of players who are helping other teams win, that's the tipoff. The description comes close to fitting Kies.

Look at his track record. He got rid of Ed Modzelewski, a Maryland fullback from New Kensington who went to a better team, the Browns, and performed well. He had a chance to draft Jim Brown and he took Len Dawson. He had a chance to draft Lenny Moore and he took Gary Glick. He had a chance to draft Joe Schmidt in 1953, but took a lineman who couldn't make it through training camp.

Joe Schmidt was a home-town boy, an outstanding linebacker at Pitt. Injured during most of his senior year, he was still on the board after five rounds. Joe Bach was the Steelers' head coach at the time, but Kiesling picked the defensive players, and two Schmidt boosters, Ed Kiely of the front office and Pat Livingston, the *Pittsburgh Press* writer, were making a case for their man. AJR told them, "If you want this guy, keep your mouths shut. You're turning Kies against him. Don't you know how stubborn Kies is?" AJR was correct. In the sixth round, Kiesling took a nose guard from Clemson called Black Cat Barton – who couldn't make the team. In the seventh round, picking just ahead of the Steelers, the Detroit Lions drafted Schmidt and had themselves a Hall-of-Fame linebacker.

Kies underrated players like Lynn Chandnois, who was not, in his opinion, "tough," and overrated players like Fran Rogel, who had about one-tenth as much ability as Chandnois but would carry a football into machine-gun fire if that was the game plan. In most ways, Kies was a hard man to satisfy. At the mention of a player or coach he disdained – there were dozens – he would turn his head to one side and go through the motions of expectorating.

The year the Steelers drafted Johnny Unitas, 1955, was during Kies's third time around as head coach. Unitas had played quarterback for a small parochial high school on Mount Washington, St. Justin, and had beaten out my brother Dan, the North Catholic quarterback, for a place on the City of Pittsburgh's all-Catholic team. No major-college coach wanted Unitas, because he weighed only 130 pounds, but the University of Louisville gave him a scholarship and he bulked up enough to have a career that may have deserved closer attention. The only reason Kiesling drafted him was that AJR wanted some Pittsburgh kids on the training-camp squad.

It didn't take Kies long to decide he didn't think much of Unitas. "He's too dumb to play quarterback," Kiesling said – words that are still used against him. If Unitas's IQ failed to match up with – well, Kiesling's – it forever casts doubt on the importance of brain power in football.

Jim Finks was the first-string quarterback that year, with Ted Marchibroda backing him up. The number three man was Vic Eaton, a rookie as obscure as Unitas. His one advantage in their competition was the fact that he could punt. Pat Brady was gone, and if the Steelers kept Eaton there would be no need to pay a salary to a kicking specialist.

In the pre-season workouts at St. Bonaventure, Finks and Marchibroda took all the snaps. There was never enough time, it seemed, for Unitas. Kies would look at his watch and blow his whistle and the drill would be over. Meanwhile, the coach of the St. Vincent Prep team, Bill Rafferty, was telling me good things about Unitas. "We played against him," Rafferty said, "and even in high school his hands were so big he could wrap them around the ball. And he can throw from one goal line to the other."

I started watching Unitas with greater interest.

He was lean and raw-boned and bandy-legged, and, for someone his age, surprisingly stoop-shouldered. From what I got to see of him, he moved around in the pocket OK, but not with the niftiness of the shorter Marchibroda, who was being likened to Frankie Albert of the Forty-Niners and Eddie LeBaron of the Redskins, the most successful little guys playing quarterback in the NFL. All Unitas did was drop back, step up, and throw with a lot of zip. He never scrambled. Like all the great ones up to then – Sid Luckman, Sammy Baugh, Bob Waterfield, Otto Graham – his object was simply to get the ball to the receiver as accurately as he could.

His problem was that Kies had arbitrarily written him off. So when practice was over Unitas would throw to Tim, Pat, and John, and to some of the other kids who were helping out in camp. He'd have them running patterns – deep patterns, mostly – and put the ball in their hands, or, more often, bounce it off their heads.

Pat and John told AJR that Unitas was the best quarterback in camp but had not been given a chance to show what he could do. Tim had similar thoughts and put them into a twelve-page letter. After reading it, AJR remained skeptical. "Tim can be a wise guy," he said to Fran Fogarty. "I don't pay my coaches to be second-guessed."

Before the regular-season opener, Kiesling cut Unitas and kept Eaton. Unitas went to work on a construction job and played semi-pro football that year with the Bloomfield Rams for six dollars a game. Somehow the Baltimore Colts heard that this was a player they might be able to use, and for a 65-cent telephone call solidified their offense for years to come.

In every game Unitas played for the Colts, the kid who was "too dumb" to make it with the Steelers called his own plays. When Unitas died, at the age of 69, the great linebacker Sam Huff said, "One time when I was playing for the Redskins I called nine different defenses. Unitas beat all nine of them. Nothing worked against him." Pat Summerall, the placekicker for the Giants, said this: "Unitas was a gambler, and he had an unconventional way of calling plays. Tom Landry, our defensive coordinator, never could figure him out."

Though Finks, like Unitas, ended up in the Hall of Fame, it was not, as I have said, for his football playing. Marchibroda fell short of being another Eddie LeBaron, much less another Frankie Albert, but developed into a first-rate coach. Vic Eaton was the Steelers' punter for one less than memorable season and then disappeared.

Some time after Unitas had signed with the Colts, AJR was in a car with John the twin and Kiesling. They stopped at a red light, and John honked the horn at the driver of a car next to theirs. Just then the light changed, and the car alongside pulled ahead. "Who was that, John?" asked AJR.

"A guy who tried out with us – Johnny Unitas."

"Catch up with him," ordered AJR. John did as he was told. The cars were side by side again at the next light.

AJR was up front, in the passenger seat. He rolled down the window and called out to Unitas, "I hope you become the greatest quarterback in football."

By the time Unitas retired in 1973 with almost every passing record – most completions, most yardage, most 300-yard games, most touchdown throws – that is exactly what he was.

Chapter 25

The Teetotaller

In his late forties or early fifties, AJR gave up drinking entirely. He never in his life had indulged very heavily. He'd have a beer with the sportswriters or in the country-club bar after a golf match. As I have written earlier in these memoirs, he tolerated drinking by his friends and business associates, but preached against it to his sons with great vehemence.

To his sons and even his nephews, he would say, "Don't be saps. Stay out of those joints [any bar was a 'joint.'] Only jerks and losers go to places like that."

Of course, it didn't take long to figure out that "joints" had been a part of his and Father Dan's early environment.

Kass was an occasional beer drinker. At the advice of a doctor, Aunt Alice drank stout, to "build up" her blood. Stout is a popular Irish drink, but to me it always tasted like medicine or tar. Aunt Alice would drink a bottle or two of the stuff every day; then in late middle age she switched to beer.

On the big holidays, such as Christmas and New Year's, all of us had champagne – for my brothers and me, just a sip. Kass would also allow us to sip wine or beer, thus removing the lure of the forbidden. Her theory seemed to work for Dan and me, but not for the twins or our cousin Trish Fiske, who lived off and on at 940 North Lincoln Avenue.

Late in life, Kass switched from beer to Canadian Club highballs – two a day at the most. I saw her tipsy only once. It was a hot summer night. We'd been to Monmouth Park, where AJR had a horse running, a horse he had named for Pat Livingston, the sportswriter. Pat Livingston came in first and, as AJR would say, he "paid a buster." AJR won more on his bet than the purse for the race was worth. So we all went to a restaurant not far from the track, and we were all very excited. Instead of her usual highball, Kass ordered a martini. Apparently she drank it too fast. The bartender gave her another, and after taking one sip she said she could drink no more. Almost immediately, the alcohol turned her into a zombie. She stared straight ahead; she couldn't speak. We got her from the bar to the table, where some food and a cup of coffee fixed her up. That was it. She never had trouble with booze.

As for Aunt Alice ... well, let's just say that sometimes she overindulged.

Ladies Last

It never occurred to me until I had learned more about life, but at 940 North Lincoln Avenue our dinner-time protocol was that of a social order pre-dating the feminist revolution.

Only the males in the family were seated. The women–Mom, Aunt Alice, and when she happened to be staying with us, Trish Fiske – served them, having first prepared the meal.

It was certainly not a case of anyone being denied equal rights. For reasons of their own, I am sure that Mom and Aunt Alice wanted it that way.

Our dinners were always robust – salad, bread, sometimes soup; steaks or chops or spaghetti or stews; vegetables and potatoes in the old Irish tradition. When tea or coffee and dessert were set before us, Mom and Aunt Alice would take their places at the table with the menfolk. I never thought much about it, but up to then they had probably eaten on the run, at the kitchen counter.

Mom was a specialist at baking apple pies. All her fruit pies, in fact, were outstanding. She made a splendid coconut cream pie as well. How she learned to bake I don't know. Her mother may have taught her. More likely, she taught herself, just by following the recipes in a cook book.

Mom's cakes were good, but not in the same class with her pies. She liked to put sherry in her pies – Harvey's Bristol Cream. Just a dash was enough.

Kass earned considerable praise for a tossed mixed vegetable salad. The Italian dressing gave it that something extra, she said. The recipe for the dressing came from a bookie and fight manager who had been a professional fighter himself. Before he would tell Kass the secret of the blend, he ordered everybody else out of the kitchen. "This is just between the two of us," he said. Kass, though sworn to silence, let it slip that "a real good olive oil" and "a dash of white sugar" were two of the ingredients.

That is all she would ever say.

The Shamrock Room

Aunt Margaret's husband, Johnny Laughlin, borrowed money from Dad to open a little saloon on Western Avenue, and it prospered. John was a hustler. Once when he was remodeling, he continued to operate by setting up a makeshift bar. It consisted of two barrels and a plank.

Shutting down for any reason was something he hated to do. During a siege of the flu, unable to be up and around, he persuaded Aunt Margaret to tend bar. Though she could handle the job as well as he could, this was not a good business decision. Many of John's customers, as it happened, were alcoholics; on their way to work in the morning they would stop at his place for "a hair of the dog that bit them" and get a lecture from Aunt Margaret on the evils of drinking before noon.

"You should be thinking of your jobs and your wives and your kids," she would tell them. Then, reluctantly, she'd pour them a shot and a beer.

Johnny Laughlin was ambitious. He moved across Western Avenue into slightly larger quarters and added a kitchen. In addition to wet goods, he was now serving food. It was the kind of bar and grill that AJR called "a sawdust joint." People started going there to talk about politics and sport.

Encouraged, Johnny borrowed more money from AJR after the end of the Second World War and bought the warehouse-type building next door. Into it, he put an upscale restaurant he called the Shamrock Room.

AJR doubted the wisdom of this venture. The North Side, he said, was not the right location for upscale dining. He advised John to try Mount Washington, with its magnificent view of the downtown skyline. But John could be obstinate at times, and he had made up his mind to stay on Western Avenue.

To the rummies and hard-bitten working-class guys his old place had attracted, the new restaurant's dining room was off-limits. They had to go somewhere else or eat in the bar. Most of them could not have afforded the prices he now charged anyway, and though feelings were hurt and a few of the old regulars drifted away, his exclusion policy was all to the good. The Shamrock Room gave him a steady income for years, which meant that the Laughlins now had financial independence. The food was not bad – steak and chops and broiled chicken were the most popular items on the menu – and the knowledge that John was related to AJR drew a sports-minded clientele.

Dad would take his pals there for casual dinners, and every Christmas he threw a big ham dinner for the St. Peter's and Rooney Reds football teams. Billy Conn and some of the Steelers would say hello to the kids and sign autographs. In a modest way, the Shamrock Room acquired a name. Jack Palance, the movie actor, stopped by one night, a tall, scary-looking guy, and John introduced him to AJR. They talked about the fight game, Palance having started out as a boxer. (In a sparring session somewhere with Billy Conn, he failed to land a single blow. Conn, Palance said, "was like a feather in the wind.")

Just as AJR had foretold, the North Side was not the place for an upscale restaurant. The kind of patron his brother-in-law wanted would show up once or twice and seldom return after that. John's lunch business was good, but at night time, when a restaurant owner has a chance to cash in, the crowds did not come.

By doing a lot of favors for people and keeping up his political contacts, John stayed afloat in a deteriorating neighborhood longer than anyone thought possible. In the end, though, he was forced to unload the place and go to work as a lobbyist in Harrisburg.

John liked to eat and drink; over the years, he put on weight. He was in his seventies when the rich food caught up to him. Heart disease and a stroke were the official causes of death.

Chapter 26

Big Spender

So that Uncle Jim would have something to do – something constructive – AJR put him on the football team's payroll as coach of the punters. That year the Steelers had a marvelous punter named Pat Brady, and Jim watched him kick on his first day in camp. There were oohs and ahs from the spectators as the ball soared into the air, high and far. When practice was over, Jim spoke a few quiet words to Brady. Later, someone asked what he had said. In his familiar stage whisper, Jim answered, "I told him to keep doing what he was doing. I told him not to change a thing. Coaching," Jim added, "would only screw him up."

In effect, Jim had talked himself out of a job. Before the start of the regular season, Special Teams Coach Jim Rooney was ex-Special Teams Coach Jim Rooney and back in the job he had always had – "being with Arthur."

At some point, Jim and George Quinlan opened the Allegheny County Sportsman's Club, a place to meet and drink after 2 a.m. "We had a corporation," said Quinlan. "With zero funds. I'd ask Jim, 'How's your bankroll?' 'I've got four bucks,' he'd say."

Jim's accounting procedures were not widely accepted in the financial community. He believed that on Chinese New Year's Day all debts were wiped out. If you owed somebody, it was canceled. If somebody owed you, it was canceled. One of Jim's creditors was a guy named Sal, who kept hundred-dollar bills in his right hip pocket, fifty-dollar bills in his left hip pocket, and twenty-dollar bills in his vest pocket. When Jim was in need, he knew where to go. "Sal," he would say, "give me a couple from your right kick."

His rule was never to go to bed until he had spent or given away all his cash. "He'd give it to the bellhop," said Quinlan. "He'd give it to the hatcheck girl. He'd give it to the doorman. He'd give it to the elevator operator. Then he could sleep."

One day when Pop Rooney boarded a streetcar, the conductor, an acquaintance, told him of a strange occurrence. "A man in a blue suit handed me a ten-dollar bill and said, 'Keep the change.'" The fare at that time was a nickel. Conductors wore change belts with compartments for coins and currency. "What did the guy look like?" asked Pop. The conductor gave him a full description, and Pop said, "I know that fool."

It was Jim.

In the Fort Pitt Hotel, while drinking at the bar, Jim would smoke a cigar. When the cigar stopped burning, as it frequently did, Cap, the black waiter, would strike a match and re-light it. Jim would then hand him a dollar. Somebody figured out that for every cigar Jim smoked at the bar, Cappy made an average of eight bucks. Jim drank there maybe five days a week, so his smoking added forty dollars a week or roughly two thousand dollars a year to Cappy's take-home pay.

In restaurants, Jim sometimes tipped coming and going. He borrowed ten dollars from Dago Sam one night – they had not yet placed their order – and immediately gave it to the waiter.

"What's the idea?" demanded Sam.

"You don't want him to spit in our food, do you?" said Jim.

In Scranton a few days after AJR struck it rich at Empire City and Saratoga, Jim checked into a small hotel with Quinlan. The room clerk glanced at his signature and asked if he happened to be from Pittsburgh. Jim said that was correct. "Are you *the* Mr. Rooney from Pittsburgh?" asked the clerk. Jim acknowledged that he was. The clerk passed the word to the manager. *The* Mr. Rooney from Pittsburgh, who had just cleaned out the bookies at two race tracks, was a guest of the hotel.

"Show him to the presidential suite," said the manager. "Extend unlimited credit."

Uncle Jim Rooney
(McGinley Collection)

Jim threw a party that night, a big one that filled the suite and moved into the ballroom downstairs. There was music (a piano player). There were girls. Later in the evening, a friend of the family named Dan Odom checked in. "Mister Rooney from Pittsburgh is here," the room clerk proudly informed him. "He's having a big party."

Odom's eyebrows went up. "Are you sure you have the right Mister Rooney?" he asked. It was now the room clerk's turn to look surprised. "Is there more than one?" he wanted to know. Yes ... there was more than one.

Jim's friends had to smuggle him out the back door. AJR, of course, got the bill.

When he was flush, Jim's favorite drink was champagne laced with Hennessy brandy. At other times he drank Old Granddad bourbon with Miller's High Life beer. He would then buy a small tin of aspirin tablets and take all twelve at once to prevent a hangover.

"We had a guy at the Fort Pitt Hotel named Kalski," George Quinlan recalled. "He'd have a doughnut and a cup of coffee for breakfast – fifteen cents. One morning Jim came into the dining room at 10 o'clock, and Kalski said, 'Sit down, Jim – have a little breakfast.' And Jim had a tripleheader of Granddad and a bottle of Miller's – three dollars and something. The next day they took Kalski to the hospital."

Exchanging banter, Quinlan and Jim were like a vaudeville team. The subtlety of their humor, with its reliance on irony and understatement, demanded a certain amount of sophistication from listeners. Adolescents, by and large, tend to lack this requirement. So it was that when Richie McCabe and Jim Boston, training-camp ball boys at St. Bonaventure in the 1950s, drove with the garrulous old sidekicks to an exhibition game in northeastern Pennsylvania one Saturday morning, the Quinlan-Rooney act did not play well. After twenty minutes or so, McCabe looked at Boston and mouthed the word "Bullshit." Boston giggled. Soon there was open mockery. And sarcasm.

When Quinlan, the driver, pulled up at a wayside fruit store around noon, the kids in the back seat snickered. They knew what the game was. Camp manager that year, Quinlan had the meal money; he and Jim were sots; by economizing on lunch, they could finance a Saturday night bender. To the ball boys that seemed hilarious. A laughing jag seized them. They went into the fruit store doubled over with mirth. The customers, not knowing what to make of it all, stared at them. By contrast with the imposing natural dignity of Quinlan and Jim, their behavior seemed all the more mystifying.

Up the road a piece was a hospital for the deranged. Quinlan, looking grave, addressed the little crowd in the fruit store. "These unfortunate boys," he said, "are from well-to-do families in Pittsburgh. As legal advisors to their heartbroken parents, we have agreed, my friend and I, to bring them here for confinement and treatment at your justly renowned mental institution. We only hope they are not too far gone to be helped."

There were pitying glances and understanding nods. With all the feigned sincerity he could muster, Quinlan had cast the ball boys in parts which, to the naked eye, suited them perfectly. Richie McCabe was a tall, thin, geeky-looking youth; Boston – called "Buff," short for "Buffalo" – had a big balloon head on a large, ungainly frame. Strangers were apt to take him for a good-natured oaf.

Actually he was shrewd enough to be promoted from ball boy to the front office and entrusted with the job of negotiating player contracts, while Richie McCabe had a successful career as an NFL player and coach. But in taking on two such masters of repartee as George Quinlan and Uncle Jim they miscalculated badly. They were kids, yes. But they were North Side kids. And as North Side kids they should have known better.

Buff

Before there was air conditioning, people left their windows open in hot weather. Because our North Side neighborhood was a quiet one, voices traveled great distances on the soft summer breeze, allowing the nuns who lived at the Sisters of Mercy convent to learn, as one of them put it, all they needed to know about life.

Jim Boston grew up in this neighborhood. His friendship with the Rooney brothers was lucky for him and lucky for us. At an early age, he went to work for the Steelers, and from the 1950s into the 1990s he served the organization well.

Jim's parents owned a mom-and-pop grocery store near the police station. He was a pudgy, undersized, sports- crazy kid, always pleasant, always ingratiating. As soon as he was old enough to drive, he had the use of an old jalopy, a 1939 roadster his uncle had kept on blocks during World War II, when gasoline was in short supply. Jim ran the wheels off the thing, chauffeuring schoolmates all over town. He delivered AJR to the Duquesne Club one day and learned that no good deed goes unpunished. The Duquesne Club's members were the rich and the powerful. They arrived for lunch or for business meetings in shiny black limousines driven by uniformed flunkies. Boston's neighborhood pals seized on this. "Why doesn't Jim wear a uniform?" one would ask. With the callous levity of the young, another would say, "Because he can't find a chauffeur's cap big enough for his head."

At Steeler training camp when Boston was a ball boy, Jim Rooney made the remark that his head was the size of a buffalo's. Others repeated it. Jim Finks and Bill Walsh, two of the players, started calling him Buffalo. Then they shortened it to Buff, and the nickname caught on. He was Buff for the rest of his life.

Too small to play football, Boston became manager for the team at North Catholic High School. Before the start of the season, a ruptured appendix laid him low. During and after his long convalescence, a physiological miracle occurred. The rest of Jim Boston caught up with his head. Suddenly he was 6 feet 3, and growing sideways as well. The cops at the neighborhood police station started recruiting him for lineups whenever they had a crime, a suspect, and a witness or witnesses. Jim was always picked as the "perpetrator" – the guy who did it.

In spite of his bulk he was an excellent dancer and a pretty good pickup-game basketball player. He was not proficient at schoolwork. Because of his weak eyes, reading may have been difficult for him. He was smart, but lacked discipline and patience. AJR gave him a job as a ball boy, and he made himself useful in the trainer's room, the equipment room, and the ticket office. It seemed there was nothing he wasn't able to do.

Only once did he run afoul of AJR. At a pre-season game with the Philadelphia Eagles on a sweltering afternoon in Franklin Field, he was wearing a T-shirt and sweat pants. Jim had a nervous habit he appeared to be unaware of – lifting the front end of his T-shirt and putting it into his mouth, which left his ample paunch completely bare. His sweat pants, secured by a worn-out elastic band, kept slipping; Boston kept pulling them up tight, which outlined his genitals. Sitting with the Chief, NFL Commissioner Bert Bell found the display offensive. "Art," he said, "look over there by the Steeler bench. Who is that big fat kid with the thick glasses, the big belly, the big round head, and the big balls?"

From then on Boston had orders to tighten the waist of his sweat pants with tape and to wear two T-shirts or two sweat shirts – one to chew, as AJR explained, and one to cover his midsection.

Irish Brewmaster

George Quinlan said of himself, "I was born in March, a windy month, in Chicago, a windy city, and I'm a windy guy." Tall and gray-haired, distinguished in appearance, he looked like an actor, the kind of actor who is cast as a senator, judge, or district attorney in the movies. He was an expert story teller whose timing, voice inflection, and body language would have been right for the stage or screen, but his actual occupation during the years of Prohibition was something quite different.

"I was sent to Pittsburgh," he said once, "because I had a degree in brewing. I was an Irish brewmaster. "

At different times, Quinlan ran breweries in Millvale and Knoxville. "I was young," he said. "I could hustle and I think I had some belly." His partner was a man called Shine, from Panther Hollow. Quinlan told a story about Shine: "One day as he was getting ready to unlock the door from the outside and let me drive through from the inside with a truckload of beer, he heard an automobile coming. He thought it was the police, and he ran like hell. He ran away and left me locked in the damn brewery. I had to chop my way out through a window with a bung pick. An hour later I found Shine in Oakland, telling a bunch of guys about the Prohibition men. I asked him, 'Where the hell's the key?' 'Oh, I threw it in the river,' he said. So I went back to the brewery and chopped off the lock."

In Chicago, Quinlan had a brother on the police force and a brother who was killed by the mob. He had an uncle named Paddy McNamara who killed a guy in a saloon fight, pleaded insanity, and spent thirty-eight years in a Cook County mental institution. "He *was* insane," Quinlan said. "From whiskey. That was the curse of the Irish – drinking. In Illinois, you couldn't sell the Indians a drink, and I always thought they should put the Irish on that list, too. 'Don't you like the Irish?' someone asked me. I said, 'I love the Irish, and my love is intensified by knowing how weak some of them are, including myself.'"

Another uncle, Barney Birch, was a political boss. "Barney Birch made four trips to four penitentiaries and ended up with a ton of money," Quinlan said. Barney Birch introduced Quinlan to Al Capone. "I met him just twice. He had the whole second floor of the Lexington Hotel. A big, tough dago, and I didn't go for him. He weighed about 290 pounds, and he grunted. You couldn't understand him. He ended up with cirrhosis of the liver. I'm never proud to say that I knew Al Capone."

Quinlan was an Irish tenor. As a young man in Chicago he sang in Clark Street saloons. An Irish tenor named Dion O'Banion, an acquaintance but not a friend, also sang in Clark Street saloons. Later, O'Banion went into the racketeering business and died at the hands of Al Capone's gunmen. In 1926, Quinlan sang at Carnegie Hall in Pittsburgh and he sang on the radio. "I could sing in Italian and Hebrew," he said.

John McCormack gave a concert in Pittsburgh at the Syria Mosque. "In the second row that night," Quinlan said, "there were eighteen Catholic priests and a hoodlum named George Quinlan. Father O'Connor from St. Mary's of the Point was sitting next to me. He said, 'George, the honey has left John's voice.' I said, 'What do you think caused it, Father?' He said, 'The whiskey, George, the whiskey.' "

When Lily Pons, the French opera singer, gave a concert in Pittsburgh, Quinlan was introduced to her. "And she put out her paw," he said. "She expected me to kiss her hand. The only other French girl I ever met was a very beautiful movie actress" – who, for purposes of this narrative, shall be nameless. "She was brought into Johnny Laughlin's Shamrock Restaurant by Jackie Conn. We sat in a booth, and I asked her if she knew Jackie's brother Billy. She said, 'Yes, but Billy says bad things about me. He told some people in New York that I was a French pig.' 'Well,' I said, 'Billy makes very few mistakes.'"

During the run-up to the stock-market crash of 1929, Quinlan invested heavily. He said, "In 1928 I had a hell of a year. I made ninety thousand dollars. I took it all into Morris, Lloyd and Lynch. I went in there and started buying stocks. I couldn't even read the damn symbols. I bought five hundred dollars of this and four hundred dollars of that. I was a big shot. President of a brewery. Oh boy, was I something. And then the market crashed. I must have lost a hundred and fifty thousand dollars. I had RCA. I don't remember what I paid for it. I told my broker, 'Sell the RCA,' and he said, 'Who'd buy it?' I had Graham-Paige. Bought it for eight dollars. I sold it at sixty-five cents."

The repeal of the Eighteenth Amendment in 1933 completed the financial undoing of Quinlan. His illegal brewery – "Bootlegging may have been illegal," he used to say, "but it wasn't illicit" – shut down, and he worked for a while in the slot-machine business with Uncle Jim.

In the 1950s, when the Steelers prepared for the season at St. Bonaventure, Quinlan was camp manager. The job was not difficult. For the most part it consisted of keeping an accurate count of the camp population for the cooks and the mess-hall workers. Up to a point, the players, coaches, and newspaper reporters found Quinlan's stories entertaining. He did not have much of a formal education but had read a lot and knew how to express himself. By the last day of camp, however, his performance had usually lost some of its charm. I would say that most people dismissed him as an Irish version of Falstaff.

Undeniably, Quinlan had strong ties to the Rooneys of his generation. He knew Anne Jackson's father, the coal miner from Harmarville who believed in Communism. "Old Dan Rooney and I used to have arguments with him," Quinlan said. "Old Dan was one of the greatest men I ever met. His son Jim called him 'Square Paper.' No con. He never screwed anybody. He couldn't. He was a tough old man but an honorable old man and very outspoken. I remember one time after the Steelers lost a ball game he was on the front porch with Art and Jim. The Steelers had been slaughtered that day, and Art said it was terrible the way the people booed Kiesling. And his father said, 'Art, take Kiesling to the Duquesne Brewery and get him a job.'

"I met Art's brother Dan when he was studying for the priesthood. Dan was a great man. As a missionary, he had to learn Chinese. A lot of Chinks didn't think he understood it, but they were wrong. Dan didn't talk much about China. He didn't talk much about anything. He could have been an outstanding baseball player. He could hit. He hit a couple over the fence against the Homestead Grays. But he had no arm. All in all, Dan was a very strong character. He got in his rough work in life early. Ran a crap game, drove a beer truck. A pretty solid fella – quiet and very, very hot-tempered."

Quinlan and Uncle Jim were close. Quinlan told stories about Jim's proficiency as a fighter. "One night Jim got into an argument with Billy Conn's father-in-law, Greenfield Jimmy Smith, and Jim asked Jimmy Smith to get out of the automobile they were in. Jimmy Smith was tough, but he didn't get out of the automobile. Jim Rooney's daddy taught his kids to fight. He taught them all, and they fought with each other for the fun of it. I took Duke to the hospital one day after Jim knocked him unconscious.

"Jim could fight, Art could fight, and Dan could fight. There was a big, tough lieutenant of police named Henninger who hung out at an engine house on the North Side. He weighed about 200 pounds and he was flattening everybody. One day a young guy who weighed about 170 came in. He put on the gloves with Henninger, and *boom*! Henninger went out. The young guy was Dan Rooney.

"One time out at Forbes Field, Bert Bell got into an argument with Buff Donelli, and Buff was going to slug him. Father Dan was sitting three seats away, and he was wearing his collar. He jumped over the rail and grabbed Buff. And Buff didn't slug Bert Bell."

Quinlan recalled that when Uncle Jim was born – in 1905 on March 16th – his parents intended to name him Patrick James. "But nobody was hiring Irish Catholics at the time, and his mother said, 'We'd better call him James Patrick. If he's Pat Rooney, he'll never get a job.' The way it turned out, getting a job was the last thing Jim ever wanted to do."

Old age was not kind to George Quinlan. He was indicted for perjury when the police discovered – it must have been shocking to them – that there was illegal gambling at the Sportsman's Club, the after-hours place run by Quinlan and Uncle Jim. Although Jim was a full partner, the indictment did not mention him. Political pull? I'm not sure. At any rate, Quinlan was never brought to trial. AJR continued to send him money – a generous sum every Christmas – but they were never again very close. Another benefactor was Buck McArdle, a lawyer friend of Ed Kiely and Jack McGinley, who gave Quinlan a job as an investigator to keep him afloat. Bedridden after a stroke, he spent the last two years of his life in a rented room in Dormont.

"Doc," he said to the physician taking care of him, "how do I stay mentally alert? How do I keep from going nuts?" "Communicate, George," the doctor said. Quinlan had mistrusted newspaper reporters all his life, but now, using the telephone, he became friendly with two or three, including Kathy Kiely, Ed's daughter. A year or two before he died, Quinlan sent her a Christmas card. On it, he wrote:

With rheumy eyes, Sans teeth,
With concrete ears [he was partly deaf], *And one dead wing* [he was paralyzed on the left side],
I'm close to being a dead thing.
Merry Christmas to you and yours.
As for me, at 91 [actually, he was 81], *I'll take a small beer.*

Prankster

You either could not abide Owney McManus or you loved him. AJR was among his devoted friends. Although we did not get acquainted until Owney had seen his best days, I counted myself lucky to have known him, and so did my brother Tim.

Owney McManus was a round-faced little man with a red complexion, very Irish and very Catholic. There were those who appreciated his humor and his prank playing and others who found him abrasive. He talked a lot, and often it was possible to believe what he said. Until old age forced him to change his habits, he liked to drink. He liked women – his first wife died young – but practiced serial monogamy.

Owney was a World War I veteran. If he distinguished himself at all, it was on the troop ship going to France. The enlisted men, crammed below deck, mistook a loud noise for a torpedo hit from a German U-boat one night and panicked. In the bedlam, little Owney took charge. Fearful of being crushed in a stampede to the hatch, he shouted in the voice that in years to come would dominate many a bar-room argument, "Quiet! Take it easy! We haven't seen any water coming in! Let's get out of here one at a time! Don't do the Germans' job for them!" Reaching deck in an orderly fashion, the frightened recruits could see that nothing had happened. The ship was steady and the ocean was calm. And a lot of big, brave soldier boys who had lost their heads were embarrassed.

Anyway, that was the story.

Owney's saloon on Fourth Avenue resembled a fun house at times. Some of the games that he and his henchmen – and henchwomen – would play were elaborate, not to say juvenile and sadistic. If a stranger who looked like a rube walked in, a waitress from the bar might go to a room the boys kept in the nearby Pittsburgher Hotel. Owney would sidle up to the pigeon and ask if he wanted a girl. Often the answer was yes, and, following instructions, the fellow would go to the hotel room, knock in a certain way, and ask for "Gertie." Or "Mabel." Or whatever name Owney had mentioned. The waitress would let him in and close the door. A moment later it would fly open, and a man with a gun would be shouting, "So you're the guy who's trying to ruin my home life!" He'd be waving his pistol in the air. The waitress would shriek. And the "John" would take off and run down the stairs, not waiting for an elevator, and out onto the street, where Owney and his friends could see how successful their machinations had been.

A variation of this scam involved the firing of blank cartridges by the man with the gun and the sudden appearance of blood — actually ketchup — on the waitress's blouse.

In such ways did Owney and his pals get their kicks. The hotel-room caper had to be dropped after one victim, running for his life, tripped on the Fourth Avenue streetcar tracks and broke a leg.

In the year when a song called "Deep in the Heart of Texas" was popular, a cop named Al Quaill, who had been a middleweight boxer, patronized Owney's bar. Even if Al was off-duty, he carried his police revolver. "Deep in the Heart of Texas" always seemed to be blaring on Owney's juke box, and in one verse the lyrics went:

The stars at night
Are big and bright
Deep in the heart of Texas...

After the word "bright" there was a pause in the beat. From the juke box you would hear the sound of hands clapping four times, and people listening in Owney's bar would join in, either clapping or banging their glasses and bottles on the table. One night everybody did that except Quaill, who had tossed off a few stiff ones. Keeping perfect time with the others, he pulled out his revolver and fired four shots into the ceiling.

Furious, Owney ushered Quaill to the door. "You could have broken one of my overhead pipes!" he kept saying. The shots might have killed one of the customers, too, but McManus was only concerned about the pipes.

Another policeman — the beat cop working Fourth Avenue — often stopped in for a free meal. It was one of his perks, but Owney disliked the guy. McManus's was a ham-and-cabbage joint, and the cop was always asking for something exotic, like rabbit. One day when he asked for rabbit, Owney was prepared to teach him a lesson. A friend of his had ended the life of a stray cat, and a butcher carved it up. Owney cooked the pieces that looked like rabbit and served them to the cop, who complimented him on an excellent meal. "Best rabbit I've ever tasted," he said. "This place is finally getting some class."

One night around closing time Owney got into a drunken argument with a judge. The judge was attacking Mayor Lawrence, and Owney was defending him. Goaded beyond endurance, Owney picked up a whiskey bottle and hit the judge on top of the head. An ambulance came and took the judge to the hospital. Sobering up, Owney began to evaluate the trouble he was in. Would he lose his liquor license? Would the escapade put him out of business? Would it put him in jail? The next afternoon the judge walked into the bar. He had come to apologize, he said. He was a judge, and his actions had been injudicious. He'd made a complete fool of himself. As for his injuries, they were minor, a slight concussion and a lump on the head. Owney sighed with relief and agreed to let bygones be bygones.

Owney shocked me one day. He said he'd been playing golf at the Wildwood Country Club and his drive had hit the side of a car that belonged to a fellow club member, a Catholic priest, who happened to be in it at the time. He said the priest got out of the car and berated him. "Can you imagine that old S.O.B.?" Owney demanded. "What a miserable guy." Never before in my life had I heard a Catholic speak ill of a priest. I had been taught by my parents and the nuns and the brothers at North Catholic High School that you always showed deference to priests. It took me a long time to get over such a display of irreverence.

But Owney was no respecter of persons or of Roman collars. He made no secret of his antipathy for Father James Cox, the priest from the Strip district who in 1932 led an army of the unemployed in a march on Washington. It seems that as a shepherd of the Lord, Father Cox had once seen fit to criticize Owney for his lifestyle. Instead of listening meekly, Owney lashed back, pointing out to the noted clergyman some shortcomings of his own. McManus knew the dirt on everybody, Catholic priests included.

Owney did have a lot of friends who were priests, and he could impersonate a priest if need be. Once when AJR and a few of his pals were driving to Canada for a week or two of fishing, they ran out of booze in upstate New York. Prohibition was still the law, so replenishing their supply would be a problem. Opportunity suggested itself, however, as they passed a mom 'n' pop drug store with an Irish name over the door. "Stop here!" someone said. With a prescription from a doctor, you could legally buy whiskey at a drug store, and though the requisite medical OK was lacking, the man who had said "Stop!" had an idea. He went into the drug store and explained to the owner that he and some fisherman friends were driving to Canada but thought they would have to turn back. A priest in the group, who was over here from Ireland, had been suddenly taken ill. A bad cold. What might help was a bit of whiskey. They had no prescription, of course. On the grounds that this was an emergency, could the druggist possibly oblige them?

"Well, now," said the druggist. "A priest from Ireland, you say?" He could let them have a pint, but with one stipulation. He would have to see this priest and hand over the whiskey himself.

Owney, unaware he had been nominated for the role of sick priest, was asleep in the back seat of the car. Aroused from slumber to meet the druggist – "Father, I know you're not feeling good, but wake up!" the idea man said to him – he caught on at once. It was twilight and rapidly getting dark. Owney pulled up the collar of his coat. He started to cough. The fact is that in appearance he resembled Barry Fitzgerald, the Irish movie actor often cast in those days as a priest. He was introduced to the druggist as Father McManus. He coughed again and wiped his nose.

"Father, I think you might need this," said the druggist, offering the whiskey. Owney accepted it with a look of saintly gratitude. A pint wasn't much, but it would get the carload of Pittsburghers to Canada. "Bless you, my son," he said, and coughed. "I will pray for you." There was the hint of an Irish brogue in his voice. The druggist refused payment.

Owney was a dedicated Steeler fan. In the days when Steeler teams did not amount to much, he created a following for them with his Ham-and-Cabbage Specials to out-of-town games. Sometimes the trains Owney ran would be hooked onto the train that carried the players and coaches, arriving at the scene after an all-night trip. "Ham and Cabbage" was a metaphor. The only food served was the railroad's standard fare. Once when Owney showed up at the Pennsylvania Station in Pittsburgh with a ring of bologna, everybody hooted at him. But the club car turned out to be oversold for dinner, and the people who had laughed at Owney were begging for some of his bologna. He would share it only with Kass, who had said he was wise to bring provisions.

Owney and AJR were great card players. When they played at 940 North Lincoln Avenue, almost always with a priest or two in the game, Kass would cook for them. Owney at such times would be on his best behavior. In fact, when AJR was around, he refrained from off-color jokes and from pranks like the one involving the waitress in the hotel room.

Owney's girlfriend, Marie, co-habited with him for a while, and AJR disapproved. After this liaison came to an end, Owney courted a more conventional matronly woman who took an interest in the bar business and made suggestions to improve its profitability. For one thing, she helped him to cut down waste and employee theft. The woman's name was Jean, and eventually Owney married her.

Sometimes it almost seemed that Owney was more concerned with AJR's affairs than his own. He kept urging AJR to develop business interests other than the football team. "You have to think about your sons," he would say. "All five can't work for the ball club."

AJR would answer, "They're little boys."

"They won't always be," Owney reminded him. This was before AJR acquired the race tracks in New York and Florida. Did Owney plant the seed? I tend to think so.

Like Uncle Jim, Owney burned the candle at both ends, and his health began to wane before he was out of his fifties. He sold or closed his restaurant and moved to Fort Lauderdale with Jean.

Owney Junior had just finished law school at Pitt. In contrast to his old man, he was staid and strait-laced, a serious, hard-working, overachieving young guy. He had always been a special favorite of Kass, who feared that Owney Senior was bringing him up in a poor home environment – an apartment above the saloon in a household that included Marie. One summer while Owney Junior studied for his bar exams, Kass put him up at our cottage in Ligonier. Before too long he was on his own and doing very well, and his father may have been an embarrassment to him at times. He was married to a girl of similar tastes and temperament, and when they entertained corporate big shots Owney Senior could be present but with orders to stay in the background. The trouble was that Owney Junior's lawyer friends would congregate around Owney Senior and coax him to tell stories about the sports people he knew.

"What was I supposed to do?" Owney Senior asked. "Play deaf and dumb?" For several years, Owney Junior was our football team's lawyer, but then the business became so big that one man no longer could handle all the legal problems – an entire firm was needed – and AJR had to replace him. Owney Junior was heart-broken.

Whether Owney Senior was still alive I don't remember. I know that his twilight years were anything but reposeful. He did stop drinking. As a diabetic with heart trouble, he had no alternative. He got some rest for a while and watched his diet. Though unable to break his cigarette habit, he succeeded in cutting back. But as soon as he realized that he was not about to die, he plunged into Fort Lauderdale politics. He was the Owney McManus of old, minus the booze and the pranks. Fort Lauderdale was full of transplanted Pittsburghers – former associates of Owney among them – and there were some, chances are, who found the moderated McManus more to their liking. Fort Lauderdale transformed him into something of a moralist. On a football trip to the Miami area, AJR was approached by the owners of the local jai alai frontons. They asked him to intervene for them with a tough little politician from Pittsburgh who was campaigning hard against a referendum to allow jai alai in Fort Lauderdale. (Jai alai is a Cuban court game similar to handball in which the players wear wicker baskets on their hands instead of gloves; in Florida there was lots of betting on jai alai, making supervision by each municipal government necessary.) AJR immediately guessed that the tough little politician from Pittsburgh was Owney McManus.

Without tipping his hand, he asked the jai alai promoters if they could get this fellow on the telephone. They could and did. Confident that Owney would recognize his voice, AJR took the phone and went straight to the point. All he said was, "I'm with the jai ali folks. They tell me you're giving them some grief. Well, they're OK guys. Lay off them ... OK. We understand each other." With that, he handed the phone back to one of the jai ali men and heard him say, "Yes ... Yes ... I'm glad you think that this can be worked out, Mister McManus. Thank you very much. I'll see you real soon." In the eyes of the jai alai guys from then on, AJR was a miracle worker.

Homesick after just a few years, Owney called Dave Lawrence in Pittsburgh. "I'd rather die around friends and family than down here," he said. "Can you get me a job?" Lawrence placed him in the state auditor's office.

Back where he belonged, he became an old uncle to the Rooney boys. One day at lunch time we brought him a sandwich from the Roosevelt Hotel, and he gave us a glimpse of his Merry Prankster persona. He picked up the telephone and called the cops who policed the Liberty Tunnel. "Hello," he began, "I'm calling about my airplane. Yes, my airplane. I landed it by mistake at the county airport last night. I meant to land it at the Greater Pittsburgh Airport, but the traffic controllers misdirected me. So I have to get my plane to Greater Pittsburgh, but I'm not allowed to fly there. I'm having it towed. Yes, towed. Now, wait a minute. Be patient. This is why I'm calling you. I got to your tunnel about three in the morning and couldn't get my plane through because the wings were too wide. Your guys told me to leave it there – park it off to the side – and come back and pick it up this afternoon, and they'd see what could be done ... What do you mean; you've never heard of anything like this? How about going outside to see if my plane is OK ... I'm not kidding, dammit! Please go out and see if it's OK. It won't hurt you to put your head out the door."

Glancing up at Tim and me, Owney chortled, "I've got the poor sap looking out the door. I hear him yelling at someone about an airplane that has to get through ..."

Another call Owney made was to the manager of the Hilton Hotel. Assuming a Polish accent, he demanded to know why the Hilton's American flag was not at half mast. An important public figure who was Polish had died – and Owney came up with a fictitious name full of Z's and K's. There were lots of Poles in Western Pennsylvania, he said, and they deserved as much respect as the Irish, who had their St. Patrick's Day parade. My brother and I were rolling on the floor.

When Rudy Bukich, a Steeler quarterback from the University of Southern California, asked AJR to finance a bowling alley, Owney took it upon himself to conduct an investigation. He visited many of the bowling alleys in Pittsburgh and took me along. His conclusion: "Bowling alleys are now like drug stores. They're at the point of saturation. That Bukich fellow is a pretty nice guy from what I hear, but how much does he mean to the Rooney family? If this thing works, he'll be sitting pretty. If it doesn't work he has used your money and contacts and good name. You are left holding the bag, while Rudy is still a nice guy and no longer around. He is back in Southern California."

It was a good lesson I have always remembered: what is the other guy bringing to the party?

In the 1950s Tim was a stockbroker. One day when I was in my early twenties I had a date to play golf with Tim and his boss and Owney. The three of them came to 940 North Lincoln in a car – I was still living at home – and when I did not make an immediate appearance, Tim ran up to the porch. He started giving me hell for causing a delay; I lost my temper; so did he; punches were exchanged, and Tim went down. The upshot of it was that they drove off without me – I no longer wanted to be a part of the golf outing.

A day or two later, I had a meeting with Owney. He told me that Tim and I must always remember who we were. If we insisted on fighting we should be careful to pick our spots. It was not a good idea to act like roughnecks in front of Tim's boss. This from an old brawler like Owney. I told him I hadn't meant to humiliate Tim. He was tougher than I was and a better fighter. It just so happened that I nailed him with a lucky punch. "Maybe," said McManus. "But when it ended you were standing over him. Don't sell yourself short."

We did not always appreciate Owney's words of wisdom. There were times when my brothers and I tested his patience with what Owney called "smart-ass remarks," but clearly he liked to be in our company.

As the old guard died off, AJR was going to five or six wakes every week, and in Owney he now had a companion. I was with them once when somebody said of the corpse that he "looked good." Owney shook his head in disgust. "NO ONE," he said turning to me, "looks good in the box."

The last wake he attended was his own. While playing pinochle with AJR and some others, he died of a heart attack. At the funeral home, I just had to say it: "No one looks good in the box." I meant this as a fond, sincere tribute to Owney, one of Pittsburgh's great unforgettable characters.

Chris

If you made a pig of yourself at the dinner table with Dad or one of his brothers present, they would say you were eating like Chris McCormick.

Chris was the guy who needed special accommodations at the Kenyon Theater because of his enormous rear end. So that he could watch the movies there in something like comfort he paid to have two seats in the back row converted into one.

Uncle Jim spoke highly of Chris. "Wonderful fella," he told me. "Must have weighed over four hundred pounds. He lived with his two sisters; they were almost as big as he was. They'd have Dan, Art, and me out to dinner on a Sunday afternoon. Dinner was one o'clock sharp. And, boy, did they put on a feed. Chickens. Roast beef. Ham. Everything king-sized. Huge bowls of mashed potatoes with lots of gravy. Huge pitchers of buttermilk. Different kinds of dessert. Filled you up for a week. They were real nice people, Chris and his two sisters."

Chris McCormick was a professional man – an accountant – but in all ways a rough-hewn North Sider. On Federal Street one night he got into a fist fight. An old sandlot football player named Jim Westerling gave me a blow-by-blow description. Come to think of it, no blows were actually struck, at any rate not by Chris. "He grabbed hold of the guy," Jim said, "and fell on top of him. Then he laid there, holding the guy down. He just about crushed the life out of that guy. Flattened him like a pancake."

As a mark of esteem, AJR named one of his race horses after Chris. I don't know how close their friendship was. I do know that Chris was part of the gang, included on at least one trip to a championship boxing match in New York. AJR used to talk about it. He said that after the fight, learning that their train would be late, he and the other Pittsburghers went for a midnight snack to a place near the Pennsylvania Station. Everybody ordered a big steak.

The moment the steaks arrived at their table, a friend from back home came rushing into the room. "Hey, Art!" he yelled. "You guys better get going! The train to Pittsburgh is ready to pull out!"

No one had had a bite of steak. But, leaping out of their chairs, they took off en masse for the station. AJR paid the bill on the run. Only Chris lagged behind momentarily. Snatching up the tablecloth, he twisted it into a bundle with the steaks inside, threw the bundle over his shoulder, and joined the stampede. No morsel of food would be wasted while Chris was around.

He died before his time, as gluttons often do. "Poor Chris," said Uncle Jim, ad-libbing a sort of epitaph. "His belly button exploded."

Part Two: Bit Player 1956-1965

Chapter 27

Stagestruck

When AJR, pulling strings, got me admitted to Georgetown Law School in 1957, my history professor at St. Vincent College, Father Hugh Wilt, played devil's advocate.

"You can't spell," he reminded me.

"Your handwriting is unreadable." he reminded me.

I stared at him, puzzled. What did spelling and handwriting have to do with the practice of law? "But, Father," I said. "I'll have a secretary to type all my letters." His reply was: "Artie, you will find there are times when a handwritten note is more appropriate than a letter typed by a secretary."

He was pouring cold water on Georgetown Law School, and I didn't mind. AJR had a low opinion of lawyers anyway. And Uncle Jim told me, "They're a dime a dozen. All the lawyers I know are starving." (His acquaintanceship among lawyers must have been limited.)

There was something else that deflected me from the law. I remembered, or thought I remembered, a quote from Winston Churchill: "Youth is the time to take chances." Secretly, what I wanted to take a chance on was acting. I had just turned 21. "Go for it!" I could hear Churchill advising me.

I forgot about Georgetown Law School and started thinking about Carnegie Tech's renowned Drama School. Sure, actors were all fruits – sissy boys (my thinking back then had not yet begun to evolve). Even John Wayne. Well ... maybe not John Wayne. As Raoul Walsh, the director, once said, "The son of a bitch looks like a man." What was good enough for the Duke, I figured, was good enough for me. So I applied at Carnegie Tech and was told I'd be given an audition – or, in football parlance, a tryout. Did my name help? Possibly. Or possibly not. But, though I didn't know it at the time, the woman in charge, Edith Skinner, was a Steeler fan. I don't think that hurt.

Miss Skinner and two or three other instructors judged the auditions. I was asked to recite two short monologues – or were they soliloquies? – one from a serious drama, the other from a comedy. I chose a passage from "Macbeth" –"If it were done when 'tis done, then 'twere well it were done quickly ... " (Macbeth is about to murder Duncan) – and reporter Hildy Johnson's telephone call to his editor from the Ben Hecht-Charley MacArthur play, "The Front Page."

In the scene from "Macbeth," I took as my model the English actor Sir Ralph Richardson. I had a recording of Richardson as Macbeth and I copied every nuance of his delivery. Not very original, but it worked. I made a tape recording of my own interpretation and listened to it, and it seemed to be all right. I had to do this on the Q.T., because if AJR or my brothers were to overhear me, they would think I had gone queer.

With the Hecht-MacArthur scene, I was more comfortable. Having been around sportswriters all my life, I thought I could mimic their speech patterns and body language.

Waiting to go on, I was scared stiff. I was older by two or three years than the other applicants and self- conscious about it. The boys all had pimples, the girls had big noses. But they could act. Quite a few auditions preceded mine, and I was able to watch. I said to myself, "Boy ... those geeks are good!"

My turn came, and by then I had settled down. I started off with "Macbeth." There was a four-legged stool on the stage, and I put my foot on it, as I had seen professional actors do. I had a pretty fair theatrical voice, and I was letting 'er rip. So far, so good. Then my leg began to shake. I leaned on it. The shaking continued. I took my leg off the stool and tried to keep focused. At last it was over. I had remembered all the words, which was something.

Doing Hildy Johnson was easier for me. For some reason, though, I started to move sideways across the stage as I spoke my lines, forgetting that Hildy was supposed to be in a telephone booth. By a stroke of good luck, I finished before I ran out of stage.

All of us waited nervously for the verdict of the judges. The others, I saw, though more experienced than I was, were even less confident. Time passed. My name was called. I stepped before the judges to be told what I already knew: "You are more than raw!" But Miss Skinner said, "Your voice is a gift!" I was in!

Classes began, and a teacher named Bess Keeley made acting sound simple. "Just speak in a loud voice," she said, "and don't bump into the furniture." Alas, she was only kidding. Miss Skinner gave me constant encouragement. "You have a great voice. Learn to use it."

Another teacher took me aside and suggested I major in set design. "You *might* get a good job as an actor, but I say might. Major with me, and be *sure* to get a good job." Well, I hadn't passed up Georgetown Law School to be a set designer. All we seemed to do in those first few months, though, was build scenery.

By the end of the semester I'd had enough. I dropped out of school and left for New York City to study the Stanislavski Method of acting.

New York

AJR's first cousin, the actress Anne Jackson, was living in New York when I finished up at Carnegie Tech, and I wrote to her, inquiring about teachers. She gave me a list of names from which I selected the one with the most syllables in it, Tamara Daykahonova.

Madame D. had studied with the great Russian director Constantine Stanislavski at the Moscow Art Theatre. In 1917 she fled the Communist Revolution and came to America. Times were hard. She kept body and soul together, as she put it, by doing makeup – at first for just a handful of actors, then more, and at last for all the members of a cast. As her reputation grew, she found herself doing makeup by mail for entire theatrical companies on the road. Is such a thing possible, you ask? For the time being, let's not get into that.

Once Madame D. became established, she opened her New York actors' studio and made a nice living for years. She taught through improvisation, through character study. She expected us to interpret the playwright's intentions. We took diction lessons, dancing lessons, voice lessons. We learned to apply makeup.

Madame's husband – we knew him as "Mr. V." – was also a Russian. He escorted the whole class on trips to the great art museums of New York City. Right from the start, the old boy sort of took to me. He was impressed by the fact that I had gone to college and played football and that I read good books. I underestimated Mr. V., mistakenly supposing that he worked for his wife because that was the only job he could get. In truth, he had been a White Army general during the Russian Revolution, knew a lot about aeronautics, and held an important position with a big engineering firm on Long Island. Beyond all that, he had written a critically acclaimed paper on the Impressionist painter Gauguin. By the time I discovered these things, we were pals, and it was too late for me to be intimidated by Mr. V.

Madame Daykahonova gave me special attention. When I stopped going to dance classes – dancing, I thought, was "effeminate" – she did not object. Dancing lessons, she explained, were helpful to an actor because actors should be able to walk and move gracefully. (As Miss Keeley importuned us at Carnegie Tech, "Don't bump into the scenery.") Madame D. excused me from the class but made it clear I would not get my money back. She said I should take more interest in art, in classical music, in drama.

One day when AJR, Kass, and Ed Kiely happened to be in New York, I cut all my classes to go to Aqueduct with them. "I'm sorry," I told Madame D., "but my father has a horse of his running and he wants me to be there." Regretfully, she said she understood, but added in a meaningful way, giving my first name a vaguely Russian pronunciation, "Ar-tur, these classes are important."

The horse from the Shamrock Stables was the colt named for *Pittsburgh Press* writer Pat Livingston, and this was the day that AJR won an even $100,000 on him by placing bets at different windows through Kass, Kiely, and myself. As an afterthought he told me to bet "a couple of bucks" for Madame D. "She let you miss school. Show your appreciation."

I put twenty dollars on the horse for Madame D. It paid seven to one, so her winnings came to a hundred and forty. After that if she knew I was going to the track she would say, "Does your fart-er have his horse running good? Here's five dollars. Get it down for me."

I hated makeup class as much as I hated dancing. The makeup instructor, observing my indifference, gave me some good advice: "Even if you land an acting job on Broadway, you'll have to do your own makeup. To hire somebody would cost twenty-five dollars a night. That's one hundred and seventy-five dollars a week – a lot of money for an actor who plays supporting roles, even on Broadway. Instead of Broadway, chances are, you'll be acting in summer theatre learning the craft. You'd make a nuisance of yourself if you asked the other actors to do your makeup." So I didn't drop out of makeup class. My attendance record, however, was less than one hundred percent.

Makeup class was educational to me in still another way. The girls in the actors' studio were far from beautiful. They wore blouses and slacks or jeans and didn't bother much with their hair – just pulled it straight back and tied a ribbon around it. I thought, "Hey, these are just average-looking kids." I guess I expected actresses to be glamorous. But all of that changed as soon as they started going to makeup class. By the middle of the term, those plain little girls with the mouse-colored hair had started to remind me of movie stars. Cosmetics, I saw, could make a difference.

'Tommy, How Was I?'

My best friend in New York was Tom Bodkin, an old Pittsburgh associate of AJR. Tom had been a fighter, a fight promoter, and a referee. On Broadway, he worked in theatrical production. A theatrical company putting on a play would hire Tom as its business manager. His duties were similar to those of Fran Fogarty with the Steelers. That is to say, Tom paid the bills, negotiating with the actors, directors, stage hands, electricians ... everybody, in fact, who had anything to do with the show.

Thomas V. Bodkin was even older than my dad, which put him, I thought, in his dotage. In 1958, remember, I was not completely dry behind the ears. Actually, Tom was a big, well set-up man who looked almost handsome in his Homburg hat, dark blue suit, white dress shirt, and polka-dot tie. His clothes were well-tailored and up to date. Unlike other old men, and I include AJR, he disposed of his suits when they went out of style. AJR would keep a suit in his closet for thirty years.

I saw that with actresses and women in general, Tom's manner was urbane. My mother he addressed as Kathleen, never Kass, and she liked him a lot. An excellent raconteur, he put me in mind of George Quinlan, one difference being that Tom had more ... I don't know, call it self-respect. He believed that a man ought to work.

Tom's background in the fight game was something I had no inkling of. It was not until recently that I was able to fit the pieces together. Had it not been for Tom, writes James R. Fair in his biography of Harry Greb, "Give Him to the Angels," the great champion's career might have ended while he was still just a preliminary boy. In Greb's first year as a pro, 1913, he was matched with the more experienced Joe Chip. Tom Bodkin was the referee. In the second round, Chip had Greb badly hurt. Greb later said he was out on his feet. There were referees who would have let the fight continue until Chip had put Greb on the floor for a count of ten, writes Fair, but Bodkin alertly stopped it, awarding Chip a technical knockout. As soon as Greb got the cobwebs out of his brain, relates Fair, he told Bodkin, "One more hard punch could have ruined me. I won't forget this. Thanks."

Old newspaper clips reveal that Bodkin actually did count Greb out, but Jimmy Fair was an author with a lively imagination.

After Greb whipped Tommy Gibbons in his first big New York fight in 1922, Bodkin organized a parade for him in Pittsburgh. He then talked the manager of a burlesque wheel, Maurice Cain, into a thousand-dollar-a-week contract for Greb. (Cain threw in one hundred and fifty for Bodkin, to which Greb added another hundred dollars out of his thousand.)

They opened at the old Gayety Theatre, Downtown. Greb, reading from a script Tom had prepared for him, began his monologue by saying, "It was right here in Pittsburgh that I got my start in the ring by defeating ... "

The next week the show jumped to Detroit. Greb's monologue was unchanged except that he said, "It was right here in Detroit ... " Three or four other cities remained on the tour, each one, as Greb told the audience, the place where he had his first fight. In Montreal, where the tour ended, he lost his bearings.

"It was right here in Toronto ... " he started out, and was interrupted by boos. From behind the curtain, Tom Bodkin hissed, "You're in Montreal, you dope, not Toronto." When the boos stopped, Greb laughed and said, "Oops, I made a mistake. It was right here in Montreal that I won my first fight."

"He carried it off so beautifully," Bodkin declared afterward, "that the audience was taken in. They thought the whole thing was a wonderful gag."

Red Mason and sometimes George Engel managed Harry Greb in his role as a fighter, but Bodkin, for a time, managed Frank Moran, who was also from Pittsburgh and fought twice for the heavyweight championship, losing to Jack Johnson in Paris and Jess Willard in New York. In 1920, Bodkin arranged a fight for Moran with Denver Jack Geyer at Duquesne Gardens.

Among the spectators was Battling Nelson; from his seat far back in the auditorium the old lightweight champion plied Moran with advice. He dispatched an usher to Frank's corner at the end of each round with a note, telling his friend what to do. Moran put up with it for as long as he could, and then he sent back a reply. He said that if one more message came he would stop fighting Geyer, get down from the ring, and fight Nelson. There was no further help, and no need for any, from his counselor.

Nelson by this time was "strange in the head," a euphemism for pugilistica dementia, the ailment old fighters commonly develop in their fifties, sixties, or seventies. Just one year before, on the eve of the July 4, 1919 heavyweight championship fight between Willard and Jack Dempsey on the shores of Maumee Bay outside Toledo, Nelson's odd behavior gave rise to an oft-repeated story in which Bodkin played an important role.

As I heard it from Tom himself - there are several other versions – Tex Rickard, the promoter, had leased him the rights to the lemonade concession. It was hot weather that week in Toledo, and he figured to make a big score. On the night before the fight, he stored the lemonade in six vats, which he covered with gauze. To keep watch over these vats, he employed Battling Nelson. But the night was so unbearably hot that, looking for a way to cool off, Nelson got out of his clothes and took a dip in one of the vats.

Early the next morning, when Tom arrived on the scene, Nelson was crawling out of the lemonade. Tom was furious. "Has anyone else seen you?" he demanded.

"No one, Tommy. No one. That's the truth."

Thus reassured, Tom went ahead and sold the lemonade. Parched fight-goers – thousands of them – unknowingly slaked their thirst on Battling Nelson's bath water.

Bodkin's partner was a man named Billy McCarney. In addition to the lemonade concession, they also had the rights to sell sandwiches, ice cream, cigarettes, opera glasses (for the fans a long way from ringside), mildly alcoholic but still legal near beer, and, most important of all, seat cushions, and they subleased all of these contracts. The man who bought the seat-cushion concession planned on cleaning up, because Tex Rickard had built an 80,000-seat arena with green lumber, and the heat brought out the sap in the unseasoned pine planks, which fairly oozed.

Alas, the word got around, and people were showing up at the ticket office with cushions from home.

Jack Dempsey won the title on that historic July Fourth when Willard, knocked down seven times in the first round, failed to answer the bell for the fourth. In New York forty years later, Bodkin introduced me to Dempsey. We had gone to Dempsey's Broadway restaurant for lunch. "Come over here, Artie," said Tom, catching sight of the owner, "and say hi to Jack Dempsey. Jack, say hello to Art Rooney Junior of Pittsburgh. You know his dad ... " Dempsey, in his high-pitched voice, greeted me with "Oh, yeah, sure I do. Art Rooney. Hi, kid. Welcome to New York."

Bodkin seemed to know everybody. At Toots Shor's restaurant, he introduced me to Stan Musial, who recognized Dad's name with more alacrity than Dempsey had shown. Shor himself I had known for some time. AJR first met him when Shor was a bouncer in Philadelphia. Shor took me around his "joint," as he called it, while Tom had a drink. We stopped for a few minutes at Gordon MacRae's table. MacRae was a singer and a movie actor. Another time, Shor introduced me to Jackie Gleason, the best-looking fat man I ever saw – impeccably dressed and as funny in person as on television reciting a script. My brother Dan was with me, and Gleason asked, "What do you guys do?" Shor broke in to say, "Why they're here in town with the Steelers." Gleason responded quickly. "Well, how did I know? I thought they were here with a monkey act." Somehow it seemed hilarious.

Usually, Tom and I went to dinner at Moore's Restaurant. It was there that I met Joe DiMaggio, a polite, dignified man, comfortable, surprisingly, to talk with.

Thanks to Tom, I saw the big Broadway shows. At times, I had to sit on a wooden folding chair in the aisle, but the tickets were always free. He would take me backstage, and there I met Helen Hayes. "Art Rooney," she repeated. "What a great Irish name! And you're a nice-looking guy, too," she added graciously. I met the great English actor, John Gielgud. Is it possible, I asked myself that Tom Bodkin, graduate of the fight racket, could know John Gielgud, whose tastes were more, shall I say, on the decorous side? My doubts quickly evaporated. "Ohhh, Tommy!" cried the thespian, "its s-o-o-o-o good to see you! After all these years!" He then turned to me and said, "Tommy managed my first show here in America." Looking on in his dark suit, Homburg in hand, Tom was beaming.

Our meeting with Gielgud gave Tom an inspiration. I should study acting at the Royal Academy of Dramatic Arts in London. He knew a chap from the Academy who happened to be in New York. Very cultured, with an upper-class accent. We got together at Moore's, where Tom, all duded up as usual, proceeded to get drunk.

The Englishman was talking about the Royal Academy; Tom kept interrupting – and straying off the subject. He had some observations to make about the Royal Family, and they were far from complimentary. His friend at first dismissed them with a laugh. Tom persisted, and the Englishman's laughter began to sound forced. Then it ceased altogether.

Tom ranted on – "Elizabeth Rex? She's a prune!" – and the Englishman ignored him. Before we had finished our coffee, he rose to leave. "If you are truly interested in the Royal Academy," he said to me, "I shall see that your application is taken care of." As it happened, I was not truly interested. The whole idea had been Tom's, and I promptly forgot all about it.

AJR came to town with Jim and Dago Sam, and Tom gave them tickets to the show he was managing, Eugene O'Neill's "A Touch of the Poet." I had seen it four times and was certain that our visitors would hate it. They sat about ten rows back in the center section. best seats in the house. I attended a play that night across the street, intending to meet them afterward. Unaccountably, they were not in the crowd leaving the theatre. I went looking for Tom, who took a circuitous way to explain their absence.

He said that when the curtain came down on "A Touch of the Poet," Eric Portman, the star - who also happened to be English – had summoned him to his dressing room. "Tommy," he asked, "how was I tonight?"

"Real good – as usual. Why do you ask?"

"Well," answered Portman, "something happened to me tonight that never happened before. There were three gentlemen ... in very good seats ... who ... well, they just got up and walked out. They left at the first curtain, before the end of the first act. Tom, nobody – I mean *nobody* – has ever walked out on me before."

Tom assured Eric Portman that his performance had been up to snuff. "Those people who walked out," he said, "are not gentlemen. They are ignoramuses. I know them. They're from Pittsburgh, my home town. I should never have given them tickets. They are philistines, Eric. No culture at all. None at all."

In today's market, Tom's fifth-floor apartment, overlooking Central Park, would be worth several million dollars as a condominium. The antique furniture reminded me of 940 North Lincoln Avenue. Late one afternoon, as we sat gazing down at the park, he talked to me of his wife.

"A wonderful girl, Artie," he said. He spoke of how grateful he was for their life together, even though they never had children. He spoke of how well they'd been doing ... "Lots of money then. We had a nest egg – one hundred and fifty thousand dollars. And then she came down with cancer. It was deeply rooted. I went all over, looking for help. Nothing could be done. I ended up taking her to Mercy Hospital in Pittsburgh. She suffered a long time, Artie. I buried her out in Calvary Cemetery." His wife's illness, I gathered, had wiped out their nest egg.

Darkness had fallen, and we left for Moore's Restaurant. In the taxicab, he told me of another disappointment, the death of a friend. The man was an actor – "an entertainer,'" Tom called him. "I was his manager, Artie, and we almost hit it big – real big. Hollywood! Funniest man I ever knew. And a good guy on top of being talented. Broadway? He had it in the palm of his hand. This was in the 1930s. We had a radio show and a movie contract in Hollywood. 'Hollywood's the future, Tommy,' he said. 'We'll knock 'em dead out there, wait and see.'

'"But you're knocking 'em dead in New York,' I told him.

"'Never mind. Hollywood's the future.'

"He was right, too. Anyway, it was all set. We'd be going West in a few weeks. Meanwhile, we had some New York engagements to finish up. It was fall, and my friend owned a boat. We'd go for cruises up and down the East River, up and down the Hudson, with our wives. He loved that boat. But the weather that fall was brisk. A chilly wind always seemed to be blowing. He had the sniffles. It developed into pneumonia. Poor guy, he died real quick. We never even got to the railroad station.

"And do you know who took his place in Hollywood?" Tom said. "Do you know who it was?" He paused for effect. "Jack Benny!" The taxi pulled up at Moore's, and there were no more reminiscences that night.

Footnote: On the night before my wedding, Tom came to my bachelor party. Patsy Scanlon and Owney McManus were there – old fighters – and the three of them had a great time. Sadly, though, Tom was down on his luck. Too old to work, he could not pay the rent on his Central Park apartment. He spoke to AJR, asking him for advice. The Friars Club ran a home for retired actors in New York, and AJR suggested that he apply for admission. "It's just the place for you," Dad said. The actors' home took him in, and a few months later Tom Bodkin died among friends.

Mr. Lunt

When AJR had a horse going he tried to avoid people he knew. Casual acquaintances would pester him for tips. "Say, Art, if you've got something good at Monmouth Park today ... " His standard reply was, "Gee, one of our horses is almost ready, but there might be a last-minute change. Time is so short that if I had to get back to you I don't see how I could do it."

Better to travel incognito. On trips to New York with a race coming up – "cloak-and-dagger" trips, I called them – he would stay at an out-of-the-way uptown hotel. Under wraps in this place, he asked me to meet him there once. "Go to Moore's Restaurant," he instructed me. "A Mister Lunt will be waiting for you with a package." The name Lunt was a pseudonym which AJR had chosen on the spur of the moment. We were standing in front of a theatre where the husband-and-wife acting team of Alfred Lunt and Lynne Fontanne were appearing, and he had happened to glance up at the marquee. The "Mr. Lunt" who would have a package for me was a runner for a big-time bookmaker named Erickson. AJR had won a whopper of a bet from Erickson, and Mr. Lunt was going to give me the money.

I went to Moore's Restaurant and I found him. I was very nervous. Everybody was looking at me, I thought. Mr. Lunt turned out to be an undersized Irishman. He took me into the kitchen and counted out twelve thousand dollars. I started to leave, but he called me back. "Tell your dad the district attorney is shutting us down. We won't be able to handle your dad's business any more," Lunt said.

When I delivered the message, AJR cut through the double talk. "They're saying they can get along without me. I've been beating them too often this year. They'd rather take bets from suckers who don't know what they're doing."

I gave him the money, and he counted it. "Eleven thousand eight-hundred dollars," he said. "Lunt shorted you."

I felt like a fool. I flared up. I heard myself shouting, "That crook!"

"No. Lunt's a good man. I've known him for years. It's just a mix-up," said AJR imperturbably.

Sure enough. A month later we saw Mr. Lunt in Moore's Restaurant. He came to our table and handed me two hundred dollars. "Hey, Artie, I've been looking all over for you. I miscounted," he said.

I have no idea whether AJR resumed doing business with Erickson and Lunt, but he was one of their oldest customers. He told me the story of a wager he made with Erickson in the late 1940s.

They had gone to the men's room at a track in New York and were standing side by side at the urinal. Undistracted by the music of the waterfall, AJR bet $100,000 against $500,000 on a horse in the next race. He repeated this tale many times. "Oh, and my horse lost in a photo," he would add, making it sound like an afterthought.

It was his custom to name the horses he owned - quite a few of them, anyway – after football players and sportswriters. As an extension of this, he proposed to name a horse for a friend somewhat closer to God – Our Lady of Mount Carmel. Not unexpectedly, the Jockey Club disapproved. So AJR merely shortened the name to Mount Carmel. In his own mind and in his own way, he was honoring the Blessed Mother.

The foal developed into a speed horse and he quietly got it ready to win a big race at Aqueduct, in New York City, a race on which he would make a big bet. Meanwhile, at the Mount Carmel Church in New York, a weekend retreat was being held. After a devotional service and a sermon Friday night, the retreatants had time to themselves. There were horse players among them, and they used their leisure hour to study the Racing Form. In the next day's entries at Aqueduct, they noticed, was this horse named Mount Carmel. A horse from a stable called the Shamrock. Owned by a man named Rooney – without the shadow of a doubt an Irish Catholic.

It was like an omen. The horse players' excited talk spread to the other retreatants – confirmed non-gamblers, for the most part, but believers in signs from above. Somebody, it seemed clear, was telling them something. Even the reverend fathers caught the fever. The next morning – Saturday – New York City's bookmakers found themselves taking an unusually large number of bets on a long shot named Mount Carmel. Even so, the horse went off at good odds. And at the Saturday evening prayer service the retreatants got word of the miracle they anticipated. Praise be to Our Lady! Mount Carmel had won!

AJR later told me that for the next few years on his visits to New York, men would come up to him and say with an air of sly satisfaction, "Mister Rooney, I won a small bet" – it was always "a small bet" – "on a horse of yours one time. A horse named Mount Carmel." Having learned of the circumstances from several different sources, he would nod understandingly.

Best Man

I interrupted my stay in New York to be the best man for Tim when he married June Marraccini at St. Andrew's Church in Pittsburgh.

June Marraccini was an attractive brunette from Clairton whose family owned and operated a string of supermarkets. Tim had met her - and fallen hard - while both were attending Duquesne University.

The nuptials, performed on a typically bleak, gray, wet, cold day in March, were private. Except for a few family members, including the bride's parents and the groom's parents, the church was empty. Tim and June had chosen St. Andrew's, on Sherman Avenue in Manchester, because Father Jim Campbell, AJR's closest friend, was the pastor. Out of loyalty to him, AJR, Kass, and Aunt Alice had been going to daily Mass at St. Andrew's instead of St. Peter's.

A few hours after the exchange of vows, Tim and June flew to New York and checked in at the Manhattan Hotel, where Tim had reserved the honeymoon suite. The Steelers always stopped there on trips to New York, and management gave Tim a special rate. When I returned to drama school, on the following day, Tim called with an invitation to dinner. "Pick out a top restaurant," he said, and I suggested a fancy place I had been to as the guest of an NFL bigwig who was entertaining Dad and Mom.

From the lobby of the Manhattan, I buzzed Tim on the house phone. "Come up to the room," he said. When I got there, he had not yet put on a shirt and tie. June, I could not help noticing, was still in her negligee. As I have said, June was a good-looking girl - so good looking, in fact, that I caught myself staring. I was young and single, remember. "I think I should wait for you downstairs," I said to the unembarrassed newlyweds.

Laughing, June said she would only be a minute. "Only a minute" turned out to be twenty, but there was no great rush. A good table awaited us at the restaurant.

The next day Tim insisted on seeing my apartment, a fourth-floor walkup on West 90th Street at Central Park West. The "Central Park West" in the address was real-estate hype. Between Central

Park and my apartment stretched a full city block. We climbed the stairs and went in, and Tim shook his head. Although he held his tongue, his body language, which was eloquent, declared, "What a dump." Under oath, I'd have had to admit that I was not the most fastidious housekeeper. June, concealing her true reaction, appeared to be lost in thought. She said to us, "Why don't you two go for a walk? I'll stay here and read a magazine and maybe watch some TV."

So Tim and I sauntered over to Stillman's Gym on Eighth Avenue, where the heavyweight Tommy "Hurricane" Jackson was training for a fight. Stillman's, I perceived, was like the gyms we were taken to as kids, only more so. This shrine of professional boxing was airless, moldy, unhygienic, and malodorous. I attempted to identify the various smells. Stale sweat predominated, but with liniment in the mix, and cigar smoke.

Fighters sparred in each of two rings. Others skipped rope. Still others rattled the speed bags. A big guy worked on the heavy bag, making it thud. The managers, stubby middle-aged men in shapeless brown suits, all wearing wide-brimmed fedoras, monitored the activity. They looked a lot like the denizens of AJR's former offices in the Fort Pitt Hotel. At one end of the gym, close to the entrance, a concession stand offered sandwiches and coffee. Customers who did not eat the crusts simply threw them on the floor.

Hurricane Jackson was taking the day off, so in less than a half-hour we made our way back to the apartment. At the top of the stairs, Tim mumbled something to the effect that there was little or no difference in ambiance between the place I called home and Stillman's Gym. While I groped for an answer, I unlocked the door, and there was June, running the vacuum cleaner. She had my bedroom slippers on her feet and was wearing my trench coat over her slip.

Turning off the sweeper and glancing up from her labors, she said, "Well, I've done my best with this old carpet, but it needs professional help."

June's best, it seemed to me, had been pretty darn good. The improvement in the looks of the carpet was unmistakable, and she had dusted all the furniture. More wonderful still, the kitchen now sparkled. June had cleaned the stove and had washed the dirty dishes I habitually left in the sink.

In my head, I composed what I now understand was a thumbnail scouting report on the newest member of our clan. "No question about it," I was thinking, "my brother Tim has picked himself a winner."

I didn't know it at the time, but making assessments of that nature in a completely different field – some just as accurate and others less so – was to be my life's work.

Semper Fi

After three semesters at Madame D.'s actor's studio, I joined a summer stock company and worked at theaters in Delmont, PA, and Belle Vernon while waiting for my call from the draft board.

In the late 1950s every young man in America faced military service. My stint at Carnegie Tech had earned me a deferment, but having passed the physical examination, I was due to report for basic training in just a few months. Dan, Tim, and John were husbands and fathers by now and therefore exempt; not so Pat and I, the only remaining bachelors in the clan.

Fran Fogarty had a contact in the Army Reserve, but was told there were not any openings. Two years of training and active service lay ahead for me. .Then Fran or Ed Kiely or AJR – I'm afraid I can't be more specific – got in touch with Joe O'Toole, who handled problems of this kind for the Pirates in addition to his regular duties as traveling secretary. O'Toole said he could get me in the Marine Corps Reserve. It would mean boot camp – three months at Parris Island and three months at Camp Geiger.

"Hold off," people warned me. "An opening may turn up in the Army Reserve. You'd be nuts to go into the Marine Corps. Parris Island is hell. You couldn't take it down there."

The more they talked that way, the more determined I became to give it a try. I'd see if I was still tough. With O'Toole's help, I joined up.

I joined up and found out I had never been tough. The Marines, though, were tough. Every single one of them thought he was John Wayne. In truth, the guys at Parris Island were what John Wayne only pretended to be – the real thing.

My education started when I got off the train with the rest of the recruits in Yamassee, South Carolina. The troop handlers got into our faces, screaming their heads off. They herded us onto a bus and told us to sit up straight and be quiet. On the 45-minute ride to Parris Island, nobody spoke above a whisper. All the confidence I had acquired from my upbringing, from my years at North Catholic and St. Vincent, from my time in New York, and from the knowledge that I was a Rooney went out the window.

Three tanned, trim, closely-shorn drill instructors wearing starched khaki uniforms and wide-brimmed Smokey Bear hats met our bus. They screamed, they yelled, they barked, and they bellowed. It was "Move, move, move – that means you, Pimple Face. Come on, there, Fatso – get the lard out of your ass. Move! Move! What's-a-rnatter, Jelly Belly? You retarded? Move! Move! Move! This yer first time away from Mommy? Hey, you – Scurnbag! Down on the ground and give me some pushups. *How many?* You askin' me how many? Listen, boy, don't EVER talk to your DI that way. You say 'SIR' before you address me. And I want it loud and clear."

The DIs did their best to intimidate us, and they succeeded. We were "turds"– civilian turds, scumbag turds, idiotic turds, pimple-faced turds, every kind of turd, but always turds. We found ourselves standing at attention in a building of wood and tin and being hectored by a sergeant who was not a DI. He was telling us how to fill out a form of some kind. "Understand me?" he yells. Murmurs of assent. "I CAN'T HEAR YOU!" So we shout back in unison, "We understand you!" The sergeant hollers, "SIR, we understand you!" "SIR, we understand you!" we repeat.

After that we were ordered to take off our clothes and given sheets of brown shipping paper to wrap them in. Naked except for a towel worn amidships, we moved down the hall to the shearing room. Barbers equipped with electric clippers shaved off our hair close to the skull. From there we proceeded to the quartermaster building to be issued duffel bags (called seabags), underwear, socks, "utilities'" (green work clothes), and three pairs of shoes – high-top boots, low-cut boots, and dress shoes.

So it went until the processing was over. It was late September and beastly hot. We took an IQ test. Stripped down, we took our physical exams. As I waited in line, a tough-looking old master sergeant confronted me. "Rooney?" "Yes, sir." He looked like Victor McLaglen – not quite as big but even tougher. "I'm a friend of your Dad's," he said. "I was in China with your Uncle Dan, the priest, before the war. He's a great man. He used to put boxing matches on between the Navy and Marine guys. Good luck to you." I never saw him again.

The orthopedic doctor looked for a long time at my left leg, which was half an inch shorter than my right leg. Still another doctor came to look at me. They conferred, shaking their heads. One of them finally asked if I had participated in sports. "High school and college football," I said. They smiled, and the first doctor said, "Good. Once you get into shape, you won't have any problem with this program."

They measured and weighed me. I was a quarter of an inch over six feet tall and I weighed exactly 214 pounds. To a DI, the doctor said, "Moderate obesity. He'll have a tough time with training."

I couldn't believe my ears. No way was I fat. Big and strong, yes. But strength with the bar bells, I soon discovered, was not what these people wanted. They wanted stamina. They wanted lean and hungry guys who could run all day and never for a minute fall behind.

That "moderate obesity" tag clung to me. "Front and center, Fat Ass – double time," a DI ordered, and I was stood at attention before the senior DI and several others. They were sitting in judgment of me.

"How'd you get to be such a fat ass? Drink a lot of beer?"

"No, sir. Sweets, sir."

From the DIs, mocking laughter, laced with obscenity. I was a lazy rich kid, I could see. They could "set me back" – place me in a motivational platoon or a physical-fitness platoon, which would mean an extra month on Parris Island. But I passed inspection. They would not set me back.

"You'll have to work harder and eat less than anyone else in the platoon," they warned me.

"Sir, thank you, sir," I said, and I really meant it.

We were marched to the squad bay, yelled at every step of the way. Every morning at 5:30 our "alarm clock" sounded. A DI came into the squad bay and rolled a large, empty garbage can down the middle of the floor. We had from seven to ten minutes to make up our beds – tightly – answer the call of nature, shave, and get dressed. "Move! Move! Move!" the DI would be yelling, and then he would march us off to the chow hall, where we stood at attention until another DI called out, "Ready! Seats!" Somehow, I had no appetite.

On the second day, the training began — close-order drill, trips to the obstacle course. There was never any letup in the yelling, never any letup in the stream of derogatory language. The aim of the DIs was to separate us from any vestige of polite civilian life. They were vulgar, mean, sadistic, their object being to take away all your self-worth and rebuild you in the image and likeness of a U.S. Marine.

At night as we lay in our bunks, we prayed together. Our prayer was mandatory and got immediate feedback – not from the Lord, but from the drill instructor who had forced us to sing out in unison, "God bless my Marine Corps home." He would then scream, "I can't hear you turds!" So we'd do it again – and again and again, until many minutes after the lights had gone out.

Another DI gave us the "gung-ho" speech one night. Looking back, I'd compare it in tone to the opening scene of the 1976 movie "Patton," in which the pistol-packing World War II general, as personified by George C. Scott, stands on a stage with an oversized American flag behind him and delivers some plain talk to the men he will lead into battle. The Marine drill instructor was even more blunt. He told us what our rights were – we didn't have any – and what would happen if we ever disputed an order – first, we would get our posteriors kicked from one end of the squad bay to the other; after that, we would spend an unpleasant six months in the brig.

His unvarnished way of linking cause to effect certainly focused our attention. So did an accidental glimpse of what life in the brig could be like. We saw some prisoners on a work detail; they were guarded by a corporal armed with a shotgun – a shotgun that could have brought down an elephant. Their heads were shaved bald; on the back of each man's utility jacket, a large white "P" advertised his status. All this made it evident to us that crime does not pay. Boot-camp training lasted three months, and nobody in our squad bay with one exception, which I'll get to very soon, ever talked back to a noncommissioned officer or complained about the hardships and humiliations inflicted on us day after day.

I had thought before the Marines tried to reshape me that nothing could be more punishing than football practice at North Catholic High School and St. Vincent College, and that nothing could be more psychologically stressful than the demands of my teachers at these strict Catholic educational institutions. Little did I know. Football practice and final-examination week were child's play compared to the Marines.

The "obesity" tag I wore like a scarlet letter meant that I had my own private taskmaster. "I'm going to work with you every minute," one of the drill instructors said, and he kept his promise. From five o'clock in the morning until eight-thirty at night, he was on my case. "Give me five more pushups," he would shout when all the others had finished. "Do it again!" he would yell if I couldn't get over the wall on the obstacle course. And then if I failed a second time, he would call for help from the recruits next in line: "Boost that piece of crap over that wall." At the chin-up bar, he would warn me, "No jump starts." When I had chinned myself to the point of exhaustion, he would not let me quit. "Dangle there for a while!" he would bellow.

I had my own special diet: no bread, no dessert, no second helpings. To ensure that I wasn't cheating, the DI followed me through the chow line and monitored my tray. At the mess-hall door after every meal, he would frisk me for hidden cookies, hidden pieces of cake. I went from 215 pounds to 155, disconcerting the mess officer. "Are you getting enough to eat, private?" he asked. Glancing at my tray, he said, "Aren't you hungry? The DIs work you very hard. You need food. You need calories." Something seemed out of whack here. Marines didn't talk this way. They just didn't. Yes, I told him, I was getting enough to eat, and, no, I was not hungry. And that was the truth. I wasn't hungry, but I seemed to be constantly tired. Even so, I could now do eleven chin-ups — ten more than I had managed the first day. We had a chin-up bar in the squad bay, and at night, after lights-out, I used it on my own while the other recruits slept. I envisioned myself as a lean, mean fighting Marine.

But then came a fall from grace. My friends in platoon 172 took it upon themselves to save me from anorexia. At great personal risk, they smuggled contraband cookies and brownies out of the mess hall. They hid them in their pants pockets, their blouses, their utility hats. Proud of my new silhouette, I refused these offerings for a while; then my will power crumbled, and I gave in as haplessly as Adam taking a bite of the apple. In no time at all I weighed 170. It was amazing how rapidly I put on the pounds.

It was even more amazing that my stamina held up. Near the end of our stay at Parris Island, we were taken on a run with rifles at order arms. Sometimes at double time, sometimes at triple time, we ran the length and the width of the vast Parris Island drill field; we skirted its four sides; we ran up and down the company streets, every one of them. All this while the DI berated us, saving his cruelest sarcasm for the drop-outs.

I came perilously close to being one of them. Weakening, I slowed to a walk with the DI nearby, and he directed a stream of profanity toward me. I lost my temper. In a low voice, but loud enough to be heard, I cussed back. The adrenaline renewed my energy: I got back in line and continued to run. And the DI, to my astonishment, started laughing. His reaction seemed all wrong, but then it hit me. I felt accepted ... in some odd way, I now belonged to a brotherhood. There I was, running and cussing, letting a DI see my frustration, but not to the point of incurring his wrath. Just like the real Marines!

I had another small epiphany in judo class. On the teaching platform one day, the instructor came up behind me and encircled my neck in a choke hold. Instinctively, I grabbed his left arm with my right hand, bent over double, and threw him four or five feet into the air, head over heels. He landed on his back with a thud.

This was big trouble for me, I knew. I had made the instructor look bad. He jumped up, took me down with a swift move called a Yokoshiro leg toss, sat on my chest, and seized me once again by the neck. Until he abruptly eased his grip, I thought I was going to be strangled.

The next time we assembled for a lesson, he asked in a loud voice, "Where is the recruit who flipped me the other day?"

"That was Rooney," someone said. All heads were now turned in my direction.

"Oh, there you are. Well, congratulations, Rooney. Keep up the good work. If you last long enough, you may learn something."

Unexpected praise from an unlikely source. It was as near as I came to winning the Medal of Honor. Drill instructors, when you got right down to it, were not unlike human beings.

Some of them, anyway. When our platoon lost a tug of war to a rival platoon, the trip from the fitness field back to the squad bay was a silent death march. Our DI refused to call cadence, going on ahead. "Stagger back by yourselves, you quitters!" he sneered. As we passed the memorial statue of the flag raising on Iwo Jima, he stopped and called out, "See those guys raising that flag? Now, *they* were *Marines*! If they'd been quitters like you, guess what. Your mothers and sisters would be sleeping with Japs." When we arrived at the squad bay, he grabbed the scarlet platoon flag we carried with us and threw it into a urinal. Our platoon guide, putting loyalty to his mates ahead of hygiene, carefully fished it out.

For many weeks, the DIs had been talking about the real test that awaited us – the Slide for Life. On the appointed morning, we climbed into buses – "cattle cars," we called them – and traveled two and a half miles over the South Carolina countryside. The buses stopped in a wooded area, where a framework wooden tower three stories high rose up at the edge of a pond. From the top of this structure a bull rope extended downward at a 45-degree angle to a stake five feet high on the opposite side. I'd say the pond was about forty yards wide. Wearing light gear – helmet liners, utility belts and boots – we were to climb up the tower on ladders, take hold of the rope, curl our feet over it, and ease ourselves all the way down, hand over hand.

The instructors were patient and relaxed, but the possibility of falling was in everybody's mind. Just ahead of me at the top, an unusually large Chinese kid started down. Halfway across the pond he lost his grip. Arms waving and legs thrashing, he plummeted into the drink, going under with a tsunami-like splash. The rest of us let out a yell, half in derision and half in alarm, but he bobbed right up and dog-paddled his way to dry land.

Now it was my turn. I made the descent smoothly and quickly.

Thirty minutes later, as we prepared to get back on the cattle cars, I heard someone say to someone else, "Rooney fell. He couldn't do it." You can be sure that I lost no time in setting that knucklehead straight.

When our last march was completed, when the last round had been fired at the rifle range, when we had gone through our last inspection, I felt a sense of exhilaration. I hadn't washed out. A few days before graduation, I was called to the drill instructors' quarters off a corridor in the middle of the squad bay. A tall, trim, good-looking sergeant whose last name was Harms said to me. "Private Rooney, you and I are going over to the medical center, but first let me see you do some pull-ups."

He led me to the chinning bar, and I pumped out twelve.

"Not bad at all, Rooney," he said. "That's only average, but, for you, pretty good."

I cherished every compliment, even left-handed ones.

"Okay,' Harms continued, "I want you to put on your cleanest utilities – starched ones. Make sure your boots are shined. And gargle. You can't talk to the doc with stinky breath. I'll meet you when you're ready."

We marched all the way to the medical center in step, Private Rooney detoxified and wearing his clean utilities. Neither of us spoke.

My examination by the doctor was entirely oral. He started with a question for Harms. Had I kept up with the other recruits?

"Yes, Doctor. Private Rooney is one of our hardest workers," Harms told him.

The doctor then asked me how many pull-ups I could do. Before I could answer, Harms said, "Eleven, sir. And Private Rooney started with only one."

He was giving me a short count – I had just done twelve – but how could I not like the praise, coming, as it did, from a drill instructor?

That was it. There were no more questions, and we marched back to the squad bay, Harms and I, the way we had marched over – wordlessly and in step.

Years later I would hear that Sergeant Harms had been badly shot up in Vietnam.

Making it through Parris Island was the hardest thing I ever had done, and I felt emotionally and physically drained when I boarded one of the buses that would take the boot-camp graduates to Camp Lejeune, a stopover on the trip to our ultimate destination, Camp Geiger. Camp Lejeune is a long drive from Parris Island. It's in North Carolina. But the distance is short between Camp Lejeune and Camp Geiger, and our buses were almost luxurious – nothing at all like the Parris Island cattle cars. The DIs were still yelling at us, but with a difference. They called us Marines now, where before we'd been scumbags, and their screaming made no impression on me. I found a seat and flopped into it. I was worn out, yes, but I was saying good-bye to Parris Island and therefore at peace with the world.

A rather quiet Marine I knew as an acquaintance asked if he could sit next to me. I said, "Sure," and for an hour we rode with just the barest minimum of talk. The others in the bus were whooping and hollering, glad to have seen the last of Parris Island. I was too contented to be annoyed. Then the guy next to me spoke up.

"Hey, Rooney," he said, 'do you mind if I tell you something?"

"Go ahead."

"Well, I think you're the toughest guy I've ever met. And lots of others feel the same way. I couldn't believe what those DIs put you through, but you took it. You took it and you didn't break."

All I could manage to say was, "Thanks."

I knew I had never been tough. I'd been able to stick it out. But I wasn't tough.

Maybe, instead, I was the next thing to it – hardened. In consequence, the training at Camp Geiger, though arduous, was not the test of manhood for me that Parris Island had been. I thought of it as a harsh post-graduate course. In any case, my three months at Geiger passed swiftly. And at the end of that time, every notion of an acting career forever dismissed from my mind, I was ready, and more than ready, to come home and start learning the football business.

Chapter 28

High-Maintenance Coach

Buddy Parker was a truly brilliant coach whose Detroit teams were NFL champions in his second and third seasons, 1952 and 1953. In 1954 the Lions again won a conference title but lost to the Cleveland Browns in the playoff. Injuries and retirements then forced Parker to rebuild, which he proceeded to do without delay. After a 3-9 season, Detroit was once again a contender, finishing second to the Bears in the 1956 conference race.

Management rewarded Parker with a two-year contract extension, but two days before the first pre-season game in 1957 he flamboyantly resigned. At a "Meet the Lions" banquet, he made a speech that was startling in its content and brevity. "I'm quitting," he said, going straight to the point. "I can no longer control this team, and when I can't control a team I can't coach it."

What had brought this on was the sight of his star players drinking with the owners, a group of wealthy Detroit "socialites," at a cocktail party before the banquet. For obscure reasons, Parker disapproved of such fraternizing between bosses and hired hands. It was certainly not the drinking that bothered him. Emulating the team leader, charismatic quarterback Bobby Layne, the Lions did plenty of that.

Parker himself was a problem drinker. Alone or in the company of his assistant coaches, he drank under stress and he drank when the Lions lost. He drank as much, when the mood was on him, as Layne did, but he differed from Layne in his ability to handle the stuff. Once after an embarrassing defeat he put the entire team on waivers, infuriating Commissioner Bert Bell. When the Lions lost on the road Parker would be drunk by the time they arrived home, and often the results were unpredictable, as when he ordered assistant coach Buster Ramsey to get on the public-address system at Willow Run Airport in Detroit and announce the outright release of the players in Parker's doghouse at the moment.

As soon as he heard that Parker was now available, AJR made him an offer. Because of their mutual interest in horse racing, they were friends. Parker was a bit of a head case, yes. But he could coach. In AJR's opinion, he could do as much for the Steelers as Jock Sutherland had done. He could give the team the sense that it was going somewhere. He could bring hope and excitement to the fans.

Apart from all that, he was not a bad guy when he was sober. He was smart, with a sense of humor. He was close to his wife and son. His assistant coaches liked him, or seemed to. Parker was from Texas, but had gone to Centenary College in Louisiana. Few Centenary players ever make the NFL. Parker did, as an undersized fullback (about 5 feet 11 and 170 pounds) for the Lions and the Cardinals from 1935 to 1943.

In their contract negotiations, Parker made one thing clear to AJR: he would be a high-maintenance coach. When it came to bringing in players, he would need a free rein. He would need a taxi squad, which the Steelers had done without up to then. "The way I operate costs money," he warned. AJR said the money would be there.

In Detroit, Parker's salary was $30,000 a year. The deal he worked out with AJR, in all of its ramifications, netted him more than twice that amount. Parker brought two of his assistants to Pittsburgh, a payroll increase partly offset by a reduction in Walt Kiesling's pay. Off and on, either as head coach or assistant, Kiesling had been with the Steelers since 1939. Accepting a demotion, he would remain on the staff as an assistant until 1961. According to Pat Livingston, who covered the Steelers for the *Pittsburgh Press*, the hiring of Parker was actually Kiesling's idea "He cared more about Art Rooney's welfare than his own," Livingston said.

A man who believed in wasting no time, Parker immediately traded two first-round draft choices and linebacker Mike Matuszak to San Francisco for quarterback Earl Morrall and rookie lineman Mike Sandusky. From the Redskins he acquired scatback Billy Wells. In 1957, Morrall passed for 1,900 yards and eleven touchdowns and Wells led the Steelers in rushing, punt returns, and kickoff returns. Goose McClairen, the long-armed end, caught forty-six passes, third highest total in the

NFL. Jack Butler had eleven interceptions, which tied the club record. But the won-and-lost record that year – 6-6 – was no great improvement over 1956.

Giving Parker the benefit of the doubt, AJR was optimistic. His confidence in his coach was unshaken. So far, their relationship had been a good one. It was not to continue that way.

Garden Party

When Parker came over to Pittsburgh, one of the assistant coaches he inherited was Lowell Perry, who had been a member of the team, and a rookie at that, just the season before.

He was a wide receiver and defensive back from the University of Michigan, earmarked for success not only in football but in any occupation he chose to follow. I became a believer in Lowell Perry the first time I saw him return a punt. It was in a pre-season game in Toledo. Returning a punt is always a better measure of talent than returning a kickoff. With a burst of speed, Perry cut, juked, and hurdled tacklers all the way to the goal line. And what I saw was no fluke. That night and in subsequent games, Perry made other fine plays.

But what set him apart was more than just football ability. He had the indefinable quality known as class. He came from a black family of mostly professional people, and his behavior did credit to his upbringing. More than anything else, Lowell Perry was a gentleman. He was also something special as a football player, or might have been. Running with the ball in the sixth game of the season, against the New York Giants, he took a simultaneous hit from Emlen Tunnell and Rosey Grier. It shattered his hip.

The attending physician said he had only seen such injuries during naval engagements in World War II. Perry lay in the hospital for quite some time. His football career was over, but AJR enrolled him, at the Steelers' expense, in Duquesne Law School. He then broke the news to Walt Kiesling that Perry would henceforth be an assistant coach. Kiesling did not object; he went out of his way, in fact, to keep Perry involved as the season wound down and in training camp the next summer. It is accurate to say, I believe, that Perry was the first black coach in the NFL since Fritz Pollard's day, the early 1920s.

Buddy Parker wasn't known for his sympathetic treatment of black athletes. He could be abusive toward all of his players, but abusive toward blacks in a way that was shockingly racial. Taking over from Kies, he consulted with AJR about Perry. It would not be easy, Parker said, for Perry to coach while attending law school. He suggested making him a scout, which satisfied AJR – and Perry, too, as far as I was able to tell.

Perry's stay in Pittsburgh was a short one. He left to finish work on his law degree at Michigan. He did become a lawyer and also the manager of a Chrysler plant in Detroit. He kept in touch all this time with AJR, and when President Ford appointed him chairman of the Equal Employment Opportunity Commission in 1975 he invited his old boss to the induction ceremony in the Rose Garden.

The weather that May was perfect for a ceremony outdoors. Four months earlier, the Steelers had won their first Super Bowl championship, and everywhere AJR went he was recognized. ("It must be the cap or the cigar," he used to say.) So he was not especially surprised when the guard at the south gate of the White House greeted him warmly. The guard, it turned out, had grown up on the North Side.

Ushered into the Rose Garden, AJR and Ed Kiely stood in the back row of a semicircle while Perry took the oath. President Ford was at Perry's side, and he spoke a few words, recalling that, twenty-five years apart, both had played football at Michigan. Then the President stepped down to where the spectators were gathered. It was time to shake hands. Kiely, from the back row, heard an aide whisper to Ford, "There's Art Rooney!" As though he were blocking for the ball carrier in a short-yardage situation on third down (he played center at Michigan), Ford cut a path through the crowd.

"Art!" he said, "I've been wanting to meet you," and for the next five minutes (or maybe ten; AJR felt embarrassed about taking up so much of the President's time) they talked about football.

AJR had met every president since Franklin D. Roosevelt up to then. He liked Ford, he later said, the best of them all. Ford impressed him as "a regular guy, a guy you would meet walking down the street." He felt that Ford "really wanted to talk, that he was really interested."

Before they parted company, AJR mentioned Perry.

"You made an excellent choice," he said to the President.

And Ford answered, "I know I did."

I don't know how you evaluate EEOC chairmen, but I would bet that Lowell Perry was good at his job. At least I never heard anything to the contrary. He lived for only about twenty more years, dying of cancer in his sixties.

Bobby Layne

Buddy Parker once told me that above all else a football team needed a great quarterback and some topnotch pass catchers – along with that other indispensable component, "defense, defense, defense." Earl Morrall was not Buddy's notion of a great quarterback, so two weeks into the 1958 season Parker made a deal with his old team, the Detroit Lions. He traded Morrall and two draft choices for Bobby Layne.

Parker felt comfortable with the quarterback who had helped him win championships. Layne was now 31, with some wear and tear showing, but he could lift a team up by what appeared to be mostly will power. In 1958 the Steelers had lost their first two games. So had Detroit. The Lions without Layne continued to lose; the Steelers finished 7-4-1, their best showing in eleven years, and Layne was the difference. For his primary receiver, he had a talented rookie end from Georgia, Jimmy Orr, and in another deal with the Lions, Parker had added the veteran running back Tom (the Bomb) Tracy.

Layne was still a pinpoint passer who ran the two-minute offense at the end of a half with more skill and confidence than anyone else in football except perhaps Johnny Unitas over in Baltimore. Listed at 6 feet 2 and 190 pounds, he may not have been that big. He was certainly not that tall by an inch or more. But when you talked about Layne, you forgot inches and pounds. You talked about his competitive fire.

I remember a game between the Steelers and Lions when Layne was still with Detroit. He took a cheap shot from Ed Meadows, one of our defensive ends – and a guy his own teammates disliked – that left him motionless on the ground for several minutes. After first aid from the trainers, he wobbled off the field, but not before addressing a few words to Meadows. My brother John was on the sideline, close enough to hear what Layne said. He said, "You son of a bitch, somehow I'm going to get you for this."

Whether or not he ever did get Meadows I have no idea. I can only tell you I am positive he never stopped trying. Layne himself would have been no match for some of the real bully-boys in the NFL, but wherever he played he invariably had "protectors" around him – combat-ready infighters like Ernie Stautner, the hard-as-nails Steeler defensive tackle, who claimed that if the Marquis of Queensberry rules allowed him to wear boxing gloves on his elbows he would be the heavyweight champion of the world. Observe that in his warning to Meadows, Layne used the modifier "somehow." Revenge obtained by proxy is sometimes as sweet as the regular kind.

On or off the football field, Layne was a fearless tough talker. The year my brothers and I joined the Fraternal Order of Eagles, at the insistence of our dad, he also prevailed on Layne and Stautner and two or three other players to affiliate. The initiation rites were held in the old Arbuckle mansion off East Ohio Street on the North Side. No sooner had we assembled than a rumor began to circulate that the ceremony featured a paddling, with the inductees on the receiving end. I knew all the officers – they were all from the North Side – and I said to myself "Some of these old boozers would like nothing better than to brag that they smacked the Rooney kids and Bobby Layne and Ernie Stautner on the ass with a board." Thoughts of that nature must have also occurred to Layne. When the lights went out and we were ordered to move forward in single file, he was right behind me. Loud enough to be heard all over the room, he announced what he would do if "any of these bastards" laid a hand on him. We became Eagles that night without a single swipe from a paddle.

Layne was such a dedicated football player - during work hours, I mean; on his own time, he was dedicated to other activities – that he actually liked to practice, which is rare. At South Park one day in 1962 our first-round draft choice, a fullback named Bob Ferguson, arrived for practice a few minutes late.. I was serving my apprenticeship as a scout that year and I was standing near Layne on the field. As soon as Ferguson approached us, he got an earful in Layne's Texas drawl – high-pitched and rasping, a "whiskey voice" – about rookies who let their teammates down and were taking money from the owners under false pretenses.

Not only was Layne on time for practice every day, he made it a point to be at least ten minutes early, often bringing along a receiver or two and maybe a backfield guy to catch his warm-up tosses. And he would stay for fifteen minutes after practice was over, again with someone to run routes and catch the ball.

One sacrifice he would not make was to deny himself the pleasures of night life. He liked to keep late hours; he liked to party; he liked to drink. And when he did these things he wanted lots of company. Layne had an inner circle on the team, made up principally of the very best players. To be one of the favored few was a sought-after distinction. "Let's go bowling," he would say, but when the last pin had fallen, the carousing began. Jack Butler belonged to the gang but dropped out after one or two evenings that did not end until dawn. Butler was not a boozer, and for another thing he came to believe that the establishment of a clique, its members anointed by the quarterback, fostered dissension.

Layne had an off year in 1959, throwing twenty-one interceptions. In 1960 the Steelers were out of contention by October, and Layne missed part of the 1961 season with a shoulder injury. Then in 1962 he got it back together. The Steelers had their best season up to then, winning nine games and finishing second to the Giants in the Eastern Conference. Layne, though, went down with another injury and sat out the last three weeks. He never played again. Before the 1963 season he announced his retirement. He held the NFL career record for touchdown passes (196) and passing yardage (26,768) and would soon be elected to the Hall of Fame.

Len Dawson, drafted out of Purdue, was a backup quarterback during Layne's first two seasons, his presence barely acknowledged by Parker. He's in the Hall Of Fame now with Layne, but not for anything he accomplished as a Steeler. Traded by Parker and cut by the Browns, he flourished in the AFL and later the NFL. However, let's not get into that. In the short time he spent with the Steelers, something about him caught the attention of Layne, and Dawson became one of his Night Riders.

AJR was a hands-off owner, but there were times when he put aside his reluctance to interfere. Mom, answering the doorbell at 940 North Lincoln Avenue one morning, beheld an athletic-looking guy in a Steeler jacket. "He seemed so young," she said later, "young enough to be out in the back yard playing touch football with the twins." The kid was acting a little sheepish, she thought. "Mister Rooney asked if I'd drive him to practice," he said. It was Lenny Dawson, and AJR had a purpose in asking for transportation. On the long trip to South Park he delivered a lecture to Dawson on the evils of drink and on the importance of choosing the right companions. "You have a future," AJR told him. "Don't jeopardize it by getting into trouble."

Again I don't know how the story played out. What it illustrates best is AJR's ambivalent attitude toward Layne. He saw the good in Layne and admired him as a football player and competitor without condoning his lifestyle. He kept Layne on as an assistant coach after his retirement. Unaccustomed to being a second banana – actually, he wasn't even that – Bobby went back to Texas in no more than a year or two.

Layne put so much of himself into football that there wasn't a great deal left for anything else except drinking and mischief. He died before his time, of acute alcoholism.

Quarterbacks

At a football luncheon in New Orleans one year, AJR, who did not like to speak in public and always kept it short when he did speak, began with the following preamble:

"Number one, if you're going to ask me any questions I'm going to disappoint you, because I don't know that I'm able to answer your questions. So, better that you don't ask any. But if you insist on asking questions anyway, ask me about quarterbacks. I can tell you all about quarterbacks because in Pittsburgh we're experts on quarterbacks. We had Sid Luckman, we had Johnny Unitas, we had Earl Morrall, we had Len Dawson, we had Jack Kemp, and we had Bill Nelsen. Now, those are all quarterbacks you know about, and we traded them all. They were all with our ball club and we got rid of them. "

Morrall and Dawson, as I have said, were traded on Buddy Parker's watch. Morrall had some success in Baltimore. In 1968 he led the NFL in passing, was the league's Most Valuable Player, and took the Colts to the Super Bowl, where they lost to Joe Namath and the New York Jets. Four years later, in his football dotage at 38, he was sitting on the bench in Miami when a broken leg sidelined Bob Griese, the first-string quarterback. The Dolphins up to then had won all their games, with three left. Morrall kept them undefeated and won the playoff game for the division title. Then with Griese again at the controls, they knocked off the Steelers in the AFC championship game and the Redskins in the Super Bowl, becoming the first team in the history of the NFL to go undefeated in 17 games.

Lenny Dawson went from Pittsburgh to Cleveland and from Cleveland to the AFL. His old coach at Purdue, Hank Stram, picked him up for the Dallas Texans. In 1962 the Texans were league champions and Dawson was player of the year. They became the Kansas City Chiefs the following season, and, with Dawson still at quarterback, played in two of the first four Super Bowls, losing to Vince Lombardi's Green Bay Packers in 1967 and beating the Minnesota Vikings in 1970.

Another good quarterback whose existence Parker ignored was Jack Kemp. The Steelers drafted Kemp out of Occidental College in 1957. By 1960 he was in the newly created AFL, passing the Los Angeles Chargers, later the San Diego Chargers, to a divisional championship. In 1962, while Kemp was out of action with a broken hand, Coach Sid Gillman put him on waivers. Claimed by Buffalo for one hundred dollars, he was half of a Siamese Twin quarterback combination, sharing the position in the Bills' first two AFL championship seasons with Daryl Lamonica. Kemp is today better known as the long-time Republican congressman from upstate New York who ran unsuccessfully for vice president when Bob Dole headed the GOP ticket in 1996.

Johnny Unitas ... well, there is no point in beating a dead horse. Sid Luckman was the first great T-formation quarterback. He'd been a tailback in the single wing at Columbia. In 1938, the Steelers surrendered their draft rights to Luckman for Eggs Manske, an end with the Chicago Bears. Luckman was all-pro six times and quarterbacked the Bears to four championships. He of course is in the Hall of Fame. Eggs Manske's only distinction was his memorable nickname. After one season, AJR returned him to the Bears.

Parker had Bill Nelsen, too, finding no use for him, but it was Bill Austin, the coach from 1966 to 1968, who traded Nelsen to Cleveland. A believer in plain talk, Nelsen was on the outs with his backfield coach, Don Heinrich. The Steelers got Dick Shiner in the deal. He was a part-time starting quarterback on Austin's worst team and Chuck Noll's worst team. Nelsen, although not exactly another Unitas, prospered for a while with the Browns. They were divisional champions in 1968 and 1969, when he still had some cartilage in his knees.

To give Buddy Parker his due, he recognized the ability of the quarterbacks he unloaded, but correctly judged that they were not yet ready to pull their own weight in the NFL. Parker was a coach who wanted immediate results. He insisted on working with experienced players, and to get them he traded away prospects, he traded away slow learners, he traded away draft choices. For short-term gain, he was mortgaging the Steelers' future, as AJR eventually came to realize.

Chapter 29

Change of Scene

It was Buddy Parker who convinced AJR that the Steelers could not remain in Forbes Field. To begin with, there were not enough seats in Forbes Field; to make matters worse, the overhanging upper deck and the massive iron girders supporting it greatly reduced the number of good seats. Forbes Field was a baseball park, admired for its intimacy and charm, and for the view of Schenley Park beyond the ivy-covered outfield walls, but poorly configured for football.

During the Depression years of the 1930s it was not unusual for AJR to move a home game from Forbes Field to an out-of-town location – Latrobe, say, or Youngstown, or as far away, even, as New Orleans. Pittsburgh in the 1930s was more of a baseball town and a fight town than a football town. In the minds of the public, Pittsburgh's only football team was Pitt, never mind that Pitt sometimes lost to Carnegie Tech and Duquesne. Pitt had a stadium; Tech and Duquesne, like the Steelers, rented Forbes Field. Tech and Duquesne were Pitt's poor relations; the Steelers were more like the hoboes who knocked at back doors, begging for handouts.

Barney Dreyfuss, an immigrant German Jew, owned the Pittsburgh National League baseball team, the PIrates. In 1909, with his own money, he built Forbes Field (named for the British general whose expeditionary force chased the French out of Western Pennsylvania). Forbes Field, expansively described as "a symbol of civic pride and a monument to the national pastime," was nothing less than that, but for football games it contained only 12,000 seats with unobstructed sightlines, and on special occasions – an appearance by the Chicago Bears and Bronko Nagurski, or by the Washington Redskins and Sammy Baugh – 12,000 were not enough. It was then that Joe Carr, the Steelers' ticket manager, practiced his wiles.

"Right on the fifty-yard line," he would tell a customer, taking his cash. Sure enough, the seats might be at or near midfield; what Carr was certain not to have mentioned, though, was their proximity to a huge iron pillar obliterating most of the view. A misanthropic North Sider who radiated gloom, Carr had been on the payroll for as long as the Steelers had one. There were people he liked – just a few – and people he did not like. He saved the best seats for the people he liked and took vindictive satisfaction in putting those he did not like – almost everybody else– where they'd need a periscope for a glimpse of the action. A game with the Chicago Cardinals brought Marshall Goldberg's father from Elkton, West Virginia, to see his son perform in the Cardinals' defensive backfield. He went home with a stiff neck. Joe Carr had seen to it that his seat would be directly behind a pillar.

Carr's roots on the North Side gave him license to do as he pleased. If AJR was aware of how his ticket manager dealt with the public, he did not interfere. Whatever he knew or did not know, the question became moot with the hiring of Jock Sutherland in 1946. The new coach's mystique sold out the park for every game. When the good seats were gone, his worshippers clamored for bad ones. They happily paid their money for standing room. But by 1948 Sutherland was dead, interest in the Steelers back to normal, and the Forbes Field issue on the table once again

There were problems in addition to the sightlines. Parking was one. In the years before the Second World War, people came to the park by trolley car. But now they drove their automobiles – nobody seemed to be without one – and overcrowded Oakland, filling up with cultural, educational, and "health-care" institutions, couldn't cope. Such was the shortage of parking lots that enterprising residents sold space on their lawns, in their back yards, in their driveways. Two or three householders tore down their front porches to accommodate more cars.

Fran Fogarty, our business manager, complained of another aggravation. When Carnegie Tech played at Forbes Field on Saturday afternoon and the Steelers had a game on Saturday night, he spent the time in between searching the toilet stalls in the rest rooms and flushing out would-be gate-crashers. The only non-paying spectators Fogarty tolerated, aside from the players' wives and their girlfriends, were the hundreds of Catholic priests on the deadhead list.

Carnegie Tech games and high school games denuded the field of grass. When it rained there was deep mud. When the weather turned cold and the mud froze, razor-like ridges cropped up. I have told you how Johnny Grigas, the league's leading ground gainer, took one look at those ridges before the final game of the 1944 season and caught the next train home to New England – and how somebody else won the rushing title.

AJR would say, "Aw ... it's the same all over the league." He would say, "Other teams have to play here, too. At least we have the advantage of knowing where the bad spots are." He would say, "Don't lose any sleep over something you can't control." An attitude of hopelessness pervaded the front office., Naysayers like Walt Kiesling, Ed Kiely, and Joe Carr encouraged AJR to drag his feet. Until Buddy Parker tried it, no one could make him see that the team's financial future depended on finding a more customer-friendly playing venue. Television, in the late 1950s, was creating new fans for the pro game, but had not yet begun to generate big money. Gate receipts were still the critical factor.

Inconveniently, the one acceptable alternative to Forbes Field was Pitt Stadium. The political tug of war that would one day result in a new publicly-financed stadium for both the Steelers and the Pirates had only just begun. There were chances to move the franchise out of town. Because of AJR's loyalty to Pittsburgh, however, the only option was Pitt. And at Pitt a major obstacle presented itself.

Admiral Tom Hamilton, U.S. Navy retired, was Pitt's athletic director, and Hamilton saw the NFL as both disreputable and threatening. The followers of pro teams were in his opinion rabble; admitting them to the sacred grounds of Pitt Stadium was unthinkable. Furthermore, it would be an unwise business decision. Why help the Steelers compete for the football dollar and for media attention? The NFL itself, Hamilton thought, was like the camel peering into the tent. Once its nose was inside, the neck, legs, and hump would follow, leaving no room for the tent's original occupants – which of course would be exactly what happened. Tom Hamilton was a visionary. Over the next twenty years, in all the cities where professional football had taken hold, the college teams lost their support base, the general public. Already, New York was more devoted to the Giants than to Army or Columbia; Philadelphia preferred the Eagles to Penn; Chicago belonged to the Bears, not to Northwestern.

Admiral Tom was a big, bluff, strong-minded authority figure who commanded the aircraft carrier Enterprise in World War II. Very much accustomed to getting his own way, he reckoned without the political savvy of AJR. Pitt was an institution partly supported by state funds and therefore dependent on the good will of the State Legislature. Every Democrat in Harrisburg took his orders from Pittsburgh Mayor David Lawrence, soon to be governor, and AJR was by now the boss's best friend. One word from Lawrence set in motion a predictable chain of events, which ended with Edward H. Litchfield, Pitt's chancellor, converted to a-live-and-let-live point of view.

It was then that AJR, having cleared the way for the move from Forbes Field, started second-guessing himself. In 1958, Buddy Parker's second season, the Steelers played all of their home games at Pitt Stadium. The following year, and for the three succeeding years, they were back in Forbes Field. In 1963 there were games in both venues, but from 1964 until 1970, when Three Rivers Stadium opened, home sweet home was Pitt Stadium exclusively.

Pitt Stadium had 58,000 seats, all with good sightlines, and AJR needed the extra income this generated. He needed it because of Parker's contract. Clark Gardner, a financial advisor who worked for AJR, told me long after Parker was gone that his base salary with the Steelers had been eighty thousand dollars a year – top dollar at the time in the NFL – plus incentives. Gardner did not know what the incentives were. I did. But I had thought that Parker's base salary was closer to thirty thousand dollars. No, Gardner said - the eighty-thousand figure was correct.

Over and above that, Parker got a percentage of the profits, as Jock Sutherland had. The move to Pitt Stadium and a new TV contract with the National Broadcasting Company guaranteed that the profits would be higher than they ever had been.

And there were still more add-ons for Parker. This is hard to believe, but AJR cut him in on a percentage of his race-track and stock-market earnings, which were sizable. For one thing, he was betting heavily and successfully on the horses in those years. The real bonanza, though, was the killing he made in soy-bean futures, the result of a tip from Father Dan. There had been a huge crop failure in China, Dan learned. After the Communist takeover, the Franciscans had all left the country, but they were not without sources of information. Father Dan told AJR about the soy-bean shortage, and before the news could spread, raising prices all over the world, he invested enough for a hundred-thousand-dollar profit. The other Dan – my brother – raised the question of whether part of this money should go to Parker. He did not see how Buddy was entitled to it. AJR put the issue to rest by telling him, "Your word is your bond."

All in all, Parker made out pretty well with the Steelers. On AJR's side, there were no regrets, either, for the first couple of years. It is hard to tell at just what point misgivings began to set in. Parker was impulsive and eccentric. AJR had known that. Whether he foresaw the extent of the trouble this would cause is open to doubt. Personally, I got along with Parker very well. He was easy to talk to and friendly toward my brothers and me. Before his departure, I had started to learn the scouting end of the business, and he gave me some helpful advice. One thing he said was: "When you visit a college campus, conduct yourself in a way that will not keep anybody from wanting you to come back the next year." He saw that we needed more scouts and better scouts and was instrumental in the development of the Blesto concept, in which four or five teams would share the cost of tracking down and evaluating the NFL prospects among thousands of college players. It was ironic but typical that in his eight years with the Steelers he managed to trade away all of the team's high draft choices.

Footnote: AJR knew that Parker's first name was Raymond but always addressed him as Clarence. One day I asked why. "Because his middle name is Clarence," AJR said. I corrected him – something I did not often do. "I think his middle name is Kemp," I said. "Look it up to be sure." AJR looked it up and discovered that I was right. From then on he called the coach Buddy.

Uneasy Alliance

I think there was mutual dislike and mutual suspicion when the Steelers gained access to Pitt Stadium. The Pitt people seemed to think they were working with a pack of racketeers. Our own front-office people felt as out of place in Pitt Stadium as Irish Catholics in a Presbyterian church.

What Joe Carr felt was a loss of control. At Forbes Field he could parcel out the 12,000 seats with good sightlines to the customers he favored. At Pitt Stadium there wasn't a bad seat in the place. There wasn't a comfortable seat, either; all 58,000 were backless, but the fans who objected were the ones, for the most part, on Joe Carr's priority list.

They complained that their new seats were too narrow; that they were sacroiliac destroyers; that they bristled with butt-piercing splinters. They complained about the lack of cover: Forbes Field had a grandstand roof; Pitt Stadium was open to the elements. They complained about the climb up DeSota Street – called Cardiac Hill – from the bus stops, streetcar tracks, parking lots, and parking garages on Fifth Avenue.

For another thing, Pitt Stadium had no lights, which meant we could not schedule night games there. Joe Carr, making capital of all this, campaigned for a return to Forbes Field. Pitt Stadium had stripped Joe of his power. The old baseball park, with its vision-impeding iron posts and girders, its dankness and dirt, its odors of spilled beer and decay, was his source of power. He prevailed on AJR to authorize a survey – let the ticket buyers decide where we should play. And of course the outcome was never in doubt. Polling only his favored 12,000, ticket holders for life who bequeathed their seats to relatives when they died, Carr found that, overwhelmingly, the fans were for going back to Forbes Field.

AJR was taken in. After the 1958 season, we did not play at Pitt Stadium again until 1963, and then for only part of the schedule. In the end it was Dan who convinced him to make a clean break with Forbes Field. Joe Carr's hold on the Chief had been broken at last.

One of Fran Fogarty's concerns about the move to Pitt Stadium was the prevalence there of gate-crashing. Every male Oakland native, as Fogarty knew, having grown up in Oakland himself, considered free admission to the stadium almost a birthright. Working with Kenny George, the ticket manager at Pitt, Fogarty attempted to plug the leaks, aware that complete success would not be possible. A short, white-haired man, serious and strict, George had a reputation for tough-mindedness, but the equally tough-minded Fogarty won his confidence and, in the end, his cooperation.

On the upper administrative level, my brother Dan earned the respect of the Pitt people for his competence; AJR won them over with an irresistible combination of friendliness and good faith, proving once again that he was able to make connections with anyone. In doing so, he deliberately underplayed his sharp intelligence. High flyers who thought they were outsmarting AJR, and ended up being outsmarted themselves, rarely even knew how it happened.

A minor example of this was his psychological tussle with Beano Cook and Jim O'Brien.

Beano Cook, Pitt's sports information director, rubbed me the wrong way. In my view, he was too opinionated. Media members, I subsequently learned, admired him for his honesty and forthrightness. He said what he thought - overdoing it, I believed. But New York columnist Dan Parker called Beano "the greatest publicity man since Barnum - and, on second thought, Bailey too," and Frank Carver, who succeeded Tom Hamilton as Pitt's athletic director, pronounced him "the best press agent in the business." His allegiance, of course, was to college football. Beano's one stint with a pro team - the Miami Dolphins - coming after a decade or more at Pitt and a job with the American Broadcasting Company in New York, lasted just twelve months. Later, hired by the all-sports radio and television network ESPN, he developed into an on-the-air personality and something of a pundit.

Jim O'Brien, a brash Irish kid from Hazelwood, had been sports editor of the *Pitt News*. Before graduation, he started a newspaper of his own, a tabloid called *Pittsburgh Weekly Sports*. Beano, Jim's patron, was listed on the masthead as co-publisher. It was a lively publication. O'Brien reprinted columns and articles by some of the talented young writers on big-city papers in the East, papers with sports sections more interesting than those of the stodgy, uncreative Pittsburgh dailies. He himself covered the local scene with a critical boldness absent from the *Press* and the *Post-Gazette*. The paper's style reflected Beano's journalistic credo. "I know what I like to read – controversy!" Beano would say. "I don't care if the writer is Ernest Hemingway – he's got to write some controversy."

Controversy, of course, makes for hard feelings, and O'Brien's bumptiousness offended both the objects of his scrutiny and the city's older, less adventurous sports reporters and sports editors, whose policy it was to sweep controversy under the rug. O'Brien was especially hard-fisted in writing about the Steelers. To my astonishment, that did not prevent Beano, his partner, from asking AJR for a favor. O'Brien, I believed at the time, was no more than a mouthpiece, putting into words what Beano, because of his affiliation with Pitt, couldn't prudently say on his own. Yet here Beano was, before a Steeler game at Pitt Stadium, coming uninvited into AJR's box and making what I thought was an outrageous proposition on behalf of *Pittsburgh Weekly Sports*. He wanted AJR to give the paper an exclusive story – no particular exclusive story, just the next big story that broke. It could be a story about a trade or a coaching change or a lineup shuffle – anything at all that the dailies wouldn't have.

To be truthful, I expected my dad to slug Beano. *Pittsburgh Weekly Sports*, remember, was a paper that consistently found fault with Dad's football team. But, instead, he was patient and courteous, explaining in a reasonable way that the *Press* and the *Post-Gazette* had large circulations, that their reporters covered the Steelers day in and day out, and that it could never be right to withhold something from them in order to make O'Brien's paper look good.

Beano persisted, showing none of the deference I had come to expect from people who had dealings with AJR. "Give us just one exclusive." Jack Butler was in our box, and I thought maybe *he* would punch Beano. Still under 30, Beano was six feet tall, or close to it, and weighed about 200 pounds. He was therefore, I thought, fair game. But though I knew Jack was steaming, he made no move – which left it up to me. I had recently finished my year in the Marine Corps and was still feeling gung-ho. Like Jack, though, I held off. Sucker-punching guys was not my style. And AJR, while never losing his composure, had made Beano see that he was pushing things a little too far.

I was surprised at how quickly Dad forgot the whole incident. No doubt to him, as to many others, Beano was a Pittsburgh character, outspoken and assertive but knowledgeable, humorous, and likable. As for me, after all these years, my temper still rises when I think of his demand for an "exclusive."

Though Jim O'Brien, with good cause, continued to take shots at the Steelers, AJR did not seem to mind. In fact, he placed ads in the paper. Publishing on a shoestring entails risk, and there were rumors, finally, that the little upstart tabloid was going broke. O'Brien eventually folded the paper, but did it, he says, to accept a job offer from the *Miami Daily News*. From Miami he went to the *New York Post* and then came home to work for the *Pittsburgh Press*. Halfway through the 1980s he unexpectedly turned up in Cook's old job, that of sports information director at Pitt. Another career change quickly followed. By the time he was 45, a mellowed 45, he was writing and publishing sports books, among them a laudatory memoir of AJR called "The Chief." Pieced together after his death, it's a collection of interviews with people who knew him. "I love and admire [AJR] more than ever," O'Brien writes at the end of the introduction.

A Pittsburgh character who ingratiated himself with me was Leo Chester Czarnecki, the Pitt athletic department's head groundskeeper. Thick-set, square-shouldered, and immensely strong, Czarnecki acquired his nickname – Horse – from Torn Hamilton, who watched him pull an iron-wheeled cart across the football field one day. The cart had a heavy tarpaulin in it. "Who's that horse?" Hamilton asked.

Czarnecki had a spiky blond crew cut and baby-blue eyes. He hit it off immediately with AJR, who always hit it off with people who were down to earth. Horse's humor was not for stuffed shirts. On the canvas-back chair he occupied at Pitt basketball games he stenciled a sign that read "Reserved: Field House Atzerverator." To those who inquired what "atzerverator" meant, he explained, "When I came here, they called me a janitor. I needed a more impressive title to scare off the walruses who plopped themselves down in my chair. So I threw a handful of alphabet cereal on the breakfast table and it spelled out atzerverator." In a year when the Pitt football team was scoring few touchdowns,

Horse gave the offense some needed direction. Across the top of the goal-line markers he painted the words "Pay Dirt," with an arrow pointing into the end zone. A device that got better results was the sprinkler system he installed at the base of the goal posts to repel the mobs bent on tearing them down. Activated at the end of the game – if Pitt won – the sprinklers were more effective than the Pittsburgh police at protecting the goal posts from destruction.

Horse's greatest feat, the achievement that made his reputation, dated back to the big Thanksgiving Day snow of 1950. With the whole city immobilized, there was no way to disconnect the plumbing in Pitt Stadium. Commandeering a crew of five, Horse spent four days and four nights in the stadium's recesses, flushing toilets to keep the pipes from freezing.

"From now on," Hamilton told him, "you're a foreman."

As far as those of us with the Steelers were concerned, he was something much more than that – namely, Pitt's most successful good-will ambassador.

South Park

When the Steelers played their home games at Forbes Field they practiced there, too, on the outfield grass. With the move to Pitt Stadium, a difficulty arose. The stadium itself was out of the question as a practice site. Not even the university team practiced at Pitt Stadium but on a nearby field only eighty yards long, which was either unavailable to the Steelers or unsatisfactory.

As he usually did, AJR turned to his political friends for help. South Park, owned by the county, had a football field where the team from a small high school in the area played some of its games, and the Steelers became seasonal tenants.

Comprising almost two thousand acres of what once had been farmland, much of it reforested in the 1920s and 1930s, South Park was a pastoral extension of Pittsburgh's South Hills. With assistance from the Civilian Conservation Corps, a government-funded Depression-era haven for jobless young men, the talented landscape architect Paul B. Riis had planted and transplanted maples and oaks, beeches and dogwoods, cherry trees and pear trees. By the time all the work was finished, the park's attractions included a golf course, a "bathing" pool (four feet deep), tennis courts, baseball diamonds, nature trails, bridle paths, picnic groves, and dance pavilions. The county fair was held at South Park. Until attendance tapered off in the 1960s, half a million spectators came every year for the livestock judging and home-cooking exhibits, for the harness-horse races and high-school band competitions.

Once the summer was over, activity ceased. Off and on, the county's mounted police troop trained in one of the horse barns. The cow barns and sheep pens were empty. In 1927, a buffalo herd and a band of Native Indian caretakers had been trucked in from the West. No trace of either remained. There had been thirty-six buffalo all told, but Chief Wild Eagle's braves, instead of protecting the shaggy creatures, gunned them down for their meat and their hides. When all the buffalo were gone, the Indians went home to the Great Plains. Their reason for leaving, they said, was the weather. Winters on the prairie, which are famously long and hard, had not prepared them for Western Pennsylvania's icy Decembers.

So the Steelers worked out in isolation. Buddy Parker, obsessed with privacy, liked it that way. Parker and all or most of his assistant coaches lived in the South Hills, and they took the back roads to the park. One day a week, conveniently for Buddy, they met for a strategy discussion in his game room.

Halfback Ray Mathews, who also lived in the neighborhood, sometimes came to practice on horseback. Between workouts, he galloped his steed. Kicker Bert Rechichar kept a shotgun in his car and used it to wing pheasants until the chief of the county police, Monk Ketchel, reported him to AJR. Using Torn the Bomb Tracy's car, Bobby Layne was stopped by Ketchel for "irregular driving." Ketchel opened the trunk and found an entire arsenal of shotguns, rifles, and pistols – "enough hardware," he said, "to start a revolution."

All things considered, Parker's wild Steelers made Wild Eagle's wild Indians look like Cub Scouts. One of the quarterbacks working out with the team was a strong-armed walk-on named Dan Nolan. He had an M-l rifle for an arm, but never knew where his passes were going. Sometimes he bounced them off various body parts of the county police or their horses if they were anywhere near the practice field. For a night on the town, Mike Sandusky and Joe Krupa, veteran Steeler linemen, took Nolan with them as a safety valve. At their first stop, they informed him that he was not to imbibe. His job, they explained, was to drive them back to the South Hills, and he had to be sober. When Nolan tried to object, he could not make them listen. At the end of the evening, thoroughly soused, they handed him the keys to the car. He sat down behind the wheel, stepped on the accelerator, and took off, Krupa recalled, "like a bat out of hell." He rocketed across the Liberty Bridge and tore through the Liberty Tubes at ninety miles an hour. "Slow down! Slow down!" his terrified passengers shouted. Finding the brake at last, he pulled up on the side of the road. "Where in the hell," demanded Krupa, no longer under the influence, "did you learn how to drive?"

"That's what I've been trying to tell you," answered Nolan. "I never did learn to drive."

Nolan did not make the team. The next Krupa heard of him he had been ordained as a Catholic priest.

The Steelers' locker room at South Park was housed in a ramshackle clapboard structure of one and a half stories, painted white. During the heyday of the county fair, it had served as a first-aid station. At other times, the county stored supplies and equipment in the building or rented it out for parties.

County workmen did what they could to keep the place in repair, but it was close to falling down from old age. A small porch led to the front door; another door opened into the basement, where the players dressed. No more than three or four at a time could use the showers. Those who did not mind waiting played cards, but Parker had a rule against crap games. A "cheesy rug" – as Joe Krupa put it – camouflaged the cement floor.

The meeting rooms and the trainer's room were upstairs. There were three meeting rooms all told – one for the offense, one for the defense, and one for the whole squad. When the whole squad met, there was not enough space for all the players. Some had to sit outside in the hallway, along with a coach or two. The others huddled together on chairs that were too narrow for bulky tackles, guards, and centers.

In the absence of a kitchen and lunch room, the players chose to eat at the nearest fast-food joints instead of brown-bagging it. At least once a week, a local optometrist, a celebrity hound, drove to a good delicatessen and got take-out for Buddy Parker and his staff. Parker showed his gratitude by letting the guy hang around. He survived the Mike Nixon and Bill Austin administrations, but one of Chuck Noll's first moves was to bar him from the premises.

Steelers Andy Russell and Ray Mansfield, whose avocation in later life was after-dinner speaking, worked up a routine they often repeated. They told a story that went like this: Parker (they would say) complained to AJR about conditions at South Park and obtained a promise from the Chief to do something. After several days there were still no changes. So Russell and Mansfield took it upon themselves to remind AJR that the situation had not improved. "It's all being taken care of," he assured them. "Improvements are certainly in order. I know that you fellows have to put on the same underwear and use the same towels twice a day – once after the morning practice and again after the afternoon practice. We're going to end that. From now on when the afternoon practice is over, you two will change with each other. After the second workout, Mansfield, you put on Russell's underwear and use Russell's towel. Russell, you put on Mansfield's underwear and use Mansfield's towel."

The story was neither true nor very funny, but Russell and Mansfield liked to tell it, and I must say that it caught the flavor of our years at South Park.

Low Point

There was never a more passionate Steeler fan than Joe Chiodo, a short, wide-bodied tavern keeper from Homestead. At Pitt Stadium one rainy Sunday, I saw him shed his blood in defense of the team and its owners.

Chiodo's bar was on Main Street in Homestead, not far from the gates of the Homestead works of U.S. Steel, where many of his customers earned the money they spent at his place on whiskey, beer, and the specialty of the house, a "mystery sandwich," the mystery being that nobody knew what was in it. If you ordered one, you could only be sure that you never had eaten anything quite like it, or would do so again, for the contents differed each day.

"Sports bars," as such, did not exist back then, but Chiodo's came close to looking like one. Call it a cross between a sports bar, a junk yard, and the Hanging Gardens of Babylon. Suspended from the ceiling were all kinds of artifacts – everything from rare (and not so rare) antiques to the most ordinary household items. An equally eye-catching decorative touch was a collection of brassieres. How they ended up hanging from Joe Chiodo's ceiling I don't know. There was also a photo gallery. Pictures of sports figures covered every wall, football players predominating. Steelers past and present gazed down from these walls on the beer drinkers and mystery sandwich eaters.

For many reasons, Chiodo revered my dad. It would take me thirty minutes to list them all, but the one that he talked about most often was a commonplace courtesy the Chief seldom neglected. "When my father died," Joe would say, "Mister Rooney came to the wake. Can you imagine a guy like Art Rooney paying his respects to a poor Italian immigrant who could barely speak English?" What he probably didn't suspect was that Joe Carr or Ed Kiely or someone else in the Steeler office routinely checked the obituaries every day and notified AJR of wakes and funerals it might please him to attend.

Jack Butler nicknamed Joe Chiodo "The Little Tycoon" because he organized bus trips from his bar to our home games and also to certain games on the road. When we played in Cleveland, Washington, or Philadelphia, Joe and his busloads of steelworkers would form a boisterous Pittsburgh cheering section. For me at least, they revived fond memories of the Ham and Cabbage Specials run by Owney McManus to Steeler games in New York and to Billy Conn's championship fights. All the more unsettling, then, was the scene that took place on the Sunday Joe fought for our honor.

To start from the beginning: a crew from NFL Films was in town to do a segment on Chiodo's bar. Its uniqueness and its fame as a shrine to the Steelers was attracting a lot of attention from the media. When Karl Malden, the noted character actor ("Patton," "On the Waterfront," "A Streetcar Named Desire"), made a television movie about working in a steel mill, he chose to do his research at Chiodo's. All of this, I'm afraid, went to Joe's head just a little. Old customers who may have been a trifle uncouth found themselves barred from his place as undesirables. Joe's high-handedness in deciding who could or could not be served with a drink reminded me of no one as much as Pop Rooney.

On the day that NFL Films was in town, the camera crew finished shooting interiors – football fans juicing up for the game – and then the buses took off for Pitt Stadium, the movie people following in rented cars. What happened at the game ruined Chiodo's day and mine. The clouds hung low, the rain never stopped, the field was a swamp, and our football team, a very bad one that year, could not have been worse. Five minutes into the second half, most of the crowd had departed. Chiodo's guys – wet, cold, drunk, and unhappy – stuck it out. For shelter from the downpour, they huddled under the eaves of the press-box roof, growing mutinous. The foulness of their language matched the foulness of their mood. From our seats in the owner's box, we could hear all the words.

"Fuck the Steelers!" they were shouting. "Fuck the Rooneys!"

Only Chiodo himself was sober. Angrily, he tried to shut them up, and they turned on him. One yahoo lunged for his throat. He had a choke hold on Joe and wouldn't release it. I suppose the camera was recording the whole ugly spectacle. If so, it ended up on the cutting-room floor. No lasting harm came to Chiodo. Just in time, a few of the bus riders who still had some sense converged on his attacker and pulled him off. Joe was bloodied and bruised, but more embarrassed than hurt.

In all of our years at Pitt Stadium, this day was the low point.

Chapter 30

'Don't Knock Friendship'

Richie McCabe was a kid from The Ward, cut from the same environmental and educational swatch as the Rooney boys: St. Peter's grade school, North Catholic High School, the University of Pittsburgh. There was never a more unlikely looking football player. Tall and thin, he weighed 165 pounds at the most. He wore thick-lensed glasses that seemed to dominate his pale, narrow face. He was the temperamental opposite of the Cowardly Lion, the Bert Lahr character in "The Wizard of Oz." His courage and ferocity were all on the inside, camouflaged by a scarecrow exterior.

When we were kids at North Catholic, Richie played basketball for the neighborhood YMCA team. There was a game one night with a team from the Nike missile base at the Greater Pittsburgh Airport. One of the GIs singled out the scrawny kid with the thick glasses as someone he could push around. Richie let him have it with five quick punches, the last four landing on his hasty descent to the floor.

Intelligence and speed were Richie's main assets on the football field. From a distance, he could not see the goal line, but he knew where it was and how to get there. He played the game with a passion and learned the fine points so well that even at North Catholic High School he was telling his teammates what to do. The coach, Bob Hast, encouraged him to an extent. "Just don't get full of yourself," he would say.

Richie and my brother Dan played in the same backfield. "I was a hotshot offensive back – I thought," Richie said. "I could have gone to twenty or twenty-five schools." He went to Pitt – "and to be honest about it," he said, reminiscing, "I didn't do anything there. I mean I played – I played a lot – but I weighed 145 pounds and they never ran me around end. They ran me on dive plays and off tackle."

The Steelers, for old time's sake, took McCabe in the twenty-seventh round of the 1955 draft. No one gave him a chance to make the team, but deep down he felt he could play. When Dewey McConnell, the safety man, got hurt, Richie took his place in an exhibition game. He intercepted two passes, recovered a fumble, and scored a touchdown. He was the scrawniest defensive back in the NFL, but fast enough and tough enough to win a place on the roster in three of the next four years. Buddy Parker described him to AJR as "a player who makes a contribution." So AJR was a little surprised when Richie asked to be traded or released.

Pressed for an explanation, he said that he wanted to prove something. "Everybody in Pittsburgh is saying the only reason I'm on the team is my friendship with the Rooney family. I'd like to show them I can play for any team in the NFL."

"Look," AJR told him, "don't knock friendship. In this life you are lucky to make five really true friends – and that includes your wife. All the others are just acquaintances."

But Richie's heels were dug in. AJR traded him to Washington, and for one season, anyway, he proved he could play there. In1960, he went to an AFL team, Buffalo, mainly because Jack Butler was on the coaching staff. It was the AFL's first season, and Richie described the caliber of play as a joke – better than college football, but not that much better.

He retired after two years. Bad knee. Back home in Pittsburgh, he found a teaching job at Mount Oliver High School, but what he really wanted to do was coach. "No one would have me – I couldn't even get an interview," he said. "The North Catholic job was open, my own school. I wrote a letter and nobody answered it."

Another two years went by and then Joe Gasparella, himself a former Steeler, invited Richie to be his assistant at Carnegie Tech – to "help out," as Joe put it.

"I'll be honest with you," Richie said. "I don't think Carnegie Tech can be helped."

But he accepted the offer and "turned out to be a good coach – a great coach," according to Joe. "He was very dynamic with our kids," Joe said. "He straightened some of them out, I'll tell you that. He had a little different vocabulary than we usually heard on our campus."

One day out of the blue a call came from Joe Collier, the Buffalo Bills' coach. He was asking McCabe to be his defensive coordinator, and it launched him on a second pro career. Coaches, especially assistants, change jobs a lot, and Richie was no exception. He went from Buffalo to the Jets to Denver.

The Richie McCabe I remembered was shy around girls, but in Buffalo he had married a secretary in the Bills' front office. Meanwhile, we were hearing good things about him from people like Babe Parilli, who had come here from the Jets to be our quarterback coach, and Joe Namath, the Jets' first Hall of Famer. In Denver, McCabe was the number one assistant to Dan Reeves. His future at this point looked as cloudless as a future could be.

And then, very quickly, the picture changed. He developed cancer. When he learned that it was terminal, he methodically called his friends to say good-bye. His call to me interrupted a meeting with some scouts. What he wanted to talk about, going all the way back to his childhood, was my mother. He said that from time to time when he was growing up, she would offer him money for a movie or a snack, knowing his family could not afford such luxuries. Always he had refused. The other kids would find out and make fun of him, he admitted to her at last. "Richie," she assured him, "it will be a secret between the two of us."

He asked if she ever had told me about this conversation. I said no.

Then Richie said, "I loved your mother very much."

They were his last words to me, almost.

Helping Hand

In the division of labor decreed by AJR, my brothers Tim, John, and Pat were not involved with the football team. They ran the horse racing and later the dog racing end of the family business. Because the tracks were so distant from Pittsburgh, outsiders seemed to be unaware of this. The Rooneys, they knew, owned the Steelers. As individuals, all five brothers were therefore accountable for every decision, no matter how trivial, made by either management or the coaches. Even the players' wives, or at any rate one player's wife, held to that view.

We had a wide receiver and kick returner from Michigan State, Gary Ballman, who was big and fast but lacking in the ability to improvise on the field. Buddy Parker used him sparingly, influenced, perhaps, by the perception then in vogue that Michigan State players were slow to catch on. As a Blesto scout put it, "You could toss them all into a bag and then throw Duffy Daugherty in" – Duffy Daugherty was Michigan State's highly successful coach – "and their IQs wouldn't add up to a hundred and ten."

However unfactual that may have been, Gary Ballman spent most of his Sundays on the bench.

Anyway, during Ballman's second year on the team, his wife was in the maternity ward at Mercy Hospital at the same time as my brother John's wife. One day after visiting JoAnn, John decided to call on Mrs. Ballman. He did not get quite the reception he anticipated.

Going straight to the subject of her husband's limited playing time, she gave him a thorough tongue-lashing. John listened quietly and departed.

The next weekend, for some reason, Parker had Ballman in the starting lineup, and he made some spectacular catches. On Monday morning, John was back at the hospital to pick up JoAnn and the baby. In the hallway or somewhere, he encountered Mrs. Ballman.

"Oh, Mister Rooney," she said. "How can I ever thank you enough for talking to Coach Parker about Gary? All he needed was a chance to show what he could do, and you gave it to him."

John had said nothing about Mrs. Ballman's complaint to anyone, Parker least of all, but told her he was glad to have been of service.

Gary Ballman became a good, productive player for the Steelers. The other wide receiver was Buddy Dial, which didn't hurt. Dial attracted double coverage every week, making it easier for Ballman. After the Steelers traded Dial to Dallas – handed him over for a draft choice we failed to sign – Ballman was still a decent performer but considerably less effective without his running mate.

Cannonball

On Interstate 95 in Florida where it passes through Jacksonville, there's a sign that says "Edward Waters College," with a big black arrow pointing west. Whenever I see it, I think of Cannonball Butler.

Edward Waters was a nineteenth-century Baptist minister, and the college that bears his name is affiliated with the Southern Baptist Church. No doubt the Rev. Mr. Waters was fully deserving of the honor his church bestowed on him, but as far as I am concerned the wording on that sign along Interstate 90 should be "Cannonball Butler College."

For those of us connected with the Steelers, it was Cannonball Butler who put Edward Waters on the map. In his senior year at Edward Waters, 1964, he played on an undefeated football team, scoring twenty-eight touchdowns. Against one opponent, Friendship College, he scored a touchdown every time he carried the ball, for a total of six. Edward Waters won that game 142-0.

Although our scouts had seen Cannonball only on film, we drafted him in the fourteenth round. He was not very big – just 5 feet 9 and 180 pounds – a matter of concern to some of our coaches. Ken Stilley, who signed Butler, advised them not to worry. Cannonball was compact, Stilley said, and would be able to block. In Buddy Parker's system, the halfbacks had to block, but what Cannonball did best was run. And he could run like ... oh, I don't know, like a shot out of a cannon, I guess you'd say. That was the reason for his nickname, after all. The nickname seemed to embarrass him a little, but nobody including his parents ever called him by the name he received at birth – James. "I have four sisters," he said, "and I'm the only boy in the family, so they call me Brother."

Getting back to the way he ran, his speed excited everybody at our training camp in Rhode Island. He got loose for some long runs in the intra-squad scrimmages, and against a minor-league team called the Rhode Island Indians he sprinted eighty yards for a touchdown.

Buddy Parker believed we had something. Cannonball, he said, was certain to be "a terrific running threat" for the Steelers. Parker wasn't around to see if his prediction held up (that was the year he resigned before the start of the season), but Mike Nixon, the assistant coach who succeeded him, liked Cannonball too. "Give him that much room in the open," Nixon said, holding a forefinger and thumb an inch apart, "and he's gone."

Nixon saved a place on the roster for Cannonball. "He's short, yes," Nixon told me, "but look at those shoulders and arms. He's all man. His thighs are huge. And he can cut on a dime. We have to get him into the game as much as we can. He may not be a starter, but there's so many good things he can do. We have to get the ball to him on pitchouts and screens and flares. He can outrun defenders to the corner. We have to use him on quick openers and draws. Why, he'll drive people crazy."

As it happened, the only people Cannonball ever drove crazy were the coaches and some of his teammates. Not that he was in any sense disruptive. Personally, he was quiet and well behaved. The trouble with Cannonball was that he lacked football intelligence. Despite multiple repetitions in practice, said his coaches, he simply could not remember the plays. After the 1967 season, Bill Austin, who had taken over from Nixon the previous year, traded him to Atlanta.

Cannonball's speed notwithstanding, Chuck Noll would have cut him in two weeks. Noll often said, "The dummies will kill you." When Noll took over as coach in 1969, he recognized the need for team speed. "But there was something we needed even more – team intelligence," he said. "And I saw that we needed it very badly."

Chapter 31

Owls Hoot, Eagles Fly

Even as an assistant coach, Bobby Layne continued to be the Steelers' off-the-field leader. He led them most often to Dante's, a popular hangout in Brentwood. A Detroit Lion teammate aptly summed up Layne's influence on everyone who ever played with him: "When Bobby said block, you blocked. When Bobby said drink, you drank."

If you drank all night, you blocked the next day – no excuses accepted. "Don't hoot with the owls unless you can soar with the eagles," Layne used to say. He applied this code rigidly to himself.

On his way home from Dante's one night, having hooted perhaps to excess, he met with an accident. "I was hit by a parked, swerving streetcar," he explained to the police. The next day was a game day, and Bobby soared. He soared even higher than usual.

Punter Frank Lambert, one of the more intellectual types to play for the Steelers, described the culture of the team as "hard-hitting, hard-drinking, blue-collar masculinity." Jim Brown, the punishing Cleveland running back, said, "I hear their coach puts beer on their bus. But when you play against them," he added, "your body is sore for days. They leave you black and blue."

Buddy Parker wanted players who could do that – tough guys in the mold of Ernie Stautner, John Henry Johnson (acquired from the Detroit Lions), and Big Daddy Lipscomb (acquired from the Baltimore Colts). Parker stocked his teams by trading draft choices; one of the few draftees who made the grade was Red Mack, a slight but ferocious pass catcher from Notre Dame. Mack's right hand was a lethal weapon. Teammate Lou Michaels, a defensive end/placekicker who was sixty pounds heavier than Mack, tested it twice. Both times the Notre Damer stretched him.

Parker's 1963 Steelers, even without Layne and even without Big Daddy Lipscomb, who had died in the off-season of a drug overdose, retained their character. Jim Brown called them the NFL's version of the Gas House Gang. The quarterback was Ed Brown, a big, shaggy-haired ex-Marine. Acquired from the Bears, Brown had been Layne's backup in 1962, and Parker had great confidence in him, or seemed to. He said that Brown "could throw the ball about as well as you'll ever see anyone throw it." That's an exact quote.

From the middle of the season until the final week, the Steelers were undefeated, winning a number of close games on fourth-quarter touchdown plays and getting a tie with the Eagles on Lou Michaels' last-minute field goal. All they had to do to be the Eastern Conference champions was close out the schedule by knocking off the Giants in New York. At home, they had beaten the Giants by thirty-one points.

This time they lost, decisively, and Myron Cope thought he knew why. In a story for *Sport* magazine, Cope blamed the Steelers' 33-17 defeat on Ed Brown's decision to give up booze. Brown dismayed the patrons at Dante's, Myron wrote, by taking the big game too seriously. It seems that "on the Wednesday preceding the showdown battle, he disappeared from his favorite saloon" and "went into training."

Consequently, according to Cope, he "lost his sang-froid," overthrew receivers all day, and "gave the most miserable performance of his career."

A neat theory, except for the fact that, resuming his old habits the next year, Brown gave a series of equally miserable performances. The Steelers descended to sixth place, and that was the end of Brown. Make of it what you will.

A Cuckoo's Nest

As Roy Blount described it in "About Three Bricks Shy of a Load," the Steelers' dressing room at South Park was "the basement of a dilapidated building [that] had six showers, four of which worked. The toilets didn't have seats; you had to sit on porcelain." The dressing area was dingy and cramped, with battered tin lockers. A network of bare pipes covered the ceiling.

At the start of his first year on the job, 1957, Coach Buddy Parker noted with disapproval that there was always a long line outside the trainer's room. Injuries couldn't explain it; it was early in the season, the team was in pretty good shape. Investigating, Parker discovered that the players were lining up to get rubdowns.

Parker's attitude toward rubdowns was similar to that of Luke Carney, an old boxing manager, who said, "A good fighter don't need a rubdown and a bad fighter don't deserve one." Parker at once had the door to the trainer's room padlocked. The next thing he did was tell AJR that the trainer himself should be fired. In his place Parker wanted a man with enough backbone to resist the players' demands and entreaties. In his opinion, they were being coddled.

Instantly, AJR thought of Doc Sweeney. A New England Irishman whose first name, like Parker's, was Raymond. Sweeney had been the trainer for the Brooklyn Dodgers when Jock Sutherland coached them. He had come to the Steelers with Sutherland in 1946 and had stayed on after Sutherland's death for as long as John Michelosen was coach. Tough and self-assured, he ran a tight ship. There was a story about his fearlessness that preceded him to Pittsburgh.

During his years in Brooklyn, the story went, he worked on the players with his shirt off, and one of the owners, Shipwreck Kelly, who was also the first-string tailback for the Dodgers, developed an annoying habit. He would sneak up behind Sweeney and slap him resoundingly on the back. Sweeney warned him to "cut out the foolishness." Kelly didn't listen. There came a day when he delivered one slap too many. Sweeney wheeled around and crashed a right to Kelly's jaw, putting him on the floor. To the surprise of everyone the trainer did not lose his job.

Sweeney was a bona-fide doctor, with a degree in osteopathy. In Maine, where he practiced, he was authorized to write prescriptions, deliver babies, and even perform appendectomies. It annoyed him to be called Mr. Sweeney or Ray instead of Doc. Then in his late forties, he was a bear of a man – six feet tall with massive shoulders and arms. As a trainer, he knew what he was doing and was tireless in doing it.

After Sweeney's return to Pittsburgh, I became his particular friend. At South Park, he would stand on the sideline and appraise various players in a word or two. This one had "lots to say" but wasn't much on performance. That one had talent but would never use it to the fullest extent. "There's something twisted in him." Nine times out of ten, Doc's assessments were right on the mark.

Parker, he quickly discerned, had much more wrong with him than just his addiction to alcohol. "He's a very backward person," Doc said. "Bipolar problems, I suspect." He considered Buster Ramsey and one or two others on the coaching staff a bad influence on Parker. They were "egging him on."

Ramsey, it seemed, was giving Sweeney "a lot of crap" in the meantime. "I came here to work for your dad and Parker – not that guy," Doc told me. "I've never taken anything from anybody, but I'm an old man now with no wife [she had died young] and two kids to raise, and I need this job."

He could stand for only so much, however, and one night when the team was on the road he resolved to have a showdown with Ramsey. He waited in the hotel lobby for Buster to come back from dinner, knowing the hour would be late. "I'm old and fat," Doc said to me later, "but Buster, I figured, would have a snoot full. I planned to go after him – invite him outside and let him have it."

It was not to be. When Ramsey arrived, half-drunk, his wife was with him. "Wonderful lady," Doc said. "Everybody liked her. And she hadn't been well. How did she ever marry a bum like that?" Instead of challenging Ramsey, Doc just said "hi" and went up to bed.

An incident in Dallas was "the last straw" for him, Doc said. The Steelers had gone there to play the Cowboys and were staying at the airport motel. Unlike the downtown hotels, the airport motel was not segregated. Neither were the Steelers, but black players and white players went their separate ways off the field. In Dallas on the night before the game, the blacks had gone off to a blacks-only night club and were late getting back to the motel. Ramsey, in charge of bed check, was "egging Parker on," as Sweeney related it to me, letting him know every few minutes that the black guys were not in their rooms.

"Buddy was drinking," Doc said, "and Buster was getting him upset. They came to my room and pounded on the door. When I opened it, Buddy says right away that he wants his hands taped. 'Like a boxer.' I ask him what for. 'I'm going to punch out Johnson and Lipscomb,' he tells me.

"Buddy and Buster were blaming John Henry Johnson and Big Daddy Lipscomb for keeping the rest of the black guys at the night club. There was no use arguing with Buddy, I realized that, so I taped his hands, but I taped them so tight that in twenty minutes the blood would stop circulating.

"Well, he's running up and down the hallway, punching his fist into his open hand and yelling, 'I'll beat the hell out of that black son of a bitch Lipscomb, and then I'll beat the hell out of John Henry.' This goes on for a full twenty minutes, until his hands went numb and he was back in my room asking me to 'cut the damn tape off.'"

Sweeney had worked with Jock Sutherland, a formal, dignified, larger-than-life sort of personage who tolerated no monkey business from either his players or his assistant coaches. The undisciplined ways of Buddy Parker were more than Doc could put up with. When Mike Duda, the president of California State College of Pennsylvania, offered him a trainer's job that also involved teaching, he jumped at the chance to leave the Steelers. He felt that California, PA, a little college town, would be the perfect environment for his children.

Footnote: After the Vietnam War ended, a cousin of mine told me that through the efforts of "a wonderful man who had once been connected with the Steelers" he was able to enroll at California State as a freshman and avoid being drafted into the Army. Immediately I knew that he was speaking of Doc Sweeney.

Up in the Air

The Steelers had played an exhibition game in Miami, losing to the Dolphins, and now their chartered jet was ready to take off. Fran Fogarty, who doubled as the team's traveling secretary, counted heads. Everybody was on board except Parker, the head coach, and Dick Plasman, his close friend and assistant.

They were not to be found. At the little building on the field where the aircraft was parked, away from the main terminal, there was no bar or restaurant. The plane's big motors were going, and Lou Kroeck of United Airlines, who always flew with the Steelers, warned Fogarty that the tower was pressing them to get on the runway.

Kroeck and Fogarty huddled with the pilot and his crew, after which Fogarty went to my brother John, who was 20 years old, and said, "Stand by. You are going to fetch the coach." The plane then taxied to a gate near the terminal, and the pilot lowered the back steps. Fogarty laid one hand on John's shoulder and placed the other against his back. "Go into the bar," Fran said. "That's where he'll be. Tell him he's got five minutes to get on the plane or his ass stays in Florida." With a gentle shove from Fogarty, John set off on his mission.

"I was scared to death," he later told me. After all, he was still just a kid. And Buddy Parker was a famous head coach with two NFL championships on his résumé.

As Fogarty had predicted, Parker was in the bar with Dick Plasman. Informed that the plane was about to take off, they made a beeline for the gate, with John at their heels. Actually, there was more time before takeoff than Fogarty, knowing Parker's habits, had led John to believe.

Parker had been downing whiskey, as he usually did after a defeat. When the plane was in the air, and the seat belt sign went off, he roamed the aisle, drunk. Jack Butler, Ray Mathews, and two or three other players were having a card game. "Ahh," said Parker. "Card players. Well, you'd better be card players, because you sure as hell aren't football players."

Somebody, for once, had the temerity or bad judgment to talk back. It was Mathews. "And you're the guy who was going to make us winners," he said. "Well, we haven't won yet." (He would soon be traded to the Cowboys, in those days a second-division team.)

Parker glared at Mathews, but held his tongue. Turning around and heading the other way, he stopped at the row where John Nisby and Billy Ray Smith, two big linemen, were seated. "Nisby," Parker sneered, "you're not black, you're yellow. Smith, you're always hurt. We got you from the Rams. You're supposed to be great, but you're a dud."

Nisby said nothing; Billy Ray spoke up. "Dammit, I *am* hurt," he protested. "And I didn't even play today."

"Just what I said – hurt and on your ass!" was Parker's comeback.

Smith had a bad temper. He started up from his seat, but Nisby restrained him.

Next, Parker turned on Ray Campbell, a quiet linebacker called "Soup," for obvious reasons. Since his days at Marquette, the Jesuit college had dropped football. "Campbell," Buddy screamed, "you're not even a player. That school you went to don't even have a football team any more. You're so bad you put them out of business."

Thus did Head Coach Buddy Parker comport himself when AJR was not with the team.

His most memorable scene was at the airport in Houston after a meaningless exhibition game with the Bears. First, though, a digression: To stop some hanky-panky that teams like the Bears and, yes, the Steelers were up to, the NFL had instituted a new rule. In those days it was possible to hide, stash, or stockpile a player by means of a phony, and temporary, "trade." Players would go from one team to another and be returned, by prior agreement, before the next game. Under the new rule, a team had to keep the "borrowed" player for two full weeks. Meanwhile, the player would take part in non-contact drills and calisthenics — nothing more. During games, he would sit on the bench but not play.

Two weeks before the exhibition game in Houston, Parker and George Halas, the owner of the Bears, had agreed to one of these bogus in-name-only exchanges. Consequently, there were two players on the Steeler bench who belonged to the Bears and two players with the Bears who belonged to the Steelers.

One of the Steelers in Bear's clothing was Rudy Hayes, a linebacker from Clemson. Immediately after the game, the so-called trade having been officially reversed, the four players turned in their gear and rejoined their original teams. Parker, living up to the unwritten code, had not used the Bears masquerading as Steelers, but Halas had used his Steelers on special teams. Near the end of the game the Bears went ahead by a field goal. The ensuing kickoff went to a Steeler who broke free and was seemingly on his way to a touchdown. At the Bears' 20-yard line, he had only one man to beat. That man was Rudy Hayes, and he brought down the runner with a desperate, diving, game-saving tackle.

An hour and forty-five minutes later, the team buses pulled up at the Houston airport. The Steelers' charter and the Bears' charter were sitting nose-to-nose on the tarmac, each with its back steps lowered. One by one, the players boarded the planes, Rudy Hayes and the other spurious Bear with the Steelers again and the two counterfeit Steelers back with the Bears. On the Steelers' plane, Buddy Parker, drunk already and brooding about the exhibition-game loss, was up near the front of the cabin. Looking around, he noticed Hayes, who had taken a seat toward the back and was trying to make light of his spectacular flying tackle.

"You traitor!" screamed Parker. "What are you doing on this airplane? Get off! GET OFF! Go over to the Bears' plane. You're no Steeler, Hayes. You cost us the game!"

Hayes was dumbfounded. With Parker standing over him, he got up out of his seat. Slowly, he moved to the back exit, looking at Parker over his shoulder, disbelief written on his face. He made his way down the steps, hesitated, and climbed the back steps of the Bears' plane. Going straight to George Halas, he explained his predicament.

Later, Halas said, "I thought my old friend Buddy had finally blown a gasket."

Halas escorted Hayes back to the Steeler plane, where he spotted Fran Fogarty with some airline people at the steps. "Do something with this young man; we're getting out of here," Halas said to him.

The ever-resourceful Fogarty solved the problem. He led Hayes up the steps once more and pushed him into a lavatory. "Stay here," he said, "until five minutes after we're airborne." Parker, his thoughts on the game, remained none the wiser, and the Steelers enjoyed a tranquil flight home.

Ordinarily Buddy watched himself when the Chief was on board. Only once did he lose control, but once was enough. The Steelers had lost a squeaker to the Giants, and the coach emerged from the airport bar with his usual post-defeat buzz. On the airplane, dropping into a seat next to AJR, he poured out a string of complaints. "I made an awful mistake when I came to this team," he said.

AJR had heard the stories about Parker. Abruptly, he ordered him to shut up. This was a side of AJR that Parker never had seen. Not another word was spoken until the wheels of the big aircraft touched down on a runway in Pittsburgh. Turning then to the Chief, who was looking straight ahead, Parker said, "We have to talk."

"Not now," the owner snapped. "You're in no condition to talk. I'll be in your office tomorrow at lunchtime."

That was all. They debarked from the plane and went their separate ways. Early the next morning, Parker called AJR and apologized. He said he knew he was out of line and would just as soon forget about their lunchtime meeting. "Let's put the whole thing behind us," he suggested.

"No," the Chief said. "It's important to get this straightened out. I'll see you today at practice."

On the long ride to South Park, I was AJR's driver. He asked me questions about Parker. The answers he got were consistent with his own observations. He rehearsed the speech he intended to deliver.

As it happened, the meeting was cordial. Parker was feeling contrite, and AJR was conciliatory but firm. He said to Buddy, "You walked out on a great championship team in Detroit. You're like the guy who had a beautiful wife. He loved her, but found her cheating. He took a walk – and pretty soon was wishing he hadn't. Deep down, he wanted go back to the woman he still loved. But he couldn't. It was too late.

"Buddy," the Chief went on, "you're in Pittsburgh now. Make the best of it. This is the only job you have. We're still friends, and believe me when I say I'd still like to have you as my coach. But I'm putting in some rules, and they have to be followed."

Henceforth, he continued, there would be no drinking on chartered flights. That meant everybody – from the head coach down to the equipment men. Assistant coaches, players, and front-office people, newspaper reporters, broadcasters, and invited guests traveling with the team were included. If a player or coach boarded the plane drunk he was fined $10,000. If a player or coach got drunk after the plane was in the air, he was fined $10,000. Anyone seen to be drunk while the plane was still on the ground would be left behind. He would be responsible for getting to the game or getting back to Pittsburgh on his own. For a second offense, players, coaches, and other employees would be fired. Everyone concerned had to sign a piece of paper acknowledging that he understood these terms and accepted them.

Parker did not object. He said that all of his coaches would sign the statement and that he would be the first. AJR promised to make sure that everyone else signed. Everyone did. On flights from then on, the Steelers were perfect gentlemen, the most circumspect team in the NFL. Even Buddy Parker was a model of good behavior

But in other ways – disastrously – he continued to make a fool of himself.

Chapter 32

Turmoil

Parker had many idiosyncrasies. The number thirteen was anathema to him. His fear of that number, in various manifestations, was almost comical. He refused, of course, to stay in a hotel room if the number on the door began or ended in thirteen, which was never a problem for traveling secretaries. What they were forced to guard against with equal vigilance, though, was assigning him to a room with a number that *added up* to thirteen.

His despair after defeats, even after defeats in exhibition games, often seemed almost psychotic. First he would look for a bottle, or a bar. Then came the ranting. Then, alone or with only his coaching assistants nearby, he would find a knife or a pair of shears, lie flat on his back, and cut off his necktie directly below the knot. Finally, re-playing the lost game in his feverish mind, and assessing blame, he would shake up the team, threatening cuts, trades, or lineup changes, and even, on occasion, putting them into effect.

Parker was a gifted coach, a gifted strategist. In 1964 the Steelers won five games, and coaching won two of them. He threw the Cleveland Browns into confusion with an unorthodox defense and got the Washington Redskins out of sync with an unorthodox offense.

But he relied too often on desperation measures, which became necessary, in part, because Parker created problems for himself. He made spur-of-the-moment decisions with a grand disregard for the consequences.

There was the Buddy Dial-for-nobody trade. In exchange for the draft rights to Scott Appleton, a tackle from the University of Texas, Parker sent Dial, his best wide receiver, to the Dallas Cowboys. What he failed to anticipate was that Appleton would sign with an AFL team – namely, the Houston Oilers.

There were other, less obviously misbegotten trades and releases. There was his stubbornness in the face of criticism from fans and sportswriters. Before Parker was ready to change quarterbacks in 1964, the fans wanted Ed Brown replaced, and the press backed them up. As the call for Bill

Nelsen increased, Parker's obstinacy mounted. Correctly, he reasoned that his knowledge of football was superior to the knowledge of the fans and the reporters. Therefore, if the fans and the writers preferred Nelsen to Brown, they must be wrong.

Brown's failures at the end of 1964 and in the early pre-season games the following year forced his hand. He gave in to the mob by starting Nelsen a couple of times, but what he really wanted to do was trade for somebody else's backup quarterback. All that deterred him was AJR's stipulation after the 1964 season that he and my brother Dan, who was taking over the day-to-day operation of the team, had to be consulted on personnel moves.

King Hill of the Eagles was the quarterback Parker coveted. "What would you think," he asked AJR, "of trading Ben McGee or Chuck Hinton for Hill?" McGee and Hilton were promising second-year defensive tackles from all-black schools in the South.

"I wouldn't do it," the Chief told him. AJR's thinking was: Why weaken your defensive line to get a second-string quarterback who might not be as good as the quarterbacks we already have? "But go ahead and do what you believe to be best for the team," he said.

Parker did nothing. But two weeks later, after the Steelers had lost an exhibition game to Baltimore, he proposed a different trade with a different team. Calling Dan's room in the training camp at the University of Rhode Island from his own room, he suggested trading McGee and a draft choice for two grizzled veterans, a lineman and a linebacker. It was late on a Saturday night, and Parker was drunk.

"Let's talk it over in the morning," Dan said.

"Are you questioning my judgment?" Parker asked.

"No," Dan replied. "But I don't believe in making trades in the middle of the night after a loss."

Parker then declared that he was quitting. Dan said, "I'll get back to you tomorrow morning," and called AJR in Pittsburgh.

Down through the years, after galling defeats, Parker had made a habit of quitting. "He quit twenty times," said AJR when the dust had settled. "He quit twenty times, and I got him back twenty times. This time I didn't get him back."

Accept his resignation, he said to Dan. So on Sunday morning Dan was prepared. The first thing Parker said to him was, "I don't think I can handle this team any longer." Dan said with finality, "I don't think so, either."

And that settled it.

The previous December Parker had signed a three-year contract extension. AJR agreed now to pay him for two of those three years. Roughly, the amount came to $160,000. If the Steelers had fired Parker, he'd have been entitled to his pay for the full duration of the contract – $240,000 or so, plus the extras it called for. But he quit, and legally they owed him nothing. Quitting turned out to be a luxury he could well afford.

Footnote: Parker flew home to Texas from the Greater Pittsburgh Airport. A newspaper photographer snapped a picture of him as he headed for his plane. It was leaving from Gate 13.

Power Struggle

By the time Buddy Parker left the Steelers, my brother Dan and I were sold on building and maintaining the team through the draft. It was an unintended consequence of the way Parker operated. His way was to trade draft choices for veterans, or to pick up players who were not under contract to some other team. If there were bad actors, drunks, and oddballs among them, no problem. Using such misfits, he had won in Detroit, and he held to the view that what worked in Detroit would work with the Steelers. He was wrong.

Parker's attitude toward blacks – the fewer the better – was still another crippling mistake. Deep down I knew this, but I also knew that my opinions carried no weight. Too young and too green to speak with any authority, I held my tongue and bided my time.

Dan, on the other hand, was coming into his own. He had gone through a form of executive training – not that AJR or anyone else would have called it that. After starting out as a go-fer in what passed for our personnel department, he had worked with Joe Carr in the ticket department, with Ed Kiely in P.R., and with Fran Fogarty in the business office.

At Duquesne University, meanwhile, he studied accounting. And he had married Dad's secretary, Patricia Regan. His coming of age entitled him to certain perquisites. For one thing, he now had full use of the Steeler station wagon. That was nice – he had a wife and a kid to haul around, with other kids undoubtedly on the way. Better yet, AJR handed over the program concession to Dan.

The program concession had belonged since the 1930s to a man named Eddie Bernhardt, and losing it put his nose out of joint. From sales and advertising, the programs generated roughly $20,000 a year, half of it going to the team and half to the concessionaire. Eddie Bernhardt was a dapper little guy who tended to be officious and could rub people raw.

When Johnny Blood coached the Steelers, his exasperation with Bernhardt drove him to the point of committing ritualized murder. Bernhardt sat in on a meeting one day and attempted to do all the talking. Blood remained silent for as long as he could and then, picking up a yardstick, he cradled it in his shoulder, pointed it rifle-like at Bernhardt, and shouted, "Bang! Bang! Bernhardt, you little son of a bitch, you're dead!" A bullet from a yardstick Bernhardt could survive. Turning over the programs to Dan was a mortal blow. Did he need ten grand? Probably not. He worked full-time at a job in some other field. Far, far more than the money, he valued his Steeler connection. Deprived of it, he was visibly changed – perpetually downcast instead of cheerful to a fault. His visits to the office became much less frequent, and then, after a while, we saw him no more.

For Dan, gaining stature, the program concession was a springboard. Working with advertising agencies, local business people, and his NFL counterparts, he developed an identity of his own. He went from being Art Rooney's kid to a bright young guy who did his homework, asked intelligent questions, and offered original insights. He made some important friends – notably Pete Rozelle, an up-and-coming P.R. man soon to be tapped for the commissioner's job, and Art Modell, the Cleveland Browns' new owner. The three of them, forming a team, persuaded national advertisers to buy program space on a league-wide basis. AJR's oldest son was acquiring a reputation for wisdom beyond his tender years.

Buddy Parker, observing Dan's rise in the Steeler organization, felt threatened. By 1964 he was slipping over the edge. AJR continued to indulge him, moving the team's training base to the University of Rhode Island, for example, because of Parker's complaints about the "lousy practice fields" in Western Pennsylvania.

Down through the years the Steelers had been nomads. Under Jock Sutherland they had trained at Alliance College in Cambridge Springs. When Joe Bach was the coach, they trained in New York, at St. Bonaventure. There were summers when they trained at California State in California, PA, at Slippery Rock State, north of Pittsburgh, and even at West Liberty College near Wheeling, West Virginia. None of these places suited Parker. They were too close to Pittsburgh, too close to the fans and the media. Parker was publicity-shy. The fans in his mind were necessary evils, the media more like evils he could do without.

It was Ken Stilley, assistant coach and head scout, who suggested Rhode Island to Parker. The facilities and the practice fields, Stilley volunteered, were first-rate. Parker, convinced, told AJR, "It sounds pretty good. Maybe this is just what we need."

AJR was hesitant. He sent Stilley back for talks with the Rhode Island people and ordered me to go along, too. Stilley had been right about the facilities. They were clearly superior to anything we had seen up to then. Privately, I wondered about the practicality of it all. It would be a logistical nightmare, I thought, to get a jockstrap, much less a blocking sled, to Rhode Island, but the university was eager to have us as tenants and I knew that Buddy Parker's wishes would carry the day in the end.

He wanted greener pastures and he wanted them far away with no one looking over his shoulder. Dan would be there, having rented a house in Kingston, the university town, but AJR's other business interests tied him to Pittsburgh. Parker was free, as he supposed, free at last, and he gradually lost control of the team. More to the point, he lost control of himself .

It happened over the course of two summers, starting with the first week of practice in 1964, when perpetual troublemaker Lou Michaels badly beat up a smaller defensive back, Jim Bradshaw. Parker solved the problem by shipping Michaels off to Baltimore (where a few years later he was kicking field goals and extra points for a Super Bowl team), but the turmoil never really abated. There was the day police came, with questions about a player they identified as a Peeping Tom.

There were flare-ups and fights and disciplinary lapses that did not get into the papers, there was the unpredictable behavior of Parker.

A pre-season game with the San Francisco Forty-Niners was scheduled for a Saturday afternoon at the Brown University stadium in Providence. Long beforehand, Parker announced that the players would then be off until Monday. On Saturday, however, they lost the exhibition game, and he angrily rescinded their furlough. "I want you back tonight for dinner and meetings," he told them after the game. Rushing to a telephone, Fran Fogarty called the Rhode Island people with the news that in just a few hours there would be a football team to feed. Impossible, they said. There wasn't any food in the kitchen and the help had been sent home. There were no cooks, no waiters, no dishwashers.

Parker canceled his meetings and opened a bottle of booze. Only the injured players, then, would report back to camp, he told the squad. As he said this, he looked at John Henry Johnson, who had spent the whole game on the bench, explaining that his leg was sore. Treatment after a game for casualties was standard procedure, and John Henry Johnson by his own account was a casualty.

On the trip from Providence to Kingston, Parker got drunk. He went directly to his office and sent an assistant coach to John Henry Johnson's room. "Tell him I want him to see me right now," Parker said. The assistant coach returned in five minutes. He had knocked at John Henry's door and no one had answered. He had then tried to open the door. It was locked.

"He's hiding in there!" Parker exclaimed. "Go back. Break the lock. Kick the door down." Forcing his way in, the coach found an empty room. John Henry, it appeared, had gone AWOL. No doubt he was in the arms of some golden-hued temptress, all thought of football banished from his mind. Parker abruptly called for a large, rectangular piece of cardboard and a staff member adept at lettering and dictated the following manifesto:

TOO SORE TO FIGHT
BUT NOT TOO SORE TO FORNICATE

"Fornicate" was not the exact word Parker used, but close enough. Continuing to follow orders, the staff member took his artwork to Johnson's door and tacked it up as a sort of greeting. It would be the first thing John Henry saw when he returned from wherever he had wandered. Very quickly, Fran Fogarty learned of these developments and without wasting a minute he got in touch with Pittsburgh by telephone. "The coaches," he said starkly, "are running amuck."

AJR was by no means astonished. He had known for some time that Parker was on the verge of a crack-up. There had been an incident not long before that greatly disturbed AJR. The Steelers had played a pre-season game at Forbes Field, and some of AJR's North Side friends had arranged for a welcome-home dinner at the North Side Elks club, the mansion once occupied by the Arbuckle family, industrial pioneers. Its faded magnificence failed to impress Parker, who remarked in an aside that if this was the best the city could do there was not much hope for the old burg. That did not sit well with AJR, and his coach then rankled him further. On the front porch, as they were leaving, Parker delivered an ultimatum, or what sounded to his boss like one. With characteristic bluntness, he informed AJR, "I came here to work for *you*. I didn't come here to work for Dan."

Well, now. AJR had heard something like that from Doc Sweeney, but with Parker's stooge, Buster Ramsey, as the object of the trainer's disaffection. Whatever answer he gave to Parker carried no warning. But In the Roosevelt Hotel the next day a meeting took place, attended by AJR's sons and his front-office staff. His sons were full-grown now and eager to make themselves heard. At the dinner table after Steeler defeats we'd been trying to raise our voices for years. We would criticize the players, criticize the coaches, and criticize AJR. Shutting us up, he would bark, "That 's enough! There will be no talk of football at our table when we lose!" Soon afterward it became: "There will be no talk of football during the season." Then finally: "There will be no talk of football in this house unless I bring up the subject myself." The turn-around may have begun when all of us lobbied for Johnny Unitas, and AJR listened to Kiesling. The success of Unitas with the Colts was our wedge. From that time on, we had freedom of speech. When we sounded off, there were no more reprimands, as long as we did not overdo it. And Dan, the heir apparent, assumed a title also held by Jack McGinley – vice president. He was making decisions, preparing to take over the reins.

As for AJR, he appeared to be phasing himself out. At the meeting in his office he did a curious thing. In effect, he deputized the whole staff. As we all knew, he told us, every game the Steelers lost provoked a crisis. Parker, despondent, would offer to resign. AJR would talk him into changing his mind. Never again. The next time Buddy resigned, said AJR, it would be for keeps. If he resigned in the hearing of Fogarty, Ed Kiely, Dan, myself, or Jack McGinley, we were authorized to take him up on it. Our instructions were to say that his resignation was accepted.

The idea frightened me. I was 29 years old but everybody's junior, it seemed. Tell Buddy Parker good riddance? Somehow I couldn't see myself doing it. I'd have to run to a telephone and call AJR. But there was never the need. Routinely, the Steelers lost another exhibition game. Once again in the usual way Parker said he was quitting. Only this time he said it to Dan, not to the Chief. And this time, he picked the wrong guy.

Coming of Age

Dan's wife, Patricia Regan, was the older sister of Mary Regan, who succeeded her as Dad's secretary. Mary and Patricia were first-generation Irish girls from St. Peter's parish. Both had red hair. So did their sister Gerri, the Steelers' ticket manager after the death of Joe Carr.

Patricia and Dan had met in grade school at St. Peter's. A pretty fair quarterback despite his lack of size, Dan played football as a freshman at Duquesne, but in his sophomore year the university abandoned the sport. At North Catholic High School, Dan was a good student but not at the top of his class. At Duquesne, where he majored in accounting, his grades were never below A. Being married and the head of a family had changed Dan's priorities.

So obsessed was he with football that he coached the St. Peter's grade-school team just to keep his hand in. The players were dirt-poor North Side kids who loved the game with a passion and showed up for practice rain or shine. But his real career was in the administrative side of football, and it would take him all the way to the Hall of Fame.

Boots

A sidelight: Buddy Parker was the only coach in the NFL who had his own personal valet, or body servant. The go-fer was "Boots" Lewis, a medium-sized, old-looking, gray-colored black man who had evidently once been a shoe-shine boy. They had first met each other when Parker played football at Centenary College and Boots was a campus maintenance man.

It seems that he was also one hell of a craps shooter, which apparently struck a chord with Parker. They were together from the time that Parker got into coaching. The only real work that Boots ever did was to fetch and run for his boss – or, more accurately, fetch and walk. Boots had arthritis and always gave the impression of being tired.

Their partnership was an odd one if you took into account Parker's typically Southern racial views. In a way it harked back to the ante-bellum plantation days, with Boots as Old Black Joe and Parker in the role of benevolent white massa.

At training camp and on the practice field, Boots was a tolerated fixture. The football players, white and black, teased but did not torment him. To an onlooker, their bantering seemed affectionate, although Boots, no dummy, would not have agreed. The white players, he told Parker, didn't want him around and the black players accused him of being a spy. "I'm a man without a country," he said.

He accepted jocular remarks with good grace, but would let the players know, when they pushed him, that he was Buddy Parker's man, first and always. One year when the Steelers trained at Slippery Rock, in northwest Pennsylvania, Boots felt uncomfortable because the environment, he complained, was "too woodsy." On an early-morning errand for Parker, he imagined he heard a bear thrashing around, and Parker picked up on this. Finding a costume supplier somewhere, he rented a bear suit. One of the training-camp functionaries put on the disguise and made a juvenile attempt to frighten Boots. The joke fell flat when Boots refused to play the fool and pretend to be taken in.

At the time of Parker's resignation, Boots had a stroke and a heart attack. AJR paid the hospital and medical bills. Boots had some money put away and wanted AJR to be its custodian, for he trusted no one else. From his hospital bed, he would ask in agitation, "Where's mah munnah?" Reassured that "Mister Rooney" was holding it for him, he would settle down. When he was ambulatory again, AJR offered to keep him on the payroll for life. Showing more class than some of Parker's coaches, he said, "I worked for Buddy. When he goes, I go."

Friends in the scouting business would tell me years later that Boots was shining shoes in the Los Angeles International Airport. Many times when I flew in there I looked around but could never find him.

Logical Choice

Only two weeks were left before the start of the season when the Steelers parted company with Parker, so AJR could not afford to dilly-dally. The logical choice to replace Buddy as head coach was Mike Nixon, who had been on the staff, except for a brief hiatus, since the Jock Sutherland era.

Mike was AJR's man, not Parker's. As a stubby little halfback called Mike Nicksick, he had played for Sutherland at Pitt, for the Steelers when the Steelers were the Pirates, and during World War II for the Brooklyn Dodgers, the NFL team Sutherland no longer coached, having wangled a Navy commission. When Sutherland took over the Steelers, Mike returned also, as one of his assistants, and after Sutherland's death he stayed on, leaving in 1959 to become head coach of the Redskins. Two seasons later – unsuccessful seasons for Mike and the Redskins – he was out of work, and AJR obligingly brought him back to Pittsburgh. Somewhere along the way, probably out of deference to Sutherland, he had Anglicized his name. Sutherland liked to have ethnic Slavs and Italians on his football teams but wanted the public to think they were WASPs.

Parker's resignation, if that is the right word, took place on a Sunday morning. Notified by Dan in a telephone call, AJR told me to pack an overnight bag. We were leaving right away for Rhode Island, he said, and we were going to fly. En route, he bounced ideas off me, reviewing his options, running over in his mind the deal he intended to offer Nixon.

Simply put, it was this: the head coaching job is yours for the asking, but I strongly advise you to turn it down. If Mike accepted that advice, there would still be a vacancy to fill, though not for long, AJR was quite certain. Everybody he knew would have a candidate. In the Pittsburgh airport we had happened to meet an old friend, Bishop Vincent Leonard, and he suggested one. "Don't forget Ernie Hefferle," the bishop said. Ernie Hefferle had been an end at Duquesne (he caught the winning touchdown pass when Buff Donelli took the Dukes to the Orange Bowl), an assistant coach at Pitt, and an unsuccessful head coach at Boston College. He was just the man, Bishop Leonard seemed to think, who could clean up the mess Buddy Parker had left.

The good prelate was unaware of what AJR proposed to do. Whoever succeeded Parker would in all likelihood be nothing more than an interim coach. Once the 1965 season was over, AJR expected to make a complete overhaul – to "get the broom out," in Uncle Jim's borrowed metaphor, "and sweep the joint clean."

I was present when he talked to Mike Nixon. "I'm going to offer you this job," AJR said, "but I don't think you should take it. The situation is such that I don't think it can be turned around in one year. In that case I'd have to let you go. If you've been the head coach I don't feel I could keep you on with the new head coach. But if you tell me you don't want this job, I can pretty well promise that you will be with the Steelers for the rest of your working days."

Nixon listened impatiently. He had made his decision and could not be talked out of it. "Look, I'm from Pittsburgh, " he said in a placating voice. "To be head coach of the Steelers is something I've always dreamed of. I just can't bring myself to pass up an opportunity like this." Much more was said on both sides, but only to work out details. I remembered something Jack Sell, the *Pittsburgh Post-Gazette* sportswriter, once told me: "All football coaches are crazy."

Buddy Parker had lost the team, and it was impossible for Nixon to find it. With young Bill Nelsen at quarterback, the Steelers had a miserable season, winning only two games. John Henry Johnson was hurt most of the year and carried the ball just three times. Out came the broom, sweeping Nixon away with all the deadwood.

He coached for many more years in the NFL, but always as an assistant and never again in Pittsburgh. At the end of his career, when he was in player personnel, I would see him on scouting trips, a man with no regrets – or should I say with none that he confided to me?

Bargain Hunting

Rival football leagues had been competing for talent with the NFL as far back as AJR could remember. Always, he had managed to hold his own, but in the 1960s he was up against owners like Lamar Hunt, who was making a lot of money in the oil business and spending big sums on his AFL team, the Dallas Texans. Told that Lamar had squandered ten million dollars on the Texans, his brother Bunker drawled, "Gee, what a shame. Now he's only got a hunnerd and sixty-four million left."

There were other rich owners besides Lamar in the AFL. The Steelers traded Buddy Dial to the Dallas Cowboys for the draft rights to Scott Appleton and then couldn't sign him. They were outbid by the Houston Oilers. Our top draft choice in 1966 would have been Francis Peay, an offensive tackle from Missouri. If we selected him, he told us, he would play in "the other league." So the New York Giants, an NFL team with deeper pockets than ours, drafted Peay. We thought we still had a chance to sign Tom Mack, an offensive tackle from Michigan whose father was on the police force in Cleveland. On the telephone, he agreed to sign for the money we could offer. It would be an honor to play for the Steelers, he assured us. Alas, the team drafting just before we did took Mack. He remained with that team, the Los Angeles Rams, for thirteen years, earning himself a niche in the Hall of Fame

After Peay and Mack got away from us, AJR said, "Let's pick a guy we can sign." As it happened a guy we could sign was within arm's reach at the moment. His name was Dick Leftridge and he had dropped in to mingle with the pathologically curious draft-day crowd that assembled in our offices at the Roosevelt Hotel every year. Actually, the NFL had put Dick up at that hotel to hide him from the AFL. An underachieving fullback for West Virginia, he was big and easy-going and when he opened his mouth to laugh he displayed a shiny gold tooth. We knew of his reputation for irresponsibility and laziness, but we were desperate. And he did have the makings of a football player, if only some coach could get him to show a little interest.

Well, sure, he'd sign with the Steelers, he said, which was all we needed to hear. Bowing to the dictum that beggars can't be choosers, we went ahead and drafted him. "Steelers Go Shopping in the Bargain Basement" was the headline the next day in one of the newspapers. We couldn't dispute it.

Dick Leftridge played one season – not very well – and was never heard from again.

When it seemed that the NFL was losing the war for talent, Commissioner Pete Rozelle came up with a battle plan. Just before draft time in 1966, the league had hired "handholders." Each handholder or pair of handholders was assigned to a prospect, such as Leftridge. They were not to let him out of their sight. Kidnappers lure children with promises of candy and toys. The handholders lured football players with promises of lavish entertainment. Keep the player busy, show him a good time, and stash him away in a hotel room if necessary. He must not be allowed to see anybody or talk to anybody. Fence him off completely from the AFL's coaches and scouts.

Sometimes it worked and sometimes it didn't. While Jack Butler and I had one player on the telephone, an AFL representative was signing him to a contract. We took another kid to one of our games. He was not impressed with the team and he was not impressed with Pitt Stadium. Prudently, no doubt, we kept him away from the Roosevelt Hotel and our practice facilities at South Park. He signed with an NFL team other than the Steelers.

One of Butler's future Blesto scouts, Jerry Neri, was handholding a huge black lineman from Los Angeles State in a hotel room. The kind of portly Italian who looks and acts like a moody old man before he is out of his thirties, Neri had been a player and coach but never a handholder. Rooming for three nights with a Nubian behemoth, he said, was more than he had bargained for. Very quickly, they ran out of things to talk about, so from then on they watched television, listened to the radio, read the newspapers. Or Neri did. What the player did, mostly, was eat. Neri ordered freely from room service – gigantic breakfasts, double hamburgers for lunch, hot fudge sundaes for snacks, the biggest steak in the kitchen for dinner. In the end the player signed with the NFL. The downside was that he lasted only one season.

Combined, the two leagues spent seven million dollars in signing bonuses that year, a lot of money at the time. This, more than anything else, was responsible for the merger that took effect in 1970. Under its terms, the NFL would absorb the AFL. There would be two conferences in the league

– a National Football Conference, made up of teams from the NFL, and an American Football Conference, made up, for the most part, of teams from the AFL. To achieve balance, three NFL teams would have to be switched to this presumably inferior hybrid conference. Making it easier for them to swallow, the commissioner and the owners agreed on a "compensation fee" of three million dollars apiece.

Tempting, thought AJR. He asked some questions. If the Steelers and the Browns, traditional rivals by now, were willing to make the change (he was promised), they would be placed in the same division and continue to play each other every year. That assurance, plus the three million dollars, was incentive enough for both AJR and the Cleveland owner, Art Modell. When the two leagues became one, Pittsburgh, Cleveland, and Baltimore moved to the AFC.

One Steeler fan who found it hard to accept the new arrangement was Kass. "It's like a death in the family," she lamented. "Don't be foolish," responded AJR. "We've got three million bucks. We'll still be playing the Browns. And in five years no one will even remember the American Football League. It will all be the *National* Football League."

He was absolutely correct.

Chapter 33

Superman

One of Buddy Parker's more irrational moves in his last full year with the Steelers was the firing of Ernie Stautner as defensive line coach. In 1964, Stautner had worked very hard with the unschooled rookies and fading veterans at his disposal, but the Steelers lost nine games, and in 1965 he was gone.

Nineteen sixty-four was his first year as a coach after fourteen as an all-pro defensive tackle and future Hall of Farmer. On the first day of pre-season practice, he gathered the Steelers' defensive linemen around him in a semi-circle and explained some of the fine points of line play.

"We hit with these," he said, thrusting out a huge pair of forearms. "That's where you get your power. Not from your legs or your belly or your head. If they'd let me use my elbows, I'd put on the boxing gloves with anybody."

The Steeler linemen, listening silently, accepted these last words at face value.

"The major thing about Pittsburgh Steeler football," Stautner went on, "is that we've always had the smallest line in the league. We'll be small this year, too, but we intend to be rough and tough. Everybody in the past has hated to play us, and it's still going to be the same way. There'll be times out there, especially for you rookies, when you'll forget all the things you ever learned, but remember this: with the snap of the ball, move. Move and be rough."

The fact that Stautner could stand in front of people like John Baker (6-6 and 270), Chuck Hinton (6-5 and 260) and Ben McGee (6-4 and 255), urging them to compensate for their lack of size by being rough, told a volume about the course of evolution, for when Stautner was a rookie in 1950 he reported to camp weighing 213. Although short for a tackle at 6 feet 1, normally in those days he weighed 220. What accounted for the seven-pound difference was that he and his brother-in-law, with one ax and one saw, had cut down a forest around Saranac Lake, New York, that summer and replaced it with a drive-in theater. There were few better ways back then to achieve a firm silhouette.

Even in that remote age, Stautner was not considered a full-grown tackle. He had gone to Notre Dame as a 219-pound freshman, and Frank Leahy had cut him from the squad. "You're too small and too slow," Leahy told him.

Without adding an ounce of weight or subtracting a tenth of a second from his time for the forty-yard dash, Stautner played four years at Boston College for Denny Myers, every minute of every game on both offense and defense unless he was hurt. John Michelosen, then the Steelers' head coach, drafted him in the second round.

All through the 1950s and into the sixties, he practiced what he preached about roughness and aggressiveness. Quarterbacks and their blockers thought they were being charged by a rhino.

When Stautner retired as a player – the truth was that Parker retired him – he claimed to be 38. Ed Kiely, the Steelers' publicity man, guessed that he was fudging by several years. Born in Bavaria, he had come to this country at the age *of* four with his parents, who were fleeing hard times. In the Germany of the 1920s, ruinous inflation had paralyzed the economy. By the time Stautner was 17, America was at war with Germany and Stautner was a U.S. Marine fighting against the Japs in the Pacific.

Coming into the NFL, he was all muscle and bone. He played with tremendous leverage and quickness. He was as quick off the line of scrimmage, in fact, as anyone who ever played the game. His first pop could devastate a blocker, and he rang the bell of so many opposing linemen with his slap to the head that the NFL ultimately outlawed that move. When he tackled, he tackled for keeps, hitting through the ball carrier and almost never losing his hold on the guy.

Stautner's habit of showing up late at training camp was annoying to his coaches and teammates. One year when he arrived a rookie named Ernie Cheatham had taken his place in the line. Both were ex-Marines. Both were from Jesuit colleges — in Cheatham's case Loyola of Los Angeles. Cheatham was much bigger than Stautner and seemed to be every bit as strong. Anticipation built up. Would this big, powerful West Coast kid teach Stautner a lesson when he finally straggled in from Saranac Lake?

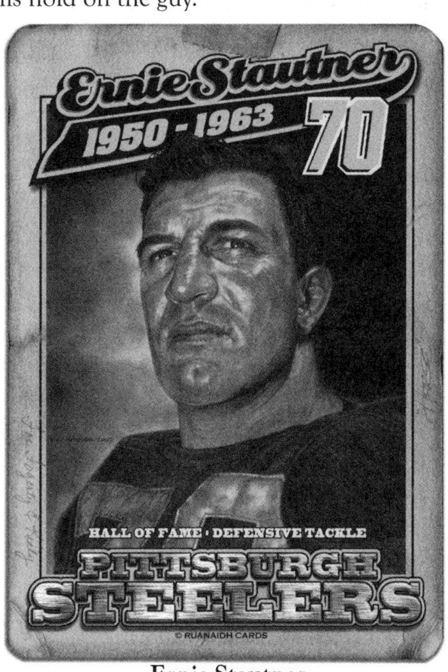

Ernie Stautner
(Drawing by Denny Karchner)

The day of the showdown came, and Stautner looked lean and mean, not bulky and slow, as expected. He lined up opposite Cheatham in a scrimmage. Cheatham's foot was shaking the way my leg did when I recited Shakespeare at Carnegie Tech. The first time the ball was snapped, Stautner completely wiped him out. Cheatham played high, allowing Stautner to get leverage and upend him. The next few times it was more of the same. Stautner was still king of the hill. Before the season ended the Steelers had let Cheatham go. Baltimore then gave him a chance, but he quickly moved on into football oblivion. Cheatham rejoined the USMC and retired as a general.

Another ex-Marine who came to the Steelers as a rookie years later decided that the best way to make his reputation was to pick out the toughest veteran on the team and challenge him to a fist fight. He saw himself winning the fight impressively and reigning from then on as the team's undisputed alpha male. As logic dictated, the kid chose Stautner to be his stepping stone. At a post-game party in the Roosevelt Hotel — Buddy Parker had a theory that post-game parties during the exhibition season created team harmony, with lasting results — he offered to take Stautner on. Both were well-oiled. Stautner at first could not believe the guy was serious. Realizing, finally, that nothing else would do, he followed him downstairs and into the alley between the Roosevelt Hotel's trash dump and the emergency exits of the Harris Theater. Those who saw the fight said it was evenly matched and vicious. The kid turned out to be a handful for Stautner. They kicked, they kneed, they head-butted, they rabbit-punched. They kept at it for thirty minutes or more, with the outcome in doubt until Stautner picked up a big metal garbage can — the whole can, not just the lid — and used it to beat the kid senseless.

Management, of course, meaning Parker and AJR, found out what had happened and who the instigator was and lost no time in sending the youthful tough guy on his way.

Implausibly, Stautner had a taste for the finer things in life. He aspired to play the piano. He took lessons one year, borrowed an old Steinway, and moved it all by himself into an unused office at the training camp. During lunch hour, when his teammates were trying to nap, he would practice. The man's fingers, misshapen from all the head slaps he had delivered, were less than ideal for making music, but he got to the point where he could pound out a current favorite or two. After pre-season games, he would play at the parties, with everybody present clustered around the piano for sing-alongs. Fran Fogarty's voice, trained in operettas at Duquesne University, rose above all the rest.

If the Steelers had a leader, it was Stautner, and then in 1958 Bobby Layne joined the team. Here were two living legends brought together. How would it work out? Was there room enough on one team for two such dominant personalities? The answer, as it happened, was soon apparent. Almost from the first day, Stautner subordinated himself to Layne, becoming his sidekick and bodyguard. Some people thought that under Layne's too powerful influence Stautner went over to the wild side.

In all of his years with the Steelers, there would never be a championship for Stautner. When Buddy Parker dropped him from the coaching staff, he immediately caught on with the Redskins. He remained at his next stop, Dallas, for almost a quarter of a century, a valued assistant to Tom Landry and to several of Landry's successors. After his NFL career was over, he returned to Germany, his native soil, as the head coach of a so-called spinoff team. He still spoke the language and he looked like an aging Superman. So the Germans idolized him. And why not? At last they had found a Superman who had won most of his wars.

McPeak

It was heavy weather for Steeler coaches in the 1950s as John Michelosen made way for Joe Bach and Bach made way for Walt Kiesling and Kiesling made way for Buddy Parker. Stability, such as it was, came from a small nucleus of veteran players, Elbie Nickel, Jack Butler, Ernie Stautner, and Bill McPeak among them.

McPeak, along with Stautner, anchored the defensive line. He played end, as he had at Pitt, and the coach who drafted him, John Michelosen, was a Pitt man, too. McPeak had something in common with Billy Conn. They were tough-as-nails Irishmen who misled people by looking like pretty boys.

Off the field, McPeak was a ladies' man. He liked a good time. In pads and a helmet, he attended strictly to business. He could make life miserable for blockers and quarterbacks and ball carriers. Nothing, in fact, gave him more pleasure, and if the inclination seized him he could make life miserable for a teammate.

Bill Krisher, an All-American guard on Bud Wilkinson's great Oklahoma teams, was a rookie with the Steelers in 1958. McPeak by then was past 30, a little overweight, a little slow, but hoping to play one more year and make it an even ten in the NFL. Buddy Parker, the head coach, considered that a dubious proposition. There was an opening for McPeak on the coaching staff, he said. Still a warrior at heart, McPeak dragged his feet, so Parker compromised. "For the time being," he told the old fire horse when training camp opened, "we'll call you a player-coach."

McPeak went along with the fiction that his title actually meant what it said, but perhaps he knew otherwise He may have therefore needed an outlet for the frustration he probably felt. At any rate, he took an immediate dislike to the inoffensive Krisher. Big and blond, as handsome as McPeak, Krisher was a nice enough guy. He was also a leader of the Christian Athlete movement on the team, and this, more than anything else, settled his hash with McPeak. The Christian Athletes were high-minded fellows intent on setting a good example for sinners. They met for prayer and meditation and were ready at all times to profess their faith in the Lord. McPeak, an acknowledged sinner, disdained them as pious frauds. From the first day of practice he took a special interest in Krisher. College All-American though he was, Krisher had run-of-the-mine ability. For someone like that to excel as a pro would require extra effort. I did not believe Krisher wasn't trying, but neither did I think he was going all-out. It may be that the adulation he received at Oklahoma had made him complacent. Or possibly football never was all that important to him.

So McPeak became his personal motivator. Krisher, he decided, would need some hands-on attention. I watched them one day when he lined up opposite Krisher for a one-on-one hitting drill, and the instruction he dished out was brutal. McPeak understood leverage and he knew all the tricks of the trade. In their first collision, he knocked Krisher's helmet off and bloodied his face. Krisher was ready for Doc Sweeney's ministrations, but McPeak said, "Let's do it again. I want you to work a little more on your blocking technique." Krisher put on his helmet and they did it again. And again. And again.

When Parker told McPeak to forget about playing and made him a full-time coach, which meant that he would have to turn in his pads, there was nobody happier than Krisher. He lasted out the season and then was gone, resurfacing two years later with the Dallas Texans in the AFL. By 1962 he was through with football entirely.

McPeak, after just three years as an assistant in Pittsburgh and then Washington, became the Redskins' head coach in 1961. The ex-Steeler and Pitt man he succeeded, Mike Nixon, left him with nothing much to build on, and five straight losing seasons brought his career to a turning point. He went into scouting and did a good job for the New England Patriots. When he retired, he was only 62. Three or four days later, with cruel and astonishing swiftness, he died of a stroke.

Return to Latrobe

As far back as the Depression years of the late 1930s, AJR made up his mind that St. Vincent College in Latrobe was the ideal site for his football team's pre-season training camp – ideal, that is, in all but one respect. The facilities were inadequate.

St. Vincent had two dormitories, but the Benedictine monks sponsored a retreat every August attended by large numbers of men from everywhere in Western Pennsylvania. Among those who never passed up this chance for spiritual enrichment was AJR. Since the retreat filled both dormitories, leaving no room on the campus for the football players, his solution was to practice at St. Vincent but to quarter the team at the Mountain View Inn, ten minutes west of the college on Route 30.

The Mountain View Inn looked out on the Chestnut Ridge of the Alleghenies in a setting of great natural beauty. On a clear summer day you felt that by extending your hand you could touch the sides of the ridge. But in rain and mist or even overcast the hills always seemed to be miles away. How much the players appreciated this, or what the coaches thought, I don't know. It may be that the coaches would have preferred a more Spartan-like atmosphere. Vacation resorts contrast oddly with the rigors of pre-season football practice.

The monks at St. Vincent, putting first things first, considered the football team a distraction while the retreat was going on. Accordingly, after one or two years, the Steelers began looking for other practice sites. They became nomads, moving from place to place. AJR, meanwhile, never lost hope of returning to St. Vincent.

At last the opportunity carne. In the 1960s the Benedictines built two new dormitories, and now there was room, with adequate separation, for both the football players and the retreatants. There was a new recreation center, a new gymnasium, and a weight room. There were new classrooms, new training and dressing facilities. St. Vincent had dropped football, and the stadium I once played in was torn down and replaced with science buildings. But there were two practice fields now instead of one.

St. Vincent's maintenance director, a Father Connell, worked out the logistics of our move with Fran Fogarty. I heard that the athletic director, my old phys ed teacher Dodo Canterna, gave me credit for selling the idea to Fogarty and AJR. The truth is that no selling was necessary. They both thought St. Vincent suited us to a T and they were right. We moved back there as soon as Buddy Parker was gone.

The Hypocycloid

From time to time people ask about the Steeler emblem that appears on the right-hand side of our helmets. It's a hypocycloid, defined in one of the dictionaries as a "curve traced by a point on the circumference of a circle rolling internally on the circumference of a fixed circle."

Do you get the picture? No? Let me try again. The Steeler hypocycloid – not a true one, perhaps – is a circle with a rim the color of gun metal and nothing on its circumference "rolling internally". The rim the color of gun metal encloses three diamonds against a white background. There's a yellow diamond at the top of the circle, an orange diamond on the right-hand side, and a blue diamond directly below the yellow diamond. That leaves a space on the left-hand side, which is filled with the word "Steelers" lettered in black.

Except for the lettering, this was the logo developed for the American steel industry. The diamonds represent ingredients of steel – yellow for coal, orange for iron ore, and blue for scrap metal. You say that coal isn't yellow, iron ore isn't orange, and scrap metal isn't blue? I'm only telling you what I myself have been told.

In 1962 Republic Steel of Cleveland took credit for suggesting this insignia to us. My own recollection is different. As I always heard it, the logo was John Reger's idea. Reger was a local kid, a linebacker from Pitt who made the team as a walk-on with only one year of college experience. By 1955, his first season, decorations had begun to appear on the helmets of other NFL teams – the Rams had their horns (very Hollywood), the Redskins their war bonnets, the Eagles their wings, and so on – and Reger proposed that we adopt and adapt the American Iron and Steel Institute's logo. The word to the left of the diamonds on that one was "Steel." Getting the AISI's permission to use the logo in the first place and to modify it in the second place took time. There was opposition to overcome and red tape to untangle. Nobody then foresaw the media exposure those Steeler helmets would bring to the AISI.

On the gold helmets the team had worn up to 1955 the logo did not stand out. Therefore, the color of the helmets was changed to black. Along with "What the heck is it supposed to be?" there's another question we get about the logo: "Why is it worn on only one side?"

Every other NFL team wears its logo on both sides. The answer is that Jack Hart, the Steeler equipment manager in the 1950s, was attempting to cut his work load. Hart had the job of attaching the logos – pasting them on – and of re-attaching them when they were knocked off during a game. Using one instead of two was a labor-saving device.

Chapter 34

Mama's Boy

After old Dan Rooney – Pop – passed on, Uncle Jim continued to live with his mother on Perrysville Avenue. One morning as he sat in his favorite parlor armchair, reading the *Post-Gazette* and smoking an after-breakfast cigar, she asked if he would please come to the kitchen and kill a fly. "It's a big one," she said. "It's driving me crazy."

Without looking up from the paper, Jim took a puff at his cigar. "Okay," he grunted. "In a minute."

A minute went by. Then another. And another.

Grandma Rooney reappeared in the parlor. "Jim! Are you coming?"

Jim was still absorbed in his newspaper. "In a minute." The minute turned into five. ..ten ... fifteen. Grandma Rooney called out from the kitchen, "Jim! Are you ever going to kill this fly?"

Jim stood up, tossed the paper aside, and placed the stub of his cigar in an ash tray. He took a step toward the front door. "I'll kill it tonight," he said, leaving the house.

Grandma Rooney lived to be 88. She died of a sudden heart attack, and Jim took it hard. He was now all alone, and he knew it. Teary-eyed, he said to me, "You can be a real tough guy, but when you lose your Mom ..." He stopped and looked away. Then he said it again: "You can be a real tough guy, but when you lose your Mom ... "

Leaving Perrysville Avenue, he moved to the Roosevelt Hotel, where the football team had its offices. By this time he was drinking heavily. On many a night some friend or acquaintance, with the help of a bellboy, would get him into the lobby and up to his room.

He returned once from McKees Rocks – don't ask what he was doing in McKees Rocks – by taxicab. Rummaging through his pockets to find money for the fare, he discovered that he had spent his last cent, or, more likely, given it away.

"See Arthur," he said to the driver

"Arthur" in some way learned about this - perhaps from the night clerk at the hotel, perhaps even from Jim. In some way he found out who the cab driver was and got in touch with him. "How much do I owe you?" he asked. "Look, Art," said the cabbie, "I've been driving Jim around Pittsburgh for years. When Jim had money, he always took real good care of me. So this one is on the house." As repeated over and over by AJR, the story became a part of Jim's legend.

Al Quaill, a cop who had been a pretty good middleweight boxer, described how Jim drank. "He drinks to get drunk," Al told me. "He doesn't enjoy drinking and he doesn't enjoy socializing when he drinks. He just drinks the stuff as fast as he can, for the effect."

That was also my own impression. I never saw Jim feeling euphoric when he drank. If he wasn't stone sober, he was either stupefied or delirious. Earlier in these memoirs, I wrote of a night on the road when he and I roomed together. I remember his screams that night. He'd cry out, "*Ma*-ma!" Then he'd mumble the Hail Mary. Then he'd be quiet for a spell, and I'd start to fall asleep, and suddenly there would be another shrill scream. My night with Uncle Jim sold me on the evils of booze.

In his cups he would borrow money from people. "Can you let me have five until I see Arthur?" "Can you let me have ten until I get a check cashed?" I don't think these loans were ever repaid. He hit me up only once or twice, but I was present many times when Jim put the arm on somebody else.

To him, asking people for money was like asking for a match, or asking what time it was. He put no value on money or on any other material possession. Everyone on the 1929 Pitt Rose Bowl team received a commemorative pin – something to remind him for the rest of his life that he had played in this important college football game. Getting off the train at Penn Station after the trip back home from Pasadena, Jim handed his pin to a girl he knew – not a special girl, just a student who was there to welcome the players.

I have said that I never saw Jim when liquor made him euphoric. I must now tell a story contradicting that statement.

The Roosevelt Hotel was where the Curbstone Coaches held their weekly football luncheon, a tedious affair at which the speakers always talked too long. The Steelers had a table in the back of the room, filled every Monday with front-office people who had to be at the luncheon or answer to AJR. One week Uncle Jim sat with us. He was wearing a dark suit and a necktie and looking his best. It took me a few minutes to see that he had a buzz on. Alex DiCroce, the hotel's banquet manager, came to our table with a guest – Guy Lombardo, the orchestra leader. They were friends of long standing. Alex, in fact, had worked in some capacity for Lombardo. Proudly, he introduced the musician to each of us, identifying Jim as AJR's brother and "a fine football, player" for Jock Sutherland at Pitt. Lombardo was an ardent sports fan, according to Alex, and he appeared to be impressed.

"Jim," Alex said, "you know who Mr. Lombardo is. The big band leader. He has the New Year's Eve show from Times Square in New York every year." Lombardo's credentials meant nothing to Jim, who had not been sober on New Year's Eve since the night (or day) he lifted his first shot glass. In any case he was only half listening. Out of the corner of his eye, he was measuring the distance from our table to the door. His plan was to make an unnoticed getaway and hobble across Sixth Street to one of two or three bars he patronized.

But now he was being asked to acknowledge an introduction. "Coach Lombardi," he said after a pause, "it's an honor and a pleasure to meet you. You've been doing a great job with the Packers."

DiCroce and Lombardo were speechless. Finding his voice, Lombardo said, "No, Jim, I'm Guy Lombardo, not Vince Lombardi – the band leader, not the football coach."

Jim seemed oblivious to this distinction. He was still sizing up his escape route. Lombardo sat down, at a place near Jim, and everybody started to eat. Jim broke off a piece of his hard roll. Turning to Lombardo, he said, "Coach, I like the way you're using Paul Hornung. He's a triple threat. He can run, pass, and kick, and you're taking advantage of all these things." The rest of us, embarrassed, concentrated on our food. Lombardo forced a smile. "Jim," he repeated, "I'm the music man."

We tried to muffle our laughter. By this time Jim was into his soup. Looking up, he addressed Lombardo again as "Coach." We were laughing openly. Lombardo was laughing too. There were stares from the other tables.

His words drowned out, Jim had no more to say. He lurched to his feet and started toward the door. Passing Lombardo's chair, he said, "Coach, it was nice to meet you. Keep up the good work in Green Bay."

We watched him until he limped out of sight, and then we waited to hear from Lombardo. Not knowing Jim, what would he think? That he had somehow been played for a sap? That we'd been making him the butt of a practical joke? Not at all. He was flattered, he said, as soon as he could stop laughing, to be mistaken for the concert master of a championship football team – his *paisano*, the great Vince Lombardi.

Saying Goodbye to Pop

Some time after the fact I learned that the cause of Pop Rooney's death was prostate cancer. The adjective "prostate" had been omitted in all of the talk I had heard up to then – another example of the Rooney family's prudishness.

AJR, for one, never put a name to a private body part or to a bodily or sexual function. Instead, he employed euphemisms. I recall an incident when a daughter-in-law (not Kay) offended him by wearing hot pants (extremely tight, abbreviated shorts). "If you prance around like that," he told her, "you're going to get grabbed." By "grabbed" he meant raped. "And I'll be a character witness for the guy who does it," he added.

In the beginning, Pop Rooney's sick room was his upstairs bedroom in the old brick house on tree-lined Perrysville Avenue. The house was built on a terrace, and I never understood how Pop or, for that matter, Uncle Jim made the climb up the steps from the street to the big front porch. Perrysville Avenue had deteriorated a little, but Pop and Maggie were not pretentious people, a trait their son Arthur inherited. One of Pop's nieces, Helen O'Keefe, lived in Mount Lebanon and regarded the North Side as a slum area. "Well, they could certainly afford to live where they want to," she said of her uncle and aunt, "but they do have their ways, you know." Pop and Maggie, for their part, thought that Helen O'Keefe was someone who put on airs.

For a number of years before his death, Pop had suffered from what we now call depression. He had lost his youngest son – Tom – in the war. His son John had died in early middle age of alcoholism, and his son Jim had a drinking problem. Like Jim, Pop had a gimpy leg, the result of a fall. His brewery business had failed and he was too old for any other kind of work – too old and too infirm. All of these things had combined to make him "nervous," Maggie and the daughters, Margaret and Marie, would say. No one ever used the word "depression" back then. Not many people knew what it was.

Pop's grandsons were well aware that he was dying. Every few days we would troop into his bedroom – sent there, perhaps, to remind him that the bloodline would continue. This was old Irish stuff, I believe. Illness or maybe the pain killers he took had reinforced his natural cynicism. Walt Kiesling was still the coach of the Steelers, and Pop said to me one day, "That fella" - he had never been an admirer of Kiesling – "that fella should be tending bar in Milwaukee. And if it weren't for Arthur he *would* be!" Told that Luby DiMeolo had been made a United States marshal for Western Pennsylvania, he sputtered, "Luby? Why, if Luby can be a federal marshal, Jim could be a U.S. senator."

When they moved Pop to Mercy Hospital, all of us gave blood. We gave blood again and again, and afterward we would stop in his room to say, "Hello, Pop," and make a quick exit. In his bedroom at home we had lingered. Now it was best to get in and get out.

One day I noticed Margaret or Marie pouring him a stiff drink of whiskey. AJR was there. Driving us home, he said, "Boys, your grandfather was not a drinker. He was in the whiskey business and sold the stuff – but he never drank it. He'd take a sample out of the barrel and rub it on his hands. Men like your grandfather could tell the quality of whiskey from the aroma. If a customer offered to buy him a drink when he was tending bar, he would say, 'No, but let me pour you a drink." He'd give the man a free one to keep from having to take one himself."

And so Pop left his family and Pittsburgh. He died at Mercy Hospital, where many years later his son Arthur would die. It was a place where Rooneys came into the world and a place where they said goodbye.

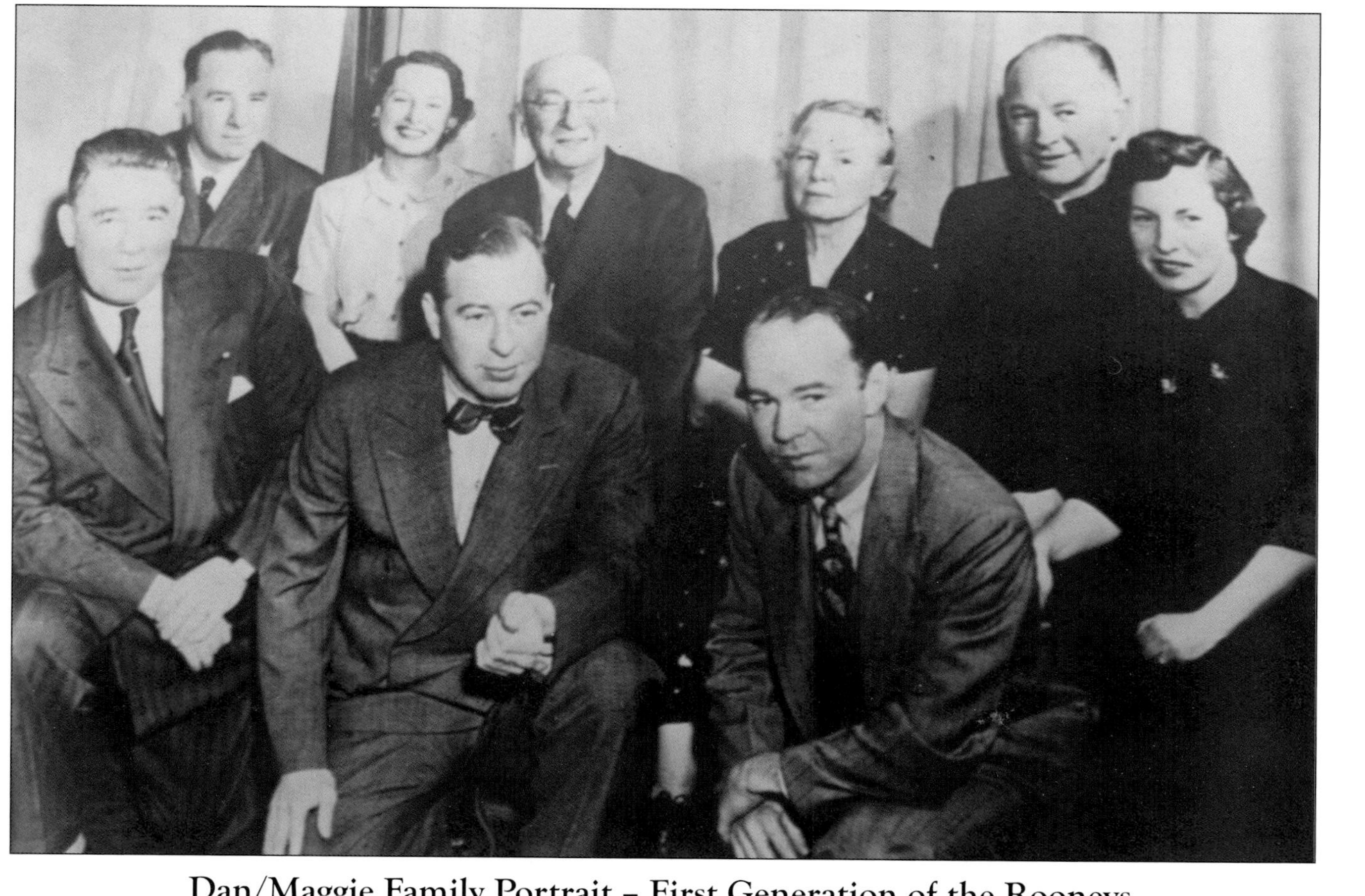

Dan/Maggie Family Portrait – First Generation of the Rooneys
Top Row: Jim, Marie, Pop, Maggie, Father Dan (Silas) O.F.M
Bottom Row: Art Rooney, John (Red), Vince (Duke), Margaret
(Courtesy of Vince/Kathy Rooney Collection)

Second Generation of the Rooneys

Top row: Art Rooney, Bottom row: Art, Jr., Pat, Mom, John, Tim, Dan

(Dan Rooney Collection)

Rooney McGinley Military

Left to Right: Barney McGinley, Jack McGinley (US Navy),
Tom Rooney (USMC), Art Rooney
(Jack McGinley Collection)

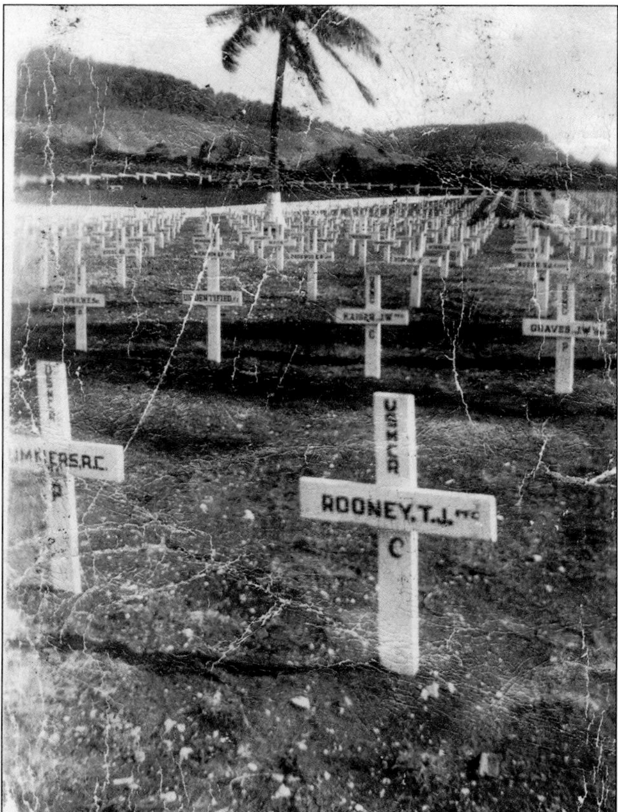

Tom's grave on Guam.
(Courtesy of Carl Wincalowicz)

Father Dan (Silas) in field in France
(Vince/Jamie Rooney Collection)

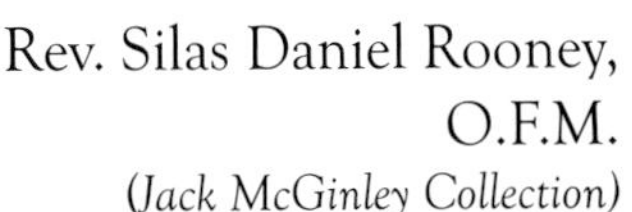

Rev. Silas Daniel Rooney, O.F.M.
(Jack McGinley Collection)

Dan, Art, Jr., AJR, Pat, John and Tim at Yonkers Raceway.
(Tim Rooney Collection)

AJR and Kass cir. 1975 at Yonkers Raceway
(Tim Rooney Collection)

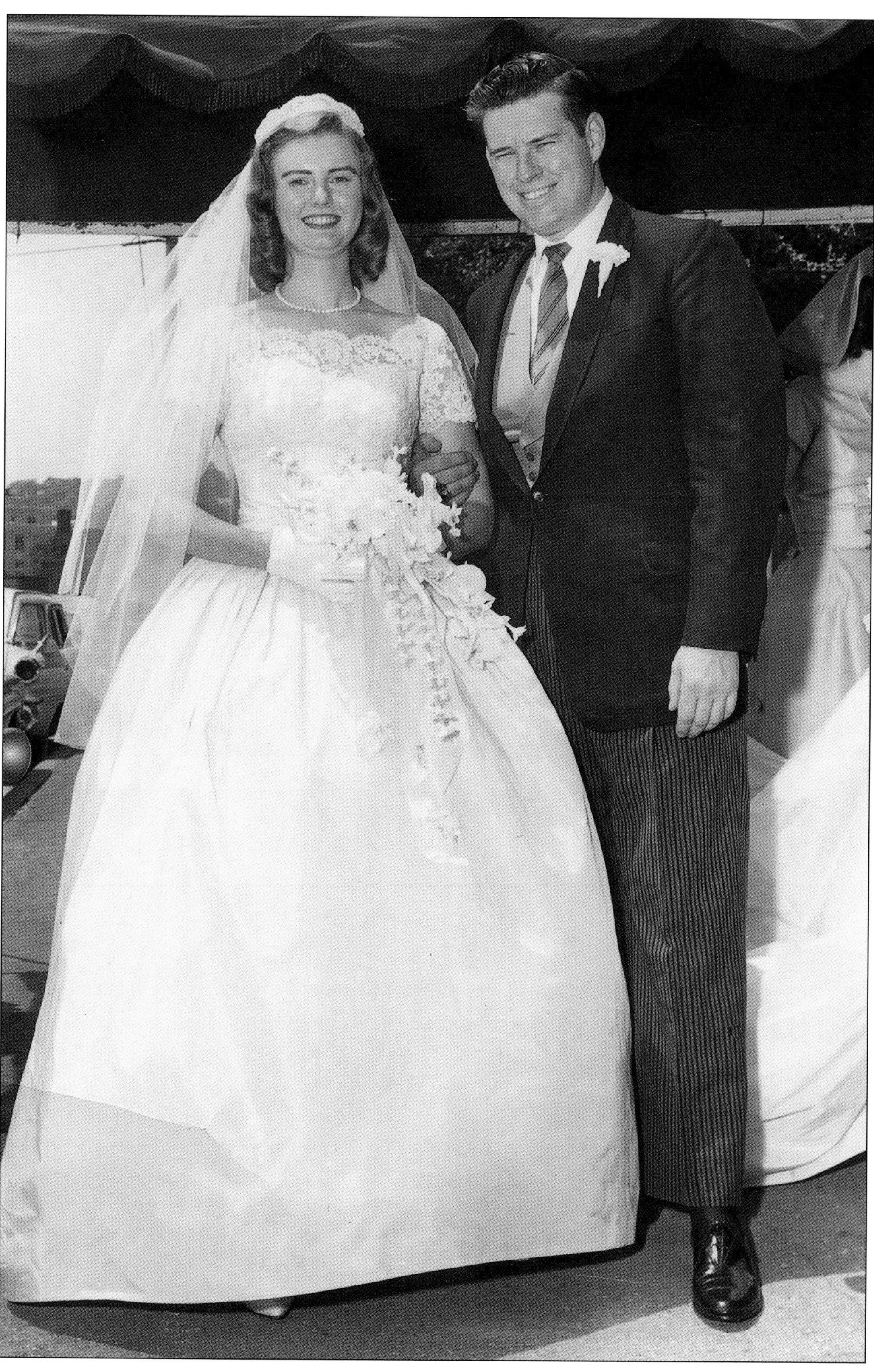

Kay and Art Rooney, Jr. July 1, 1961, St. Paul Cathedral
(Kay Rooney Collection)

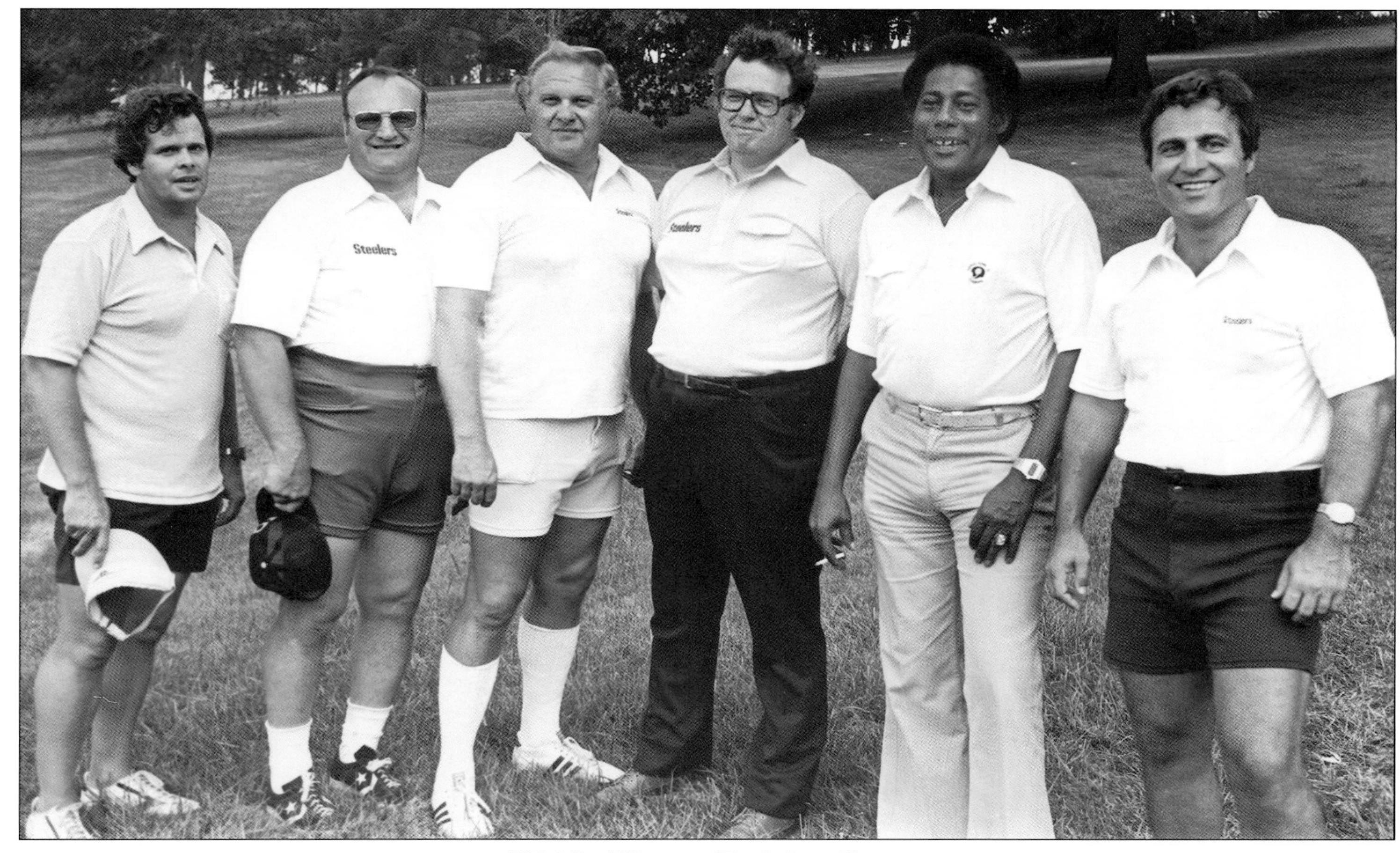

1986 St. Vincent Training Camp

(Left to Right): Dick Haley, Joe Krupa, Bob Schmitz, Art, Jr., Bill Nunn, Tom Modrak

(Steelers Collection)

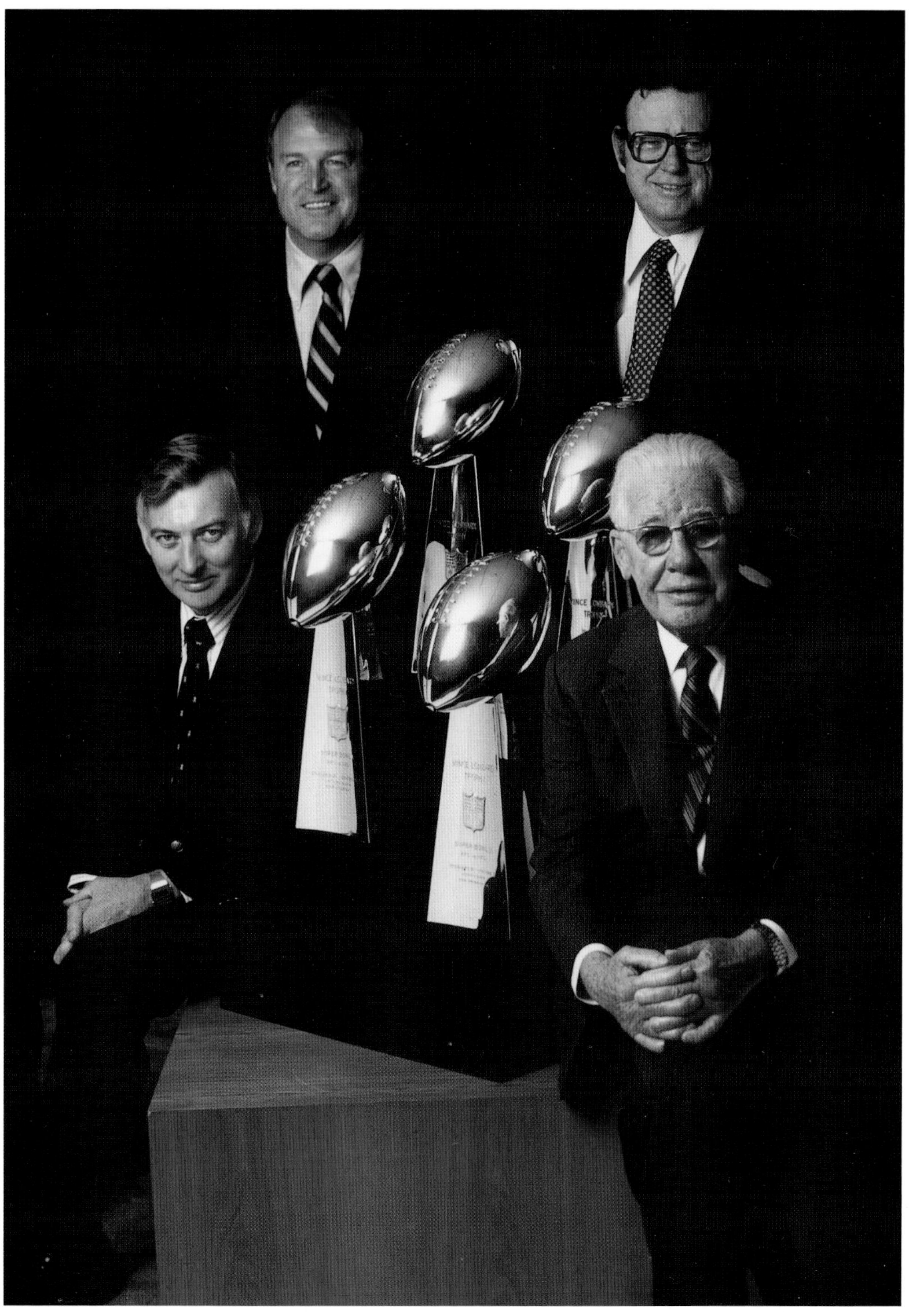

Back Row: Chuck Noll, Art Rooney, Jr.
Front Row: Dan Rooney, Art Rooney, Sr.
(Steelers Collection)

Franco Harris (above), Rocky Bleier (below)
Merv Corning Paintings *(Art Rooney, Jr., Collection)*

Terry Bradshaw (above), Mike Webster (below)
Merv Corning Paintings *(Art Rooney, Jr., Collection)*

John Stallworth (above), Lynn Swann (below)
Merv Corning Paintings *(Art Rooney, Jr., Collection)*

Joe Greene (above), Jack Lambert (below)
Merv Corning Paintings *(Art Rooney, Jr., Collection)*

Mel Blount (above), Jack Ham (below)
Merv Corning Paintings (*Art Rooney, Jr., Collection*)

Dan Rooney (above), Chuck Noll (below)
Merv Corning Paintings *(Art Rooney, Jr., Collection)*

Art Rooney, Sr. (above), Merv Corning Paintings *(Art Rooney, Jr., Collection)*
Art Rooney, Jr. (below), Merv Corning Paintings *(Art Rooney, Jr., Collection)*

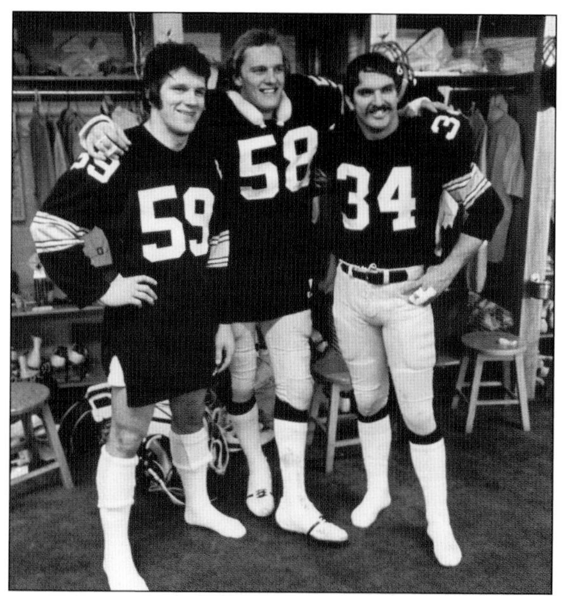

Ham, Lambert, Russell, 1976

(George Gaadt Collection)

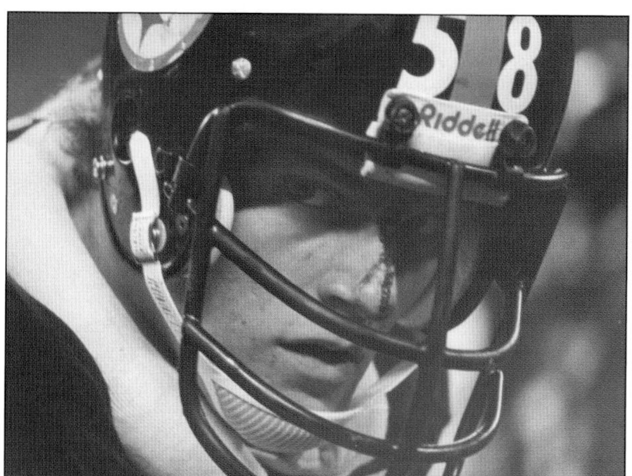

Jack Lambert, 1970s

(George Gaadt Collection)

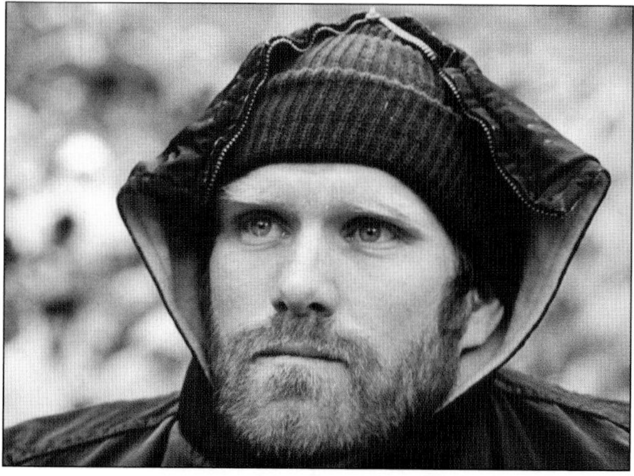

Terry Bradshaw, 1970s

(George Gaadt Collection)

Right: Roy McHugh

Below: (Seated) Roy McHugh, Art Rooney, Jr., (Standing) Dee Herrod

(Meg Herrod Collection)

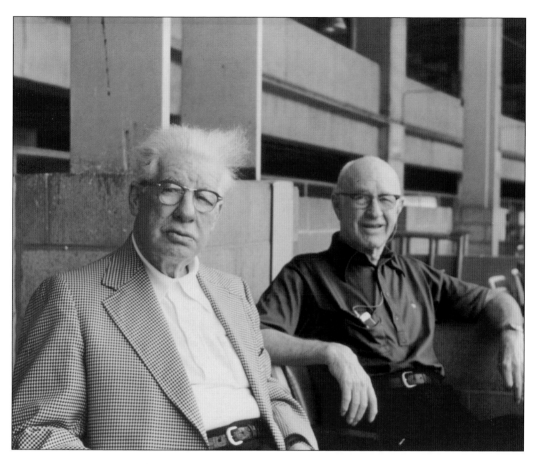

Art Rooney, Sr., and Rev. Silas Daniel Rooney, O.F.M. at Three Rivers Stadium.
(Steelers Collection)

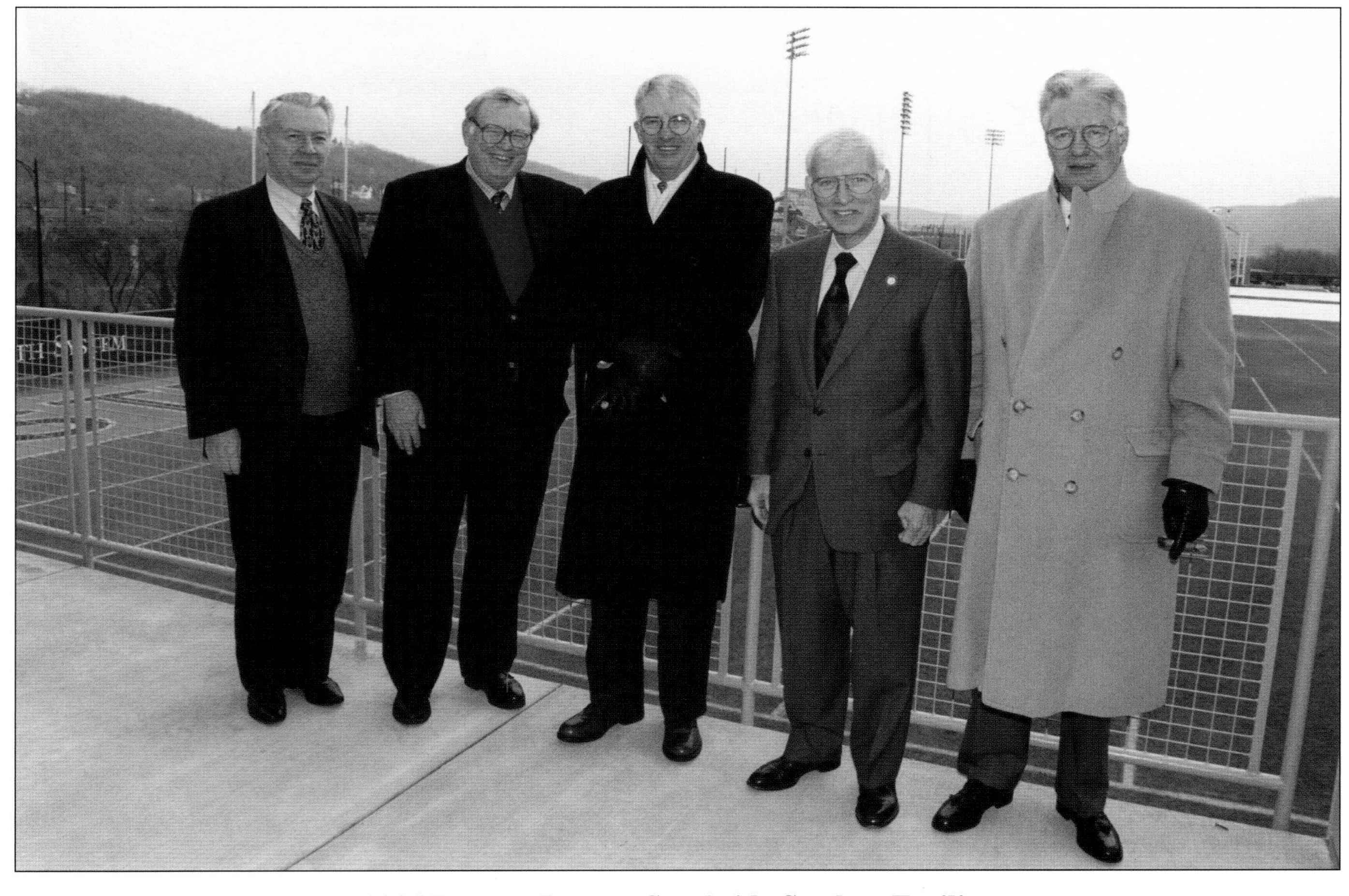

2004 Rooney Boys at Southside Steelers Facility
Left to Right: Tim, Art Jr., Pat, Dan, John
(Steelers Collection)

Third Generation of Rooneys in Palm Beach, Florida, 2005
Front Row (Left to Right): Kyle Lewis, Jack Lewis, Alex Rooney, Heather Rooney, Brian Rooney; Back Row (Left to Right): Susan Rooney Lewis, Mike Rooney, Kay Rooney, Art Rooney, Jr., Art Rooney III, Christine Rooney, Art Rooney IV
(Kay Rooney Collection)

"There Will Never Be Another You"
Kay Rooney
painting by Merv Corning

Death in Dealey Plaza

Our ticket manager, Joe Carr, always seemed to have a radio turned on. Around 1 o'clock in the afternoon on Friday, November 22, 1963, he was listening to it as usual when a voice interrupted the regular programming to announce that President Kennedy had been shot.

Carr bolted from the ticket office (a very small room partitioned by a counter) into our main office, gasping out the news. Ed Kiely reacted like a newspaper reporter. He ran into his private office and picked up the phone to make a call. Steeler defensive back Brady Keys broke off a conversation with Mary Regan at her desk and started shouting obscenities. He was raging at "all the nuts in the world." There were others in the room, but names and faces elude me. All I know is that I followed Joe Carr back into the ticket office.

By the time we learned that the President was dead, a big crowd had gathered around the radio. No one spoke. After a little while, I walked to St. Mary of Mercy Church on the Boulevard of the Allies at Stanwix Street. It was full by then, and people were standing on the sidewalk outside.

The next day — Saturday — no college football games were played except for a few in the South. Blesto scout Will Walls came into the office and kept explaining to everybody that even though he had gone to college at Texas Christian he was really from Arkansas. Because the assassination took place in Dallas and because the man who had fired the shot lived in Dallas, Texans that weekend were being stigmatized through guilt by association.

With the whole country in mourning, Commissioner Pete Rozelle decided that the NFL would go ahead on Sunday with its full slate of games, a ruling he never lived down. AJR felt uncomfortable about it, and Buddy Parker was flat-out perturbed. The Steelers were playing the Bears at Forbes Field, and Buddy, who was paranoid anyway, expressed the fear that a sniper in the stands would be gunning for him. "Everybody in Pittsburgh hates Texans right now," he said to AJR, "and I'm the only Texan available."

A few minutes before the kickoff I was down on the field, talking with my brother Tim and Jack Butler, when we heard from one of the twins that a small-time Dallas racket guy named Jack Ruby had blown away Lee Harvey Oswald, the suspected assassin, in the Dallas police station. Will Walls later said that he had been in Ruby's strip joint two or three times.

The football game ended in a 17-17 tie, memorable still for a Hall-of-Fame play by the Bears' Mike Ditka. With up to half a dozen Steelers hanging onto him, he carried them a good twenty yards, maybe farther, before they could drag him off his feet. Ditka was an all-pro tight end drafted by George Halas out of Pitt. The game served one purpose, I thought. For a short while, at least, it took some minds off the national trauma.

Two weeks later, the Steelers played the Cowboys in Dallas. Fran Fogarty had a friend from Pittsburgh who was working and living there, and he offered to take Fran on a tour of Dealey Plaza, the assassination site. I went along with them, and so did AJR. Fogarty's friend pointed out the Texas School Book Depository and the window from which Oswald aimed his rifle. Our guide's small, nondescript car seemed to please AJR. The more unpretentious a car was, the better he liked it. When we returned to the hotel, he invited the Texan from Pittsburgh to dinner, but Fogarty had made plans for them that couldn't be changed.

For the rest of his life, AJR was ill at ease in Dallas. He never went back except on a "need-to-go" basis — a Steeler game of exceptional importance or for an NFL meeting at which major issues would be discussed. He conducted this partial boycott quietly. None of the other owners seemed aware of it. If the Steelers were playing in Dallas and it was just another game, there would be a wake or a funeral he had to attend, or business at Shamrock Farm to be taken care of, or a horse of his would be running in a race he couldn't miss, or it was time for his annual visit to the shrine of St. Anne.

I remember something Owney McManus once said: "There will never be a Catholic president, or if there is he will never finish his term." It may be that what happened to John Kennedy was for AJR sufficient proof.

Chapter 35

A Slight Misunderstanding

In the beginning and for many years afterward, the Steelers were just a hobby for AJR. His primary interest was betting on horses. The public tended to forget this, and his grandchildren, most of them, were ignorant of it.

For example, my son Artie. Delving into family history, he put a question to Kass:

"What did grandfather do before he owned the football team?"

"He had an office in town," Kass replied.

"What did he do at the office?" persisted Artie.

"Well," said Kass, "he had a lot of phones there."

"What did he do with the phones?"

"He answered them," Kass said, and that was the end of it.

When Artie was older, he found her to be a willing storyteller. The locale for one of her tales was Moore's Restaurant in New York, where she and her husband were having lunch. Tim Mara, the owner of the New York Giants and a bookmaker on the side, came to their table and informed AJR that such and such a horse was running at such and such a track. Would he like to place a bet?

Offhandedly, AJR told him, "Yeah. Fifty on it to win."

Kass was furious. When Mara left, she reminded her spouse that she was pregnant and that fifty dollars was money they'd need. It was risky to be betting so much on a horse race.

AJR said nothing for a while. He broke his silence when the lecture continued.

"Will you please stay out of my business?" he said. "And I'm not betting fifty dollars. I'm betting fifty *thousand*."

Pretty soon Mara returned. The horse, he told AJR, had won. Even for a bookmaker of Mara's stature, paying off on fifty G's was no small thing. AJR understood how he felt.

"I hate to do this to you," he said, "but I'll tell you what. If it's a boy, we'll call our baby Tim."

And that was how the Rooney brother in charge of the family's horse-racing business got his name.

A long time later, Tim Rooney's daughter Kathleen married Tim Mara's grandson Chris.

Cocoa Beans

At some point in his life – I am not certain when – it seemed to me that AJR began to bet more money on grain futures than on race horses. His partner was a man named Jerry Nolan, who worked in (or out of) the Chicago Board of Trade. AJR may have met him through one of his Chicago football pals, George Halas or Charley Bidwill.

Jerry Nolan was in on the soy-bean deal I referred to a while back. Down through the years the team of Nolan and Rooney brought off successful transactions by the dozen, but in the market, as in football and horse racing, sometimes you win and sometimes you lose. After AJR sold the cottage in Ligonier, which belonged to Kass, he promised to double or maybe triple her money in futures. He lost every cent of it – about $30,000. Most memorably, AJR and Jerry Nolan took a whacking from cocoa-bean growers.

Much of the world's cocoa comes from West Africa. However it happened, AJR got a tip that the crop there had failed, and he instructed Nolan to buy cocoa contracts. Accordingly, Nolan bought cocoa contracts the way Jim bought drinks in any bar. Then the two high rollers sat back comfortably and waited for the price to go up. Hadn't soy-bean prices gone up after AJR was told by Father Dan about the failure of the crop in China? They certainly had, but the analogy didn't hold. Where Father Dan's information had been accurate, the hot tip on cocoa turned out to be a scam.

Far from being scarce, cocoa that year was abundant. The native growers in Africa – Harvard Business School graduates, no doubt – were manipulating the market. Instead of taking their cocoa beans to the middle men, they stashed them away in their huts, to be sold when the price was right and not before – a time that never came. There was cocoa enough, from whatever source, for cocoa drinkers everywhere, it seems, and the cocoa market collapsed. The native growers lost their shirts

— or their dashikis, if that was the case. Meanwhile AJR and Jerry Nolan scrambled to unload their contracts.

No one was buying. "We'd better write this off as a loss," suggested Nolan. "Whatever we do, we can't take delivery of the beans." It was good thinking. But AJR and his accountant, Fran Fogarty, had one last card to play.

Fogarty called friends at the Hershey Chocolate Company and explained the situation. The advice he received was the same as Jerry Nolan's: Don't get stuck with those beans. You now own more cocoa — raw cocoa — than we have or are going to have here in Hershey, his friends added.

In the end, the Chief faced reality. There was no way out. He was stuck with the beans - or would have been if the seller had not agreed to take them back. Of course there was no refund. AJR had learned that cocoa can leave a bitter taste.

Branching Out

In the late 1950s or early 1960s AJR formed a business partnership with Dan Parish, a contractor and a friend of Mayor Lawrence. Dan Parish was from Youngstown, a self-made man who had Anglicized his Italian surname, Parisi. He told me once that he and his brother Mike got their start as cement layers. Many houses in Youngstown still had cellars with dirt floors; the Parisis, riding to work on streetcars, wearing unwashed overalls and carrying their equipment, transformed these cellars into basements.

By the time Dan Parish came into our lives he never wore anything but business suits. Well-mannered and intelligent, he was of average height and build and had a high, squeaky voice. Like Dan Hamill and Owney McManus, he prodded AJR to expand from football into other avenues. "Give your boys something to make a living at," he would say.

An earlier experience with a contractor named Martin Wise, whose wife was related to the McNultys, had left Dad with cause to be hesitant. The Chief was a third-interest partner, putting up the capital and using his political clout to get construction jobs. All seemed to be going well until Mr. Wise surreptitiously bought out the other equal partner. He now owned two-thirds of the business. To be a minority shareholder went against Dad's principles, a fact I am sure he conveyed to Mr. Wise when he ended their relationship. "I've done business with tough guys," Dad later said, "and all I ever needed was a handshake. This 'legitimate' businessman — married to a relative of my wife — turns out to be a sneak and a crook. If they're all like that, I want no part of them."

Dan Parish, of course, had Lawrence's endorsement, the ultimate seal of approval. With a man like Parish as his partner, AJR used to say, he could have made millions in the construction business. As it was, they got into the race track business. But first let me interject one last word about Wise: his health failed, his wife's health failed, their son developed a drinking problem, and they ended up losing their company.

AJR and Dan Parish, having reason to believe from what Lawrence had told them that legalized horse racing in Pennsylvania was a certainty, bought Randall Park, a dilapidated old track in Shaker Heights, Ohio, a suburb of Cleveland. When they applied for a license in Harrisburg, they theorized, a background in ownership would give them credibility.

I watched them research this deal with John Joyce, an associate of Parish, and couldn't help but be impressed. The football business, especially as conducted by AJR's generation, was in many respects like a game. AJR and his fellow owners thought of it as fun, and from a dollar-and-cents point of view this had always been a weakness, I felt. Getting ready to own and operate a track was different. Parish and Joyce could laugh at a good story, but levity had its time and place. When it carne to working out the details, financial and otherwise, of starting a race track, they couldn't have been more in earnest. Business was business and they never forgot it. In the Steeler organization, after Jock Sutherland died, only Fran Fogarty took the same deadly serious approach. Among the Rooneys, only my brother Dan and later Tim seemed temperamentally fitted to run a tight ship.

AJR had no trouble adjusting as long as he left the grunt work to Fogarty and Dan — or even to Tim. Oh, he hollered and screamed now and then, but would ultimately defer to their business judgment. To people he had dealt with when there were no set rules, and who were taken aback to find that things had changed, he would say, "What you're asking for is the way I used to do it. But my boys — with their high-powered educations — tell me I have to do it the modern way." Not that he ever became rigid. When his instincts told him to deviate from business-school methods, he did so. And he would be right. And people loved him for it.

There had been no big money in pro football until the 1950s. AJR, along with pioneers such as Joe Carr (the NFL's first commissioner), Bert Bell, George Halas, the Maras, the Bidwills, and George Preston Marshall, had seen the game's potential long before the fans or the newspapermen wised up. With a common goal spurring them on, they had the foresight to pull in the same direction, so that when television gave their league a showcase and generated piles of cash they were able to agree on revenue sharing, which allowed small-market teams like the Steelers to compete with the Giants and the Bears and the Rams and with the handful of teams owned by men of unlimited wealth. However, this was not something that happened overnight. There were anti-trust issues for Congress or the courts to decide. And teams were making deals on their own with the networks, for example the one involving the Steelers, the Colts, and NBC. The league had not reached the point of "united we stand." But it was getting there. The days were not far off when the Steelers would be a valuable property.

Even so, and whether or not he realized it, AJR had a problem. As Dan Parish pointed out to him, there was only one football team and there were five Rooney sons. How to keep them equally occupied and equally happy, once they were ready to join the work force, was a question that would soon need an answer. Dan Parish now seemed to be offering one: throw a couple of race tracks into the mix.

'Not You, Art!'

AJR was a great one for writing postcards and thank-you notes. Over the years he sent thousands of them in his large, beautiful script. Msgr. Francis Rooney (no relation) once let me see a letter from Dad in which he stated that Catholic priests were his heroes.

All through his life Dad went to Mass and Communion every day. As I have said, I never once heard him use profanity and when it carne to sex he was puritanical. The only women in his life were the members of his extended family. In college, at Indiana Normal, he'd had a girlfriend, and later he dated Imogene Coca, the actress, but except for those two I don't believe that he ever spent time with women other than Kass, Aunt Alice, his mother, and his sisters.

The pastor at St. Mary's of Mercy on the Boulevard of the Allies, Downtown, was a tough old Irishman named Lawless. He ruled his congregation like a drill sergeant, issuing orders from the pulpit which he expected to be obeyed without question. At the early Mass on a Friday morning, he announced a re-routing of Communion traffic. Instead of coming up the middle aisle and returning to their pews by the side aisles, the parishioners were to reverse that procedure. "You're to approach the Communion rail by way of the side aisles and go back by way of the middle aisle," he instructed them. "In preparation for the big crowds on Sunday," he added, "we'll give it a trial run today." As our friend Father Bob Reardon told me the story, chaos resulted. Almost everybody started up the middle aisle, including AJR, who often attended Mass at St. Mary's and was always a big contributor at the offertory. Msgr. Lawless, standing behind the rail with the chalice, became incensed. At the top of his lungs, he shouted, "Up the side aisles, I told ya. Go back and start over." The parishioners were milling around – turning left, turning right, and bumping into one another. And AJR was in the middle of all this. Just then the monsignor spotted him.

"Art! Art!" he called out, "Not you, Art! Come right up the center aisle."

Some time later AJR confided to Father Reardon that he was never in all his days more embarrassed.

On a visit to New York City he was the unwitting cause of a traffic accident in St. Patrick's Cathedral. Toots Shor, the celebrated restaurant owner, was with him. A Jewish guy married to a Catholic, Shor attended Mass now and then but always as someone out of his element. He followed Dad into the cathedral and was looking around for familiar faces, since many of his customers were Irish or Italian. At this moment Dad genuflected. As his right knee touched the floor, his right foot became entangled with Shor's left foot. Shor was as big as an NFL tackle and he hit the deck with a thud.

At a testimonial dinner for AJR at the Hilton Hotel in Pittsburgh, the restaurateur did an encore. He went up to the dais and gave a speech extolling Dad's virtues, and then he started back to his table. Misjudging the steps, he crashed to the floor. The crowd let out a gasp. Falls like this had been known to kill people. But we underestimated Toots Shor. He was on his feet again in a minute, smiling and waving and proclaiming himself unhurt.

Could he have passed a sobriety test? I doubt it.

Two of a Kind

Exaggerating only a little, AJR used to say that his friend Davey Lawrence was a Democrat in Pittsburgh when nobody else was a Democrat. Because Senator Jimmy Coyne's Republican machine was unbeatable for a time, Democrats at heart, like AJR, grudgingly entered its ranks. In no other way could they escape irrelevance. Liberals who believed in giving a break to the poor, they worked from the inside. David L. Lawrence never joined them.

He studied politics at the feet of Bill Brennen, Allegheny County's Democratic chairman from 1901 to 1918. A lawyer who had been an ironworker and labor activist, Brennen hired Lawrence as a clerk-stenographer when Lawrence was 14 years old. At 29, he succeeded to the party leadership. "As a young guy," said AJR, "he ran errands. Later, he made the big decisions. And he was incorruptible."

Fastening onto that "incorruptible" tag in the years when Lawrence was mayor and then governor, my brothers and I would put a mock-serious question to Jerry Lawrence, his son: "How much graft money has your dad tucked away in Switzerland?" Having been close to Jerry Lawrence for most of our lives, we were sure we could take liberties that from anyone else would be a challenge to a fist fight. Jerry, as I have noted, had charge of the press-relations department at the Rooney-owned William Penn Raceway. "If I knew where that money was," he would answer good-naturedly, aware that the Rooneys were with him one hundred percent, "I'd be living high on the hog instead of working for you guys."

The local history books tell us how Lawrence and Richard King Mellon saved Pittsburgh from the ash heap in the 1950s and how they cleaned up the rivers and brightened the skies. So much has been written about Lawrence, in fact, that I can only put down the stories I heard from AJR and the things I observed at first hand. I understand that when AJR ran for register of wills, Lawrence made no objection. Realizing better than anyone the futility of such a race, he saw the potential for humor in it. Chances are Lawrence was not a man much given to laughter, but the combination of an inept candidate, AJR, and a buffoonish campaign manager, Owney McManus, must have tickled him. Certainly it was droll entertainment.

There is no doubt whatever that Lawrence enjoyed sports. In particular he liked baseball, football, boxing, and, after AJR had given him a sort of tutorial, horse racing. As mayor, Lawrence did what he could to help the Steelers. Several times a year he attended practice. On one such occasion, striking up a conversation with Jack Butler, he offered to get him a liquor license. Butler had no real intention of going into the bar business, "but here was the mayor of Pittsburgh," he said, "ready to be of assistance. I knew a lot of people who'd have traded one of their eyes for a liquor license."

I've described how Lawrence put pressure on the University of Pittsburgh to share Pitt Stadium with the Steelers. Tom Hamilton, Pitt's athletic director, was bitterly opposed to the idea. You'd have thought by the way he acted that he was selling his soul to the devil. Lawrence also played a part in making Three Rivers Stadium politically possible, and but for him we would not have had a harness-racing franchise.

Dad, Lawrence, and Dan Parish attended football games, baseball games, and boxing matches together, went out to dinner together, and played cards together. If I was present during their card games, the governor made an effort to include me in the conversation. He told me once, off the record, that obduracy on the part of our steel makers, who wanted the labor market all to themselves, kept the automobile industry out of Pittsburgh. With two such titans competing for workers, the cost of hiring them would be bound to escalate. As a result, Lawrence said, Pittsburgh lost out to Detroit. Something else that prevented us from being a diversified manufacturing center was our topography, he argued. There were too many hills and valleys and rivers, which are enemies of economical plant construction.

Being David L. Lawrence had its downside. I was in the visiting owner's box at a football game between the Steelers and the Browns in Cleveland when two rowdies nearby, spotting Lawrence and AJR, began to heckle them. They started on Dad, telling him what they thought of his lousy football team, but quickly shifted to Lawrence, calling him a crook and telling him what they thought of his lousy state. With us was Richie Easton, a *Pittsburgh Press* truck driver who was AJR's personal chauffeur at the time. Richie happened to be the strong, silent type. He took it all in for a while and then abruptly got to his feet. He was holding a pair of binoculars – mine. "If you don't shut up," he said to the two drunken loudmouths, "I'm going to shove these glasses right down your throats. And then," he went on, "I'm going to throw you out of your seats, all the way down to the ground."

In our boxes, we were maybe three stories high; the players below looked like ants. Sizing Richie up, the two louts could sense that he might be in earnest. For the rest of the afternoon, they held their tongues.

This time with Richie out of the mix, the same kind of problem arose at a College All-Star game in Chicago. Besides Lawrence, AJR's guests were two young owners of the Pick Hotel chain, husband, and wife. An adjacent drunk, overhearing Lawrence's name mentioned, took it upon himself to abuse the old politico unmercifully. Richie, as I have said, was absent, but sitting unnoticed a row or two back was the Pick Hotels' chief of security, who now intervened. He got hold of the pest by the coat collar and ushered him out of the stadium.

When his days in elective politics were over, Lawrence went to work for the Kennedy administration in Washington and stayed on after JFK's assassination put Lyndon B. Johnson in the White House. He said that my dad would have loved the Kennedys because they were Irish Catholics. But they were also, in contrast with President Johnson, bluebloods. Lawrence himself preferred LBJ, "a real man of the people," and wished that AJR could have known him.

Lawrence's son Jerry, after leaving William Penn Raceway, moved up to an executive position – general manager of our track in Yonkers, New York. The governor's nephew, Tom Donahoe. was in the Steeler organization as director of football operations from the early 1990s until the turn of the century. In the end, he could not maintain harmonious relations with the coach, Bill Cowher, and resigned (one of them had to go, and it was Tom). Later, Tom became president of the Buffalo Bills. Both he and Jerry were great guys, and they excelled at what they did.

The Misfit

If I may repeat myself, AJR was a Democrat at heart, but out of loyalty to Senator Jimmy Coyne, he always had been and would continue to be a Republican. Most other Republicans in Western Pennsylvania were rich Presbyterians. AJR had money, but most of it came from betting on horses, and not even the Pope was more Catholic.

He differed greatly from your typical Republican in still another respect – his admiration for labor people. He spoke of Philip Murray, the steelworkers' revered leader – buried in the graveyard at St. Anne's Church in Castle Shannon – as a truly great man.

Grandma Margaret Rooney, herself born a Murray, was not related to Phil, but all the men in her family were coal miners, and AJR knew the head of their union, John L. Lewis. Returning from the race tracks in New York or from Shamrock Farm, Dad used to see John L. Lewis having dinner in a restaurant at White Sulphur Springs, in West Virginia, and they would talk. Despite his forbidding appearance – the shaggy black eyebrows gave him a sinister look – Lewis was never anything but cordial.

Then there was Pat Fagan, a coal miners official and a Pittsburgh city councilman. Pat Fagan would stop to visit with AJR at the Steelers' office in the Fort Pitt Hotel and later at the Roosevelt Hotel. He was a friendly, unassuming old guy.

Out of an interest in the Russian Revolution – I had a history degree from St. Vincent College – I asked him once if he had known Leon Trotsky. "Know him!" Pat said. "We ran that guy out of Western Pennsylvania. He was a Commie, and up to no good."

Not only labor leaders but politicians as well were looked on with favor by AJR. He introduced me to Jim Farley, who was Franklin D. Roosevelt's postmaster general and a man who reputedly never forgot a face or a name. Farley and Dad were busy conversing, and though Farley addressed his remarks to AJR, I could see that he was pleased to have somebody young and impressionable for an audience.

What he was saying surprised me. He claimed that FDR had lied to him several times, and that in consequence he watched his step around the President.

"I was careful never to be alone with Mr. Roosevelt," Farley said.

The Murrays and the Lewises and the Fagans, the Farleys and the Davey Lawrences – people of this sort, not football players and baseball players, should be our heroes, Dad told us. And then of course all priests were heroes - his friend Father Campbell in particular. If we modeled ourselves after men such as these, there was no way we could ever go wrong.

A Positive Product

According to John and Pat, AJR was against any and all forms of pleasure. We thought of him as a rigid disciplinarian but a fine man, the best we would ever know. His sense of honor was acute. He did not lie or cheat and he lived by the golden rule.

Publicity – favorable publicity, the only kind he received after the Steelers won their first Super Bowl trophy – was pleasing to him, but he knew how to act as though he disdained it. He liked sports and the people in the business of sports. He took a pragmatic view of the horse racing industry but believed that most sporting events, horse races included, were on the level. In many respects, he tended to be a romantic about sports, and I admit that I am one, too.

In moments of anger, he could tell someone off without cursing. People who aroused his ire were bums, or rotten bums, or dirty rotten bums, or greasers and the like. His epithets, although harsh, were safely within the bounds of the Second Commandment: "Thou shalt not take the name of the Lord thy God in vain."

He attended three institutions of higher learning – Indiana Normal, Georgetown, and Duquesne – and was none the worse for it.

His vocabulary neither changed nor increased. It was free of vulgarisms and free of obscenity. His slang never emerged from the 1920s. In fact it seemed quaint. He spoke Pittsburghese with a certain pride, although at some point he stopped saying "yinz." He pretended that words of more than two or three syllables were over his head, implying pretentiousness on the part of those who used them. He talked the way he did for a reason. Besides expressing his personality, it kept the people he dealt with off-balance. It gave them a misleading impression, which I think was the main idea. In practical terms, he was smarter and much shrewder than most intellectuals, and if the fact wasn't obvious to them, so much the better.

There were many Art Rooney wannabe's, copying this or that characteristic but failing to understand the uniqueness of AJR. My dad was tough – not the kind to back down from anyone – but soft on the inside, and on the outside too when it wouldn't be misinterpreted. He controlled his passions. He controlled his baser instincts. He had spiritual depth. Leadership came naturally to him, but he did not seek it out. Extremely generous, he could also be close with a buck. He appreciated humor, which he found in the give and take of life, but he could not tell a joke without messing it up. The men who tried to imitate him lacked the gift he was born with and cultivated – his ability to connect and interact. He was a positive product of his heredity and environment, profiting from the one and rising above the other.

Except for Father Dan, even his own brothers could never get a fix on exactly who Art Rooney was. Father Dan, like AJR, heeded the better angels of his nature. He was no less intelligent than AJR, and if a good big man always has the edge on a good little man, the superior athlete. He devoted his whole being, and not just a part of it, to the service of God.

Together, they made a phenomenal pair.

Chocolaholic

After Dad gave up booze he developed a gigantic appetite for sweets, in particular chocolate. He could eat it by the pound. If there's a connection of some kind – if chocolate addiction replaces alcohol addiction – medical science has not yet confirmed it. Kass was always able to combine chocolate and alcohol. While eating a Hershey bar, she would drink a glass of beer. "This is really good," she would say. I was never persuaded.

Dimling's and Reymer's made excellent chocolate candy here in Pittsburgh. The chocolate buttercups from Dimling's were irresistible. During the Korean War, people sent boxes of Dimling's candy to relatives in the service. The demand became extraordinary – and this was why Dimling's went out of business.

I am telling you the story as I heard it from Kass. Just when the orders peaked, according to Kass, the union boss at Dimling's called a strike. It dragged on for weeks. Angered, the owners closed all of their stores except one – the Downtown location on Liberty Avenue near the Stanley Theater. By the 1960s that store also was gone.

One day a man came into our offices in the Roosevelt Hotel and presented Dad with a large box of Clark bars from the Clark candy factory on the North Side. After he left, Dad told us that this was the candy chef who worked out the recipe for the Clark bar. The main ingredients seemed to be chocolate and peanut butter. At any rate, the Clark bar was now the company's best seller, but the man who created it had received nothing more than a bonus and a raise in pay, Dad said. Was he bitter about that? Yes, but in Dad's opinion, anyway, he had not been treated unfairly. "After all," Dad explained, "coming up with new ideas was part of his job. It was what the company hired him to do." Dad was a firm believer in capitalism.

Sometimes Dad went on eating binges. The once compact lightweight was rounder in the midsection now; his face had a softer, more benevolent look. Every year for most of his life he paid a visit to the shrine of St. Anne de Beaupre in Quebec, and on all of these trips he stayed at the Chateau Frontenac. Because he tipped so well the staff gave him special attention. One time when Pat and his wife Sandy were with him, a huge silver tray full of chocolates, the best that Quebec could offer, was sent to Dad and Mom's suite. At a single sitting, he ate every piece except one. "He got woozy," Pat said, "and then all of a sudden he fell over backwards onto the bed." Kass called the head porter, who called the house doctor. "We thought Dad was down for the count," Pat continued. "He appeared to be unconscious. Then I saw him reach out and grab that last piece of chocolate and pop it into his mouth. I couldn't believe it."

Indulging Dad's taste for chocolate was only one of the ways in which the people who worked at the Chateau Frontenac expressed their deep affection for him. He took care of them, as they say – that was part of it. What weighed more heavily was his personal touch. By always having time for them, he made the doormen and the bellhops and the waiters and the busboys feel important. Returning from Mass in the morning, he would say to one or the other, "Come on and sit down and have a cup of coffee with me."

And he could do these things – I don't know what the secret was – without seeming phony. I'm a pretty good tipper myself, but it was always a fight to tip anybody at the Chateau Frontenac. "No, no, no," they would tell me. I was Art Rooney's son – in their minds his little boy, I suppose – and for that reason their services were not to be bought.

One of Dad's close friends was a police inspector from Lawrenceville named Ignatius Loyola Borkowski. Iggie's looks, which were unremarkable, belied his professional skill and intelligence. A bachelor with time on his hands, he put himself and his car at the Chief's disposal, becoming, in effect, an unofficial chauffeur. Dad always paid for the gasoline but never gave a thought to such broad-based incidentals as wear and tear. In time, as cars will, Iggie's broke down, and his suggestion that Dad should replace it led to a brief estrangement. They were pals again by the next Shrove Tuesday, when Iggie drove Dad to Sarris Candies, in Canonsburg, a confectionery noted for its unsurpassable chocolate and ice cream.

Predictably, Dad gorged himself. After eating all he could hold, he made it as far as the parking lot and then threw up profusely. Iggie got him into the car and to Mercy Hospital, back in Pittsburgh, at speeds you may be sure were illegal. Dad spent two days and two nights there, taking tests. "They dried me out like an alcoholic, and I don't even drink," he complained. The tests revealed that his sugar was high, but he continued to gobble up sweets. Alcoholics and chocolaholics have one thing in common: they don't know when to quit.

In the last decade of his life, Dad went to Ireland with Tim. Something about being on vacation stoked his appetite, it seemed, and he put away a lot of candy in addition to the regular fare. "One night he zonked out," Tim said. "I called a doctor." All of this happened in Waterville, a little seaside resort, but the doctor, a young guy, turned out to be very good. He made the right diagnosis. It was not an attack of diabetes, as Tim thought, but congestive heart failure. Dad was so full of liquid that his heart couldn't pump it out of his system. The doctor gave Dad some medicine, and it straightened him out quickly.

Meanwhile, Tim had called Pittsburgh. "This time Dad may not make it," he told us. Thanks to the young doctor, he lasted for another five years.

Generation Gap

Because AJR, Father Silas, and Uncle Jim were such outstanding athletes, my brothers and I felt like underachievers, and with good reason.

Three of us – Dan, Tim, and I – played football at North Catholic, and I lettered for two years at St. Vincent. Tim and Dan were good high school players. John went out for track at St. Mary's College of Emmitsburg, Maryland, and competed successfully in the pole vault. The unusual thing about this was that he never had vaulted before, since North had no track team. John could box, too. In that respect, he and Tim were most like their father and uncles. Pat, the other twin, was on the tennis team at St. Mary's.

In short, we had nothing to be ashamed of. Compared with our forebears, though, we did not measure up, and we knew it. More to the point, AJR knew it – and allowed his disappointment to show.

John's pole vaulting gave him no pleasure. It reminded him only of a track story that featured himself. AJR was a sprinter – exceedingly fast at short distances. So when one of his friends entered a marathon race of twenty-six miles and a fraction he agreed to be the "rabbit," he told us. He would set the pace for awhile, pulling along his friend to a start that might enable him to break the course record, and then he would drop out. "But when the time came," he said, "I felt pretty good. I felt good enough to keep going, so I ran some more and some more. In fact I kept on going and won the race."

We had learned over the years that when AJR talked this way he did not exaggerate. He really was as good at sports as he claimed to have been. Old newspaper clippings document most of what he said. Father Silas was almost his equal. And at football, if nothing else, Uncle Jim may have been the best of the three.

As for my brothers and myself, blessed with ordinary ability, we were doomed to fall short of the standard these older Rooneys had set. We not only failed to satisfy AJR, what was worse, we failed to satisfy ourselves.

Chapter 36

Liberty Bell

Pennsylvania legalized standard-bred racing in 1963. Standard-bred horses do not, in the technical sense, run. Harnessed to little two-wheeled carts called sulkies, they trot or they pace. The driver, equipped with reins and a whip, sits low in the sulky and maneuvers for position on the rail.

In the nineteenth century and during the first half of the twentieth, harness racing was popular at county fairs but nowhere else. Arc lights, which made night racing possible, parimutuel betting, and the invention of the mobile starting gate moved the sport off the fair grounds and into the big money. What the starting gate did was make it easier for the entire field of horses to get off at the same time. Uncle Jim and his friends – and AJR, too – still preferred thoroughbred racing, but that is beside the point.

Through their relationship with Dave Lawrence, who was governor by then, AJR and his partner Dan Parish obtained a license to operate at the Liberty Bell track, a newly-built facility in northeast Philadelphia, just inside Bucks County. It was owned by a group that included Jim Clark, as powerful a man in the Democratic party as Lawrence was. Besides Parish, the Chief's associates included Herb Barness, a real-estate developer from Philadelphia's Main Line. In John Macartney, they had a brilliant lawyer and spokesman.

The Kelly family of Philadelphia was also somehow involved. Jack Kelly, Sr., who started out as a bricklayer and worked his way up to construction-company owner, had been the gold-medal winner in single sculling at the 1920 Olympic games. A scull is a light racing boat propelled by one oar or two and by either one oarsman, as in single sculling, or four. Kelly's son, Jack Junior, was perhaps an even better sculler than his father but never an Olympic champion. Three straight times – at the games of 1948, 1952, and 1956 – he finished third and had to settle for bronze instead of gold.

The Kelly my brothers and I were most interested in, of course – not to deprecate scullers and their sport, as little as they excited us – was Jack's sister Grace. Jack merely looked like a movie star; his sister triumphantly became one. With her arresting blend of refinement and sex appeal, she was the actress every director wanted, and then she gave it all up for a royal wedding.

Monaco, the domain of her prince, a man named Rainier, wasn't much bigger than the Paramount lot in Hollywood - or, for that matter, the Beaver Valley steel town of Monaca – but the crown jewels and the palace were real. To our disappointment, none of us ever met Grace, who seldom returned to America.

Jim Clark was the principal owner of Liberty Bell. He got along very well with AJR and Dan Parish, who leased the track from him for fifty-day meets twice a year. All three men had come up the hard way, Clark as a one-time trucker. He now owned much of the stock – the majority of it, I believe – in the Philadelphia Eagles. Herb Barness had a smaller piece of the Eagles. He was a big help later on – the details are unimportant – to me and my family.

Politically, financially, and in the shifting sands of human relations, there was more to the Liberty Bell arrangement than I can put down on paper, but let me say this: AJR looked after our interests so shrewdly that fifteen years after his death the race-track business was as profitable to his family as the football team. Clark, Barness, and Macartney were out of horse racing entirely.

We operated at Liberty Bell as the William Penn Raceway. Without leaving Pittsburgh, I did some work for William Penn before the track ever opened, but horse racing never appealed to me. It fell to the twins, Pat and John, to represent the Rooneys at Liberty Bell, with Johnny Laughlin, Aunt Margaret's son, and Jerry Lawrence, the governor's son, as their associates.

Pat left a job selling copper for a Pittsburgh manufacturing company and served a brief apprenticeship at the Brandywine track in Delaware before making the move to Philadelphia. He was now a husband, having fallen in love with one of the copper firm's secretaries, Sandy Sully. John and Johnny Laughlin had been teachers, John at Plum High School, where he also coached track, and Johnny Laughlin at North Catholic. John the twin was married also, to his long-time girlfriend Jo Ann Wallace, a hot-shot basketball player from Spring Hill.

For Jim Clark's group, the Rooney-Parish participation was a sweetheart deal. To start with, it required us to make a two-million-dollar "security deposit." Clark's people ran the place and got about half of the profits. Even so, we made out all right, as AJR would remind us whenever we complained about getting the short end of the stick.

Pat and John and their families – they had children by now – lived in apartment complexes, huge places a few miles from the track. There was nothing ostentatious about these complexes, which suited Dad perfectly. Dad disapproved of ostentation. Mom disapproved of apartment living. She was happy when Herb Barness's real estate company put the twins and their wives and kids into nice big substantial houses.

John's first house had a back-yard swimming pool, and he tried to conceal it from Dad. A back-yard swimming pool was "putting on the dog." Also, Dad thought, swimming pools, and young children didn't mix. So whenever he came around, John and Jo Ann made sure that the curtains were drawn. If the kids raced in, dripping water, the parents would lie. They'd say the neighbors next door had a pool.

John's new Cadillac was harder to account for. Looking at it distastefully, Dad put John to a test.

"What kind of car is that?" he asked

"Oldsmobile," John replied

"Don't kid the kidder," Dad barked. "And don't be putting on the dog to impress these people in Philadelphia. That's a Cadillac."

Harness racing is such a sedate sport - compared with thoroughbred racing, anyway - that something I heard from John about the intensity of its patrons came as a shock. He said that deaths at the park from heart attacks and strokes were not uncommon. For every meeting, Liberty Bell had to hire a full-time physician and a full-time nurse.

Curious, John asked a doctor about typical last words. Before losing consciousness, what did these poor unfortunates usually say? Did they enter eternity with a prayer on their lips? With a farewell message to their loved ones? Hardly ever. Most often, according to the doc, they died wanting to know if the horse they had bet on had won.

When AJR was in Philadelphia, he would drive out to Liberty Bell early in the morning, right after Mass, and have breakfast at the kitchen in the backstretch – pancakes, bacon and eggs, and coffee. Then he would talk at length with the trainers, drivers, grooms, warm-up boys, hot walkers, and miscellaneous flunkies. All of them spoke his language. They knew he was some kind of big shot but not much else.

Each year the racing people held an awards banquet which our Philadelphia contingent was expected to attend. At one such event a troop of dancing girls, stark naked except for G-strings, came out from the wings and ran into the dining area. They circulated among the tables, gyrating salaciously. AJR turned his chair around and sat facing the twins, Jerry Lawrence, and John Laughlin, Jr.

"He started a business meeting," Pat told me later. "He said, 'Pat, how are things going in the mutuel department?' Then he asked, 'What was the handle last week?' After that, he had questions for the others: 'John, are you getting top horses in here?' 'Johnny, how are the programs selling?' 'Jerry, what about the publicity department?'" On and on it went until the dancing was over. The twins, making a heroic effort, were able to keep their faces straight. Johnny Laughlin and Jerry may have been too frightened to laugh.

At another banquet one of the men who ran Liberty Bell made a disparaging remark about AJR from the dais. Del Miller, respected throughout the harness-racing world as both an outstandingly successful driver and the owner or the Meadowlands track near Pittsburgh, took umbrage. When the speaker passed Miller's table on the way back to his own, Miller got up and punched him, saying, "Nobody insults my friend Art Rooney."

All in all, his friend Art Rooney, and Art Rooney's sons, were doing pretty well. The football team was out of the red and phenomenal times in the racing business were not far over the horizon.

Foot in the Door

My aim all along was to work for the Steelers, preferably as a scout. The man in charge of our scouting at the time was Ray Byrne, better known as Digger. For more than one reason the name fit, because in addition to digging up football players, he buried the dead.

By profession an undertaker, he buried the dead in a grimly literal sense. When I say that he dug up football players I am using a figure of speech. Scouting methods in Byrne's day were primitive; to identify prospects, he dug through press guides, newspapers, and magazines.

Until the 1960s the Steelers were never able to spend more than a pittance on scouting. Assistant coaches doubled as scouts and there were one or two men on the road.

Byrne was the coordinator. He worked in the front office, too, helping Fran Fogarty with some of the minor bookkeeping chores. Byrne was short and slight, with the polite, deferential, gently accommodating manner that morticians acquire from daily inter-action with the bereaved.

I remember hearing him tell AJR on a train ride to Cleveland for the 1953 league championship game that Detroit University quarterback Ted Marchibroda, who had played at St. Bonaventure until Father Silas scrubbed the football program for economic reasons, was probably too short to be successful in the NFL. AJR, I could see, disagreed. Marchibroda's St. Bonaventure connection – and the fact that Father Silas was the school's athletic director – weighed heavily with AJR. Not that Father Silas had ever lobbied for Marchibroda. He told us that Ted was a good guy, nothing more.

In Cleveland, and again on the return trip, AJR discussed Marchibroda with Wellington Mara, the owner of the New York Giants. He then confronted Ray Byrne. "Ray," he said, "dooo ... you ... know ... who we are going to draft first? Well ... it's Teddy Marchibroda." He paused for a moment to let that sink in. "I just talked to Wellington Mara," he continued. "Wellington Mara knows more about drafting than anybody in the NFL, and he says if he gets the chance he will take Mar-chi-bro-da." For emphasis, AJR pronounced each syllable distinctly. "He will take Marchibroda *first*."

Byrne's job with the Steelers was only an avocation, but he treasured it. Meekly, he answered, "Yes, Mister Rooney."

The Steelers had given the Giants a 63-7 pasting that year, and perhaps this was Mara's revenge. They were friends, these two owners, but all's fair in love, war, and football. Drafted by the Steelers in the first round, Marchibroda proved to be an exciting, strong-armed little scrambler who was never quite good enough to unseat Jim Finks as the starting quarterback.

For several years after Byrne parted company with us – reluctantly but voluntarily; he and his family were moving away from Pittsburgh – we had no personnel director as such. My first job, given to me at the insistence of Kass, was in group ticket sales.

In a way, I was qualified for sales, and in another way I was not. Upon leaving the Marines, I had taken the first offer that came along: I sold advertising for WEDO, a radio station owned by Uncle Jim's old football teammate at Pitt, Eddie Hirshberg. Hirshberg seemed to think he could teach me all about salesmanship, but I knew better. Salesmanship was not in my blood. Football was. I believed I had a future with the Steelers.

I hoped it would also include a beautiful red-haired lady from Seton Hill College in Greensburg. She had the same first name as my mother, Kathleen, and my mother loved her. But what I needed now was a game plan. Step one would be to get out of radio, a move made more urgent by Eddie Hirshberg's desire to expand his business – acquire a station in Las Vegas and go on from there. In the picture he painted for me, I was to be his partner, with AJR putting up the capital. Somehow I couldn't see myself proposing this idea to my father. So I turned Eddie down.

In group ticket sales, I was a one-man department: no assistants, no office, and no secretary. I had the inescapable feeling that no one was taking me seriously. My job was to sell tickets in blocks, and I used the door-to-door method, visiting large corporations, small businesses, and even bars. It was hard going; the Steelers in those days were not exactly a hot item. In our thirty years of existence, there had been only four winning seasons. "Better things are corning," I would say. "Bullshit" would be the answer on the faces of the people I was trying to sell. Some of them even said it out loud, and I knew they were right.

Occasionally Art (Pappy) Lewis, our head scout, came with me to help with the sales pitch. Lewis had been a coach, most recently at West Virginia University, and Buddy Parker had brought him to the Steelers because college coaches everywhere knew him and liked him. He was a cracker-barrel humorist, capable of spinning tall tales.

Not long after we first teamed up, Pappy had a heart attack. I called the hospital to see how he was doing.

"Not too well," the nurse told me.

"Can I come to visit?" I asked

"If he gets better," she replied

"What do you mean by 'if'?" I wanted to know.

After a pause, the nurse said, "Well ... he probably won't make it."

Pappy Lewis died the next day.

I no longer remember which of our scouts replaced him. It may have been Will Walls or it may have been Ken Stilley. I do remember that Stilley would come with me when I was making my rounds, just as Lewis had done, and we talked at great length about "recruiting" college players in competition with the new American Football League.

If we were ever going to win, I decided, we had to find more good players we could sign, the kind of players other teams were overlooking. We could not let a player like Johnny Unitas slip through our fingers because of a coach's misjudgment. In an operation like ours, there was no room for error. We could not afford to carry any deadwood. Given our limited financial resources, every player had to be a good one. You could lose with good players, yes, but without them you never could win.

Something else I decided was that I did not have the persuasive power to be a ticket salesman – not as long as we played our home games at Forbes Field. "These seats," a prospective customer would say. "Where are they?" When I told the unavoidable truth – "Behind a pole" – my prospect lost interest every time. I went to AJR and asked if I could work with the scouts. Reluctantly, he agreed.

"You're brand new," he told me, which was something he often said to all of his sons. "Brand new" meant green, naive, wet behind the ears. In my own opinion, I wasn't completely brand new. There were some big truths I was figuring out, and winning with good players, as simple as it sounds, was one of them. I had another idea that was mean-spirited and wrong. "Let's get so many good players," I would say to the other scouts, "that the coaches can't screw them up." As I matured, I put that one in mothballs. Football, after all, is a team endeavor. It was true, nonetheless, that you had to work very hard at your job and be self-reliant.

Starting out, I realized I was still an apprentice, with many things to learn from experienced old-timers like Stilley. Ken had been a lineman at Notre Dame. In the movies he'd have played a judge or a senator or the head of a corporation. Real life miscast him as the mayor of Clairton, a coal and steel town on the Monongahela River near Pittsburgh. Finding himself involved in a nasty campaign for re-election one year, he came to AJR for advice. A local bar owner, he complained, was bad-mouthing him all over town. "Close the guy down," AJR suggested. "He has to be violating some code or regulation or ordinance." Stilley was dumbstruck. That political power could be a weapon had apparently never occurred to him.

P.S. He was not re-elected.

Stilley helped me a lot while he was still with the Steelers and continued to help me as the first executive director of the Blesto scouting organization. He taught me how important good relationships are. There were college coaches and athletic directors who looked upon scouts as a nuisance. "Behave the right way when you go around to these schools," Ken reminded me, "and you'll always be welcomed back."

Stating the obvious, was he? Couldn't anyone with a brain have figured that out for himself? Well, yes, but it's surprising how rare a simple thank-you can be. I learned from Ken Stilley the value of sending follow-up notes and postcards. All right – so Ken was a politician, at least on a small scale. Was he giving me a lesson in the art of casting bread on the waters? A politician's trick? Or is there still such a thing as plain old-fashioned common courtesy?

In Charge

I am sometimes referred to – undeservedly – as the guy who invented Blesto. As a matter of fact, the idea came from Buddy Parker, Russ Thomas of Detroit, and Vince McNally of Philadelphia. When they were putting it together I attended all the meetings as a go-fer. While having fun, I enriched my knowledge of football.

Blesto was my big break. The following year, 1965, the Bears came into the organization and AJR put me in charge of the Steelers' scouting department. Our collaboration with the Lions, Eagles, and Bears gave us coverage from nine or ten scouts instead of three, and coverage was exactly what we needed. Just as crucial, it seemed to me, Blesto's executive offices were under the same roof as ours. Working and talking with so many capable scouts, I learned from the bottom up. They taught me the rudiments – everything from the importance of not leaving home without your foul-weather gear to the proper method of running a movie projector.

Besides me, our only scouts were part-time assistant coaches. They would coach a position in camp and then hit the road. Thanksgiving came and went before we saw them again. Although on paper I was now their boss, they answered to the head coach, not to me, an annoyance until the end of my tenure. As scouts, some of these coaches were good, some were OK, and others just simply didn't give a damn. They wanted to spend all their time on coaching, which was all right with me. Good riddance, I thought. We had coaches who were bad judges of talent and one coach who seemed allergic to work. On the day before the draft he would call somebody, get a recommendation, and then push that player real hard.

When I went on the road myself I kept my eyes and ears open and asked questions. Because of AJR, everybody treated me well. Constantly in the back of my mind was a small voice that said to me: Don't act like too much of a big shot.

In-house, there were changes to be made. Our bookkeeping was primitive. I had to fight for a full-time secretary. I angered a lot of people when I announced that scouting records were not to leave the office. And of course I heard the grumbling: "Artie's new job is going to his head."

Even if that was so, I intended to do things my way.

Will Walls

One of the more colorful Blesto scouts was Will Walls, a big, rangy guy, part Indian and all Texan. Or maybe not. After President Kennedy's assassination in Dallas, Walls disavowed his Texas heritage. "You know, Artie," he said to me once, "I'm really from Arkansas."

Wherever he was from, Walls had been the primary target for Sammy Baugh's passes at Texas Christian. Apparently the Indian blood that flowed in his veins qualified him for membership in a fraternal organization he belonged to – Wigwam Wisemen of America, who held their meetings in a telephone booth.

After college, Walls played for the New York Giants from 1941 to 1943. His next stop was Hollywood, where he presented himself for a screen test and earned a bit part in "Thirty Seconds Over Tokyo." Returning to Texas, he coached a junior-college team and helped to put on an all-star high school game; this enabled him to make contacts that were useful in his scouting career.

Will Walls
(Steelers Collection)

When Walls beat the bushes for Blesto, he averaged 50,000 miles a year on the road. He carried so much baggage – hot plates, coffee makers, movie projectors, still cameras, and what not – that the springs in his car gave way, and he drove at such a high rate of speed that he came very close to killing himself in a series of head-on crashes. An accident that sent him to the hospital knocked out all of his teeth and lacerated an ear. It may have given his face character – the producers of "Gunsmoke" had a part they thought he'd be right for, but Walls wasn't interested, which was television's loss.

In addition to the items listed above, Walls carried hundred-watt bulbs everywhere he went (the light bulbs in the hotel rooms were too dim to read by, he said), big bars of soap (the tiny wafers you got in hotels were next to worthless), and a .38-caliber revolver. It was Buddy Parker who advised him to include a still camera. Parker wanted a photograph of every top prospect – black prospects in particular. "If I'd known how ugly that Bob Ferguson was," he said to me once, "I wouldn't have drafted him." Ferguson was a fullback from Ohio State who played for the Steelers in 1962 and 1963.

I liked Walls a lot – almost everyone did – but learned to discount his reports just a bit. His judgments were sweeping and final. At the University of Colorado one day, we watched some film of a player we were checking out for the draft. "Artie," Walls said to me at the end of the reel, "did you see that feller flinch'?"

"Yeah, Will, I saw."

I was wasting my breath. To make sure that I saw, he ran the film again and again and again – ten times altogether.

"Once a flincher always a flincher. Remember that, Artie," he said.

On-the-Job Training

In the spring of 1965, Buddy Parker sent me on my first scouting trip – to an all-star game in Buffalo with Walls. We traveled in the ancient Packard he drove, and the trek took eight or nine hours (there were still no Interstate highways). Because I scarcely knew Walls, I wondered starting out what we would talk about – if anything. Walls, after all, was part Indian, and Indians were notoriously tight-lipped. In the cowboy movies I had seen as a kid, they muttered "Ugh" now and then but otherwise had little to say.

Walls lived up to the stereotype only part of the time, alternating between silence and loquaciousness. He was only part Indian, remember, his reddish brown complexion augmented by exposure to the sun. In his silent moments he fiddled constantly with the radio dial. When I relieved him at the wheel of the car, he practiced taking pictures with an unloaded camera. He would half turn around from time to time and fish something out of the back seat. As I have said, he carried enough equipment to outfit a department store.

His Packard went back to the 1950s, when ordinary cars were almost the size of the SUVs that became popular forty years later. At one point, in his deep Southwestern drawl, he said to me, "Art, big guys like us need these big boats. We've got to have cars with strong springs. There's pretty good safety in these babies, too. Ya know, I almost got kilt once – up in Colorado. I must of hit a deer; it happened so fast I couldn't tell. All I remember is that I laid there on the ground a long time. Another car was involved, and there were bodies all over the place, so I've been told. Like I say, I don't remember a thing."

The longer he talked, the harder he pressed down on the accelerator. "Pissant roads!" he grumbled. "They're nothing but wagon trails – farm to market. Gawdam!" We were doing about eighty.

I thought, "In a minute or two, I'm going to be dead! We both are! And me with a beautiful redheaded wife" – I had married Kay Kumer – "and a lovable little kid at home. I'll never see them again!"

Whoever looks out for daredevils – St. Christopher? – kept our four wheels underneath us.

And now Walls was back on the subject of his accident. "I heard someone say, 'This guy here is done for.' He meant me. I was alive, but I couldn't speak. I couldn't move. I was all broken up. My biggest fear right then was that they'd take me to the morgue and have me embalmed." He shook his head. "It was months before I could work again."

To lighten the mood – and take my mind off how fast we were going – I told a few stories about AJR. Walls smiled as he listened and once or twice actually laughed. He was quiet for a while, and then, out of the blue, he switched to a new topic: his football career. "I went to TCU. Over in Fort Worth, ya know. Played with Sammy. Caught a lot of his passes. Never anyone better."

"Sammy?" I was revealing my ignorance.

Walls sat still, scrutinizing the windshield. Then he said, "Baugh." That was all.

Uncomfortably, I recalled what AJR had been telling me: "You're brand new" – words I resented. I was 29 years old and full of myself. I was a college graduate. I had studied acting. I had lived in New York City. I had been through a course of Marine training at Parris Island. I was a husband and a father. How could I be brand new?

But I was. There are memorable football people, some of them great ones and others merely colorful, we know by their first names or nicknames: Tuffy, Bronk, Fido, Peahead, to mention a few. And Sammy. Slingin' Sammy Baugh was a great one. Walls himself belonged to a subdivision of this species. When his fellow scouts spoke of him, they used both his first name and his last. Will Walls, they called him, never just Will or just Walls. The full name had a ring to it. "Will Walls" was both alliterative and assonant. He started talking again as we drove into Erie. "After TCU, I went to the Giants. Well Mara – Duke." He was using Wellington Mara's two nicknames. "Good man. Then I went out to Hollywood. Made some movies – mostly Westerns. Action things. Had a nice little part in a Wallace Beery movie."

He reflected for several minutes. "Spencer Tracy. Now, there was a good guy. And he could act." I thought of some Tracy films I had seen and of Tracy's reputation as a drunk. "Tracy had a deaf child," Walls was saying. "Brought his wife over to the sound stage one day to talk to me. Real nice lady." Another pause. "My mom and dad were deaf mutes," he went on. "I told them what they wanted to know. I can use sign language as good as any deaf person. Sometimes I run into a panhandler who's passing out a card that instructs you how to use sign language. I'll sign to them, and if they don't sign back I know they're phonies. I go after them."

Much later I saw this actually happen. Walls did go after the kind of impostor he was talking about, and the fraud took off on the dead run.

By then Walls had shown me how adversarial he could be. Checking us in when we arrived at our hotel in Buffalo, the desk clerk remarked that the place was sold out, adding, "You're lucky to get a room." Sharply, Walls answered, "No we aren't lucky. We made a reservation." The desk clerk had no further pleasantries to offer.

We were both laden down with Walls' paraphernalia but needed a bellboy with a dolly to get the rest of it to our room. Walls closely supervised the whole operation. "Here, Art," he said, "you take the tape recorder. I'll carry the cameras." Noticing my amusement, perhaps, he intoned, "You can't be overprepared."

Walls was in charge of the expense money, and I watched him reward the bellboy with a handful of small change. Having overheard the dialogue between Walls and the desk clerk, the bellboy concealed his disappointment. Accusingly, Walls said to him, "Damn hot in this room." The bellboy answered, "It cools off at night, mister. This is Buffalo, you know." Then he left, rattling the change in his pocket.

I had wanted two rooms, but Fran Fogarty, as usual, was squeezing nickels. At least there were two beds. Across the street from the hotel was a park; if Fogarty had known how to arrange it, we'd be over there in that park sharing a pup tent, I thought.

The first thing Walls did after stowing away all his gear was hook up a tape recorder to the telephone.

"Is that legal, Willie?" I asked.

"Who gives a fuck?" Walls said. "The law's got too much on its hands to worry about a pissant tape recorder."

He complained again about the heat. The hotel seemed to lack air-conditioning. "Ya know, Art," he said, "lots of times on trips like this I've slept in my car. And lots of times when I didn't sleep in my car I wished I had. You'll never know what hot is, Art, until you've tried to sleep in some of those West Texas fleabags. There were nights when I'd toss and turn in some poor excuse for a bed and then go into the bathroom and turn the shower on cold and jump in for a few minutes and then jump out as wet as a duck and run back into the room and take a flying leap into the sack. I'd do that all night – as many times as I had to. Then towards dawn I'd take the bed sheets into the shower with me. Wrap myself up in 'em and let the cold water soak through. Then I'd run back into the room and jump into the bed again and get about an hour's sleep."

The lobby, when we were ready to go down, was full of scouts, coaches, and football players. Buddy Parker had wanted me to tag along with Walls for a reason: "You'll be able to meet all these guys and do some networking." Walls knew all the coaches from the South and Southwest and introduced me to them. "Billy Bob, say hi to Art Rooney Junior. His daddy owns the Steelers, and he's going to be one of our scouts." A majority of the Billy Bobs were wearing cowboy boots. Privately, Walls told me that "every asshole in Texas" had a pair of cowboy boots. I was glad I never wore mine. When I got back to Pittsburgh I gave them to our equipment man, Pinky Freyvogel.

It surprised me, although it should not have, that many of Will's friends knew AJR. "Glad to meet ya, Rooney. Knew yer dad from when I was with the Eagles. He took us to a place in yer town called the Lotus Club. Art paid for everything. Good guy. Drop by and see us the first time you come to Southwest Texas State."

To the Eastern coaches, most of them, Walls was a stranger. Fortunately, I ran into Bill Daddio, the former All-American end from Pitt, who had just gone to work for Blesto. Daddio got me acquainted with his friends from the East and the Big Ten, giving Walls an opportunity to head for the bar with his Southern and Western pals.

I didn't know at the time how much booze he could tolerate. When we returned to our room at the end of the evening there seemed to be no cause for alarm. He allowed me to use the bathroom first, and I came back wearing my P.J.'s, ready for bed. Walls then used the bathroom and came back in only a pair of undershorts. "A real pro," I thought. So many of the coaches and football players slept that way. Later, to Kay's annoyance, I acquired the habit myself. It made me feel – I don't know – like a true NFL guy.

Just as Walls had done, I kicked off the bed covers and pulled up one sheet. Walls had a book or maybe some scouting reports and left his reading light on; I turned mine off and faced the wall. Our windows were wide open, admitting too much light from the street below, and I slept fitfully, dreaming of Queequeg and Ishmael at the Spouter Inn. Will Walls, a part-Indian Texas cowboy, looked as exotic to me back then as any Polynesian harpoonist. I knew that Daddio and Jerry Neri, of the Philadelphia Blesto contingent, had very little use for Walls. Buddy Parker liked him, but Parker also liked the bombastic Fido Murphy (who will make an appearance farther on in this narrative).

After Walls turned off his light, all was quiet until about 1:45, when I heard him jump out of bed and quickfoot it into the bathroom. He moved with such lightness and speed I could see him breaking clear of a defensive back and snagging a pass from "Sammy." He did not, as far as I could tell, get under the shower. Returning, he literally dived into bed. He tossed, turned, farted, and went back to sleep. Maybe two hours later, he jumped out of bed again and made another trip to the bathroom. I thought, "His kidneys are processing all the liquor he's had to drink." He made one final bathroom run at 6, when I was just about to get up.

We had a practice to cover at 9:30. One of the all-star teams was working out at the Buffalo University field. The first player Walls pointed out to me was a big stud from Grambling, defensive lineman Alphonse Dotson, who had gone to the Kansas City Chiefs of the AFL in the second round of the draft. "I seen that feller play a few times," Walls said. "When the goin' gets tough, he's more of a Jane than a Tarzan." It was a half-speed workout – no pads, only helmets – but Dotson kept roughing up the guys in the offensive unit. "If he tries that cheap-shot shit against one of the Bears' kids," Walls said, "he'll get smacked in the choppers."

I made it a point to follow Dotson's career. He played a year in Kansas City, a year in Miami, and two years in Oakland, never with great distinction. Whether anyone ever smacked him in the choppers I couldn't say.

When we went to the other team's practice, the best-looking athlete I ever had seen caught my eye. A running back, 5 feet 11 and a little over 200 pounds, he was perfectly configured from head to foot. He was quick-quick, with absolute control of his movements. I mean he could cut without losing a fraction of speed. When this guy ran sideways, he was faster than Steeler backs like Tom Calvin and Popcorn Brandt going straight ahead. He caught the ball a few times on pitchouts and short curling routes; without breaking stride, he sucked it right into his hands. "Mister Smooth," I said to myself. His right name, I learned, was Gale Sayers. George Halas had drafted him out of Kansas.

Will Walls sidled over to me. "Look at him, Artie. He'll never hold up. All that dancing and jitterbugging – he'll get killed. The way I see it, he'll have to be a flanker. Bit of a risk there."

I was shocked. If this guy couldn't play in the NFL, who could? The Bears, who were not yet in Blesto, had taken him in the first round. This was my first look at Sayers in the flesh. What was I missing? Bill Daddio, standing nearby, had overheard Walls, and later he said to me, "Artie, I don't know what your man was looking at, but nobody has to be a scout to tell that this guy Sayers is special. What the hell – he was the best running back in the Big Eight, and the Big Eight isn't exactly a push-and-pull league."

A long time ago, I watched a comet as it streaked across a dark Hawaiian sky. Sayers' career in the NFL was like that comet – brilliant, but not long-lasting. For five years he set ground-gaining records; in his sixth and seventh seasons, he was hurt most of the time.

So, yes – in a way, Walls was right. Sayers didn't hold up – not like some of the indestructible if otherwise ordinary workhorse backs. But to say he didn't hold up is like calling Alexander the Great, who died at 32, a flash in the pan.

As Walls and I drove back to Pittsburgh, I thought about what I had learned on this educational tour, this field trip. I learned that big guys should ride in big cars. I learned who "Sammy" was. I learned that Spencer Tracy was a good guy and Spencer Tracy's wife a nice lady. I learned that beggars who claim to be deaf mutes are not always trustworthy. I learned how to survive on hot nights in West Texas fleabag hotels. I learned that Texans who wear cowboy boots are not necessarily cowboys. I learned that Will Walls could hold his liquor.

But what had I learned about my profession? I learned that two people looking at a football player don't always see the same thing. And what had I learned other than that? Not much.

Part Three: A Seat at the Table 1965-1969

Chapter 37

Kass

If Dad and Mom had a spat, Mom would jump in the car and drive to the summer cottage in Ligonier, an arduous trip in the days before Interstate highways. When you're driving a car you're in control, or imagine you are, and control was something Mom needed at such times.

She was one of the best drivers I knew. With Mom behind the wheel, there was no reason not to feel perfectly at ease unless her temper caused problems.

As I have said, she could cuss a blue streak. When another driver in some way annoyed her, she never hesitated to let the offender hear about it, and in language that will not bear repeating.

Before cars were air-conditioned, I must remind you, people drove with their windows rolled down except in the coldest months of the year. The comments Mom directed at lane-jumpers, tailgaters, cut-off artists, and slowpokes were clearly audible, and they sometimes provoked violent reactions.

Twice, as she related it to us – and I admit I have trouble believing this – paranoid drivers threatened her with guns.

The first time it happened was on the Manchester Bridge. There had been an exchange of words, and at the ramp to Galveston Avenue the man in the other car flashed a pistol. Mom planted her foot on the accelerator. Up the steep cobblestone hill she flew, outrunning her pursuer. She made a left onto Lincoln and was safe.

The experience left her "in a state," as she used to say. We were just as well pleased that Dad was not at home – he'd have jumped in his car and gone out looking for the guy with the gun.

Mom hated going through tunnels and always slowed down to a crawl. In the Fort Pitt Tunnel one evening she incited road rage in the driver behind her. After leaning on his horn for a while, he pulled out into the other lane, a serious infraction of the traffic laws. Mom had a passenger – Aunt Alice. "Kass," she said as the man in the other car passed them, "he's waving a water pistol at us." Kass had been watching him, too. "Water pistol, hell," she replied, setting Alice straight. "That's a real gun."

In a minute they were out on the Parkway West. Eager to get beyond firing range just as quickly as possible, they took the first exit the gunslinger passed up.

Call it flight at the end of the tunnel.

Mr. Marshall

Kathleen McNulty Rooney had a quiet elegance about her. The way she dressed and the way she furnished her house reflected it. There was no reason, ever, for AJR to complain about "putting on the dog." Mom's inborn good taste and the advice of a decorator kept her from overdoing things.

The decorator, a man named Bill Marshall, worked at the Joseph Horne Company, which at least in the judgment of my mother was Pittsburgh's finest department store. I was partial to Kaufmann's myself, but deferred to her superior expertise.

She had clerked at Horne's as a young girl and spoke of having waited on Lillian Russell, the extravagantly endowed stage actress whose career pre-dated the movies. Miss Russell and her husband, Alexander Moore, publisher, of the *Pittsburgh Leader*, lived for a while in the North Side neighborhood called Millionaire's Row.

Horne's was Downtown, near the Sixth Street Bridge, just across the river from the old First Ward. You could spend hours in Horne's, or even days if you were able to spend more than time. In the days before and just after the Second World War the department stores sold everything anyone could want. I remember the aroma that hit you as soon as you walked into Horne's. Overdressed, overcoiffed sales girls stood near the entrance and sprayed perfume on every woman in sight. Kids unaccompanied by adults received an entirely different kind of welcome. Floor walkers – store detectives, actually – gave them the bum's rush.

Marshall, the decorator, was a dapper young guy with a neatly trimmed mustache. Mom and Aunt Alice never used his first name. Present or absent, he was always "Mister Marshall." There were times when his objectivity took me by surprise. If Horne's did not have what Kass was looking for, he would send her somewhere else. "I think you can find it at Kaufmann's," he would say. Or perhaps he would tell her about "a little antique store in Squirrel Hill," where she could buy exactly the right table, exactly the right lamp, exactly the right chair.

Between them, Mr. Marshall and Mom had 940 North Lincoln Avenue looking like a place out of Architectural Digest. Dad, although he acted indifferent to all this, was proud of the results, I think. By the purchases Kass made, you could tell how successful, or unsuccessful, he had been at the race track. Years later, the broker he dealt with in the Chicago commodities market told my son Art that his own family went through decorating binges or periods of retrenchment according to the way Dad's investments turned out.

Mr. Marshall and Mom refurnished Dad's den to give it a very masculine look. There were leather couches and chairs, a bookcase filled with books on sports and religion, a telephone, a portable radio, and in later years two television sets – placed side by side so that Dad could watch the news and a football or baseball game at the same time. It was not unusual for both TV sets and the radio to be going while he talked on the telephone and kept up a conversation with a visitor. Inexplicably, he did not have any need for a desk.

When Mr. Marshall was in his eighties and officially retired he did some work for my wife Kay in Florida. "Your mother was a delight – lots of fun," he said to me one day. "She had taste. I didn't really know your father, in spite of all the time I spent at his house, but one thing about him I remember: he always paid in cash and right away."

After Mr. Marshall's wife died, he found a sort of replacement – a boyfriend, whose name was Don. Their relationship lasted longer than most marriages do. Sometimes Mr. Marshall and I talked about life. He said to me once, "Do you know what I'm most sorry about?" and I thought, "Here comes the baloney." But not for the first time, he surprised me. "I'm sorry I wasn't nicer to people," he continued.

Bill Marshall was about the last person I could have imagined saying this to, but I told him, meaning it, "You sound just like my dad."

Loyalty

In 1954, AJR's old friend and political godfather, Jimmy Coyne, lay dying in Mercy Hospital at the same time Kass was there for a rather serious operation. Every now and then Dad would steal away from Mom's room to visit Senator Coyne on another floor.

That didn't bother me, although I think I expected him to be constantly in attendance on Kass. What did make me angry was his focus on getting the race results every day. He borrowed a small portable radio from a nun and allowed nothing to keep him away from it when Joe Tucker came on with the sports news. Couldn't he give up the race results for just one or two evenings while Mom was recovering from surgery?

The nun who had loaned him the radio sensed my displeasure. She explained to me that when some men are worried about their loved ones – wives, children, parents – they try to hide their emotions. Feigning an interest in race results or baseball scores or the stock market, or in anything else of a similar nature, would be one way to do that, she said.

I was not entirely convinced.

Apart from his nearest relatives, Senator Coyne had few visitors other than Dad. Where were all the people he went out of his way to help when he controlled Republican patronage in Allegheny County? Dad wondered. It makes me think of something Dave Lawrence once said about AJR. I heard it from Carl Hughes, who covered the wartime Steelers as a young sportswriter for the *Pittsburgh Press*. He quoted Lawrence as follows: "Art was a Republican, and always able to do political favors until Roosevelt was elected and we Democrats took over. So when someone would ask his help he would write me a note: 'This is a good guy.' But when he really wanted to help someone the note would read: 'Dave, this guy will be with you when you lose.'"

"Art," Lawrence added, according to Carl, "will be with you when you lose." Then Carl asked me, "Could any of us ever have a testimonial greater than that?"

In later life, when he was president, chief executive officer, and chairman of the Kennywood corporation with responsibility for the four amusement parks it comprised, Hughes put loyalty, the kind exemplified in Lawrence's tribute to AJR, at the top of an ethics system he informally laid out for himself and for Kennywood's employees.

Senator Coyne drifted in and out of consciousness. In his lucid moments, Dad said, he would pray for his political enemies and for anyone he might have done injury to, inadvertently or otherwise.

Dad made sure that this message got back to his "boys," whose own prayers were only for their mother's quick recovery. We wanted her back home at 940 North Lincoln Avenue cooking our meals.

Chapter 38

Mr. Clean

Offensive linemen are the working stiffs of football – drudges unnoticed by the spectators. Have you ever seen an offensive lineman jump up and down and thump himself on the chest to celebrate a block? The notion is ludicrous. "Most people – most fans – don't even realize we're out there," said Charley Bradshaw, a Steeler offensive tackle who played from 1961 through 1966. "They don't even know our names."

With one exception, he might have added. They knew Bradshaw's name. They knew it well, but they seldom used it. Derisively, they called him "Mr. Clean." In any kind of weather he could play an entire game and never get his uniform soiled. The fans, accustomed to the down-and-dirty, give-no-quarter, all-or-nothing effort demanded of Steeler linemen by coaches like Walt Kiesling, Jock Sutherland, and John Michelosen, jumped to the conclusion that all Bradshaw did was stand around. They wanted to see football players with grass stains, mud, and preferably a little blood on their uniforms.

When Ray Downey, the Steelers' public-address announcer, introduced the offensive unit at the start of a home game, calling off the names one by one, there would be perfunctory applause for everybody but Bradshaw. What Bradshaw heard, Sunday after Sunday, would be boos, and with each game during the miserable twelve-defeat 1965 season, the boos increased in volume.

That Bradshaw had been chosen for the 1963 and 1964 Pro Bowls meant nothing to the fans. That his coaches – he played for Buddy Parker, Mike Nixon, and Bill Austin – consistently gave him the highest efficiency rating in the offensive line after watching game films meant nothing. That in a magazine poll of all the coaches in the league he was picked as the lineman who blocked straight ahead most effectively meant nothing. He was always on his feet, the fans complained, and so he obviously couldn't be giving the game everything he had. The logic of Austin's observation — "You're no good on the ground" — failed to register with them. "He should be putting the other guys on the ground," his critics argued.

Bradshaw "played tall," with his legs straight, and in fact he actually was tall — 6 feet 6, which made him easy to single out on the field, for his teammates in the line were mostly fireplugs half a foot shorter. What the fans did not perceive was that besides playing tall he played smart. He knew how to use his hands and he knew how to slide with the pass rusher, skills that could be appreciated by a quarterback in the pocket.

In or out of uniform, Bradshaw was destined to be recognized. Allowing for the difference in their ages, he was a dead ringer from the neck up for John Nance Garner, a much-photographed congressman who spent a single contentious term as Franklin D. Roosevelt's vice president. Garner had a shock of white hair; Bradshaw's hair was so blond it might as well have been white.

Besides looking like Garner, Bradshaw resembled a leaning tower. By habit he stood and walked with his head forward and his shoulders stooped, a posture he developed in the East Texas country town where he was born. "Back home," he explained, "all of my friends were little guys. I had to bend over to talk with them." Going off to Baylor University on a football scholarship, he fell for and later married a girl who was 5 feet 2.

Bradshaw accepted the hazing he took from the fans with good grace. "People watch the ball," he said. "Then they look back and see me standing up and think I wasn't blocking. I wish they'd watch me the whole play. One of these Sundays I'll get a bucket of mud and a brush and have the equipment manager paint me before the game. Then I'll roll back to the huddle after every down."

AJR used to say that when Bradshaw's playing days were over, no one would have to hold any benefits for him. While he was still with the Steelers, he earned a law degree and had an office in Houston. He was the only practicing attorney in the NFL. During the 1966 football season he appeared in Allegheny County Criminal Court, granted impromptu admission to the Pennsylvania bar by Judge Gwilym Price, Jr., under the jurisdictive equivalent of the free-substitution rule. Looking as immaculate as ever, he wore a sharply creased banker's gray suit, a radiantly white shirt, and a perfectly knotted tie. His client was charged with "malicious mischief" – throwing an empty beer bottle through the window of a doctor's office.

The switch from offense to defense was no problem for Bradshaw. Good offensive linemen "fire out," as the coaches then called it, and Bradshaw fired out in defense of the accused. With a series of objections, he kept the prosecution from showing that the window had cost fifty dollars or more. Mischief costing less than fifty dollars was not by definition malicious, which meant that it therefore was subject to a lighter sentence. Unable to produce a witness who could testify that the window had in fact cost fifty dollars or more, the prosecution asked for a delay of two hours in the trial. Judge Price, upholding Bradshaw's objection, denied the request, whereupon Bradshaw jumped up and asked him to dismiss the charges. The judge said, "I sustain the demurrer."

With that, Mr. Clean had won the case. And there wasn't a speck of dirt on his unwrinkled banker's gray suit.

Him Tarzan

In the first few Tarzan movies there was always a scene in which the ape man comes upon his future mate.

"Me Tarzan," he says.

"Me Jane," she replies.

The Tarzan series lived on, year after year. It never aged. Leading men and leading ladies were not as durable. Like Steeler coaches in the 1950s, new Tarzans replaced old Tarzans and new Janes replaced old Janes with clockwork regularity. The actor who played Tarzan had to be young, well-built, good-looking, and agile. It helped if he could swim (the best-known of all the Tarzans, Johnny Weissmuller and Buster Crabbe, won Olympic gold medals in the freestyle events). The Janes who came and went were held to the same high standards. Even in the Legion of Decency era, Tarzans and Janes swung from treetop to treetop, or splashed in the crystal-clear water of jungle lagoons, with hardly any clothing to impede them.

It was toward the end of the 1960s when Mike Henry took his turn at being Tarzan. Mike was a former Steeler and also a former Los Angeles Ram. As a linebacker he ranked in the middle of the pack. For good looks, he was up near the top. "Ruggedly handsome" would be an accurate way to describe him, an assessment concurred in by AJR's pretty secretary, Mary Regan. Hearing that Mike was to be the next Tarzan, she glanced up briefly from the letter she was typing and enhanced her reputation for laconic witticisms.

"Me Jane," she announced.

Mike Henry grew up in Hollywood – he came from a family of film cutters – and played college football at Southern California. The scout who discovered him was Fido Murphy, an outlandish character hilariously profiled in *Sports Illustrated* by a young Pittsburgh freelance writer named Myron Cope, for many years afterward the color man on Steeler radio broadcasts. After Henry's third season with the Steelers, Buddy Parker traded him to the Rams. He was now back in movieland, where another kind of talent scout discovered him. A screen test followed, and Mike was the next Tarzan.

Playing Tarzan does not require the acting skill of an Olivier or a Brando, but I saw Mike once in a somewhat demanding role. I forget the name of the film, but Jackie Gleason and Burt Reynolds had two of the leading parts. Gleason was a father and Henry his idiot son. He played off Gleason in a sure-footed, believable way, revealing a modest flair for comedy.

Most of the Steelers I have known, when they were through playing football, became coaches or teachers or salesmen or sportscasters. Just as Byron White was the only Supreme Court justice, Mike Henry was the only real movie star, if not for long.

Prematurely cast aside by the studios, he went into the old established family business – film-cutting.

Rock of Gibraltar

Rick Roberts, a black man who wrote sports for the *Pittsburgh Courier*, talked AJR into hiring Bill Nunn, Jr., another *Courier* sportswriter and the son of the paper's managing editor, as a part-time scout. I was pissed purple.

Nunn had near-perfect contacts. One of his beats for the *Courier* was college football – Negro college football. More than six feet tall, he had gone to a black college himself – West Virginia State – and had been an outstanding basketball player. He picked the all-star and the All-America football and basketball teams for his paper. I knew we needed a scout and I knew how important the black schools were to our future success. But I wanted to hire the scouts myself. He was not my guy.

Aware of how I felt, AJR got us together one night. Nunn seemed all right – well-spoken and polite. He did not try to B.S. me. I could see that he had a good attitude and I gave Dad a qualified OK – not that it mattered. Dad's mind was made up and could not have been changed.

Very quickly Nunn became a Rock of Gibraltar for me. Often I have wished I could say that I was the one who "discovered" him. He scouted part-time for us in 1968 and 1969 and became a full-fledged member of the organization in 1970. This I can claim to be my idea, but getting AJR and Dan to fall in line was no problem.

Nunn spent seventy percent of his time with me and the remainder in "community relations." He continued to work in the *Pittsburgh Courier* sports department, which he was able to do by doubling up. On trips to the black schools in the South he scouted football players for the Steelers and gathered material for his newspaper articles. Because the *Courier* appeared only once every week, he had some leeway in meeting deadlines. The Steelers and the paper shared his travel expenses.

I thought of the *Courier* editors and reporters I got to know through Nunn as pretty nice guys who seemed to like sports. It would be years before I developed a true appreciation of what a tremendous crusading newspaper the *Courier* was. Bill Nunn's merits, on the other hand, were obvious to me from the start.

At first it was only his contacts that made him valuable to us – his contacts and his insights – but as time went on I saw that he could scout football players of any color whatever – black, white, blue, green, you name it. In fact he tossed Dad an Irishman now and then, much to our amusement.

Like Jack Butler, he cut through all the baloney. There was a big murder case in Pittsburgh one year. "The broad did it," Nunn told me. I said, "Dammit, Bill, you're too cynical. She isn't even a suspect." "Just wait," Bill said. A few years later, big headlines in the morning paper confirmed what he'd been saying. The broad did it.

"It was there for you to see." Nunn said,

I found that to be a general principle. You could apply it to football players, to coaches, to scouts. The truth was always there for you to see.

We had this great young player Joe Greene – a defensive tackle, the cornerstone of our success. But he was also a loose cannon, thrown out of three games in his rookie year, infamous as far as the press was concerned for spitting in the face of a sportswriter, Pat Livingston. What could we do with this wild man?

Bill Nunn came up with the answer. We had a player named John Brown, a very good offensive lineman and a civilized human being. "Have Brown and Greene room together," Nunn suggested. "Brown is the one who can settle that kid down." He was right. Brown and Greene, both black, were the ideal color combination.

In the first few years after integration, color was all-important in the assignment of roommates at training camp. Black roomed with black; white roomed with white. A Hawaiian player, a rookie, stormed into the camp manager's office: "Get that black son of a bitch out of my room." The Hawaiian was moved in with a white guy. So now the white guy had a complaint; "Get that Chinaman out of my room." Everybody was angry at everybody else. So Bill Nunn took over the management of the camp. "From now on," he announced, "the rookies will be assigned to their rooms alphabetically, like it or not. Next year if you're on the team you can pick your own roommates. But while you're rookies you'll do as we tell you." It worked. There was no more turbulence.

Jake Gaithers, at Florida A. & M., and John Merritt, at Tennessee State, were two of the great coaches I met through Nunn. He advised me to take Merritt a box of my dad's cigars, which I did, and from then on we were friends. It was Merritt who told me, confidentially, "Never trust a black man with gray eyes." The task of checking out eye color wearied me so much that I soon gave it up. Nunn himself used to say, "Never draft or sign a big kid with small feet." I thought it made sense. On scouting trips, I would say in a deliberately casual manner, "By the way, Coach, what's the shoe size of ol' Smith over there?" At last I got tired of it. I said to Nunn, "Heck, Bill, I'm a size nine and I weigh two-fifty." I had left myself open for a counter punch. "From what I hear," Nunn drawled, "you couldn't run, either."

As camp manager, Nunn was in charge of the payroll. He made a trip each week to the Mellon Bank in Latrobe and withdrew enough cash to pay the coaches, players, scouts, equipment men, and ball boys. A coach from a black college was in the office one day when Nunn returned from the bank with a satchel full of money. Watching him empty the bag on a table, the coach was transfixed. When Bill had sorted everything out and left the room, the coach said to me, "You Rooneys would let him do that?" I knew what the sub-text was. "You Rooneys," he was saying, "would let a *black* guy do that?"

Of course he was black himself. I said, "Coach, that job is a pain in the ass."

He shook his head, and it was clear what his thoughts were: "You'd trust a *black* dude with all that money?"

Every one of us, I guess, has some learning to do.

Chapter 39

Dog Pound

Back home from a trip to the West Coast, I heard myself telling somebody, "I saw Fido out there, and he said he's seen Bow-wow." My wife Kay heard me, too. With a look of disgust, she said, "When are you going to get a real job?"

Fido Murphy and Bow-wow Wykevicz were scouts. Fido worked for the Steelers, the Bears, and Blesto, alternately, and Bow-wow for the Eagles.

In Myron Cope's book, "Broken Cigars," a collection of his magazine stories, there's a profile of Fido, whose facial resemblance to a bulldog, Myron wrote, was not the origin of his nickname, as most people assumed. According to Fido, its derivation went back to the way he ran with the football as a halfback for Westbrook Seminary of Portland, Maine, in the early 1920s. His speed of foot was such that Boston sportswriter Bill Cunningham likened him to a greyhound, Fido explained. "And when we played in hostile territory after that," he went on, "the fans called me Fido."

If there's an explanation for Bow-wow's nickname, and there must be, I've never heard it.

Fido Murphy was a little guy, no more than 5 feet 8 inches tall. He claimed to have played football at Fordham when Major Frank Cavanaugh, noted for his heroism in the First World War, was the coach. "Cavanaugh called me 170 pounds of dynamite," Fido informed Cope. It was as a strategist and innovator, however, that, by his own account. Fido left a permanent imprint on the game.

Again according to himself, he invented the modern T formation while coaching at Samuel Johnson Academy in Connecticut. It seems that Marchmont Schwartz, an assistant to Clark Shaughnessy at the University of Chicago, saw the Samuel Johnson team play, and he let Shaughnessy in on the details of what Fido was doing. Shaughnessy then indoctrinated George Halas, and presto! Halas's Bears rode the T-formation to instant success.

The next thing Fido invented, as a consultant for the Detroit Lions, was the red dog, or blitz, and then he conceived the five-man line, middle guard and all. This was why George Halas hired him as a scout. Having given the Bears their offense, he told them how to prevent Sammy Baugh from completing short passes ("Back up your tackles and back up your secondary kids deeper. Baugh won't run, and if he overshoots the short stuff we'll pick 'em off.") Result: Bears 73, Redskins 0 in the 1940 title game. Later – still advising Halas – Fido imparted the secret of stopping the San Francisco Forty-Niners' shotgun offense. The Bears stopped it cold, winning by a shutout, but Shaughnessy, who was now their defensive coach, "again got credit for Fido's brainwork," related Cope with amused skepticism.

Revealing to Cope the source of his genius, Fido declared modestly, "It isn't that I'm smarter than everyone else in football. It's just that I know more."

Actually, there was sometimes a grain of truth in Fido's assertions. Buddy Parker once told my dad and me that Fido had "a real good eye for formations – where guys lined up and where they moved on the playing field." This was very important before game films came into use and were readily exchanged, Parker said. Up till then I had thought – erroneously, I now decided – that Parker kept Fido around just for laughs. I know that Fido had a feel for scouting quarterbacks. "Look at their feet, how fast they set up and move around and how well they escape the pressure," he told me. It was pretty good advice.

Overall, he was not an astute judge of talent. His scouting reports were always late and disorganized and his expense accounts exasperated the meticulous Fran Fogarty. I saw Fran take a punch at him one day in Parker's office. Like others who were present, I wanted to see Fogarty clean Fido's clock, but Parker quickly jumped to his feet and got between them.

For some time afterward, Fido went around telling people that Parker had saved Fogarty's life. Uncle Jim then took Fido aside and warned him that he was playing with fire. He said that Fogarty had fought with the French underground during World War II and had killed more Germans than Commando Kelly.

"Who is Commando Kelly?" Fido asked.

"A North Side kid who won the Congressional Medal of Honor for wiping out a whole German regiment. He killed a lot of those krautheads barehanded, and Fogarty is even tougher than Kelly was."

Fido swallowed all of this, even the exaggerations. From then on he was more prompt with his expense accounts (but not his scouting reports). He wrote friendly letters to Fogarty and spoke of him admiringly to mutual acquaintances. When Fran dropped dead of a heart attack several years later, Fido proclaimed that he had lost his best friend in football.

Fido lasted only two or three years with Blesto before Jack Butler sent him back to the Bears. Butler would have fired him, making no bones about it, but Fido was Halas's guy and therefore untouchable. This way, it was simply a case of goods being returned to the sender, and not even Fido took exception. He stayed with the Bears until his retirement, and wherever NFL scouts gathered, Fido would be there. After the Steelers had won a Super Bowl or two, he made a great point of introducing me to people. "Meet Art Rooney Junior," he would say. "I taught him everything he knows."

In truth, Fido did teach me a lot – how not to act, how not to present myself. It was typical of Fido that when Buddy Parker left the team he immediately called AJR with a recitation of Parker's shortcomings. Cutting him off, AJR handed me the telephone. "Fido," I said, "Buddy Parker was your sponsor, and now you're the first to tell us good riddance."

My portrayal of Fido may be a little one-sided. There were those who must have shared his good opinion of himself – for example, his wife. Fido's wife was an actress named Iris Adrian –"a Ziegfeld queen, the belle of Broadway," her husband told Myron Cope. For a guy with a mug like his to snag a Ziegfeld queen did not seem unusual to Fido, who saw nothing wrong with that mug. "The dolls loved Murphy in those days. He was a handsome devil," Fido confessed to Cope. As for Iris, she held her own, I understand, in the looks department. Her specialty as an actress was dumb-blonde parts. On the Jack Benny television show, she played a telephone operator with a Flatbush accent and an impudent tongue. She called Fido Raymond, or Ray, never using his nickname. He spoke of her always with pride, and they lived contentedly, as far as I know, in their Hollywood crash pad.

Bow-wow Wykevicz, a native of New Kensington, was tall, slim, and distinguished-looking. In the late 1940s, he surfaced on the Pacific Coast and ingratiated himself with Tommy Prothro, the coach at UCLA. Bow-wow would do anything for anybody. He ran Prothro's errands, baby-sat for him and his wife, and picked up their kids after school. Whenever he did a favor, he expected two in return. But Prothro genuinely liked Bow-wow and hired him as a scout upon leaving college football to coach the Eagles. The title, I suspect, was an honorific. Actually, he continued to serve Prothro as a glorified odd-jobs man.

Bow-wow had a bizarre sense of humor. From Los Angeles, he sent a telegram to his mother in New Kensington informing her of his death in an automobile accident. The next day he sent her a second telegram, instructing her to disregard the first.

While Prothro was still at UCLA, Bow-wow transported a Hollywood starlet to the coach's front door on his birthday, rang the bell, and ducked out of sight. The young lady was gift-wrapped in cellophane, a red ribbon securing the package. Underneath the cellophane, she was completely bare. Prothro's wife came to the door and let out a shriek. That Bow-wow remained a friend of the family indicates how much he could get away with.

For money or love, or maybe both, the bimbos he knew in the motion-picture business were willing to be his accomplices. He would get them to pose nude in some kind of football stance for a photographer, and then he would send the pictures – inscribed "To my dearest friend So-and-so: Hope to see you again when you come West. Yours ever, Trixie [or whatever]" – to various coaches of his acquaintance. How often such keepsakes fell into the hands of the coaches' wives I can only guess.

In communicating with AJR, and also with me, Bow-wow was much more discreet. Knowing the Chief's aversion to anything off-color, he sent us holy cards depicting St. Anne or the Blessed Mother.

Almost all coaches eventually lose their jobs, and after the Eagles got rid of Prothro, Bow-wow returned to his beloved California. His greatest triumphs were now behind him, but out there during his heyday he may or may not have been married to Hollywood columnist Sheila Graham. If there is proof that actual vows were exchanged I am not aware of it. Miss Graham writes extensively in her memoirs of a documented love affair with F. Scott Fitzgerald; she alludes only in passing to a "relationship," its nature undefined, with "a person who is not worth mentioning." Presumably this was Bow-wow. Those of us who knew him and followed his career would like to think so.

Brian and Brucie

With our drafting completed in 1966, we were signing free agents to fill out the roster when my telephone rang.

A man with a strong Italian accent introduced himself and said, "Why you not draft my son?"

I was taken aback. Still fairly new to the business, I never had heard a question like that from a parent. Without being rude, I tried to make our conversation a short one. It was no easy matter.

"Why you not draft my son? He's-a good-a football player," the stranger persisted. He seemed hurt. His tone of voice got to me, and I patiently explained that we were limited in the number of draft choices we could make. What was his boy's name? I asked.

Brian something. The last name I failed to catch.

Had anyone else drafted him?

No.

Where did he play?

Wake Forest

What position?

He ran with the ball.

It occurred to me suddenly that I was giving myself away. The mind of a scout who was worth his salt would be a repository for information like this. I came up with what I thought was a plausible excuse. I said, "I have to ask about these things because I'm not at my desk. So many names have been going through my head I'm in a bit of a fog right now."

He could fill me in, the man said. His boy had been a starter for the last two seasons at Wake Forest. He had run for a lot of yardage and had caught a lot of passes. Why had nobody drafted such a player? The man did not raise his voice and there was no animosity in it.

"Hang on for a minute while I get your boy's records" I said. I found the reports on Wake Forest, checked out a running back whose first name was Brian ("Very productive. An overachiever. Lacks size and speed. May have already reached his potential"), and went back to the phone, half expecting the line to be dead. But my caller was waiting.

"Well, the probable reason Brian was not drafted," I began, "is the lack of great size or speed ..."

"Yes, but he's a top-a player." The man's pleading tone softened my response. I agreed that Brian had good credentials. "Let me talk with a scout who has seen him," I said, "and I'll call you back."

I spoke to the scout, Ken Stilley, the next day. He told me that in his opinion the kid should have been drafted in one of the late rounds, having led the nation in rushing with more than 1,000 yards in 252 carries. Then Stilley added, "He probably did reach his potential in college, but he's a fine individual and won't embarrass you in camp. Go for him." On the telephone again with the father, I said we would like to offer Brian a contract. Hardly able to contain his happiness, he promised to have Brian call me.

When Brian did call, he was somewhat apologetic. He respected his father greatly but explained how difficult it was for someone not born in this country to have a clear understanding of National Football League protocol. Fathers did not call personnel directors to lobby for their sons.

I told him not to worry about it. I said I liked what I heard from my scouts and would send him our standard free-agent contract. There would be a signing bonus of a few hundred dollars and another small bonus if he succeeded in making the team.

"Sounds good," he said. "I'll let you know my decision very soon." I had done this on my own, without consulting our head coach or anyone else, but I was comfortable with the thought that we were giving an opportunity to a young man who deserved it. For the rest of his life, whatever happened in camp, he could say that he'd had a tryout with the Steelers.

It wasn't long before Brian called back. He was grateful for our offer, he said more than once, but had made up his mind to sign with the Bears. I reflected that most free agents who accepted another team's offer rather than ours never bothered to let us know. I thanked him and wished him good luck.

The kid's full name was Brian Piccolo. He played in the Bears' backfield for four seasons and then died of cancer. Brian Piccolo had but a few months to live when his friend and teammate, the great runner Gale Sayers, was voted the Most Courageous Player award by the Professional Football Writers Association in 1970. Sayers had come back from a serious knee injury to lead the NFL in ground gaining. At the presentation ceremony, he said the award should have gone to Piccolo.

Sayers had much to tell about Piccolo in an autobiography he wrote with Al Silverman. Its title – "I Am Third" – was taken from a sign on the desk of his track coach at the University of Kansas, Bill Easton. Sayers had asked what it meant. "It means the Lord is first, my friends are second, and I am third," Easton told him. The book became the basis for a television movie – "Brian's Song" – its main theme the friendship between Sayers and Piccolo.

When Piccolo died, and when the movie came out, I thought of the telephone call I received from his father and of the question that haunted me: "Why you not draft my son?"

Brian's father and Brucie's aunt were two of a kind. Brucie's aunt was a cleaning lady who worked for my mother-in-law. "Tell Mister Rooney not to forget about my nephew, Brucie," she kept reminding her. In our occasional face-to-face encounters, the cleaning lady would ask if I had seen "Brucie" yet. Dismissing her as a pain in the neck, I resolutely ignored these entreaties.

Brucie, I gathered, went to college at Davidson, in the Carolinas. Davidson was a member of the weak Southern Conference and not exactly a noted producer of NFL talent. Besides, how was it possible for anyone called Brucie to be a football player? Like Mr. Piccolo, my mother-in-law's cleaning lady would not be put off. She started hounding my wife about Brucie. At last for the sake of peace in the family I went to our scouting book, and found just a single entry for Brucie. I learned that Brucie played for Davidson, all right. A better way to put it would be that he did the field-goal kicking – "which accounts for his sissy name," I said to myself. Next I went to the report book and found another single entry for Brucie. Real prospects were written up six times, seven times, eight times. Brucie was a big, strong kid with a live leg, the report said, but "inaccurate."

"Tell your mother's cleaning lady that I looked up the scouting report on Brucie. The verdict is that he's not a good enough kicker for the NFL," I instructed my wife.

I heard nothing more about Brucie until the following spring. Pausing in her work one day, the cleaning lady told me that he had signed as a free agent with the Rams. I wished him the best of luck and got away quickly. A month later, with the season under way, my mother-in-law informed me that, according to her cleaning lady, Brucie made the team. "She must be mistaken," I thought. I checked out the rosters, and sure enough — a rookie free agent had won a job with the Rams as their field-goal kicker.

It was Brucie, and he played for several years.

He taught me something, a valuable lesson for a scout: listen to recommendations and follow them up — especially recommendations from cleaning ladies.

L. C.

Late in the football season of 1968 I was planning to scout a running back who played for Arkansas A. & M. Because I had a bad cold, I was tempted to stay at home and send for the team's game films. My wife had a cold and our kids all had colds, but though I caught hell from Kay for doing it, I flew to Little Rock, rented a car, and drove to the A. & M. campus in Pine Bluff.

The A. & M. coaches were considerate and friendly. First they let me look at the films, sitting in as I watched. I forget the name of the halfback I was down there to see, but they talked him up. "Look at that move," they would say. "Did you notice the way he broke that tackle? Run that play back again. See how big the defensive back is ... " They were certain the kid could play in the NFL.

I had another A. & M. guy on my list, a defensive end named Clarence Washington. "He's big and strong, and he has good movement," the coaches told me. "Let's watch him. He'll make it as a defensive tackle."

So we looked at the films of the defensive unit, and I liked Washington as a project. But somebody else caught my eye, a kid who appeared to be about 6 feet 6.

"Who's the guy making that pass rush?" I asked.

"Oh. That's L.C. We knew you'd spot him. He's special."

"L.C.? Spell that out for me."

"L.C. Greenwood."

I looked at my list, and he was on it. Too tall for his weight, the notation said.

"Well ... that's what they all say. He has growth potential, though. Wait till you see him in practice." The coaches were trying hard to reassure me.

On a dusty, hardscrabble practice field, we watched him in practice. He was so tall and thin he reminded me of the Masai warriors in the movie "King Solomon's Mines." But nobody pushed him around. Defensive tackles that tall aren't supposed to have leverage. Greenwood was different. He could break down and get under blockers.

This one could be a ruby — a sleeper — I said to myself.

When we met to prepare for the 1969 draft, our new head coach, Chuck Noll, said he was looking for guys who could make something good happen. I mentioned Washington and Greenwood from Arkansas A. & M., and we drafted them both. The halfback whose name I've forgotten did not fit into our plans.

Washington hung on for one season. Greenwood did more than hang on. He helped the Steelers of the 1970s win the Super Bowl four times and is nominated every year for the Hall of Fame.

Those initials — L.C.— used to bother me. What did they stand for? L.C. himself would never say. Eventually I learned that they stood for nothing. In the South, somebody told me, it is not unusual to have initials instead of a first name and a middle name.

"L.C.," from then on, was O.K. with me.

Chapter 40

Lombardi Lite

When the time came to replace Mike Nixon as coach, there was certainly no shortage of recommendations. Everybody, it seemed, had a candidate. Even Nixon's old boss got into the act.

Buddy Parker had resigned in a huff, and he had done it abruptly at the worst possible moment – several weeks into the exhibition season – but AJR was still Buddy's friend. Buddy knew, as all of Pittsburgh did, that the Steelers were glad to see him go. A severance package of handsome proportions undoubtedly eased his pain. So, being helpful, he called AJR from Texas and told him about the coach at John Carroll, a Catholic university in Cleveland the size of Duquesne. "Get yourself a good young student of football who's an expert on defense," was Buddy's advice. "Look at what that young guy Don Shula has been doing with the Baltimore Colts. John Carroll has a defensive-minded coach named John Ray who's the same type. I'm not saying Ray is your man, but that's the kind of guy you want. He knows defense." Parker believed the importance of defense could not be overestimated.

I asked Ken Stilley about Ray, unaware that they were personal friends. Stilley concurred with Parker, telling me that Ray understood defense, was a man of good character, and would go places. (He later became head coach at Kentucky.) Stilley then made a prediction. He said that AJR would consult Vince Lombardi before he did anything at all and that Lombardi would recommend his former assistant, Bill Austin. "Remember this about Austin," Stilley continued. "Austin has a poor personality. He's a lot like Buster Ramsey, with one difference. Austin is not as smart as Ramsey." I relayed Stilley's warning to AJR. He said that with all due respect to Stilley, a capable scout, this was Vince Lombardi that he was going to call. There was no need for further discussion.

Ernie Stautner, meanwhile, applied for the job. After leaving Parker's staff, Ernie had caught on with the Dallas Cowboys. Jack Butler applied because I urged him to. Embarrassed about it, he asked for the job in a note I hand-delivered to AJR. "Tell that Butler to come over here and see me," he said. The Blesto offices in the Roosevelt Hotel were just a few steps away from Dad's, and, as fearless as he could be on the football field, the walk was a long one for Butler. Feeling responsible – the whole idea had been mine – I tagged along. AJR did not order me out. He said to Butler, "Jack, you're a top man and you're one of us. You have ability. But you need experience, and that knee of yours is so bad you can hardly stand. For you to think about coaching ... well ... this just isn't the time." Now Jack was even more embarrassed, but if he blamed me for putting him on the spot he kept it to himself. In hindsight, getting the brushoff from Dad was a lucky break for Butler. His promotion to the executive directorship of Blesto followed soon afterward.

Through Mary Regan, AJR placed a call to Lombardi in Green Bay. Nobody told this to Lombardi, but Dan listened in on Fran Fogarty's phone and I was hooked up at Ed Kiely's. Lombardi came on the line and greeted Dad heartily in his normal tone of voice – loud and gruff. Dad told Lombardi the purpose of his call, and the coach brought up a few names. In two or three minutes they were talking about Austin. Austin had left the Packers to take an assistant's job with the Rams the year before. "I didn't like that," Lombardi said, "but it was something he had to do. Talented people like Bill Austin get antsy when they're waiting for a head coaching position to open up."

At the end of the conversation, both Dan and I felt, as AJR did, that Austin was our guy. Lombardi had praised him extravagantly, had said we couldn't go wrong with Austin. And who would know better? Besides, Lombardi was Dad's old friend; he would never intentionally give us a bum steer.

Fleetingly, I thought once again of Ken Stilley's words. They lingered uncomfortably in the back of my mind. If Austin was a clone of Buster Ramsey ... But no – it couldn't be true. Vince Lombardi had spoken, and that was enough.

'Now Is Now'

Bill Austin was a big, blond, ruggedly good-looking guy, standing 6-1 or 6-2 and weighing 225-230 pounds. He had been an offensive lineman at Oregon State and had played for the New York Giants' championship teams in the 1950s.

His off-season hobbies were handball and aviation. Austin was pretty good at handball and considered it the ideal training for interior linemen. Handball compelled a player to stay low; at the same time, it sharpened his hand-to-eye coordination, Austin believed. Aviation seemed to fascinate him. He flew his own airplane and often spoke of his brother, a Navy pilot shot down in Vietnam. Once when Austin asked me for a scouting assignment, I sent him to a game at Bowling Green because the Bowling Green stadium was next to an airport.

It became apparent to us right away that, like his mentor Lombardi, Austin was going to be a control freak. In his own mind, he ruled the entire organization. Joe Bach had been the same way, but whereas Lombardi was a winner and Bach a nice guy, Austin fell short in both respects. His manner was sarcastic and he offered "suggestions" freely. Ticket sellers, publicity men, accountants, and most especially the personnel director – me – were the objects of his attention and criticism.

Not far into his first season, Austin had all of us on edge, including AJR, who did not like Austin's habit of chastising his players and assistant coaches in public. After Austin gave one coach a dressing down in front of his two young sons, AJR warned him never to repeat such an insensitive act.

The understanding between Dan and me that we would build the team through the draft meant nothing to Austin. His first move as coach was to trade our top pick to Green Bay for Lloyd Voss, a defensive tackle. Voss was hard-working and likable and still a pretty fair lineman, but the feeling was that Lombardi had given up on him. When the chance came to unload Voss, he took advantage of it. In fairness to Austin, we had not been able to sign the best available college players since the American Football League had come into the market, a state of affairs that would continue until the merger the following year. But I was still a personnel man first and foremost, and Austin's high-handedness put my nose out of joint.

Austin maintained that even with Blesto our scouting coverage was insufficient. I felt that our coverage had been good and would get better. When the Vikings joined the Blesto group in 1967 we would have more scouts in the field. "Next year is next year. Now is now," Austin said, and he had a point. To satisfy him, our assistant coaches were scouting college games on Saturday. It caused logistical problems because most of our own games were played on Sunday afternoon. The coaches resented the trouble this made for them, but Austin prevailed.

Our perceived shortage of scouts was the reason for the Bowling Green trip. The Steelers were not scheduled that weekend, and Austin had taken an interest in a guard named Jon Brooks who played for Bowling Green's opponent, Kent State. This Brooks was a top-rated blocker who would be a good fit, we thought, for Austin's "run-to-daylight" scheme, which required a lot of pulling by the guards.

Back in the office on Monday, Austin asked to see me. The trip had gone well, and I got my first look at a different side of him. There was nothing of the smart aleck in his behavior that day. It was man to man, scout to scout.

"Artie," he said, "I know that you and the Blesto guys are pretty high on Brooks, but he really doesn't have it as a top-of-the-line prospect. First of all, there's his size. He isn't tall enough for his weight, and most of his weight is in his thighs and ass. He can pop out on a man block. He comes off the ball well on the down block. The quick pass rusher who has some movement is going to be a lot of trouble for him. He's supposed to have good pulling ability. Check it out on the films again. He has nice short-pull quickness, but loses so much on the deep pulls ... and that's what we'll be asking him to do."

And so on and so on. When he was finished, Austin had convinced me of something without giving offense. The Blesto scouts were pushing Brooks hard, but I re-studied the films, as Austin wanted me to do, and they bore out his assessment. Brooks went to the Philadelphia Eagles in the second round of the draft. He had gained so much weight that somebody gave him a nickname – the S.S. Brooks, meaning he was as big as a ship. After his rookie season, the Eagles had no further use for him, nor did Brooks ever play again in the NFL. The scout who had been his staunchest supporter found himself in very hot water.

Austin tried to copy Vince Lombardi's methods the way that John Michelosen had imitated Jock Sutherland. His practices were long and hard. But a counterfeit is a counterfeit and never the real thing; he can't be. Just as Michelosen had not been another Sutherland, Austin was not a second Lombardi.

His first Steeler team ended up with a 5-8-1 record, a big improvement over Nixon's 2-12 and marginally better than Buddy Parker's 5-9 the year before, but insubstantial grounds for expecting Austin to be our messiah.

Battered and Bloody

Bill Austin never understood that conditioning and toughness were just a means to an end, and not ends in themselves. In his second year, 1967, the Steelers regressed, winning only four games, with one tie.

Austin looked and acted like a coach, but that was all. In one game, the Steelers lined up to punt with ten men. The quarterback was calling signals before Cannonball Butler, the fleet little running back, realized he was part of the coverage team. Frantically, Butler dashed onto the field. He crossed in front of the kicker as the ball was snapped, intercepting its flight. Like a guided missile gone wrong, it bounced off his helmet.

In the history of football, has there ever been a more ludicrous special-teams play?

Pat Livingston of the *Pittsburgh Press* had sized up Austin immediately and did not shrink from putting the coach's feet to the fire. Austin never forgot or forgave. A good while later, when Vince Lombardi was coaching the Redskins, and Austin was back where he belonged, coaching Lombardi's offensive line, Livingston strolled into the Redskins' dressing room after a Pittsburgh-Washington game at Pitt Stadium, and Austin saw red. Showing the speed that had made him one of the NFL's quickest guards, he had an arm around Livingston's neck in a split second and with his free hand he punched Pat in the ribs. Lombardi needed help to separate them.

If AJR had listened to Dan, Austin would not have returned for the final year of his contract. "Austin must go ... now!" Dan said, asserting himself with new forcefulness. "Not yet," answered AJR. "We'd be the laughing stock of the league. And remember," he added, "we'd have to pay the guy. We'd have to pay his assistants. In full. For not working. No way."

Austin's obtuseness had kept him from noticing that he was close to the edge of the cliff. He put a rule in, on his own, barring visitors from the dressing room before a game. AJR had not been notified. On a Sunday before the Steelers played the Giants at Yankee Stadium, he was with the New York columnist Jimmy Breslin and invited him into the dressing room, along with his kids. Austin, glaring at them, made it clear they were unwelcome. So they left, but AJR had some words with his coach the next day. "Bill, I didn't know the dressing room was closed," he began. "Otherwise, I wouldn't have taken Breslin and his kids in there. I keep the rules. Now, Breslin is a guy who can walk into any dressing room in the league. But he picked ours. Let me tell you this, Bill. I said I keep the rules, and I do – if I know them. But there's something I want you to remember: I own this team. I don't care if you're playing the biggest football game in the history of the world. I own the team. And if I want to, I'll bring Alexander's ragtime band into the dressing room. I hope I'm making myself clear."

AJR always told his five sons: "Treat everybody as you would like to be treated yourselves. But don't allow anyone to mistake kindness for weakness."

In Austin's last year, AJR hired a new trainer, Ralph Berlin from the University of Kentucky. The coach there, Charley Bradshaw, had played at Kentucky for Bear Bryant. That he patterned himself after Bryant was therefore not surprising. John Michelosen had played for Jock Sutherland and tried to be Sutherland II. Austin never played for Vince Lombardi, but he coached under Lombardi and mimicked Lombardi.

Charley Bradshaw was a stern-faced ex-Marine and a combat veteran of World War II. His biographer in the Kentucky publicity department described him as "inwardly tough." Bryant, of course, was inwardly tough and outwardly tough. Bradshaw's inward toughness found expression on the practice field. In his first year at Kentucky, twenty-nine players quit the squad. "Some things," he said, "have to be paid for in blood, sweat, and tears. And sacrifice." One Kentucky player sustained a broken neck in a hitting drill, and it proved to be fatal. Another owed his life to Berlin's prompt treatment before the ambulance arrived, but was permanently crippled. The new trainer came to Pittsburgh, then, wise in the ways of demanding coaches.

On a hot day at the Steelers' pre-season training camp, Berlin watched from the sideline as Austin put the team through a "grass" drill. In full uniform, the players jogged in place until Austin blew his whistle. Then they dropped to the ground and immediately jumped up again, repeating the process *for* what seemed like forever. After the grass drill came a nutcracker drill, sometimes called the Oklahoma drill. In the nutcracker, offensive players and defensive players line up and slam into each other. This one lasted longer than the grass drill.

Next on the agenda was a scrimmage, the first offensive unit versus the first defensive unit. It was uncommon in the NFL, once the exhibition season had begun, for teams to scrimmage, and the Steelers had played two or three games, but Austin had a point to make. He was teaching his guys to be tough.

Heard from up close, the sound effects of contact give you a keener appreciation of what a violent game football is. The animal noises, the grunts, the thud of pad against pad tell the story. Five minutes into the scrimmage Berlin was watching came a sound of a different character. A cry of "Trainer! ... Ralph! "sent him hurrying onto the field. A starter was down; it looked serious. Almost at once, Berlin called for the "wagon." Off went the injured player to the dressing room, and then the scrimmage resumed without a pause.

And soon another player was down. A nose-and-mouth injury, front teeth knocked out, blood pouring onto his uniform. More work for the ambulance/station wagon, but no halt in the scrimmage until still another player collapsed.

This time there were curses from the players ... intermingled with the calls for Berlin. "Damn fool!" "Fucking asshole!" "He's ruining our season before it starts."

Right there, Berlin later said, was where the bottom fell out of Austin's last season. The Steelers lost their first six games and their last five. In between those losing streaks there were two wins and a tie. While the defeats were piling up, I attended a dinner of some kind at the Roosevelt Hotel with AJR. He asked me suddenly if I knew the coach at Notre Dame, Ara Parseghian. I said I did, but not well.

"But he knows who you are?"

"I think so."

"Well, go call him now," AJR said, "and ask if he'd like to talk to me about coaching the Steelers."

I was startled. Stalling for time, I said I'd have to go to the office, look up Parseghian's number, and use our own telephone.

Dad said, "Don't worry about that. Do it now! Go to the pay phone." There was one in the room. "Call information in South Bend. You can probably get him at home." I protested that Parseghian's home number was undoubtedly not listed.

AJR cut me off. "Just try it! Now!" I went to the pay phone.

To my astonishment, the call went right through. Parseghian was at home. Yes, he recalled meeting me. "To talk to your father about coaching the Steelers? Well, I'm flattered," he said, "but, you know, I'm very happy at Notre Dame. I hope to spend all of my coaching days here ... " He was very nice. He sent his regards to Dad. The whole conversation was over in three minutes.

To AJR, it was not a rebuff. "Coaching's a shaky business," he said. "Today you're on top. Tomorrow you're looking for a job. It doesn't hurt to ask."

The search for Austin's replacement had begun. From that time on, it was Dan's responsibility, which suited me to perfection. I had a mission of my own – to get so many good players the coaches could not screw them up.

Austin's firing took him by surprise. The Steelers' final game that year was in New Orleans. The day before, in a conference room at the team's hotel, Austin met with his coaching staff – "to talk about next season," as one assistant put it. Minutes after the meeting broke up, Austin got the news that he was through. He'd be spending "next season" he knew not where.

The Steelers lost to the Saints, 24-14, and on Monday morning AJR announced Austin's dismissal. While answering questions from the media, Austin choked up.

A few weeks later, I met him on the street. He was finishing up some business in Pittsburgh, he said. He asked about my wife and kids. On one of the radio stations that evening, the host of a sports talk show interviewed Austin. "How do you think the Steelers will do next season?" the radio guy asked. "Well," answered Austin, "as long as Art Rooney Junior is working in scouting the team will get better and better."

I was completely dumbfounded. After all, the man hated me – or so I thought. Over the next dozen years, we would meet by chance here and there, and he was never anything but friendly and courteous. To this day I wonder if I had the guy wrong – misjudged him as a person, I mean. I know with certainty what kind of coach he was, because his record speaks for itself.

Chapter 41

Fran Fogarty

The Forgartys and the Rooneys were distantly related. Fran Fogarty's father, John Fogarty, had been the head groundskeeper at Forbes Field for many years. Temperamentally, father and son were somewhat alike – quiet, laconic, and undemonstrative.

Fran rarely smiled or raised his voice. He was short and stocky but athletic enough to have played on the hockey team at Duquesne University in the heyday of hockey as an intercollegiate sport. He went from Duquesne to the Army and eventually into combat against the Germans in France. He was either a first or second lieutenant. I don't know any of the particulars or what kind of outfit Fran was in, but at some point the Germans took him captive.

Here are the rough details as he told them to me:

The German soldier who captured him – when and where and what the circumstances were I can't tell you - was a big, good-looking guy who spoke almost flawless English.

"I was sorry to hear about Chicago," he said.

"About Chicago?"

"Yes, that it's bombed out."

He'd been misinformed, Fran told him. "Neither Chicago nor any other American city has been bombed by the Germans, by the Japs, or by anyone else." Instantly, the German soldier's friendliness evaporated. With anger in his voice, he accused Fran of "propagandizing." From then on, Fran kept his mouth shut, which was never much of a problem for him.

With other captured Americans, he was herded onto a cattle car. The doors slammed shut and the train began to move – headed toward Germany, the POWs assumed. Before it had gone very far, Fran noticed a GI with a pen knife at work on a screw in the floor of the car. Fran asked him what he was doing.

"I'm gonna get these floorboards up, so we can escape."

"Escape? Through the floor? Don't you know we'd be killed by the wheels?" Fran said. "If we're going to escape we have to make a hole in one of the doors."

And that is exactly what they did. How it was possible, using only a pen knife, to remove enough bolts or carve an opening large enough for a man to slip through I'm not sure. Nor do I know how many escapees there were. Nor do I know if they jumped from the train while it was moving, not to mention if they all made the leap without being hurt or killed. Nor do I know if it was daytime or nighttime. At any rate, they escaped from the train and got into the countryside. Whether Fran was alone or with others when the French underground picked him up is something else I don't know. Characteristically, Fran just never talked about it a lot, and so I can't even guess at how long he remained with the underground or whether he took part in any sabotage. I know that in some manner he worked his way back to the American lines and was personally interrogated by General Patton.

He came to work for the Steelers immediately after the war. You could see right away that he was tough and smart. He looked and listened but never blabbed. It always surprised people to hear him break into song, this taciturn little bookkeeper who would fight for a dime. In the musical shows at

Duquesne, he'd been a part of the cast and he remembered the words to some Gilbert and Sullivan airs. Actually, his voice was not bad.

He dealt with the coaches and scouts in ways that AJR was disinclined to, reviewing their expense accounts minutely. "That's too much for gas," he would say. Or "That's too much for meals." An item like "miscellaneous" was certain to raise his hackles.

And yet there were coaches and scouts and players who regarded him as their friend. Others, like Fido Murphy, hated him. He could be curt with all of them, but he was AJR's man, doing AJR's bidding. The joke was that when he visited Shamrock Farm he counted the horses, the cows, and even the chickens. (Speaking of chickens, they disappeared from the farm after Jimmy McGee left. McGee was the trainer who bred and fought gamecocks.)

When Fogarty first came on board, the boxing club was still in existence and we also had a piece of a motorcycle raceway out in Heidelberg. Fogarty kept the books for everything. The motorcycle raceway was meant to be a dog track, but the man who laid it out miscalculated. The distance between the turns was so short that in a practice race before the track was to open, the dogs couldn't negotiate them. They floundered all over the place. Dad's interest in motorcycles being limited, he relied on Fogarty to make decisions for him. Motorcycle racing was not a part of our sports conglomerate very long.

More and more, Fogarty got to be AJR's alter ego, even to the point of looking after his stock-market investments. If there were money matters to be straightened out between AJR and one of the other NFL owners, Fogarty was empowered to act. George Marshall (who called him by every name but his own) wanted to trade somebody in the Redskins' front office for Fogarty, the way he would trade a football player. "That fellow," he said to AJR, "is so good he could work for me!"

He was so good that with Dad's approval he had a say-so in every aspect of the business, and he worked anonymously. Sometimes in newspaper stories about the signing of this player or that player, Fogarty's name would appear. But never once in all the years he was with the Steelers did anyone write a column or feature story about him.

As you might expect, Fogarty knew Forbes Field like the back of his hand. The son of the head groundskeeper would have a certain familiarity with the place, but Fran's expertise exceeded the bounds of the ordinary. On the few occasions we had a sellout at Forbes Field, and needed temporary stands to accommodate the crowd, Fogarty was in charge of measuring the seat space. He believed that fans of professional football were wider in the beam than fans of high school or college football and he factored that into his assessments. If the weather was cold he made an allowance of two inches for overcoats and heavier clothing. In September and October the seats measured eighteen inches across. In November and December the figure was twenty inches. I remember hearing him call down from the end of a row at the top, "The guy who gets this seat better be half-assed – there's only fifteen inches left for him."

Fogarty's caustic side came out when he negotiated player contracts, but there were players he liked – Fran Rogel, Joe Krupa, and Jack Butler; anybody who gave one hundred percent. Not, heaven forbid, that they got more money than the others. His esteem for them paid off in respect, which was something.

After his wife, a fine lady, developed heart trouble, he made a thorough study of all the health-insurance plans, talked at some length with everybody concerned – the insurance agents, the team doctor, the Internal Revenue Service – and worked up a better deal for our players and front-office people.

The team doctor, John Best, looked like Robert Mitchum in a white smock. He was gruff; he smoked and drank. During a pre-season game a player was smacked in the mouth and had to be taken to the dressing room. Doc Best would need help, he could see, but the game was still in progress, requiring the presence of the trainers on the field. So Doc called for Fogarty and gave him a short set of instructions: "Don't worry about anything – just do as I tell you." With Fogarty's assistance, Doc gave the player some painkiller and stitched up his cuts. "Fran Fogarty," he told everyone afterward, "is by far the best nurse I've ever had, and I mean it. I'd like to have him in my operating room when I perform major surgery."

Is it any wonder we came to believe that Fogarty could do anything?

Among the many hats he wore was that of traveling secretary. For games out of town, he made the airline and hotel reservations and arranged for the ground transportation. His network of hotel managers and food-service people was vast. Fogarty and Lou Kroeck, the United Airlines representative, made an efficient team that functioned especially well during the years when our preseason schedule took us to places that were off the beaten path – places like Shreveport and Fresno, Salem, Oregon, and Omaha. One shot and you're out, never to return.

On all trips, there were petty thieves and petty politicians and venal policemen to deal with. In towns and large cities, the cops could be as worrisome as the thieves, stealing footballs and jerseys and anything else they could get their hands on. Of course, the politicians always wanted tickets. So did certain cops, and in some towns they expected to have their palms greased.

Getting seriously injured players back to Pittsburgh was another problem, and then along with the official team party you had the hangers-on and the relatives, not to mention the players' girlfriends. On occasion even a coach or two had a girlfriend to be looked after. Somehow Fogarty handled all this and made it look easy.

If sufficiently provoked, he would lash out at the hangers-on, unless their degree of intimacy with the Chief protected them. Special cases received special treatment. One year our first draft pick, Art Davis, a halfback from Mississippi State, was joined by his wife, a former Miss Mississippi, in a Southern tank town. Fogarty assigned me to pick her up at the hotel in a taxi, and he saw to it that our tickets to the game were the best available. "Forget about your other duties," he said. "Just take care of Mrs. Davis." Well, Mrs. Davis's personality and charm matched her looks. Her husband was never much of a football player, but in the matrimonial department he could not be faulted.

There were also women of a different type, for whom the players would demand rooms and tickets. "What am I," Fogarty would yell, "a pimp?" – and not without reason. Delivering tickets to one of these bimbos, he found the door of her hotel room ajar. He tapped it gently. "Mister Fogarty?" a voice called from within. "Come right in." Fogarty opened the door a little wider. "Mister Fogarty? I'm in the bathroom. Just bring the tickets in and put them on the dresser." He did so, and turned to leave, when "out jumped the devil," as he put it. The player's dream girl emerged from the bathroom in the skimpiest underwear obtainable. Fogarty flew out the door. "That girl was a photography nut," he explained to some of us later, too shocked to keep silent about it. "She might have had a camera with her. She might have been trying to blackmail me."

He did not hear the last of the ribbing for some time to come.

On another trip, Fogarty shared a suite with one of the coaches. There was a knock at the door. Alone for the moment, Fogarty opened it, and the coach's sweet patootie stormed in. She was looking for her boyfriend to complain about the way he'd been treating her. With nobody else to chastise, she turned all her wrath on Fogarty. She grabbed his briefcase, containing tickets, cash, keys, and documents, and flung it across the room. Papers and heavier objects landed everywhere. "She spilled all my 'brains,'" Fogarty said. Before the irate lady could trash the rest of the room, he hustled her out into the hall. Then and there in Fogarty's mind, that particular coach was finished. "He isn't our kind of guy," Fogarty declared to a few of us.

At the end of the season the coach got his walking papers.

Meanwhile, the winds of change were blowing hard. Dan, who had an accounting degree from Duquesne just as Fogarty did, and was taking over as a sort of chief executive officer, wanted a big national firm like Arthur Andersen to audit the books every year. Perhaps the time had come, Dan thought, for the Steelers to modernize their accounting procedures. And that was all right with him, Fogarty said. But how would it suit AJR to have a group of outsiders poking their noses into his football affairs and all of the other things he controlled?

Fogarty wondered about that. He'd been the man with the books for twenty years or more. Like it or not, though, professional football was becoming big business. In just another year the Steelers would be in a new, publicly-financed stadium. Fogarty did not live to see it. He appeared to be imperturbable, but the pressures he must have felt were building up. At the age of 51, on the day he attended his daughter's wedding, Fran Fogarty died of a heart attack.

Go-Between

Fran Fogarty's death left a void in the organization, which Ed Kiely proceeded to fill. From 1969 on, he was AJR's sounding board.

Ed had been an intelligence officer in the South Pacific during World War II and a reporter in New York City for the now defunct International News Service. He came to the Steelers as a public relations man. Other PR guys churned out statistics and bits of factual information for the sportswriters. Ed saw his job a little differently. Statistics, the condition of injured players, lineup changes, press releases, and so on were never his top priorities. Ed was much more of a big-picture guy. The commodity he chose to sell was not the team, it was AJR. And the place to do that, he believed, was on the road.

Long before everybody else caught on, he saw that AJR had a special brand of charisma. From over-familiarity, the Pittsburgh writers and broadcasters took the owner of the Steelers for granted. Among themselves, they agreed that he was down to earth, generous, straightforward, a man with a colorful, adventurous past. In the world he inhabited, high rollers, finaglers, cut-throats, and con artists had attempted to outsmart him and had failed. The reporters had heard all the stories, heard them too often. Where was the news value, anyway? And, besides, to mention Art Rooney in any favorable context was to infuriate large segments of the public.

This was because, year after year, the Steelers kept losing football games. As the owner of such a team, then, how could Art Rooney be the warm, intelligent, philanthropic, completely likable person the media sometimes dared to portray? It wasn't possible.

Even if Art Rooney did have good qualities, the disgraceful things that happened to his team on Sunday afternoons in the fall made them irrelevant, his detractors seemed to feel. Since about 1955 or 1956, pro football fans everywhere had been investing their own self-esteem in the fortunes of whatever team they identified with. Each defeat was a slap in the face, a personal affront. When the team lost, the fans lost. And who was to blame? Management, obviously. In the case of the Steelers, there could be no question about it. Management – in other words, AJR – was either too cheap to pay the salaries of good players or too dumb to recognize who they were. Too cheap AND too dumb, the chances were.

Aware of this attitude – how could he not be? – Ed Kiely ventured afield. Kiely was from Morningside, a Black Irishman, so-called, dark rather than fair, one of the Irish whose ancestry goes back, if the fabulists have it right, to shipwrecked sailors from the Spanish Armada, cast up on the shores of Ireland at the end of the sixteenth century. Ed's years in the Army and in New York City had given him an air of sophistication. He knew how to dress. He knew how to deal with maitre d's at high-priced restaurants. He knew how to meet people and he knew the kinds of people it was worthwhile to cultivate. If they were media people, they worked in New York. They remembered Ed Kiely from his time with the International News Service. They sat still for his presentation of AJR, and through him they got acquainted with the subject himself, and that's all it took.

At winning over the press, there was never a sports figure more effective than AJR. His secret was being one hundred percent natural. He genuinely liked people, even newspapermen, and they responded in kind. When Roy Blount, who prided himself on his objectivity, wrote an Art Rooney story for *Sports Illustrated*, his colleagues at the magazine – strangers to AJR – derided it as saccharine. Later, in his book "About Three Bricks Shy of a Load," Blount admitted having looked for discreditable things to say about the Chief to sort of balance the scales, but none of it turned out to be damning, and so the book merely added to the legend.

New York being the communications capital, if you could make it there you not only could make it anywhere, you could and did make it everywhere. Writers in the hinterlands take their cue from the writers in New York. Kiely understood this and expertly set the process in motion.

My first impression of Kiely, I have to say, was negative. He came across as condescending, I thought. Well read and well informed, he appeared to regard the coaches as his mental inferiors, "kidding them on the square" about their phys-ed degrees. In truth, there were coaches with master's degrees, whereas Kiely himself had left Pitt before earning a bachelor's degree.

For another thing, I felt that he considered me an upstart – the owner's son with no appreciation of what the older front-office people were contributing. He had the Walt Kiesling mind-set on Steeler culture: "Sure, we like to win as much as anybody does, but there are limitations to what we can do here, you know ..." Offering many good reasons why something could not be done rather than one good reason why something had to be done, the Kieslings and the Kielys were in my view holding us back.

"You're too tough on Kiely," AJR would tell me, and the longer I knew Ed the better I liked him. Whatever our differences may have been, I came to think of Ed Kiely as a real fine person and a gentleman.

By the 1970s, Kiely was out of publicity. His hand-picked successor, Joe Gordon, brought energy to the job – more than we ever had seen. Kiely, moving up in the hierarchy, became, in effect, AJR's right-hand man. When the Chief was into his seventies, Kiely read and sorted his mail and answered some of the letters. He wrote AJR's speeches and stood in for him, on occasion, at dinners and public affairs. "Art," I would hear him say, "you should look into this," or "Art, here's something you should take care of right away."

Around the NFL, people knew that Kiely had AJR's ear. Using him as a go-between, they could get things back to the Chief, and this was now one of his major functions. No further need existed to keep the name of Art Rooney before the public. Thanks in large part to Kiely, he was one of the best-known football men in America. Thanks to his own personality – and in no small measure to four quick Super Bowl victories – he was better known than he ever had been. His thoughts about this he kept to himself. He liked the good publicity but never once lifted a finger to encourage it, I am sure, having too much sense to believe that people came to the games to see the owners and not the football players.

Kiely's attractive, talented wife, Pat, was the first woman in Pittsburgh to anchor a television news show. She developed mental and physical problems and died before reaching old age. This was difficult for Ed, but he sent his daughter Kathy and his sons Tim and Kevin to excellent universities and all three had successful media careers, Kathy in journalism, the two boys in television.

After AJR's death in 1988, Kiely no longer had a niche in the organization, but he continued for a while to spend three or four days a week at his desk, not the last of the original front-office cadre but the last of the generation that followed.

Chapter 42

A Sense of Belonging

At our St. Vincent training camp one hot August day in 1969, the *Pittsburgh Post-Gazette's* Jack Sell flagged me down.

"Hey, Artie," he said, "I've been interviewing Bob Adams." I knew that to interview Bob Adams, a rookie tight end from a college called University of the Pacific, standing in line was not required. We had signed the kid as a free agent, and he had come to St. Vincent unheralded. But he was tough and smart and mature beyond his years and had caught Sell's eye in practice. "He told me you scouted him out in California," Sell went on. "He said you gave him a lot of encouragement." Which was true. When I heard that Adams was undrafted, I had called him and consoled him and offered him a contract. All of this seemed to astonish Sell. "You know, Artie," he said, "I owe you an apology. I thought you were on the payroll for family reasons. Because your dad wanted to keep you off the streets. I had no idea you actually worked – went out on the road as far away as the West Coast and scouted these guys, actually saw them play and sent in reports."

I could tell that the revelation pleased him. I was pleased that he was pleased, for Sell was a crusty old skeptic, but less than flattered to think that though I had been in charge of scouting since 1965 – four years – I was just now beginning to acquire some credibility with a sportswriter covering the team.

Adams turned out to be a good tight end, if not a great one. What he had that we liked was character - both off-the-field character and football character. As I define football character, it's a product of intelligence and heart, which are difficult for a scout to evaluate. All you can do is watch and wait.

You look for a moment of truth. Bob Ferguson came to the Steelers in 1962 with a big reputation that earned him a big paycheck – what we thought of as big money back then. In the Woody Hayes offense at Ohio State – "three yards and a cloud of dust" – Ferguson had been the ideal fullback. He could get three yards when they were needed, and there was nothing more that Buddy Parker wanted from him. Though he was built like a little bull, he couldn't block. He couldn't catch passes. But doing what he did best – hitting into the line of scrimmage – he kept his short, thick legs churning and was hard to drag down.

The fullback position appeared to be his for the taking. Then came a telltale incident. Ferguson skipped a meeting and was late the same day for practice, antagonizing Parker's quarterback, Bobby Layne. To antagonize Layne, the team leader, was bad news, but Parker gave Ferguson playing time the next week against Detroit, and at one point, after picking up his usual three yards, he broke free, which he did not often do. Coming on fast to meet him, linebacker Carl Brettschneider delivered a perfectly executed rising blow.

When his playing career had ended and Brettschneider was a scout for Detroit, we got to be friends. The hit on Ferguson, he told me, was "under and up." He meant that he came in under Ferguson's shoulder pads with tremendous momentum and leverage and drove them up into his face. The ball went one way and Ferguson another. According to Brettschneider, as Ferguson lay on the ground, dazed, he recited scripture.

Apparently convinced that the meek shall inherit the earth, he was never again much of a football player. Not far into his second season, 1963, Buddy Parker traded him to the Vikings. The year after that, he was back in Ohio, operating a skid loader on a construction job.

For the scouts who recommended Ferguson, it would not have been easy to foresee that one hard thump would be his complete undoing. Most often it's the intangibles, the psychological stuff, that scouts are unable to fathom.

I was in my first year on the job when we drafted Larry Gagner, and I agreed with all the reports, which told us he couldn't miss. A guard from the University of Florida, Gagner was big, fast, and strong. He was something else, too – over-impressed with his own ability, as we discovered too late. Florida played in a bowl game that year and lost. When Jack Butler met with Gagner afterwards to sign him, Gagner put the blame for Florida's defeat on his teammates. Because of their shortcomings, his valiant one-man effort had gone for naught, as he told it.

Wait a minute, Butler said to himself, do we know what we're doing here? In fact we didn't. Gagner made it through four full seasons with the Steelers (1966-1969), but, lacking heart for the pro game, he was never the player we expected him to be.

On our teams in the 1960s, journeymen like Gagner could prolong their careers by staying out of trouble off the field. That was about all it took. We had a veteran defensive tackle from a mid-level conference in the West, a big, good-looking guy, who, as big, good-looking guys sometimes do, got enmeshed with a girl. It was what in those days we called a predicament (I am trying not to be blunt). Even as late as the sixties, that sort of thing could be serious business. Compounding the offense, AJR had heard about it from the girl's employer, a close friend. He summoned me to his office and said, "That guy from out West. What a yegg. Is he any good? Can he play?" We were changing coaches, and I told my dad what I thought – that the guy had been getting by up to then on size and strength, but was too slow for the new system about to be installed. AJR said, "All right. We don't need him."

At St. Vincent that summer, the veteran defensive tackle failed to survive the cut.

Go-To Guy

Long before the end of the 1968 football season, AJR had made up his mind to get rid of Bill Austin. I therefore wanted no help from Austin or anyone on his staff in preparing for the 1969 draft.

Scouting had for years been a haphazard business with the Steelers. We relied for much of our information on assistant coaches, part-time bird dogs, and tips from old friends. This was work that belonged in the hands of full-time professional scouts. A man whose reputation and livelihood depend on the quality of his judgment will do a better job for you every time.

The reports of Jack Butler's Blesto scouts were available to us by now, but available also to the Bears, Lions, Eagles, and Vikings. Technologically, Blesto was miles ahead of us. Its computers broke down the information on prospects in ways and in combinations of ways that would answer many of the questions a personnel director might have. We were doing some of these things ourselves, but doing them "by hand," a slow, tedious, outdated process I was ready to junk.

Meanwhile, with Austin as good as gone and no one yet hired to take his place, I would be organizing, evaluating, interpreting, and then reorganizing the data we needed for the upcoming draft on my own. I had the Blesto material, yes. And Austin's assistants would be fanning out to the post-season all-star games. AJR, out of the goodness of his heart, was giving them a chance to network for new jobs. They would turn in reports; I would read the reports and debrief the coaches, yes. But their observations, I knew, would be of limited usefulness.

Nor did I want any input from the new coach, whoever it might be, and his assistants. I made this clear to AJR and I made it clear, profanely, to Dan. I was fully prepared and in charge. I had the prospects rated by position; more important, I had them rated, best to worst, regardless of position. Of course you didn't waste much time on the players at the bottom of the list – the rejects – but the rejects were part of it all. Dan Towler and Johnny Unitas were rejects who became all-pros. I had served my apprenticeship, I knew what I was doing. I was 32 years old and self-confident to the point of obnoxiousness.

But I'm getting ahead of myself.

My "go-to" guy for information and guidance would be Butler. He knew how to evaluate the reports of his scouts. In Butler's opinion, the critical factors in the makeup of a prospect were toughness, production, and NFL-type athletic ability, the little bit extra that separates the pro from the college player. Jack could look at a kid from Grambling or Alcorn or North Texas State and recognize that he had what it takes to make the transition, and he could look at an All-American from the Big Ten or Pac Eight and foresee a short, undistinguished NFL career. As Paul Brown said of the great Jim Brown, "When you have a gun, you shoot it." That was how I felt about leaning on Butler.

While it was true that the other Blesto teams I have mentioned also had access to Butler and his people, I perceived a difference between my attitude – I can't be modest about this – and theirs. Ralph Kohl, Butler's national scout, told me that some of the Blesto subscribers he worked for did not even know how to interview him.

"They'll ask me a question and then not wait for the answer," Kohl said. He described a meeting in the office of the Chicago Bears that opened with Abe Gibron, the head coach, asking about a player Kohl had scouted. Before Ralph could get two words out, George Halas, the Bears' owner, and Muggsy Halas, his son, interrupted him to offer their own opinions, Gibron countered with his, and the three men started shouting at one another. Presently Gibron's assistants chimed in, and the babble continued for ten or twelve minutes, becoming steadily more obscene. When at last the disputants ran out of breath, Gibron, turning to Kohl, said, "Good report, Ralph – nice job," and ushered him to the door.

"Don't get me wrong – I love those guys," Kohl said. "It's just that they're wasting their investment in Blesto."

There would be none of that in the Steelers' draft room, I resolved. We would prepare, prepare, and prepare some more. We would be organized and organized some more. The arguments and the bickering would take place at the draft development meetings. At the draft itself, unless Dan, AJR, or the head coach asked a question, only one voice would be heard – mine.

Looking and Listening

In the fall of 1968 I was doing double duty as a scout. Primarily, my job was to evaluate football players. Acting on instructions from AJR and Dan, I also scouted head-coaching prospects. Everywhere I went, I made discreet, low-key inquiries.

Even before the start of the season, we knew that Bill Austin would not be returning. Dan, in fact, had wanted to fire him at the end of the 1967 season, but AJR counseled patience. None of this had leaked to the media.

Meanwhile, in my conversations about coaches with other NFL scouts, I kept hearing one name again and again. It was that of a young assistant with the Baltimore Colts, Chuck Noll. The scouts all gave me the same feedback: "Real decent guy ... Smart as can be ... Gonna be a top NFL head coach some day ..."

I would sometimes ask my informants for the best two or three prospects, and the name Chuck Knox frequently came up. Knox, an assistant with the Detroit Lions, was a Western Pennsylvania guy from Sewickley. But whereas *most* of the scouts mentioned Knox, *all* of the scouts mentioned Noll.

Upton Bell, the Colts' head scout, and his brother Bert Junior recommended Noll in the strongest possible terms, not only to me but to Tim (a close friend of theirs) and to AJR. I don't doubt that Joe Paterno of Penn State was Dan's first choice and could have had the job if he wanted it, but when Joe indicated he was not interested, Noll's name went to the top of the list.

Subject to AJR's approval, Dan would make the final decision. As personnel director, I did not have a vote, but I was forceful about stating my views. I emphasized two things. I felt that our new head coach should be absolutely color blind and absolutely committed to building a team through the draft.

Bill, Ralph, and Rhoda

When I say I had no help from anyone in preparing for the 1969 draft, I am doing a disservice to three important friends – Bill Nunn, Jr., Ralph Berlin, and Rhoda Duffy.

Since 1966, Bill Nunn, Jr., had been covering the small Negro colleges in the Southeast and Southwest for the Steelers. He was not a football guy, but a newspaperman – sports editor of the *Pittsburgh Courier*. Moreover, he had not played football in college. His game was basketball, and he must have been pretty good at it. While Nunn was at West Virginia State, the team hardly ever lost, and he missed no chance to remind me that the Harlem Globetrotters had tried to sign him up.

I could not hold his résumé against him, not when I compared it with mine. After all, I had been just a so-so football player on a college team in the second or third tier, and I owed my job to my mom and dad. Joe Krupa remembered watching me tutor Nunn in his first year with the Steelers. "Artie, you taught him everything," Krupa said. If that is true, I would call it a classic case of the blind leading the blind. All I knew about scouting in 1966 I had learned from picking other people's brains, including Krupa's.

At our first meeting, Nunn told me that he never had been around a loser and was "not about to start now." I could have put that down to braggadocio, but he reminded me in certain ways of myself. We both had something to prove, Nunn and I. In a time of deep racial prejudice, Nunn was a black man, with all the baggage that being black entailed. And I, of course, was "the owner's son," which carried its own kind of baggage. We knew there were skeptics eager to see us screw up, and we were equally determined that it wasn't going to happen.

As the 1969 draft approached, I asked Nunn to help me get our Blesto reports in order. I still had my cubbyhole in the Roosevelt Hotel, and we met there one day. Ralph Berlin, the trainer, was lending a hand, too, as he sometimes did between the end of one season and the start of the next. I needed all the assistance I could get, having recently lost my secretary. Her departure was unexpected. Pleading stress and her forthcoming marriage, she had simply walked out. The timing of her resignation puzzled me just a little. Why had she not waited to collect her Christmas bonus? I wondered. Anyway, we were minutes into our task this January day when Berlin looked up from the files and said, "Art, a lot of reports from Blesto seem to be missing."

"Reports missing?"

"Yeah, we've got spring reports on a lot of these guys, but no follow-up reports in the fall."

Thoroughly nonplussed, I got in touch with Jack Butler. All the fall reports had been sent to us, he told me.

I said, "Well, they're not here."

As chief scout, I was constantly on the road. I took meticulous notes at the Blesto meetings. I took meticulous notes of my conversations with Nunn. But it just wasn't possible for me to keep an eagle eye on the Blesto reports that came to the office. That was the job of my secretary, the one who had left.

Instead of calling her to ask what she had done with those reports, I procrastinated. Frankly, I had been glad to see the last of her, and our relations were such that I was fearful of losing my temper. Berlin, meanwhile, took me off the hook.

His fetish for tidiness, acquired in the military, impelled him one day to declare that my office was a mess. "I'm going to sweep the floor," he announced. "Where's the broom closet?"

I pointed to a door in the corner of the room. Berlin pulled it open, and out tumbled all of the missing Blesto reports. In her haste to get to the altar, my secretary had streamlined our filing system.

The incident opened my eyes. I could handle the 1969 draft without any help from our coaches, but not without an efficient office manager, I now realized. A call to the Kelly Girls brought Rhoda Duffy of Homestead into my life.

Rhoda Duffy was not a "girl," but a mature married woman. She was with us until she retired, in 1978, and there were no further breakdowns in clerical procedure. Rhoda Duffy loved the Rooneys and she loved Bill Nunn and the feeling in both cases was mutual. Her presence gave me comfort because it proved that I could learn from my mistakes.

Chapter 43

Out of the Loop

The 1969 draft was scheduled for late January. In the middle of the month I attended a Blesto meeting somewhere and got back to our offices in the Roosevelt Hotel at a little after noon on the following day. Ed Kiely or Fran Fogarty – I am unable to be more precise – informed me as soon as I walked through the door that AJR and Dan were with Chuck Noll in the Sylvan Room.

Noll, it appeared, had the inside track for our vacant head coaching job, but neither my father nor my brother had bothered to clue me in about the interview. Just a few months earlier, neither Kiely nor Fogarty would have bothered to do so, either. Not without a feeling of gratification, I reflected that someone, at least, believed I had a stake in all this.

My determination to exclude the new coach, whoever it might be, from taking part in the draft was no secret. I had told AJR again and again that I wanted full authority in making our selections. Actually, I was hoping the draft would be out of the way before the new coach came on board.

AJR dismissed all my arguments. "I'm not saying the job is too much for you," he said. "I'm not saying you couldn't handle it alone, and handle it well. But there are other issues involved here. There'd be trouble from the press and the public. I've been in this business a long time. Just get it into your head that we are going to do things my way."

When I saw he was adamant about hiring a coach as soon as he could, and giving him a strong voice in the draft, my heart sank. If the new guy resembled Bill Austin – an iron-willed, hard-headed commanding-officer type with firm ideas of his own – all my work and preparation would go to waste.

The approach I favored was a simple one: Draft the best athlete available. The hell with drafting to fill a certain position. There were NFL coaches who looked at positions where they were thin and tried to reinforce them through the draft. There was no better way, I thought, to lose the prospective superstars and pack your roster with garden-variety talent.

Catering to the fans could be just as destructive. Terry Hanratty from Butler was the star of the 1968 Notre Dame team, a quarterback and a real nice kid. We had the No.4 pick in the first round, and if we listened to our fans we'd take Hanratty. But in no sense did I consider him the fourth best player – or even the fourth best senior – in the country. The draft was not a popularity contest; it was a mechanism, I believed, for improving your team.

Something else that concerned me was the ticklish subject of racism. I remembered dialogues from the past word for word:

"Yeah, well ... we've already drafted three of them in the first six rounds."

"But, Coach, this kid is special. I don't know why he's still on the board. We have him rated higher than our third-round pick ... Trouble? ... No, he's a kid who stays out of trouble ... Injuries? No, there haven't been any. And don't worry about the military. He's safe – he has a wife and a child to support. Eddie Robinson told me in confidence he's better than that other guy from Grambling who went to the Giants last year in the second round, and Robinson coached them both. This draft is like an auction, Coach. Knowing when to draft a player is one of the secrets. Let's go for him now."

"Well, you make it sound good, but I'm looking for a defensive end, not a linebacker. I like this kid at Alabama."

"Coach, we have the Alabama guy rated as the one hundred and tenth best player in the draft. The Grambling kid is our forty-sixth best player."

"Listen, *Artie*. I'm the one who'll be coaching these guys, the one who'll be out on the field with them every day. So we're taking the Alabama kid. Maybe your ace from Grambling will be there in the eighth round. We'll talk about it then."

(Head coach turns on his heel and exits stage left.)

This and other scenarios kept playing through my mind. AJR didn't get it. Dan did. He was committed, like me, to building through the draft. But he was also committed, like AJR, to a quick resolution of our search for a new head coach. And he had worked just as hard on his interviews as I had on the draft.

Knowing the game was up, I could do only one thing. Welcome or not welcome, I was going to barge in on the Sylvan Room meeting, see what was happening, and take a stand if I had to.

Elbowing In

AJR and Dan were surprised, just a little, to see me. They were with Noll at the big round table – the Chief's table, where he liked to hold court. AJR introduced me, and Noll stood up to shake hands. We were the same height, about 6 feet 1. He had the wide, compact, thick-necked build of an offensive lineman, fair skin, a broad face, and light brown hair. I knew how old he was – 36 – from my reading in press guides.

There were three empty chairs at the table, and I took the one next to Dan. On the face of a clock, I'd have been at seven, with Dan at six, Noll at five, and AJR at four. They picked up their conversation where I guess they had left off, chatting idly about Noll's boss, Don Shula. I wondered if AJR remembered the advice Buddy Parker had offered him before parting company with the Steelers. "Find yourself a good defensive coach like that Don Shula fellow over in Baltimore," he had said. Even then, in his second year as head coach of the Colts, Shula was impressing other football men. AJR began to cultivate his friendship, and now it was Shula's recommendation, more than anything else, that seemed to have sold him on Noll.

The way Shula described Noll, they were replicas of each other. "He's your kind of guy," Shula had told AJR. "Smart. Serious. Hard-working. *A good defensive coach.*"

The similarities went even deeper. Both Shula and Noll were Catholic (being Catholic raised your status with AJR). Both were from Cleveland. Both had played football at small Catholic colleges in Ohio, Shula at John Carroll, Noll at Dayton. In the NFL, both had played for their home-town team, Cleveland, and were coached by super organizer Paul Brown. As assistant coaches, both had been in charge of defensive units.

I listened for a while to the table talk. It had turned from Shula himself to the Colts' surprising defeat in their recently played Super Bowl game with the New York Jets. When would they finish breaking the ice? Noll, in his demeanor, was reserved, almost formal. Don Shula had called him AJR's kind of guy, but AJR liked people who were friendly and open.

I took a deep breath. This job interview, if that's what it was, appeared to be going nowhere. For weeks I had lost sleep over the draft. The fear that we'd end up with another Bill Austin, or for that matter another Buddy Parker, had me paranoid. It was time to end the sparring, time to forget about niceties. Plunging in heavily, I said, "Coach, what are your feelings about black players?"

Dan let me know with a frown that I had overstepped.

AJR assumed his poker face – not a good sign.

Noll said, "What do you mean?"

I said, "Well, some coaches seem to think you can have too many of them."

Noll's expression hardened. He said, "Look, all I want are top athletes who can learn. They can be black or white or any other color. If they can learn, I won't have any trouble coaching them." His voice, which was light but assertive, for the first time had an edge to it.

AJR was glaring at me now, but I couldn't be stopped. I told of my visits to black schools in the South and of the many great athletes and nice kids I had met. Noll answered that he, too, had been to the black colleges and also had met great athletes and good people. Almost baring his teeth, he said, "I don't believe in quotas. On any team I coach there'll be none of that. With me, the quality of the person is major, but I want athletic skills, too. I've seen films of the Steelers, and there's a need for team speed."

AJR and Dan nodded in agreement, and to lighten the atmosphere AJR tossed off a humorous anecdote. I sensed that the mood was changing, so I popped another question to Noll.

"How do you feel about building a team and maintaining a team through the draft?"

AJR and Dan squirmed in their chairs. I braced myself for a kick beneath the table from Dan, but it never came.

Buddy Parker, I reminded Noll, had traded away a big piece of our future for "now." He had done OK with that philosophy, but no more than OK, and only for a while. Then the wheels fell off.

Noll said exactly what I wanted him to say – that going with top young athletes who are coachable was the right path to take. As we soon would find out, primarily Noll was a teacher.

"When I was with Sid Gillman in the AFL," he said – Gillman had coached the Los Angeles Chargers, precursors of the San Diego Chargers – "we developed a lot of good players who came to us in the draft. I don't see a problem in doing that with Pittsburgh. You only have to be patient."

This put me at ease.

Then Noll added, "But I won't be selling out to the draft. There are times when a trade is the best thing to do."

Whoa! Could this guy be a Parker in disguise? I felt my paranoia returning. But there was more that I wanted to know.

"What do you think of the Blesto group?" I asked. "Jack Butler does a terrific job ... "

Noll cut me off.

"Scouting groups have their place," he said. "They can be very good at collecting basic information: height, weights, speed. They can separate the prospects in the draft according to ability. But you need your own people to look at these players and determine where they would fit into your organization. After all, Blesto is scouting for five or six teams. Practically speaking, their scouts can't be expected to know exactly what each team is looking for. It's asking too much."

Now I was really getting nervous.

"Well, Coach," I said, sounding argumentative even to myself, "we don't have enough scouts to cover all the players in the country – cover them in depth. I mean the down-the-line guys. There are sleepers out there in the sixth to eighth rounds, and they have to be dug out." I let it go at that, unwilling to put things more bluntly. In truth, we relied on Blesto for economic reasons. We couldn't afford the big scouting staffs the rich teams had. But to say that to Noll, with AJR listening, would be a mistake. Poor-mouthing was no way to present ourselves to this man.

Like the rest of the teams in the NFL, we used our assistant coaches as scouts. I felt that some of them were capable, or at least energetic; the majority merely went through the motions. I had never seen an assistant coach fired or even bawled out for writing a bad scouting report. The year that AJR put me in charge I was going over a draft list with Buddy Parker's coaches and one of them asked why we did not have Jim Grabowski of Illinois rated No.1 among the running backs. When I started to explain, he said curtly, "How can any back who gains a thousand yards in the Big Ten not be a star in the NFL?" Before I could continue, Dick Haley, an injured Steeler defensive back who was working that year as a part-time scout, spoke up. He answered the coach in two words: "Bob Ferguson." I repeated that story to Noll, and he almost smiled. He said, "I'm an assistant coach myself. I saw Jim Grabowski, too. And I didn't like him much, either."

As far as the Chief was concerned, my probing had gone far enough. "Chuck," he said, looking at Noll but intending his words for me, "our next coach will have his assistants involved in the draft as much as he sees fit. And the final say on the draft and on trades will belong to him and nobody else." Tacitly, he was telling me to shut up. This is Dan's show, not yours, he was saying. I was like the camel who got his nose into the tent. If AJR could help it, and he could, the camel's hump would remain outside.

From then until the meeting adjourned I was silent. Clearly my performance had been annoying to AJR.

There was only one more coach for Dan to interview – Nick Skorich, an assistant with the Browns and a former assistant with the Steelers who had played guard for Steeler teams in the late 1940s. Nick was head coaching material. When his chance came in Cleveland, he would prove it. But in his interview with Dan he eliminated himself by insisting on a deal that would make him the de facto general manager as well as head coach. As far as AJR and Dan were concerned, that settled it. Chuck Noll was their man.

Knute Knowledge

Chuck Noll's home town, Cleveland, was similar in many ways to Pittsburgh. Both were northern industrial cities in various stages of decay but energetically remaking themselves. Noll came from working-class people. So did the Rooneys. Though the family was now affluent, AJR's five sons had grown up in a working-class neighborhood, a neighborhood once populated by millionaires. AJR and Kass continued to live there, occupying a well-kept-up nineteenth-century mansion. He wanted us to believe we were "salt-of-the-earth folk," said John and Pat. By salt of the earth, he meant "poor," they explained. The twins weren't falling for that line of gab, but took care not to flaunt their subversiveness. It was the state of one's mind, not the state of one's pocketbook, that counted with AJR.

He sent his sons to a Marianist high school and to small Catholic colleges, in my case a Benedictine college. Charles Henry Noll, born in the same year as my brother Dan – 1932 – attended a Benedictine high school and a small Marianist college. He devoutly subscribed to what the Marianist Brothers taught, as did we, although some of us, in our habits of speech, did not reflect it. Our zeal for football, like his, matched in fervor the zeal we all felt for religion.

So in the ways I have just enumerated it was true, as Don Shula had said, that Noll was the Rooneys' kind of guy. In other respects we could not have been much more different.

The Rooneys were gregarious. They were story-tellers, always ready with an anecdote. Perhaps I should except Dan, who was more like Uncle George McNulty, we thought, than like his forebears on the Rooney side. But I'm straying off my subject – the disconnect between a few of us, anyway, and Noll.

Our new coach was all business. Aside from football, his main interests were music – classical music – food, and wine. He was focused and self-directed. In conversation, he tended to be didactic. His coaching associates called him The Pope, because he spoke with an air of infallibility. His manner discouraged small talk. AJR, who prided himself on being able to communicate easily with anyone, from presidents of the United States to Federal Street winos, confessed that in the company of Noll he was ill at ease. Beyond matters that concerned the football team, they had little to say to each other.

At the University of Dayton, Noll was a good student as well as a good football player. In jest, I once boasted to Noll and Jack Butler that the professors at St. Vincent never had cut me a break. "I had to earn my degree," I said. "You guys wouldn't know about that. You went to school on athletic scholarships." Butler saw at once that I was being facetious, but Noll promptly rose to the bait. Dayton, he informed me, was a serious institution of learning. He said he had earned his good grades by hard work. For Butler's entertainment, and my own, I pretended to be skeptical. The longer I kept the joke alive, the more staunch Noll became in defending the integrity of his school.

Playing linebacker and guard, Noll was a Little All-American at Dayton, and Paul Brown drafted him in one of the late rounds. In addition to playing linebacker for Cleveland, Noll was a "messenger guard." Brown called every play in every game and delivered them to the quarterback by way of Noll and another lineman. Alternating, they would run back and forth between the bench and the huddle. Noll disliked this role and disliked the term "messenger boy" so much that as coach of the Steelers he entrusted all the play calling to his quarterbacks.

On a red-eye flight from the West Coast, Paul Bixler, an assistant coach with the Browns, characterized Noll for me in the following words: "Hard-working. Undersized, but tough. Smart as can be. And opinionated! Lots to say about everything. This kind of got to P.B. [Paul Brown] at times. Noll wanted to know reasons. 'Why?' he would ask. 'Why?' It was always why? why? why?"

Noll put up with his messenger-boy job for seven years (1953-1959). Then the coach of the Los Angeles Chargers in the AFL, Sid Gillman, took him on as an assistant. Gillman was innovative, intense, scientific, and thorough. In breaking down every aspect of the game, he used so much film that his photographers became full-time auxiliary members of the coaching staff. Noll brought this approach to the Steelers. In addition to being a coaching tool, it helped him to evaluate personnel and it helped the scouts to see what he was looking for in the way of talent.

Gillman, Noll once told me, required his assistants to cut all the game film into segments for painstaking study. Each segment consisted of a series of plays, which the assistant coach had to analyze. He would then tag the film and "file" it. The "filing cabinets" were trash cans Gillman had collected – one for each coach. It was a very time-consuming process, Noll said, and one morning when the coaches came to work they found that a janitor had emptied all their trash cans. The game film they had so meticulously taken apart was gone forever.

Bobby Burns – one of Jock Sutherland's ancestors – had it right: "The best-laid plans of mice and men ... " Noll, when he coached in Baltimore and Pittsburgh, continued to edit and save film, but always remembered to place a large sign on each receptacle. And I think he avoided storing the film in trash cans.

The three years Noll spent with Don Shula put the finishing touches on his football education. To Bill Nunn, he explained how an assistant coach makes progress: "You take a step up the ladder, learn what there is to learn at that level and learn it thoroughly, and take the next step."

"That's easy to say," Nunn answered. "But guys like you bring a little bit extra to the learning business."

By the way, I never heard anyone call Noll the Pope, or use his other nickname, Knute Knowledge, except behind his back. A few of the Baltimore players, I understand, addressed him as Knute, omitting the rest of it. Neither AJR, Dan, nor I called him anything but Chuck, or Coach. For a while when he was winning Super Bowls I referred to him among my scouts as Charlemagne – Charles the Great in plain English – but it never caught on, for which I am grateful. In retrospect, I can see that I was being a smart ass.

I have said many times, and repeat it now, that my brother Dan was responsible for bringing Chuck Noll to the Steelers. My only contribution was to ask some coaches and scouts what they thought of him. When I muscled into the Sylvan Room interview, I expressed a lot of forceful opinions about coaching philosophy, but the way Noll reacted, I feel sure, had nothing to do with his hiring. He'd have landed the job regardless, I believe. The decision was Dan's, with AJR concurring, and for twenty-three years there would not be any need to look for another head coach.

Guardian of the Faith

Charles Henry Noll became the fourteenth head coach of the Pittsburgh Steelers on January 27, 1969. I do not include Greasy Neale, co-coach with Walt Kiesling of the wartime Steagles, or Phil Handler, co-coach with Kiesling of the wartime Card-Pitts, but I do include Bert Bell and Buff Donelli, co-coaches for part of the 1939 season. Kiesling, who was head coach three different times in three different decades, and Joe Bach, who reappeared as head coach in the 1950s after a sixteen-year hiatus, are counted only once.

Noll joined our ranks on the day before the 1969 draft. This was how AJR wanted it, and I tried to conceal my disappointment. It was how Dan wanted it, too, but I could argue with Dan. When AJR spoke, there was no appeal. Although, unofficially, he had handed over the reins to his oldest son, he was still very much the Chief, still very much in command. He made it evident to me now that Chuck Noll would be in charge of the draft and have the final word on the selection of players and on trades. As head of the personnel department, I would make out a draft list for him and offer advice. That was all.

The Steelers did not have a table of organization, but there were clear and distinct lines of authority. On football matters, Noll, like the coaches before him, was to have a free hand. Dan would continue to run the front office. In addition, he would hire (and fire) the trainers and equipment managers, subject to approval by Noll. I would hire and fire the scouts, subject to approval by Noll and by Dan. Left unspoken was something we all knew: Noll had more latitude than either Dan or I did, but every decision made by any of us was subject to approval by the Chief.

He had not yet started telling me, again and again, "There can be only one boss." That would come later – and when he said one boss, he meant Dan. But as long as the Chief lived, Dan was never completely autonomous. Always the Chief retained veto power. Even after his death I expected him to reach down from heaven and reclaim that power whenever it suited him. So as far as I was concerned I answered to only one man: AJR. My attitude, I'm afraid, was "Fuck everybody else" – a sure-fire recipe for trouble. I didn't worry about that. My focus was always on the draft, completely.

For years I had chafed at the public perception of the Rooneys: Nice people, maybe, but stupid and cheap. I resolved to do what I could to change all that. The family honor was at stake. If no one else realized it, I did. In 1969, AJR was preoccupied with our race-track acquisitions. He was constantly on the telephone, constantly on the move. Dan's responsibilities covered so wide a spectrum that he was barely a participant until the day of the draft. Only I could protect us from the ridicule that would follow if we took the wrong players for the usual wrong reasons, as we had done so many times in the past. I would not let it happen again. I would keep the faith.

Noll's answers at his first press conference as our coach, I had to admit, gave me hope. He repeated what he had said in our Sylvan Room interview: "I'm not looking for respectability, I'm looking to win a championship." From what he had seen in the Steelers' 41-7 loss to the Baltimore Colts the previous season, they needed help everywhere. When the Steelers' turn came in the draft, he would take the best player on the board, irrespective of his position. A No. 1 draft choice at any position couldn't help but improve us at that particular spot.

It was music to my ears. Bill Nunn, Jack Butler, and I had rated the players in the draft on their ability, as we judged it, also without regard to position. We rated them from one to one hundred and sixty, and from the top one hundred we wanted as many as we could get. The Steelers had never drafted that way; now our new head coach was calling it the approach he favored. But did he mean what he said? I thought of a bromide my mother used to repeat: There's many a slip 'twixt the cup and the lip.

This was how anxious I became: Noll had been working with Don Shula on the draft list of the Colts. Would he bring that information to Pittsburgh – a serious breach of ethics? I had seen Bill Austin do something similar. It could damage a coach's reputation. It could damage ownership's reputation. I need not have worried. Noll's conduct in such matters, as in everything else, was above reproach.

Our draft room – the press called it the war room – was in the Roosevelt Hotel on the eighth floor. While Noll was involved with the reporters, I went there with trainer Ralph Berlin, equipment manager Tony Parisi, his assistant, Frank Sciuilli, and my secretary, Mrs. Duffy, to make certain that all was in readiness. On draft day I would be in that room with Noll, Dan, Bill Nunn, Ed Kiely, Fran Fogarty, and maybe one or two other front-office people, all of us seated at three walnut tables arranged in the shape of a T and laden with telephones. A green cloth covered the tables. Berlin would be in Philadelphia, where the Blesto scouts were gathered. I needed him there to keep me informed about late-breaking developments such as trades, new injury reports, and, sad to say, the existence of previously undisclosed rap sheets, and to put me on the phone with various Blesto people as the need arose. Nunn would stay with me through the first day of the draft and then hop a plane for Atlanta. There he would be in place to sign undrafted free agents and our own late-round picks from the black schools. Leaving Philadelphia when the draft was over, Berlin would get in contact with players of that type in the Mid-Atlantic region and New England. The number of free agents we corralled by being first on the scene with cash in hand could be astonishing.

But now I was in the war room to work on our draft lists. We had them on large sheets of white poster paper mounted on easels that nearly reached the ceiling. The names had been blown up to gigantic proportions, a task we deputized to a company called Buhl Optics. If there were last-minute changes in height, weight, or 40-yard dash speed reported by Blesto – and there always were – Parisi or Berlin would print the information on a narrow strip of masking tape and place it over the existing numbers. If a player went up or down in our ratings because of last-minute developments, the name itself, along with the appropriate statistics, had to be printed on tape and moved, which meant that one other name, at least, had to be moved as well. Berlin was now making a change of this kind, standing precariously on a chair. Distracted by a phone call, I hadn't been watching him, and when I saw what he was doing, I flipped.

"You're taping over the wrong name!" I shouted. Then I shouted some more. And screamed. Berlin, who weighed about 200 pounds, lost his balance on the chair. For a long, suspenseful moment, I thought he would fall over backwards. So did everybody else in the room. When he righted himself, their attention shifted to me. I knew what they were wondering, or thought I did. Would I drop to the floor and start chewing on the rug, like Adolf Hitler in moments of lunacy?

With an effort, I got a grip on myself. I counted to ten and said, "Ralph, the first thing Noll will look at when he walks into this room are those charts. If he sees a lot of mistakes, if he sees all that masking tape, our credibility will be shot. Henceforth," I added, the calm executive once again, "keep that optical company open all night if you have to. Keep it open right up to the morning of the draft, but this work must be professionally done – I don't care how much it costs."

That was how the draft always affected me. It raised my intensity level and my blood pressure. It gave me acid indigestion. On two or three previous draft days, I had run to the nearest men's room and tossed up my lunch. Berlin, suffering, I would guess, from post-traumatic stress disorder, kept the optical company open on the night before the draft for years and years to come. The cost was high, yes, but we saved a few nickels on masking tape.

From the draft room, I went downstairs. Dan wanted to see me in my office, someone said. Noll was there, too, and the drabness of the place embarrassed me. On my blackboard was a list of the players I had rated by position and Noll now suggested that we review it together. I steeled myself for whatever might be coming, but with his first few words he stilled all my doubts.

Clearly we were on the same wave length. I would read off a player's name and his statistics and then say something about his athletic skills. Noll listened carefully. He was interested above all in "playing speed." He called it the Steelers' greatest need. We discussed that a bit heavily, I remember. We talked about quickness and body control. We talked about "production," a big factor with Jack Butler. When his scouts extolled a player's talent and "growth potential," Butler would ask impatiently, "Can he play the damn game? Does he have playing smarts? Is he aware of what's happening on the field or is it all just a blur?" And here was Noll, talking the same way, telling me now that besides lacking speed, the Steelers were deficient in "football intelligence."

We kicked production and playing smarts and football intelligence around, and then we got into the specific skills needed for each position. I seldom heard him say, "Well, we had this player rated this way with the Colts." He gave me his own impressions of the players he had seen, and they were not the impressions of the Baltimore scouts. He asked me some questions which I was pleased to be able to answer. I learned for the first time of his obsession with muscle building. If a player had a good frame, Noll said, we could get some solid poundage on him through diet and weightlifting. He said we'd need barbells – the Olympic sets manufactured in York, Pennsylvania. "This stuff works. You'll see that it does," he told me.

Another thing he stressed was "playing with leverage." Playing with leverage was more important than brute strength. "Play with your legs. Hit through. Get under and up into the other guy. Deliver a blow. Don't be taking a blow." This was Noll the teacher indoctrinating a new pupil. He spoke with such sureness and enthusiasm that I couldn't help but be dazzled. Dan, too, was dazzled. But not only by Noll. Turning to me after Noll had politely thanked us and left the room, he said, "You gave a memorable performance."

I was flattered. But what gratified me most of all was how my ratings of the eleven "best athletes" conformed so exactly with Noll's. One of the players on my list was Joe Greene, a defensive tackle from North Texas State. At the mention of his name, Noll actually smiled. Scouting for the Colts, he had watched Greene in spring practice. After the NFL season, he had studied North Texas game films. And he liked Greene as much as I did, he said. Greene was black; he had not been widely publicized; he might still be available when it was our turn to draft. In that case, Noll and I agreed, we would make him our first-round pick.

Later that same afternoon, Dan told me that Shula had called. "He wants to talk to you," Dan said. "Shula feels that since Noll is over here giving us the Colts' information on college seniors, we ought to reciprocate."

I blew my top – again. "Damn! Noll hasn't given us a thing! He doesn't have their draft papers and I don't want them anyway. He only talked about the players he's seen himself. Tell Shula to go to hell!"

"Back off a little," Dan said. "It'll be OK. Shula wasn't demanding with me. Just return his call. After all, Don was the one who recommended Chuck."

So I reconsidered. Shula had received me cordially on my visits to his training camp in western Maryland. It was part of my job to look at players we thought the other teams might be willing to trade, and some coaches were barely civil when I approached them. Shula was always friendly, and now our phone conversation was friendly. He started off by praising Noll in the same terms as before. Chuck was a good coach, a good man. He was smart and hard-working. I had heard all this, but I didn't mind hearing it again. Eventually Shula asked me about ten or twelve players in the draft. How did we have them rated? It wasn't really an interrogation, I felt. Rather, I had the sense that we were talking like fellow scouts. One player we discussed was Ted Hendricks, the tall, thin University of Miami linebacker the sportswriters had dubbed The Mad Stork. It seemed to please Shula that our evaluations of this Colt-to-be and future Hall-of-Famer neatly dovetailed.

I hung up feeling good about Shula, Noll, myself, and the upcoming draft.

Chapter 44

The 1969 Draft

On draft day, as usual, I was in our eighth-floor control center at the Roosevelt Hotel by 6 a.m. Nobody else had arrived. I checked out the phones to Blesto headquarters in the Philadelphia Eagles' offices. Jack Butler and Ralph Berlin were there. It was too early to call New York, where Commissioner Pete Rozelle, facing television cameras from a dais in Madison Square Garden, would announce the selections. We had my brother Tim in New York, sitting by a telephone to keep us abreast of developments. After one last inspection of the room, I ordered coffee, tea, doughnuts, and sweet rolls from room service.

One by one, Noll, Dan, Nunn, Ed Kiely, and the others drifted in. Sidney, the bellman, came with the breakfast cart. Alex DiCroce popped in to see if there was anything else we needed. Kiely was briefing Noll on our ground rules for dealing with the media guys, who still had access to the draft room back then (the next year I put it off limits). AJR always turned up late. He'd be in and out all morning, seldom speaking, seldom making his presence felt.

It was 8 o'clock – time for the draft to start – before I knew it. Buffalo had the first pick. Although inter-league play would not begin until 1970, the war between the NFL and the AFL had ended and twenty-six teams would take part in a common draft, the team with the worst record drafting first. In late October, it had seemed that the team with the worst record would be the Steelers or the Eagles. Both were winless. Both had looked bad in losing six games. Whichever team lost when they met at Pitt Stadium, the assumption was, would keep on losing for the rest of the season and thus earn the right to draft O. J. Simpson.

Even in 1968 the name O. J. Simpson was well known – almost as well known as it is today, if for a somewhat different reason. When in the late 1990s he went on trial in Los Angeles, accused of murdering his wife and a hapless acquaintance of his wife by cutting their throats with a knife, O. J. Simpson's fame turned to infamy, never mind that a jury perhaps swayed by racial bias acquitted him. In 1968, he was college football's premier running back, the holder of every national ball-carrying record worth talking about. He was so good that Jack Butler, after watching him play, did something unprecedented, something completely out of character. He asked O. J. for his autograph.

Blesto scouts graded players from zero to five in such categories, for a running back, as power, elusiveness, breakaway speed, blocking, and pass-catching ability. The lower the grade the better. Simpson scored a zero, or close to it, in every department. "He left a little to be desired as a blocker," Butler said, "but you wouldn't want him hammering on those big defensive ends all day and slowing himself up."

I knew what Butler was talking about. Simpson played for Southern California, and on a visit to the West Coast I had watched USC game films with a scout from the San Francisco Forty-Niners. We agreed that a coach who did not take O. J. first would have to be minus some buttons. Every scout in the country – every scout I knew of – felt the same way.

And so interest built up in that late-October meeting between the ragtag Steelers and the ragtag Eagles. Sports reporters dubbed it the O. J. Simpson Bowl. The winner will be the loser, they wrote. Joe Kuharich, the coach of the Eagles, was vexed about that. "All this talk is just nonsense," he told me. "Neither one of us is going to draft O. J. Simpson. We're not the two worst teams, and before the season is over we'll prove it. Wait and see."

I didn't believe him.

The game at Pitt Stadium went down to the wire. With the score 3-3, and 1:36 left to play, the Steelers lost the ball at the Eagles' three-yard line on an intercepted pass. From the looks of things, the game would end in a tie. But on fourth down at the 10, the Eagles ran the ball – for no gain. Seconds later, Booth Lusteg kicked a field goal for the Steelers. Final score: Pittsburgh 6, Philadelphia 3. The Eagles now had the inside track in the race to draft O.J. Simpson.

Feet propped up on a bench, hands joined behind his head, Kuharich leaned back in a Pitt Stadium folding chair and complacently discussed his fourth-down call. Had he been looking ahead, maybe, to the draft? Not at all. In fact, he was more convinced than ever that the Eagles would win some games. Bearing him out, they won two of their last seven. The Steelers, meanwhile, beat Atlanta by three touchdowns and then tied St. Louis before reverting to form. They finished the season exactly as they had started it, by losing six in a row, but their 2-12-1 record was better than the Eagles' 2-13, Atlanta's 2-13, or Buffalo's 1-12-1. My old pal Harvey Johnson had won the highly coveted booby prize for his Bills. And so it was that O. J. Simpson, much against his will, ended up in the AFL.

In our room on the eighth floor of the Roosevelt Hotel, none of us gave O. J. a thought. We were hoping that neither the Falcons nor the Eagles would take the player who had gone to the top of our list, Joe Greene. Buffalo drafted quickly, and we waited with mounting tension for Atlanta's selection. While Atlanta deliberated, Buff Boston, in an ante-room, was talking with Greene on the telephone. From having heard it so often, I knew Buff's routine. "Hey, Joe," he would say, "would you like to be a Steeler? ... You would? Well, that makes us real happy. Have you had any recent injuries in workouts? Playing basketball, maybe? Horsing around? ... Good. Say, how about the military? Any change in your deferred status ... No? And, uh – are you still single? ... Oh, you're married? Any kids on the way? ... You're a dad? ... Congratulations! ... Well, we think you could help our ball club, so stay close to the phone. And, by the way, have any of the other teams called you? ... New York? Which team in New York? ... Giants? OK. And, oh yes – you haven't signed with any team in the Canadian League, have you? ... OK. Thanks a lot. Just sit tight."

Atlanta drafted George Kunz, a two-way tackle from Notre Dame. We had rated him near the top of our own list, but Joe Greene was our man. Noll and Dan were talking to him now. As for me, I wasn't interested in talking to Greene, I was interested in talking to Butler, in Philadelphia. Once again, I demanded to know if his scouts liked Joe Greene as much as we did. "Art," Butler said – Butler never called me Artie – "we think he's a good pick."

The fear that seized me now was that the Eagles would take Greene. I thought of Tom Mack, and how in 1966 Los Angeles had beaten us to him. Years later we learned that Philadelphia was extremely interested in Greene, but, drafting third, they took a running back from Purdue, LeRoy Keyes. I looked across the table at Noll and mouthed the word "Greene." Everybody in the room was staring at us. "Let's go for him," Noll said, loud and clear. He nodded at Dan, who had our man in New York on the line, the receiver cupped to his ear. "Greene," Dan said, making it official, and soon, with dramatic pauses between his incomplete sentences, Pete Rozelle was speaking into a microphone, saying:

"Pittsburgh ...

"Fourth choice in the first round ...

"Joe Greene, defensive tackle from North Texas State."

For the first time in weeks, I could relax.

An excellent beginning. No confusion. No arguing, no discussion. In my meeting with Noll on the eve of the draft, we had worked out a procedure. We would follow our list, right down the line. The chemistry between us was good. Noll liked our setup, or seemed to. I had spent a lot of time making sure that we were organized, and, so far, nothing had gone wrong. I dreaded the possibility that in Noll's eyes we would look bad – look like bumblers.

For our first pick in the second round, Noll was leaning toward a player named Ernie Galloway, a big, fast defensive end from Texas Southern. Noll had been harping on our need for team speed, and Galloway was a No. 2 on my charts. But Philadelphia took him. We then switched to Hanratty, although in doing so we deviated from our plan. He was not "the best athlete available." We took him for one reason: pressure from our fans. I had not yet matured enough to keep from being influenced by them. Our choice of Greene in the first round had come as a shock to the fans. They had wanted Hanratty, had clamored for him, and so had certain members of the press corps. Hanratty's credentials were threefold: He was from Western Pennsylvania – Butler. He had played at Notre Dame. He had broken passing records that belonged to the storied George Gipp and then apologized for it, disarmingly. "I feel like I've broken my mother's most expensive set of china," he announced.

But Hanratty, at best, was a marginal second-round pick. I knew it, Noll knew it, and even AJR, as partial as he was to players with Irish names, as partial as he was to Western Pennsylvanians, and as favorably impressed as he had been when Hanratty came to Pittsburgh for a physical examination – he had undergone minor surgery – and a get-acquainted lunch in the Sylvan Room, knew it. Drafting quarterbacks, both the Bengals and Chargers had passed on Hanratty in the first round. The Bengals, predictably, went for Greg Cook, who was big and strong-armed and had played at the University of Cincinnati. San Diego, unpredictably, chose an Ivy League quarterback, Marty Domres of Columbia. If the Steelers had done that, said a radio reporter in our draft room, the fans would be rushing over to burn down the Roosevelt Hotel. The Bears, when their turn came, had called to make us an offer. They would be willing to take Hanratty if we agreed to trade a veteran for him. Thanks but no thanks, I replied. We could have waited to take him ourselves even longer than we did – until the second of our two second-round picks, at least. But I was still too unsure of myself to gamble. (Thirty years afterward, at an Ireland Fund banquet in Palm Beach, I ran into Don Shula. Harking back to the 1969 draft, he told me how lucky we were that Chuck Noll had been around to advise us. "You were going to waste your first pick on Hanratty," he said as though stating a fact. "Chuck Noll went over there and straightened you guys out." I repressed an impulse to straighten out Shula. In the end, all I said was, "Yep, we were real lucky.")

Hanratty was by no means a dud, but during most of his seven seasons in Pittsburgh, he stood on the sidelines with a clipboard. Our second pick in the second round was Warren Bankston of Tulane, a good running back with size. He would have been a better tight end. In the third round, we drafted Jon Kolb, a center from Oklahoma State who could also play tackle. He started on all four of our Super Bowl teams, as did L. C. Greenwood, the tall, skinny defensive tackle I had scouted at Arkansas A. & M. I can pat myself on the back for landing Greenwood in the tenth round.

One other player worth mentioning was our fifteenth-round pick, Kenny Liberto, a wide receiver from Louisiana Tech. Liberto ran disciplined pass routes. He had a good pair of hands. He made all the catches. But he was small and he was slow and he did not survive training camp. Why do I bring up his name? Well, in watching Louisiana Tech game films, we could not help but notice the quarterback who was throwing to Liberto. He had a cannon for an arm and a lightning-quick release. We were getting our first look at Terry Bradshaw.

Joe Who?

Eight of our seventeen draft choices remained with the team. That is a fairly large number, but I remembered what an assistant coach under Buddy Parker said to me once: "It isn't how many rookies you keep that's important, it's how many rookies who contribute – who help you win. You don't want stiffs replacing stiffs."

By that measure, the 1969 draft was still not a bad one at all. Joe Greene played for twelve years and made the Hall of Fame. L. C. Greenwood played for thirteen years. Jon Kolb also played for thirteen years and stayed on for ten more as an assistant coach. (Greene joined the coaching staff, too, after getting out of the restaurant business.) Without Greene, Greenwood, and Kolb, we would not have gone to the Super Bowl four different Januaries, returning each time with the Vince Lombardi Trophy. Terry Hanratty, Warren Bankston, running back Bob Campbell, defensive back Charles Beatty, and linebacker Doug Fisher had much less successful but not insignificant careers, and the same could be said of tight end Bob Adams, an undrafted, underrated free agent.

We were making a break with the past, I felt, building for the future through the draft. We were getting it all together, and Joe Greene was the cornerstone.

Not that anyone in Pittsburgh thought we had done the right thing by drafting him first. The headline the next day in the *Post-Gazette* was derisive: "STEELERS SELECT ... JOE WHO?" But then the know-it-all newspaper guys had not seen Joe Who? in action, as I had. Scouting North Texas State, I saw him dominate every third-down situation. He was 6 feet 4 and 275 pounds and seemed to push the entire offensive line back toward the quarterback on pass plays. In the 1960s Greene was big for a tackle, and though smaller linemen can often beat larger ones with quickness and speed, it was Greene's own quickness and speed, and not his size, that made him so hard to handle.

After his first couple of games as a Steeler rookie, the fans stopped calling him Joe Who? They adopted his North Texas State nickname, which he disliked. The school color at North Texas was green, and the defensive unit, collectively, was known as the Mean Green, and so of course its best player could not have escaped being Mean Joe Greene, no matter what.

The funny thing was that he thought of himself as a teddy bear. There was nothing ogre-ish in his looks or his manner, and on the football field he conversed in a pleasant way with the other team's center, sometimes asking hopefully, "You gonna run the ball at me?" True, he could show meanness under stress. Early in the 1969 season he leveled the New York Giants' quarterback, Fran Tarkenton, with an unnecessary forearm blow and the officials ejected him from the game. Other expulsions were to follow. The Steelers were losing every week – after beating Detroit to start the season, they lost thirteen times in a row – and he was taking it badly. He was like an uncontrolled oil-well gusher, spewing his talent into the wind. Near the end of one game, as our opponents came out of their huddle, he picked up the ball and threw it into the stands.

There was also the deplorable spitting incident. Greene let fly in the face of the *Pittsburgh Press* reporter Pat Livingston because Pat wrote a column defending the team owners' position during a short-lived player strike. For that, and for his other transgressions, Greene was suitably contrite, but he had to be reined in. I think he'd been spending too much time with Roy Jefferson, a militant member of the players' union. Previously, I have written how Bill Nunn put John Brown on his case, rooming them together in training camp. Older and wiser than Greene, Brown was a calming influence. A heart-to-heart talk with Chuck Noll did some good after Greene let his unhappiness show because the Steelers had cut Charles Beatty, a close friend. "You have a long career ahead of you," Noll said. "You will see many teammates and friends move on. I can understand your concern, but learn to deal with it."

Brown and Noll between them re-directed Greene's talent and energy. If he was never a perfect gentleman on the football field, Noll did not mind. "Make something happen," he liked to tell his players, and no one responded more willingly than Greene. To reach the playoffs for the first time, in 1972, we had to beat Houston, and he absolutely crushed his side of the Oilers' offensive line. The defense held Houston to three points, and our nine were enough to win. In that '72 season the Steel Curtain came into being, with Ernie Holmes joining Greene, L. C. Greenwood, and Dwight White as the final component of a fearsome front four.

There came a time when injuries and age reduced Greene's effectiveness, but he adapted. He mastered all the nuances of team defense. Greene was a special favorite of AJR. Their rapport had increased year by year. Often the Chief would hand Greene a fist full of expensive cigars, huge ones that were shaped like baseball bats. In Joe's mouth, they looked as insubstantial as toothpicks. But Greene was getting into his thirties, and AJR worried about him.

"Have you been watching Joe lately?" he would ask me.

"Yes," I would say.

"How is he doing?"

"OK."

"Just OK?"

"He's been great."

"Yes, he's still good. He still plays fine team defense, doesn't he?"

"Yes, he does."

"He should be able to keep it up for years. Don't you think so?"

"Yes, I think he can," I would say.

I wasn't lying, exactly – Greene did keep it up for a very long time. I never admired him more than in his last year at our training camp, but not because of his football playing. One afternoon my son Art was filming practice from the top of a high steel tower. Suddenly an electrical storm blew in. There was lightning, thunder, heavy rain. Everybody ran for cover – everybody except Art and me. And Joe Greene. He was standing at my side, shouting at Art, "Don't jump! Climb down quickly! Be careful!"

Art – concerned about his equipment – was calling, "I have to take care of the cameras. They cost a lot of money."

"Fuck the cameras!" yelled Greene. "You get off that tower right now!"

Placing his cameras on the platform he'd been using, Art Rooney III climbed down as fast as he could. The lightning flashed, the thunder pealed, and the rain fell in torrents, but one of our team cars was pulling up near the tower and all three of us hopped safely inside.

There was a scene in a movie about El Cid, the intrepid Spanish soldier who made life difficult for the Moors, in which he single-handedly killed a dozen would-be abductors of a prince of Castile. Call it far-fetched if you will, but Joe Greene, to me, was his modern-day counterpart. EI Cid stood up to the Moors. Joe Greene, just as defiantly, stood up to offensive linemen and thunderbolts.

Our third draft choice, Jon Kolb, was a blond, open-faced, square-jawed country boy. At 6 feet 2 and 225 pounds, he appeared to be too short and too light to play center in the NFL, but he was strong, tough, durable, and willing to learn. On the surface, he had nothing in common with AJR. Kolb grew up in rural Oklahoma, AJR in a raffish urban neighborhood. Where they resembled each other was in their common philosophy of treating others as they would like to be treated themselves while allowing no one to mistake kindness for weakness. For Kolb, that was especially true on the playing field.

He was not an immediate success. In a game at Wrigley Field in his rookie season, Dick Butkus, the Chicago Bears' Hall-of-Fame linebacker, roughed him up shamefully – "kicked his ass," line coach Bob Fry told me – and it was shortly thereafter that Chuck Noll moved Kolb to tackle, where he gradually came into his own. His tenacity, consistency, discipline, and attention to physical condition made him an iron man.

Lifting weights tirelessly, he gained close to fifty pounds, and he mastered all the blocking techniques, the little tricks of the trade, as well as the textbook moves.

Here is one last thing to be said about Kolb: year after year, the fans and reporters took him for granted. There are not many higher compliments.

Chapter 45

The Media

Most of our fans paid little attention to the players we selected on the second day of the draft. Their names might come up in water-cooler talk at the office or in casual conversation over cocktails at the golf club or over beers and shots of whiskey at the neighborhood bar. Even the sportswriters and sportscasters who covered the draft seemed to feel that nothing of importance was taking place on the second day.

I noticed three of them on the far side of the room, forming a tight little group with AJR. There was Pat Livingston of the *Pittsburgh Press*, the first paid scout the Steelers had ever had. In 1946, just out of the Navy, Livingston went to work for Jock Sutherland. "You're my personnel director," The Great Stoneface informed him. "But Doctor Sutherland," protested Livingston. "I don't know a thing about scouting." "You'll learn, Pat, you'll learn," answered his boss. There was Jack Sell of the *Post-Gazette*, a North Sider of my father's generation. There was Joe Tucker, called The Screamer, the play-by-play announcer on our radio network for twenty-five years but who was then in poor health and semi-retired. All three were argumentative, Livingston as relentlessly as a trial lawyer (he had a law degree from Duquesne), Sell with sardonic amusement, Tucker if called upon to defend or denounce some coaching decision.

I noticed them standing with AJR, and I noticed something else: they were looking at our scouting reports. We had just drafted Doug Fisher, a linebacker from San Diego State, and now Livingston called over to let me know he approved. "Hey, Artie," he said. His voice came from deep in his throat, emerging in a series of barks. "Your reports on that Fisher were pretty accurate. You had him pegged as a late-round pick and he was right where you expected him to be."

Scouting reports were private information, but I wasn't touchy about it. I liked Pat Livingston. I liked Jack Sell. I liked Joe Tucker. I had nevertheless promised myself that from now on we would run a tighter ship, at least in the scouting department. John Troan, the editor of the *Press*, would never have opened his board room to Chuck Noll and Art Rooney and Art Rooney's sons while he and some department head were discussing the pros and cons of hiring a new reporter. I made a mental note to talk with Ed Kiely and Dan about changing our policy. More restrictions were needed on access to the draft room.

I wanted Ed and Dan in my corner before I approached AJR because I knew exactly what AJR would tell me: "This is the way I do business. It does us good to have the newspaper guys feel they're a part of the organization. It will all work out for the best." And so on and so on. Ed and Dan, to my relief, saw things as I did. There were more reporters now from the radio stations and television stations, more reporters from the papers in the Beaver and Monongahela valleys. Letting them all have the run of the place was impractical.

Surprisingly, when we put it like that to AJR, he gave us an unqualified OK.

AJR's liking for, and rapport with, sportswriters went back a long way. Like Richard Nixon, he had hoped in adolescence to be one.

Recall that his first mentor was Dick Guy, half sportswriter, half sports promoter. Why, then, couldn't AJR have become a sportswriter? He had an expert's knowledge, certainly, of football, baseball, and boxing. Developing reliable news sources would not have been a problem for him, either; he was born with the gift of putting people at ease, of getting them to talk. Could he have learned how to write – acquired the necessary skills and techniques? I believe so. There are different kinds of intelligence, and his may not have been literary, but America's press boxes were not overflowing with Hemingways, Joyces, and Fitzgeralds. Very few literary artists gravitate to the profession. But as much as I respected my dad's capabilities, I never thought he was tough enough to have been a good sportswriter.

Granted it contradicts all that we know about him to say such a thing. If anyone or anything ever intimidated AJR, it remains a secret. In moments of anger, he could and did use his fists. He had a frightening facility for taking the starch out of people with a scowl and a few caustic words. But these moments of anger were sporadic. He had a temper, and he lost it now and then. Hurting someone's feelings, or, worse, the feelings of that person's close relatives – his wife, his mother, his children – and doing it publicly, cold-bloodedly, was different. Sportswriters are not just reporters, but critics as well. They have to assess blame for the failures and mistakes and bonehead plays endemic in any type of sports competition. They have to write about the side issues that come up – scandals and scrapes and even felonies. Though less common back then, and more frequently hushed up, felonies occurred, and they had to be written about. I don't think my dad could have brought himself to be the instrument. He was too soft inside.

Let me give you an example of his thought processes. Back around the dawn of the twentieth century, two brothers who had murdered a grocer and a policeman sawed their way out of the Allegheny County Jail, assisted by the wife of the warden. Infatuated with one of the killers, she provided them with guns and joined them in their flight from justice. They headed north in a horse-drawn sled (it was January, and there was snow on the ground), but the sheriff and his deputies caught up with the unlikely trio. In the shootout that ensued, both brothers were fatally hit. More than eighty years later, Hollywood turned the escapade into a movie, which AJR refused to attend. "I knew that warden's family," he explained. "Some of them are still living. I think that movie will be embarrassing to them."

There was also the time he ordered Dan to remove a story that mentioned Tim Mara's gambling background from one of our game programs regardless of the expense. Mara was a bookmaker; it never had been a secret, but to say so in print wouldn't do.

Yet my dad's true vocation, he continued to insist, was sportswriting. What appealed to him about it was the life: sitting in the press box and eating free hot dogs while being paid to watch a baseball game or a football game. It pleased his fancy to believe that I enjoyed the same perks in my own job. "Scouting those Big Ten games must be great," he would tell me. The Big Ten, I would answer, allowed no scouts in the press box. At halftime, there was no free lunch. AJR never bought that.

For as long as I could remember, sportswriters and media people were always a part of his entourage. He named a few of his best race horses after sportswriters – Livingston, Sell, Al Abrams. He named one for Kathy Kiely, Ed's daughter, when she was only 14, too young to go to the track and see the horse run. Kathy grew up to become a fine journalist, a Washington correspondent for the *Pittsburgh Press*, the *Houston Post*, the *Arkansas Gazette*, and *USA Today* (though not all at once).

Sometimes Dad would talk about meeting big-name writers like H. L. Mencken, Ring Lardner, and Damon Runyon. Mencken never wrote about sports, but liked to bet on the horses, Dad said. Lardner and Runyon were sportswriters who graduated to fiction. AJR always spoke of them with awe.

He appeared to regard the local writers and broadcasters as cronies. Even though he would take them on junkets to the Kentucky Derby, to New York, or out to the Pacific Coast, he never gave the impression that he was buying them off. In Las Vegas one time, he sent Joe Tucker and me to a horse room with seven thousand dollars to bet. When we tried to get it down, we were told that four thousand dollars was the limit. Well, Tucker went into liftoff. He more than lived up to his nickname – The Screamer. At the top of his lungs, he shouted for the manager. "This is Las Vegas! The big time! You're supposed to take all the action!" Quietly, the bookmaker informed us it was almost post time. "Would you like to bet four thousand or not?" he asked. Tucker placed a bet for four thousand.

My dad's horse finished out of the money, so we saved him three thousand bucks – or, rather, the bookmaker did.

Dad, Tucker, Jack Sell, and I were staying at Milton Jaffe's hotel and casino, the Stardust, and Milton was picking up the tab. On the day we left for home, Dad won seventeen thousand dollars at a craps table in the Stardust. "Darn it!" he said. "I was trying to lose a little to pay Milton back for his hospitality, but then I happened to get on a roll. And craps isn't even my game."

In retrospect, I can see that the old-time writers and broadcasters knew things about AJR that the public did not know and that AJR would not have wanted the public to know. He was one of the most successful gamblers in the country, but to the people of Pittsburgh he looked like a loser, because the Steelers were losers, and the writers did nothing to enlighten them.

After Sell, Tucker, and Livingston had passed from the scene a generation gap existed between AJR and their successors, young journalism-school graduates with a more serious, businesslike attitude. No longer was AJR a friend and companion to the "newspaper guys," his all-inclusive term for print reporters and broadcasters alike. Instead, they regarded him as almost an object of worship. They were largely unaware of the past, unaware of a time when Art Rooney took the blame for everything that seemed wrong with the Steelers. Chuck Noll had turned the chronic losers into winners, and now the owner was receiving the accolades long denied him.

AJR's knack of remembering not only names but home towns and neighborhoods dazzled these journalistic tyros. As Ed Kiely put it, he could make the lowliest cub reporter feel like Red Smith. But there was never any personal relationship, never any hanging out. AJR's age and eminence discouraged familiarity. The new guys listened to his stories, but went to Joe Gordon or to Dan for information about the team. And there were many more beat reporters than ever before. Regional papers and radio stations had joined the two large Pittsburgh dailies and the three Pittsburgh television channels in providing their readers and viewers with constant, extensive Steeler coverage.

AJR, in his dealings with the press, was never adversarial. According to Ed Kiely, he would pick up the paper, read a story about the team that he didn't like, and fume. He would then denounce the author as a knucklehead, a dummy with no knowledge of football or anything else. Thirty minutes later, the knucklehead himself might show up, strolling into AJR's office unannounced, as Mary Regan allowed most reporters to do. AJR would offer a welcoming handshake, Kiely said, and compliment the guy on an insightful piece of reporting.

Still, AJR was sincere, I believe, when he said that he liked newspapermen. He liked to talk with them, and not about football, necessarily. I was discussing college prospects one day with Vito Stellino of the *Post-Gazette* when AJR made an unexpected appearance. "What's up? Whaddaya hear?" he asked Stellino. A tall, rather gaunt young man who resembled the illustrators' renditions of Ichabod Crane, Stellino had more than the usual sportswriters' understanding of X's and O's and was highly regarded by his colleagues and I think the coaches as well. He'd been taping our interview and did not turn off the recorder, I noticed, as AJR took a chair and began chatting with us.

Almost at once the conversation turned to boxing – I don't remember how. Boxing was not a sport that I followed very closely, but I had learned to appreciate the stories the Chief could tell about fights and fighters and managers. He was in rare good form – unaware of the tape recorder and hence not the least bit self-conscious – and Stellino seemed to be mesmerized. Even I was mesmerized, as often as I had heard all the tales. In fact, when AJR finished, I felt like applauding. He stood up to leave, said goodbye, and was out the door. I turned to Stellino. "Well, Vito," I said, "I got you one for the history books." I was proud of my Dad and happy to have been the agent for giving Vito, a nice guy who had treated me well in the *Post-Gazette*, access to a special kind of feature story.

But, alas, he was looking at me sadly. "There was only fifteen minutes on that tape," he said. "I used twelve of those minutes on your stuff, leaving only three, and Mister Rooney must have talked for half an hour."

After Stellino returned to Baltimore, his home town, Ed Bouchette became the *Post-Gazette's* pro football writer. One day in the 1980s he was typing up a story in the Three Rivers Stadium press room when AJR wandered in, chewing on a big fat cigar, the kind that looked like a baseball bat. He started talking about the old days, with no other purpose than to socialize with a newspaper guy. "At first," Bouchette said, "I tried to think of a way to cut your dad off. I was on deadline and in no mood for interruptions. But then I thought, this is Art Rooney, a man who's already a legend. He wants to give me some of his time. So to hell with my story. I'm going to take fifteen minutes, or even thirty minutes, and listen to him. That was what I did, and I don't regret it."

AJR was well up into his eighties now. Not long after the incident related by Bouchette, he asked if I would like to drive to the farm with him. "We could maybe take a few days and go on up to Quebec City," he said. "We could visit the Shrine of St. Anne."

"I'm sorry, Dad," I replied, "but I'm pretty busy right now. Let's do it some other time."

"OK, but time's running out on me, Artie," he shrugged – kidding on the square, as he would put it.

"Some other time" never came.

Unlike Bouchette, I do have cause for regret.

Al Abrams

Only once did I ever hear AJR address a harsh word to a newspaperman. The sports editor of the *Post-Gazette*, Al Abrams, wrote a notes column every Saturday that was captioned "A Whirl Around the World of Sports." It consisted of gossipy little items separated by dots. Abrams picked up his subject matter wherever he could find it. I know that Ed Kiely supplied him with notes and would write an entire column for him once or twice a year. But what I started to say was that in his notes column one week there appeared the following line: "Art Rooney's box at Forbes Field is filled at every Pirate game with priests and racketeers."

In the 1950s, when I was still in college, the *Post-Gazette* published an early, pre-dated edition, called the "bulldog," that hit the streets at about 6 p.m. Reading Abrams' Saturday column at home on a Friday night, while the rest of us watched television, AJR became very animated. "Why, that greasy bum!" we heard him say. He picked up the phone and called Kiely. "Have you seen the bulldog yet? Have you seen what Abrams wrote? He says my box at Forbes Field is filled with priests and racketeers. Do you have his telephone number? ... No, I won't wait till tomorrow. Give it to me right away. If you don't have it, get it ... OK. Let me write that down."

All eyes in the room are fixed upon him now, and he has noticed. We notice that he has noticed, and our heads swivel back to the television set. Now he is dialing Abrams. "Al? This is Art Rooney." His voice is hard, menacing. The eyes of his sons have switched again from the television screen to the Chief. "I just read your column in the morning paper. What are you talking about, priests and racketeers? That isn't funny. How do you think those priests feel? They read the paper too. You're way out of line, Al, way out of line." He is yelling into the phone. "I thought you had more sense than that ... Calm? I AM calm. And when I read something I know what it means. I'll talk to you later." The next sound heard is the receiver slamming down. We pretend to have been watching television all this time.

I had met Al Abrams as a kid, but our conversations had been brief and perfunctory. "How's school?" he would say. That sort of thing. Lebanese by extraction, Abrams was a short but substantial looking olive-complexioned man whose slicked-back, pomaded black hair was as shiny as the Guys and Dolls suits he always wore unless he was wearing a sport jacket. Dark, soulful eyes and sagging jowls gave him the melancholy expression of a basset hound.

A year or so after the telephone call, on a trip to the West Coast for a Steeler game, I was hanging around the hotel swimming pool with my brothers when Abrams turned up, dressed in a sport shirt, slacks, and loafers. Recognizing that we were Rooneys, he greeted us. His manner was as casual as his apparel. I admit I didn't know what to make of him. Al Abrams was the guy who had suggested in the paper that Art Rooney, Sr., was a racketeer, the guy Art Rooney had yelled at on the telephone. He was the best-known Pittsburgh sportswriter, a celebrity in his own right, the MC and organizer of the big Dapper Dan sports banquet, of which Owney McManus had said, "You could back up all the paddy wagons in town to the hotel where that affair is being held and you wouldn't have room enough for all the bums and con artists who deserve to be taken to the hoosegow." I recalled that AJR had named a race horse after Abrams. But AJR named his horses after all kinds of people. Should I give Al Abrams the benefit of the doubt or be hostile?

In a soft-spoken, good-humored way, he was telling us of a side trip he had made to Las Vegas. His outlook on Vegas, his outlook on life in general, seemed to be cynical and jaded, but indulgent. He reminded me of AJR's North Side friends, of the people he knew in boxing, of Uncle Jim, of Dago Sam. Over the next twenty minutes or so, Al Abrams completely disarmed us. From then on when I saw him he would always say, "Hi. What's up? How are things going?"

I decided he was not a greasy bum.

Jack Sell

Jack Sell and my dad played with and against each other on sandlot football and baseball teams in the early 1920s. Jack was a strict German Lutheran from the North Side neighborhood of Fineview. Higher than Troy Hill, Fineview looked down on the Allegheny River and the Pittsburgh skyline on the opposite side. He had a full head of iron gray hair and his perfectly tailored suits were the same color, which gave him a monochromatic look. He was stocky, like Pat Livingston, but several inches taller. Friendly but distant with the training-camp ball boys, he would take them on fishing trips to privately-stocked lakes near Olean. In the coaches' room at camp, he put away gargantuan amounts of beer without ever showing the effects.

Every Saturday night he went bowling, even when a Steeler game was scheduled. In Jack's day the *Post-Gazette* had no Sunday edition, and thus he was free to make a choice. That he preferred to go bowling amazed me. When I conveyed this to Ed Kiely, he said, "You have to understand Sell." Ed's theory was that year after year of covering Steeler teams that always fell short had left Jack professionally numb. He felt no emotional involvement with the team. Going to the games was a job, nothing more.

Jack's reporting on the Steelers was methodical and bland. Kiely and Dan often joked about it. I thought his straightforward, focused style of writing gave the reader the essential facts of a story without any attempt at fanciness, and AJR seemed to feel the same way.

Sell had a special relationship with the Chief. In fact, Sell, Tucker, and Livingston belonged to what I thought of as an inner sanctum. There seemed to be a tacit agreement among them that no one would break a story that made the team or the organization look bad. At our pre-season camp in Olean one year, I thought that Sell overstepped the line. Shockingly – to me and, I am sure, to the *Post-Gazette's* readers – something he wrote was actually quite critical of Walt Kiesling and his assistant coaches. On behalf of the whole Steeler family, I felt betrayed. The headline over the story seemed particularly nasty. Pat Livingston, noting my distress, explained to me that copy editors in the office wrote the headlines, sometimes distorting the information contained in the story itself.

"Take another look at what Sell wrote," Livingston advised me. "It's not as hard on Kies as the headline suggests. You have to remember, Artie, that we're supposed to do our jobs no matter how tight we are with your dad. Sell doesn't dislike the coaches. Just the opposite. But a reporter has to tell it like it is."

A few days later AJR drove up from Pittsburgh, and I saw him conversing with Sell as if nothing had happened. It was then that I first began to alter my thinking about sportswriters. Maybe Livingston had it right, after all. Over the years, for personal reasons, I came to appreciate Pat's sensitivity, but that is another story.

Jack Sell never covered our NFL championship teams. After the 1973 season, he retired – too old and too set in his ways to meet the changing demands of his job, or so it seemed to the *Post-Gazette* brass. The brass pushed him out, and he resented it. On January 12, 1975, he was our guest when we won the Super Bowl game for the first time. After that, I don't remember seeing much of Jack. One day in the mid-1980s, AJR collected Dan, Kiely, Uncle Jim, and me for a trip from Three Rivers Stadium up Fineview Hill to the Lutheran church. We were going to Jack's funeral, all of us. No questions or excuses accepted.

When my brothers and I were young, we had known Jack's son, Jack, Jr., a good-looking kid and a better athlete, I secretly felt, than any of us. Except for a blown-out knee, Jack, Jr., would have played college football. It sobered me at the funeral to observe how grief-stricken he was. The tears ran down his cheeks and he sobbed inconsolably. Tough old German Jack Sell, I reflected, had a gentler, less buttoned-up side invisible to us. It was there all the time but we were simply not looking.

The Screamer

In 1936, when the Steelers were still the Pirates, AJR hired a Jewish guy from Canada, Joe Tucker, to broadcast their games on the radio. Fitting in was no problem for Joe. He liked to play the horses, idolized AJR, took undisguised pleasure in the camaraderie associated with his job, exulted in each of the Steelers' rare victories, and agonized over their defeats.

A tall, jovial man verging on fatness, Tucker had no affectations, but took considerable pride in his tennis game. He competed in local amateur tournaments, always with success if you took his word for it. His great friend Jack Sell had a different story to tell. Assigned by the *Post-Gazette* to cover the West Penn championships (a bit of a comedown, he thought), Sell was on hand to witness Tucker's most embarrassing moment. A sizzling forehand drive from his opponent eluded Joe's racket, made contact with a most sensitive part of his anatomy, and left him writhing on the court in an anguished heap. Sell never tired of rehashing that incident.

Chronic bad luck at the race track provided Tucker with a punch line for one of his running gags. In the airport before traveling to a Steeler game, he conscientiously bought flight insurance – a $10,000 policy on his life, payable to Mrs. Tucker if the airplane went down. The ticket-sized receipt went into his pocket. When the plane landed safely, he would take out the receipt, tear it in half, and mutter to Livingston or Sell, "Another loser."

Because of his partisanship in the broadcasting booth, most listeners regarded him as a shill or a mouthpiece for AJR. He was in any case a loyal employee. He worked with a "color" man, usually Bill Burns, who interspersed comments during lulls in the play-by-play, and a "spotter" who helped him identify blockers, tacklers, ball carriers, pass receivers, and so forth. One Sunday in the absence of his regular spotter, he asked me to fill in. The lineups of both teams were spread out before us, and as each play developed my job was to point with a pencil to the names of the players involved. But though familiar with all the Steelers, and with the other team's personnel to at least some degree, I was still in my teens, and more of a fan than a professional observer. A spotter must not lose his concentration. Caught up in the fortunes of the Steelers, I frequently lost mine.

At halftime, Tucker gave me a cram course in the art of spotting. It was useless. By the middle of the third quarter, I had forgotten my lessons completely. Tucker did not reprimand me, or show any trace of annoyance. When he handed me my fee – ten dollars – I felt reluctant to take it, but I took it.

Tucker never asked me to spot for him again, but there were visiting broadcasters who did. All of them concluded, as Tucker had, that once was enough.

AJR's contract with the radio station allowed him to handpick the play-by-play announcer, and year after year it was Tucker. When professional football went national on television, the league and the network combined to pick the announcers. They looked first to the veterans of the radio booth, and Tucker perceived this as the chance he'd been waiting for. "Stay with radio," counseled AJR, but in television the money was bigger, the public exposure greater, the prestige of a higher order. Tucker left the Steelers to go with NBC and did not do at all well.

On a national telecast, the announcing must be objective. Screamer Joe, conditioned to root for the home team, failed to adjust. A second difficulty was that he found himself talking too much. Each play on television unfolds before the viewer's eyes. Detailed descriptions are therefore superfluous. Ray Scott, a Pittsburgh guy who also had learned his craft on radio, made the transition more smoothly than Tucker. His opportunity came when Bill Stern, another blabbermouth, had a meltdown on the air while broadcasting a Pitt-Georgia Tech game and couldn't continue. Ray Scott stepped in as his backup and revolutionized the calling of television games. He was terse and informative, never intruding on the action. "Let me set the defense: Left end, Jones, number ninety-two. Left tackle, Smith, number seventy-seven ..." "It was Sam Huff, from West Virginia, who made that tackle ..." From the day he took over for Stern, he was able to write his own ticket.

Tucker, with the help of AJR and Kiely, hung on for a while at NBC and did some telecasts for CBS, but they were using him mostly on color. His assignments began to come less and less often until at last there were none at all. Meanwhile, he continued to work in Pittsburgh for radio station WWSW, giving the race results and a commentary each night. To make extra money, he dabbled in stocks and bonds. Red Donnelly, a young announcer from Steubenville, was broadcasting the Steeler games on WWSW, with Tom Bender doing color, and there was never any thought of replacing them.

I was in AJR's office one day when Tucker came in and began to talk in a discouraged way about the turn his career had taken. AJR was surprisingly unsympathetic. He said, "Well ... I advised you to stay in radio. Remember what they called you? The Voice of the Steelers. You threw that away." This was where it seemed to me that AJR should have stopped. Instead, I heard him saying, "You're Jewish, Joe. A Hebe. Hebes are supposed to be smart. You should be the owner of that radio station by now."

What am I doing here? I wondered. I wanted to turn myself into a fly and buzz right out of the room. Tucker had not been looking for charity. He was an old and dear friend, almost a member of the family. His reception from the Chief put an end to all that. He got up to leave, and they mumbled something about seeing each other later. I walked out with Tucker and we paused for a minute. Smiling ruefully, he said, "Your dad doesn't get it. Owning the station because I'm Jewish ... Not all Jews are gifted businessmen, you know."

In the next few years, Tucker had a series of heart attacks. He and Frances, his wife, retired to Florida. With her encouragement, he wrote a couple of books about his time with the Steelers. "It helps him beat depression and his feeling of disconnectedness," she explained to some of us. AJR bought hundreds of Tucker's books and sent them to friends. Jack Sell once told me that he would never even think of writing a book. He said the risk of hurting people he had known well was too great. Tucker's books were harmless. As in his broadcasts, he was careful to avoid being critical of anyone. He wrote about himself and Jack Sell and AJR and Walt Kiesling, but not revealingly. The real Sell, the real AJR, the real Walt Kiesling, and even the real Joe Tucker were much more interesting and human than the cardboard characters in Tucker's books.

AJR used to tell me that his biography would have to be written twenty years after he died. "After all, I touched all the bases," he said. Tucker may not have touched all the bases – not the way AJR did – but they were running the bases together at times. If Tucker had just told his story, letting the chips fall where they might, he could have written a more interesting memoir.

Pat Livingston

I was 11 years old, or maybe 12, when I first met Pat Livingston. On the morning after a Steeler game in Washington, D.C., Kass, Aunt Alice, and all five Rooney boys – jammed into the family's Buick Roadmaster – were waiting for AJR in the driveway of a big hotel. A young, black-haired man came up to the car and spoke to Kass. He called her Mrs. Rooney. She introduced him to the rest of us, one by one, as Pat Livingston.

When the introductions were finished, he said, "Just a minute, I'll be back," and disappeared into the hotel. While he was gone, Kass said to Aunt Alice, loud enough for the rest of us to hear, "Pat works for the Steelers." In no time, he was back at the car with two bags of candy – Hershey kisses. AJR arrived, got behind the wheel, and we pulled away. Pat Livingston, I remember, stood in the driveway watching us depart.

I thought of him after that as the Candy Man. A few years later I came to know him as one of the toughest but fairest sportswriters ever to cover the Steelers.

In 1946 and 1947 Livingston was the team's press agent, a part-time scout, and an errand boy for Jock Sutherland. One day the frugal Scotsman sent him to pick up a suit at the dry cleaners'. Livingston returned with the suit and twenty-five cents in change from the dollar Sutherland had given him. Sutherland was not in the office, so Livingston put the change in an envelope and handed it to assistant coach John Michelosen, whose desk was next to Jock's.

Michelosen chuckled. "The Doctor won't want this quarter," he said. "Yes he will," Pat replied and went back to his own office. In a few minutes Sutherland appeared. "Did Pat come with my suit?" he asked Michelosen. "It's right here, hanging up," Michelosen told him. "Oh," Sutherland said. "Where's my change?"

To save carfare, Sutherland walked from the PAA in Oakland, where he lived in one room, to the Steeler offices in the Union Trust Building downtown, a distance of five miles. This was not out of character for him, but at the time of the dry-cleaning incident his behavior was growing bizarre. He accused Livingston of planning to keep the change he had put in the envelope. Years later Pat talked to me about it. The thing that seemed to bother him most was that both he and Sutherland had been Navy officers during World War II. "And now he's telling me I tried to steal his change – twenty-five cents. I knew it was time to move on," Pat said.

Shortly after that, he resigned. It was not until Sutherland's death from a brain tumor the following spring that we all learned the reason for the inexplicable way he had been acting.

Pat never used his Duquesne University law degree. The fact that his brother Tom was one of the most successful trial lawyers in Western Pennsylvania may or may not have been a factor. Shortly after joining the sports staff of the *Pittsburgh Press*, Pat got the Steeler assignment. He covered three winning teams in twenty-two years. As a beat reporter, he kept his eye on the story – on the performance of the players, on the way they were coached. He was willing to ignore a lot of off-the-field carrying-on by Buddy Parker, Bobby Layne, Ernie Stautner, and others.

I was present at our training camp in Latrobe on the day of the Joe Greene spitting incident, but all I saw was the aftermath. Interrupting a conversation we were having, Bob Reiland, an old high-school friend of my brother Dan, exclaimed, "Oh, this is terrible!" He was looking over my shoulder. I turned to see Joe Greene walking away and Pat wiping his face with a handkerchief.

At least a dozen people had been witnesses, but Pat made an effort to suppress the story. He prevailed on all the media people in camp to write nothing and say nothing about it. Even John Troan, editor of the paper he worked for, accepted Pat's argument that if the story were printed it would hurt his relations with the other players, shutting off valuable sources. The next day, after Greene told a *Press* columnist and a wire-service reporter that if he had it to do over again, he would, Troan changed his mind and wrote a blistering page-one editorial, which broke the media silence. There were follow-up stories in Pittsburgh and elsewhere without the consequences Livingston had feared. Not a single Steeler, including Greene, stopped talking to him.

Pat was a perceptive writer, I thought. In the 1950s and '60s, everyone said the Steelers were cheap and dumb. What Livingston saw was a lack of organization. He wrote long, analytical stories on how Paul Brown, in Cleveland, had organized his team from the ground up. Brown kept tabs on the training room, the equipment room, the conditioning program, the scouting, and the psychological and intelligence testing. He coached his coaches as well as his players. All of them knew where they stood, knew what Brown expected from them.

He did not throw money around. Instead, as Livingston pointed out, he emphasized doing things right. My brother Dan and I read Pat's stories about Paul Brown closely and often discussed them. We felt that AJR's approach was in many ways not compatible with Brown's, but when AJR decided at last to modernize his operation he asked a former Brown, Don Shula, for advice, and hired another former Brown, Chuck Noll, as his coach. The system Noll installed was a lot like the one that Pat Livingston had touted a decade before.

Pat encouraged me in my work and was kind enough to compliment me now and then in his columns. In my office one day we were talking about the way that new and sophisticated scouting methods had become commonplace since Sutherland's time. "That stuff," Pat said, "is baloney."

I challenged him to a test. We turned down the lights and turned on the movie projector and watched a University of California quarterback. Using our current scouting forms, each of us graded him as a prospect. It was serious business, lasting forty-five minutes. Little was said, other than, "Run that one back again ... " When we were finished, I turned up the lights and pushed our final scouting form at Livingston. "We've scouted the same quarterback," I said. "Let's each write him up and see what we have."

It took us another twenty-five minutes. And our reports were almost identical. We agreed that the prospect could improve with time and play in the NFL, that he should develop eventually into a starter, although perhaps not a starter for a winning team, that he was worth a second look. Both of us rated him a second- or early third-round draft choice. We compared what we had written about his size, speed, quickness, body control, toughness, football smarts, position skills, running ability, release, vision, awareness, throwing accuracy, and arm strength. Pat wrote much better than I did, but, over-all, our conclusions were similar. Our final summing-up was similar, too.

"Well, Pat," I said, "this shows me that even a newspaper guy can do what I do. I guess you learned something from Sutherland after all. Come out for a plate of spaghetti and some chocolate cake with me and Kay and the kids. She'd love to have you. You'll be an Irishman eating home-cooked Italian food served by a red-headed German girl while a bunch of half-Irish, half-German teenagers are running around. "This plain-talking reporter who'd been barred from the Steeler locker room, pushed or thrown out of the Bears' locker room, and punched in the ribs while being held in a headlock by one of Vince Lombardi's assistant Redskin coaches was a mellow fellow in our dining room that night.

After Pat became the sports editor of his paper in 1972, Phil Musick covered the Steelers. Pat continued to write columns about the team, but seemed to be more interested in golf.

On a perfect summer night in 1980, AJR and Kass marked their fiftieth wedding anniversary with a party at 940 North Lincoln Avenue. Only two media people were invited – Bill Burns and Pat Livingston. Dad and Mom were still in good health. Chuck Noll had given them a winning football team and I don't think they could have been happier. Pat by then was calling Mom "Kass" instead of "Mrs. Rooney." She said she never read anything that Pat or Jack Sell had to say about AJR for fear of jeopardizing her friendship with them. If what they wrote wasn't "nice," she would prefer not to know it.

I thought that Pat would write a column about the anniversary celebration. He chose not to. He had come to the party as a friend and not to report on it. From AJR and Kass on down, all of us Rooneys had a true affection for Pat.

In my case, it went back to the Hershey kisses.

The Mighty Atom

Toward the end of World War II, the pro football writer for the *Pittsburgh Press*, Les Biederman, went into the Army, and Carl Hughes, a kid just out of Geneva College, took his place. Carl was from South Fork, in Cambria County, where Barney McGinley had once tended bar. McGinley and AJR were still promoting fights, and Chet Smith, Carl's boss, informed him that in addition to covering the Steelers and Pitt, he was now the paper's boxing writer.

"But I've never seen a fight in my life," Carl protested.

"Don't worry about it," Smith advised him.

Carl never had written a news story, either, but he turned out to have quite a flair for the job. His reporting uncovered the fact that without an OK from the university the Pitt coach, Clark Shaughnessy, was moonlighting on Sundays as a consultant to the Washington Redskins. Incensed, Shaughnessy called the editor of the *Press*, Ed Leech, and demanded that Hughes be fired. Leech's response was to give Carl a five-dollar raise, increasing his pay to the munificent sum of thirty dollars a week.

AJR, unlike Shaughnessy, took a liking to Carl. In the 1920s the world flyweight champion, a Welshman named Jimmy Wilde, had been known as The Mighty Atom. Carl Hughes was Welsh and also diminutive in size. Accordingly, AJR bestowed Jimmy Wilde's nickname on Carl, abbreviating it later on to "Atom."

When the Steelers played out of town, AJR would take the writers and broadcasters to dinner. In Detroit one Saturday night, he piled them all into a taxicab and asked the driver to recommend a good place for fried chicken. As Hughes told the story, the driver said there was only one good place but added, "No use going there, because you couldn't get in." AJR said, "Well, take us to that place anyway. I'll make it worth your while."

Grunting "OK," the cabbie drove them to what appeared to be an ordinary house – a private residence - deep in the black ghetto. The writers and broadcasters exchanged looks with one another, but followed AJR up the steps of the front porch to the door. AJR rang the bell. Nothing happened. He rang again. Another long wait. He rapped on the door with his knuckles. No one came. He rapped a second time, harder. At last a door panel which was little more than a peephole slid open. A black face peered out. "Whaddya want?"

"Some fried chicken," said AJR.

"We don't let strangers in."

"Do me a favor," AJR told him. "Go tell your boss that Art Rooney is here. If he doesn't know who Art Rooney is, ask him to call Gus Greenlee in Pittsburgh." Gus Greenlee, as I have said before, was the numbers king of Pittsburgh and the owner of the city's Negro League baseball team, the Crawfords.

The sergeant at arms disappeared. In a minute a different man came to the door and pulled it wide open. He was short and fat and beautifully dressed and he had a big cigar in his mouth.

"Art Rooney!" he said. "Come right in! You look exactly how Gus Greenlee described you to me."

The fried chicken, according to Hughes, was excellent, and the dinners were all on the house.

The Groundling

Tom Birks, the pro football writer for the *Pittsburgh Sun-Telegraph*, was an untidy man in his sixties who came from somewhere in the British Isles and talked with a Scottish or North of England burr. Tom never flew with the team to out-of-town games. Instead, he would travel by railroad or bus or drive his own car, sometimes missing out on important stories.

"Mister Birks," I once asked him, "why do you refuse to fly?"

"Young man," he replied, "when I was a cub reporter I had to cover an airline crash. This was in the early days of aviation. When I got to the scene, I looked at all the mangled, compressed corpses, and the body parts lying around, and said to myself, 'From now on I'm staying close to the ground.'"

I wished I had not been so curious.

Mort Sharnik

In the early 1960s, Mort Sharnik of *Sports Illustrated* showed up at our training camp in Rhode Island and asked Ed Kiely if he could speak to "Mister Rooney." Whether or not Kiely knew of Sharnik's reputation as a top-flight investigative reporter I have no idea. If he did, it might have given him pause. In any case, he arranged the interview. Off and on, Sharnik and my father talked for several days. Before their last meeting broke up, Sharnik said, "Mister Rooney, you are known by football people as a good loser. I don't believe it. From what I've seen and heard about you, I think you are anything but a loser."

After I got to be friends with Mort, he told me that AJR choked up with emotion. He clenched his teeth, biting off the end of his cigar. And then with his voice cracking he said, "I hate losing! I've won as a baseball player and a baseball manager. I've won as a football player and a football coach. I've won as a boxer. And you know that I've won at the race track. With the Steelers, I'm trying to win. Just remember that. I'm trying! I hate losing!"

That particular story never made *Sports Illustrated*, but Mort kept in touch with the family. "It's only a matter of time before Art finds a winner," he would say. Art did find a winner, and Mort was with us as a friend, and not in his capacity as a *Sports Illustrated* writer, at all of the Steelers' Super Bowl games.

He accompanied us one time to a mid-season game between the Steelers and Bengals in Cincinnati. A constant theme in the sports pages just then was quarterback Terry Bradshaw's supposed lack of intelligence. The Steelers won that day in Cincinnati, but not because Bradshaw had distinguished himself, and in the dressing room afterward the writers were subjecting him to an unending string of blunt, not to say insulting, questions. Before the interview was over, we were ready to board the bus for the airport. "Wait a minute," Mort said. He took a few quick steps to Bradshaw's locker and penetrated the crowd to introduce himself. "Terry, I'm Mort Sharnik from *Sports Illustrated*." On such and such a play, in such and such a situation, Mort went on, "I thought you did exactly the right thing." Bradshaw looked up, and Mort proceeded to ask him questions of a much more positive nature than the ones he'd been getting from the other reporters, who were taking it all in and writing it all down.

After they scattered, Sharnik and Bradshaw stood by themselves for a while, talking and laughing and having a good time. Mort then rejoined us, and I gave him a quizzical look. He smiled, shrugged, and said, "Well, you've been telling me that Bradshaw just needed some self-confidence. So I thought I'd try to make him feel good."

Part Four: New Broom 1970-1973

Chapter 46

Three Rivers

On April 25, 1968, after twenty years of political bickering, ground was broken for the city's new baseball and football stadium. "Hallowed ground," the speakers kept calling it – this clearing in a junk yard on the north shore of the Allegheny River where Exposition Park and Pop Rooney's tavern once stood. Five civic leaders with five silver spades dug five little holes in the hallowed ground, and Pittsburgh had started building a $28 million playpen for the Pirates and Steelers.

AJR was one of the ground breakers. For public- relations purposes, there were goal posts on the site, and he placekicked an extra point, with my brother Dan holding the ball. It was pure symbolism – getting the project off on the right foot, so to speak. Afterward, AJR told reporters that he had not tried a placekick since 1921, when his sandlot team, the Hope-Harveys, played the Canton Bulldogs. As I don't have to remind you if you've been reading this memoir closely, a Canton lineman blocked that kick, allowing Jim Thorpe to pick up the ball and run for the only touchdown of the game.

It takes forever in Pittsburgh to get something done, and Three Rivers Stadium, as the structure would eventually be named, had been pie in the sky since the late 1940s. There were vague plans for a stadium during what came to be known as Renaissance I, the massive cleanup and construction project launched by Mayor Dave Lawrence and banker Richard King Mellon, but bridges, tunnels, the Hilton Hotel, the Gateway Center office-building complex, and Point State Park had priority. Finally in 1958 the University of Pittsburgh, gobbling up real estate in Oakland, bought the Pirates' outdated ball park, Forbes Field, with the object of tearing it down. Pitt needed land for classroom buildings and a library, so Forbes Field had to go – not right away, but eventually. Pirate owner John Galbreath, in consenting to the sale, was sending Pittsburgh a message: without a new, taxpayer-financed, state-of-the-art facility, the Pirates might pick up and leave.

For both the Pirates and the Steelers, there were greener pastures elsewhere. America's population was shifting to the South and the West, creating boom towns that hungered for major-league baseball and professional football, and they were offering unheard-of inducements to established but troubled franchises. Among these inducements was the latest and gaudiest in free public housing: new stadiums at no cost. AJR, who spent his entire life in the same North Side neighborhood, wasn't tempted. "We're Pittsburgh guys," he admonished his sons. "I want you to keep the team here. But if the time ever comes when you see that you can't make a living," he added, "get out."

There was never the need. Just the mere possibility that one day it might come to that – that Pittsburgh would find itself without a baseball team or a football team – concentrated the minds of the politicians. Lawrence, the expediter, was in Harrisburg now, his energies channeled into governing the state, and though the Lawrence wannabe's attempting to fill his shoes squabbled endlessly over every little detail, they agreed in principle that a stadium should be built. How, and with whose money, were more difficult questions to deal with.

The Republican county commissioner, a dentist named Bill McClelland, was the main obstructionist. Getting him to play along with the two Democratic commissioners was like pulling teeth – harder than pulling teeth, in fact, because McClelland held out to the end. A private business, he insisted, should pay for its own workplace. Maybe so. John Galbreath, with his real-estate millions, could have managed it; AJR's resources were not as great. In any case, when the give and take was over, and the last speech had been made, the politicians found a way out. They floated a bond issue.

The site of the new stadium, within walking distance of 940 North Lincoln Avenue, was never a point of contention. AJR could not have been better satisfied, but his knowledge of past events made him apprehensive as well. "We'll be right in the middle of a flood plain," he warned the architect,

Dahlyn Ritchey, repeating the old story of how he almost drowned in Exposition Park on the long-ago day when Squawker Mullen upset the canoe. No cause to worry, Ritchey assured him. All the new dams on the Allegheny River had made flooding a thing of the past. AJR worried anyway. Not two years after the stadium opened, Tropical Storm Agnes careened into the area, the Allegheny overflowed its banks, and again there was high water. "A once-in-a-life-time occurrence," Ritchey explained, to the Chief's amusement.

Ritchey's first model for Three Rivers, presented in 1966, was a gem – graceful and crescent-shaped, with a multi-level concourse around it, and open at one end. It offered a view of Mount Washington and the skyline nearest the Point. Everything about it seemed right except the price tag – $38 million. Go back to the drawing board, the Stadium Authority instructed Ritchey.

The cheaper design he came up with, a concrete cylinder indistinguishable in any way from the cookie-cutter stadiums going up all over the country, lacked intimacy, lacked character, lacked charm (which Forbes Field had in abundance, despite its shortcomings). None of this bothered me. I felt that any new stadium would solve our problems if only we could put a winner on the field. The seating capacity was the same as before – 52,000 for baseball, 59,000 for football – but there were fewer seats close to the action and fewer seats covered by a roof. One other thing: with the usual overruns, the cost turned out to be more like $40 million than $28 million, the estimate. Adding the cost of new roads to the total, it came to at least $55 million. Thirty-three years later, when the stadium itself had ceased to exist, the bond issue was still unredeemed.

Both the Steelers and the Pirates wanted a glassed-in restaurant from where diners – and drinkers – could watch without leaving their tables, but they differed on its placement. The Stadium Authority listened to Galbreath, with the result that the Allegheny Club, as it was called, overlooked the football field between the twenty-yard lines – premium seating space – instead of from an end zone. AJR would tell his people, "Do you know how many good football seats we lost?"

Even so, Three Rivers was a better stadium for football than for baseball. Oval-shaped now, rather than crescent-shaped, it gave every football fan the best possible view for his money. Some of the baseball seating might as well have been in Saskatchewan. Dan, looking at the model, spoke for us all (with the exception of Joe Carr) when he said, "We're pleased." We preferred Three Rivers to Shea Stadium in New York, to the stadiums in Washington and St. Louis, and for sure to the circular Atlanta stadium.

Long after we had moved in, knowledgeable people would say to me, "The Steelers have the best of it. This place was built for football, not baseball." Undeniably true. However, John Galbreath and his son Dan owned the corporation that held the lease, collected all the rent from the motorcycle races, rock concerts, and circuses held at the stadium, and owned the air rights, which meant that only the Galbreaths could develop the adjacent land. They developed nothing – and they were builders. Eighty-one baseball games and only ten football games were played at the stadium every year, and yet the football team generated almost as much revenue as the baseball team.

No ... the Pirates, not the Steelers, had the best of it.

In the months before construction began, we were hearing loose talk about financial and political shenanigans. Innuendos like "How much is Davey Lawrence getting out of this? ... Nothing? ... Aw, come on." A suggestion that the stadium bear his name met with ferocious resistance. Inevitably, I suppose, the Rooneys and the Galbreaths were said to be the owners of the land Three Rivers would occupy. A title search disposed of that particular canard, but revealed something else: much of the housing property displaced by the stadium had belonged to families we knew from St. Peter's parish – the McCabes, the Yuhaszes, the Boyles, and various others. Just for the record, the buyouts they received did not make them rich.

On the site of their demolished houses, a scrap heap had risen: piles of gravel and coal and rusty wrecked cars, all destined to be bulldozed into stadium landfill. And rising weirdly above the bleak panorama was the unfinished north end of the double-decked Fort Duquesne Bridge – "the Bridge to Nowhere," *Post-Gazette* writer Mel Seidenberg called it. In time the bridge would carry Pirate and Steeler fans across the Allegheny River to the parking lots. For now, it hung uselessly above the shore, dead-ending in the sky because the Urban Redevelopment Authority had run out of funds. Drivers who were either drunk, insane, or recklessly macho would maneuver their cars onto the bridge and keep going until they plunged into space. There were not as many deaths as you might expect.

Predictably, work stoppages and slowdowns kept the stadium from being finished on time, and featherbedding expanded the construction costs. Under the terms of the labor contract, if a delivery truck arrived at the gate to the chain-link fence surrounding the work site, it could not pass through. Only the builders' trucks were allowed to transport cargo from that point on, and the driver had to be paid for an eight-hour day. Once when Burrell Cohen, the project coordinator, arrived at the gate on foot with a package under his arm, a package that weighed about a pound, he was halted. A union truck driver relieved him of the package, took it through the gate, and handed it back. For that, he received a full day's pay.

Outsiders who had business at the work site were being systematically shaken down by the gatekeeper, a man named Brown. He was charging people an admittance fee. Everybody knew what he was doing, but for reasons I can't explain he was able to get away with it. One day when I intended to show a few friends of mine how the work was coming along, Fran Fogarty called ahead to alert the construction foreman. I had a name that opened doors – I was Art Rooney, Jr., the son of Art Rooney, Sr. – but Brown, I had heard, was an arrogant little bastard and no respecter of persons. Afraid of being turned away at the gate with my friends looking on, I requisitioned a football from the Steeler equipment manager and presented it to Brown in lieu of payment, I am sorry to say. Admittedly, though, we were treated quite well on our tour of the work site.

Either the union bosses or the Stadium Authority eventually put an end to Brown's scam. He was arrested, tried, convicted, and sent to jail. Later on, there was trouble with the painters. Jim Lally, a labor leader and city councilman, was also a member of the Stadium Authority. The painters who had been on the job, Lally told me, tried to "blackmail" the Authority shortly before the stadium opened. Instead of giving in to their demands, the Authority took Lally's advice and hired a crew of painters from the union hall to replace them.

Our move to Three Rivers would be total. The team would practice there, abandoning South Park. Executives, coaches, secretaries, scouting department, and the ticket office would be headquartered there.

Overseeing all this was Dan, who could look for no help from the rest of us. On the eve of the changeover, we had lost our irreplaceable business manager, Fran Fogarty. to a fatal heart attack. AJR, at 69, had become very involved in our race tracks. Ed Kiely's P.R. duties kept him sufficiently occupied. And, speaking for myself, I was focused on player personnel and only that. I headed for Latrobe when training camp opened, hit the road at the start of the season, and did not return home, except for fresh laundry, until after Thanksgiving.

In short, my older brother had his hands full. Overworked and on edge, he discovered one day that Joe Carr and his assistant, Jim Boston, had messed up the ticket manifesto. Season ticket holders at Pitt Stadium expected comparable seating at Three Rivers, and something had gone wrong in making the switch. Dan was irate. He wanted to fire Carr and he wanted to fire Boston. AJR was at Liberty Bell, with John, and Dan put in a call. "Our whole organization will look stupid," he raged. "The public thinks we're incompetent as it is. We are seen as incapable of making a move like this, and now here's the proof."

AJR de-escalated him. Joe Carr, he reminded Dan, was like an old family retainer. Not only that, but he was still in mourning for his son, who'd been killed in Vietnam. Allowances had to be made. Jim Boston needed self- discipline, but he was bright. Jim and Joe were our kind of people, North Siders. Give them a break this one time. Everything will be OK. We can get this straightened out. Just make it clear that there will not be any further mistakes.

Joe Carr, Jim Boston, and everybody else in the ticket office were out in the stadium counting seats the next day. Dan was there, too, riding herd. Joe Carr remained on the job until he retired, but with gradually decreasing responsibility. Buff Boston was made traveling secretary and acquitted himself to Dan's satisfaction in the unenviable task of keeping owners, players, coaches, and influential hangers-on appeased. He also negotiated contracts, in the process dealing with players, their agents, their wives, and even their mothers-in-law. His years with the Steelers taught him to be a diplomat.

The move into Three Rivers was a definitive moment in our history. Under the iron hand of Jock Sutherland, we had known success for a time in the 1940s. Just his name was enough to fill the stands. When he staggered out of a Kentucky swamp, ready to die of a brain tumor, the Steelers died with him, on the field and in the counting house. Three Rivers Stadium brought back the crowds and the fan interest. Season-ticket sales took off, and never thereafter was the stability of the franchise in doubt.

It's trite to say this, but in 1970 we turned things around. In 1970 the balance between major-league baseball and professional football had shifted; more Americans now preferred football, and Three Rivers positioned us to catch the incoming tide. The new stadium was the showcase we needed. The product itself, the football team, soon would be worthy of its packaging. Dan, who was now in charge, and Chuck Noll, the young coach he had hired, were giving us fresh, imaginative leadership, with AJR presiding over the transition. At last the stars in the heavens were lining up perfectly for us – either that, it seemed to me, or the coal dust was blowing the right way.

Chapter 47

Golden Boy

In the fall of 1969, convinced from our scouting reports that Terry Bradshaw, the quarterback at Louisiana Tech, would be a first-round draft pick, I flew down to Shreveport, rented a car, and drove to the Tech campus in Ruston on Interstate 25, not far south of the Arkansas border. I was traveling east and passing through hill country, a rustic landscape of cow pastures and ponds grotesquely overhung with pipelines. There is oil in Louisiana, and natural gas. The traffic consisted mainly of pickup trucks. They were arsenals on wheels, a rifle or shotgun in every rear window. Up North, it was getting cold; in Louisiana, green leaves still clung to the trees, and for comfort I turned on the air conditioner.

Grambling, where Eddie Robinson coached, is just outside Ruston, so I stopped there to say hello. "Wait till you see this guy Bradshaw. He's the greatest thing going," Robinson told me. Thus reassured, I drove into Ruston with pleasant expectations.

At the Holiday Inn, the desk clerk recognized my name. "Rooney," he said. "The Pittsburgh Steelers. Pro scouts have been coming through here for weeks. Everybody wants a look at that big blond kid over at Tech."

The Tech coach, Maxie Lambaugh, received me affably. Two months earlier, for a Steeler exhibition game in Shreveport, I had taken care of his whole staff's ticket needs. Lambaugh set up a movie projector for me, and in a stifling room with just a chair and a table for furniture, I watched game films of Bradshaw. Nothing in them surprised me. I had seen him on film in his junior year and I knew what the Blesto scouts thought. Jess Thompson had called him a "dinger" – a pro all the way. Jim Palmer declared that he "had it all – size, mobility, quick release. And a cannon for an arm." In high school, Palmer noted, Bradshaw had been a javelin thrower and in fact held the national record. Will Walls compared him with "Sammy" – to Sammy's disadvantage. He said that, for strength, Bradshaw's arm was actually superior to Baugh's.

At practice the next day I examined the flesh-and-blood Bradshaw. He was big, all right – 6 feet 2 or 3, 215 pounds. And he could move. Even in the NFL, he'd be a quarterback who ran like a halfback. As for the quick release, it was something to behold. He got rid of the ball *right now*. And for sure he could lay it out there. At the same time, he was not a "mad bomber." Arm strength, Chuck Noll and backfield coach Don Heinrich maintained, was less important than accuracy and the quick release; Bradshaw's accuracy gave me no qualms. His short and medium passes were catchable and his deep throws came down in "the area of reception" (scoutspeak for "close enough to the target"). He could use some fine-tuning, that much I recognized, but the basics were solidly in place. I learned at first hand about the strength of his arm when an incomplete pass ricocheted off the ground and hit me on the leg. Two days later, the black and blue mark had not yet disappeared.

A Tech student manager, tall and dark-haired, was gathering up footballs and putting them into a bag. Student managers, if they're not afraid of the coach, will tell you things that you otherwise never would hear, so I introduced myself. "What kind of a guy is this Bradshaw?" I asked. He paused in his task and straightened up. Beaming, he answered, "Wonderful guy."

The kid was so willing to talk that I decided to probe him for headshrinker stuff. I remembered a few questions from Psychology 101 at St. Vincent. Did Terry respect his father? Very much, which meant he'd be coachable. Did he drink? He'd take a beer, and I had no objections. Most good athletes don't abstain. What about girls – did he like them? Absolutely! Nothing wrong with that, either, nothing at all.

I asked about Bradshaw's character, and the student manager described to me an All-American Boy, possessed of so many virtues I couldn't help but be skeptical.

"You sound like a relative," I said.

"I'm his brother."

His name was Gary. Two years older than Terry, he'd been a football player himself, he said, until he fell from a tree, breaking his back. I thanked him for his help and sought out the team's quarterback coach, Mickey Slaughter.

Chuck Noll had made a point of asking me to interview Slaughter, an acquaintance from the days when Noll was an assistant on Sid Gilman's San Diego staff and Slaughter played quarterback for the Denver Broncos. A persistent story that Baylor and L.S.U. had stopped recruiting Bradshaw because of his SAT score was troubling to Noll. Were we wasting our time on a physically gifted dunce? If not, it seemed odd that a quarterback with NFL potential, "a pro all the way," had chosen a middle-of-the-pack college like Tech in preference to a Southwest or Southeastern conference school. Sure, the Denver Broncos had drafted Mickey Slaughter out of Tech, but that was in 1963, when Denver was in the AFL and the AFL was still very much a fledgling league. So, to ease Noll's concerns, I asked Mickey Slaughter about Bradshaw. "Listen," he said, "don't believe the rumors. The guy's plenty smart enough to figure out a pro team's offensive schemes."

I went back to Pittsburgh completely satisfied. Everything I had seen, everything I had heard, made me a full-throated member of the chorus, singing Bradshaw's praises with Thompson, Palmer, and Walls. Not that I envisioned him yet as a Steeler. Somebody else would draft him ahead of us, I was sure. In our opening game, Noll's first as the Steelers' coach, we had beaten Detroit; now we were losing week after week, but there was still no way, I believed, that we could possibly end up with the NFL's worst record and thus get the No. 1 pick.

Bad guess.

In November, when we lost to the previously winless Chicago Bears, my brother Dan, for one, saw the writing on the wall. We finished the season 1-13. So did the Bears. To decide which team drafted first, there would be a coin toss in New Orleans during Super Bowl week.

On December 10th, Jack Butler's Blesto scouts, meeting in Pittsburgh, arrived at their final evaluation of one thousand college seniors. Bradshaw, the ratings said, was most likely to succeed, making him the theoretical No.1 pick.

Or so I believed. Our coach, Chuck Noll, was not as certain. One thing that bothered Noll was the quality of the competition Bradshaw had faced – Northeast Louisiana and Southeast Louisiana, Northwest Louisiana and Southwest Louisiana, McNeese State and East Carolina, not exactly seedbeds of professional talent. The post-season all-star games, Noll predicted, would test Bradshaw's mettle. At the Senior Bowl game in Mobile, he'd be playing for Don Shula, running the Baltimore Colts' offense, or one that resembled it, against top-flight pass rushers and top-flight defensive backs. "We'll see how he picks up the teaching," Noll said.

"Gawwd," I replied – under my breath. I was like a kid who has fallen madly in love and is getting disagreeable feedback from his parents. (My own parents, happily, were just as smitten with Kay as I was.)

At the North-South Bowl, in Miami, and the All-America Bowl, in Tampa, Noll's assistants had scouted Bradshaw. The head man himself went to Mobile. Noll was a Doubting Thomas. He had to see to believe. He attended three practice sessions, watching Bradshaw run the forty-yard dash in 4.7 – fast time for a quarterback – while pulling a hamstring. Shula, considerate as ever, offered to send him home, but Bradshaw refused to hear of it. He played the whole game, and Noll was impressed. Still he reserved judgment. Noll could be maddening.

What decided the issue, for me, was the I.Q. test. I.Q. tests for football players were not yet standard procedure, but Jack Butler sent Dick Haley to Mobile, and Haley persuaded Bradshaw to take one. Actually, Bradshaw was more than willing, Haley said. There were twenty-five math questions and twenty-five that dealt with vocabulary. Bradshaw measured up, or I don't think we'd have drafted him. Given Noll's priorities, the I.Q. test was important.

Questions about Bradshaw's reputed lack of brainpower followed him throughout his career. Jim Palmer had seen him as Li'l Abner, the Al Capp cartoon character from the mythical redneck village of Dogpatch. For a fact, there were similarities. Bradshaw had deep-set blue eyes and a square-jawed, snub-nosed, ingenuous face suggestive of Li'l Abner; he had the same massive upper torso, developed through weightlifting and summertime ditch-digging. The analogy ended there. Bradshaw was neither dumb nor naive. He came from a Deep South back-country culture unfamiliar to Eastern sportswriters, so they misunderstood him, or some of them did, baffled by his cracker-barrel witticisms. Sometimes to amuse himself, Bradshaw played games with the sportswriters, giving different answers to different reporters when they asked him the same silly question. Bradshaw knew, if the writers did not, that what football players say to newspapermen is seldom of any great consequence.

Even among his fellow athletes Bradshaw was known as a dimwit. Hollywood Henderson's infamous gibe – "He couldn't spell 'cat' if you spotted him the 'c' and the 't'" – appeared in newspapers all over the country during Super Bowl week in 1979. Henderson played for the Dallas Cowboys, whose coach, Torn Landry, was a certified football genius. In the championship game between Dallas and the Steelers, Landry called every play for his quarterback, Roger Staubach. Bradshaw, for the most part, relied on his own oft-disparaged intellect. Amazingly (or maybe not), Bradshaw came out on top. When his playing career was over and his blond hair was gone, he raked in more money as a public speaker and television personality than he ever had made in football. (It may be that the ability to spell "cat" is overrated. As one for whom spelling has always been a struggle, I'd like to think so.)

The coin flip took place on the day before the Senior Bowl game. Under the eyes of witnesses gathered around a cloth-covered table, Commissioner Pete Rozelle tossed a 1921 silver dollar into the air. Ed McCaskey of the Bears called out "heads" and made a face when the dollar came up tails. Dan, smiling broadly, said, "I have no idea who we'll take."

There was never any doubt what the Bears would have done. In a conversation about Bradshaw years later, Ed McCaskey told me, "That coin flip made such a difference to both of us."

I lobbied hard for Bradshaw with Dan and with Noll. Buddy Parker had always preached that when you're putting together a football team you start with the great quarterback. To me, it made sense. Whatever Noll may have thought was not clear; in any case, he wanted to think some more. There was game film, he said, to be studied and re-studied. And if we did take Bradshaw, what then? Already the telephones were ringing at the Roosevelt Hotel, bringing trade offers. AJR had decreed that the final say on the draft belonged to Noll, and presumably this meant he was free to make deals, but the Chief himself, I noticed, was taking every call, which terrified me.

I was violently opposed to any kind of trade. We were notorious – weren't we? – for giving quarterbacks away. I could roll the names off my tongue: Luckman, Unitas, Dawson, Kemp, Morrall, Nelsen. We had cut them all loose or traded them and they all had won championships elsewhere. Would history repeat itself with Bradshaw?

The owners and general managers who took us for fools, and were making ludicrous offers ("Same old Steelers"), worried me only a little. But there was one proposal, from our old friend Frank Wall, general manager of the Atlanta Falcons, that struck me as halfway worth considering, and AJR seemed to be interested. Wall was offering multiple draft choices and a handful of veterans for Bradshaw, veterans who were close to being stars. Instead of calling Noll or Dan, he talked to the Chief directly, and it gratified AJR's ego. It seemed to me that they talked every day.

Back from my last scouting trip before the draft, I went into crisis mode. I had to make my dad see that we must not even think of letting Bradshaw go. But for that I would need one-on-one time, and AJR was never alone. He shared an office at work with Fran Fogarty; if he and Fogarty were not together, he and Kiely were together. During business hours, it was impossible for me to isolate my dad. Newspapermen, hangers-on, close friends, acquaintances, the Catholic clergy, and even complete strangers had seemingly unfettered access to him. He was almost incapable of turning people away, convinced it would hurt their feelings. To hurt anyone's feelings – anyone's, that is, except his sons' – was unthinkable. I could ask for a private meeting, but it would bring out all of his stubbornness. The approach had to be an oblique one. And then it came to me – the solution. He liked to be chauffeured to and from work. I therefore volunteered to transport him. Each morning I picked him up at 940 North Lincoln Avenue and drove him across the river to the Roosevelt Hotel; in the late afternoon I returned him to Kass. Twice each day, for fifteen minutes at the most, the

Chief was my captive audience. There were no cell phones back then, and no car phones. I prayed for heavy traffic on the Sixth Street Bridge.

Sometimes John the twin, who in 1970 was a schoolteacher, would be with us, but he sat in the back seat and kept his mouth shut. On our first trip, I decided to go slow with the Chief. I said, "Dad, Noll is not saying that Bradshaw's a bad first-round pick. He's saying we have to weigh everything out. These quarterbacks we have now" – Terry Hanratty and Dick Shiner – "are not the kind who can take us to a Super Bowl. I think eventually Bradshaw could do that." AJR remained noncommittal. It seemed clear that I was not getting through, and I knew the reason why. "He's warming up to the Atlanta deal," I said to John.

Gradually I began to harangue him. His response was to chew his cigar and say very little. And then one morning as we were headed toward the Roosevelt Hotel, I made a spur-of-the-moment suggestion. I said, "If Frank Wall is serious, if he really wants Bradshaw, ask him to throw in Claude Humphrey with the rest of those veterans he's offering."

Claude Humphrey was a dominating defensive linemen for Atlanta, one of the new breed of NFL player the small black colleges in the South had been developing. In Humphrey's case, it was Tennessee State. AJR had hoped we could draft him and was not unaware of the impact he had made in his first two years as a pro. "Ask the Falcons if they're willing to trade Humphrey," I repeated. From the way the Chief looked at me, I was certain I had caught his attention.

When we were back in the car at quitting time, the first thing he said was, "I heard from Frank Wall again today."

Faking coolness, I said, "You did?"

"Yes. I asked if he'd let us have Humphrey. He didn't answer me right away."

Get to the point! I was thinking.

"Then he said, 'Art, we can't do that.' He said, 'You don't win championships by getting rid of your great young players.' And I told him, 'That's what my son Artie says about Bradshaw.'"

So there would not be a deal with the Falcons, I understood, and I was elated. But now a different concern replaced my fear of losing Bradshaw to Atlanta. I disliked what I was hearing from Noll. He spoke of "offers" from other teams, offers he would have to evaluate after taking into account the views of his assistant coaches.

Wait a minute, I said to myself. Had he forgotten our agreement to build through the draft? In a state of agitation, I took up the matter with Dan. Calmly, he reminded me that Noll had the right to keep or trade draft choices. "Well, I know how to settle that," I blurted. "We were one-and-thirteen last year. Fire him! If he refuses to go for Bradshaw, fire him!"

In hindsight, I can't believe I said that.

Temperate words from Dan brought me back to my senses, but I was not giving up. With only twenty-four hours left before the draft, I appealed once more to the Chief. I was driving him from 940 North Lincoln to the Roosevelt Hotel as usual, with John in the back seat. Many years afterward, John's recall of the pitch I made that day was better than mine. As he told it, I said, "Dad, you gave me a job to do, and I've worked at it. Now I am telling you that we've got to keep Bradshaw, regardless of what the coaches decide. Who are you going to believe – them or me?"

The Chief's answer – if there was one – left me in the dark. But as soon as we arrived at the Roosevelt Hotel, he went to the eighth floor. The coaches and Dan were up there. John, for some reason, tagged along, and he told me what happened. First, the Chief called everyone together. Then he delivered a speech. He said, "I've given this draft a lot of thought. Here's what we are going to do with our first choice: we are taking Terry Bradshaw. And we are NOT going to trade him." There was no further discussion. Case closed.

All I could think of when John brought me the news was "Mission accomplished."

Control Freak

On draft day, having decided in advance that we would use our first pick to take Bradshaw, we could immediately start thinking about the sixteen rounds that were left. Steeler drafts in years gone by had been a disorderly process. Under Buddy Parker and Bill Austin, a lot of mischief could happen. Their assistant coaches were the source of the trouble. We'd be ready to go ahead with a selection when one or the other of them, barging into the draft room, would call out excitedly, "We can make a trade for so-and-so!" I promised myself I'd put an end to these disruptions.

For the most part, that is what I did. Chuck Noll was all business, which suited me perfectly; I was all business myself – to a fault. There was this routine I fell into of writing down in chalk on a blackboard the names of the top four athletes in the draft, regardless of position. I had a long list of players ranked numerically, and as names disappeared from the board I added new ones. Meanwhile, we'd be discussing our options, but even after Noll took over, an assistant might interrupt to bring up the name of some marginal prospect, and I'm afraid I would let my annoyance show. "Hey," I would tell him, laying down the law, "we've already decided this."

In the eyes of the coaches, I suppose this made me a control freak. One year on draft day when I was out of the room, an assistant took the liberty of putting a few names on the board. I considered it an act of insurrection. Demanding silence, I announced, "Only one person can write on this blackboard – me!" There were hoots of derision from the coaches. "Listen," I continued, "you guys will be allowed to write names on this board when you allow me to call the plays during our games." With that, I grabbed an eraser, wiped the board clean, and chalked up my own names, three of which duplicated the names I had just taken off.

For the rest of the draft, the coaches carried on like schoolboys tormenting a teacher. They would write down players' names on pieces of paper and contrive to let me see them. One taped his names to the inside of his coat lapel and flashed it at me whenever I walked past. Another attached a list to the sole of one shoe and sat across from me with his feet on the table. It was all in good fun, no hard feelings on either side. They were making their point just as I had made mine, but with humor rather than passion.

The 1970 draft was even better than the one the year before. In Bradshaw, we now had a passer, and Noll's first thought was to give him a target. Unexpectedly, Ron Shanklin from North Texas State – Joe Greene's school – was still on the board in the second round. We'd been watching him for three years and none of us doubted that Ron was our man. Though never a great player, he turned out to be a very good one, voted the MVP by his teammates in 1973. The following season, Ron was a starting wide receiver on the first Steeler team to play in and win the Super Bowl. He made the Pro Bowl, too, but by that time Noll had Lynn Swann and John Stallworth, rookies with Hall-of-Fame skills, and he traded Shanklin to the Bears. When his playing career was over, Ron did some scouting for me. He was still a fairly young man when he died.

In the third round, we improved the defensive backfield. Noll was certainly not a disciple of Buddy Parker, but in some ways their values were similar. Your first need, Parker always said, was a quarterback who could throw, and then you had to get him some receivers. "Everything else is defense," he would add.

A cornerback we liked, Mel Blount, played at Southern University, an all-black institution in Louisiana. He was tall, handsome, and ebony-colored, with sharply-sculpted features and no hair on his head, and he could run about as fast as the quarter horses he liked to ride. One of Southern U.'s assistant coaches, Ron Brown, told me that Blount was (a) a great defensive back, (b) the very best horseman in Louisiana, and (c) a fine person. The first two of these claims turned out to be indisputably true, and I never doubted the third one, although I differed in that respect from certain NFL players – ball carriers, tight ends, and wide receivers who in years to come would let their feelings be known. Having taken hits from Blount, they feared and despised him. In time, his aggressiveness prompted a change in the rules. So successful was he at bumping receivers to keep them from running their pass routes that the NFL officially made this tactic illegal.

The drafts of 1969 and 1970 and the signing of Jim Clack, a free agent, added seven players to the roster who would start against the Minnesota Vikings in Super Bowl IX. The draftees were Joe Greene, L. C. Greenwood, Jon Kolb, Terry Bradshaw, Mel Blount, and Ron Shanklin. Greene,

Blount, and Bradshaw were future Hall of Famers. Eight players in all from the 1970 draft made the roster, which included four eventual Super Bowl starters Noll had inherited from Austin – Andy Russell, Ray Mansfield, Sam Davis, and Rocky Bleier.

We were getting our act together.

Labor of Love

Bradshaw's "legal representative," a lawyer from Shreveport named Robert Pugh, was tall and lean, with strawberry blond hair and a soft Southern drawl. "Please un-da-stand," he informed us. "I am not an agent. I want the best for my client, of course, but I think we can work something out that is fair to both sides."

Doing business with Mr. Pugh was a pleasure. He took an immediate liking to AJR, and said so unabashedly. "Youah fathah," he told me, "is truly special. I am honored to call him mah friend." AJR was equally honored. He made a generous offer to Bradshaw, who quickly accepted it, and the signing took place in an atmosphere of mutual good feeling.

Our association with Mr. Pugh continued for many years. A large glass case in his Shreveport office held autographed Steeler footballs, photos of Bradshaw, photos of AJR, and personal letters from AJR. When our Philadelphia lawyer, John Macartney, got us into the oil and gas business in Louisiana, Mr. Pugh represented the family down there. To judge by the difficulty we had in persuading him to send us a bill, he was doing it as a labor of love.

Our team physician, Dr. John Best, performed surgery on Bradshaw to remove a calcium buildup on his hamstring. It was "no big deal," according to Best, but required a stay of a few days at Divine Providence Hospital. Thinking a visitor might be welcome, I went to see Bradshaw. He's alone in a strange city, I said to myself. Up here in the frozen North, where the faces are all unfamiliar. But I needn't have worried. There was somebody else in the room – an attractive brunette with a honeysuckle accent and a million-dollar smile. She was fluffing his pillows and paying him all sorts of little bedside attentions.

"Terry," I said, "you sure have a nice girlfriend. Is she from back home in Shreveport?"

With a straight face, he answered, "She certainly is. Let me introduce you. Mister Rooney – meet my mom."

Chapter 48

Sunrise

Except to get a line on rookies (and veterans who were dealing with injuries), exhibition football games, or, to use what is now the preferred nomenclature, "pre-season" games, are meaningless affairs, quickly forgotten. But on August 21, 1970, the Steelers and the New York Giants played a pre-season game of transcendent importance to the Rooney family. It was our first game ever at Three Rivers Stadium.

Never mind that the Pirates had been installed there for more than a month – had opened the place with great fanfare on July 16th (losing, by the way, to Cincinnati). Still another month would pass before our first regular-season game at Three Rivers (with Houston; and we, too, were destined to lose). Nothing mattered except that at last we were putting a team on the new civic stadium's brilliant green Tartan Turf. Nothing could detract from the moment; nothing could detract from the excitement we felt.

It was perfect summer weather. Pat and John flew in from Liberty Bell. Tim came up from Palm Beach. The two Kathleens, looking gorgeous, were dressed for an opening night. I had a bounce in my step which I hoped was not evident. It wouldn't do to look "brand new" – AJR-speak for acting like a rube. Never wear your emotions on your sleeve. Never show dejection. Never show jubilation.

The crowd came early and filled the tiers that rose up to a clear, deep sky. When darkness came and the lights burned bright, 59,000 spectators gazed down on the dazzling scene. Of course, the circumstances called for the Steelers to win, and they did.

There was confusion – on our family's part, at least – about the parking. AJR, it goes without saying, had spaces reserved in Stadium Circle, a step or two away from the door to the Steelers' office suite. Of these, there were not enough. Less privileged Rooneys parked where they could – in the lots for the general public, which were teeming with cars, on the streets around 940 North Lincoln. Kay, though, was able to do neither. August 28th would be my mother's 66th birthday, and Kay had the cake for a party in Kass's private box. Pulling up at the gate to the preferred-parking area, she turned on her smile for the guard.

"I'm Kay Rooney. We're having a surprise party for my mother-in-law, Mrs. Art Rooney. I have to deliver this cake ... A parking pass? No, sir, I don't have one. But what am I to do with this cake? ... Oh, yes sir. You're very kind, sir. Just tell me where to park and I'll drop off the cake and come right back and move my car. Thank you so much."

"Well, you see, sir," she explained three and a half hours later, "my mother-in-law wouldn't hear of my leaving her box with the party and the game going on. I'm s-o-o-o-o sorry. Thank you for understanding."

Kass's box, No. 341, was on the fifty-yard line (where else?). It had a carpet, or rug, a wet bar, leather swivel chairs for fifteen people, a counter at each row for programs, purses, and so on, and, most special of all, a private rest room. Only this box and Pirate owner John Galbreath's box had private rest rooms. A black waiter dressed in a tuxedo served the birthday cake with glasses of champagne. This was Sidney, a bus boy at the restaurant in the Roosevelt Hotel. Sidney looked magnificent, and he went about his work with the aplomb of an English butler. He bowed and scraped; he hovered over Kass. Sidney added much to the elegance of the occasion, but after his first year on the job a nondescript woman attendant succeeded him. It seemed to AJR that, with Sidney, we were "putting on the dog." Sidney was too flamboyant – and too free-handed with the liquor. He poured such generous drinks that by the time the game ended Box 341 was like a night club at 2 a.m. Get rid of him, ordered AJR.

Box 341 was the owner's box, actually, but AJR sat with Richie Easton and Father Mark Flanagan or Father Jim Campbell in a bare-bones box near the press box. A priest named Reardon sat in my box, an open-air eight-seater next to the visiting owners' box. Father Flanagan and Father Campbell did not have long to live. After both had died, AJR approached me and said, "That Father Reardon – does he keep his mouth shut?" Father Reardon, I told him, was as quiet as a mouse. "All right, then," said AJR. "From now on, he can sit with me."

Impressed by his elevation from my box to AJR's, Father Reardon's friends started calling him Monsignor, or so he alleged.

Iggy Borkowski, who sometimes occupied the fourth chair in AJR's box, said that sitting there was no fun. "You're not allowed to say a word." AJR himself rarely spoke. "The only time I ever heard him sound off," said Father Reardon, "was to second-guess Chuck Noll. 'Chuck's a good man,' he began. 'A fine coach. But he's bound and determined to set up the run. No matter what, he has to establish the ground game. Even with a passer like Bradshaw throwing to the best receivers in the league. He'd rather prove that we can run than win the game."

My box was close to the press box, where fat Harry Kalson served up the best Jewish hot dogs I ever have tasted. More than once I missed a big play near the end of the half because I left my seat early for a good place in line at the hot dog grill. Never first in line – that would be too obvious – but up toward the front.

AJR never had women in his box, and neither did I except in emergency situations. At one game, a young lass came into my box and said her boyfriend had told her she'd be "warmly received." Her boyfriend, it turned out, was the *Sports Illustrated* writer Roy Blount, who was working on a book about the Steelers. It was December; she was lightly dressed. Until a good-hearted usher brought her a folding chair, she sat, looking uncomfortable, on a cold concrete step.

Box 341 was on the other side of the field, but Kay always carne with binoculars, and she spotted my visitor. That night at home, we had a dialogue. If a sportswriter's girlfriend could sit in my box, asked Kay, why was it off-limits to her? I pointed out that Dan's wife, Pat, never sat with her husband in his box, an argument Kay rejected. Finally I said, "Look – when I watch a football game, I'm at work. Does your father take women to his wool mill?" (Roy Kumer owned the Pittsburgh Wool Company). Kay had no answer for that, but made it clear she did not accept my analogy.

Only one other woman ever made it into my box — the girlfriend of a scout for the Kansas City Chiefs, Lloyd Wells. Lloyd flagged me down one Sunday to complain that she had been barred from the press box. "You're a big shot, Rooney," he said — smiling. "Whuddaya gonna do about it?" What I did about it was have an extra chair sent to my box. Both Lloyd and his girlfriend, I should note, were African- Americans. Perhaps I should mention also that the girlfriend was very beautiful. Conscious of Kay's binoculars, I placed her next to Father Reardon, an arrangement that pleased my other two regulars, Bill Nunn and Jack Butler. "She's a very sweet girl," said Father Reardon after the game, "but it bothered me a little that she didn't stand up for the national anthem."

Lloyd Wells ended up in Muhammad Ali's retinue, by the way.

Inevitably, I suppose, Kass's box, 341, became a catch-all location for guests of the management who did not have a seat — governors, mayors, bishops, college presidents, state legislators, movie actors, Hall-of-Fame football players, Hall-of-Fame coaches, and, yes, a Supreme Court justice, Whizzer White. Not only the VIPs, but even the no-names, Kass said, had to be treated with respect, because you never knew. The mild-mannered priest might be in charge of marriage annulments somewhere, and in a large family like the Rooneys it didn't hurt to have a friend in court. The politician you never heard of might be voting on a race-track bill that affected Liberty Bell.

Other than AJR, and sometimes Dan, the most tireless proponent of using Box 341 for our overflow was Joe Gordon, the Steeler publicist. Joe was a can-do guy. If you had to rush somebody to the airport, Joe could get a taxi or limousine right away. If you had to transport a whole football team, Joe could have a bus at the door in five minutes. There were those who resented his aggressiveness. I had some negative moments with him myself when my scouting agenda clashed with his drive for publicity, but I could be aggressive too, and I made allowances. Joe was Dan's hire and extremely loyal to him. He had come to the team while Three Rivers was under construction, and very soon we realized that he belonged in the top rank of P.R. men. One guy in his corner was AJR. Gordon had been a baseball player at Pitt and spent hours with the Chief talking about the Pirates, talking about the Wheeling Stogies, talking about long-ago sandlot teams.

But on Sunday afternoons during the football season, he made life difficult for Kass. Mom, Kay, and especially Aunt Alice valued their privacy. The guests who were showing up for the free lunch and free booze at halftime upset them. After Sidney's departure they had a security guard posted outside the box. AJR considered this "uppity." The guard followed Sidney into oblivion, and halftime became an open house. Decorative fixtures — Steeler memorabilia — began to disappear. Visitors walked away with Steeler cocktail glasses, a black and gold Steeler throw rug, a waste basket with the Steeler insignia. Old-time Steeler photographs vanished from the walls. One of Kay's touches was a supply of Steeler-embossed hand soap for the private john. It lasted approximately two hours. Returning from an inspection tour, she announced that "even the goddam soap" had been taken.

"This is your father's fault," Kay and Kass would tell me. But the problem, Kass knew, could only be controlled, never eliminated. Even during the off-season, Box 341 was perceived as a hospitality suite. One year on May 10th, the eighth or ninth birthday of our son Art, Kay had a party in the box, and almost before she knew it there were strangers present — middle-aged men, helping themselves to the hot dogs. If AJR had sent these men to the box from his office below, it seemed odd. Were they friends of his? Kay had no clue, so she asked. Well, ma'am, someone explained, they were friends of a friend of Mr. Rooney. They were friends of Dago Sam.

Politely — she said "please" — Kay invited them to leave.

Dan replaced the missing photographs with new ones and had them securely bolted to the wall. The centerpiece was an oil painting — AJR and Father Silas in their Wheeling Stogie uniforms. The Wheeling Stogies played baseball, not football, a discordant note in keeping with AJR's notion of irony. Bolted down like everything else, the painting was safe from the pillagers — souvenir hunters, let's call them. The new cocktail glasses, a gift from Charley Affif, liquor salesman and former middleweight boxer, they disdained as lacking in uniqueness. A plain gray wall-to-wall carpet had replaced the black and gold Steeler throw rug, and there were no fancy emblematic waste baskets. Box 341 had been stripped of its ornamentation.

There came a Sunday when Kass was gone, too. I looked across the field and saw Kay, with her red hair shining in the sunlight. Beside her I saw Aunt Alice. The third chair was vacant. I lowered my binoculars and pretended to watch the game.

A Link to the Past

Our post-office address at Three Rivers was 300 Stadium Circle. We had an office suite on the ground floor that followed the curvature of the oval-shaped superstructure for something like three city blocks. If you walked from Dan's office past the other offices, past the dressing rooms, and on through the runway to the field, and then walked back, you were exercising.

I remember one day the scouts used a gently curving stretch of corridor to measure the forty-yard dash speed of Jim Haslett, a linebacker prospect from Indiana University of Pennsylvania. Haslett's entire playing career was with the Buffalo Bills, but we added him to the coaching staff during Bill Cowher's regime, the final step in his progression to the head coaching job at New Orleans.

A commercial decorator, hired by the Stadium Authority and Dan, picked out the gun-metal gray carpeting and palomino brown furniture. There were no windows in any of the rooms – none – but the incandescent lighting was easy on the eyes. AJR tried to hide his satisfaction with the looks of the place by protesting that, for his taste, everything was too fancy.

"I'm just a yinz guy," he would say.

"Now that you've arrived," the decorator would answer, "your new home should reflect your higher status." AJR reveled in that kind of talk.

His own private office had dark wood paneling, a black couch, modernistic chairs, and potted plants. AJR wanted pictures on the wall – photographs. The decorator quietly demurred. "It's really not that kind of an office," he suggested. AJR paid no attention, insisting, "I want my old friends around me." Up on the wall went Johnny Blood and Whizzer White, Jack Butler and Ernie Stautner, George Halas and Big Kies – and, directly overlooking AJR's desk, Honus Wagner. Another baseball player in foreign surroundings. To his own surprise, I have no doubt, the decorator approved of all this. The office, he said, mirrored AJR's personality.

Flesh-and-blood old friends were less numerous at Three Rivers. Hangers-on found the atmosphere inhospitable. Uncle Jim was still a fixture and Dago Sam too, but not many others. Patsy Scanlon and Doc Sekay dropped in now and then.

Mort Sharnik, my *Sports Illustrated* friend, remarked to me once that our digs at the Roosevelt Hotel reminded him of Times Square – the crossroads of the world. Three Rivers was off the beaten track, which suited Dan and me perfectly. Good riddance to all the characters, we thought. The environment now was more businesslike, a change I considered long overdue. On scouting trips I had visited big universities with big budgets, and I saw how important ambience could be. Neither Dad nor even Dan seemed as sensitive to this as I was. The Union Trust Building had been an improvement on the Fort Pitt Hotel, and the Roosevelt had been an improvement, if only a slight one, on the Union Trust Building, but the two hotels were dumps and we knew it. Because we had to, we made jokes about them. We made jokes about our practice field at South Park and the dilapidated frame house where the players changed into their workout gear. But now that was all in the past. We were moving up in class.

And at first it was too rich for my blood, I'm afraid. Glancing disdainfully at AJR's picture gallery, I said to Dan, "We'll get so many good players he'll forget about these guys." Well, I give myself credit for being half-right. We did get good players, Super Bowl-quality players. But I was a jackass, I confess, for minimizing a legacy that meant more to my dad than I could understand.

Backwater Moses

I always see, in my mind's eye, Pitt Stadium and Forbes Field as gray, cold, wet, gloomy places and Three Rivers Stadium glowing with color, the Tartan Turf a vivid green, the plastic seats a painter's palette of blue, orange, and yellow (for yellow, an ex-Marine would say gold; yellow is not a shade the Marine Corps recognizes). In reality, of course, there were dismal days and nights at Three Rivers, and the stadium itself was a huge gray pile of concrete, as dreary in the rain as a penitentiary. So much of life is perception.

Three Rivers stood for hope. It stood for the future. It stood for a new beginning. After that first exhibition game, the team's outspokenly confident, awesomely athletic, ruggedly handsome rookie quarterback came out with a manifesto. Everybody, he said, was to forget about the past, forget the losing seasons, forget that in 1969 our 1-13 record had been the worst in professional football.

That was then, this was now. We were starting from scratch – a new team in a new decade in a new stadium. The Steelers would get the job done, for sure.

Terry Bradshaw was young and immature then, with a full head of blond hair. (Later on, he'd be middle-aged and immature, with some remnants of blond hair behind his ears.) Cynics in the press and cynics in the stands often ridiculed his artless big talk. But Bradshaw was on to something, never mind that it would be 1972 before the Steelers and their fans caught a glimpse of the Promised Land envisioned by this backwater Moses from Shreveport, Louisiana.

The biggest believers were Dan Rooney and Art Rooney, Jr. There were two things the people knew about the Rooneys – they knew we were dumb and they knew we were cheap. What Dan and I knew was that the Rooneys had something to prove. It became a shared passion. Let the skeptics make fun of Terry Bradshaw. The Steelers would get the job done, he said, and we took those brave words as a challenge.

We would see to it ourselves that they got the job done.

The Allegheny Club

The Allegheny Club in Three Rivers Stadium, which took up space that otherwise would have been occupied by four hundred of the best seats for football, was where the baseball team, the Pirates, wanted it. The Pirates – or, rather, John Galbreath, the Pirates' owner – called the tune when it came to the design of the new facility. AJR was so desperate to have a stadium of any kind that he never questioned either the location of the club or whether there should even be one. Three Rivers, after all, was a publicly-funded stadium, and the Allegheny Club, after all, was a private eating and drinking place, accessible only to dues-paying members and their guests.

It never occurred to the Chief, I am sure, that inside of five years, with thousands of would-be customers on the waiting list for season tickets, the Steelers would need those four hundred seats and need them badly. A sellout at a Pirate game was as rare as an eclipse of the sun. But the Pirates played eighty-one times at Three Rivers every year and the Steelers played ten or eleven times - twelve at the most.

One wall of the Allegheny Club, on the side overlooking the field, was a huge sheet of virtually unbreakable glass. With unobstructed sight lines, diners watched the game from tables placed on terraces. It was a tastefully decorated place and had a breathtaking view of the stadium's interior. Visitors were bound to be impressed.

In the first few years of the club's existence, a strict dress code was enforced. Steeler scouts grumbled that when they brought a draft-eligible player to lunch, and he was wearing a sport shirt with no jacket, the maitre d would turn them away. "You have to be dressed like a U.S. Steel executive," one scout complained.

Mom, Aunt Alice, and Kay dressed for the Allegheny Club like U.S. Steel executives' wives. The upscale atmosphere suited them. So did the service and the menu. It pleased them to see AJR's likeness – and mine and Dan's – among the mahogany-framed portraits of sports celebrities on the wall of the corridor between the foyer and the restaurant. No Rooney men ever patronized the well-stocked bar.

The restaurant's back windows looked out over the conjunction of the Allegheny and Monongahela Rivers and up to Mount Washington on the opposite side. Kay preferred this view to the view of the playing field. A decorative touch that appealed to every Pittsburgher had historical connotations. It was a section of brick wall from Forbes Field. With the score tied in the ninth inning of the seventh and last game of the 1960 World Series, Bill Mazeroski of the Pirates hit a pitch from Ralph Terry over that wall for the home run that beat the New York Yankees.

The Allegheny Club was where Kass – "Mrs. Art Rooney" – became a personage of sorts. To the functionaries and waitresses, she was someone special – "the owner's wife." Aunt Alice, the more diffident of the sisters, found such attention uncomfortable. At lunch, she ordered the same thing that Mom ordered, or that Kay ordered. Kay once asked me if Aunt Alice could read. I said, "Sure." "How do you know?" Kay demanded. After a moment's reflection, I said, "Show her something negative about the Rooneys or Terry Bradshaw in the newspaper. You'll learn that she can read, all right."

Aunt Alice had met Terry Bradshaw when he came to see AJR at 940 North Lincoln Avenue. Printed allegations that Bradshaw was "dumb" infuriated her. "The dumb one," she would say, "is the simple son of a bitch who wrote that story." Now, this was a woman who went to Mass and Holy Communion every day and who wore out rosary beads and prayer books.

The Allegheny Club did not show a profit for some time. Our representative on the board of control was Ed Kiely, who had turned over his P.R. duties to Joe Gordon and who liked to work at the upper levels of the power structure. "Hey," he'd report to AJR, "we might have to come up with some dough to keep this place afloat." AJR would hit the ceiling. We were underwriting the club's indebtedness on exactly the same basis as the stadium's principal tenant, the Pirates. "These guys ..." the Chief growled. "They're too darn high-toned. They should hustle up some business in the off-season, when there aren't any games." Parking at such times was plentiful, and where else in town, apart from the Duquesne Club, were the amenities superior?

What was needed, decided AJR, was a manager with pizzazz. He thought of Alex DiCroce, who ran the Sylvan Room at the Roosevelt Hotel. Kiely and Dan were pushing for him, too. Alex took the job, filled the club's open dates with weddings, banquets, and corporate parties, and pulled it out of the red.

He was equally skillful at human relations. If AJR was in the club, Alex knew when he could take a visitor to his table and when it was best not to bother him. AJR, regardless of the circumstances, would never be less than courteous, Still there were moments when a private business discussion might be going on. Alex had a feel for these things.

With the waitresses, busboys, bartenders, cooks, and bottle washers, AJR was his approachable self at all times. He knew their first names; he knew the intimate details of their lives. They brought him their family snapshots to look at, brought him news of a son or nephew in the military, kept him up to date on their relatives' health problems. "How's your mother?" he would ask a waitress. "Did that medicine do her any good?"

The Allegheny Club's membership cards were numbered according to rank. My recollection is that John Galbreath – who could have walked into the dining room without being recognized – had Number 001 and AJR Number 002. The mayor, Pete Flaherty, rated 003. My number, in which I took a certain vainglorious satisfaction, was 009. I felt like a big shot.

But then the system had to be changed. Low numbers were easy to remember. On nights when the bar was crowded, a patron ordering drinks would call out his number and name. Even in a high-class joint, and the Allegheny Club was high class, there are always unscrupulous people. The next time the bartenders were busy, someone of this type, having overheard a number and name, might call out, "Johnson, oh-oh-seven" (let's say), and in the hubbub get away with it.

Of course it was only a matter of time until new cards were issued. From 009, my number went to something like 2761, ending an ego trip I had rather enjoyed.

Whatever may have happened to AJR's number, he probably gave it no thought.

Chess Board

P. T. Barnum or someone said that people will come to see the elephant, but to keep them coming back the elephant had better learn to do tricks. So it is with a new stadium. For a year or two, the fans will buy tickets just to see it. After that, they demand a winning team.

To build a winning team, you need good players, good coaches, and good management. I mention management third, but management's job – to put all the pieces together – is by no means the least important.

Management is responsible for scouting, drafting, and signing the players, an ongoing process. The pipeline must never run dry. Management hires the coaches. And management must give them the tools they require to do their work – first-rate practice facilities, first-rate locker-room facilities, and first-rate training facilities.

Everything, in other words, that South Park notably lacked.

With plenty of justification, Steeler coaches had complained about South Park for years. "You play as you practice," they insisted. And at South Park, they argued, practicing in the rain or the snow was impossible. There was too much mud. Too much slop.

Uncle Jim gave the faultfinders no sympathy. "Players and coaches are all the same," he would say.

"They're looking for a reason to flop. A reason to fail." Chances are he was quoting Jock Sutherland. But in Chuck Noll's system, the condition of the practice field really mattered.

It was linebacker coach Denny Fitzgerald who clarified this for me. We were going over my list of college prospects one day. "Art," he said — only the old-time coaches still called me "Artie" — "those linebackers you're looking at — they'd better be able to think on their feet as well as move. We change our damn defensive scheme three times a week. For the players, it's like a chess board. They have to be smart enough to pick up the changes and get to the right place on the chess board."

Finding the right place in the mud could be difficult.

Three Rivers Stadium, with its artificial turf, was ideal for Noll's version of chess. There were other advantages, too — the spacious locker-room area, for instance. The locker room at South Park was a joke if not an outright disgrace. Three Rivers had locker rooms with carpeting thick enough to serve as a bed. There were players who took naps on it, recovering from an arduous workout. The atmosphere was so pleasant and home-like that AJR would go there to relax. Wearing his cashmere sweater and chewing on an unlit cigar, he would circle the room with his hands behind his back. He might stop for a conversation with someone, but not necessarily. For AJR, the locker room was a quiet retreat.

In the trainer's room, Ralph Berlin had a taping table big enough to hold three football players, even if they were linemen. The whirlpool tubs - there were two — occupied an area up against the wall. Hot-water treatment for injuries was popular with the players but disdained by the team physician, Dr. John Best. In his deep voice he would cackle, "I suppose it helps if you think it helps."

Ralph Berlin's office, which adjoined the trainer's room, contained a desk, his locker, and two examining tables. Over two large windows separating the office from the rest of his domain he had hung a heavy pair of draw-string curtains. I asked about them one time. "Why the curtains, Ralph? Why the need for so much privacy?" "Well," he told me, "I had a player in here whose chin had been split open from contact with a helmet, and he needed a lot of stitches. Blood all over the place. It was halftime, so Big John" — Dr. Best — "sewed his face up right there on that table. One of the other players, his best friend on the team, was looking through the window, and his eyes got as big as saucers. I thought for sure he was going to faint. So I went over and pulled the curtains together, but it was locking the barn door after the horse is out. Do you think that guy was worth a damn in the second half? Ever since then, I keep those curtains drawn when I'm working on an injured player."

The weight room was Noll's innovation. He imported a body builder and judo expert from New Orleans, a guy named Lou Riecke, to install the equipment. Lou was small but of course muscular, a one-time Olympic silver medalist in weightlifting. The silver medal matched the color of his perfectly coiffed silken hair. Noll wanted free weights — dumbbells and barbells — "not those useless machines." Free weights, Noll thought, built what he called "gross strength." He said that when he coached as an assistant with the San Diego Chargers in the AFL, a lot of "skinny-assed kids" the NFL had rejected were able to gain from fifteen to twenty pounds through a combination of weightlifting and diet. "And they'd be just as fast. We'll do it here, too," he promised.

He was right. But, ever the teacher, Noll always had to demonstrate. Lifting more than he could handle, he damn near ruined his back. That was Chuck, a man who would stop at nothing to prove a point.

Bean Counters

After Fran Fogarty had been taken from us, my brother Dan talked AJR into signing on with the nationally known, highly respected accounting firm of Arthur Andersen. This was thirty years, more or less, before Arthur Andersen's fatal involvement in the Enron scandal, a house-of-cards collapse that left thousands of defrauded investors holding the bag when the high-tech stock-market run-up of the late 1990s came to an end.

Fogarty had been "a one-man dog," answering only to AJR. Arthur Andersen's representative, Dixon Rich, worked more closely with Dan, the former Duquesne University accounting major. Dan knew how to speak the current language.

AJR, you should understand, was still the big boss. Over many years of dealing with race-track sharpies, his common-sense approach to money and finance never had failed him. He was dismissive, even scornful, of people who needed accountants and lawyers. Give him Fogarty, who could keep the books straight and smell a rat. Doing business with a handshake satisfied AJR.

Which was good enough for the old days, perhaps, but now things were different. The NFL had grown beyond recognition. There were all kinds of rules to comply with – federal, state, and local. You had the IRS looking over your shoulder. Dixon Rich treated AJR with the greatest respect, cluing him in on the discussions he was having with Dan, but to put it plainly, the Chief had become a sounding board.

It was Dan's job to supervise the numbers crunchers in the office. Besides the Arthur Andersen people – Dixon Rich, an assistant, and a secretary – we had a "controller." The way it looked to me, a controller was a sort of super accountant. Buff Boston had been acting as Dan's liaison with Arthur Andersen, and he could not have been more relieved when Dan hired our first controller, Terry Jacobs.

All of us liked Terry. Our compensation for accepting membership in the supposedly inferior American Conference after the merger between the NFL and the AFL had been three million dollars, a considerable sum at the time, and Terry wanted to put this money into a real-estate tax shelter. High finance was out of my line, but he and Dan would ask me to sit in on their conversations with the real-estate people. I'd stay for thirty minutes – forty-five at the most – look at my watch, and say, "I have some reports to make out and some game films to watch," an excuse that did not fool anybody. Dan being all business, Terry had the notion that the real-estate guys were eager to talk football with me. At lunchtime, when they moved from the conference room to the Allegheny Club, he would urge me to come along, and I did now and then, but mostly then. I never looked at myself as a public-relations man or a greeter. If I could make a contribution, it would be as a scout.

After leaving us for opportunities elsewhere, Terry remained a friend of the family and continued to work on the real-estate end of our business. His successor as controller, Bob Quinn, devoted all his time to the football operation. Recommended by Dixon Rich, Quinn carne to the Steelers from Arthur Andersen. He was the second in a series of people who held the controller's job for two or three years and then departed. The anxiety-and-stress quotient must have been higher than I realized.

We were slow, for some reason, to computerize. Although Dan was a believer in modern business methods, he "outsourced" the work that could most efficiently be done by computers. At the risk of antagonizing everyone, I begged, pleaded, and even groveled a bit for an in-house system. In the scouting department, I told AJR, we needed computers for the ever-increasing volumes of information we were gathering, but he appeared not to listen. He'd shake his head as if to say, "The kid wants another new toy."

It was like Christmas morning when at last he gave in.

Our oldest scout, Will Walls, scoffed at computers. "What a crock," he would sneer. But computers eliminated much guesswork. They quantified everything, helped us put a number beside a prospect's athletic potential. Will Walls belonged to the past; whether we like it or not, the world keeps spinning on its axis. Still, I considered myself fortunate to be a scout instead of a bean counter. A scout's activities, it seemed to me, were part of the main show. Scouts went places, saw people, and evaluated football players. Accountants sat behind desks and juggled figures. Ours, overseen by Dan, kept the business office running like a fine machine. Because of them, the Steelers got value for every dollar they spent. And yet, compared with Dan, I thought I had the best of the bargain.

Chapter 49

VIPs and Others

Dad's partners at Liberty Bell – rich men, patricians, swells – gathered in the track's VIP room and took in the races from there. It was also where Dad stopped for dinner on his way back to Philadelphia after watching the thoroughbreds run at Delaware Park. His driver would be with him and sometimes an extra guest, a horse-player friend he had casually invited. The bigwigs in the VIP room thought this was presumptuous. The VIP room was for VIPs, and neither Richie Easton nor Iggy Borkowski – AJR's drivers – qualified. The others, guys from Delaware Park, were even less welcome.

Nothing of this was ever put into words. The job of weeding out undesirables belonged to the black doorkeeper, a man who resembled the butler on a Cream of Wheat box. He had the tuxedo, the gray hair, the dignified, forbearing look. Known as "Mr. Lee," this well-turned-out functionary was a bit of a snob, but AJR's method of dealing with such people never failed. It was called "duking" them, and from years of experience he duked with great skill.

AJR's business partners were not the only ones who could see that the tone of the place was being lowered. Even Kass sometimes noticed. Addressing no one in particular, she might ask, "How did that stiff get in here?" whereupon a woman at the next table would be as likely as not to whisper, "Shhh! He's a friend of Mister Rooney's." To the annoyance of the waiters, Iggy Borkowski had a habit of going to the bar and pouring himself a drink. His explanation to my brother John, our man on the scene at Liberty Bell, would be that after driving AJR from Pittsburgh to Philadelphia to Camden, New Jersey, (where Delaware Park was located) and back to Philadelphia, he needed the sedative of alcohol.

There were times when AJR traveled by himself and other times when he would fly. One of the Liberty Bell stockholders, Herb Barness, had a private plane, but AJR would not allow our own corporation such a luxury. He patronized the commercial airlines or, when that wasn't feasible, chartered a small four-seater.

In one of these light planes, he was caught in a heavy storm with a pilot who seemed to be panicking. "You could see the fear in his eyes." And you could hear it in his voice as he said, "We're in trouble, Mister Rooney. It looks real bad up ahead. I believe we should turn back."

The guy was in no shape to make life-or-death decisions, AJR realized. Soothingly, he told him, "I flew as a young man. Here's how I look at it: We know what we've been through. What's up ahead might be better. At least there's a chance. There'd be no chance, though, if we turned and went back. Keep going."

Dad said that the weather ahead was not good, but neither did it keep them from landing without mishap. A few years later, flying the attorney general of Pennsylvania somewhere, the same pilot crashed. The pilot, the attorney general, and all of the other passengers were killed.

AJR said, "I never did think that fellow had any judgment."

Like the social committee at Liberty Bell, AJR categorized people. It was just that his standards were different.

People Person

AJR was drawn to politics and politicians. He followed elections closely and looked forward with great interest to election day. Always he was backing some local candidate and supporting him financially, too. His contributions, I think, were modest except when a particular issue excited him, and then he would dig deep.

He liked aldermen, constables, and ward heelers. He liked state legislators. He liked justices of the peace. He made all of these people feel like big-timers, and when some of them actually did get to the big time they remembered that AJR had been their friend when they were nobodies.

Whatever came along he could handle. He took care of himself, took care of his family, took care of his extended family, and took care of his friends. He abided by certain rules. If you asked for a favor, you gave one in return. He was a great one to send postcards – postcards to say thank you, postcards to say hi. He sent them from places like the shrine of St. Anne, in Quebec, to places like race tracks. His handwriting was wide open and beautiful. In that way it resembled his sisters' handwriting and did not at all resemble his sons'. It may be that our father's generation learned penmanship as part of the educational process, but in his case I think it was something more. As a young kid, I would find doodles and signatures on his scrap paper. Penmanship was an art that he practiced.

He remembered names and he remembered home towns. Bumping into the most casual acquaintance, he would always have something to say. "Oh, you're from St. Clairsville, aren't you? ... I used to play baseball over in Wheeling ... We played in St. Clairsville a few times ... Is that landmark still there? ... Our second baseman, Joe Doakes, was from St. Clairsville ... Did you know him? ... " And so on and so on. If a bond of some kind existed, he could find it.

In later years I'd be with him at Steeler training camp. He wanted me within earshot whenever an obscure new player approached him. As the player drew near, he would ask, "What's this kid's name?" I'd say, " Walter Smith." And Dad would call out to him, "Hi, Walt," or "Hi, Smitty," and throw out his hand as though greeting a top draft choice or a veteran. As likely as not, the player would soon be cut. Then on more than one occasion when I made the rounds of the colleges to scout spring practice I would hear from the coach that Walt Smith had told him what a fine gentlemen Mr. Rooney was.

In his old age he would not come to practice until after the cuts were made, because then there'd be fewer names to remember, and remembering names was important to him.

AJR was a "people person." There was nothing phony about it. He actually *liked* people. They say in drama school that if you play a part long enough the mask will become the face. With AJR, it was different. You got exactly what you saw.

In the 1940s, when AJR was in his heyday as a horse player, the walls of his office in the Fort Pitt Hotel were covered with a hodgepodge of photographs. There was a big one of Twenty Grand, the great Kentucky Derby winner, inscribed in AJR's flowing hand, "Champion of Champions." AJR said that in 1931, the year Twenty Grand won the Derby, he had made more money betting on the horse than on all of the other races that year put together.

When the Steelers moved their headquarters to the Union Trust Building and then the Roosevelt Hotel and eventually to Three Rivers Stadium, AJR took the pictures along, too – everything from autographed photos of big shots to little plastic-framed group shots of a Cincinnati sportswriter's children. The sportswriter, Pat Harmon, had ten or eleven kids; one of the daughters grew up to be a television actress, best known for her role as the mother in "Everybody Loves Raymond."

In our splendid new digs at Three Rivers Stadium, the disorder of Dad's office seemed incongruous. The haphazard arrangement of the pictures drove a lot of us nuts, but meant nothing to AJR. What did mean something was that they were there.

At home, the pictures on the walls of his den were neatly hung. Kass saw to that. There was a story behind every face. These were photographs of people he liked. How well off they were, or how high in the world, was of no account. The people he did not like were bums, yeggs, and con men. I said to him once, repeating something I had heard in a movie, that an honest man couldn't be conned. "Bunk," he replied. He disliked mean people and people who had no compassion. Once in AJR's presence the head Steeler coach berated an assistant in front of the assistant's kids. At the end of the (losing) season, without a touch of remorse, AJR told the head coach he was fired.

This was the same coach who embarrassed John Baker, a huge black defensive end, with hundreds of fans watching a training-camp drill. In the off-season Baker worked at a North Carolina penitentiary, and one day the coach yelped at him, "Baker, if you don't get off your backside you'll be back in that prison." AJR was furious. He thought that to the fans it must have sounded as though Baker had been a jailbird. In truth, John Baker was a high-class fellow who went back home at the end of his playing days and served for years in the elective office of sheriff.

Insensitive people like this coach were the kind that AJR had no use for.

Going To Bat For Joe

In the beginning, AJR liked to deal with Jim Clark. They worked out any problems between Liberty Bell and our William Penn Racing Association on a man-to-man basis, bypassing the lawyers. This arrangement suited them both; unfortunately, Clark was in failing health and died at about the time the track started flourishing. From then on, Liberty Bell's lawyers and John Macartney handled almost everything, with Macartney reporting to AJR.

A company owned by the Sullivan family of Lowell, Massachusetts, printed our tip sheets and programs. The Sullivans did the printing for almost every important race track from Narragansett, near Boston, to Pimlico, in Maryland, and had a special tie with the Rooneys. Old Joe Sullivan, the patriarch of the clan, was a cousin of Billy Sullivan, the Boston Patriots' owner. Joe had loaned Billy the money to buy the franchise and had placed his own son, Walter Sullivan, on the Patriots' board.

The Sullivans transported their printing presses in an eighteen-wheel tractor trailer, moving from track to track. After the last race at Liberty Bell one night, Walter Sullivan, Pat the twin, and a Liberty Bell employee whose name I've forgotten went pub-crawling, with Walter at the wheel of his monstrous rig, which happened to be a new one. They stopped at every after-hours bar within a ten-mile radius of Liberty Bell, Walter said. "We had a devil of a time parking," he added, "but somehow we managed."

In later years, both Walter and Pat joined Pathfinders, an Irish-American temperance organization.

While Billy Sullivan's football team prospered, Joe Sullivan's printing business fell on hard times. With the advent of computers, the race tracks the company serviced could do their own printing. The Sullivans no longer were needed, and a Liberty Bell official, speaking for the William Penn Association as well as for Liberty Bell, told them so, bluntly.

"Wait a minute," said AJR. "Who gave you the right to make decisions on behalf of William Penn?" He went on to tell the official that Walter Sullivan, big truck and all, would continue to do the printing for the Rooneys. Economically, it wasn't feasible to bring the rig and the presses into the park for only one race meet, so Liberty Bell had to back down and the Sullivans stayed in business a while longer.

AJR had a soft spot for the Sullivans because of old Joe's generosity to Father Silas and other Franciscan missionaries. In the 1930s, Joe Sullivan had made a practice of giving each Franciscan five thousand dollars on the eve of his departure for a foreign land. Throughout Massachusetts, many a Catholic priest said Mass before an Italian marble altar paid for by Joe. He was AJR's kind of Catholic.

When the old man died, the Chief saw to it that all five Rooney brothers attended the wake and the funeral. His loyalty to the Sullivans was a lesson to us, one of many.

Keeping Up Appearances

AJR never lost his love for Shamrock Farm. It was one of many ways in which we differed. As far as I was concerned, Shamrock Farm belonged in the same category as Parris Island. When I took my kids to the farm for a visit, we stayed at the nearest hotel.

Shamrock Farm was on a beautiful piece of land, its rolling hills and pastures sectioned off with black wooden fences. The springs and streams fed the water supply of Baltimore, a half-hour drive to the east on Interstate 70. On Interstate 270 the farm was just a forty-minute drive from Washington, D. C. AJR always predicted that easy access to these interstates and to a good state highway, 26, would make the price of the farm soar. It never happened.

My brother Tim shared Dad's interest in the farm and in horses. The only horses on my radar were the two-legged kind to be found up the road on the football team at the University of Maryland. In football terminology, a horse is a guy who stands well over six feet tall, weighs at least 250 pounds, and runs about a 4.7 forty.

At judging horses, buying them, breeding them, and selling them, Tim had better success than the Chief did, and nothing could have pleased the Chief more. At one of our William Penn or Yonkers meetings in the 1970s, he was going on and on about Tim's expertise. Our lawyer, John

Macartney, listened quietly, smiling. When Dad paused for a moment, Macartney interrupted. He said, "If Franco Harris, Terry Bradshaw, Joe Greene, and some of your other football players had four legs instead of two, they'd be Kentucky Derby winners, maybe even Triple Crown winners."

I had scouted and recommended those guys, and I could not help showing the satisfaction I felt at hearing Macartney's indirect praise. As we left the meeting room, he fell in step with me and said, "Artie, I meant every word of that." I was momentarily too flustered to make an adequate response.

In its austerity, Shamrock Farm resembled Jimmy Coyne's farm in the hills north of Pittsburgh. Coyne sold his land for a lot of money. Property values in Carroll County, Maryland, never went high enough to make selling a worthwhile option for AJR or his heirs. Coyne, a born rustic, liked to plow and plant and harvest and look after the livestock. AJR thought of Shamrock Farm as a place to get away from it all. On his visits, he never lifted a finger. The Rooney womenfolk avoided the farm as much as possible.

One of AJR's earliest pair of custodians, Charles Clayton and his wife, resembled the stern-faced couple in "American Gothic," the painting by Grant Wood that shows a man wearing overalls, holding a pitchfork and standing side by side with a woman in an apron, the two of them guarding, or seeming to guard, their farmhouse, a narrow white clapboard structure with a high-pitched roof. Clayton was called Johnny Bill, never Charles. By any name, he was not much of a caretaker. Shamrock Farm's buildings and grounds suffered greatly from inattention. Tim, embarrassed by the looks of the place, pushed for improvements, but Fran Fogarty, AJR's financial watchdog, held fast to his purpose of spending no money that didn't absolutely have to be spent, and AJR backed him up.

Despite the rumpled suits, the cloth caps, and the studied air of unpretentiousness, AJR was not without vanity. The role of gentleman farmer was one that he liked. It was how he wished to be seen by his NFL colleagues. To appear unsophisticated in the eyes of these people – "brand new," as he always put it – would have bothered him much more than he wanted you to think.

One of the few NFL guys who had actually set foot on Dad's farm was Harvey Johnson, the Buffalo Bills' head scout and a close personal friend of the owner, Ralph Wilson. In their dependence on one another, they reminded me of Walt Kiesling and AJR. Twice when Wilson fired his head coach, Johnson filled in as interim head coach. He then would return to the personnel department. On the side, he dabbled in thoroughbred racing. With a man named Breezie Reed, he bought a filly they thought could "run some." After racing the horse at two of the Maryland tracks, Bowie and Laurel, they put her up for the winter at Shamrock Farm.

Johnson was something of a story teller. He had a resonant tenor voice that could penetrate the thickest wall. The more he got involved in a story, the higher his voice would climb. One tale he was fond of went like this:

In 1972, after a 1-13 season as interim coach, he was back in scouting. Arriving at War Memorial Stadium in Buffalo for a meeting, he found himself confronted by a rent-a-cop behind a locked gate. The cop asked Johnson for his I.D. card.

"I don't have one," Johnson told him.

"Then I can't let you in," the cop said.

"But I'm Harvey Johnson."

"You're who?"

"Harvey Johnson, the head scout. I'm here to attend a meeting."

"You're who?" the cop repeated.

At this point, Johnson lost his temper.

"Were you working here last season?" he yelled at the cop.

"Yeah."

"Well, do you remember the head coach who fucked up the whole team?"

"Yeah, yeah."

"Well, that asshole was me!" Johnson yelled. "Now, open this damn gate!"

"Yes, sir, Mister Johnson. I remember you now," said the cop.

It was in his usual uninhibited, clamorous way that Harvey accosted me at a Blesto gathering the year he had boarded his filly with the Claytons.

"Hey, Artie," he said, "when's the last time you were over to your dad's horse farm?"

"It's been quite a while, Harv. My brother Tim is into that stuff."

"Well, you'd better get over there and take a look." His voice was in the fortissimo register already. "You know that filly that belongs to Breezie Reed and me? The one we took to your farm? We only took her there because of your dad. Great guy. But that farm! It's a pig-sty!"

I glanced around. Everybody in the room was tuned in. "Breezie and I went over to see that horse," Harvey continued. "Hell! The fence rails were down! Horseshit everywhere you looked! And our filly had lost weight.

"I want you to tell your dad about it. I can't believe he knows how bad the place is," Johnson finished, every syllable reverberating.

Of course, as soon as I got back to Pittsburgh, I dutifully reported what Harvey had said. AJR looked stricken.

"Who was there – who heard him say that?" he demanded.

"A lot of scouts and some general managers – all the football people."

I could see that Dad was upset.

Not too long afterward, renovations began at the farm. Johnny Bill Clayton and his wife were sent on their way, replaced by a couple named Shaw. Dad was now listening to Tim's recommendations. They had the Winfield Volunteer Fire Department burn down the old, dilapidated farmhouse and the old, dilapidated cow barn. "Good practice for our boys," said the fire chief. Fran Fogarty was gone, and our real-estate advisor, Terry Jacobs, closed a deal with an advertising firm to put up a larger, contemporary farmhouse.

Don't ask me about the particulars. Preoccupied with football, I paid no attention.

A little later, new stables were constructed, attracting more business from horsemen with brood mares. Shaw, the new tenant, had worked at other stud farms and knew horses – unlike Clayton. A couple of new stallions, one named for St. Bonaventure, the other for Pat's son Christopher, helped pay the bills.

Tim, justifiably, took credit for all the refurbishment. He had forced AJR to recognize that changes were necessary. Everybody said so. But if you want my opinion, raucous ol' Harvey Johnson had quite a bit to do with it, too.

Chapter 50

Man of LaMancha

By 1970, the year we moved into Three Rivers Stadium, I was representing the Steelers at the Blesto meetings. I had had my first shouting match with a Steeler head coach (Bill Austin). I had argued with my wife over the inordinate amount of time I was spending on the road. And I had clashed with my brother Dan over territorial rights.

The Steelers' front office had always been understaffed. During my first few years as personnel director, I worked without an office or a secretary. Buddy Parker's departure left his back-room cubbyhole in the Roosevelt Hotel vacant, and I lobbied for it. To Dan, it may have seemed that I was making a power grab. Once installed, I asked for help with my correspondence and filing.

There was nothing at all grand about this hole in the wall I had seized. *Sports Illustrated* writer Mort Sharnik came calling, took a look at my new digs, and said it confirmed his belief that the Steelers ran a no-frills operation.

I introduced Mort to some of our office fixtures – Uncle Jim, Dago Sam, Patsy Scanlon, Doc Sekay, our eccentric team dentist, and Radio Rich, a toothless, jobless, mentally challenged sports nut who walked in on us one day with a transistor set clamped to his ear and soon had the status of a permanent hanger-on. Mort was mesmerized. "This place," he told me, "is like something right out of a Damon Runyon story."

The thought made my father uneasy.

"Hey," he cautioned me in a private conversation, "I don't want these press guys talking to Jim or Sam or any other Damon Runyon character." They were loose cannons, he was saying.

My brother Dan's view of the Steeler organization was much broader than mine. He looked at all aspects of our business. My one concern was to build a good scouting system. I became obsessed with player procurement: "Build through the draft." And I was obstinate about that – pigheaded, some people thought. But I knew I was right and would take on anyone who differed with me. Mort Sharnik would say, "You're on a quest." I didn't know the definition of "quest" and was too proud to ask. So did I look it up in the dictionary? No. I learned the meaning years later at a Broadway musical – "Man of LaMancha."

Don Quixote would say it was an honor and privilege to be on a quest, and that is how I felt about my job in the Steeler scouting department. Pursuing my aims single-mindedly, I antagonized the entire front office and coaching staff. AJR would tell me, "Nobody likes you." I wanted to be liked – I really did. But if not being liked was the price of doing what had to be done, I was willing to pay it.

Soft Sell

In the spring of 1969 I arrived at Wake Forest on my swing through the South with a list of prospects from Blesto and instructions to look up Beattie Feathers, an assistant coach. Although we never had met, I knew all about him. Thirty-five years earlier, as a rookie from Tennessee in the backfield of the Chicago Bears, Beattie Feathers had gained 1,004 yards, averaging 8.4 yards a carry. At a time when there were fewer games, and when officials stopped the clock less often, reducing the number of plays, and when running backs also played defense - back in those days, to gain one thousand or more yards was extraordinary, and no one before Feathers had done it.

He was now in his late fifties, but I expected to see a big, rugged, powerful-looking guy. Instead, he just missed being undersized. He was affable in his greeting and said he remembered AJR. I had been told he would give me a good appraisal of the Wake Forest players on my list, and he discussed each one thoroughly. Then he asked with an air of puzzlement, "Why did you leave off our best prospect?"

"Your best prospect?" Now it was my turn to be puzzled. "And who might that be?"

"His name is Jimmy Clack," Feathers said. "Nobody drafted him. Even though he won't be back next fall, he's working out with the kids who will be." Clack, Feathers told me, was a center. "He's too tall for his weight - six-five – and that's what scared you guys off. But take a look at him. He's strong and he's as smart as they come. Heck, Jimmy won the Bill George Award as the best blocker in the Atlantic Coast Conference. Played basketball and track, too. Fine student. You can watch him on film when you're lookin' at the other seniors."

I had heard this type of story before. It would turn out in the end that the player was a relative of the coach – maybe a son-in-law. Or else the kid had a police record. Drugs were not yet a problem back then, but he may have been a boozer. Whatever it was, you could be sure that a coach who talked in such flowery terms about an undrafted player almost certainly had a hidden agenda.

Feathers, though, didn't sound like the kind of guy that Ken Stilley referred to as "a high ambassador of bullshit." From his matter-of-fact tone, I did not get the impression that he was making a sales pitch. "You can check Jimmy out for yourself on film," he repeated.

This, I thought, was the least I could do, if only as a courtesy to one of the game's most respected old-timers. Feathers set up a movie projector – when I traveled by air, I did not bring my own – and put on a game film. As we sat there watching it, he quietly called attention to everything Clack did. Coming from other coaches I could name, but will not, this might have been aggravating. But Feathers remained low-key, and I saw with my own eyes that Clack was good. In fact, he was more than good. He was dominating.

Still, I did my best to resist going overboard. Once when I was praising an undrafted player to Jack Sell, the old *Post-Gazette* football writer, he asked me why no one had wanted him, suggesting that there had to be a reason. This was now the question I put to myself about Clack. What bothered me was that besides being undrafted he had failed to catch on as a free agent. Why? You needed bodies – cannon fodder, if you like – for training-camp scrimmages, after all.

We watched another film – Wake Forest-North Carolina. Playing opposite Clack was a tackle expected to be an early-round selection in the upcoming draft, a tackle named Smith. As Feathers kept pointing out to me, Clack won every round of their contest. His height was not a handicap because he went in low, getting up and under the Tar Heel. After taking care of Smith, he would then go looking for others to block.

"Coach Feathers," I said, "there has to be something I'm missing. I haven't seen anything not to like about this guy."

"Well, Jimmy is on the practice field now. I'll go over there with you," Feathers answered. Tall and skinny, just as Feathers had described him, Clack was in shorts and a T-shirt. His legs were muscular and he had a deep chest. He was all smiles – a yes-sir and no-sir lad. Chuck Noll had warned me to watch out for Southern kids who said yes sir and no sir. "That's just the way they're brought up – it doesn't mean anything," he said. However, as far as I could determine, Clack seemed genuine. He made it a point to let me know he had been a basketball player, and I remembered that Noll was partial to basketball players, basketball being a movement sport. Noll wanted offensive linemen who could maintain a block while they were moving.

Clack's playing weight during the 1968 season, he told me, had been 215 pounds. He knew that 215 was too light for the NFL, but he was lifting barbells and other weights, he said. He went on and on about that, which would have been pleasing to Noll.

I watched Clack run a little, and noted that he was fluid, showing quickness and body control. Something else I observed was the way he got along with the other players. He was very much a part of the gang, and I liked that.

As soon as the workout ended, I said to him, "Jim, would you like to sign a contract with the Steelers?"

"By golly, yes!" he answered, a wide grin creasing his face. Before Jim Boston and Bill Nunn took over the job of negotiating with our late draft choices and free agents, I always carried a blank Steeler contract with me; this was the only time I ever used one. Agents had not yet begun to proliferate, and we could deal with most players directly. All that was to change. Even the free agents would say, "Well ... you'll have to see my agent." In the late 1960s and early '70s, Dan or Fran Fogarty signed the high-enders; the rest of us had parameters within which we could operate. We might offer someone like Clack five hundred dollars to sign and another five hundred on top of his salary – eleven or twelve thousand a year – if he made the team.

Clack, to the best of my recollection, did not receive a bonus. I placed the contract on the roof of a parked car, handed him a ballpoint pen, and in just a few seconds the ceremony was over. The only thing we guaranteed him was a tryout, and he was happy to sign for that. Despite his lack of bulk, he could be assured of fair treatment from Noll, who believed in the benefits of diet and weight training. Noll wasn't looking for redwood trees – he favored short, compact linemen with mobility and quickness – but I once heard him say of a player, "Hey – he's a midget!"

In any case, Clack's performance that summer in pre-season camp made a strong impression on Noll. Clack wasn't ready for the NFL, but Chuck farmed him out to a minor-league team in Norfolk, Virginia, the Neptunes. His coach there was George Hughes, a former Steeler, in whom we all had the utmost confidence.

The next year Clack returned to us heavier and stronger. George Young, head scout for the Dolphins at the time, saw him doing his stuff in an intra-squad game at Jeannette and said to me, "Arthur, are you guys trying to hide that kid?" You couldn't hide a good prospect from a top scout like Young, but before the season started Clack disappeared into the Army.

Fran Fogarty, making use of his contacts in the National Guard, got him assigned to a local unit. It may be that, unlike Rocky Bleier - there'll be more about him as we proceed – he was thus spared the fate of the Vietnam veterans I saw when we played a pre-season game in Norfolk, the site of a large military hospital. Sailors and Marines were looking on from wheelchairs or gurneys, some of these young kids bandaged like mummies while others had missing arms or legs.

After his year in the Army, Clack was bigger and stronger still, but with no loss of quickness. Once the game was under way, he knew how to "make things happen," Noll used to say. Noll's system was intricate, featuring traps, sweeps, down blocks, and slides (to pick up pass rushers), but it gave Clack no trouble, and in 1971 he cracked the starting lineup. He could play anywhere in the offensive line except at tight end. In fact, he started at guard in two Super Bowl games, IX and X.

Clack remained with the Steelers until 1977, when he was traded to the Giants. There he developed into a team leader and had five more good seasons. Not bad for a kid the pros would have ignored without the understated intercession of his college coach.

Frank and Peahead

Most NFL scouts headed south early in March, checked out the teams in the Southeast Conference, and worked their way north, from Florida up into the Carolinas and Virginia. By the end of the month they would be in Pennsylvania, New York, and New England, fanning out from there to the Midwest, to Texas, to the Rocky Mountains, to the Pacific Coast.

As late as the 1970s there were still assistant coaches who doubled as scouts. Some had bright futures; you could pick out the assistants who would one day be head coaches. Some of the scouts were real sharp guys also. I can think of three – George Young of the Colts, Ron Wolf of the Raiders, and Bobby Beathard of the Chiefs - who became general managers and Hall-of-Fame nominees.

Scouting was a chance for me to meet and establish friendships with such men. I had a passion for my work, and I could not understand why there were scouts who felt differently. I recall a cold, wet spring in Utah; I was sitting in a darkened room with two other scouts I did not know well, watching game films. One of the two started whining about the unpleasant weather, about the unpleasant reception the coaches we came to see had given us. Then the second scout chimed in, saying, "Yeah, you're right. While you and I are out here in the boondocks seven days a week, the personnel directors sit around drinking coffee and talking on the phone. They don't hit the road until Thursday. They're home again on Sunday and back in the office Monday morning."

Well, I happened to be a personnel director myself. It was Tuesday, not Thursday, and I was four thousand miles from my wife and kids. Like the two complainers, I preferred sunshine to rain. Like the two complainers, I had not been made to feel welcome by the coaching staff at this college. I thought, "Hell – I don't have to worry about competing with these guys. It doesn't matter how smart or how experienced they are. They don't like their jobs. And I couldn't be more satisfied with mine."

There were coaches who looked down on scouts and there were coaches like Frank Howard of Clemson who went out of their way to be cooperative. When I met Frank Howard he had been at Clemson for years and was also the athletic director. Even the unfriendliest coaches provided us with game films, a room, and a movie projector. Howard did more than that. He allowed us to watch practice; he allowed us to interview his assistants; he allowed us to time his players in the forty-yard dash.

We were timing the forty at Clemson one spring on a day that began with the air damp and raw. Then the sun came out, and by mid-afternoon it was warm. I took off my trench coat and draped it across my shoulders like a cape. I put on my sunglasses. To complete the picture, I may have been smoking one of Dad's big cigars; Howard did not forbid smoking or even chewing on his practice field. In any case, I was making myself conspicuous, a violation of scouting protocol. Cape effect, shades, and cigar (if there was one) had not escaped Howard's attention.

"Rooney boy," he said, "is that the new look for the well-dressed scout these days?" My answer came from out of the blue, unpremeditated. "Only if his father owns the team." Howard laughed uproariously. Given their cue, his assistants laughed uproariously too. (When Howard laughed, his assistants laughed; when Howard frowned, his assistants frowned.) Even the other scouts and the Clemson players were chuckling. I felt like Bob Hope. As we walked off the field when practice was over, another scout fell in step with me and said, "I think Coach Howard likes you."

I did what I could to keep on the good side of Howard. At Christmas I would send him a box of expensive cigars. He had long been out of coaching but was still athletic director and still an important figure on the campus (Clemson had named its big new stadium after him) when I asked if he could help a nephew of mine, Pat Rooney, enroll at the university as a freshman.

Sarcastically, he demanded to know if Pat could at least read and write. I vouched for the young man's literacy. "Well, then, Rooney," Howard assured me, "I'll get him in. Hell, boy, the president here is one of my former student managers. He'll do what I tell him."

Howard had a penchant for practical jokes. His friend Peahead Walker, at one time the coach at Wake Forest, but a scout for the New York Giants when I first encountered him, told me of a joke Howard pulled that he did not soon forgive. Arriving with his Wake Forest team for a game at Clemson one year, Peahead recalled, he stepped off the bus to find a pair of South Carolina state troopers waiting for him.

"You're under arrest," one of them said.

While Walker's players and assistant coaches looked on with their mouths hanging open, the no-nonsense enforcers of the law hustled him into their patrol car and drove away. At the local police station, he was put in a cell, screaming, "What's going on here? I'm Coach Walker! I have to be with my team! Call the president of the college – Wake Forest! Call the governor of North Carolina! Damn! I just know that old bastard Howard's behind this! Take my word for it, there'll be hell to pay! You jackasses! I'll have your jobs!"

Back at Clemson Stadium, meanwhile, the Wake Forest squad was out on the field, loosening up. At last the troopers let Peahead out of his cell, explaining that – ha-ha – it was all in good fun. They got him to the stadium just before the kickoff. He spent the entire first half yelling across the field at Howard, calling him names I would rather not repeat.

"Aw," Howard retorted, only making matters worse, "your players and coaches didn't miss you."

In football the rule is that anything goes, and Peahead himself was not above practicing trickery. As you may or may not know, Wake Forest is located in Winston-Salem, North Carolina. Its original campus, in the Raleigh area, was nothing special, I understand. I heard that Peahead would show high-school prospects the more opulent Duke University campus in Durham, giving them the impression that this was an extension of Wake Forest. When they turned up the next fall to enroll, they'd be puzzled.

"Gee, Coach," they would say, "this place looks different from when we visited last spring."

"Well, son, it *is* different," he would tell them. "See, you have to prove yourself here before you can go to our big main campus as a sophomore."

Walker and Howard had thick cornpone drawls. Howard was a big man, Peahead quite a bit smaller. His tasteful clothes, silver hair, and courtly manner gave him the air of an ante-bellum aristocrat. Recruiting coal miners' sons and steelworkers' sons from Western Pennsylvania, he exuded Southern charm. Mamas and grandmas never doubted him for a minute when he said, "Ma'am, if this fine boy of yours comes down to play football for us at our splendid college, we'll take real good care of him."

Peahead was partial to Western Pennsylvania football players but resented it, he told me, when Wake Forest recruited a Western Pennsylvania golfer one year.

"This fellow would take a short cut across our practice field to the golf course every day," Peahead said, "and he seemed to know a lot of our kids. He'd stop and talk with them, interrupting their work, and I could see that they were just a little bit jealous because of how easy he had it. He was getting a free ride just to hit that little white ball while the football players were taking bumps.

"So do you know what I did? I told him he couldn't cut across the football field any more. I said, 'You're distracting my players. From now on, use the same path to the golf course that everybody else uses.'

"Good Lord! If I'd a known he was going to be Arnold Palmer, I'd have asked if I could carry his golf bag."

Peahead's wife bought a parrot to keep her company in the house, and he hated the squawking creature. In Mrs. Walker's absence one day, he found a way to silence it. He poured a fraction of an ounce of Kentucky bourbon into the bird's drinking water.

It had a tranquilizing effect, and Peahead continued the treatment. Half-stewed, Polly was much less of a nuisance. As time went on, Peahead became fond of the parrot. Surreptitiously, he started teaching it a new vocabulary – locker-room talk. At first it was just "hell" and "damn." Kindergarten stuff, Peahead thought. He added "shit" to the bird's repertory, then "son of a bitch." When Mrs. Walker got wind of what was happening, she was horrified, but Polly's language lessons could not be unlearned and Peahead now had a drinking buddy, so to speak.

Most parrots live a long time. This one died fairly young – perhaps of acute alcoholism, though I hope not. It is horrible to imagine a parrot in the throes of delirium tremens, and I know that Peahead would have been devastated. I heard him say to someone, "I have lost a real friend."

Several years later, at an NFL meeting on the West Coast, the owner of the Giants, Wellington Mara, came to me and said, "I just had a telephone call from New York. Peahead Walker is dead. I know you liked him."

It was true, and I thanked Mara for remembering. Somehow, all I could think of for the next few hours was Peahead getting that parrot drunk and teaching it to swear.

'Why Do You Hate Me?'

For professional reasons, politicians, traveling salesmen, and football scouts must be able to woo. Politicians court voters. Salesmen shine up to their customers. Scouts curry favor with college coaches.

Getting off on the right foot makes everything else so much easier. Whenever I could, I laid the groundwork beforehand. In 1969, we played an exhibition game in Baton Rouge, Louisiana. Southern University, a small black school, is in Baton Rouge, and I took care of the coaching staff's ticket needs. It paid off. Later, I got good information on Southern U.'s gifted defensive backs, in particular Mel Blount.

It was equally important not to aggravate a coach. For the preservation of harmony, there were times when you had to bite your tongue. The head coach at Texas A. & M., Gene Stallings, was a Bear Bryant disciple who patterned himself after his teacher. On my first visit to College Station he invited me into his office, indicated that I should sit down, and proceeded to tell me why the Rooney family had no one to blame but itself for seven losing seasons in seven consecutive years under four different coaches: it was our slipshod organization.

Recollecting that I was a guest – an intruder, almost – obligated to Stallings for the access I needed to do my job, I managed to curb my temper. Besides, what he was saying made sense. So instead of arguing with him I listened in silence until he had come to the end of his lecture and led me out onto the practice field.

What awaited me there was a demonstration of Bryant-like efficiency: so many minutes allotted to this drill, so many minutes to that one. At intervals timed to the second, a horn sounded. Groups of players and coaches would then disintegrate; new groups would form somewhere else. The players' jerseys were color-coded – one shade for the offense, another for the defense, a third for the injured, a fourth for the teams of specialists. There was no lost motion, no indecision, not a tick of the clock wasted in idleness.

On one side of the field stood a tower reaching into the sky. From this lofty eminence Stallings surveyed the scene and issued orders, like an admiral on the bridge of an aircraft carrier. He headed for it now. "Come along, Rooney," he said. "I'll show you what we're doing." I followed him to the base of the tower and we started our climb up a ladder of sorts. Stallings went first, as easily as a steeplejack. For five feet, ten feet, twenty feet, I was right behind him.

And then I missed a step. I lost control and was falling backward. Stallings, informed by some sixth sense that I was in trouble, glanced down at me over his shoulder. I saw his face – he was thinking: "Oh, my God!" Racing through my own mind were thoughts of a broken leg, a broken back, a fractured skull. But then I felt two strong hands firmly placed on my rear end. They were pushing me up and in. A young graduate assistant had been right on my heels. Maintaining his balance – I can't imagine how – he pushed until I recovered mine.

Quite literally, the guy saved my ass.

I made it to the platform above, all in one piece but embarrassed – so embarrassed that while Stallings pointed out the players he regarded as NFL material, detailing their strengths and weaknesses, I couldn't concentrate. Though I had risked life and limb to get my interview, his words went unheard.

Texas A. & M. 's facilities were magnificent. Not so the facilities at the small black colleges, and yet these segregated schools, back in the days of separate but unequal, held the same attraction for scouts that the Klondike had held for an earlier generation of prospectors.

Future all-pros were to be found in such places, and I valued all the help I could get with their coaches. Accordingly, when John Baker, a one-time Steeler defensive end, offered to ride shotgun for me on a trip to North Carolina A. & T. one year I gratefully accepted. Based in Raleigh, Baker was the county sheriff. AJR had given me orders to look him up, and as we talked in his office I mentioned casually that the all-black college a few miles down the road in Greensboro would be my next stop. "I'll drive you over there," he said, jumping to his feet. "I know all the coaches."

I knew the head coach, Hornsby Howell, myself. Hornsby was a guy who made life easy for scouts, but with the tall and impressive Baker at my side, dressed completely in black and wearing his star, the A. & T. people outdid themselves. It was all the more dumbfounding, then, to be shunted off from the others by one of Hornsby's assistant coaches and asked in aggrieved tones, "Why do you hate me?"

I had no idea how to answer. "Hate you?" I said. "I don't even know you. Why should you think I hate you?"

"All white men hate all black men," he explained.

I said I would like to hear why he believed that.

"Because you're afraid of two things about us," he said. "First, you think we enjoy sex more than you do. Second, you're afraid we'll take jobs that would otherwise go to white men."

"Well, Coach," I said, "if you enjoy sex so much I admire you for it. And I'm not a bit worried that you're going to take my job. My daddy, you see, owns the football team I work for."

Instantly, this made us friends. From then on, I couldn't get away from him. He asked where I was staying, and I named a motel in Raleigh. He said, "Well, give me a call the next time you're here. They have a lot of these big furniture conventions in North Carolina, you know, and sometimes it's hard to find a motel room. If there aren't any vacancies, you can always stay with me and my wife. We have a nice house just off the campus."

There would never be the need to call on his hospitality, but I was flattered and touched.

Scouting at colleges like A. & T., where usually I would be the only white man in a room full of blacks, never made me uncomfortable. I liked the ambience; I liked the humor you always could count on; I liked the coaches. Before the word got around, I heard about Mean Joe Greene at a small black college in Texas. The coach there had films of North Texas State, and he said to me, "Hey, Rooney, you'd better see this. North Texas has a defensive tackle who is gonna be great!"

At one school I visited, there was plenty of film on hand, but no projector. The only projector the coaches had was being repaired.

"When will you have it back?" I asked.

"Oh, it's been ready for two or three days now. We're waiting for the check from the accounting office, so we can pick it up."

Where I was from, I said, we'd call that getting it out of hock. I asked how much the repair bill would come to.

"Thirty-five bucks."

I was with Jerry Neri, a scout for the Detroit Lions, and I suggested that each of us could throw in seventeen-fifty to reclaim the darn thing. I said we were eager to look at the films.

Everybody waited for the head coach to answer. "OK," he said after a pause, "but there's one other problem. We're all too busy to go after it. Now, if you two guys are that interested ..."

So Neri and I drove to the repair shop. We felt that back in the coaches' office they were laughing at us, but we also knew that if we left without watching the films, another Sam Davis, Ernie Holmes, or L. C. Greenwood might forever remain undiscovered.

Mormon Country

At St. Vincent College in the summer of 1969, Bill Nunn and I spent hours at a time with Chuck Noll. He repeated to us again and again that there were three things he looked for in a football player – athleticism, intelligence, and character. Our job was to learn how to recognize these qualities. Even though there are nuances to be considered, almost anyone can tell if a prospect has the requisite physical ability. Identifying character and intelligence – football intelligence – is not quite so simple.

When Noll and his assistant coaches studied film, he invited us to sit in. As they endlessly dissected the performance of each player, we watched and we listened. He was cloning us, in a sense – transplanting his vision and his values. Or trying to.

That year in camp we had something like one hundred players. All wore jerseys with numbers, which made life easier for Nunn and me. In the future Noll would order Tony Parisi, the equipment manager, to get rid of the numbered jerseys and substitute plain ones. It seems that at practice one day a Steeler coach had noticed a little-known scout from another pro team looking on. "We don't want those guys to spot the talented young players we're bringing along," Noll explained to me.

"And turn down any requests you may get for practice games," he added. "Hell, they film those scrimmages and see who our best young free agents are. Then they grab them on waivers for a hundred bucks."

I was miffed, because practice games were helpful, I believed. In retrospect, though, taking into account the overlooked free agents and late-round draft choices who developed into starting players for us, perhaps Noll was right. As usual.

Every year after Labor Day, I hit the road. As head scout, I followed Wellington Mara's advice: Do a good, accurate job when you visit the colleges in the spring and then hold a meeting with the other scouts to map out an itinerary for the fall.

For myself the routine was to stay on the road until Thanksgiving. I had permission to take Kay with me, and when I was going to sun-belt places like California, Arizona, or Florida late in the season I frequently did. AJR insisted that I attend every Steeler game, both at home and away. He also instructed me to telephone Kay every day and telephone Kass once a week at a minimum. Returning to Pittsburgh for our games allowed me to recharge my batteries, keep the home fires burning, and catch up on administrative work. I had no office help except for a secretary, which meant that she had to be competent (over the years, not all of them were).

Making it to the games away from Pittsburgh became a chore, but I obeyed Dad's orders unthinkingly. As I have said, I felt that I worked *with* Noll and Dan, but *for* AJR, and for AJR alone, an attitude that would get me into trouble. Years were to pass before AJR began telling me, "There can be only one boss." What could he mean by that? AJR was my boss. Did he suppose I needed reminding? It hadn't registered with me somehow that by then he was in his eighties, and slowing up. At the start of the Noll era he was still very much in charge.

So was I, in my own mind, when I took off from Latrobe that September and headed west. There were colleges in Utah worth visiting, and I planned on hitting them all. At Utah State, my first stop, the head coach was not at all friendly. "Hell, man," he grumbled, "we haven't played a game yet." Practice was about to start, and he grudgingly permitted me to watch. He considered my presence an imposition, I could see. We were sitting in his office and he was puffing on a cigar. It looked like a burning piece of rope and smelled the same way. So from the inside pocket of my sport jacket, I whipped out a Bance Aristocrat.

"Here, Coach, try this," I said. "It's one of my dad's cigars, and he smokes the best. Before I go on the road, I grab as many of these as I can."

The coach's face lit up like the smoldering end of the weed in his mouth. "Hey, thank ya," he said. "Ya can't buy or steal a good cigar in Utah. Mormons, ya know." The coach himself was from Los Angeles, where his wife, a nurse, had stayed on to work in a hospital. "She sends me a box of my regular cigars once a month, but they haven't come yet," he said, tossing aside his rope and striking a match for the Aristocrat I had given him.

After that, I received special treatment.

I got my Bance Aristocrats from a guy named Jake who ran a cigar stand in the Jenkins Arcade, a Pittsburgh landmark on Liberty Avenue back then. Jake sent the bill to AJR, and he always paid up without a word. Tobacco, as compared with booze, was the lesser of two evils, he believed. As a parting gift for the head coach at Utah State, I entrusted a box of Aristocrats to one of his assistants. "Pretty smart move, Rooney," he said. "As long as Coach stays here, or wherever else he goes, you'll be welcome."

Actually, this was more of an R.A.K. – a random act of kindness – than a calculated smart move. I was never a guy who consistently made smart moves. I remember giving Rip Engle, the Penn State coach who preceded and groomed Joe Paterno, a tin of licorice. Mike Nixon, scouting for the Philadelphia Eagles, happened to be in State College at the time, and he told me, "That was very nice. And very smart. Old Rip loves his licorice." Which I hadn't known.

The coaches in Utah much preferred contraband cigars. I discovered, to my chagrin, that not many natives were so disposed. At Brigham Young I found myself with time to kill and wandered around the campus smoking a toby. I have told you what tobies are – black, tightly-rolled cigars that give off the odor of musk. AJR bought them for twenty-five cents apiece at a cigar store in Squirrel Hill, and I helped myself to his ample supply. I thought of tobies as a good change of pace. AJR liked to bite a toby in two and chew it, one half at a time. I did my chewing bit by bit. The taste was acrid, but not unpleasant.

Because a religious convocation, attended by all the students and faculty, was going on in the field house, I had the Brigham Young campus all to myself. It's at the foot of the mountains on the Provo side of the boundary between Provo and Orem. I walked for thirty-five minutes and then slowly headed toward the athletic department's building. Approaching the field house, I lit another toby; I had smoked and chewed the first one down to a stub. Just then the convocation let out, and I stopped to take in the scene – scores of clean-cut Mormon kids streaming in my direction from the exits. In the warmth of a sunlit September afternoon, I stood there puffing and spitting, smiling and saying hi to the fresh-faced boys and the uniformly pretty girls passing by.

But hold on – something was wrong. They were giving me sour looks. They were glaring at me. Instinctively, I reached for my fly; it was zippered up completely. Puzzled by this show of hostility, I continued on my way to the football coaches' domain. And when I told them the story of my misadventure, including the detail of the cigar, they spelled out what should have been obvious to me. "Certainly they were glaring at you," one assistant coach said. "These are Mormon kids. Smoking is against their religion. You were lucky they didn't run you off the campus." The head coach, as it happened, was a friend, an old NFL guy. "Look here," he said, pulling open the bottom drawer of his desk. "See all these ash trays and matches? This is where I have to keep them. If I didn't hide this stuff, I'd be in trouble."

I scouted football players in Utah that year, and maybe we signed one or two. I don't remember. What I do remember are the inconsequential occurrences.

Driving into Ogden, where Weber State is located, I looked at the fuel gauge and saw that I was low on gasoline. Against my better judgment, I had rented a sports car – a Cougar. Getting into and out of the damn thing was a chore, for I had gained a lot of unneeded weight. "You can't eat like the football players unless you work as hard as they do," one of our trainers had warned me. At the filling station in Ogden I wedged myself out of the door, putting a heavy strain on my clothing, unscrewed the gas cap, and then dropped it. I bent to pick it up and heard a ripping noise. All the way down to the crotch, I had split the seat of my pants. Underneath, I was wearing white skivvies, which now were on public display. I finished gassing my car and, red in the face, went inside to pay up, all the while cursing the Avis gal who had talked me into renting a Cougar.

"Mister," said the guy at the cash register, "there's a tailor and dry cleaner right across the street. They can help you."

I was almost too embarrassed to say thanks.

Weber State had a player the Blesto scouts regarded as a "keeper." Although I scouted him, I do not recall his name, his position, or whether he ever made it to the NFL. I don't remember the names of his coaches. But I can tell you about Weber State's student manager.

We were watching the team practice, and he was talking up the prospect, as student managers tend to do. But then the next thing I knew he had changed the subject. He was giving me the most intimate particulars of his personal life.

He came from a strict Mormon family, he said. His grandfather had died and left him more than five million dollars. There was a caveat, however. The will provided that by his twentieth birthday the kid would have to be married – and married to a good Mormon girl. No wedding, no dough. The grandfather's money would in that case go to the Mormon church. He was 19, the kid said, which didn't leave him much time. Plus he did not have a steady girlfriend.

He knew he could easily find someone who met the will's specifications and would jump at the chance to marry five million dollars. That was by far the least of his worries. The thing that bugged him – the thing he resented – was the sense of being manipulated, of being squeezed. He was ready to tell the lawyers who drew up the will and the matchmakers in his family to go to hell – where it's possible he suspected his grandfather might be.

As he spoke, I asked myself what to make of all this. Was he giving me a line of bull? I didn't think so. As far as I could determine, the kid seemed sincere. I believed he was telling the truth.

Any last doubt evaporated when he turned to me and said, with anguish in his voice, "Mister Rooney, what should I do?" Unprepared for such a question, I thought it over carefully. I understood how Solomon must have felt when people with large problems came to him. Then I offered my advice. I said, "Kid – you'll have to solve this one yourself."

I never did find out if he took the money.

Emergency Landing

Intent on leaving no stone unturned, domestic or foreign, I decided to take a look at the Canadian League. Football players were where you found them, even in Canada. In addition to the home-grown talent, such as it was, you came across promising American players the NFL had somehow overlooked or players at odds with their NFL teams as an aftermath of failed contract negotiations.

Because of the fierce winters in Canada the football season started while we were still in our summer workouts and it finished around Thanksgiving time, when the NFL division races were just heating up. The Canadian League's equivalent of the Super Bowl was a championship game called the Gray Cup.

Canadian teams played on fields that were wider and longer than ours. Instead of four plays to make a first down, there were three, enhancing the importance of punters and punt returners. Our great punter Pat Brady, who came to us in 1952 and played only three seasons before an injury put an end to his career, was scouted in Canada.

The early onset of cold weather required Canadian teams to play twice a week. I planned to spend a day in Montreal, meeting with coaches and front-office people, catch a mid-week game the following night, and fly from Montreal to Southern California, where I could scout USC on Saturday afternoon and San Diego State a few hours later. AJR had instructed me to fly first class on long trips; interpreting these directions liberally, I booked a first-class flight to Montreal as well as to Los Angeles. Any flight that took me west of Cleveland, east of Harrisburg, or south of Morgantown was to my way of thinking a long trip. My duties as our team's personnel director encompassed more than scouting. I had to study reports, organize reports, and write reports, and I could get a lot of work done on airplanes. In first class, this part of the job was much easier.

The Montreal team was called the Alouettes, alouette being the French word for skylark. Everybody in the organization seemed overjoyed to make my acquaintance. They were bringing people out of the woodwork for me to meet, and some of them said things like "I met your father at the Frontenac in Quebec City," or "I knew your dad from the race track in Toronto." I even attended a party they were having that night, a sort of old-timers' reunion. It was a positive first trip for me, and I resolved to get up to Canada once a year or to send one of our scouts. I wondered if Jack Butler might be willing to expand his Blesto group's Canadian coverage.

On the morning after the Alouettes' game, I boarded a Canadian-Pacific flight to Los Angeles. Canadian planes were very comfortable: upholstered leather seats, excellent meals, flight attendants who looked like the actresses selected for "nice-girl" parts in the movies. This was before the feminist revolution, when there was no such thing as a homely or middle-aged stewardess. The ones with Canadian-Pacific were wholesome rather than seductive, and slim enough to fit their uniforms well. They indulged all of our wants with perfect propriety.

I had a seat on the aisle. Shortly after takeoff, I got my charts out and brought them up to date on the players I had scouted since the start of the season, discouraging conversation from the nice but talkative elderly couple in the two seats to my left. I then reviewed statistics on the players I'd be watching in California. I remember a flight on which a stewardess asked me what I was doing. When I told her, she asked how often I flew. I said, "I'm on nine or ten airplanes every week." Not even airline crews traveled that much, she exclaimed. "Our union rules don't allow it."

I laughed and replied, "Just routine."

On this flight to the West Coast, we were zipping along at about thirty-five thousand feet. I could hear the sounds of lunch being prepared in the galley – heavy silverware and expensive china clinking, stewardess talk in modulated, ladylike voices. Lunch was always elaborate on the Canadian-Pacific, and today we were having prime roast beef. I gave the attendant my drink order – ginger ale – and settled back in anticipation.

Across the aisle from me sat a pleasant-looking gray-haired gentleman. A conservative banker, I guessed. The stewardess, however, informed me that he was the Canadian-Pacific Airline's chief pilot, en route with his wife to a conference in Los Angeles. Minutes later, the man left his seat and walked up the aisle to the cockpit. While the door was open, I saw him shake hands with the pilot and pat him on the shoulder. Soon afterward, he was coming back, all smiles. Before sitting down he paused and said something to the stewardess, holding her by the arm.

I returned to my scouting reports. When I looked up again, I saw the stewardess bending over his seat, talking earnestly. She moved on, and he took his wife by the hand, whispered briefly into her ear, got up, and made his way to the cockpit once more. My only thought, meanwhile, was, "When are they going to serve lunch?" The carts with the food had been out in the aisle, but now they had disappeared.

Then I noticed that the plane was descending – not abruptly but gradually. We were slowly losing altitude. I looked at my watch. We had been in the air for just a few hours. No way we were close to Los Angeles. We'd been flying due west and had not yet turned to go south. The airplane dropped through the clouds and even from my seat on the aisle I could see that the ground below us was flat. We were still over Canada's great wheat plains. North of us, I saw the skyline of a city. But what city? Winnipeg? Saskatoon? Wherever we were, it seemed clear that a landing was imminent.

Next I became aware that the pilot who looked like a banker was still in the cockpit. And now the flight attendants were going from seat to seat, saying politely but firmly, "Put everything away. Fold up your tray. Carry-on luggage under the seat, please."

I said to one of the girls, "We're not in California."

Smiling, she answered, "I know. We're in Saskatchewan."

Over the airplane's P.A. system came the voice of the captain. "We must make an unscheduled landing in Saskatoon. Follow the instructions of the cabin attendants without question. I will speak to you again in a matter of moments." The attendants, moving about serenely, were giving soft-spoken orders. They reminded me of the nuns at St. Peter's School. "Do not remove the personal belongings under your seats for any reason. Seat belts must be tightly fastened."

Through the porthole I caught a glimpse of ambulances, police cars, and fire trucks gathering on the runway. Red lights were flashing. The flight attendants, patrolling the aisles, kept reaching down to tug at loose seat belts. "This must be tighter. Stay calm. Everything will be OK." There were no smiles. The passengers, unnaturally silent, asked no questions.

A different voice on the P.A. system, that of the co-pilot: "We're about to land. So far, everything looks good. We will slow the airplane with our engines. Do not be alarmed. Continue to follow the instructions of the cabin attendants." We touched down softly and smoothly. The pilot reversed the engines and we came to a sudden stop. An attendant's firm voice was urging us to our feet. "Leave your belongings and proceed to the nearest exit." We did as we were told, but the chief pilot's wife, I observed, went straight to the cockpit, where her husband was waiting.

On our shuffle toward the first-class service exit, I stepped back to let a woman of mature years go ahead of me. Curtly, the flight attendant said, "Keep your place in line, sir. Continue to move forward." When I arrived at the exit, another attendant was saying, "Step out onto the slide. Then sit. And do not grab hold. Just slide. Do not hesitate." Lemming-like, we followed one another through the door. The slide was rubber, I noticed, and slick. I went down to the bottom swiftly. When I hit the tarmac I heard someone calling, "Don't bunch up. Step away from the slide." The voice was masculine. In contrast to the voices of the flight attendants, it sounded panicky. "Get away from the airplane!" It was coming from a man in a green uniform – a policeman, I thought, or maybe a soldier "Run!" he was shouting. "Get away from the airplane!" Huffing and puffing, I joined a stampede that included weak-kneed old men and women in high heels.

It was more like a marathon than a sprint. The terminal buildings and hangars were off in the distance. If the airplane exploded, nothing else would go up.

The cop's voice now directed us to buses that were parked with their motors running. They were not as far away as the hangars but safely removed from the plane. The one I boarded took off when it was only half-full. The driver, it seemed to me, was in a god-awful hurry to leave the area. Only then did I notice that my heart was beating faster than normal, and not from our gallop across the runway.

It was a two- or three-mile ride to the terminal, a cookie-cutter affair of cement, glass, and marble which appeared to have been recently built. Two policemen at the entrance directed us into a roped-off section. I asked and received permission to visit the men's room and the cigar stand. Both were nearby. When I returned, I had a gift for AJR: Havana cigars, unobtainable in the United States because of our differences with Castro.

Later I went to a pay phone and called home. When Kay answered – she'd been getting lunch for the kids – I blurted, "Guess what just happened to me ... " Interrupting, she said, "Are you all right?"

"Yeah, but my plane just made an emergency stop in Saskatoon, Saskatchewan." Everything, I repeated, was fine, and she said, "Thank God. You damn nut, you – flitting and flying all over the place. You need your head examined."

Which ended the conversation.

I still didn't know why our flight had been aborted, but I could guess. Although Canadian politics held no interest for me, I had read newspaper stories about the clash over language and customs between the French-speaking Roman Catholics and the English-speaking Protestants in Quebec. Quebec is a province in which the French make up the majority. Elsewhere in Canada, the non-French outnumber them overwhelmingly. The French in Quebec wanted secession. In fact, they had forced a referendum on the issue, or would do so shortly (it failed by a narrow margin). Outside of being a Roman Catholic myself, I couldn't see that I had a dog in this fight. I understood, however, that the French Roman Catholics were inclined to be passionate in their beliefs and belligerent when it came to asserting them, and I assumed that some out-of-control separatist faction had planted a bomb in our airplane.

After a wait of three hours in the terminal, we learned that it was all just a hoax. There'd been a phone call while the plane was in the air, an anonymous warning that we would all be blown to bits. But now security people had gone through every piece of luggage on our plane, and no explosives were found. We boarded another plane, identical to the first one, and resumed our flight. There was lots of drinking. Then lunch, or by this time dinner, was served: succulent roast beef, fine china, fine wines. The drinking continued almost all the way to California. So did the excited babble. We were veterans of a slide-for-life, and eager to talk about it.

In Los Angeles the next day I searched the newspapers for an account of the bomb threat. Nothing. It was not a story. Among the people who'd hit the slide with me were men and women in their sixties and seventies. Some, I imagine, had heart problems; a few of the women could have been pregnant. In our first-class compartment, I had seen a man with an artificial leg. He'd had a hell of a time, he told me later, getting up on his feet after our slide. But to the newspapers this was not a big deal. And when I told of my adventure back in Pittsburgh, or on subsequent scouting trips, I could sense that most listeners were bored. Other scouts always seemed to have a story of their own that topped mine.

In later years, I did not, as I had planned, make annual expeditions to Canada. I returned, I think, twice, but when our staff became larger I sent a scout up North every year. I never was able to persuade Jack Butler that Blesto's time would be well spent in Canada beyond an occasional visit. In the end, I came to agree with that judgment. We were sold on developing our Steeler teams with college talent from the good old U.S.A.

The relative danger quotient of airplane travel in the U.S. and Canada had nothing to do with this decision. Now that it has shifted dramatically, though, I sometimes recall with a certain wistfulness a half-hour of suspense in the clouds above Saskatchewan and fifteen harrowing minutes on the tarmac in Saskatoon. The threat, I had believed at the time, was real. But fortunately for me and my fellow travelers, those French-Canadian cultural rebels were pussycats by comparison with Osama bin Laden's homicidal and suicidal Islamic fundamentalist hit men.

Chapter 51

Training Camp

Midsummer, for as long as I can remember, has meant training camp. It's a time when the Steelers come together to hit and hurt, a time when nervous, untested rookies measure themselves against veteran pros — veterans in their prime, veterans just hanging on. It's when the baseball season goes into retreat and Latrobe is the capital of Steeler Nation.

There are rigid specifications for a training camp, and St. Vincent College in Latrobe fills the bill. It's off the beaten path — rustic but not without amenities, removed from big-city distractions but accessible to the Steelers' fan base. In searing heat or soaking rain, zealots in gold and black crowd the hillsides that overlook the practice fields. They come in two major sub-species — critics and followers. The critics are there to judge and to argue, firm in the belief that their knowledge of the game is more profound than that of any coach. The followers seek a religious experience. They hunger for a blessing of some kind from the demi-gods in shoulder pads: a word, a smile, an autograph. A *Post-Gazette* reporter named Rebekah Scott has written that training camp is the start of their "liturgical year." For everybody concerned it's a time of renewal and preparation and hope, like Advent.

The followers, during the years I was personnel director, included a group of decorous middle-aged women, all good friends, it appeared. They did not seem to want any attention but attracted it anyway from the players, coaches, and scouts, who would greet them with a wave or stop to chat. There was something different in their behavior that set them apart from the hero worshippers and autograph hounds.

Back in 1933, when AJR took his first Pirate team to the wilds of North Park for pre-season training, it was largely a non-event. Public and press barely noticed. Early on, AJR realized that colleges offered better facilities, and he switched to St. Vincent in 1934 or 1935. As I have written, he put the team up at the Mountain View Hotel, which was closer to Greensburg than Latrobe. Room and board at the Mountain View, like everything else in the 1930s, was cheap, because, for one thing, no one had money. After the Second World War, when the Mountain View was thriving, AJR would speak of a lost opportunity. "The owner of that place," he said, "tried to give it to me for back taxes. I wasn't interested, and look at it now."

There were years when he shopped around for a camp. He moved from St. Vincent to St. Francis, a small Catholic college in Loretto. The first camp I can say I remember was in Hershey, where the sweet smell of cooking chocolate permeated the town. It comes back to me now as I write this. And Hershey had a wonderful amusement park.

It was too much of a resort town for Jock Sutherland. He preferred Alliance College in Cambridge Springs, an hour north of Pittsburgh near the Pennsylvania-Ohio state line. Sutherland's camps made Parris Island look like Club Med, but in any camp brutality is the norm. With my brothers, I watched the vicious hitting from up close. We saw the players bleed, saw them sweat, heard them swear, listened to the screaming of the coaches, and thought nothing of it. This was routine training-camp stuff, all in the day's work. "Smash-mouth football," people called it approvingly, and we were hardened to it, excited by it. I can still hear one of Sutherland's assistants yelling, "Get those kids the hell out of here! They're gonna get run over!" It happened once to Tim, who was knocked flat.

In the 1950s, while Father Dan was athletic director at St. Bonaventure, the Steelers trained nowhere else until Buddy Parker took over as coach. He said that Olean, New York, was too far from Pittsburgh. He said the weather up there was too cold. "We need the hot sun to get these guys in shape," he complained, and that was it for St. Bonaventure. Owney McManus accused him of being devious. "It's not the location or the climate he doesn't like, it's the monks," McManus said. "All those Franciscans in their long brown cassocks."

Parker coached the Steelers for nine years and moved the team around like a band of gypsies – from St. Bonaventure to West Liberty College in West Virginia, where the practice field was "too dry," causing "shin splints and sore legs," and then on to California State of Pennsylvania, where the facilities were unsatisfactory, and then on to Slippery Rock, where "the people in charge" weren't friendly enough, and finally all the way to the University of Rhode Island. There at last Parker found contentment of a sort. He liked the dressing room and the trainers' room, he liked the coaches' offices, he liked the thick green grass on the practice field, and most of all he liked the isolation. When the Steelers took leave of Parker, they also took leave of Rhode Island. Our coach the next year, 1966, was Bill Austin, and he rejected Rhode Island as "too far away and too cold."

We had heard that song before, I remember thinking.

So back to St. Vincent we went, and the union now looks to be permanent. The Benedictines are good landlords, and I am sure they can use the income. Over and above the rent, the Rooneys as a family have paid for a million-dollar campus renovation program – money well spent, I would say. St. Vincent, after all, is my old school.

All of us – the old-timers, I mean – have our favorite training-camp stories. It was Ralph Berlin who told me about the unsigned free agent recommended by the Lord.

On Saturday nights and Sundays when Chuck Noll was coach, the players were not required to stay on the campus. Until a team meeting Sunday night, their time was their own. Noll and his whole staff would normally absent themselves too, and even Bill Nunn, the camp manager, sometimes went home to Pittsburgh, leaving Berlin at the head of a skeleton crew. There would be no one else around except a handful of players with injuries that needed attention and a dozen or so rookies with nowhere to go.

Late one Saturday night, Berlin was in Nunn's office when a neatly dressed young black man walked in. He was wearing a white shirt with a button-down collar, dark slacks, and loafers. Calmly and pleasantly, he announced that this was where he'd been "ordered to report."

"Well, the coaches and scouts have gone home for the weekend, but maybe I can help you," said Berlin. "Are you a player?"

"Oh, yes sir. A very good one. By the grace of God."

A strange way to put it, Berlin thought. Neither Nunn, Noll, nor anyone else had told him to expect a late-arriving prospect. "Well, who sent you here?" Berlin asked. It was not unusual for AJR himself to promise tryouts to the relatives and acquaintances of his friends. Even Tip O'Neill, the Speaker of the House in Washington, had once called the Chief about a football player. So Berlin took care to be polite, but the answer he got was unsettling.

"The Almighty One sent me," the kid said. "He who is ..." He was not allowed to finish the sentence.

Berlin, breaking in, said, "Wait a minute. Just what are you talking about?"

"God Almighty has sent me to play for the Steelers."

"God Almighty?"

"Yes, and I am his humble messenger."

"OK, OK," said Berlin. "Look – come back tomorrow evening when the coaches and scouts are here."

God's humble messenger was not to be so easily dismissed.

"He told me to come NOW!"

It crossed Berlin's mind that religious freaks can be dangerous. "I'm just the plumber," he said, using his standard disclaimer. "Please come back tomorrow, when everybody is here. I'm just the guy who answers the phone."

"NO!!!" God's messenger thundered. "He said TONIGHT!"

With all the diplomacy at his command, Berlin now asked him to step outside the office while he put in a call to his bosses. The ruse worked. Berlin then called the state police. They arrived within minutes and led the young man away. He was screaming, "I am the Paraclete of Kaborgia – God's messenger and prophet! I am here to take my place as a Pittsburgh Steeler!"

The next day when Bill Nunn returned, he asked Berlin casually if anything had happened over the weekend.

Shrugging, Berlin answered, "Nothing out of the ordinary."

The best trash talker in camp one year was a huge defensive lineman from a small black college in the South. "I'm gonna send you to your grave!" he would yell as he started after a ball carrier.

He lasted two scrimmages before being cut.

"Hasn't made a single good hit since he got here, you know," explained an assistant coach. "He should go back home and become an undertaker," the coach suggested.

A Greyhound bus took the players who were cut to the railroad station or the airport. They called it "the Big Grey Dog."

A free agent from one of the black schools came to St. Vincent with a label. Our scouts had pronounced him "the fastest wide receiver in the Southwest." He was every bit of that, but nothing more. He could not catch a pass or be taught to catch one. Embarrassed by his failures, he went out one night and got drunk. When he returned to camp, he wandered out onto the practice fields instead of going to his room. All alone in the night, he just stood there, surrounded by darkness and empty real estate. Teammates implored him to end his self-imposed isolation and get some sleep. It was simply no use. So then a few of the camp assistants were told to corral him. Even drunk, he was much too fast to be caught. The coach, Bill Austin, now sent for his four fastest rookies and told them, "Go get that guy." Working in concert, they encircled him, bagged him, and dragged him back to the dormitory.

Before noon the next day he had a window seat on the Big Grey Dog.

At Texas Southern one year I scouted a football player who could jump over cars. I saw him warm up on a Volkswagen and then jump over a Cadillac. He'd take a running start from the side, lift off, and easily clear the top. Even if the car was in motion he could do this.

The gazelle was a wide receiver, with good moves and good hands. Though not very big, he was fearless. Nobody drafted him, so I suggested to Bill Nunn that here was a free agent we ought to sign. "Who knows, we might get lucky," I said. Nunn had some doubts, but went along with the idea. To get him, we outbid two other teams.

He did not have a successful training camp. Yes, he could run, and yes, he could jump for the ball. What he could not seem to do was free himself from defensive backs. As he came off the line of scrimmage, they would bump him, and then bump him some more, disrupting his patterns. No fool, he sensed that his days in camp were numbered. Once, rather pathetically, he offered to jump over my car, or even Noll's car, to attract the attention of the coaches. They would see that he was an athlete and allow him more time to develop. But the coaches had made up their minds, and soon he was climbing aboard the Big Grey Dog.

Later I heard that Norm Van Brocklin of the Atlanta Falcons had given the car jumper a tryout. For the same reason we did, I can only assume, the Dutchman let him go. I mentioned to Chuck Noll once that the kid was an exceptional athlete. Again I described how amazing it had been to see him jump over cars.

Noll answered me tersely.

"Save that kind of stuff for the halftime show," he said.

Noll had little patience with car jumpers, but would willingly take a chance on a basketball player. I know we drafted a couple and invited several others to camp. Noll also liked wrestlers. "They work low and understand leverage," he would say. Late in his coaching career, he drafted a wrestler named Carlton Haselrig from the Pitt campus in Johnstown. Haselrig developed into a good offensive lineman but had problems with alcohol and drugs. A Pitt basketball player who got away from us was Sam Clancy. The Seattle Seahawks drafted Clancy and turned him into a capable defensive end. None of the basketball players Noll or I brought to camp ever actually played a down in the NFL.

What most of them seemed to lack was the temperament needed for football. By temperament, I mean a form of toughness. I remember a tough-looking basketball player from Gannon College in Erie who worked in a gin joint up there as a bouncer. He was 6 feet 4 and 240 pounds, not quite big enough for the NBA but adequate for professional football. The day he reported to camp he had a black eye, a fat lip, and various other facial bruises, sustained the night before when he broke up a fight in the gin joint.

My heart soared. Here at last was a prospect with the smooth agility of a basketball player who would not shy away from physical contact. Could we have found a defensive end – another Sam Clancy? The way he handled himself in the drills was encouraging. He moved well and picked up his assignments easily. Then the hitting began. This was rookie camp; the big boys were not yet in practice togs. Our basketball player's stance was too high, natural for a kid of such limited experience, but he did not back down, even while getting the worst of it. He may just be OK, I thought. And then one day after lunch he came looking for me in Nunn's office, where I was talking on the phone. "*Mister* Rooney!" he exclaimed when I put down the receiver. "You gotta get me out of here! They're bouncing my ass around like a basketball. I can't see where they're coming from!" I tried to explain that this was part of the learning process. He refused to listen. I never again wasted time on a basketball player.

Two or three years after we discarded John Unitas, one of the free-agent quarterbacks in camp was a kid from the University of South Carolina whose name I forget. Like most rookie quarterbacks, he did not immediately distinguish himself. After the first week, though, he was showing a lot of arm strength and making accurate throws. Still later, he was firing pinpoint passes. He could see the whole field and put zip on the ball or lay it out softly. Everybody in camp was impressed.

But then that old Gray Dog began yelping. Cutdown time came, and we were forced to release him. My brother Dan drove the kid to the bus station, listening all the way to his cries of anguish. "How could they cut me? Did you see me in practice these last two days? How could they do it?" the unhappy victim of oversupply kept asking. I suppose he went home to a job teaching school or selling insurance. A lot of ex-jocks made a pretty good living as salesmen. But for those with real talent, like the quarterback from South Carolina, not to play football was the same thing as going into exile.

With the creation of more teams through expansion, more young players got better and longer looks from bigger coaching staffs. In fact, when the Steelers became valid contenders, a lot of our cuts were picked up by other teams. The feeling was that we had more talent than we could use. Because of Chuck Noll's reluctance to part with the aging stars of his great teams from the 1970s, sometimes we did. I directed our more promising castoffs to the New York Giants, where my friend George Young was the general manager. Once before a game between our teams, the coach of the Giants, "kidding on the square," thanked me for my help.

The Giants didn't always listen to me. When I saw that Dwaine Board, a rookie defensive end from North Carolina A. & T., was about to be cut, I hurriedly called Young and said, "Offer us something for this guy – a used jockstrap, your last pick in the draft two years from now, anything at all. He's good."

Young said, "Well, Arthur, our team has improved so much that we may not be able to find room for him. I'll talk to the coach."

"Hey, George," I persisted, "I'm telling you not to pass on this guy."

The Giants passed on him; the Forty-Niners did not. Board was a starter on their championship teams in the early 1980s and ended up as a coach.

Driving from Pittsburgh to Latrobe on treacherous Route 30 one day, I got a little past Greensburg when a torrential rainstorm came up. Unable to see very far, I slowed to a crawl. A car with a man, a woman, and two children in it passed me. It was not going unusually fast, just too fast for conditions. A few minutes later, at the bottom of a hill, I saw the wreck of this same car ahead of me. The driver had skidded into a bridge abutment. I stopped and got out. It was raining so hard that the instant I stepped onto the concrete I was soaking wet. The woman I had noticed sat motionless in the passenger seat. I saw that she had bounced off the windshield and was obviously dead. The man behind the steering wheel was unconscious, but moving a little and groaning. The kids in the back seat, boys of about 10 and eight, appeared to be in shock.

Looking me in the eye, the younger one pleaded, "Save me, save me." I said, "Stay in the car. You will be OK." With the rain still coming down, I knew that nothing would catch fire. Just then Warren Bankston, a Steeler fullback, pulled up in his car. I told him, "Go back to the gas station over the hill and ask them to call an ambulance. This is bad." As he drove away, some people came out of their houses off the highway and stood in the rain. "Call an ambulance," I shouted.

Very quickly, an ambulance arrived. Then another one. Paramedics were bending over the woman and shaking their heads. They put the injured man on a stretcher and whisked him away to a hospital. The little boy in the back seat who had begged for my help continued to follow me with his gaze. He kept repeating, "I don't want to die," and I kept assuring him he was not in any danger. He talked to me that way until he and his brother were removed from the wreck and carried off in the second ambulance.

In the paper the next day I found the story of the crash on an inside page near the back. It was short and to the point. The mother had been killed. The father and one of the sons – the older one – were seriously hurt.

Just a few years later Route 30 took the life of a red-haired Steeler rookie named Randy Fritsch, a big lineman from a school in Missouri. The minute I heard about it, I thought of the little boy who lost his mother on that same stretch of road and was looking in desperation for a guardian angel.

I was far away on a scouting trip when the Benedictines at St. Vincent held a memorial Mass for Fritsch, but somebody told me that Fats Holmes, one of the football players who were present, had received Holy Communion. Fats was not a Catholic. Later that season, he joined some Catholic teammates at a Mass in a hotel room the night before a game on the road. Being on fairly good terms with Fats, I whispered to him as we took our seats that in order to receive Communion you had to be a baptized Catholic. He nodded and said he understood. When it was time for the distribution of the Host, he did not participate. Immediately after Mass he grabbed me by the arm. "I have to talk with you," he said. Fats had been having emotional problems and I was not sure what to expect. Just a few days earlier, he had said something odd to Bill Nunn: "Please tell Artie not to forsake me." But we went to my room, and all he had to say was, "I know I am not a Catholic, and I know I am not to receive Holy Communion. But Randy Fritsch was a real nice kid and I thought if I received Communion for him that one time, God would not get mad at me."

"Ernie," I said, using his alternative nickname, "I think you are right."

One hot day as I was heading for afternoon practice, I noticed a car pulling up in the parking lot near the dormitory that housed the camp manager's office. Two young men in dark suits and conservative ties got out and went into the building. The only people I knew of who dressed so circumspectly in the summertime were Mormons doing missionary work and plainclothes law-enforcement officers. These men, some instinct told me, were not Mormons.

Bill Nunn, the camp manager, almost never was late for practice. On this day more than an hour had gone by when he appeared. He came over to where I was standing and said, "We've got trouble." Indicating one of our linemen, a big white kid, he explained, "I have to talk to that guy and to Noll."

My response was a single word: "Cops."

Nunn's response to my response was also a single word: "Yup."

I watched him go down to the practice field and walk up to Noll. They talked for five minutes or so. There were lots of hand gestures and shrugs. Noll kept taking his visor cap off and putting it back on. They parted, and Nunn spoke briefly to the lineman he had pointed out to me. A whistle blast signaled that practice was over, and the players now headed for their weightlifting stations - all except the lineman, who was trudging up the hill toward the locker rooms in Kennedy Hall. Nunn and I, meanwhile, headed for his office, walking swiftly. On the hill, I was huffing and puffing.

The men in the suits, Nunn told me, were narcotics police. They were there to pick up the player Nunn had talked to and take him away for questioning.

"In cuffs?" Nunn said he had asked them.

"That's the procedure," they replied.

"Hey, you can't do that," Nunn objected. "His teammates down there on the practice field aren't gonna like it."

"Mister Nunn," one of them said, "that's the law. If anyone tries to interfere, we can handle it."

"Are you telling me you could handle Joe Greene and the front four?" Nunn asked. "Look," he went on, "let's use our heads here. The kid you want is not a violent criminal. Let him shower and change clothes and meet you down in the parking lot. I promise you, it'll be OK."

There was much more palaver, Nunn said, including a telephone call to Dan in Pittsburgh, before the drug agents reluctantly gave in. Nunn and I watched them wait in the parking lot while the player, showered and dressed, slowly made his way to their car. He got into the back seat with one of the lawmen. The other one slid behind the steering wheel and drove off. It was all done so quietly that nobody other than Nunn, Noll, and I knew what had happened. This was Nunn at his best. He had managed the situation perfectly.

AJR never forgot a player's name. Ralph Berlin told me about a kid on the injured-reserve list who spent the whole season in the trainer's room and was there one day when the Chief came in. Berlin introduced them. Eventually the player was cut, never having appeared in a game, and he dropped out of sight. A few summers later, finding himself near Latrobe, he drove to camp for a visit with his old friend the Plumber. While they were talking, Berlin said, AJR came by. He recognized the ex-player at once and called him by name. He asked how his wife was, referring to her also by name. He then wanted to know what the fellow had been doing and listened to the answer with evident interest.

After AJR went on his way, the former player was awe-struck. "Imagine him remembering me. And I was just an injured-reserve guy!" he exclaimed.

AJR came and went unpredictably, never remaining in camp for more than a day or two. He knew what he wanted from the coaches and from everybody else, and his word was law. I remember a punter sent to camp by a friend of his, a horse trainer. AJR made it clear to me and to scout Dick Haley that the kid was to get a fair tryout. Just to be sure, he sat on a bench a short distance from the practice field and watched.

No walk-on ever received a more thorough inspection. One of the scouts snapped the ball to this guy. Haley and Nunn recorded the hang time of his punts with their stopwatches. Other scouts with notebooks stood in various locations and jotted down their impressions. One of them marked the line of scrimmage, the goal line, and the spot where the ball came down with towels. In no way were we mocking the Chief by such overkill. As Haley put it, we were just making sure that his orders were carried out.

The punter, by the way, was a dud — a humpty-dumpty.

Over time, the Chief's visits became a great deal less frequent. He would customarily drop by on his way to or from the race track or Shamrock Farm, generating excitement among the media hordes, players, and fans. "Art Rooney is here!" went the buzz. "That's him over there. Look at the cigar!" Instead of his cloth cap from Ireland, he'd be wearing a Steeler visor cap. The collar of his shirt would be open and his tie would hang loose. To protect his weak eyes, he'd be wearing sunglasses. He would pull off his cap from time to time and run a hand through his bushy white hair.

Like his football team and its training camp, he was now an institution. Taken all together, they created a way of life for the Rooneys.

The Spectator

During batting practice and infield practice before Pirate games, AJR liked to sit behind the visiting team's dugout on the third-base side of the field. The Pirates all knew him or recognized him; to most of the visiting players and management people, he was an elderly guy in a tweed cap who chewed incessantly on a cigar and seemed to have the run of the place.

AJR never met a stranger. Especially if the people around him were baseball men — scouts, ex-managers, and the like — he would start a conversation. At some point he would say, "Want a cigar?" and since most of the old ball players were addicted to tobacco, having picked up the habit of chewing it early in life, they would seldom refuse. An instructor at the Pitt dental school — I'm not sure how he knew this — told my son Art III, "Your grandfather has no enamel on his teeth. He wore it off with his chewing." No doubt the baseball guys who sat with AJR at Three Rivers Stadium observed that he could spit cigar shreds and tobacco juice with the best of them.

Something else they must have noticed was that he could talk baseball. He could talk about Honus Wagner and Pie Traynor from the old days; he could talk about Branch Rickey; he could talk about the Pittsburgh Crawfords and the Homestead Grays. He knew all the technical stuff, too. One day the New York Mets' first-base coach said to the team's manager, whoever it may have been at the time, "See that old-timer over there behind the dugout? The one with the cap and the cigar? That guy knows more about baseball than most of our players do. He knows as much about the game as we do." The manager replied, "Why, that's Art Rooney. He owns the Pittsburgh Steelers. He used to play and manage in the minor leagues."

When the Steelers were practicing, AJR would get right down on the field. He knew how important it was to stay alert. Keep two big steps away from the sideline. Never take your eye off the ball. But one day his attention wandered. He took his eye off the ball for some reason. And *wham*! A quarterback overthrew a receiver, and the receiver, Mike Collier, heading for the sideline and reaching for the ball, crashed into the Chief at full speed and sent him flying.

Instantly, a crowd of players, coaches, and functionaries surrounded their fallen leader. Trainer Ralph Berlin was kneeling at his side. Collier stood dumbfounded, not knowing what to say or do. The usually imperturbable Chuck Noll never had looked more agitated. There were cuts on AJR's face and head. Berlin applied bandages and tape. The injuries, he could see, were not serious. He helped the Chief back to his office. Mike Collier followed them, eager to apologize. AJR cut him off.

"Don't worry, Mike. I'm OK. I've been around a long time, but I forgot one of the rules.

"I took my eye off the ball."

Chapter 52

Shakedown

"The majority of you," Chuck Noll warned his squad of about one hundred on the first day of pre-season practice in 1969, "will not be with us very long. Keep your bags packed."

New brooms sweep clean, and Noll was a new broom. The 1968 Steelers, he knew, both from first-hand observation and the films we had watched together, were lacking in speed, "athleticism," and "football intelligence." There would be a complete overhaul, it was clear. "We need better athletes to fit the schemes I intend to put in," he kept telling me.

If you spend much time around coaches, you'll hear them talk about their "schemes" — football jargon for the various components of a particular offense or defense. Noll had three teachers - Hall of Famers Paul Brown, Sid Gillman, and Don Shula; mixing and matching, he took the schemes they had taught him and tinkered with them, refined them, added things, subtracted things. What emerged was a system of his own.

To make it work required a certain kind of player. He wanted top athletes who were smart. By definition, a top athlete is strong, tough, coordinated, and fast. For Noll's purposes, you could be a top athlete with only a moderate amount of football intelligence, or you could be a very smart player with moderate athletic ability, and make the team. If you were unacceptably deficient in either or both of those qualities, he immediately crossed you off his list.

Historically, up to then, our principal sources of talent had been the major conferences and the major independents. But from everything I had seen I knew that more top athletes were to be found somewhere else — in the small black colleges of the South. And though the players from these colleges may not have been as thoroughly tutored as the white players in the Big Ten, Pac Ten, Southeast Conference, and so on, where integration was just getting into gear, they were teachable.

So I brought them to camp by the carload, and Noll welcomed them. His prejudices — and they were keenly felt — had nothing to do with skin color. "I'm prejudiced against bad athletes," he said to the scouts. "I'm prejudiced against slow guys, dumb guys, bad actors. Get us people who can think on their feet, who are tough, strong, fast, people of good character, and I will teach them. I will teach them."

And teach them he did. His practices were not brutal, in the Bill Austin tradition, but St. Vincent College never had seen their like for intensity. There in the foothills of the Allegheny Mountains, where I had lost a front tooth in the service of the St. Vincent Bearcats, the black players more than held their own.

One of the white guys from the South, looking around, exclaimed, "Have you ever seen so many blacks?"

From the first day it was evident that Noll played no favorites, black or white. Clendon Thomas, who was white, had been an All-American halfback at Oklahoma, one of the quick, slashing runners coached by Bud Wilkinson in the 1950s. AJR liked him a lot, liked him for his personality and attitude and liked him because they could talk about horses. To Dad it was all the same that Thomas raced quarter horses, not thoroughbreds. He had come to the Steelers in 1962 from the Los Angeles Rams, and Buddy Parker asked him to make the switch from running back to defensive back. The rangy Southwestern type, Thomas was not ruggedly built and had taken a pounding as a ball carrier. He changed positions uncomplainingly and continued to give his all for the team. When tight ends were in short supply, he played some tight end. Nature had not designed him to be a tight end, but he made the adjustment willingly.

By 1969, when Noll arrived, Thomas had been in the league for eleven seasons. On our first day at St. Vincent, unaware that different rules were now in effect, he set out for the practice field wearing a railroad engineer's cap. It was his trademark – like Billy Johnson's white shoes and Harp Vaughan's headband, a sartorial touch that set him apart. Very quickly, he learned that Noll made no distinction between eleven-year veterans and rookies.

Stopping him before he had taken a dozen steps, Noll said, "We all wear the same uniforms here, Clendon."

I could hardly believe what I was hearing. I said, "Hey, Coach – this is one of the good guys. Cut him a break." But I said it to myself.

I realized later that Noll was setting a tone. All of our players were starting out from scratch. Veterans, as well as newcomers, had to prove they belonged on the team. And Thomas, despite his skills and versatility and know-how, no longer could get a jump on the ball, no longer had the speed to cover the younger, faster, more agile wide receivers. I am unable to tell you what Thomas may have been thinking when Noll warned his players that most of them would not be around long, but before we left camp he was gone.

A defensive back still in his prime, Marv Woodson, was another short-term guy. In 1964, Woodson had been a high draft choice. In 1968, he played in the Pro Bowl. None of this helped him to master Noll's defensive schemes, and he suddenly found himself in New Orleans.

His departure, like that of Thomas, was uncontroversial. Thomas, the fans knew, could not last forever, and they never had thought of Woodson as a star. It was Paul Martha's failure to please Noll that grieved and disappointed them.

Martha was a home-town hero, a celebrated high school player from Wilkinsburg who became an All-American halfback on a 9-1 Pitt team famous for missing out on a bowl bid. The reason was simply that on November 22, 1963, an assassin in Dallas murdered a president of the United States. Anticipating an invitation from the Orange Bowl, Pitt had turned down the not quite as prestigious Gator Bowl and maybe some other bowls too. A game on Saturday, November 23, remained; it was with Penn State, and Pitt was heavily favored. Then the rifle shot that killed John F. Kennedy transfixed the entire country. All college games on November 23, except a few in the South, were postponed. It was two whole weeks before Pitt and Penn State could reschedule their game, and the Orange Bowl, meanwhile, had settled on Auburn and Nebraska. In refusing to take it for granted that Pitt would beat old rival Penn State, the Orange Bowl was only being prudent. Pitt won the game, all right, but by the ultra-thin margin of an extra point.

I throw that in as an almost forgotten bit of Pittsburgh lore. What I started out to tell you was that we drafted Paul Martha in 1964. At Pitt, he had been a breakaway runner, but running backs in the NFL had to carry enough weight to absorb punishment, and Martha was as sleek as a greyhound. So for Buddy Parker he caught passes and returned punts, or tried to. Alas, his hands were made of stone, and he ended up playing defensive back.

In the 1960s I subscribed to the theory that superior college running backs who were too light or too slow to be great athletes could make it on defense in the NFL. Chuck Noll changed my thinking. He convinced me that you needed great athletes on defense to stop the great athletes on offense. Paul Martha had played defense as well as offense at Pitt and was certainly not without athletic ability. He was fast and he was smart; he got to the right spots on the field. But Noll, after one season, gave up on him, explaining, "He's not a tough enough hitter."

When we traded Martha to Denver, AJR, along with most of our fans, was sorry to see him go. An unmistakable rapport had developed between them, partly because of their Pittsburgh heritage. AJR called him "The Star." In football matters, however, Chuck Noll made the decisions, and AJR adhered to his policy of rigid non-interference.

Noll's assertion that Martha did not have the will to make shattering tackles was not for publication, but, somehow, Martha got wind of it. The slur was uppermost in his mind when Denver came to Pittsburgh in 1971 for a late-season game with the Steelers. On that day, Martha hit everything in black and gold that moved. He was the second coming of Jack Butler, and, due in no small part to his ferocity; Denver beat us, 22-10.

As time went on, the Steelers acquired defensive backs with the athletic traits Noll demanded – defensive backs like Mel Blount, Glen Edwards, and Donnie Shell from the small black colleges in the South. Martha had his moments both on the field, with Denver, and off the field. He married the daughter of the chairman of U.S. Steel, obtained a law degree, and was president for a while of the Pittsburgh team in the National Hockey League, the Penguins.

I don't think he ever forgave Noll, but his friendship with AJR ended only when the Chief passed away.

Senior Citizen

At Noll's first training camp, one of the few returning Steelers whose efforts seemed to satisfy him was Ben McGee. Five years earlier, before the start of the 1965 season, McGee had played an unwitting role in the philosophical clash between Buddy Parker and Dan Rooney that culminated in Buddy's resignation.

McGee was a 6-foot-4, 255-pound defensive end from Jackson State, in Mississippi, this at a time when weight training, steroids, growth hormones, advances in nutrition, and various other factors had not yet produced a race of behemoth linemen. With help from assistant coach Ernie Stautner, he had shown considerable promise in 1964 as a rookie. But Parker wanted to trade him, along with a draft choice, for two more experienced players.

Dan (as I have written before) counseled patience, telling Parker, "We can't continue to mortgage our future by trading away young guys for players nearing the end of their usefulness." The upshot of it was that McGee stayed with the team and Parker left, his departure unmourned by either Dan or AJR. Noll was McGee's fourth coach, and his last. He played through the 1972 season, in which the Steelers won more games than they lost for the first time since 1963.

A holdover running back who looked "interesting" to Noll was Don Shy. He was big, strong, and fast, and could catch passes. Shy had come to us well schooled in the pro sets used by Don Coryell at San Diego State, but in his first two seasons he was inconsistent. Though capable of making big plays, he lacked the steadiness a coach likes to see.

I had urged Bill Austin to draft Shy despite the reservations expressed by Ken Stilley. The fact that Shy had been a track man prejudiced Stilley against him. "Beware of those guys, they're in the training room all the time," he warned me. Then he added, "You can't coach heart."

"What about Bob Hayes?" I asked. "I've never heard anyone say that Bob Hayes doesn't have heart." Hayes, of the Dallas Cowboys, had won the 100-meter dash in the 1964 Olympic games, lowering the record to ten seconds flat, and yet there were few wide receivers as productive or as durable.

"Hayes is an exception," Stilley argued. "He's a football player first and a track man second."

Noll said, "We're looking for exceptions," and went on thinking – at least for a while – that we had one in Shy. Upon closer inspection, he changed his mind, and Shy spent the season in New Orleans. His accomplishments there were so minuscule that the Saints got rid of him, too.

Noll initially misjudged Shy, overestimating him (as we both did), and he initially misjudged Dick Hoak for the opposite reason.

Hoak had been one of our running backs – usually our primary running back – since 1961. He was dark and somber-looking, short, chunky, and slow. Every summer in training camp, he had fought off competition for his job. "We know what you can do," the coaches would tell him. "Now we're trying to see what these other guys can do."

"These other guys" were rookies like Don Shy – younger, bigger, faster, and flashier than Hoak. They would come to camp, get their opportunity, and fail. By the time the season started, unspectacular, reliable Dick Hoak would be the first-string running back. In his eighth season, 1968, he was the Steelers' old man – the player with more seniority than anyone else on the team.

And the stereotype he never could shake – "too small, too slow" – had become a burden. Normally, Hoak kept his mouth shut, but finally one day he spoke out. To a reporter, he said, "I'm tired of this stuff about not being big enough, not being fast enough. A lot of guys who can run fast don't know where they're going. You have to get to the hole in the first four or five steps, and then it's not how fast you run, it's what you do when you're there."

He was making what, for him, was a speech. "That's the big thing about some of these kids coming out of college," he went on. "They're not that smart. It takes a little brains to play this game. Plays are changed at the line of scrimmage, you have to recognize different defenses. If you don't know where you're going, it doesn't do you any good. In a football game, you never run in a straight line. You never run a forty-yard dash, and usually you're following a guard. On most of your plays you have a guard pulling out in front of you, and if you go full speed it doesn't help you."

At full speed or half speed, Hoak always knew where he was going. Hoak always got to the hole in four or five steps, and it was always the right hole. We had drafted him out of Penn State, where Fran Rogel once played, and in some ways he ran like Rogel, with tenacity and a willingness to sacrifice his body, scratching for tough yards when they were needed. But, slow or not, surprisingly, he could make the occasional breakaway run - seventy-seven yards against the Saints, eighty yards against the Giants, seventy-six against the Eagles, seventy-six against the Forty-Niners.

It was not Hoak's fault that penalties wiped out all of those runs except the one against the Saints. On the way to the goal line, Hoak said after the New Orleans game, he resisted an impulse to turn around and look for a yellow flag.

Hoak had other credentials more highly esteemed running backs did not. He could block, he could pass – at Penn State, he had been a quarterback – and he could catch the ball. So why did he have to keep proving himself, year after year – with Parker, with Nixon, with Austin, and now with Noll?

"I know you like him, and he's a good player," Chuck told me on the second or third day in camp, "but he's far from a great player." And then he said something that put my nose out of joint. He suggested I go to the next Pro Bowl game "and see what a great running back looks like."

Come again? I hadn't said that Hoak was a "great" running back. In the NFL at the time, there were not too many of those. But I knew he was better than Noll gave him credit for being, and now I seemed to hear our coach imply that I did not have the know-how to recognize a great back, never having seen one.

Well now. I had been a scout for five years and had a fairly high opinion of my ability to assess and evaluate. I had seen Jim Brown, an old teammate of Noll's in Cleveland. Most people, I thought, would agree with me that Jim Brown had been a great back. Besides, didn't Noll realize that Hoak himself had played in the Pro Bowl the previous January? That he was one of our all-time statistical leaders, right up there with John Henry Johnson, a Hall of Famer (and another great back I had seen)?

I never did get to the Pro Bowl. Kay, I am sure, would have welcomed a winter-time trip to the West Coast, but my work kept me busy. Meanwhile, Hoak's good showing in camp silenced Noll on the subject of who was and who wasn't a great running back. Hoak played two years for Chuck and then retired – voluntarily. He had run out of gas, he explained.

Lindley Military Academy, in Wheeling, West Virginia, hired him as its coach in 1971. From AJR down to Jack Hart, the equipment manager, everybody in our organization hoped that Noll would bring him back to fill the next vacancy on his own staff. Never once did Noll acknowledge that he might. But when rumors of an offer to Hoak from Pitt began to circulate, Noll immediately called him. They quickly came to terms without haggling, and more than three decades later Hoak was still with the Steelers, an assistant to Bill Cowher.

He had seen Buddy Parker go berserk, Mike Nixon and Bill Austin flop, Noll briefly flounder and then win four Super Bowls, Bill Cowher win a Super Bowl, AJR become a demi-god, and Steeler football arouse passions that in 1961, his first year with the team, were beyond imagining. Through it all, he remained as unobtrusive as ever, a model of dedication and efficiency.

The Agitator

A player whose days were numbered when Noll took over as coach was Roy Jefferson, his best wide receiver. "We aren't going to have any troublemakers on this team," Noll had promised AJR, and Jefferson made trouble. Though never quite openly insubordinate, he was a "tester" – assistant trainer Bob Milie's term for a player who tested his coaches. Jefferson tested Bill Austin, Noll's predecessor, by asking sarcastic questions in team meetings; he tested him by demanding water, ice, and wet towels on the practice field when he saw that teammates were suffering from the heat. Here, I believe, Jefferson had a point. Austin, like a majority of coaches in the 1960s, thought of dehydration as a training aid; Noll came to realize how dangerous it was. But Jefferson, right or wrong, could be a pain in the ass with his yelling and screaming and carrying on.

He had come to the Steelers in 1965 as Buddy Parker's top draft choice, a number two pick from the University of Utah. Normally, Parker traded his top choices for over-the-hill veterans. What predisposed him in Jefferson's favor was the strong recommendation of Fido Murphy, our West Coast scout. For some reason Parker had great confidence in Murphy, and certainly Fido did not overestimate Jefferson. The kid's physique – his nickname was "Bird Legs" – belied his strength. He was tall and fast, with exceptional body control, and he ran the kind of routes that caused directional problems for cornerbacks. After Jefferson had been in the league for a while, Ray May, a teammate, described how he came off the line. "Man, he's slithering like a snake. Everything's moving – his arms, his feet, his head, his legs. He's running in seventeen different directions," May told a writer for *Sport* magazine, Tom Dowling.

That Jefferson had gone to college in Utah was strange. When you think of Utah, you think of conservative white Mormons. Jefferson was a black guy from inner-city Los Angeles – an anti-establishment black guy. I'm not sure how he adjusted out there in Salt Lake City. With the Steelers, he was always an agitator.

Parker, who accepted blacks grudgingly, did not have much inter-action with Jefferson. The year we drafted him, Parker resigned before the start of the season. I don't recall any problems with Mike Nixon but there was friction all the time between Jefferson and Austin. Given Austin's facade of toughness, and his blunt way of dealing with black players, it surprised me how much he put up with from Jefferson.

Noll sort of bided his time. Jefferson, he knew, was not a good influence on Mean Joe Greene and the other young blacks. Still he did not intervene. At St. Vincent, Jefferson flouted minor regulations – parking his car in a no-parking zone (Noll and Dan scrupulously obeyed the rule), tossing aside his helmet during practice. In meetings, as he had with Austin, he tried to play word and mind games with Noll, coming out second-best more often than not. And then in Montreal, before an exhibition game, he went too far. Noll fined and suspended him for missing curfew.

Dispassionately, Jefferson agreed that justice had been served. It was not, however, the end of his complaining. The season got under way, and he said the quarterbacks never threw him the ball "when it meant something." From her seat in Pitt Stadium, his wife kept statistics. They demonstrated, Jefferson said, that the quarterbacks passed to him "mostly in the second half, when we've already lost the game."

After winning their opener from Detroit, the Steelers were losing every week. Losing teams are not happy teams, and Jefferson burned with discontent. When he "did something good," the fans, the press, and the coaches ignored him. When he "messed up" – dropped a pass – he was castigated. Of course he saw prejudice as the reason.

At the end of the season, Noll traded him to Baltimore for two fourth-round draft choices.

Objectively, it made no sense. We were giving Jefferson away. But Noll – and Dan, too – wanted nothing more to do with the guy. "It's not a black-white thing," Dan told *Sport* magazine. "But with Roy around, there would have been confusion. Uncertainty. Chaos."

There was no connection, Dan said, between the trade and Jefferson's role as a militant leader in the player strike the previous July. The underlying problem, he thought, was pretty clear: "Roy wants to be in the limelight. He wanted to be the Steeler superstar. And the truth is, if we had kept Roy, he wouldn't have been number one. Joe Greene and Terry Bradshaw" – the Steelers had just drafted him

– "were going to get more publicity than Roy. We talked about it, and Roy was not pleased with the lack of attention he was getting in the press."

Whatever. The end result was that Jefferson went to the Colts, and in 1970 he caught fewer passes than he'd caught the year before with the Steelers. The explanation was that everybody double-covered him, helping the other receivers. The Colts won their division title, and Jefferson caught passes when it meant something, twice for winning touchdowns with time running out. It didn't hurt a bit that Johnny Unitas was throwing to him.

After the 1970 season, Baltimore traded Jefferson to the Redskins. He was with them until he retired, in 1977, and Washington never failed to make the playoffs during his time there. In 1972 they got as far as the Super Bowl, losing to Miami.

The Steelers by then, without Roy Jefferson, had been to two Super Bowls themselves – and had won both of them.

Trip Ticket to Texas

Right from the start, my choice of an occupation baffled Kay. The way it looked to her, I was Don Quixote chasing windmills, but now I had the guidelines I needed. Chuck Noll's specifications made it easy to identify the particular type of player he wanted, and Blesto's scouting reports were my compass and my map.

They led me to places like North Texas State, where in 1969 we had found our number one draft choice, Mean Joe Greene. The head coach there was Rod Rust, formerly an assistant at Stanford and destined to join Noll's staff toward the end of the 1980s. He could not have been more helpful to the Steelers and to Art Rooney, Jr. Other coaches gave us access to game films. Rust gave unlimited access. He allowed us to meet and talk with his players.

North Texas State under Rust was one of the first Southwestern schools to break the color line in football, hastening the move toward integration. From the Rio Grande Valley to the cane brakes of Georgia to the Florida Everglades, a vast pool of talent had been going untapped. North Texas State's success was helping to change all that. Coaches and administrators were facing a new reality. In order to stay competitive, you hauled down the Confederate flag.

Tipped off by Blesto, I knew that, for NFL scouts, North Texas State was a happy hunting ground. In the 1968 lineup, there were others beside Greene: defensive back Charles Beatty, wide receiver Ron Shanklin, and defensive end Cedric Hardman, to name three. All were black; all were prospects who couldn't miss. In 1969 we drafted Beatty along with Greene. In 1970 we drafted Shanklin. We'd have drafted Hardman, too, if the Forty-Niners hadn't taken him first. North Texas by then was no longer our little secret.

On my occasional visits, Rod Rust always put me at ease. Everywhere I went I presented myself as a working stiff, and not as the pampered son of the man who owned the Pittsburgh Steelers. At North Texas this was no problem. I had the run of the place, thanks to Rust. I could roll up my sleeves and watch game films with the players – let people see that I knew what I was doing. Alas, there came a day when my self-assurance betrayed me.

A player I was looking for did not seem to be in the film. Surrounded by members of the squad, I decided to show off my knowledge. "Where's so-and-so?" I demanded. For an answer, I heard a ripple of nervous laughter. Then a voice drawled, "Have you really been scouting him?" "Sure I've been scouting him," I replied. "Hey! We've got some good reports on that guy." More laughter – laughter with an undercurrent of strain. In the darkened room, I could not distinguish faces. I asked, "Is there something wrong?"

"No, sir. Not at all."

Those Texas kids, black or white, always said "yes, sir" and "no, sir."

I let it drop for a while. The film kept rolling, and I mentioned a good play by one of the guards. It prompted a humorous jibe or two from his teammates. And then I asked again, "Where's so-and-so? I can't find him."

Silence, broken only by a cough.

"Is he still on the team?" I persisted.

"No," someone finally said. "Just before the start of the season, he was killed in an automobile accident."

I had my answer.

After that, for what seemed like a long time, the only sound was the whirring of the movie projector. Then, with muttered excuses, the players started to leave, scraping their chairs. "Gotta go see the trainer," the first guy remembered. Another said quickly, "Me, too." A third one bailed out with, "Time for my class." And there were those who said nothing at all. In a matter of minutes, I found myself alone, staring blankly at the screen.

The embarrassment of that moment comes back to me now whenever I think of North Texas.

Chapter 53

Growing Pains II

September, 1970. A new season, a new stadium, a new quarterback. A new feeling of hope for the fans. Filled to the top row, the stadium dazzled them. Initially, so did the quarterback. Their satisfaction with the stadium never waned; but soon they were disillusioned with the quarterback.

In every Steeler crowd, maybe half of the ticket buyers are men who played football in high school. One and all, they consider themselves expert appraisers of talent. And they perceived after two or three games that Terry Bradshaw, his strong arm and quick release notwithstanding, simply wouldn't do.

By the time we were 0-3, the verdict was in, and it was scathing. The talk was the same wherever you went. "Yeah, he's big and he can move, but he doesn't see the field. He doesn't know where his receivers are. He doesn't know where the defensive backs are" ... "Chuck Noll can't allow that guy to keep on calling his own plays. He doesn't understand the offense" ... "What do you mean, calling his own plays? The center calls the plays. Ray Mansfield has to do it because Bradshaw's too dumb." ... "That country bumpkin is killing the offense, and he's killing the defense, too, with all those interceptions."

There wasn't any letup, and it only got meaner. And though Bradshaw came across in his lighter moments as a classic self-confident extrovert, he was not cut out to take criticism. This unflawed physical specimen with the gleaming blond hair and square-jawed good looks was insecure. He wanted to be loved. He wanted to be admired. Instead, he was booed and reviled. The coaches in the stands called him a redneck ... a hick. He was not one of our own, like Terry Hanratty. The minute he opened his mouth, you could tell. Guys who said "yinz" and "dahntahn" made fun of his locutions and his accent.

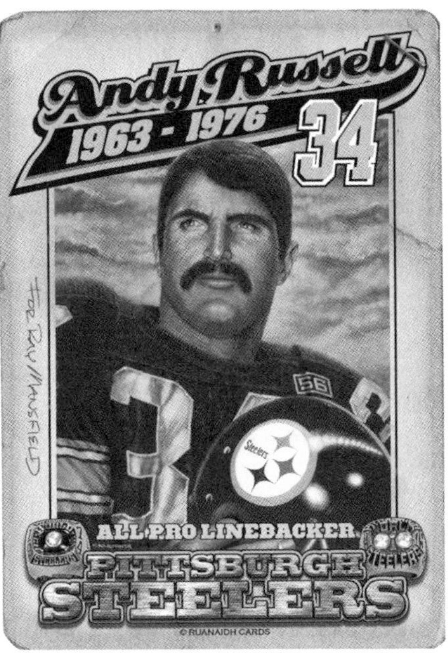

Andy Russell
(Drawing by Denny Karchner)

The hostility toward him bewildered Bradshaw. He was not unpopular with his teammates, but none were close friends or companions. He did have a girlfriend, Melissa Babish, a minor celebrity in Pittsburgh. Just a year or two before meeting Bradshaw, she had reigned as Miss Teen-Age America. In short order, they were married. It didn't last. From the Chief came some fatherly counsel. "Terry," he said, "marry a girl from Shreveport. A farm girl. A girl who milks the cows. A girl who believes you're the most important man in the world."

"And you are," the Chief always added. When all of Western Pennsylvania seemed to be down on Bradshaw, AJR would remind him that "everyone has bad days. I do," he said. "Your coach does. Babe Ruth struck out a lot. Man O' War lost a race. Jack Dempsey lost a couple of fights. Forget those yeggs who are booing you. They don't know how lucky they are to have you in Pittsburgh. You're a once-in-a-lifetime player."

Bradshaw's staunchest supporters were Kass, Aunt Alice, and Mary the maid. He was often a dinner guest at 940 North Lincoln Avenue. No one could say a word against him. Especially after the breakup of his marriage, he may have needed all the solace he could get.

Terry Hanratty predicted – correctly – that Bradshaw would be married "at least three times." Over the next thirty years or so, he was married three times and divorced three times. His second wife, Jo Jo Starbuck, was a figure skater, the star attraction of the Ice Capades.

Certainly Bradshaw's best friend in the Steeler organization was AJR. They talked about football; they talked about boxing; they talked about horses. Bradshaw shared a passion for quarter horses with Mel Blount, who was also from Louisiana. As soon as they could afford it, each of them had a stable of sorts. AJR invited Bradshaw to Shamrock Farm and gave him a thoroughbred horse for breeding purposes.

Like many others, including even AJR, Bradshaw could not communicate easily with Noll. The coach's extracurricular interests – music, wine, food – were too sophisticated for Terry. Noll dismissed the allegations that Bradshaw was "dumb," but considered him "flighty." AJR believed, as I did, that he suffered from low self-esteem. Looking back, I wonder how I could have felt sorry for him, considering all the things he accomplished.

Bradshaw liked cigars, and he conducted bold raids on AJR's well-stocked brown humidor, following my example. The humidor sat on the front edge of the Chief's desk. When the Chief was out of the office, Bradshaw would walk past a dismayed Mary Regan and fill his shirt pocket with the choicest Havanas. Mary's boss knew what both of us were doing, but did not make an issue of it. "Once in a while is OK," he allowed me to understand. Placed beside the humidor was a stainless steel sculpture of two upraised hands with the fingers intertwined, an award from a human-rights organization. It stood about twelve inches high. One day Bradshaw stopped for a moment as he started to leave with his cigars. He took a crisp dollar bill from his wallet and tucked it into a space between the fingers.

The dollar bill, or *a* dollar bill, stayed there for years. Every time somebody filched it, AJR would insert a new bill of his own. When people asked why those metal hands were holding that dollar bill, he would eagerly tell them the story.

Getting to Know Chuck

Even though our cultural interests overlapped to some extent, encompassing music, theater, and the fine arts, I can think of only one non-football conversation I had with Chuck Noll. And I'd just as soon forget it.

Noll, like almost every other coach I have known, was conservative politically. I considered him slightly to the right of Attila the Hun. On a day in 1971, when the Vietnam War was still very much in the news, he made an unexpected foray into my office while Bill Nunn, Dick Haley, and I were going over scouting reports with our charts spread out on the floor. He appeared to be highly agitated, and since the draft was coming up in a week or two I wondered if we had somehow displeased him. But no. His concern was about the massacre at My Lai – not the massacre itself, but the public's reaction to it.

Three years earlier, American soldiers under the command of Lieutenant William Calley had slaughtered more than five hundred noncombatants suspected of having ties of some kind to the Viet Cong. They were mostly old men, women, and children, and now Seymour Hersh, the great investigative reporter, had broken the story. It was all over the airwaves, all over the newspapers, and Noll was disturbed. He thought that Calley and his men were being maligned. "You have to see their side of it," he argued. "Strange things happen when you're at war. In the stress of the moment, any of us might be capable of doing what Calley did. I know I could have done it myself."

I was shocked. I said, "Bullshit! You're too good a person to shoot down women and children and unarmed old men in cold blood. I don't believe you."

Without replying, he turned to leave. Apparently I had offended him. Before reaching the door, he stopped and called back, "If that's what you think, you don't know me very well."

"Like hell I don't know you!" I shouted. Now we had both lost our tempers. He started for the door again, and I yelled, "Watch out! You're stepping on our charts!"

He instantly countered with, "No, I'm NOT stepping on your charts!" It was beginning to sound like a playground squabble. I don't know what kept me from saying, "You are too!"

Later, I reflected, "Why did he get mad? I was showing him esteem. No way in the world he could have shot those helpless villagers."

I suppose that war stirs the passions like nothing else, not even football. It makes us say ridiculous things.

Tempest in a Teapot

The 1971 draft was our first in Three Rivers Stadium. Nothing about the draft room itself was different. Same wall charts, same easels, same T-shaped table, same telephone bank, same swivel chairs. The most important chart was our list of the 220 best players regardless of position.

There was one innovation. Our accountants had informed us that it would actually be less expensive to leave the telephones connected the year round than to keep installing them for the draft and taking them out afterwards. Tony Parisi, our street-smart equipment manager, foresaw trouble with the new arrangement: everyone from the coaches and players to the go-fers and janitors would be placing long-distance calls at the team's expense, he predicted. I forget who came up with the solution, but it was really quite simple. Between drafts, we would hide the phones – there were four or five – in the space between the layers of the ceiling. It worked well over the years except for one glitch. At times the draft room served as a meeting room, and it had not occurred to us that people are apt to dial wrong numbers. It happened more than once, inopportunely, when Chuck Noll was addressing his squad. To the mystification of the players, the unseen phone in the ceiling would ring for minutes at a time.

Once during a draft at the Roosevelt Hotel we used a magic marker to cross out the names of the players who'd been selected and were horrified to discover that the lines had bled through the chart and onto the wall. Never again, I vowed, but after the first draft in our beautiful new home, sure enough: there were black, red, and gold ink marks on the wall. Parisi and his helpers were able to cover them up with paints that blended in with the wall paint.

We had an expensive gray rug in the draft room. To protect it from cigar and cigarette smokers, Parisi placed ash trays everywhere and would personally pick butts off the floor. His tender loving care went for nothing when, as AJR had warned the stadium architects, the flood waters came. In the spring of 1972 they invaded our magnificent offices and destroyed every rug we owned.

The area for the scouts at Three Rivers consisted of a reception room and work station for our secretary, Rhoda Duffy, a room for Bill Nunn and later Dick Haley, and my T-shaped office. After the boiler room I inhabited at the Roosevelt Hotel, I felt that I was now in the Taj Mahal. Behind my desk and chair, next to the bookcases filled with scouting reports, was a pair of big, square boards. On one, I had the names of all the players in the NFL, listed alphabetically. On the other, they were grouped by position, listed as we rated them in the order of their ability. Stuck to the board magnetically, these names were moveable.

Draw curtains covered this board when it was not in use, but eventually I started leaving the curtains open. The players who came to my office wouldn't look at the board anyway, I reasoned. And then one morning a young linebacker stopped by for a chat. During our short talk he did not, as far as I could tell, even glance at the board. Getting up to depart, though, he casually reached out to his own name – it was close to the top but slightly askew - and straightened it. As he left, he gave me a quick little smile.

On or off the football field, nothing escaped Jack Ham.

From then on I made sure that the curtains were drawn.

In the scouts' office were two blackboards, one on each of the side walls, and a white screen on the wall at the far end. We wrote on the white screen with dust-off magic markers except when we absent-mindedly used regular magic markers. The dust-off markers left no trace on the wall behind the screen; the regular markers created a mess. It was Mrs. Duffy's job – and she hated it – to find a solvent that removed the permanent ink.

Our unintentional vandalism greatly disturbed AJR, who was proud of his new domain. I had a habit of dropping cigar ashes on the rug, and he constantly took me to task for my carelessness. Worse yet, I would rest a burning cigar on the edge of my vast, gorgeous desk, with its blond wood top, and forget about it while taking a phone call. Another of my sins during a phone conversation was to write the names of prospects on the desk top instead of using a scratch pad.

"Who do you think you are, anyway?" the Chief would roar. "Cigar burns! Scribbling on the desk! Ashes on the rug!" He never called me a slob or an ignoramus, but that is what he was thinking, I knew. He would end these tirades with what I felt was a non-sequitur – "Get a haircut!" maybe, or "Go on a diet!"

I've been told that years after I left the organization the names and the cigar burns were still on that desk. Somehow, my conscience remains clear. Any damage I may have done, it seems to me, was an unfortunate but forgivable side effect of the zeal with which I went about my work.

When I reported what was going on to Kay, she bought me an enormous ash tray for the desk. Dan, who considered himself the guardian of our office furniture, was displeased with my carelessness but at the same time consoling. "A tempest in a teapot," he told me. "Remember, the Chief always gives us hell about the little things, but cuts us a break on our major crimes."

'What About Ham?'

The Steelers' 5-9 record in Noll's second season gave us the eighth first-round pick in the 1971 draft. My only scout was Bill Nunn, a full-time employee by now. Necessarily, I looked at all the prospects myself and relied a great deal on Blesto. After the NFL season, our coaches got involved, evaluating prospects at the all-star games and on film. This was around the time when I came in off the road and went to Blesto meetings with Noll. Between Christmas and New Year's, working both at home and in the office, I reorganized the scouting reports and studied game films endlessly.

We drafted at the end of January back then, which for most teams was too soon after the season. Physically and mentally exhausted, the assistant coaches who doubled as scouts had a hard time refocusing. Not so Chuck Noll. For him, the transition was seamless. He never preached to his assistants, but would tell them, "The more you can do for the club ..." and let the sentence tail off. As his coaches understood, he was saying, "Get off your asses and do something useful." Noll led by example. With the head man so fully energized, how could the others lay back?

I had always felt driven, but I know that because of Noll I felt more driven than usual. Bill Nunn and Jack Butler seemed to share this attitude, and Butler's intensity rubbed off on his scouts. In my opinion, we were the only team getting its money's worth out of Blesto. I interviewed the scouts and I interviewed Butler. Every piece of paper that came across my desk from Blesto I scrutinized thoroughly. I made a pest of myself, badgering the scouts for more and more information. "I'm a slow learner," I'd say. "Would you do me a favor and discuss that report with me again? Can I take you to dinner tonight and talk about some of these players?" I would ask to spend a few days on the road with a scout. When we looked at a player, I'd say, "Would you take this kid on the first or second round if your job depended on whether or not he was worth it?" I became a pain in the neck to everyone everywhere, but the Blesto people didn't mind. "Artie," they would tell me, "you're the only personnel guy who's listening to us."

Mort Sharnik, the *Sports Illustrated* writer, thought I was "on a quest." "You have a passion," he said. Actually, I was afraid of being typed as the boss's lazy son. I dreaded failure. For years we had been "the same old Steelers." Scouting was a low-priority job. Uncle Jim could have handled it – his football résumé was much more impressive than mine – but early in life he had formed an antipathy to work. Ray Byrne, the Digger, acquired his expertise from magazines and newspapers. Byrne was an undertaker, a bookkeeper, and an organizer, but not a scout. With just one assistant, a dedicated football man beating the bushes, Byrne could have made a difference. But he and Uncle Jim belonged to the past. Now, thanks to Mom and Dad, it was my turn.

Just before our first draft meeting in my still new office, Chuck Noll buttonholed me.

"Artie," he said, "my coaches and I have a big request to make."

"Sure, Coach. What can I do for you?"

"Please limit yourself to just one of those big green baseball-bat cigars a day."

He was serious. So was I.

"I'll try, Coach," I promised. "I'll try."

And I did.

Our meetings always began the same way. Alternating, the assistant coaches, Nunn, and I would read the scouting reports aloud. Noll did not read, but took notes. One thing I never failed to notice was the difference in reading skills the coaches exhibited. Some coaches read the reports very well; others read poorly, even the former school teachers among them. As the years went by, and we hired more coaches and scouts, I proposed a change in the routine. Let the scouts do all the reading, I suggested to Noll. And let the coaches take notes, but only about the players they would be supervising. If a scout read a report about a cornerback, for example, only the defensive backfield coach would take notes. The other coaches need not even be in the room. The offensive line coach could make better use of his time watching films of offensive linemen; the backfield coach could make better use of his time watching films of halfbacks and fullbacks. And so on.

Noll did not like this idea. He said, "We all have to be part of this as a team." I agreed in principle but said I had observed during these meetings that some of the coaches always seemed to lose interest unless they were directly engaged. Their minds tended to wander.

Flaring up, Noll demanded, "Just who is not paying attention?"

"Hey, I'm not a squealer," I said. "But look around."

There the matter rested until the following year. We covered only two positions a day at our draft meetings, one in the morning and one in the afternoon, which meant some hours of near boredom for certain coaches. In the middle of one report, a coach who was not a bad guy and no dumbbell started nodding. Soon his chin dropped down to his chest. He had dozed off for all of us to see. Over the next couple of days, the same thing happened again and again. He would catch himself, stay alert for a few minutes, and then stop fighting it. To the horror of his colleagues, he started to snore. No one laughed. We were all too embarrassed. Noll, characteristically poker-faced, kept his eyes on the scout who was reading the report. At last I nudged Rip Van Winkle, waking him up, and said, "Please don't sleep on my time."

I was to learn shortly afterward that the coach had narcolepsy; he would fall into deep slumber at any time of the day without warning. Properly medicated, he was soon back to normal. Meanwhile, he had settled the issue between Noll and me. "Come to think of it," Noll admitted, my suggestion made sense. Henceforth only the coaches whose positions were being discussed would attend the draft meetings.

Noll himself missed a full week of meetings in 1971. Late on the morning of the first day, Dan walked into the room and asked if he could see Chuck alone. While they were gone, we continued, at Chuck's request, with our work. He returned after fifteen minutes or so. "I've received some bad news," he announced. "My father has just passed away." There was silence, and then an outpouring of murmured condolences. "I'll be leaving right away for Cleveland," Noll said. "Just go on without me."

I considered it a tribute to Noll that his absence did not set us back. The meetings were conducted as smoothly as if he had been on the scene: no short cuts; no joviality. When he was with us again, Nunn and I brought him up to date, and now we were ready for draft day.

Anticipating, I had written the name of Frank Lewis, a wide receiver from Grambling, on the blackboard and underlined it three times. Both Nunn and I had seen him on film and in games. We liked him a lot, and so did the Blesto scouts. He was very fast, with stop-and-go movement besides. He could see the whole field and knew the location of everybody on it. We had talked with Eddie Robinson, Grambling's long-time legendary coach, and everything he told us was positive. Lewis, he said, was a nice kid, a quick learner, easy to coach. These traits, along with his athleticism, made him exactly the kind of player Noll wanted. Grambling was not far from Shreveport, Terry Bradshaw's home town, and I had visions of Lewis and Bradshaw working out together in the off-season. The thought of Bradshaw throwing to Lewis and Ron Shanklin, the wide receiver we had drafted in 1970, excited me.

While the seven teams picking ahead of us announced their selections, I was on the edge of my seat. Our own turn came, and no one had taken Lewis. With a nod of assent from Noll, I reached for the phone, becoming aware, in the same instant, of a voice that bounced off the walls. It belonged to an assistant coach, who was calling out, "Hey – what about Jack Ham?"

I went rigid. Jack Ham, from Penn State, was the player we hoped to draft in the second round. Turning on the assistant coach, I said, "Look: we have worked on this list together. So now I suggest that we take these players the way we have them rated. If Ham is out there in the second round, we'll grab him. But first we're taking Lewis."

For the record, I have said that no one we ever drafted was more of a disappointment to me than Lewis. If I could, I'd retract those words. Actually, Lewis turned out to be everything we expected. He worked hard in practice. He was never seriously hurt. He made some important plays in big games. Once when we were up against a good Houston team in the Astrodome, the Oilers' head scout came rushing through the press box, headed for the Houston coaches' booth and shouting at the top of his voice, "He's coming into the game! Back 'em up, back 'em up! He's in the fucking game!" Noll had inserted Lewis, and the head scout was spreading the alarm. Look out! he was warning the Houston defensive coaches. Back up your cornerbacks and safeties. If Lewis gets behind them it's a touchdown.

The scout was right to be fearful of Lewis. Speed kills, and Lewis had speed in abundance. He was a starting wide receiver the first time we went to the Super Bowl. Eventually, though, we traded both Lewis and Shanklin. The more productive wide receivers we drafted in 1974, Lynn Swann and John Stallworth, had made them expendable. Sitting on the bench, Lewis was wasted. With Buffalo in 1981, near the end of his career, he had a Pro Bowl year, catching seventy passes. I took this as vindication for Nunn and myself. A great athlete and a good guy, Frank Lewis was one of my favorite Steelers.

Getting back to 1971, we drafted Ham in the second round. My hunch that he would still be available was correct after all. Inexplicably, the coach who had thought we should draft him ahead of Lewis was urging us now to take a linebacker from Bowling Green, Phil Villapiano. I looked at the guy to see if he was being facetious. Villapiano became a very good player for Oakland, but Ham made the Pro Bowl eight years in a row and is now in the Hall of Fame.

After we had taken him, my good friend Upton Bell, director of player personnel for the Baltimore Colts, had a question for me: "Where are you going to play the guy? He's an undersized linebacker and an oversized strong safety." I had seen Ham in games, I had seen him on film, and I had seen him practice, and I felt sure he had the size to be a linebacker. I had not, however, seen him in street clothes. We had an orientation meeting for rookies and free agents in the Downtown Hilton that year, and just as we were ready to get started I heard a knock at the door of our suite. I opened it, and there stood a slight-looking young man wearing a blue zipper jacket, a white shirt, blue slacks, and loafers.

"Is this the Steelers' room?" he asked.

"Yes," I said. "What do you want?"

"I was told to come here."

"Yes?" This time I made it sound like a question. "Do you have a message for us?"

Bashfully, the kid said, "I'm Jack Ham."

Upton Bell's question came back to me. Could this be the linebacker we had picked in the second round?

The next morning, when the rookies took their physical examinations at Three Rivers, I watched them being weighed and measured. They were wearing only shorts. It would be going too far to call Ham emaciated, but from the waist up he was certainly fat-free. Though his frame seemed big enough, he'd be a project for Noll and Lou Riecke, his strength coach, I told myself. Then I looked at his legs. They were long and muscular.

Before the start of the season, Ham pumped iron and put on twelve pounds, mostly in the shoulders and chest. I came to regard him as the perfect football player for the 1970s. He was a wonderful athlete with exceptional leverage, excellent vision, and unerring anticipation. Moving to the ball, he could not be blocked. He covered passes with the agility and speed of a defensive back.

The first time Ham played in the Pro Bowl, it happened that Noll was his coach. During the week devoted to practice, my cousin Tim Rooney, who was helping Noll as a go-fer, found himself on an elevator with some of the players. They were speaking freely of their discontent with Noll's hard-to-grasp defensive scheme, and Tim, under the cloak of his anonymity, was an interested listener. "Nobody," said one guy, "can make this coverage work. It's too complicated." Another player, Tim reported, promptly took issue with that. All he said was, "Ham. Ham will make it work." To which the first guy responded. "OK. OK. Ham. It'll work."

After Ham's eleventh year with the Steelers, a foot injury sent him to the team's orthopedist. "You can continue to play," he was told, "but you'll be slower." Ham tested the foot, and sure enough – he'd be able to play but had lost a full step. Unwilling to lower the standard he had set for himself, he retired.

We came out of that 1971 draft with twelve players who would make the team. Seven of the twelve were starters in Super Bowl games. Four would play in the Pro Bowl. One – Jack Ham – would become the fourth Hall of Famer we drafted in Noll's first three years. All in all, our 1971 draft was one of the best in the history of the league – the fourth best, actually, according to a recent poll of the statistical wizards who evaluate such things.

We had two picks in the fourth round. Both made the team. We had four picks in the fifth round. Three made the team. Our three picks in the eighth round included Fats Holmes, who made it big. Our eleventh and thirteenth picks made the team, and one outstanding free agent, Glen Edwards, was a starting defensive back for seven years, MVP of the 1974 team, and a Pro Bowler in 1976 and 1977. Edwards had come to the team from Florida A. & M. as a running back. He was tough, fast, and smart, but trouble off the field. After the 1977 season, we traded him to the Forty-Niners.

The eleventh-round pick was Mike Wagner, a defensive back from Western Illinois. "Hey," Noll said to me, "how come this guy is still on the board after ten rounds?" I suggested that early in the season he'd been hurt. Noll said, "If he's smart enough maybe we can do something with him." An accounting major, Wagner was smart enough. But I confined myself to saying that he hit hard and seemed to be a nice kid. Noll laughed. "Nice kids make good son-in-laws, but I'd rather have tough guys." Wagner was tough enough, it turned out, to play in our first four Super Bowls and also a couple of Pro Bowls.

Let me sum it all up: Fifteen of the players who were starters on one or more of the Super Bowl teams had been drafted since Noll's arrival or signed as rookie free agents. You could call that striking it rich.

One of our fourth-round picks, Gerry Mullins, from Southern California, was an offensive lineman who could be plugged in almost anywhere. In a career that lasted nine years, Moon played guard, tackle, and tight end. The other fourth-rounder, defensive end Dwight White, was one of my lucky scouting finds. Blesto, for some reason, hadn't rated him high, but in my opinion he was everything Noll looked for in a player. Moreover, White's coach at East Texas State had spoken well of his attitude and intelligence. White used his intelligence after ten seasons of football to start a successful career as a stockbroker.

Fifth-round pick Larry Brown was a tight end from Kansas, a better blocker than pass catcher at 6 feet 4 and 225 pounds. But in Super Bowl IX he caught a touchdown pass from Bradshaw that finished off the Minnesota Vikings. Eventually Noll moved him to an offensive tackle position, and in 1983, his thirteenth season, Brown went to the Pro Bowl. He played one more year and then ran a chain of restaurants after dropping out of dental school at Pitt. Neither the public nor the press ever gave him his full due. Nominated for the Hall of Fame, Brown fell short of receiving enough votes for induction.

Players like Steve Davis, a running back from Delaware State; Mel Holmes, offensive tackle from North Carolina A. & T.; and Craig Hanneman, defensive end from Oregon State, were cut before we ever went to a Super Bowl. Hanneman, a big farm boy, was born tough; the other defensive linemen – Joe Greene, L. C. Greenwood, Dwight White, and Fats Holmes – simply happened to be better football players. Hanneman earned his place in Steeler lore on the afternoon of November 11, 1973. The Steelers were beating the Oakland Raiders in Oakland for their eighth victory in nine games, and Hanneman was in his usual place on the sidelines. Next to him stood Roy Blount, who'd been gathering material for a book about the team. As the Steelers scored the touchdown that assured them of a 17-9 win, Hanneman uttered the words that gave Blount's opus its title. "We're about three bricks shy of a load," Hanneman said. It could not have been put more strikingly, Blount thought. With all the bricks in place the following year, the Steelers began their Super Bowl run. Hanneman, sad to say, was by that time a New England Patriot.

Fat Man

My first glimpse of Ernie Holmes in the flesh was on a rainy night in Texas in 1970. I had seen him on film and he had caught my eye (he'd have caught anybody's eye). So, for an up-close look, I flew down to Houston and drove my rental car to Jepson Stadium, where his team, Texas Southern, played its home games, usually under the lights. On this night Texas Southern was playing ... oh, forget who Texas Southern was playing. It's beside the point. Arriving at Jepson Stadium, I found a seat in the stands. There were no booths for pro scouts, and the raindrops kept falling on my head. As I waited for the kickoff, thoroughly wet and thoroughly miserable, I heard a baritone voice calling, "Hey, Artie!" It was Red Almond, a Washington Redskin scout and the only other white guy in the stadium. From the track that encircled the field, he hollered, "Come down here. I've got something important to tell you."

Red had gone to college at Mount St. Mary's with my twin brothers John and Pat and our cousin Johnny Laughlin. The information he had for me concerned the Texas Southern coach. Aware that two scouts would be in the stands, he had changed the numbers on the jerseys of all his seniors. His motive was anger – not at us, but at his players. Unhappy with the way the season was going, he had labeled the whole team "a bunch of quitters."

"What a jackass," Red growled. The teams on the field, their pre-game loosening-up exercises finished, had gone to their respective benches. "Come on," Red urged me. "Let's walk over to the Texas Southern bench and see if we can figure this out."

The first guy to spot us was Holmes. Waving his arms to get our attention, he pointed to his number and shouted, "Fats! This is me! Fats!" All of the other seniors were doing the same thing – pointing to their numbers and calling out their names.

But I was interested mostly in Fats. He showed his enormous strength that night. I remember a luncheon in the Allegheny Club for Bill Nunn's black college all-stars at which Muhammad Ali was the main attraction. Americans were still fighting in Vietnam, and his refusal to put on a uniform still rankled with supporters of the war. To show how he felt, an NFL scout who had been a colonel in the Army boycotted Nunn's Steeler-sponsored affair and ate his lunch in Ed Kiely's office. I wasn't too crazy myself about having Ali for a guest, but I shook his hand and called him "Champ" and I must say that he was certainly a presence. I'm digressing, however, so let me start over. Fats Holmes crashed the luncheon in order to meet Ali (they engaged in a duel of wits, which Fats lost) and Kay was on hand with Susie, our three-year-old daughter. Fats, in greeting us, picked Susie up and held her in the palm of one hand. I do not exaggerate. He was that big, that powerful. The instant he put Susie down, Kay swiftly hustled her out of sight.

To become a functioning part of the Steel Curtain, the Steelers' front four, Fats needed guidance. He got it from Bill Nunn and assistant coach George Perles. They curbed his flamboyant individualism. Fats himself looked to Joe Greene for leadership. One time when his feelings were hurt – Greene had ordered him off the field for freelancing instead of playing within the defensive scheme – he refused an order from Perles to go back in. "Not till Joe tells me it's OK." Somehow, Perles got word to Greene, and he came to the sideline. Pointing a finger at Fats, he bellowed, "Get your ass in here!" Did you ever see an elephant fly? The elephantine Holmes fairly flew off the bench.

During the 1976 season there was a stretch of five games in which the Steeler defense did not give up a touchdown. Houston then pushed one across, and an argument broke out in the dressing room over who was at fault. Fats and his idol Greene exchanged angry words. None too soon, trainer Ralph Berlin alerted Noll – "It was getting real bad," he told me – and Noll had to step between the combatants. It may be that Fats now considered himself a rival of Greene. Frank Gifford, the Hall-of-Fame running back turned broadcaster, was calling him the best defensive lineman in the NFL. There even came a time when Noll, who measured his words, would say that for two years, 1976 and 1977, Fats was a better lineman than Greene, L.C. Greenwood, or Dwight White.

That is possible. But he was also a very troubled soul, an alcoholic with bipolar disorder. On a memorable afternoon in the off-season one year, news reports came in over the radio that a Steeler player had gone berserk; from his car; he was firing a revolver at truck drivers on the Ohio Turnpike. "Couldn't be true," we told ourselves in the Steeler offices. "Must be a case of mistaken identity."

The news flashes continued; in fact, they got even worse. The Steeler was now shooting at a state police helicopter. A bullet had gone through its floor and hit the pilot on the foot.

More details quickly followed. The rampaging football player was being chased by the cops across Ohio. One by one, the tires on his car were blowing out. Now he had left it on the Turnpike and had disappeared into some woods. Then came the news of his capture. He was being taken to jail in Youngstown, but not in handcuffs, which were too small for his wrists, the police said. For the first time, they gave him a name: Ernie Holmes.

Dan, Joe Gordon, and our lawyer, Jack McGinley, Jr., were swinging into action. Mrs. Duffy, my secretary, put in a call to the Youngstown jail and got me on the line with a lady cop. I wanted to be sure that the man they had locked up was Fats, and not an impostor. What did he look like? I asked. The description she gave me was as thorough and exact as a scouting report; when she finished I knew there had been no mistake.

Doc Best, our representative at the court hearing for Fats, got him committed to Western Pennsylvania Psychiatric Hospital in Pittsburgh. An early visitor, Buff Boston, told us, "He's there with all the nuts – and he's one of them." The assessment seemed harsh, but I welcomed it. Nothing less than an insanity plea could keep Fats from going to prison. I went to see him after Boston did, and he was moved by my gift of a prayer book. He appeared to be the king of his unit. The other patients looked up to him, and he related quite well with the nurses and orderlies. He told me that during the car chase in Ohio one of the pursuing state troopers had a "direct bead" on him with a pistol. Fats, who was out of his car, heard the trigger snap, he said, "and nothing happened." A truly lucky misfire.

According to one of his doctors, Fats was a man who "behaved like the people around him." Good company influenced Fats for the better, bad company influenced him for the worse. After his release from the hospital, he was put in the custody of his girlfriend.

Fats was a Steeler for several more years. In January of 2000 he came to our twenty-fifth anniversary Super Bowl party weighing 415 pounds. From the dais, he talked incessantly of having found redemption in "Christ Jesus our Lord," belaboring this theme until his teammates induced him to shut up by tapping with knives, forks, and spoons on their water glasses. At this same party, the only player I asked to sign my team picture was Fats. Yet for all he contributed to the success of the front four, it was painful to think of how great he might have been except for his personal problems.

Far less physically gifted than Fats, another player we drafted in 1971, Al Young, was his opposite also in level-headedness and character. Young was a wide receiver from South Carolina State. He developed sickle cell anemia, which affects mostly black people, after just two years with the team and never played again. Looking for a way to keep Young in the organization, I offered him a chance to become a talent scout. He thought about it, and even scouted some games for us, before deciding that what he really wanted to do was work with adolescents as a teacher and coach.

"Do you know what I mean?" he asked. I said I did.

Chuck Noll had assured us when we interviewed him for his job that he placed no importance on the color of a player's skin. Could there now be the slightest doubt? In that 1971 draft, three of our first five picks and seven picks altogether were from schools in the South with all-black enrollments. I know that Bill Nunn and I helped to bring that about, but Noll had the final say. As our draft picks and free-agent signings demonstrated, his commitment was to winning with the best players available. Down through the years, I have never heard him even hint that he deserved any credit for this. And I can say just as much for myself. At least I think I can.

Frank O'Harris

The Blesto scout was telling me about a sophomore running back at Penn State who had the talent to be a big-time star. His name, as I heard it, was Frank O'Harris.

Ordinarily, I paid little attention to scouting reports on sophomores. We had a thousand seniors to think about, after all. But as the 1969 season moved along, everyone kept praising this Frank O'Harris. Penn State's opponents couldn't contain him.

"One for Dad," I said to myself. There weren't that many good Irish players any more. I felt we should keep an eye on this guy.

But then I saw his name in print, and it wasn't actually Frank O'Harris. There was no capital "O." There was no apostrophe. Thus rearranged and altered, the letters spelled Franco Harris. No way he was Irish, I realized, not with a first name I had seen on spaghetti cans. His mother, I learned, was Italian — an Italian war bride — and his ex-GI father African-American. Franco Harris came from a town in New Jersey. He was tall, maybe 6 feet 2 or 3, and he weighed about 215 pounds. He could run over tacklers or run away from them. But he was still just a sophomore and hardly more than a blip on my radar screen.

I did not scout Franco in person until his senior year, 1971, when I made the drive from Pittsburgh to State College twice, first with my family and later with Dick Haley. Even though it was always a distraction, taking Kay and the kids along on scouting trips eased my conscience. As I have said, I was spending too much time on the road. While Kay kept the kids occupied — she took snapshots of them climbing all over the granite Nittany Lion sculpture - I slipped away to meet with the coaches in their office, study film, and then watch practice.

It was early in Joe Paterno's long run as Penn State's major domo. Our relations with him were excellent, as they had been with Rip Engle, his predecessor. In fact, when we were looking for a coach after ridding ourselves of Bill Austin, Paterno had been Dan's first choice. He was interested, too — very much — but his roots in Happy Valley were too strong and too deep and he decided to stay put. It was only after Paterno turned down the job that Chuck Noll moved to the head of the list.

When I talked to Paterno and his assistants about Franco Harris, I was in for a surprise. None of them really bad-mouthed Franco, but they diverted the conversation to one of the other running backs, Lydell Mitchell. I watched a game film and saw that while Mitchell was a pretty good player in a big-time program he did not have his teammate's size, power, speed, or mobility.

For a close look at Franco, I cadged an invitation to practice. On a gorgeous fall day, the hills that enclosed the campus were blazing with color. Somehow this background seemed perfect; it was just the right setting to view an athlete who might have been carved out of marble by, oh, Michelangelo, let's say. Later, describing Franco to Kay, I remarked, "There's something classical about him."

"That's nice," she replied, "but can he play?"

I was certain of it. "He has all the tools," I said, "and he's made the big plays in big games."

Pure football talk. There never was much of that between Kay and me. On the drive back to Pittsburgh, we stopped at a famous eating place called Erculani's and found that we didn't like it at all; neither did the kids, who wanted hamburgers instead of Italian food. Situation normal again, I thought. Afterward, in the car, the kids fell asleep, and Kay brought up the subject of my job. I was being consumed by it, she felt, and the evidence backed her up.

Scouting had gotten to be an opiate with me. Always there was more to do — more players to check out, more coaches to interview. Though we had hired Dick Haley to relieve me of certain duties, psychologically I was not yet prepared to give them up. I would have to achieve a balance between work and family — I knew that. The strain that my long and frequent absences were putting on Kay had become a matter of great concern to everyone most important to me. Kass and Aunt Alice were saying rosaries, making novenas, attending Masses every day. They were asking God to show me the light.

AJR was more direct. I should be going to Mass every day myself, he let me know. If he and Kass and Aunt Alice could do it, what was my problem? Unconvincingly, I tried to explain that in most parts of the country, and particularly in the South, where the football players I was tracking seemed to be concentrated, Catholic churches were few and far between. Of course, when Jerry Neri was traveling with me, excuses were not acceptable. Jerry Neri would drag me to Mass. In the Northwest that year, during Lent, we never missed a day. The church he took me to might be a one-room wooden building in the boondocks or a chapel in some college or university's Newman Club quarters. No matter where it was, this hard-bitten little Blesto scout would find it. "I know about you and your family," he would tell me. "So get your ass in gear."

Before my next and last trip to State College, the one with Haley, AJR cautioned me to avoid Route 22. "It's a death trap since they made it three lanes," he said. "That middle lane is supposed to be a passing lane. They should call it a suicide lane. All the nuts and drunks think they can pull in and out whenever they want to. Take the Turnpike. Or, better yet, fly."

I did neither. Winter comes early in the Allegheny Mountains, and I had driven Route 22 in November snowstorms – real white-outs; this time it was merely cool and damp. We had some rain, and in places the road was slick, but we arrived safe and sound on a game day.

Our seats in the press box were good ones. Harris, we knew, had been having a sub-par year. He was lackadaisical in practice, the coaches complained. As on my earlier visit, they dwelt on the abilities of Mitchell. A coach in the press box, cupping a hand over his mouth, confided to me that Harris "sulked." "He's moody, Won't work hard." I decided to trust my own instincts.

Afterward, when Haley and I were by ourselves in the car, we agreed that Harris was still an outstanding NFL prospect. Taking into consideration the things a scout looks for, there was just no comparison between Harris and Mitchell. Somehow Harris gave you the feeling that here was a great football player. Mitchell for some reason did not.

On New Year's Day, from a seat on the bench, Harris watched Penn State beat Texas in the Cotton Bowl. He'd been late for practice one morning, and Paterno removed him from the starting lineup. Stubbornly, I continued to think of Franco as the guy we should draft in the first round if we could.

The Steelers had won more games than in 1970, but it was still a losing season. Even so, we would pick rather late – thirteenth. Chuck Noll attended the Blesto winter meetings and listened to all the scouts give their lengthy presentations. He took a few notes but asked no questions. He did ask questions, under his breath, of Haley, Nunn, and me, making sure he was not overheard. It was all very hush-hush, an approach that, for reasons of my own, I disdained. I had a whole list of questions for the scouts, and I asked them openly. My manner was low-keyed but persistent.

After the first couple of days, Noll said he wanted a word with me – in private. "I like the way you've prepared for this meeting," he began. "You've put a lot of time into it. But you're tipping off the people who are here from the other teams. All they have to do is listen to the Blesto scouts answer your questions. You're doing their work for them."

Without showing disrespect, I nodded and turned away. Chuck's perception that other personnel directors were eavesdropping was correct. I could not have cared less. Whether or not we had an audience, I continued to interrogate the scouts. I was unabashedly out to prove something – that I did not owe my job to nepotism. Call me obstinate. Call me hard-headed. Say I was putting my own interests ahead of the team's. But more than anything else I wanted my competitors to realize that Art Rooney's son was not a lazy, over-indulged rich kid. If I was doing their work for them, let them all see that no one had to help me do mine.

Was I being immature? Perhaps. Was I being smart? Maybe not. Was I antagonizing Noll? I suppose so. But as the coming years were to demonstrate, we ended up with a better draft than any of the other Blesto teams could claim. In fact, our 1972 draft was one of the best in the NFL.

Back in Pittsburgh, Nunn, Haley, and I studied and re-studied our reports. We shuffled our ratings and carne up with a new list of top players for every position and another new list of our top two hundred regardless of position. It took us a full week. For two weeks after that, we met with Noll and his assistant coaches every day, which resulted in more new lists.

We moved to the draft room for "discussions," as Chuck called them. I called them "heated" discussions.

"You know, Art," he said to me, "this all has to be like your teeth."

"Teeth?" I didn't get it.

"Yes, teeth. I have read," he explained in his best professorial tone, "that all animals – humans included – must work their upper teeth against their lower teeth. It has the same effect as exercise. Keeps the gums healthy and the teeth themselves firmly in place. It's like our scouting meetings, where we have a clash of opinions – weigh the pros against the cons, so to speak. It keeps us sharp."

"Oh," I replied. "Yes. Like your teeth."

After chewing on it for a while, I guess I could see what he meant.

I have said that our discussions were "heated." When we got around to discussing the running backs and fullbacks, they were more than heated. Pure emotion took over, especially in my own case. Let's say I was carried away.

Even before the Blesto meetings, Noll had made it plain to the scouts that he was biased against big backs. "If they're more than 6 feet 2 and 220 pounds," he said, "they can't change direction.

They're not flexible enough at the hips and knees. And their forward lean is too pronounced, because they lean from the waist instead of the hips and legs. Give me the strong short guy – 5 feet 10 and 205. Short guys have balance, quickness, control. They hit it in tough. They can bounce to the outside and cut back. They can set up the arm tackle with a sudden move. Put 'em in a pass pattern and you have a guy who can run after making the catch. All those big guys can do is run straight ahead. They're one-dimensional."

It seemed to me that Noll preferred two good backs who could run and catch to a backfield with one great runner and a fullback who does all the blocking. "Two backs who produce fifteen hundred yards between them and catch sixty passes are just as valuable as one star," he maintained. It made sense. Years later, I would hear George Young of the New York Giants, the winners of two successive Super Bowls, echo Chuck's remarks.

Coming up in the same draft as Harris was a good little big man at the University of Houston. Short, strong, productive, and willing to give his all for the team, Bobby Newhouse had every virtue that Noll said he admired in a running back. I liked him a lot myself, but I happened to like Franco more. That was where we differed – vociferously.

Noll seemed just as concerned about Franco's height as with the reports about his moodiness and his aversion, in the eyes of some of the Penn State coaches, to hard work. While our draft talks were going on, I got support from an unexpected source – my good friend George Young. A big, corpulent, erudite man with two master's degrees, he said to me one day on the telephone, "Arthur, you sound gloomy. Are you having trouble with Chuck? Is he giving you a hard time again?" George and Chuck were friends, too, by the way. In need of a sympathetic ear, I explained that Chuck and I were at loggerheads about the relative merits of Newhouse and Harris. Young answered, "Well, that argument, tell him for me, was settled more than six thousand years ago when Socrates said, 'A good big man will beat a good little man every time.'"

The epigram sounded more like something from the mouth of a twentieth-century fight manager than that of an ancient Greek philosopher, but I repeated it to Noll. "Just like George," he said with a chuckle, and went on arguing with unabated fervor that Newhouse belonged at the top of our list.

Sometimes Noll would put us on notice that no matter how high we may have rated a certain player he wasn't going to draft him. Never once did he say this about Franco, which gave me hope. Though our discussion of running backs ended with Noll unshaken in his support of Newhouse, and though we would start to evaluate offensive linemen the next morning, the game wasn't over.

On the previous evening I had called Jack Butler and asked him to compare Newhouse and Harris. He must have thought I was losing my marbles. We had talked about them as prospects again and again. What Jack didn't know was that on this occasion he was being tape-recorded. After my conversation with Jack, I proceeded to call every Blesto scout who had seen Newhouse or Harris or both. My plan was to add their opinions to the tape and put together an audio for Noll and his staff.

I talked to Alex Bell, Ralph Kohl, Jess Thompson, and Will Walls. Bell, the former head coach at Villanova, had scouted Harris for two years. "Take him if you get a chance," he urged me. Kohl had scouted both Franco and Newhouse. "Don't worry about the squabble between Franco and Paterno," he said. "Franco will be a better pro than Newhouse because of his size." I had not told Bell or Kohl about the tape recorder; I did tell Jess Thompson (I'm not sure why). He didn't mind. Thompson scouted the Southwest Conference for Blesto and knew a lot about Newhouse, but had watched Franco play only once – in a post-season all-star game. He was therefore unwilling to compare them. "Well, would you take Newhouse with the thirteenth pick?" I asked him. He hesitated. "Need gets into it," he said. Then he added, "Bobby won't let you down." Walls, like Thompson, was more familiar with Newhouse than with Harris but had scouted them both. When I asked him the same question I'd put to Thompson – was Bobby Newhouse a legitimate thirteenth pick? – he answered, "Uh ... say hi to your dad, Artie." It was all I needed to hear, but I pushed for just a little bit more. "If your life depended on it, Will?" Cornered, he said, "I don't know." I told him, "OK, Will, thanks. You've been a big help."

Taping these guys, the ones who hadn't given their consent, was unlawful, I suppose, but nothing to bring up in the confessional. Still, I am glad I did not let the newspapers in on it for a good long time.

On the morning after my phone calls, Mrs. Duffy was in the scouts' office, passing out lists of offensive tackles. Besides Noll and his staff, Haley and Nunn were present. Haley, on paper, was our personnel director now, but he had taken no part in the debate between Noll and me. The fact that I presumed to argue with Noll surprised him, I think. I am not putting Haley down. He was new on the job and had a newcomer's reluctance to assert himself.

These morning meetings started with coffee and doughnuts. Before we had drained our cups, I took out my tape recorder and placed it on my desk. It was plugged in and ready to go. Addressing Noll, I said, "Chuck, I've come up with some more information on Franco and Newhouse. How about giving it a listen?"

He nodded, more expressionless than usual. For thirty minutes, the whole room listened quietly. The voices of the scouts were unnaturally loud and clear. When it was over, no one spoke for what seemed like a long time. Finally Noll, betraying no emotion, said, "You asked the Blesto scouts leading questions. They had to answer in the way that you wanted them to. Let's move on here." He was telling me his mind had not been changed. "OK, Coach," I said, but I still had a card to play.

Dan Radakovich was a Western Pennsylvania guy who had been on Noll's staff in 1971 but resigned to take a coaching job in college football. Because of a misunderstanding of some kind – I can't be more specific because I don't know the details – it turned out that the job would not be open, and he was helping me now with the 1972 draft, watching game films and writing reports.

What I wanted him to do for me was make the case for Franco with Noll. My interviews with the Blesto scouts may have eaten away at Noll's certainty just a little. But in spite of his denials, were the stories about the trouble between Franco and the coaches at Penn State in the back of his mind? The label they had fastened to Franco was that of a shirker. The "intangibles," so-called, had always been supremely important to Noll. He wanted players who were "teachable," who worked hard to improve themselves, who came to practice and meetings on time. If this was his problem with Franco, I thought that Radakovich, who had been on the Penn State coaching staff when Franco was a junior or sophomore, might be qualified to offer a second opinion.

We had talked about Franco previously, and I knew what Rad would say: "He's not a troublemaker. He's not a bad guy. He comes from a good family. There were some misunderstandings with the coaches – he has some sensitivities – but this is a good person. If you draft him you won't regret it."

Rad did speak to Noll, and it made a difference, I could sense. It wasn't anything Noll said, it was everything he did not say. On draft day, the first twelve teams to make their selections were agonizingly deliberate, but at last it was our turn. "The Steelers are on the board." To my relief, with some apprehension mixed in, Franco was still out there. I waited for Noll's decision. Would it be "Let's go somewhere else"? We had fifteen minutes to decide, but Noll didn't vacillate. From his seat at our T-shaped table, he was looking at me. "Let's take the big back from Penn State," he said.

I held myself in check. Jim Boston was on the phone, maintaining contact with NFL draft headquarters in New York. Calmly, I said to him, "Franco Harris." It was like touching a match to a short-fused Roman candle. "FRANCO HARRIS!" Boston thundered, splitting eardrums at both ends of the line. "RUNNING BACK FROM PENN STATE."

Joe Gordon raced out of the room to notify the media. Dan left with Boston to call Franco. As for me, I put on an act. Hiding my elation, I glanced at Haley and then at Nunn in lieu of a thumbs-up. I then called Jack Butler. "Good move," he said, and that was about the extent of it. At Gordon's request, I spoke with a newspaper reporter. I took pains not to gloat, and I excused myself quickly. We had eighteen more players to draft.

Before the 1970s were over, Franco Harris gave us reason to congratulate ourselves on our astuteness that day. By serving as Franco's advocate, it was Radakovich, I still believe, who converted Noll to the cause. Rad himself was not loath to suggest the same thing. He told a story to the effect that AJR had kept him around as an odd-jobs man for no other purpose than to lobby Noll. I don't remember it that way, but if I'm wrong – if AJR really did play the role of silent manipulator – then all I can say is "thank God."

Bad Rad

Tall, lean, and blond, a center in his playing days, Radakovich had coached our offensive line. "Bad Rad," we called him – a tribute to the hard work he demanded from his charges. He had a genius IQ and the absent-mindedness that extraordinary brain power sometimes engenders.

Bad Rad lived in a neighborhood where the streets and the houses looked pretty much the same, and one night returning home (as he thought) from practice he let himself in through the unlocked kitchen door and sat down at the table with his playbook, his mind on the following Sunday's game plan. The next thing he knew, a small boy he never had seen before was staring at him from a few feet away.

"Mommy," the kid called out, "there's a strange man in our kitchen."

Seconds later, Mommy appeared. "What are you doing in our house?" she demanded.

Slowly, Rad began to realize that he had made a mistake.

Even in his own house, Rad found himself out of bounds once, to use a football metaphor. This was in Cincinnati, one of his coaching stops. The Radakoviches had house guests, another married couple, the husband a former Penn State teammate of Rad's. They were using the master bedroom, where Rad and his wife normally slept. Doing their best to be hospitable, host and hostess moved into the guest room. Not long after dinner, the friend's wife, tired out from a day of traveling, excused herself and went to bed. An hour passed and then Rad said good night. "Gotta get some sleep for our game tomorrow," he explained.

He did get some sleep, but it was soon interrupted. Not half an hour later, his friend was standing over him and shaking him awake. "Hey, Rad," he was saying. "You're in bed with my wife."

Whenever Rad told the story, and he told it many times, he was careful to emphasize that he had gone to the master bedroom out of habit and forgetfulness, an understandable lapse.

"Nothing bad happened," he would say.

Turning Point

Historians of the Second World War point out that before the U. S. Navy destroyed the Japanese fleet at Midway, American forces never had won a battle, and that from then on they were never to lose one. Franco Harris was the counterpart of Midway for the Steelers.

Before he carne to Pittsburgh, we had not had a winning season since 1963. After he arrived, the Steelers went thirteen years without a losing season.

In the second round of the 1972 draft, the Dallas Cowboys took Robert Newhouse, the "fine little running back" from Houston. He had a praiseworthy career with a great team but was never a Hall-of-Fame-type player. Franco Harris did make the Hall of Fame. In his first season, he gained more than one thousand yards, was the NFL's Rookie of the Year, and was voted MVP of the Steelers by his teammates. In his third season he was the MVP of Super Bowl IX, a 16-6 win over the Vikings. He rushed for one thousand or more yards eight times and played in nine straight Pro Bowls. I found it interesting that Harris and Jack Ham, who were teammates at Penn State, had parallel careers with the Steelers.

The second player we took in the 1972 draft, Gordon Gravelle of Brigham Young, was a tall, smart offensive tackle. After five years with the Steelers, he lasted another three seasons with the Giants and Rams. Gravelle and our No.5 pick, defensive tackle Steve Furness of Rhode Island, became Super Bowl starters. Furness got his chance when we shipped Ernie Holmes to New England after the 1977 season. Eventually we traded Furness to the Detroit Lions, but not until 1981. Like Joe Gilliam, the exceptional but ill-starred quarterback we drafted the same year, Furness died young, of coronary problems. After his playing days were over, he had taken up coaching and served for a time under Bill Cowher.

While they were with the Steelers, no player we took in that 1972 draft would ever experience a losing season. Except for defensive back J. T. Thomas, who came on board in 1973, and Jack Lambert, who arrived in 1974, the starters on both offense and defense in our first Super Bowl game were now in the fold, and Franco Harris was the catalyst.

Footnote: Our third pick in 1972, a tight end from Clemson named John McMakin, showed up at Latrobe as a raw-boned, crew-cut Southern kid who yes-sirred and no-sirred everybody in camp. Returning in 1973, he was unrecognizable. He had hair that was longer than Robinson Crusoe's. He carried a purse, hanging from his shoulder by a strap. I was in Bill Nunn's office when McMakin checked in. Poker-faced, Bill sent him off to a room in the dorm. Then he said to me with a look of disgust:

"That guy won't even make the squad this year."

Nunn's vehemence took me by surprise. I said, "Gee, Bill, he did very well as a rookie."

Nunn said, "Well, look at him now. He's in the 'cute' bag. That long hair. That purse hanging over his shoulder. Last year John was a biter and scratcher. Not anymore. He thinks he's a finesse guy. He won't make it."

As usual, Nunn was right.

He went up another notch in my estimation.

The Kid from Idaho

On draft day, AJR was forever getting phone calls from cronies all over the United States, cronies bent on giving him tips. This kind of intrusiveness made me more paranoid than ever. I wanted no help from friends of my dad, and I wanted no help from the assistant coaches, who always seemed to be pushing some overlooked player of rare ability. "We know about that guy, we have detailed information on him," I would say, stamping out another brush fire. On draft day I had to have order, and now as the fourteenth round of the 1972 draft came to an end, here was AJR with a tip from an old pal – in his race-track lingo "a tip right out of the barn."

"A kid from Idaho – Idaho U.," Dad was telling me. "Plays linebacker. And the best part of it is, he's an Irish kid."

The name was Linehan – Ron Linehan. "My friend out there knows athletes, and he says this guy is a steal," continued AJR.

I thought of times in the past when the Chief had accused me of "just throwing darts at the names on the board." He would stand then and listen to my lecture about the work we put in on our draft list. The reaction I got was always the same. First he would shake his head. Then he'd puff at his cigar, chuckle sarcastically, lock his hands behind his back, and walk away.

In the fifteenth round, I did not draft the Irish kid from Idaho, making Bill Nunn and Dick Haley nervous. "Hey, Artie," said Nunn, "your dad owns the team." Haley said, "I think you'd better cut him a break."

I dug in my heels a little deeper. An important principle was at stake: my independence. In the sixteenth round I drafted a wide receiver – Nate Hawkins by name – from Nevada Las Vegas. One pick was left.

AJR returned to the room and stood with a cigar in his mouth and his hands behind his back, staring at the board. It was almost too much for Nunn and Haley. Even Chuck Noll felt the tension. He was glaring at me. One of them – either Nunn, Haley, or Noll – said to me under his breath, "Last round. Loosen up."

When our turn came to draft, I was tongue-tied. In a quiet voice, Noll said, "Linehan."

Just as softly, I repeated, "Linehan."

He was our seventeenth pick.

At training camp the next summer, Linehan did not make the cut. Neither did Nate Hawkins.

AJR kept his thoughts about this to himself, and so did I.

Chapter 54

Paper Promotion

By 1972, the Rooney family – primarily Kass - had decided that Art Rooney, Jr., personnel director and head scout of the Steelers, was spending too much time away from home.

"It's endangering his marriage," Kass said to AJR.

At her instigation – the word is not too strong - he came to my office in Three Rivers Stadium for a talk, father to son.

"You're on the road too much," he began.

I knew what he was getting at, but my job had become a passion, an addiction, a cause. "Same as you," I replied, "when you were following the horses."

"That was different," he said.

"How so?"

"I had to make a living for your mother and your brothers and you. The race track was where I worked. Anyway, I got home more often than you do. When I gave you this job, I didn't mean for you to be gone as much as you are."

I played my trump card. "Dad, this job is important. It's the most important job in the organization. You cannot win without good players. And I'm the one who's supposed to make sure we have them."

AJR wasn't buying it. "You're forgetting Blesto, aren't you?" he said. "Jack Butler does a fine job there."

"Yes, he does. But Blesto is rating players for half a dozen teams – not just the Steelers. Chuck Noll has specific things he's looking for, and the Blesto scouts aren't as familiar with them as I am."

I had hit on an argument that gave him pause. He puffed at his cigar, thinking of how to respond, and then he said, "OK. I understand. Maybe you need some extra help. Besides Blesto."

Extra help was the last thing I wanted. "We have Bill Nunn," I reminded him.

"Yes, and he's good. But Nunn only scouts the Negro teams."

I said, "He's ready to start looking at all the teams." It was no use. AJR put an end to the discussion.

"You still need more help. I'll talk to you later."

Even Noll had been urging me to cut back. After scouting a college game on a Saturday afternoon, or sometimes on a Saturday night, I would fly to wherever the Steelers were playing. If their game was on the road I'd return to Pittsburgh with the team. At least twice Noll suggested that I was covering too much ground. "You don't have to be flying all over the map. You can study film, read scouting reports, go to the post-season all-star games." I would listen patiently and say, "I do study film. I study enough film to go blind. I do read scouting reports. I do see the post-season all-star games. There's more to it than that. If you're a scout, you have to watch practice. You have to talk with the coaches and trainers." From the Dick Guy Book of Clichés, I resurrected a mixed metaphor. "You have to touch all the bases ... leave no stone unturned."

Down deep, no matter what I said, I knew that further resistance was foolish. My parents were correct. What sense would it make to put a football team ahead of my family life? Could there be a way, I wondered, to have both? There had to be a middle ground somewhere.

Extra help. That was the answer. On the Blesto staff was a young guy scouting the Southeast. He was from Western Pennsylvania, which, for AJR, always seemed to be a definite plus. At Pitt, during John Michelosen's tenure, Dick Haley had been a halfback, playing both ways. Buddy Parker drafted him in 1959 as a defensive back and traded him to the Redskins, who traded him to the Vikings, who traded him back to the Steelers in 1961. His pro career was over by 1965 and then he had gone into scouting.

I had traveled with Haley and considered him very organized. He was also, I thought, a terrific person. Given my choice, the assistant I would have picked was Jack Butler, whose lofty status as Blesto's executive director of course ruled him out. Even with Haley, we had a problem. So many NFL teams had been raiding Blesto for talent that a sort of gentleman's agreement among the owners became necessary: no Blesto scout could be hired away from Butler unless the move was a promotion.

Thus if we offered Haley a job, it could not be as an ordinary scout. To make it look right, we'd have to give him a title.

But what title? The only title in the scouting department – personnel director – belonged to me. It was Kass, I believe, who came up with a solution. Dick Haley would join the Steelers as personnel director, and my new title would be vice president. There were two other vice presidents – Jack McGinley and Dan. On paper, at least, I was now their equal.

Exactly how much my brother and my father had to do with all this I'm not sure. Forever after, I would say that I owed my new title to my mom, infuriating Kay.

"Don't say that! You *earned* the position," she would tell me.

"I'm kidding," I'd answer. To myself, I would add, "On the square."

Until Haley got his bearings, I continued to do my job the same as before. In other words, I spent too much time away from home. After that first season, though, I changed my modus operandi. (If AJR could read that sentence, he'd say I was putting on the dog.) I traveled less and coordinated more, letting Haley do the bulk of the field work.

He remained with the Steelers for nineteen years. As a matter of fact, he outlasted me.

Cousin Tim

After the 1972 draft, I pestered AJR, Dan, and Chuck Noll to let me branch out. I wanted a subdivision within the scouting department to evaluate and keep track of the players on other teams in the NFL.

It would help us make trades and, even more important, avoid trades. For reasons like injuries, poor performance, and undisciplined behavior, teams were always looking to unload somebody.

As I expected him to, AJR raised objections. "We hardly ever make trades," he pointed out. Our philosophy, after all, was to build through the draft. Although he never actually bought into the idea, he allowed me to hire another scout.

My first pick was Chuck Klausing, the dean of high school and small-college coaches in Western Pennsylvania. He agreed to take the job and then, on the grounds that he could not give up coaching, reversed himself, and I understood. If a football man preferred coaching to scouting, it was all right with me – just as long as he did not give the impression that to be a mere scout was somehow degrading.

The scout I ended up with was my cousin Tim Rooney. AJR seemed to hesitate when I mentioned Tim. There were limits, he believed, to the number of family members the Steeler organization could accommodate.

"I know that," I replied. "But Tim would be working somewhere else in the NFL except for the fact that he's a Rooney. The other teams ask me why the Steelers don't hire him. It makes them question his ability."

For once, I had struck the right note. "If he's the guy you want," said AJR, "then it's all right with me. Our name shouldn't keep him from getting a decent job."

Tim was an assistant coach at Villanova. I called him immediately and said that if he'd like to be a full-time scout for the Steelers he should get to Pittsburgh as soon as possible. The time was about 10 a.m. At 4 in the afternoon, Tim walked into my office.

I expressed surprise that he was able, on such short notice, to catch a plane.

"Catch a plane? No way," Tim said. "I jumped right into my car and hit the Turnpike. I thought if I waited too long you might change your mind."

Tim's work for the Steelers was first-rate. After seven years, he left to become head of the Detroit Lions' scouting department. From Detroit, he went to the New York Giants.

The way I look at it, the lift that Tim needed to start his very successful career as a scout came from AJR. Tim was Duke's son, remember. And AJR's relations with Duke had been anything but brotherly. They disliked each other, in fact. Tim, of course, wasn't Duke, but AJR's ability to disassociate father and son said something I had always believed about his essential good will. It was not just a job he was offering Tim; he was giving him a chance to start a new and more satisfying life.

'He's Got an Agent!'

Franco Harris got off on the wrong foot with AJR by immediately hiring an agent. AJR liked to negotiate contracts directly with the player, one on one. But now we were hearing that Tony Rossano, a Western Pennsylvanian from New Castle, would do all the bargaining for Franco.

Rossano was a friend of Bill McPeak – had played football with him at New Castle High School, I believe. He followed McPeak to Pitt, but was never more than a bench-warmer. After college, they kept in touch. McPeak spent nine years with the Steelers and Rossano went into coaching. When McPeak became coach of the Washington Redskins, he found a place for Rossano on his staff.

Jack Butler's opinion of Rossano, in contrast with McPeak's, was unfavorable. I'd be leery of anyone who failed to meet with Butler's approval, and yet in some respects Rossano impressed me. I liked his "go-get-'em" attitude and I respected his knowledge of football. These same qualities may have been apparent to the San Francisco Forty-Niners, who made him their head scout in the 1980s.

In 1972, AJR had not yet accepted agents as a fact of life. When he saw that there was no getting rid of them, he tried to adapt. Sitting across the table from an agent, while Dan did the negotiating, he could turn on his Irish charm, although not without difficulty. Whether Irish charm prevented any agent from getting the best deal possible for his client I couldn't say.

As time went on and there was still no agreement between the Steelers and Rossano, AJR's testiness increased. I was with him one day at 940 North Lincoln Avenue when the telephone rang. The call was from Dan, about Franco. Greatly agitated, AJR began shouting. As soon as he hung up, I got the full benefit of his anger. He swiveled around in his chair, gave me the kind of look I had come to dread, and spoke just two words. "Franco!" he said. "Rossano!" Nothing else. Making Franco our No. 1 draft pick had been entirely my doing, and now I had to answer for Rossano's intransigence.

Faster than Joe Greene could slash between two offensive linemen, I was out the front door and headed for home.

One of Chuck Noll's innovations was a get-acquainted session with our rookies every spring. They would come to the city, visit Three Rivers Stadium, take a physical examination, meet Noll and the other coaches, get a brief tutorial on the system he'd be using, and listen to him talk about the training program he expected them to follow. They'd meet the Chief, they'd meet Dan and Ralph Berlin and Tony Parisi. They'd go to dinner that night at LeMont, a restaurant on Mount Washington with a panoramic view of the Golden Triangle. They'd watch our highlight film - action shots from the previous season. (The fact that cynics had stopped calling our highlight films "lowlight" films attested to the progress we were making under Noll.) The next morning, on the Tartan Turf at Three Rivers, there'd be a light non-contact workout.

When the rookies from the class of '72 checked in, only Franco Harris was missing. "He's late," someone said, but then a scout, my cousin Tim Rooney, summoned Noll to the telephone. The call was from Dan, who had heard from Rossano. It seemed that, instead of being late, Franco wasn't coming at all.

According to Tim Rooney, Noll gave vent to his outrage in a voice that may have reached Happy Valley, where Franco was holed up. He then slammed down the receiver. The tour of Three Rivers, the physical exams, the introductions, the lectures, and the dinner on Mount Washington proceeded with Franco still absent. But in the morning, lo and behold, there he was at the team's workout.

Like every other player, he was wearing a light gray sweatsuit. I saw him standing alone for a minute or two, which gave me an opening to say something. It wasn't much – just that he'd be doing the things we knew he could do best. With that, our conversation was over, interrupted by a call from Dick Hoak, the backfield coach, for Franco to walk through a play.

I don't know how it happened that Franco came in for the workout that morning. Dan, I assume, got to Tony Rossano. The give and take between them continued in the days that followed until they finally settled on a contract. I could not have been more relieved. If we were going to win – if we were going to be successful – we had to sign our top picks. Dan understood that. His antipathy toward agents equaled AJR's, but he knew when to compromise and when to stand firm.

With help from Jim Boston, Dan had been our chief negotiator even before Franco's signing, but in more ways than one it turned out to be a watershed moment.

Vindication

I had stuck my neck out for Franco, and no one allowed me to forget it. Later that spring on a tour of the Southwest, I traveled with another scout, an outspoken, abrasive type. We were watching practice one day at Arizona State when he told me, for no apparent reason, that drafting Franco had been a terrible mistake. "He won't be there when things get tough – he's a front-runner," the scout said.

After nine years on the road, I could listen to such blowhards without wanting to fight.

At St. Vincent, in July, Franco dispelled the myth that he saved all his effort for game day. He practiced as willingly and intensively as Chuck Noll and the other coaches could have wished. When the team finished running a play, he would keep going downfield for twenty more yards. In the post-practice conditioning drills, he skipped rope for what seemed like hours. He was good at it, too, as graceful as any heavyweight boxer with the exception, perhaps, of Muhammad Ali. And though Franco was not an effusive person, his teammates accepted him as one of the gang.

It helped that Dick Hoak, another Penn State man, was the backfield coach. Franco and Hoak had confidence in each other and were temperamentally alike – quiet and retiring. Typically, Chuck Noll treated Franco with even-handed reserve. Noll was first and foremost a teacher; his players were members of the student body. In a Chuck Noll classroom, there were no teacher's pets.

I watched the early exhibition games nervously until Franco's first breakaway run. Then I said to myself, "He can do it." But how consistently? Consistently enough, it turned out, to satisfy Noll. When the regular season opened, Franco was the team's starting fullback.

All great athletes have uncanny vision. It was why Franco could see a hole when it opened up and could sense the location of every other player on the field. Cutting back to a hole was easy for him because of his quick feet. He could pick his way through the debris of a broken field and turn on a burst of speed that would take him all the way to the goal line. Instead of blocking, he positioned himself in front of the runner (or the quarterback), and most of the time, anyway, his size kept the tackler at bay. Used primarily as a runner himself, he seldom was called on to block. At catching the ball, we were to learn that we had a miracle worker in Franco.

Size and quick feet are an unlikely combination. Here's a training camp story: Franco had a brother, a defensive back named Dino, and we gave him a tryout one year. On his first day at St. Vincent he was working with the other rookies in a basic drill for defensive backs – backing up and turning – when Franco sauntered over to take a look. Maybe somebody dared him to join in the fun. At any rate, that was what he did, moving his feet so adroitly and swiftly that the rookies, Dino included, were made to appear hopelessly inadequate. Sabotaged by his well-meaning older brother, Dino's NFL career never got off the ground. The brothers' DNA, although it came from the same source, differed in crucial respects.

Quick feet, vision, strength – these were the qualities that would take Franco Harris to a coveted destination, pro football's Hall of Fame in Canton, Ohio.

The French Connection

As successful as he was at squeezing through holes, Franco needed a teammate who could block, and in Frenchy Fuqua he had one. Of Frenchy's myriad skills, the ability to impede big defensive linemen or to mow down linebackers, safeties, and cornerbacks was most eye-catching.

He came to the Steelers in a trade with the New York Giants, a trade engineered by Chuck Noll. Frenchy was short but well put together. He was quick and hard to knock off his feet. He was strong – much stronger than he looked.

His Frenchness, as he explained it, derived from an earlier incarnation. He'd been of royal birth – a count, no less – but while sun-bathing in the nude on the French Riviera one day, he fell asleep and woke up as a black man.

Disowned by his aristocratic relatives, he carne to the United States.

That was Frenchy's story, related in a broadly humorous vein to anyone who asked about the origin of that nickname.

He spoke with a faint lisp. "My French accent," he called it. He wore a cape and a wide-brimmed hat. His accessories included a cane with a silver handle. But to appreciate Frenchy's sartorial uniqueness, you had to look at his feet, as everyone did. Frenchy's shoes – black pumps with four-inch high heels of transparent unbreakable glass – were twin aquariums. Each of those heels was full of water, and in each of them swam a pair of goldfish.

The fish had short lives. Inexpert marine biologists, Frenchy and his shoemaker did not understand that fish need fresh water and oxygen. In two or three days, the little fellows would be belly up – dead. Others replaced them and met the same fate. Over the course of a single football season, the casualty rate was enormous.

As far as I know, Frenchy never did get the problem resolved.

Play of the Century

With few exceptions, the twenty-two starters on the 1972 team were players we had either drafted or signed as free agents. The Steelers were now ready to roll, and it was Franco Harris who got them under way. No Pittsburgh team since 1963 had won more games than it lost. From 1972 until 1985, no Pittsburgh team would lose more games than it won. Let me put that another way: in the nine years before we drafted Franco, there were no winning seasons; from the beginning to the end of his career as a Steeler – twelve years in all – there were no losing seasons.

Right from the start he was clipping off one hundred yards a game. By NFL standards, his blockers were undersized but quick, smart, and durable. Through a process of addition and subtraction, Chuck Noll had rectified the Steelers' most obvious deficiencies: team speed and team intelligence.

The 1972 team won eleven of its fourteen regular-season games, putting us into the playoffs for the first time since the Jock Sutherland era. In a matchup at Three Rivers Stadium, our opponent was Oakland, which worried me sick. The Raiders had a lineup of skilled, veteran bruisers, capable, I thought, of making us look bad.

To my considerable relief, we held our own. With time running out, Oakland led, but by the narrowest possible margin, one point. I was ready to accept an honorable defeat. So was AJR. Leaving his box, he headed for the elevator. He would get to the Steelers' dressing room before the usual tidal wave of newspaper reporters and radio/television crews and be there to offer condolences and congratulations. This team, he intended to say, had played better and won more games than any other in the history of the franchise.

I was still in my own seat, watching the game clock: only twenty-two seconds left and no way to keep it from moving. The Steelers had the ball at their own 40-yard line and were lining up for one last play. I whispered a Hail Mary.

Certainly we needed help from on high, for whatever call Terry Bradshaw had made wasn't working. He dropped back, looking frantic. Not a single receiver was open. Dodging pass rushers, he scrambled to his right. An Oakland defensive end got a hand on his jersey. Pulling free, Bradshaw stopped and anchored himself and zipped a bullet pass in the direction of the one teammate he could spot, diminutive Frenchy Fuqua.

The Frenchman leaped skyward, his back to the Raiders' goal line. Simultaneously, and just as the ball arrived, Jack Tatum, the NFL's most fearsome defensive back, slammed into him. *Oof!* The ball now reversed its direction. It traveled in an arc toward an oncoming Steeler – Franco Harris.

Instinctively, Franco had started downfield to block for the pass catcher, if any. As his backfield coach, Dick Hoak, pointed out later on, in the heat of action he was always around the ball. Stretching forward now, and bending from the waist, he scooped this one up no more than eight or ten inches above the turf.

Between Franco and a touchdown there were forty-two yards. Knees pumping in a race with the Oakland defense, he angled toward the extreme left corner of the field. At the ten-yard line or thereabouts, he stiff-armed his last pursuer. With exactly five seconds on the clock, he was loping into the end zone.

On the most written-about, talked-about, argued-about play in the overcrowded annals of football, a play that Franco's employer, imprisoned for the moment in the press-box elevator, did not see, the Steelers had won a landmark victory, 13-7.

To the present day, the ending remains controversial. Had the pass from Terry Bradshaw bounced off the person of Tatum or Frenchy Fuqua? Under the rules then in effect, if Fuqua last touched the ball, Franco's touchdown was illegal. Referee, umpire, and back judge conferred on the field, after which the referee called the press box to speak with the NFL's supervisor of officials. And then, dramatically, he lifted both arms.

The roar of the crowd must have shattered many eardrums. In a downtown bar, The Interlude, a man named Michael Ord climbed onto a chair and silenced the other patrons, who were whooping it up. "This day," he announced, "will forever be known as the Feast of the Immaculate Reception."

A few hours later, preparing to do a commentary on the eleven o'clock news at radio station WTAE, Steeler broadcaster Myron Cope received a telephone call from a friend of Ord's. Did the name Ord had given to Franco's catch strike his fancy? Cope hesitated – "for fifteen seconds," as he subsequently acknowledged. Shared with his listeners, would the phrase be perceived as offensive – "sacrilegious, even?" He decided it would not, and over the next days and weeks, not only Cope's large audience but football fans everywhere were repeating the words gleefully.

AJR was one of the holdouts. To him, a pun on the doctrine that the Mother of God had been born without original sin violated good taste and by extension the Fourth Commandment. But gradually his attitude softened. He learned to accept the fact that the Immaculate Reception had changed the Steelers' image. It had made them "winners." More to the point, it had changed their owner's image. He, too, now was a winner. Besides, if everybody insisted on using a blasphemous term to describe a football play, there was nothing, after all, that he could do about it.

In the American Conference championship game the following week, the Steelers again played well, but lost to the undefeated Miami Dolphins, 21-17. Significantly, Miami went on to win the Super Bowl, beating the Redskins, 14-7, for a clean sweep of their seventeen games.

Franco Harris ended the season with more than one thousand yards rushing and was Rookie of the Year. I wasn't shameless enough to go around reminding people of the trouble I'd had in convincing Chuck Noll of Franco's merits, but on one occasion, anyway, Noll himself raised the subject, at least indirectly. Not long before the 1973 draft, Noll, some assistant coaches, and I were checking out the fullbacks available. One of them, Chuck Foreman, had impressive credentials, most of us thought; watching him on film, we were all the more surprised when Noll abruptly stopped the projector.

"I'm not crazy about this kid," he said, "but I suppose I'm wrong." He got to his feet and then continued. "Just like I was wrong about that big fullback from Penn State last year."

As we looked at each other, withholding comment, Noll left the room. An assistant coach broke the silence. "Art," he said to me, "that's as close as you'll ever get to hearing Chuck say, 'You were right and I was wrong. '"

I allowed myself just a flicker of gratification. Another new draft was in the offing, and all of us had work to do.

Fighting Back

By the time Rocky Bleier was a senior at Notre Dame in 1967 all the NFL scouts had sized him up. He was captain of the team, a guy who consistently made good plays, not a great athlete but not a bad one. His quickness and speed were OK rather than eye-opening. He ran the forty-yard dash in 4.8 seconds. We saw him as "an overachiever who had reached his physical potential." If he gained the twelve pounds he needed as a pro, we thought, his time in the forty would be 4.9 instead of 4.8. Not up to par for an NFL running back.

We were lucky to have Don Heinrich, our backfield coach, scouting Bleier. A quarterback for the University of Washington and later the New York Giants in his playing days, Heinrich had been a scout when Bill Austin hired him, and he knew what to look for. In the hours we spent over scouting reports, I gained an appreciation of Heinrich's acuteness. He stressed what we called in the jargon of our profession the intangibles – toughness, intensity, character, football smarts. Discussing a prospect, he would ask, "How much does he love the game?" He believed that regardless of how talented a player might be, "if football is not the most important thing to him, he will let you down somewhere along the line." This sort of thing may sound like hogwash, but it helped us to evaluate Bleier.

Rocky's glass, you could say, was only half full talent-wise, and, for most scouts, half-full was not enough. Heinrich chose to analyze the contents of the glass, not to dwell on how much was in it, or how little. "Yes, the kid's limited," he told me. "But let's look at it this way: He was playing big-time college football and was in on all the action; he produced; he is willing to sacrifice his body. If this kid gains the twelve pounds he needs for the NFL and stays at a four-eight forty, he will be a valuable special-teams guy and can play some as a running back, though he will always be pretty much of a straight-ahead runner. He catches the ball in a crowd and I think he can learn to block. He won't embarrass us for lack of effort. We've done worse. Let's try to get him as a late draft choice."

We drafted Rocky Bleier in the sixteenth round. Exceeding expectations (a habit of his, we were to learn), he lifted weights that summer at Notre Dame and reported to training camp not twelve pounds heavier, but twenty pounds heavier. And, at 205, he still ran a 4.8 forty. His toughness impressed Bill Austin, and his attitude – infectiously positive – impressed all of us.

For the first eleven games of the 1968 season, he made a significant contribution on special teams. But America was at war in Vietnam, and the lives of young men were being put on hold – or in some cases violently extinguished. The Steelers, like every other team in professional sports, tried to keep their personnel on the home front. This was Fran Fogarty's job, and he did what he could for Bleier, working through friends in the military. Late in November, the National Guard unit in nearby Washington, Pennsylvania, found an opening. Bleier was in.

But then his home-town draft board in Appleton, Wisconsin, was heard from. What Bleier had done at Notre Dame, and what he might possibly do for the Pittsburgh Steelers, made no difference whatever to the woman who served as its chairman – or chairperson, if you prefer. Special treatment for athletes, she believed, was grossly unfair. Men without athletic ability and men without connections were doing their part to the fullest extent, and so should Bleier. Period. Ordered to report for induction into the Army irrespective of any arrangement with the National Guard, he missed the last three games of the NFL season.

He went into the Army uncomplainingly, let it be said. On a moral and ethical level, he agreed with the draft board's point of view.

He did have a grievance, a minor one. In accordance with league rules, he was entitled to be paid for only eleven games. Believing that the Steelers shouldn't dock him for his time in the Army, he took up the matter with Fran Fogarty while on furlough in April. When he arrived at our offices in the Roosevelt Hotel, AJR had greeted him with a handshake and then wandered off. Instead of chaining himself to a desk, he liked to circulate. Fogarty, ever mindful of the balance sheet, told Bleier there was no way he could be compensated for the entire season. They argued about it a little, back and forth, and Fogarty, as usual, was adamant. Suddenly, from the next room, a voice rang out.

"Give him anything he wants!"

Stubbornly, Fran held his ground. "We can't do that, Art," he protested. "The league won't allow it."

"Then give him his bonus."

Bleier's contract called for a bonus of $1,500 if fifty percent of his playing time was at running back. He hadn't come close to earning it, but the Chief ordered Fogarty to write out a check.

From Fort Gordon in Georgia, where he had taken his basic training, the Army shipped Bleier to Vietnam, a private first class in an infantry battalion. Four months later, in a firefight with North Vietnamese Communist troops, he was hit twice, taking a rifle bullet through his left thigh and hand-grenade shrapnel that did severe damage to the ligaments, tendons, muscles, and bones in his right foot.

A fellow GI, a black man whose name he never learned, half-carried him to the helicopter evacuating the wounded. He was flown to an aid station and then to a military hospital in Tokyo. There he asked a doctor the question that had been on his mind all along:

"Will I be able to play football again?"

"No," the doctor said. "It's impossible."

To accept that verdict was the impossibility for Bleier. He wrote a letter from Tokyo which AJR read to me aloud, something I never before had known him to do. In the letter, Rocky said he'd been badly hit. "But don't worry, Mr. Rooney, I'll be back. I'll be back as good as ever," he promised.

His optimism, I thought, sounded genuine. AJR, who had been around a lot longer than I had, was more experienced at reading between the lines. "Yeah, Rocky, you'll be back," he said in a disconsolate voice, and tossed the letter onto his desk.

A few years after the war ended we heard from the helicopter pilot who evacuated Bleier to the aid station. Rocky's foot, the pilot said, had appeared to be hanging onto his leg by the tendons alone. The medics had given him morphine and he started babbling, telling everybody he would soon be playing football again. "I admired Rocky's spunk, but couldn't see how he'd ever walk again – walk normally," the pilot told me. "As for playing football ... I thought the chances against that were a million to one."

October 26, 1969, was Steeler Alumni Day. Before the game with the Redskins at Pitt Stadium, Rocky limped onto the field, and the crowd of 46,500 gave him a standing ovation. He was many pounds underweight and using a cane. Not for a minute believing it, AJR told him, "I'm sure you're coming back to the team," adding, "I'll take care of the rest."

It would be another thirteen months before Bleier was eligible for discharge. At Fort Riley, in Kansas, he underwent an operation on his foot. He ran laps on the track (it was agonizing, he said). He lifted weights. He ran the steps of the Kansas State football stadium with weights attached to his ankles. A friendly personnel officer hastened his release from the Army and by the summer of 1970 he was in Pittsburgh, determined to resume his football career.

Training camp opened with the NFL players' union on strike, creating a dilemma for Rocky. His decision was not to cross the picket line, and it seemed to inflame every Steeler fan. Pittsburgh always had been a union town, but though a small percentage of talk-show callers praised Rocky's stand, the majority excoriated him. He was showing ungratefulness to his team and to AJR. Letters to the newspapers were similar in tone. Almost nobody thought that Rocky would ever play again, but the Steelers were giving him a chance. It was known that AJR had assumed the full cost of his rehabilitation. On Myron Cope's popular radio show, he appeared one night as the union's spokesman. Driving Dad home from the office, I listened to the calls and was shocked. The comments phoned in were blistering. I glanced at AJR and saw that he was greatly disturbed. At last he began to talk. He said he could not understand why Rocky's teammates had put him in such an awkward position. "All the work and pain he has to go through ... " To a degree, the Chief blamed Cope, one of our broadcasters. He "shouldn't have let Rocky do this."

I went into the house with the Chief instead of dropping him off. The first thing he did was call Joe Gordon, our publicity guy, and ask him to get in touch with Rocky. "Tell him I'd like to speak with him," AJR said. Minutes later (Gordon worked fast), Rocky was on the phone. In my life with my father there were times when I took him for granted, times when I was furious with him, and times when I held him completely in awe. Hearing what he said to Bleier, I was in awe. He let Rocky know he had listened to Cope's show. "I thought you handled yourself very well," he said. He went on to tell Rocky he owed the Steelers nothing and should do what he felt was right. One thing he should not do was worry about the opinions of the herd.

I remember wondering at the time how I could ever live up to the standards my father had set for me. To this day, years after his death, I wonder how he would feel about the things I have done and have not done. In the end, Bleier reported for practice. At a meeting of the Steeler veterans, he had asked for, and received, permission to join the rookies in camp because of his "special circumstances."

As it turned out, that was the easy part. Though he had gained back all his lost weight, he was slower, even, than the linemen, limping and running flat-footed. He could not get up on his toes, he said, because it hurt too much to bend them back. After watching him for a while, I said to my brother Dan, "He's going to get hurt. He can't protect himself. One of these afternoons when he's really tired, he's going to get killed on a sweep."

Doc Best, our team physician, felt the same way. So did Ralph Berlin, the trainer. "Why is he doing this to himself?" some of the other players were asking. Rejecting advice to quit, advice to have another operation, Bleier told his well-wishers, "There's only one man whose opinion counts." That man was our coach, Chuck Noll.

In short order, Noll made up his mind. He called Bleier into his office and said he was putting him on waivers.

"Driving home that night, the tears blinded me. I could barely see the road," Bleier wrote in his autobiography, "Fighting Back."

Early the next morning Rocky's telephone rang. It was Dan. He had talked things over with his father, he said. The Steelers were putting Rocky on the injured reserve list instead of on waivers. And now it was AJR who suggested a second operation.

"How soon do you want me in the hospital?" Bleier asked.

Doc Best performed the surgery. There were two Doc Bests – the martinet who cracked down on inattention or levity in the operating room and the big, loud, jovial, chain-smoking, two-fisted drinking man. Diagnosed with cancer and told that only the removal of his prostate could save him, he declined, explaining, "I intend to leave this world with all the parts I came in with." Ultimately, he did leave this world with all his parts, but he was spared sufficient time to work on Rocky, and the Doc Best who went about it was the skilled orthopedist. The military surgeons had left some shrapnel in Rocky's foot. Best dug it out. In therapy sessions, he pulled and stretched Rocky's tendons and ligaments. Ralph Berlin pulled and stretched. This second, more painful round of treatment and exercise, Rocky said, was sometimes pure hell. But his foot had begun to improve.

AJR gave instructions that Bleier should receive a full year's salary – $19,000. That taken care of, he said to me, "Rocky's got a long way to go. I want you to keep him busy. Make him one of your scouts. In case his foot doesn't get better, let's see if we can find a place for him in the organization."

Rocky's conditioning program and the frequent team meetings he had to attend cut drastically into his time, but on weekends I could send him to college games. His scouting reports, a bit ragged at first, quickly improved. Rocky didn't mind being kidded. "I can tell who your friends are," I would say when he reported on Notre Dame players. "You're making them all sound like Heisman Trophy winners." Half-serious, I would advise him, "If your comeback doesn't work out for you, Rocky, you can always be a scout. Don't look down your nose at scouting. It's the scouts who make this game go. Hell, anybody can play."

In "Fighting Back," Bleier wrote, "I laughed with Art because he knew what I was thinking – that I'd rather be a third-string special-teams player than the greatest scout in the world."

After the season was over, Rocky sold insurance in Chicago and worked out hard at the YMCA. My brother Dan tried to discourage him from returning to the team, but he insisted on giving it a try. He asked to report with the rookies that July, and Dan consented. On the first day, loosening up, Rocky pulled a hamstring. At the urging of Noll, Doc Best advised him to retire. Rocky paid no attention. He wrapped up the hamstring and played in a few of the exhibition games. Noll then put him on the taxi squad. Reactivated to fill a vacancy created by an injury, he was hurt in his first game. He appeared in only three games all season and failed to distinguish himself on special teams. AJR, people said, was keeping him around for three reasons: he was Irish, he went to Notre Dame, and he was a war hero.

Dick Haley asked, "Does anyone actually think he can play? He can't run. He can't do anything." And I am quoted in Rocky's book as saying, "Last year he was a cripple. This year he's just bad."

Over the winter, Rocky practiced yoga. He ran up the fire escape on the side of the apartment building he lived in – eight stories, bottom to top – eight times in a row every day. He worked at the conditioning program Ralph Berlin had given him: five consecutive 350-yard runs in sixty seconds apiece with twenty-five seconds of rest in between.

In July, when training camp opened, I couldn't believe what I was seeing. Rocky looked big. He looked strong. We lined him up to run the forty-yard dash and I was even more surprised when I checked my watch: 4.6 seconds. He was two steps faster than he'd been at Notre Dame. I checked with the other scouts and the coaches. Everyone had either 4.6 or 4.65.

I said, "I've never seen anything like this." How could a guy who'd had most of his foot destroyed pick up so much speed? "Guts ... perseverance ... good physical therapy ... Doc Best," I told myself. "And the prayers of all those nuns and moms and grandmoms throughout the United States."

Rocky again was a special-teams player in that 1972 season, but with a difference. He tackled and ran back kicks like a whirlwind. We drafted Franco Harris that year, improved from 6-8 in 1971 to 11-3, and won our division title before losing in the playoffs to Miami. Harris was the rookie of the year. Terry Bradshaw was learning to be the kind of quarterback Noll wanted. Through the draft, we were building a defense to match the offense.

And, with Rocky Bleier an unexpected addition, our Super Bowl lineup was gradually taking shape.

Chapter 55

Airlift

First Dan and then Noll flew their own airplanes, small twin-engine four-seaters. On short trips to NFL meetings, they would ask other members of the Steeler organization to be their passengers. I never flew with Dan unless he had a co-pilot, but I would and did fly with Noll even when his co-pilot was his wife, Marianne.

Noll liked to fly to the Blesto physicals in Philadelphia because the football team's offices in Veterans Stadium happened to be near the airport. Each time, he offered to take the scouts along. Bill Nunn and Dick Haley begged off. Not me. I thought that flying with Noll was an excellent way to save time. Since Noll kept his plane at the Allegheny County Airport, there would be no standing in line at the much larger Greater Pittsburgh Airport.

The Blesto physicals were held in mid-winter, but if the weather was clear it never worried me. Returning to Pittsburgh, a trip of about an hour and a half, I would take a back seat and work on my reports. Meanwhile Noll would be busy on the radio or occupied in making instrument adjustments. There was no small talk. None was needed.

The first of these trips was uneventful. On the second, I noticed that Noll kept in contact with the radio tower as we approached the airport. By now I had made many landings with Noll, but this one seemed different. Although weather conditions were perfect, he started to curse. We descended almost to the runway, and then he pulled up and gained altitude. The twin engines were making a racket.

"I missed the [expletive deleted] approach," he said to me over his shoulder. "I'll have to go around again." This had happened previously to me with other pilots, and it was never a big deal. However, Noll was berating himself the way I had heard him admonish Terry Bradshaw for bonehead decisions on the football field.

I wasn't especially frightened, but I did what the Sisters of Mercy at St. Peter's School had trained me to do. I said a hasty Act of Contrition. I said it silently: I had no wish to distract Noll as he circled around for a second landing attempt. After my Act of Contrition, I started in on the rosary. I was halfway through the Sorrowful Mysteries when he brought the plane down very softly.

Noll sometimes said that any flight you could walk away from was a good one. He may have said it this time. I don't remember. What I do know is that this was a flight we never talked about afterward.

Uncle Miltie

On AJR's trips to Las Vegas, there were times when Kass went along. "In small doses," as she put it, Kass enjoyed the company of Ruth Jaffe, Milton's wife. Milton owned a piece of the Stardust Resort and Casino, and Ruth could dish the dirt about the big-time performers who came to Las Vegas. Her gossip entertained Kass, but only up to a point. "Too much of a good thing," she would say after one of Ruth's talkathons.

When Ruth and Milton first moved to Las Vegas they lived in a suite of rooms at the Stardust. However exciting that was, Ruth told Kass, she wanted them to have "a place of their own," and they found one away from the Strip. Even after Ruth's death, Milton remained there. AJR would see him often, stopping off on his way to or from the West Coast, where football and race track meetings were most frequently held. The NFL, for obvious reasons, never met in Las Vegas itself, the nation's gambling capital, but the players' union would meet there in spite of the league's disapproval. Under the terms of the bargaining agreement there was nothing the league could do about that.

With Ruth gone, we thought that Kass might curtail her visits, but she liked to see the shows, for which Milton obtained tickets, refusing to be compensated for them, and she liked to play the slot machines. Milton was always happy to have her around. Reminders of Ruth seemed to comfort him somehow.

AJR, Milton's old partner, took an academic interest in the show-business side of Las Vegas, but what drew him to the place was the gambling. When any of his sons were in town, he and Milton would go their own way, hanging out with friends from the Pittsburgh-Youngstown-Steubenville area – friends like Nick the Greek – while one or more of the boys and their wives looked after Kass.

I remember an evening at a Ziegfeld Follies-type show in Las Vegas with Kass, Kay, and the Butlers, Jack and Bernie. Up on the stage was a chorus line of beautiful girls - every one of them bare-breasted. We of course had expected something like this, but seeing it in the flesh, so to speak, was a little overwhelming. Though we tried to act blasé, our jaws fell open. Kass, with a chuckle, guessed that not even George Jaffe, Milton's brother, would let the strippers at their burlesque house in downtown Pittsburgh display quite so much of themselves.

It got so that Kass preferred the games in Las Vegas to the shows. On one of the last times she went out there, AJR gave her a hundred dollars for the slot machines, already a major attraction on the Strip. To women especially, the blinking lights and the sound effects seemed irresistible. As Kass told the story herself, she was merrily feeding coins into her favorite machine when she dropped one. Bending down to retrieve it from the carpeted floor, she noticed an alligator shoe on the foot of the person playing next to her. A tuxedo trouser leg grazed the top of that shoe. It was just barely visible beneath a long fur coat – mink, Kass thought, or maybe sable.

She looked up to see who was wearing this outfit. A smiling, wavy-haired, middle-aged man with powder and rouge on his face. In a singsong effeminate voice, he said to Kass, "Don't you just love these toys! My mother always loved to play them."

Kass was too startled to reply. The man pumped the handle of his slot machine a few more times and then walked away. And Kass went running to AJR, who was having a conversation with Nick the Greek.

"Art!" she exclaimed. "Art! I've been playing the slots with Liberace!"

AJR was not in the least surprised. He immediately understood what had occurred.

"Milton Jaffe," he said, "put him up to that."

A Kiss from Mary Ann

Clint Eastwood, the old cowboy actor, made a boxing movie called "Million Dollar Baby" that was popular with the critics and the public. It took me back to a time when AJR and the McGinleys promoted fights at Forbes Field, Hickey Park, and Duquesne Gardens and when the drivers who picked up my brothers and me after school were often ex-pugs or their managers.

"Do you remember those days?" I asked Tim.

"Sure do."

Tim then wanted to know if I remembered Gus Camp, a middleweight club fighter in the 1920s. Camp, Tim thought, was on the after-school pickup crew. "Nice guy. Owned a bar. When Dad's office was in the Fort Pitt Hotel, Gus would drop in to say hi once in a while."

I remembered Camp well. And I knew a story about him.

Frank Moran, an Irishman from the North Side who boxed twice for the heavyweight championship, losing to Jack Johnson in Paris and to Jess Willard in New York, had a fight coming up at Duquesne Gardens with somebody named Jack Geyer. Moran was approaching the end of his career but still carried a knockout punch in his right hand. He had a name for his right hand – "Mary Ann." Opponents who were kissed by Mary Ann became instantly weak in the knees.

As George Quinlan told it, with the date of his appearance at Duquesne Gardens impending, Moran needed sparring partners and there were none to be had. He was his own manager, usually, but on this occasion was being handled by Luke Carney, who in years to come would manage Pittsburgh's colorful welterweight champion, Fritzie Zivic. Looking around in the gym one day, Carney spotted Gus Camp.

"Wanna make ten bucks?" Carney asked.

"Doing what?" Camp replied.

"Boxing a couple of rounds with Moran."

Moran was 6 feet 2 and weighed 215 pounds; Camp weighed 160.

"He'll throw the right hand and kill me," Camp objected.

"I'll tell him not to use the right."

Camp then agreed to spar. They got into the ring, and he was having an easy time of it. Moran was a fighter who could hit with only one hand; deprived of that hand, he looked helpless. All the punches were being landed by the smaller, quicker Camp.

At the end of the round, Moran went back to his corner unhappy.

"You're letting that guy show me up," he said to Carney.

"Use the right hand then," Carney answered. In round two, Moran did. Camp hit the deck, unconscious. Carney, in an access of guilt, bent over the stretched-out fighter and passed smelling salts under his nose. Gradually, Camp came to.

"Gus!" Carney said. "Are you all right? Shall I call a doctor?"

Camp's eyes were now beginning to focus. He lifted his head a few inches. "Hell, no," he said. "Call a priest."

This was one story that Tim never had heard. There were dozens of others like it, and AJR knew them all.

On Second Thought

After Ralph Berlin had been with us for several years, he approached me about changing jobs. Since coming to the Steelers as trainer during the Bill Austin regime, he had done a little scouting for me. Now he was interested in scouting full-time, as long as extended road trips would not be necessary. I expressed my willingness to give him a try. Berlin was easy to work with, a subscriber to the doctrine passed on to Chuck Noll from his mentors Paul Brown and Don Shula: "Whatever it takes."

All the things a trainer must do were wearing Berlin down. His knees hurt, making it difficult for him to tape ankles, which required a lot of stooping, and to help injured players get back on their feet before they limped off the field. He was not in a position, financially, to retire, and he loved football. Scouting, therefore, would be an ideal situation for him, he thought.

"You can scout the Mid-Atlantic Conference teams – Bowling Green, Kent State, Miami, Ohio U., Youngstown, Marshall," I told him.

Initially, it worked out fine. His reports were well written and he got them in on time. He knew the technical aspects of the game. His opinions were OK. And he represented the Steelers in a high-class way. Early on, I advised him to keep at it. He had the makings, I said, of a first-rate scout. His response to this, I must admit, was unexpected.

"Thank you, Arthur," he said, "but scouting is not for me. Too much time on the road. I'll stick to taping ankles and taking care of the wounded as long as I can."

All told, Berlin was with the Steelers for more than twenty-five years. From time to time, he continued to give me help when I needed it. In retirement, he helped Dan, working at part-time jobs in the scouting and ticket departments and also on occasion as a driver.

"The Plumber," he called himself. "Jack of all Trades or "Handy Man" might have been closer to the mark. There was nothing he couldn't do, it seemed, and nothing he couldn't do well.

'That One's a Cop'

If I had followed through on my youthful ambition to be an actor, I could have played any character part. Without makeup. Without a disguise.

Do you doubt that? Read on.

In New Orleans one time on the morning of a football game, I went to the hotel coffee shop with my brother John and assistant coach Woody Widenhofer. The place was packed. We spotted three open seats at the counter, but only two of them were together. John sat with Woody, and I took the single. The counter was in the form of a square, and I could see, but not hear, John and Woody. Seated next to Woody was a young woman, attractive in a rather flashy way. I saw him turn to her and say something, and I saw that she answered him. Later, John filled me in.

"Woody whispered to me, 'Watch this, '" John related. "Then he said to this lady, 'How much?'"

According to John, she told him to keep his voice down, explaining, "I can't talk now. That one over there is a cop."

"She meant you," John went on.

"And you do look like a cop," he said. "An Irish cop from the North Side."

It must be that I have an air of command. At Parris Island one day, I walked into the squad bay wearing my summer dress uniform – khaki pants, shirt, and tie. Someone shouted, "Officer on deck!" and everyone else snapped to attention.

Almost immediately, one of my fellow enlisted men, recognizing me, called out, "Aw, that's no officer; it's just that damned Private Rooney."

A long time afterward, when Kay and I were in Aspen, Colorado, for a wedding, I was pointed out to my brother Tim by another guest. We were outdoors, near the ski slopes. "See that big guy with the redhead?" said Tim's acquaintance. "The one with the Irish cap on? That's Victor McLaglen's son."

Victor McLaglen was an old-time character actor with an unmistakable Irish brogue. A heavyweight boxer in his younger days, he co-starred with John Wayne in "The Quiet Man." They engaged in a memorable bare-knuckle fight, which McLaglen would have won in real life.

The man who told Tim that McLaglen was my father went on to say that I had used this connection to land a job as a Hollywood movie director.

At another gathering, somebody confided to my nephew Sean Rooney that he had seen me often on television. I mostly played cowboys, the man said.

Sometimes even Kay could be fooled.

At a big social affair in a high-class nightclub, she told me I looked very handsome in my new tuxedo.

I'm as willing to accept compliments as most people are, but this was overdoing it.

"Dear," I replied, "I look like the bouncer."

A Special Relationship

When "On the Waterfront," a movie about union racketeering, played the Stanley Theater in 1954, Billy Conn went to see it. The scene that everybody remembers from "On the Waterfront" is the one in which Marlon Brando, as the washed-up prizefighter Terry Malloy, has a long conversation with his older brother Charley, the union's lawyer, in the back seat of a taxicab. They discuss, among other things, Terry's ill-starred boxing career, and Charley says, "Kid, when you weighed 168 pounds you were beautiful. You could have been another Billy Conn."

At that point, according to Conn himself, someone in the audience at the Stanley called out very audibly, "He's a big enough bum as it is."

Conn had a mordant sense of humor and was capable of inventing a story like that. And yet it has the ring of truth; in the way they treat their celebrities, Pittsburghers are notoriously irreverent.

Conn was anything but a bum in the ring. Light-heavyweight champion of the world at 21, Conn beat every good fighter he ever went up against except one – the great Joe Louis. On the other hand, he fastidiously avoided work, which was something he had in common with AJR if work is defined as the drudgery of a 9-to-5 job. AJR made his living with his wits; Conn earned more than a half-million dollars with his fists; he sustained himself and his family from then on in ways that were not clearly visible.

He was prudent enough, I believe, to have invested wisely. And AJR once said that he had "made a ton of money" for Conn by giving him advice at the race track. It was a favor he rarely did for anyone else, which tells a great deal about the special relationship between them.

Another of Conn's special relationships was with Milton Jaffe, his business manager. Jaffe owned a piece of the Stardust Casino in Las Vegas and would pay Conn handsomely to go out there now and then and make himself agreeable to the customers. Conn being Conn, this was sometimes difficult for him.

The newspaperman Gene Collier wrote in Conn's obituary that he was "as blunt as a fist." It's a statement for which plenty of documentary evidence existed. In the early 1970s, thirty years after Conn's first fight with Louis, AJR was taking him on a tour of Three Rivers Stadium. He introduced Billy to several white players in the locker room, and they admitted they never had heard of him. Irritated, Billy called over to a group of black players in another part of the room: "Hey, blackies." In unison, their heads swiveled toward him. "Do you know who Joe Louis was?" he asked. The black players nodded. Conn turned again to the white players. "And you knuckleheads don't know who *I* am," he said.

Conn was from East Liberty, and like everybody else who grew up in tough big-city working-class neighborhoods before World War II he used all the ethnic slurs so common back then. There was nothing malicious about it – it was just the way people in that time in those places talked.

An example: While waiting for the bell on the night he won the light-heavyweight title from Melio Bettina, who was from Beacon, New York, Conn noticed a group of the champion's hometown Italian fans in the front row at Madison Square Garden. They had unfurled a banner imploring Bettina to "Bring Back the Bacon to Beacon." Conn looked down at these high-spirited partisans from the camp of the enemy and said, "There's gonna be a lot of hungry dagoes in Beacon tonight."

He was just as irreverent toward the Irish. On his only visit to the land of his ancestors, a newspaper reporter said to him, "Billy, you're a god over here. Everybody loves you. Now, what do you think of Ireland?"

And Billy answered, "I'm glad my mother didn't miss the boat."

Then of course there was also his unforgettable "What's the use of being Irish if you can't be dumb?" – this after he was foolish enough to slug it out with Louis in the thirteenth round of their first fight.

Billy Conn was a Pittsburgh guy. He could have settled in Las Vegas with a well-paid sinecure at the Stardust. Instead, after just a few weeks out there, he could hardly ever wait to get home. He believed that God had in mind the same fate for Las Vegas that was meted out to Sodom and Gomorrah. Returning for the last time, he announced he was home to stay,

But then he always had felt drawn to home in whatever part of the globe he happened to be. Johnny Ray, his manager, sent him down into the Ozark Mountains of Arkansas to prepare for a big fight, and he took no pleasure in the scenic splendor, the pure air, the company of the birds and bees.

"Why, Billy," admonished Nate Liff, who was training him, "this is God's country."

"God's country?" said Billy. "I wouldn't give you an alley in Pittsburgh for it."

Conn took $17,000 from his purse for the first Louis fight and bought a house in an upscale section of Squirrel Hill. For the rest of his life, he lived there with Mary Louise. Their four kids, three boys and a girl, grew up in that house. His purse from the second Louis fight, $325,000, plus the money that Milton Jaffe, AJR, and other financially-wise pals were able to funnel in his direction, enabled him to keep the wolf from the door without scrimping.

His aversion to anything like actual work had been apparent from the time he was 13 years old. William Conn, Sr., who worked as a steamfitter at Westinghouse, took him to the plant in East Pittsburgh one day and said, "This is where you're gonna be as soon as you're old enough, son."

"It scared the hell out of me," Billy later recalled. Soon afterward, having left Sacred Heart School in the eighth grade by request of the nuns, he presented himself at Johnny Ray's gym and asked to be taught how to box.

"You've got to be nuts to be a fighter," Conn said at the end of his career, "but it was better than working in a mill."

Or working almost anywhere at all. Budd Schulberg offered him a supporting actor's role in "On the Waterfront" – Schulberg had written the screen play – but Conn turned him down, saying "One stink bomb is enough." In 1941, after his first fight with Louis, Billy had gone out to Hollywood and played the part of a fighter based on himself in a movie called "The Pittsburgh Kid." The film was so bad, Conn thought, that when people he didn't like came to his house he made them watch the video.

Conn may have been a wooden actor but his boyish good looks impressed casting directors. There were offers from several studios – they wanted Mary Louise to audition for them as well – but Conn wasn't interested, so neither was Mary Louise. He did have a role, for which he received no screen credit, in "Gentleman Jim," a film about the nineteenth-century heavyweight champion, Jim Corbett. The only parts of Conn the audience could see were his legs from the knees down. Errol Flynn played Jim Corbett, but his footwork in the fight scenes was not quite satisfactory, so the director substituted Conn's.

Unlike other ex-pugs, Conn was never reckless with money. Whether or not he had it, he turned to AJR or to Milton Jaffe for advice. Once when Conn lost his driver's license, AJR used his political influence to regain it for him, but declined to pay the twenty-five dollar fine. "I've done enough for Billy," he told the magistrate. "Let him pay it himself." Weeks went by, and Billy still wasn't driving. AJR called the magistrate to ask what had happened. He was told that Billy had refused to fork over. AJR simply shrugged and wrote the magistrate a check.

On the other hand, there was this: Over the Mediterranean Sea during the war, Billy was in an airplane that developed engine trouble. He made a promise to the Lord that if the plane landed safely he would give five thousand dollars to Father Silas for the Franciscans' missionary work and a statue of the Blessed Virgin to Sacred Heart Church in East Liberty. The plane landed with no casualties, and Billy was as good as his word. The five thousand dollars in cash went toward the construction of a church and a school in China.

Billy's gruffness masked a streak of sentimentality. He was devoted to Mary Louise. When he spoke of his mother, his eyes filled with tears. Told that Father Silas had died, he said, "I know this: I've got a friend up in heaven today." Father Silas and AJR, he confided to Aunt Marie, had kept him from being what that real or imaginary movie critic in the Stanley Theater suggested he was – a bum.

As for AJR, he smiled from ear to ear when he talked about Billy, regardless of how exasperated with him he might have been at the time. And yet it amused the Chief that Milton Jaffe, in his will, left nothing more than a fountain pen to Billy. They had flown to Las Vegas for the funeral together, Billy anticipating a five- or six-figure windfall.

A few years later, Billy died of a fighter's occupational ailment as destructive to the brain cells as Alzheimer's – pugilistica dementia. But in his early old age, shortly before going to the Veterans' Hospital where he ended his days, he made the newspapers and newscasts one last time. He was in a convenience store with Mary Louise when a hold-up man came in. Billy knocked him down with a left hook, whereupon the guy crawled to the door, scrambled to his feet, and ran off into the night.

Chapter 56

Horse Sense

Our experience with Ken Phares reminded me of a story that Kass used to tell about one of Dad's race horses. We were kids the first time I heard it. According to Dad's trainer, this particular horse was unbeatable. It couldn't lose. Kass did not believe in sure things, and she said so. "Take my word for it," the trainer assured her. "This horse can't lose. No way it can lose." Still not convinced, Kass said she could think of a way. "Suppose it breaks a leg," she suggested.

At this point in her narrative, Kass would say to us, "And do you know what happened to that poor animal?"

We could guess, but we always asked, "What?"

"Broke its leg. Right in the middle of a race. In front of where we were sitting that day. One of those big green horse vans came onto the track, and a man with a pistol got out. He went up to that horse and shot him in the head, the poor thing – shot him dead. Then they got him into the van and off the track and the races went on just as usual."

Ken Phares, a defensive back from Mississippi State, was our second selection in the 1973 draft. Phares was a "can't-miss" prospect. He had size, speed, and mobility. He liked to hit. In the draft room, we were still congratulating ourselves when AJR came around. "Hey, you guys," he said, "I just had a phone call from a good friend of mine in Atlanta. He's a top sportscaster who used to be a coach, and he said we never should have drafted this Phares kid. He said that Phares has a real bad knee. It kept him out for part of the season and may not hold up very long."

We immediately pulled our scouting reports on Phares and showed them to the Chief. They were unreservedly positive. The player's coaches all downplayed his knee injury. There was no reason to worry about it, they insisted.

AJR barely glanced at the reports. "I can read this stuff," he said, "but my informant is very well connected. He'd never give me a bum steer."

"It's OK, Dad. It'll be OK." I was telling him we could do without advice from outsiders. Ken Phares came to camp in perfect condition. He looked, moved, and conducted himself exactly the way our scouts had promised he would. The team doctors examined his knee and pronounced it as good as new. "A nice repair job," they agreed.

So what happened? On the second play of the first drill in which he took part, Phares re-injured his knee – badly. He never played football again.

And the Chief? He reminded us frequently of the mistake we had made. Our successful 1972 season meant that in 1973 we would draft near the end of each round. The system set up by Bert Bell, with AJR backing him all the way, ensured parity. It prevented the more prosperous teams from cornering the market on talent. Drafting lower now, we had to juggle our rating list just a little, but still we came up with a couple of worthwhile picks.

In the first round, ahead of Phares, we drafted cornerback J. T. Thomas from Florida State. A fine athlete with leadership qualities, J. T. was a starter on our first two Super Bowl teams. He missed the 1976 season because of illness - sickle cell anemia – but returned to the starting lineup, this time as a safety, for one more Super Bowl. The season after that, Thomas was a Pro Bowl selection. In the 1980s, like so many of his fellow ex-Steelers from the Super Bowl years, he distinguished himself as a businessman and community leader.

Besides Thomas, three other players we drafted in 1973 made the team. Two of them, Dave Reavis, defensive tackle from Arkansas, and Glenn Scolnick, wide receiver from Indiana, didn't last long. Scolnick, nicknamed "Tomatoes," was a vegetarian. He could catch the ball and was fast, but lacked the physicality to cope with the bump-and-run defense, which made me wonder about the muscle-building power of spinach.

Our eighth-round pick in 1973, linebacker Loren Toews, was more typical – a meat eater, or so I presume. Toews (pronounced Taves) hung around for ten years and started in one of our Super Bowl games. I blush to say that the scout who called my attention to Toews was not a football scout, but a Boy Scout, perhaps 16 years old. Seated high in the stands, I was watching the 1972 intra-squad game at the University of California when the kid approached me. The Boy Scouts of Berkeley were acting as ushers, their good deed for the day.

'What are you doing'?" he asked, taking in my notebook, binoculars, and other paraphernalia.

I told him I was scouting talent for the Pittsburgh Steelers.

"Oh. Are you watching a player named Toews? He's my brother."

I consulted the Blesto list I always carried. Loren Toews was on it. Six feet two and a half, 205 pounds. Blesto had him rated as a "prospect," nothing more.

From then on I took pains to notice what Toews was doing. He made a few stops. He could hit and move and he played with confidence.

I put the guy's name on my "must-watch" fall list. During the season I happened to catch the California-Oregon game in Eugene. Toews was bigger and just as fast. He had a faculty for being in the right place at the right time. I gave him a decent "can make it" grade.

When I got back to Pittsburgh, Dick Haley said to me, "You know that Toews kid you liked last spring'? I had a chance to see him. He's OK. We have to look at him again."

I chuckled and said, "I just did look at him again."

We had found ourselves a sleeper – an undersized, underappreciated player who would not go high in the draft All we had to do was put some more weight on the guy. He was one of the late picks we made in the 1970s who contributed to those Super Bowl wins.

Footnote: Toews' brother Jeff, the Boy Scout, grew up quickly. The University of Washington recruited him out of high school as an offensive lineman, and from 1979 to 1985 he played in the NFL for Miami, sometimes going up against Loren.

California

New title or not – in our table of organization I was now a vice president – I continued to think of myself as a scout, first and foremost. And to the detriment of my marriage, I continued to spend weeks at a time away from home. Partly to placate the various family members who were telling me to get my priorities straight, I decided, in the fall of 1973, to take my wife and our five-year-old, Susie, on a scouting trip to the West Coast.

We would fly to San Diego, where Don Coryell had installed a pro-type offense at San Diego State, drive from there to Los Angeles – Kay could visit relatives, and I could scout UCLA and USC – and then proceed north on U.S. A-1-A to San Francisco, arriving in time to catch a Stanford home game in Palo Alto. Berkeley was nearby, too, and there I'd be able to learn if there were any decent prospects at "Cal" – the University of California.

Kay and Susie would be free to take in the sights. San Diego had mountains spilling into the Pacific and a breathtaking coast line, its somber browns and brilliant greens a perfect match for the blue of the ocean and the sky. There were fine hotels and many good restaurants and a harbor that was home to the U.S. Navy's Pacific fleet. In Los Angeles a tangle of freeways awaited us, but the drive to San Francisco is a scenic wonder, and San Francisco itself offered us Telegraph Hill and the Golden Gate Bridge. Berkeley, in those days of student unrest over Watergate, Vietnam, civil rights, and whatnot, was an interesting freak show, a gathering place for the nonconforming rebellious young in all their ragtag, bearded and long-haired, unwashed outrageousness.

I was their staid sartorial opposite, dressed at all times in a dark suit, white shirt, and conservative necktie. Other scouts, our own included, went to work in more casual attire. They were not the obedient offspring of AJR. No Rooney, the Chief insisted, must ever appear in public looking slovenly.

Some years before, on my first trip out West, Jerry Neri had sent a friend of his to pick me up at a USC practice scrimmage. These practice scrimmages were major events. I was watching from the bleachers, one individual in a crowd of at least two thousand, but Neri's friend, a man I never had met, identified me at once. "Rooney!" he called out. "Hey, Rooney!" "He'll be the only guy wearing a suit," Neri had told him. "He dresses like he's going to the office."

In about my fifteenth year on the job, I at last felt secure enough to switch from a suit jacket or dark blue blazer to a golf shirt. When it came to those "athletic shoes" with foam-rubber soles and white canvas tops, I drew the line.

Jerry Neri lived in Los Angeles and was well acquainted with all the coaches in the area. Of course by 1973, introductions were the last thing I needed. Don Coryell at San Diego State was a football genius, highly regarded for his passing schemes. "Our receivers will know what they're doing when they get to your camp," Coryell had assured me, "but don't let their training fool you. They still must have talent to compete in the NFL." A friendly tip that I found to be useful. John McKay, at Southern California, hailed from Western Pennsylvania. His parents, West Virginians, had farmed him out to relatives in rural Greene County when he was still in his teens because Western Pennsylvania's brand of high school football was superior.

McKay and I had some reference points in common, and perhaps for that reason he gave me a lot of help. I recall that on my West Coast visit in 1973 we sat on a bench not far from the USC practice field and discussed the seniors on his team who were pro prospects. One player he talked about – "a wonderful person who comes from a good family and is just big and fast enough to be a winner for you" – was Lynn Swann.

McKay drove around in a golf cart, and he asked me to hop aboard. "I'll show you the kids," he said. Out on the field, he would stop the cart to instruct a player in some technique and for brief consultations with an assistant coach or a trainer. Meanwhile he'd be calling my attention to the seniors, Lynn Swann in particular. I noticed how smooth in his movements Swann was and how well he could jump. Most especially, I liked his cheerful, spirited demeanor.

I felt out of place on the golf cart – a little embarrassed, in fact. When practice was over, two of the assistant coaches had some fun with me. To be a passenger in the USC counterpart of Air Force One meant that I had "arrived," one of them said.

On our second day in Los Angeles, I watched USC film and met with McKay's backfield coach, Craig Fertig. When I told him that Kay and Susie and I would be driving to San Francisco, he said we had to stay at the elegant Del Monte Lodge in Monterey. "I know the manager, I'll call him for you. It's a tough place to get into," he said. That it was, but Fertig delivered on his promise. By the time we checked out of our hotel the next morning, we had a room, thanks to Craig, at the Del Monte Lodge.

So far the trip had been a success, but now our luck changed. A few miles north of Los Angeles, Kay became very ill. Under the circumstances, going on to San Francisco in our rental car was out of the question. I turned around and drove to the airport. How easy it was before September 11, 2001, to travel by air. At the ticket counter, I asked about a night flight to San Francisco. We could rent a car there, I figured, and backtrack to Monterey. "Won't be necessary," the airline agent informed me. A direct flight to Monterey was leaving in half an hour. "A Hertz car will be waiting for you there," the agent said.

By this time, Kay was feeling better. At the Del Monte Lodge, we were affably greeted and shown to a spacious room. It had a wood-burning fireplace, a king-sized bed, and a rollaway bed for Sue. Flying from Los Angeles instead of driving had been a good idea. There were still a few hours of daylight left, and Kay suggested going for a ride. The scenic Seventeen Mile Drive would take us past Pebble Beach and one of the world's most beautiful golf courses.

All of it lived up to our expectations. There were oohs of appreciation from Kay. So we agreed to take a trip after breakfast the next morning – south to the Big Sur. On the two-lane highway, up in the mountains, we came to a bridge that crossed a deep, wide gorge. At the bottom of the gorge, a stream rushed into the ocean. Kay said, "You're driving too fast." The altitude and the sheerness of the canyon walls were making her queasy. I lost no time in putting the gorge behind us.

A few miles farther on, we stopped for lunch. Kay couldn't eat, which worried Sue. "Mommy's not feeling well, Daddy," she announced. Still we drove on, with stops here and there to take snapshots. I was ready to turn around and head back to the lodge when Kay said, "Stop here! This is a great place for a picture." Though I could see nothing special, I pulled off the road and got out of the car. "Where's the picture?" I asked. "Over there," Kay said, directing me to an ordinary-looking rise in the ground.

Dutifully, I walked to the little hillock and took a shot of a nondescript view. When I returned to the car, Kay was ensconced behind the steering wheel.

"Hey!" I objected.

"I'll drive," she said.

"You're too sick to drive."

"No I'm not. I'll get us back alive. No way do I want you driving Susie over that bridge again. This isn't Indianapolis."

Actually, Kay handled a car better than I did. We crossed the bridge – the Bixby Bridge, it was called – at a moderate rate of speed and arrived at the lodge safe and sound.

That night was a downer for Kay, so much so that I canceled out of the Stanford game and called off the rest of my scouting trip. On our way to the San Francisco airport, we drove past the Stanford campus. Because the Steelers were good customers of United Airlines, booking a mid-day flight to Pittsburgh, non-stop, was no trouble.

On the way home, it struck me that Susie's concern for Kay was greater than my own. I'm ashamed to say it, but I gave as much thought to the scouting opportunities I had missed as I did to the condition of my wife. I must further confess that during her illness and convalescence I went about my work with just as much intensity as before. Kay had good doctors, I told myself. They were taking good care of her.

Besieging heaven for Kay's recovery, Kass and Aunt Alice renewed their novena campaign. One day Kass lectured me. "Your wife is not *well* ... don't you see that?" she said. "Don't you appreciate what it is to wake up in the morning beside a woman as nice and as beautiful as Kay?" Kass thought, and so did AJR, that perhaps I should leave my job with the football team and move with Kay and the kids to Palm Beach. There I could work at the dog track we had recently acquired. Even Father Silas joined the chorus. The man who was running the dog track, he told me, was very old. Soon there would be an opening for me. "In just a few years," he said, "a smart guy like you could be ready to take over down there." I wasn't flattered; I wasn't interested. Football still was my passion. "Anyway," Father Silas went on, "you've done a great job with the team. But there will be problems in the future about who's in control, I believe. Keep that in mind."

In the years to come, after Kay had recovered, we made return trips to the West Coast again and again. Susie and Art and Mike would be with us. We'd drive from San Diego to San Francisco and even farther north, most of the time with me at the wheel and most of the time with no adverse comment from Kay. But on side trips out of Monterey, whenever we approached the Bixby Bridge, she would say, "Look, kids. This is the place where your father almost killed Sue and me, going ninety miles an hour over this dangerous bridge."

Lambert

Late in the fall of 1973 I decided to take a look at a Kent State linebacker named Jack Lambert. Just 110 miles west of Pittsburgh by way of the Pennsylvania and Ohio turnpikes, Kent State was an easy trip. I could eat a leisurely breakfast, see the kids off to school, skim through the morning newspapers, watch an early newscast on television, call the office, and kiss my wife goodbye before departing. Once I arrived, there was time to interview the coaches, study films, watch practice, and still get home (a little late) for dinner.

Kent State football teams did not compete at the top level but played some top-level opponents and had to be scouted. As my old drama coach in New York, Tamara Daykohonoa, used to say, "For every ten students I accept, only one has a true chance of making it as an actor. But I do not accept people who have no potential. That would be dishonest. I look for people with the capacity to act and re-act with each other. If they can do that much, I will take them."

That is roughly the way it was at Kent State. In fact, a shocking event connected with the Vietnam War had served indirectly to upgrade the university's football program. In the spring of 1970, National Guardsmen assigned to keep order on the campus had fired point-blank into a group of war protestors, killing four of them and wounding thirteen. Subsequently, in the hope that success on the football field and basketball court might divert the student body's attention from matters of life and death in Southeast Asia, Ohio government officials earmarked more money for Kent State athletics. Anyway, that is how I heard it from one of Chuck Noll's assistants, Denny Fitzgerald, who had been a Kent State coach at the time of the shooting.

Jack Lambert, as a senior, was the Kent State captain. The question about him had nothing to do with ability or toughness. It was whether he could put on enough weight for the NFL. Lambert stood 6-3 or 6-4 but was all sinew. Dick Haley, my cousin Tim, and even Ralph Berlin had scouted him. One and all agreed that he could get to the ball, had moxie, and was mean as hell.

The definitive story about Lambert came from Tim. It seems that the Kent State quarterback missed bed check or something and would not be allowed to play in one of the season's biggest games without doing penance. He must run, roll, and crawl the length of the practice field, one hundred yards, one hundred times. Sure that he wasn't up to it, the quarterback demurred. If he sat out the big game, Kent State undoubtedly would lose, and thus fail to qualify for post-season bowl consideration. Kent State never had gone to a bowl; as far as Lambert was concerned, missing out on this one could not be tolerated.

"Look, asshole," he said to the quarterback. "Do the drill. I'll do it with you. It may be tough, but not as tough as it's going to be if you don't do it or don't finish it. Because I'll kill you."

Taking Lambert at his word, the quarterback did the drill. At about the halfway mark he stopped to puke, and from then on he had to be dragged and pulled by Lambert, but he completed the ten thousand yards. As he lay on the ground, totally exhausted, Lambert looked down at him and snarled, "I think I'll kill you anyway, but not until later. Right now I'm too tired."

Whether the quarterback lived to win the big game I don't know.

On my visit to Kent State in 1973 I studied film, talked to the coaches, and watched practice, just as I had planned to do. Heavy rains that week had soaked the practice field, so after wading around in the mud for a while the players moved over to the cinder-coated stadium parking lot and worked out in shorts. There was just enough activity to give me a good look at the prospects on our list, primarily Lambert.

I liked the depth he was able to get on his pass drop. I liked his peripheral vision and his lateral movement. I liked his awareness; he was quick to anticipate both the pass and the run. I liked his leadership qualities – the way he communicated with his teammates and coaches. In short, I was feeling that my time had not been wasted. And then something really memorable happened.

Coach Don James was putting the team through a touch-tackle drill. Cutting through the line, a running back broke free. Lambert went after him but appeared to be a step and a half short. So instead of reaching out to make the two-handed touch, he launched himself into the air and got his two hands on the ball carrier's back. The ball carrier, stumbling, kept his balance. Lambert went face down into the cinders.

For the rest of the workout he was picking cinders out of his epidermis. His face, arms, and legs were scraped. Not by a single outward sign did he show that any of this bothered him even slightly. All business every minute, he concentrated on doing his job.

There was nothing more I needed to see.

Inducting Sinatra

Notwithstanding injuries to Terry Bradshaw, Franco Harris, and Frenchy Fuqua, the Steelers returned to the playoffs with a 10-4 record, good for the wild-card berth, in 1973. The playoff game was in Oakland against the Raiders late in December. A week beforehand, to escape the cold weather in Pittsburgh, Chuck Noll took the team to Palm Springs.

He had done the same thing the year before, when the Steelers ended the season with a must-win game in San Diego. Acclimated to temperatures in the high seventies or low eighties, they had beaten the Chargers easily, 24-2, despite a major distraction – Frank Sinatra's appearance at practice during the week.

I wasn't there, but I heard about it and read about it and can piece together all the details.

Unquestionably, Steeler broadcaster Myron Cope, inspired by his involvement with a Franco Harris fan club, orchestrated the whole thing. The fan club, called Franco's Italian Army, consisted of twenty or so members headed by Tony Stagno, a baker, and Al Vento, a pizza maker. I know that Franco thought of himself as a black man, like his father, but his mother, you may recall, came from Italy. In any case, Stagno, Vento, and their followers attended Steeler games wearing battle helmets. One guy proudly waved an Italian flag. Stagno and Vento were generals in the Army, Stagno with five stars and Vento with four. Cope, the only non-Italian so honored, was a one-star general. Under orders from Stagno, he had gone to Palm Springs on a mission.

"Frank Sinatra lives there, you know," Stagno reminded him. Cope's job would be to track down the singer, bring him to practice, and induct him into the Army as still another general of the single-star variety.

Nothing, it turned out, could have been easier. Cope spotted Sinatra one night in a high-class restaurant and sent him an invitation, delivered by a waiter, to be present the next day at practice and receive his commission. With surprising affability, Sinatra joined Cope and his friends at their table and agreed to cooperate.

After Sinatra left the restaurant, Cope excitedly called Stagno in Pittsburgh. He must fly to Palm Springs with Vento as soon as possible, Cope urged him. This the commanders did, arriving just in time to officiate at the induction ceremony. They were wearing their battle helmets and carrying baskets laden with Italian wines and foodstuffs. Sinatra was on hand, taken in charge by Cope, newspaper photographers trailing along as they moved toward the sideline. Out on the practice field, Noll had become aware that he was losing the attention of his players. He looked unhappy. Cope then did the unthinkable. Boldly setting foot on Noll's turf – sacred ground – he shouted, "Franco! Get over here!" Sinatra was waiting. Stagno and Vento were waiting.

Franco glanced uneasily at Noll. "Can't do it, Myron, I'm practicing," he apologized. First things first. The onus now was on Noll: would he humiliate Cope and openly "diss" Frank Sinatra? The suspense seemed to last forever; then he ended it by echoing Cope. "Get over there, Franco," he said, and the ceremony proceeded with much fanfare.

Allow me now to digress. At some point that day, Sinatra met AJR and was much taken with him. They were to meet again and again over the years. Sinatra made a ritual of sending gifts to his friends, and for AJR it was always a fine box of cigars, dispatched like clockwork every six months.

Getting back to the Italian Army caper, its effect on the team had been harmless, but sideshows of that nature did not amuse me. So when Noll opted again for a week in Palm Springs before the playoff game with Oakland the next year, I was looking for reasons to be worried. A newspaper photograph of two Steeler players at poolside, hovering lasciviously (I assumed) over a voluptuous young miss wearing a barely noticeable bikini, turned the trick.

I asked myself unsettling questions. Was a pleasure resort the right place to get a team ready for so important a game? In such an atmosphere, did the players have their minds on football or on babes? Strange business, it seemed to me, with puritans like Dan, AJR, and Chuck Noll on the scene.

Months later I was to learn that my suspicions were groundless – even silly. The girl was no temptress but a child-woman of 15 or 16, physically mature for her age. Her parents, it turned out, were not football fans; unaware that the team was in Palm Springs, they had booked themselves into the same hotel. Moreover, my informant told me, they kept their daughter under non-stop surveillance. And in the second place, Palm Springs was actually quite staid. When they weren't on the practice field, there was little for the players to do.

Not knowing this, and looking on from a distance, all I could do was judge by what I took to be the evidence. There was still another reason – the big one – for my foul mood that week and beyond. Noll and his coaches had gone to Palm Springs with every last one of our movie projectors. When I was told about this, I blew my stack. "Don't those people realize that life has to go on for the scouting department?" I bellowed. Here we were, three weeks before the draft, without an essential tool.

All we could do was rent and borrow projectors – if possible. Dick Haley scrounged one from Pitt, trading on the fact that he had played there, but we were still far short. Seething, I bought an expensive Bell and Howell projector and had a nameplate attached to the top of it. "For the personal use of Art Rooney, Jr.," the nameplate proclaimed. "Not to be taken from the scouting department." For months and years to come, this would rankle the assistant coaches.

My grievances against Noll peaked on game day. We lost to Oakland disgracefully, 33-14, and I blamed this catastrophe on the frivolous week in Palm Springs that existed solely in my mind. Two days after the trouncing, Noll walked into the room where I met with the scouts. He was rubbing his hands together in what struck me as a self-satisfied way. His first words – something to the effect that he and his assistants were ready now to do some real work on the 1974 draft – lit my fuse.

"Coach," I blurted, "that was some performance your team gave in Oakland Saturday. We were not just defeated, we were embarrassed. I never imagined I'd see a Chuck Noll team play so poorly."

Taken by surprise, Noll was speechless. All of my scouts were speechless. Mrs. Duffy, my secretary, was speechless. Breaking the quiet that hung over the room, someone finally mentioned the scouting assignments for the post-season bowl games we were to cover.

This set me off once again. "Coach," I resumed – I never called him Chuck – "some of your assistants take scouting seriously and do a good job and some of them have a so-so attitude and do just a so-so job. Still others don't give a damn, and it shows in their reports. I'll give you an example. One of your coaches wrote that a prospect he had seen at a bowl game was 'a little fat guy who rolled around in the mud.' Period."

With that, Noll found his tongue. He came up close to me, baring his teeth. "Tell me who that coach is," he said. "Just tell me which of my coaches doesn't give a damn about scouting, and I'll fire him. Right now."

We were practically face to face. I said, "Coach, I'm not going to tell you. The coaches are your responsibility. The scouts are mine."

Noll turned on his heel and left the room. Dick Haley, Bill Nunn, Tim Rooney, and poor Mrs. Duffy were looking down at the floor. As for me, I was shaking with rage, indignation, and self-righteousness. I had never stood up to Bill Austin like this. Now I was making amends.

Of course I came to regret my impetuosity. There's a time and a place for letting off steam. This was neither. But then I had always been one to hold things in when I should have spoken up and to lash out intemperately when I should have kept my mouth shut. I was right about the assistant coaches – I still believe that – but my treatment of Noll was inexcusable. Reflecting on it, I remembered how I felt when AJR would reprimand me in front of scouts, coaches, secretaries, and whoever else happened to be listening.

There's a postscript to this. Years later, Noll hired an assistant coach with dubious credentials. I knew the guy's history at second hand, but kept it to myself. Noll in time grew dissatisfied with his work; during a conversation between us in my office one day, he said so, and this was my cue to lay out the information that had come to me.

"Art," Noll said, "when you hear something like this, you should tell me right away."

I repeated that our areas of authority did not overlap.

Half an hour later, the coach with the problems in his résumé no longer was employed by the Steelers. I thought of how Noll had promised to fire any coach I accused of taking scouting assignments lightly.

And I said to myself, "He'd have done it."

One thing more: never again did Noll take a team to Palm Springs or anywhere else for a week of warm-weather practice.

Weights and Measures

After Kenny Phares went down on the second play of his first practice at St. Vincent, we looked to our medical staff for some answers. In addition to a serious knee injury, we were told, Kenny had rheumatoid arthritis, which "never really gets better." On top of that, "the problem migrates from one part of the body to another."

There was more to understanding sports injuries than we knew at the time, it seemed. When we lost Kenny Phares we not only lost the money invested in him, but the draft pick as well – a high one. Our investment in scouting and draft selection was now so substantial that it made a lot of sense to have better information about injuries. Scouting reports and interviews with trainers were not enough. I don't mean to say that the college people were intentionally deceiving us. But they were not our employees, after all, and there was no incentive for them to be as uncompromisingly forthright as we might have liked.

The situation with Phares and others like him convinced us to spend a little more money on physical examinations. Why couldn't the fifteen or so top prospects who were injury risks come to Pittsburgh every year for checkups? It would be more work for trainer Ralph Berlin and my secretary, Rhoda Duffy, not to mention the front office, but everybody pitched in with great enthusiasm. The outcome was so pleasing that we added more players to the invitation list and set up a branch in Los Angeles, where Kay's cousin, Dr. Don Gaylor, a Pitt medical school graduate, put together a team of orthopedic and neurological surgeons to examine the West Coast prospects with physical problems.

And we didn't stop there. We arranged to swap injury information with the other four Blesto teams. Television revenue and sold-out games at Three Rivers Stadium made all of this possible. AJR never liked to throw money away, but Dan argued persuasively that money for such a purpose was well spent. As Dan reminded him, he always had said that the most overpaid player a team could have was the guy who "sat on the oak." The medicals were helping us avoid that.

Not long after the other Blesto teams had adopted our idea, Carl Peterson, personnel director of the Eagles, suggested, rather forcibly, that Blesto as a group bring *all* of the top-rated prospects to a central location for physicals, I.Q. tests, and psychological evaluations. Blesto bought into the concept, and in deference to Peterson the central location we agreed on was Philadelphia. Two or three years later, we moved the operation to Detroit, where the new domed stadium gave us room to bring in even more players and work them out. My cousin Tim Rooney, by that time the head of player personnel in Detroit, got together with Peterson and Dick Haley, and the three of them organized a series of drills: a long jump, a high jump, a change-of-direction run, a bench press to measure strength, and of course the forty-yard dash – all in addition to basic drills set up by the coaches for quarterbacks, receivers, defensive backs, and linebackers. The running backs had their own set of drills, and it was easy to make a judgment on the kickers.

Many college administrators protested that we were taking these "student-athletes" away from the business of getting an education. So, to appease them, we compressed all of our testing into a single long weekend, a tremendous organizational feat for the scouts, coaches, trainers, doctors, and secretaries (who never received enough credit).

Meanwhile, the rest of the teams in the NFL had also started a camp, and league officials agreed with the colleges that too much time was being demanded of the players. The solution we reached was to combine the other teams' camp with the Blesto camp, which eliminated duplication. We now had a supersized operation. There were media people who called it a "meat market" and others who likened it to the slave markets of the antebellum South. In my opinion, that was baloney. We were not putting price tags on slaves, but appraising young men who were going to be extremely well paid.

The testing was done in mid-winter, making it necessary to move back the draft until spring. I had always felt that a hard-working, knowledgeable, well-organized scouting department – ours, for example – could outdraft the teams that were slower to prepare, but now we were all on equal terms. Even the late starters could get their act together with an additional two months of leeway.

Another result of the testing was that scouts and coaches were putting more stress on athletic skills, so that the camp itself had become a showcase for players with exceptional speed and agility. Jack Butler of Blesto, for one, thought it was misplaced emphasis. "You'd better evaluate a kid on how well he plays the game of football rather than how well he hops, skips, and jumps in his underwear," Butler said. And Chuck Noll repeated the line he had used about the rookie who could leap over cars. "These workouts," he said, "are all well and good in their place, but are we looking for football players or auditioning for the half-time show?"

After a while, I started to feel that Butler and Noll had it right. During a film study of the workouts, I told Dick Haley, "I could send you guys to scout the Olympics. You'd see the greatest athletes in the world there, but half of them will be girls and the men won't like football."

Not that it makes any difference, for these mid-winter circuses are now a permanent part of the landscape, their popularity undiminished by the passing of time.

Name Game

In the early 1970s, Blesto, under Jack Butler, entered the computer age. With the help of high-tech professionals at companies like Sperry Rand, Butler developed a program that could take the information his scouts had assembled on a football player, put the various pieces together, and measure his potential as precisely as technology allowed.

I said to Butler, "That's fine, Jack, but how did you pay the bills for all this? Sperry Rand guys don't work for nothing."

"We got lucky," he told me. "One of the top men with that outfit has a Pittsburgh background and loves football. He was so interested in our scouting procedures he gave us a special deal."

"Hey, Jack," I reminded him, "don't forget what the Chief always says. If something looks too good to be true it probably is. What is the catch here? What does your Pittsburgh friend want in return? And just who is he, anyway? You haven't told me his name."

"It's John Butler," Jack said.

"No, I asked you what *his* name was, not your own."

"His name and my name are the same: John Butler."

For a long time I wondered if Butler – Jack Butler – was putting me on. But a year or so later – this would be 1975 – Jack called me and said, "Remember that John Butler guy who helped me computerize our scouting? You asked if there was going to be a payback. Well, the answer is yes. His company wants to do a TV commercial for an NFL game, a TV commercial with a Blesto angle. When they shoot it, I'm going to be a consultant."

I heard from Jack later that the set for the commercial was a mockup of an NFL draft room. "You can't believe the detail that went into it," Jack said. "Everything was absolutely authentic except the names on the charts. The names of the players and the schools were made up. I think it'll work."

As an afterthought, I asked if all the teams in the Blesto organization had given Jack permission to do the commercial.

"Yes, quite a while ago."

I said, "You didn't ask *me*."

"I didn't think I had to," Jack sort of explained.

There were actually two commercials. One was a full minute and the other a half minute. The actors, pretending to be coaches and scouts at a draft meeting, were sporty looking guys, a little too pretty for their roles. One actor yelled, "Pittsburgh is up!" Another one, playing the guy in charge, but too sharp-looking to be Chuck Noll or me, said, "Hold on. We're looking for the best athlete available." He was hunched over a computer, with everybody else crowded up behind him as a name appeared on the screen.

"Here it is!" the Noll/Rooney figure exclaimed. "Defensive back ... Six-two ... Two hundred pounds ... Four point six forty ... Butler – Jack Butler ... Saint Bonaventure University."

"Yep, that's our man," said an actor who was playing an assistant coach. "Jack Butler. He'll be great."

All in all, it was not a bad commercial. The next time I saw Jack, I had only one question: "'Best athlete available.' Did you give them the idea for the name?"

The look on his face said, "How could you think such a thing?"

Out loud, he said, "No, not at all. The name wasn't supposed to be mine. It was the other Jack Butler's. The guy from the computer company. *John* Butler, he calls himself. But that was supposed to be him, not me."

"Oh. My mistake," I said, but not out loud.

Chapter 57

A 'Yeah, But' Player

To the old-timers in my department, the Blesto computer program was an irritant. The younger scouts acknowledged its usefulness, and my own point of view was the same as theirs. If aircraft and automobile companies could test products still in the planning stage on simulated tracks and landing strips, why couldn't we do something like that with football players?

Computers were not infallible, however. Where they sometimes went wrong was with players you couldn't pigeonhole – players like Mike Webster, a center from Wisconsin. The Blesto computer took into account the intangibles Webster possessed. It gave him high marks for desire, toughness, stamina, effort, awareness, and football intelligence. But his height, 6 feet 2 1/2, his weight, 225 pounds, and his forty-yard dash time, 5.25, were substandard. With a center that small and that slow, the computer said, you could not win a championship.

I'd have said so myself, I am sorry to say, and the Blesto scouts would have concurred. Mike Webster was not a "computer player," a guy who jumped off the screen. Neither was he an obvious reject. He was simply the kind of player who might easily get lost in the shuffle.

But this time good fortune attended us. I thought of AJR and his belief in the importance of luck. An assistant coach at Wisconsin had kept in touch with our defensive line coach, George Perles. I've forgotten the Wisconsin man's name. It was Irish, I know. And I know that he called Perles to tell him about Webster – "the best offensive lineman in the Big Ten if not the whole country."

I had an up-and-down relationship with Perles. To be frank, I considered him a Neanderthal type. In the coffee room at Three Rivers Stadium one day, he told me bluntly that the only reason Chuck Noll put up with me was the fact that my father owned the team. Mustering all the self-control I was capable of, I answered without raising my voice. I said, "George, I have learned a lot from Chuck and from each of his assistants, but I don't think it's one-sided. I can offer them a lot in return."

In the back of my mind – I can't shade the truth here – was the realization that if I blew up at Perles and we duked it out, he'd have taken me. Enviably, AJR was always sure that, like John L. Sullivan, he could lick any man in the house.

Perles and Noll complemented each other. Perles was outspoken and passionate, Noll understated and cerebral. "Football," Perles would tell his defensive linemen, "is a violent, emotional game, and it has to be played that way." He deserves a tip of the hat for developing L. C. Greenwood, Fats Holmes, and Dwight White, three of the components in our Steel Curtain, and later John Banaszak, Steve Furness, and Gary Dunn, starters, like the others, on Super Bowl teams. I omit any mention of Joe Greene. Sister Mary Vincent from the Little Sisters of the Poor could have coached Joe Greene.

Perles lacked the temperament to be of much use as a scout. He hated those long days and nights alone on the road. Mike Webster, in a sense, was dropped right into his lap. Before the 1974 draft, George's friend at Wisconsin sent him game films, and we were able to judge Webster on the way he performed against Big Ten players we had earmarked as prospects. Not only did Webster hold his own with these guys, he was dominant. Dick Haley and our offensive line coaches agreed that while he came up short when we looked at his numbers, there were "compensating factors" – namely, the intangibles I have referred to, plus the unbelievable leverage he could generate.

What we had here, we thought at first, was a late middle-round pick who could hang on for a while as an adequate special-teams player. He would be what we called an "exception," just as bumblebees are exceptions. The laws of aerodynamics tell us that bumblebees are not built to fly. Yet, somehow or other, they do. Another law, one that football scouts ignore at their peril, says you can go broke taking chances on exceptions. The trick is to spot the real thing, which of course requires superior drafting know-how.

I think an awful lot of NFL teams had a "yeah, but" attitude toward Webster. "Yeah, he was good in college, but he's just not big enough for the pros." This kind of talk played into our hands. We could hold off drafting him until a very late round. Given the general feeling of apathy toward Webster, even a free-agent signing might not be out of the question. But then we saw the films from the post-season all-star games.

Dick Haley would run into my office after watching them. "Ya gotta see this Webster!" he'd exclaim, and see him I did. I saw him knock a prospective first-round pick, 275 pounds of muscle and beef, halfway back to where he came from. "Look at Webbie get up under his face mask. *Wham!* He hits like Rocky Marciano," Haley chortled.

My cousin Tim Rooney came around with a reel of film, and we expressed our amazement at Webster's complete mastery of blocking techniques. "Look at his feet!" Tim enthused. "Look at him slide! He pops one rusher and slides over to pick up another guy. Do you know how many years of NFL experience a center needs to make that move look so easy?"

"Great work," I replied, "but let's not go overboard yet. We can still get the guy in the late middle rounds."

As it turned out, he was the fifth player we drafted. Though I believed my own words, I couldn't wait any longer.

Senior Bowl

Senior Bowl week in Mobile, Alabama, was not the ideal time to scout a football player, and Mobile itself was not the ideal environment.

There was Mobile's weather, as fickle as a Southern belle. A January day in Mobile could be springlike; it could be oppressively hot; it could be cold, wet, and windy. Old-timers packed their bags to be ready for anything. I had a big fleecelined coat that I sometimes wore to practice when the temperature dropped. A sudden storm rolled in from the Gulf of Mexico one day and it covered my coat and me with ice. Twenty-four hours later, I thought I would die from the heat. On one of Chuck Noll's first visits, a wind came up, the sky clouded over, and a freezing rain started to fall. Noll took his staff to an Army-Navy store and the whole gang returned wearing galoshes and waterproof jackets.

The competing all-star teams practiced at different sites – a Catholic military school and a field near the Senior Bowl stadium. Our understanding was that the coaches would stagger their practices so that the scouts in attendance could see both teams twice a day. Because of the weather, it didn't always work out that way. Rain could muddy a field and make it necessary for a practice to be moved. Then the scouts and the visiting coaches would have to scurry around in search of the new location.

Still another impediment was the presence of agents and news media. When the players weren't practicing, their agents would whisk them away or the sportswriters and sportscasters would be after them. Getting time with the players alone was always difficult. Renting a car was difficult. Finding a place to park was difficult. As necessary to the success of these post-season all-star games as publicity is, and as much a part of professional football as agents had become, my perspective was that of a scout, and the sheer profusion of such supernumeraries, as I thought of them, made a scout's job anything but pleasurable.

There were distractions unconnected with football, too – distractions like Wentzel's Oyster House. We were drawn to Wentzel's at lunchtime every day by the blue points, the clams, the fish sandwiches, the cold beer – I took a pass on the beer – and the likelihood of hearing football stories from 350-pound Don Joyce, a scout for Blesto and later the Indianapolis Colts. Without ever repeating himself, Joyce could hold us spellbound all week. In the early evening hours, we assembled at the Senior Bowl's nightly cocktail party for NFL people only. The "bar food" at these functions was so abundant that the scouts would pocket their meal money and hang around to pig out. Then at the end of the week came the super pig-out – a mammoth fish fry, called the Seafood Jamboree, at which tons of aquatic creatures and gallons of truly excellent gumbo would be consumed.

Royal entertainment, without question. "But is that why we are down here?" I asked myself. It went against the work ethic I had carefully developed. As much as I enjoyed the Gulf Coast cuisine, the shop talk, and the companionship, my conscience hurt. I could have been studying game film, after all.

At the 1974 Senior Bowl, the Steeler contingent was interested in one player above all the others, a wide receiver the public never had heard of. Nor, as far as I could tell, had more than a handful of scouts become aware of him. His name was John Stallworth, and he played in obscurity at Alabama A. & M., a little-known black college.

But not in total obscurity. Bear Bryant, the football coach at Alabama's state university and in that part of the country a figure of Olympian proportions, was threatening to break the color line. Without black players, Bryant realized, Alabama no longer could win. Though it would take a little time, he therefore intended to recruit them. To everybody's surprise, he had publicly regretted that there were no John Stallworths catching passes for the Crimson Tide.

The Blesto scout who alerted us to Stallworth's potential was Joe Bushofski, a teammate of mine and Tim's at North Catholic High School and later the head coach at North Catholic. In college, Joe played at North Carolina State. Joe and his brother Jack, another North Catholic guy, had parallel careers as scouts. Both worked for Blesto after I recommended them to Jack Butler, and both ended up as personnel directors in the NFL, Joe with the Detroit Lions, Jack with the Baltimore Colts and Carolina Panthers.

Joe's report on Stallworth at the fall Blesto meeting in 1973 placed him among the top wide receivers in the nation, and we immediately got Bill Nunn on the case. Because of Nunn's connections with black college coaches, he could get access and information denied to most other scouts. The films he brought back included a game in which Stallworth was a one-man highlight show. He appeared to be a tall, skinny kid who caught every ball that was anywhere near him. Our time for Stallworth in the forty-yard dash was 4.6; he looked a bit faster than that. He separated himself from defenders quickly and made over-the-shoulder catches on the dead run.

Chuck Noll took a look at the films and pronounced Stallworth a definite first-round pick. "If he's going to the Senior Bowl, there's no way of hiding him," Noll said. "Everybody will see how good he is. These scouts for the other teams in the league aren't idiots, you know." Dick Haley and I counseled restraint. "Let's calm down a little," I suggested. "At this point, we can get him on the third or fourth round." Noll shook his head. Stallworth, he repeated, was a first-round pick.

Alabama A. & M.'s coach had exacted a promise from Nunn to return all the game films we had seen. The coach wanted to circulate them among the other NFL teams for Stallworth's sake. The films would move him up in the draft-selection process. Nunn sent back all except one – the film in which Stallworth evoked memories of Don Hutson, an end from Alabama who played for the Green Bay Packers from 1935 to 1945 and set pass-catching records that remained in the books for decades. It seemed to me that every time I walked past our projection room, Nunn and Dick Haley, or Haley and Chuck Noll, or Nunn and Lionel Taylor, the receivers coach, or all of the above would be watching that film. In the interest of complete truthfulness, I must admit that I joined them on occasion. Even AJR would sometimes be in the audience. In later years, when we had the technological ability to do it, we'd have made a copy of the film and returned the original to Alabama A. & M. As it was, we kept the damned thing until the eve of our departure for the Senior Bowl, when I at last said to Nunn, "Look, Bill, you promised that coach you would send back all of those films. If we hang onto this one any longer, we'll be getting a bad reputation." I then repeated the same warning to Haley.

Well, Senior Bowl week came and went, and I noticed one day that we still had the film. Nunn and Haley were looking at it again. In college at St. Vincent, I learned about "pragmatism" – the theory that whatever works is OK. I also learned that getting away with anything you could was *not* necessarily OK. Going back on our agreement with Stallworth's coach was the first and last time we were guilty of such a trick during my tenure as head of the scouting department.

Noll's fear that the Senior Bowl game would be a showcase for Stallworth, revealing the extent of his talent to every other team in the NFL, turned out to be groundless. I was reminded of AJR's belief in the importance of luck. He used to say that no matter how smart you were, no matter how well-prepared, it could all go for nothing if luck was against you. This time, luck was on our side. Uncertain of what to do with Stallworth, his coaches kept moving him back and forth between two positions – wide receiver and cornerback – so that he never had a chance to display his pass-catching skills. Having already observed them on film, we didn't mind. We could see that Stallworth in the flesh was a gifted athlete, and when our emissaries talked to him they liked his good-natured acceptance of the way he had been misused. Evidently he was not a prima donna.

Hall-of-Fame Haul

In the NFL, success had a downside. To ensure parity – balanced competition – losing teams drafted early, winning teams drafted late. The Steelers, under Noll, had started to win. Accordingly, the first player we selected in the 1974 draft would be the twenty-first who was picked overall.

Personnel directors lived by the saying "Don't screw up when you have those real early choices." In making some real early choices since 1969, the year we drafted Mean Joe Greene, we hadn't screwed up. But now all of a sudden we'd be "reaching" – taking a chance on a player with what Noll aptly referred to as "impediments." As AJR put it, we would have to get lucky.

As he also put it, you never counted on luck. He spoke from the perspective of a horse player. For a visit to the race track, you prepared as if there were no such thing as luck. Approach a draft the same way, was his counsel. To borrow again from Noll's terminology, we'd be looking for "exceptions" – players deficient in size and/or speed but with qualities not as easy to assess, qualities like intelligence, tenacity, an instinct for the game.

Everyone liked Lynn Swann, a graceful wide receiver from the University of Southern California. His lack of height – he was barely 5 feet 9 – and his time in the forty-yard dash, 4.65, worked against him. When our turn in the first round came, he might still be available.

Interested, I spoke to Jack Butler about Swann. He said that Howard Slusser, Swann's agent, had agreed to let a Blesto scout time him in the forty in Los Angeles a week before the draft. Butler did not like Slusser. In Jack's opinion, the agent was overbearing and glib. The adjectives I'd have used were "sharp" and "verbal." Slusser's clients esteemed him, I understood; he delivered for them in contract negotiations. Slusser was a short, red-haired guy on the somewhat corpulent side. AJR had a favorable opinion of him, but was uncomfortable with the presence in his stable of "too many Steelers." Trouble would come of it, he predicted. As it happened, none did, other than "mental aches and strains." Dan and Jim Boston dealt with Slusser honestly and fairly, and AJR treated him like a human being, this at a time when NFL owners in general looked upon agents as vermin. The result was that we never lost a player represented by Slusser. Many of them, in fact, helped us win championships. "Tell Howard for me," I said one day to his good friend Jim Boston, "I wish we could give him a Super Bowl ring."

Blesto's Howard White re-timed Swann in the forty at 4.54, nearly a tenth of a second faster than his previous best time. One of our assistant coaches had said of Swann, using a commonplace putdown, "He's small, but he's slow." He was still small, but no longer slow. He now had a timed speed to go with the playing speed we knew he possessed from our studies of USC film. Later, if we asked Swann to run a forty in training camp at St. Vincent, he'd consistently do 4.61, but in a match race with John Stallworth, losing by a nose (as AJR would say), he'd run a 4.55 to Stallworth's 4.54. Swann had what we called competitive speed. The fact that his extracurricular activities included ballet dancing was something we were willing to forgive. Ballet dancing is good for a player's footwork and equilibrium.

In Swann, Stallworth, Jack Lambert, and Mike Webster, we now had identified four good draft picks we believed the rest of the teams had underrated, or, in Stallworth's case, overlooked. In previous drafts when we had singled out such players, they would disappear from the board while we waited to claim them. On this occasion the stars in the heavens were properly aligned for us. We took Swann in the first round and Lambert in the second. Someone – I forget who – suggested an alternative second-round pick, a linebacker from the West Coast. Assistant coach Woody Widenhofer saved the day. He stood up and said, "Look, this West Coast guy is a fine player. No question. But our defense, don't forget, is very, very sophisticated. Both of these guys will take a long time to learn it, but Lambert, while he learns, will be a heck of a player on special teams. The other linebacker ... I don't think so. Let's go for Lambert." Providentially, Widenhofer's logic prevailed.

I had fought for six years to keep our assistant coaches out of the draft process. Now at last I could see the merit in Noll's argument that pulling together was necessary. "Coaches, scouts, trainers, everybody, even the secretaries and equipment men ... we all have to work as a team," he would say. I remembered how an assistant coach named Walt Hackett insistently beat the drum for Moon Mullins in 1971. At tight end, the position he played for Southern California, Mullins was not a prospect. "Never mind that. He'll make an outstanding offensive guard," Hackett kept telling us.

At offensive guard, Mullins became a starter. He would continue to be a starter on our Super Bowl teams. I remembered how Don Heinrich encouraged us to draft Rocky Bleier in 1968. And how Dan Radakovich gave me so much support in my lobbying on behalf of Franco Harris. Maybe, after all, there were times when it paid to listen, regardless of the source.

The third-round pick we had traded brought us defensive tackle Tom Keating from Oakland. In the fourth round, as Haley and I had promised, we were able to get Stallworth. Selling our head coach on the idea that we could wait that long had been no easy task. "If he's not there," I said to Haley, "we're going to hear some screaming." When Stallworth fell into our clutches, I was not too polite to gloat.

So far, so good, I said to myself. Drafting twenty-first and without a third-round pick, we had timed the big auction perfectly. With our second fourth-round pick, the result of a trade with New England, we chose a defensive back from UCLA, Jimmy Allen. Jimmy Allen was a street kid from Watts, the black ghetto in Los Angeles. As remote as Watts is from the surfboard culture, swimming, rather than football, may have been his best sport. He was good enough, I had heard, to consider trying out for the U.S. Olympic team, but football punched his ticket to UCLA, where the long arms that propelled him through the water bedeviled pass receivers. He was tall and flexible, with a hawk's eye for tracking the ball and magnetized fingers for snatching it out of the air. And, by the way, he could also return kicks.

Allen's most striking personal characteristic was fearlessness combined with a hair-trigger temper, evident for all to see in the mess hall at St. Vincent on one of his first days in camp. He had taken his place at the table when Mean Joe Greene, the toughest Steeler of them all and the one most universally deferred to, reached out in a spirit of playfulness and grabbed something from Allen's tray – a shrimp, or a piece of fruit. Instantly, Allen lifted his tray and banged Greene over the head with it. Allen's lunch flew in every direction. He'd have mixed it up with Greene then and there except for the intervention of teammates. In any case, the rookie had served notice that he was not to be trifled with.

Allen was a part-time starter and a full-time contributor on the championship teams of 1974 and 1975. After the 1977 season, we traded him to Detroit, where he distinguished himself one year by intercepting ten passes. Eventually, the ghetto reclaimed him. In the 1980s I heard that he had dropped out of sight, a homeless vagabond.

Luck remained with us as the draft moved into the fifth round. We had rated two or three offensive linemen ahead of Mike Webster, but now they were off the board. That much conceded, luck played no part in the choice we then made. "Catching lightning in a bottle," someone called it. I disagree. Our decision to take Webster was the result of considerable spadework. After George Perles had mentioned him to us, we studied film and asked questions. For very long stretches of the next twelve years, Mike Webster was the NFL's most dominant center.

Distressingly, and for reasons I will not at the moment explore, he came to the same end as Jimmy Allen.

The first five rounds of the 1974 draft produced a result we could not have imagined. Of the five future Hall-of-Fame players in the draft, the Pittsburgh Steelers came away with four – Swann, Stallworth, Lambert, and Webster. Dave Casper, the Oakland Raiders' tight end, was the fifth. Chuck Noll pronounced it "a draft of exceptions." There was Swann, who was "too small and too slow;" there was Stallworth, a hidden jewel from a small agricultural school in the South; there was Lambert, whose "growth potential" raised questions; there was Webster, the unappreciated overachiever.

The credit for this draft does not begin and end with the scouting department. Dan Rooney and Jim Boston got the players signed. Chuck Noll and his assistant coaches brought out the best that was in them. Finally, as an old talent hunter once reminded me, I owe a debt to their "mamas and papas." Why did they grow up to be football players at all? Because they had the right genes. and, in most cases, because they had the right training at home. In football, as in the construction business, everything starts with the bricks and mortar.

Add-Ons

In the remaining rounds, we drafted sixteen players. Three of them – Jim Wolf, defensive end from Prairie View; Rick Druschel, offensive lineman from North Carolina State; and Charley Davis, defensive tackle from Texas Christian – survived the weeding-out process at St. Vincent and were with us for one season.

One season isn't much, but what a season it was. They suited up for a Super Bowl game, something to cherish for the rest of their days, something to tell their children and grandchildren. Twenty-five years later, at an anniversary celebration, I spoke with Druschel, a successful coach and athletic director in the Western Pennsylvania high school world. He expressed profuse gratitude to me and to Dan and to our entire organization for "a year that changed my life." It made me feel that scouting for the Steelers had been a worthy occupation.

We drafted still another player from North Carolina State in 1974 – Alan Sitterly, who had gone to high school at North Catholic. Our scout Tim Rooney told me a story about Sitterly. It seems that his coach at North Catholic decided one day that Sitterly's toughness needed testing. He tossed the player into his car and drove him to North Park. There, on one of the dusty back roads, he tied Alan Sitterly to the car's rear bumper and dragged him around the park for the next sixty minutes. Thus inured to the bumps and bruises of football, Sitterly more than held his own at North Carolina State.

It has been said that our 1974 draft was the best in the history of the NFL. And beyond the draft, there were free-agent signings of consequence. We had picked up two free agents in the 1960s who opened my eyes to a way of improving the team that required a lot of intensive bird-dog work, but was cheap. Both were from schools below the radar. Sam Davis, offensive lineman, had played at Allen University in Columbia, South Carolina; Jerry Simmons, wide receiver, came from Bethune-Cookman on the east coast of Florida. By the time that Chuck Noll was in charge, we were making a real effort to dig up more athletes of their caliber. Noll, I had learned, would spend as much time with promising free agents as with top-five draft choices. Exhilarated, I put my scouts on a year-round free-agent alert.

Noll didn't want any "stiffs" in camp – third cousins of front-office people, politicians' nephews, "friends of friends." We had moved away from cluttering St. Vincent with "nice-guy" candidates for the team. Pre-season practice was for prospects only, and this, on occasion, put AJR's nose out of joint. At his insistence, we'd be forced to make an exception now and then. He was the Chief, after all; he paid the bills. Moreover, every one of us had been guilty to some degree of bending the same rule. "Just this once," we would tell ourselves, and grant a tryout to somebody's kid, saving a friendship.

On a warm summer day in the 1980s, Kay and I were cooling off on the porch when a neighborhood kid named Peckish, like our son Art a former wrestler at Mount Lebanon High School, showed up. He also had wrestled at the University of Cincinnati and punted, he said, for the football team, and now he was proposing that I allow him to try out for the punting assignment with the Steelers. I admired young Peckish; he was as tough as old shoe leather, I had heard. But to punt for the Steelers was something else. I suggested reasons why Peckish would be wasting his time. And then Kay jumped in.

Right in front of the fellow, she called me "the meanest old coot" she had ever known. "Give the boy a tryout," she said. "It won't hurt anything, and he'll be better than those other hopeless cases you bring to camp."

Peckish got his tryout. Hard-edged from wrestling, he was in wonderful shape. Whether or not the coaches knew that Kay was his patron, they let him dress for the first pre-season game. It was at Three Rivers Stadium, and he kicked the ball once when the third- and fourth-stringers were on the field.

By the following afternoon his football career was over. He was free, as Noll always put it, to "get on with his life's work."

Several months later, driving to a restaurant one evening, Kay and I came to an unexpected four-way stop. Just ahead of us, a work crew was repairing the road, and we took our place in a long line of cars, Kay at the wheel of her big black Caddy. We were stuck for an agonizing length of time, inching forward slowly as a man with a red flag moved the cars through, one by one. Suddenly he caught sight of Kay. He approached us, smiling. "Hello, Mrs. Rooney, how are you?"

Only then did we recognize him: Peckish.

Vigorously waving his red flag, he held up all traffic for a minute, pulled us out of line, and sent us through.

Deluded would-be punters like Peckish turned up in camp every year. One of them, a young married man, had resigned from his job as the pro at a nearby golf club. How he obtained a tryout I never knew. He had a beautiful wife who came to watch him punt. While he chased his fantasy, she would stand by her parked car and gaze out over the practice fields, and her eyes would be full of affection for him. But then at times I would catch a look that betrayed the dismay she had to be feeling. The punter had no chance of making the team, and she realized it. "You crazy nut," she seemed to be thinking, "why have you walked out on a steady job and a decent paycheck for this?"

Greenfield Jimmy Smith's grandson, also named Jimmy Smith, was another of our undrafted free agents. I forget who his sponsor was – Billy Conn, perhaps. Billy was married to the grandson's aunt, Mary Louise. Young Smith had been a linebacker at Penn, in the Ivy League. He had the Irish pugnacity of his baseball-playing granddad, along with fiery red hair, but was not exactly NFL material. Few Ivy Leaguers then were, or now are. Young Jimmy was smart, and not without talent, and the coaches were willing to "get a picture" of him, as Noll used to say. "The question is," Woody Widenhofer asked, "will he be tough enough?"

During practice one day at St. Vincent, Widenhofer got his answer. One of our first-round draft choices, Baylor running back Greg Hawthorne, decided that the one hundredth and last kid invited to camp, an Ivy Leaguer in the bargain, could be pushed around, and he gave Smith a late bump. Then a second late bump. It was one too many.

Football fights are usually just pushing and shoving, and only an idiot would take off his helmet in order to fight, but the story I heard was that Greenfield Jimmy Smith's grandson flattened Greg Hawthorne. It may even be true. Smith never denied it and Hawthorne never talked about it. Noll, when I asked him one time, professed not to remember the incident. All he would say was that Hawthorne, a superior athlete who lasted five years with the Steelers, could have used some of Jimmy Smith's combativeness.

Jimmy did not make the team. Instead, he made money – as a banker. I ran into him once, I forget where. He still had his red hair, all of it. He was wearing a banker's blue suit with a red tie. "Jimmy," I said, "I got you that tryout, and you made me look bad by beating the crap out of my first draft choice." Jimmy smiled and said, "Thanks for the tryout."

In the space I occupied at the Roosevelt Hotel I received word one day that a lawyer had come to see me. Envisioning a lawsuit of some sort, I felt a small, brief tremor of apprehension. The man who presented himself might have been 35 years old. He was very good looking and unusually well dressed. "What can I do for you?" I asked. For an answer, he recited his curriculum vitae in a nutshell: college, law school, the bar exams, a job in a law firm. He was happily married with two children. Yet none of this had brought him fulfillment. "You see, in college I played football," he said. "And it was always my ambition to play for the Steelers. I've stayed in good physical condition, and I think I could help the team."

I spent the next fifteen minutes talking sense into the guy.

When someone applied for a tryout by mail, I never failed to answer. Recently I became aware that a letter of rejection I wrote in 1965 had turned up on eBay, the network auction site. It was written by hand; I did not yet have a secretary. As Kay pointed out, my penmanship back then was the same barely legible scrawl that it is today, but at least there were no misspellings.

Re-reading the letter, I looked for some trace of historical value. None was evident to me. The name of the person who had asked for a tryout did not at first glance ring a bell. Then I came to my closing sentence: "Drop by to say hello some day." Inviting these romantics to look me up was something I had resolved never to do. Why, in this case, I changed my policy I don't recall. This particular letter of application may have struck a chord with me. At any rate, as a result of my suggestion, a short, heavy-set guy in his early-to mid-twenties came walking into my office.

The first thing he said to me was that he always had been a big Steeler fan. I asked him about his background. He'd played college and semi-pro football in Ohio, he said. He spoke of his semi-pro team reverently, the way I had heard old-timers reminisce about the Canton Bulldogs and Jim Thorpe. He went on to say that he was also a wrestler and a judo expert, which had been an advantage to him in football. "Leverage, you know." He was sure he could help "turn the Steelers around."

"Well," I replied, hoping to discourage this kind of talk, "our roster is pretty well solidified, and, anyway, I don't know what kind of shape you are in, or how fast you are. We time our players now in the forty-yard dash. Speed in today's game is very important."

He understood that it was, he said. Being timed in the forty-yard dash was something he would welcome. "Let's go outside and get it done right now," he said.

I did a double take and saw that he was serious. He was proposing to run the forty-yard dash on Sixth Street, downtown, in street shoes, in the middle of a weekday afternoon.

Stalling, I said, "Gee ... it's hardly the time or place. There's too much pedestrian traffic ... "

"OK. But let me show you what kind of an athlete I am. That desk of yours ..." He was sizing it up. "I think it'll hold me. I'll do a squat jump from the floor up onto your desk. I'll do it ten times."

He was slipping out of his blazer. "Hey, wait a minute," I protested. "This desk isn't built for gymnastics. I'm afraid you'd wreck it." In truth, I was afraid he might wreck his knee or his ankle. With the promise that I'd get in touch with him later – in a few weeks, maybe – I persuaded this bulldog to be patient.

I never saw him again.

By the way, my letter on eBay was sold to the highest bidder for eleven dollars and six cents.

Part Five: Full Speed Ahead 1974-1980

Chapter 58

Jefferson Street Joe

In the eleventh round of the 1972 draft we took a young black quarterback from Tennessee State, Joe Gilliam. The main reason, as I recall, was that Bill Nunn kept insisting, "He's a steal."

Nunn had Chuck Noll convinced, too. Gilliam's father coached the defense at Tennessee State and was known for his football savvy. He had handed down a lot of it to Joe, we had heard. "Gilliam," Babe Parilli once told me, "is smarter than either Bradshaw or Hanratty." Parilli was the Steelers' quarterback coach and therefore qualified to judge, I suppose.

Not five minutes after we drafted Gilliam, my telephone rang. A football man I regarded as well informed was on the line with a warning. "Don't you know this guy's into drugs?" I let it go. With an eleventh-round pick, what did we have to lose? Gilliam wasn't getting big money. We could take a chance.

They called him Jefferson Street Joe, for the street that wended its way through the Tennessee State campus in Nashville. He was tall and thin and he played with a sort of devil-may-care flamboyance that seemed to captivate Noll, who discouraged such tendencies in Bradshaw. He moved around quickly in the pocket; he got rid of the ball quickly; he had a strong arm, good peripheral vision, uncanny anticipation.

Gilliam made the team, but spent his first two seasons watching Hanratty start when Noll was dissatisfied with Bradshaw. There were sports reporters who wrote that Gilliam's talent exceeded Hanratty's *and* Bradshaw's. They were half-wrong, anyway – Bradshaw was our best quarterback but the fact that he continued to struggle reinforced the belief that Noll should be using Gilliam.

By 1973, the Steelers' defense was among the best in the league. All the offense had to do was control the ball. Its overriding mission was: don't get the defense in trouble with too many interceptions. Ron Shanklin and Frank Lewis, a player we had drafted in 1971 for his speed, were top receivers. Franco Harris was a big, powerful, deceptively fast running back. In the offensive line there were quick-thinking men with quick feet. For Bradshaw, then, it should have been all so simple: give the ball to Franco; throw short, high-percentage passes, going deep only in rare situations; do those two things and let the defense kick hell out of the other guys' offense.

But to Noll's ill-concealed annoyance, Bradshaw was making it complicated. He appeared to be throwing passes blindly. As the interceptions multiplied, critics asked if by any chance he was color-blind, or needed glasses. An ex-coach said to me, "Everything on the field is a blur to Bradshaw."

Only Kass, Aunt Alice, and Mary the maid seemed to give him their unquestioning love. Even AJR began to have doubts. Meanwhile Gilliam, the third-stringer, was looking better and better to Noll.

When the players' union called a strike before training camp opened in 1974, Gilliam saw his opportunity. He was one of the few veterans who crossed the picket line. Surrounded by rookies and a scattering of older guys, marginal players in fear of losing their jobs, he performed with confidence and style in the early exhibition games, and he was lucky as well. Three of the incoming rookies, wide receivers Lynn Swann and John Stallworth and center Mike Webster, were earmarked for the Hall of Fame. Another rookie, Randy Grossman, would in time be the starting tight end. And Rocky Bleier was in camp, recovered now from his war wounds. Though he considered himself a defector, his striking teammates did not. They knew that after four years of painful rehabilitation, Bleier had reached the make-or-break point.

With four exhibition games left, the strike ended. Bleier hadn't broken. Swann and Stallworth had established themselves, foreshadowing the ultimate departure of Shanklin and Lewis. Rookie Jack Lambert at middle linebacker and rookie Donnie Shell at strong safety had made the defense even more frightening. And Terry Bradshaw no longer was the No.1 quarterback. Joe Gilliam had replaced him.

Along with the other veterans, Bradshaw had to feel some bitterness toward Gilliam. Did they use the word "scab" in referring to him? I don't know. What I do know is that Bradshaw went back to his religious roots. In college, he had belonged to the Fellowship of Christian Athletes and was youth director at his Baptist church. Even earlier, he felt called upon to enter the ministry, but decided in the end that God would rather have him play football, as he expressed it. Now that he wasn't playing at all, he consulted God once more through the scriptures. He carried around a Bible almost constantly, looking into it whenever he could. He would come by himself, Bible in hand, to the stadium every morning and lift weights. No later than 8 o'clock he would be in the coffee room, wearing sweats. After drinking a cup of tea – Constant Comment – he would head for the field and throw passes to anyone he could find, usually ground-crew workers or front-office people. "Run as fast and as far as you can, and I'll get the ball to you," he would tell them, and off they would go. He reminded me of Johnny Unitas in Olean.

During our mornings in the coffee room, I felt I was learning what made Bradshaw tick. We never were pals, but I frequently spoke with his parents and I knew his three brothers at least casually. Craig, the youngest Bradshaw, was a quarterback at Utah State in the late 1970s, and one day Terry asked me – just kidding, or maybe kidding on the square – not to write Craig off without taking a look at his scouting reports. I assured him I would do as he asked, but when I took up the matter with Noll, his reaction was: why bother? We weren't going to draft Craig, he said. I answered, "No, we're not. But I gave my word to Terry. Let's look at the reports." And we did.

The Houston Oilers drafted Craig, but kept him for only one season.

Terry by then - the late 1970s, remember – was a certain Hall of Famer but still having problems with Noll. In the weight room one day I was watching some of the younger players work with barbells when Terry came up and stood next to me and started talking about his coach in the most unflattering terms. They were oil and water, these two, incapable of understanding each other. Terry believed, erroneously, that Noll disliked him, which made it mutual, he said. As he spoke, he kept his eyes on the weightlifters. So did I, but my attention was focused on Terry's diatribe. When he had finished, I said, "You know, Terry, I haven't gotten along with Noll myself. I don't worry about it, though, because we're here to do a job, and with players like you, we've won big. Because of that, people really think I know what I'm doing. Try to look at your own situation the same way. You're a great player on a great team. That's the important thing – getting a job done, being part of it. Whether we like our boss or not is beside the point. Furthermore, whatever you might think, Noll's not a horrible guy. He's just tough."

Bradshaw had listened in silence. Now he said, "See ya later" – that was all – and drifted away. I was left with the impression that my attempt at imparting wisdom had been a failure.

Some time later, I caught him being interviewed on television one night. The interviewer was asking about the team, about Noll, about the Super Bowls he had played in, and Bradshaw's answer left me dumbfounded but gratified. He repeated, almost word for word, everything I had told him in the weight room.

But the rift between Terry and Noll lasted for years. After his retirement, in fact, Bradshaw nursed a grudge against the Steeler organization as a whole and the entire city of Pittsburgh, a grudge that lasted for years. Launched on his second career, that of broadcaster, motivational speaker, pitch man, comedian, and movie actor, he never came near us. He boycotted player reunions, he refused to accept honors and awards. During much of that time, we have learned, he was suffering from clinical depression. And then, declaring bygones to be bygones, he returned for a testimonial dinner, a lovefest attended by most of his surviving Super Bowl teammates and by Noll. It was Bradshaw who had made the first move, and he of course was the star of the televised reconciliation. He gave a virtuoso performance, by turns sappy and droll, flippant and serious, plain-spoken and sentimental. As a student of acting, I had always seen in Bradshaw this talent for show business. I am glad it has served him well.

Lucky Strike

The NFL players' union called it a "work stoppage." Our fans, Western Pennsylvanians, were more concise. They had a word for what happened that went back in history, a word that went back to the railroad riots of 1877 and to Homestead in 1892. The word was "strike."

Nobody died, nobody bled. The players' union, after negotiating for weeks with the club owners in that summer of 1974, turned down their proposals for a new collective bargaining agreement. A peaceable boycott of the training camps followed. Peaceable or not, the fans didn't like it one bit.

How could these "pampered athletes" hold out for more money? They were lavishly paid (the fans thought) for playing "a kids' game" six months a year. The argument that football is a dangerous occupation, that football players risk serious injury, was unacceptable to Western Pennsylvanians. And why wouldn't it be? Coal miners and steelworkers risk serious injury and worse. The fatality rate was higher and the wage scale lower than in the NFL. So *gittahta* here, the fans said. In bars and on talk shows, the players' defenders were few.

When the training camps opened, the union miscalculated fatally by allowing the rookies to report. Imagine the plumbers' union calling a strike and letting the plumbers' apprentices go to work. A scenario just as unlikely was playing out in the NFL. While the veterans picketed, the rookies who came to camp were trying to take their jobs. And many of these rookies could play. That is why they'd been drafted or signed as free agents. They were not quite finished products, but they were getting there.

Our own rookies, it turned out, were the best of the lot. Draft scholars – the people with strange one-track minds who devote their entire lives to studying and analyzing and researching this subject – still say that our 1974 draft never has been surpassed.

On the first day of camp, the veterans set up their picket line at the entrance to our training facilities. The AJR who had dealt with his players face to face would have talked them into moving away from the main gate by appealing to their common sense and loyalty. But now things were different. The pickets included "union representatives" – agitators, some called them. We turned the problem over to our downtown law firm. That we could do this was entirely because of Dan. He had replaced Fran Fogarty with a team of accountants, and he had replaced lawyer Owney McManus, Jr., the son of AJR's longtime crony, with what amounted to a legal department of our own – after considerable soul-searching, I should add. Invoking arcane labor laws and, for all I know, the Constitution of the United States, our counselors got the picket line transferred to an unpaved farm-to-market road that wound its dusty way through corn fields and a cemetery to the back door of St. Vincent College. From then on, there was absolutely no contact between the strikers and the pared-down football team, or, for that matter, the front-office people and coaches.

Chuck Noll, in public, was stoic and noncommittal. "I try very hard not to worry about things I can't control," he would say in response to questions from the media. On the subject of the absent veterans, he would say, "I can only coach the players who are here." And coach them he did. When Noll could coach – that is to say, teach – he was never happier. With a camp full of rookies, he could teach to his heart's content. The veterans, as far as Noll was concerned, had ceased to exist. Out of sight, out of mind. There was work to be done (two-a-days in the hot sun, weightlifting sessions, flexibility drills); there were meetings to be held – meetings with the players, meetings with the assistant coaches, meetings with the scouts. From all appearances, Noll and his coaches had gone to football heaven.

We were well prepared for the strike. Along with our draft picks, we had signed an unusually large contingent of free agents and walk-ons, giving the coaches enough players for full-scale practices. Most of the other teams, it was clear, had taken the threat of a boycott less than seriously. The decision to go ahead with the pre-season schedule, using rookies and any veterans who crossed the picket lines, took them by surprise. Caught shorthanded, personnel directors went looking for bodies.

The Steelers' only need was at quarterback. Woody Widenhofer had sold us on drafting Frank Kolch, a marginal prospect from Eastern Michigan, one of Woody's coaching stops, but after showing up for the indoctrination get-together, he refused to sign a contract. Perhaps he knew that we needed arms. So when Jim Trimble, a scout for the New York Giants, called and asked if we had a running back we could spare - the Giants were desperate for one - we sent them Doug Kotar, a rookie free agent, in exchange for a quarterback named Leo Gasienica. Kotar was from Canonsburg and had played at Kentucky. In letting him go, we presented the Giants with a back who served them well until a brain tumor seven years later ended his football career and his life. And Leo Gasienica? In the short term, he helped to alleviate our quarterback crisis but is chiefly remembered for something else.

It was late at night when he reported to camp, and my cousin Tim had to find him a place to sleep. There happened to be a dormitory room with two beds and only one occupant - another rookie, Tim supposed - and that was where he stashed Leo. Morning came. Leo woke up first. He went to the lavatory and showered and shaved. When he returned, ready to dress for the day, his roommate was up and moving around. The first thing Leo noticed about him was his age. He must have been 60 at least. "This is no football player," Leo realized. He then did a double take. At Rutgers, Leo had majored in literature. "Hey, I've seen you before - your picture, anyway," he blurted. Then it came to him.

"You're James Michener! I've read your books!"

The best-selling author was doing research for a scholarly work about the cultural role of sports in America. Upon meeting him earlier in the week, AJR, who had *not* majored in literature at Indiana Normal or Georgetown or Duquesne, had taken him for an ordinary "newspaper guy."

Assigned by Bill Nunn to room with another player, Leo demurred, asking if he could stay with Michener. "It's as close as I'll ever get to a famous writer," he explained. And with Michener's enthusiastic approval, the arrangement continued for as long as Michener remained at St. Vincent.

Besides Leo, there were two or three others in camp who could at least throw the ball, and we had some promising receivers: John Stallworth, Lynn Swann, Randy Grossman, Nate Hawkins, Reggie Garrett. Those last three, under different circumstances, might have been more appreciated. Chuck Noll had nothing but praise for this crew. The only real quarterback, though, was Leo. And then, unexpectedly, Joe Gilliam reported to camp, breaking ranks with the strikers, and our troubles were over.

This was the same Gilliam who had made an impassioned pro-union speech at the outset of the strike, excoriating management. It appears that after giving the matter some thought, he had seen on which side his bread was buttered. Noll watched him throw and was visibly excited. He walked with a light step on the first day Gilliam practiced. And Bill Nunn, who had scouted Gilliam and recommended him to us, was all smiles.

Gilliam's sharp passing changed the tenor of the workouts, and Gasienica's presence kept him from wearing out his arm. Stallworth and Swann were going deep for the first time and making beautiful over-the-shoulder catches. Not only Nunn and the coaches were pleased. The other scouts, ecstatic, couldn't believe their eyes. "Did you see that?" they were asking one another. Training-camp blossoms often die with the first frost, but this new fleet corps of receivers looked like hardy perennials.

(With defensive backs Jimmy Allen and Donnie Shell putting hits on them, life for the receivers wasn't easy. Jack Lambert's Kent State teammate, tight end Gary Pinkel, made a good catch one day, and then, *wham!* A killer hit by either Allen or Shell - here, again, my memory fails me — knocked him senseless. The crash could be heard from one end of the practice field to the other. Up went the cry for first aid — "RALPH!" — and out trotted Berlin, pumping his bad knees. Just for the record, Pinkel did not make the team. In another end of the business, he did make it, becoming a good assistant coach at the University of Washington and elsewhere.)

Someone else in camp who could throw a football was Lionel Taylor, the receivers coach. Taylor had a drill in which the receivers would form a circle around him. Picking up footballs from a collection at his feet, he would fire them at the players. He would go clockwise to start with, and then throw passes randomly, so that no one could tell whose turn it might be. From time to time he would call out a warning: "Keep your eyes on the ball, not my face." With either hand, he would throw hard passes and soft passes, behind-the-back passes and between-the-legs passes. He could put a tight, perfect spiral on the bail or make it travel end-over-end, like a placekick. His dexterity was amazing; it reminded me of the Harlem Globetrotters' famous Meadowlark Lemon and his sleight-of-hand tricks with a basketball.

A player who muffed a pass dropped out of the circle. When only three or four players were left, the competition became intense. The eliminated players would cheer for their particular friends, creating a hubbub. At last it would come down to Taylor and one survivor – often enough, but not always, Stallworth or Swann. It might be Grossman, it might be Hawkins, it might be Garrett. It might even be, and this was not out of the ordinary, an unknown free agent. Draftee or long shot, the last man would stay on the firing line until one of Taylor's passes eluded his grasp. Or until Taylor himself, soaked with sweat after fifteen strenuous minutes, called an end to the drill.

I tried to guess, as I watched Joe Gilliam, what Bradshaw and Hanratty were thinking. How resentful did they feel? Gilliam's – what would you call it, naked opportunism? – must have rankled. Noll did not say so, but I could sense that Gilliam had moved ahead of Hanratty and now was the second-string quarterback. Then came the first pre-season game, and after Noll and the other coaches had made their evaluations, there could not be the slightest doubt: even Bradshaw's job was in jeopardy.

"Pre-season game" was the new terminology. The league's marketing geniuses had decided that "exhibition game" conveyed the wrong message. Football was serious business now. We were charging the same price in the pre-season as in the regular season, combining both sets of games in one inseparable ticket package, and how could you ask the fans to dig that deep for "exhibitions"? In the second place, or maybe the first place, the television networks were voicing concern. The networks had to think about ratings. And that word "exhibition," was a turnoff, the networks believed. Who would tune in to watch an "exhibition"? Not as many viewers as profitability required. So there was general agreement that the word wouldn't do. Orders went out to eradicate it. None of which meant that in "pre-season games" the coaches would not pull their starters very quickly and let the players on the fringe compete for jobs.

A Very Good Year

Some teams, I believe, thought the strike would be settled before the pre-season games got under way or that the pre-season schedule would be cancelled. The picketing players held to this view, I am sure. But on July 27, the annual Hall-of-Fame game took place as usual at Canton, Ohio, the officially designated birthplace of professional football. From St. Vincent, I watched on television as the Cardinals and Bills, traveling by bus, approached Fawcett Stadium. The whole thing resembled a military operation. Police cars escorted the buses and stood watch at the overpasses. Helicopters looked down on the side roads for union members lying in wait with sabotage in their hearts. But nothing happened. There were no disruptions. When the Cardinals' rookies kicked off to the Bills' rookies (or it may have been the other way around), I knew there would be a pre-season.

The Steelers' first game was with the Saints in New Orleans. Joe Gilliam was spectacular, and, as AJR used to say in his race-track vernacular, we won going away, 26-7. Back in Pittsburgh, we trounced the former Monsters of the Midway, the Chicago Bears, in front of a large, enthusiastic crowd. The Steeler aerial circus, with Gilliam once more the ringmaster, ran up the score. It stood at 50-21 when AJR got up from his seat looking embarrassed and sought out his old friend George Halas to apologize. "But Dad," his sons reminded him, "what about all the times that Halas did the same thing to us?" AJR took a savage bite out of his cigar. "Aw, you wise guys ... you ... you just don't get it," he growled.

We understood this much: the Steelers' image was improving. Fast. For two years in a row, Chuck Noll had put us in the playoffs. And now the early success of this makeshift team of rookies and retreads was attracting favorable attention. As I had learned to expect, much of it rubbed off on the family. After the Saints and the Bears, we played the Eagles. In Philadelphia. Where our race-track operation had not been well received by the power structure. Initially, the Main Line bluebloods had been disposed to regard us as agents of Davey Lawrence, the evil, conniving political boss whose object in life was to grind them under his heel. Worse, even, than being interlopers, we were hoodlums and racketeers. Not any more. AJR had become "Mister Rooney," no longer a shady character but a "sportsman," welcome now in the most elevated circles. "Funny thing," he said thoughtfully. "Wherever I go around here, people are asking me all kinds of questions. What do I think of this, what do I think of that. As if I was some guy whose opinion mattered, a guy with the inside dope. And you know something? I'm starting to give them answers."

Our newly acquired popularity had its drawbacks. All of our friends wanted tickets to the game. Free tickets, of course. And not just any free tickets, but good ones. The job of satisfying their demands fell to Jim Boston and Dan. I was glad, once again, to be the scouting director.

Buffered by the return of the veterans – the union had given in and the strike was over – we won from the Eagles in overtime, 33-30, and Gilliam was still the big story. Every night on the talk shows you heard the admonition: Bradshaw had better watch out. One fine old veteran, linebacker Henry Davis, didn't last long. Davis lost his job to Jack Lambert and was cut. Other experienced players who were kept on the roster found themselves suddenly demoted. To his evident chagrin, Bradshaw was one. The unwritten rule that an injured player kept his starting position did not, as far as Noll was concerned, apply here. It was one thing to be hurt, something entirely different to strike.

The next game we played was with the Giants, and there were scouts all over the place. I could guess what they were thinking: *The Steelers have too many good young players. They can't possibly keep all these guys. And who knows? Maybe Gilliam will be available. He's too good to be a number three.*

Our game with New York was a 17-7 win. Against the Giants' regulars, Gilliam performed as brilliantly as he had against rinky-dink defenses. We beat the Redskins in Washington, 21-19, and the Cowboys in Dallas, 45-15, for a 6-0 record. Gilliam was still the ace. He had played every minute on offense, and now, for the first time ever, we had finished the pre-season undefeated. It would happen again, often enough, but never with such an overabundance of rookies in the lineup. Six of those rookies plus Rocky Bleier became starters on Pittsburgh teams that won Super Bowls. They were Swann, Stallworth, Grossman, Webster, Lambert, and Shell. To paraphrase some lyrics from an old Frank Sinatra tune, 1974 was shaping up as a very good year.

The Only Thing

My scouts and I, although buoyed by the success of our young players in the pre-season garnes, kept reminding ourselves that it didn't mean a whole lot. Pre-season results can be misleading.

So we were not uncontrollably euphoric. We thought we had a playoff team, yes. After winning a division title in1972 (our first in forty years) and landing a wild-card berth in 1973 despite some truly inopportune injuries, we expected something similar in 1974. The playoffs were now a sort of benchmark for us, and of course I felt good about it. This was my tenth year in the scouting department; I had shown that I belonged, that I was not just the owner's son, an undeserving rich kid. The respect I had wanted from my peers was coming to me now, along with words of caution from tutors like George Young. "Arthur," George said to me once, "you have done well. But please remember — the only real prize is the Super Bowl. And getting to the Super Bowl is not enough. You have to *win* it."

The gospel according to Vince Lombardi. Chapter and verse. Winning isn't everything, it's the only thing.

Looking back, I still don't see how we managed to go all the way. The players' strike helped us by hastening the development of our rookies, but it also created a huge problem — the quarterback controversy that was almost the team's undoing. Joe Gilliam's arm strength and pizzazz, so evident from his first day at St. Vincent, seemed to have Noll entranced. Bradshaw, consigned to a backup role, couldn't believe what was happening. He sulked and popped off to the media. Hanratty, the new low man on the totem poll, accepted the situation dispassionately. Aware of his limitations, Hanratty was content to be the backup to the backup.

In 1974, we did not yet realize that Bradshaw suffered from clinical depression. Knowing about it, we could have dealt more understandingly with his moodiness and his juvenile behavior. That he did not completely blow his cork was due not only to his reliance on Holy Writ but to AJR's influence, I thought. AJR studied people the way he studied race horses. He talked with Bradshaw, listened to him, kept him from forcing a showdown with Noll.

The first game of the regular season, at home against Baltimore, was a 30-0 win. So far so good for Gilliam. Next, it was off to Denver, where Gilliam's exposure to the thin mountain air seemed to bring on an attack of giddiness. He forgot that, with Franco Harris, we had a powerful running game, and he never stopped throwing passes, too many of them caught by the guys in the wrong uniforms. We should have won easily; instead, we were lucky to get a tie. The score was 35-35 after a fifteen-minute overtime, the limit back then under the rules.

Inevitably, Gilliam was now the focus of talk-show debate. Noll's assistant coaches had questions of their own. "Damn it, anyway," one of them grumbled, "we can't throw away a victory like that." The subject came up in meetings with their boss. George Perles and others lobbied for a shutdown of the aerial circus. "Those interceptions can kill you," they said. "Control the ball with the run."

The Oakland Raiders came to Pittsburgh and shut down both the aerial circus and our running game. Oakland 17, Steelers 0. Making his third start, Gilliam couldn't get the offense in gear. Still Noll kept him at quarterback, a move that paid off in road wins over Houston and Kansas City. Then at home against Cleveland, Gilliam misfired on thirteen of his first eighteen passes, and Noll replaced him with Bradshaw. We won the game, 20-16.

After that, no one knew whether Bradshaw or Gilliam was the starter until Noll made up his mind with the season nearly over. Let me just say that Bradshaw won out in the end by subordinating his ego. Gilliam threw far too many passes, and they were deep passes, mostly. He was hell-bent on showing off his arm. Bradshaw gave the ball to Franco and threw medium-distance passes to his agile receivers. Bradshaw kept the defense off the field, adding to its effectiveness as the best defense in the league. After the Cleveland game the Steelers beat the Falcons and the Eagles, with Bradshaw now the starter, but lost at Cincinnati, and once again it was Gilliam's turn. Wins over Cleveland and New Orleans followed, but then we lost to Houston, 13-10, and that was the end for Gilliam. Noll reinstated Bradshaw with the promise, "I'm sticking with you for the rest of the year, no matter what happens."

What happened was that the Steelers won their last two regular-season games, knocked off Buffalo and Oakland in the conference playoffs, and, in their first trip to the Super Bowl, overpowered Minnesota, 16-6. The defense put pressure on Fran Tarkenton, intercepting three of his passes and deflecting four others. Franco Harris, meanwhile, rushed for 158 yards, a Super Bowl record.

I never have figured out whether Gilliam started on drugs – hard drugs – before Noll benched him or afterwards. We knew that in college he had used marijuana. As a Steeler, no doubt he continued to use it. He remained with the Steelers through the 1975 season, nothing more than a supernumerary until the meaningless final game. Bradshaw was banged up and the Steelers had their divisional championship won, so Gilliam relieved him against the Los Angeles Rams on the road. At once it became apparent that he was high on drugs. Noll took him out, and he never again played in the NFL.

His life after football was that of a junkie. He died at 50 of natural causes brought on by his addiction.

Not the Howling Type

After the win over the Vikings in the Super Bowl game in New Orleans you'd have thought that AJR, instead of Franco, was the MVP. In the locker room, where he accepted the championship trophy from Commissioner Pete Rozelle with television looking on, the print reporters scrambled to get near him. He was irresistible copy, the lovable loser transformed into a winner at the age of 73. The reporters threw questions at him. They were smiling and laughing, reveling in the occasion and all but ignoring Dan.

AJR, wearing his overcoat, a yellow cashmere polo shirt buttoned at the neck, and a checkered woolen cap brought back from Ireland by Tim, was affable but poker-faced. The reporters kept asking him how he *felt*. Unexcitedly, he said he felt good. The reporters weren't satisfied. They wanted emotion, they wanted exuberance. "Well, at the end of the game," one of them prodded, "did you let out a little howl?" AJR explained that he wasn't the howling type. "If you were standing alongside of me at the race track," he said, "you wouldn't know I was betting." The reporters were acting nonplussed. The millions watching on television ate it up.

Later, talking with friends, the Chief unburdened himself. He said, "It may not look like it, but I'm every bit as happy as a guy who hollers and whoops and jumps up and down. I just hoped I could get through this without starting to cry."

A lot of other people had started to cry – people in the television audience. As unlikely a sentimentalist as mean old Bear Bryant had tears in his eyes. Coach John McKay of USC told me so; he watched the game with Bryant. I know that more than a few stragglers in the Sugar Bowl were blubbering.

My description of the locker-room scene is gleaned from the accounts of it I have heard and read. I had watched the game from the stands, and for some time afterward I remained there with Mom, Kay, Jack Butler, and Bernadette, Jack's wife. New Orleans in January can be as frigid as any Northern city, and Mom, shivering, said she could use a shot of whiskey. From out of nowhere, bottles and flasks appeared. On this day, anyway, the Pittsburghers in our vicinity were not going to let Mrs. Arthur J. Rooney feel the cold.

A confession: I had learned from my sixteen years of Catholic schooling never to try to barter with the Lord. But I bartered with Him in the fourth quarter. "Let us win this game," I proposed, "and I'll give up ..." Give up what? An image of the Chief came to me. Ah! Cigars! "I'll give up cigars," I said to the Lord. "For a month." And I kept my word.

Bud Carson, our defensive coordinator, said after the game that he had looked for me at the trophy presentation. Then in words I have never forgotten, he continued, "If any one guy deserved to be in that locker room, it was you." I told him that, on the contrary, I thought I belonged with Kay. "Making up for all the time I spend on the road every year." Bud Carson had nothing to say about that, but I can tell you what Kay's reaction was. "Well, sweetheart," I said as the final minutes of the game ticked away, "wasn't it all worthwhile?" Looking beautiful in her mink coat, she turned the question over in her mind. It didn't take long. Flatly and firmly, she answered, "No."

The Kipling Ideal

From the Sugar Bowl, all of us returned to our hotel in the Latin Quarter. As AJR was about to enter his suite, his bodyguard, 6-foot-3, 270-pound Joey Diven, said, "Just a second, Mister Rooney," and flung himself through the door like an undercover narcotics agent leading a drug raid. One by one, he gave the sitting room, the bedrooms, and the bathrooms a quick eyeball job. No interlopers were lurking under the beds or behind the shower curtains. The Chief didn't know what to make of all this. As puzzled as the rest of us were, he was staring at Joey.

"Mister Rooney," Joey explained, "I wasn't worried about crooks or bad guys. It's those crazy fans. So many of them want to shake your hand I thought I'd better check the place out. To be on the safe side."

AJR's ticket for the game dangled from his lapel. He tore off the ticket and flipped it onto a desk. Picking it up, I asked if he wanted me to save it for him. He did not. The ticket was marked: "Super Bowl IX. Official. Art Rooney." A week or so later, I asked him again if he'd like to have it. He said no, I could keep the darned thing. "Would you sign it?" I asked. He took a pen from his pocket and wrote "Art Rooney" on the ticket. Back in Pittsburgh, I had it sealed in plastic.

Not long afterward, I gave this memento to a doctor, Frank Reda, who had taken care of Kay. Thirty years went by. The doctor was now an old man. One night when Kay and I attended a party at his house, he gave us a look at his curio cabinet. And there, among his precious possessions, was AJR's Super Bowl ticket.

The Chief's apparent lack of emotion after the game carried over into the victory celebration, a large but private gathering in the ballroom of our hotel. There was absolutely no change in his demeanor. I thought of Kipling's famous verse:

If you can meet with Triumph and Disaster
And treat those two impostors just the same ...

Well, then, according to Kipling, you're a man.

I doubt if AJR was a really devoted reader of Kipling, but he embodied the Kipling ideal. In victory or defeat, in good times or bad, there was never the slightest difference in the face he presented to the world. His claim that if you stood right next to him at the race track you wouldn't know if he'd made a bet was accurate. More than once I had seen him win a hundred thousand dollars on a single race and give no sign of elation or even satisfaction.

But now as we made our way to the victory party, he could not help looking pleased. For the first time since the end of the game he was smiling ... letting his humanity show.

I wondered if Kass was responsible. Had she told him to lighten up? She was capable of it, certainly. But on reflection I think it was just the sense that he had of knowing exactly how to behave.

Chuck Noll's reaction to the game was similar to AJR's, and Chuck's wife Marianne resembled Kass in the way she conducted herself. They were cheerful, but low-keyed. Neither the owner nor the coach was a back-slapper.

At one point in the evening, Chuck and Marianne came to our table and asked if they could join us. Kay and I were with Mom and Dad. "Sure, sure. We'll make room. Sit right down." Noll's chair, as it happened, was next to mine, and a funny thing happened. Here was the man who had taken our team to the pinnacle of football a few hours earlier, and I could not find the power to speak. I was tongue-tied. Struck dumb. Don't ask me to explain it. I can't.

Most of us went to bed early that night. At 5:30 a.m., we'd be leaving for the airport. At 6:45 a.m. I'd be thirty thousand feet above the ground and thinking very hard about the 1975 draft.

All Hail

For the trip to New Orleans with sixteen of his friends, Mike Kearns had rented a big mobile trailer. I don't know the route they took. I don't know who drove. I don't know when they left Pittsburgh or how long it took them to get to their destination. I asked Mike only one question: "Was anyone in the expedition sober?"

At least two of the travelers were – a young man named John Clayton and his mother. They will reappear in this narrative later on. Mike Kearns himself was among the imbibers. It was his last real alcoholic fling. He gave up drinking shortly afterward, cold turkey, and never again swallowed a drop.

Mike's luggage on the trip included a huge cardboard sign reading: "A.J. Finally Has His Day." He took this sign into the Sugar Bowl and kept it under wraps, I don't know how, until the outcome of the game was no longer even slightly in doubt. Then he broke through security and got down onto the sidelines and, holding the sign aloft, circled the field. He was wearing a steelworkers' hardhat, which he had painted black and gold. Rising from its crown was a battery-powered, spinning red light. All the television cameras recorded Mike's one-man victory parade for the viewers back home.

The initials "A.J." referred, of course, to the Chief. Every Pittsburgher understood this, and many others in both the crowd at the game and the television audience could deduce as much from the context of the message on the sign.

A bigger, more boisterous celebration awaited us all the next day. As soon as our plane, dubbed Steeler One, landed at Greater Pittsburgh Airport, we were herded into buses. Along the Parkway West, between the airport and Downtown, it seemed that every inch of space was packed with cheering, waving Steeler fans. Car horns were blowing in the outbound lane of the Parkway. In the distance, we could hear the whistles of railroad trains. Our escort of fire trucks and police cars sounded their bells and sirens.

In the press of humanity there were small children, teenagers, fathers, mothers, and grandparents. Thousands among the tens of thousands wore black and gold, and thousands fanned the air with Terrible Towels. Conceived, designed, and popularized by broadcaster Myron Cope, the black and gold Terrible Towel was the Steelers' new battle flag.

The day was cold and bright, with some snow on the ground. When our buses emerged from the Fort Pitt Tunnel, we entered a black and gold sea. Daredevils were hanging from the girders of the Fort Pitt Bridge; people were massed in an unbroken line between the exit and Market Square. They screamed, they shouted, they lifted clenched fists above their heads. It was Rome welcoming Caesar back from the wars. And we were part of it, every one of us – not only the coaches and players, but the scouts, the trainers, the equipment men, Dan, Jim Boston, Ed Kiely, Joe Gordon, the secretaries and, most of all, AJR. He was having his day and then some, smiling and waving but at all times keeping his composure. As for Kass, I can only say she was beaming.

In Market Square, the coaches and players climbed up onto a platform and surveyed the noisy, ebullient throng. Cope, the master of ceremonies, called Chuck Noll to the microphone and demanded an ovation. "All hail the Emperor Chaz!" he cried out, and the Emperor's subjects broke into a roar. The celebration continued with speeches and ovations for the stars of the game. At last the platform emptied, and slowly, reluctantly, the worshippers dispersed. It would be six months before the coaches and players returned to Latrobe, and I know they could hardly wait. And neither, to be honest, could I.

Prize Catch

On the 1974 Steeler team that defeated the Minnesota Vikings in the Super Bowl there were five undrafted free agents. Five may not seem like a lot, but it's an extraordinary number, believe me. Remember also that nine of the players we drafted that year were with us all season. Probably no team before or since ever went to a Super Bowl with fourteen rookies.

Ray Mansfield and Sam Davis in the offensive line, Rocky Bleier in the backfield, and linebacker Andy Russell were the only significant leftovers from the Buddy Parker and Bill Austin regimes. The 1974 team was almost entirely put together by Chuck Noll through the draft, a few trades, and free-agent signings.

Two of the free agents – Reggie Garrett, wide receiver from Eastern Michigan, and Dickie Conn, safety from Georgia (and no relation to Billy) – played very little. Marv Kellum, linebacker from Wichita State, was not a starter but contributed. Randy Grossman, tight end from Temple, became a starter eventually. In 1974 he was our go-to guy in tough-yardage situations. He could track the ball, separate himself from defenders, and twist his body into unbelievable shapes to make a catch. His hands were like grappling hooks. If the ball came anywhere near them, it was his.

After eight years with the Steelers, Grossman got into the investment banking business full-time. Intelligent and affable, he rode the economic boom of the 1990s to a successful career. AJR, foreseeing how well he would do, always said, "They'll never have a tag day for Randy." (Tag days were once a staple of Pittsburgh's downtown civic life. Awarded a tag day by City Hall, a charitable organization would post collectors on every street corner to hand out lapel tags in exchange for donations.)

Our prize free agent in 1974, and, along with Jack Butler, one of the two best free agents the Steelers ever signed, was Donnie Shell. In his four years at South Carolina State, an all-black school in the lowlands near Charleston, Shell had had two head coaches, a man named Banks and a man named Jeffries. Both had praised him to our scouts, using nearly identical words: "He'll knock a ball carrier's jock off." He was also, they told us, a high-class individual.

For a linebacker, Shell lacked size. He was only six feet tall, or a little over, and 205 pounds. In the NFL he would have to be a defensive back. Bill Nunn tried to get him on our draft list, but without success. The transition from linebacker to safety would be "too tough," everyone said.

In the draft, there were no takers for Shell. Afterward, as in previous years, Nunn headed South with a briefcase full of contracts and blank checks. His job was to sign draft picks and free agents in the area, including Shell. None of us, except possibly Nunn, held out much hope for him, but Noll, we knew, was a brilliant developer of talent. Given the athleticism Shell possessed, and his reputation for being coachable, there was always a chance.

Shell signed, as we expected he would. Then fate took a hand. Just before training camp opened, the players' union called its strike, and the rookies had the place to themselves, opening the door for Shell. In short order, he proved himself to be a top special-teams man while developing into a very good defensive back.

In many ways Shell reminded me of Jack Butler. Both were free agents who had played college football in the sticks, so to speak. Butler, like Shell, was a "projection" – a defensive end and receiver at St. Bonaventure but a defensive back in the eyes of our coaches. Both he and Shell were hard hitters.

I remember a ferocious hit Shell delivered on the Houston Oilers' powerful fullback, Earl Campbell. The Steelers were playing Houston in the Astrodome in 1978. As Campbell bulldozed his way through the line, Mean Joe Greene got a piece of him. Campbell managed to stay on his feet, but was slightly off-balance when Donnie Shell came up fast from the secondary. Dipping his hips, he exploded "under and up." It was a textbook rising blow into Campbell's neck and jaw. Knocked flat, the NFL's most punishing runner was through for the day. I had seen Mike Ditka make a pass reception and shake off four Steelers who had climbed onto his back, an unforgettable Hall-of-Fame play; I had seen the hit Chuck Mehelich put on Leon Hart; but nothing that ever happened on a football field is more vivid to me than Shell's hit on Campbell.

Butler, in a nine-year career, had fifty-two interceptions; Shell had fifty-one in thirteen years and many more games. Butler played in four Pro Bowls, Shell in five. The fact that Shell made it to four Super Bowls, as against none at all for Butler, doesn't mean a thing. It was Shell's good fortune to have exceptional teammates; Butler came along at a time when the Steelers were also-rans. Like Butler, Shell remained in football after his playing days, a front-office executive with the Carolina Panthers.

Barefoot Boys

There was a time in the early 1970s when our trainers, to make things easier for themselves on road trips, taped the ankles and feet of the rookies before we left the hotel. They would then be able to give the veterans more attention at the game site.

I remember an incident in an Alabama hotel during John Stallworth's first year. Bob Milie and Ralph Berlin were taping the rookies in the lobby. Walking through on my way to the team bus, I caught sight of Stallworth, alone and half-hidden in a corner by the door.

I stopped and asked why he was not with the other players, who were clustered around the trainers some distance off in an open part of the lobby.

He glanced at his bare feet and told me politely that he would prefer not to be seen in so public a place without shoes on.

"I don't want to look like I'm from Alabama," he added.

I said, "Hey, it's no big deal. All of those other barefooted guys are being taped over there in full view. And, anyway, you *are* from Alabama."

"I know it," Stallworth answered. "I just don't want to *look* like I'm from Alabama."

An unimportant happening that told me a lot about Stallworth. His sensitivity was a trait I admired.

Stallworth became a successful businessman, the president and CEO of an information technology company based in Huntsville – Huntsville, *Alabama*. The firm had 650 employees with offices in nine cities and yearly revenues way up in the millions.

Chapter 59

Too Much Too Soon

Late in 1974 our Philadelphia lawyer, John Macartney, apprised the Rooney family of a business opportunity that had nothing to do with football.

Macartney had worked out a deal that would give us an excellent chance to acquire the Avis Rent-a-Car company. Avis was then a subsidiary of the International Telephone and Telegraph corporation, which had somehow run afoul of the anti-trust laws. The courts had ordered IT&T to divest itself of certain holdings, Avis chief among them. And IT&T had to get this done by a certain date; otherwise, outside receivers would take over Avis.

From our point of view, the timing could not have been worse. The "certain date" would coincide with the Steelers' preparations for Super Bowl IX. But Macartney wanted us to think very hard about branching out from football and horse racing into other entrepreneurial ventures.

He had talked to "the right people" at IT&T, he confided, and had found them receptive. He said that AJR's reputation for integrity was already well known to these movers and shakers. Macartney, who was also a mover and shaker, had set up the necessary financing with the same banks that had handled our Yonkers Raceway acquisition, and AJR was his hole card.

For estate-tax reasons, AJR himself would not be officially involved in the transaction. If everything fell into place, ownership would reside with his five sons and Macartney. By this time, Macartney was one of the Chief's "boys," as my father always referred to my brothers and me. No one believed for a moment, of course, that AJR would not have a key role to play.

Macartney belonged to the exclusive Sailfish Club in Palm Beach, and all of us met there with the general manager of Avis. I've forgotten this gentleman's name, but he did not come across as an "old-money" guy. Rather, I deduced that he had made his considerable pile the old-fashioned way, by earning it. Still, there was something Ivy Leaguish about him. "Did you dig that fellow's suit — classic

Brooks Brothers," said Pat to me after the meeting. "It might be ten years old or six months old. Doesn't show its age."

Like Macartney, this man was low-keyed and focused. He knew what questions to ask us, and he knew what the answers ought to be. Mainly, he was interested in our intentions. Were we determined to keep Avis in business? AJR quietly made it clear that we did not have a hidden agenda.

I remained perfectly silent until the confab was winding down. Then I mentioned to our inquisitor that I had been using Avis cars for years and that my dealings with the company had been very satisfactory. On his part, there was no reaction to this until I went on to say that as the head of the Steelers' scouting department I rented Avis cars in the spring, fall, and winter, and even on summer vacations now and then. I pinpointed the cities and towns where the Avis service had been good and also some places where the service had been not so good. When I observed that most of the company's young female employees were ladylike and attractive, and added that the turnover rate among them must be high because of their desirability as marriage partners to the young, single, upwardly mobile businessmen who travel in rented cars, the Avis man broke down and laughed. Up to then, and we'd been talking for three hours, he hadn't cracked a smile.

"That's an inside thing at Avis," he said. "The young ladies we hire do tend to be pretty. And they do get to meet successful young businessmen. But more often than not they end up marrying the guys who deliver the cars."

My playful little digression was an ice-breaker. Since I was such a good friend of Avis, this very professional higher-up continued, he would send me a special credit card.

He kept his word, and one time when I used it, an Avis station manager said to me, "Hey, where did you get this? Are you some kind of VIP?"

The way things turned out, our meeting at the Sailfish Club led to nothing. With the Super Bowl coming up, we didn't have time to make a concerted pitch for Avis. Macartney stayed hot on the deal and kept telling us it was far from dead, but we just couldn't give it our full attention.

In the lobby of our hotel in New Orleans on the day before we played the Vikings, my brother Dan told me Macartney had called. "He said, 'If you mean to go through with this, you have to do it now. Tomorrow at the latest, or Avis will be in the hands of a New York law firm acting as receivers or controllers.'" In Dan's opinion, all we could do was hold off. AJR had waited forty years to be in a championship game, and the Avis deal would take "too much away" from his moment. I said, "I agree. The Super Bowl is more important to Dad than Avis."

Just then I heard myself being paged. It was Kay. She said, "Get up here to the room right away. John Macartney is on the phone and desperate to talk to you." When Macartney and I spoke he repeated his words to Dan. I then repeated what Dan said to me and what I said to him. Macartney answered, "I thoroughly understand. But please believe me when I say we can get Avis now. Next week we'll be dealing with an outside controller."

Tim, Pat, and John looked at this dilemma the way I did, the way Dan did. The Super Bowl came first. We told Macartney to hold off, and sure enough, the court turned Avis over to an outside controller, a New York law firm.

A month or so later, Macartney invited me to New York for a meeting with the head of this firm, who turned out to be a stuffed shirt. After we had cooled our heels in his waiting room for a while, he listened to Macartney's proposal. "We have enough money. Our business concept is good," Macartney assured him. The stuffed shirt was completely unresponsive.

During our wait for the meeting, I had noticed a collection of elegant model railroad trains in a big glass case. I asked the receptionist about them. The law firm, she explained, was the outside controller for a railroad that happened to be in financial trouble.

I said, "Oh? How long have you been the railroad's controller?"

"About fifteen years."

As Macartney and I left the stuffed shirt's office, I nodded in the direction of the model trains, reminded John of my conversation with the receptionist, and said, "I don't think these people will be in any hurry to let us take Avis off their hands."

I was right about their way of operating. They held onto the reins for many years, and we never came close to getting another smell of the deal.

"How much," I once asked Macartney, "would Avis have meant to us money-wise?"

He said, "Oh, if we had held it for just a couple of years, with the old guard at Avis running the business – if we had held it for two years and then sold it, the six of us – you and your brothers and I – would have made at least a million dollars apiece."

Winning that first Super Bowl had its price.

Standing Up to the Chief

Something else important in the strike year of 1974 took place on the administrative side of our business. My brother Dan became much more active in league affairs.

The players' union had been gaining strength and giving ownership a lot to think about, and one thing that helped Dan when it came to dealing with labor problems was the legacy of AJR. Going all the way back to the 1930s, AJR's reputation with the players was that of a straight shooter. Joe Krupa, the one-time Steeler Pro Bowl tackle who joined my scouting department on a part-time basis after his playing career was over, summed it up for me one day. The trade that sent him to Los Angeles in the mid-1960s heightened his appreciation of the time he had spent in Pittsburgh, he said. Los Angeles was a first-class operation, but Krupa found the personal touch lacking. "Your father," he said, "always treated me like a friend. With Mister Rooney, you always knew where you stood." Dan wisely built on that trust; he knew where the players were coming from and would listen when they voiced their concerns.

Like Tim, Dan spent more time with AJR than I did, or than the twins did. Dan's link to the Chief was the managerial responsibility they were sharing; Tim's was their mutual interest in the horse racing business, local politics, and the stock market.

At standing up to the Chief, Tim was braver, even, than Dan. Tim's arguments with the Chief never seemed to end until the Chief told him, "Get out of here!" Tim would then disappear for a while, but he always returned to the wars. "He has a hide like an elephant," said John (or maybe Pat). "He can take what the Chief dishes out and come back for more."

I held Tim in awe. The thought of displeasing the Chief terrified me. When I was unlucky enough to cross him, I retreated to my office or hurriedly arranged a scouting trip. In my dealings with AJR, with college coaches, and with NFL general managers, I wanted no trouble. I wanted above all to be liked. With Noll and his assistant coaches, and with anyone who got in my way when I was trying to do my job, I could take off the gloves. I surprised even myself at how roughly I sometimes treated Noll. I couldn't figure Noll out. My verbal attacks on him seemed to make no impression. He actually thought I was too diffident, too unassertive. "Polish up those brass balls," he would tell me.

As good as the advice was, I just couldn't bring myself to slug it out with the Chief. "Artie doesn't talk to me," the Chief would say to my brothers. It was true. I seldom did. But I listened to him, and I listened to him closely.

Folk Hero

The start of AJR's elevation to folk-hero status is hard to pinpoint. Perhaps it went back to a luncheon he gave at the Allegheny Club before the Steelers' first football game in Three Rivers Stadium.

He was saying thank you to the people who in his opinion got the stadium built – the politicians, the bankers and lawyers, the newspaper editors and broadcasting executives. The main speaker was Howard Cosell, the newest television celebrity. Due in no small measure to his obtrusive personality and crisp judgmental attitude, Monday Night Football on the ABC network was attracting a larger audience every week. Ed Kiely, I assumed, had been responsible for his presence on the dais. Kiely had a way with the media stars from New York. His goal was to make the whole country aware of AJR, and to make the country aware you first had to make New York aware. Home-town coverage of the Steelers could meanwhile take care of itself. In Kiely's view, the local writers and broadcasters had no need of a P.R. guy to feed them information and attend to their every wish. They were being paid by their employers to do a job. Let them do it.

Whoever persuaded Cosell to be on the program, granting that any persuasion was necessary, the words he spoke were his own. He spoke in his familiar New York staccato, high-pitched and nasal. He spoke with authority, and he spoke of AJR in terms that were almost effusive.

The public up to then had known the man called the Chief as the owner of a chronically unsuccessful football team and some race horses that didn't amount to much. He had bet on more winners than would ever come out of his Shamrock Stable. But Cosell now spoke of him as "one of America's most distinguished sportsmen," deserving of honor, a man who had turned down every chance to name his own price for moving the Steelers to some other town. Pittsburgh was where they belonged and Pittsburgh was where they would stay. Such loyalty, Cosell went on, put the money-hungry baseball owners to shame. To the shakers and bakers in the Allegheny Club that day, this was a new way of looking at AJR. Perceptions were being changed almost tangibly. You could feel it.

Four years earlier, the speakers at his sixty-fifth birthday party were preaching to the choir when they showered AJR with accolades, and even in that audience you had his mother attempting to keep everybody's feet on the ground. Using Father Silas as her mouthpiece, she reminded the crowd of mainly long-time friends that AJR was "not yet a saint."

Canonization, or something very nearly like it, would come later, in stages. Cosell's talk was the beginning; the Immaculate Reception – the miraculous catch and run by Franco Harris that won a playoff game with the Oakland Raiders – greatly accelerated the process; the first of the four Super Bowl championships, and the televised presentation of the Lombardi Trophy, with AJR looking humble and almost sad instead of elated, set his transformed image in concrete.

During the bad times, the public used to believe that the Steelers lost because AJR wanted them to lose. Losing was less expensive than winning. It kept the payroll within bounds. Every Steeler failure, every Steeler defeat, was AJR's fault. But in the 1970s all of that changed. The Rooneys weren't dumb or cheap any more, and AJR, as I have said, was a folk hero, a folk hero so accessible that anyone at all, it seemed, could walk past Mary Regan, his personal secretary, barge into his office, and settle down for a conversation.

A cub reporter from the *Pittsburgh Press*, 24 years old, recorded his first impression of AJR. "There is something captivating," he wrote, "in meeting so great a man with so little sense of his greatness." Another young sportswriter said it was like visiting Mount Vernon and finding George Washington still in residence. Not only did the great man welcome you like a friend, you learned that he knew your uncle or your grandfather and could tell you a funny story about him.

Now and then the rumors linking AJR to the rackets resurfaced. At a New Year's Eve party, a local business executive was talking to me with a drink in his hand. His friends in New York, he said, regarded AJR as a "mystery man." Here in Pittsburgh, he went on, he had heard that mob money financed the Steelers and the racing stable. I held my tongue, even though his, loosened by liquor, was flapping irresponsibly.

Somebody else, an old retired guy who had married into money, cornered me at another gathering. He and his friends, he confided, just knew that AJR had made his money on the fringes of the law. He then revived the shopworn accusation that AJR had saddled Pittsburgh with losing teams as a cost-control measure. Next, in the belief that he was giving me a compliment, he said the Steelers had started winning in the 1970s for one reason only: because Dan and I were calling the shots.

Politely, but coldly, I said it surprised me to hear a purported gentleman spreading such mischievous gossip. His wife, who was listening, looked hurt. I felt sorry for her, mainly because she was stuck with this viper until one of them died.

There were times when it seemed that everybody in town had the lowdown on AJR. A retired North Side police detective told Rob Ruck that AJR was in the numbers business. Even Kay's dentist spoke of this as a fact. During my courtship of the beautiful redhead, he shared his information with her parents. AJR, he assured them, was the "numbers king" of Pittsburgh, raking in one thousand dollars a day. Not long after our marriage, Kay reported this to me. With a straight face, I reminded her that one thousand dollars a day, or three hundred and sixty-five thousand a year, wasn't much when you considered the overhead.

It is true that AJR had friends and maybe relatives who were numbers men, but he was not in the business himself. He told his sons he was not, many times, and I believed him. He was in the slot-machine business and he never denied it. He and Milton Jaffe operated the Showboat, where you could gamble illegally and buy liquor illegally, and there was never any secret about it. If he indeed had been in the numbers business he'd have said so, without hesitation.

For his book about AJR called "The Chief," Jim O'Brien interviewed Frank Bolden, entertainment editor and later city editor of the *Pittsburgh Courier*. Bolden referred to numbers writers as "digitarians." It was more respectful, in his opinion. As to whether AJR had been a digitarian, Bolden considered it unlikely. The reason people thought so, he explained, was AJR's association with Senator Jimmy Coyne. In Coyne's organization, there were digitarians, all right, but AJR wasn't one of them. Bolden seemed to be positive about that.

Rob Ruck's North Side police detective may have come to a different conclusion. During my freshman year at North Catholic High School, a teacher asked a silly-sounding hypothetical question: "Is it a sin to break a numbers writer's pencil?" At supper that evening I posed the same question to Dad. "Of course it's a sin," he answered emphatically. "Some good men write numbers for a living. They have to take care of their kids like everyone else."

AJR believed that human beings are weak by nature and that attempts on the part of government to legislate morality always fail (Prohibition comes to mind). People will gamble, he said, no matter what. Consequently it was better to have a lot of small-timers writing numbers on their own than for one powerful crime boss to be soaking up all the cash. When crime became big business, the corruption of elected officials was certain to follow.

In my civics classes at North Catholic High School and St. Vincent College, theories such as this were never discussed.

The snobs who liked to insinuate that AJR's fortune came from the numbers underestimated his prowess as a horse player. The fights he promoted gave him an income for many years, and in the 1970s television revenue and sellouts at Three Rivers Stadium turned the Steelers into a money maker. Shamrock Farm, a hardscrabble, no-frills place, probably didn't pay for itself, but whatever losses there may have been were negligible. Fran Fogarty, you can be sure, took advantage of every tax-saving opportunity. Overall, the racing operation more than broke even because AJR knew how to bet.

According to Pat Livingston, AJR made his money in the Chicago grain market. I disagree. He had one big score in soybean futures, but the grain market wasn't something to be counted on. By the time he was in his seventies and eighties, the football team and our race tracks – Liberty Bell, Yonkers, and the Palm Beach Kennel Club – kept the wolf a long way from the door. His days as a plunger were over.

My brothers Pat and John, as adults, often said that AJR got the best out of life. Everything he wanted, he had – the football team, the boxing club, a hideaway horse farm where females did not intrude, his own stable of thoroughbreds running at nearby tracks, the jockeys in Shamrock silks, the horses named for particular saints and for his friends, not all of them saintly; pals like Kies and Father Jim Campbell to hang out with; brothers like Jim, for all his faults, and Father Silas; a great wife who believed him when he told her the Depression hadn't ended; five sons he put through the Catholic educational system from grade school to graduate school (no Ivy League costs there, and we all stayed out of the pokey). Never less than one hundred cents for every dollar he spent. On a higher plane, faith in God. And almost everybody loved him.

Who could ask for anything more?

Don't Kid the Kidder

Nineteen seventy-two was the year of the Immaculate Reception and the year of AJR's de facto canonization. Overnight, Pittsburgh embraced the Steelers and their suddenly popular owner. Forgotten were four decades of almost continuous ineptitude. Under Chuck Noll the Steelers had started to win, and there were no more losing seasons until 1985. The public's scorn gave way to a Terrible Towel-waving giddiness. Steelermania was born. And though the fans could appreciate Noll, and though they knew, or at least were told, that Dan was responsible for bringing him here, and though a few sportswriters mentioned that the scouting department had helped put the pieces together, the accolades went to AJR.

Reviled for so long as a bumbling loser, he was now unexpectedly a civic treasure, a man who had weathered the bad times with fortitude and grace, never losing heart, refusing all inducements to move the franchise. Sometime in the late 1960s, thanks mainly to television, professional football had supplanted baseball as the national pastime, and the Steelers were now the champions of the

NFL. In the glare of the television lights, AJR gave a virtuoso performance. He was always himself, plain-spoken, humble, and unaffected. He had a down-to-earth type of charisma, he connected with everybody, high or low, and America ate it up. All over the country, sportswriters and broadcasters – on cue, it almost seemed – were calling him as though with one voice, "the most beloved figure in sports."

His humility and unaffectedness were real, but let there be no mistake – he liked this new perception of himself. His wife knew it; his sons knew it; Ed Kiely knew it. My brothers and I caught on slowly; Kass was never fooled for an instant.

Of course, when she heard that Johnny Laughlin, Aunt Margaret's husband, had referred to AJR as a prima donna, she sprang to her husband's defense. "Prima donna, is it?" she said, sounding like the Maureen O'Hara spitfire character in "The Quiet Man." "Coming from that one! Everything he has he got from Art." But she saw very clearly, and his sons gradually learned, that the accusation was not totally false.

We are all prima donnas in the sense that we want recognition and approval. It was obvious to me from my scouting work that even the greatest football players need a certain amount of praise. It's a universal trait. AJR simply happened to be adept at masking this need.

When Pat Livingston or Ron Cook of the *Post-Gazette* or someone from out of town wrote a favorable newspaper story about him, he read it with evident enjoyment. When he expected to be on television, he watched. One night at the supper table, as the 6 o'clock news came on, he demanded silence. He'd been filmed that day with Governor Dave Lawrence and Mayor Joe Barr at the funeral of an important politician, and their exit from the church was shown twice – the second time when we were having dessert. "Wait!" he ordered us, putting a stop to the table talk. "Here it comes again." But we were much more interested in Mom's great apple pie. He pushed back his chair and jumped to his feet in a swift athletic move not often seen in an overweight fellow nearing 60. "Well, if you people don't care about this, I'll watch it myself in the front room," he said as he stalked to the door.

He was passing up a slice of the best apple pie ever baked for his cameo appearance on the news.

As soon as he was out of hearing range, we looked at one another and laughed. Even Kass was amused – something rare. It was her habit at such times to remind us that, collectively, we would not make a patch on our father's ass. (Kass rarely sugarcoated anything.) This was one night she kept quiet.

"Don't kid the kidder," AJR always said, and though his foibles entertained us, we were careful not to let on. We felt we could recognize his human failings with no loss of respect. There was genuine affection between us, and yet we were not a demonstrative family. AJR was a Rooney. His love for Kass and his love for his "boys" – that was what he called us, his "boys," never his sons – did not have to be constantly proclaimed. We were sure of it, as Kass was. His brothers, except for Dan and Tom, might have wondered at times where they stood. He loved them all, I believe, including the three reprobates - Jim, Red, and Vince.

When I was in New York City studying drama, AJR would come in from Pittsburgh. We would meet at his hotel and go to Moore's Restaurant in a taxicab, an exciting trip through the night-time sounds and sights of Manhattan. One night on our way to the restaurant he suddenly reached over and took my hand, an overtly intimate gesture so uncharacteristic it shocked me. I was 23 years old; I thought, "My God – he's dying! Or, no – Mom's dying! He's getting ready to tell me. Or, wait – maybe it's Aunt Alice who's dying. Or else – could it be? – he's lost the Steelers."

But we finished our ride without speaking, and then he released my hand. It was over – for me, an uncomfortable experience. And it was never to happen again.

Yankee Doodle

From 1921 through 1964, the New York Yankees won twenty-nine American League pennants and almost as many World Series championships. In 1964, a television network, the Columbia Broadcasting System, bought the team. It made no sense, except that owning the New York Yankees was a can't-lose proposition.

The Yankees had two inherent competitive advantages – the biggest fan base and the biggest TV market. Their minor-league farm teams routinely delivered an endless supply of talent to the parent club. When age caught up with Babe Ruth in the 1930s the Yankees had Lou Gehrig; when Gehrig passed on just a few years later, they still had Joe DiMaggio; when DiMaggio turned up lame at the outset of the 1950s, Mickey Mantle was ready. The Yankees' pre-eminence seemed as permanently fixed as Manhattan Island itself. Then the ownership of the team passed to CBS, and everything changed.

Overnight, the Yankees stopped looking like a dynasty. Instead of winning pennants, they were thrashing around in the second division. In 1966, before the two major leagues split up into divisions, they ignominiously finished tenth. Improvement after that was only marginal, and, by 1974, CBS wanted out.

It could not be admitted, of course, that the difficulties of operating a baseball team were more than the network's top brass could handle. After all, CBS had its image to think about. The official line, therefore, was "conflict of interest." CBS was in the news business as well as the entertainment business; to get rid of a team it "reported on" became necessary "for the good of the game."

And bringing it off without fanfare was desirable. Quietly, somebody from the network got in touch with AJR. He was now a man of acknowledged prestige and integrity. Years of picking winners at the race track – and of not picking coaches who were able to win football games – didn't make you an "American sportsman." It took a Super Bowl victory, televised and publicized and celebrated as never before, to do that. The owner of the football team that won the Super Bowl was deemed worthy of owning a tradition-rich baseball team like the Yankees.

"Make a legitimate offer for the ball club, and it's yours. You'd know how to run it," he was told.

The Chief spent some time in deep thought. Would his background as a horse player make such a venture controversial? Until John Galbreath bought the Pirates, baseball had been off-limits to anybody connected with a sport whose lifeblood was the parimutuel window. And Galbreath made his living in real estate, not at the race track. Owning thoroughbreds was his avocation. If he ever placed a bet – and who could doubt that he had? – it was not as a professional gambler. AJR, as everyone knew, had built his fortune on gambling.

There was also the NFL rule against owning more than one major sports franchise. You could not own two football teams in the same league. You could not own two football teams in competing leagues. You could not own a football team and a baseball team, or a basketball team, or a hockey team. You could own a football team and a racing stable, but the NFL preferred that you did not.

AJR wore two hats, but he was careful about donning a third one. Milton Jaffe, his old business partner, approached him once as a representative of the casino owners in Las Vegas. How would he like to be the commissioner of gambling out there? There'd be a lot of money in it and also a lot of power, Milton promised. AJR turned him down. "I'm a Pittsburgh guy," he said. "And I'm a football guy." He wasn't tempted.

Neither did the offer to buy the Yankees interest him for long. It never got out of the conversational stage.

Later, the Chief second-guessed himself. "I didn't use my head," he told me. "I had three boys" – always, we were his "boys" – "who weren't involved in football. I could have bought that team for Tim, John, and Pat."

The price tag on the Yankees was six million dollars, a pittance. When John Macartney learned that the Chief had taken a pass, he shook his head. "We could have borrowed six million from a small local bank," he lamented. Not long afterward, George Steinbrenner, a filthy rich shipbuilding impresario, bought the Yankees. He paid, as I recall, eleven million dollars. By the turn of the century they were worth well over a billion.

Postscript: Sometime during the late 1960s, Tim and I had dinner one night with AJR at Toots Shor's restaurant on 52nd Street. AJR left us money enough to pay the check and went off to take care of some business. Shor carne to the table, said that dinner was on him (he insisted), and called for his car. We were going to the ball game, he said.

The game was at Yankee Stadium, where we were ceremoniously ushered to a V.I.P. box. An attendant served hors d'oeuvres, and though we protested that we were not at all hungry, having so recently finished our dinners, Shor wasn't listening. "Both of you bums eat something," he said, using the epithet he reserved for friends, friends of friends, or relatives of friends. "Act like this is a big deal."

After watching us force down the snacks, he took us on a tour of the private boxes and introduced us to people whose names he was sure we would recognize. "Meet Art Rooney's boys from Pittsburgh," he'd say.

For the Yankees, these were the lean years, and the occupants of the boxes made up a large share of the crowd. Tim and I, adept at counting heads, thought that no more than three thousand paying customers were present. Shor seemed to read our minds. In a barely audible voice, he muttered, "CBS has really screwed this up. Now, I ask you, how could anybody screw up the Yankees?"

We watched a couple of innings and returned to the restaurant. It was my first and last visit to the House That Ruth Built, which I also like to think of as The House That Art Rooney's Boys From Pittsburgh Almost Fell Heir To.

Chapter 60

Overcoming Oakland

Traditional rivalries come and go. From the 1930s into the 1960s, geography ordained that the Steelers' bitterest rival would be the team at the other end of the state, the Philadelphia Eagles. When Jock Sutherland's Steelers had a shot at the Eastern Division title in 1947, it was the Eagles who beat them in a playoff game.

Mostly, however, the Philadelphia-Pittsburgh rivalry was for blood, not championships. There was a game at Forbes Field in 1954 so ferocious that it left both teams badly crippled, destroying their seasons at the halfway mark. Although the Steelers came out on top, 17-7, they lost their quarterback, Jim Finks, with a fractured skull and a fractured jaw. Various other Steelers, notably guard Dale Dodrill, who took an unmerciful going-over from Philadelphia's Bucko Kilroy, ended up in the trainer's room with injuries almost as severe. The Eagles had a casualty list just as long. Conspicuously missing from it was the indestructible Kilroy.

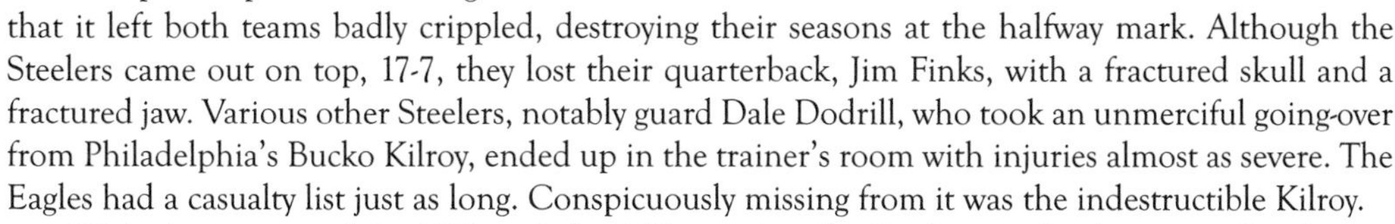

With the merger of the NFL and the AFL, putting the Steelers in the American Conference and the Eagles in the National, the rivalry died. Cleveland became the team the Pittsburgh fans chose to hate. Pre-game and post-game brawls between Pittsburgh fans and Cleveland fans resulted in more mayhem than anything that happened on the football field. The rivalry with the Browns has persisted, in a way, but with much lower intensity since Art Modell, who owned the Cleveland franchise, moved it to Baltimore, filling a vacancy created when the Baltimore owner moved the Colts to Indianapolis. For a couple of seasons there was no team in Cleveland. The league then brought forth the expansion Browns, who were too weak, at least in the beginning, to be thought of as anyone's deadly enemy. And the original Browns, transformed into Baltimore Ravens, don't arouse the same passions as they did wearing Cleveland uniforms.

Rivalries in professional football can't be shuffled around, or arbitrarily called into existence. Paul Brown was so dominant a personality that as coach and general manager of Mickey McBride's new All-America Conference team in 1947 he selected the uniform colors and agreed to the nickname — Browns — suggested by a fan. His accomplishments and renown, as much as the cultural resemblances between Cleveland and Pittsburgh and their accessibility to each other by automobile, gave our rivalry with the Browns its special cachet. But when Modell, weary of playing second fiddle to Brown, unceremoniously fired him, and Brown became the owner and coach of a startup team in Cincinnati, the Bengals, not much of his name's magic rubbed off. As far as Pittsburgh was concerned, the Bengals were just another opponent. Their games with the Steelers at Three Rivers Stadium drew capacity crowds, but only because all Steeler home games drew capacity crowds.

Paul Brown had a cold formality that not even the Chief could penetrate. The Chief was affable toward Brown, but had to work at it. George Halas, George Marshall, the Bidwills, and other owners were friends. Brown was never more than a respected business acquaintance.

This absence of a close relationship embarrassed the Chief once in a California airport. It was back before the days of credit cards. AJR paid for everything by cash, whatever it was, and he always carried several thousand dollars in his kick. On this occasion, after an NFL meeting in Los Angeles, he discovered that he was carrying less than one hundred. His traveling companions, Ed Kiely and Fran Fogarty, couldn't help. They were running almost on empty; when you traveled with AJR, money was not a necessity. But this time the Chief had broken his own rule, which was never to be caught with "short paper." By his own extravagant standards, one hundred dollars and change would not get the three of them back to Pittsburgh. And their flight was about to take off. What could he do?

Looking around the airport, he spotted Paul Brown. There was no other choice. He would have to approach Brown and ask for at least two hundred bucks. It would not be like going to Halas or Marshall or Charley Bidwill or Milton Jaffe. For favors, you went to your pals, and Brown was not exactly a pal. In truth, he may have been nobody's pal. The Chief tried to imagine what Brown would be thinking about these unpolished, unsophisticated Pittsburgh guys. Nothing irked the Chief more than to be taken for a rube, for a greenhorn right off the boat. But, with an effort, he swallowed his pride. "Hey, Paul ..." It must have been excruciating to put that request into words.

"Brown was real good about it," the Chief told me later. As far as I could make out, he did not see the incident as humorous. I thought it was like the time he mistakenly poured vinegar on his pancakes and pretended he liked them that way. To admit the truth wouldn't do. It would be humiliating. Taking money from Brown was humiliating, too, all the more so because the Steelers, in their rivalry with the Browns, were the underdogs then, just as they had usually been with the Eagles.

By the 1970s, when the Oakland Raiders were up there with the Browns as the team we most wanted to beat, as well as the team our fans most wanted us to beat, the situation was different. The Raiders had great teams, yes, but so did we. In Buddy Parker's time as coach, we could beat the great teams now and then. After Chuck Noll had the players he wanted, our chances were never worse than even.

The man who built the Raiders brick by brick was Al Davis. Like Paul Brown in Cleveland and Cincinnati, he controlled the entire operation, including every insignificant detail. Like Brown, he was a student of the game, whose knowledge did not derive from first-hand experience on the playing field but from sharp observation. Ted Dailey, one of the ends on the 1933 Steeler team, was a coach at Syracuse University when Davis attended school there. "He came to practice every day, just to watch," Dailey told me. "And he watched with an eagle eye." After graduation, Davis applied for a high school coaching job. "You know, a lot of guys named Davis played football here," Dailey went on. "What Al did, he wrote on his application that he was 'Al Davis of Syracuse.' In his interview they asked if he was *the* Al Davis of Syracuse. And he finessed it. He didn't say yes and he didn't say no. That was clever. He got the job."

Cleverness served him well wherever he coached from then on. One place was The Citadel, in South Carolina. "Al was just an assistant," said a scout I knew, "but you'd have thought from the way he talked and the way he acted that he ran the whole show." It led to better job offers elsewhere.

Davis was from Brooklyn, but he picked up his Southern accent at The Citadel. A Southern accent is for some reason one of a football coach's most valuable assets. Players from the South find it reassuring and Northerners imitate it.

Along with his Southern accent, Davis picked up organizational skills. He knew how to put a team together. Chuck Noll had coached with Davis in the AFL and said he was not to be underestimated.

The guy was a fitness freak. He brought his barbells with him to league meetings, and I saw him a time or two when he was bare from the waist up and wearing sweatpants. He was fairly tall, about 6 feet 1, and moderately well-built.

AJR "kind of" liked him, or did until Davis began to sue the NFL whenever he wanted to move his team from Oakland to Los Angeles or vice versa. After that, the Chief would say, "You know, there is something sinister about Al." Davis used to wear a black leather trench coat, and AJR once said to him, meaning no harm, "You look like one of those storm trooper guys in that coat." Davis was Jewish, and he told AJR later on that the remark had been hurtful. AJR said, "Gee, Al, I'm sorry. I never thought about that."

AJR looked with favor on the coach Davis hired in the 1970s, John Madden. I liked him, too. Madden was from California, but he reminded me of guys I had played with at North Catholic. In college, he'd been a defensive tackle of barely enough promise to be signed by the Eagles. He spent an entire season on the injured-reserve list and made the best of a bad situation by studying game films. Norm Van Brocklin, the Eagles' veteran quarterback, noticed how focused and intent Madden was, and gave him a lot of useful advice.

When Madden went into coaching, he never had played a down in the NFL. During the off-season, he worked as a sporting-goods salesman, and somehow this added to my good opinion of him. It was what a regular guy would do, I said to myself. Jack Butler had sold cemetery lots between seasons. I was happy for Madden when Al Davis made him the head coach of the Raiders, but I wondered at the same time how he would ever manage to survive. Already Davis was known as a hard man to work for. He was a martinet, a second-guesser, a tyrant.

Madden did more than just survive. He thrived; he won championships; he made it to the Hall of Fame. I credited Al Davis with brilliance for having picked so successful a coach.

It was during Madden's time with the Raiders that our rivalry grew discordant, even violent. On the evening before a playoff game at Three Rivers Stadium, a Raider tight end, returning to the hotel from somewhere, roughly pushed his way through several dozen Steeler fans who were gathered near the entrance. He may have given some lip to a Pittsburgh cop assigned to the job of keeping order. At any rate, the cop used his billy club on the player, hitting him upside the head and heaping fuel on a raging inferno. When the Raiders played in Pittsburgh or the Steelers played in Oakland, there was always the threat, sometimes acted upon, of fisticuffs or worse.

The football teams were evenly matched. In the 1970s and early '80s, the Steelers and Raiders split even in ten games. One year the Raiders beat us to go to the Super Bowl; another year, we beat the Raiders to go to the Super Bowl.

After a Monday night game we had lost to the Raiders by three points, I sat with Dan and Danny Ferens, our No. 1 numbers cruncher, in the Oakland press box, motionless. We were not sore losers, we were stunned losers. Sportswriters passing our seats offered condolences. "Tough one," they'd say. "Get 'em next time." We were giving our well-wishers one-word answers. Don Meredith, the former Dallas Cowboy quarterback who was doing commentary on the Monday night broadcasts, said hi as he passed us, but stopped and turned around after taking a few more steps. He walked back and stood in front of us and said, "It's all over, boys. They're not gonna play any more. You may as well pack it up." With that, he continued on his way once again.

Dandy Don's summation had broken the spell. All three of us started to chuckle. We slowly got to our feet and went to the locker room.

On the night before our playoff game with the Raiders in 1974, I attended a big party in an Oakland hotel, everything paid for by the NFL. I was with a fair-sized contingent from Pittsburgh, but the Oakland mob outnumbered us by at least ten to one. Their whole organization seemed to be present, from the guys who picked up jockstraps in the dressing room to Al Davis himself. It was while talking to an Oakland scout at this party that I realized how overconfident the Raiders had become. The scout was Al LoCasale, Davis's administrative assistant. Davis was Big Al and LoCasale was Little Al. He was short, gruff, smart, talkative, opinionated, "a bit of a rogue," as my brother Tim's friend, Father Duggan, characterized him. "We have a problem," this scout was telling Tim and me. "We can take only so many people to the Super Bowl, and it's gonna be tough to leave the others behind. A lot of people have worked hard all year and deserve to go. But we can't take them all."

I saw the disdain Oakland felt for us in such an unwary admission, but let it pass. Tim's reaction was more like outrage. Until LoCasale had left us, he held his tongue. Then he said, "That little friend of yours, saying, 'Who can we leave behind?' Those S.O.B.'s think they have the game already won. I'll tell you what. If *we* win tomorrow ... not *if* we win, but *when* we win ... we'll take everybody on our payroll."

He paused and then added, "Like 'Giant.'"

I was mystified. I said, "What do you mean, like 'Giant'?"

"'Giant,' the movie," Tim explained. "Remember the movie about the Texas oil people? With Jimmy Dean? Liz Taylor? Rock Hudson? Remember how they flew to the big party in Dallas? Remember all those planes coming in at the airport? We'll do the same thing. We'll charter a bunch of planes and take everybody we can think of to New Orleans."

We actually did do something like that. Tim chartered a big jet for our New York and Philadelphia people and a smaller one to fly from Palm Beach. And we put a lot of people on commercial flights and private planes leaving from Pittsburgh.

First, of course, we had to beat the Raiders, which we were able to get done. The score was 24-13, maybe not as one-sided as Tim could have wished, but clear-cut.

Happily for the Raiders, it solved their problem. They flew no jets to the Super Bowl and therefore left no one behind.

Best to Worst

I hold these truths to be self-evident, that our 1974 draft, as people who study these things have concluded, was and still is the best in the history of the NFL, and that our 1975 draft was a bust.

Think it over.

The first four players we picked in 1974 are now in the Hall of Fame. Conversely, except for Dave Brown and Mike Collier, who were used as kick-return guys, nobody we drafted in 1975 made the roster.

Yes, I know: in 1975 we drafted last. Super Bowl champions always do. But in 1974 we drafted very late and found riches at the bottom of the barrel.

Jack Butler pointed out that 1975 was not an auspicious year to be a brand new Steeler in training camp. Both on offense and defense, the lineup was set, full of talent not yet at its peak. On the team that had beaten the Minnesota Vikings in the Super Bowl, only Ray Mansfield, the center, and Andy Russell, an outside linebacker, were anywhere close to retirement.

If I went along with that, I'd be rationalizing. I know what a rationalization is because the Benedictine monks at St. Vincent explained it to me. It's "a good reason for the real reason" – plausible enough, that is, to sound convincing.

The real reason our 1975 draft turned out to be a dud was not that there weren't any openings for newcomers. It was not that our scouts hadn't worked hard. We were just as well organized and just as well prepared as in 1974. We collected as much information, fine-tuned it as carefully, and presented it to the coaches in as orderly a fashion. The real reason we drafted so poorly was the absence of the passion I had brought to this task since the hiring of Chuck Noll. In 1974 and the five previous years, getting ready for the draft had been an obsession with me. In 1975, the flame did not burn quite as high. I did what I had to do, yes; there was nothing I shirked, nothing I overlooked. It was just that I was somehow less than fully engaged. Success breeds contentment, it breeds complacency. Was I resting on my laurels? Possibly. I can't be sure.

In fairness to my staff, not everybody we drafted was a stiff.

Our first pick, Dave Brown, had been an All-American defensive back at Michigan. There's an adage to the effect that you can't judge a draft until after the third season. Dave Brown was gone after one season, taken by Seattle in the 1976 expansion draft. On his last day in Pittsburgh, he came into my office for a handshake. He thanked me for the Super Bowl ring he was wearing and for giving him a chance to be a Steeler. In a ten-year career with Seattle, Brown intercepted sixty-two passes, five more than Hall of Famer Mel Blount's lifetime total with the Steelers. After his playing days, he remained in Seattle as an assistant coach.

Mike Collier, a running back out of Morgan State, looked like a steal as our fourteenth-round selection. Collier was the player who ran out of bounds in practice one day and accidentally pancaked a spectator – AJR. That is the only thing he's remembered for. We cut him before the start of his second season. Later, he caught on with the Buffalo Bills and played for another three years – returning kicks.

Our second-round pick, Bob Barber, defensive end from Grambling, washed out in training camp, but played for a few years with the Green Bay Packers. Our third-round pick, Walter White, tight end from Maryland, found a haven in Kansas City after we cut him. Until an injury laid him low, White was productive, catching 160 passes for sixteen touchdowns in four seasons.

But that was the extent of it. Except for Collier, the players we drafted from the fourth through the seventeenth rounds quickly dropped out of sight. Bob Barber was an example of what Chuck Noll referred to as the superior athlete with an "impediment," the superior athlete who "lacks something." Performers of this stripe can make the big play, but not consistently. "Yes, we see the problem," Noll would say, and try to correct it. The problem was usually an "intangible" - insufficient toughness, insufficient "football intelligence," insufficient zest for the game. I don't recollect how Barber fell short, but Noll clearly regarded him as one of the "exceptions" he was always talking about, a player whose undoubted natural ability could be brought to full flower with coaching and a customized strength program. Alas, in Barber's case the "impediment" was too deeply ingrained.

So many high draft picks turn out to be disappointments that some NFL teams – the New York Giants were one – looked for help in the realm of the behavioral sciences. The man who was running things for the Giants, my good friend George Young, hired a psychologist to interview his players, and, with George's permission, I asked the guy to visit our training camp.

Jack Butler, for one, didn't think much of this idea. "More paper and pencil testing?" he asked. Any scout with a lick of sense, Butler thought, could glean as much information as he needed by poring over game films and talking to the people who knew the player best – coaches, trainers, equipment men. You had to talk to these people selectively, Butler added. There is always a "right" coach, meaning the coach who is most insightful. It's the job of the scout, Butler stressed, to identify that coach. He may or may not be the coach at the top, but stay away from assistants who merely parrot what the head man is saying.

The shrink the Giants sent to us, Neil Goldberg, did not dispute Butler's assertions. "You have first-rate scouts; your record proves it," he told me. And they collect valuable data, tons of it, he conceded. All the same, he went on, there was information in our files that we might not know how to interpret, information we were probably misreading.

Predictably, our scouts were not pleased to hear this. Our West Coast guy, Bob Schmitz, was openly scornful, arguing, "I played here with Bobby Layne. At practice sometimes, he'd be half-loaded. He drove his car into a streetcar one night, and played the next day. And won the game." Schmitz's point seemed to be that Layne would have flunked any psychological test ever conceived. Therefore, everything we were hearing from Goldberg was hogwash.

To which the headshrinker responded, "I'm only saying you'd get more out of the information you've compiled if you knew what to look for and listen to, and if you asked better questions of the coaches." He explained how we could learn invaluable lessons about a player from his body language, his tone of voice, his willingness or unwillingness to make eye contact. This was just the tip of the iceberg, or the Goldberg, if you prefer. Every word, every gesture, every quirk, it seemed, was loaded with meaning. To hear Goldberg tell it, a player's psyche was just as important as his physical dimensions and his time in the forty-yard dash.

I told the good doctor we'd get together with him later. And we did. Some of his ideas could be helpful to us, I thought. "Bullshit," grumbled Bob Schmitz. All Jack Butler said was, "How much are you going to pay for that stuff?"

Again I dredged up a maxim I had learned from the Benedictines: If you could state a problem correctly, you were well on the way to solving it. Our problem was that, because of "intangibles," too many high draft choices never became the football players we expected them to become. Every team in the league had this problem. Decades later, it still exists. Despite the efforts and advice of all the behavioral gurus, high draft choices continue to fail.

Not even the Benedictines have an answer for everything. The way it turned out, the best new player we acquired in 1975 was a free agent who looked like a misfit. A linebacker from Eastern Michigan, he was "too big," the scouts said, for his position. They meant he did not have the agility to cover pass receivers. On the other hand, he was "tough as hell," and could put a good rush on the quarterback, shedding blockers right and left. Let's bulk this guy up with a barbell program and see how he looks in a three-point stance, someone suggested.

We gave my cousin Tim a blank contract and dispatched him to Ypsilanti. He called back quickly to tell us, "The kid won't sign. Says the Steelers are loaded and he couldn't make the team."

With Eastern Michigan prospects, our trouble shooter, if we needed one, was Woody Widenhofer. Woody called the player on the telephone and went into his spiel. He said that as someone with Eastern Michigan connections, having coached there, he would personally see to it that the kid got a chance to show what he could do. We'd move him from linebacker to defensive end. The coaches would work with him patiently. He'd be a special project. Five minutes into the conversation, John Banaszak was ours.

Of the twenty-one players we selected in the 1975 draft, nineteen never played for the Steelers. Banaszak was on the team from 1975 through 1981. He suited up for three Super Bowl games and started at defensive end in two. Impressed with Banaszak's progress in his rookie season, Jack Lambert remarked to a teammate, "Those scouts of ours must be pretty smart guys to dig up a free agent that good."

In my twilight years, I accept all compliments even if they're only half-true, so let me say I am grateful to Lambert for his comment. I am even more grateful for his kindness in overlooking the nineteen draft picks who flopped.

The Steel Curtain

In the years between 1972 and 1980, the Steelers under Chuck Noll redefined defensive football. His formula was so simple: Run the ball. Play the hell out of special teams. Keep Terry Bradshaw from getting a case of happy feet, throwing off balance, and putting the ball up for grabs. Let the Steel Curtain do the rest.

There was never a better defense than the Steeler defense of 1975. When I use the term Steel Curtain I include the linebackers, the cornerbacks, and the safeties along with the front four. Many times when the offense fumbled or the kick returners left us in bad field position and we had to punt, the defense pulled the fat out of the fire. Joe Greene and the other linemen could destroy an opponent's offense. Collectively, our linebackers were unsurpassed. Andy Russell had lost a step but couldn't be faked or fooled. Jack Lambert played with controlled ferocity. Jack Ham was a coach's dream. If there were flaws in his game, I couldn't name them. The defensive backfield looked to Mel Blount, big, strong, and frightening, for inspiration and leadership.

This was the kind of football that Pittsburghers admired. It was in the DNA of all who had breathed the soot-filled industrial air of Western Pennsylvania. Bradshaw kept the defense out of trouble and made judicious use of his fleet and elusive receivers. Lynn Swann alone caught eleven touchdown passes. In the 16-10 win over Oakland for the AFC championship, defensive back George Atkinson put a hit on Swann that knocked him out. Swann left the field in the arms of Joe Greene, who picked him up like a baby. He had a brain concussion, and spent the next few days in a hospital bed. Would he be able to play in the Super Bowl? No one knew.

Getting back to the regular season, Franco Harris scored eleven touchdowns on runs, equaling Swann's total on pass catches, and gained 1,246 yards, a Steeler record. Rocky Bleier was Franco's blocker and picked up important yardage as a change-of-pace runner. Blount led the league with eleven interceptions. The Steelers lost to Buffalo in the second game of the season and then won eleven straight. (Eleven, you will notice, seems to have been our lucky number.) We finished the regular season 12-2, and beat the Colts as well as the Raiders in the playoffs.

The venue for Super Bowl X, Pittsburgh vs. Dallas, was the Orange Bowl in Miami. By contrast with New Orleans, Miami seemed cut off from history and tradition. Miami and New Orleans were very different cities. Early twentieth-century real-estate speculators cleared away the tropical jungle and filled in the mangrove swamps to create Miami, from then on a haven for snowbirds drawn to the sun. Pre-Katrina New Orleans was redolent of its Creole past, a collection of old neighborhoods, unchanging and faintly mildewed, wrought-iron balustrades enclosing the second-floor balconies. Miami in January was warm, New Orleans close to frigid. The skies over Miami were bright and cloudless, New Orleans was overcast. Everything in Miami looked white, or salmon-colored. Even before the levees broke, everything in New Orleans looked brown.

New Orleans was a long trek for Steeler fans. They could get to Miami in a hop, skip, and jump. And Miami was full of Pittsburgh expatriates, pensioners who remembered when the Steelers were chronic also-rans, fair game for ridicule and scorn. They had joined in the vilification, but now they decked themselves out in black and gold and trumpeted their undying loyalty.

The NFL had booked the football team and its front-office cohort into the Miami Lakes Hotel – partly owned, we understood, by Don Shula, coach of the Dolphins. For reasons I couldn't make out, the players all seemed to dislike it. Fats Holmes was dissatisfied with the hotel and everything else about Miami, "a place," he declared, "where old people come to play golf and die." If Fats could maintain his bad temper until kickoff time it might be helpful, I said to myself. He might re-direct his animus toward the Cowboys.

One day in the hotel restaurant my brothers John and Tim were sitting with Senator Ted Kennedy and some other people when Jack Butler and I walked in. I heard John mention our names, and immediately a rich baritone voice called out, "Hi, Art. Why don't you guys join us?" We accepted Kennedy's loud invitation willingly, and for the next half-hour fielded questions about football. Surprising me, Kennedy seemed to know without being told, although John did tell him, that I was head of the Steelers' scouting department. A big, Irish-looking guy whose hair was still dark and whose waistline was still well contained, the Senator reminded me of the scouts and assistant coaches I usually hung out with.

While we were talking, my son Artie appeared. Running up to the table, he asked if he could rent a motorbike, and Kennedy beat me to the answer. "Don't let him do it, Art. My brother Jack rented motorbikes in Bermuda when he was just that little guy's age. There was an accident, and one of Jack's friends was terribly hurt."

No motorbike for you, Artie, I said.

The conversation switched from football to stories about the Kennedy who'd been president. When it was time to break up, I called for the check. "Hold it!" The resonant baritone again. "I'm paying!" Best not to argue, I decided.

The next day a little earlier, here came Kass, presenting me with a crisis to handle. It seemed that AJR had set up a luncheon for still another Kennedy – Ethel, Bobby Kennedy's widow. Somehow Ethel and the Chief had met and hit it off. To Kass's consternation, he would not attend the luncheon himself – league business prevented it – and neither would Dan. "Your father got me into this, and I don't know what to do," Kass was telling me.

I attempted to put her at ease. Nothing to worry about, I said. We made a reconnaissance excursion to the dining room. It was ready for the party, with everything in order. "All you have to do, Mom, is sit there and smile."

All right, she said, but I must be at the luncheon, too, in the place right next to Ethel Kennedy. I asked what I'd have to say that might interest the lady.

"Oh, you'll know what to say. You read a lot of history books. Talk about history."

A better idea came to me. "Mom, you can be on one side of Ethel and we'll put George Young on the other side, with me next to George. George has three history degrees and he used to be a teacher. He can keep this luncheon going until it's over."

"Damn!" George said upon hearing my plan. "Why, hell, I've never even voted for a Kennedy. I don't like their ideology."

Many football people are staunch Republicans, but George, though he didn't talk like one, was a Democrat.

"Well, you're going to sit next to Ethel. Turn on the charm," I instructed him.

It worked out. I could hear them go back and forth, and Ethel seemed totally engaged. There was animation, there was laughter, and there were serious moments as well. "We have to meet again and continue our conversation," Ethel said to George as we were leaving.

Kass was relieved and happy. And George, forgetting he did not like the Kennedys' ideology, was ecstatic. He had met the wife of a figure in American history and had held his own. But then he always held his own, in any company.

The Steelers, it seemed to me, had a sound, no-frills way of doing business. The Dallas Cowboys were glitzier. The package they sold included a leggy chorus line of cheerleaders. In their calf-high boots, ultra-short skirts, and skimpy tops, they were part of the show, an important part. AJR had done away with the Steelers' cheerleaders after just a few years. We gave our people football, and that was enough.

On game day, while the Cowboys loosened up before the kickoff, their cheerleaders did some rehearsing. I stood on the field with Dan, watching them. Up close, they looked like the girls you might see on any college campus, only prettier.

"In thirty minutes," said Dan, "a preacher will give the invocation, a band will play the Star-Spangled Banner, and then the game will start."

"That's how it is all over the South," I reminded him.

"Yeah," Dan agreed. "Football in the South is sex, prayer, patriotism, and violence."

Kay, my son Art, and I sat with Mom and Dad in our box near the rim of the stadium. AJR, uptight and irritable, was wearing his game face. In the first quarter, Art III began to film the action with a brand new, motor-driven, 35-millimeter Nikon camera. The click-click-click of the shutter was continuous, and AJR could endure it for only so long. Then he swiveled his head and snapped, "No more pictures!" If Artie never had understood why everyone called his grandfather the Chief, he did now.

AJR liked to watch football in silence. Once in a great while he would make a pronouncement of some kind. Or he would ask me a question and answer it briefly himself. Mom and Kay sat dutifully quiet, "seen but not heard," as Kass would say. In spite of his desire to concentrate on the game, AJR wanted us with him. I was like a dictionary – there to be consulted, but only if necessary. Which suited me fine. I was into the game as much as the Chief was.

Early in the first half our punter, Bobby Walden messed up a kick, and the Cowboys scored. Their object was to shut down our running game. At times they succeeded, but Franco Harris and Rocky Bleier combined to gain 133 yards, enough to keep the defense honest and give us opportunities to pass.

Of the first ten Super Bowl games, this was the best-played. At one point Jack Lambert exhorted his teammates as no one else could, shouting, "We're supposed to be tough guys, but they're bringing it to us!" He then made an effort to change the momentum. When our stubby placekicker, Roy Gerela, missed a field goal we badly needed, a Dallas defender mockingly patted him on the helmet. Lambert flew at this Cowboy, knocked him to the ground, and stood there screaming over him. It got us going again.

Roger Staubach, the Dallas quarterback, took a pounding. We sacked him time after time. Chuck Noll had warned Bradshaw that he could not throw short passes. The Cowboys' defense prohibited short passes. "Go at 'em deep," Noll ordered him, but Randy Grossman got into the clear for a touchdown pass of a mere seven yards. Lynn Swann, meanwhile, was having a Hall-of-Fame day, completely recovered from Atkinson's hit. Defensive back Cliff Harris persisted in thinking that he could get into Swann's head and intimidate him, but Swann said after the game that he never had felt so loose. He caught only four passes, but they were long ones. A jumping, twisting catch at a critical moment silenced the trash-talking Harris. Another catch by Swann went for a touchdown. By vote of the sportswriters, he was the game's most valuable player.

In the last few minutes, the Cowboys made it exciting. With a four-point lead to protect, Noll put his trust in the defense. It was the only time I ever had seen a "prevent" defense work. We covered their receivers downfield while giving them short gains. On the last play, Staubach passed into the end zone, and Glen Edwards came up with an interception. The final score was 21-17.

Two officials from the NFL stepped into our box. They'd be taking AJR to the dressing room for the presentation of the Lombardi Trophy. One of them asked if I was coming along. "Naww," I replied. My heart was still beating too fast.

At our second victory party in twelve months, the Chief and Chuck Noll were just as low-keyed as at the first one. Celebrations in the end zone after touchdowns were anathema to Noll. "Act like you've been there before," he would counsel his young receivers and running backs. That was the approach he took now. It was also the Chief's approach. They "acted like they'd been there before." Following their lead, so did I.

Everybody who missed the victory party in New Orleans, and everybody who did not, seemed to be in the crowd at this one. I don't know why, but when I think of that party I think of John Troan, editor at the time of the *Pittsburgh Press*. With swarms of people around us, he happened to be alone for a moment, and I spoke to him. "Art Junior!" he said, recognizing me. We could not have met more than once or twice before, and then very briefly, but Troan remembered. Something else he remembered, and repeated to me, was the story of how AJR had picked him up on the Pennsylvania Turnpike when he was hitch-hiking home from a Naval base in Maryland during World War II. AJR always had liked John Troan.

Again we had a victory parade from the Greater Pittsburgh Airport, witnessed by cheering thousands. I rode in a limousine with Kay, Art III, Kass, and AJR to 940 North Lincoln Avenue. No sooner had we settled down than Artie said to me, "I'm bored. There's nothing to do here."

He was taking Noll's strictures about keeping one's cool a step too far. Bored? Nothing to do? "This," I told Artie, "is a time in your life you'll never forget."

In February, Kay invited Dad, Mom, and Aunt Alice over to Mount Lebanon for a big roast beef dinner. When the dishes were put away, Artie set up a screen, got out the slide projector, and displayed the "transparencies" he had taken from our box in the Orange Bowl. AJR, who had been so abrupt with the kid when the camera was running – "Put that thing away!" – watched intently. Time after time he would ask for a replay. "Can we see that one again?" Was he perhaps showing remorse for his treatment of Artie in Miami? I couldn't say, but for one evening, anyway, he made the youngest Art Rooney feel like a big shot.

Chapter 61

Wising Up

Credibility comes with success. When the Steelers were chronic losers, the reason had to be that the Rooneys were dumb. As soon as we started winning championships, our IQs climbed up to the Einstein level. We were geniuses, all of us, including Tim and the twins, whose connection with the football team was marginal.

Almost overnight, the sports world readjusted its outlook on the Rooneys. For close to forty years, we'd been hopeless bumblers. Now we had the know-how to rescue floundering franchises.

CBS renewed its offer to sell us the Yankees, this time sounding out Tim. Again there was no deal. Shortly afterward, we heard from Ned Irish, the man who popularized basketball in New York City by promoting college doubleheaders in Madison Square Garden and later became the founding owner of the New York Knicks. The San Francisco team in the National Basketball Association was for sale, and AJR could buy it to be overseen by Tim and the twins. Basketball before Irish got involved had been outside the scope of the national media. Now even the pro game was going big-time, but not fast enough to suit the Chief.

He dispatched his brother-in-law, Jack McGinley, to an NBA contest in Cleveland. McGinley talked to people and crunched a few numbers and concluded that the NBA at the time did not have the venues, the marketing, or the television exposure to make it a powerhouse professional sport. Owning a franchise in the league, McGinley advised the Chief, would be fiscally unwise.

But that was many years ago. The franchise we could have acquired, the Golden State Warriors, survived and eventually prospered.

NASCAR got in touch with us. NASCAR was wasting its time. We did buy a soccer team, the Philadelphia Spartans. The twins and even the Chief had some fun with it, but when our losses in just a few years reached half a million dollars there was nothing to do but bail out.

Football and horse racing were the only things we knew about. John Macartney discouraged me from buying a Mount Washington condominium with a spectacular view of the downtown skyline. My plan was to be a landlord, leasing it for "good money," as I explained to Macartney. "Good money," he said, "is nice. But it's not big money. Put up a whole condo building and lease it. You spend as much time and effort on those little deals as you do on big ones." We explored the subject no further.

In search of a big-money proposition for us, Macartney went on a wild goose chase to Zurich and Jakarta. He was bent on getting us into the oil business. In Conoco tankers, we would transport oil from Indonesia. He came home without a deal but with a nasty case of malaria. Having been infected before, as the pilot of a PT boat in the South Pacific during World War II, he was only too familiar with malaria. That little foray cost us about one hundred thousand dollars, an unexpectedly high price for a sniff of oil. Big deals, we were learning, didn't come cheap.

Our next purchase, Green Mountain Raceway in Vermont, set us back millions. Like the soccer team, it turned out to be a dud. We tried to race the year round, but winters in Vermont were brutal. Think of Napoleon's retreat from Moscow, and you get the idea.

AJR was against the Green Mountain project from the get-go. The job of running the place, a thankless one, went to Pat. Later, he added our dog track in Florida to his responsibilities.

And there was trouble at the dog track, too. The dog owners were making demands that we considered unreasonable. Looking for a way to deal with them, we consulted Macartney, and he predictably had a brainstorm, another one. "Buy your own greyhounds from all over," he advised us. "They breed them in Ireland, you know. Race your own dogs, and you won't have to fool around with outsiders."

We tried it. The operation was a success, but the patient eventually died. The dog men proved to be hard-fisted adversaries. They planted explosives under the car hoods of people they didn't like, someone warned us. That kind of talk could be largely discounted, but it would have been foolish to ignore the risk we were taking.

We had a meeting at Green Mountain to discuss the whole dog-track issue one day, and I remember it for one tell-tale incident. Macartney tossed his keys to young John McNulty, who was up there learning the business. "Go fetch my car, will you, John?" Macartney asked. Unthinkingly, John headed for the door. Then he stopped and turned around and tossed the keys back to Macartney. "Start your own car," he said.

We operated the dog track independently for a couple of years and then returned to the old status quo. Nobody's car was ever blown up.

Business deals, I reflected, were like the draft. Sometimes you had a good one and sometimes you had a bad one. And, whichever it was, you worked hard.

Thanks But No Thanks

More and more often, AJR would be required to attend a function of some kind at the Duquesne Club, where the coal and iron barons of the nineteenth century, Pittsburgh's WASP aristocracy, isolated themselves from Catholics, Jews, and of course Negroes. Women were admitted only as guests – women with the proper ethnic and socio-economic credentials. Irish males could be doormen or porters or waiters. Italians, and maybe one or two blacks, toiled out of sight in the boiler room.

With the passing of the years, the Duquesne Club lowered its barriers just a bit. Hesitant steps toward ethnic, religious and gender diversity were taken. One thing remained constant: members still had to have money. But new money, as well as old money, was perfectly acceptable now.

And so the membership committee offered AJR a chance to join. Never one to forget or deny where he came from, he refused the bait. What he could not avoid, for business reasons, was the need to be present from time to time at the small, exclusive civic luncheons and dinners for which the Duquesne Club provided a venue. On one such occasion – a meeting of NFL and NBC officials, as I recall – he directed Buff Boston to chauffeur him there in a broken-down Oldsmobile on loan from Buff's uncle. As they pulled up in front of the club's majestic sandstone building, a uniformed factotum hurried down the steps. With practiced ceremony, he opened the jalopy's battered door. AJR was a man who had a fine sense of irony.

The Duquesne Club went in for dark, austere, wood-paneled elegance. Murky portraits of dead capitalists hung on the walls. Up the street a few blocks stood the William Penn Hotel, where gatherings a shade less important than the ones at the Duquesne Club took place.

Having left a meeting at the William Penn on a bright spring day in the late 1970s, AJR obeyed an impulse. Instead of jumping into a taxi, he decided to walk. But he was getting along in years and the Steeler offices at Three Rivers Stadium were no short distance away. Approaching the Sixth Street Bridge, he began to tire.

A passing bus slowed down. The Steelers had lately won their third straight Super Bowl, and AJR was a frequently photographed, incessantly feted, easily recognized folk hero. In the middle of a block, the bus driver came to a stop and opened his door.

"Mister Rooney – where are you going?"

"Over to the Stadium."

"Wanna ride?"

AJR did not deliberate. "Don't mind if I do."

Climbing into the bus, he said, "I hope this won't take you out of your way." The driver glanced over his shoulder. There were maybe half a dozen people on the bus. "Would you folks mind if I dropped off Mister Rooney at Three Rivers Stadium?" he asked them.

Their answer was a chorus of no's and not at all's, and then the riders were calling out, "Hi, Mister Rooney," or, more boldly, "Hi, Art." The Steelers' mantra that year was "One for the thumb," and undoubtedly someone invoked it.

Across the Sixth Street Bridge on Federal Street, the driver turned left, making a detour. A few minutes later he was in Stadium Circle, parked at the door to the Steelers' suite of offices. "No charge, Mister Rooney," he said.

I don't have any documentation for this, but the passengers, I'm inclined to think, gave the driver - and AJR — a round of applause.

Bidwill's Burg

The Chief called Chicago "our kind of town." He said it was "Pittsburgh — only bigger." Carl Sandberg called Chicago "the City of the Big Shoulders, Hog Butcher to the World," and so on. All of us felt a kinship with Chicago, one reason being that it was Charley Bidwill's home town. Charley Bidwill owned the Chicago Cardinals. He owned a piece of two race tracks, Sportsman Park and Hawthorne. He was AJR's kind of guy.

Chicago had the Board of Trade, where fortunes were made and lost in the blink of an eyelash. Chicago was where "killers could kill and go free to kill again." The Chief knew the stock traders; he knew the killers — a few of them, anyway. He himself was a sportsman — a horse player, a football guy, an investor in grains and soybeans.

Aunt Harriet had lived in Chicago when she was married to Max Fiske. "It's where the wind always blows. That's why they call it the Windy City," she told me. Chicago, I concluded, was many things to many people.

My first look at Chicago came when I was 13 years old. Dad and Mom took me there, leaving all of my brothers at home with Aunt Alice. How come? If I ever knew, I've forgotten. We traveled by train, on the Pennsylvania Railroad. "*Dinner in the diner, wake in Carolina* ... "Over the radio, I had heard Tex Benecke sing "Chattanooga Choo Choo;" with just a slight change in the lyrics, I imagined myself waking in Chicago. I thought the telephone lines that whizzed by our coach were bull ropes, attached to the poles to keep them from blowing away.

AJR was taking us to the Chicago All-Star game, the brainchild of Arch Ward, an enterprising Chicago sports editor. Every summer since 1934, the champions of the National Football League had played a collection of the previous fall's best college seniors. Ward's paper, the *Chicago Tribune*, sponsored the game. Everything over expenses went to charity.

This annual extravaganza was popular with football fans and the NFL owners for the first thirty years of its existence. The game in Soldier Field was a showcase for the league, the owners thought. But after about 1960, with the NFL in the ascendancy and baseball losing its dominance as the national pastime, their attitude changed. They became paranoid about the injury factor, and so did I in my role of personnel director. In what the league now perceived as a glorified exhibition game, top draft choices could get hurt; high-priced established veterans could get hurt. Beyond that, the game was no longer competitive. From 1934 to 1958, the College All-Stars frequently won; from 1958 until the promotion was discontinued in 1977, the pro champs lost only once.

The pro champs were always the Chicago Bears or the New York Giants or the Green Bay Packers or the Detroit Lions — any team but the Steelers. On that first exciting trip to Chicago, in 1949, I saw the Philadelphia Eagles manhandle the All-Stars, 38-0, before a typically large crowd in mammoth Soldier Field.

It would finally be our turn in 1975. We represented the league in the last two All-Star games ever played, winning both. The score was 21-14 in 1975, with Joe Gilliam passing for two fourth-quarter touchdowns. In 1976, we were leading 24-0 toward the end of the third quarter when a storm from Lake Michigan hit. The special effects were spectacular: thunder and lightning, torrential rain, cyclonic winds. Play was suspended, and the crowd, wet and unruly, spilled onto the flooded field. After about fifteen minutes of anarchy, Commissioner Pete Rozelle called the game.

George Halas was still alive in 1976, but so many others of the old guard were gone. What I remember with most pleasure about that All-Star week was a visit to City Hall. "Come on," the Chief said to Dan, Tim, and me. "Mayor Daley wants to meet us. Put a tie on."

Ed Kiely and Jack McGinley were with us when we entered the mayor's office, which looked as spacious to me as Soldier Field. Richard J. Daley, a short, heavy-set man in a smartly-tailored business suit, got up from his high-backed chair with green leather upholstering, walked with a firm step around a shining mahogany desk, and offered his hand to the Chief. The Chief then introduced the rest of us, one by one.

Daley at the time was the best-known mayor in America. In Chicago, he was all-powerful; in the Democratic Party he still had great influence, even after the tumultuous 1968 presidential convention. The Democrats met in Chicago to nominate Hubert Humphrey that year, and Daley's police turned the streets of the Loop into a battleground, beating up demonstrators against the war in Vietnam, beating up newspaper reporters, beating up innocent bystanders.

De facto leader of the Illinois delegation, Daley himself created an uproar on the floor of the convention hall, jumping up in the middle of Senator Abe Ribicoff's nominating speech on behalf of George McGovern and shouting something at Ribicoff, his exact words in dispute to this day. Were they obscene, as lip-readers watching on television claimed? "I've never used language like that in my life," he insisted irately.

Daley's hold on his followers survived the convention. It even survived his depiction in Mike Royko's 1970 best-seller, "Boss." Royko, a newspaper columnist as king-like in Chicago as Daley was, described how the mayor had built up an unstoppable political machine through deception, dirty tricks, patronage, and vote-buying.

Well, I can only speak for myself, but I found this ruthless manipulator to be not without wit and charm. He made us all feel like big shots. He asked intelligent, pertinent questions about our lives and our various enterprises, and he listened to our answers with what seemed to be genuine interest.

A year or two later on, Dad and Mom sat next to him at a dinner of some kind. Mom's take on the mayor was as favorable as mine. "He's so nice. Made me feel at ease. Talked about you kids. It was like being with Davey Lawrence or Joe Barr [the genial ex-Congressman who served as mayor of Pittsburgh after Lawrence moved up to the governor's office]."

I rest my case.

Chapter 62

A Different Approach

Before the 1976 draft, AJR called me into his office for a lecture. "Chuck Noll," he began, "is the best coach in the NFL. We could never get lucky enough to find another coach as good as Chuck is, and if by some chance we did find a guy like that, we couldn't afford him. Don't cause Chuck to leave us. In your dealings with him from now on, I want you to just take it easy."

I said, "I understand," and that was it. Nothing more remained to be said.

AJR's edict reinforced a conclusion I had already formed in my own mind. I had been thinking for some time that my turbulent confrontations with Noll had to cease. Every year when we prepared for the draft, our discussions would turn into disagreements and our disagreements would turn into altercations, in which I was always the aggressor. The Chief, Dan, and even Noll himself would tell me, "You take everything personally." And it was true. But how did they expect me to take things? They were like the Mafia figures in the "Godfather" movies, explaining actions that issued from lethal differences of opinion with the phrase, "It's just business." To get your own way, you did what you had to do, they seemed to be saying, but in an unruffled, dispassionate manner.

Unruffled dispassion wasn't my style. I had too much McNulty in me.

But losing my temper with Noll would get me nowhere, I could see. His was the last word when it came to the draft. AJR had made that exceedingly clear. My job, then, was to collect, organize, and evaluate information and present it to the coaches in a thoroughly professional manner. A modus operandi of this sort would be something that could go on for decades.

By 1976, friends and media people were referring to me as "the guy who drafted Franco Harris over Chuck Noll's objections." I didn't want that. Rather, I aspired to be known as the guy who put together the best scouting system in professional football or any other sport. We had the basics in place for such a system: Blesto; Dick Haley as head scout; cousin Tim Rooney tracking NFL players along with some of the college players; Bill Nunn scouting everywhere instead of just the African-American institutions (which is what the black colleges were now being called). Haley, Tim, and Nunn winnowed out the top seniors, and I made it a rule to look at them all.

We had an unfulfilled need – another scout to cover the West Coast with Bob Schmitz. A Steeler linebacker in the 1960s, Bob Schmitz had come over to us from Blesto. I thought there were just too many teams in California, Oregon, and Washington for one scout to keep tabs on. Building up our coverage had been a long, hard fight. When I first took charge of the scouting department in 1964, it was not uncommon for our scouts to turn in one-line reports. Sarcastically, the assistant coaches would say things like, "Hey, Artie, what did that scout of yours do – stop at a gas station when he was driving by the campus and call somebody on the telephone?" Now we were getting reports so comprehensive it created a different kind of problem. A professor from Penn State, a statistical expert, went through our files and said to me, "You have more information about these players than the mind can take in. It all runs together and just becomes words, words, words. Break it down. Computerize."

Three years were to pass before I could sell this idea to the Chief, Dan, and the accountants. Tom Modrak, who joined the scouting department in 1979, said to me that the best thing I ever did was set up our computer program.

Again in 1976, we drafted dead last, but with much more success than the year before. "Don't screw this up!" I kept telling myself. I was able to control my intensity, avoiding passionate encounters with Noll. As in 1975, players we had our eye on disappeared from the board one by one – all but Bennie Cunningham of Clemson. A powerful tight end, he lasted until the end of the first round, and we snapped him up.

We were looking for a tight end who could block like a tackle, and Cunningham, we thought, might be the type. As it turned out, he developed quickly, allowing Noll to make a move he had long envisioned. He shifted Larry Brown to tackle. Brown had started two Super Bowl games at tight end. In Super Box XII, against Dallas, he'd be lining up next to Cunningham.

At Clemson, Cunningham had been a good pass-catching end. We expected him to develop into an equally good blocker, and he did. But in the nine years he played for some great Steeler teams, he thought of himself as a pass receiver who blocked, and not the other way around. One summer at St. Vincent, Bill Nunn began suggesting that Cunningham's true position, when you considered his ability to block, might be tackle. Getting wind of it, Cunningham was incensed. The next day Nunn attended a controlled scrimmage. He stood behind the huddle, watching, and Cunningham went after him. He chased Nunn around the field, shouting, "Bill, you just keep your mouth shut. No more crap about moving me to tackle. I'm a tight end, Bill. I'm a tight end." Back with his teammates, he would line up and run through a play or two, and then it would start all over, Bennie advancing, Nunn retreating, Bennie commanding Nunn to mind his own business.

At last Nunn removed himself to another part of the field, and Bennie now focused his wrath on me. "Mister Rooney, he works for you. Get him in line. None of this offensive tackle stuff. I'm a tight end."

He certainly was, and he finished his career as a tight end.

Ironically, when critics suggested in years to come that we had wasted a first-round draft pick on Cunningham, Nunn was his stoutest defender. "On a passing team like the Raiders, Bennie would have been all-pro," Nunn declared.

We had two second-round picks in 1976. First we took Ray Pinney, from the University of Washington, who became one of the good Steeler centers whose game Noll improved. Like Jimmy Clack and Jon Kolb before him, Pinney could play any position in the offensive line except tight end. Although not overly strong, he used his head. He knew all the tricks, and it kept him on the team for eight years. The second round also yielded us Mike Kruczek, quarterback from Boston College, who played for the Steelers through the 1979 season, but more about him later.

In the sixth round, we drafted Gary Dunn. He'd been a linebacker at Miami, where his father was president of the university, but Chuck Noll turned him into a nose tackle. Dunn was a stalwart on excellent Steeler teams for the rest of the decade, including two Super Bowl winners.

All in all, I was satisfied with our choices. The draft had gone smoothly, and I had not clashed with Noll. I thought we were back on track.

Bottom Line

AJR lived to see his 1974, 1975, 1978, and 1979 teams win Super Bowl games. Which of those four, then, did he consider the best Steeler team of them all? When he was asked, he would answer: None of the above. Or words to that effect.

AJR thought his 1976 team was the best.

The 1976 team lost four of its first five games. One of those defeats, in the season opener, came at the hands of our hated and hateful rivals, the Oakland Raiders, which was doubly hard to take because of off-the-field repercussions from the 1975 AFC championship game between the two teams.

To recapitulate: There had been bad blood between us for several years. It reached the boiling point in that title game when Oakland defensive back George Atkinson slammed into the Steelers' Lynn Swann just as Swann caught a pass on a cross-over pattern. "It was a quote-unquote *legal* hit, up around the head," Atkinson told Frank Deford of *Sports Illustrated*. And it put Swann in the hospital with a brain concussion.

For a time, he considered getting out of football, citing far too many "intentional acts of violence." Earlier in that '75 playoff game, another Oakland defensive back, Jack Tatum, had flattened Swann in the end zone, hitting him from behind when he was "nowhere near the ball." Swann played the second half in a daze, he said.

Built like the ballet dancer he might have been, rather than the all-pro football player he was, Swann risked annihilation every week by running pass routes over the middle that exposed him to blind-siding defensive backs. He could take deliberately vicious hits and still hang onto the ball. Nonsensically, Atkinson accused him of being "gutless." Chuck Noll, meanwhile, had been talking to reporters about a "criminal element" in the NFL. "Are you referring to Atkinson?" somebody asked. Correct, answered Noll. He was also referring to Tatum, his listeners inferred, because Tatum and Atkinson were two of a kind.

Atkinson sued Noll for defamation of character, and in cross-examination when the case went to court, Noll was led to admit that, by his own criteria, Steelers Mel Blount and Joe Greene were part of the criminal element, too. Well, now. If Greene had any objections, he kept them to himself. Blount, however, was ticked off. He threatened a lawsuit of his own against Noll, with the Steelers as co-defendants. He'd been bickering with the team about a raise he did not think was sufficient. Eventually, Blount dropped the idea, but I blamed our slow start in 1976 on the distractions resulting from the controversy itself, the trial in San Francisco, and Blount's displeasure at being tarred with the same brush as Atkinson.

The trial took place while the Steelers were encamped in Latrobe. During Noll's absence to testify, George Perles took charge of the team, and though Perles was a competent football man, we missed the head coach. But even after the trial, in which Noll was acquitted of slander, we could not get untracked.

Our fourth defeat of the regular season left me shaken. Besides losing away from home to the Browns, we lost Terry Bradshaw – for how many weeks or months, no one was sure. Turkey Jones, a 6-foot-9 Cleveland defensive end, had corkscrewed Bradshaw head-first into the turf. Only luck and Bradshaw's great physical strength saved him from a broken neck.

When he boarded our flight back to Pittsburgh on a stretcher, a crisis arose. Where on that crowded airplane could we put him? Ernie Holmes had the answer. He picked up the stretcher with Bradshaw still in it and carried the whole cargo – Bradshaw, remember, weighed about 220 pounds – to the last row of seats. Depressing the armrests, he gently laid the stretcher across the row. At Greater Pittsburgh Airport, Doc Best had an ambulance waiting, and off Terry went to the hospital.

In the coffee room at Three Rivers Stadium Monday morning, I said to receivers coach Lionel Taylor, "Four out of five down the tube. Have you ever known a team to recover from a start like this? We won't make the playoffs." Too despondent to answer, Taylor could only give me a vacant stare.

Bradshaw missed the next six games. Rookie Mike Kruczek replaced him and engineered a miraculous turnaround. The Steelers won every game he started. All he did, really, was give the ball to Franco and Rocky. In our first game without Bradshaw, a 23-7 win over Cincinnati, Kruczek handed off to Franco forty-one times, an NFL record. After Bradshaw's return, the Steelers kept winning. The Cleveland game was the last one they lost in the regular season. They finished 10-4, with five shutouts in their last nine games. In the four that were not shutouts, they held their opponents to twenty-eight points. Over one stretch, the defense did not allow a touchdown for twenty-three consecutive quarters. Eight of the starters on that 1976 defensive unit went to various Pro Bowls and four ended up in the Hall of Fame.

For years people asked me if Kruczek deserved to be a second-round pick. I always said we were drafting for the type of guy we needed at the time. Kruczek had good size, and he moved fairly well. Terry Bradshaw felt that he lacked a strong arm. Maybe so, but he could get the ball to receivers on short and medium pass routes. And he was intelligent — a student of the game.

Bradshaw considered Kruczek his friend. I hope he was right, because Bradshaw needed friends. Once at a practice I was watching, Bradshaw delivered a very poor pitchout to a running back, who fumbled it. Another player, a second-stringer, walked over to Kruczek on the sideline and mockingly pantomimed Bradshaw's awkward underhand toss. Kruczek turned his back and walked away. He wasn't interested in making fun of Bradshaw.

I recalled that incident years later when Bradshaw spoke warmly of Kruczek in a television interview. A couple of paragraphs back, I referred to Kruczek's size. Bradshaw used to call him the strongest quarterback in the league, a believable assertion. "Mike followed the weightlifting plan Noll gave him to the letter," Ralph Berlin told me. "Golly, he could push those barbells around."

As either a person or a passer, there was not a bit of Joey Gilliam in Kruczek. In the six games he started, he put the ball in the air only eighty-five times for an average of fourteen passes a game. None went for touchdowns, but fifty-one were complete. Do the arithmetic: it's not a bad percentage. Of course, he had two Hall-of-Fame receivers, Stallworth and Swann, plus the speedy Frank Lewis and short-yardage specialist Randy Grossman.

Mostly, though, he simply did as he was told, which was to keep the defense out of trouble by handing off to Franco and Rocky. When the defense took the field, it was always fresh. Franco and Rocky each gained more than one thousand yards rushing in 1976. "A lot of the credit," said Bleier long afterward, "goes to Kruczek."

The offensive line was pretty efficient, too, I reminded him.

Kruczek played very little while backing up Bradshaw. He stayed in Pittsburgh long enough to get a couple of Super Bowl rings and spent one final season with the Washington Redskins. Thereafter, at the college level, he went into coaching. Let Kruczek's detractors remember two things: (1) we had a number of more talented second-round picks who did not even make the team, and (2) he kept us in the hunt in 1976.

The Steelers ended the regular season looking unbeatable. In their last two games, they shut out Tampa Bay and Houston while totaling sixty-three points. A large contingent from Western Pennsylvania followed them to Baltimore for their AFC playoff game with the Colts, who never knew what hit them. On the third play of the first quarter, Bradshaw threw deep to Lewis, who took advantage of double coverage on Swann to break free. The play covered seventy-six yards for a touchdown.

Bill Nunn and I had been waiting six years to see Bradshaw hook up with Lewis like that. Bradshaw said afterward that he couldn't believe Noll would allow him to cut loose so early in the game. AJR was just as surprised. Noll's concern with establishing the run before he would let Bradshaw pass reminded him too much of how Walt Kiesling stifled his quarterbacks.

Bradshaw had a marvelous day against Baltimore, completing fourteen of eighteen passes for three touchdowns and 264 yards. Two of his touchdown passes went to Swann. Franco Harris gained 132 yards in two and a half quarters, and the offense as a whole amassed 526 yards, a divisional playoff record. The defense sacked Baltimore quarterback Bert Jones five times and forced two interceptions.

At the line of scrimmage, the Colts were calling Dwight White a "bush-leaguer." Bad mistake. White gave their linemen and backs such a going-over that Dick Szymanski, the Colts' general manager and a close friend of mine, came to me several times with complaints about his allegedly "dirty play." I let it pass.

The final score, by the way, was 40-14.

Only a few hundred stragglers from an original crowd of 60,000 witnessed the afternoon's most exciting moment. Twenty minutes after the game, a pilot who'd been buzzing Memorial Stadium in a single-engine Cherokee flew it right into the empty upper deck. "Look, it's a bird," wrote Glenn Sheeley in the *Pittsburgh Press*. "It's a Terry Bradshaw pass. It's the Steelers soaring toward the AFC championship game with their tenth straight win." And then: "No, it's a plane." Somehow the pilot survived.

At the time of the crash, I was just outside the press box, talking with Mort Sharnik. June, my brother Tim's wife, was with us, waiting for her husband, who had detoured into the press box to say hello to a Baltimore sportswriter he knew. She was seven or eight months pregnant. Fearing an explosion, Mort and I grabbed her, each of us taking an arm, and hustled her all the way down to the parking lot, three ramps below. "My feet hardly touched the ground," she said later. Tim, who'd been looking all over for June, was more annoyed with us than grateful. "There wasn't any danger," he insisted.

On Monday, when Ralph Berlin turned in his casualty report, we got the butcher's bill for that tenth straight win. Franco Harris had taken a cheap shot in the ribs from Joe Ehrmann, a Baltimore defensive tackle, and would miss the AFC championship game in Oakland the following Sunday, the day after Christmas. Bleier was hurt, too. Even Roy Gerela, the team's placekicker, had not come back to Pittsburgh unharmed. Worse luck that we were going to play Oakland, of all teams.

Before fanning out to the post-season college all-star garnes, our scouts spent Christmas at home every year. It was one of my steadfast rules. Kay and I and our kids and my in-laws exchanged gifts that year on Christmas Eve in our new house on Washington Road in Mount Lebanon. After a big breakfast the next morning, I flew to San Francisco with Jack Butler, Tim, and Harry Harvey, a devout Steeler fan who drove and trained harness horses. On our cab ride from the San Francisco airport to Oakland, I assured my three companions that the dining room at the Hyatt Hotel would be open. It wasn't. In fact, every good restaurant in town seemed to have closed its doors, so we settled for a fast-food Christmas dinner at Denny's. The team had been served an early catered dinner in private.

Bleier and Gerela, as well as Harris, had to sit out the game the next day. Oh well, I said to myself, maybe Bradshaw, his three great receivers, and the defense could pull us through. Maybe Reggie Harrison, who had done well as Franco's replacement in limited action against the Colts, would amaze everybody. Full of confidence, he vowed to take up the slack. Then there was Noll, our equalizer. Surely he would think of some answers. He always did.

During our pre-game warm-up, I noticed Al Davis and his coach, John Madden, watching Ray Mansfield kick field goals. They looked skeptical. I imagined I could hear them telling each other, "This is some kind of trick, a mind game." If only it was. What Davis and Madden saw was what Davis and Madden got. Without Harris and Bleier, we did not have an offense. The Oakland defensive line easily wrapped up Harrison. All the Raiders had to do was defend against the pass. Putting up little resistance, we lost, 24-7. Mansfield, by the way, kicked our extra point.

Monday morning, Butler and I rented a car and drove to Stanford University in Palo Alto, where the East and West college all-star squads were practicing. As I accepted condolences from the other scouts and the coaches on hand, I spotted Davis and Al LoCasale some distance away. I started toward them, and a few of my well-wishers called out, "Don't do it, Artie! Come back!" They knew what my intentions were. Disregarding them, I continued on my walk of shame. I went up the field a way and cut over to the other side, where Davis and LoCasale were standing. First I held out my hand to Davis. "Congratulations, AI." Then I nodded to LoCasale, including him, too. Davis, the bad loser, proved he could be a gracious winner. "We beat a great Steeler team," he said. Then he said it again. "A great team."

Great, but just how great? AJR, as I have written, called it the best Steeler team of them all. I know of coaches, players, and media people who agreed with him. Ralph Berlin said he agreed.

I beg to differ. Injuries and luck are part of the game. In 1976, the Steelers had too many injuries and not enough luck. I repeat: injuries and luck are part of the game. To me, the best Steeler teams were the teams that won Super Bowls.

Fear of Flying

Lionel Taylor's only phobia – the only one as far as I knew – was fear of flying. He especially feared to fly with Chuck Noll. I had flown with Noll myself and appreciated Taylor's point of view, but my scariest minutes in an airplane occurred on a flight in a private four-seater from New Orleans to Jackson, Mississippi.

Everett Marks, a Louisiana oil man, was with me. About halfway to our destination, an electrical storm caught up with us. There was thunder, there was lightning, there was wind. Marks ordered the pilot to turn the plane around and go back to New Orleans. The pilot obliged, but now we were flying into the teeth of the storm. We were low enough to see a two-lane asphalt highway, and Marks screamed at the pilot to set the plane down on the road. "Like hell," he called to us over his shoulder. "I could wreck the plane. That would cost you guys a lot of money." To say nothing of our lives, I said to myself. Out loud, and profanely, Everett Marks expressed the same thought. I don't know how, but we made it back to New Orleans and landed on the airport runway.

But I was talking about Lionel Taylor, the second black coach AJR had ever hired. Chuck Noll brought him in for the 1970 season. He had a fine way with the players and was popular, in fact, with everyone, which meant that the satisfaction was mutual, because Taylor liked the Steelers as well as the Steelers liked him. His only complaint, as far as I could see, was Noll's insistence on taking the other coaches with him when he flew his own plane to NFL meetings or on scouting missions. Taylor was not alone in feeling like this, I can assure you.

At any rate, in January of 1977, Noll flew most of his staff to the Senior Bowl game in Mobile in a small chartered plane. Whether Chuck took over the controls, as he sometimes did, I'm not sure; I never asked. I know that on the way to Alabama they met with foul weather. It was like hitting a stone wall, someone told me. The passengers were lifted out of their seats, and Dan Radakovich dropped the cigarette he was smoking. "Put it out!" the others yelled at him. Then they yelled, "And don't even think about lighting up another one!"

When Noll and his shaken assistants checked into our motel after "a white-knuckled, sweaty-palmed, nail-biter of a flight," as one coach described it, I happened to be in the lobby. There were those who tried to make light of the experience, but Lionel Taylor was still upset, and he let it show. He took me by the arm and led me outside, where we could not be overheard. "Art," he said, "the Rooneys have always been more than fair to me. You have a first-class organization." He stopped, almost breaking down. With a tremor in his voice, he resumed, "But I don't like those plane trips. Why do I have to travel that way – because the head coach tells us, 'Let's go'?"

With that, Lionel turned on his heel and strode back into the lobby. I hadn't uttered a word, but it made no difference. What could I have said? Here was this strong ex-football player, a fearless pass-catcher who had set receiving records with the Denver Broncos, in such an obvious state of distress that he could hardly hold back the tears.

Before the next season, instead of renewing his contract with the Steelers, Taylor joined the staff of the Los Angeles Rams. No doubt he had personal and professional reasons for doing so, but I can't help but think the plane ride to Mobile was a factor.

His replacement, Tom Moore, was a true, hard-working professional, the first coach to show up at Three Rivers Stadium every morning. Once when we pulled into our parking places at roughly the same moment, I jumped out of my car and ran to the door for no better reason than to say I was there before Tom.

Lionel Taylor's departure and the retirement of Andy Russell and Ray Mansfield would alter the makeup of our 1977 team. I hated to see them go. Russell, like Jack Butler, deserved a Hall-of-Fame nomination and never got one. Mansfield was a team leader who had the ability to laugh at himself. He died before his time – of a heart attack in the Grand Canyon, where he and his son Jim had gone for an extended backpacking hike. The end came at sunset, while Ray was taking in the gorgeous view.

There was tragic irony connected with the death of Everett Marks, my companion on the aborted flight we were certain would be the last for both of us. A few years later, Everett and his wife, Mary Anne, were killed when a flight taking off from the New Orleans airport suddenly lost altitude and crashed.

Total Recall

One of our three choices in the fourth round of the 1977 draft was Ted Petersen, a center from Illinois, 6 feet 6 with a frame that would carry 285 pounds. He was Chuck Noll's kind of athlete: intelligent.

To be a center, you had to be smart. Everything starts with the center, he's the switch that turns on the motor. Often he must call the offensive blocking schemes. On every play, he must know what his teammates in the line are expected to do. Petersen, in that respect, was the equal of Steeler centers like Bill Walsh and Ray Mansfield and Mike Webster. Perhaps I also should mention Tunch Ilkin and Jimmy Clack, who were centers when they came to us.

On a day almost thirty years after we drafted Petersen, I met him for lunch at the St. Clair Country Club. A Steeler alumnus who had chosen to remain in Pittsburgh, he was athletic director at Upper St. Clair High School, where high academic standards and success in competitive sports co-existed. As soon as we sat down, he started talking about the 1977 draft. "I want to congratulate you on that draft," he said, and I accepted the compliment gratefully. I have learned it's the only way. As I remembered it, nine guys we drafted that year made the team, a team that had won two of the last three Super Bowls, and three of those nine – Robin Cole, Dirt Winston, and Cliff Stoudt – became starters.

Cole and Winston were linebackers. Cole, our first-round pick, developed into a Pro Bowl player. Stoudt, one of Terry Bradshaw's successors at quarterback, took the Steelers to the playoffs in the 1980s.

The player we drafted in the second round, Sidney Thornton, unearthed in one of those Louisiana colleges named for a point on the compass, had many good games and made occasional big plays, but was never going to beat out the running back ahead of him, Franco Harris. In the third round, having given up a player to the Jets, we drafted twice, coming up with Tom Beasley, who turned out to be a good support guy in a strong defensive line, and Jimmy Smith, a wideout and kick returner from Michigan, as friendly an environment for wideouts and kick returners down through the years as you will find. How good was Smith? Let me just say that he made Frank Lewis expendable.

And now to hear Ted Petersen recall these old teammates, the names and all the circumstances rolling off his tongue, gave me a lift. At one point, he switched the conversation to Chuck Noll and his emphasis on fundamentals. "He was always on my tail about run blocking, pass protection, weightlifting," Petersen said. Noll's inscrutable exterior mystified Ted. "I never quite knew what he was thinking. Maybe he liked me and maybe he didn't. I couldn't tell."

"If he didn't like you," I said, "he wouldn't have pushed you so hard. You were his prototype offensive lineman."

I had noticed that Petersen's back was giving him trouble, a legacy of his days with the Steelers. "Comes and goes," he said now in answer to my question. "When I played, it hurt all the time. This back cut short my career."

Nodding sympathetically, I told him what Walt Kiesling used to say about injuries. They hurt like hell initially, but then you put some ice and heat on them and ran them off and forgot them. "But after you're retired," Kies would go on, "the pain comes back. About the time you hit 50 you're hurting constantly. You remember when you got that injury, and then you remember where you got it, and a little while later you remember the name of the bastard who hit you." Petersen forced himself to smile. "My Uncle Jim," I went on, "used to say that betting on the horses was a hard way to make easy money. Well, professional football is like that, too." Uncle Jim was the philosopher I quoted most often.

The talk of injuries turned Petersen's thoughts to Laverne Smith. "Remember him?" he asked me. "The fast kid from Kansas? He was our other fourth-round pick in 1977."

"Yes, a great talent," I said. "We hoped he would be a guy who could change off with Franco." But Smith was unlucky. "He took a bad hit. Busted up his wheels. Never the same runner again."

Our third fourth-round pick in 1977, Petersen remembered, was Dan Audick, an offensive guard from the state university in Hawaii, a state that exports a lot of pineapple but very few football players. "Hawaii, beautiful Hawaii. I'll bet you scouted Audick yourself," Petersen said.

"Unfortunately, no. Bob Schmitz went out there. My only look at Audick was in a game on the mainland. In person, I mean. Of course I saw him on film. And, oh yeah – Audick was in one of those all-star games we scouted."

"Noll cut that guy, and then he played in the league for eight years – mostly with the Raiders," Petersen recalled.

"The Raiders," I said "Our hated rivals."

"We took three guys in the fifth round," Petersen resumed. His mind seemed to work like Google or America On Line.

"Cliff Stoudt, he was the first!" I blurted, my competitive instincts coming to the fore. "Noll and Bill Nunn went to Youngstown State to watch him play, and they went in Noll's plane. Hell, you could *drive* to Youngstown in an hour and a half. Anyway, Noll and Bill were favorably impressed. Stoudt was a big tall kid, like you, and he had a strong arm. No dumbbell, either. But he lacked something."

I have trouble defining exactly what it was that he lacked. Consistency at placing his long passes, I'd say to start with. Beyond the physical demands of a quarterback's job, the ability to generate a feeling of confidence is needed, and there again he fell short. Our fans, with the fervor of a lynch mob, loathed him, and one reason seemed to be that he wasn't Bradshaw. He escaped them by jumping to the USFL – the United States Football League – one of those fly-by-night conferences that seemed to come and go for so many years.

As I said, Stoudt passed his audition with ease, but what Nunn and even Noll recalled most vividly about their visit to Youngstown was the return flight. Nunn likened it, I remember, to a World War II bombing mission over Berlin, the turbulence was so bad.

"Steve Courson, fifth round." Petersen said, bringing us back to the 1977 draft.

I cut him off. "We don't have time to talk about Steve Courson."

"OK, Mister Rooney."

"Call me Art."

"OK, Art. But Steve has matured." I did not respond. Moving on, Petersen said, "After Courson, we took Dennis Winston — Dirt. From the University of Arkansas. Gosh, he was tough."

"Sure was."

We had covered the first six rounds, and I mentioned again how remarkable it was that nine of our draftees made the team.

"Ten," Petersen said, correcting my arithmetic. I'd forgotten Dave LaCrosse, a linebacker from Wake Forest who hung on as a special-teams player. We kept a walk-on that year, too – Tony Dungy. I had scouted him myself at the University of Minnesota. Dungy was a quarterback, but Tom Moore, the assistant coach who signed him for us, said he could be a defensive back, Tony's lack of speed notwithstanding. With the Steelers, he played both positions, and he used his time here constructively, asking good questions and increasing his knowledge of the game. Although he would not like to hear me say so, I felt all along that his abilities were more suited to coaching than to playing. After three years in the league, two with the Steelers and one with San Francisco, and a year on the coaching staff at Minnesota (the university), he came to us as an assistant to Noll. It was easy to see, at least for me, that he was cut out to be a head coach, and in fact he got to be one, first at Tampa Bay and then at Indianapolis, where his assistants included Tom Moore. Under Dungy, the Colts were Super Bowl winners in 2007.

We parted, Ted Petersen and I, with no discussion of the season we had in 1977, which uncannily resembled the 1976 season. The team lost four of its first eight games, then won five of the next six. Our 9-5 record put us into the playoffs, but we made a quick exit, losing in Mile High Stadium to Denver, 34-21. Red Miller, the Broncos' head coach, and George Perles, our defensive coordinator, were long-time antagonists, and they almost got into a fist fight down on the field before the kickoff. The game itself was played in the same spirit, with lots of hard hitting and some intermittent displays of good old-fashioned animosity. The Broncos beat us, you might say, at our own game, Steeler football.

Steroids

My thoughts about Steve Courson are so mixed that I can only express them on paper. In conversations like the one with Ted Petersen, I don't trust myself to be sufficiently even-handed.

Anyway, by the time we scouted Courson intelligence tests had become a part of the process, and he passed them with high scores. Athletically, he measured up just as well. He could run, jump, and change directions with great agility for an offensive lineman. But he was flighty and lacking in common sense, it seemed to me, and prone to make questionable decisions. Electing to use steroids was the worst decision he ever made, and one that he came to regret.

Like too many others gone astray in the drive for excellence, he believed that he needed an edge. Weight training and large intakes of protein were not enough. To improve his performance, he juiced himself up.

What the source of his advice was I never knew, but at pre-season training camp in 1984, which would have been Courson's eighth year with the team, Chuck Noll perceived that something was wrong and told us to get rid of him. "I don't want the guy around here," Noll said. We traded Courson to Tampa Bay, and he played for another two years.

The steroids eventually ruined his health. A decade or so after his retirement, he confessed to having taken them and revealed that he was suffering from damage to his heart. He was on the waiting list for a transplant, he said, but time went by and there was no further word about a transplant, and finally Courson announced that his heart had repaired itself, crediting the improvement to radical changes in his lifestyle.

When Courson made public his use of steroids, he said there were many other users in the NFL. Some of them, he added, naming no names, had played for the Steelers when he did. He wrote a book; he appeared before Congressional committees. I was surprised at how well he expressed himself, I admit, having always considered him a blowhard.

Even before the trade, Noll banished Courson from training camp. On the day of his departure, my son Mike, a teenager then who washed the players' cars for pocket money, saw Courson climbing into his SUV. Mike always had liked Steve; whether he knew what had happened is doubtful. At any rate, he chose this moment to remind him of a promise. "You said you'd give me a ride in your truck. Let's do it now."

"Sure, kid," answered Steve. "Hop in." Later Mike said that Steve gave him a tour of the St. Vincent campus. They drove to the Benedictine cemetery and down the steep hill to the terrace from where our fans watch the workouts and then out onto the practice fields and on up to Kennedy Hall, the building that houses the dressing rooms and showers. There Mike got out, saying, "Great ride, Steve. Thanks a lot."

"OK, Mike, take care of yourself," Steve told him and was off down Fraser Purchase Road and onto Route 30 – out of our lives, we mistakenly thought, for good.

I had been taught about redemption in grade school at St. Peter's, high school at North Catholic, and my four years at St. Vincent College. The Good Thief stole heaven on the cross next to Christ. I wish I had known Steve Courson after he turned his life around with strict diet, exercise, and medical care. He became an advocate of clean living. He lectured young people on the dangers of drugs and steroids. He wrote about it and led by example.

Steve died trying to save his old Labrador retriever from a falling tree. It could have been a teammate or a child. He reached out to a friend in danger. Courson saved the dog and lost his own life.

Were there Steelers besides Courson taking steroids during the Super Bowl years? I couldn't say yes and I couldn't say no. Certainly Mike Webster was open to suspicion. What I can say unreservedly is that Chuck Noll would not have knowingly tolerated steroid use. In meeting after meeting, attended by assistant coaches, scouts, and trainers, he inveighed against steroids in the strongest language. The marching orders he gave to our scouts went something like this: "Guys who take that crap are destroying themselves. Their balls will fall off. They have to grow beards to hide the blemishes and lesions on their faces. I don't want anybody like that."

He felt the same way about drugs. Every rookie we signed went directly from the Greater Pittsburgh Airport to Divine Providence Hospital, where he took a physical examination that included a urine test for steroids and controlled substances. One year when my other son, Art III, was studying dentistry at Pitt, he had a summer job with the team that required him to pick up the new players and take them to the hospital. Then he monitored the tests.

His instructions were to stand by and watch the players urinate into plastic cups and make sure there was no switching of samples. After one week of this, Art came to me and said he had had enough. He was pissed off, if you will pardon the expression. "This job is dehumanizing, Dad. It's not respectful to me or the players," he said.

I asked if he knew why having an overseer was necessary. "You're a medical person," I reminded him.

"Yes," he replied, his demeanor turning one hundred percent professional. "That is true. I do understand the motivation for what you are doing. But my focus is on dentistry. The mouth. May I suggest that you engage a urologist for this work?" Then and there, Art's duties as a urine watchdog came to an end.

The Little Architect

After the 1977 season, two more staff members defected. Offensive line coach Dan Radakovich and defensive coordinator Bud Carson followed Lionel Taylor to the Rams. Their reasons for leaving were unclear, at least to me. Perhaps they believed they were putting themselves in a better position to become head coaches. Or maybe they looked at the way the Steelers had regressed since their two straight Super Bowl victories and jumped to the conclusion that the wheels were coming off. Possibly the California weather seduced them. No doubt they were getting upbeat reports from Taylor on life in the Golden West. I could only guess.

Bad Rad's departure bothered AJR, who predicted, "He'll be back." For the next twenty years Rad wandered all over the coaching landscape, professional and college, going from job to job. Like Ulysses returning home from Troy, he did come back to Pittsburgh as an assistant to Joe Walton at Robert Morris University, but AJR had not lived to see it. Lionel Taylor meandered around the NFL for a while and then came to rest at Texas Southern University. He was still the head coach there when he retired. Essentially, Taylor and Radakovich were nomads. The Bud Carson case was not quite the same.

In my opinion, this bright and able football man left the Steelers at least partially because of a power struggle he was losing, a power struggle with George Perles, the coach who was closest to Chuck Noll. Perles coached the defensive line and I thought he resented the credit that went to Carson for certain innovations in the development of the Steel Curtain, the name the sportswriters gave to the Steeler defense in its entirety. My own impression was that Chuck Noll developed the Steel Curtain, but Carson, I would say, contributed. Woody Widenhofer, a good friend of Perles, sarcastically referred to Carson as "the little architect" of the defense. If Bud had a fault, and I think he did, it was an inclination to be impatient with young, physically gifted players like Mel Blount who had not yet mastered all the techniques.

Los Angeles was not the last stop for Carson. In fact he ended up, several jobs later, as head coach of the Browns. Losing him, I believed, was a blow to Noll. With Tom Moore and Rollie Dotsch as their replacements, Taylor and Rad could be spared. Dotsch had some theories about offensive line play that were not in accord with Noll's, but it never became a problem. Noll was the boss; nobody disputed it, least of all the affable Dotsch. Taylor and Radakovich versus Dotsch and Moore was a wash. The assistant Chuck really missed, whether or not he would say so, had to be Carson. Perles and Widenhofer could install Noll's defensive system and get it operative, but the new defensive backfield coach, Dick Walker, seemed unable to communicate with the four very exceptional Pro Bowl performers he inherited. All he had to do was oversee their conditioning and make sure they understood the game plan every week; it was still too much for him. Even so, he remained on the staff for four years, and to say that three of them were good ones for the team would be understating it.

Moore, Dotsch and Walker had one thing in common: George Perles and his ally Widenhofer were the employment agents who had orchestrated their hiring. I don't mean to imply that this was harmful, necessarily. But Perles and Walker were not very good at evaluating talent, which made the work of the scouts more difficult. Dick Haley and I had to be constantly on the lookout to keep them from getting into mischief.

We would see the effects of their meddling in future drafts.

Chapter 63

Too Many Cooks

In 1978 the league moved the draft from early in the year, late January, to spring. The thinking was that playoff teams would have more time to prepare and coaches would have more time to assess the condition of veteran players who had suffered injuries late in the season.

Selfishly, I didn't welcome the change. The early draft, I had always believed, gave us an edge. We made some hurried decisions, and hurried decisions could result in mistakes, but I felt that we were always more successful than the teams that did not put manpower and, yes, money into the draft. I was proud of the organization we had developed. In my opinion, only Dallas and Los Angeles had scouting departments equal to ours. Never mind that the public considered us penny-pinchers. We outspent most of the other teams and got more bang for the buck than all of them. The proof was in how well we had done with low-end selections and free agents.

With the draft moved back to April, Chuck Noll seized the chance to get his assistant coaches more deeply involved. He dispatched all seven on a two-week mission to scout the college teams engaged in spring practice. A saying among coaches went like this: "If we have to cook the stew, we should help pick out the ingredients." That was how it seemed to Noll, and he insisted on sending his kitchen workers to the produce market.

Each assistant coach would visit nine or ten schools and in that way get to observe almost all of our top-rated prospects. Ordinarily at this time of the year our scouts would be looking at younger players, rather than the ones we had already evaluated, but to monitor the situation I assigned a scout to each coach as a traveling companion. As I have said before, some of the coaches were very good at scouting and some were OK; the others, and there is no reason to name them again, did not have a feel for the job.

And so it was that in spite of the scouting department's reservations, we wasted a second-round pick on Willie Fry, defensive end from Notre Dame. Our scouts had him rated considerably lower, but the assistant coach who visited Notre Dame was susceptible to the mystique of the place and to the sales pitch of the Notre Dame staff. Swayed by his report, Noll remained a believer until Fry's weak performance in training camp gave him buyer's remorse. Before the season was under way, he traded Fry to San Francisco.

Our first pick that year was a cornerback, Ron Johnson, another Eastern Michigan guy. One of our regular cornerbacks, the competent and experienced J. T. Thomas, had been diagnosed with sickle cell anemia, obliging us to shore up the position. Johnson, like Thomas, was strong enough to cope with the supersized receivers who could trample "pissant corners" (as Bud Carson called them) and fast enough to keep up with the more elusive type. Thomas made a complete recovery; meanwhile, Johnson was in the starting defensive backfield and even after J. T.'s return he more than earned his keep as a backup.

In the third round, we drafted again for insurance purposes. Punter Bobby Walden, a holdover from the Bill Austin era, had retired; his legs were gone. To replace him, we took a chance on Craig Colquit from Tennessee, and he was our punter for the next four years.

Of the players we drafted in rounds four through twelve, four made the team. Larry Anderson, a cornerback and kick returner from Terry Bradshaw's old school, Louisiana Tech, came to us in the fourth round. Our eighth-round selection, running back Rick Moser, was a long shot. Moser had played at Rhode Island, a school not noted for its football tradition. He hung around long enough to pick up a couple of Super Bowl rings. In the eleventh round we took another cornerback, Nat Terry from Florida State. His time was even shorter than Moser's, one year, but he, too, experienced the euphoria that goes with a Super Bowl appearance.

We drafted a Pitt player, Randy Reutershan, in the sixth round. Reutershan was a wide receiver, but Noll preferred to use him as a special-teamer and part-time defensive back. Shortly before my wife Kay turned 40, Noll flip-flopped Randy to his original position, wide receiver, and I saw my chance to requisition the number 40 jersey he had worn as a defensive back and give it to Kay for a birthday party I was planning. We had recently cut a free agent named Kay, and the idea was for Tony Parisi, our equipment manager, to take Reutershan's name off the number 40 jersey and substitute this guy Kay's.

One thing worried Parisi. "You know how upsetting it is for women to hit 40. They don't like to broadcast it," he reminded me. "So, remember – this came from you, not me. Old Tony isn't looking to get on the wrong side of Kay."

But it pleased Kay to see her name on the black Steeler jersey with the big gold 40 front and back. Reutershan was a sort of streamlined fellow, and Kay looked just fine in the still loose fit. Her red hair blended perfectly with the jersey colors and the flaming fall foliage.

Then came an unexpected hitch. Chuck Noll had changed his mind again. Reutershan was being returned to the ranks of the defensive backs and would wear his old number once more. There was no time before the next game to dig up another number 40, so Parisi would have to come to the house and retrieve Reutershan's jersey.

I broke the news to Kay. She had surprised Parisi by raising no objections to the advertisement of her age, and now she startled both of us. She said a birthday gift was a birthday gift; no one was taking it from her - not Parisi, not Noll, and not Reutershan. I explained that league rules left Parisi and the team with no choice. As a defensive back, Reutershan could not wear his receiver's number, 87. Kay refused to listen. "This jersey is a present," she said. "It's mine! The Rooneys own the team, and I'm a Rooney. Let Randy Reutershan wear 87. All he does is go down under kicks anyway." The beautiful redhead's temper was flaring. She had her own set of rules, and they superseded the NFL's.

It took a lot of persuasion, but at last I got her out of Randy Reutershan's jersey. Tony Parisi returned it after the game, and it has been in Kay's possession ever since.

There's an unhappy postscript to this story. With the1979 season barely under way, an automobile accident put an end to Randy Reutershan's football career. Kay was saddened even more than I normally would have expected her to be. After all, they had worn the same jersey, she and Reutershan, in the glorious season of 1978.

Never Better

To this day I call it the greatest of all Steeler seasons. In 1978 there were questions about the team after an indifferent showing in the exhibition games. As no one seemed to realize, Chuck Noll was reconfiguring his offense. This was to be the year he turned his quarterback loose. The receivers, he knew, if no one else did, were better than ever. John Stallworth was showing himself to be as talented as the flashier Lynn Swann and now for the first time as productive, and Jimmy Smith was an able replacement for the departed Frank Lewis. Injuries limited Bennie Cunningham's effectiveness, but Noll was letting Terry Bradshaw throw the bomb, ignoring the tight ends as never before. What came of it was twenty-eight touchdown passes.

In every way, it was Bradshaw's finest season. Possessed of new-found confidence in the huddle, he quieted the chatterers. He alone would decide whose pass play he would call. The countrified Southern boy with the unruly temperament had become a team leader at last.

Don Shula had told me that the Mel Blount Rule, as it was now being referred to - the restriction that kept defensive backs from manhandling pass receivers running their routes - would not cramp the defensive unit's style. I think it did, but only a little. The new guy, Ron Johnson, was fresh clay, easily molded. There was less freelancing now, and more cohesiveness. As for the linebackers and front four, they had lost nothing physically and were bringing one more year of experience to their work.

The offense was at its pinnacle, I thought; the wide-open passing game kept defenses off balance for Franco and Rocky. We looked unstoppable, in short, and for the first seven weeks of the season, which started auspiciously with a 28-17 thumping of the Buffalo Bills (who had O. J. Simpson in their backfield), that was the case.

To my bemusement, AJR seemed embarrassed by the fact that in going undefeated over that seven-game span, we had beaten Cleveland twice. The win at Three Rivers Stadium, 15-9 in overtime, was our ninth in a row in games there with the Browns. We never had lost to them in Three Rivers, and it seemed to weigh heavily on Art Modell, the Browns' owner.

Starting from scratch, Modell had become successful in the advertising business (radio and TV commercials). He was smart and sharp-witted and he openly worshipped AJR. At a league meeting one year the Chief was seated at our table, a rosy-cheeked, white-haired, benevolent-looking patriarch. Just as he deposited his chewed-up cigar in the ash tray, Modell approached him and, bending over, cupped the older man's face in his hands. That was Modell's greeting. For an instant I thought he was going to kiss the Chief on the forehead.

Any doubts I may have had about Modell's good faith vanished then and there.

The Pittsburgh-Cleveland game at Three Rivers was our fourth of the season. Just when the Browns appeared to have it won, a 36-yard field goal by Roy Gerela tied the score, 9-9. The game went into overtime, and Bradshaw called one of the "gadget" plays which Noll half-reluctantly allowed him to use now and then. Designated in the playbook as "fake 84 reverse gadget pass" (I had to look that up in an old newspaper story), it was nothing more groundbreaking than the ancient "flea flicker." Bob Zuppke, if I'm not mistaken, originated the flea flicker at the University of Illinois in the 1920s. For all I know, he may have copied it from some even earlier coach. Anyway, at the Browns' 36-yard line, Bradshaw handed off to Bleier, who handed off to Swann, who lateraled to Bradshaw, who floated a high-trajectory pass to the overlooked Cunningham, all by himself in a corner of the end zone. And that was the death blow. Flea bites can sometimes be fatal.

Modell, I understand, was in agony, but he pulled himself together, concealing his chagrin, and said something congratulatory to AJR and Dan. I could be wrong, but I think that in this moment of what should have been elation, or satisfaction at least, the Chief felt genuine sadness for his friend. "Art," he said consolingly, "you beat the tar out of us for fifteen years. Things are just evening up." Maybe. My own point of view was that nothing could ever atone for what Paul Brown's Cleveland teams did to us in the late 1950s and all through the '60s.

I was never very adroit at either winning or losing graciously. It just isn't part of my nature. I liked Bum Phillips, the Houston Oilers' coach and the best of the good ol' boys; he wore boots and a ten-gallon hat, and he spoke in the lazy idiom of the cowpuncher. Besides, he knew football. I liked him, but when his Oilers handed us our first defeat of the season, 24-17 at Three Rivers in another overtime game, I was in no mood to tell him the better team won, or that losing to nice guys didn't hurt.

Actually, the better team had not won, as events were to prove. Our record after the loss to the Oilers was 7-1. We lost one more regular-season game, 10-7 at Los Angeles, and won all the rest to finish 14-2. In the Astrodome on December 3rd, we hogtied Earl Campbell and squared accounts with the Oilers, 13-3. That was the game in which Donnie Shell flattened Campbell with one of the hardest hits ever delivered. Running smack into Campbell in the open field was like meeting a locomotive head-on and derailing it.

We were to play Houston a third time in the AFC championship game, and win much more easily.

At 77, AJR was feeling the effects of age. His over-all health seemed OK, but his hearing had deteriorated and his vision was poor. Cataract surgery on both eyes had not been altogether successful. I remember that after the first operation he was flat on his back in Mercy Hospital for a week with his head immobilized between sandbags. For the rest of his life he would wear Coke-bottle glasses and complain that his peripheral vision was gone. "I can see the games better on TV," he said, and had one installed in his box at Three Rivers. Meanwhile, he was spending thousands of dollars on unsatisfactory hearing aids. At NFL meetings, he could read the printed agenda but only pretended to hear what was being said.

Although he delegated more work to Dan now, he wanted the rest of us to know that he was still very much in charge. His state of mind worried Kass. "Your grandfather," she told us, referring to Pop Rooney, "went into a funk at about your father's age and never really got out of it." AJR, deaf to the conversation at the dinner table, would silently recite the rosary, using a metal wheel the size of a man's ring. It contained only one decade – ten beads. He held it under the table cloth as he prayed. If the others at the table were laughing, he would smile; if the others looked serious, he matched his expression to theirs.

The way the football team was performing brought him out of his depression. Nobody called it that, but the term was not then in general use. Depression had certainly darkened the last few years of Pop Rooney's life. AJR overcame it. He could see, after all – not perfectly, but well enough to manage. And perhaps he had found a good ear doctor: his hearing seemed to improve.

Early in the season he had watched all the road games from Pittsburgh, but he accompanied the team to Kansas City the week after Houston had beaten us. More encouraging still, he invited Ed Kiely and me to have dinner with him at the Kansas City Hilton the night before the game with the Chiefs, which was not at all customary.

An invitation from AJR wasn't an invitation, precisely. It was more like an order, meant to be obeyed without demurral. I was scouting a college game in the afternoon — Kansas was playing in nearby Lawrence — and had arranged to meet George Young for dinner. He, too, was scouting in the area. Turning down AJR would have been unthinkable, but I could mention my appointment with George, and I did. For a very long second or two, AJR thought about this. Then he said, "George Young. Oh, yeah, the scout ... your friend." Reaching a verdict, he continued. "Well, bring him along ... George is OK."

At dinner, although I sat between them, AJR seemed to hear Young's every word. He asked questions, laughed at the stories George told, and left no doubt that he was having a good time.

Wins over Kansas and New Orleans sent us to Los Angeles with a 9-1 record. Our expatriate coaches – Taylor, Carson, and Radakovich – had Los Angeles ready for us, and though the Steel Curtain did well, our offense did not. Lionel, Bud, and Bad Rad knew what to expect from Noll and Bradshaw.

If they tried to conceal the pleasure they took in the outcome, I was not aware of it. On the other hand, Perles, Widenhofer, and their confederates smoldered for the better part of a week. As for Noll, he was his usual imperturbable self. My respect for the Rams' scouting department tempered my own disappointment. However, I still viewed L.A. as a team that would never win a league championship in spite of the great talent its scouts routinely identified, and this failure, I thought, could be summarized in a single word. "Chinatown, Jake," a detective says to the Jack Nicholson character in the cult movie called "Chinatown" to explain why municipal crime went unpunished in the Los Angeles of the 1930s; "Tinseltown" was the reason I gave for the Rams' chronic failure to end up on top. Partying with the Hollywood crowd was not the best way to condition one's self for a game of football.

Again the following Sunday the Steeler offense could muster just seven points, but the defense held Cincinnati to six. In the Bengals' own stadium, we had beaten them by twenty-five points. At Three Rivers, they put up the kind of fight we had come to expect from a team with Paul Brown in command.

Paul Brown and AJR were men of contrasting personalities, but with the passing of time the similarities between them increased. As club owners and in all of their business dealings, both got full value for their money ("one hundred cents for every dollar spent"). Both were devoted family men. And Brown, like AJR, had two sons working in positions of responsibility for his football team. Mike Brown was the assistant general manager and Pete Brown the personnel director. If Pete and I happened to be scouting the same team, we would often get together for lunch or dinner. From Pete and from all that I observed on my own, I learned that Paul Brown the driven perfectionist had a mellower side: he could be an indulgent father.

The week after the Cincinnati game, the Steelers flew back to the West Coast and pummeled San Francisco, 24-7. San Francisco had a young coach named Bill Walsh — sarcastically dubbed "The Genius" by envious rivals — but a few more years would elapse before his brain power came close to bearing fruit.

Our win over Houston in the Astrodome the following Sunday all but made it certain we'd have the home-field advantage in the playoffs. Any questions on that score were answered in the last two regular-season games, a victory at Three Rivers over Baltimore and one in Mile High Stadium over Denver. The traveling our team had done since the second week in November – two flights to California preceding the long trip to Denver – seemed to worry Noll. "We've spent so much time in airplanes we can't get ready for the games," he said. The notoriously thin air in Denver worried him, too. His recourse was to "get out there early and acclimate ourselves." He had the right idea, but the 21-17 score was a little too close for comfort.

We had ended the regular season with our best won-and-lost record, and now there would be a rematch with Denver to start the playoffs – Denver, the team that eliminated us in 1977. I blamed myself to some extent for that defeat. One play near the end of the game did us in – a 34-yard touchdown pass caught by Jack Dolbin, a free-agent wide receiver I had unsuccessfully tried to sign. Back in 1970, when I visited Wake Forest and corralled Jimmy Clack, he told me about Dolbin, an undrafted teammate. "He's faster than fast," Jimmy said. I looked at film of Dolbin and watched him romping around on the practice field and offered him a contract. Politely – all Southern kids were polite – he insisted on a bonus that was five hundred dollars more than I had offered, and Dolbin ended up with the Broncos. In the aftermath of our playoff defeat, I reconsidered one of the certitudes I had been taught. Holding out for "one hundred cents on the dollar" is not invariably good economics.

Pittsburgh in late December is cold and forbidding – good Steeler weather. On the next-to-the-last day of 1978, an icy rain was falling and the temperature had descended into the lower thirties. In the back of my open nine-seat box in Three Rivers Stadium, I could see the gray-brown shank of Mount Washington and the roiling black waters of the Monongahela-Allegheny-Ohio confluence. I had come to the game bundled up. So had Bill Nunn, but the rain and the frigid air chilled our bones. Jack Butler, always the stoic, made only one concession to the cold. He wore gloves. His sport jacket and raincoat were more suitable for September, and he was characteristically hatless. Into this bleak environment came the Broncos, looking out of their element. "We felt like turning around and jumping on our buses and going back to Denver," defensive lineman Bernie Chavious confessed later on to his old South Carolina State teammate, Donnie Shell.

Three Rivers in December could do that to a team. The fans, dressed in black with just a sprinkling of gold, set up a din. They roared and screamed and stamped their feet till the stands shook. The kickoff, and what followed it, only intensified the noise. The thumping, cheering, and howling just never let up.

Two weeks earlier in Denver, the hard-charging Steeler pass rush had put Craig Morton out of commission. Replacing him, fleet-footed Norris Weese gave us fits. Again the Steeler defense knocked Morton out of the game; again he made way for Weese, and I nudged Bill Nunn. "We'd be better off with Morton still in there." Nunn, it turned out, was thinking along the same lines. When Weese led the Broncos to a touchdown, we threw up our hands. But then the defense started getting to him. Joe Greene forced a sack. He blocked a field-goal try. There were two or three Denver fumbles and six sacks of Weese all told.

And Jack Dolbin? He wasn't a factor. Bradshaw passed for 272 yards. John Stallworth had ten catches for 156 yards and a touchdown. Lynn Swann caught a touchdown pass in spite of double coverage all afternoon, and Franco Harris ran like Franco Harris, scoring twice. What all of this added up to was sweet revenge, 33-10.

Our third meeting with Houston, also at Three Rivers, would be for the AFC championship. It was cold again – even colder than the week before – and raining again. Jack Butler had a cap on, a cap he had got from Ireland. I wore my fur-lined trench coat, a tassel cap borrowed from Tony Parisi, and my good-luck talismans, the high-top shoes in which I had watched our Super Bowl wins over the Vikings and Cowboys. The shoes and a pair of heavy woolen socks did not keep my feet warm.

In the run-up to the game, the normally easy-going Bum Phillips had been almost belligerent. He publicly declared war on the Steelers. Houston would get even, he promised. But as they waited in the rain for the kickoff, the Oilers seemed anything but warlike. Rather, they stood petrified during the minute or so it took a brainless Steeler fan, naked except for a Terrible Towel loin cloth, to burst out onto the field and race through their kick-return formation, waving another Terrible Towel above his head.

The rain, the slush, and the cold affected both teams, the difference being that the Steelers found ways to adapt. There were twelve fumbles, and the Steelers recovered almost all of them. Earl

Campbell fumbled three times. Franco Harris fumbled three times. Rocky Bleier fumbled three times. But when Harris and Bleier weren't fumbling they were ripping off pretty good gains, whereas the Steelers held Campbell to sixty-two yards.

In common with everybody else, he was slipping and sliding on the drenched Tartan Turf. Dan Pastorini, the Oilers' quarterback, complained that he couldn't get a grip on the ball, his hands were so numbed from the cold. We intercepted four of his first six passes in the second half, but by that time the game was as good as over. Scoring seventeen points in the last forty-eight seconds of the second quarter, the Steelers had leaped ahead, 31-3. At the finish it was 34-5.

The one-sidedness of the game provoked some late hits by the Oilers, which in turn led to some scuffling, but good ol' Bum Phillips discouraged any talk of animosity between the two teams. "Aw," Bum said, "you couldn't do a lot out there 'cause it was wet." Still, Jack Ham, the best outside linebacker in the NFL, was hitting so hard that he cracked his helmet. Ham started fast, dumping Campbell for a two-yard loss on the first play from scrimmage. He recovered two fumbles, intercepted a pass, and accounted for one of the sacks on Pastorini.

So we were back in the Super Bowl for our third appearance in five years. "And this time," Kay informed me, "we're taking all three of our kids."

"What about their schoolwork?" I asked.

"I talked to the principal. The principal and their teachers feel that this is an educational and life experience that can't be passed up. The teachers just wish they could go with us. I don't know how many times I've heard one of them ask if we needed a baby-sitter."

I said I'd work things out, but I didn't have to. So many Rooney grandkids and so many young children of other people connected with the team were looking for an "educational and life experience" that Joe Gordon and Buff Boston made special arrangements to include them all in our traveling party. Once we arrived at the Super Bowl site— Miami – their entertainment needs would be provided for.

Aunt Alice was staying in Pittsburgh, she told us, impervious to the coaxing of Kass, AJR, and just about everybody else in the extended family. "Not me! I don't like those crowds," she kept repeating. Uncle Jim felt the same way. A few days before the game, an elderly woman approached him in the coffee shop of the Webster Hall Hotel, where he had taken a room. "Why, Mister Rooney," she said, "I thought you'd be in Miami for the Super Bowl." Jim's answer, as he related it to me in cadences echoing W. C. Fields, went like this: "My dear friend – I don't think you appreciate the marvels of modern technology. I am now at a stage of life where travel wearies me and big crowds annoy me and unnecessary hoopla drives me up the wall. On Super Bowl Sunday, you will see me having breakfast in this room. Then a limousine sent by Arthur will whisk me to the Allegheny County Airport, where the corporate jets land and take off. I will board one, sent by Arthur, fly to Miami, proceed to the Orange Bowl in another limousine, and watch the game in Arthur's box. Afterward, another limousine will take me back to the Miami airport and another corporate jet will fly me home. That night you may see me right here at this table, having a late-evening snack. Ah, these modern-day marvels."

"And do you know what?" he went on. "That lady believed every word of it."

Earlier in the week, as I was driving to work, I noticed cut-out figures of all the Steeler players, AJR, and Chuck Noll in the windows of the Washington grade school building on Washington Road in Mount Lebanon. The cut-outs were the work of the school kids. AJR's had a big cigar in its face. The hold of this football team on Pittsburgh and all of its suburbs was astounding, I thought, but how were Susie, Mike, and Art III going to cope with the attention they were getting because of it? How were they going to keep their heads screwed on right? Next, I wondered what AJR would do in my place. It wasn't long before I had a general idea. I was driving him, along with Kass and Aunt Alice, to our house for dinner, and I stopped to let them see the cut-outs. As tickled as one of the kids would have been, AJR made me park there illegally for minutes on end while he gawked at those silhouettes – chewing on a long green cigar.

Foster, the grade school that Susie and Mike attended, was not to be outdone by Washington. The kids in Susie's class designed and put their signatures on a banner, a huge one containing black and gold images of individual Steelers. We were to take this banner to Miami with us, I learned, and make certain to have it placed where the television camera would pick it up. "Well," I told Susie and Kay, none too enthusiastically, "I'll deal with that problem when the time comes."

To myself, I added, "But not if I can find a way out."

Spelling Lesson

In the media buildup for Super Bowl XIII, the Steelers were portrayed as rough and ready guys from a shot-and-a-beer town, the Cowboys as slick and sophisticated. Football teams in the eyes of the public took on the properties of the metropolitan centers they happened to represent. Pittsburgh was steel mills and coal mines; Dallas was office buildings populated by the millionaire businessmen Big Oil had created.

Journalistic hot air, signifying nothing. Our players were tough, yes, and Steeler teams historically hard hitting, but not because steelworkers and coal miners are tough. Tradition and coaching and their God-given physical and emotional singularities made our teams what they were. Geography ... the environment ... may have contributed something, I don't know. But you could find as many native Texans, I believe, on the Pittsburgh roster as on the Cowboys'. In college, Joe Greene had played at North Texas, Dwight White at East Texas, and Ernie Holmes at Texas Southern. L.C. Greenwood (Arkansas A. & M.) and Mel Blount (Southern of Louisiana) came from the same neck of the woods. And didn't the Cowboys feature a running back bred in Aliquippa – Tony Dorsett, who in four years at Pitt had broken every national collegiate ground-gaining record worth talking about?

Both teams were loaded with Pro Bowlers and future Hall of Famers, and both teams had cultivated their own gardens. Of the forty-five players on the Steeler squad, we had drafted all but three – the place-kicker, a second-string tight end, and a second-string linebacker. Dallas was our mirror image, the prototype drafting team in the National Conference.

The Super Bowl team that Chuck Noll put together in 1974 was no longer intact. We had eleven new starters – six on offense and five on defense. We had a different punter. All in all, there were twenty-three new faces. Dallas was back in the Super Bowl for the third time in four years. Most conspicuously absent from the team we had beaten in Super Bowl X was Bob Lilly, the Hall-of-Fame tackle. For both teams, the dynamics were moving forward.

At Super Bowl X in Miami, AJR had asked – that is to say, ordered – Kay, Art III, and me to keep him company in the owner's box. This time, to our relief, we three plus Susie and Mike were seated with the Steeler entourage in the stands. We were ten rows up from the twenty-yard line, high enough for a good overview of the action but close enough to the Steeler bench to see and hear what was going on. For Kay and Susie, the first order of business was to get the Foster School's banner displayed in a location where the television cameras would be sure to zoom in on it. Kay had the banner tightly rolled up, and now she handed it to me, saying, "You and Artie have field passes, and Mike can be helpful without going onto the field. Here is some masking tape." We marched down the steps and went to work, unfurling the banner and taping it to the barrier between the field and the crowd while Kay called down instructions from above. It was, Do this, do that. And, No, not that way, it will never hold. Standing in the aisle, all she needed was a bullhorn.

I was mortified but obedient. At these post-season games, I felt superfluous, my self-importance shredded. As Kay liked to put it, when we went to the Super Bowl the coaches coached and the players played, but the scouts were as useless as tits on a bull.

"Where did you learn that language?" I demanded.

"From the North Side Rooneys," she answered. "Before we met, remember, I was a convent girl at Seton Hill."

Packed in the former convent girl's luggage, I knew, was a pair of lacy, vulgar, salacious black panties, with the obscene exhortation PULL 'EM DOWN PITTSBURGH lettered on the backside in gold. Bernie Butler, Jack's wife, had a pair in her luggage, too; so did the wives of my brothers. Would I be obliged, as a corrupter of innocence, to bring up the matter in confession?

Art III had a problem of his own. Neither his camera nor his field pass obscured the fact that he was 14 years old. Nobody mistook him for Neil Leifer, the *Sports Illustrated* photographer, least of all the security guards. "Hey, kid, where'd you get that field pass?" they would ask. Then they'd pick up the name on the badge, an attitude changer. "Oh, from your granddad!" The tone of voice would sweeten, suspicion giving way to solicitude. "Need film or anything? Just let me know."

Names can be magic, but I could now open doors on my own. Having mastered the technique of looking as though I belonged, I wandered around unchallenged, even venturing onto the Cowboys' side of the field. At one point, talking with a fellow scout, I stood near the Dallas cheerleaders, oblivious, I thought, to their manifest charms. Ten minutes later, back in the stands, I was shocked to hear Bernie Butler suggest something different. Giving me a look, she said, "I saw you checking out those cheerleaders." My rejoinder, I'm afraid, was brusque. "No, you didn't. I was over there on serious business." How sharper than a serpent's tooth is a false accusation.

That's what I thought at the time. Reliving the moment as I write this, years and years later, something tells me that Bernie was correct. These are memoirs, and I have to be truthful; involuntarily, I may have stolen a peek or two.

Now for the game itself. The Steelers kicked off, and Dallas started feeding the ball to Dorsett. When Dorsett was at Pitt, he weighed 170 pounds; in the NFL, he couldn't possibly take the punishment a running back must absorb, it seemed to me. I envisioned him as a combination running back/wide receiver, a speedier Frank Gifford, a more compact Lenny Moore. Gale Sayers was Dorsett's size, and crashing into gargantuan defensive linemen week after week had shortened his career. Dorsett, however, surprised me. In his first two NFL seasons he had gained more than 2,300 yards in heavy traffic. And now with Super Bowl XIII barely under way, he was penetrating the Steelers' line and racing around their flanks. In four plays he moved the ball deep into Steeler territory.

But then the Cowboys got cute, or rather, their coach did. Tom Landry called a reverse. Messing up the handoff to Drew Pearson, Dorsett lost the ball. Defensive tackle John Banaszak fell on it, and the day's first change of momentum had occurred. It was not to be the last.

In a drive that covered eighty-one yards, Terry Bradshaw quickly passed the Steelers to a touchdown. On the last play, from the Dallas 28, his target was John Stallworth, who made a move that fooled the Cowboys' defensive backfield and left him open in a corner of the end zone.

We had seen the best first quarter in Super Bowl history. The second quarter was no less exciting. It started with Bradshaw throwing an interception. On our next possession, he fumbled, and Dallas tied the score. He fumbled again, under pressure from the insufferable Hollywood Henderson, and Dallas took the lead when Mike Hegman picked up the ball and ran thirty-seven yards for a touchdown.

Henderson, the trash talker, was putting his athleticism where his mouth was. On the sideline, he yakked at the camera. Bradshaw needed help, and he got it immediately from Stallworth, who turned a fairly short pass into a 75-yard touchdown play. And then toward the end of the half, with the Cowboys driving again, Mel Blount made a Hall-of-Fame move. One of Roger Staubach's receivers was open in the end zone until Blount came out of nowhere to intercept the pass. A penalty on the play put the ball in Cowboy country, and Rocky Bleier, never known for his leaping ability, went up high to make an impossible-looking catch for another Steeler score. Meanwhile, on the Cowboys' bench, Staubach and Landry were discussing with evident acrimony the reason for Blount's interception.

I watched the first half in near silence, trying hard to concentrate on the game and resenting the flow of questions from the boisterous Steeler fans in our vicinity. Butler and I were the authorities here, it seemed. My curt one-syllable answers got a rise out of Kay. "Be more pleasant! This is fun! Fun!" I begged to differ. "Fun? Like hell it's fun! It's life and death!"

The Steelers were out in front. 21-14, but still there was reason to be wary. Dallas had blanketed Franco and Rocky on the ground. And from the locker room came alarming news; leg cramps would keep Stallworth from returning for the second half. Far worse from Susie's perspective, a strong wind was ripping the Foster School's brown paper banner to shreds.

The third quarter was a vicious slugging match. Dallas got down to our 10-yard line, where, on third and three, Staubach threw a little too low to his tight end, Jackie Smith, all alone in the end zone. Smith was a hard-luck guy. He'd been a first-rate player on a third-rate team, the St. Louis Cardinals, before a serious neck injury bumped him into retirement. Offered a chance to come back, he saw the Cowboys as his ticket to a Super Bowl. Balanced against that was the very real risk of permanent disability, of life as a paraplegic. He took the gamble. And now a Hall-of-Fame career had come down to one play. Staubach, as I said, threw low, but the pass was catchable; Smith had hung on to many a throw just like it. This time, though, instead of using his meat-hook hands, he encircled the ball with his arms. Bouncing off his chest, it fell to the ground, and the Cowboys had to settle for a field goal. Going into the last quarter, Pittsburgh led by four points.

"Luck," I remember hearing Chuck Noll tell his players, "is being prepared to take advantage of your opportunities." If good luck is being prepared, then bad luck is its opposite. In the biggest game of their season, the Cowboys couldn't do what they had to do. They missed a shining opportunity, but for some of our Dallas friends there was much more to it than that. General manager Tex Schramm, in particular, never stopped talking as though Jackie Smith's failure to bear-hug a football was an undeserved stroke of misfortune.

The way I looked at it, there were fifteen minutes left in the game, more than enough time for the Cowboys to regroup. The fourth quarter had everything. There was suspense; there was controversy. Lynn Swann made a catch to put beside Rocky Bleier's. Hollywood Henderson got his come-uppance. The Steelers stretched their lead to eighteen points and ended up winning by only four, the margin they started the quarter with.

And yet the final result was decisive enough. Landry and Schramm, in the aftermath, talked incessantly about luck - about the unforced incompletion in the end zone, about a fourth-quarter call that went against the Cowboys. Swann, going out for a pass, tripped over the legs of a Cowboy defender. An official just a few yards away did not react. Another official dropped a flag, calling pass interference. Landry and Schramm yelled bloody murder. The tripping was not intentional, they screamed. Doesn't matter, the official informed them. According to the rules, even accidental tripping is not to be countenanced. The penalty stood. I thought that by harping on a legitimate call and a dropped pass, Tom Landry and Tex Schramm detracted from their own team's valiant performance.

The interference penalty prolonged a 94-yard Steeler drive that ended with one of the most memorable runs in a Super Bowl setting. The incentive for it was a routine late hit on Bradshaw by Hollywood Henderson – who else? All afternoon, the Cowboy linebacker's over-the-top behavior had been an irritant to the Steelers. Franco Harris, in his own quiet way, was seething. In itself, the roughing up of Bradshaw with the ball dead was nothing too far out of the ordinary by NFL standards. But Henderson couldn't leave it at that; he added a few expletives, which was going too far. Face to face with Hollywood, Franco was telling him off. Observers who thought they knew our mild-mannered fullback were stunned. Open displays of anger, or emotion, were foreign to his nature. Bradshaw, seizing the moment, discarded a play he intended to use. He could see that Franco was bursting with adrenaline and changed the call to a tackle trap. Our quick, almost undersized offensive linemen were excellent blockers "in space," by which I mean on the move. As the team advanced to the line of scrimmage, I caught a glimpse through my binoculars of Franco's face. I've been to Florence, in Italy; I have seen Michelangelo's David. This may sound nutty, but Franco just then was David ready to slay Goliath. At the line of scrimmage, everything went perfectly. Franco took the handoff and bolted straight up the middle on a 22-yard touchdown run. Nothing could have stopped him, and nothing did.

OK, an official helped out by partially shielding Franco from a tackler. It was still an extraordinary feat. Bobby Newhouse, the fullback we might have drafted in Franco's place, was watching from the Dallas bench. Could Newhouse have made such a run? Never in a million years.

Momentum brings luck, as Chuck Noll has probably said. On the subsequent kickoff, Roy Gerela lost his footing and squibbed the ball directly to the Cowboys' all-pro tackle, Randy White, who had a cast on one hand. A split second later, Tony Dungy was climbing all over him, and White fumbled. Dirt Winston recovered for the Steelers. Up in the stands, our fans were pummeling one another in a demonstration of pure joy.

Without delay, it got better. The graceful Swann jumped up for a pass, reached it with his fingertips, and came back to earth with a touchdown. The difference between this catch and Bleier's was that from Swann you half-expected these miracles of levitation. They were the rule, not the exception, or seemed to be. On the sideline, Bradshaw slapped backs and high-fived, but cut the celebration short when he remembered how Staubach had rallied the Cowboys in Super Bowl X, keeping them in the game until the very last play. The same thing could happen again, and it did – passing on almost every play, Staubach took Dallas eighty- nine yards to a touchdown.

With under two and a half minutes remaining, the Cowboys were eleven points behind. So, predictably, they tried an onside kick. And Dungy, the opportunist who had made an accidental onside kick work for the Steelers, gave us a scare. He fumbled, and Dallas recovered. Starting from the Pittsburgh 48-yard line, Staubach threw nine passes in a row, and Dallas had still another touchdown. After the extra point kick, the score was 35-31.

Time was nearly up. Dallas of course took the onside-kick route, but Rocky Bleier put a death grip on the ball, and the Steelers just waited for the clock to run out.

Bradshaw was the game's MVP. His seventeen pass completions in thirty attempts were good for four touchdowns and 318 yards, a Super Bowl record. Impatient with any talk of statistics, the gentlemen of the press, gathered in the Steelers' locker room, wanted human-interest stuff. Relentlessly, they asked about Hollywood Henderson, attempting to draw Bradshaw out. "He said you couldn't spell cat," a persistent fellow reminded him. "Maybe not," answered Bradshaw, "but there's one word I can spell, and that's w-i-n – win."

On a chartered bus outside the Orange Bowl, waiting to make the trip to the hotel, where we all would attend another victory party, I felt contentment. In the afterglow of a game like the one we had just witnessed, how could any Pittsburgher – any Pittsburgher with the right kind of values – be susceptible to life's petty annoyances? It wasn't all that hard, I soon learned.

The bus was almost full, and still the driver sat there, making no move to depart. My fellow passengers seemed to be on a timetable. They were eager now for the evening's festivities. Voices were raised, demanding, "Let's get the show on the road!" The driver sat motionless, ignoring them.

I became aware that Merle Gilliland, the president of PNC Bank, had left his seat and was standing next to mine. "Say, Art," he said, bending over confidentially, "can't you do something about this? Can't you show your authority?" Beneath his banker's self-control was an unmistakable note of urgency.

Stirring myself, I got up and walked to the front of the bus and said to the driver, as nicely as the circumstances allowed, "Hey, let's pull out of here. We're nearly full."

"Sorry. I have my orders." His tone was polite but determined.

"Who gave you the orders?" I asked.

"That big guy. The one they call Buffalo, or Buff."

"Yeah, Buff Boston. He works for me."

The driver said nothing. He was forcing my hand.

"Listen," I told him, "if anyone asks you for an explanation, just say that Art Rooney Junior said to get out of here."

He turned on the ignition and hit the gas pedal. We were on our way to the hotel.

Have I mentioned that names can be magic? Tranquility restored, I went back to my seat and resumed my enjoyment of the afterglow.

Chapter 64

Father Jim

Father Jim Campbell was a golfer and pinochle player. He liked sports. He liked to hunt and fish. He liked a good smoke but never tasted alcohol except each morning at Mass. Originally from Scranton, in Pennsylvania's hard-coal region, he entered the lives of the Rooney family when his order assigned him to St. Peter's Church.

Father Jim was much loved by the poor people of the parish. He had dark hair and looked like an athlete and became a dedicated horse player and stock-market investor, but AJR used to say that you never could mistake him for anything other than a priest. Long after I got to know him, he told me that he was trying to make enough money to support himself in his old age. If he could help it, he would never be a burden on his friends, his family, or the diocese.

As it happened, the problem never arose. He died at the age of 60, his financial situation unclear, at least to me. With AJR telling him how to bet on the horses and stock market, I am sure there were more ups than downs for Father Jim, but like all good priests he gave so much of his money to the poor and unfortunate it is hard to say if any was left.

It seemed to me that in Father Jim's day the pastors of Catholic churches remained on the job too long. They would do magnificent work in their prime, but grow old and feeble as the years went by. Some who were lucky had a dynamic young assistant like Father Campbell. Those with enough sense would let the young assistant take over. Others, due to bullheadedness, lack of intelligence, or simple jealousy, would cling to their authority. This was the case at St. Peter's.

World War II allowed Father Jim to get out from under a boss who had outlived his usefulness. He served in the Philippines during MacArthur's campaign to recapture the islands, and when at length he came back to St. Peter's the setup was different. A fine old Celt named MacPherson was now the pastor, and he loosened the reins on Father Jim.

In time there came a transfer to St. Andrew's in Manchester, a tough blue-collar neighborhood. St. Andrew's and St. Peter's were equidistant from 940 North Lincoln Avenue, so Dad, Mom, and Aunt Alice started going to daily Mass at Father Jim's church. Manchester back then was similar in many ways to the old First Ward. Father Jim understood his parishioners and knew how to communicate with them.

A man who worked at the bingo game (every Catholic church had a bingo game) got drunk one day – not for the first time – and Father Campbell gave him a temperance lecture. "How long are you going to make a fool of yourself and break the hearts of your family?" he demanded. Contrite, the fellow took the pledge; he swore to Father Campbell that he would never take another drink as long as he lived.

Of course in no time at all he came to work drunk again. Father Campbell told him he was fired. The boozer asked why.

"Because you're not trustworthy. You took the pledge and went back on your word."

"Oh, that?" said the drunk. "I took the pledge, all right, but it wasn't official. It didn't count."

"What do you mean, it didn't count?"

"When you made me say I'd never drink again, you weren't wearing your collar, your Roman collar."

If Father Campbell had an answer, it is lost to posterity.

Father Campbell was a man's man, but, like AJR, he frowned on off-color jokes. When you were with him, said AJR, you knew you were with a priest. Even so, he willingly went along with the cloak-and-dagger games that AJR's race-track companions had to play. Once on the train from New York City to Aqueduct, Father Jim and I rode in one car, AJR in another. You could not be seen with Dad because professional gamblers, eager to know how he was betting, would in that case follow you to the parimutuel windows. On the train that day, Father Jim tried to recruit me for Holy Orders. He urged me to think very seriously about the possibility of going into a seminary. I was flattered. I also reflected that never before, in all likelihood, had there been a conversation such as this on a train that was headed for a race track. Here we were, our pockets filled with money to bet on a horse, a man of the cloth and a teen-age boy he regarded as suitable material for the priesthood, earnestly discussing the religious life.

We were having dinner after the races at Moore's restaurant in New York. Now, AJR was a people person. If he had met someone two or three times he was just as apt as not to call him a friend. At Moore's he spoke of a certain public figure as a friend. Father Campbell interrupted him, which no one else except Mom ever did. He fired a series of questions at AJR: "How well do you know this man? ... How long have you known him? ... Under what circumstances did you meet?"

AJR was flustered. "Because that is a bad guy – a killer," Father Campbell went on. Defensively, AJR was saying, "Well, I don't know him that well ... I was introduced to him at the track ... " Father Jim interrupted again. "I should hope so. Don't ever say that guy is your friend! Forget that you ever met him!"

There was a silence, and then, mercifully, one of us changed the subject. We relaxed and enjoyed the rest of our meal.

It was the only time I can ever recall hearing anyone aside from Kass give AJR such a talking-to, but the Chief told me later that on their long drives together he and Father Campbell would now and then have a difference of opinion. If the argument grew heated, Dad said, Father Campbell would turn off the radio in the car and suggest that they recite the rosary.

AJR and Father Campbell were together so frequently at the race track and ball park that Kass felt left out. She often said she begrudged the time they spent with each other. Had Father Campbell realized this, he would have quietly backed off, I am sure. His sensitivity would not have allowed him to become a problem. It was exactly this quality that enabled him to work so successfully with the down-and-out poor of St. Andrew's. He understood their problems, but could not be deceived or imposed upon.

To raise money, he had started a street fair with Las Vegas-type games of chance. Schooled by AJR, he knew how to run them. All went well until a fleet-footed thief grabbed a stack of bills from a table one night and took off. Father Campbell gave chase. He was neither young nor swift; by one account, a heart attack felled him while he was still in pursuit. Another story, less plausible, is that through perseverance he ran the guy down, subdued him, brought back the money, and *then* collapsed.

The heart attack took years off his life. Transferred to St. Margaret's in Greentree, a prosperous neighborhood that was growing in size, he had a difficult time adjusting. He felt closer, he told me, to the poor folks at St. Peter's and St. Andrew's than to the well-off parishioners at St. Margaret's. Thinking, perhaps, of his Greentree flock, he said that as people got older they became less susceptible to boozing and to sins of the flesh but never seemed to lose their love of money. For all that, he was every bit as popular with the rich as with the poor.

Father Campbell knew when the end was near. In a conversation between us at Three Rivers Stadium one day, he confided matter-of-factly that his heart was worn out and he was operating on reserve, as he put it. A few weeks later I was driving out of the stadium as Father Campbell was driving in. We stopped and lowered our windows and he asked how I was doing. He asked about Kay and the kids and then he asked me to say hi to Kay. That was his way of sending her his love and his way of saying goodbye to us both. He did not last much longer.

Doc Sekay

Art Sekay, commonly referred to as Doc, was a man of compact build and average height or less. He had a round, partly bald head, a bulbous nose, a thick neck, heavy shoulders, and the beginning of a paunch. He wore ill-fitting clothes in need of cleaning and pressing. At a football convention in Florida, Sekay was standing outside the Hollywood Beach Hotel when I drove up with relatives in the car. My mother-in-law said, "Look ... there's a bum near the entrance."

Just then Doc happened to spot me. I waved and said hi. He waved back, calling, "Hi, Artie ... I'll see you later." My mother-in-law was astonished.

"Who is that?" she asked.

"He's our team dentist," I replied.

In all candor, Doc's appearance and behavior could not have inspired much confidence in the people who sought his professional help. The constant use of chewing tobacco had worn down his own teeth and stained them a bilious yellow. When he was not chewing tobacco he was smoking cigars.

He had played football at Pitt, where Jock Sutherland, also a dentist, was his coach, and, like other Pitt players, Sekay had gone on to dental school, graduating near the top of his class. "When he puts his mind to it," one leading dentist told me, "Doc can be one of the best. He has great strong hands." At the mechanics of the business, Sekay was more than adequate. At the hygienic end, his methods were sometimes alarming.

Whenever he dropped an instrument on the floor – and though his hands may have been strong, they did not exactly stick to the tools of his trade like glue – he would pick it up, wipe it off on his smock or a pair of dusty curtains that hung on the window of his office, and go immediately back to work. That was what happened when Soup Campbell, a Steeler linebacker, needed Doc's ministrations.

Another time, Jack Butler's son John was having a tooth capped by Sekay. While affixing the cap, he dropped it, and the cap just disappeared. Sekay told John to get out of the chair and help him look for it. John was crawling around on his hands and knees. The search continued for I don't know how long, and then Sekay found the cap in the tread of one of the football shoes he always wore. He pried it loose and stuck it back – unsterilized – in John's mouth.

Doc was a low-handicap golfer, and his second-floor office in a building on Forbes Avenue in Oakland wasn't far from the nine-hole course in Schenley Park. He did a good business with young people for some reason, and if the weather was fine, and he had a teen-age boy in the chair, he might say to him, "Hey, kid. Would you like to learn something about golf?" Unaware of what Sekay was getting at, the kid would usually nod, or say, "Sure." Sekay's bag of clubs would be handy, and saying, "Come on," he would lead the way to the golf course and play two or three holes with the kid as his caddie.

Sekay always said he could beat any other dentist in town who played golf, and do it with three clubs – a driver, an iron, and a putter.

His football background – he and Uncle Jim were teammates at Pitt – was why AJR selected him to be the team dentist. Furthermore, AJR had a weakness for characters, and in that respect Sekay certainly qualified. He was completely without tact. During Chuck Noll's first season, 1969, Sekay was in my office telling me the new guy coached "sidewalk football." In the middle of his tirade, Noll walked in. I introduced them, and Sekay took up where he'd left off, directing his comments this time to Noll. Instead of taking offense, Noll listened politely and then suggested that the three of us have lunch together. Afterward, I said to Doc, "Well, what do you think of Chuck Noll now?" They had seemed to hit it off over lunch. "He's no dumbbell," Doc conceded, "but I still think he coaches sidewalk football."

Doc never played much at Pitt before his senior year, but he considered himself an authority on football and did not have to be pressed for his opinions, which were mostly negative. Fran Fogarty attributed Doc's sour attitude to his own lack of success as either a player or coach. Where and when he coached, I couldn't tell you; he'd been a part-time assistant somewhere, I think. I know that he spent more time on the golf course than as a coach or a dentist.

John Michelosen, a fellow Pitt man, he dismissed with the phrase "dumb-ass." Buddy Parker he sort of liked. Buddy was one of the few. Jack Barrett, a craft-union boss who knew Sekay, said the only people he liked unreservedly were AJR, Jack Butler, a local high school coach named Joe Moore, and me.

Sekay was in the military during World War II and resented it when his number came up for service during the Korean War also. He went back in as a lieutenant colonel, but rank was not important to him. In company formations he would wear his cap with the bill turned around. Saluting, he would bring up his hand to the back of his head. "What is the meaning of this?" asked the company commander. "I'm saluting the enlisted men," answered Sekay. "They deserve a salute more than the officers do."

Doc told me that when a soldier came off the front line for dental work he would pull one of his teeth, whether or not it was sound.

"Why would you do that?" I wanted to know.

"Because if one of these kids had an extraction it kept him out of combat for twenty-four hours. Any other procedure, they went right back to their unit. I gave a lot of kids an extra day of life."

I heard from Fran Fogarty that while Doc was in Korea both his wife and his daughter died and that Army red tape kept him from returning in time for either funeral, which embittered him further.

AJR was patient with Doc, but only up to a point. Complaints from the players about his unkempt looks, slovenly behavior, and disregard for sanitation at last became so numerous that the Chief had to act. He instructed Fran Fogarty to give Doc the word that his services were no longer required.

The last time I saw Doc – we met by chance on the street one day – he said he was working in the office of another dentist. "All I have to do," he told me, "is put on a white smock, wash my hands, and pull teeth."

He asked me where I was going. When I said, "To the bank," he reached in his pocket and brought out a large roll of bills. "How much do you need? I'm making a ton of money," he said.

I told him, "Thanks, Doc, but I'll be OK."

A year or so later I was reading Doc Sekay's obituary.

Butch

Butch was a big kid from the First Ward who seemed to have a future in football. A standout lineman at North Catholic High School, he attracted the attention of college scouts in his junior year. He attracted the attention of the girls in the neighborhood, too. With pretty little Betsy Sue, the attraction was mutual.

Soon they were going steady. Not long afterward, Betsy Sue was in an unwanted condition. Butch did not hesitate to do the right thing. Without a second thought, he married the girl.

At North Catholic in those days, there were certain inflexible rules. The Marianist Brothers could have expelled Butch; showing lenience, they encouraged him to save them the trouble. He transferred to Allegheny High School and continued to play football so well that two or three college coaches with scholarships to offer came calling. All bets were off, though, when they learned that a wife and child would be part of the deal, with still another child on the way. (College athletic departments had not yet begun to change with the times. In fact, the times themselves had not yet begun to change. Butch was ahead of the curve.)

So Butch went to work instead of to college. His father, a dispatcher for the Exhibitors Trucking Line, got him a job as a driver. In due time, he was driving a Pepsi-Cola truck. Pepsi-Cola drivers doubled as salesmen, and Butch had a salesman's personality. When the money started coming in, he, Betsy Sue, and their kids moved from the First Ward to an upscale part of the North Hills.

Betsy Sue had gone through nursing school and worked at various hospitals. Her salary helped pay for the arrival of a third child – born, unfortunately, with a physical disorder. In their search for a cure, the parents traveled far and wide, consulting with specialists and spending every dime of their savings.

One thing kept Butch's spirits up. As a First Ward kid who'd played football at North Catholic, he was not unknown to the Rooney family, and his connections landed him on "the chain gang," a highly coveted distinction.

The chain gang performed, and still does, at Steeler games. It consists of only three men. They carry a ten-yard length of chain attached to sticks at either end, the chain that is used to measure for first downs. At the top of one stick are the down markers – metal signboards numbered one through four, which are flipped after every play. Stick holders wear the uniform required by the NFL – white cap, white shirt, white knickers, black knee socks, and football shoes.

Butch gloried in this job. It brought him prestige, and the envy of his friends. It was a time when the Steelers were winning Super Bowls, and he had what is called high visibility. A lower profile, as it happened, might have kept him from getting into trouble.

When the Steelers played at Three Rivers Stadium the game officials went to their private dressing room for the fifteen-minute halftime intermission. The chain gang and the field crew had soft drinks and sandwiches in one of the two baseball dugouts. But soft drinks and sandwiches were not Butch's notion of a satisfying snack.

He started venturing into the stands and making his way to the concession area for a brewski or two and a hot dog or two. Butch liked people and liked to talk. It was not too long before friends and complete strangers were competing for the honor of buying him his beer and his dogs. He never once got drunk or out of line. It is natural, however, for people to spread tales, and the tales people spread about Butch were reaching NFL headquarters in New York – tales to the effect that officials at Steeler games were consorting with the fans and guzzling beer in the stands. Was it any wonder they were blowing so many calls? An investigation resulted, and the finger of blame pointed at Butch.

He must be fired, the league office insisted.

It was a staggering blow – the loss of psychic income more damaging to him than anything else. The Steelers had a great team, elevated to demi-god status, and Butch was a part of it. And now his comedown had turned him into a laughing stock. At work and at the neighborhood bar he patronized, Butch endured joke after joke. Outwardly, he affected indifference. "I'll make more money pushing soda pop than some of these football players will when their careers are over and they're has-beens," he said, fooling no one. Privately, he berated himself. To go up in the stands the way he did had been stupid. And he felt he had let down the Rooney family.

But it was true just the same that his soda pop business was thriving. His route was in the Hill District, and black people sure liked their Pepsi. They drank more soda pop, Butch used to say, than all of the other ethnic groups combined.

Betsy Sue, meanwhile, continued to work as a nurse. All three children went to college. The son who was born while Butch and Betsy Sue were still in their teens finished pharmacy school at Duquesne and found a well-paying job with one of the big drug-store chains. Butch himself was putting on too much weight. Betsy Sue worried about it and pestered him continually to diet, but life couldn't be better, he thought.

And then on a cold March night he was roused from his sleep by a telephone call. His son the pharmacist had died from an overdose of prescription drugs.

Butch was in shock. He could not understand it. Over and over he said that this was a boy who never had been a problem. Increasingly, he leaned on Betsy Sue, the more resilient of the two. He was drinking no more than usual, but seeking comfort in food.

Spring departed and summer came. At a family picnic on the Fourth of July, Butch again ate too much. Getting up from the table to greet a relative, he checked himself for a moment, collapsed into his chair, and lurched forward. His face in his third helping of fried chicken, baked beans, and potato salad, he was dead of a massive stroke. Those who really knew Butch, his closest friends, were convinced there had been a much deeper cause.

What he died of, they said, was a broken heart.

Political Pals

Even after Jimmy Coyne's downfall in the 1930s the North Side continued to be an assembly line for politicians, with the difference that now they were Democrats. Tom Foerster and Pete Flaherty, the most successful, had close ties with AJR. Foerster made some noise as a state legislator, but for most of his career was a county commissioner.

Finding ways to keep AJR's name before the public seemed to be Tom's avocation. He was a tireless organizer of award banquets and testimonial dinners. Pete Flaherty got his start as the attorney for the Steelers. Successively, he became a city councilman, mayor of Pittsburgh, deputy United States attorney general, and, like Foerster, a county commissioner.

Bob Colville – public-safety director, district attorney, and judge – had been another North Side kid who regarded AJR as a patron. Jim Flaherty, Pete Flaherty's brother, preceded his older sibling as a county commissioner but returned, after one term, to the practice of law. Jim was a sort of maverick commissioner, teaming up with the Republican minority commissioner, Bob Peirce, to neutralize Foerster, the chairman. There was never any kind of association that I know of between Jim Flaherty and AJR. Foerster, a big, curly-haired endomorph, had been a football player, a tackle, at North Catholic High School and Slippery Rock State Teachers College. While serving in the State Legislature he coached his neighborhood kids team, the Perry Atoms, and a Catholic grade-school team that competed with my brother Dan's team at St. Peter's. Tom distinguished himself in the legislature by working hard for the passage of environmental and conservation laws.

In the shifting power struggles of county government, he was always at the center of things, gaining, losing, or vying for control. The politics could often be tortuous. After Jimmy Carter's election to the presidency, everybody knew that he would offer Pete Flaherty a job in his Justice Department and that Flaherty would resign as mayor to accept it. In circumstances such as these, the president of City Council served out the departing mayor's term. At the time Flaherty left, the president was Jeep DePasquale, head of the ushers' union at Three Rivers Stadium. Foerster and his henchmen forced or persuaded Jeep to step aside for Dick Caliguiri and forced or persuaded Caliguiri to promise he would not be a candidate in the next primary election. Caliguiri kept his word; he did not run in the primary, and the nomination went to Foerster, as planned. But then in what looked to the Democratic power structure like a double-cross, Caliguiri ran as an independent in the general election. Having done well in his year as the incumbent, he won from Foerster hands down

It was never quite clear why Foerster wanted to be mayor, given the influence he could exercise, and the good he could do, as chairman of the county commission. He was largely responsible for

Allegheny County's community college system and for the billion-dollar expansion of the Greater Pittsburgh Airport in the 1990s – not a bad legacy.

Pete Flaherty came from a typical Irish family in what AJR considered "the right" part of town. He had a sister who married Jimmy Smith, the son of Billy Conn's father-in-law, Greenfield Jimmy Smith. Pete, a World War II veteran, went to a Pittsburgh girls' college, Mount Mercy, and to Notre Dame Law School as a beneficiary of the GI Bill. Right from the start, AJR recognized his potential.

What impressed the Chief most after Pete came to work for the Steelers was the *way* he handled a sensitive assignment at Shamrock Farm. It seems that the wife of the tenant farmer had been taking retarded children to live there in return for monthly payments from the state. In AJR's view, a house full of retarded kids was an accident waiting to happen. At the same time, he wanted them taken care of. He turned the problem over to Flaherty, who talked to the woman and gave her a lease on the farm house for a dollar a year with the understanding that as soon as she was able to move somewhere else and take the kids, she would do so. The lease, I suppose, put AJR in the clear if there was trouble with the state in the meantime. Flaherty's kindness and tact made the solution he came up with as agreeable to the woman and her husband as to everybody else.

Tall and somewhat shambling in the Jimmy Stewart manner, with an unruly forelock and photogenic blue eyes, Pete had uncommon political charisma. As mayor, he proved to be a ruthless cost cutter. He cleaned the deadwood out of City Hall and stood up to the featherbedding truck drivers' union. When Pete was in office in the 1970s other cities like Pittsburgh were going bankrupt. He kept it from happening here. But as "Nobody's Boy" – the label under which he campaigned – he made enemies, and his reclusive personality turned off many friends who at least by their own lights had helped him.

Being nobody's boy meant a freeze in his relationship with AJR. As disappointed as he may have been, AJR understood. He looked upon Pete as "one of our own" – Irish, Catholic, born and raised on the North Side. Enough said.

Chapter 65

A Kindly, Aging Guy

At his specialty, betting on horses, AJR was as good as they come. He knew every betting system, knew every scam, and knew all the schemers at all the tracks. I am quoting Pat Lynch, turf writer for the Morning Telegraph. He knew the horses, AJR did, knew the jockeys, knew the trainers, knew the touts, knew the bookies, knew the guys the bookies went to when they were looking to lay off a bet.

He considered race tracks his second home. At race tracks he could always feel good about himself. At race tracks his name commanded instant respect.

But at NFL meetings, with a new generation of businessman-owners taking over – sharp and self-important entrepreneurs – AJR the race-track legend seemed to be oddly diminished. He was looked on, it appeared, as just a kindly, aging guy in a rumpled dark suit – a little too nice and a little too easy-going to stay in the swim.

Certainly he appreciated irony and certainly he could laugh at himself. He understood where talent and where luck came into play. But maybe this was too much. AJR prepared for a horse race as thoroughly as Paul Brown prepared for a football game. In a world far tougher than the NFL, not only had he survived – he had flourished. To see how little that counted with men such a world would have eaten alive must have nettled him, and yet it's hard to be sure. If he ever felt patronized no one could tell. Behind his gambler's poker face, his feelings were not for public display. Even the way he dressed was part of the mask.

But he could put almost anybody, stuffed shirts not excepted, at ease. I recall a business luncheon in fancy surroundings – a private dining room in the William Penn Hotel if I'm not mistaken – at a time when we were starting to look at things other than football. On this occasion we met with some people from the Consolidated Coal Company, good ol' West Virginia boys who had risen in the corporate hierarchy and were now big executives dressed for the part and acting the part and very much aware of their hard-won eminence. In just a few minutes, the Chief softened them up.

Exactly as he did with everyone – waitresses, bus boys, parking attendants, elevator operators – he asked one of the men where he was from. Reluctantly, the coal company honcho mentioned a little town in the West Virginia panhandle. "Been there," said AJR. "You know, I used to play center field for the Wheeling Stogies in the Middle Atlantic League. When we played in your town we got into a big fight. My brother Dan – he's a priest now – was our catcher, and he laid out a guy on the other team. You had a big, fat sheriff, I remember. I'll never forget him."

Interested suddenly, the coal company man forgot he was wearing a Brooks Brothers suit and broke in to say, "He died just this year, that sheriff did. I knew him well." Then the others chimed in with their own reminiscences. Three of the four, it turned out, had played baseball in West Virginia themselves, and now they were dredging up ancient games and ancient anecdotes, kindred spirits, for the moment, with AJR, and he was having as much fun as anyone else at the table.

His stories were contagious – they got the ball rolling. They were never about sex and he always mangled the punch line, if by some chance there happened to be one, but people listened. At Toots Shor's Restaurant in New York, AJR and Bert Bell would start telling football stories and keep on going until Shor chased them out of the place at two or three in the morning with just the waiters and a handful of sportswriters still hanging in and eager for more.

This was AJR the spellbinder. At home we got AJR the sermonizer – hellfire and brimstone. And we listened as raptly as the waiters and sportswriters did. We listened because we had to. For us, there was no other choice.

Dirt

Trainer Ralph Berlin recalled that when the Steelers played home games at Pitt Stadium, AJR would spend the hours before the kickoff in their dressing room, seated on an equipment trunk and absorbed in conversation with Horse Czarnecki, the Pitt groundskeeper. Much of the time he'd be laughing and gesturing, waving his cigar like a band leader's baton, Berlin said.

AJR would have liked to bring Horse to the new stadium with us, but Czarnecki by that time was a permanent fixture at Pitt. In any case, the same ground crew that worked at Forbes Field had moved to Three Rivers with the Pirates.

Headed by Eddie Dunn, who had learned the business under John Fogarty, Fran's dad, the ground-crew members were spirited, obscene, opinionated, inbred (nepotism dictated the hiring), and unionized. They could make life difficult for an employer, but AJR was on good terms with all of them. He knew their relatives, he knew their politics, and he knew their frailties, which he excused.

AJR had the common touch. The hot walkers and stable boys at the race tracks we operated in Philadelphia, Vermont, and Yonkers idolized him. So did their counterparts at our greyhound track in Palm Beach. This rapport between AJR and people who worked with their hands for low wages was something that Pat, John, Tim, and I used to discuss. Our father's attitude seemed to be "We're all in this together, but some of us are luckier than others." He understood how these "others" felt and could make them see that he understood. The odd thing, of course, was that he never had worked a day in his life. He worked a half-day, in a steel mill, and then quit.

My relations with the ground crew lacked the same intimacy as my father's. One time when he invited the whole bunch, wives and all, to a week of Super Bowl fun in Miami, we were lining up after a pre-game party to get on the bus. Kay, our kids, and Father Bob Reardon were with me. As the bus door swung open, one of the young ground-crew guys jumped ahead of us, bumping my little girl Susie out of his way. I followed him onto the bus, grabbed him by the neck, and pinioned him against a support pole. Neither of us said a word – we just looked at each other – and after a few seconds I released him.

Father Reardon, I think, was in shock. My kids were very obviously in shock. I expected AJR to castigate me. Ground-crew guys were sacred cows, and I had over-reacted. For whatever reason, he let me off the hook. I was reprimanded instead by one of the ground-crew wives. At the end of the bus ride, when we were filing into the hotel, she came up beside me and said, "You have to understand that we're people. We have little kids just like you do." It was then that I experienced full remorse. I said to myself, "You'll never be the man your father is."

The sequel to this embarrassing incident was strange. From then on, the ground-crew guys would go out of their way to say hi, and the new head man of the crew, Dirt DiNardo, made a special effort to strike up conversations. "Come around and hang out with us," he suggested. I was still too mortified to take him up on it.

One of the football players – L.C. Greenwood, I believe – gave DiNardo his moniker. Dirt was a loud, heavy-set, dark-skinned Italian, quick to speak up in any situation. AJR liked his boldness and humor, and he spent as much time with Dirt as he had with Horse Czarnecki. Once when Dad and I were returning by air from a trip to Yonkers, the stewardess asked for our drink orders. I said, "Coke." I'm a total abstainer. Dad, who had been on the wagon for years, said, "Ginger ale and Canadian Club." He then told the stewardess to bring me some Canadian Club too. When she had left us, I gave him a look. He said, "We're in first class. The booze comes with it. Always pick up the drinks." They were served in small three-ounce bottles with the seal unbroken. "Bring them home to me." For Mom and Aunt Alice, I thought he was going to explain. But no. He said, "I'll give them to Steve."

Steve? Who was this Steve, I asked.

"Steve DiNardo – Dirt. On your scouting trips, you travel all over the country. Always pick up the booze for Dirt."

Of course I complied. If I neglected to – purposely at times – more than likely I would hear from AJR.

"Did you get the whiskey for Dirt?"

One day at Three Rivers when I took a free agent onto the field for a workout, Dirt and his crew were rolling up the big, heavy tarpaulin. At one end, I noticed a little white-haired guy with a cigar in his mouth. AJR was in his seventies then, and pushing as hard as everybody else. It staggered me to see my father engaged in what could only be called manual labor.

He would sometimes watch practice from the vantage point of Dirt's tractor, contentedly smoking his cigar. The tractor had two massive wheels in back and two small ones in front, behind a power brush for removing snow from the field. Dirt's proudest moment with the tractor came on a December afternoon in 1978, when the Steelers played the Baltimore Colts in a blizzard. Ordered by the officials to keep the yard lines visible, he did just that, racing back and forth across the Tartan Turf and leaving pale green strips on the snowy surface. He worked during timeouts and he worked while the game was going on. The teams would be at one end of the field and DiNardo at the other. He was more of a threat to Baltimore's defensive backs than Terry Bradshaw was, sometimes coming within a foot or two of mowing them down. They shouted at Dirt, and Dirt shouted back. "I've got a job to do!" he let them know.

Dirt was never shy about protecting his territory. After a cold-weather playoff game with the Oakland Raiders at Three Rivers, Al Davis, the Raiders' owner, accused him of conspiring with AJR to let the Tartan Turf near the sidelines freeze. The purpose of this nefarious scheme, Davis said, was to make it difficult for the Raiders to run their sideline pass patterns.

Dirt's professional pride would not allow him to forget such an affront. The next time the Raiders came to Pittsburgh, he took his revenge. Waiting until John Madden, the Raiders' coach, had led his team onto the field for a Saturday workout, Dirt gruffly ordered them to "get the fuck off." Madden was about the size of the legendary Bigfoot and accustomed to being spoken to with a lot more civility. "Do you know who I am?" he demanded. "I don't give a fuck who you are," answered Dirt. "My men have some work to do on this field." The Raiders didn't practice that day until Dirt and his crew were finished with their chores.

Madden went to AJR for a rundown on Dirt and concluded that feuding with him would not be productive. "I'll win the guy over with kindness," he said. From then on when the Raiders played here, Madden always took time for a visit with Dirt and brought his name up frequently at press conferences, referring to him as "my good friend." Apparently it was more than just fence-mending. Years afterward, when he was a well-known member of the Monday Night Football broadcasting team, if Madden encountered someone with a Steeler connection he would ask to be remembered to Dirt.

In their game uniforms – shimmering yellow acetate shirts and white duck pants the first year at Three Rivers – the ground crew looked like a mariachi band. These outfits were provided by the Pirates. When the ground crew was actually at work they wore castoff Steeler regalia – T-shirts, old game jerseys, old warm-up jackets, discarded tassel caps. Tony Parisi and Jack Hart, the equipment managers, had instructions to be generous with the ground crew. While AJR was alive, it would not have surprised me to see them show up in Steeler helmets and knee pants.

Even the trainer's room was available to the ground crew if one of them needed first aid. Bumps and bruises went with the job, and the Steelers' trainers worked on these men as conscientiously as they attended to the players.

At least once a year, AJR would have a party for Dirt and his boys in their quarters at the stadium. He would buy the best ham for the cooks at the Allegheny Club to bake, order Jewish rye bread and New York cheesecake from a place in Squirrel Hill, and supply the booze, large quantities of it. To imagine John Galbreath doing something like this would be impossible.

For heavy-lifting chores at 940 North Lincoln Avenue, Dad would send DiNardo and some of his men to help Mom, Aunt Alice, and the maid, Mary Roseboro. I saw them in action just once – at Christmas time. Mom, impeccably dressed and ladylike, was still a North Sider, issuing crisp orders as they put up the tree. "Barry, you're tall," she would say. "Please put the star up on top ... Now, that looks just right ... Steve, don't worry about the bulbs. Mary will take care of it ..." And so on. Dirt and the others, striving to be gentlemen, kept their voices carefully subdued.

Sometimes on summer nights if AJR saw the lights on at the stadium and knew the Pirates were out of town he would hop into his car and make the short drive from North Lincoln to see what was happening. Usually Dirt and the gang were getting ready for an event of some kind – a rock concert, perhaps. Cigar in hand, AJR would watch them set up the stage. And then he might stay for the performance, looking on from the dugout with the crew. "Hey, Dirt," he might say, "what kind of music is that?" Or, "Say ... what's that sweet smell? The more I sniff it, the better the music sounds."

After AJR's death, I made a sentimental journey to my boyhood home and took ten cigars from his humidor. I gave five of them to Ralph Berlin. The other five were for Dirt DiNardo.

Chapter 66

High Noon

After the 1978 season Chuck Noll's mantra, reiterated time and again in his conversations with the press, was: "This team has not peaked." Noll said what he thought and thought what he said, but I didn't see it that way.

Granted, we were still getting stellar performances from our best players, nine of them future Hall of Famers and two others good enough to be nominated for the Hall several times. The center, Mike Webster, never seemed to age, and his career was not yet half over. Franco Harris had lost a step for sure, but was still a quick, powerful runner with the savvy derived from years of big-game experience. He was still cranking out the thousand-yard rushing seasons that would make him, next to Jim Brown, the most productive ball carrier in NFL history at the time of his retirement. Rocky Bleier had been a thousand-yard runner in 1976 and was coming off an excellent Super Bowl game. Terry Bradshaw, maturing late, had come into his own. There was never any question about his talent. As long ago as 1969 we had known what Bradshaw could do, and now he was doing it. At the other end of his passes, John Stallworth and Lynn Swann were the best receiving tandem in the NFL. The foundation of our defense, Mean Joe Greene, was showing a few cracks, but the combination of Greene, L. C. Greenwood, Dwight White, and John Banaszak gave us a truly formidable front four. In the defensive backfield, there was Mel Blount, whose disruptive pass coverage had forced a change in the rules. Blount was as good as ever – better, in fact; he had learned the principles of team defense and was playing with more discipline. Mike Wagner gave us stability at the safety position. Like Blount, and like Donnie Shell, he could rattle a pass catcher's teeth. Going on down through the roster, I could talk about Moon Mullins and Sam Davis, who had started all three of our Super Bowl games at guard; Hall-of-Fame nominees Larry Brown and Jon Kolb; backups like Ted Petersen, Steve Courson, Jimmy Smith, and Sidney Thornton.

But so many of these players were now more than 30 years old. AJR believed, as Noll did, that they hadn't peaked. I was the lone Doubting Thomas, and it made me uncomfortable. More than anything else, I wanted to be wrong. It was not that I expected our team to dry up and blow away, following the example of other Super Bowl winners in the past. I thought that, with no important changes, we could have good teams, playoff teams, or winning seasons, at least for another five years. Meanwhile, I told myself, Noll would be artfully rebuilding, piecing together his next Super Bowl team. If we could draft and develop three good players a year we would stay on track.

It sounded good. The fallacy was that three new quality starters a year would keep the machine running but not allow us to win big. To win really big, you needed three *great* new players every year, people who could not just make the good plays consistently, but make the great plays consistently – and do it in big games. It would come as a bonus that great players elevate the performance of good players – "catapult" them, Lynn Swann used to say.

As winners, we'd be drafting late. In the NFL, this was a fact of life, and not, in my opinion, an excuse for mediocrity. There were other ways, I thought, to explain the difficulty of staying on top. I knew that on the good teams the players lost their edge. Successful and well paid, they went into every game a little too complacent, taking it for granted they would win. Players on championship teams forget how they got to where they are. A scout from a great team in decline once told me that when your players show up with Wall Street Journals instead of The Sporting News tucked beneath their arms, you know you're in trouble. I wondered if the agents who hustled endorsements for their players understood that endorsements could be a pitfall. These were the things that Noll called "distractions." "We have to get back to the basics," he would say.

And draft even better than we had been, I added silently. I asked Doc Best if a football player past 30 was over the hill. He shook his head. "Naw. That idea is a lot of bunk, especially for quarterbacks. With a good training program, a guy can go on and on. But I'll tell you something that happens to those nine-and ten-year vets. Since high school, they've been taking hits; they enter the injury phase of their careers. Formerly, they would get banged up on Sunday, rest, shake it off, and be practicing again on Wednesday. But now they need more time to recover. Instead of practicing three or four days a week, they're practicing one or two days. And then before you know it they're hardly practicing at all. They play on Sunday, and that's it. There's an old saying, Artie – 'practice makes perfect.' Pretty soon those guys are missing a game here and there. Then they're missing more than just a game; they'll be out for several weeks. They're hurting like hell every day, and they don't like football any more, don't like the whole package: summer camp at St. Vincent, the practices, the meetings, the aches and pains. The money's good and the attention's good, but the price is too high. They chuck it in – or they *should* chuck it in."

Too many Steelers had reached that stage, it seemed to me, but there I disagreed with Noll, and I hoped Noll was right. My job would be to draft the way we had from 1969 through 1974 while sticking to Noll's guidelines; my scouts were to look for the kind of player Noll could motivate, the ones with football smarts and recognizable, if unrefined, athletic ability. It was easy to say, "We want the great athlete." The great athlete who had fully realized his potential was out of our reach; we were drafting at the bottom, remember. Consequently, we had to hold our mistakes to a minimum and reel in the players Noll and his assistants could teach. Noll was a football genius; with superior playing schemes, he could make us win and win big. So our work was cut out for us in the upcoming 1979 draft.

It would be more challenging, even, than I thought. Jack Butler kept urging me: "Go after guys who are tough and who play with consistency. Toughness and consistency can't be taught." In other words, leopards don't change their spots. Still, we believed that if a kid had exceptional athletic ability, coaching would bring out whatever else may have been lacking.

We continued to rely on Blesto as the base of our scouting system, but Blesto's past success was taking a toll. Too many of the scouts who had made it possible were leaving the organization for better-paying jobs with NFL teams either affiliated or unaffiliated with Blesto. Butler kept bringing in promising young scouts, molding them into the finished product, and then losing them. Blesto, nonetheless, continued to be a valuable tool for us.

I have said that pushing back the draft from late January or early February to the beginning of spring was not advantageous to the Steelers, the Rams, or the Cowboys. These were the three teams, I thought, with the most highly developed scouting systems. In my opinion, the time, money, and resources we put into scouting had given us an edge. Now the rest of the field had a chance to catch up with us. They were getting their coaches involved.

So were we, and in our case this was causing problems. Noll and his assistants were swamping us with their reports. Added to the necessity of scouting the post-season all-star games, there were meetings with Noll and his staff to attend. All of this called for substantial amounts of time – time we had previously spent on the road, on interviewing coaches, watching practices, comparing notes, picking up information. In the staff meetings, there were questions to be answered – questions from Noll and his coaches, questions, even, from AJR and Dan. Much more film had to be watched, much more information had to be processed.

In my mind, the ancient bromide that too many cooks spoil the broth was sounding more and more like a priceless bit of wisdom. I was now making judgments that were based more on other people's opinions than my own. Whether this was good or bad, I didn't like it. I was spilling out answers like the history major I had been at St. Vincent in the early 1950s. When I talked about a prospect it was not with my former fervor. I was repeating what others had told me. In the years when I was free to spend weeks on the scouting trail, weeks that began on Labor Day and kept me busy until after Thanksgiving (at the sacrifice of my family life, I'm afraid), I could speak from first-hand, personal observation.

Even so, I was ready to go to war for my beliefs. Only now I had to be temperate. I was part of a team effort. Never mind that I had no respect for the input from certain assistant coaches. "No complaining," I said to the scouts. "Let's just get the job done. We're after the best athletes we can get who are smart enough and coachable enough to pick up Noll's system."

One week Noll requisitioned Dick Haley and Dick Hoak and flew them to Texas in his private plane. For us, this was something new, a departure from our modus operandi. The reason, it seemed, was the presence at Baylor of a running back who could be the perfect fit for us. His name was Greg Hawthorne. He had the football intelligence Noll demanded. He was in every way a solid citizen. And he was the best athlete likely to be available when our turn came to draft. Here was a player who just might be one of the great ones we would need very soon as replacements for worn-out parts.

Hawthorne stood 6-2 1/2 and weighed 218 pounds. He was fast – a sprinter on Baylor's track team. With his fleetness of foot, he could get outside on sweeps; with his size, he could go up the middle and move the pile. One thing kept him from being an early first-round pick: a chipped bone in his hip. Because of it, he had missed a large portion of the 1978 season. Noll was flying to Waco with Haley and Hoak to see for himself how serious the injury might be.

Auditioning in T-shirt and shorts for this jury of three, Hawthorne was impressive. He demonstrated running ability and catching ability. He ran flawless pass routes. Hawthorne was a lad who excelled in the world of drills. The game films we studied – films, for the most part, from 1977, his last full season – revealed that he could make good plays with consistency and great plays every so often. Will Walls used to say, "If a guy can do it once, he can do it all the time." I had decided that this was malarkey, but now we all seemed to be falling for it, especially Noll. Woody Widenhofer argued that except for Hawthorne's hip he would be a high first-round choice. Well, we all make misjudgments.

The trouble was that Hawthorne was only the forerunner. For the next few years, drafting late, we'd be taking flashy kids who were not consistent when we might have helped ourselves more in the first and second rounds. Noll had always wanted a running back with the speed to get off tackle, the size to hit for the tough yardage inside, and the hands to catch all kinds of passes. He wanted a running back who could beat the strong safety in man-to-man coverage, and Hawthorne appeared to be the guy. He appeared to be a mixture of Paul Hornung and Frank Gifford.

Noll had seen all these things in Preston Pearson, and when Pearson was with the Steelers he lived up to expectations but not consistently. Pearson seemed to think that blocking for Franco Harris was somebody else's job – Rocky Bleier's, to be precise – and there were too many times when he failed to hang onto the ball. His shortcomings made him expendable, and after the 1974 season we shipped him to Dallas, where he did quite well, becoming a good, productive player on a championship team. Noll may have come to believe that he had given up on Pearson too soon; if so he never admitted it. And yet I'd swear he was hopeful that in Hawthorne we'd be getting another Pearson. This would undo the mistake he may have feared we had made.

All right, I'm speculating; in any case, Hawthorne was the first player we drafted. I didn't argue. In the second round we took a linebacker from North Carolina State. Purely as an athlete, Zack Valentine resembled the "perfect" linebacker, Jack Ham. And we thought he might grow into a pass rusher on the order of Dwight White. Could be a real good one, we assured one another. *Should* be a real good one. We were wrong.

Our third-round pick was the one the so-called shoulder-pad incident – a violation of a widely disregarded rule — had cost us. The shoulder-pad incident will be fully explained as we move along. Suffice it to say for now that we had put the whole thing behind us. Certain sportswriters guessed that the penalty imposed by the NFL kept us from taking, as our third-round choice, Joe Montana. Montana was a Western Pennsylvania kid who had quarterbacked Notre Dame. He threw a soft short and medium-range pass that was very accurate and very easy to catch. It was also easy to intercept. Dick Haley had him pegged as a third-round selection, but I must tell you again that we were drafting last. When the Steelers' turn came in the third round, Montana was long gone. The Forty-Niners had taken him.

Why, then, hadn't we moved the guy up to the second round? Because we didn't have him rated that high. Neither, may I point out, did the Forty-Niners or any other team. At Notre Dame, Montana had been the quarterback who came off the bench. The Notre Dame alumnus who recruited him was Fritz Wilson, Jack McGinley's partner in the beer business; Carl Hughes remembered that every week during the football season, Wilson would get a call from Montana's mother. "Why isn't Joe playing?" she would ask. Sure, Montana's in the Hall of Fame now, but in 1979 this was largely unforeseeable.

With our two fourth-round picks, we went for Russell Davis, a fullback from Michigan who had size, strength, and willingness, and Calvin Sweeney, a fast wide receiver from USC who made the difficult catches look easy. In that respect, he was similar to Lynn Swann. Unlike Swann, he also made the easy catches look difficult. Sweeney gave us one good year out of eight with the team. Davis, envisioned as a replacement for Rocky Bleier, lasted four years but never came close to taking over the role. During much of that time, he was on the injured reserve list.

Rounds five through twelve yielded just two players who were helpful to us – Dwayne Woodruff, defensive back from Louisville, and placekicker Matt Bahr from Penn State. Woodruff became a longtime starter who was our MVP one season. In later life he practiced law, ending up as a judge. Bahr replaced Roy Gerela, whose performance had deteriorated with age. Bahr's kickoffs left something to be desired, but he converted field-goal opportunities from forty yards or less with great accuracy. As long as we had Bahr, we could almost count on getting three points whenever our still tenacious defense forced turnovers or punts in enemy territory.

Along with Zack Valentine, two other rookies hung around for one season. They were linebacker Tom Graves of Michigan State, an eighth-round pick, and running back Anthony Anderson of Temple. The 1979 team won another Super Bowl championship, and these three supernumeraries were part of it. They had their big winner's bonuses, their Super Bowl rings, and a wealth of recollections to share with friends and family for the rest of their lives.

Greg Hawthorne played five years for the Steelers but reminded no one of Paul Hornung or Frank Gifford. For that matter, he did not even resemble the Preston Pearson who disappointed us in Pittsburgh, let alone the Preston Pearson who played so much better for Dallas. His story was the same as it had been at Baylor: too many injuries, not enough consistency. Taking him off our hands, the Patriots thought he could be a tight end; the experiment lasted until 1989 with only moderate success. AJR had taken a liking to Hawthorne and wrote a letter of recommendation to the Sullivans, the Patriots' owners. Learning of it, Hawthorne from then on was one of the Chief's worshippers, an ever-growing multitude.

Calvin Sweeney led the Steelers in receptions one year. Sweeney and Hawthorne were great guys but not great football players. We got rid of the likable Bahr, after just two seasons, because of a rap pinned onto him by one of Noll's assistants: "He's killing us with those short kickoffs." Bahr's subsequent NFL career went on for another sixteen years. His older brother Chris, also a kicker, played for fourteen years.

We failed to achieve our goal of drafting three new starters every year, three new starters who could play for a winning team. In my time with the Steelers, we never again drafted a Hall-of-Fame player. We had some very good players, such as Louis Lipps, wide receiver from Mississippi Southern, but no catapults, to borrow Lynn Swann's figure of speech. Gabe Rivera, the defensive tackle we drafted out of Texas Tech in 1983, might have been such a player, but an automobile accident in his rookie season left him permanently crippled. Other than Lipps and Rivera, our first-round picks over the seven years after 1979 were either average players or not even that. There were top-level performers on those teams of the 1980s, but not enough of them to put us into a Super Bowl.

Nineteen seventy-nine was to be our last hurrah during the reign of Chuck Noll, but a cherished last hurrah that continues to resonate.

Sidney

Running backs don't last long in the NFL. Wear and tear comes with the job. It is doubly burdensome to be a running back who blocks when he doesn't have the ball, and by 1977 Rocky Bleier's exertions were beginning to tell.

Bleier's history was well known: Drafted out of Notre Dame in 1968. His rookie season cut short by a call from the draft board in Appleton, Wisconsin. Horribly shot up in Vietnam. More than two years of arduous rehabilitation. His unlikely return to the Steelers, detailed so well in "Fighting Back," a blockbuster autobiography. He had not reached the end of the line, but it behooved us to look ahead. Sidney Thornton, our second-round draft pick from Northwestern Louisiana, was the running back we hoped would be his successor.

Chuck Noll worked him into the lineup gradually. Filling in at first for Franco Harris now and then, he did not do badly at all. He would block, or perhaps I should say at times he would block. He could hit the line hard and break a tackle. He made some big runs – when he found the right hole. On the debit side, he was too much inclined to fumble.

There were other things we learned about Sidney. "He's not the sharpest knife in the drawer," I'd been warned. But on a ninety-minute flight from Louisiana to Pittsburgh, he conversed with me quite sensibly. When I reported this to Dick Haley, he laughed and said, "Art, you could talk to anyone that long." Any good listener, I think Haley meant.

"Let's see if he has football smarts," Haley added. Well, Thornton did have football smarts – sort of. What he also had was a propensity to get hurt and to pick up avoidable illnesses. For example, food poisoning once caused him to miss a stretch of games.

"What did you eat?" Ralph Berlin demanded.

"Oh, just some pizza. I had it in the ice box."

Berlin couldn't see any harm in eating a little reheated pizza. As an afterthought, he asked, "How long was it in the refrigerator?"

"About three weeks" said Thornton, clearing up the mystery.

Sidney always seemed to have a sprained ankle; for big running backs, sprained ankles can take a long time to heal. In desperation, he consulted a voodooist from the bayous of his home state. The witch doctor was an old woman. She concocted an emollient for Sidney to use, its main ingredient being human urine. Whether Sidney applied the stuff to his ankle was something I never wanted to know.

It was Sidney of whom Chuck Noll aptly declared, "His problems are great, and they are many."

Mr. Peepers

Between the end of one football season and the start of another, coaches have too much time on their hands. In the way that nature does, Coach Noll abhorred a vacuum, and he filled the empty days with sessions like the one he instituted in the spring of 1970; he invited (read: ordered) all the rookies and free agents, together with the quarterbacks, the players who had been on the injured reserve list during the previous season, and the players whose chances of making the team were in question, to an "indoctrination period" at Three Rivers Stadium. For the better part of a week, the rookies and free agents would acquaint themselves with our offensive and defensive schemes, the quarterbacks and bubble players would learn the new plays Noll intended to put in, and the injured reservists would undergo conditioning tests.

Noll was always in search of a "good picture," as he put it, and this, he believed, would provide one, but not if all of these guys were simply "running around in their underwear" – i.e., wearing T-shirts and shorts instead of football gear. Inconveniently, NFL rules prohibited any kind of equipment at these mini-camps except helmets. The idea was to discourage contact, which league rules also prohibited. In Noll's mind, the regulations made no sense. To put twenty or thirty football players on a football field and expect them to refrain from bumping into one another was unrealistic. On his own, he decided to stretch the rules and allow them to wear shoulder pads. Pittsburgh was not the only team to hold a mini-camp in the spring, and most of the others ignored the shoulder-pad rule, so why not the Steelers? With helmets and shoulder pads, the players would feel protected, Noll reasoned. They would move faster, show off their skills to better effect.

In the spring of 1979, I watched the first day's workout with Dick Haley and Bill Nunn. As we were leaving the field, I said to Haley, casually, "Of course, we're breaking a rule with the shoulder pads." All of us knew this. All of us knew that other teams broke the rule. And all of us felt, as Noll did, that we could not let these others get the jump on us, regardless of how trivial the advantage might be.

Admittedly, a rule is a rule. But the NFL, it seemed to me, had been turning a blind eye to the rule against shoulder pads. Don't ask, don't tell. So I did not think our rule-breaking was anything really scandalous.

I was at the Blesto meeting in Florida with my fellow scouts when I heard about the controversy that erupted. A young reporter from the *Pittsburgh Press*, John Clayton, had been present at one of the "indoctrination" workouts – or perhaps he had merely caught a glimpse of the players on their way from the locker room to the field. At any rate, he started to ask questions. Was there not a league rule against shoulder pads? There was? Then why were the players wearing them? Because other teams did it? To find out what the official attitude was – like Noll, he wanted a "good picture" – Clayton put in a call to the commissioner's office in New York, and the fat was in the fire. Once notified that the Steelers were wearing shoulder pads, the commissioner's office would have to take steps.

I think that in 1979, Dan, Noll, and I regarded sportswriters who came to practice as our "guests." What was seen there was to be kept there, we thought. Later on, I realized how immature that notion is. When I was sounding off on the subject, Bill Nunn said to me, "Art, I was a newspaperman myself. Newspapermen have a job to do, just like coaches and scouts. The people connected with the team may be their friends in a way, but you can only protect your friends up to a point. Then you're risking your own job, because if you sit on a story as a favor to the owners or the coaches or the players, somebody else on some other paper will report it."

AJR either had already learned this or knew it instinctively. He would tell me, "Don't talk to the press. You don't have a knack for it, like I do. All you're going to do is get in trouble." I think he was mostly right, but partly wrong. Talking freely to the press has hurt me in some ways and helped me in others. Wherever the truth lay, I resented the implication that I was "brand new," a slur I'd been hearing from AJR all my life.

Noll and Dan, aware that Clayton was going to write a shoulder-pad story, attempted damage control. If the story got into print, there'd be "hell to pay." The NFL would have no choice but to impose the proscribed penalty - a fine and the loss of a draft choice. Indirectly, through Pat Livingston, they contacted the editor of the *Press*, John Troan. Troan was a Steeler fan. He was immensely fond of AJR. He respected Noll and Dan. But he stood behind his reporter. The story would appear in the next day's *Press*. "If it's a bad rule," he suggested, "then the NFL ought to change it."

Not long afterward, we were fined – I don't recall the amount – and deprived of our third-round choice in the 1979 draft. I was furious. I did not blame Noll, I blamed Clayton. An outsider, a newspaper guy, was impeding my effort to keep our team on top through the draft.

The story and its repercussions turned a spotlight on Clayton. Outraged Steeler fans attacked him for his perfidy. So did a majority of the radio and television sportscasters. The newspaper guys all defended him: he had handled the situation in a fearless, professional manner.

I had known John Clayton a long time. As a high school kid, he covered our pre-season training camp for one of those shopping center "green sheets." It wasn't much of a paper, but Clayton obtained access to the practice field and locker room. His mother, I remembered, drove him to St.

Vincent every day. If the perception that he was still a mama's boy embarrassed him, he gave no hint of it, and his *sang froid* impressed me. I was even more impressed by the willingness of his mother to encourage his ambition.

Nothing about Clayton's looks was impressive. A pipsqueak, he was short and thin. He wore glasses. He was nerdy-looking, a youthful Mr. Peepers. I imagined him as the smartest kid in his class at school. He was always respectful and asked intelligent questions. After graduation from Duquesne University – his choice of a college gave him a leg up with the Rooneys – he landed a job at the *Press*. Over time, I found out that I had underestimated this guy.

The *Press* underestimated him, too. Taken off the Steeler beat after Troan had retired and Russ Brown had succeeded Livingston as sports editor, Clayton moved on to a newspaper in Tacoma, Washington, and became a stringer on the side for the cable television network ESPN. He had a face made for radio, as they say, but established himself in just a few years as ESPN's most knowledgeable pro football correspondent. Nobody else in his field was breaking more big stories than Clayton, whose competence has earned him a place in the writers' wing of professional football's Hall of Fame.

From the shoulder-pad incident, I learned the truth of something AJR had observed – that newspaper and radio-TV reporters no longer conformed to the Jack Sell-Joe Tucker-Pat Livingston mold. Among the newer breed, the competition was fierce. No longer did anyone worry that something in the paper might make us look bad. It was "out of my way or a leg off." If the reporters smelled a story we wanted to cover up, they'd "gang up on us – operate in packs," I heard Dan complain.

"They'll ask the trainer a question about an injury the coach would rather conceal from our next opponent. Ralph Berlin will throw them a bone. He'll say just enough to get off the hook. What they do then is take the little bit of information Berlin has given them to Tony Parisi. 'Player A has a knee problem. will he suit up for practice?' Tony, he figures they already know how bad the guy's knee is. So he tells them, 'I can't say much, but no – the player won't dress.' Then with that information they go to Dick Haley. 'We hear that this guy has a bad knee. Won't dress. Might need surgery.' Haley thinks they know the whole story, so he confirms it. The only thing I'm saying is: be careful. They're tricking us into giving them stories we don't want in the paper."

Dan's new rules cramped my style. In dealing with reporters I tended to say more than I should. Wariness wasn't my strong suit. It would be better, I decided, if I simply kept my mouth shut, never the easiest thing for me to do.

My anger at John Clayton subsided when I saw that AJR was treating him like an old and trusted friend. I followed the Chief's lead and became very comfortable with Clayton. Meanwhile, though, deep inside, a little voice told me to watch my step. Clayton's agenda was different from mine, after all, and I don't think I ever forgot it.

At the draft meeting that year, we referred to the pick we didn't have in the third round with a mixture of ruefulness and humor. There were those who called it the shoulder-pad pick and still others who called it the John Clayton pick.

'A Great American Sportsman'

Even before our third Super Bowl victory, AJR was everlastingly in demand for speeches and public appearances. He liked the attention but pretended not to. His "speeches" rarely lasted more than three minutes. He knew how to get to the point quickly and he knew how to infuse his remarks with humor in perfect taste.

Sometimes it seemed that he lived to accept honors and awards. He was constantly being asked to attend some banquet or luncheon, if only to stand and take a bow. Invitations came from civic organizations, social organizations, fraternal organizations, and athletic organizations. The Catholic Youth Association sold one thousand tickets every year to an awards banquet called the Art Rooney Dinner. Even today, with the name unchanged, it's the CYA's biggest money-maker.

AJR was at the same time gregarious and shy. He overcame what I think was a natural reticence by seeming genuinely interested in everybody he met. After his rise in the public eye to a level just short of deification, the mere sight of him could overawe the unsophisticated – young football players, young sportswriters and broadcasters, many ordinary people aware of his status as a legend.

Then he would show, with the ease of a skilled actor, his unpretentious side. "How are ya?" he would say. "What's your name? Where ya from?"

Displayed to strangers familiar with the name but not the image — strangers who never had seen the man on television or pictured in a newspaper — this unaffected informality was sometimes confusing. At Three Rivers Stadium, AJR had a habit of leaving his office and wandering around sort of aimlessly, his arms behind his back, a cigar in the corner of his mouth. More often than not he'd be wearing a dark cashmere polo shirt with a necktie. The polo shirt would have a pocket in it for his matches and hearing aid. He was in the lobby one day, emptying an ash tray, when a brand new Steeler rookie walked through the door. The player didn't recognize AJR. He was there to see Dan, or maybe Chuck Noll, and asked for directions. AJR, after telling him where to go, detained the kid briefly for the usual interrogation – "What's your name? Where ya from?" and so on. Later, when the rookie was told he'd been greeted by Art Rooney, he exclaimed, "My God! I thought I was talking to the janitor!"

AJR would not have been offended by this. Still, there was something in his demeanor that commanded the utmost respect. Old friends addressed him as "Art," new friends and everybody else as "Mister Rooney." Just once did I hear him called, to his face, "Chief." A newly-employed secretary committed that indiscretion. She never repeated it.

The polo shirt with the inappropriate necktie was my Dad's only sartorial eccentricity. On formal occasions, he wore a necktie that never called attention to itself with a well-fitted white dress shirt and a conservative dark suit. His pants were always creased, his shoes were always shined, and he was always neatly barbered. Kass, his superintendent in such matters, saw to that. Once when my wife happened to read a description of me as "an overweight man who has little regard for grooming," she took me to task. "Where did you come from?" she demanded. "You look too much like your father to be a bastard. There's a missing gene in you — the grooming gene!"

If Fran Fogarty had been the watchdog of AJR's purse, Mary Regan and Ed Kiely were the guardians of his time. Given free rein, their boss was accessible to everybody, from bankers and cardinals and high-ranking politicians all the way down to street beggars. In the absence of Mary Regan, anybody known or unknown could walk right into his office. Mary Regan — Patricia Rooney's sister— converted her desk into a checkpoint.

Mary was a good-looking redhead. Politely or tartly, depending on the circumstances — depending, sometimes, on her mood — she turned away bores, pests, and callers who lacked the proper credentials. Her standards of admission were rigorous, and only AJR could change the red light to green. Peering out from his office while a disappointed visitor pleaded for a hearing, he would give the nod, the safe-conduct, the sign of approval: "He's OK, Mary, he's OK." Usually, though, Mary Regan's word was law. "Sometimes I don't know if Mary works for me or if I work for her," AJR used to say.

Ed Kiely found his proper niche as the Chief's indispensable alter ego after Joe Gordon took over the public-relations job in 1969. Ed liked to deal with the upper echelon; responding to the needs and demands of the media was never one of his strengths. During the last ten years of AJR's life, Kiely was often his stand-in, chauffeur, and traveling companion. "We were more like friends than anything else," Kiely told a reporter a long time afterwards. "He was still the boss, but we had grown really close. His kids said I was like part of the family" That was correct. Kiely knew the Chief's mind and in certain situations could speak for him. The Chief was therefore enabled to pace himself. Once he had reached his late seventies, the celebrity whirl became exhausting, but it pained him to refuse invitations. Using Kiely as a surrogate lessened the guilt he invariably felt.

He was still making decisions on issues connected with the football team and the horse-racing business. When it came to horse racing, my brother Tim was a big help. In addition to running Yonkers, he supervised Shamrock Farm. AJR was breeding and raising standardbreds as well as thoroughbreds there. He would sometimes describe Tim as an "ignoramus," but proudly relate, in the next breath, that son number three had made and given to charity thousands upon thousands of dollars.

My own relations with the Chief were not as close as Tim's or Dan's and not as contentious as Tim's. In that respect, I felt like Ensign Pulver, the lowest ranking officer on the World War II Navy tub created by author Tom Heggen as the setting for his novel "Mr. Roberts," which became a Broadway play and then a Hollywood movie. Ensign Pulver tried very hard to avoid being noticed by the captain of the ship; in the same way, I wanted as little as possible to do with the Chief.

And yet at times, when we traveled together, I thought we achieved a kind of intimacy. He entrusted me with two of his possessions, and I treasure them. One was a limited-edition copy of Richard Nixon's autobiography, numbered and inscribed to "Art Rooney, a great American sportsman." Admittedly, Richard Nixon had his flaws, but he was a twice-elected president of the U.S.A. My other prized memento is a key to the city of San Francisco, presented to the Chief by Dianne Feinstein, San Francisco's mayor at the time and later a U.S. senator.

When he was alive I wondered often what AJR thought of me, and I wonder what he would think of me now.

Distractions

Chuck Noll hated distractions. They caused his football players to lose focus, which caused them to lose concentration. And without concentration the learning environment was in jeopardy.

Distractions came with success, and distractions were the enemy. After the Steelers' third Super Bowl win, Joe Greene and Terry Bradshaw had bit parts in movies. A distraction. These two and other marquee players – Swann, Stallworth, Lambert, Ham, and Blount – were getting offers to endorse commercial products on television. A distraction. Less publicized players, including part-time starters and special-team guys, were making paid appearances in the Tri-State area. A distraction. Loaner cars and golf outings were suddenly available for everybody: assistant coaches, trainers ... all the way down the pecking order. Another distraction.

Media guys were almost as worrisome as the advertising people. They hounded anyone with the team who would talk to them – even me. I was one of their favorites, in fact, because I said things. My attitude was that we had nothing to hide. And, besides, publicity was an agent of the NFL's popularity. It made no difference. The Chief, Noll, and Dan considered me a blabbermouth. Even some of the media guys wondered if I knew what I was doing. "You're so candid," one of them told me. A friend with my best interests at heart said, "Hey, you don't owe those reporters anything. Be more circumspect." So I was a big distraction, too.

I've told you how AJR seemed to welcome certain distractions (although not the one he attributed to me) and how Kiely and Mary Regan protected him from them. They grew concerned about the infirmities that come with the years. The Chief had some health problems (eyes, ears, gall bladder), but professed to be in "pretty good shape." Physically and mentally, he was better than pretty good. It would have angered the Chief to know that people who worked for him thought that he had to be watched over. His astuteness in all matters personal was unimpaired. Let me give you an example: The distillers of Smirnoff vodka had a proposition they brought to Ed Kiely. They wanted a distinguished looking older man with a recognizable name to appear in a magazine ad pushing their brand of booze, and AJR was made to order for the part. All he had to do was pose for one of America's leading photographers and be well recompensed. A sum in five figures was mentioned.

I think he felt honored – or maybe just amazed. "But I don't drink – haven't for years," he reminded Kiely. "I don't really approve of drinking. You know that. I'd be a real hypocrite, doing this."

So Kiely told the ad men, No sale.

Ask him to reconsider, they answered. "We'll give all the money to any charity of his choosing."

The Chief was tempted, but wouldn't budge.

Of course, Kass looked after him as much as she could. He made an effort to attend the horse owners' and dog owners' conventions, viewing it as part of his job, and Kass would go along to make sure that he took his medications and always had clean shirts to put on. Her own health, I'm afraid, was something we tended to forget about.

Chapter 67

Last Hurrah

On the St. Vincent practice field in the rainy, sweltering summer of 1979, the heat would build up all through the day, creating a mist that obscured the Chestnut Ridge of the Allegheny Mountains off to the east. Then the wind would start blowing and the thunder would crackle. The thunder reminded me of the artillery exercises at Camp Lejeune, but the Emperor, Chuck Noll, made light of it. "Thunder never hurt anyone," he would say. I'd been hearing that from Noll for ten years. Lightning was a different story. Even Chuck Noll feared lightning. With thunder came lightning and rain, and then the crowds on the hillsides would scramble for safety and Noll would lead the charge to the Kennedy Hall gym, where his players took refuge from the wicked atmospherics.

Sometimes it rained or drizzled for two or three days without a break. Then the fields so carefully tended by Benedictine Brother Pat Lacey would turn to mud, causing Noll and his assistants distress. Time was short, and you couldn't practice in such conditions. Buff Boston would canvass the area high schools in search of a dry field. If none could be found, Noll would herd his players into the St. Vincent gym. Looking ahead to the regular season, he foresaw difficulties but remained unshakeable in his conviction that even with twenty-two Steelers above the age of 30 the team had not peaked.

New rules designed to protect the quarterback would help rather than hurt, Noll thought. Despite the changes of a few years before, designed to protect pass receivers, the defense had caught up with the offense. The NFL was now a television league, and the millions of fans who watched from their living rooms preferred high-scoring games to the knock-'em-down, drag-'em-out trench warfare of professional football's formative years. The quarterback was the star of the show; to keep him on the field, the rule-makers imposed penalties for late hits, penalties for spearing, penalties for blows to the head. Disgustedly, Jack Lambert grumbled that quarterbacks ought to wear dresses. He was too young to remember Charley Seabright, the quarterback in Jock Sutherland's single wing. Seabright was just a glorified pulling guard; all he did was call the signals and block. Well, Noll had Terry Bradshaw, who could throw the ball a mile. With Bradshaw feeling safe in the pocket, how many passes would Lynn Swann and John Stallworth and Jimmy Smith and Ben Cunningham be able to haul in?

One of Bradshaw's idiosyncrasies – his latest – bothered Noll. Bradshaw had taken up country western singing. He was more than raw, but I liked his stage persona. Having been exposed to the theater in my youth, I saw that he had a talent for self-abasement. Right: self-abasement. He could laugh at himself, which tends to draw laughs from the audience. I thought the critics who said "Boy, does he stink" were missing something.

Lynn Swann's aborted career as a ballet dancer never had been an issue, but now he was missing practice for a reason that forced even Noll to hold his tongue. He was suing the San Francisco Police Department for racial harassment. A few years previously, with his brother and some friends, he'd been accosted by the police without provocation, he charged. The case had come to trial, and no one was saying that Swann should be in Latrobe. He remained on the West Coast to testify – persuasively, it seemed, for the verdict went against the cops. In his absence I expected some of our young wide receivers to strut their stuff, just as Swann himself had done as a rookie in 1974 when the veterans went on strike and skipped the first few weeks of the pre-season. I was disappointed. Nobody came to the fore.

Center-guard-tackle Ray Pinney, a bright light in the offensive line, suffered complications after an appendicitis operation and was lost for the season, but there were no other ailments or injuries of any real consequence and, despite the wet weather, the team left St. Vincent pretty well prepared for the season.

Everybody said it had been a hard-hitting camp. Compared with Sutherland's camps, and John Michelosen's and Bill Austin's, it had been a walk in the park. Noll was a coach who believed that pre-season camp should be a learning experience. He kept his players constantly on the move, but nothing was left on the practice field, as in Sutherland's day, or Michelosen's or Austin's. After all these years, the players were sold on Noll's system. It was tested and successful. His veterans were experts at putting his schemes into practice; in addition to being great athletes, they were artists at the game of football, pliable and smart.

Twenty-two veterans – the over-thirties, for the most part – had played in the 1974 Super Bowl, and they were not yet ready for the ash heap. I would like to mention also that everybody on the roster was home grown, which gave me a lot of personal satisfaction. Not one of these players in his pro career ever had worn a jersey other than Steeler black and gold. To the best of my knowledge, this had never happened before in the NFL. Nor has it happened since, I think it is safe to say.

Our pre-season record was 3-1. We took the measure of the Bills, Jets, and Giants (thereby winning the championship of New York state) before losing by two points to the Cowboys. Our first-round draft choice, Greg Hawthorne, came to life against the Giants; at a critical moment he made a spectacular catch. "See? See?" I exclaimed to our scouts. "He has what it takes." Again, I had made a bad guess.

We won our first four regular-season games. Three of the four were what AJR and the sportswriters called cliffhangers. The other, versus the Oilers in Houston, was a romp. During the 1979 season the Steelers played seven close games and won five of them. Great teams with great players could rise to the occasion.

Houston had replaced the Oakland Raiders as our designated bitterest rival, but there was nothing like enmity between the Oilers and the Steelers. In 1977, after a win by the Oilers over one of our division opponents had put us into the playoffs, every Steeler chipped in to buy every Houston player a handsome briefcase. Our games with the Oilers were hard-hitting but relatively clean. There may have been more rough stuff, actually, in our loss that year to the Eagles, one of four regular-season defeats. The first four times we got the ball we gave it back on fumbles, and Philadelphia won by the margin of a field goal.

Our 12-4 record did not impress a segment of Steeler fans, who asked what had become of Noll's aerial circus. Bradshaw was still completing passes, but not with as much regularity as in 1978. What did the fans want? I asked Nunn. How we won and by how many points never concerned me. As Al Davis used to say, "Just win, baby, just win." And in 1979 we won when it mattered.

The loss to the Eagles came in our fifth game. It was a setback Noll blamed on mistakes and injuries. Recovering, we proceeded to blow out Cleveland, 51-35, but in Cincinnati the next week there came a relapse. Nine Steeler turnovers added up to a 34-10 embarrassment. For the second time in three weeks, the offense had disappeared, and AJR joined the multitude wanting to know why. Earlier in the season he had questioned Noll's game plan. "Chuck will establish the run if it kills us," he grumbled to a crony in his private box. After the Cincinnati debacle, he said the Steelers had become a "herky-jerky" team, alternating good games with bad games. Then they went out and won their next four.

The aerial circus was back against Denver, with death-defying catches by Stallworth, Swann, and Smith. Bradshaw that day passed for more than three hundred yards in a 42-7 victory. Dallas, the team we had beaten in Super Bowl XIII the previous January, was in Pittsburgh the following week, and the Steelers came out on top in an epic defensive struggle, 14-3.

One week after that, the offense was reasserting itself when Bradshaw took a blow to the head and had to be pulled from the game with Washington – through for the day, it appeared. Shortly afterward, the Redskins fumbled on their own four-yard line and Pittsburgh recovered. Off the bench, where he'd been attended to, hustled Bradshaw. He threw a touchdown pass to Randy Grossman, and the Steelers were back in overdrive. At halftime their lead was 27-7. In the locker room during the intermission, Bradshaw's eyes were glazed, but Noll sent him out for the second half, in which the Steelers outscored the Redskins 14-0.

"I want a tough quarterback," Noll used to say, and in Bradshaw, he most certainly had one. Mike Webster, I understand, called every play for Bradshaw from the second quarter on. In thirty-two minutes of action, Bradshaw passed for 311 yards and four touchdowns, and I doubt if he remembered doing it.

His head was clear enough in our game the next week in Kansas City. We won it easily, 30-3. Bradshaw passed for three touchdowns, and Sidney Thornton, a.k.a The Bull, broke off some big runs as the backup to Bleier and Harris. Thornton's career would eventually fall apart, but in 1979 he answered our needs.

Military historians say an army is no better than its reserve strength, and this was a year in which the Steelers had to call upon every available man. It became difficult, because of injuries, to keep our Super Bowl warriors on the field at the same time. We were thinnest in the offensive line, where the battle-hardened Old Guard was showing signs of erosion. The Old Guard included old guards – aging ones, anyway; younger guards – Ted Petersen and Steve Courson – were fast acquiring game experience. "Make good things happen" was Noll's oft-repeated battle cry; young linebackers Robin Cole and Dirt Winston were making things happen, and so was Tom Beasley, a backup who played tackle or end. Like Petersen and Courson, all three had been drafted in 1977 or 1978. J.T. Thomas, who played a lot of safety and wing that year off the bench, was of a slightly earlier vintage.

Going into the San Diego game out West, the Steelers' passing attack looked unstoppable. San Diego stopped it, and stopped the run, too. The Chargers had our offense well scouted. Instead of moving up their defensive backs to deal with Harris, Bleier, and Thornton, they dropped them even deeper than usual and intercepted Bradshaw five times. Their own offense, meanwhile, tore the Steel Curtain apart in a 35-7 stunner.

A humbled Pittsburgh team was back in Three Rivers Stadium the next week to play the Browns, who never had won there and came to town with blood in their eyes. Although he was sacked seven times and had L. C. Greenwood putting pressure on him all afternoon, Brian Sipe, an underrated quarterback, kept the Browns in front most of the way. When the score was 20-6 and later 30-20 the Steelers seemed to be out of it. But great players will find a way to win. Greenwood, Joe Greene, and Jack Lambert never let up. Franco Harris, taking hit after hit, gained 151 yards on the ground, all in short chunks, caught nine passes for an additional eighty-one yards, and scored three touchdowns. Steve Furness, the extra man in the front four, had the best day of his career up to then. But three-point plays were the difference. Near the end of the fourth quarter, rookie Matt Bahr tied the score with a field goal and near the end of the fifteen-minute overtime he kicked the game-winner, his third of the season.

This was a game that had everything, not excepting great defense in spite of the 33-30 score. Pat Livingston, who'd been covering the Steelers for thirty years, expressed amazement at the behavior of the normally raucous, Terrible Towel-twirling crowd: as the suspense intensified in regulation time and then in overtime, a hush came over the stadium. When the final gun sounded, Lambert threw his arms around Bahr and hoisted him into the air. Bahr didn't weigh much, even for a kicker, but it was all Lambert could do to lift him up. Lambert, Greenwood, Greene, and Harris had played themselves into exhaustion, and 35-year-old Sam Davis said he felt like a zombie. George Perles was drained just from watching. I was worn out myself, voiceless and happy and dazed. Leading Houston by one game in the Central Division, we were ready now for the stretch run.

The hangover all of us thought was coming did not materialize. Before another home crowd the next week, the Steelers got even with Cincinnati, 37-17. Lynn Swann's five catches were good for 192 yards and a pair of touchdowns. Then it was on to Houston. The Oilers had to beat us to stay in the race, and they did, 20-17. For the first time in his life, the great Earl Campbell battered our defense, rushing for 100 yards. The Houston people – owner, management, coaches, and players – celebrated the outcome in Super Bowl style. From several different sources, I heard the locker-room scene was something out of a Cecil B. DeMille spectacle.

But the season wasn't over. One week later, at Three Rivers Stadium, a 28-0 whacking of Buffalo gave us our sixth straight division title. Houston, with an 11-5 record, got into the playoffs as a wild card. The home-field advantage, though, would be ours.

We'd be playing without Jack Ham, whose season ended in the Buffalo game when an ankle injury put him out of commission. Jack Ham, it was generally agreed, did not have a weakness as a linebacker. He would play three more years but never again at the same high level of proficiency. Filling in for him, Robin Cole and Dirt Winston helped to shut down the Bills. Our defense forced them to punt ten times, an NFL record, and their total yardage for the game was not quite the length of a football field. When it came to giving up yardage, the Steelers that year were the stingiest team in the American Conference.

Ten of our players made the Pro Bowl, seven were named to the all-NFL team, and Franco Harris had his seventh straight thousand-yard season, tying Jim Brown's record. Had the Steelers finally peaked? As a matter of fact, we were on the way down, but there was still another Super Bowl to be won.

Over the Hump

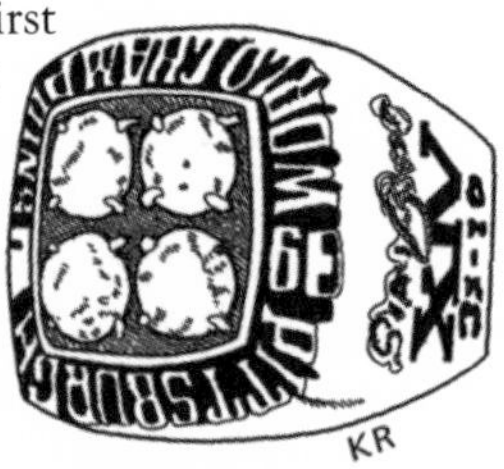

On the last day of 1972, at Three Rivers Stadium, Chuck Noll's first Steeler playoff team had lost to the Miami Dolphins in the AFC championship game, 21-17. The Dolphins were coached by Don Shula, the man who had hired Noll to be an assistant on the coaching staff of the Baltimore Colts and later recommended him to AJR when we were looking for a successor to Bill Austin. Noll's young team gave the Dolphins all they could handle, but Miami was on its way to a 17-0 season climaxed by a Super Bowl victory and came up with the big plays.

Now the situation was different. After seven years, almost to the day, Shula's current Dolphins would be the Steelers' first opponent in the 1979 playoffs, and this time the edge in experience and skill belonged to Pittsburgh. The pupil had a great team, the teacher merely a good one. Fog enshrouded Three Rivers Stadium at the kickoff; by the time it lifted, at the end of the first quarter, the issue was decided. With Stallworth and Swann catching touchdown passes from Bradshaw, Pittsburgh had the lead, 20-0. From then on the Dolphins held their own, but the final score, 34-14, correctly measured the disparity between the two teams.

Except for a missed extra point by Matt Bahr, the Steelers came close to playing mistake-free football. Said the normally low-keyed Noll: "We were outstanding in all areas of play." He did not exaggerate. The Dolphins, according to their coach, were overmatched. "We never challenged them," Shula conceded. "They totally dominated us." The Steelers, he said, were "the best team of the 1970s." He was taking the whole decade into account and not admitting that his 1972 Dolphins were inferior to any single championship team of Noll's.

"Everywhere we looked," a Miami player said to Bob Milie, the Steelers' assistant trainer, "we saw future Hall of Famers." With so many of our future Hall of Famers hurt, I was pleased, as a scout, to see our recent draftees perform well. On the Steelers' first-quarter touchdown drives of sixty-two, sixty-two, and fifty yards, Steve Courson was a terror getting out on sweeps and traps. And Sidney Thornton, with the help of a killer block by veteran guard Sam Davis, pounded the ball across for one of our scores.

It was amazing only in retrospect that a few of the most self-confident Steelers – Joe Greene, Mike Webster, Robin Cole – had been sleepless with worry before the game, and not entirely without reason. On certain Sundays, the 1979 Steelers underachieved. To put it bluntly (as Joe Greene did), they were blown out a couple of times and had no business losing the other two games that got away from them.

The four defeats, and Greene's relentless harping on the subject, concentrated their minds for the playoffs. Something else that may have helped was the outcome of the Houston-San Diego game. The Oilers, like the Steelers, had finished the regular season with certain key starters out of action. But they upset San Diego, 17-14, giving the home-field advantage to Pittsburgh in the AFC championship game. If the Chargers had won, a flight to the West Coast would have been necessary. Out there during the season, remember, San Diego had beaten us, and though our records were the same, 12-4, that head-to-head result would have broken the tie.

So Bum Phillips, the Oilers' coach, had it right: Pittsburgh was the door to the Super Bowl – the pearly gates, so to speak. And Houston stepped onto the threshold when defensive back Vernon Perry, who had intercepted four passes in the Oilers' win over San Diego, picked off one of Bradshaw's with the game barely under way. He ran it back seventy-five yards for a touchdown. There was a time in Bradshaw's career when a reversal like this would have rattled him. Not now. Before the first half was over, Bradshaw had hit Cunningham and Stallworth for touchdown passes, and the Steelers were out in front, 17-10.

The Steel Curtain, meanwhile, was taking care of Houston. Slanting and stunting on their pass rush, the Steelers gave Dan Pastorini no room to operate, and they stopped Houston's running game in its tracks. In seventeen carries, Earl Campbell gained only fifteen yards. Except for two field goals and Perry's runback, the nearest thing to a score the Steelers allowed was a pass caught by Ray Renfro deep in the Pittsburgh end zone. Out of bounds, was the call, disputed by the Houston players and coaches.

Meanwhile, our offensive line was a fortress protecting Bradshaw. And the running game produced a touchdown when Rocky Bleier, back in the lineup because Sidney Thornton was ailing, crossed the goal line from four yards out after the Steelers had recovered a Houston fumble. Final score: Pittsburgh 27, Oilers 13. The Oilers had lost to the Steelers for the second time in three games, prompting Bum Phillips to declare that, on this day, no other team in the NFL could have done any better against Pittsburgh.

What was there to fear, then, from our opponents in Super Bowl XIV, the Los Angeles Rams? Their record was 9-7, and no team with seven defeats had ever lasted this long in post-season play. They had won the NFC championship game without scoring a touchdown, but their defense was impregnable, holding Tampa Bay without a score of any kind, and their offense moved the ball just enough to get Frank Corral within range for three successful field-goal attempts. That defense, coached by ex-Steeler Bud Carson, was one of the best in the NFL. Let me give you a for-instance: in a 24-0 win over the Seahawks, it had held them to minus seven yards. There was also this to consider: the Super Bowl game would be in the Rose Bowl, home territory for the Rams.

Carroll Rosenbloom, the team's owner, had died several months before the start of the season in a drowning accident. While Georgia, his wife, watched from the beach, the 75-year-old daredevil had gone swimming in rough surf off the coast of southeastern Florida. He never returned alive. Officially, "the undertow got him," but there were far-fetched rumors of foul play. In any event, his widow, a blond former showgirl, inherited the team. Steve Rosenbloom, her stepson, was the executive vice president who ran things, but Georgia quickly replaced him with Don Klosterman, on the face of it a more capable football man.

Ray Malavasi, promoted from assistant the year before when the elder Rosenbloom fired George Allen after two pre-season defeats, remained as coach. In 1978 the Rams got to the playoffs and almost made it to the Super Bowl, losing to Dallas for the conference title. In 1979, although Malavasi had heart problems, and a broken finger sidelined Pat Haden, their first-string quarterback, they reached the playoffs as a wild card, and this time they beat Dallas, 23-21. With under two minutes left in the fourth quarter, Haden's backup, Ray Ferragamo, completed his third touchdown pass for the winning points.

Partly because of Carson, I did not underrate the Rams. When it came to understanding defenses he was just about as good as they come. Still, we were ten-point favorites, and deservedly so.

Beating Bud

We'd be playing Los Angeles in the Rose Bowl, twenty or thirty miles of freeway travel from the Coliseum, which had been the Rams' home field since Danny Reeves moved his team out of Cleveland in 1946. Reeves was long gone, but his pioneering spirit had changed the face of professional football. Where once there were no teams west of Chicago or south of Washington, D.C., by 1979 the league was far-flung.

There also had been an unintended consequence — the disappearance of a de facto color line. In agreeing to take Reeves as a tenant, the board that ran the Coliseum had insisted on an unusual quid pro quo, that the Rams must offer contracts to Kenny Washington, who had been an All American halfback at UCLA, and Woody Strode, an end from the same school. Washington's NFL career lasted only three years and Strode's was even briefer, but they were Southern Californians, popular with the fans, and their signing opened up the NFL to other non-white players. By the time of Super Bowl XIV, blacks, or African-Americans, as the preferred usage now has it, were well-represented on both teams, although not in the numbers we have since grown accustomed to see.

Forget that the Rose Bowl is in Pasadena: this would of course be a home game for the Rams. It was Chuck Noll's wish to keep the Steelers in Pittsburgh, working out in cold weather, for half of the two-week interval between the end of the playoffs and the Super Bowl itself. As usual, he wanted no distractions. "Enjoy yourselves," he told his players when they reached the West Coast, "but remember what we're here for. Don't blow it."

The logistics of transporting the team and its support structure and getting everything set up at the Super Bowl site fell to Dan, Joe Gordon, Buff Boston, and Dennis Thimmons, our controller, but they were experts at it by now. My own preoccupation was with the 1980 draft. Following Noll's lead, I gave a talk to the scouts: Have a good time for the few days we'll be out here, but re-focus quickly after the game.

What was driving me nuts, and the same thing went for everybody else connected with the organization, were the calls from our friends, if the word fits them, for tickets – tickets that in many cases, we knew, would end up in the hands of agents and scalpers. They could be sold for ten times their worth and then sold again for twenty times their worth, while fans who had backed us all season long were shut out.

I was fuming about this. Unabashedly, one of our assistant coaches approached me and asked for "help" in obtaining tickets. In his mind the Super Bowl was a "once-in-a-lifetime chance" to "make a nice buck" for his family. The coach was not a sleazeball, just an ordinary nice guy who didn't get it. I discussed the situation with Dan, who told Dennis Thimmons to wise up the poor sap. Dennis explained to the coach that scalping tickets was illegal; he mentioned the IRS; he mentioned our loyal ticketless fans. The coach did not take this well, and for some time afterward the displeasure he felt was directed toward me. It may be that he changed his outlook when a man of importance in the Rams' front office went to jail as a tax cheat for Super Bowl scalping.

Game day was sunny and bright – normal, in other words, for Southern California. Driven onto the field in a 1933 model touring car, 1933 because that was his first year in the league, AJR called the coin toss. He was famous now, the biggest winner in sports, and universally beloved, and yet he managed, as he always did, to look humble. Affection poured down from the 103,000 spectators; an estimated sixty million others were watching the telecast. In all the pre-game hoopla, Dad was a necessary presence. Seemingly reluctant, seemingly embarrassed by the attention, he went along with it, never for a minute fooling his wife or his sons. These were the best years of his life, we knew, a sort of grand culmination of all that had gone before.

The Rams won the coin toss. AJR was consistently successful at the race track, but ten years earlier, in New Orleans, we'd had better luck with Dan making the call. I'm talking about the coin toss between the Steelers and the Bears for the first selection overall in the 1970 draft. The prize then was Bradshaw, who'd be starting his fourth Super Bowl game as the Steelers' quarterback. Could we have come this far without him? The answer, I suggest, is self-evident.

Up in the stands, near the middle of the stadium, I nervously awaited the kickoff. The Super Bowl is a spectacle, a pageant, and rightfully so, but I was saying to myself, "Get it on, get it on." There had been enough ritual, too many bells and whistles. Even the panoramic background scenery was losing its charm for me. How long can you look at palm trees and eucalyptus trees and mountains that change to a different shade of purple every few minutes?

I had on my game face; I was ready for the action to start. In our section of seats there was lots of black and gold. We'd been placed with an assortment of Pittsburgh-area big shots and just a tiny sprinkling of AJR's hangers-on. Mom and Dad were seated above us, in one of the VIP boxes. A limousine and a chauffeur had been provided for their transportation to the game, but AJR had insisted on riding in the team bus with the players. ("I guess he wants to get his ankles taped," Bernie Butler theorized.)

When Kass found out that she would be in the limousine all alone, she decided to join the rest of us in the Rooney family's bus and ordered Kay to telephone her father and stepmother and any other relatives who had tickets to the game and have them come to the Newport Beach Marriott, where AJR had reserved a suite. "Now, don't argue with me," Kass said. "We've got that big car, and it's going to waste. Tell your folks they might as well use it. The driver will take them to a parking place right next to the entrance gate." No question about it, Kay was always Kass's favorite daughter-in-law.

In an offhanded way, I'd been wondering about the silver-foil trim attached to all the seats. Now I saw what the purpose was. The sun, on its downward arc, had reached a calibrated point at which the angle of the rays lit up the stadium and the silver foil. I admired the stage-managing. A brilliant effect had been achieved, but it temporarily blinded me. "When, oh when," I muttered, "will the bullshit come to an end?"

In due time, was the answer. The Steelers took the field without their two most seriously injured starters. Jack Ham and his wife were watching the game from AJR's box; Mike Wagner had a seat outside with the rest of us. Twenty-two holdovers from Super Bowl IX were still in uniform, but outnumbered now by the players we had added since 1974. To me, this meant that the scouts had been doing their job. The draft was the pipeline that kept our tank full.

Chuck Noll's game plan was for Bradshaw to stretch the field. The three assistant coaches who had defected to the Rams – Bud Carson, Lionel Taylor, and Dan Radakovich – would know how to stop, or at least hinder, our running attack. The best way to respond, Noll felt, was to put all our chips on Bradshaw. Throw the ball downfield, let Stallworth and Swann do the rest. How well the three of them executed would determine the outcome. No defensive scheme was a match for perfect execution, and Noll had full confidence now in Bradshaw's ability to deliver. As for Stallworth and Swann, there never had been a time when they were anything less than consummate pros.

On the first possession after the kickoff (another short one by Matt Bahr), Los Angeles had to punt on fourth down. And then, game plan or no game plan, the Steelers ran the ball. It was business as usual, with Franco and Rocky biting off yardage. There was one pass completion, thirty-two yards to Franco. But all-pro defensive end Jack Youngblood made a couple of good stops, and we settled for a field goal from Bahr.

Two weeks earlier, when the Rams beat Tampa Bay for the National Conference championship, Youngblood had broken a leg. "Damn! The guy's inhuman," I said to no one in particular. "How can he keep this up?" He couldn't – couldn't possibly, I assured myself. I was wrong, it turned out, but meanwhile the Rams were completing a 59-yard touchdown drive on which their ball carriers punctured the Steel Curtain. What was going on here?

Larry Anderson, a second-year special-teams player from Louisiana Tech (since finding Bradshaw there, we had kept going back), reversed the momentum for us with a 45-yard kickoff return, and now Bradshaw mixed up his play-calling. On a 53-yard drive that ended with Franco bucking over from one yard away, the pass supported the run and the run supported the pass. Just three minutes into the second quarter, we had taken the lead, lost it, and taken it back.

Negative thoughts entered my mind. How could I have expected anything other than the kind of game I was watching – a tough one? These Rams were the same team, pretty much, that had beaten us the year before in a regular-season game. We never had won from them here in their home surroundings. I wondered if Bud Carson was right when he said that the Rams (meaning himself) had our number.

Bahr's next kickoff carried to the 10-yard line, a bit of an improvement. The runback took the ball to the 19. Five and a half minutes later, Frank Corral kicked a field goal. Pittsburgh 10, Los Angeles 10.

Another long kickoff return by Anderson, this one for thirty-eight yards, gave us a chance to score again before the half. It had been a sub-par second season for Anderson, but he was having his greatest game, both as a runner and tackler on kickoffs, a game of the kind he was never to replicate. Anderson was a guy who could make both good plays and bad plays; against the Rams he was making only good plays. This latest one, though, got us nowhere. The offense couldn't muster a first down, and another field goal by Corral gave Los Angeles a 13-10 lead.

Believe me when I say I felt relief. But for a dropped pass or two, it could have been 17-10. After the field goal, Anderson took the kickoff past midfield again, but the half ended before we could score.

A group of singers and dancers - hundreds of them, it seemed, all vibrantly youthful and excessively clean-cut - performed during the long intermission. Among them, I now recalled, was the daughter of a friend who had asked me to look for her. Finding a needle in a haystack might have been easier.

"Help me out," I said to Kay.

"All right, but you'll have to describe her for me."

"Well ... she's pretty and she's athletic."

"Pretty and athletic? Every one of those girls is pretty and athletic. You've been sent on a fool's errand," Kay said.

I forgot about looking for the daughter of my friend. These young entertainers were full of what the French call *joie de vivre*, but I thought they never would get off the field. We were three points behind in a game that could go either way, and I was anxious to see what tactical alterations Noll had in mind.

Down in the Steeler locker room, Joe Greene and Jack Lambert were berating their teammates on the defensive unit. "We're letting them push us around!" The offense had problems of its own. Almost every time Bradshaw audibled – changed a play at the line of scrimmage – the Rams knew exactly how to adjust. This was Bud Carson's doing, some of our assistant coaches believed: the Rams knew our signals; Carson had cued them in. My own guess was that unaided anticipation on the part of the Rams' defensive players was hurting us more than any signal stealing.

Either way it was no time to panic. Right on schedule, the sun descended into the Pacific, the lights in the stadium came on, and the second half started. And now the Steelers, I could sense, had fire in their eyes. Los Angeles kicked off, and Larry Anderson did it again: another nice return, thirty-seven yards. Five plays later, Bradshaw went deep. From the Rams' 47, he launched a touchdown pass to Swann, who went up high, splitting two defensive backs, to make the catch. So here it was at last: Noll's game plan remembered.

But Malavasi had a game plan of his own. In fact, it resembled ours; a pass good for fifty yards, Ferragamo to Billy Waddy, put the ball on the Pittsburgh 24, and the Rams then caught us off-guard. Ferragamo handed the ball to Lawrence McCutcheon, but instead of blasting into the line he swept right, stopped, and threw a touchdown pass to Ron Smith. Our defensive backs, looking for the run, had been overly aggressive, and Smith got behind them in the end zone. It had taken the Rams less than a minute to cover seventy-seven yards in four plays.

Shockingly, Corral missed the extra point. With Los Angeles leading by only 19-17, a field goal would put us ahead once again. This time we started a little deeper, from our 28, and moved to a first down on the 44. Then came one of those "what-if?" plays. Bradshaw fired a pass that missed the intended receiver; its trajectory took it straight into the arms of defensive back Norm Cromwell, a Hall of Famer to be. And he dropped the ball.

Afterward Cromwell said that all he could see in front of him was "green grass and the goal line." All I could see, in a flashback to Super Bowl XIII, was Jackie Smith, the Dallas Cowboys' most dependable receiver, dropping a pass in the end zone. Fate, once again, had been kind to us, by which I don't mean to say we were not a better team than either the Cowboys or the Rams. Norm Cromwell and Jackie Smith, excellent players, dropped the ball in big games, but that's why we call them games. As Kass once reminded AJR when he boasted of having bet on a sure thing at the race track, there is no such thing as a sure thing. The horse could break a leg, she cautioned. That's what the horse did, and they shot the poor animal. At least Smith and Cromwell lived to tell about the passes they dropped, Kass said.

Time and again you've heard the old truism that everybody makes mistakes. The difference between the Steelers and the Rams in Super Bowl XIV was that the Steelers overcame their mistakes. It's what great teams usually do. In any case, not long after the failed interception Lynn Swann caught a short pass over the middle and was knocked silly. Our doctors would not allow him to finish the game. A bad break. Swann had been making routinely fantastic catches. Injured earlier, his sub, Theo Bell, was already out of the game, leaving no one to take Swann's place except Jimmy Smith, who was taking Bell's place as our punt-return man. Carson's defense had been stuffing our run. "Now all we have to do," he was telling his guys, "is shut down Stallworth." He made it sound easy. Too easy.

Despite the near interception and an interception by Eddie Brown that changed the flow of the game temporarily, Bradshaw kept throwing the bomb. Time was when an interception like Brown's would have unsettled him, but when the Steelers got the ball again, on their own 27, he was calm and efficient, setting up play-action passes with the run. We were soon on the Rams' 16, close enough now for a go-ahead field goal. Then on third-and-ten, instead of setting it up with a safety-first thrust into the line, Bradshaw threw toward the end zone, where Stallworth was open, and Rod Perry intercepted on the four.

Damn, damn, damn! Why didn't we kick the easy field goal? Why didn't we play the percentages? Now, with the fourth quarter under way, we were still two points down.

But the Rams were slowly fading. Under pressure from Robin Cole, Jack Lambert, and Steve Furness, their offensive line, a very good one, was beginning to crumble. Ken Clark, their punter, pushed us back with a 59-yard kick, but we still had time. On second-and-eight, with the ball on our 27, Sidney Thornton dropped a pass. "Get Rocky in there," I grumbled, sending a telepathic message to Noll – whose mind was on something else.

"Go for the big one," he instructed Bradshaw, calling for a play that had not worked in practice, a pass to Stallworth on a hook-and-go route. Bradshaw, I later heard, was dubious; even Stallworth wasn't sure they could bring it off. But Bradshaw put the ball in the air and Stallworth caught it. He caught it at the Rams' 32 and never broke stride as he kept on going into the end zone. The pass and run covered seventy-three yards. After Bahr's extra point, our lead was 24-19.

Bud Carson, I understand, did some powerful emoting on the sidelines. The sportswriters still referred to Bud as the architect of the Steel Curtain. Bud was a smart coach, but the Steel Curtain's only architect had been Charles Henry Noll — who was proving himself now to be an architect of some distinction when it came to offensive football, too. The pass to Stallworth was Noll's call; nobody else, not Bradshaw, not Stallworth, and not the assistant coaches in the spotter's booth, had a whole lot of faith in that call, but it worked. Bud Carson said it shouldn't have worked. "All we needed to do was double-cover Stallworth," he explained after the game. His defensive plan, he said, had provided for double coverage. Somehow, the Rams were remiss. They didn't execute. Or simply got beaten on a game-busting play by a Hall-of-Fame quarterback, a Hall-of-Fame receiver, and a Hall-of-Fame strategist.

It was odd, when you think about it, how Super Bowl XIV had come to be viewed by so many of the actual participants as a duel of wits between Carson and Noll. Noll himself was caught up in it: "I know how to beat Bud," he had said to Marianne, his wife, before leaving Pittsburgh. Not "I know how to beat the Rams," but "I know how to beat Bud." Coaches don't win or lose games; players do, we are told. Undeniably, however, coaches have their moments. The hook-and-go call was one such moment, and something similar happened with five and a half minutes of the fourth quarter remaining. Los Angeles had the ball on the Steelers' 32, first-and-ten. Wendell Tyler had been running hard; Ferragamo was hitting his passes; our five-point lead appeared to be none too secure. In front of the Steeler bench, linebacker coach Woody Widenhofer shouted to Lambert. "It's coming, Jack – this is it!" "It" was a pass from Ferragamo to Ron Smith. Lambert, judging the trajectory of the ball with scientific exactitude, intercepted. And up at the top of the stadium, AJR got to his feet and headed for the elevator. "Where are you going, Dad? The game's not over," called out Dan. "Yes, it is," answered AJR. "Lambert just ended it."

That was not how it looked from where Kay and I were sitting. Five minutes in a football game can be a long time. Bradshaw handed off to Franco and then to Thornton for a net gain of three yards. Third-and-seven on our own 33. "OK, run the clock out," I urged Bradshaw silently. But somebody had other ideas. Again he went deep to Stallworth, on the same hook-and-go pattern that had given us our come-from-behind touchdown. Again there was no double coverage.

This pass took us to the Rams' 22, from where Bradshaw threw to Jimmy Smith in the end zone. The defensive back climbing all over Smith was flagged for interference, and though it took three tries from the one-yard line, with Rocky and then Franco and then Franco again hitting straight ahead, the penalty set up a touchdown.

Now it was Steelers 31, Rams 19, and it stayed that way. In a dying-gasp effort, Ferragamo passed the Rams to the Pittsburgh 27 before J. T. Thomas dumped him seventeen yards behind the line of scrimmage, effectively ending the threat, if that's what it was.

Larry Anderson got the game ball for his 162 yards on five kickoff returns, a Super Bowl record. Bradshaw, though, for the second straight year, was the MVP. In football, as in warfare, it's the bomb that can do the most damage. And yet this best of all Super Bowl games up to then was in one sense a vindication of Noll. Bud Carson was sure he could double-cover Stallworth. Noll had a hunch his old assistant was mistaken about that. So where did all this leave Ray Malavasi – Carson's boss? Out of it, I guess you'd have to say.

For Noll and his assistants and each of our players, the winner's share of the Super Bowl jackpot was thirty-two thousand dollars. Neither Dan nor I, after previous Super Bowls, ever had taken a cent, but now I went to him and suggested that perhaps we owed something to our wives and kids. I never asked how it happened – did Dan argue the case with AJR? – but both of us received a full share. To this day I don't know if the Chief ever cut himself in.

Filling In

Alex DiCroce was in charge of the post-game party at the Newport Beach Marriott, and he had told me ahead of time that Kay and I would have our own table. I reminded him that after Super Bowls IX, X, and XIII, we had sat with Mom and Dad. "I know," Alex said, "but you're as much a part of the Steelers' success as your father is, or as Dan is. You should have your own table, and I'll see that it's right next to the Chief's." Whatever distinction there was in being put at a separate table pleased me, of course, but not half as much as Alex's compliment did.

In any event, we sat with Dad and Mom after all. It was Kass's idea. Dad's race-track cronies spent their winters on Florida's east coast; very few of them had come to Pasadena, which meant that his table would not be full, Kass said. And he wanted no walk-ons. The solution Kass proposed was for Kay and me and the friends we had asked to sit with us – the Butlers and the Youngs – to occupy the empty spaces. That would leave Kay's father and step-mother and her other relatives to keep an eye on young Susie at our table. Meanwhile, Art III and Mike would be happy to pal around with their numerous cousins. It worked out, I think, to the satisfaction of everybody concerned.

These victory parties were elegant affairs. There was music, good food, and - yes – lots of liquor. But no one ever got boisterous. No one misbehaved. The presence of AJR and Noll had a moderating influence, I believe. All the wives and girlfriends looked beautiful to me. All the children did credit to their parents.

We flew back home to another big welcome. Once it was over, I quickly turned my thoughts to the draft. So many of our players were getting long in the tooth. They were still superior athletes, with great experience and moxie, but age was catching up with them. Since 1974, I had drafted many good players, but no great ones. It was time to rectify that.

Nowhere To Go But Down

I didn't' know it then, but we were full of ourselves, dangerously so. Winning inflates the ego. Everybody seemed to be on a high, everybody except the head coach, Chuck Noll. Like the traveler in Robert Frost's poem, Noll had miles to go before he slept, but it was not in his nature to pause and reflect on where a change of direction might take him - or to revel in Super Bowl glory.

As for AJR, he had reached his destination in life, by this time content to play a largely ceremonial part in the Steeler hierarchy. Over the previous six years the fans and the sportswriters had coroneted, then canonized him. The former vagabond scatback, amateur boxer, minor-league batting and base-stealing marvel, ward boss, sandlot football impresario, up-by-the-bootstraps NFL pioneer, and immensely successful race-track plunger had become a "great American sportsman," so designated by nobody less than a president of the United States. Expunged from the Chief's past were his rough beginnings - the days of hey rubes and fist fights, of illegal booze and illegal gambling aboard the Showboat, of speakeasies and all-night card games, of an easy familiarity with hoodlums like Bill Duffy and Owney Madden. In the public consciousness, nothing remained of that time but mythology – nostalgic recollections of the NFL and its origins. With George Halas and George Marshall and Johnny Blood and Whizzer White, AJR was a symbol of an age perceived as golden and romantic.

The Chief's reputation was important to him, and carefully guarded. He wore his persona like a monk's habit. Puzzled over a quotation attributed to the philosopher Jacques Maritaine - something to the effect that artistry is "the habit of practical intellect" - I asked my teacher at St. Vincent, a Father Erik, for amplification. "Well, a habit, you see, is like a cloak," he said. "A habit is what I'm wearing right now. It's my costume. An artist wears a habit, too - the habit of practical intellect." I was now more confused than ever, but looking back, it seems clear that AJR wore humility and charm like a habit. Not that there was anything phony about this. The public now saw him as warm, kind, benevolent, and upright, and he was all of these things, a man of truly countless good deeds. Once again I repeat something that my drama school instructors used to say of an actor perpetually cast in the same role – "the mask becomes the face." In the end there is no distinction between actor and character. They are one.

In private, however, AJR was still the Chief. He could be humble and charming and generous, but also a dictator. If it was Dan who now ran the football team, Dan who made the day-to-day administrative decisions, they were not irreversible. AJR retained veto power. And it was AJR, unless he waived the privilege, who accepted our championship trophies from Pete Rozelle, the NFL commissioner, while Dan stood quietly in the background, a secondary figure.

When I say that all the Chief's sons feared his reprimands, I speak from experience. As vice president in charge of personnel, I had some status, I supposed, in the organization. Thus when AJR ordered me to appear in his place at a public function I had no wish whatever to attend, I offered the valid excuse that I was trying to spend more "quality time" with my neglected wife and children. Such opportunities for me were rare; even as the scouting department's "coordinator," I continued to go out on the road. But AJR was unsympathetic. In front of the whole office staff, he gave me a fiery dressing down.

Of course I went to the affair. I spoke. Word that I had done well filtered back to the Chief. Genially, he observed, "You should do more of this." Although the topic never was alluded to, my years at drama school in New York had cost him a lot of money. If I could now use my training, it would be a return of some kind on the Chief's investment, but I was quiet about this. My interest in acting, I knew, had made me, for a spell, the family's black sheep. "Don't ever mention it," Kay often counseled me. All the time I had logged in Madame Daykahonova's version of the Actors' Studio was in Kay's opinion – and AJR's – something best hushed up, like a jail sentence.

I was wise, as it turned out, to abandon any notion of a theatrical career. Working for my father had its drawbacks; but in no other job could the rewards have been as great. Just the personal associations that were open to me enriched my existence. By virtue of being Art Rooney's son, I was frequently in contact with the social, political, and economic elite, but I'm talking about something else.

I wasn't comfortable with the elite; I preferred ordinary, grass-roots football people – scouts and coaches, administrators, team doctors and trainers. Most but not all of my friends had played the game. Those who hadn't included even sportswriters. I liked to entertain, both at home, where Kay was unsurpassed as a hostess, and at our club. When I entertained at the club, Kay excused herself. She knew the story-telling would last for hours, with waiters and bartenders gathered around to hear the yarn-spinning, a mixture of fable and fact.

There was also the work itself. Since 1974, we had won four Super Bowls, and I think I can claim without boastfulness that the scouting department was entitled to some of the credit. Since the move to Three Rivers Stadium in 1970, there had been only two losing seasons. But now it was 1980, the start of a new decade, and I recalled, from the scriptures, a warning, a reminder that mortality spares no one. With the passing of the years, certain changes occur. Muscles weaken, strength wanes, reflexes atrophy. As reluctant as we were to recognize the truth, our football team was getting old.

Part Six: Winding Down

Chapter 68

Executive Privilege

On a wet, chilly morning in February of 1980 the Pittsburgh Steelers, reigning Super Bowl champions, and the Pittsburgh Pirates, reigning World Series champions, flew in a chartered jet to Washington, D.C., for a visit with President Jimmy Carter.

Pittsburgh, at the time, had a sports-page moniker – Title Town, U.S.A. Unable to choose between Terry Bradshaw, the Steelers' quarterback, and Willie Stargell, the Pirates' first baseman, *Sports Illustrated* had designated both as its Sportsmen of the Year. For the magazine's cover, they posed side by side in their uniforms, outlined against the silhouette of a steel mill.

Never mind that by the end of the 1970s steel mills producing steel were hard to find around here. Closed forever, all but the Edgar Thomson Works in Braddock awaited the wrecking ball. Gone from the river banks was the flare of the open-hearth furnaces that lit up the night with a demonic red glow. The U.S. Steel Building stood watch just as always over the Golden Triangle, but it had a new name – the USX Building. What did X mean, anyway? It was certainly not a synonym for steel. And who remembered that the decoration on the side of the Steelers' black helmets, three stars enclosed in a circle, was the industry's insignia?

We had won four Super Bowls, but the invitation to the White House was our first. Kay and I would be going in Chuck Noll's twin-engine six-seater with Buff and Janet Boston. On the big chartered jet, with a football team and a baseball team to accommodate, extra seating was limited. AJR, down in Florida with Kass, elected to pass up the trip. He made decisions like this on a unilateral basis. The thought that his bride of forty-nine years might perhaps take some pleasure in seeing the White House, in meeting the President, would not have occurred to him. In my inner ear, I could hear him saying, "Kathleen, you don't want to go to that thing, do you?" And it would not be a question, but a statement. "I've been to the White House, Kass," he would say. "It's nice but a real hassle. Let's stay here. We'd be taking away attention from the team."

On the day of our departure a low-hanging fog was in the air. Kay, under the best of conditions, did not like to fly. "If we have to go – and, frankly, I'd rather not – let's drive," she proposed.

"Kay," I said, "it's too late to drive. We wouldn't get there in time."

"Then go by yourself." was her answer.

In the end, after much vacillation, she relented. Chuck Noll's little plane took off from the County Airport. We had a pilot from the Westinghouse Corporation, a good one named Ralph something. The fog was still heavy, but Ralph said the sky would be clear above four thousand feet. As we fastened our seat belts, Kay whispered to me, "Headline tomorrow in the newspapers: 'Art Rooney Junior and Steeler associate Jim Boston killed when airplane crashes in Allegheny Mountains.'"

We rose above the clouds at three thousand feet and were flying in sunshine – but not for long. Over the Chestnut Ridge of the Alleghenies we were back in pea soup. Kay and Janet Boston were getting panicky. Even Buff, by nature a fatalist, had started to sweat. Our plane was bouncing around like one of those teacup-shaped bumper cars at Kennywood Park. Ralph the pilot, jabbering non-stop, gave us his word that there was no cause whatever for alarm. To myself, I said, "Right. You can be sure if it's Westinghouse."

Kay wasn't buying any happy talk, especially not from Ralph. We'd been holding hands. Now she released hers and dug the fingernails into the flesh just above my knee. "You!" she hissed. "You made me come on this goddam pissant excuse for an airplane!" The Bostons were quiet but looked paralyzed. They could both use a drink, I thought, and I was worried about Kay. The buffeting worsened the closer we got to Washington, but finally Ralph turned around and said, "Not long now until we land. We only have to get clearance."

Descending through fog, we could not see the ground. And then all of a sudden there were lights. We landed almost gently, and I recalled one of Noll's original epigrams: "Any landing is a good one if you can walk away from it."

On the tarmac, Kay said, "I don't care how we go back to Pittsburgh as long as we don't fly. I don't care if we rent a car and drive. I don't care if we take the train. I don't care if we go by Greyhound bus. I don't care if we hitchhike. I don't even care if we walk every step of the way. But I'm not getting back on that goddammed airplane." She paused to let her ultimatum sink in. Then she added," Do you understand me?" I did. When a redhead lays down the law, there is no ambiguity.

On the buses that were to take our group to the White House, we learned that President Carter, who was having a busy day, would not be able to see us at the appointed time. So, first, there would be a tour of FBI headquarters in the building named for J. Edgar Hoover. The explanation that Carter was in a meeting that had not yet broken up evoked cynicism on our bus. "Overtime meeting my ass," someone chirped. "We're going to the FBI building so they can check us out. They think there might be subversives in our midst. Buff Boston looks like a bomb tosser for sure. Once they eyeball Buff, they'll think he's gonna blow up the White House."

Everybody laughed, but those were innocent times. After September 11, 2001, remarks of that nature ceased to be humorous.

Actually, the tour was quite interesting. And before very long we were back on the road. As soon as we got to the White House, I headed, with many others, for the restroom. It was all black marble and polished brass. Just like the Duquesne Club, I reflected. When we had reassembled, a White House guide took us through the corridors, which were lined with the portraits of the presidents ... Washington, Jackson, Lincoln, Wilson, FDR, Harry Truman, Jack Kennedy. The furniture was French Provincial and the trimmings were gold – one of Thomas Jefferson's legacies, I suppose. Jock Sutherland's 1929 Pitt team, national champions that year, had been here in the 1930s, having their picture taken in the Rose Garden with Herbert Hoover. Uncle Jim was in that picture, as big as life. And now it was our turn. There's a lot to be said for being a winner, I told myself smugly.

I had left home full of nonchalance. Now my mouth was hanging open and my head was on a swivel. There was so much to see and to think about. Big-time football players accustomed to the hoopla that went with Super Bowl games and their victorious aftermath were gawking and chattering like schoolboys. With smiles on their faces, they were taking it all in. So was I. So was Kay. So was everybody.

We were ushered into a room for coffee or tea and pastries (the best I have ever tasted, and I'm a connoisseur of sweet stuff). There were presidential seals on the cups, saucers, and silverware and predictable jests about taking them home with us for keepsakes. One of the wives – a lovely strawberry blonde – suggested a perfect place for the women to stash away the cups. I am sure you can guess where it was.

"Too obvious," someone said, and I recalled a story Dick Szymanski, one-time general manager of the Baltimore Colts, had told me, confirming George Young's account of the same incident. Once when the Colts were Super Bowl champions, the governor of Maryland, Spiro Agnew – later the only vice president forced to resign from office for taking bribes – invited them to dinner at his official residence in Annapolis. Toward the end of the evening, Agnew and several members of the Baltimore coaching staff adjourned to the billiards room, where they were sipping brandy, smoking cigars, and shooting pool. All had removed their jackets except for one coach. Agnew urged him to loosen up. "You look uncomfortable," he said. "Maybe if you take off your coat you can make a few shots. Ha ha." So, feeling pressured, the coach took off his coat. Where to put it? He spotted an empty chair and was draping the garment over the back of it when, *crash*! Knives, forks, and spoons, each one bearing the Maryland state seal, fell out of the pockets, landing with a clatter on the hardwood floor.

"It was embarrassing," said Szymanski. He didn't tell me how Agnew reacted. When it came to thievery, of course, Agnew turned out to be fully as inept as the Baltimore coach.

President Carter, standing next to a tall Marine captain at the end of the White House reception line, looked diminutive. He was wearing a beautifully tailored dark suit. When Kay and I, moving forward, found ourselves facing the Marine officer, he said to me, "Your name, sir?" I gave him the information. Turning to the President, he passed on our IDs in an undertone.

Jimmy Carter now addressed us in his Georgia drawl. "Come over here, Art," he said, smiling toothily, "and have your picture taken with me. And bring Kathleen." He shook my hand. As we posed for the photographer, he put his arm around Kay, at the waistline. When the picture session was over, we exchanged a few pleasantries and Carter returned to the business of welcoming his guests.

The greeting and smiling all done with, he led us to a stage at the far end of what appeared to be a ballroom. There we all gathered for a group photo with Carter. Then Chuck Noll and Dan gave him an NFL football with the players' and coaches' signatures on it. The Pirates gave him a memento of some kind, too, but I don't know what it was. When Carter left us, he had our football cradled in his arm.

To Kay's delight, the Steelers returned to Pittsburgh by bus, and two of the seats were for us. It was a warm, pleasant ride. At one stop along the way, Noll and Dan, noted oenophiles, bought a case of expensive wine, and when we stopped at another place for dinner they had the waiters bring the wine to all the tables.

On the bus as we were pulling into Pittsburgh, Kay spoke privately to me. In a whisper, she said, "You may not believe this, but it's true," and waited for me to respond.

"What's true?" I asked.

"Well ..." Again she hesitated. "Well, when we had our picture taken with President Carter, he ..."

"Yes, go on."

"He pinched me on the backside."

I have to admit I was speechless.

"On the upper part of my bum," Kay went on.

As she had predicted, I couldn't believe it. "You're nuts!" I exclaimed.

"It's true," Kay said.

"No! Not the President!"

"It's true," Kay repeated. "Now I'll say no more about it. But it's true."

And there, for the time being, we let the subject drop.

Several years passed. In my office at Three Rivers Stadium early one morning, I was talking about the draft with one of our coaches. We were drinking coffee. The conversation somehow shifted from football to our White House visit in 1980. The coach put his cup down and said, "You know, that Carter was a feisty little guy."

Feisty? I nodded as though I understood.

"Can I tell you something?" the coach said, leaning toward me confidentially. "When we were getting our picture taken, he pinched my wife on the ass."

I said, "Oh, my God!" Then I jumped up and ran to the telephone and dialed our number at home.

"Darling," I said when Kay answered, "you once told me a story I didn't believe, but I believe it now. And I apologize for ever having doubted you."

Some time later I got to thinking about the label our coach had for Carter – "feisty" – and a different, more suitable adjective occurred to me, one that, like "feisty," ends with a "y."

It was "horny."

Change or Die

When Moon Mullins signed a long- term contract sometime during the 1970s he announced to his teammates (I overheard him say it), "I'm a Steeler forever." Mullins was a man of his word. After the 1979 season, Chuck Noll arranged a trade that would have sent him to the Cleveland Browns; instead of going along with the deal, Mullins retired. He had played for the Steelers since coming into the league and would play for nobody else.

We had drafted Mullins in 1971 out of Southern California. For nine years, Mullins and Sam Davis, an undrafted free agent from Allen University in South Carolina, gave us quickness and mobility at the guard positions. Davis, the team's "old man," was a survivor of the failed Bill Austin regime, but, like Mullins, he possessed the attributes needed to jump out in front of the ball carrier on Noll's sweeps and traps. And now he, too, would be gone – finished as a player because of injuries accrued over thirteen backbreaking seasons.

We owed them a debt, Mullins and Davis, and their departure would leave a void. They took so many intangibles with them. But a football team is an organism, and an organism cannot remain static.

It must change or it must die. Baldly stated, Mullins and Davis were worn-out parts. Replacements had to be ready, supplied by our scouts.

So in the 1980 draft we were looking for offensive linemen. In the fifth round we took Craig Wolfley, from Syracuse, and in the sixth round Tunch Ilkin, from Indiana State. Ilkin was a center, but adaptable enough to play tackle. In that way he was similar to Ray Pinney, our second-round choice in 1976. Although Pinney had been a center at the University of Washington, Noll used him mainly as a fill-in for Mullins and Davis.

Wofley, Ilkin, and Pinney had long, productive careers with the Steelers, maintaining the standard of offensive line play established by their predecessors. Wolfley, in fact, made one of those Steeler all-decade teams for the 1980s. Ilkin had a more difficult time of it. He was cut before the season started, but when Rollie Dotsch, his position coach, expressed misgivings to me about this, I instructed one of our scouts, Tom Modrak, to keep us from losing track of Ilkin. Tom called Tunch every week and urged him to stay in shape. With just a few games remaining, his chance came. An injury left us short-handed in the offensive line, and Ilkin rejoined the team. He was a Steeler for twelve years, captaining the offensive unit at the end of his career, and he played in two Pro Bowls.

All in all, the 1980 draft was not a bad one. We took a quarterback, Mark Malone of Arizona State, in the first round. A fellow scout I knew and respected had a theory about Malone: his above-average passing ability, according to this scout, blinded us to the fact that he was playing out of position. Malone was a reasonably good quarterback who never developed into a great one. As a halfback, the scout said, he could have been another Frank Gifford or Paul Hornung. (I'd heard that before about, oh, any number of talented individuals whose accomplishments fell short of their potential.) "If Malone hurt his arm," the scout told me in all seriousness, "it would be the best thing that could happen to him."

Actually, my friend may have had a point. Terry Bradshaw was going to be our quarterback for another three years, but, recognizing Malone's versatility, Noll found ways of getting him on the field from time to time. When we played Seattle during Malone's second season, Noll lined him up at wideout because his ranginess and speed created coverage problems for the defense. While the Seahawks were wondering what to do about this, Malone, who was positioned off to the right – something like Army Coach Red Blaik's "lonesome end" – caught a pass from Bradshaw and streaked down the sideline all the way to the end zone, a distance of ninety yards. Years and years later, it was still the longest pass play in Steeler history.

Malone never hurt his arm, but he did hurt his knee, badly. With his mobility diminished, quarterback from then on was the only position he could play. After taking over from Bradshaw's successor, David Woodley (obtained in a trade with Miami), he finished the 1984 season strongly, and we won a playoff game for the first time in five years. Against Indianapolis the next season, he tied Bradshaw's single-game team record by passing for five touchdowns, but that, I am sorry to say, was his high-water mark.

Four other players from the 1980 draft made the squad. Linebacker Bob Kohrs, who had been Malone's teammate at Arizona State, lasted six seasons, but always seemed to have an injury of some kind. Aside from Wolfley and Ilkin, we made our best pick that year in the eleventh round. Continuing our search for a running back to replace Rocky Bleier, we drafted a kid from Baylor, Frank Pollard. Faster than Rocky, he could block just as well and catch just as well. In Kass' phrase, Greg Hawthorne, the Baylor running back who had been our first-round pick the year before, "lived in hope and died in despair," by which I mean that he ultimately disappointed everyone, himself included. Pollard never had a thousand-yard rushing season, but came close a couple of times in a nine-year career. He was an unselfish player who could have been a starter on our great teams of the 1970s in a role similar to Bleier's. In the role that circumstances forced him to take, one that was similar to Franco's, he could not quite fulfill the requirements. In other words, Pollard just wasn't a franchise player, but of course there are not too many of those.

Making late picks has been likened to throwing darts at the draft board. During my tenure as head scout, we had remarkably good luck with late picks. "Why do your scouts do so well from the fourth round on down when the top picks tend to be so-so?" Dan used to ask. Well, it wasn't by throwing darts at the board. We rated our late picks as carefully as the ones higher up, and it frequently paid off. In the NFL, drafting toward the end of every round is the price you pay for success, and no matter how well you may do, it isn't often you get the real superstars.

To state the obvious, great players are the stuff that great teams are made of, and great teams win the close games. In 1980, a lot of our great players were either aging or hurt – sometimes both. The result was that Cincinnati beat us twice by one point, Cleveland beat us by two points, and Houston beat us by six. We finished the season with a 9-7 record, missing out on the playoffs for the first time since 1971.

Golden Anniversary

For Mom and Dad's fiftieth wedding anniversary – June 11, 1981 – the late-spring day was picture-perfect: golden sun, pale blue sky, air that sparkled like Waterford crystal. The only reminder of how Pittsburgh had looked when the couple first met was the soot-blackened exterior of St. Peter's Church. No farther away than Terry Bradshaw could throw a football were the main-line tracks of the Pennsylvania Railroad, and decades of smoke from the coal-fired locomotives had left the building blocks of the church – originally some color no one remembered – with a coat of obliterating grime. Since the anniversary Mass would be at St. Peter's, a touch of old Pittsburgh was not amiss, for, in fundamental respects, AJR – and by necessity Kass – had kept to the old ways. They had aged with St. Peter's and the old crumbling neighborhood that once had been Millionaire's Row, content to stay on at 940 North Lincoln Avenue, the well-preserved architectural relic dating back to a time when houses like theirs were called mansions.

On this milestone anniversary there would be a twilight garden party, "orchestrated," as Kay put it, by Dan, with his usual thoroughness and efficiency. But first the Rooneys and McNultys and McGinleys and Laughlins and Millers, brought together from wherever life had taken them, converged on St. Peter's for the Mass. The occasion demanded it; any such gathering without this expression of our Catholic faith was unthinkable. From the time of Maggie and Pop, Rooneys had gone to Mass at St. Peter's, and to St. Peter's a penitent AJR and his bride had returned for the wedding that authenticated their mysterious civil union of the year before.

This detour from the straight and narrow was now long forgotten. At the anniversary Mass, Bishop Vincent Leonard, Father Bob Reardon, and Monsignor Bassom Pierre officiated. Father Reardon had obtained a papal blessing from John Paul II – Dan's inspiration – and he solemnly read its text from the altar. Father Henry McAnulty, speaking with his expected eloquence, put into words what so many of us felt about the man and the woman we were honoring.

Accustomed to being made much of, AJR, I must say, was not exactly carried away. For one thing, a year in advance, there had been an "anticipatory" anniversary party for family and close friends in the rectory of Duquesne University's Holy Ghost fathers, which occupied the entire fourth floor of the on-campus Holy Childhood Building. "We have the octave of Christmas and the octave of Easter, so why not an octave for Kathleen and Arthur's anniversary?" said one of the good priests who taught at Duquesne – AJR's alma mater of choice. It may be that events too long foreshadowed become anticlimactic. Unless they don't. Either way, AJR had been bluntly dismissive when asked if he and Kass were planning to renew their vows at the anniversary Mass, a tradition his daughters-in-law favored. "Certainly not," said the Chief. "The vows we took the first time still work. Vows don't wear out."

Whatever Kass may have thought, with those words the issue was settled. And then to a priest who spoke of the papal blessing as something a bit special, AJR replied rather airily, "Well, you know, Father, I've heard from all kinds of important people about this – cardinals, bishops, governors, mayors, top business executives. I've had cards, letters, phone calls, and they've come from all over." Repeating this dialogue later, with an understanding smile, the priest was a little bemused. AJR's cloak of humility had parted, revealing the pride that lay hidden.

It was a pride his accomplishments justified, a pride his wife and five sons were aware of and happily shared. Through the exercise of self-discipline, he concealed this minor weakness from the world at large, but he was human, and at rare moments it surfaced.

For Kass, however, his seeming contrariness on this day of all days was too much. Back home after the Mass, with only Kay and another relative in the room, she started to sob. And then, with sudden vehemence, she exclaimed, "I'll divorce that little bastard yet!" Kay, astonished, cried out,

"What are you talking about? You've been married for fifty years!" "It's not too late, dear, it's not too late," answered Kass, and now the three women were laughing, the built-up tension of a stressful episode released.

For the garden party, the immense back yard at 940 North Lincoln was strung with Christmas lights and Chinese lanterns provided by Kay. Votive candles flickered on the twelve large circular tables that were spaced around the lawn. The tablecloths and napkins – black and gold, of course – came from the Allegheny Club. Kay, recalling the affair a long time later, wrote that "Kass looked elegant in her azure blue cocktail dress. She wore a necklace of gold set with a cluster of diamonds that Sandy and Pat gave her and a diamond pin that Art and I gave her the year before."

Her anniversary gift from the family was a set of twelve gold and white Picard serving plates, with an inscripted "R," hand-painted, in the center of each. On the back were the words "Kathleen and Art" and, under the names, the dates: "June 11, 1931-June 11, 1981," (It was Kay, by the way, who drew the design for those plates and who ordered them from the upscale jewelry store Bailey, Banks and Biddle.)

Aunt Alice, Kay said, "looked great in her traditional black." Kay herself was never more beautiful. Her red hair, I remember, caught the rays of the setting sun. Aunt Alice and Kass – I'm quoting Kay again – were "coiffed to perfection" by Angie, the hairdresser. Angie was present as a guest – partly to keep an eye on Alice and Kass, in case their plumage should need attention – and Mary Roseboro, too, was a guest, a guest who insisted on pitching in to help the caterers. "Mary," we kept urging her, "please sit back and enjoy the party," but she could not leave the serving and "redding up" to Alex DiCroce's staff. In her own mind, Mary was still the Rooney family's loyal and vigilant maid.

Two media people were there – Bill Burns the news anchor and Pat Livingston the sportswriter, but with an unspoken condition attached: no publicity. AJR wanted nothing on the society pages. None of us did. The guest list of dozens included few outsiders. Relatives and the Steeler gang predominated. The most notable absentee was my brother Tim, who felt that his duties at Yonkers Raceway during the biggest week of the standardbred season took precedence, a decision I am sure he came to regret. June, Tim's wife, and their children represented his branch of the family. I remember seeing only one politician – Tom Foerster, the longtime county commissioner. Most of AJR's old political friends were under the sod.

His grandchildren – regiments of them – seemed to be everywhere. In the early afternoon they had stormed through the house like a herd of frightened antelopes, racing in from the back yard and up the back steps, gathering speed as they rushed from one end of the upstairs hall to the other before risking their slender necks in a bouncing descent of the steep, carpeted main stairway, a pastime my brothers and I invented as kids. We had torn up the back yard with our war games, football games, and hockey games, churning it into mud when the weather was wet, but now, as Kay said, it looked amazingly pristine.

Under Kass's garden canopy, Bob McCartney, our young film director, had set up a projector and screen for a continuous slide show – still pictures and moving pictures of the Rooney family, going all the way back to when AJR and Kass were honeymooners. Probably there was music of some kind; after all these years I'm uncertain. The dinner, I know, was an appetizing buffet. Afterwards, the conversational hum and laughter were stilled as Mom and Dad cut the wedding cake, and then came the singing of "Happy Anniversary." Finally, Kass opened the gifts. One gift Kay admired was a gold Picard serving bowl with scenes painted on it. Kass, she said, "seemed thrilled by it all." AJR was embarrassed by all the attention but smiling, his earlier show of offhandedness put aside.

Nobody drank too much, and the grandchildren, sequestered in a corner of the yard, were peaceable – or maybe just exhausted. I found myself thinking of North Side garden parties from the storied past, the kind the Fricks and the Phippses and the Thaws and the Joneses and the Mooreheads and the Byerses — the custodians of high society at the turn of the twentieth century — must have staged. Ours, I imagined, was just as grand. And in conformance with AJR's wishes, we hadn't really "put on the dog."

I know that this night, for Kass, was as good as it would get. She had made her marriage last through fifty years, not all of them golden. To hear me say this would displease her, but it's true. Though she had threatened, out of pique, to "divorce that little bastard," AJR was, in her opinion, the greatest man who ever lived.

Some time before, in this same comfortable house, there had been a fiftieth anniversary party for Maggie and Pop. The old saloon keeper soon would pass on. Maggie was nearing the finish line, too, but not quite as fast. How much longer, I asked myself, would Mom and Dad be around?

With an effort, I turned away from such thoughts. Maggie and Pop had looked old. Tired. Mom and Dad were still full of life. Snap out of it, I said to myself. In a few more spins of the earth, the football team would be encamped at St. Vincent, starting a new season. Nineteen eighty was a disappointment, but 1981 would be different. We had hope. We were winners. We were Rooneys. All was well.

Slipsliding

In retrospect, my parents' golden wedding celebration was the best thing that happened to the Rooney clan in 1981. The football season turned out to be a downer. In clusters now, we were losing important pieces of the mechanism that had brought us our championships. Nineteen eighty was the last time around for Rocky Bleier, Dwight White, Mike Wagner, and Steve Furness. Bleier, White, and Wagner retired; Furness, disposed of, was picked up by Detroit. He would play only one more year. We got rid of Matt Bahr as well – his weak kickoffs, anathema to the coaches, had shortened his time with the Steelers – but Matt, unlike the others, was still in his prime. Super-accurate field-goal kicking would keep him in the league for another ten seasons.

The loss of Bleier – and, to a lesser extent, of White, Wagner, and Furness – took away part of our ambience. I remember something that Lovey Young said on the night before we played a pre-season game in 1981 with the New York Giants. Lovey and her husband, George Young, the Giants' general manager, were having dinner with Kay and me, and Lovey remarked that the team's younger players, not all of them rookies, seemed to be over-awed by the Steelers. She had heard them talking about Joe Greene, Jack Lambert, and Mel Blount as if they belonged to a race of superhumans. "Our guys are licked before the game starts," Lovey said, and perhaps this was true, for on the following day the Giants lost to us. But even then they were on the way up, while the Steelers, with their fading superstars, were on the way down.

Rocky Bleier's value to the Steelers derived just as much from its inspirational nature as from anything he was able to do on the field. A player who was neither big, fast, nor agile, one whose battlefield wounds might have crippled him for life, he epitomized strength of will. To no one's surprise, he prospered as a motivational speaker when his football career was over. I thought that, if so inclined, he could have been an exceptional coach. Frank Pollard, our second-year running back from Baylor, filled the bill as Rocky's replacement, but only by the measuring stick of performance. To the fans and the media, what Bleier stood for could not have been duplicated.

Dwight White, after leaving the Steelers, was an overnight success in the brokerage business. He revealed an unsuspected talent for making shrewd transactions in stocks and bonds. With White gone, only Joe Greene and L. C. Greenwood remained from the original Steel Curtain; at the end of the 1981 season they would follow White and Ernie Holmes into retirement. Furness, a late comer to the brotherhood, had started at defensive tackle in Super Bowl XIV and many other big games. Then there was Wagner, a total player who used his head, heart, and athletic skills to "make things happen."

We would miss all four of these veterans, miss their experience and attitude. That Matt Bahr would also be missed was largely unforeseen. Coaches make the mistake of thinking kickers are where you find them. Well, the kicker we signed in 1981 couldn't kick, requiring the expenditure of quality scouting time to find a new one.

Dick Haley and I had always maintained that we could stay near the top by drafting three new starters of top-flight ability every year. We thought that any other team with a core of good players could do this, too. There was nothing wrong with the concept, nothing obviously wrong, but in the 1981 draft, picking seventeenth in each round, we came up a player short. I can offer no excuses for the 1981 draft, none at all. I bungled it.

Our first-round selection, Keith Gary, a defensive end from Oklahoma, seemed to have all the tools. We thought he could step in right away and fill one of the holes in the line; and the truth is that he played some good games. His trouble was inconsistency. Along with the good games, there were just as many not so good games. As for the rest of our top four, all of them rated among the top one hundred in the draft, they were not worth a hill of beans, and the same could be said for my analysis of the information about them delivered to me by our scouts.

Summing up, I did not do my part to keep our defensive front four intact. The two rookies who became starters were linebackers – Bryan Hinkle, from Oregon, and David Little, from Florida. Continuing a trend, we took Hinkle in the sixth round and Little in the seventh. Our best picks of late seemed to come, as Dan had observed, from the middle of the pack, or even lower. Little had good bloodlines: he was the younger brother of the Dolphins' great offensive lineman, Larry Little. In his eighth year with the Steelers, 1988, David was the team's MVP, and three years later he went to the Pro Bowl. Hinkle was MVP in 1986; both he and Little were still on the roster in 1992, when Bill Cowher succeeded Noll as head coach.

Again in 1981 we failed to make the playoffs. Another sign of regression was that we lost as many games as we won. And again we lost the close games, the kind we had won in our playoff years. In six of our defeats, a touchdown or a field goal was the difference. Football indeed is a game of inches. It is also a game of intensity and focus, a game in which the hungry prevail. To complete the metaphor, age dulls the appetite. Our players from the years I speak of would be upset with me for saying this, but they were swiftly becoming superannuated.

Their coaches wouldn't like to hear that, either, which makes it none the less true.

What is equally accurate, and the blame falls on me, is that our draft did not help the situation. For example, Swann, Stallworth, and Cunningham were still catching passes, but not quite as many as before, and the wide receivers we drafted in the fourth and fifth rounds were absolute duds. Under certain conditions Noll would use Ray Pinney, a center, guard, and tackle, as an emergency receiver, lining him up at tight end. In one game, he actually caught a touchdown pass.

Speaking of Pinney, Joe Gordon overheard him remark at the end of the season that an 8-8 record "wasn't too bad." When Joe repeated that to me, saying, "It shows how far the attitude of those young guys has slipped," I shook my head in consternation but made no reply. After all, I had drafted those young guys. A lot of them, like Pinney, were good players. They were not, however, the game-breakers we needed.

In the first forty years of the franchise's history, an 8-8 record would have been satisfactory, or even at times something to celebrate. But the 1970s had changed that way of looking at things. The 1970s had raised our expectations, and in 1980 and 1981, we failed to meet them.

Chapter 69

Patchwork

Retirements were changing the face of our team. After the 1981 season Joe Greene and L. C. Greenwood, the last two charter members of the Steel Curtain front four, retired. John Banaszak, a backup and sometime starter at defensive tackle and defensive end, retired. So did J. T. Thomas, who had given us years of service at defensive back. From the offensive unit, we lost Jon Kolb, a durable, highly valued tackle, and Randy Grossman, one of the better pass-catching tight ends.

Joe Greene's jersey number also went into retirement. Greene's 75 and Ernie Stautner's 70 were the only numbers that would never again be worn by a Pittsburgh player. Selecting jersey numbers for retirement is a ticklish business. Rosters are so large that to retire every number that belonged for a while to a Hall of Famer would cause a shortage. Greene, though, was a special case. Starting in 1969, his rookie season, he'd been the cornerstone (if I may mix a metaphor) of the Steel Curtain front four. The day we drafted Greene was the day we turned the franchise around.

But now he went home to Texas and opened a restaurant – three "family-style" restaurants, actually. Chuck Noll's advice to every departing Steeler was: "Find your life's work and get on with it." Joe Greene's life's work, as he soon discovered, was not the restaurant business. Which left football, something he knew about. In 1987, at the suggestion of Joe Gordon, Noll made room on the coaching staff for him, and he remained with the team as long as Noll did. Moving on in 1992, when Bill Cowher took over from Noll, he was with the Dolphins for a while and then the Cardinals. Finally Dan brought him back for the second time – not to coach but to be a scout.

Even without Greene and the others, we were not quite ready for the graveyard. We still had Terry Bradshaw. We still had Franco, who had lost a step but reported to pre-season training camp in fine fettle. We still had Stallworth and Swann. We still had Mike Webster. We still had Larry Brown, one of the most underrated offensive tackles in the NFL. We still had Ben Cunningham. We still had two of the top linebackers in the game – Jack Ham and Jack Lambert, plus Loren Toews. We still had Mel Blount, Donnie Shell, and Ron Johnson in the defensive backfield. We still had Gary Dunn in the defensive line. Frank Pollard had become an able replacement for Rocky Bleier. Ray Pinney was becoming a Noll-type offensive lineman – smart, quick, versatile. And we had filled one of our greatest needs by acquiring a place-kicker, Gary Anderson.

We had wanted Gary Anderson since we scouted him at Syracuse, but on draft day in 1981 we fell into an easily avoidable trap. "We can get this guy on the next round, we're the only ones who have him rated this high." we kept telling ourselves. It's a mistake that coaches and personnel directors repeatedly make. The waiting game had worked when we drafted Stallworth, but Buffalo beat us to Anderson.

"We'll have to trade for him," I said to Dick Haley. "Hold on," he answered. Anderson was a prospective free agent, and Haley believed we could sign him. "No. We have to trade," I insisted. "Trust me," Haley said. Haley got his way and, just as he had foretold, Anderson signed with us in 1982. In his second season he was our MVP. He remained with the Steelers until 1994, when Cowher changed kickers, and was one of the most consistent performers in the league for many years afterward with other teams.

The credit belongs to Dick Haley for landing this prize catch.

We prepared for the 1982 draft in the same manner and the same spirit as always, but with more people involved – assistant coaches, that is to say – and more gadgetry. Computers had become an indispensable help in sorting and qualifying the raw information we gathered. I was trying to set up models that would give us a complete list of draft-eligible players who met certain minimum height and weight standards and minimum time standards in the forty-yard dash. In addition, we were looking for such things as growth potential, body control, prehensile hands (which wide receivers must have), quickness off the ball (a requirement for pass rushers), the ability to block and to shed blockers, strength, toughness, and so on, all hard to measure. Counting free agents, we had seven hundred or more names in the computer. Fewer than half were legitimate prospects.

As a result of our 8-8 record in 1981, we'd be picking twelfth. With the thirteenth pick in 1971, we came up with Franco Harris. With the twenty-first pick in 1974, we drafted Lynn Swann. We were therefore not without hope. We thought we could possibly draft someone who could lift the whole team, who could make the big play when the occasion demanded. And Walter Abercrombie, we believed, was such a catalyst.

He was still on the board when our turn came, and we grabbed him. Walter Abercrombie would be the third Baylor running back we had drafted in four years. In the first round of the 1979 draft, we had taken Greg Hawthorne, who underachieved. In the eleventh round of the 1980 draft, we had taken Frank Pollard, who overachieved. Abercrombie, it seemed to us, had Greg Hawthorne's talent and Frank Pollard's intangibles. "Can't miss" was a phrase I had learned never to use. But Abercrombie could run, catch, and block. He could make the big play. He was consistent. He was productive. He was a splendid athlete with all the intangibles.

Of course, there is always a "but." In his senior year, Abercrombie had hurt his knee. Accordingly, our medical people gave him an especially thorough physical examination, which he passed to their satisfaction. His knee, they informed us, was "playable." And they were right. Abercrombie played six years for the Steelers and seven years in the NFL. He made some big plays and some good plays. There were years when he was our second-best rusher and pass receiver. But none of this made him another Harris. As Rocky Bleier's successor in the backfield, Frank Pollard was everything we expected, and more. As Franco's successor, Abercrombie fell short by about the distance from Pittsburgh to Waco.

Watching game films of Abercrombie after he left the team, I noticed something that escaped me while he was with us: he favored his "playable" knee. George Allen, a Hall-of-Fame coach, once said to me, "The good ones" – the good running backs – "have that burst." When Abercrombie ran, he couldn't shift to a higher gear. He could not turn a good run into a great run.

Our second-round pick, offensive tackle John Meyer of Arizona State, had two sound knees when we drafted him, but only one by the end of his first and only training camp. Seriously injured, he never played a down for the Steelers or for any other pro team. In the third round, we had much better luck. Mike Merriweather, linebacker from Pacific, became a team MVP and a Pro Bowl player. Our fourth pick, defensive back Rick Woods of Boise State, was a Steeler for five years. He started at times and could make an interception. We drafted a number of other players who were able to contribute, but the 1982 crop wasn't among our better ones.

We did have some luck with free agents. Besides Anderson, there was Keith Willis, a defensive end from Northeastern University in Boston, where scouts seldom ventured. He played nine years for the Steelers. In six of those years we won more games than we lost and in four of those years we went to the playoffs. Willis was one of the guys who popped up in our computer listing of lower-rated players deserving of consideration. Bill Nunn made a trip to Boston, watched him work out, watched a few game films, and told us he looked like a prospect.

In camp, he confirmed Bill's judgment. Little else of a positive nature was happening. Before the season started, George Perles, who had the title of assistant head coach, bailed out on us. Perles always had wanted to be the commander-in-chief somewhere, and one of the fly-by-night teams in a brand new – and short-lived – pro league gave him the opportunity. Then came an offer from his alma mater, Michigan State, and Perles bailed out on the pro team to be the Spartans' head coach. Perles did well at Michigan State. He had a series of winning seasons and took the team to the Rose Bowl one year. Even the most successful coaches usually end up being fired – they're fatalistic about that – but when Perles left Michigan State he left on his own terms: he retired.

The Steelers missed Perles. He provided a sort of counterbalance, I thought, to Chuck Noll's cerebral approach. George was a down-and-dirty type of guy, by which I don't mean to say that he taught dirty football. I mean that he implanted a rambunctious mind set. Particularly in the NFL, line play is hand-to-hand combat, and Perles had the temperament to coach it as such. He also helped Noll choose assistants. Perles lobbied for Woody Widenhofer, Tom Moore, and Rollie Dotsch. They were three of the best we ever had. I thought the best assistant that Noll himself actually hired, aside from Perles, was Tony Dungy.

Rollie Dotsch left the Steelers to go with Perles, his mentor, but did not make the move to Michigan State. He became the head coach of the pro team and was doing very well when he suddenly died of a heart attack. He was one of the true gentlemen in the coaching profession. Paul Uram, our conditioning coach, also departed with Perles. After that, I lost track of him. We did not have to search very far for a conditioning coach. Jon Kolb, newly retired from the playing ranks, was eager to take the job and made a seamless transition.

On the other hand, the defection of Perles and Dotsch left us high and dry, at least temporarily. And it strengthened the impression that the Steelers were falling apart.

Momentum Killer

After going undefeated in four exhibition games, the Steelers opened the regular season of 1982 like anything but a team on its deathbed. They outfought the Cowboys in Dallas, 36-28, and won from Cincinnati at Three Rivers Stadium in overtime, 26-20. Terry Bradshaw was still throwing touchdown passes. Franco Harris was still breaking tackles. Gary Anderson had given us a field-goal threat. There was nothing to suggest our imminent demise. Then the Players Association called another strike.

The timing of the walkout was calculated. The players had learned their lesson in 1974, when they went on strike before the training camps opened. It was shortsighted strategy. Draftees and free agents reported as usual. A handful of veterans, worried about losing their positions, crossed the picket line. Others who had gone along with the strike began to lose heart, and two weeks into the pre-season the insurgency collapsed.

For this strike, the planning was better. With the rookies assimilated, the union had everyone on board. Team owners, unable to fill out their lineups, suspended the schedule. They did not have a choice. Over an eight-week period in September, October, and November no games were played while negotiations with the union proceeded acrimoniously.

The players were asking that fifty-five percent of the league's gross revenue be earmarked for salaries. I remember hearing three of my brothers – Tim, John, and Pat – declare that if the owners gave in, then the NFL could just fold up its tent. "It'll kill the league," they told Dan and me. "The race-track owners gave the horsemen a percentage, and now we have a business where the return on investment is hardly enough to make it worthwhile." In the end, the football players got a percentage, but not the fifty-five percent they demanded. That would come later, as the outcome of a strike in 1993. The NFL not only survived, but seems to be doing fine.

During the 1982 strike, AJR continued to pay the coaches, scouts, and front-office people their full salaries. The coaches studied film; the scouts carried on as they always had. There was work, I suppose, for the front-office people, but I didn't have time to pay attention.

In the talks between the owners ad the Players Association, both sides listened closely to Dan. He was taking a first step toward the leadership role he would one day assume. Unmistakably, he was now his own man, a person of true consequence in the affairs of the NFL and no longer merely Art Rooney's son. The pride the Chief took in him was barely containable.

It eclipsed by far the confidence he placed in his second-oldest son. While the strike was still going on, he called me into his office and told me to say nothing to anyone about it. "Let Dan make all the statements to the media," he said. "The strike is his show. You butt out of it."

Since I hadn't butted in, I was taken aback. I knew the importance of the part Dan was playing. I knew the limits of my authority in the Steeler organization, or thought I did. No newspaper, television, or radio reporter had asked me to talk about the strike and I hadn't intended to volunteer anything. Whether I'd have answered a question about the strike I couldn't say. I believed in being open and honest with reporters, but I didn't tell them everything I knew.

This was not quite the way the Chief would have put it. He thought I talked too much, that I couldn't hold my tongue. He never exactly said so – not in as many words. He didn't have to; he could make his opinions clear without getting into specifics. The Chief himself was a master at talking to the media. He never let anything out unless he wanted it out. Or almost never. Once in a while he slipped up. Usually, though, if that was his purpose, he could beguile a reporter who was digging for something and send him away satisfied with a humorous story. Dan tried to do this, but lacked the Chief's ability to disarm. Although he and the Chief took pains not to lie, they were good at misleading – or "disassembling," as George W. Bush would say, losing another struggle with the English language.

They were more in control of themselves than I could ever be. My big mouth helped my relations with the press, but got me in hot water now and then. One thing I came to realize: the Chief's insistence that Dan should be the spokesman for the whole organization made sense. During the strike, when I went to a college football game on a scouting trip, I sat in the stands, not the press box. That way, there was no chance I would absentmindedly give a sportswriter a quote.

While the owners and the Players Association were scratching out a new collective bargaining agreement, Paul Martha, now a Pittsburgh attorney, rendered valuable service as an intermediary. In my view, the strike hurt both sides, since the revenue lost was gone forever, but the players ended up with a minimum salary guarantee, higher training-camp and post-season pay, and an increase in medical, retirement, and health-insurance benefits.

With a rejiggered schedule, the season resumed on November 21st. Our October 24 game with Cleveland, wiped out by the strike, would be played on January 2nd. The remaining bypassed games, seven in all, were simply canceled.

Back in action, we had an easy time beating the Oilers in Houston and were now 7-0, including those four pre-season wins. But the layoff had cost us our momentum. We had an aging team that lost three of its last six games.

Because of the shortened season, the format for the playoffs was different. For one year only, the league held a sixteen-team tournament. The Steelers qualified as one of the eight teams from the American Conference by winning the postponed game with the Browns but lost in the first round of the tournament to San Diego, 31-28. On our own field, we let an eleven-point lead slip away in the fourth quarter.

Disappointing, yes. But 1982 was another winning season. We had not had a losing one since 1971. We were keeping our heads above water.

Special Delivery

What bothered me almost as much as the way our defense crumbled after Bradshaw's touchdown pass to Stallworth had given us a 28-17 fourth-quarter lead in that 1982 playoff game was the performance, leading up to it, of the Steelers' ticket people.

Unaccountably, they hadn't prepared.

I mean they hadn't printed playoff tickets beforehand. The news that our win over Cleveland on January 2nd had put us into the tournament seemed to come as a big surprise.

So when our season-ticket holders started calling for their seats, there was utter confusion.

Quickly, the utter confusion gave way to pure bedlam.

In poured the howls of displeasure.

"You don't have my tickets? What are you telling me? Is this a joke of some kind?"

And "How can you do this to me? I've been with you since the days when you were bums and losers. I sat behind the girders at Forbes Field. I walked up Cardiac Hill to get to Pitt Stadium. I sat in the rain and snow and watched you disgrace yourselves. And now I can't get tickets to a playoff game?"

And "You Rooneys will never change. You've been giving us the shaft for fifty years."

On and on it went in the same tones of outrage. Where was the good will I thought we had earned with ten winning seasons in the past eleven, with four trips to the Super Bowl and four Lombardi Trophies?

Day and night in the frigid January weather there were long lines that almost encircled Three Rivers Stadium. Inside, the scouting department worked day and night on the 1983 draft. On rare occasions, I caught a glimpse of the freezing ticket buyers and wondered if somebody in the organization was getting hot coffee to them while they stood out there in the cold. Preoccupied with the draft, I did not take the trouble to check. I had my father's strong bent for the random act of kindness but not his disposition to act on it.

In this case, the only Rooney who acted was Dan. He ordered coffee for the people in the cold at least once.

Crisis management dictated that everybody in the front office deliver tickets door-to-door, in person. We were to do this for any customers who lived in our neighborhoods. Three houses down the street from ours there resided a sour-visaged old guy of the curmudgeonly type. He never smiled, never spoke, never, in fact, made eye contact. That he was one of our fans greatly surprised me, but, tickets in hand, I rang his doorbell on a cold, dark night near the end of the week before the game.

The next thing I knew, he was standing in the entranceway. "I have your playoff tickets," I blurted, and his face suddenly lost its rigidity. With his left hand, he grabbed the tickets. With his right hand he grabbed mine, and started pumping it. I thought he would never let go. Meanwhile, he was actually smiling. "Our tickets! Our tickets!" he shouted to his wife. "Our playoff tickets are here! And Art Rooney's kid delivered them!"

Then he was saying to me, "Thanks, neighbor, thanks. Come in! Have a drink. Or, if you don't want a drink, a cup of coffee. Gosh, I've heard so many nice things about the Rooneys, and now I know they're true."

I was flabbergasted. I did not stay for coffee, but it took me a while to break away.

"Thanks," he kept saying. "This is great. Good luck in the playoffs."

From then on, whenever I saw him, he gave me a smile and a big hello, I returned his friendliness to the best of my ability, thinking that in all the time I had lived near this fellow I misread him. He was not anti-social, just reserved, or maybe shy. AJR would have quickly penetrated his shield. He'd have made the guy believe there was nobody else whose company he preferred.

Was my father born with that gift, or did he work to acquire it? Either way, it was something I felt I never would have.

A Night with the Stars

On October 9, 1982, one year and four months after the fiftieth wedding anniversary of my parents, we celebrated another significant milestone, the fiftieth anniversary of the day that AJR put up $2,500 to buy a franchise in the National Football League.

October 9th was Kay's birthday, as it happened, a coincidence important only to me. The strike called by the Players Association had been going on for three weeks. Even so, there was no thought of postponing the big public shindig we had scheduled for that date at the David L. Lawrence Convention Center or the private party the night before at LeMont Restaurant up on Mount Washington.

The party at LeMont would honor the all-time Steeler all-star team selected in a poll of its readers by the *Pittsburgh Post-Gazette*. More than a third of the players voted onto that team – Terry Bradshaw, Franco Harris, Jack Ham, Jack Lambert, Mike Webster, John Stallworth, Larry Brown, Mel Blount – were participants, willing or otherwise, in the strike, but everybody came except a handful who did not live nearby. Only AJR could have dealt with the social awkwardness inherent in such a gathering. His person-to-person skills, as I knew they would, instantly put the strikers at ease.

If there was any disharmony at all, it had to do with the fiftieth-anniversary team's makeup. No one could even quibble about many of the selections – Bradshaw, Harris, Joe Greene, Blount, Lambert and Ham, Stallworth and Swann, Jack Butler, Ernie Stautner, L.C. Greenwood, Pat Brady as the punter. And Bill Dudley belonged – there was general agreement about that – but where? As a running back? He led the league in rushing one year, after all. Conveniently, he led the league also in pass interceptions. So Dudley ended up in the defensive backfield, leaving room on the offensive unit for John Henry Johnson as well as Harris.

My own feeling was that, while John Henry Johnson was a true Hall-of-Famer, he did not do as much for our teams in the 1960s as Rocky Bleier had done for the teams that won Super Bowls. When we drafted John Henry in 1953 he refused to sign with us and went off to Canada. His best years in the NFL, actually, were with San Francisco and Detroit. He came to Pittsburgh in 1960 and had two exceptional years and two good years. Then he got hurt, and after that he did nothing.

In the voting for center, there were pockets of support for Chuck Cherundolo, who played both ways in the 1940s, and Ray Mansfield, a favorite with the fans and the media. But Mike Webster was beyond any doubt the logical runaway choice. And though without Ben Cunningham our Super Bowl record might have been 2-2 or 2-0 instead of 4-0, Elbie Nickel deserved to be the tight end. Nickel paid a price for every pass he caught, but in a career that lasted eleven years he caught more passes than any other Steeler tight end and seldom missed a game or even a down.

It is no easy matter to judge an offensive lineman's performance except by looking at film and then rerunning it. So the choice of Jon Kolb and his teammate Larry Brown at the tackle positions reinforced my belief that no fans anywhere knew as much about football as ours did. The third linebacker, with Lambert and Ham, was Andy Russell, an equally pleasing selection. Russell, like his good friend Ray Mansfield, came to the Steelers in the 1960s, when times were tough, and played on into the Super Bowl years. That Russell, Mansfield, and Jack Butler have never even been nominated for the Hall of Fame is an injustice I don't understand.

To be with all these men who were sharing a special award for excellence was exhilarating. At the risk of going overboard, let me say it reminded me of certain Marines I got to know at Parris Island, veteran instructors who had fought in places like Guam, Iwo Jima, Guadalcanal, and the Chosen Reservoir. They seemed to be saying, "We have been there, and we survived." So did the Steeler all-stars. I hope the analogy I am making is not too far-fetched.

LeMont Restaurant on Grandview Avenue offered better-than-adequate food and a stunning view of the rivers and the Downtown skyline. Next to the view from Nob Hill in San Francisco, the urban panorama that lies before you is unrivalled in all of America. Whenever we drafted a player we wanted to impress, we took him to LeMont.

On the night of the party the skies were clear and everything sparkled. I looked around me and took in the magic. There I was with these Hall of Famers – the Chief, Johnny Blood, Bill Dudley – plus future Hall of Famers like Dan, like John Henry Johnson and so many of the still-active all-stars. There were also the players I knew would be nominated for the Hall. I'd be nominated myself one day. How lucky I am, I thought, to be Art Rooney's son and to have some involvement in the creation of what the Steelers had become – a championship team and a civic institution.

There were no formal speeches, but at the end of the dinner Andy Russell, who was always so at home on occasions such as this, tapped a fork on an empty glass. The clink-clink-clink brought us all to attention. "Let's go around the room," he proposed, "and give everyone a chance to tell what it means to be a Steeler – everyone who wants to, that is." Almost everyone, as I recollect, did want to.

Fittingly, AJR went first. With the simple straightforwardness for which he was known, he spoke of his good fortune in having guided his team through the lean years we thought would never end. He said that every player and coach connected with the Steelers in times gone by had helped us get to the top of Mount Washington on this night.

Johnny Blood, still looking like a movie star pushed into grudging retirement or like a U. S. senator at the zenith of his career, gave us a refresher course on the history of the NFL. Bill Dudley expressed his affection for AJR. Speaker followed speaker, each with a perspective of his own. Smart enough to keep quiet, I sat back and listened. Waiters and busboys and I think a few of the cooks listened too, from inconspicuous vantage points along the fringes of the room. They were all as transfixed as I was.

Each all-star left the restaurant with a foot-high bronze sculpture of a defensive player colliding with a ball carrier. The artist had somehow compressed all the dynamism and force of a spectacular open-field tackle into his creation. The image of Chuck Mehelich's hit on Leon Hart in a game at Forbes Field came back to me.

Hart was with the Detroit Lions, a huge tight end from Turtle Creek who had won the Heisman Trophy at Notre Dame. Mehelich weighed 180 pounds at the most. Knocked end over end, Hart was carried off the field on a stretcher. Mehelich got up and walked to the bench, his eyes glazed. Then he staggered into the arms of the trainer and a helpful equipment man. Snapped in two by the violence of the tackle, the leather belts attached to Mehelich's hip pads, the belts that held them in place, were dangling free. That scene, for me, epitomizes Steeler football.

I was so moved by the sculpture's symbolism that I thought of finding out if there were replicas left over, so I could buy one. It would nicely enhance a collection I had started – water-color paintings of our greatest players, past and present, by Merv Corning, a talented West Coast artist. Then I dismissed the idea. You don't buy an award meant for someone who has earned it.

My paintings had been put on display at the LeMont affair, and Joe Gordon told me that after it was over he spotted a female guest walking out with the likeness of Rocky Bleier. These paintings are originals, not copies, and my investment in them was more than sentimental; there had been times in the not-so-distant past when their cost put a squeeze on my finances.

Joe stopped the woman before she got to the door.

"Where are you going with Rocky?" he asked.

"I'm taking him home," she explained. "I just have to. I want him to be mine."

"Impossible, lady. He belongs to Art Rooney Junior," said Gordon – and, thanks to Joe's protectiveness, he still does.

I continued to collect Merv Corning's work, by the way. I have an excellent study of AJR, one of Chuck Noll, another of Billy Conn, and a beautiful portrait of Kay, with her glorious red hair accentuated.

Only the still-new David L. Lawrence Convention Center could have held the crowd that attended the big open reception on the night after the party at LeMont. I remembered how, when Lawrence was alive, public outrage killed a suggestion that Three Rivers Stadium be named in his honor. Now that he had gone to whatever place in the hereafter is reserved for politicians, it was OK to put his name on the convention center. But that was how we treated the American Indians – first we tried to exterminate them and then we gave Indian names to cities and rivers and national parks and sports teams and everything else under the sun.

Howard Cosell – "Mr. Monday Night Football" – emceed the televised celebration at the convention center. He introduced Myron Cope as "the diminutive one" (Cope loved it) and he introduced all the football players. His introduction of AJR was effusive. AJR repeated much of what he had said the night before and expressed hope that the strike would soon end. He introduced Kass, who looked elegant.

But of course she always did.

Burglarized

There was excitement afterwards, of a different kind, for the Art Rooney, Jr. family. When we returned to Mount Lebanon, Kay and I were worn out; our two sons, Mike and Art III, were hungry. While they snacked on her apple pie in the kitchen, Kay went upstairs, with Sue. In a minute, she called down, "Art, get up here immediately. Something's wrong." As she was putting away her long strand of pearls, she had made an unsettling discovery: her short strand was missing. Then she had looked into her jewelry boxes. They were empty. Everything in them was gone, including her Super Bowl X necklace. The only other such necklaces belonged to Kass, Mrs. Noll, Patricia Rooney, and Aunt Marie McGinley. The thief had even taken some of my cufflinks. I'd had the foresight to stash my Super Bowl rings in a safe-deposit box at the bank. My St. Vincent class ring had not been worth stealing, apparently. It was untouched. "Thanks, pal, you son of a bitch," I said between gritted teeth. Under Kay's bed was a jackpot the burglar had overlooked – her best silverware, lots of it.

Some on-the-spot detective work revealed that the guy was a second-story man. He had climbed up on top of an awning and entered Art III's room in the back of the house. We guessed that he had turned on the TV and watched the convention-center doings to judge how much working time he would have.

The stolen jewelry, by the insurance company's estimate, was worth about twenty thousand dollars. There had not been any cash in the house. On the window sill where the thief broke in, Art III had left a Rubik's Cube he'd been trying unsuccessfully to master. Now, glory be, it was solved.

The police identified the burglar when they picked him up later for another crime. Among the many houses he had looted was one that belonged to a relative of Kay's. The bum never confessed but went to jail for a short time. Kay's jewelry – and my cufflinks – were never recovered.

For the rest of the year, when the Steelers had a game at Three Rivers Stadium, we hired an off-duty cop to watch our house. AJR said, "You're locking the barn door after the horse has been stolen." And then he said, "You fancy dudes in Mount Lebanon who put on the dog, you're asking – just begging – to be taken."

Chapter 70

Put in Our Places

Like all of us, AJR had his faults. When he said hurtful things to Mom, I sincerely hated him. He appeared to believe that since he was the linch-pin of the family it gave him certain prerogatives. If he saw the need to be brusque with the rest of us, that was his right.

Father Silas, of course, who worked for Christ Almighty, was exempt from this sort of hazing. Father Silas would not have put up with anything like that except perhaps from the head of the Franciscan order and most certainly from the Pope.

I have said that when Dad and Mom had a spat, Mom would drive all the way to Ligonier, cooling off. After one of these blowups, when there were visitors in the house, she asked me to come with her as she started out the door. Instead of driving to Ligonier, she got no farther than St. Peter's Church. There, sobbing and crying, she remembered her guests and turned back.

AJR's wrath could be shattering to Pat, John, and me. In the Steeler offices he might put you down in front of an intern or a secretary. Only Tim was bold enough to talk back.

I made a suggestion once that I thought was in Mom's best interest, and her reaction surprised me. Because Dad was out of town so much, I told her, she should have her own credit cards and belong to a country club. To Kass, this sounded like criticism of Dad. She fastened me with a look and said: "You and your four brothers put together would not make a patch on your father's ass."

And she was right.

Ordinarily, AJR did not berate his football players, but I was in the office one day when he picked up a telephone and called Steeler guard John "Bull" Schweder a "no-good greasy bum." It seems that Bull was asking questions about the team and its finances, which Dad thought was none of his business. Another time, on a street corner, he took a swing at a heckling fan. It was perhaps just as well that the punch did not connect.

I don't want this to be one-sided. Dad could compliment your work and make you feel super. He was an exponent of the R.A.K. – the random act of kindness. The part-time workers at Three Rivers Stadium – the press-box crew, the security people, the spotters for the radio announcers – were frequent beneficiaries of these R.A.K.'s. Let me give one example. Hearing that Ralph, a member of the ground crew, was in Palm Beach on vacation one winter, and knowing that he was seriously ill with kidney trouble and liver trouble, Dad invited him to dinner at our dog track. He also invited Curt Gowdy, a big-time television sportscaster. "Ralph's with our organization," Dad said to Gowdy after introducing them. As far as Gowdy knew, Ralph might have been the trainer or he might have been the controller – the man in charge of investments.

"Mister Rooney made me feel like a million bucks," Ralph said.

He could make perfect strangers feel the same way. Checking out of a motel in Frederick, Maryland, I found a note to call the head of security. It crossed my mind at once that my car had been stolen. But no. The man wanted to tell me about the time he had gone to Pittsburgh for a Steeler game at Pitt Stadium in the 1950s.

"My young son was with me, and we were waiting for the ticket window to open when this guy came by," the cop said. "He was short and portly. Had a big neck. Glasses. Big cigar in his mouth. He was wearing an old topcoat. And a hat. Somehow we got to talking. The guy asked my boy where he was from. 'Frederick, Maryland.' 'Frederick? I have a farm near Frederick.' The ticket window opened and I pulled out my wallet. 'Save your money,' the guy said. 'Come on with me.' Well, he took us through the gate and down to the field. When we got there, the boy and I hung back. This older man said, 'Come on,' and we followed him out to where a few of the players were loosening up early. He introduced us to them and he introduced us to some of the coaches. Then he pointed to a section of the stadium and said, 'Go up there and find yourselves a couple of seats. There'll be a lot of them open, because we're not sold out.' That man was Mister Art Rooney."

Certainly Dad mellowed with age. In the 1970s and 1980s there were only occasional eruptions. One that I recall took place in the coffee kitchen at Three Rivers Stadium when Myron Cope, the color man on Steeler radio broadcasts, learned what it was like to displease AJR. A streaker, naked except for a jockstrap, had been making a spectacle of himself at our games, dashing out onto the field and running around madly until the cops chased him down. Myron seemed to regard this as harmless entertainment. On Steeler broadcasts and on his radio talk show, he mythologized the guy – "When will he strike next?" – and other media people picked up on it.

AJR, meanwhile, was smoldering. He blamed Myron, the most popular and most listened-to sportscaster in town, for egging the halfwit on. The chance to say so before an audience came one morning in the coffee room, a gathering place for coaches, scouts, and front-office workers. Myron was with them, shooting the breeze, when AJR strolled in. He was wearing his gray cardigan sweater with a white shirt, sharply-pressed dark slacks, and well-shined black loafers, a fashion plate now in contrast to the way he had dressed before our move to these bright new surroundings. He poured himself a cup of coffee and then, without preamble, gave the unfortunate Cope a blast right out of the old days.

"Myron," he began, "you're making a hero out of that streaker. What you're doing is just going to encourage other nuts. They'll be trying the same thing. The cops will be after him, and it could easily cause a riot one of these Sundays. I thought you had better sense than that."

Simply repeating the Chief's words doesn't fully suggest how withering they were. It was the tone of his voice and the look on his face that conveyed the extent of his anger. Having spoken, he turned on his heel and quickly walked back to his office. Myron called after him, "Mister Rooney ..." but Mister Rooney paid no attention.

The coffee room fell silent. Ten or fifteen seconds that seemed like an hour went by, all of us staring into our cups, and then I said cheerfully, "Well, Myron, welcome to the family. The only people he talks to like that any more are his sons!"

'Gone'

On a morning two or three weeks after the Steelers' anniversary party and a day or two before the end of the players' strike, I was at Three Rivers Stadium as usual – the strike hadn't changed my routine – when Mary Regan came into my office, looking perturbed, and said, "You'd better get over to your dad's house right away."

Then she continued, "Your mom hurt herself on the steps."

Kass was 78, and visibly slowing down. She was no less elegant, no less ladylike. At the anniversary party, beautifully dressed as always, she had sparkled, making all of us proud. Though she had instantly recognized such long-absent friends as John Blood McNally, Bill Dudley, and Ernie Stautner, her short-term memory was failing. She had stopped driving her car, the big, high-powered Buick replaced for her every two years by AJR. Now she relied on the chauffeurs he recruited: Iggy Borkowski, Richie Easton, and her favorite, Ed Kiely. Ralph Berlin helped out between football seasons, and of course there were always sons and grandsons.

"Hurt herself on the steps," Mary Regan had said. I made the trip from Three Rivers Stadium to 940 North Lincoln Avenue in less than five minutes. That Victorian stairway was treacherous. When my brothers and I were young, and addicted to racing back and forth in the upper hall, a barricade had been placed at the top to keep us out of danger. Kass, while descending those steps, had twisted an ankle. Instinctively, she reached for the banister, saving herself from a fall to the ground floor. And now she could not stand, or move from the steps, where I found her awkwardly seated.

Aunt Alice, I think, was the one who had called Mary Regan. AJR was at home, but seemed helpless. "These damn steps!" Kass said to me. They were steep, the distance between them hard to judge. From Aunt Alice, or AJR, or Kass herself – I'm no longer certain – I learned that Ralph Berlin was on his way. Kass would be getting the same quick first aid as a Steeler disabled on the football field.

Ralph Berlin and Kay arrived in a dead heat. Kay had just sent the kids off to school when Aunt Alice called her at home. Nobody – not the fastest driver on the NASCAR circuit – could have made better time between Mount Lebanon and the North Side. Berlin was his capable self. With help from the rest of us, he moved Kass off the steps and into a chair with rollers. He called the paramedics. Then he called Dr. Paul Steele, the football team's orthopedic specialist.

It took the paramedics a full twenty minutes to get to the house, greatly annoying Kay. When the ambulance left for Divine Providence Hospital, where Dr. Steele was waiting, all of us piled in except AJR. "Aren't you coming?" asked Kay. To her consternation, he answered, "No, I'm not much good in situations like this."

At the hospital, Dr. Steele ordered X-rays. They revealed a broken bone in the lower part of Kass's leg. All the while she was calm – "mostly mad at herself for causing such an uproar," Kay remembers. Dr. Steele ordered a cast. We did not get a look at it until some time later, and Kay was not pleased. It covered the entire leg from the foot (every bit of it) to the upper thigh.

"All this for a turned ankle?" Kay said to Dr. Steele.

"We have to immobilize these older people," Steele replied. There was also a fracture, he reminded her.

The top of the cast cut into Kass's leg, making her "miserable," she said. So the next morning, Kay asked Dr. Steele if he could shorten the cast "by at least five or six inches." He shortened it by one and a half inches.

More confident in Dr. Steele than Kay was, I believed Kass to be in good hands. In about a week and a half, she was out of the hospital. Dan engaged round-the-clock private nurses, and Mary Roseboro moved in to help with the work. In Dan's opinion, Mom, AJR, and Aunt Alice had all reached the stage where they "needed keepers." The house was extremely crowded, but Dan could organize and operate anything, it seemed to me.

Thanksgiving arrived. There would be no big family dinner for upward of fifty-five people at the St. Clair Country Club, our traditional way of celebrating. Kay, who'd been visiting Kass every day, cooked and delivered to 940 North Lincoln Avenue a sumptuous repast of turkey breast, stuffing, giblet gravy, cranberries, mashed potatoes, corn, peas, and a pumpkin pie with fresh whipped-cream topping.

By this time the football strike was over and the Steelers were to play the Seahawks that Sunday in Seattle. Saturday, on my way to the airport for the flight to the West Coast, I made a stop to see Kass. She was in bed in my old room, with its view of the back yard, the garden, and the church steeples on Western Avenue. I thought she looked old and gray, but otherwise "not bad." Dan thought differently. He told me on the plane that, to him, she looked "like death." I knew that Kay was apprehensive, too. She and Susie also had gone to see Kass on Saturday, and Kay was overcome with "a strange feeling." Would this be the last time? she found herself wondering.

I watched the game in Seattle from the Kingdome press box with Dan. At some point, I was called to the telephone. "Art, this is Jim Laughlin. Your mom is in bad shape. She's been taken to the hospital ..." He stopped talking. Then: "Wait." Another few seconds of silence. "I'm just getting something ... She's gone, Artie. She's gone."

After a heart attack at home, Mom had died in the operating room while Dr. George Magovern was installing a pacemaker.

Dan was now beside me in the Kingdome press box. "Let's get out of here," he said. We waited below, in a private office, until the game was over. On the long plane ride home, players, coaches, trainers, and equipment men came to us with murmured condolences. I thought of what Uncle Jim said to me after Grandma Rooney had died: "You can take a lot, Artie, but when it's your mother ..."

Now I understood. Completely. All I can say is that my dad never meant as much to me as Kass did. I thought of them differently. He was Art Rooney. She was Mom.

Devlin's

At Devlin's Funeral Home, we were in for a shock. As Kay expressed it years later, in writing, the Devlins "had actually laid Kass out WITH THAT !@#$% CAST STILL ON HER LEG!!!!!"

Kay spoke to the head mortician. She told him to get the cast off or he would never again bury anyone from the Rooney family. "Kass *hated* that thing." she added.

"We don't have a saw," the man replied.

"Then you'd better *find* one," Kay said.

"Which they did, by God," she wrote in her reconstruction of the incident.

Kay still feels that by impeding Mom's circulation the cast was what hastened her death.

So many flowers were sent to Devlin's that nobody knew where to put all the baskets. It was customary, in cases like this, to send the extra flowers to nearby hospitals, but AJR had a different solution. In another room at the funeral home, the 93-year-old father of a firefighter he knew was laid out. At AJR's behest, this room was soon full of floral arrangements with cards bearing well-known names - names of football players and coaches. When the players and coaches came to pay their respects to Kass, they were urged by the Chief to visit the old man's casket and sign the condolence book. All the Rooneys in sight were requested to do the same thing, and they knew the request was an order.

A random - and typical - act of kindness. Even in this hour of grief, it was second nature with the Chief to think of others.

St. Peter's Church was too small for the crowd at Kass's funeral Mass. There were twenty or more priests and concelebrants. Friends of Kass and the Chief from every NFL team came, and they joined the long procession to the North Side Catholic Cemetery, a cortege of automobiles that stretched out for miles.

As I was pulling away from the church with Kay and the kids, I caught a glimpse of Mort Sharnik, the *Sports Illustrated* writer from New York, standing alone on the sidewalk bordering West Park. He looked lost. I stopped at the curb and called out to him. "Need a ride?" He did. "Squeeze in," I suggested, and after hesitating a little, he complied. "You're with the main mourners," I told him, " but don't be embarrassed. We're all glad to see you."

Once we had put him at ease, he told us of having said to a taxi driver at the airport that morning, "I'm here for Mrs. Rooney's funeral, but I don't know where it's going to be." The driver said, "Don't worry about it," and took him straight to St. Peter's Church.

I thought of how many lives of strangers my parents had touched. Mort, as though reading my mind, said, "Your mother was such a wonderful lady."

Later he reminded me of a promise I had made to write down everything I could recall about the Rooney family. "Your mother is gone," he said, "and soon a lot of others will be gone. Believe me, your memory will grow dim. Do it for all your kids. Do it for your grandchildren. Do it for your nephews and nieces."

Here is one last memory – Kay's – from the cemetery. She noticed AJR wandering off, away from the crowd at the gravesite, and going behind a tree – in order to cry without being seen, Kay presumed. "But then my Art walked down to find him 'taking a whiz,'" she continued. "Strange what comes to mind when one thinks back."

A Time to Grieve

For about a month after the funeral, our family would drive to 940 North Lincoln Avenue every evening to visit AJR and Aunt Alice, who continued to make her home there for as long as she lived. AJR had promised Kass he'd "take care" of Aunt Alice, but in some respects it was just the reverse: Aunt Alice took care of him. None of us ever knew her actual age, but she was well over 70 – old enough, Dan said, to need help. AJR, who was 81, believed they could get by with only Mary Roseboro's assistance; artfully, Dan persuaded him that some of the extra staff people who were looking after Kass should be kept on.

With his wife gone, AJR spent more time than ever at Three Rivers Stadium. The Steelers, more than ever, became his family, Mary Regan more than ever his protector, Ed Kiely more than ever his right-hand man. His infirmities increased, but his mind remained sharp. He was still the Chief, and everyone knew it.

At Three Rivers, his routine seldom varied. Every morning he walked the gray carpets, from the kitchen past Dan's office and the accounting department, down past the scouting department, out to the front desk and Joe Gordon's office, on through the meeting rooms and the coaches' area, then into the dressing rooms to play a hand or two of poker with Ralph Berlin and any players being treated for injuries. Even now I encounter players who speak of these card games as the most vivid memory they retain of their days with the Steelers. They are players whose injuries cut short their careers, who may never have worn a uniform on a Sunday afternoon. AJR embodies the whole experience for them. "He always remembered my name," they tell me, finding it hard to believe.

There was never any change in the way he dressed: red, brown, or tan polo shirt, with or without a necktie, cardigan sweater, dark gray slacks. The big green cigar, protruding at an angle from the corner of his mouth, was an unneeded badge of identity. "Doing your laps, Mister Rooney?" asked the people who passed him in the corridor. And unfailingly his answer was the same: "Yep. At my age, it's all you *can* do."

In good weather, he would venture out on the field to watch practice, or to chat with Dirt DiNardo and the grounds crew, getting them to talk about themselves and their families. When he asked how the wife and kids were, he really wanted to know.

At home, he would sit every night in his black leather reclining chair, one leg dangling over the side. An arm's length away, he kept the blue cashmere lap robe we had bought for him in Scotland. The big brass spittoon that Mary Roseboro still attended to would be on the floor at his feet. Two television sets would be blaring. Yes, blaring: his deafness had increased. While he listened to the news, he'd be saying the rosary.

Alice, who always before had remained in the kitchen with Kass, now sat in the den, keeping him company. Sometimes Dan and his family would be there. Aunt Margaret's son Jim seemed to be always around. He referred to himself as AJR's driver and "go-fer."

Kay and Susie and I would stay for a half-hour, stretching it out at times to forty-five minutes. Susie had a special way with her grandfather. Somehow she knew how to comfort him, silently holding his hand. Years later, she endeared herself in much the same fashion to Kay's father, Roy Kumer, who was then in his nineties. How did she do this – establish such an easy rapport with these two strong men? I could only wonder. It was not a skill she inherited from her dad. Communication with the Chief was always difficult for me. As a mark of his fondness for Sue, he gave her Kass's rosary, the one she had held in the coffin.

Friends and relations were allowing the Chief time to grieve. There were interruptions in our visits while he answered brief telephone calls. When it was Jack McGinley or Ed McCaskey of the

Bears on the line, the conversation would last a while longer. Over time, the telephone calls gradually lengthened and AJR's life returned to normal. He listened more closely to the televised news and sports. On visits, we found ourselves drifting back to the kitchen, where Alice had resumed spending most of her time. We no longer made the trip every evening. Then AJR's name began to reappear in the newspapers. He was back in circulation. "I'm going to the farm with Iggie and Richie," he would say. Or, "I'm flying to New York to see Timmy."

The mourning period had come to an end.

Chapter 71

'Let's Take Rivera'

I don't have much to say about the fourteen players we drafted in 1983. No, the player who stands out in my memory, and I am not alone in feeling this way, is a guy we could have taken but didn't.

Dan Marino was eligible that year. Pittsburgh born and bred, Marino grew up in lower Oakland and played quarterback at Central Catholic High School. He was good – very good. Another game he played well was baseball. The Kansas City Royals, convinced that he had the makings of a big-league third baseman, drafted him early, but Marino chose to play college football. At Pitt, a short walk up the hill from his working-class neighborhood, he passed for 8,597 yards and seventy-nine touchdowns in three and a half seasons. Both were all-time Pitt records and still are.

As a freshman, Marino became Pitt's starting quarterback in the seventh week of the season. The Panthers then won their last five games and beat Arizona in the Fiesta Bowl. In his sophomore year, Pitt won ten of eleven games and then beat South Carolina in the Gator Bowl. In his junior year, Pitt won ten of eleven games and then beat Georgia in the Sugar Bowl on Marino's 33-yard touchdown pass with thirty-five seconds to play.

When Marino was a senior, Pitt lost two regular-season games, while winning nine, and lost to Southern Methodist in the Cotton Bowl, 7-3. It was one of the few times ever, possibly the only time (I haven't researched this), that a defense had kept Marino from throwing any passes for touchdowns. He appeared to have slipped just a little but was still the best quarterback by far in the 1983 draft. He was 6 feet 4 and solidly built, a dropback passer in the NFL mold who didn't move around much in the pocket. He didn't have to: he could put a lot of zip on the ball and he could get it away instantaneously. His arm may have been as strong as Bradshaw's. He could pinpoint receivers and his passes were easy to catch.

But we were hearing rumors about Marino, rumors we didn't like. Word had gotten around that he was sniffing cocaine. Other scouting directors would say to me, "Hey, Artie, what's the story on Marino? Is he or is he not a cokehead?" There's no proof of it, I'd tell them. But I resolved to find out, if I could.

As it happened, one of the players on our injured-reserve list was Steve Fedell, a linebacker who had been Marino's teammate at Pitt. He was smart and proud-spirited. Told he'd continue to be paid while he was hurt, he said to my brother Dan, "I don't want money for doing nothing. Give me a broom. At least I could sweep the floors." Dan then suggested to me that Steve might be useful as a part-time scout. Rocky Bleier had helped in that way while recovering from his war wounds, Dan reminded me. I made a phone call or two, learned only good things about Steve, and put him to work. He was an excellent judge not only of football talent but of character, it seemed to me, and so I asked him about Marino.

"Is he into dope? No," Steve said. Marino's only fault, he told me, was excessive loyalty to certain friends of long standing – friends who were not good guys, according to Fedell. I thought of how AJR remained close for a long time to the hangers-on he collected the way a ship collects barnacles. They were people he knew from the race tracks, from the fight game, from the North Side, from Las Vegas. Father Silas would shake his head and say, "It's amazing how much good there is in these men" – he never used the word "hoodlums" – "but there's something flawed about them. They can't take that big step, the big step away from their impediments." AIR could step away. He could separate himself from dubious companions and do it with such finesse that there were no hard feelings.

I don't think he knew Marino at all, but he loved him – saw some Billy Conn in him, perhaps. I didn't know Marino, either. I had watched him work out for us on a windy day between the 1982 football season and the 1983 draft, but our conversation afterwards was brief, and I remember only one thing he said to me: "I'd sure like to play for the Steelers." I may have replied that we'd sure like to have him. Certainly Tony Dungy, our defensive coach, was impressed with Marino's arm strength. I have said that the day was windy. Actually, the wind was more like a gale, and Marino was firing missiles into its teeth.

Just as Steve Fedell had assured me, the rumors about Marino were untrue. Three or four weeks before draft day, the Chief called me into his office. Two men wearing dark suits and nondescript neckties were with him. Neither of them cracked a smile. They were very tough-looking in an unmistakable Irish way and I immediately recognized them as cops – plainclothesmen. I could see the clear-enough outline of their shoulder holsters. "Close the door," the Chief ordered. I did as I was told. Then he said to the detectives, "This is my boy Artie; he's in charge of our scouting." He introduced his visitors, but their names have slipped my mind. "These men," he went on, "have something to tell you about Danny Marino."

It was this: "We've been looking into the rumors about him, and we find no evidence that he is using, selling, or transporting hard drugs like cocaine. There aren't any maybes about this. He may have puffed on some marijuana. Most college kids nowadays do."

The one who did the talking asked if I understood. Wondering what he had said that I could possibly misinterpret, I nodded. AJR then dismissed me with the injunction, "Say nothing about this to anyone except Noll and Haley." I did tell Noll and Haley – and no one else.

Steve Fedell came with me to the Senior Bowl game in Mobile, and we kept an eye on Marino during practice. He appeared to be moody and distracted. Is it any wonder? I thought. When you're the subject of innuendo and scandal mongering, when you're constantly under a microscope, what does that do to your peace of mind? One day when we were watching from the stands he walked off the field looking disgusted and headed for the North team's bus. He climbed inside and sat there alone until Fedell joined him. As Steve told me later, he said to Marino, "Hey, Danny, you can't behave like this. No matter how you feel. This is your showcase. The scouts and coaches from the pro teams are down here to learn who you are."

These words from an ex-teammate may have done Marino some good. I saw him that night in the hotel lobby with Don Shula, who was coaching the Miami Dolphins by then, and he was noticeably more cheerful and relaxed.

We had the twenty-first pick in the first round of the draft, our penalty for having won twice as many games as we lost in 1982. Dick Haley wanted to move us up by trading this first pick and a couple of extra picks we had somehow acquired in the middle rounds. By doing so, we could get a higher-rated player, but Noll and I felt that we needed every pick available to us. We were looking for smart, coachable players with the capacity to improve, players we could develop into the kind you must have to keep winning. There was always a supply of gifted natural athletes who had not performed up to their ability. To think we could bring out the qualities in them that were lying dormant may have been arrogant, but, damn it, the concept had worked wonders for us in the past, so why would it not continue to be successful?

One reason, hindsight informs me, was that the other teams in the league were pulling even with us. They were doing as good a job of identifying these overlooked diamonds in the rough and either scooping them up in late rounds or signing them as free agents. Maybe, in fact, they were doing a better job. Perhaps we had lost an edge we once had, but in 1983 it was not yet completely evident.

Ordinarily when we were picking as far down as twenty-first, we watched the players we had rated one, two, and three disappear from the board. But as the teams drafting ahead of us in 1983 made their picks, we didn't see this. There were three players we wanted badly, and everybody was passing them up. One of these was Marino. Another was Gabe Rivera, nose tackle and defensive end from Texas Tech. The third was Dave Rimington, a center from Nebraska, who in our opinion was one of the best offensive lineman in the draft. Team after team left them unclaimed, and our optimism grew steadily. "Hey," Noll said to Haley and me, "it looks like we've got a shot at one of these guys."

It turned out that Noll was correct. All three still could be had when our turn came. AJR was hoping we'd take Marino, I knew. Noll seemed to lean that way too. He spoke of Marino in superlatives, stressing his size, his strong arm, his quick release, the accuracy of his throws, his excellent field vision. "He has it all," Noll said. "He's going to be a good one."

I agreed with every word of this, but I was low-keyed about it. On draft days in the past, I had been an unabashed partisan. It would be the end of the world, I believed in 1970, if we did not draft Terry Bradshaw, the end of the world in 1972 if we failed to take Franco Harris. This time I controlled my emotions. Don't let the fact that Marino's a Pittsburgh guy influence your judgment, I said to myself. Go about your job in a professional, impersonal manner.

Haley and I huddled with Noll. The first thing he said was, "Let's decide between Marino and Rivera." Our information was that Rimington had been playing with two bad knees, and though he had played very well it was still a negative. It explained why twenty other teams had stayed away from him, we surmised. "He'll have a short pro career," Noll predicted, with perfect foresight. The Cincinnati Bengals drafted him, and in three years he was finished. "Both of you know how I feel about Marino," Noll continued. "He's a marvelous talent. But look – we're overloaded with quarterbacks. We have Bradshaw. We have Malone. We have Stoudt." Cliff Stoudt had been with us since 1977, but all he needed, Noll thought, was a chance. Furthermore, it might come a little sooner than anyone expected, for though Mark Malone was next in line after Bradshaw – now a thirteen-year veteran – Malone, too, had a bad knee. Bad, but not alarmingly bad. "It could be OK," Noll allowed.

"Anyhow," he said, having finished his review of our quarterback situation, "let's go the way we started." The way we started, back in 1969, was by drafting a great defensive lineman, Mean Joe Greene. "Let's take Rivera."

I didn't argue. I didn't ask questions. I didn't prolong the discussion. Chuck Noll had given his reasons for making Gabe Rivera our number one pick, and I thought they were sound reasons.

So without further ado we drafted the defensive lineman from Texas Tech instead of Danny Marino.

And the whispered allegations that Marino was using drugs had nothing to do with it.

Déjà Vu All Over Again?

Twenty-six of the twenty-eight teams in the league had kissed off a chance to take Marino when the Miami Dolphins drafted him. We were one of those twenty-six, but here in Pittsburgh there was no great outcry; picking Joe Greene before Hanratty back in 1969 had been more of an issue with the fans. Multiple Super Bowl championships can do a lot for a team's credibility.

The parade of great quarterbacks spurned by the Steelers is a long one, and Marino fell into step right away. In the very first game of his rookie season, he passed for more than three hundred yards. From that time on, in seventeen years with the Dolphins, Marino did not often *fail* to pass for three hundred yards.

The analogy I draw between Marino and Johnny Unitas is that both were home-grown and both might have played for the Steelers instead of for Don Shula. We drafted Unitas, yes, but cut him before the start of the season and then watched him break the following NFL records as a Baltimore Colt: most passing yardage, most completions, most touchdown passes, most 300-yard games. When Marino retired, he held all the records Unitas had set and thirteen others besides, which I hope you will not expect me to list.

Of course, the relative ability of football players from different eras cannot be measured entirely by the statistics they leave behind. Changes in the rules, the help a player gets from his teammates – these and other factors, lots of them, contribute to the breaking of records. Unitas is still thought of by many NFL historians as the quarterback who could do the most to win a game for his team. With Unitas at quarterback, the Colts were league champions in 1958 and 1959, before championship games were called Super Bowls. The one time Marino took Miami to the Super Bowl was in 1984, his second season. He dueled it out with the Forty-Niners' Joe Montana, still another product of the Western Pennsylvania quarterback hatchery, and Montana prevailed, 38-16.

Bradshaw, just in case you've forgotten, was the winning quarterback in Super Bowls IX, X, XIII, and XIV. (Don't ask me why Super Bowls get the Roman numeral treatment, a prerogative once reserved for popes, emperors, and kings.) When we drafted a defensive lineman instead of Marino, we had no idea that Bradshaw would start only one more game for the Steelers. During the 1982 season, even in our post-season loss to San Diego, he had played as well as ever, or almost as well. For a quarterback, he was not yet an antique – just 33 or 34 years old. The elbow on his throwing arm had been giving him pain, but our orthopedic specialist, Dr. Paul Steele, counseled that surgery would be foolish. Cortisone shots in the affected area, coupled with a program of physical therapy, should keep him playing for several more years, Steele believed. We called upon our highly-regarded neurosurgeon, Joe Maroon, for a second opinion, and he backed up Dr. Steele. Cortisone shots and therapy were all that was needed; Bradshaw could "play through the pain."

Bradshaw himself was not convinced. At home in Louisiana, he went to a Shreveport doctor who sold him on undergoing surgery. I heard about this from our trainer, Ralph Berlin. "If you let me operate," the doctor promised Bradshaw, "you can be playing pain-free for a long time to come."

What the operation actually did was wipe out the first three months of the 1983 season for Bradshaw. He was back in the lineup on December 10th for our game at Shea Stadium with the Jets – a game we had to win to reach the playoffs. In the first quarter, he efficiently directed two long drives that ended with touchdown passes. On the second touchdown pass he blew out his arm and never played again for the Steelers or any other team.

Crack-Up

Gabe Rivera was friendly and likable, a Mexican-American from Crystal City, Texas, who spoke with a barely perceptible Spanish accent. At Texas Tech, he acquired a media nickname – "Senor Sack." Getting to the quarterback – bringing him down, making him scramble, or forcing him to throw a hurried pass – was his specialty. He measured 6 feet 2 or a little over and weighed 290 pounds. In 1983, even for a defensive lineman, that kind of size was extraordinary. Despite his bulk, he was quick off the ball; no one could hold him up at the line of scrimmage – at any rate, not for long. Keeping low to the ground, which wasn't easy considering how big he was, he used his strength to shed blockers on the move.

The 1983 season opened, and week by week Senor Sack was showing improvement. We were all quite content with the No. 1 draft choice we had made. In Bradshaw's absence, the inheritor of the quarterback job was Noll's favorite, Cliff Stoudt. Mark Malone's trick knee had so impaired his mobility that all he could do now was back up a few steps and throw the ball. Stoudt, when he had to, could pivot away from tacklers or sometimes knock them over. He was tall, maybe 6 feet 5, and no beanstalk. For another thing, he had a better arm than Malone did. In his own estimation, his arm was the equal of Bradshaw's. For a guy who had spent his first six years in the league as an understudy, he did not lack self-confidence.

Calvin Sweeney was more of a realist. "I'm not a Hall of Famer like Swann and Stallworth," he would say, just in case there was any question about it, which there wasn't. But with Swann gone and Stallworth on the injury list, fun-loving Cal became our go-to pass receiver.

The running game, though, was our bread and butter. Franco Harris, for the eighth time in twelve seasons, would gain one thousand yards. Frank Pollard continued to run and block effectively and Walter Abercrombie was everything Noll had hoped he would be as a runner and pass catcher – maybe not quite everything, but close. Right here let me say that a tenacious offensive line (Webster, Brown, Wolfley, Ilkin, and Cunningham) undergirded the success of the running game.

After seven weeks, our record was 5-2. I thought, "Hey – this could be the start of something big!" On October 16th, in a 44-17 win over Cleveland, Stoudt at one point completed thirteen passes in a row. He was taking pressure off Sweeney by throwing just as often to Cunningham or Harris. I had to admit it: he reminded me of Bradshaw when Bradshaw was coming into his own. In another way, too, he mirrored the youthful Bradshaw. He was throwing a lot of interceptions – momentum killers.

They hadn't hurt us all that much because of the defense. There were times when Mel Blount or Donnie Shell or the upstart Rick Woods, our 1982 fourth-round pick from Boise State, would get us back on offense with an interception. Jack Lambert was still hell on wheels, a threat to the other team's quarterback whether leading the pass rush or climbing all over a receiver. In the defensive line, Gary Dunn and Keith Willis were having good years. And Gabe Rivera – Senor Sack – was doing his part and more.

To sum it all up, the future looked promising. Then came a blow from which we never fully recovered.

Friday night, October 21st. It was raining a little. Enough to make the streets slick. Gabe Rivera was having "one for the road" at a popular North Side tavern owned by a man named Wiggins. Before that, he had evidently had five or six for the road somewhere else. I knew that Gabe liked to drink, and I should have factored that little item into the data we had used in reaching our decision to draft him, but I didn't. His appetite for food bothered us more. Told he must keep his weight under 300 pounds or thereabouts, and that one way to do it would be to substitute fish – tuna, perhaps – for a Tex-Mex diet rich in saturated fat, Gabe went along with the program. He started to eat tuna — by the can. He was eating, we learned, twenty-eight cans of it every day. I fear that his consumption of alcohol was equally unrestrained. When one of our assistant coaches came into the Wiggins place on the night of October 21st with a friend, he saw that Gabe had a snoot full and told him he'd better get home. The team was flying to Seattle the next day, but first there would be a light practice.

Bitterly, the coach blamed himself for letting Gabe drive, for letting him go out to the parking lot and wedge behind the wheel of his modified sports car. Gabe was used to driving on the Texas prairie, where the roads are straight and flat. Speeding along Babcock Boulevard, he came to a hill. At its crest he lost control of his car, and it hydroplaned.. No doubt he was going too fast; no doubt the asphalt was wet; no doubt all the alcohol had deadened his reflexes. He skidded out of his lane and crashed head-on into a bulkier car driven by an elderly man. The force of the collision sent Rivera through the large rear window of his car, which had no back seat. Except for minor cuts and bruises, the driver of the other car was unhurt.

The paramedics called for a helicopter. Alive, but badly injured, Gabe was lifted in and flown to Allegheny General Hospital, a few miles away. One of the orderlies at the hospital told me, "I helped carry Gabe from the chopper to the emergency room. He was huge – so big we had to call for extra guys."

Instead of getting on the plane to Seattle the next day, I stayed behind with AJR to monitor Gabe's condition. The previous November, I had gone with the team to Seattle while Kass was in Allegheny General. To my everlasting sorrow, she died there before we got back to Pittsburgh.

On our way to see Gabe, the Chief had me park his Buick near the hospital's main entrance. We started walking, and a flower vendor reached out and thrust a bouquet into AJR's hands. "Mister Rooney," he said, "please give these fall flowers to Gabe." AJR seemed embarrassed. He carried the bouquet to the hospital entrance and then turned it over to me, explaining, "The nurse can take care of this."

Right away we were told that Gabe had a very severe spinal-cord injury. In the recovery room, mingled with the smell of the antiseptics, was another pungent odor. Blood. Gabe Rivera's blood. We saw him hoisted up in his bed, motionless. Several nurses bustled around him, doing busy work. He was wearing one of those ridiculous, bib-like hospital gowns – light blue, I think – and he was conscious but heavily tranquilized.

"Gabe," a nurse said to him, "Mister Rooney is here to see you. And his son, too." I had spoken with Gabe a number of times after the draft and the pre-season camp, but AJR seemed to know him better than I did. The Chief went out of his way every year to make himself acquainted with all the rookies. Approaching the bed, he took this helpless hulk of a man by the hand.

"Remember me, Gabe? I'm Art Rooney. And this is my boy Artie." On the opposite side of Gabe's bed, I had taken his other hand. It was immense, and he was hanging on tight. AJR kept talking. "We came over to make sure you're OK. The nurses say that you're not in pain now."

Dazedly, Gabe was staring at AJR, looking into his eyes. He glanced over at me with what I thought was a faint, fleeting sign of recognition. He would not let go of our hands. Did he realize, I wondered, how alone he was, a long way from Texas in this dark, cold, strange northern city? He must have sensed that we were his lifeline, or that AJR was.

"Gabe, your mom will be here very soon," the Chief was saying to him softly. "And I'm here. I'll make sure you're OK." Again, he added, "That's Artie over there. This is a good place here – very good. They'll look after you. I'll make sure that they do." The Chief's voice was low and assured. At this sort of thing no one equaled him. For the hundredth time I was tremendously impressed. If I had gone to see Gabe by myself, I would have been absolutely tongue-tied.

Gabe's mom did come very soon. His wife came, too. When Gabe left the hospital, weeks later, we knew he would never walk again. He was paralyzed from the waist down but had movement in his arms and upper body. Dr. Huber, our team intern, told me, "In cases like this, you never regain the use of your legs. Lots of work is going on in the area of paraplegics, but the big breakthrough is still years away. There is no hope for Gabe as an athlete."

Nor was there much hope, in Huber's opinion, for Gabe's marriage. Top athletes who are permanently and totally disabled at the outset of their careers have a difficult time adjusting, Huber said. "They're young, strong, and active. It takes a lot of mental and emotional resilience to keep going on. Rivera faces a complete change in life-style. His mother can help – she's a comparatively young woman – but often the changes in the husband are too much for the wife. His marriage is in real jeopardy."

I talked with Dad and Dan about Rivera's situation and suggested that he could work with me in the scouting department, as Rocky Bleier and Steve Fedell had done. Both Rocky and Steve rendered valuable service and could have been successful in the administrative end of football had they so desired. I thought I could teach Rivera to be a capable scout. He was in a wheelchair, but there were reports to analyze and masses of film to review. Even by watching games on television you could learn a great deal about a prospect. Even by getting on the telephone it was possible to collect information. Gabe came to my office four times, as I recall, and would stay for a half-hour or forty-five minutes. Then he would have to leave for a doctor's appointment or physical therapy. Of necessity, we were taking it slow, but he appeared to be bright and willing. Together, we went through our scouting manual, and I gave him a tutorial in the jargon we use.

I met his mother and his wife. The mother, as Dr. Huber had noted, was young-looking, the wife tall, fair-haired and attractive. She had married Gabe while both were in college. On one of her visits she brought their little boy. I was upbeat for a while, and so was Gabe. But in the end Dr. Huber was correct. Rivera, preoccupied with his physical condition, lost interest in being a scout – or, rather, just sort of stopped coming around – and when the doctors at the hospital had done all they could for him, he went home to Texas.

AJR bought him a customized van, which he learned to drive but eventually wrecked. His marriage, as Dr. Huber had feared, did not endure. But he pulled himself together, married again, and has a job down in Texas working with kids. The last I heard, he was getting along surprisingly well.

Destry Rides Again

The Steelers beat the Seahawks, 27-21. Forgive me if I'm being sentimental, but they won it, I think, for Gabe Rivera. After beating Tampa Bay, San Diego, and Baltimore, they took a seven-game winning streak and a 9-2 record into their November 20th date with the Vikings at Three Rivers Stadium. Minnesota was a team they should have been able to handle. But something happened. Maybe the rest of the league, by this time, had us figured out. Whatever it was, we lost, 17-14. Then the Lions embarrassed us in Detroit, 45-3. The following week, Cincinnati – a team we had beaten earlier, rather easily – won the return game at Three Rivers rather easily.

For reasons that were hard to fathom, the bottom was falling out. It wasn't just the loss of Rivera – Senor Sack – although without him the pass rush had suffered. Both the run blocking and pass blocking were less efficient. Our wide receivers were not getting open and Cliff Stoudt was being hurried. Often his only recourse was to take a sack. Or to dump the ball off to a running back. There were so many broken plays that Stoudt ended the season as our third leading ground gainer with 479 yards. Interceptions increased, and so did fumbles. Inside the 20-yard line, the offense stalled so consistently that Gary Anderson, the field-goal kicker, was our leading scorer that year.

None of which meant we were out of the running for a playoff spot. We had two games left, with the Jets in New York and with the Browns in Cleveland, and the Central Division of the AFC was so weak that no one could catch us unless we managed to lose both. Providentially, the one guy who could spark us – Terry Bradshaw – would be ready to play against the Jets. It seems that where ice packs, heat pads, pain killers, cortisone shots, and Aunt Alice's novenas had done him no good, a myna bird worked its magic.

The myna bird was a pet he had taken in. Perching on Bradshaw's sore arm, his little feathered friend had brought about a miraculous cure, he announced. Not since another Louisiana native, Sidney Thornton, bathed his sprained ankle in a bucket of piss, provided for him by a witch doctor, had we witnessed such a marvelous recovery.

Having Bradshaw back lifted our flagging spirits. Against the Jets, he'd be making his first appearance on a football field since the previous January, when, through no fault of his, we lost to San Diego for the AFC championship. It was Wyatt Earp getting off the train to clean up Dodge City. Or maybe it was "Destry Rides Again." (For those of my readers with a limited frame of reference, I'm invoking a 1939 Western with Jimmy Stewart in the title role). But could one player, even if that player was Bradshaw, make a difference?

The game with the Jets would be the last in Shea Stadium before their move to the Meadowlands (formerly just a swamp) in New Jersey. While the two teams warmed up, I wandered around taking in the scene. Many of the players I was gawking at, Jets as well as Steelers, I had scouted in college. Now I was feeling anxiety. The Jets had won their last three games. The Steelers had lost their last three and were floundering. Mike Webster had said that the Jets' defensive line was the best in the league.

So much would depend on whether Bradshaw was the gunslinger of old. He'd been doing just fine in practice, although his elbow continued to bother him. The operation in Shreveport the previous March was a mistake that could not be undone. And now at last the time had come to see if old Number 12 still had it.

Lining up to take the first snap, he was nervous, I could sense. But then he threw his first pass, a completion to Ben Cunningham, and it was just as if he never had been on the shelf. "We're going to have some fun," he said to his teammates. Of his first six passes, he completed three. On the last of these, it was third and ten. He scrambled and threw a touchdown pass to Gregg Garrity, a rookie from Penn State and a Pittsburgh kid. Something for Gregg to tell his grandchildren.

My elation was tempered by a change in Bradshaw's delivery. Early in the drive he'd been throwing without effort. Now there was evidence of pain. On our next possession, we ran much more often. From our 29-yard line, Harris and Pollard moved us to the New York 10. Once on third down, Bradshaw hit Pollard with a screen pass for a seventeen-yard gain. From the 10, in the face of a heavy blitz, he passed to Sweeney in the end zone for a touchdown, and though we didn't at the moment suspect it, that was the last pass he ever threw.

He went to the bench looking troubled. His arm was now useless. Cliff Stoudt came in and played as he did before going into a three-week slump. With the ground game churning out yardage, the Steelers added to the 14-0 lead Bradshaw had given them. Our offensive line played its best game of the season and Sweeney caught a second touchdown pass. The final score was 34-7.

We came back from New York on a high, thinking Bradshaw would be ready for the playoffs if not for our last regular-season game with Cleveland. "I proved I can do it. I proved I can throw the football," he assured everybody. He threw no footballs in practice that week and he threw no footballs against the Browns the following Sunday. This time Stoudt, who had regained his form in the win over the Jets, was not the same quarterback, and we lost to another team we had beaten earlier.

My reaction was: Oh, well. A meaningless game. Surely the extra week of rest would be all that Bradshaw needed to play on New Year's Day in Los Angeles against the Raiders. We were shutting our eyes to reality.

Whacked Out

On New Year's Eve, an old fried of AJR's, a man named Ray Heffernan, invited all the Rooneys to a fancy dinner party at a fancy Hollywood restaurant. Heffernan lived in Rye, New York, but took his family to Pasadena for the Rose Bowl festivities every year. He had made a lot of money in the shoe business and was putting on the dog with a will.

Before we had finished our dessert, we found ourselves in the middle of an elaborate costume party. Dozens of after-dinner guests, presumably Heffernan's, streamed into the restaurant. They had raided the wardrobe departments at the movie studios to outfit themselves, it appeared. One guy was dressed like General MacArthur, right down to the corncob pipe and the sunglasses. Another fellow came as the Little Tramp, Charlie Chaplin: derby hat, mustache, too-tight jacket, baggy pants, oversized shoes with holes in them, and a cane. And he could waddle like Charlie Chaplin. There were John Wayne impersonators, of course, and women from the court of Louis XVI, the Hollywood version, with piled-up blond hair and low-cut gowns that showcased their boobs. Unfortunately, Kay, who had chosen to stay in Pittsburgh, missed the fun.

Explaining to our host that we had to make bed-check, we left for our hotel before the new year arrived.

As it turned out, Ray Heffernan's party was the highlight of our trip. For the game with the Raiders, we had Stallworth back in the lineup. We did not have Terry Bradshaw, whose myna bird had lost its healing power. He could barely raise his arm to comb what was left of his hair, and neither all the king's horses nor all the diocesan holy oil from St. Anne's in Quebec would have helped. It was over for him. We would have to face the Raiders with Stoudt.

And for part of the first quarter, it looked as though Stoudt might be up to the task. Our tried and tested formula was working: establish the run; pepper the other guys with passes when they tried to clog the holes with linebackers and cornerbacks; rely on the defense to get the Raiders' offense off the field. We drove to their 17-yard line. Fourth and inches. Chuck Noll took the field goal, which was automatic with Gary Anderson kicking. I thought it was sound football. Watching from the press box in the Los Angeles Coliseum, full to the brim with more than 90,000 spectators, I felt we had made a good start.

The coach of the Raiders, Tom Flores, looked at it differently. If we were satisfied with three miserable points, he had us where he wanted us. To Flores, it proved that the Raiders could stop our ground game. Our passing game didn't worry him much, not with Stoudt instead of Bradshaw under the center. The next time we had the ball Lester Hayes picked off a pass from our 18-yard line and sauntered into the end zone.

It was only the beginning. On touchdown drives of eighty, seventy-two, fifty-eight, and sixty-five yards, Marcus Allen cut through our defense like the future Hall of Famer he was, and the Raiders whacked us out, 38-10.

Would it have mattered if a vigorous, strong-armed Bradshaw had been in there? Yes, I believe so.

We'd have lost by fewer than twenty-eight points.

Chapter 72

The Blacklist

The NFL had a blacklist of restaurants and bars with connections to the mob, real or imaginary. They were off-limits to everyone in the league – owners, front-office people, coaches, and players. In the NFL, there was always this fear of a betting scandal. The best way to keep from being tainted was to avoid all the places where gamblers hung out, or were likely to hang out, or were thought by the sportswriters to hang out.

Neither Dan nor I felt that such a precaution was unreasonable. AJR understood why prudence might be necessary, but would jokingly say, "You should see the kind of yeggs I came up with." He said that the restaurants on the list, or at least some of them, were by his standards forbiddingly upscale.

Of course, AJR was so sure of himself, and so sure of exactly who he was. In fact, when the NFL commissioner's office was in doubt as to whether a particular place belonged on the index, it would frequently ask for his advice.

I have to say that sometimes I thought it was Dad who needed guidance. I remember being apprehensive once when he suggested a family dinner at a restaurant in Bethel Park called The Living Room. Appointing me the host, he said, "I hear they have fine steaks. Take us all out there next week – your mom and Kay and Aunt Alice and me."

I said, "Well, Dad, people do say it has fine steaks and chops. Pat Livingston and some of your other friends go there a lot. But the owner, you know, is Tony Grosso."

Tony Grosso was a numbers guy who had recently served time.

"I realize Tony Grosso is the owner," Dad replied, and that was the end of the discussion.

So we went to The Living Room and enjoyed ourselves. The maitre d' and the waiters made a fuss over Dad; he knew, or seemed to know, a few of the patrons; the service was good and the steaks were good and the fruit plate served for dessert looked like the work of an artist. Pat Livingston was nowhere in sight.

AJR asked the maitre d' if "Tony" had been around. "Not lately, Art. He comes in once in a while, but he don't own the place any more. His wife does."

AJR just nodded. The information came as no surprise. On the way to the parking lot, he said, "I was never close to Grosso at all. He was sort of a loner who did his own thing. Those guys" – the real bosses, Dad was saying – "keep guys like Tony in line. They're the ones who have control."

We walked another five yards before Dad spoke again. "So his wife owns the joint, does she? Hah!"

He never said, "Don't go back there," but his vocal inflections got the message across.

For obvious reasons – just because something's a stereotype does not mean it's false – most places on the index were Italian-owned. Out on Route 88, beyond the South Hills, I knew an Italian restaurant where the food was not only good but cheap. Kay and I and the kids would go there early; we liked the spaghetti. There was nothing sinister about this joint, which was called, if I'm not mistaken, Mama Lena's. It was bright and clean, a nice place to take the whole family.

On our first few visits, no one recognized us, but then one night a presentable young guy at the cash register noticed the name on my credit card. He said, "You must be Art's son."

I admitted I was and added a word of praise for the food.

While he was thanking me, the man who owned the place walked through the door, and the other one introduced us. I was accustomed by now to being Art Rooney's son. Kay was accustomed to being his daughter-in-law. Artie and Mike and Susan were accustomed to being his grandchildren. Reflected glory is sometimes hard to put up with, but it's better than reflected notoriety, better than having someone like – oh, John Dillinger, let's say – for a relative.

The boss was now telling me, "A lot of sports people come in here, but they don't come this early."

I said, "Well, ya know, with the kids, we don't like to eat too late."

"Sure. Sure. Come back. You're always welcome."

And we did go back, bringing Kay's parents with us now and then. In the Steeler offices one day, someone who overheard me talking about the place said it was on the forbidden list – "a real den of iniquity," as I later told Kay. "The hell with that," she said. To her way of thinking, the list was far too inclusive. "Anyway," she went on, "the devil shows up after nightfall, you know. By that time, we're in and out."

At her insistence, we kept returning. "Good to have you," the owner would say. "We like families. Next time bring the Chief. We'll make something special."

Though my demeanor, I hope, didn't show it, I was nervous. All through dinner I'd be looking over my shoulder for gangster types, characters I could spot from having watched Francis Ford Coppola's "Godfather" movies. In the meantime, Kay was losing patience with me. "There is absolutely nothing to worry about," she said. "Nobody else in Pittsburgh goes to supper as early as we do. We open the place up."

So we continued to eat at Mama Lena's, opening the place up and leaving while it was still almost empty. But finally one evening when we arrived we had company – a table of at least a dozen men in the back of the room. All but one of them were young: early twenties to mid-thirties. Two, as I recall, were black; only a few looked Italian. I thought, well, the Mafia recruits all kinds and all ages these days.

The one older man – short, round, bald, and definitely Italian – was in charge. This guy did all the talking, it seemed. He laughed, he pointed, he gestured. Yep, I said to myself, he's the "don;" we have to get out of here.

Our orders came, and I urged the kids not to dawdle. "We'll get dessert at the Tasty Creme," I told them. In an undertone, I said to Kay, "The NFL was right about this place. Let's move."

I called for the check and paid in cash to save time. Pushing the kids ahead like a sheep dog, I started for the door, with Kay right beside me. We were almost free when a voice cried, "Stop!" and the owner of the joint came running after us. "Mister Rooney!" he was shouting. "Wait a minute! I want you to meet my friends."

"God deliver me," I said – again to myself.

The owner was grabbing my arm. "I wanna innerduce you to these fellows. They're special people." He dragged me toward the T-shaped table where this loud, fat take-charge guy was holding court. "Tommy!" the owner said. "Tommeee! This is Art Rooney's kid, Art Junior. Art, this is my good friend Tommy."

Possibly he mentioned Tommy's last name. If so, I didn't hear it. All I could think of was the need to get out of the restaurant. Tommy, I knew, would be asking about our football team, digging for information that guys who make bets always want. Instead, he was saying, "Your dad's a great guy!" Then he added, "I like this place. Every time we're in town I bring my boys here. The food's good, and it's out of the way."

I forget how I answered – unintelligibly, no doubt – but my interior monologue went like this: "His 'boys!' All of these mob guys call their henchmen their 'boys.'"

Tommy, still in control, was introducing them to me, one by one. Hardly listening to the names, I heard them say, "Hi, Rooney," or "How ya doin', Art?" or "Good to see ya" – things like that. I do remember thinking that, gee, in appearance and manner they were not much different from our Steeler football players. One of the mob's more pernicious aspects was its ability to change with the times.

As quickly as I could, I broke away. Kay and the kids hadn't waited inside. They were already out in the parking lot. The genial Tommy was calling after me, "Say hi to your dad!" And then, regretfully, it seemed, "I thought those boys of yours might have liked to meet the players."

The "players"? What the hell was he talking about?

My pal the restaurant owner escorted me to the door. "Great guy, that Tommy Lasorda," he was saying. "Always comes in here when the Dodgers are in town. Brings a whole bunch of his players with him, too."

Not until I got into the car and was pulling out onto the highway did the realization hit me: Tommy Lasorda! Manager of the Los Angeles Dodgers! I had not, after all, stumbled upon a meeting of the Cosa Nostra.

The first thing Kay said was, "Who were those men?"

"Oh, nobody," I told her. "Just some friends of my dad."

One of AJR's favorite Italian places was the Villa Rosa. It was near Three Rivers Stadium on General Robinson Street, where he had lived as a young man above his father's saloon. By the 1970s, General Robinson Street was the last of the First Ward's "bedbug rows," the name used by Aunt Alice for all the narrow, grimy, alley-like passageways that criss-crossed the neighborhood in the days before urban renewal. They reminded Ed Kiely of "something right out of Dickens." The decrepit three-story houses were all much the same: soot-covered red brick, rotting wooden doorframes, "stoops" made of dirt-darkened stone. Their owners were slum landlords, who fed off the poor.

I remember how astounded Aunt Alice was when she learned that her uncle, George McNulty, had bought a row of these squalid houses for "investment purposes" during the Hoover depression of the 1930s. Aunt Alice's brother John said that George spent nothing on their upkeep. "All he did was pick up the rent." To be sure, there was never any love lost between John and George. After World War II, with the clearing of ground for a housing project, George's bedbug row disappeared. With the building of the stadium, the others disappeared – all except the one on which the Villa Rosa still proudly stood.

About once or twice a month over this relatively short stretch of cobblestones – "hobblestones," AJR called them – he would take a carload of front-office people to the Villa Rosa for lunch. Separated from the slum houses by a parking lot, the restaurant was not in bad shape. Even so, I never went inside without looking for rats. The First Ward's rat population, I always thought, probably exceeded its bedbug population. My brother Dan disliked these trips to the Villa Rosa for a different reason entirely. He believed we were taking a chance – patronizing a place that would not have met the standards of the NFL.

The building itself had a gray stucco exterior. Not far from the front door was the cash register. A room to the right contained a mahogany bar with eight or ten stools, but we never ate there. We went to the main dining room beyond the cash register. We never seemed to need a reservation. The woman at the cash register, Frances LaQuatra, would greet AJR and ask about Kass. In turn, he would ask about "Joey," her son. Frances LaQuatra was a little past middle age and neatly but not stylishly dressed. She gave the impression of having known Dan and me a long time. When I first started going to the restaurant, I could not quite place her, but then one day it came to me. Frances LaQuatra was Mike Hogan's wife.

I remembered Mike Hogan from years gone by. But why did his wife and his sons – Joey and Jack LaQuatra – have a name that was different from his? Eventually Kass cleared it up for me. "Hogan," it seemed, was Mike's ring name. He had boxed as a pro, and AJR had been his manager. Back in the 1920s and '30s, Italian, Slavic, and Jewish boxers often adopted Irish-sounding names. Irish boxers, in the opinion of managers and promoters, were the ones who pulled in the ticket buyers.

Although vaguely aware that Mike Hogan had boxed, and later refereed, I thought of him only as an older acquaintance. Jack and Joey had boxed, too, using their own last name, but now only Joey, the head of a laborers' union, was still alive. Looking back, I think I understand why Frances LaQuatra would remark so often to AJR that her son Jack had been my age: to this well-mannered, self-contained woman, I represented something — a link with the past.

There were booths in the Villa Rosa dining room, but we always sat down at a big round table near the swinging doors to the kitchen unless the Villa Rosa "family" was occupying that table. When this was the case, Dad would quietly walk over and pay his respects and then join the rest of us at another large table on the opposite side of the room. Nothing was ever said about this, either by him or by anyone else.

If the second table was occupied, Frances LaQuatra would leave us for a minute while she spoke to the men who were eating there (it always seemed to be men). They would immediately get up and move to the bar, some with napkins tucked into their belts or shirts and carrying cups of coffee. As they passed us, they would nod deferentially to AJR, unresentful at being displaced. Then while AJR protested to Frances LaQuatra that he was putting everybody to a lot of unnecessary trouble, a waitress and maybe someone from the kitchen would come by with the unfinished lunches of the men now waiting for them on barstools.

Whether the Villa Rosa was a mob hangout I never learned. Nor did I ever learn exactly who the owners or their customers were. What I took from my visits there was the feeling that AJR could be many things to many different kinds of people. Like St. Thomas More, he was a man for all seasons.

Richie Easton

Every time we added a race track to our holdings, AJR offered his friend Richie Easton a managerial job. Richie always declined. It was not his lack of a formal education that gave him pause, but the fact that he needed only a few more years of driving a delivery truck for the *Pittsburgh Press* to retire with a good pension.

Richie was tough and smart and a true friend of my Dad. He had been in the Navy during the Second World War. Married, with two sons, he made sure they attended college. One of them, Dick, chose the academic life as his profession, becoming an English instructor at Washington & Jefferson. The other, Tom, was the owner of a prosperous surveying business.

Because of a conversation we had with Richie at a Dapper Dan sports banquet, my son Mike enrolled at Washington & Jefferson. Richie asked Mike where he planned on going to college and Mike replied that he didn't really know. "How about W. & J.?" Richie suggested. Mike expressed doubt that he could pass the entrance examination for W. & J. Richie, who was fond of Mike, said, "Well, let me look into that."

I could tell what Mike was thinking: "This is Granddad's old friend, a guy who drives a truck. How is he going to help me at Washington & Jefferson?" As it happened, there was no further discussion of Mike's future that night; hovering over us, the waitress at our table spilled a whole dish of Ranch/Roquefort salad dressing on Richie. He was wearing a gunmetal gray suit and the salad dressing now covered most of it. Flustered, the waitress took a napkin to the mess with results that were far from satisfactory. After a hurried trip to the kitchen, no doubt for a consultation with her boss, she returned and told Richie apologetically that there was no good way to rub out the stains.

"Send us the cleaning bill," she added. Richie got to his feet, slowly. He was a dignified, rugged-looking man with an abundance of silver-white hair. I knew him to be normally unexcitable, but I remembered how he had dealt with two obnoxious hecklers who were bothering AJR and Governor David L. Lawrence at a football game in Cleveland, and I felt apprehensive for the waitress. But all Richie said was, "Sure," and, excusing himself, he left the banquet room and headed for home.

It was four or five weeks before Mike and I saw him again. We had forgotten about his offer to intercede at Washington & Jefferson. "You haven't applied," he said to Mike. "Why not? Do it, Mike. Do it."

The urgency in his voice spurred Mike to act. He mailed in an application. Soon afterward, a caller from the W. & J. registrar's office invited him to come down for an interview. I drove Mike to Washington, Pennsylvania, where the college is located, and when the registrar greeted us, Richie Easton's son Dick was at his side. As soon as the necessary introductions were made, Dick left the room, and the registrar asked if he could talk to Mike alone. Their conference lasted twenty minutes at the most. The registrar then informed me that Mike's application had been accepted.

In due time, he was a Washington & Jefferson graduate. All the way through, Professor Dick Easton guided him step by step. For all this, of course, we had Richie to thank.

During his last few years at the *Pittsburgh Press*, Richie spent more and more time with AJR. Wherever AJR went - whether to Shamrock Farm, the races, Steeler games, or pre-season training camp – you could always find Richie. When he retired he took a part-time job in the Steeler ticket office. If he actually sold tickets, that was nice, but driving AJR to wakes and funerals came first.

He outlived the Chief by five years or so, continuing to work in the ticket office. As he aged, he complained of hip pain – due, he supposed, to the jostling a truck driver takes. At last he allowed a doctor to examine him, and the doctor's diagnosis was bone cancer. Tough, loyal, reliable Richie Easton lived for another six months. When he died, he was 74.

Tom Murray

Someone uniquely different among AJR's innumerable race-track companions was Tom Murray, a bank executive who worked for First Boston Corporation. Tom seldom bet. He liked to watch thoroughbreds run for the spectacle of it. The sight of these large, powerful, magnificent animals thundering toward the finish line in a pack was like nothing any other sport could offer, he thought.

Educated at Georgetown, Tom had more class than most of the Damon Runyon types who clustered around AJR. In a time of discrimination against Irish Catholics, he rose to the upper levels of the banking business, the exclusive domain of WASP aristocrats back then. If you were good at your job, and Tom was good at his, you could beat the odds. He'd take a nip of the bottle now and then, and it sometimes interfered with his work.

In appearance, he resembled Edward Everett Horton, a dapper Hollywood actor who played fussbudget parts in some of the Fred Astaire-Ginger Rogers movies. Tom had perfect manners. In restaurants, he unfailingly got to his feet when a woman approached the table, and he could open a car door for a woman without seeming awkward. His diction and grammar were meticulous. AJR, contrasting himself with his friend, would say, "Tom's a gentleman; I'm a 'deeze, dem and doze' guy." Murray, in turn, would say that AJR was a "true" gentleman.

Tom lived to be 92. Not too long before he died, my son Art spotted him one day at the Pittsburgh Athletic Club. He was living by himself in an apartment in Oakland. His neighbors, mostly Pitt and Carnegie Mellon students, kept his mind young, he told Art cheerfully. I hadn't seen Tom in years, so I called him on the telephone.

His voice was unchanged - a bit high and nasal - and his mind, sure enough, was still keen. We got to reminiscing about AJR, and Tom was reminded of a race-track story I never had heard.

"This must have been in the late 1950s or early '60s," he said. "One of your dad's horses was running at Pimlico, and he asked me to fly to Baltimore with him. Your dad was a good guy to travel with, because he always paid for everything, airline tickets and all.

"On the flight over, I noticed a couple of rugged-looking men sitting behind us. They didn't have much to say to each other, and nothing at all to anyone else.

"At Pimlico, your dad and I went to the clubhouse. In the cheap seats not far away, I saw the same two guys I had seen on the airplane. Shortly before the race your dad's horse was entered in, his trainer came to our box and said in a loud stage whisper that the horse wasn't feeling well, but could run. Your dad got up and left with the trainer after telling me to stay put.

"Near post time, the two guys from the airplane came over to where I was sitting. One of them said, 'I heard that trainer say the horse was sick. What's up?' Now I was scared. The guy said to me, 'We're with Art, too. We have two thousand dollars of his to bet on the horse. When is he coming back?' I told him, 'Well, if Art gave you two thousand dollars to bet, you'd better follow his orders.' The two guys looked confused. They stood there for a minute and then started off in the direction of the parimutuel windows.

"I had fifty dollars of my own money I'd decided to bet, but I didn't know if I should. Where was your dad? Finally I said to myself, 'Well, the hell with it. I'll take a chance.' I went to the window and put my fifty dollars on the sick horse to win.

"As it turned out, he wasn't sick after all. He won going away and paid over thirty dollars. For my fifty I collected more than fifteen hundred. Not bad interest for a conservative banker.

"When the Chief showed up I told him it was one of the most exciting things that ever happened to me. I said I was perplexed, though, when the trainer told him the horse was sick. Your dad then explained that if the trainer had announced for everyone to hear that the horse was in top shape he would have gone off at even money instead of 30-1.

"I thought, but didn't say, 'Those two friends of yours - the ones I advised to do as they were told - bet two thousand dollars for you. That's sixty thousand dollars you won today.'"

Many an old-timer could attest to AJR's genius for beating the horses. When I talked to Tom Murray, he was one of just a handful who were left.

Out of Time

After Father Silas retired — or "semi-retired," as he liked to think — he spent a lot of time at 940 North Lincoln Avenue and not much time with his sisters, Marie McGinley and Margaret Laughlin. They were openly displeased about this, but the house on the North Side had two advantages over theirs: it was larger, offering more room than ever now that all five sons had flown the coop, and it was only a short distance from Three Rivers Stadium. When the Pirates played or the Steelers played, Father Silas always sat with AJR in his private box. Gently, he turned down invitations from his sisters with the explanation that his presence as a house guest would be an imposition on them, which was part of the truth, at least.

At the behest of AJR, he attended many funerals and wakes. I went, too, if I knew the surviving relatives. I remember that on the ride to a wake for Phil Musick's father - Phil Musick covered the Steelers for the *Pittsburgh Press* — AJR and Father Silas got into a low-keyed argument about just what position an old baseball teammate of theirs had played.

"He was a second baseman," said AJR.

"No, he played shortstop," contradicted Father Silas. They went back and forth like this until we arrived at the funeral home. After paying our respects, Father Silas and I returned to the car. AJR had lingered on the sidewalk to converse with an old friend or acquaintance. While we waited for him, Father Silas said to me, "Your dad is confused. That fellow was a shortstop."

Presently AJR beckoned to Father Silas, and the twosome on the sidewalk became a threesome. A few minutes went by, and then AJR broke away. Father Silas and the other man continued to talk. AJR got into the car, and the first thing he said to me was, "Your Uncle Dan is losing it a little bit. That guy was a second baseman."

AJR grew increasingly more protective of his brother, whose health was deteriorating. Mom's niece, Kathy Milligan, lived at 940 North Lincoln for a while, and one day by accident she left a razor blade in the soap dish. Picking up the soap, Father Silas grabbed the razor blade as well and cut his hand. Kathy Milligan was a good kid, and AJR always treated her with great consideration, but when he heard what had happened he went berserk. He told Kathy off as only he could do. It left Kathy, Mom, and Aunt Alice in what I think was a state of shock.

Father Silas had a need to feel productive and busy. He was always reading newspapers, periodicals, and books. With AJR, he watched sports on television, and of course they attended the games at Three Rivers. Father Silas was even a spectator from time to time at the Steelers' daily practice sessions. Every year in late fall he headed for Florida, spending a part of the winter at AJR's Palm Beach condominium and the rest of it at the Franciscan friary in St. Petersburg, where some of his fellow missionaries from China were then in residence. Father Silas was the designated driver, taking people to the doctors, to restaurants, and to the airport.

He never lost his aptitude for driving. He told me once that he had picked up "two hitch-hikers, teen-aged girls," and had given them a ride to their homes in the North Hills. "When you do that," I said, presuming to give my uncle some useful advice, "you can't really be sure of what you're getting yourself into." He replied that they were just a couple of kids. "I knew they were OK with me," he said, "but I didn't know what might happen to them if they were with somebody else."

My cousin Jim Laughlin and I were sitting with Father Silas one day at our dog track in Florida, the Palm Beach Kennel Club. He was into his late seventies by now. He said, "You know, boys, I've been ready to meet my maker for twenty-five years." Taking off his wristwatch, he handed it to Jim. "Here. I won't need this any more. I've run out of time," he said.

It was not too long before the meeting with his maker occurred. Just short of his seventy-eighth birthday, Father Silas died at the friary. At his bedside was the priest who had been such an unruly alcoholic in their days together at St. Bonaventure that Father Silas had seen fit to apply discipline with his fists. Now the same priest was giving him the last rites.

The Franciscans offered to bury Father Silas at their cemetery in Paterson, New Jersey. AJR said, "No. At St. Bonaventure. More of us can visit his grave there."

I missed the funeral. It was on the day of the Senior Bowl All-Star game, which I was scouting, and I asked AJR what I should do. "Stay for the game," he said. "Your uncle would want you to do your job." My cousin Tim Rooney, also a scout, was at the Senior Bowl, too, and I know it eased his conscience to receive a dispensation from AJR.

It was so cold that winter in Olean that the Franciscans postponed Father Silas's burial until spring. A few years later, on a beautiful summer day, I visited the gravesite, which was near the golf course he had kept in such good condition. Lining up the family around the gravestone, I prepared to take a picture, but my daughter Sue, a junior in high school, objected. She said, "Dad ... stop! That is so Polish! Besides, Father Dan wouldn't like it."

I did not take the picture.

Before leaving, we toured the campus. An aged Franciscan approached us and asked if he could be of any help. I told him we knew our way around, and he asked what my name was.

"Art Rooney Junior."

He backed off a couple of steps, beaming.

"Then you're Mike's family'?"

At first, I thought he meant my son. But Mike was a name the Franciscans used in referring to Father Silas. They used it more often than Silas or Dan. I said, "Yes. We're from Pittsburgh."

The old friar reached out and took my hand.

"Welcome!" he said. "Welcome home!"

Chapter 73

1984

Going into the 1983 season, we had a quarterback glut. For that good reason, we did not make Danny Marino our first-round draft pick. With Bradshaw coming back, with Cliff Stoudt coming back, with Mark Malone coming back, we chose to strengthen our defensive line. That's where the need was, we thought, not at quarterback. At quarterback, we were set.

But now it was 1984 – 1984, a year made synonymous with doomsday by the crystal-ball gazing George Orwell. And our quarterback cupboard, if not exactly bare, was understocked. Suddenly we were left with only Malone, whose damaged knee would impede him for the rest of his career.

First, Cliff Stoudt had defected to the United States Football League. Stoudt believed, as most of us did, that Bradshaw would return for another season. Two or three more years on the bench was a prospect that did not appeal to him. So when Rollie Dotsch's team, the Birmingham Barons, offered him more money than he was getting from the Steelers, Stoudt had no difficulty in making up his mind.

If we were unprepared for Stoudt's departure, we were staggered by what was to follow. Bradshaw announced his retirement. Sure, we knew that his elbow was hurting. But, blindly, we had viewed it as something temporary. A little more rest, and the elbow would come around. Wasn't time the great healer?

Not in Bradshaw's case, we were to learn.

More than the media did, and more than our fans did, I regretted the loss of Stoudt. Before our playoff game with the Raiders, I was telling a sportswriter that if Stoudt had a decent day we could win. "Well, he won't have a decent day," the sportswriter said. "He's the worst quarterback in the NFL." Believe what you want to, I thought, but give Stoudt receivers like Swann and Stallworth, instead of the ones at his disposal, and then make a judgment. The fans were just as harsh as the writers. Toward the end of the 1983 season they'd been booing him. Then in 1984 the Pittsburgh team in the USFL, the Maulers, drew the only big crowd in their three-year history – 60,000, it was said – for a game with Birmingham at Three Rivers Stadium, and all of those people, if their behavior was any indication, had come to boo Stoudt. In his defense I would say we had a pretty good season in 1983 with Stoudt as our quarterback for all but a part of one game. He played well for Birmingham, too, and, after the upstart league folded, began a second career in the NFL as a backup.

As for Malone, the bad knee would prevent him from ever being more than a journeyman quarterback.

Bradshaw left Pittsburgh feeling terribly unappreciated. To his way of looking at it, he was mishandled by Noll and underrated by the fans. A couple of years after his retirement, Dick Haley bumped into him at the Dallas-Fort Worth airport. Bradshaw told Haley that he could have returned to football in 1985 – had been making practice tosses without any discomfort, in fact – but was glad to be out of it; he preferred his new life as a television personality. For a long time afterward he did not attempt to conceal the bitterness that was eating at him. He appeared to hold a grudge against both his ex-coach and Pittsburgh as a whole, never coming back for Steeler reunions, spurning invitations to return for any purpose at all.

Then came the open acknowledgement that he had suffered since early youth from clinical depression. Going public seemed to change his entire outlook. There ensued a dramatic re-enactment of the prodigal son's return, Pittsburgh version. Old grievances were buried, palsy-walsiness reigned. He buried the hatchet with Noll, he participated joyfully in a television talkathon with some of his old teammates.

Let me say that I like Terry Bradshaw. I have felt a kinship between us dating back to the 1970 draft. So I lobbied hard to make him our number one pick. He gave me some trying moments, Bradshaw did, but in the end he more than justified my confidence in him. He was a once-in-a-lifetime player. Without him we would not have won our first four Super Bowl games – or even have had the opportunity to win them, I've heard it argued.

AJR could not understand my failure to see in Danny Marino the same gifts of nature I thought were so evident in Bradshaw. "Never pass up a great one," I had preached, and AJR kept reminding me of it. My part in letting Danny Marino slip away was a malfeasance I was not to be allowed to forget.

The USFL

A few words now – or maybe a few hundred – about the USFL.

The first Steeler to defect, a year before Stoudt and Ray Pinney, who went to Birmingham with him, was Jimmy Smith. On almost any NFL team other than Pittsburgh, Smith could have been a starting wide receiver. In Pittsburgh, Stallworth and Swann had kept him on the bench. By 1985, Smith was back in the NFL with the Raiders, who were still in Los Angeles.

The USFL played its games in the spring and summer, avoiding direct competition with the NFL. Its commissioner, Curt Simmons, had been the president of ESPN and was able to land two big television contracts, one with his old network and the other with ABC. Simmons, the networks, and the founders of the USFL were betting that America's appetite for professional football was insatiable.

In every decade since the 1930s, AJR had seen rival leagues such as this one come and go. A professional football team must have a place to play, and my recollection is that no team in either the NFL or the USFL had a stadium of its own. Since the stadiums in the cities where the two leagues would be going head to head – all the big ones, anyway – were leased by the NFL, what the people behind the new league were trying to do, my dad believed, was position themselves for an anti-trust suit. Their aim, reasoned AJR, was to force a merger, as the American Football League had done in the 1960s.

There was a lawsuit, all right, and the USFL won it, but no merger resulted. The jury awarded the plaintiffs the sum of one dollar – one whole dollar – in damages. Ultimately, two USFL cities, Jacksonville and Carolina, ended up getting expansion franchises in the NFL.

Most of the new teams in the USFL drew fairly well while the league was still a novelty. Initially, no team was to spend more than $1.2 million on salaries or try to sign more than ten of the top-rated college players, but neither promise was kept. Right off the bat, a USFL team gave Herschel Walker, the swift, powerful running back who had won the Heisman Trophy, five million dollars to leave the University of Georgia after his junior year.

Walker was very good, but the team that signed him was not. Attendance throughout the league began to decline, and so did the television ratings. Players who had left the NFL were returning en masse. Every team in the USFL lost huge amounts of money. At the end of its third season, 1985, the league went out of business.

The ill will I felt toward George Perles and Rollie Dotsch, the coaches I blamed for luring Cliff Stoudt and Ray Pinney to the USFL, had long since dissipated. AJR's animosity was focused on the owner of the Maulers, Edward DeBartolo, Sr. We regarded DeBartolo Senior as an NFL colleague. On paper, the younger DeBartolo, Ed Junior, owned the San Francisco Forty-Niners, but he was still, at the time, a front man for his father. Now DeBartolo Senior had bought a USFL team – the Pittsburgh Maulers — and moved it onto the Steelers' turf, Three Rivers Stadium.

AJR felt betrayed. He was angry. Furious. Livid: He got up at a meeting of NFL owners and excoriated DeBartolo. I wasn't there, but I heard about it at second hand. His remarks, as they were reported to me, went like this.

"I'm going to talk about class. There is class among bank robbers, class among pimps, class among whores. But what Ed DeBartolo has done is completely without class. How can this man belong to our league and screw one of his partners?"

Not the kind of language the Chief ordinarily used, but I know he was boiling over.

His outburst reminded me of how Franklin D. Roosevelt denounced Mussolini – a bit more gracefully, it is true — after Italy declared war on France while the Germans were driving toward Paris in 1940. "The hand that held the dagger," FDR proclaimed, "has struck it into the back of its neighbor."

Postscript: Once the USFL ceased to exist, the Rooneys and Ed DeBartolo, Sr. resumed diplomatic relations. There never had been a rift between the Rooneys and Ed Junior.

Departures

Mel Blount's retirement coincided with Bradshaw's. We had drafted them together and now they were leaving together. Blount was the best defensive back who ever played for the Steelers, but defensive backs don't last as long as quarterbacks do, and his time had come.

There were also involuntary departures. Chuck Noll unloaded two of his most experienced offensive linemen, sending Ted Petersen to the Browns and Steve Courson to Tampa Bay. As I have said, I think Chuck knew that Courson was using steroids. One of our younger offensive linemen, Rick Donnalley from North Carolina, had the skills and the physical requirements to be the prototype of a Steeler guard, but Noll sent him packing for "failure to produce." He spent the next two seasons with the Washington Redskins and two more with Kansas City. We had drafted worse players than Rick Donnalley.

In the 1984 draft, we scored big with our first-round pick, Louis Lipps, a wide receiver from Southern Mississippi. Lipps had it all – great athletic ability, great hands, great field vision, and great speed. And he could "make things happen," as Noll used to repeat – and repeat and repeat. I believe that Lipps could have played on any of our Super Bowl teams, holding his own with Stallworth and Swann.

Our second-round pick was a rugged tight end from Wyoming, Chris Kolodziejski. When we took our new players to LeMont for a get-together dinner that year, I sat next to Chris, and he opened the conversation by saying, "Well, Mister Rooney, Jenna said she would get you to draft me, and here we are."

"Jenna?" I was puzzled.

"Yes. You know. Jenna, your niece. Lives in Santa Monica."

I wracked my brain. Then it came to me. He meant Gina – Gina Valdivia, whose mother was a first cousin of Kay's. Chris had been one of Gina's high-school boyfriends in Los Angeles, and she boasted to him that her "uncle" was the Steelers' personnel director. She would get the old boy to draft him. Never once had I heard Gina mention Chris Kolodziejski, but as soon as I caught on I went along with her tall tale.

In his rookie season, Chris played an outstanding game against the Forty-Niners in San Francisco. Afterward, the offensive coordinator, Tom Moore, came up to me and said, "We've got a keeper." He meant Chris – "Kolo," Moore called him. And Moore was a guy who measured his words. But in that same San Francisco game, Kolo had gone down with a severe knee injury, foreclosing from then on his usefulness as a football player.

The supply of quarterbacks in the draft was so limited that we waited until the seventh round to take one. Scott Campbell was a little guy from Purdue, a school that was famous then and is famous now for turning out quarterbacks. Chuck Noll liked his mechanics, and so did I, but good mechanics were not enough to compensate for his short stature. Talent-wise, Campbell reminded no one of undersized wonders like Davey O'Brien, Frankie Albert, and Eddie LeBaron. It was remarkable, I thought, that we kept him around for two years.

Knowing that Campbell was a long shot and fearing that Mark Malone could not be counted on because of his knee problems; Noll traded our third-round pick to Miami for David Woodley. As if we needed another reminder of the mistake we had made the year before – as if AJR needed another reminder – Woodley was the quarterback whose job Dan Marino had taken.

Trading for a quarterback was something we hadn't done since the tenure of Bill Austin, but Noll was desperate. When Bill Nunn scouted Woodley at LSU, he turned in a favorable report, and in fact Woodley had quarterbacked Miami to the Super Bowl in his third year as a pro. Then Marino came in and made him expendable. On film, Woodley looked better than OK to all of our scouts, myself included, but we failed to allow for the demon that possessed him – alcoholism. After his second season with us, he was finished at the age of 27. Let me say this: for as long as he lasted, he served the team capably.

One of the players we drafted before Campbell was Terry Long, a guard out of East Carolina. He played well as a starter for a couple of good Steeler teams, but did so, we were to learn, with the help of steroids. When Long tested positive in 1991 (the NFL had started to crack down), Noll suspended him. All through as a Steeler after two unsuccessful attempts at suicide, he pulled himself together and started a business. His Value Added Foods Group was a chicken-processing plant on the North Side with thirty employees, but in 2005 he died of "inflammatory meningitis" after swallowing antifreeze. Long was 41. An inordinate number of offensive linemen who played for us in the 1970s and early '80s had unusually short life spans. Ray Mansfield died in the Grand Canyon on a backpacking trip with his son. Jim Clack died at 49. The early deaths of Steve Courson and Mike Webster were highly publicized. Webster's family, in a lawsuit against the NFL Pension Fund, claimed that head injuries sustained as a football player were partly responsible for his health problems and put the onus on steroids as well. There was testimony from two doctors that Webster "experimented" with steroids. Courson, after his troubles became public, let the whole world know he'd been using them. And Clack told the author Roy Blount that steroids had helped him add muscle and weight.

There were also the quarterbacks who died prematurely. Joe Gilliam was addicted to cocaine, David Woodley, as I have said, to alcohol. Drugs, booze, and steroids. All three were anathema to Noll and to AJR, but in spite of our best intentions we did not go unscathed.

Unhappy Ending

On the eve of the 1984 season, I thought we had a pretty good mixture of youth and experience and were still on the right track. I thought we could pull something off that you did not often see in the NFL. We had an excellent chance, a kind of sixth sense told me, to rebuild a great team without hitting rock bottom.

One thing that gave me hope was our success in the pre-season games. Winning three out of four didn't mean much; what mattered was that we looked good doing it. Mark Malone and David Woodley kept the offense moving, and I came to believe that our two-quarterback system might work. In 1983, Cliff Stoudt's pass receivers had a hard time getting open and a hard time catching the ball when they did get open. Malone and Woodley were throwing to a fully recovered John Stallworth and to a young guy with Stallworth-like ability, Louis Lipps.

Replacing the worn-out parts in our Super Bowl machine was an ongoing process. Through it all, there had not been a losing season. I felt sure that for the rest of the 1980s we could keep this up – make the playoffs habitually and perhaps, with any luck, return to the Super Bowl one more time.

At St. Vincent, however, we had a distraction – the absence of Franco Harris. In twelve seasons, all with the Steelers, he had rushed for 11,950 yards, a total second only to Jim Brown's NFL record of 12,312. But now he was holding out. He wanted a two-year contract extension, and we had offered him only one year. As productive as he had been in 1983, for a running back he was entering old age. I thought that this time around we could expect him to rush for maybe five hundred yards at the most instead of his usual thousand or more. In 1983, though he was hitting the holes with as much precision as ever, he had lost some agility. Cutting back was a problem for him now, and on sweeps he was being forced out of bounds more and more. In Franco's favor, he knew the offense thoroughly; he knew what the blockers could do; he was a good pass receiver and his competitive flame burned with the same intensity. I believed that even as something less than a full-time player he could still help us win.

All of us – Dan, AJR, the assistant coaches, the other players, the medical staff, and the fans; all of us, that is, except Noll – desired what I thought of as a Hollywood happy ending for Franco. As for Noll, he seemed to feel that Franco's happy ending had already occurred. His 1983 stats — 1,007 rushing yards, thirty-four pass receptions, five touchdowns — closed the books as far as Noll was concerned.

He commissioned Dick Hoak, Franco's predecessor as a Penn State and Steeler running back and his coach from the time we had drafted him, to deliver a message: "Tell Franco to retire."

Respectfully, Hoak declined the privilege. "Chuck," he said, determination in his voice, "that has to come from you. Either from you or the Rooneys. We're talking about a Hall of Famer here."

Objection sustained.

With Noll, there was no room for sentiment. Whether or not Franco Harris overtook Jim Brown was irrelevant to Noll. What always came first was the team. Personal records counted for nothing. In fact, the nearer Franco got to Brown's record, the greater the harm. Press, fans, and even Franco himself would be focused on the record, creating difficulties. There would be pressure to play Franco when it was not the best thing for the team and not the best thing for Franco. I remembered what the coaches said about L.C. Greenwood toward the end of his career: "Let's get him out of there before he gets hurt. L. C. can't protect himself well enough any more."

In camp, we appeared to have made a lucky ninth-round pick. Rich Erenberg, who had played college football at Colgate, a seldom-visited way station for pro scouts, was showing considerable promise as a running back. Erenberg looked so good to Noll that while the team was still at St. Vincent he got rid of Greg Hawthorne, sending him to the Patriots. It raised the question: if we didn't need Hawthorne, why did we need Franco, for whom the clock was so obviously ticking?

To make the contract negotiations even stickier, Franco had an inexperienced agent. The agent and Franco's wife seemed to be unaware that his pursuit of the ground-gaining record was of secondary importance in Noll's mind to the object of winning games. Between these two and the coach there was little or no communication. Still, I felt it could all be worked out. And would be.

I was wrong for two reasons: Noll's strong belief that Franco ought to retire and the reluctance of AJR and Dan to throw away money on a player the coach didn't want. And yet, by accepting our terms, Franco could have stayed for a graceful fadeout. He could have had one final season with the Steelers.

On a morning in August Dan told me that he and the Chief were meeting that day with Franco and his agent. Dan said he was pretty certain that Franco was going to sign. Pleased, I took off for St. Vincent, where I had some business of my own to attend to – a discussion with Haley and Tom Modrak about moving Hawthorne. After that, I went up the hill to Bill Nunn's office, and while Nunn and I were talking, our assistant P.R. guy, John Evenson, rushed in.

"Art," he said breathlessly, "there's something I want to tell you before the press comes after you ..."

I broke in on him. "Yes, I know – we traded Hawthorne."

That wasn't it, Evenson started to say.

"Oh." Again I thought I could see what was coming. "Yeah, Dan told me this morning. We signed Franco."

"No, no." Evenson was more excited than ever. "Dan and your father gave Franco his release!"

I reached for the telephone and got Dan. He said our differences with Franco could not be bridged. I talked to AJR, who ordered me to keep my mouth shut when the sportswriters came around. "All you can say is that you have nothing to say."

For the rest of the afternoon I had media people shooting questions at me.

"What's your reaction? You were the one who brought Franco here."

"I'm sorry. I have nothing to say."

That was the way it went, over and over.

The Hollywood ending for Number 32, the man who, along with Joe Greene, started us on our way to greatness, the man who never played on a Steeler team that lost more games than it won, was not to be. A free agent now, Franco went out to Seattle. Having missed training camp, he was physically unprepared for the season. And of course, he was unfamiliar with Coach Chuck Knox's offense.

In his first two games, he did not do a thing for the Seahawks. The season was in its third week, and the Steelers were idle (they had played a Thursday-night game with the Jets in New York), when Kay and I met AJR for dinner on Sunday evening at the St. Clair Country Club. Because the Chief liked his privacy there, we'd have asked for a table in a secluded part of the dining room, but this time he insisted on eating with the crowd that was clustered near the television set. The Seattle game was being shown. AJR's eyes were getting weak, and when the Seahawks had the ball he would leave our table and his dinner and put his nose right up against the screen. To his unconcealed disappointment, Franco performed miserably. He looked lost.

Seattle let him go before the season was over.

With Frank Pollard, Walter Abercrombie, and Rich Erenberg running the ball, the Steelers got to the playoffs, vindicating Noll's judgment.

On a weekend afternoon in late January, I drove to 940 North Lincoln Avenue for a visit with my dad. I walked into his den, and there was Franco. He had come, as I had, to see the Chief. His young son was with him. Franco stood up and gave me a warm greeting. He introduced me to the kid. I thought, "What a special guy."

And then I corrected myself. I was in the presence of two special guys. Franco Harris and Art Rooney, Sr.

Against the Odds

I have an abiding affection for our 1984 team. In the face of what seemed like endless bad luck, it persevered. It overcame injuries, overcame obstacles, bounced back from defeat. And went to the playoffs for a third straight year.

AJR reacted to all this rather sourly. The team's performance, he complained, was "herky-jerky." The Super Bowl seasons of the 1970s had accustomed him to a steady diet of success. Bumping along – taking two steps forward and one step backward, and then repeating the process again and again – was not the kind of advancement he liked.

Right from scratch with that 1984 team, there were holes to be filled, beginning with the great void at quarterback. Mark Malone, getting his chance to start after four years as a backup, was far from the sprightly athlete we had drafted out of Arizona State. He reminded me now of Mike Kruczek, the stand-in who kept us winning while Bradshaw was sidelined in 1976: big, strong, mechanical, admired by his teammates for bringing out the best that was in them. (Kruczek's teammates, it is worth mentioning, included nine or ten Hall of Famers in their prime). Another difference: where Kruczek lacked exceptional inborn talent, Malone at one time had a ton of it. The injury to his knee would linger. He no longer could escape the rush, no longer could pick up yardage by running with the ball, which had been his most striking asset. He had a pretty decent arm, but not a gun. To see him work by the numbers – drop back, step up, throw – was disheartening.

Still, he got through the season, completing fifty-four percent of his passes for a respectable 2,137 yards and sixteen touchdowns. Stallworth and Lipps had plenty to do with these totals, of course. The silky Stallworth, our MVP, was never better, catching eighty passes. Lipps caught forty-five and was Rookie of the Year. When Malone alternated with Woodley, there was never a fall-off in production. Woodley had played for one of Chuck Noll's mentors, Don Shula; because their systems were so much alike, he made the transition easily.

In the sixth game of the season (our record going in was 3-2), we went up against Shula's Dolphins at Three Rivers Stadium. It was Dan Marino's homecoming party, and I can't honestly say that I had a good time. Unperturbed by our blitz, Marino picked us apart, 31-7. We were to play the Forty-Niners in San Francisco the next week, and I left for the Coast as soon as I could, not only because Kay was going with me, but to distance myself from the Chief.

October that year in northern California was golden. Jack Butler also had brought his wife, and the four of us took in the sights: the vistas from Nob Hill, looking out on the Bay; the Golden Gate Bridge; the cable cars; Fisherman's Wharf; Berkeley ("So many weirdos," declared Kay); Palo Alto and Stanford ("Beautiful!"); a Stanford football game. There were marvelous restaurants to go to, and wine to be sipped on a tour of the Napa Valley.

San Francisco itself was not yet as iniquitous as Sodom and Gomorrah, but getting close. Our trip coincided with an early gay-rights parade, and we joined the onlookers. Bernie and Kay were bemused, I guess you would say, by the spectacle. "Nothing like that in Pittsburgh," one of them observed.

Our game with the Forty-Niners was at Candlestick Park, better suited, unlike Three Rivers Stadium, to baseball than to football. The sky was blue and the sun was shining, but a cold wind blew in from the Bay. It goes without saying that we were underdogs to the reigning Super Bowl champions. Their Joe Montana was another Western Pennsylvania quarterback we had chosen not to take in the draft. Would he burn us the way Marino had done? I was understandably nervous.

Montana had shown that he knew how to win. The Steelers, looked upon as has-beens even though we'd gone to the playoffs the previous two years, were given no chance. What worried me as much as the Forty-Niners' proven ability to dominate was the fact that we entered the game banged up. Louis Lipps was hurt; Larry Brown was hurt; Ben Cunningham was hurt. Even Stallworth was limping. All four would play, but Brown and Cunningham couldn't do much. After Chris Kolodziejski's injury, Noll had to alternate Weegie Thompson, a slightly built wide receiver, and Tunch Ilkin, whose position was tackle, at tight end – Thompson in passing situations, Ilkin when the play called for a block. With Ilkin at tight end, a retread named Steve August filled in at tackle. He was so unfamiliar with the offense that Mike Webster finally told him to forget about the blocking assignments and simply "come off the ball."

Early in the first half, Terry Long hobbled off the field, and Emil Boures, who had been a center at Pitt, and a lowly-regarded center at that, went in to play guard. Even Blake Wingle, a late-round pick from UCLA in 1983 and a bench rider ever since, logged some important minutes at guard. And who was that guy Noll kept putting in at tackle, taking out for repairs, and putting in again? Why, if my eyes did not deceive me, it was Ray Snell from Wisconsin, another no-name.

Everywhere you looked, there were no-names, but this was to be a day on which these rag-tag offensive linemen would excel. Their blocking cleared the way for Frank Pollard to grind out 105 yards. The Steelers' offense controlled the ball most of the day and when this happened Montana could do nothing but watch. Mike Webster was a dynamo, leading the charge of the offensive line and urging his teammates on. An inspirational force if there ever was one, he elevated their level of play.

Stallworth used all of his guile to snooker the Forty-Niners' defensive backs, lining up first on one side and then on the other, designing and calling a pass play that resulted in a touchdown, a touchdown made possible by one of the jumping, twisting catches for which he was known. In attempting to cover him, the Forty-Niners' Eric Wright drew some holding and interference penalties at critical times in the game.

The Steelers won it, 20-17, on two long, time-consuming touchdown drives and Gary Anderson's field goal, set up by the defense when linebacker Bryan Hinkle smartly intercepted one of Montana's arrow-like passes and made a dodging, darting runback of forty-three yards. It was the only game the Forty Niners lost that season – a season in which they repeated as Super Bowl champions – and Chuck Noll put the victory right up there with some of our big ones in the 1970s.

From then on, there were ups and downs, and to reach the playoffs again we had to win our last two games. Which we did, just barely, edging a rival from way back, the Browns, and a hated adversary of more recent vintage, the Raiders, out in Los Angeles.

We took a 9-7 record into the post-season. Our first opponent, Denver (13-3), had John Elway, a future Hall of Famer, at quarterback, a thousand-yard rusher in Sammy Winder, and the home-field advantage. The Denver fans, who were just as crazy as ours, were hollering their heads off in Mile High Stadium long before Elway's short touchdown pass gave the Broncos an early lead. But the Steelers came back. The defense shut down Winder and got us out of trouble that was caused by Malone's two fumbles in Steeler territory and a blocked punt. We drove for a touchdown, Denver scored again, so did we, and the teams traded field goals.

Finally Eric Williams, a second-year safety from North Carolina State, made the play of his life. He slipped between Elway and the intended receiver for an interception; his return put the ball on the two-yard line and then it was Pollard up the middle for the game winner. Pittsburgh 24, Denver 17.

So many of the players we had acquired since our last trip to the Super Bowl were producing for us now. I began to think that we might be able to pull this off: beat Miami for the AFC championship – and, after that, who could tell? In Super Bowl competition, the Steelers never had lost. But we had gone about as far as we could go. For the game with Miami in the Orange Bowl, another vast crowd was on hand: 76,000-plus. Again, no one gave us a chance. Even though we had defused Montana, even though we had defused Elway, the explosive offense engineered by Marino would be too much for us, the know-it-alls decided. And they were right.

On a bright, warm sixth of January, Malone had a good day (312 yards passing and three touchdowns), and we moved the ball on the ground. When we got near the goal line we pushed it across, scoring in every period. Near the end of the first half the game was even, but while Malone was having a good day Marino was having a better one: twenty-one completions, 421 yards, and four touchdowns.

When the Dolphins had the ball it was quick-strike football, reminiscent of our games with Paul Brown's Cleveland teams in the 1950s. Back then, the Steelers would keep the ball for up to ten minutes and score a touchdown; then Otto Graham would take to the air, and the Browns would have a touchdown in two minutes. Cleveland's touchdowns came with less exertion and more frequency than ours did, and the same thing was true in Miami. We were zinged again by Danny Marino, 45-28.

It would be eleven more years before Pittsburgh went to another Super Bowl and twenty-six years between Lombardi Trophies.

Chapter 74

Overrated

After the 1984 season, the leaves continued to fall from the tree. Jack Lambert, Ron Johnson, and Larry Brown called it quits. Just four players were left from our Augustan Age, the 1970s: John Stallworth, Mike Webster, Donnie Shell, and Gary Dunn. Ben Cunningham remained on the team, but had reached the injury phase of his career. For some time now, he had not been much of a factor.

Yet in my estimation, we were on our way back. It would take a while longer – four years, maybe five – but we could win while rebuilding and possibly return to the Super Bowl. The 1984 season had convinced me of that.

There was still only one route to take. We couldn't trade for the players we needed, nor hope to shuffle them out of the deck. We had to draft them, as we had done since Chuck Noll took command. The difficulty was that again in 1985 there would be nineteen teams drafting ahead of us.

To get the special athletes who could make the big play we'd have to reach. When at last our turn came, the best available bet seemed to be Darryl Sims, a defensive end from Wisconsin. I had seen him play and had scrutinized him on film. In height, weight, speed, and quickness, he certainly measured up. Put to the test in actual competition, he could and did make big plays – once in a while. He was similar to a lot of other guys we'd been drafting for the past several years, the kind we believed we could somehow reconstruct. We could transform him, we thought, into something a bit closer to an L. C. Greenwood, a Steve Furness, or a John Banaszak. We were kidding ourselves, of course. No matter how full of wisdom our coaches were, no matter how inspirational it was to play on the same team with future Hall of Famers wearing Super Bowl rings, you could not take a Darryl Sims and train him to be consistent.

Chuck Noll would tell me that Sims was "flashy," meaning volatile, unstable, erratic: an on-again, off-again performer. Joe Greene, now a member of our coaching staff, said he was overdrafted, someone you'd hope to get in the fourth round. After watching Sims in a few exhibition games I doubted if he was even that good. I recalled that Moon Mullins and Dwight White were fourth-round draft picks, and Sims was no Mullins or White. He put in two mediocre years with the Steelers and another two years with Cleveland.

Because Larry Brown's departure left a vacancy in the offensive line, we had to draft a tackle, so Mark Behning of Nebraska was our second-round pick. Defensive linemen in the NFL were getting bigger every year; the mammoth power rushers coming into the game could run right over standard-sized tackles and guards, and Behning, we felt, had the strength and the heft to deal with them. He was a big ol' boy. Pass blocking had become more important; too, with more teams stressing the pass instead of the run, and here again Behning filled the bill. The officials were letting blockers "lock on" to the rusher with their hands and arms, which appeared to be a tactic for which Behning was well adapted.

No such luck. He turned out to be a slow learner, easily got discouraged, and gave it all up at the end of his first year.

In sum, our 1985 draft was almost a washout. Of the thirteen players we took, only five made the team, and there was no long-term help from any of them except maybe Harry Newsome, who was our punter for the next five years. A defensive back we cut, Liffort Hobley of LSU, caught on with the Miami Dolphins. We drafted a center from Wisconsin named Dan Turk. In 1974, we drafted a center from Wisconsin named Mike Webster. Nineteen eighty-five would be Webster's twelfth year with the Steelers. Dan Turk played two years for the Steelers and ten more in the NFL, most of that time on special-teams duty with the Raiders.

Our sixth-round choice in 1985, Gregg Carr, was a linebacker from Auburn who had the same characteristics as Jack Ham, Loren Toews, and Bryan Hinkle. He could move and he was smart. Too smart, as it turned out. After improving in each of his first four years, he left us to study medicine.

I thought of what Will Walls said to me once when I was breaking in as a scout: "Pass 'em up if they're too smart. Before very long, they'll find better things to do than play football."

Breakdown

Granted the 1985 draft was a disappointment. Still I expected us to play at the same level as in 1984 – to win more often than we lost and find a way into the playoffs. We were upbeat in camp, especially after a 42-27 spanking of the Tampa Bay Bucs in our first pre-season game.

I know, I know. Pre-season games are meaningless. But I was looking at how we had finished the 1984 season, with that gritty performance out in Los Angeles and the playoff win over Denver. There'd be a carryover, I was sure. We were getting some traction.

On this score I had enough confidence to let the word out wherever I could find any listeners. Once we had started playing for keeps, the feeling only grew. We hammered the Colts, 45-3, in our opening game. But if the 1984 season had been herky-jerky, the 1985 season was like a roller-coaster ride at Kennywood Park. We were up and down, up and down. We'd win one and then lose one. There was a stretch where we lost three games in a row, split the next two, *won* three games in a row, and then – going into another death spiral – *lost* three games in a row for the second time.

Up and down, up and down. To avoid our first losing season in fourteen years, we'd have to come on strong and win our last two games. But where the 1984 team, needing two wins at the end of the season for a playoff spot, was able to get the job done, this one couldn't make it to .500.

At home, we won from Buffalo, 30-24. Then we lost on the road to the Giants, 28-10. Which left us with a 7-9 record.

For me the Steeler dynasty ended on that cold December Sunday in the Meadowlands. Here we were – not even in contention for the playoffs. The incentive was to keep our heads above water. And we couldn't do it. Oh well, some would say – winning exactly as many games as you lose is like kissing your sister. If so (I'm no authority), I'd have settled for that.

There were individual Steelers who performed well statistically in 1985. Frank Pollard missed becoming our fourth thousand-yard rusher, joining Franco Harris, John Henry Johnson, and Rocky Bleier, by less than the distance it takes to make a first down. Walter Abercrombie gained 851 yards and caught twenty-four passes. John Stallworth caught seventy-five passes and Louis Lipps fifty-nine. Lipps led the league in punt returns. Dwayne Woodruff made five interceptions.

Add it all up and it still comes out to a sub-.500 record.

We lost a few games we should have won. Close ones. Good teams win the close ones. We had some injuries, but every team has injuries. In 1984 we overcame our injuries; the 1985 team lacked the bench strength to do the same thing. Lambert and Brown were gone, and we missed their leadership. But it was time for new leaders to take their place, and none did. Our drafts in recent years had failed to produce these new leaders. The assembly line was malfunctioning.

Since 1980 we had reached for players who could have been great but were not. Most of them, I am sorry to say, were not even solid, steady contributors. There were no Randy Grossmans or Bryan Hinkles or John Banaszaks among them. Forget the Pro Bowlers and potential Hall of Famers. There was not a Keith Willis, a Loren Toews, a Frank Pollard, or a Rocky Bleier in the bunch. All of these overachievers I have mentioned, none of them big names in college, were drafted below the fourth round or signed as free agents. Our aim was to acquire at least three players every year who could be starters on a winning team, and we hadn't been doing it, not consistently.

We had to go back to where we started.

We were losing sight of a big part of Noll's strategy to get what he needed in young players: football character and grit. One of his first acts as head coach was to trade Roy Jefferson, a fine athlete and performer, to the Colts for almost nothing. Noll said he would not work with players whose personal goals were put above team goals.

We had to continue looking for superior athletes who were coachable, but we had to reemphasize character – character for our game. We had been picking up too many players without the burning desire to win.

And it wasn't being instilled.

Since 1980 we had drafted at least a dozen players in the first four rounds who were useless to us. If even half of them had measured up to the low-end picks we made every year in the 1970s, then beyond any doubt we could have kept on winning.

The Long Goodbye

Bill Nunn wanted to retire. He was adamant about it, saying the only reason he had not retired earlier was his loyalty to the Rooneys. After one last look at the college teams he scouted in the spring every year, his days as a full-time member of the Steeler organization would be over.

One year earlier, in the spring of 1985, it had looked as though Dick Haley would be leaving us. Officially, Haley was our "director of player personnel." My title, since shortly after Dick came on board was "vice president in charge of personnel." Somehow, there was not any overlapping. I ran the scouting department and Haley was my No. 1 assistant. I liked Haley as a person – as a gentleman and a family man – and had great respect for his astuteness as a scout.

But now he was mulling an offer to be the top personnel guy for the Detroit Lions. In a way, it flattered me to hear that. Since 1980, I had not been pleased with our drafting. At the time of the offer to Haley, we had nonetheless gone to the playoffs for three straight years, and the Detroit people, at any rate, must have thought we were doing something right.

Haley was taking the offer seriously, he said. I advised him to meet with the Lions' executives, carefully weigh their proposal, and take a week to decide. A week but no longer. If he left, we'd have to find a replacement, with time growing short.

After Haley left my office, I went down the hall and conferred with Chuck Noll. If Haley had a chance to better himself, Noll said, there was little we could do about it, or should. He expressed satisfaction with the work of our scouts. Finally, we agreed that of the people on our staff who might fill Haley's shoes, Tom Modrak would be best qualified.

Modrak scouted the other pro teams for us. Like Haley, he was personable, responsible, and a hard worker. He knew football. He knew how we operated. When the week I had given Haley to make up his mind went by without a decision, Dan and I spoke to Tom. Would he be interested in Haley's job? His answer seemed "different," to say the least.

"Is this a situation," he asked, "where if I say no I'll be fired?"

Not at all, we assured him.

"Well, in that case," he said, "I'd just as soon stay as I am."

Replacing a good man like Haley would be no easy matter, I could see.

Another five or six days passed before Haley informed us he had made up his mind. He was turning down the Detroit job.

I was relieved, but henceforth, I promised myself, if the possibility of losing a deputy as important as Haley arose, there must be someone available who was ready to move up. And by the time I found out we'd be losing Bill Nunn I knew where to find such a person.

Young Tom Donahoe had been a successful high school coach in Western Pennsylvania. Now he was scouting for Jack Butler in the Blesto organization and responding very well to Butler's tutelage. I went to Nunn and asked if he might let Donahoe tag along on his next scouting trip; when they returned, he could tell me what he thought.

Nunn was exactly the right man for this assignment. They were gone for a week, and then he handed in his report. It confirmed what my instincts had told me: "One of the best new scouts Jack Butler has developed in years and years."

Donahoe was a grandson of David L. Lawrence. The only significance this had from the Steelers' point of view was to give Tom some identity. It had nothing at all to do with whether or not we would hire him. With Jack Butler's approval, hire him we did.

Another Blesto scout I added in the spring of 1986 was Jesse Kaye. Jesse would scout the central states, Donahoe the Eastern Seaboard, and Bob Schmitz the West, while Haley and I would look at the top picks wherever they were. Modrak, besides checking on the NFL teams, would help scout the colleges selectively.

I had a talk with Dan about Nunn. I said, "Hey, we can't let this guy get completely out of the organization. He can do special scouting assignments on a part-time basis and earn every cent of what we pay him." Dan sort of chuckled and said he'd been thinking along the same lines. Something would be worked out.

Nunn's post-retirement plans were to spend the winters in Florida with Frances, his wife. They were going down there for a week to get the lay of the land, so I arranged for them to stay in AJR's

Palm Beach condominium on the ocean. Long-range, I had a schedule in mind for Bill. He could scout the Florida schools for us from mid-October until the end of the season, help with the draft when he came back to Pittsburgh, and scout some Northeastern colleges in the early fall before heading south again.

This, more or less, was how everything fell into place. The Nunns bought a condominium of their own and spent the winters in Florida for the rest of the 1980s and the first part of the 1990s. Three of my brothers - Tim, Pat, and John - had winter homes in Florida, too, and so did our cousin Artie Laughlin. All four came to look upon Bill as their football guru. Eventually, Bill and Frances tired of the snowbird life and sold their condominium at a profit. As a full-time resident of Pittsburgh once more, Nunn continued his part-time work for the Steelers, remaining on the job into a hale and hearty old age.

During all these years our friendship would go on, but we were not any longer professional associates.

Aftermath

On Monday, December 22, 1985, the day after our season-ending loss to the Giants, Dan called me into his office. At once, we began to discuss the game and its consequence — our first losing season in fourteen years.

Both of us were upset. I had been certain we would make it to the playoffs again. I felt that with Louis Lipps in our offense and also returning punts, the 1985 team should have been superior to the 1984 team. Chuck Noll referred to players like Lipps as "weapons." This was a team that had outscored its opponents, 379 points to 355, and yet the striking power mostly generated by Lipps was not reflected in our over-all performance and 7-9 record.

To a considerable extent, I felt responsible. After the Battle of Gettysburg, somebody asked a general on the losing side to explain the Confederate Army's defeat. "There were many reasons," he said, "and I contributed to them." So it was with me. I had been the one, after all, who promised to get so many good players into black and gold uniforms that the coaches would not be able to mess things up. I had matured since making that unwise (and unfair) assertion, but our failure in 1985 to win as many games as we lost could in large part be laid at my feet. Our scouting department had not given our coaches the players I had said we'd provide.

I knew this better than anyone else, but now my brother Dan was saying it to me, and his words were hard to take.

Our discussion became an argument. Then a heated argument. When I left Dan's office, I was angry and remorseful. The anger was directed mostly at myself - in the first place because we no longer were drafting players of the kind who had kept us going to Super Bowls, and in the second place for losing my temper. I resolved not to do that again, and I never have.

In a little over two weeks - on January 11 — Art III was to marry Christine Swanson, a tall, lovely blonde he had known since grammar school. Art had a degree from Boston College in biology and was in his third year of dental school at Pitt (where some of his instructors, he told me, remembered Jock Sutherland and Art Sekay). Christine was a Duquesne University graduate. Certain family members, among them Kay's father, Roy Kumer, thought that marriage and dental school combined would be too much for Art to handle. Kay and I had some misgivings, but Art was a good student and in fact would receive two awards on graduation day.

Father Bob Reardon tied the knot for the young couple at St. Louise de Marillac Church in Upper St. Clair. There followed a bounteous reception at LeMont arranged by Christine's parents. The wedding put a cap on a very pleasant Christmas season, and my spat with Dan seemed a thing of the past.

Last Draft

With the wedding out of the way, I turned my thoughts full-time to the draft. We'd be picking ninth, which gave us our best shot since 1971 at getting good quality. In 1971 we drafted a Hall of Famer (Jack Ham), four Pro Bowlers, and four other really good players. "Let's get solid performers who can help us over the long run," I now told my scouts.

We came up with three.

Our first pick, John Rienstra, was a big offensive lineman from Temple. For five years, he made steady improvement. Then we traded him to Cleveland, where he played for another two seasons.

After Rienstra, we drafted Gerald Williams, defensive tackle from Auburn. Gerald Williams played nine years with the Steelers and two more with Carolina.

Bubby Brister, the quarterback we selected third, had played college football at Northeast Louisiana. In temperament, he was similar to the Louisiana Tech quarterback we had drafted in 1970, Terry Bradshaw. Both were flippant and temperamental. What Brister lacked, for the most part, was his predecessor's ability.

By which I don't mean to imply that he couldn't play, just that Bradshaw was a quarterback with skills you don't often see.

All Brister had to be was himself, not the second coming of Bradshaw. He'd been a minor-league baseball player and threw a pass from behind his right ear, with lots of zip on it. He could move around behind the line of scrimmage, avoiding defensive linemen and linebackers. Although he was not by any means a dumbbell, Noll found it best to eliminate things from the playbook for Brister – to keep the offense as basic as possible.

In 1988, the year that Brister replaced Malone, the Steelers had their worst record since 1970, Bradshaw's rookie season, losing eleven of sixteen games. The following year, for the first time since 1984, they got to the playoffs. They beat Houston in overtime, 26-23, before losing to Denver by an even closer score, 24-23. Bubby played well against Houston and played well against Denver until he lost his composure near the end of the game.

The 1989 season was Brister's high-water mark. He lost his job to Neil O'Donnell after Bill Cowher succeeded Noll in 1992. That same year, his refusal to enter a game in relief of O'Donnell earned him a one-way ticket to the Steeler boneyard. His words to Joe Walton, the offensive coordinator – "I'm not mopping up for anybody" – became Bubby's epitaph.

His epitaph in Pittsburgh, that is to say. The repercussions of the incident taught Brister humility, and he ended his playing days as a backup, first with the Eagles, then with the Jets, and finally with the Broncos – mopping up when the need arose.

His NFL career covered fifteen or sixteen seasons and brought him a Super Bowl ring as the backup in Denver to John Elway.

A tight end who came to us in 1986 out of Santa Clara but never made it through training camp ended up with no fewer than four Super Bowl rings. Noll cut Brent Jones before the season started. He was a pass-catching tight end, not a blocking tight end, the only kind Noll liked to use. The misfit caught on with San Francisco and flourished for ten years in Coach Bill Walsh's "West Coast" offense, with its premium on passing.

Another tight end we released, Cap Boso of Illinois, signed with the Bears and had a six-year pro career. Boso was our eighth-round pick. I didn't know it at the time, but I would never again be involved in the drafting of a player whose name you will find in the NFL Encyclopedia.

Out

There was a different atmosphere that summer at Latrobe. We had finished the 1985 season with our worst record in fourteen years. It took away some of our charisma, some of our swagger.

And there was trouble right at the start. Frank Pollard went down with an injury, leaving us short-handed in the offensive backfield. For very little – almost nothing – we acquired Earnest Jackson from the Eagles, a small stroke of good fortune. Jackson was not a bad pickup. Twice with San Diego and once with Philadelphia, he had rushed for more than one thousand yards.

Our performance in exhibition games – one win, three defeats – was not encouraging. Then in our first three regular-season games, we lost to Seattle, Denver, and Minnesota. Two more defeats followed an overtime win over Houston. We lost to Cleveland by three points and to Cincinnati by two.

Back in July or August, I had been told by Dan that he wanted to meet with me in October to discuss some organizational ideas for the scouting department. "That's fine. I'll be ready," I said. Meanwhile, my scouts and I met with Noll, as usual, to hear what he felt was needed in the way of player personnel for 1987.

On October 14th, the day after the Cincinnati game, Dan let me know it was time for our get-together. In preparation, I sat down with my secretary, Bev Zavodni, widely regarded as the very best secretary in the entire Steeler organization, and developed three or four sheets of talking points. When I entered Dan's office, he was looking rather pale, I thought – pale and serious. Occupying leather-upholstered chairs with ultra-modern cast-iron silver frames, we faced each other on opposite sides of his desk. I don't know why, but I was sharply aware of the furnishings in Dan's office that day: the desk in the shape of a football flattened on the topside; the document for which AJR had paid $2,500 in 1933 – the Steelers' NFL franchise – hanging in a frame on the wall behind the desk; the familiar gray carpeting. Dan barely glanced at my outline, which I had set down in front of him. He pushed it aside and said, "This is not what I want to talk about."

I waited.

Then he said, "I want you out of the day-to-day business."

He continued to speak, but I don't remember his words. There was something about my going into one or another of the family's various enterprises, where I could write my own paycheck. The message I most clearly retained was that I was finished with the football team. Out.

Since my terrible display of temper the previous December, I had vowed never again to lose control. And on this occasion, as on all other occasions ever since then, I succeeded. When I left Dan's office, I walked down the hall to AJR's office, passing Mary Regan, who kept watch outside his door, without a word. Calmly, I told the Chief what had happened. I couldn't make out if the news surprised him. He did not know it was coming, he said. He told me to go back to the scouting department and "do my job." When we parted, he said evenly, "There can be only one boss."

Back in my office, I reviewed the events of the previous half-hour. Do my job, AJR had said. But how? There was no way I could concentrate on football, study film, evaluate scouting reports. So I sat. And I thought.

I have no recollection of what Kay and I said to each other that night.

The next day, for the first time ever, I closed the door to the personnel department. I called my three younger brothers Tim, John, and Pat. They were surprised but not shocked to hear that I had been fired. I went to see Dad again. I never had seen him looking more frail and tired. Sadly, he told me, "I can't make things happen any more." Later, he repeated, "There can be only one boss."

And of course that boss was Dan. Who wanted me out. That was it. Humpty-Dumpty sat on a wall, Humpty-Dumpty had a great fall.

It would be a change of lifestyle for me and Kay and the kids. I was concerned just a little about our future financial well-being until AJR called me at home and said, "You will never have to worry about money."

For the remainder of the 1986 football season, I went through the motions of "doing my job." The Steelers ended up with a 6-10 record. Our fans were not chanting their "one for the thumb" mantra that year.

On January 8th it was publicly announced that I would have nothing further to do with the scouting department. I was to stay on as vice president, but without any duties except to attend meetings of the board. Dick Haley succeeded me as head of the scouting operation. He remained with the Steelers until Chuck Noll retired after the 1991 season. Haley then took a job with the New York Jets and Tom Donahoe moved up to become scouting supervisor of the Steelers. Later, Jesse Kaye and Bob Schmitz joined Haley in New York and Tom Modrak left Pittsburgh to accept a very good offer from the Eagles. Modrak ended up with the Buffalo Bills, but Schmitz stayed with the Jets for fifteen years and then retired.

Kay and I got on with our lives. Nothing was more important to us than family and religion, and the Steelers were family. Beyond the pain of separation, my job had been more than a job; it had been a passion. With Kay's help, eventually I refocused.

A couple of NFL teams sounded me out: would I be interested in continuing to work? Jack Butler, Bill Nunn, and my high school coach, Rip Scherer, advised me to disregard these overtures. "You set the standard here," they told me. "Let the guys who follow you try to live up to it."

In 1993 Chuck Noll was elected to the Hall of Fame in Canton, joining seven of the players he had coached. Over the next nine years, Mike Webster, Lynn Swann, and John Stallworth were chosen. Dan Rooney was elected in the first year of the new century, joining AJR.

Other Steelers coached by Noll – L. C. Greenwood, Dwight White, Donnie Shell, Jon Kolb, and Larry Brown – have been nominated to the Hall of Fame. For whatever it may be worth, two Steeler scouts have also been nominated:

Bill Nunn and Art Rooney, Jr.

Chapter 75

Vigil at Mercy

Dr. Ted Gelet still made house calls – for one patient only: AJR. During the horribly hot summer of 1988 he examined the Chief in his offices at Three Rivers Stadium. "Art," the doctor said after looking him over, "everything seems to be pretty good."

For some time now, the Chief had been wearing a pacemaker. Toward the end of May he'd had a blood clot removed from an artery in his upper left arm. But he had cut down on cigars (to one a day, and he chewed only half of it). He was laying off sweets (except in moments of weakness). He had cut down on salt. "How many years will this buy me?" he asked Dr. Gelet. "A few," he was told. "A few? I guess that means three." The tradeoff, he concluded, wasn't worth it.

And yet for the most part he followed orders. He was living alone now, except for a daytime practical nurse and a nighttime practical nurse; Aunt Alice had died in 1986. The practical nurses were holdovers from Mom's last days. "I don't need help," AJR had insisted once she was gone, but he did need help, all of us knew, only that was not the way to make the case. "You need help for Alice," Dan explained, and AJR, never the easiest man to be taken in, was taken in.

Or pretended to be taken in. Again after Alice's death, he argued against keeping the nurses on, but Dan overrode his objections once more, this time encountering less resistance.

Mary Roseboro still cooked, dusted, and vacuumed, and Aunt Margaret was often on hand to see that AJR did not over-exert himself. "Remember," Dr. Gelet had warned him, "these are the dog days. Don't go outside in this heat. Before you get into your car, make sure that your driver has turned on the air-conditioner. Your car must be cooled off completely, because a car can be just like an oven. Go straight home when you leave the office. In the office and in your house, have the air-conditioner going full-blast. What I'm telling you is very important."

Not important enough, though, for AJR to change his most ingrained habits. There were wakes to attend, and funerals. There were sick friends in hospital rooms to be visited. And he could not miss Mass for even one day. If hot weather was a danger, he had to risk it.

On August 17th, Kay, Mike, Susie, and I retreated to the Laurel Mountains. Kay's father, Roy Kumer, was generous in letting us use his lakeside house in Deep Creek, Maryland, and we had gone there for relief from the deadening heat of the city. While Susie and Mike, who were college students by now, zipped around the lake in a speedboat, Kay and I immersed ourselves in the cool, shallow water near the shoreline.

In the evening, we had a cookout. Darkness came, and we went inside. After skimming through the newspapers, I looked at my watch. Eight-thirty – for us, almost time to turn in. Then the telephone rang. It was Dan.

He spoke calmly, but in tense, clipped tones. "I'm calling about Dad. He had a dizzy spell at the office this afternoon. We called 911 and got him to Mercy Hospital. At first he wouldn't go, and then he said he'd drive. We talked him into the ambulance. On the way to the hospital, he almost fell asleep. The doctors gave him tests. A brain attack of some kind. Don't rush home now, but come back tomorrow."

When I told all this to the family, Sue was the most upset. Granddaughter and grandfather had developed a close relationship. I called Art III in Pittsburgh. Art was a dentist, not a physician, but with more than just a layman's knowledge of medicine. AJR, he conjectured, had suffered a stroke. He advised us not to wait. "Come now. Right away."

By 10 o'clock we were speeding westward on Route 40. The gas tank in my oversized Cadillac was less than half full, and all I could think of as we passed a series of darkened service stations was how AJR would reproach me now for "putting on the dog." Cadillacs were gas-guzzlers. Everybody knew it. At the foot of Chestnut Ridge, to my immense relief, a station owner in the act of turning off the lights allowed me to pull in and fill up. Laconically, he said, "You just made it."

We were home before 1 o'clock and, after a short night's sleep, at the main entrance of Mercy Hospital by 6.

Already the television people were setting up their equipment. Mercy Hospital's information director, a competent young woman, told us that calls had been coming in from all the news organizations. A nun who worked in the intensive care unit spoke of how AJR had apologized for "causing trouble." He was "out of it" now, she said, but "not in a full coma."

We approached his bed. I said, "Dad, this is Artie," and took his hand. I felt him put pressure on mine. His eyes were closed, but he turned his head toward me. Holding his other hand, Kay said, "Art, I am here, too." He turned his head now in Kay's direction. She relinquished his hand to Susie, who took it in both of her own hands. Later, Susie recalled how white everything was – the walls, the bed, his hair. Everything but his eyes, which he suddenly opened. And his eyes, she said, were blue.

"So blue. Just those blue eyes looking up at me."

When he closed them, he was never, as far as I know, to open them again.

In the next day or two, my brother John and his wife flew in from Philadelphia, my brother Tim and his wife from New York, my brother Pat and his wife from Palm Beach. Rooneys and Rooney relatives from everywhere flew in. People from all walks of life and from every ethnic group came to the hospital: the rich and the poor, upright citizens and low-lifes, priests by the dozen and bishops, too. An Army private who was stationed in Iceland showed up. On the second day, as I sat with my four brothers in a restricted section of the hospital lunchroom, the information director came to our table.

She said, "There's a man out there who says he must see Art Junior and Dan. Just has to. He's quite insistent. A nice-looking fellow. Well-dressed. He says he is one of your dad's best friends."

Maybe, I suggested, it would be a good idea to show him in. She glanced at Dan, who simply nodded.

In a minute, she was back with our visitor, a clean-cut, middle-aged black man who was wearing a suit and tie. He greeted me in a familiar way and Dan somewhat formally. I thought I recognized him, but from where? He had excellent manners. He appeared to know Dad very well. "He was always nice to me," the man said. "You, too, Art Junior," he went on, and I searched my memory. Where had I seen this fellow? He'd been a boxer, he said. A football player. A cop. For some reason, he used the word "airport," and then I remembered. This was Jerry the redcap – a porter at the Pittsburgh International Airport. Without his uniform on, he might have been almost anyone.

AJR, he had said, was one of his best friends, a declaration we had long been accustomed to hearing. Most people, when they first met the Chief, felt instantly connected. By the second or third time, he was someone they had known all their lives.

Dan and I were urging Jerry to sit down, have some coffee, have a sandwich. We introduced him to Tim, John, and Pat. "This is Jerry, from the airport. Real good friend of Dad's." Jerry volunteered to make himself useful to us in any way he could. Did we need a driver? Whatever it might be, all we had to do was just ask.

We heard a hundred Art Rooney stories that week, all of them touching or humorous. Ron Cook of the *Pittsburgh Press* assembled two full pages of Art Rooney stories. He interviewed relatives and friends; he interviewed people the Chief had helped in a financial way – more often than not without being asked. It's a common journalistic practice to gather obituary material on important public figures who are getting along in years, and Cook had started this project earlier in the summer, careful to state his purpose when he asked somebody for an interview. Art III was still attending Pitt Dental School when Cook interviewed him. Wearing his starched white laboratory coat, he sat with Ron in the end-zone seats at Pitt Stadium. Ron tried to interview Mary Regan, but she turned him down with the utmost decisiveness. "For an obituary? While he's alive and not even sick? God forbid!"

Mary was loyal and wonderful and as Irish as Aunt Alice.

My brothers and I had sealed ourselves off from reporters. "Not now," we would say when somebody with a microphone came near. The information director did her best to protect us from media people, well-wishers, gawkers, and pests, and she was mostly successful. The gifts pouring in, hand-delivered or mailed, were something else. There were holy medals, scapulars, prayer cards, pictures of the saints. Somebody sent me rose petals from the shrine to St. Rose of Lima. Or was it the shrine to St. Theresa of Avila, the Little Flower? The rose petals were too fresh to have come from any great distance. I delivered them to the head nurse in the intensive care unit. They would end up in the trash, I supposed. Then I noticed on one of my visits that she had pinned them to the top of Dad's bed, with a scapular and a likeness of St. Rose completing the arrangement. Smiling, I said to myself, "God bless these good people at Mercy Hospital. They're looking out for Dad's spiritual welfare along with his bodily needs."

Dr. Oliver Turner called on me at home. Retired now, he had been AJR's personal physician in years gone by. He was a former chief of staff at Mercy Hospital and still had the run of the place. He had read Dad's charts and talked to his doctors and nurses, and he gave me the kind of report any football scout would have envied for its thoroughness and professionalism. The details were harrowing, the prognosis even worse. There had been a stroke, extensive bleeding, and total destruction of the brain. "You and your brothers should know this," he said.

(As time went by, Dr. Turner and I got to be pals. I called him Ollie, the difference in our ages notwithstanding. He told me something I never had known – that in the weeks after my dismissal from the football team AJR had come to him and said he was worried about me. My "mental outlook" and health were much on his mind. "He asked me to look after his 'boy,'" Ollie confided.)

Like Father Silas before him, AJR was ready to meet his maker. He believed in the sacraments and he believed in the promises of the Roman Catholic Church, and now his hour had come. Very early on the morning of August 25th, the five Rooney brothers and their wives were called into a meeting room and told that the Chief could only be kept "going" (not living) by artificial means. All of us agreed that survival without consciousness was not an acceptable option, and we were taken to his room for a last good-bye.

We gathered around the bed in a shuffling semi-circle. As we stood there, the silence became heavy. Then Dan's wife, Patricia, spoke some necessary words. "Let's all hold hands and say a prayer for Art." We said an Our Father, a Hail Mary, and a Glory Be. Patricia Rooney impressed me that day. She gave us an image to take away from our last few minutes with the Chief.

Reunited

And so once again the Rooney-McNulty clan would be making the trek out U.S. Route 19 to West View, where the Devlins had moved their funeral home from a deteriorating North Side. Three times in the previous six years the Devlins had buried family members – first Kass, then Dan's daughter Kate, who departed too young, and most recently Aunt Alice.

I remembered how Alice used to talk of the "three-two plan – three days in Divine Providence Hospital and two days at Devlin's." That is the way it was with Alice herself and Kass, but we had taken AJR to Mercy Hospital, not Divine Providence, and he had lingered there for a week. At Devlin's, he was to stay for only a short while and then be transported to St. Peter's Church for a full day's visitation before the funeral.

Visitation at Devlin's was restricted, supposedly, to the immediate family, a dictate that proved impossible to enforce. Kay, when she arrived there, noticed a black limousine in the parking lot and caught a glimpse of "a sinister-looking old fellow" heading towards it. The old fellow was Ed DeBartolo, Sr., who had driven over from Youngstown.

On arriving, he had greeted me with a hug and described AJR as "a most special man, a man of his word." Had I misjudged Mr. D., as I had misjudged so many other things in my fifty-three years? It was possible.

Something else Kay noticed at the funeral home was that "every politician in Pittsburgh" seemed to consider himself immediate family. Politicians, gate-crashers, and relatives we'd never heard of joined the unending line that filed past the casket. The Devlins were overwhelmed. But AJR had been going to wakes and funerals for decades, and now it was payback time.

This wake and this funeral would be the biggest in the history of Pittsburgh, surpassing Davey Lawrence's sendoff in 1966. Bursting with flowers, Devlin's and the church looked like the Phipps Conservatory. In AJR's opinion, flowers were the way to memorialize the dead. "I don't want any of that 'in lieu of flowers, contributions to this or that charity are suggested,'" he had said after Mom died. In his lifetime, he gave more to charity than many a nonprofit foundation ever did, but he was thinking of all the flower-store owners he knew; a wake was their chance to "make a few bucks," he explained. So it was somehow fitting that only hours after he died, a florist on Western Avenue converted the front window of his store into a shrine to the Chief, whose portrait, enlarged and bedecked with lilies and black and gold ribbons, looked out on the street from an easel.

As for what he might have thought of the sentence that concluded his voluminous newspaper obituaries – "The family requests that donations be made to the St. Vincent DePaul Society" – I refuse to guess.

The doubleheader wake was Dan's idea. He called the transfer of the casket from Devlin's to St. Peter's a "removal ceremony." As verified for us by Monsignor Charles Owen Rice, a native of Ireland, removal ceremonies are an old Hibernian custom. This one, fortuitously, gave my brothers and me a chance for some time to ourselves; from Devlin's, we took a detour to 940 North Lincoln Avenue, John and Pat in one car, Dan, Tim, and I in another.

When John, driving the lead car, went through a red light a momentary crisis ensued. An officer in a patrol car, his siren blaring, ordered John to pull up at the curb. Driving the second car, I pulled up behind them. The policeman asked John for his driver's license. He looked at it, handed it back, and poked his head through the window of the car. First he shook John's hand, then he shook Pat's. He did not write a ticket. John drove off, and I followed with Dan and Tim. As we passed the cop, who was standing outside his patrol car, he waved.

The visitation at St. Peter's was open to all. What we saw there, once again, was true diversity: the young and the old, the rich and the poor, the black and the white, the high and the low. Friends and people who considered themselves friends converged on the church. A woman named Flo Swinski told a *Pittsburgh Press* reporter, "I didn't know Mister Rooney personally, but I've read and heard so much about him I felt he was part of my life." She was dressed in black and gold. There were men and women in shorts (the August heat), there were men in coats and ties, and there were all kinds of people in blue jeans. They arrived in their cars; they arrived on foot and by bus. A few, like Ed DeBartolo at Devlin's the night before, came in chauffeured limousines.

By the time the doors opened at 2 p.m. a line had encircled the block. It was Friday, a work day. Police estimates were that three thousand people came in the afternoon and two thousand more at night. More than half of the two thousand remained to say the rosary.

The newspapers listed the NFL owners who attended the wake, the funeral, or both. There were eight or nine, plus the commissioner, Pete Rozelle, and the supervisor of officials, Art McNally. My close friend George Young was among the mourners. Al Davis – hard-crusted Al Davis – referred to the Chief as "someone I loved." Billy Sullivan of the Patriots added, "This may be sacrilegious, but I'll say it anyway: God was having a good day when he made Art Rooney."

Our coaches and players – all of them – came on Friday afternoon and went directly from the church to the airport. There was no thought of canceling their game the next day in New Orleans. "Mister Rooney," said Chuck Noll, "would expect us to play." Superdome officials arranged for a likeness of the Chief to be shown on the scoreboard during a minute of silence preceding the kickoff.

At least two dozen Steelers of an earlier vintage, the majority from the Super Bowl years, joined the throngs at St. Peter's, and there was even an original Pirate – Angelo Brovelli, a quarterback on the 1933 team. George Perles, Noll's one-time top assistant, who was still the head coach at Michigan State, flew in from East Lansing.

The Chief liked politicians, having been one himself on the ward-boss level, and there were plenty of those: Governor Bob Casey; former governor Dick Thornburgh, by that time the U.S. attorney general; County Commissioners Tom Foerster and Pete Flaherty; Mayor Sophie Masloff; Sheriff Gene Coon, on crutches (hit by a car as he was crossing a highway at night, he had recently lost a foot); County Controller Frank Luchino, who was Jack McGinley's good friend; and many smaller fry.

Jimmy the Greek Snyder came from Las Vegas. All of AJR's special cronies – the ones still living – were there. The kids from St. Peter's grade school came in a body. Two of them – boys – entered the church eating ice cream cones. It was in tune, everyone thought, with the spirit of the occasion.

There was talk of moving the service from St. Peter's to the cathedral in Oakland. We wouldn't hear of it. Jack McGinley said, "If we buried Art from another church, I don't think he'd go." St. Peter's Parish went back to 1849. The church building itself was one hundred years old. Throughout his long life, AJR had gone to Mass there. His parents had gone to Mass there. During the bleak Depression days of the 1930s the Chief raised money for St. Peter's in every conceivable way. "No one who lives in this parish," went a saying attested to by many of his neighbors, "will ever go hungry as long as Art Rooney is around."

To accommodate the funeral crowd on Saturday morning, the North Side farmer's market was canceled so that its parking lot could be used. Flags in the city flew at half-mast. A small airplane circled above the church, trailing a banner that read:

"BLESS YOU CHIEF – GLASSPORT."

The funeral was scheduled for 11 o'clock. According to the *Pittsburgh Press*, Blanche Furtwangler, a North Side native who lived in Bellevue, came in by bus to be first in line. She arrived three hours ahead of time. "I only knew Mister Rooney to say hello," she told a reporter, "but I felt like I'd known him all my life." The church's main sanctuary, which had a seating capacity of 1,100, was packed. "Standing room only," as Joe Carr would have put it. An overflow crowd of three hundred watched the service on four wide-screen television sets in the basement.

Only the closed-circuit camera was allowed upstairs. Anxious to save room for family, friends, and VIPs, Ed Kiely restricted the television stations to before-and-after coverage outside the church. As much as he might have wanted to, he could not show favoritism even to our friend from KDKA, Bill Burns. Three radio stations, their announcers unencumbered by camera crews and ponderous equipment, carried live broadcasts of the service.

The funeral Mass was extended to eighty minutes. Two soloists, both women, led us in four hymns. "On the altar," recalls Kay, "were what seemed like one hundred priests, bishops, and archbishops." Actually, there were four bishops, one auxiliary bishop, and two priests – Father Henry McAnulty, who may or may not have been Mom's distant relative, and Father Daniel Dixon, the pastor of St. Peter's, a man with the dimensions of an offensive tackle long retired. Bishop Vincent Leonard and his assistant, Bishop Donald Wuerl, gave eulogies. Bishop Wuerl had cut short his vacation, hastening back to Pittsburgh when he learned of the Chief's stroke.

Art Rooney was not a saint, just a near-saint, declared Bishop Leonard from the pulpit. "A devil's advocate," he said, "could have a field day with a man who took his wife to the race track on their honeymoon. He knew good people and he knew evil people, but he never let the evil embrace him."

One of the Chief's most frequently quoted remarks – that there never had been a Steeler he didn't like – made a deep and lasting impression on him, Leonard continued. He himself could not have said the same thing about some of his fellow bishops and priests, the old prelate admitted with a smile.

Our son Art III was one of the readers and did a good job. When the service was over, all of us filed out behind the casket. AJR had wanted an inexpensive one; in this respect, we disregarded his wishes. Six of the Chief's grandsons were pallbearers.

As we headed for the cars, I looked around. There were people I had not seen in years. So many, from so far away. The funeral cortege, by Kay's estimate, was "four miles long at least." Close to St. Peter's, the crowds on each side of the street stood shoulder-to-shoulder, three deep. Farther along, they gathered at every corner, silently watching. I caught sight of familiar faces here and there. All the way out Perrysville Avenue, people in Steeler jerseys were waving Terrible Towels. It reminded Kay of our trips from the airport to town after Super Bowl wins. Down in New Orleans, the Steelers and the Saints were going at it. I turned on the radio and listened for several minutes.

Near the gate to the North Side Catholic Cemetery the masses of spectators thickened again. An old man standing next to his car – stiffly at attention – held his hat over his heart and saluted the hearse as it passed. Resting on the car's hood was a large framed photograph of AJR. The old man, the salute, and the photograph form a tableau still emblazoned in my mind.

The graveside ceremony was brief. A few final words from Bishop Leonard. A sprinkling of holy water. Spoonfuls of earth tossed onto the casket. And AJR reunited with Kass. On their granite tombstone, three feet wide, were carvings of the Savior and a shamrock.

For the funeral luncheon, we adjourned to the Allegheny Club, where the solemnity of the morning gave way to lightheartedness. Among the guests were two women from Philadelphia, well dressed, well coiffed – and mortal enemies, or so I had heard. But now with their heads together they were all smiles and giggles, chatting away like schoolgirls. John and Pat knew the two women, and I asked if it wasn't true that they despised each other.

"Yes," answered Pat, "they certainly do."

John said, "But not today."

Bishop Leonard had declared from the altar that AJR was not a saint. And yet ... for canonization, according to the Catholic Church, it must be shown that a saint-in-waiting has performed three miracles. If that is true, I reflected, AJR had made a start. It was one down and two to go. Under the spell of his aura, two very dedicated antagonists had buried the hatchet.

Yes, indeed – I had witnessed the Chief's first miracle.

940 North Lincoln

Not long after the funeral, the five Rooney brothers met at 940 North Lincoln to decide what should be done with the old place. Tom Foerster had told us that Allegheny County wanted to make the house a historical site. The County Community College, the Catholic Diocese of Pittsburgh, the Holy Ghost fathers from Duquesne University, and two or three charitable foundations also had expressed an interest in taking it over.

For our part, we agreed that we would prefer to see it turned into rubble than fall into disrepair and perhaps become a crack house or worse. "Don't sell the old homestead after we're gone – burn it!" Kass used to say. I envisioned a sort of Viking funeral pyre – a real spectacle.

When we finally got down to business, Tim and I offered to buy the house from the estate, turn the ground floor into an office for the family enterprises, and keep the bedrooms upstairs in good repair so that relatives from out of town could use them on visits. In the end, it was Dan who bought the house. He and Patricia fixed it up and eventually moved in from Mount Lebanon. They are still there as I write this, happily ensconced.

Mary Roseboro and Georgia Flaherty, one of the housekeepers who attended to AJR, Aunt Alice, and Kass, continued for many years to be a part of the ménage.

What all of this caused me to realize was that I had come to think of the house as a person, almost. I was intensely concerned with its well-being. I gave the fifteen thousand dollars Dan paid me for my share of the purchase price to Bishop Wuerl, who had succeeded Bishop Leonard as head of the diocese. It was his to use as he pleased. Tim, Pat, and John did something similar.

Having been left one million dollars by the Chief, none of us needed the money. A stipulation of the will was that we should each give one-fifth of our two hundred thousand to charity. I divided my own share among worthy recipients in Western Pennsylvania.

A short time before his death, AJR had told me that he was handing down equal shares of the football team to his sons, but that he wanted Dan to run it. He was very emphatic about who was to be in charge. People I knew – some of them relatives – predicted that our joint ownership of the Steelers would fall apart in from five to seven years. They assured me family businesses never endure. This one, I think it is safe to say, did.

Mary Regan, AJR's loyal secretary, and Ed Kiely, his loyal lieutenant, remained with the Steelers until they retired of their own volition. Mary's great value was her ability to judge character, to weed out the frauds and the phonies who ingratiate themselves, or try to, with prominent figures like the Chief. She had the additional advantage of being Dan's sister-in-law, which gave her a personal investment in the welfare of the organization. And, like Kiely, she never lost track of people. Where AJR and later Dan might have been at a loss, she knew the whereabouts and the circumstances of friends and acquaintances and one-time business associates who had slipped off the radar screen. I always said I would like to have Mary Regan's Rolodex. Ed Kiely helped to settle the Chief's affairs and made himself useful in other respects. Just his presence on the scene was an asset to the Steelers. Like Jack McGinley, he connected the team's past with the here and now.

Chuck Noll retired after the 1991 season. He had a playoff team in 1989 and two other teams after 1987 with winning records. Bill Cowher, his successor, twice took the Steelers to the Super Bowl and came home with the trophy in 2006.

As I write this, the Chief's five sons are healthy, wealthy, and wise. Or healthy and wealthy, at any rate. All of us are married to the wives we first accompanied to the altar. Good things have happened to us. We give the credit for that to AJR and Kass.

Bishop Wuerl, at AJR's funeral, said in his eulogy that everyone he addressed had walked "in this big man's shadow." I walked in the big man's shadow during the last fifty years of his life, and I walk in his shadow even now.

Epilogue

At a time when life was mistreating Uncle John McNulty, I heard Uncle Jim say to him, "Your luck is going to change. And when it does," he continued, "I hope you are at the race track." Then he added, "And I hope I am with you."

In the grip of an impulse to wish someone well, Jim could do so with style. He liked and felt grateful to Kay, who remembered to send him a gift on his birthday and on other occasions and who frequently invited him to dinner, along with Grandma Rooney. Spotting Kay one day in the lobby of the Roosevelt Hotel, where he had taken a room after the death of his mother – they had been living together in the house on Perrysville Avenue – he limped across the distance between them to greet her. "Kay," he said in his best confidential stage whisper, "I don't know what you want in life, but I hope you get it."

His wants for himself, beyond the next drink, were hard to fathom. He led a solitary existence, an aging and lame alcoholic with no one looking after him. AJR was now a very old man; Uncle Dan, like Grandma Rooney, was gone; Margaret and Marie were getting no younger and in any event had families of their own to keep them occupied.

Small accidents bedeviled him. Crossing the streetcar tracks near the Roosevelt Hotel, he tripped and fell. An elevator door slamming shut too fast broke his arm. AJR, alarmed at these signs of decrepitude, made arrangements for the Passionate priests at St. Paul of the Cross Monastery to take him in.

St. Paul of the Cross overlooked the South Side from a hilltop. The dwindling number of priests in the Passionate order left them with enough vacant rooms for an old folks' wing. AJR, having gone to many retreats at St. Paul's, was friendly with the administrators and a generous contributor to fund-raising drives.

Uncle Jim's one request was for a large-screen television set, which AJR provided. Jim always preferred to watch the news and the sports in privacy, rather than in the monastery's common room. He had to do without booze unless Iggy Borkowski, John Joyce, or one of his other friends came to see him. Off they would then go, all three of them, for a visit with AJR and the rest of us at Three Rivers Stadium and maybe to watch a few innings of a Pirate game. Nothing wrong with that, you might think, but when Jim went back to the monastery he would usually have with him a bottle of contraband whiskey. Taken to task by AJR, his suppliers stoutly denied their complicity.

Physically, Jim thrived in his new surroundings. Mentally, he had started to slip. One day when Jim Laughlin drove AJR to the monastery, they arrived to find him having soup with some other old men in the dining hall. Suddenly one of them fell face forward into his lunch, dead of a heart attack. Seemingly unconcerned, Jim went on spooning up his soup.

The incident depressed Jim Laughlin for days, and AJR began to talk about the grim possibility of living too long.

Uncle Vince was the fourth of the brothers to die. Accompanied by John Joyce, Jim showed up at the wake. His hair had turned white and he looked old and pale. He knelt at the casket. He asked for "Arthur." No one else who was present seemed to interest him. He was worried about "Arthur," he said, having heard he was going "balmy." As it happened, "Arthur" was still fully functional – he remained so, in fact, until the day of his fatal stroke.

Uncle Vince's wake was Jim's last appearance in public. On one of my visits with Kay to the monastery, he informed us as though it were news that his brother Tom had been killed by the Japanese. At other times, his language would turn into gibberish.

Six months went by. Perhaps a year. I no longer was working out of Three Rivers Stadium. A newspaper story appeared, stating that I had been absent from the Steeler office for weeks. Someone called me from St. Paul's. Uncle Jim was frantic. He had to see me. A telephone call would not suffice. He was demanding that a taxicab be sent for him so he could get to me. It was urgent. He could not be settled down. He had to see me in person.

I told Kay about this, and we drove to St. Paul's, bringing candy for Uncle Jim. The Passionist brother who took us to his room said he never had seen him so upset. He thanked us for coming quickly. But, face to face with us, finally, Jim was perfectly calm. He smiled all the time we were there. He thought Kay was our daughter Sue. He told us again that his brother Tom had been killed in the war. As before, he ended up babbling nonsense.

Some time later word came to me that Jim wasn't going to make it. He'd been taken from St. Paul's to a hospital on the South Side. I decided to put off seeing him until the next day, but then for some reason I changed my mind. I found him alone in his room. He was dying, the nurse said. He would be moved to a hospice to wait for the end. I stayed for a while and talked to him. He looked at me blankly, and I told him who I was. I used his Irish name – Seamus – but there was still no response. I said some prayers and then departed.

I was the last of the Rooneys to see Jim alive. He died at the hospital before they could move him. On a glorious summer day he was buried at the monastery. A second cousin, Father Utz, officiated at the funeral Mass. Laid out in a blue suit, Jim was a handsome corpse. His sisters were there, along with nephews, nieces, and friends, and everybody said nice things about him. "He must have been made of steel," someone marveled, "to live as long as he did after putting away so much liquor."

It was indisputable. He was into his eighties and had outlasted all five of his brothers. And now he would be "with Arthur" again. Believe it.

***

Soft lights. Subdued Christmas decorations. White table cloth, good silver. Trusted old friends.

The waitress asked for our drink orders, and Kay said, "I'll have a highball – C.C. and water with a lemon twist. Kass drank that all the time. I guess I got that from her."

Dee Berlin, responding to the memory, said, "Yes, yes – I'll have the same thing. Kass was so special. She'd say, 'Hi, Dee, it's so nice to see you,' and you knew she meant it. She made me feel special, too."

"Dee, you are special." Kay said. She patted Dee's hand. Meanwhile Ralph Berlin was telling the waitress, "Scotch and water for me." Now it was my turn. "Too cold outside for a soft drink," I said. "What I'd like – if you have any – is one of those non-alcoholic beers."

The waitress assured me it would not be a problem.

I explained to the others that I had tried the stuff before and it wasn't bad. "In fact it almost tastes like the real thing." Not only tastes like the real thing but looks like the real thing, I could have added. My St. Clair Country Club friends – and the dining room seemed to be full of them – would think I had given in to John Barleycorn.

Ralph Berlin said, "We went to see 'The Chief' – that play about your father. It brought back old memories. Kay, did you ever hear that one of my first jobs with the Steelers was to fish your Uncle Jim out of Frenchy's, across the street from the Roosevelt Hotel? He was over there tying one on, and Fran Fogarty said, 'Hey, Berlin. Go get Jim. Get him up to his room.' Jim had a room in the hotel."

Ralph was smiling. "I came here to be the trainer, but I soon found out there were lots of other things I had to do."

There were indeed. He was the odd-jobs man in our organization, or, as he himself put it, "the plumber." "I'm just the plumber," he took to saying, and "The Plumber," in time, became his more or less self-bestowed nickname.

The drinks had arrived. We lifted our glasses and wished one another a Merry Christmas. Ralph took a swallow of Scotch. He said, "I knew all those people Gene Collier wrote about: Father Dan ... Dago Sam ... Patsy Scanlon ... Remember Patsy Scanlon, that little old white-haired bookie, Art?"

"I sure do. He could fight. Patsy Scanlon boxed some world champions."

"So many characters," Ralph said. "We were lucky to be a part of it, Dee and I." Helped along by the Scotch, the reminiscences started to flow. "The Berlins were Philadelphia people. Somehow we got out to Los Angeles. The Depression was on. My father must have thought he could get a job out West. We lived in Watts, Kay – that's the tough black section of L.A. Heck, I never really got to know my dad. The war started, see ... and he was gone for five years. He came back and died. Went to the Vets hospital and died. I knew I should feel bad, but he'd only been back about a year, and I couldn't grieve.

"Art" – Ralph never called me "Artie" – "I felt more sorrow when my dog was killed by a car."

In our relationship of thirty-five years, I never had heard Ralph talk this way. The guy was an ex-Marine. His coach at Iowa State in the late 1950s had called him one of the toughest interior linemen on the team. But now on this cold December night almost half a century later, the season, the warmly festive atmosphere, the Scotch, and most of all, perhaps, the sentiments awakened by the play he had recently seen were having an unexpected effect.

"Your dad," he said to me earnestly, "was the father I never had."

We were starting on our second round of drinks. "Remember all those years you sent me to work those Blesto draft meetings in Philly? Sometimes your dad would drop by. He liked to hang out with the scouts and coaches from the Eagles. 'Ralph,' he said to me once when he was there, 'I need a cab – I'm going to the airport.' I was waiting at the phone for a call from Pittsburgh, but I grabbed one of the Blesto scouts and told him, 'Take over for me here. If Art or anybody from Pittsburgh calls, they'll let you know what to do.' And I picked up the Chief's bag and said to the receptionist, 'Call Mister Rooney a cab. He's going to the airport. '

"Well, the next thing you know, here comes Leonard Tose rushing out of his office – the owner of the Eagles himself. The receptionist must have tipped him off. 'Arthur,' he says, 'I hear you'd like to go to the airport. My driver is outside with the limousine.' And the Chief says, 'No, no. Berlin here will take care of it.' And Tose said, 'Arthur, I insist.' He snatched the Chief's bag out of my hand and gave it to this guy in a chauffeur's uniform, cap and all. 'Take Mister Rooney right to the gate,' he tells the driver. 'If that isn't possible, park right next to the entrance and get Mister Rooney to his gate.' He turned to the Chief. 'The police know our limousine, Arthur. Give my regards to Kathleen and have a good flight.'

"I am now going to tell you the difference between your dad and phony big shots like Leonard Tose. While the driver was putting his bag in the trunk, the Chief said to Tose, 'Do you know our trainer, Ralph Berlin?' 'Oh, yes,' Tose says, 'I've seen him around here before.' The truth is he hadn't even known I existed. And after our introduction, if you can call it that, he never looked at me again.

"I'll tell you another thing about your dad. When former players of ours – guys who'd been with us for only one season, or maybe half a season – would drop by the training room years later to say hi, the boss would sometimes happen to come in. And nine times out of ten he'd remember the player's name. I'll never know how he did that."

I said, "Neither will I, Ralph. I saw that, too. It was certainly not a talent passed down from the father to the son."

"Oh, Art, you have a wonderful memory – all of those stories about the old days," said Kay, letting the air out of my false-modesty balloon in the gentlest way imaginable. "He's a Civil War expert, too," she informed the Berlins.

As much as I liked the attention, I felt I was upstaging Ralph. To keep him going, I said, "I interrupted you," and that was all it took.

"Another time in Philly," he resumed, "I shared a room with the Chief at this big fancy hotel. In the morning your dad says to me, 'I plan on going to Mass, but I don't know this section of town very well. Go down to the desk and ask where the Catholic church is. And, while you're at it, see if you can find out the schedule for the Masses.'

"I was so excited about doing this job that instead of stopping to check with the head bellman I ran right out into the street and started asking whoever passed by. People were on their way to work, and to judge by the clothes they were wearing, they all seemed to be going to construction jobs. There must have been a lot of construction around the hotel. Anyway, I was asking them, 'Where's the Catholic church? What time are the Masses?' and they're looking at me like I'm a nut. I'm getting no answers, but at last I see a cop. I ask him where the church is, and he points to it.

"'Right across the street.'

"Well, it was easy to miss, that's all I can say. It didn't look like a church. It looked like an old library or bank. It had gray stone columns, and there were empty lots on both sides – empty lots full of rubble. I go inside. There was nobody there except a priest in one of those long black robes. He had a big old black dog with him – a Labrador or something. I said, 'Hey, Father – when's the next Mass?'

"'Not till noon.'

"Oh, my. I said, 'Gee, Father, my boss wants to go to Mass. My boss is Art Rooney from Pittsburgh.'

"'Art Rooney? The man who owns the Steelers? I'll say a special Mass for him. Right here.' He indicates a side altar close to where we're standing.

"'What time, Father?'

"'Right now. As soon as he gets here.'

"Fifteen minutes later we're having the Mass. The priest is up on the altar and I'm in a pew with your dad. Two Catholics and a Lutheran. And oh, yes – the black dog. I don't know if the dog was a Catholic or not."

Ralph said he had been to so many Masses and funerals with the Chief that he knew some of the prayers. "But of course I kept my mouth shut. I was only the plumber. Still, you'd be surprised at how much the same the Lutheran services are to a Catholic Mass."

That night Berlin went with the Chief to a testimonial dinner for a Philadelphia boxing promoter named Herman Taylor. They left from Liberty Bell with my brother John in his Cadillac (the car which he had tried – without success – to make our dad believe was an Oldsmobile). "The dinner was at a restaurant in South Philly," Ralph said, "and John had some trouble finding it. When we finally got there, the parking lot was full and all the parking places on the street were taken. South Philly is all Italian, and a little Mediterranean guy was standing in front of the restaurant. He recognized your dad. 'Park here,' he says, waving us up onto the sidewalk. He put us right up against the steps to the front door.

"Inside, it looked like a Mafia joint. The place was packed with Italians. Everybody made a fuss over your dad, which was old stuff to him. He did his thing, the same as always, and he knew just the right time to leave.

"When we got out to the car, John said, 'I'm still lost. If you can get me to Broad Street, I'll know where I am. From Broad Street I can take you anywhere in Philly.'

"The Chief said, 'Ralph, you're from Philly. Where's Broad Street?'

"I couldn't answer. I was as lost as John, I had to tell him.

"Then the Chief saw some kids pitching pennies on the sidewalk. He goes to the biggest kid, whips a five-dollar bill out of his kick, and says, 'This is yours if you can get us to Broad Street.'

"The kid grabs the bill. He says, 'Get in your car and follow me. It's not far at all.' With the three of us close behind him, he runs down the middle of the street, takes a couple of turns, and there we are – right on Broad Street. In no time, John has us back at the hotel.

"'Mister Rooney, you da man,' I said to myself. Believe me, I was in awe of that guy."

"Ralph," Dee said, "tell the one about Rico's."

I remembered Rico's well – an old roadhouse off McKnight Road.

"We'd go to dinner there – Dee and I and your dad," Ralph said. "One night Joe Greene came with us. Well, when Mister Rooney showed up at Rico's, he owned the place. We got the best table, and the only thing we ordered were the drinks. Your dad would have ice tea. Then they just brought out the food. Salad. Hors d'oeuvres – all kinds. The good stuff – crabmeat, shrimp. I had no idea what it was. Then pasta. All kinds of fish and veal. When we finished eating, your dad didn't wait for the bill. He left a tip – a good one – and then stood up and said, 'We're going.'"

Dee broke in to say, "Joe Greene was so surprised."

Kay asked, "What did he do?"

"Do?" said Ralph. "He got up and walked out with the rest of us – still looking baffled.

"But the best – the very best – was on a trip out West with the football team. We went to this restaurant, Saturday night before the game. There were five or six of us. The bill comes, and the Chief grabs it. 'Mister Rooney,' I said, 'I have the Steeler credit card.'

"'Not when I'm here.' He puts his hand in his pocket – and comes up empty. 'What a sap,' he says. 'I forgot to bring my money.'

"'We'll have to use the card,' I tell him.

"'No way!' He says to the waiter, 'I'll give you an I.O.U.' and pulls out a ballpoint pen. He takes his napkin – a big white linen napkin, because this was a nice place – and writes in big, bold letters on the napkin: 'I.O.U. – X amount of dollars.' Then he signs it 'Art Rooney, Pittsburgh Steelers, Three Rivers Stadium, Pittsburgh, PA., 15212, telephone 412-323-1200.'

"What a man!" Ralph said. "The father I never knew."

***

After Marie McGinley's death in 2003 the only surviving Rooney of AJR's generation was Aunt Margaret Laughlin. At the age of 90, suffering from congestive heart failure, she made a special effort to see the play about her brother by Gene Collier, a *Pittsburgh Post-Gazette* columnist, and Ron Zellers. In reality Collier wrote the script, or most of it; Zellers' contribution was to get the play on-stage. Called "The Chief," it had a successful month-long run at the O'Reilly Theater on Liberty Avenue, downtown. There was only one part – the title role – played by a very good local actor named Tom Atkins, who delivered an unbroken ninety-minute monologue.

With her son Jim, Aunt Margaret attended a matinee. She was so moved by the performance of Tom Atkins, she said afterward, that she laughed and cried all through the show. When it was over, she attempted to meet the actor backstage, unsuccessfully. So as soon as she returned to her house on the North Side she wrote Mr. Atkins a letter. Her calligraphy was like AJR's – strong, but at the same time flowing and elegant. Both learned the art of penmanship from the nuns at St. Peter's School. Atkins responded at once, with a telephone call. "We had a nice, long, warm conversation," Margaret told me. From Atkins later on, I heard the same thing.

Aunt Margaret died in her ninety-first year. Late one night she asked her son Jim to fetch some ice cream from the kitchen. "And don't forget the chocolate sauce," she called down the steps while Jim was on his way. Aunt Margaret liked to have the last word. If "Don't forget the chocolate sauce" qualifies, she had the last word right up to the end, for when Jim returned with her bedtime snack, chocolate sauce and all, his mother had left us.

Jack McGinley, Aunt Marie's husband, was the next to go. He died in 2006. Jack McGinley, along with men like Father Silas and Byron White and Jack Butler, had been someone I was taught to emulate, or try to. They were models of upright behavior.

With AJR's death in 1988, his sons had become the patriarchs of the family. In March of 1987, sensing that his time was short, the Chief wrote a formal letter addressed to all five of us. After expressing his "love and respect" for our wives and children, he told us we should "make every effort" to buy back all of their stock in the football team, the stock we had put in their names. If we failed to do this, he predicted, there would be lawsuits and strife "down the road." He wanted us all – sons, wives, and children – to be fairly treated, and this was the best way to ensure it.

As we always had done, we honored the Chief's request. We bought back the stock. Twenty years have gone by, and we are all still in business together. Through some trying times, we have kept the ability to communicate with one another. Even more to be celebrated, the same thing holds true for our wives.

Lately the third generation of Rooneys has entered the picture. Dan's son Art joined him some time ago in the day-by-day operation of the Steelers. None of Dan's brothers are involved. In accordance with AJR's wishes, however, all five of us own the same amount of stock in the team as I write this and we are all on the board of directors. In the table of organization, I'm the only vice president listed. We have kept the Steelers and our other businesses under family ownership since the 1930s and are hopeful this third generation can hold things together as successfully.

I don't play golf. I don't play cards. I never have hunted or fished. But in one respect I'm a hobbyist:: I value my collection of Merv Corning art - the water color paintings I've commissioned of great Steeler players from the 1970s and earlier. Merv Corning died in 2006. Portraits of athletes were his specialty, and he was preeminent in his field. I was fortunate to have counted him as a friend.

One of the advantages of a more anchored existence is the time I've been able to spend with my family. Almost from the day I was married, my work as the football team's personnel director obsessed me. I was committed to building up a first-class scouting organization, and nothing seemed more important. Perpetually on the move, I touched down often at home, but only between trips and eager to be off again, insensible to the burden this was putting on Kay. Alone, she was taking care of our children.

Art III was the oldest, then came Karen, Mike, and Susie. Karen, born in 1964, was a strikingly beautiful child - blue-eyed, with her mother's red hair. But with good cause we were troubled. We had noticed, when she was still in the cradle, that Karen did not respond to the sound of our voices, or indeed to the ordinary sounds of a busy household. Pediatricians advised us not to worry. As time passed, all would be well. We were to learn, instead, that Karen's hearing problem was permanent, and "profound." We were to learn as well that there were problems of a far more serious nature, with "strong features," said the doctors, of that mysterious affliction known as autism.

We needed help. Thank heaven for the Sisters of Charity at DePaul Institute, the good nuns of the order that taught at Seton Hill College when Kay was a student there in the late 1950s. Kay's mother had recently died, but Kass and Aunt Alice gave us their support. And yet the stress on Kay, as our daughter's condition worsened, was enormous.

Desperate, we were taking Karen to specialists everywhere, not only in Western Pennsylvania, but in Washington, D. C., Philadelphia, the Menninger Clinic in Topeka, Kansas, and Children's Hospital in Baltimore. And in all of these places we were told the same thing. Our daughter could not be "cured." She would require full-time professional care for the rest of her life.

Throughout this ordeal my extended absences on football business frequently left Kay on her own, coping heroically. In the words of an old song, she was "the wind beneath my wings."

Karen, now in her forties, is in good physical health. She receives the best and most devoted attention that one of the topmost facilities in America can provide. There she will live out her days, visited often by her parents for as long as the fates allow.

Before his death some time ago, Roy Kumer, Kay's father – who lived to be 95 – gave Kay a fine piece of property next to his lakeside home in Maryland, and on it I have built her a weekend retreat. We go there in the spring, summer, and fall. From January to April, we're in our Palm Beach condominium in the ocean-front building where AJR and Kass spent a part of each winter. I can still see them walking up Grace Trail every morning on their way to St. Edward's Church for early Mass.

And now I am following in their footsteps. It's a ritzy neighborhood for sure, but if I'm putting on the dog, so was the Chief. I look around and say to myself – sometimes I even say it out loud – "Thank you, Dad. Thank you for making all of this possible."

1974 PITTSBURGH STEELERS

Bottom Row: Field Manager Jack Hart, Terry Hanratty, Roy Gerela, Terry Bradshaw, Joe Gilliam, Rocky Bleier, Dick Conn, Mike Wagner, J. T. Thomas, Ron Shanklin, Preston Pearson, Equipment Manager Tony Parisi.

Second Row: Head Coach Chuck Noll, Glen Edwards, Donnie Shell, Franco Harris, John Fuqua, Andy Russell, Steve Davis, Ed Bradley, Bobby Walden, Frank Lewis, Jim Allen, Defensive Coordinator Bud Carson.

Third Row: Offensive Backfield Coach Dick Hoak, Mel Blount, Jim Clack, Loren Toews, Mike Webster, Marv Kellum, Jon Kolb, Ray Mansfield, Sam Davis, Jack Lambert, Jack Ham, Defensive Assistant Bob Widenhofer, Flexibility Coach Paul Uram.

Fourth Row: Defensive Line Coach George Perles, Jim Wolf, Ernie Holmes, Steve Furness, L. C. Greenwood, Gordon Gravelle, Gerry Mullins, Rick Druschel, Dave Reavis, Joe Greene, Receiver Coach Lionel Taylor.

Top Row: Offensive Line Coach Dan Radakovich, Charlie Davis, Dwight White, John Stallworth, Randy Grossman, Reggie Garrett, Larry Brown, Lynn Swann, John McMakin, Trainer Ralph Berlin.

With many good wishes for the holidays and the coming year

Mother - Dad - Grandmother &
Grandfather
We are grateful to you for
your kindness to us. We
are proud of you. You have
made us very happy by
the way you live your life.
Be good and stay a close
knit family -

PITTSBURGH STEELERS
300 STADIUM CIRCLE
PITTSBURGH, PA. 15212
412/323-1200

March 18, 1987

Mr. Daniel M. Rooney
Mr. Arthur J. Rooney, Jr.
Mr. Timothy J. Rooney
Mr. Patrick J. Rooney
Mr. John J. Rooney

Dear Sons:

Time is starting to run out on me. I am concerned, just as you are, about my Will, particularly my Stock in the football club. I would like to reach some kind of an understanding so that there will be no questions or complications regarding my Estate.

You are all fine men; I love all of you and I am proud of you just as your Mother was. I love and respect your wives and children. I believe that you should make every effort to buy the football Stock that is in their names. I want them all to be treated fairly. I believe if this does not happen, down the road, there's going to be nothing but lawsuits. I do not want this to happen. I want you to start working on this immediately and try and come to a fair conclusion.

With all my love,

Dad

Dad

Managers/Coaches/Scouts

DAN ROONEY
HOF 2001

BERT BELL
1941 HOF 1963

BILL NUNN
1967

WALT KIESLING
PITTSBURGH PIRATES
1937 HOF 1967

ART ROONEY
HOF 1964

ART ROONEY JR.

COACH BUDDY PARKER
1957

DICK HALEY
1972

"JOCK" SUTHERLAND
1946

CHUCK NOLL
1969 HOF 1993

JOHNNY "BLOOD" MCNALLY
PITTSBURGH PIRATES 1937
HOF 1963

Design by Kathy Rooney, www.krooney.net